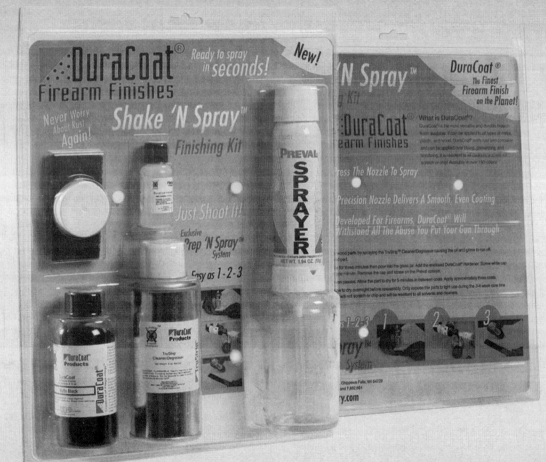
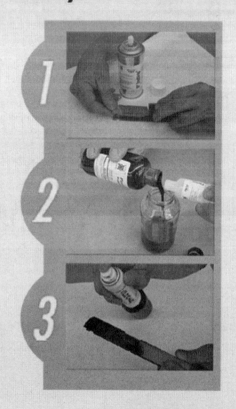

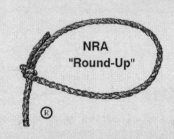

SHOTGUN◉NEWS

GUNSMITHING PROJECTS

Edited by
ROBERT W. HUNNICUTT

SHOTGUN◉NEWS
GUNSMITHING PROJECTS
Table of Contents

Introduction
by Robert W. Hunnicutt............................8

Restore That Military Rifle
by Steven Matthews..............................10

Screw Slot Blues
by Reid Coffield................................14

Cutting and Crowning a Rifle Barrel
by Reid Coffield................................18

What's This 4140?
by Steven Matthews..............................22

Just Park It Yourself
by Steven Matthews..............................26

Give Your Gun a Coat
by Steven Matthews..............................30

Can You Blue it Yourself? Yep!
by Steven Matthews..............................34

Wallhanger? No Way!
by Paul Mazan...................................38

Two-Piece Stocks Need Love, Too
by Reid Coffield................................41

Upgrading AK Furniture
by George Spafford..............................44

Gunsmithing Tools: Make Your Own! Part 1
by Steven Matthews..............................48

Gunsmithing Tools: Make Your Own! Part 2
by Steven Matthews..............................52

Machining For Beginners, Introduction
by Clayton E. Cramer............................56

Machining For Beginners, Engine Lathe 1
by Clayton E. Cramer............................60

Machining For Beginners, Engine Lathe 2
by Clayton E. Cramer............................64

Machining For Beginners, Vertical Mill
by Clayton E. Cramer............................66

Police Automatics: Are They A Bargain?
by Reid Coffield................................70

Reclaiming a Rent-A-Cop Revolver, Part 1
by Reid Coffield................................76

Reclaiming a Rent-A-Cop Revolver, Part 2
by Reid Coffield................................82

The Basic Black Rifle
by Jeremy Clough................................86

Why Retro?
by Jeremy Clough................................90

Back to the '60s: Building a Classic AR-15
by Steven Matthews..............................94

An Accurate AR For Less Than A Grand?
by Steven Matthews.............................100

M14 Maintenance & Inspection
by Gus Norcross................................105

The Weekend Garand
by Reid Coffield...............................108

Baby at the Gates: Building a .22 Mosin-Nagant Sniper
by Richard Parker..............................114

Budget Building the Model 1911
by Steven Matthews.............................118

Fixing a "Non-Repairable" Pistol
by Reid Coffield...............................122

Dummy Up! Part 1: the Sten Mk 2
by Steven Matthews.............................126

Dummy Up! Part 2: the Beretta 38A Submachine Gun
by Steven Matthews.............................130

Dummy Up! Part 3: the Finnish Suomi m/31
by Steven Matthews.............................134

Dummy Up! Part 4: Building an AK-47
by Steven Matthews.............................138

Scratch-Made Dummy M1919A4, Part 1
by Steven Matthews.............................142

Scratch-Made Dummy M1919A4, Part 2
by Steven Matthews.............................146

Build Your Own AK? Yes You Can!
by Steven Matthews.............................152

New Life for a Martini Cadet
by Reid Coffield...............................160

Installing a Barrel Liner in a Martini
by Reid Coffield...............................164

Restoring a Veteran Firearm for a Returning Veteran
by Steven Matthews.............................170

Resurrecting A Citori, Part 1
by Reid Coffield...............................174

Resurrecting A Citori, Part 2
by Reid Coffield...............................178

Resurrecting A Citori, Part 3
by Reid Coffield...............................182

Resurrecting A Citori, Part 4
by Reid Coffield...............................186

Resurrecting A Citori, Part 5
by Reid Coffield...............................190

Kathmandu to Columbia: Reviving a Nepalese Martini, Part 1
by Reid Coffield...............................196

Kathmandu to Columbia: Reviving a Nepalese Martini, Part 2
by Reid Coffield...............................200

Gunsmithing the Russian Nagant Revolver, Part 1
by Reid Coffield 206

Gunsmithing the Russian Nagant Revolver, Part 2
by Reid Coffield 212

Building A 10/22 Garand, Part 1
by Reid Coffield 216

Building A 10/22 Garand, Part 2
by Reid Coffield 222

Enfield? Martini? Or Both? Part 1
by Reid Coffield 228

Enfield? Martini? Or Both? Part 2
by Reid Coffield 233

The .22 Cal. No. 4 Lee-Enfield, Part 1
by Reid Coffield 238

The .22 Cal. No. 4 Lee-Enfield, Part 2
by Reid Coffield 242

The .22 Cal. No. 4 Lee-Enfield, Part 3
by Reid Coffield 246

Building The Sten Mk 2.5, Part 1
by Steven Matthews 250

Building The Sten Mk 2.5, Part 2
by Steven Matthews 254

Home-Building the FN FAL, Part 1
by Steven Matthews 260

Home-Building the FN FAL, Part 2
by Steven Matthews 264

VZ-58: a Real Easy Wallhanger
by Steven Matthews 270

Dummy Up a PPSh-41
by Steven Matthews 274

Building a Semi—Automatic PPSh-41, Part 1
by Steven Matthews 278

Building a Semi—Automatic PPSh-41, Part 2
by Steven Matthews 283

Building the SGN-22, Part 1
by Steven Matthews 288

Building the SGN-22, Part 2
by Steven Matthews 292

Building the SGN-22, Part 3
by Steven Matthews 296

Building the SGN-22, Part 4
by Steven Matthews 300

Building the SGN-9, Part 1
by Steven Matthews 304

Building the SGN-9, Part 2
by Steven Matthews 310

Building the SGN-9, Part 3
by Steven Matthews 313

Building the SGN-9, Part 4
by Steven Matthews 316

Building the Rapid Fire VZ-58, Part 1
by Steven Matthews 322

Building the Rapid Fire VZ-58, Part 2
by Steven Matthews 327

Semi-Auto Suomi from Scratch, Part 1
by Steven Matthews 332

Semi-Auto Suomi from Scratch, Part 2
by Steven Matthews 336

Semi-Auto Suomi from Scratch, Part 3
by Steven Matthews 339

Semi-Auto Suomi from Scratch, Part 4
by Steven Matthews 344

I Want My Belt-Fed! Part 1
by Steven Matthews 350

I Want My Belt-Fed! Part 2
by Steven Matthews 356

Building the Poor Man's Browning Belt Loader
by Steven Matthews 360

What Can You Do With a Drill Rifle? Part 1
by Reid Coffield 364

What Can You Do With a Drill Rifle? Part 2
by Reid Coffield 368

What Can You Do With a Drill Rifle? Part 3
by Reid Coffield 372

Straight-Pull Sporter
by Paul Mazan 378

Mosin Nagant? Sporter?!? Part 1
by Reid Coffield 384

Sporterizing the Russian Mosin-Nagant Rifle, Part 2
by Reid Coffield 388

Sporterizing the Russian Mosin-Nagant Rifle, Part 3
by Reid Coffield 392

Sporterizing the Russian Mosin-Nagant Rifle, Part 4
by Reid Coffield 396

Sporterizing the Russian Mosin-Nagant Rifle, Part 5
by Reid Coffield 401

Sporterizing the Russian Mosin-Nagant Rifle, Part 6
by Reid Coffield 406

Sporterizing the Russian Mosin-Nagant Rifle, Part 7
by Reid Coffield 410

Sporterizing the Russian Mosin-Nagant Rifle, Part 8
by Reid Coffield 414

Build Your Own Bren Gun! Part 1
by Steven Matthews 420

Build Your Own Bren Gun! Part 2
by Steven Matthews 424

Build Your Own Bren Gun! Part 3
by Steven Matthews 428

Build Your Own Bren Gun! Part 4
by Steven Matthews 432

Build Your Own Bren Gun! Part 5
by Steven Matthews 436

Build Your Own Bren Gun! Part 6
by Steven Matthews 440

101 Gunsmithing Projects On One Gun?
by Reid Coffield 444

SHOTGUN ◉ NEWS

An Unexpected Calling

I don't know that I intended gunsmithing to be a major feature of SHOTGUN NEWS when I took over the helm almost 14 years ago. I knew I wanted to do a lot about surplus military arms and an AR-15 category that was at that point stunted by the Violent Crime and Law Enforcement Act of 1994.

Gunsmithing was no more than an afterthought until I was approached by Reid Coffield, an old coworker from my days as technical editor of the *American Rifleman*. Reid is a veteran of more than 30 years in the trade, and worked for many years on the technical staff of Brownells.

He suggested a gunsmithing column and a program of feature articles on the subject. As I was at the time publisher of *Shooting Times*, I happily took him on for both titles.

He occupied himself for the first months with pieces covering the basics, as you would expect. But in the summer of 2003, he approached me with a plan for a multi-part series on sporterizing a 98 Mauser. To say I was underwhelmed would be a thorough understatement. I thought such a series would have been great in 1963, not so much 40 years later.

But Reid's enthusiasm cut through my skepticism and I relented. In those days I hadn't yet learned to refer in each article to the previous installments, and our phone rang constantly with calls from readers who'd come into the series in midstream and were looking for the back issues. We quickly ran out of spare copies and wound up putting the whole series on a CD that is still for sale on the SGN website.

That series taught me that while we are told Americans are losing their mechanical skills and can't be expected to operate anything more complicated than battery-powered gizmos whose name starts with "i," there are still a surprising number out there who know how to weld, operate machine tools and shape wood. And they are looking for ways to use those skills.

Shortly thereafter, I started getting submissions from Steven Matthews, an industrial maintenance man from Ohio. He wasn't a trained gunsmith, but had a native knack for mechanics and a determination I've rarely seen matched. There's no pile of junk too rusty and torn up for him to turn into some sort of gun. He turned in stories of ever more ambitious projects, some of which I thought were far too labor-intensive for readers to try. Again, I was wrong. Matthews likes to bring his creations to the SGN tent at the Knob Creek Machine Gun Shoot, and when he does, there's always someone examining them with an "I can do that" expression.

So without any particular plan for it to happen, gunsmithing has become a vital part of SGN, with projects I think you'll agree are unlikely to be seen elsewhere. The stories we've run have inspired a whole subculture of builders who exchange ideas on the Internet and compete to build the most outlandish projects.

Home gun building has made parts kits a coveted commodity on the gun show circuit, and you can buy the best of them in SGN. Determination and imagination can turn a greasy, rusty pile of parts into something all your own.

I decided that the best gunsmithing stories could be compiled into a useful book, and this volume is the result. In it, you can learn about the tools and techniques you need to know to build your own guns, and you'll be inspired by the products of imaginations like Coffield's and Matthews'. It's a great time to "roll your own," so get out to the shop and start building!

Robert W. Hunnicutt
General Manager
SHOTGUN NEWS

> " Determination and imagination can turn a greasy, rusty pile of parts into something all your own."

SHOTGUN◎NEWS

SHOTGUN NEWS PRESENTS...

SHOTGUN NEWS
GUNSMITHING PROJECTS

Editor	Robert W. Hunnicutt
Group Art Director	David Kleckner
Art Director	Bill Smalley
Designers	Ashley Dale
	Luke Bouris
	Kelly McCarty
Photographer	Mike Anschuetz
Production Manager	Terry Boyer

Shotgun News Gunsmithing Projects

First Edition
Second Printing

ISBN: 1-934622-54-0

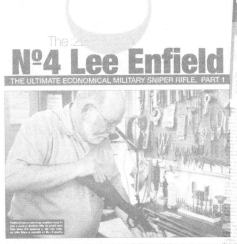

Restore that Military Rifle!

Whether it's for fun or profit, you can turn that beat-up old military surplus rifle into an attractive piece of military history.

By Steven Matthews

Matthews says good-looking surplus guns can be enjoyed on a lunchpail budget if you are willing to do the work yourself. It can be rewarding and fun as well as cheap!

The first thing you notice when you get interested in military surplus firearms is that most of them are really beat up. They generally are scraped, dinged, dirty and have seen years of abuse. If you are looking for military surplus guns in good to excellent condition, they are few and far between.

On those rare occasions when they can be found in good shape, fine guns can command prices two to three times the cost of one in typical condition. I have been collecting for more than 25 years and have found only a few in really good shape that I could afford on my industrial mechanic's wages. This poses a problem for me since I am the kind who likes good-looking guns but am really frugal with a dollar.

Fortunately, I am also the kind of collector who values condition over originality. I prefer a nice-looking refinished gun to a well-worn one in original condition. I don't care about cartouches, original bluing or wood finish; I want one that looks nice.

A lot of "true collectors" really look down on this type of collecting, since it isn't historically accurate. However, the marketplace has indicated that there is a market for good condition refinished guns. There are a multitude of companies out there that refinish military arms.

Some will restore to original condition with traditional methods and others will use modern economical methods to return them to very attractive firearms that may not be historically accurate but still look good and appeal to many less discriminating collectors. I believe there is room in the collecting market for both types.

The economical solution to this problem for me has been the do-it-yourself refinish option, since I won't pay someone else to do what I can do for free. I have refined some basic refinishing methods down to the bare essentials to return these average-condition guns to very good-looking examples. For very little expense that old warhorse of yours can be returned to its former glory!

The methods I use will allow you to refinish a military surplus arm to good shape for as little as $25 if you can do a couple things to spread out the cost.

At this point I should mention I am not advocating refinishing historically significant and rare guns but only basic run-of-the-mill military surplus guns that were made in great numbers and

are readily available. You don't want to ruin the value of something like an all-original M1D Garand that is worth many times the price of a common example Garand. Leave those rare and desirable guns alone and focus on the common ones.

When looking for a gun to restore/refinish you must learn to look past the scrapes, dings and grunge and look at what lies beneath that rough exterior. When most dealers place military surplus guns on display, they generally just take them out of the box and put them out.

It just isn't economically feasible for these dealers to put any work or effort into these guns, since the profit margin just isn't there. This can work to your advantage, because somewhere in almost all those guns is a diamond in the rough.

It's important to pick a suitable gun for refinishing, since not all are good candidates for refinishing. In the last 25 years, I have probably refinished 50–75 guns using these methods and have refined it down to the bare minimum effort that will produce excellent results.

I can restore an average military surplus gun to good shape with only about two to four hours of total time invested, and so can you if you follow my methods. They may not be traditional, but they do work. I have kept most of the guns I have refinished for my own collection, but I have sold a few, and almost every time I sell one, the prospective buyer comments on how good it looks.

It isn't unusual to double your money when selling if you did a good job. This little bit of profit can then be used to further your collecting efforts.

Only certain firearms are suitable candidates for refinishing and must meet some minimum standards to be worth the effort. It makes no sense to put a lot of work into a gun, only to sell it for the same price. Here are the things I look for when buying a surplus gun.

1. The very most important issue to me is bore condition. If it doesn't have a good shiny bore with sharp rifling, all else doesn't matter. Rough stocks and exterior metal finish can be corrected, but a bad bore is reason to avoid a gun. Rebarreling a cheap military surplus gun is not economically feasible. The only exception to this may be a case where it is a very difficult model to find and you are primarily interested in it for display

purposes rather than actually shooting it. If you want a nice wall-hanger go ahead, but don't buy one for resale, as any gun with a bad barrel will never have good resale value.

2. Make sure it is complete! This may seem to be obvious but even small parts missing can drive up the cost. A simple screw on some of the more uncommon guns can cost several dollars after you pay shipping and handling charges. Replacing a major component such as a bolt, trigger assembly or a magazine is usually cost-prohibitive. A perfect example here is a Russian SVT40 rifle I saw for sale that had the magazine missing. The dealer had it discounted a few dollars since the mag was missing. What the dealer didn't say or maybe didn't know was the magazines for this rifle are extremely hard to find and when they can be found, they bring $75–100! A small price reduction doesn't make up for a major expense!

3. Metal condition (bluing or Parkerizing) must meet a minimum standard to avoid the cost of complete metal refinishing. A professional hot tank rebluing can easily cost more than $100, which would be a very large part of the original purchase price on the cheaper guns. I can reblue a gun for less than $25 using an improvised hot tank bluing system I built for about $200 (see

Matthews' M1 started out as a Greek-issued M1 sold by the Civilian Marksmanship Program. It was scarred, dented and covered in 60 years' worth of grease and grime.

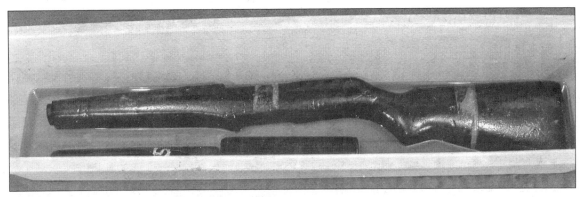

Matthews recommends a thorough dunking in mineral spirits to remove grease and oil from the rifle stock. Water-based solvents can get in the wood and cause warping.

There's often some attractive walnut lurking just beneath the grime and paint. Careful chemical stripping and wood repair can make it look factory-new again.

August 10), but unless you have a complete bluing system, the cost to have someone else do it is prohibitive. I recommend at least 75% finish remaining. With that amount of finish remaining it can be touched up with cold blue and still look acceptable if you do a good job. Stay away from guns with rust and pitting, as the work involved to remove pits and refinish isn't worth the effort. *Very* light rust that hasn't caused pitting may be acceptable, but keep it at a minimum.

4. Stock condition is probably the easiest to restore. Greasy, dented, dinged, scraped and dirty stocks can refinish very well if they aren't extremely bad. Stay away from cracked or broken stocks, unless the faults are minor. Minor cracks can be repaired; big ones will greatly affect value even if repaired. One thing I look for in stocks that I am going to refinish is "fat stocks." Manufacturing tolerances mean some stocks are slightly larger than others and these give you a little more room to work with. Any stock that is slim enough that a little wood removal will cause it to look "thin" should be avoided.

5. *Price!* If you are obtaining them for your own collection, price isn't so much an issue as if you are buying them for resale. If you want to resell, you have to buy them cheap enough that you still make money when your time and costs are figured in. I have bought Mosin-Nagants for as little as $40 and resold them for $120, which is a marginal profit for your time unless your time isn't worth much (sometimes mine isn't!). On the other hand, I have bought M1 Garands for $300 and after four hours' work resold them for $625, which *is* worth the effort. The laws of economics apply to guns just as anything else, buy low and sell high!

Do recall that if you buy and sell guns often, you can cross over into what the BATFE regards as "engaging in the business" and may need to think about getting an FFL. I recommend you keep it very safely on the side of "hobby level". If you are setting up and selling at gun shows, selling several per month, taking orders for future sales, printing business cards, etc., you may be considered by the authorities to be dealing in firearms without a license.

For the purposes of this article, I have chosen a surplus rifle that has the reputation of being one of the rougher guns on the surplus market. I obtained a Greek-issue (but U.S.-made) M1 Garand from the Civilian Marksmanship Program (website odcmp.com) for $295. These M1s are mechanically sound, but have suffered years of abuse from Greek soldiers way beyond what is tolerated by most military services.

The stocks are especially rough, and it isn't unusual to have the soldier's initials carved in the wood. Metal finish usually

runs from 50–80%. I found one that wasn't too bad, but it still looked pretty rough (see picture). The big selling point of these rifles is that no matter how bad they look, they are functional. Even in this condition, it did have potential.

Once you have found a suitable candidate for restoration/ refinishing, you are going to need some basic tools and supplies. Listed below are some of the items needed for my style of refinish job.

• Large assortment of sandpaper, 100-, 150- and 220-grit
• 1/2 or 1/3 sheet electric finishing sander. This is the most valuable and timesaving tool I have ever had for stock refinishing. With coarse paper, it will remove material fast and with fine it will gently smooth the wood. The large flat work area will allow you to remove material without gouging and dishing out the wood as you would with a disc or belt type sander. It also keeps you from rounding off edges and corners like you would by hand sanding. With practice you will get to the point where you can remove just the right amount of material and only have to do a minimal amount of hand sanding.
• A good set of gunsmithing screwdrivers for disassembling the rifles. Common screwdrivers may get you by, but some of the very thin slots found on gun screws will be very difficult to remove with common screwdrivers.
• 36-inch planter or window box or any other long, narrow container to hold solvents to clean your stocks and rifle actions. It needs to be made of material that will stand the solvents that you will be using.
• Common paint thinner (mineral spirits) 1–2 gallons, 1 quart of lacquer thinner or acetone
• Oil-based stain if you want to color your wood (I do *not* recommend any water-based stains or finishes, they have never given me satisfactory results)
• Spray can of fast-dry satin polyurethane varnish
• Spray oil such as gun oil, 3-in-1, CRC Power Lube, etc.
• Oxpho-Blue Cold Blue from Brownells (brownells.com)
• Rags, Q-Tips, 0000 steel wool, 2-inch paintbrush, coat hangers for hanging parts to spray.

Now that you have your materials and gun, let's get started. You need a workbench or table someplace with adequate ventilation, since you will be using flammable solvents and varnishes. Remember *no smoking* when working with solvents, varnishes and sawdust!

First, you must disassemble the gun into its major components. All metal parts should be removed from the wood stock.

Unless it is packed with hard grease, you shouldn't have to disassemble subassemblies like bolts, triggers, etc. Place all your small parts in a suitable container because you won't believe

how easy it is to lose them. Place all your metal parts away from the work area, because we are going to do stock work first and you will be making a lot of sawdust that will stick to those oily/ greasy parts.

If your wood is very oily and greasy, you are going to have to clean/degrease it before sanding. Most military arms have been exposed to a lot of oil, so even if it doesn't look oily on the surface, it should be cleaned. Over the years the wood has absorbed a lot of oil and this will affect how your final finish dries if not removed.

There are a lot of ways to clean these stocks, but what I have found to be the easiest is to soak them in solvents. The solvents cut the oil better than most cleaners and it will also soak into the wood some and cut some of that soaked-in oil.

Fill your container with enough solvent (mineral spirits) to cover at least one side of your stock. Place your stock in the container and let it soak for a while, then scrub it with a stiff paint brush. When one side looks clean, turn it over and do the other side. If cost isn't an issue, you can substitute lacquer thinner for mineral spirits as it cuts the grunge a lot better and dries faster when done.

Just remember this it is *extremely flammable* and appropriate precautions have to be taken. Every military surplus stock I have ever done has had so much oil and grease imbedded that the

Matthews likes to look for a stock that's on the beefy side and uses a pad sander to sand out the dents and scratches. Don't remove too much stock, however.

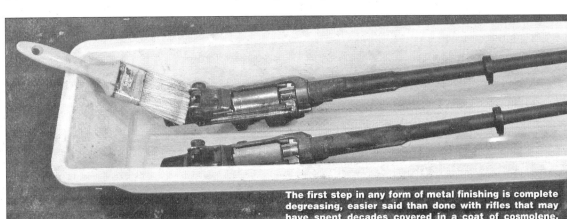

The first step in any form of metal finishing is complete degreasing, easier said than done with rifles that may have spent decades covered in a coat of cosmolene.

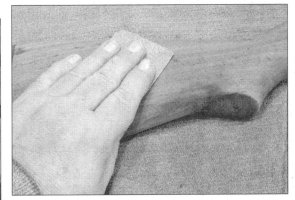

You can stop at 150-grit paper for an authentic military look, but Matthews likes to hand finish-sand with 220-grit paper for a more commercial grade of finish.

Furniture-making books won't recommend this, but Matthews likes to scrape up the solids at the bottom of the stain can and apply them directly for a thorough fill.

Matthews has written previously in these pages about hot bluing and Parkerizing, but says simple touch-up with cold blue will often do the job on most surplus rifles.

Applying cold blue with 0000 steel wool will often give a matte finish that closely resembles the original factory blue. He says color is a bit lighter this way.

Often, Matthews says, metal finish is OK except at wear points like the protective ears of this M1 rear sight. Cold blue is perfect for touching them up a bit.

solvent starts looking like root beer after a while. I specifically don't like water-based cleaners because water will penetrate into the wood; that's why I use solvents.

Water can warp the wood and raise grain and cause problems when final finishing. Water and wood just don't mix in my experience. After it is cleaned, set it aside and let it dry for a few hours. If it still looks oily, repeat the cleaning process.

After the final cleaning, I like to wipe it down with a rag heavily soaked with acetone to get any missed oil or grease. Acetone is very flammable also, so use caution (warnings are on the solvent labels) appropriate for flammable solvents. Let it dry while you work on the metal parts.

Since you have that solvent still in your cleaning container, you might as well use it for cleaning off all that grease and oil from the metal parts. Just put them in and scrub just like you did with the wood, then allow to dry. These solvents are good degreasers and really cut that hard grease. If you aren't going to do the blue touch up at this time, spray a light coat of spray oil on the parts to preserve the finish.

A lot of people don't know it, but whether it is bluing or Parkerizing, a light coating of oil is needed for maximum protection. Dry bluing or Parkerizing is not all that durable. If you are going to do the touch-up bluing, now leave them dry.

If your gun has a lot (50–75%) of bluing left, then simple touch-up will give very good results. Usually, the parts that are handled and rubbed a lot are missing bluing or Parkerizing, and this amount of handling usually means that they are worn down

to bare metal. Any rust should be removed with fine sandpaper or steel wool, because you can't touch up rust! Bright shiny metal is what you want for touch-up bluing.

There are a lot of cold blue products on the market, and I have tried most of them. After years of refinishing guns, I have found that there is one brand that stands out above the rest. For ease of use and for best results, I have found that Brownells Oxpho-Blue (brownells.com) is simply the best.

It cost no more than any of the other brands but performs better than any other I have tried. It blends well with the original bluing and also blends well with most of the darker shades of Parkerizing.

To touch up the bare metal, simply soak a Q-Tip with cold blue and rub it over the bare steel. If it doesn't turn black, you probably have a little oil left on the metal and using some acetone on a rag will remove it.

An alternative to using a Q-Tip is to soak a small piece of 0000 steel wool in bluing solution and then lightly rub the bare steel. I have found that when using the steel wool method that the color is lighter but if you want it darker, just rub the part with some more bluing on a Q-Tip and it will darken more.

Don't worry about getting bluing solution on the old finish, as it won't harm the original blue or change its color. When you get the color you want, wipe off all remaining bluing solution and apply a light coating of oil to the reblued area. Continue to touch up all the other bare spots and when done give all your metal a light coating of oil to preserve it.

You will also notice that the original and touched-up parts look a lot better with a little oil on them. If you are cold bluing a larger part such as a buttplate, I have found that slightly heating the part and using the steel wool method seems to give more even and attractive finish than using the Q-Tip method.

After you have the whole part done, you can rub it with more solution on a small rag to darken it some more if it's not dark enough for your taste. I recommend being gentle with your parts while still "fresh."

It seems to me that the cold blue increases its durability after it has aged a few days. If you have done a good job, your metal should look a lot better than when you started. It won't look like

a professional hot tank reblue job, but it should look pretty good for a military surplus gun.

Now is the time to turn your attention to the stock. Since the stock is the largest part of the gun, the better it looks, the better the project will look when finished. A lot of military stocks are walnut, and once you get though all the overlying crud, there is usually pretty good wood underneath. Even stocks made from beech, maple, birch and even Chinese Chu wood can look good after staining and refinishing.

Since I am basically lazy, I prefer to use power tools such as the finishing sander; it saves so much elbow grease I can't imagine sanding by hand. If your stock is really beat and dinged up, start with 80-or 100-grit, if not, start with 150-grit. Install your paper on the sander and go to work, removing all that beat-up wood. Carefully watch how much material you are removing, especially on corners or where the contours change.

You want to keep the same shape, only remove the bad wood. Only remove enough to get down to good wood. Be especially careful sanding in areas where parts have to fit back on, only remove minimal amounts here. *Always keep the sander moving.* This is important to keep from sanding flat spots.

A certain amount of skill is required to operate a sander well, and only experience will give you the ability to do good work. One thing you will notice is that when you sand these stocks, the sandpaper will load up quickly due to the dirt, oil and grunge imbedded in the wood. Just change the paper when it gets too dirty to sand well.

Sandpaper is relatively cheap, so don't be afraid to pitch it when it gets loaded up. If you aren't sure of your abilities, practice on some scrap wood before starting on the stock. Take your time and only remove small amounts of wood until you have developed the skills needed.

Remember, if you don't take off enough, you can always remove more, but you can't put it back on if you took off too much! If you started with a coarse grade of paper, go to finer grades and go over it again until you get the finish you want.

Most military arms are on sanded with 150-grit, so you may want to stop with 150 for the most original look. But if you want a smoother finish, go to 220 for final sanding. I usually finish up by going over the whole stock with a quick hand sanding.

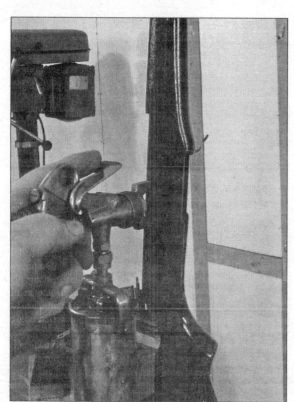

While hand-rubbed oil would be the normal choice for finishing a military stock, Matthews likes the convenience of satin polyurethane, applied with a spray gun.

The result? What looked like an old junker has a new lease of life after less than four hours of work. It's more fun to use, and will bring a lot higher price.

A lot of stocks will have dents and scrapes that are very deep, and these can't be removed by sanding. There are methods to deal with these problem areas, some of which were detailed by Reid Coffield in these pages. See the SGN special edition *Mausers*, coming in December, for those articles.

I think it doesn't hurt a military surplus stock to retain some of these minor imperfections to give it a little "character." If it's too shiny and devoid of imperfections, it just doesn't look like a military stock to me. so I leave a few dents and dings as badges of honor that reflect its past history of military use.

As a final step, I recommend wiping down again with a acetone-soaked rag to remove any oil that has found its way to the surface.

If your completely sanded stock isn't the color you want. you will now have to stain it. I prefer a little red color in my military stocks, so I use a mahogany stain. If this is used on walnut, it gives a pleasing red tint to the wood. You just rub on the stain with a rag and wipe off the excess.

One tip I have for applying stain is to use it unmixed. The solids that have settled to the bottom of the can stain a lot better than when it is mixed with the oil that has separated from the solids. Just scrape it off the bottom of the can, smear it on a rag and apply.

Your stock probably already has enough oil in it, so why put on more? If it comes out too dark, just dampen a rag with mineral spirits and rub down the stock to remove a little color. One

other benefit is that with less oil applied, the stain dries faster so you can go to the final finishing sooner.

Lots of military stocks have multiple wood colors, whether from repair inlays or from the fact they were originally made from two or more boards. Japanese Arisakas are most noted for that. The staining process is a good time to even up colors among the different pieces. Once you have finished staining, I recommend letting the wood dry for a day before applying any sprayed-on finishes.

There are many methods for a final finish. The traditional finish for most military stocks is boiled linseed oil rubbed into the stock. There are some who really prefer this method, but it does have some disadvantages such as having to apply many hand rubbed coats, *very* slow drying times and poor sealing.

If a stock is stained, boiled linseed doesn't lock the stain in well, either. Some of the more modern finishes such as tung oils and Tru Oil are considerably more durable and seal better. I prefer a very untraditional finish that when applied looks almost the same as the other finishes with a lot less work.

I prefer satin polyurethane varnish. Simply spray one or two light coats and you have a fast finish that looks almost the same as tung oil or a hand rubbed linseed oil finish without all the work. You only want one or two light coats, as more than that will cause it to start looking somewhat synthetic and painted-on.

You only want enough to seal the wood lightly, but not to fill the pores. I have also found that leaving the pores open allows any trapped oil a way out without lifting the finish if you do a lot of shooting that heats the wood enough to cause the remaining oil to come to the surface.

This gives a suitably dull finish that has the benefits of easy application yet looks appropriate for military wood. I use automotive type spray equipment but simple spray cans will give excellent results without the need for expensive equipment.

If possible, get a spray-on polyurethane finish that is listed as "fast dry," since if a finish stays wet on the wood long, it can draw the oils remaining in the stock to the surface and cause the finish not to dry properly.

I have found over the years that some stocks, no matter how much you clean and degrease, still seep oil from a few places no matter what you do. I have found fast-dry lacquer to be a better option for oily wood, since it dries so fast that as long as the

wood is dry when you start, it doesn't draw oil out of the wood. After you have the stock finish sprayed on, let it dry for a few days before reassembly.

If you have done a good job with the wood refinishing and the metal finish touch-up, once you reassemble the gun you should have something that looks so good that it is hard to believe it's the same gun. I have used this method to refinish a lot of military surplus guns and am always amazed at how good the guns look when done.

Of course, your results will depend on your skill level. I have been doing this for 25 years and it did take a few tries before I was proficient at it. Your first try may not be perfect, but with practice it will become easier each time. Once you get the hang of this, you can expect to put only two to four hours of work into a rifle to obtain these results.

I usually do a couple rifles at a time and it cuts down on the time and amount of supplies used. Most of the rifles I have reworked with this method I have kept for my own collection, but I have sold a few of them and am almost always complimented on how good the rifles look. I have tried to sell unrestored guns in the past, but I have found that restored guns always bring more and are easier to sell.

The "true collectors" always say they want the unrestored gun, but I always get more for restored arms than for guns that are beat up and grungy! Whether for your own collection or for resale, they should look good, and this method will allow you to make them look good with a minimum amount of work.

Restoring those beat up old clunkers to beautiful pieces of military history can be very enjoyable, so have fun! ◎

Screw Slot Blues

By Reid Coffield

So Junior turned a sharp slot into a ragged gash with this 79¢ Chinese screwdriver? Fix it like new with these Coffield tips.

Of all the metal parts on a gun, screws are the most likely to be damaged. This is caused in part by the design of screws and how they are made. Screws used in most firearms traditionally have a slot in the top or head for a screwdriver blade.

This transverse slot is, more often than not, fairly narrow with parallel vertical sides. This leads to a problem in that many folks unintentionally damage these screws by using screwdrivers that do not match the screw slots.

Traditional standard U.S. screwdrivers have tapered blades. That's great if your screw slot is also tapered, but keep in mind that most of our gun screws have slots with *parallel* vertical sides. The sides of the slots are the same distance apart at the bottom as at the top.

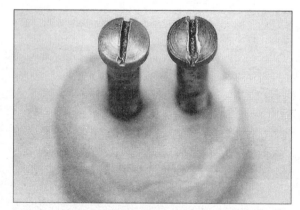

These are typical gun screws that show evidence of damage from a tapered screwdriver blade. Note the ugly raised burrs along either side of the screw slot.

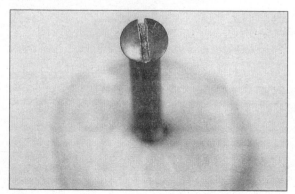

This Remington 700 guard screw can easily be restored to a "factory new" condition with just a bit of work. Again, note the small raised burrs inside the slot.

A standard tapered screwdriver blade, being narrower at the tip than further up the blade, cannot possibly provide a good uniform fit to the screw slot. Generally, only a single point somewhere on the side of the screwdriver blade tip actually contacts the edge of the screw head slot. This means that all the force or torque applied to the screwdriver by the user is transferred to that one small area on the edge of the screw head slot. Invariably the edge of the screw slot will be mashed or distorted.

In addition, the wedge shape of traditional screwdrivers causes the screwdriver to want to cam up and out of the screw slot as turning pressure is applied to the screw. When you think of it, the head or tip of the screwdriver is a ramp or inclined plane that will always want to climb up and out of the screw slot.

That's why we always apply a lot of downward pressure as we use these traditional types of screwdrivers. I could be wrong about this but it seems to me that I have to apply just about as much downward pressure as turning pressure to keep the traditional screwdriver in the screw head slot.

A gunsmith's screwdriver, on the other hand, has a tip with parallel sides so it matches the parallel vertical sides of the screw head slot. These parallel sides transfer energy or force to the screw in a much more controlled and efficient manner. With a properly fitted blade, the turning force is applied evenly to the entire side of the screw slot; from top to bottom.

There is no one single point as with a standard screwdriver tip that is the focus of all the pressure or turning force. This virtually eliminates the possibility of distortion of the top edges of the screw slot. Also, since the gunsmith screwdriver tips have parallel sides that match the corresponding parallel sides of the screw head slot, there is no tendency for the bit to ride up and out of the screw. This makes these screwdrivers easier and safer to use.

Gunsmith screwdrivers are available from a variety of sources. Both MidwayUSA and Brownells offer a number of different brands and a variety of screwdriver set sizes. You can pay anywhere from about $15 to more than $180 for a screwdriver set. MidwayUSA 5875 W. Van Horn Tavern Road, Dept. SGN, Columbia, Mo. 65203, telephone 1-800-243-3220, probably offers the largest number of different brands and sets of gunsmith screwdrivers. If you don't already have a good set of screwdrivers, check with these folks. I'd be willing to bet that they can fix you up with a set that will meet both your needs and your pocketbook.

Typically the damage most often seen with screws is distortion of the top edge of the slot. Metal from the edge of the slot may be forced up higher than the rest of the surface of the screw head, resulting is an ugly ragged ridge of metal. You will also often see where metal along the edge of the screw slot has been torn or chipped away as a wedge-shaped screwdriver tip slipped out of the slot.

Needless to say, this damage is unsightly and can potentially be so severe as to make it impossible to turn the screw in or out.

For most of us, this damage is just something you have to live with if you can't replace the screw. If it's an older gun that's no longer in production and replacement parts are not readily available, then there's little that can be done. My friends, that's not necessarily true. With just a little work you can often salvage these damaged screws. Even if you can't remove all traces of the damage, you can certainly make the screw head look a heck of a lot better.

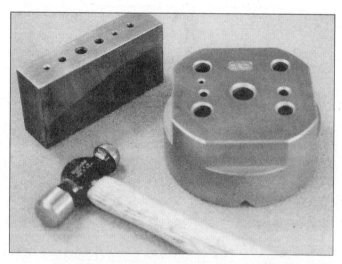

Very little equipment is required for repair of most screws. A good 4-ounce ball peen hammer and a bench block or fixture for holding the screw is just about all you need.

Fortunately very little is required for this type of work. One of the most important tools you will need is a standard 4-ounce ball peen hammer. If you're doing gun work you probably already have one. If not, you might want to add one to your tool collection. It's important that the face of the hammer should be as smooth as possible.

I go so far as actually to polish the face of my hammer. This helps me to get a smoother, more even surface to areas that I strike with the hammer face.

The next item you will need is a means to support the screws while working on 'em. I have made up a simple fixture that is no more than a block of steel with holes drilled in it of various diameters to accept the threaded shanks of screws. Some machinist bench blocks can also be used as they often have suitable holes drilled in the top surface.

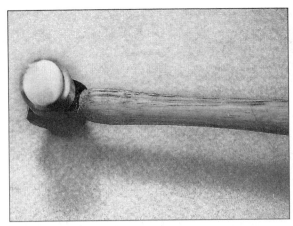

Coffield keeps at hand a 4-ounce ball peen hammer with a highly polished face just for screw repair. The hammer's polished face won't transfer marks to the screw head.

If you work on screws that have the underside of the head flat at 90° to the shank of the screw, a simple hole drilled in a piece of flat steel will work fine. However, if you're working on screws where the underside of the head is tapered, you'll need to have a corresponding tapered hole to properly support the screw head.

Repairing the screw is really quite simple. With the screw placed in our fixture with the head supported, the ball peen hammer is used to carefully swage the displaced metal back into its original location. This doesn't take a lot of force. A series of light, overlapping taps will normally do the trick. Always keep the face of the hammer moving over the surface of the head of the screw. If you strike the screw in just one spot you will more often than not create a flat that will stand out on a curved screw head like a sore thumb! So....keep that hammer moving!

Once you have hammered or swaged the displaced metal back into place on the edge of the slot, you are ready to do a bit of cleanup work. In some instances you may find that the top of the slot has been slightly narrowed by the peening. This can be corrected by opening the slot up with a modified hacksaw blade, a flat-sided jeweler's needle file, or specially made screw slot files.

This simple screw-holding fixture is just a steel block with a series of different sized holes drilled into it. It provides support for the head while peening.

A hacksaw blade will often do a great job, but you'll normally need to do a bit of modification work on it. On some hacksaw blades the cutting teeth are "set". This means that alternating teeth are bent to the right or left. This is important in that it makes sure the slot the blade cuts is slightly wider than the blade and this makes it easier for the blade to move through the steel.

That's fine for most uses, but on screw slots we generally want our slots to be fairly narrow. You'll want to measure an undamaged part of the screw slot to determine the actual width. Check the width of your hacksaw blade at the teeth. More often than not the blade will be wider than needed for the slot.

To correct this, just take your hacksaw blade over to a belt or disk sander or even to your grinding wheel and carefully remove

With the holding fixture secured in his vise, Coffield carefully works over the damaged screw head. Steady soft taps get the job done; bashing will flatten the head.

the "set" from one or both sides of the blade. You will actually have quite a bit of leeway in modifying the cutting width of the blade.

If you do use this modified hacksaw blade to recut the screw slot, do so carefully. Make darn sure that the blade is positioned so it matches the position of the slot. You definitely don't want to enlarge the slot or cut through the slot at an angle.

So far, so good! Our screw looks a lot better than it did but it still will need some work. The finish on the head of the screw has by necessity been ruined. Rather than just dabbing on some cold blue, we will want to polish it first.

Just as many screws are ruined by bad screwdrivers, a lot of other screws are ruined by improper polishing. I almost never polish the head of a screw on a buffing wheel. Generally when a screw is placed against a buffing wheel the edges of the slot, which we have worked so darn hard to restore and preserve, will be polished away. This can happen in an instant; almost faster than the blink of an eye.

I've found that I can do much better work by polishing my screws in my drill press or in an electric hand drill. Not only will I preserve the edges of the screw slot, I can if needed duplicate the original manufacturing machine marks that were on the screw head. I don't know where I first learned of this technique but over the years it has saved me many hours of work and lots of replaced screws.

All you need to do is first wrap the threaded shank of the screw with some tape to protect the threads from the jaws of the drill chuck. Once that is done, place the screw in the drill chuck with just the screw head protruding.

Next place a small piece of cloth-backed abrasive on a flat piece of soft wood such as pine. I generally have a scrap of 2x4 or similar material laying around the shop for this. Position this piece of

wood directly under the drill chuck. A drop or two of cutting oil on the abrasive where the screw head will contact it is very helpful and will give you a better polish.

Turning rate of the drill is not all that critical. Any moderate speed will do just fine. All you do is turn the drill on and lower the screw head on to the wood-backed abrasive. Use just enough downward pressure on the quill to crush or indent the wood slightly under the abrasive.

This helps to mold the abrasive to fit the curvature of the head of the screw. This is especially important when dealing with a slightly domed or rounded screw head. If the screw head is flat, then you will not need to apply as much downward pressure.

The turning of the screw head in the drill will quickly and uniformly polish it without any damage to the sides of the screw slot. I generally use a 120- or higher grit cloth-backed abrasive. If the screw was originally highly polished, I might go as high as 400-grit or so.

If you do need to put a high polish on the screw head be sure to work your way up through the various grits starting at, say, 120 and then moving up a step at a time to the next higher grit. This will actually save time and give you a much better, more uniform polish. Skipping grits will almost always result in scratches or grit marks left on the screw head.

There is one situation where you might want to leave some grit marks on a screw. Many factory screws still have circular machine marks on the surface of the head. If you are repairing one of these screws you may not want to remove all these machine marks, especially if you are trying to restore the gun or match the original metal finish.

In that case, you can duplicate machine marks by simply using a slightly coarser abrasive. A 60- or 80-grit abrasive

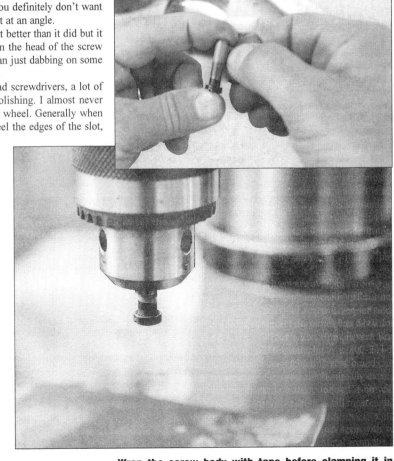

Wrap the screw body with tape before clamping it in the chuck to protect the threads. Then cloth press the head against cloth-backed abrasive on a soft pine board.

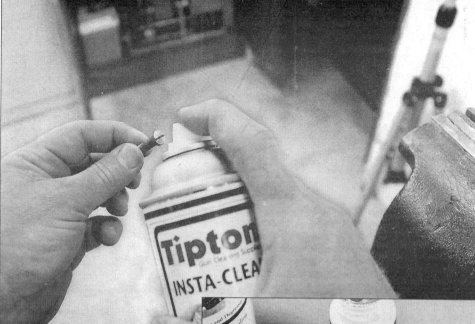

The screw head creates a dimple in the abrasive as it is pressed down. The soft pine board compresses, preserving the original shape or curvature of the screw head.

will often leave grit marks that virtually duplicate these machine marks.

Once the screw head has been polished, clean the screw head with a suitable solvent to remove all traces of cutting oil and abrasive. I generally use Tipton's Insta Clean Solvent that I get from MidwayUSA. You could also use solvents such as Gun Scrubber or even carburetor cleaner. The important thing here is to clean the screw head thoroughly. Make sure that the screw slot

is not packed with abrasive or cutting oil. If it is, use a toothpick or scribe to clean all that out.

With the screw cleaned, you can then blue it. On a small part like this, a cold blue will generally do the trick and provide a good uniform color that is acceptable. I would caution you not to simply drop the screw in the cold blue bottle.

There are two problems with this. First, if you do this you will fairly quickly contaminate your cold blue and ruin it. I have often wondered how often we have blamed a cold blue for not working when in reality we have contaminated it by dumping parts into the bottle. It is *always* best to use a clean Q-Tip or swab to apply just

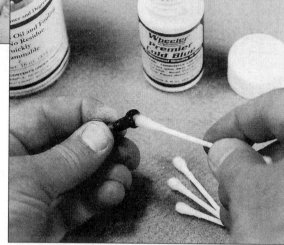

After cleaning and degreasing with a solvent, Coffield uses cotton swabs to apply Wheeler Engineering Premier Cold Blue to the screw head, completing the repair.

a small amount of cold blue to the screw head. Once the swab has been used once, don't allow it to go back into the bottle. Always use a fresh swab. This will help you to get a better color with your cold blue and make your cold blue last a lot longer.

There is also a second problem that can arise with dropping a part in the cold blue bottle. Virtually all cold blues have some type of acid in the solution. Some have more than others. If a part is just dropped in the bottle and left there, you may well find that the acid in the cold blue will literally attack the steel and create pits in the surface.

I hate to admit it, but I learned this lesson the hard way! It was quite a shock to pull a screw I had spent quite a bit of time making on my lathe out of the bottle looking like it was 100 years old!

This peening and polishing procedure will take care of most damaged screws. Occasionally you will find one that has so much metal torn from around the slot that more drastic procedures are required. From time to time I have had to use a file to cut down or lower the surface of the head of the screw to get below any damage. This can sometimes be done if the location of the screw is such that the thickness or height of the screw head is not critical. Once the filing has been completed, you then just polish and blue as you normally would.

In other extreme cases it might be necessary to weld up the screw head to repair it. If welding is done, keep in mind that you may have softened the screw and compromised its strength. If it's just a wood screw holding on a buttplate or trigger guard that may not be an issue. If, on the other hand, it's an action screw or a screw on which there is considerable stress, welding could cause problems.

For most of us, the vast majority of problem screws can be repaired with just a bit of peening and polishing. Screw slot repair is admittedly a little job but it can have a major effect on the overall appearance of a firearm.

Until next time, good luck and good gunsmithing!

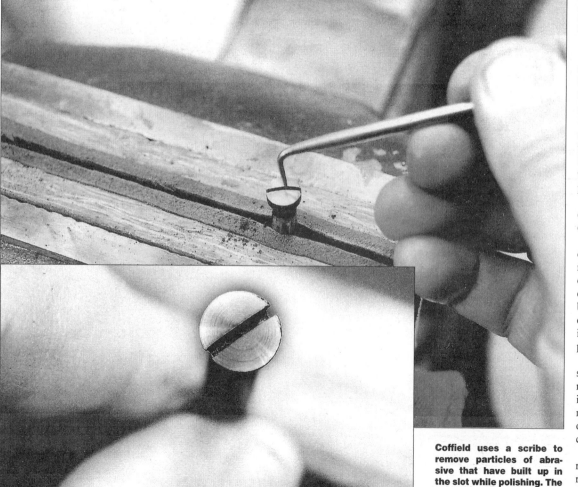

Coffield uses a scribe to remove particles of abrasive that have built up in the slot while polishing. The repaired screw head shows no signs of the earlier burrs.

Cutting and Crowning a Rifle Barrel

By Reid Coffield

Barrel crowns come in many forms, but all exist to protect the rifling. A recessed target crown can normally only be cut with a lathe. It allows easy inspection of the lands and grooves. The barrel of an M1A has a flat crown similar to the target crowns, but the flash suppressor must be removed to inspect for wear or damage. Many older 19th century rifles had flat crowns, like this very early octagon-barreled Winchester Model 94. The sporter crown of this Remington 700 barrel is the most common crown used on a typical hunting rifle.

Gunsmiths use a lathe for this job, but with a hacksaw and a few other tools, you can shorten barrels at home.

If you do an even modest amount of work with rifles, sooner or later you will need to cut or shorten a barrel. There can be any number of reasons for doing this. It may be that a shorter barrel would make for a handier more useful rifle. About the only thing a long rifle barrel has going for it with fast burning modern powders is a longer sight radius. Of course this is only applicable if iron sights are used.

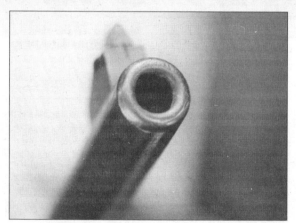

This Mauser 98 exhibits typical cleaning rod wear at the 3 o'clock position cause by cleaning from the muzzle. This barrel definitely needs to be cut and crowned.

The only other advantage I can think of for a long barrel is that you will experience a bit less muzzle blast when the rifle is fired. That may sound a bit odd, but with some of the super magnums; muzzle blast can be a major consideration.

As for accuracy, longer barrels are generally no more accurate than shorter barrels. In fact, some authorities make the case for shorter barrels being a bit stiffer and less prone to movement as they heat up. This generally means the shorter barrels will deliver more consistent and tighter groups.

In any event, there are countless reasons for cutting back a rifle barrel. It can be done because of damage to the bore or to the muzzle. It might also be necessary to cut a barrel to remove a sight or device such as a muzzle brake or flash hider. Whatever the reasons, barrels will need to be shortened from time to time.

When a barrel is cut, the muzzle end is shaped in such a way as to ensure that the point where the rifling terminates is both uniform and protected. Generally the end of the rifling is recessed. Most or part of the face or end of the muzzle is higher

than the rifling and forms a projection or crown that protects the rifling. Crowns can be of a wide variety of shapes or contours. Each style has its advantages and its proponents.

Generally most professional gunsmiths will use a lathe to cut a barrel and then to shape the crown. If you were to ask the average gunsmith why he uses a lathe for this, he would probably respond that it is the best way to obtain the most accurate and precise crown. There is some truth in this. A lathe will make cutting and crowning a barrel much faster and easier for the person doing the work but it will not necessarily give you a crown that is "more accurate."

The reality is that you can cut and crown a barrel with nothing more than simple hand tools. As for accuracy, we need to understand something about barrels first. If a barrel has internal stresses, a poorly cut chamber, a bad or oversized bore, or improperly cut lands and grooves, the best crown in the world will not make that barrel shoot accurately!

A crown is either neutral or it will diminish accuracy. A crown in and of itself will not make a "bad" barrel into a good one! True, there are good barrels with bad crowns and when those crowns are replaced the good barrels can then really perform. But you can also have bad barrels with perfectly cut crowns and those barrels are still worthless! A new crown is not an automatic or guaranteed means of making a rifle more accurate.

Another point that is often misunderstood is the effect of a damaged muzzle or crown on accuracy. It is generally assumed that any type of burr or irregularity at the muzzle is detrimental to accuracy. I know that I may well be hung in effigy for saying this, but a damaged crown is not always detrimental to accuracy.

I can hear the screams now and I am certain that there will be outraged letters to follow. Be that as it may, based on what I have seen and experienced as a gunsmith, a slightly damaged crown has not always meant that accuracy was affected. I remember a couple of rifles where there were noticeable burrs or dings in the muzzle. The owners had seen them and wanted me to recrown their barrels. No problem with that.

In the first instance, when I asked about the accuracy the owner indicated that the rifle shot very well. That got my curiosity up and I test fired the rifle before doing any work on it. Sure enough, the rifle printed its group in a nice little cluster. I don't recall what the actual group size was, but it was small for that particular type of rifle.

I contacted the owner about this but he wanted me to go ahead and recrown the barrel anyway so I cut and crowned the barrel and shot the rifle again to check for group size. There was no difference! The only change was in the point of impact. With the new crown the rifle shot about an inch or so, as best I remember,

away from the original point of impact. Again the group size was the same.

The same thing happened with another rifle not too long after this first instance. Again the damage to the crown was not severe, but it certainly was noticeable and did extend into the rifling.

The lesson for me was that just because a crown looked bad, it did not necessarily have to be replaced. Granted, the far majority of barrels I have recrowned have needed it and the new crowns have almost always enhanced accuracy. But there are always exceptions to any rule and if it had not been for a bit of luck, I would simply have recrowned these rifles and never been the wiser. You might want to keep this in mind as you cut and crown barrels.

OK you say, just how do you tell if you should recrown a barrel? Obviously if there is major damage to the muzzle there should be no question about this. If you see numerous pits, scratches, or dents extending into the rifling, cut that barrel and recrown it!

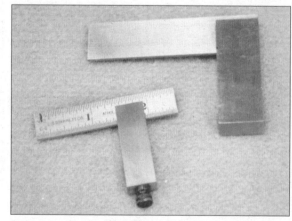

The most essential tool for cutting and crowning a barrel is a machinist's square like the non-adjustable square and small Starrett adjustable square shown.

Another type of damage that is sometimes a bit more difficult to spot initially is muzzle wear due to cleaning rod abrasion. Not everyone cleans a rifle from the breech, or if that is not possible, uses a rod guide at the muzzle. Consequently, the cleaning rod is allowed to rub against the end of the rifling as it is pulled back and forth when cleaning the bore. The end of the bore at the muzzle can literally be worn away.

For many years I thought this was just something I would see in older military rifles where soldiers were using jointed steel rods under less than ideal conditions. The rods would sometimes pick up sand or dirt and this mixed with oil created a slurry that was ideal for cutting steel. Unfortunately the steel being cut was at the muzzle of the rifle.

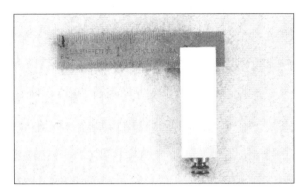

The knurled nut on the bottom of the moveable leg of the Starrett square allows it to be moved along the rule. A useful square can be bought for as little as $10.

After gunsmithing for a few years I learned that this type of damage was not limited to just old military rifles. I have seen quite a few civilian rifles, mostly lever-actions and semi-automatics, where the end of the barrel bore was slightly tapered or sometimes ovaled and the rifling was worn away at the muzzle. The damage to the barrels was due entirely to improper use of a cleaning rod.

This type of damage can be obvious or it can be subtle. One darn good way of spotting this is to use a plug or pin gauge. When I first opened my shop I was strapped for cash, so I couldn't buy all the tools and items I wanted. I remember considering a pin gauge set, which consists of a series of precisely ground pins about 2 inches long ranging in size from .061" to .250" and from .251" to .500" in increments of .001". At that time I thought these sets were just too limited in their usefulness and also they were too darn expensive.

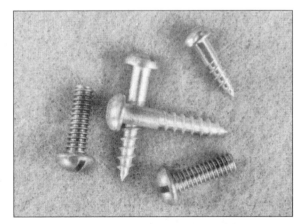

Simple brass round head machine or wood screws, readily available at any hardware store, can be used to lap the edge of the lands and grooves on a muzzle.

After many years I finally got a set, and believe me, they have been incredibly useful especially for barrel work. Also with the importation of Chinese-made tooling, they are not all that expensive. Since the pins are sized in increments of .001", it is easy to first find a pin that will just slip into the bore. That is the basic measurement of the bore size or distance from the top of one land to the opposite land.

While you have the pin gauge in the muzzle look at the end of the rifling to see if it terminates evenly all the way around the pin. If there has been cleaning rod damage, it will not be even, and with a bit of light and perhaps a magnifying glass, you will easily see this.

Another darn handy use of pin gauges is to check for tight spots in the bore. To do this, first make sure the bore is clean. Then just take the pin gauge that is the largest that will slide easily into the bore and carefully and ever so slowly gently push it through the bore with a wooden dowel. If you have a tight spot of at least a .001", the gauge will stop.

For goodness sake, *do not* try to push the gauge on through! Immediately insert the dowel from the opposite end of the barrel and remove the gauge. If you pick up a set of pin gauges and check out a number of barrels I would be willing to bet that you will be surprised at some of the things you discover.

For example, in several rifles I have found tight spots caused by sight screws that were literally pushing down into the bore. The screw holes did not extend into the bore and there was no visible irregularity when viewed through the bore. The screw holes were so close to the bore that when the screws were tightened they actually caused the wall of the bore to bulge inward.

I have also seen several M1As where the gas cylinder lock was on so tight that the barrel was literally constricted. I have also seen a few revolvers where the threaded shank of the barrel was constricted by frames that were too tight, and consequently the bore was constricted right beyond the forcing cone. All of these unusual situations were discovered or verified with pin gauges. Needless to say, none of these conditions were conducive to accuracy!

Having decided to cut a rifle barrel and recrown it, the first thing you need to do is make sure that it is unloaded. I know that sounds dumb but believe me, loaded rifles will show up where you least expect them. Check every firearm to ensure that it is unloaded before you do any gunsmithing work. It takes only a minute and it can literally save your life.

Next I would encourage you to disassemble the rifle so that you are dealing only with the barreled action. It will make your work easier and you run less chance of accidentally damaging other components.

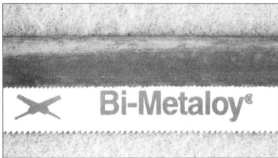

When you cut a barrel don't just grab that hacksaw you used last for cutting rusty pipe! The cut will be smoother and faster with a brand-new, lightly-oiled blade.

Clamp the barrel in a horizontal position in a padded vise. At approximately the point where you wish to cut the barrel, wrap some masking tape around the barrel. This will allow you to have a surface on which you can make marks with a pen or pencil that will be readily visible.

Coffield has found a pin gauge set to be very useful in his shop when doing barrel work. Imported sets of this type can often be purchased for less than $75.

I might add here that there are legal limits as to how short a rifle barrel can be. According to the information I have from the federal boys, you can not have a rifle with a barrel length of less than 16 inches. That, my friends, is darn short and in most high-powered rifles such as a .30-'06 would result in one hell of a muzzle blast.

The length of the barrel is measured from the face of the breech bolt in its locked position. It is not measured from the end of the receiver or necessarily from the breech end of the barrel.

I would caution anyone even contemplating cutting a minimum-length barrel to assume that any authority that might someday measure that barrel would have a ruler that was slightly worn or inaccurate. Consequently it would make sense to me to always have your barrel at least a half-inch longer than the absolute legal minimum. It certainly won't make that much difference in how the gun handles, etc. but that little half-inch could spell the difference between no problem and a major legal hassle.

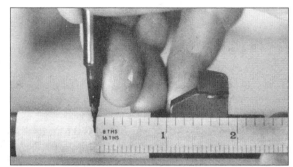

Wrap the barrel with masking tape for clear marking of the cut point. A new sharp blade properly adjusted in the hacksaw frame results in a clean, straight cut.

When you mark the spot for your cut, give yourself at least a quarter-inch for the width of the hacksaw blade and for removal of material from the muzzle in order to square it and crown it. If you want a 22-inch barrel, cut it at 22¼ inches; if you want a 24-inch barrel, cut it at 24¼ inches; etc.

Mark the spot where you want to cut the barrel with a pen or pencil on the masking tape. Make more than just one mark. In fact, it is a darn good idea to draw a line completely around the barrel. The reason for this is that it will make cutting the barrel evenly a lot easier if you have a line to guide you as you make the cut.

After marking the site of the cut, take a cleaning rod and lay it alongside the barrel from the muzzle end and have the end of the rod at least 1" below the cutting point. Make a mark on the cleaning rod shaft even with the muzzle.

A little time spent installing a fresh blade and in laying out the guideline for the cut saves a lot more time that would be required to file the muzzle flat.

Now take one or two cleaning patches and push them into the barrel from the muzzle. Push on down until your mark on the cleaning rod is even with the muzzle. Remove the rod, leaving the patches in place. These patches will serve to keep metal chips and filing from falling into the barrel and into the action as the barrel is cut and crowned.

Check the blade on your hacksaw and make sure that it is in good condition and has the proper number of teeth per inch. Generally for cutting barrels you will want a blade that has 18 teeth per inch. It is very important that the blade be in good shape. If it is like most used hacksaw blades, there will be teeth missing and the teeth that remain will be dull. If you don't have a good blade, drop by your local hardware and pick up a couple. A good blade will definitely make the job easier and it will make the cut smoother.

When you use your hacksaw, make sure the blade is held securely and firmly in the handle. Again, a loose blade will not cut straight and that will just mean that you will have more work squaring and crowning your barrel. Also, to make the blade cut more efficiently, use a couple of drops of cutting oil on the barrel as you make the cut. The cutting oil will help the blade cut quickly and smoothly.

After you cut the barrel, use a medium cut flat file to remove any major burrs around the outside edge of the barrel. Now coat the end of the barrel with a machinist layout fluid such as Dykem. This will color the end of the barrel and let you know where you are actually filing as you square it up. Also, change the position of your barrel so it is held vertically with the muzzle up in your padded vise.

The Starrett square is used to check the end of the muzzle. Note that the masking tape has been removed to make sure the reading is as accurate as possible.

You will need a machinist's square to square up the end of the muzzle. A machinist's square is nothing more than two flat pieces of metal that are joined at precisely 90°. Some squares are adjustable in that one leg of the square can be moved; others have both legs permanently fixed in place.

If you do not have one of these little tools, pick one up. As you do more gun work you will need one from time to time. They can be very helpful in making sure sights and sight bases are mounted properly and in a host of other metal working situations.

A small, good-quality imported machinist square can often be picked up for less than ten bucks. Again, I would encourage you to add one to your tool collection if you don't already have one.

When you use the machinist's square there is a bit of a catch you need to be aware of. Look at your barrel. Is it tapered or is it perfectly straight? Odds are it is tapered. Most barrels are in order to cut down on weight. If you use the machinist square on the end of a tapered barrel by laying one leg against the side of the barrel and the other leg across the muzzle, you will not end up with a square muzzle no matter how much you file!

Before filing, Coffield coats the muzzle with Dykem layout blue to enable him to determine precisely where he is cutting with his file. This is an important step.

When you place the long leg of the square along the side of the barrel and extend the short leg over a perfectly square or flat

muzzle, you should have a bit of light or a gap between the edge of the muzzle and the long leg of the square. That distance is basically the taper in the barrel.

The trick is to simply measure with the square on one side of the barrel, note the amount of the gap then place the square on the opposite side of the barrel and note the amount of gap. You want an equal amount of gap no matter where you position the square. When the face of the muzzle is perfectly flat, this will happen.

Of course, you also

The ends of the lands and grooves are sharp and distinct. It's time to break the edges of the lands and grooves with lapping compound and a brass screw head.

want the top short leg to lie perfectly flat across the muzzle. Chances are your hacksaw cut was not perfect and one side of the end of the muzzle is a bit higher than the other. You will be able to spot this with your square. Once you have noted this, you can use your file carefully to remove some metal from the face of the muzzle.

You will want to file only where the metal is high. Your Dykem will help to control just where metal is removed. If you don't use the Dykem or similar material, it can be darn hard to determine just where you have been filing.

The process is basically just check with the square by placing it at three or four different positions around the end of the barrel, note where the high spot is, and file it off. Check your work, then recoat the end of the barrel with your Dykem. Measure again; note the high spot and then file. Just keep doing this until the barrel is flat. With a bit of practice you should be able to true up your barrel in a fairly short time.

Once the barrel is flat and true, use your file to carefully bevel the outside edge of the muzzle. You may want to do nothing more than simply break the edge and remove any burrs. Then again you might want to remove more metal. If you choose to remove more, be sure that you remove an equal amount around the entire barrel. Here again the application of some Dykem will help you to keep track of just how much metal you have removed.

Coffield prefers using a very old hand operated drill that had belonged to his grandfather. He finds that most electric drills turn way too fast for this process.

Now for the final part of the process, which is to deal with the rifling. It would be possible to simply leave the rifling terminating flush with the flat muzzle. However, this would offer little or no protection to that important point where the rifling ends. Instead, we are going to carefully break the edge and at the same time slightly taper the end of the lands and grooves. How do we do this? Easy, we just use a round brass screw!

Years ago it was traditional to crown a barrel by using a round brass ball coated with an abrasive compound. The ball was mounted on a shaft and then turned in a hand drill. While it can be sometimes be hard to locate brass balls on shafts, round headed brass screws can be picked up at any good hardware store. Just make sure you choose one that has a head that is larger than your bore. Don't worry about the screwdriver slot, which will just help to hold the abrasive lapping compound.

By the way, for an abrasive lapping compound you can use a fine valve grinding compound, which you can find at almost any auto parts store or even some hardware stores.

Just coat the head of the screw with compound, chuck the shank of your screw in a hand drill and then place the screw head in the muzzle. By the way, I prefer an old fashioned hand crank or egg beater drill for this job. It can be done with an electric drill, but you have to be darn careful that you do not remove too much material with the electric drill. If you use an electric drill, keep the rpm as low as possible. While rotating the brass screw, move the drill itself in a figure eight pattern. This will constantly expose different areas of the brass screw head to the rifling.

You will not have to turn the drill for more than a minute or so. Remove the drill and clean away the lapping compound. You should find that the very end of the rifling is now uniformly beveled around its entire circumference. If it is not, then you need to either repeat the process or check to make sure you really have the muzzle filed flat. Once you can see evidence of a 360° bevel around the muzzle, *stop!*

When turning the brass screw, rock the drill back and forth and side to side. This ensures that the wear to the screw itself and the lapping of the barrel is even.

After this, you may want to polish the end of the barrel. If you do, use some cloth backed abrasive of at least 120 grit or finer. Lay a strip of the abrasive over a small flat piece of wood. Put a drop or two of oil on the end of the muzzle and then hold the abrasive against the muzzle. I like to turn the abrasive in a circular direction so any polishing marks will be around the bore. When you have polished it to your satisfaction, clean the end of the muzzle with alcohol or similar solvent and use a cold blue to darken the muzzle if desired.

You can now change the barrel back to a horizontal position. Push the two patches we placed in the barrel out from the breech end. The patches should come out the muzzle along with any filings and abrasive compound that might have fallen into the bore.

You can check the smoothness of the end of your rifling by running a Q-Tip inside the muzzle. If any strands of cotton are pulled from the Q-Tip you can be certain that there are some tiny burrs on the rifling. Generally these will be removed with a single pass of a phosphor bronze bore brush down the barrel and out the muzzle.

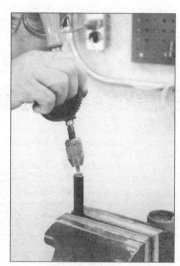

The brass screw head is coated with valve grinding compound, available at most auto parts stores. The screw slot actually helps hold the compound as the screw turns.

Basically that's all there is to it! As you can see, you can cut and crown a rifle barrel with nothing more than simple hand tools. And most importantly, if you do your part, your crown will be just as good as any cut on the most expensive and precise lathe.

Until next time, good luck and good gunsmithing! ◎

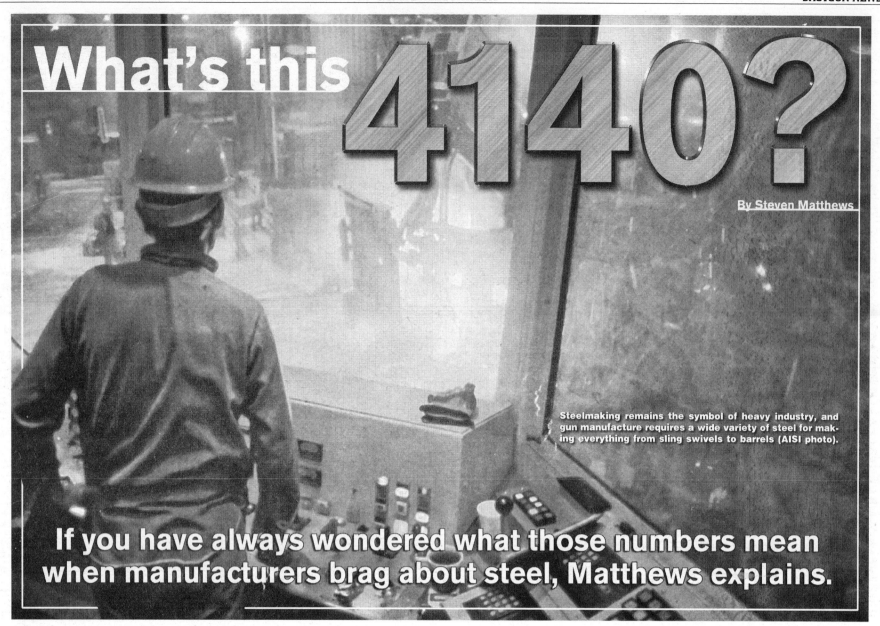

What's this 4140?

By Steven Matthews

Steelmaking remains the symbol of heavy industry, and gun manufacture requires a wide variety of steel for making everything from sling swivels to barrels (AISI photo).

If you have always wondered what those numbers mean when manufacturers brag about steel, Matthews explains.

Although many firearms today are made with high-tech plastics and aluminum alloys, the primary material for most of the 20th century was steel.

Not all steels are created equal. Firearms and their parts need to be made from appropriate steels for proper functioning and safety. Considering that a firearm must contain up to 65,000 psi, you need a strong steel to keep it from becoming a bomb rather than a gun.

Most any high-powered firearm would fail with disastrous results if it were made from common steel. Using modern high-strength steels has allowed firearm designers to build strong and lightweight firearms that were not technically possible in previous centuries.

Steel has been around in one form or another for hundreds of years, but the strength and quality was not what it is today. Excellent steel could be sometimes made by skilled craftsmen but quality was erratic and quantities were small. The difficulty in producing mass quantities of chemically identical steel in various chemical formulations kept steel from being economical and widely available until the late 1800s.

Technical advances in steelmaking in the late 1800s and early 1900s brought firearms into the modern age.

When you begin making your own guns or parts, you will be solely responsible for choosing the proper steel for your application. Using the correct steel will determine whether you make a good part or one that will eventually fail. As an advanced hobby gunsmith, I have made a multitude of parts, including triggers, chambering reamers, pins, firing pins, extractors, rifle and pistol receivers, bolts and bolt carriers, scope mounts, charging handles, sears, and complete rifles and pistols.

The only major parts I haven't made are barrels, since I don't have barrelmaking equipment. In all these cases I had to decide the proper type of steel to use for the project. When I was in my early 20s and uninformed about steel, some of my early gunsmithing projects failed dramatically!

I still have some small metal fragments embedded in my forehead from when a shotgun choke project let loose only 2 feet from my face. After digging out the metal fragments I decided I needed to learn a little more about steel before I got myself killed!

Now, 30 years of metalworking experience (both professional and hobby) has given me the knowledge to avoid those kind of

Hot work! Steel is heated, quenched, rolled, hardened, annealed, tempered and many other processes are applied to it in the mill to give it proper qualities (AISI).

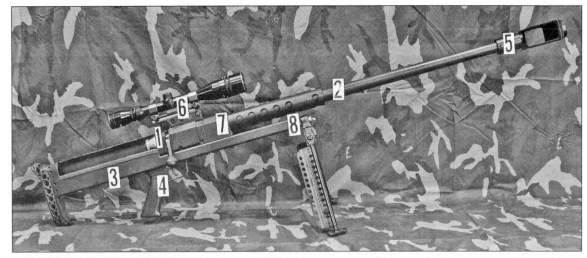

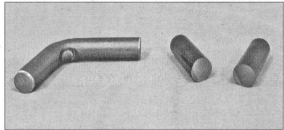

Think heat treating's unimportant? The soft pin began to bend at 12,000 pounds of force. The alloy pin held to 28,000 before fracturing, typical of hardened steel.

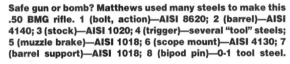

Safe gun or bomb? Matthews used many steels to make this .50 BMG rifle. 1 (bolt, action)—AISI 8620; 2 (barrel)—AISI 4140; 3 (stock)—AISI 1020; 4 (trigger)—several "tool" steels; 5 (muzzle brake)—AISI 1018; 6 (scope mount)—AISI 4130; 7 (barrel support)—AISI 1018; 8 (bipod pin)—O-1 tool steel.

explosive failures. This article will be an *introduction* to firearms metallurgy for the novice hobby gunsmith.

You will need much more information than this short article can cover and I will give you excellent sources to advance your knowledge of the subject of metalworking and metallurgy.

Hundreds of books have been written on metallurgy, most of them for engineers and skilled metalworkers. The information in them can be overwhelming for the hobbyist.

Here I will use easy-to-use terms anyone can understand to ease you into the subject. Once you have your feet wet, you can advance on to the more technical information found in the sources I will recommend.

weather it is common mild steel (also known as low carbon steel) or a hardenable high-strength steel (known as high carbon steel).

Along with carbon, several other ingredients are added to steel to create desirable characteristics.

Some of the more common additives are manganese, sulfur, phosphorus, silicone, cobalt, nickel, chromium, molybdenum, vanadium, aluminum, copper, lead, tungsten and boron. The addition of small amounts of the additives can drastically change the characteristics of the steel, including its strength, hardness, flexibility, abrasion-resistance, shock resistance and suitability for machining.

The strength of steel is measured in pounds per square inch (psi) of tensile strength. By changing the chemical composition of the steel, strength can be as low as 50,000 psi or as high as

> # Pure iron is a very soft metal and in most cases is unsuitable for firearms applications.

As stated earlier, not all steel is created equal. To understand why, you need to know what steel is made of. The primary ingredient in steel is iron. Pure iron is a very soft metal and in most cases is unsuitable for firearms applications. What makes iron into steel is the addition of several other ingredients.

The most common material added to iron to make it into steel is carbon. A very small fraction of carbon (less than 2%) turns soft iron into steel. Varying the amount will determine

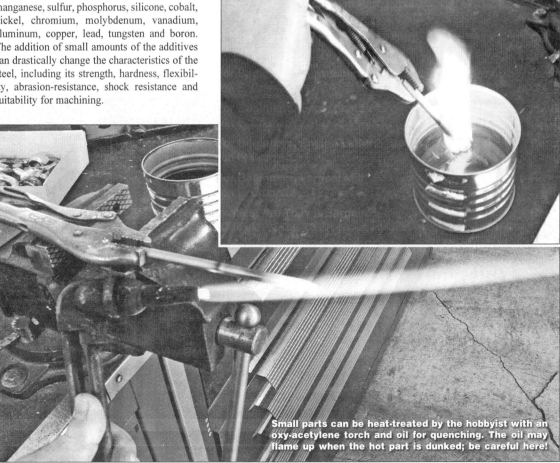

Small parts can be heat-treated by the hobbyist with an oxy-acetylene torch and oil for quenching. The oil may flame up when the hot part is dunked; be careful here!

Soft low-carbon steel can be surface-hardened with case-hardening compounds like Brownells "Hard-N-Tuff." These leave a thin layer of hard steel with a softer core.

hardness. Medium or high-carbon steel is heated red hot (1500–1800° depending on type) and then quickly cooled by quenching in oil or water, while "air hardening" steels are cooled in air. When heated to this red hot temperature, the molecular structure of the steel changes. When quickly cooled, this new structure is "frozen" in the steel and results in a stronger and harder steel. That's the broad outline of heat-treating, but the process is much more complicated in a manufacturing environment.

Once steel is heat-treated, it can be so hard it can no longer be worked with common cutting tools such as files, drills or saws. As well as being harder, the steel can be two or three times as strong, too.

> Once steel is heat-treated, it can be so hard it can no longer be worked with common cutting tools...

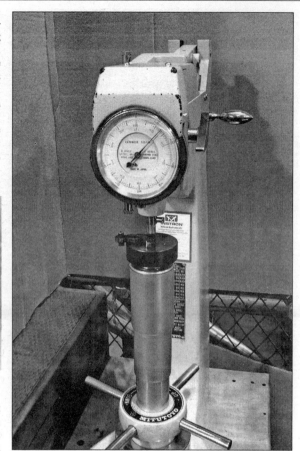

Hardness is tested with a gauge like this Mitutoyo that provides results on the Rockwell "C" scale. This AR-15 hammer tested R 45, which is about right for the application.

275,000+ psi. The hardness can also be changed from being soft enough to cut with a knife to being so hard that it can't be cut with common metalworking tools (saws, files, mills, drills, etc.).

Some of these steels are especially suitable for firearms.

Each of these steel types has to be identifiable to be of any use. You can't just call up the steel store and say "send me some good steel." The most common way of identifying/naming steel is by a numbering system. The two most common systems in this country are established by the SAE (Society of Automotive Engineers) system and the AISI (American Iron and Steel Institute).

For most carbon and alloy steels, the numbers are almost the same. The numbers represent the type or family of steel and the carbon content. The numbers are usually four digits, with the first two representing the type of steel and the last two representing the approximate carbon content in one hundredths of a percent.

For example, common low carbon mild steel is usually referred to as 1018 steel, the 10 represents the family of common low carbon steels and the 18 represents a carbon content of .18% (eighteen *hundredths* of a percent, about 1/5%). In a steel such as 4130 the 41 refers to a family of chrome-molybdenum steels and the 30 indicates a carbon content of .30%.

If you look in a steel supplier's manual, you will find a bewildering number of steels, but most all will have a SAE or AISI number. Many manuals will also give a description of the steel, heat treating procedure if applicable and its applications.

When you move on to "tool steels," the numbers are primarily in the AISI system—usually a letter and a number. Two examples are as follows: 0-1 tool steel refers to an oil-hardening tool steel, while A-2 refers to an air-hardening tool steel.

These steels are made for specific applications and are usually specified in the manuals along with the chemical composition and heat-treating procedure.

Steels are sometimes marketed under a trade name as well as an AISI number. One maker's 0-1 tool steel may be called "Badger," while the same AISI numbered steel from another manufacturer may be called "Saratoga." People sometimes become fond of a certain steel and may recommend "Starmax" as the best for a certain use even though it may be the same steel that is being marketed by another company as "Electric Tatmo."

Stainless steels are also numbered, but the AISI and SAE numbers differ somewhat. SAE numbers are usually 5 digit numbers and AISI numbers are usually 3 digit numbers. Simply by reading the last 3 numbers in the SAE system will give the same numbers as the AISI system. An example of this is as follows: SAE 51416 steel is the same as AISI 416 steel.

Both numbers refer to a heat-treatable type of stainless steel especially suited for certain applications.

These and other steel types may be found in firearms in a "soft" or "hardened" condition. Steels with between .3 and 1.8% carbon can be heat-treated, greatly increasing their strength and

One downside to this process is that the steel is now somewhat more brittle. It is much stronger but may now crack rather than bend when it fails. To reduce this brittleness it is sometimes "tempered". This process involves re-heating the steel to a certain temperature (400–1000° depending on application) for a specific amount of time. This process reduces the brittleness and increases the toughness.

A steel that when soft had a tensile strength of 60,000 psi may now have a tensile strength of 180,000 psi after proper heat-treating and tempering.

Sometimes even low-carbon steels can be hardened, but not just by heating and quenching. They can be partially hardened by a process called carburizing or case-hardening. In this process carbon is added to the surface (.005"–.025" deep) of the steel. In effect you create a piece of steel with a soft low carbon core and a high carbon "skin."

This segment probably brings up the question just how you know how hot you are heating your parts, since they require specific temperatures for proper heat-treatment.

There are several ways. The most accurate method is by using a heat treating oven that is capable of reaching over 2000°, but this method is too expensive for the hobbyist unless you are really into doing a lot of heat treating.

Once hardened, parts can't readily be worked with conventional tools and require machines like this toolroom grinder. Heat-treatment comes after parts are mostly formed.

Machinery's Handbook is the bible of the metalworking trade. It's not beach reading, but if you are making anything from metal, it's an essential reference work.

The next common method is by using a product called Tempilac. This material is available in several heat ranges that when applied to the parts allow the user to determine the high temperatures by the change in appearance of the Tempilac.

The third method is the most inaccurate but is commonly used and can be learned easily. By observing the color of the part while heating, the temperature can be guessed to a acceptable level by the skilled metal worker.

The colors are explained in most metal working books.

Once you have your parts heat treated according to the procedures recommended for the particular type of steel, how do you know how hard and strong it is? Steels are tested with a hardness tester. There are many types but the most common type is the Rockwell System. Depending on the hardness range expected you use various numerical scales to indicate the hardness.

The most common scale used for hardened steels is the Rockwell "C" scale. The number range is from about 10, which is very soft up to about 70, which is extremely hard. In this method a diamond penetrator is pressed into the steel under a standard amount of force.

For the hobby gunsmith with out access to a hardness tester, it gets into guesswork when trying to determine hardness. Steel in the 10–30 C scale range can be cut easily with a file or easily drilled with good drill bits. As you go up from there, it gets more difficult to work.

Once into the R 40c range and up, it gets pretty hard unless you have very hard and sharp tools. Over the range of about R 50–55c, you will only be able to work it with carbide tooling or grinding. Most cutting tools top out at about R 60c. So after that,

your only option is grinding, since your tools have to be harder than the material being cut.

While grinding is the most common method of working hardened steels for the hobby gunsmith, there are high-tech methods used in industry, such as laser cutting, electro-discharge machining, and abrasive water jet.

The obvious solution to working hard steels is to simply work them *before* heat-treating. It is common practice to work the parts to almost finished size soft and then heat-treat. Once hardened they are finished by light grinding to the final size.

Just what steels are commonly found in firearms? Lightly-stressed parts like trigger guards, hardware, buttplates, barrel bands, etc., may be made from common low carbon steel such as AISI 1018.

This steel may be hot or cold formed (also known as hot or cold rolled). Hot formed steel is formed to its final shape while hot. It is characterized by a somewhat rough and slightly flaky surface texture. Common examples of hot formed steel are angle iron, I-beams and some flat stock.

Cold formed steel starts out as hot formed steel, but after cooling, it is de-scaled and then worked between rollers to smooth out the surface. This surface working makes the steel very smooth and dimensionally precise; it also has the side benefit of making the surface somewhat harder. Flat stock, squares and rectangles are common shapes for cold rolled steel.

The chrome-moly steel 4140 is a traditional choice for firearms thanks to its high strength. It's often specified for barrels, and some lightly stressed receivers are also made from 4140.

One of the most popular steels for receiver applications is AISI 8620, also sometimes called "ordnance steel."

Most high strength stainless steel gun parts are made from AISI 400 series (416, 440, etc.) which is heat-treatable.

Most common stainless steel barrels are made from AISI 416. Some low stressed stainless parts are sometimes made from AISI 300 series (303, 304, etc.) due to its lower cost and easier machining characteristics. In trigger assemblies, it is not uncommon to find high strength tool steels of various types for sears and triggers.

Designers have many steels to choose from, but one factor that always concerns firearm manufacturers is cost. While it might be nice to have the absolute best steel used in all parts, it is not cost-effective to use steels that greatly exceed the needed requirements.

Common low-carbon steel may be as cheap as 50¢ a pound but some of the high strength alloys may be as high as $20 per pound. When you are making millions of parts per year, steel cost can be a major factor. One good thing about doing hobby gunsmithing is that you can use the best steels if you want, since you are only making a few parts.

There are literally hundreds of books in print on selecting and heat-treating steel. One of the best books available for the hobby gunsmith is *Machinery's Handbook*. This is the bible of the metalworking trade. It contains more than 2,500 pages of detailed metalworking information.

It covers machining procedures, selecting the proper steels, heat-treating and almost every other kind of information the metalworker needs close at hand. It is expensive ($75–$100) but worth every penny.

There are other less expensive options. AGI, Brownells and Midway have many firearm-specific books and videos that will help you improve your metalworking skills. The Internet is also a wealth of information with several gunsmithing sites available.

Don't forget the public library. Most large libraries have many books on the metalworking trade and some even have gunsmithing books. This source is free, so why not take advantage of it?

Once you have studied metalworking and metallurgy, you'll have the basic knowledge to start making parts and eventually, complete guns. With the proper know-how under his belt, even a barnyard gunsmith can do amazingly good work! ◉

SOME FIREARMS STEELS

Manufacturers have literally dozens of steels to choose from, depending on cost, machinability, and suitability for specific purposes.

AISI 1018 low carbon steel (also known as mild steel)—Non critical parts such as hardware, buttplates, barrel bands, sights.

AISI 1040 medium carbon steel—A low-cost heat-treatable steel for applications that require greater strength than mild steel. Typical applications would be parts that need wear resistance, levers, screws.

AISI 4140 chrome-moly steel—A high-strength heat-treatable steel especially useful for barrels and sometimes for low stressed receivers (.22 rimfire and other low-pressure cartridge guns).

AISI 8620 alloy steel—Commonly known as ordnance steel, it is often used for high-strength firearm receivers and bolts. May be case-hardened for a high surface hardness while still retaining a tough and strong core.

AISI 1095 high carbon steel—especially suited for springs.

AISI 400 series (416,440,410,etc.)—Heat-treatable and high-strength stainless steel used in barrels and receivers.

AISI 300 series (303, 304, etc.)—Non heat-treatable stainless steel for low-stressed parts, easier to machine than 400 series.

SOURCES

JUST PARK IT YOURSELF

By Steven Matthews

You might have thought that Parkerizing was a complicated industrial process beyond your ability. Not so; you can do it at home.

While the rest of the world's military arms manufacturers were happy with bluing, the United States and a few others were looking for a more durable military finish. The finish that they chose came to be known as a Parkerized or phosphate finish.

This finish is still in use today on many military firearms and has also gained some acceptance on sporting firearms that are exposed to extreme conditions. It is characterized by a rough, flat appearance in any of several colors ranging from light gray to near-black. Using various lubricants and cleaners on Parkerizing may yield brown or green tints.

While conventional bluing is usually very smooth, fresh Parkerizing has a rough, crystalline appearance. It may smooth up after years of use, but when new it is rather coarse. This coarse texture is one of the things that makes this finish so good. It allows oil to penetrate and stick to the metal.

Along with the actual Parkerizing coating, this makes it a very protective finish. Dry Parkerizing is good, but it gets much better when it has absorbed oil.

The term phosphate comes from the chemical composition of the finish. The light gray finishes are usually zinc phosphate Parkerizing and the dark gray to black finishes are usually manganese phosphate. Both have characteristics that make them desirable for specific applications.

Generally the type used as a final finish on military arms is manganese phosphate. One of the things that make these finishes so durable is that they are not just coatings; they are part of the steel. During the Parkerizing process a certain amount of the surface steel is actually converted to finish chemically bonded to the base steel.

As durable as these finishes are, they will eventually wear out and need to be renewed. You may think metal finishing is beyond you, but if you study the process and can purchase and improvise the necessary equipment and supplies, it's fairly easy and inexpensive.

Do-it-yourself types have been doing home Parkerizing for years. I have been hot caustic bluing firearms for 15–20 years as part of my gun collecting hobby and found it to be relatively easy and inexpensive. I decided it was time to see if I could Parkerize as easily and cheaply.

I have an improvised hot bluing system that I built in the 1990s for about $150 that has allowed me to blue guns for a cost of about $20 each (see August 10 issue). Since Parkerizing is generally considered to be an easier process than bluing, I decided to give it a try.

I already had many of the items needed to Parkerize in my bluing system, so my cost was limited to obtaining a stainless steel Parkerizing tank and the necessary chemicals. Even if you don't have any equipment, you can still do Parkerizing very economically if you are resourceful and improvise.

In its simplest form, the procedure consists of stripping off the old finish, cleaning the stripped parts, immersing the parts in a hot solution and allowing the chemical reaction to create Parkerizing. Then you rinse off the solution, dry and oil the finished parts.

I used Brownells Manganese Parkerizing solution. Other makers may have a slightly different procedure, so if you use some other brand, be sure to follow its instructions. Brownells has an *excellent* eight-page instruction manual that goes into great detail covering all aspects of the process that can be downloaded from its website at www.brownells.com.

Here I will boil the process down to the bare minimum you need to do a professional quality job. As in most DIY projects, more equipment will make the job easier, but increase cost. I went with the lowest cost setup since I only occasionally Parkerize a gun. Even though the system is boiled down to the bare minimum, don't skip steps thinking one thing or another is unimportant; everything is done for a reason. That reason is to get a good job.

I'm the kind who's always looking for a shortcut and am always trying new procedures to make it easier, but until you learn the

Matthews has hot-tank blued lots of guns, and was surprised to find that Parkerizing is actually easier. Here he starts the process by sandblasting the old finish.

Don't start right out Parkerizing that gas-trap M1. Matthews recommends a practice project to learn first. He chose a dummy Sten gun that cost only about $40.

process, follow the instructions. Some shortcuts work and others don't. Don't experiment till you know what you are doing!

Before you can start, you need to obtain your Parkerizing chemicals and equipment. The accompanying list shows the bare minimum needed to do a professional job. The largest cost is usually the stainless steel tank. I needed a large one, as I was Parkerizing a Browning 1919A4. If you don't need such a large tank, you can reduce cost considerably, both because a smaller tank is cheaper and because you'll need less concentrate.

The most commonly recommended tanks are stainless steel, though you may also use porcelain-coated steel. If you try to use bare steel, you will expend all your solutions Parkerizing the inside of your tank.

Some who practice "stovetop Parkerizing" use glass cookware but I don't recommend using fragile glassware for heating acid-based solutions. It's just too easy to break it by hitting with a hard metal gun part, and then you have a hot acid mess on your hands.

I purchased a 6x8x40-inch stainless tank for $85, but you can find less costly options. Restaurant suppliers carry stainless steel steamer pans in a multitude of sizes. These are perfect for this job and cost less than purpose-built tanks.

You can also search the scrap and recycle yards in your area and find a stainless steel container that may work for your purposes. This can result in a Parkerizing tank that may only cost a few dollars.

If you go the porcelain-coated route, you can use common kitchenware roaster pans if you can find one large enough for your needs.

Commercial Parkerizing tanks can range from $50 to $175, so the improvised options can really reduce your cost.

Whatever the tank, it will need to be heated. Parkerizing is done at about 190°, and you must have a heat source that can create and maintain that temperature.

You have several options here. Unlike bluing, which is done at 290° and is very sensitive to temperature variations within the tank, Parkerizing is much more forgiving.

My large tank system uses a 36-inch pipe burner I built from a scrap gas water heater burner for a cost of just a couple dollars. Building your own requires a working knowledge of burner construction, for obvious safety reasons. Brownells offers the parts or complete burners.

If your tank is not too long, you can easily use a two- or three-burner propane or electric hot plate that can be bought for about $35. Another option is a gas camping stove. I have even read on the internet of people using a large gas grill but this option requires you to be very careful as the solution will damage the grill if spilled.

Besides the tank and burner, you will need an accurate thermometer. I use a bluing thermometer (about $35) but a good kitchen type will work as long as it is accurate. For stirring, some common and inexpensive stainless steel cooking utensils will work fine.

Besides the heated Parkerizing tank, you will need tanks or containers for cleaning and rinsing. I have found 36-inch plastic planter boxes work fine. If you want to step up to a better tank, gunsmithing and industrial suppliers have stiff fiberglass tanks that can be bought for about $25 each.

You will also need another heat source for heating the water for in these tanks. I simply bought a couple of cheap large pots and heat the water on my kitchen stove and carry it out to my Parkerizing area to keep cost down. There is no need to buy specialized equipment just to boil water!

You are going to need several chemicals to Parkerize. First is your concentrate. Although there are many home-brew formulas

available on the internet, I recommend buying commercially prepared concentrate to obtain predictable and professional results.

If you want a light gray color, choose zinc Parkerizing and if you want the traditional dark gray to black, choose the manganese type. Whichever type you get, be sure to order enough to make enough solution to fill your tank. Check with your supplier to see how much you need, since not all concentrates mix in the same proportions.

You have to have enough for the proper mix; you can't water it down to stretch it and get good results. I chose manganese Parkerizing from Brownells, and since my tank holds more than 6 gallons, I had to buy a gallon of concentrate. If you use smaller tanks than I do, you may be able to get by with only a quart or two.

You will also need some mineral spirits (common paint thinner) for basic degreasing. It is cheap and available anyplace that carries painting supplies. For final cleaning, you will need some very heavy-duty detergent cleaner. Brownells sells a product specifically made for the gun refinishing trade known as Dicro-Clean 909. It is costly, but works well.

When finished blasting, you need to do a thorough cleaning in an approved hot solvent to remove any trace of blasting sand, grease, oil, paint or any other contaminant.

An alternative that is cheaper and works almost as well is trisodium phosphate cleaner that is available at most home centers. After your parts are Parkerized and dried, you will need water-displacing oil. Most Parkerizing suppliers offer a recommended specialty oil that's often pricey.

I personally use a product from CRC Corp. known as CRC Power-Lube. This was known as CRC 5-56 for industrial use but was renamed a few years ago for the home market. I have used this for more than 25 years for all my firearm purposes and it has always performed well. It seems that everyone has their own favorite post Parkerizing oil, some like WD-40, motor oil, 3-in-1 oil, cosmolene and the list goes on and on!

You also will need 0000 steel wool pads, some small steel rod for hanging your parts in the tank, paper coffee filters and a couple common kitchen thermometers for your cleaners and rinse water. Since you will be working with hot acid-based chemicals, you will need some safety equipment such as a face shield, rubber gloves, long sleeve shirt and possibly some paper breathing filters.

One last thing you will need for professional results is a small sandblaster and a source of compressed air. I use a 40-pound pressure feed blaster I bought at Harbor Freight for $69 and a $6 bag of blast media from our local home center.

I already had an air compressor, so that wasn't an expense for me. If you don't want this expense you can pay someone else to do your blasting. I don't think it would cost much more than $20 to have a gun commercially blasted.

Once you have all your supplies, it's time to get started. The first step is to disassemble your firearm and decide which parts need to be refinished. I normally just Parkerize the exterior parts, since the parts inside usually don't need to be redone.

Sandblasting removes all traces of the previous finish and gives the gun a uniform, slightly rough surface. You can have a machine or body shop do the blasting.

A non-reactive tank and the required chemicals are the major expense for getting started in Parkerizing. You can scrounge a lot of the other items that are needed.

I recommend cleaning your parts with mineral spirits to remove all grease and oil before sandblasting so you don't blow grease and oil into recesses or imbed it in the steel.

I scrub with a stiff brush and then do it again to get any spots I may have missed the first time. Once the parts are degreased, sandblast to roughen the metal and remove *all* the old finish. Parkerizing works best with a slightly rough finish. Extremely smooth or polished surfaces usually don't Parkerize well.

Just how rough is up to you. Different blasting media and blasting air pressures will develop different textures. One thing that needs to be mentioned here is to be careful not to blast the inside of the barrels, plugging the barrel and chambers with wood dowels will keep the media out.

One alternative to blasting off the old finish and roughing up the steel is to use a stiff wire wheel (plain steel, not stainless which will mess things up) on a bench grinder. I have never seen this recommended in any Parkerizing instructions, but it has worked well for me.

I would recommend that you try a test piece before you try this, just because it worked for me doesn't mean it will work for you! A stiff wire wheel will be very aggressive and you must be careful not to remove too much material or round off edges.

Now that your parts are blasted and roughened up, it time for a heavy-duty cleaning. Mix your cleaner according to the manufacturer's instructions. I use the planters as cleaning and rinse tanks. Brownells recommends heating Dicro-Clean 909 to 180° and aggressively scrubbing your parts after they have soaked for a few minutes. Then you should repeat.

This step is very important because Parkerizing is very sensitive to surface contamination. Any remaining oil, grease, wax or dirt will affect the final finish. The parts may not Parkerize at all or may be discolored.

After scrubbing a couple times, rinse with clean water. Rinse very well, because any leftover cleaner can contaminate your solution. If you don't want to use a rinse tank, I have found that a garden hose works well for rinsing if you are outside or have a drain close by.

Once your parts are rinsed, it is time to Parkerize, so your tank needs to be ready to go. You can't let your clean, wet steel parts lie around while you wait for your tank to get ready, because the steel will begin to rust in just a few minutes. All the operations are best done continuously, so plan to be ready for each step.

Before you use your Parkerizing tank for the first time, it needs some special preparation. I use Brownells Parkerizing concentrate so I will briefly cover its process, other manufacturers may have different procedures so *read your instructions!*

Start by mixing concentrate with water to the proper proportions and pouring it into the tank. It will be slightly green. Heat to about 140°. The fresh solution needs to be "aged" by adding a specific amount of iron (or steel). This is added in small packets

wrapped in coffee filters to keep it from making a mess in your tank.

Powdered iron is the recommended material, but I found that 0000 steel wool worked well and is what a lot of others use. This is left in the warm solution for a specified amount of time and then removed.

This is required only the *first* time and never needs to be done again unless you make a fresh batch of solution. Then bring the solution up to 195° and it is ready for Parkerizing.

Be careful when heating your tank and solution. As it gets close to the proper temperature, back off the heat for the last few degrees. Putting too much heat into the solution will create hot spots in the bottom of the tank. Little geysers will violently bubble up and make a mess.

At this point you will probably have something in your tank that looks like snowflakes; this is normal and Brownells say it won't affect your process. You should remove the flakes after you are finished using the recommended procedure.

Now place your freshly blasted and cleaned parts in the hot solution. Your parts need to be suspended in the solution without touching the sides or bottom of the tank. I use wire rod to make hooks and hang them from crosspieces lying across the top of the tank. As your parts warm up in the hot solution, they may start to fizz.

This is normal and indicates that the chemical reaction is working. For reasons unknown to me, some parts don't fizz but

still Parkerize OK. Parkerizing is a very fast process, so you won't have long to wait. The process may only take a few minutes and should never take more than 15 minutes.

When your mix is new, it is clean enough to see what's going on if the parts aren't fizzing too much. If you can't see what's going on, pull the parts out very briefly every few minutes to see if the process is completed.

If the finish looks right, the process is complete, however long the parts have been in the tank. Leaving the parts in longer than necessary allows excessive etching, which is bad for the look of the metal. When the proper finish has been obtained, immediately rinse off the solution. You don't want it to dry on the hot parts.

Once the parts have been rinsed in the cool water, I like to rinse again, but this time in a hot (180°) water rinse. This will remove any solution that may have been missed the first time plus the hot clean parts will tend to self-dry.

I use compressed air to blow out any water that may be in the cracks and crevices. After this thorough drying, spray or dip your parts in your water-displacing oil. Once this is done your parts are complete and ready for reassembly.

As you reassemble your gun, you may notice that some of the parts may be slightly different in color. This is usually noticed as slightly darker or lighter shades of the basic color.

This is one of the quirks of Parkerizing. Differences in heat-treatment, surface hardness, texture or steel chemical composition mean individual parts react to the solution differently. Parkerizing will protect the parts equally; they will just be in slightly different colors.

This is usually not a problem on guns made the "old fashioned" way with parts all made from the same steel. It usually shows up with the modern guns that may have sheet metal receivers with various parts of different types of steel welded in place. The area around the weld may be noticeably darker or lighter and the welded-on parts may be noticeably different in color.

It may also show up where parts were spot-hardened. If not especially noticeable it can be overlooked but sometimes it is so bad that it has to be corrected. If you suspect you have that sort of assembly, an option that sometimes (but not always) helps is to pre-treat your parts in an acid bath just before Parkerizing.

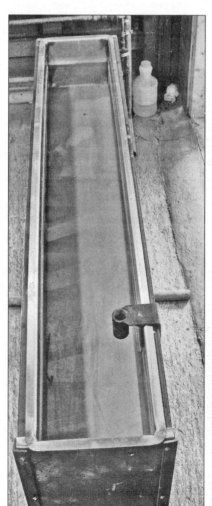

A fresh tank of Parkerizing solution is clear and green. As the solution is used, it gets cloudier and produces particles Matthews says look like snowflakes.

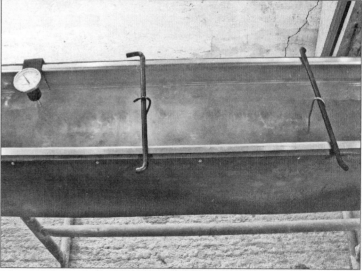

Before the first use, the solution needs to be "aged" with packets of iron in coffee filters. The parts may fizz a bit when first immersed in the hot solution.

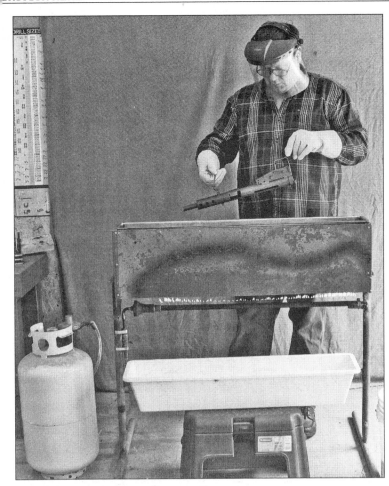

Parkerizing works quickly; Matthews says 15 minutes is a maximum. Too much time in the solution will tend to etch parts excessively. Note the proper safety clothing.

Not a bad looking piece! Matthews' Sten probably looks better than it did the day it left the factory. Parkerizing is rugged, yet quite attractive in a functional way.

I use a mixture of six parts room temperature water and one part muriatic acid (from most hardware stores and home centers). I soak the parts in this mixture for about five minutes or less and then remove and immediately rinse with clean cool water.

After removing from the rinse, go to the Parkerizing tank immediately, since these wet acid-treated parts will begin to rust in just minutes if left exposed to air. This has evened out the colors somewhat for me. Another option is to just sandblast off the poor finish and try again after a thorough cleaning.

If all else fails, there is one option that sometimes saves the day. Starting with completely dry and oil-free parts, lightly spray a fine mist of black or dark gray automotive engine paint on the parts. The Parkerizing will absorb the color and this will even out the irregularities.

After you have blended the colors, bake the parts in an oven at about 200° for an hour. This option also works well if you use one of the high-tech finishes such as KG GunKote or LCW DuraCoat instead of paint, since these finishes are meant to be applied over Parkerizing anyway.

Problems like this bring up the question of how do the arms manufacturers handle this problem? Since they are making thousands of parts, they can adjust the Parkerizing formula for the individual parts or pretreat the parts with color altering chemicals. Unfortunately, this option is not practical for the small-time Parkerizer.

As with all do-it-yourself projects, your first attempts may not be perfect. The more experience you have, the better your work will look. One beginner mistake is missing one small detail that may seem unimportant; this small detail may be the difference between a so-so job and one that looks great.

Attention to detail is the single most important issue that separates the amateurs from the pros! I recommend that you first practice on an inexpensive gun before taking on the high-dollar stuff. The gun I used in this article was a non-firing, display-only Sten gun I built for about $40.

If you don't have something cheap to work on, just Parkerizing a bare piece of steel properly prepared will be good practice and help you familiarize yourself with the procedures. Although I'm not any kind of expert on gun finishing I can offer some tips that may help the novice.

First, follow the instructions that came with your Parkerizing chemicals *exactly*. The manufacturer knows more about how to use its product than you do! The next thing cannot be emphasized enough—*surface preparation is key to all gun finishing*

projects. If it looks poor before applying the Parkerizing (or bluing or stock finish, etc.) it will still look poor afterwards.

In Parkerizing (or bluing), cleanliness is ultra important, you can't Parkerize dirt, oil, grease and crud. If there is anything between the steel and the Parkerizing solution, it will cause problems. Pay attention to the small details, that's where the problems usually hide. All this may sound complicated, but once you gain some experience, it gets pretty easy to do a professional quality Parkerizing job at a do-it-yourself cost. For me that's what makes the work worth it! ◎

Manganese phosphate provides a near-black Parkerizing. Zinc phosphate produces a lighter gray. A light coating of oil is absorbed into the finish and protects the steel.

Give your
GUN a COAT!

Spraying your own finish is easy and economical, especially if you are good at scrounging and improvising.

By Steven Matthews

Ever since firearms were invented, their owners have battled to keep the elements from attacking and destroying the metal parts. The earliest guns were largely made from brass or iron although some parts were steel.

Brass held up to the elements fairly well but the iron and steel parts were prone to rusting, requiring a regular light coating of oil. This was especially difficult for the soldier who was in combat as his highest priority during battle wasn't oiling his gun.

Some enterprising individual discovered the process of "browning" which is really just a controlled form of rusting that was stopped at a certain point. This finish, if oiled lightly was more durable than bare steel.

For many years, most firearms were finished in the "white" (bare steel) with some parts browned. Later on what we know today as "bluing" was introduced. Bluing was certainly more durable than bare steel but just as browning before it, also required a light coating of oil to be effective.

Bluing and browning added some protection and would last a long time if cared for but really only colored the steel since without a light coating of oil they would both rust in time. In the early 20th century a new and more durable finish began appearing on military arms.

This finish was known as Parkerizing or phosphate finish. The color varied according to the formulation of the finish and type of base steel alloy. It can be gray, green, black or any combination of these colors. It's a very durable finish, but its flat, low-luster appearance meant it never really caught on with sportsmen. It also required a light coat of oil, but it absorbed the lubricant rather that just letting it lie on the surface.

This oil-absorbing feature made it very resistant to rusting, but if left dry it would also rust eventually. During World War II the British experimented with what was known as "War Finish" and

guns with this finish were so marked.

To the untrained eye, this might seem to be paint over crudely finished steel, but as Peter Kokalis recently detailed in his story on the Mk5 Sten (2/1 issue), it actually was a very tough black enamel, applied over phosphated steel.

It didn't require oil for protection but it really looked poor. The U.S. military stayed with bluing and Parkerizing until the advent of the M16, which used anodized aluminium.

In the 1950s, several European manufacturers (primarily FN and HK) began experimenting with a hybrid finish.

This finish used Parkerizing as a base to apply a coating of non traditional finish. This finish applied over the Parkerizing would probably be considered paint by an average person but to call it paint would be a great understatement. It was generally a high tech polymer or epoxy type coating sprayed on to the Parkerized base.

The Parkerizing absorbed the finish and allowed it to bond extremely well. The great advantage of this hybrid was that it did not require any oil to protect the gun. It also resists dirt since it doesn't have a light coating of oil to attract the dust and dirt.

Parkerizing bonds extremely well to steel and the epoxy/polymer finish bonds very well to the Parkerizing, which results in an extremely tough finish. Over the last decade or so these finishes have become popular with sportsmen, military, police, and the average gun owner.

Due to their popularity and ease of application they have also been offered to the hobbyist gunsmith. In this article we will look at two of the more popular do-it-yourself finishes.

I choose two firearms that I recently built from parts kits and receivers, a STG 58 FAL and an AR-15. One of the reasons I choose to finish these new guns was the fact that that they were "parts guns" and as such had parts

Since DuraCoat need not be oven-baked, it was just the thing for the many plastic parts of an AR-15. LCW offers a variety of camouflage templates for the finish.

from various manufacturers and several shades of finish. By using these two products all parts were color coordinated.

When I researched the Internet, two brands were most often recommended by hobbyists: KG GunKote by KG Industries and Lauer Custom Weaponry's DuraCoat finish. Both are available in a multitude of colors, and I choose KG GunKote's gray satin moly for the FAL and LCW's DuraCoat satin black for the AR-15.

Both are sprayed-on finishes that require some form of paint spraying equipment, though KG GunKote is also available in spray cans from Brownells if you don't already have spray equipment.

Over the last decade or so these finishes have become popular with sportsmen, military, police, and the average gun owner.

They differ in their composition as KG GunKote is a baked-on phenolic resin and DuraCoat is in layman's terms a polymer finish that may or may not be baked. Both achieve similar results as far as creating a tough, durable finish, but use different chemistry to do it. In this article I will briefly explain the procedure to apply these finishes, but this is not meant to be step-by-step instructions.

Matthews overbaked the Gun-Kote finish on his FAL the first time and had to respray. The second effort worked better, leaving the rifle an attractive soft gray.

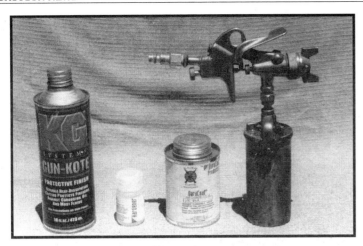

KG Gun-Kote and Lauer DuraCoat are the most popular spray-on gun finishes on the market today. Both are very thin liquids sprayed on with a touch-up gun or an airbrush.

Each manufacturer has detailed instructions and safety procedures with its products and you should follow those recommendations. Both finishes are flammable in their liquid form and should only be used away from any open flames. I also highly recommend some type of respirator or paint mask when spraying, along with gloves and safety glasses, as I am sure that these products are not to be inhaled.

The recommended method of applying both finishes is by spraying with common spray-painting equipment. A small touch-up gun or airbrush is the preferred method as a full-sized paint gun is really overkill to spray these *very thin* finishes. I bought the small touch-up gun I used for less than $25, and some airbrushes are available for under $15.

Thin paint and small paint guns mean a very small air compressor will work fine. You can find them for less than $100 and even cheaper if you shop around. With hoses and regulators, the cost can be as low as $125 if you are frugal in your spending. I already had all the equipment so my cost was $0.

KG GunKote requires baking in an oven while it's optional with LCW's DuraCoat. Some form of oven is required. Most use a kitchen oven if it is big enough. *Use the exhaust fan!* If your oven isn't large enough, you may want to find a larger scrap appliance at the salvage yard for junk price and hook it up in your garage. This method will also help keep peace in the family if you are married, as wives often look askance at guns baking in their ovens.

There are also improvised oven plans available on the Internet which will allow you to fabricate an inexpensive baking oven. Being the resourceful type I improvised my own oven from a hot bluing tank with lid. These tanks are available for about $40.

For a heat source I fabricated a pipe burner from a scrap water heater burner and salvaged pipe. Pipe burners are available for reasonable cost through various gunsmithing suppliers if you don't want to improvise. Fabricate a stand and you have your oven.

Matthews improvised an oven for baking on Gun-Kote from an old bluing tank and the heating element from an old water heater. It keeps guns out of his wife's stove.

One thing you *don't* want to improvise is a thermometer, since temperature is critical. Use a high-quality thermometer that is guaranteed to be accurate. I used a good bluing thermometer inserted into the oven through a hole in the lid.

Baking temperatures for KG GunKote are in the 275–325° range and DuraCoat range is 110–180°, so both are going to be hot enough you will need a specialty thermometer.

As a word of warning here, I will tell you on my first attempt I wasn't paying attention to my oven temperature and overbaked my parts, which resulted in the wrong finish color that required recoating to correct. Once you have your oven you must also have some way of holding your parts during spraying and baking.

You can't hold the parts while spraying and you have to support the parts in the oven while baking as you don't want them lying on or touching anything.

Fabricate some hooks from *bare* steel wire; don't use anything coated, as it might melt in the oven and get on your project. After you have made some hooks, make sure they are convenient to use; you don't want to have a painted part that you can't place in your oven without smudging the finish.

I recommend a "dry run" to be sure everything is OK. It's a lot easier to correct problems before you have a sprayed part ready to bake.

Before you can spray these finishes, the parts have to be clean and free of dirt, grease or oil. Surface preparation is the single most important aspect in getting a good finish and cannot be overstressed! Clean all parts to be coated with appropriate cleaners such as detergents and solvents.

When using solvents, follow all safety precautions, as most solvents are extremely flammable! Once you have the parts clean, do it *again*! You would be surprised at how much oil can remain in a parkerized finish even after it looks clean. I cleaned and degreased several times before I got all the oil out. Once I thought they were clean, I preheated the parts in preparation for spraying, only to notice more oil creeping out of nooks and crannies.

This oil will ruin your job, so make sure all parts are clean. Once the parts were spotlessly clean, they were ready to coat, since they were already Parkerized. If your parts aren't Parkerized, you may have to use a precoating finish or sandblast to roughen up the surface before applying the finish.

Both manufactures have instructions for surface preparation and they should be followed.

Suspend your parts in an area with adequate ventilation to reduce overspray while spraying; you don't want to breathe the vapors. These two products are very thin and will create a cloud of overspray. Prepare your liquids for spaying according to the manufacturer's instructions. Both of these finishes spray just like *very thin* paint. If you can spray paint without causing drips, runs or streaks, then you can apply these products.

Surface preperation is the single most important aspect in getting a good finish and cannot be overstressed!

I have been painting for more than 25 years and this seemed just like common everyday spray painting except for the thinness of the product. I applied several light coats of each product to each gun. I applied five light coats of KG GunKote to the FAL parts and four coats of DuraCoat to the AR-15 parts.

Both finishes dry tacky in a couple of minutes, so wait time between coats was not excessive. Be sure to spray from several angles so you don't leave bare spots or shadows.

After I finished applying the coatings, I set them aside to dry further before progressing to the next stage. Once you have the parts sprayed to your satisfaction, the hard part is done. They should look like spray-painted items. KG GunKote will look a little chalky but this is normal and will change when baked, DuraCoat will look just like wet paint and if a flat or satin color will dull as it dries.

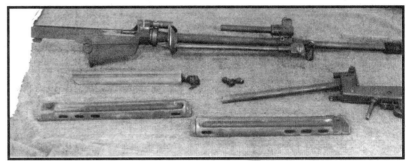

The process starts with complete disassembly of the gun, followed by thorough cleaning and degreasing. Degreasing is one of the most important parts of the process.

This is the point at which the two finishes differ. KG GunKote now has to be baked at 275–325° for one hour (more about this later). Place the coated parts in your oven and bake, watching the time and temperature. Watch the temperature *very* carefully and periodically open the oven and check progress.

Hot spots can cause uneven curing, so move your parts periodically or make sure the air is moving a little in the oven by leaving it slightly open to allow air to circulate a little. After the parts have baked for the proper time, allow them to cool, reassemble the gun and you are finished. DuraCoat may be left to air dry or may be lightly baked at low temperature (110–180° depending on time).

Since I was leaving some of the plastic parts on the AR-15, I choose not to bake and let it air dry for several days before reassembly. The instructions stated that a full cure could take several weeks if the gun were left to air-dry, and I did notice that after a few days it still wasn't as hard as I thought it should be.

I started to consider a light bake to speed up the curing. I didn't want to use the oven I had improvised, as it wasn't good for a steady low temperature. As I stood outside on a hot sunny day, an idea dawned on me when I put my hand on the hood of my truck.

The hood measured more than 140°! I simply took the assembled rifle outside and left it in the direct sun on the porch. The black finish sucked up heat so fast that in a few minutes it was too hot to handle. I let it lay this way for an hour or two for both sides.

Matthews found both products easy to spray, though he notes that the mist is very fine, leading to lots of overspray. Effective ventilation is a vital necessity.

After it cooled, the finish was a lot harder. This solar cooking duplicated the low-temperature baking without the need for an oven. Improvisation can come in handy!

This is just a brief overview of the process for applying these finishes and you should follow manufacturer instructions for a complete understanding of their individual processes.

Both finishes have their pros and cons. Your experiences may be different than mine but this is what I found out about each finish.

Pros for KG GunKote: Once baked and fully cured, this finish is very hard and durable. It dries so fast when spraying that runs are not a problem. If you apply it correctly, it is very easy to apply.

Cons for KG GunKote: The cons are primarily concerning the required baking process. At the time I chose the color for my project, I was unaware that the Satin Gray Moly color was one of the more temperamental colors available. Bake too long or too hot, and it discolors, which happened to me on the first attempt as I wasn't paying close attention to my baking temperature.

Fortunately, all that was required was to respray a new coat and rebake at a lower temperature. Also, how much and how smooth the finish is applied can slightly affect the color. I have heard from others that the other colors available are not as sensitive and that black is almost fool-proof.

Pros for LCW DuraCoat: This is very easy to apply, it sprays just like thin paint and dries like paint. It doesn't have to be baked in an oven and my improvised baking system worked perfectly with no cost involved.

Cons for LCW DuraCoat: If you don't bake, it takes a long time for full cure (up to six weeks). Although air dry was sufficient for handling it wasn't hard enough for rough use immediately. Light baking is recommended for a faster cure.

My personal opinion of these two products is favorable. Both are low-maintenance finishes that require no oil on the exterior of the gun (internal parts still need light oiling). They both appear to be hard and durable after full hardening. They are both attractive finishes, and you can have some real non-traditional colors on your guns if that's what you like.

I personally believe that KG Guncoat is somewhat harder than DuraCoat and may hold up to abrasion a little better, but from doing Internet research I found that both have their proponents. If you are like me and like the idea of not having to put much effort into the care of the gun's exterior finish, then these product might be for you.

The author would like to thank all the WECSOG engineers at falfiles.com for their valuable assistance while researching this subject on the net.

About the author: The author has been doing hobby gunsmithing for more than 25 years and takes great pride in improvising inexpensive methods to create professional results for the amateur/hobby gunsmith. His website is http://www.stoneaxe engineering.com and he can be emailed at fatmatthews2@hot mail.com ◉

Can You Blue it Yourself? *Yep!*

This home gunsmith says a bluing kit can be well worth the expense and trouble if you are working on multiple guns.

By Steven Matthews

I have been collecting military surplus firearms for more than 25 years and one of the things I have found in this quarter-century of collecting is how hard it is to find military surplus guns in very good to excellent condition at a reasonable cost.

Excellent condition guns are available, but usually at a cost that is several times the cost of a "well-used" gun. If you are on a working man's budget like I am, these excellent condition guns are out of reach unless you are willing to sacrifice quantity for quality in your collecting.

I didn't want just a few real nice guns; I wanted a lot of nice guns! This presented a problem on my budget. Most well-used guns are still mechanically sound, but the finishes suffer from years of use and abuse and these are the kind I can afford.

It's easy enough to refinish the wood, but the metal finish presents some problems. The cost to refinish a military surplus gun's metal can easily exceed the initial cost of the gun.

The most common type of finish on older military surplus guns is hot tank bluing. This was the standard finish for most of the world's military arms until the late 1950s, and still is used by many manufacturers.

There are exceptions; some British and French guns were Parkerized in World War II and U.S. military firearms have been Parkerized since the earlier part of the 20th century.

Parkerizing is a superior finish for military guns but most manufacturers and countries stayed with bluing, probably just because that's the way they always did it. Mosin-Nagants, most all Mausers, Japanese Ariskas, and most other surplus arms came blued.

Bluing is not really blue; it's generally black. You'll see a true blue finish on classic guns like old Colt revolvers, but the vast majority of blued arms come out black. Bluing offers some degree of resistance to rusting, though nothing like more modern finishes. Blued steel will rust if left to the elements, but if a light coating of oil is applied, it does have better rust resistance than bare steel.

Over the years there have been several bluing methods, but the most common is what is known as hot tank or caustic bluing. In this process, the steel is placed in a solution of very hot caustic chemicals. This causes a very thin layer of oxide to form on the steel and this oxide is the black finish.

"Cold" bluing works well for small touch-up jobs but not for complete gun refinishing, as it doesn't look or wear like the original finish. To get surplus arms back to their original appearance, there's no substitute for hot bluing.

Being cheap and resourceful, I began to look at the possibility of doing my own hot bluing. I studied up on the process and figured that if I could improvise some of the equipment, it was doable for this hobbyist gunsmith.

I was able to put together a bare-bones system for about $150. This was back in the early 1990s, but even with inflation, at today's prices it can still be done for about $300. If you have several guns to blue, this can make the cost per gun very reasonable. If you can pick up a couple jobs from your other gun buddies for pay, it will make it even more cost effective.

I estimate my cost is only about $20 per gun! If you're not much of a do-it-yourselfer, you can get a starter kit from Brownells for about $525, or if you want to go all out, their pro system is about $1,350. I'm cheap, so I improvised.

To show how it works, I blued two of my military guns, a Swiss K-31 rifle with a well-worn finish and an AK-47 pistol kit that had a painted original finish.

The basic process of bluing requires careful cleaning and surface preparation of the steel, immersing in hot bluing solution, rinsing the caustic solution off and neutralizing it, then drying and oiling.

The process requires several containers for liquids, tanks with burners for heating the solutions, several chemicals and oil, and some other easy-to-obtain equipment.

The list of supplies shown here is just about the bare minimum needed to do a pro quality blue job. I sacrificed ease of use for reduced cost. More equipment makes the job easier, but you pay for it. You have to decide whether you would rather save money or work!

Matthews says that bluing firearms yourself can make sense if you have several guns to be finished. It's too costly and too much trouble for one gun or a couple.

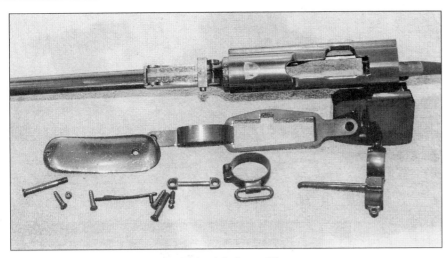

Disassembly is the first step in any bluing job. Assemblies like the barreled action can be left together, but parts that move have to be separated or they'll stick.

Excellent results can be obtained with this improvised system, but you have to be willing to work for it. You can use it for a dull matte blue job appropriate for a military gun or for a highly polished finish that would be found on a nice sporting rifle.

BLUING offers some degree of resistance to rusting, though nothing like more modern finishes.

The only difference between the two jobs is surface preparation and attention to detail. A military-style matte type blue finish is easier and is a good choice for the novice. After you get a few jobs under your belt, you can move to finer finishes.

While I scrounged a lot of parts, some items are best bought from gunsmithing suppliers. I recommend getting the bluing tank, bluing thermometer, bluing salts, specialty cleaners, neutralizer, water displacing oil, and possibly a propane burner for your bluing tank if you aren't comfortable improvising a tank burner.

Your rinse tanks can be improvised from the long (5x5x36-40") flower pots available in the gardening section of your local

home improvement store. You may already have a couple of steel buckets for heating water for cleaning and neutralizing, or can get them at a garage sale.

You can find a couple of kitchen thermometers for getting your cleaners and neutralizers hot enough at any discount store.

Each manufacturer of bluing chemicals has *detailed* instructions for their use. I use Brownells Oxynate No. 7 Hot Blue. The instruction booklet is 35 pages long and covers safety precautions, surface preparation, system setup and troubleshooting if you have problems. It explains the process in detail and tells you why things have to be the way they are.

It is absolutely the best-written "how to" manual for bluing. It even covers cold bluing, hot water bluing and polishing. It makes the job a lot easier when you have this much info available for your first job.

Brownells emphasizes safety, and it can't be overemphasized. You are going to be working with open propane flames and highly caustic and hazardous chemicals at 300°. Protective clothing like gloves, aprons and face shields is vital, as is adequate ventilation.

The centerpiece of any bluing system is the bluing tank. It needs to be least 6x6x36 inches. If you can get a larger one, all the better. I wanted to blue a Browning 1919A4 that wouldn't fit this size tank, so I bought a larger 8x8x40 inch tank from Jantz Supply.

It cost only a little more, but it needs bluing salts and takes longer to heat. You may be able to improvise a bluing tank to cut cost but it must be strong enough to support about 50 pounds of solution and should be made from mild steel at least 16 gauge thick. I fabricated a stand from scrap water pipe to support the tank and added brackets to hold the burner that I improvised.

I obtained a scrap propane burner from an old gas water heater and cut off the burner section and saved the mixer part for my burner. To this mixer I brazed a 1/2-inch coupler to which I attached a 36-inch section of black iron pipe capped at the opposite end. I drilled holes (No. 50 drill size) every 3/4 inch.

I also used a mixer orifice sized at No. 50. I mounted this several inches below the tank and added a valve to adjust flame size and a regulated propane tank connected by hose. I might add that you will have to adjust the mixer for your new burner to get the right flame.

Skirts around my tank hold in the heat for more efficient heating and to keep me from burning myself when working close to the bluing tank. If you are not comfortable making your own burner, Brownells has them at reasonable cost. You really need to know what you are doing when

making a burner or you could have disastrous results! If in doubt, just buy it!

You are also going to need a good bluing thermometer. Buy one specifically made for this purpose because temperature is *critical* for successful bluing.

You are also going to need containers to heat cleaning solutions, neutralizer, and hot water. I simply use a couple of steel 5-gallon buckets and heat them on a two-burner propane hotplate.

I heat the solutions on the hot plate, and then dump them into the cleaning and neutralizing tanks to save the cost of having heated tanks for these solutions. Get a couple cheap kitchen thermometers for measuring temperatures for these solutions, as they are both under 200°.

You will need something to use for "tanks" for cleaning, neutralizing and rinsing. I use the long planters that are available at your local garden shop. They are generally 5-6 inches square and about 36 inches long. Be sure to get heavy-duty ones because the solutions will be hot and tend to soften the plastic and make it flimsy.

I eventually bought a heavy fiberglass tank from Brownells for the hot stuff and save the lighter ones for cooler rinses. One heavy and one light tank is a bare minimum, but a couple extra ones will make things easier since you won't have to dump them to reuse for the later rinses.

Matte-finished military rifle parts can have the original finish removed using a wire wheel. Highly polished sporting arms will require more careful buffing to shine.

A source of water is needed for all these solutions and a garden hose is real convenient if you have one nearby, but if not you can use buckets and transport the water to your bluing area.

You will also need rags, cleaning brushes, hooks for hanging your parts, a stainless steel ladle for adding chemicals, a stainless strainer for removing crud from your tank, a stainless steel stirring stick, mineral spirits, steel wool or abrasive pads, plus your protective gear.

Before you can blue a gun, the metal has to be properly prepared. Surface prep is the key to a good blue job. I will say this again just in case you missed it! Surface preparation is the key to a good blue job. It doesn't matter how you do the rest of the project if it isn't prepared right. Bluing only colors the metal; it hides nothing. Your metal will look the same as before it was blued, except it will be black.

If you can see scratches or rough spots before the metal goes into the blue tank, you will see them afterwards, only they will be black. If the metal is smooth and free from defects, you will get a nice smooth defect-free blue job. As they say in the computer world, garbage in, garbage out!

Start by disassembling the gun. All parts that can be taken apart should be, with the exception of the barrel and receiver. Some loose-fitting parts can remain if they can be secured so they won't slide around and scratch up the blue job in process. Anything that is tight fitting needs to be removed because you run the risk of bluing together the parts.

A basket is convenient for small parts and keeps them from getting lost at the bottom of the bluing tank. Matthews points out that many small parts don't need bluing.

Matthews is a skilled metalworker and was able to fabricate his tank stand and burner from scrap parts. Brownells supplies the whole setup if you have the funds.

After disassembly, you have to decide which parts you want to blue. Internal parts that haven't had the finish worn off really don't need to be reblued in my opinion. Generally I just reblue exterior parts like the barreled action, trigger guard, trigger, sights, barrel bands and other external hardware.

Since I want a matte finish, I use a soft wire wheel on a bench grinder to remove the old blue and give the base metal a soft,

Bluing salts make a thick caustic slush before heating. Harsh, heated chemicals mean that safety clothing and adequate ventilation are vital parts of the process.

non-reflective texture. "Wire off" the old blue or rust: just be careful not to put to much pressure on the wheel because even a wire wheel will remove metal if pressed hard.

Be sure you get a plain, not stainless steel, wire wheel. Stainless steel can rub into the base metal and it will not blue properly because stainless doesn't blue with common bluing chemicals.

If you don't have a bench grinder and suitable wire wheel, you can also do it the old fashioned way. Use fine (400-600 grit) sandpaper and abrasive pads like the Scotch-Brite brand to remove the old finish. If you are willing to put in a lot of elbow grease, this method will work.

The sandpaper will remove most of the finish and then you can buff it a little with the pads. This is *extremely* labor intensive, so really consider the wire wheel method. You can buy a Chinese-made 6-inch bench grinder new for less than $30, so if your time is valuable, it's the choice.

If you have a blasting cabinet, it's easy to get a matte finish using a mild abrasive, but most of us don't have sandblasting equipment.

The bright shiny finishes that you see on sporting guns is obtained by polishing with various grades of abrasives on soft cloth wheels on a buffer and this is an art in itself. It is also extremely labor intensive; you can put hours into polishing a gun prior to bluing.

Now that you have your parts stripped of rust and old finish, it's time to clean them. You may think they look clean already, but trust me, they do still need cleaning as bluing is extremely sensitive to any remaining traces of oil, grease or wax that you may not be able to see. I generally start by pre-cleaning with mineral spirits (common paint thinner) to help get out any oil or grease.

Do this only away from any sources of sparks or flames and always follow the safety precautions. I just put the parts in one of the long containers and dump in some mineral spirits, scrub then dry off.

Next comes a detergent cleaner. Brownells sells a cleaner specifically for this purpose called Dicro-Clean 909. Mix, heat and use it according to the instructions. I use a 5-gallon bucket on a hot plate and then pour it into one of the long containers and really scrub it.

After you feel your parts are clean, rinse with clean water. Once these parts are clean they will be *extremely* prone to rusting since the metal is absolutely clean and has nothing to protect it from the oxygen in the air that causes rust.

I prefer to time my bluing project so that when the parts are clean, the bluing tank is ready to go. Then there is no time for the parts to sit around and rust. You can apply treatments to the parts to keep them from rusting if you aren't going to blue right away but that just adds another step and cost to the process. It's easier just to have everything ready to proceed directly to the bluing tank.

Now comes the actual bluing process. Different manufacturers have various mixing procedures for their products, but all basically require you to mix water and powdered chemicals (bluing salts) together in the right proportions and heat to the right temperature. You can't just throw some water and chemicals together and heat it. It has to be mixed in *exact* proportions and heated to an exact temperature at which it should boil.

The instructions for Brownells Oxynate 7 explain how to do this and why it must be done that way. Follow the instructions

and your results will be good; go your own way and failure will be the result.

This is probably the "touchiest" part of bluing. It isn't all that hard after you have done it and understand why it is done this way. Once you have your tank and bluing solution heated to the right temperature, you are ready to put your previously cleaned parts in the tank.

The parts can't lie on the bottom of the tank; they must be suspended in the solution. I use 1/4" wire rod hooks to hold the parts and have some rod across the top of the tank to hold the hooks.

For holding barreled actions, I recommend some Z-shaped hooks to insert in the muzzle and action to hold the parts internally so you don't have hook marks where they will show.

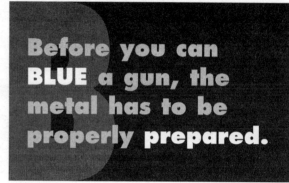

Before you can BLUE a gun, the metal has to be properly prepared.

When inserting parts into the tank always insert them at an angle and rock back and forth so that air trapped in the parts can escape. Once your parts are in the tank and totally submerged, it's time to sit back and wait.

Maybe I should say sit back and *watch* and wait. This part of the process requires your full attention. Your parts will have to be in the tank for about 30 minutes, and during this time you may have to adjust the heat and water in the tank. Bluing has to be done in a very small temperature range (about 285-300°) and requires you to pay close attention to what's going on.

Don't wander off to do something else while bluing. When you are using a fresh batch of bluing solution, it is usually clear enough that you can see what's going on in the tank if the parts are close to the top, but as you use the solution it will become cloudy enough you won't be able to see the parts without pulling them out

It's OK to check every 10 minutes or so but don't get carried away with checking, you know the old saying about a watched pot never boiling! If you did everything right, after about 30 minutes or so your parts should be done.

While kitchen thermometers are OK for some bluing operations, Matthews says there's no substitute for a high-temperature thermometer for regulating tank heat.

You will now remove your parts and rinse off the bluing solution. You can hose it off or immerse in one of your long tanks filled with clean water. Continue to hold your parts by the hooks, as I have found that fresh bluing is somewhat soft and needs some time to harden (this is not mentioned in the instructions but it has been *my* experience).

Don't be surprised if there is some caulky black residue on your parts. It may be from poor water or failure to follow procedure exactly, but it rubs off later and causes no problems.

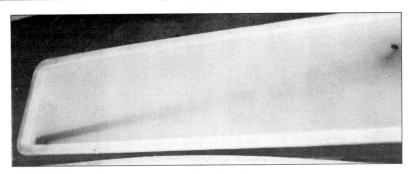

Bluing is a controlled rusting process, so it's vital to use a neutralizing solution that stops the chemical reaction when the right metal finish color has been achieved.

Even though you have rinsed the parts, there may be some bluing solution remaining in tight spots, so it should go through a neutralizing solution to keep it from "creeping out" later and causing corrosion.

The neutralizing rinse is very easy to do. Brownells sells a product for this known as B.O.N. (bleed out neutralizer). I just mix it up in a steel 5-gallon bucket, heat on my propane hot plate to the recommended temperature and then pour into one of my long plastic tanks and soak the parts for 15-30 minutes. An occasional stirring will help the process.

After soaking in B.O.N., remove and rinse with clean water (hot or cold, hot will make it dry faster when done) and then dry off the parts. I use compressed air to blow the parts dry and then

BLUING releases a lot of steam and this steam will condense on the cooler things in your area.

spray on a coating of water displacing oil and let it sit for a day or so. I like to let it cure for a day or so before taking a soft rag and rubbing off any remaining residue.

I then re-oil with my preferred gun oil and the job is done except for re-assembly.

If you have done everything right, you should now have a

Plastic planter boxes get the job done nicely as rinse tanks. Get heavy ones that will stand up to the hot water. A propane hot plate is good for heating liquids.

nicely blued part. If things didn't come out right, review the troubleshooting section of the instruction manual or contact Brownells at their technical assistance phone number. I have had some questions and they were very helpful in solving the few problems that I have had.

I don't claim to be a professional refinisher, but I do have some tips for the beginner, learned the hard way.

Hot bluing is just that, *hot* The more ventilation the better. If your bluing area is small, the heat generated by your system can be intense and the last thing you need is to be dripping sweat all over your parts. I also find the steam from the tank irritating to my lungs.

After neutralizing, rinsing and oiling, the blued part is ready for assembly. Matthews says strict adherence to the written instructions will yield a good job.

Use the recommended safety equipment. When up and running at temperature, the bluing tank can spit a little and these little bits of chemical will start burning your skin in just a few minutes. Use gloves, long sleeves, apron, and a face shield. Keep a small bucket of water with a rag close by to wipe off any splatters that you may get on your skin.

Bluing releases a lot of steam and this steam will condense on the cooler things in your area. This is mildly corrosive and will cause corrosion problems down the road. This is especially a problem with aluminum in the area. A few years ago I had a nice Harley Davidson motorcycle that I kept in the same garage that I blued in. I thought 15-20 feet away was fine to protect the bike from any splatters.

Well, a couple weeks after bluing I noticed that my highly polished aluminum parts were developing white speckles of corrosion on the top of everything. This was where the steam had settled onto the cool cycle parts and the corrosive chemicals in the steam began to corrode the aluminum.

I had to clean and polish all the parts to remove the corrosion and return the parts to their former finish. If it will hurt to be rusted or corroded keep it away from your bluing system. In gun factories, bluing is always performed in a separate room, and often in a separate building.

As you use your system a certain amount of crud will develop in the tank. This is dirt and depleted bluing chemical. Skimming it off with a wire mesh strainer will keep your tank cleaner and make it easier to use since you won't have chunks of crud settling on your parts.

The more you use your tank, the cloudier the solution will get, to the point that you won't be able to see your parts submerged in the tank. This is normal, but if you want to keep it cleaner there are bluing tank solution cleaners available.

One thing that can't be overstated is to read the instructions that came with your chemicals well. In fact read them several times before starting. The people who wrote them know what they are talking about.

One labor saving tip especially pertaining to military guns is to avoid putting too much effort into surface prep on the parts that are under the handguards or any other parts that aren't exposed to view. You can polish up the bottom of the receiver just dandy, but it will be covered by the stock and never be seen, so why bother? Put the work into the parts you see!

If you have problems with Brownells Oxynate 7, don't be afraid to call Brownells. They are pros in the use of their products and have been for years. They have probably heard of your problem before and know the solution. They want you to use their product successfully and will help you get professional results.

Like most, I always am looking for an easier way to do something and have tried a few short cuts. I have scrimped on surface prep and cleaning methods on some military surplus projects and gotten away with it a few times.

I have literally hosed off some military guns that had no rust but no bluing left with solvents and threw them in the hot tank and had good results. If you are going to try short cuts you do so at your own risk. There is nothing wrong with experimenting, but not all experiments are successful. When you go your own way you are on your own! ◎

WALLHANGER?
No Way!

By Paul Mazan

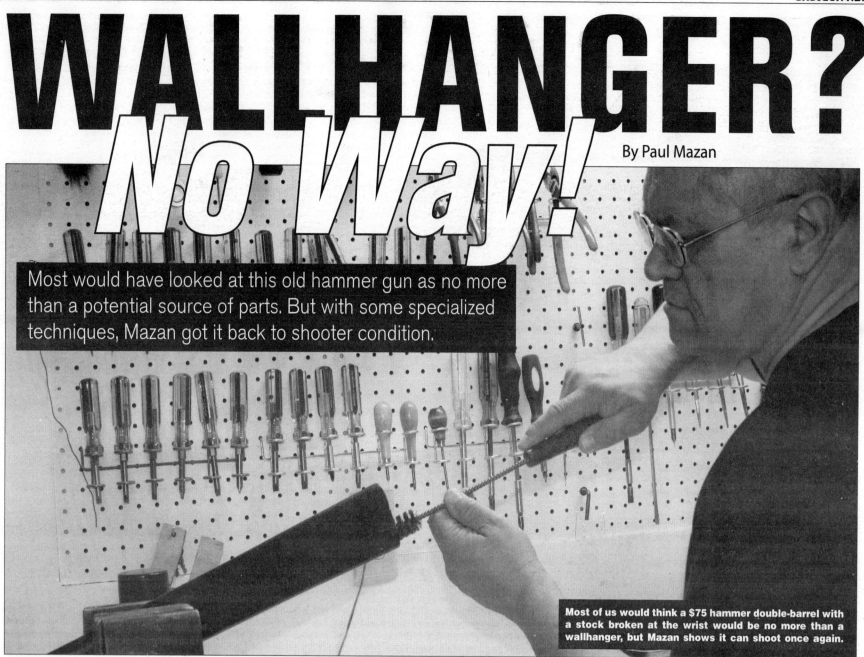

Most would have looked at this old hammer gun as no more than a potential source of parts. But with some specialized techniques, Mazan got it back to shooter condition.

Most of us would think a $75 hammer double-barrel with a stock broken at the wrist would be no more than a wallhanger, but Mazan shows it can shoot once again.

A broken stock has taken many a fine old gun out of action and you may have to repair the stock to save the gun.

Some stock repairs are easy. A new piece can be made for a chipped toe and simple gluing can often repair a split forend so well it is all but impossible to see the repair. Many popular guns are easy to find replacement stocks for and with CNC inletting, even a hobbyist can restock those guns.

Then there are those disasters that appear from time to time that look unrepairable. I recently ran into a nice English-made double that was not only broken at the wrist but was shattered, with pieces of wood missing and a homemade repair.

Then someone had attempted to repair the stock by gluing the pieces together without degreasing the oil-soaked wood and inletted and screwed two brass plates into the wrist to "fix" the damage. The repair was not only ugly, the glue didn't hold and the stock was falling apart. At first glance you might think that there isn't a chance to save this stock, but with the right techniques it can be brought back to life.

This extreme example had been stripped of many parts, including the buttplate, trigger guard and just about every screw, so disassembly was simple. Most of the pieces could simply be lifted off by hand, but to complete the disassembly I did have to remove the wedge from the forend and work the lever to remove the barrels.

A careful check showed a remarkably smooth bore with little internal pitting, solid lockwork and mechanically

excellent locks. The gun was worth some effort to save and priced at $75, I couldn't say no. The first step in repairing the stock was to remove the wood screws holding the brass strips to the stock.

With that accomplished I found I had three major oil-soaked pieces. No glue I know of will hold oil-soaked wood together, so it was important to get all the oil out of the stock. I first used the tried and true method of an application of oven cleaner followed by scrubbing in hot soapy water.

I removed the stock finish and the pieces looked very good when dried, but several days later, more oil leached out of the wood and the surface was oil-soaked again. After three more applications of oven cleaner gave the same results, I took things a step further by immersing the wood in a tank of turpentine, weighting the pieces down, and letting them soak for two weeks.

The inexpensive turpentine you get from the hardware store smells like the devil, so you will want to soak the stock out in the garage and be sure to cover the tank. That solved the problem of the oil-soaked wood. It came out of the turpentine bath free of oil but stunk so badly that

even after a bath with soap and water I had to leave it in the garage for another week before I could bring it back into the shop.

To reinforce the wood across the broken area I used Brownells Stock Repair Pins (part #080-565-093AB available from Brownells at 800-741-0015). These are 2-inch long brass alloy pins that are threaded to hold plenty of glue.

Carefully measure and align the holes so that when the broken ends of the stock are brought together, they will line

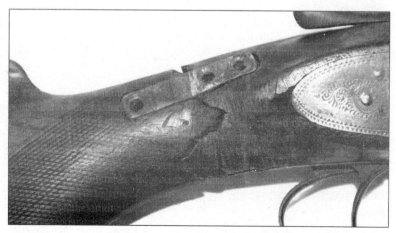

The grip area was shattered, and some gunsmith in the distant past had glued and reinforced it with a brass strip secured with screws. It was both ugly and unstable.

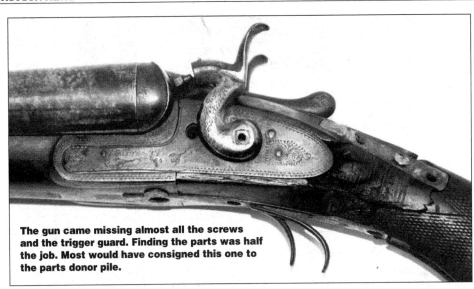

The gun came missing almost all the screws and the trigger guard. Finding the parts was half the job. Most would have consigned this one to the parts donor pile.

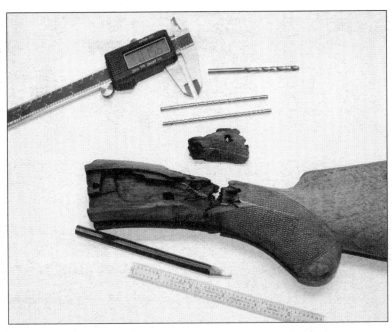

Mazan used a grease pencil to mark the layout line for positioning the repair pins from Brownells. These are grooved to retain adhesive for a strong repair joint.

Getting the oil out of the stock required a lengthy soak in a bucket of turpentine. Oil-soaked wood will not take glue or finishes, so it needs to be oil-free.

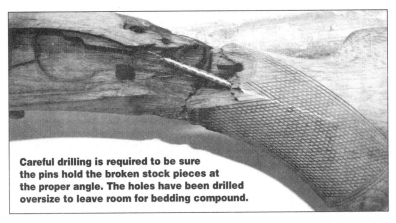

Careful drilling is required to be sure the pins hold the broken stock pieces at the proper angle. The holes have been drilled oversize to leave room for bedding compound.

up perfectly. Lining those holes up exactly on a broken stock is nearly impossible. So I drill the holes oversize, pump them full of Acraglas (also a Brownells product), and insert the pins.

Drilling the holes oversized leaves plenty of room for error in locating them and still allows the stock to be perfectly aligned. Before assembly I coated the ends of the broken stock and all the bits and pieces of wood with *Gorilla Glue* from the local home center and clamped everything together.

To hold the stock together I used a pipe clamp and to hold the broken pieces in place, I wrapped the area with surgical tubing, another item available from Brownells. The stock was left for 24 hours to allow the glue and Acraglas to set up before continuing.

Upon removing the surgical tubing, and the clamp I discovered the stock properly aligned and rigid, but ugly as sin. There were those inletted places from where the brass strips were attached as well as the screw holes and gaps where wood was simply missing and lost.

I also knew that there were substantial gaps inside the wrist where wood had broken out and was lost. To return this gun to a shootable condition, something would have to be done to fill this area or the first shot might simply break it again.

I took a piece of walnut and cut it into 1/8" thick strips and cut them to length and width to fit the inletted places where the brass strips had been and glued them to the stock with *Gorilla Glue*.

I really like the *Gorilla Glue* for several reasons. First, it sets up in 2-3 hours. Second, it expands in volume by 3-4 times and fills any voids from poor inletting or bad fit. Third, it is waterproof and your stock will not come apart if you get caught in the rain.

Starting at the bottom of the grip, I fashioned pieces of walnut to fill any gaps where pieces had broken off and been lost. In some cases, you may have to remove wood from around a broken area and fashion a walnut piece to fit into the damaged area. Don't worry about depth. It is OK to have the repair higher than the original wood surface because it can be sanded flat later. The most important thing is to get it to fit at tightly as possible and clamp the patches in place until they set.

Once all the damaged areas were repaired I had one hole I left open at the top of the stock. I mixed up another batch of Acraglas, stained it brown and poured it into the stock. This lets it fill any voids where wood is missing inside the repaired area and also allows it to flow into any cracks that did not close completely.

If you know you still have holes or cracks that will let the Acraglas leak out, cover them with masking tape. You won't be able to remove the tape but you can sand it off later. When the Acraglas sets up, you simply have to cut one more patch to cover the hole you poured it into and the repairs are done.

Sand the stock down, blending the patches into the original wood, and things start to look pretty good. You still have a patchwork quilt of walnut but a lot of that will be hidden by staining and recheckering the stock. If you have a good selection of walnut so you can match the color of the original stock and cut your patches to follow the grain, it will look even better. Once the glue has set, there should be absolutely no movement when you hold the ends of the stock and try to bend, twist, or wiggle it.

It is almost impossible to find parts for some of these old guns, and I had to measure the threads in each hole and try

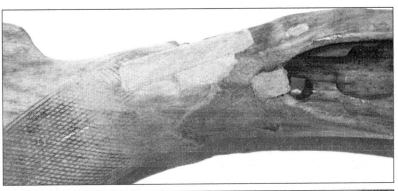

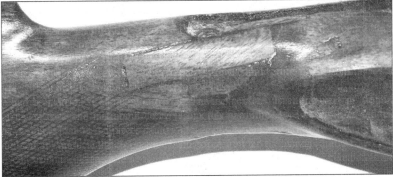

The first walnut patches are cut to size, inlaid and glued in position. You'll be unlikely to duplicate the wood's color, but stain and checkering help blend it.

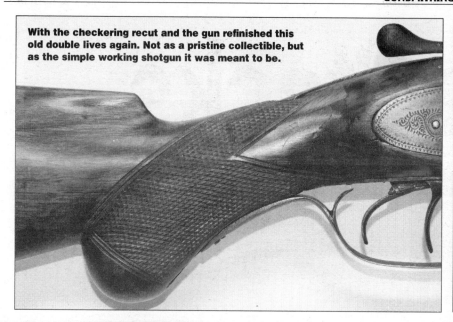

With the checkering recut and the gun refinished this old double lives again. Not as a pristine collectible, but as the simple working shotgun it was meant to be.

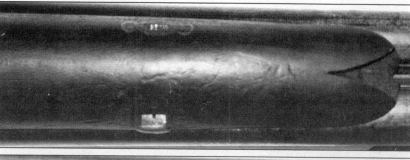

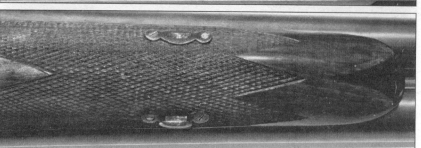

The shotgun's original fore-end tip, probably ebony, was missing. Mazan poured in black Acraglas, sanded it smooth, then recheckered and refinished the fore-end.

to find screws of the right length to fit. In some ways, this was the hardest part of the job. Being an English gun, at least none of the threads were metric, but I can tell you that no two threads were alike.

A call to Gun Parts Corp. at 914-679-2417 with the thread size did get a trigger guard on the way and I had a steel buttplate on hand that took only minor fitting. If you would prefer to install a recoil pad, now is the time to do it. You have to refinish the stock anyway, and you can sand the pad with the stock and get a perfect fit without worrying about scratching the finish.

The ebony tip was missing from the front of the fore-end and whittling one out would have been a major project. Instead, I used masking tape to build a dam around the cutout and once again poured Acraglas that had been stained black into the inletting, letting it overflow the area. Once it was set up, I removed the tape and sanded the epoxy down to the surface of the wood. It looks great and the fit is perfect!

At this point I thought all that was left was to refinish the stock and recut the checkering. Not that recutting checkering

is easy or fun, but it would hide some of the patched areas and the gun was engraved so I felt I just had to.

The gun had always seemed heavy to me, but I hadn't given it much thought until I reassembled it and discovered that the chamber swallowed a 12-gauge snap cap. Having been built long before chamber sizes were standardized, careful measuring showed the chambers to be between 12-gauge maximum and 10-gauge minimum dimensions, so effectively I had an 11-gauge gun on my hands.

Fortunately, there is a fast and easy fix for this situation. I called the folks at Gauge Mate (1-800-709-9910) and asked about the possibility of having a set of their chamber adapters made to reduce the chambers to accept 12-gauge shells. They asked for the chamber dimensions and said their 10-gauge to 12-gauge adapters would fit.

If you aren't familiar with sub-gauge adapters, let me explain that they fit into the chambers of a break-open shotgun and reduce the size to fit a smaller gauge. The best known was probably the Savage Four-tenner made back in the 70s. They were only made to fit 12-gauge chambers

and allowed .410 shells to be fired in the gun. They were discontinued by Savage many years ago, but today Gauge Mate can provide adapters to fit all the common sizes and allow them to shoot a smaller gauge shell.

If you have an old 16-gauge shotgun sitting in the closet and you are tired of hunting for 16-gauge shells and then paying a premium for them, a set of 16- to 20-gauge reducers will allow your old 16 to shoot 20s. I ordered a set of 10- to 12-gauge reducers and cut a section of the rim off so the gun's extractor would extract the shell and not the entire unit. I later found out that Gauge Mate has what they call the Gold series with this cut already made and ready to drop in.

For a little money and some shop time I now have an English hammer shotgun in 12-gauge. Before you ask, yes, I only shoot blackpowder shells in it and I bet that if I put it up for sale I can easily pay for my time. ◉

Mazan discovered the gun's chambers were between 12- and 10-gauge inside diameter. Installing Gauge-Mate 10-12 adapters allowed firing with 12-gauge shells.

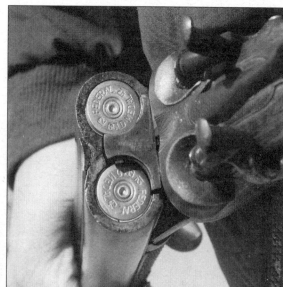

One advantage of test firing the gun is to locate unexpected problems. Metal will have to be added to the extractor to keep it from overriding the cartridge rims.

Two-Piece Stocks *Need Love, Too*

By Reid Coffield

□ ■ Glass-bedding and bolt guns just seem to go together, but Coffield says that lever-action or shotgun can need it even more.

Firearms manufacturers have produced literally millions of rifles and shotguns with two-piece stocks. Just to be clear, a two-piece stock is defined as having a separate buttstock and forearm while a one-piece stock has these two components built as one integral unit.

Whether you're talking about pump, auto, single or double-barrel shotguns, most of them use a two-piece stock. The same holds true with pump, auto, lever-action, and most modern single-shot rifles. At the same time, the vast majority of bolt-action rifles use a single, one-piece stock. There have been a few exceptions to this for bolt-action rifles over the years, the British Lee Enfields and the French MAS for example, but more often than not, the bolt-action rifle will just about always be found with a one-piece stock.

Perhaps because of the extensive use of one-piece stocks on bolt-action rifles, many have come to the conclusion that a one-piece stock is inherently advantageous and especially so when trying to achieve best accuracy.

I would tend to agree there is some truth in that. One consequence of this is that most information published over the years on bedding for accuracy and the repair of stocks has been directed towards bolt-action rifle shooters. That's unfortunate, as many guns with two-piece stocks need and can definitely benefit from synthetic bedding.

This was especially evident just recently when a nice old Marlin 336 in .35 Rem. came into my shop. This was an older rifle built in 1977. I especially like it because it

doesn't have the "lawyer" safety button at the rear of the receiver as do the currently produced 336s. I fully understand the reasoning by Marlin management for putting this safety button on these rifles. It just makes good sense to do all you can as a manufacturer to avoid lawsuits, but it still galls me to no end.

Personally, if an individual using an exposed hammer rifle has to have a push-button safety to use that rifle properly, I would question that shooter's suitability to have the rifle at all! I can get pretty hot under the collar when I see folks trying to make firearms idiot proof when you and I both know idiots will never be safe with any firearm under any circumstance.

Some of these newer safety features just seem to make the guns less attractive and user-friendly for the folks that handle their firearms appropriately. Oh well, maybe that's why older used guns are selling so well!

The 336 in my shop looked pretty good. While it had definitely been used, it was a good sound rifle. There was virtually no rust on it, the bluing was almost 100%, and the stock was in darn good shape. However, as I discovered, the buttstock had a major flaw that would just get worse were the rifle shot quite a bit.

The problem was the bedding of the buttstock. There was a noticeable gap between the rear of the receiver and the front of the buttstock on both sides of the tang. These gaps were so large that you could literally see daylight between the buttstock and the receiver. I used a feeler gauge on the gaps and measured them at about .008". This had to be corrected.

The reason for this is that it left the only contact point at the rear end of the tangs. Over time and repeated recoil, this spot would be pounded back into the wood and act just like a wedge. Eventually the stock would crack or split at these pressure points.

On this Marlin, only the rear of the bottom tang was actually in contact with the wood. To make matters even worse, the point of contact was right along a growth ring in the wood. Sooner or later the stock was going to split or crack at that point.

The solution is to use a synthetic bedding material to fill the gaps between the receiver and the buttstock. The bed-

No doubt about the gap between the buttstock and the receiver as Coffield measures it with a feeler gauge. There should be full contact between the parts.

ding will then ensure that the wood-to-metal contact is uniform and that the recoil forces from the receiver are not concentrated in one or two spots where it can lead to damage. The larger contact area will help to spread the forces of recoil and reduce compression of the wood fibers. It will also help to keep the stock to receiver fit tight and firm.

On a two-piece stock you should have as much contact as possible between the buttstock and the receiver. In addition, you want the stock to be held as firmly or tightly as possible against the receiver. It's almost as though I want to make the stock and the receiver one single unit.

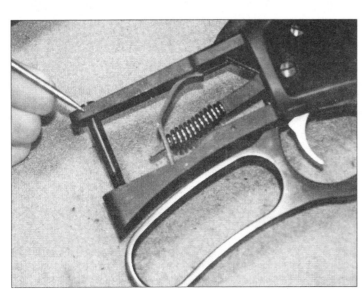

As on many lever-action rifles, the clamping force of the tangs does not draw the receiver back against the stock. This can allow a gap between the two.

The bottom rear of the tang on the Marlin 336 has the greatest potential bearing surface as well as, in this case, significant potential for cracking the stock.

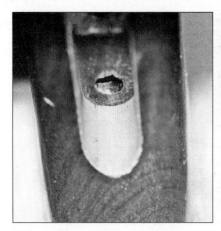

After bedding the tang inletting, the tang now had 100% contact with the stock. This will last for years and effectively prevent splitting of the buttstock.

You can't just smear some bedding compound on the wood and expect it to hold: Coffield removed wood from the front of the buttstock to allow expansion space.

Note the crack in this Model 12 Winchester stock near the middle of the receiver; This is a very commonly encountered problem that needs a solid fix.

talking about the placement of metal reinforcements inside the wood where they are completely invisible. I've always felt that when possible, a good repair should not be noticeable. That also holds true with strengthening two-piece stocks.

The metal reinforcements can be made of almost any type or shape of metal. One of my favorites is simply a piece of all-thread rod or the threaded shank of a screw. The threads in the metal give it more surface area for the epoxy or glue which helps hold it in the wood.

If I'm working on the very end of a stock or on an exposed surface inside the inletting, I'll use my Dremel tool along with a round cutter to open up a channel just a bit wider and deeper than the reinforcing metal rod.

The rod is washed with alcohol to remove any grease or oil, coated with epoxy and placed in the previously cut slot in the stock. I make sure enough epoxy is applied to fully seal the rod in place and be level and even with the wood surface. This makes for a very strong, permanent, and invisible modification.

Occasionally I'll want specifically to strengthen the wrist of a stock. As you might imagine, the wrist is relatively thin compared to the rest of the stock, and is the most vulnerable point for breaking. On more than one occasion, I've used a long drill to open a deep hole from the inletting back down through the wrist into the buttstock.

I then take a steel rod, clean it, coat it with epoxy, and place it in the hole. You have to make sure you have enough epoxy in the hole to completely coat the pin and not have any voids or open spaces. By the way, I've used both threaded and unthreaded rods for this and have not seen any difference in results.

Keep in mind that with many firearms, the pressure or force used to hold the metal work in the stock is actually at 90° to the line of recoil. In the typical bolt-action rifle, the line of recoil force is directly to the rear in line with the barrel, yet the guard screws extend up from below the barrel and receiver. All that's holding the metal in the stock is a clamping action that doesn't necessarily hold the metal against the wood.

Ruger took on this problem and dealt with it in the Model 77 rifle by having the front guard screw angled to both draw the metal back into the wood and down at the same time. On the other hand, your typical Winchester or Marlin lever gun just uses a rear tang screw to clamp the tangs on to the buttstock. There's no mechanical force at all to pull the metal back into the stock.

If the receiver is loose in the stock, it will be slammed back each time the gun is fired. This repeated battering can often bend the tang or guard screws and will definitely damage the stock.

On some guns, the buttstock is secured with a through or stock bolt. This is a large bolt that usually extends through the buttstock and pulls the metal and wood together. It's generally a better system in that it helps to ensure good solid contact between the metal and the wood. However, it's not foolproof. You will still often find damage due to poor bedding where you have uneven contact between the wood and metal.

One other problem I've found in working with older guns that employ a stock bolt is that the bolt will sometimes rust and develop scale. As it oxidizes the diameter of the bolt actually expands. This can sometimes make it almost impossible to remove or unscrew. It can, under some conditions, actually split or crack the wood. As you can see, there are no "perfect" solutions to this problem!

In the case of this Marlin 336, the application of synthetic bedding alone will probably take care of any problems both present and future. However, what if you run across a two-piece stock that has already been damaged? What can you do to repair the damage and strengthen the stock? Actually, you can do a *lot!*

First, let's talk a bit about how you can strengthen a stock before you glass-bed it. Keep in mind that more often than not, a good epoxy or glue properly applied has greater strength than the wood you are using it on. I've seen a number of cases where stocks that had been repaired with an epoxy broke again. In every case, the new break was not at the point of the epoxy repair. In short, the wood failed before the epoxy.

One of the most common techniques to strengthen a stock is to place metal pins or supports in the wood. Now don't get me wrong; I'm not advocating putting big wood screws or bolts through the stock wrist as often seen on poorly, and I mean really poorly, done repairs. Instead I'm

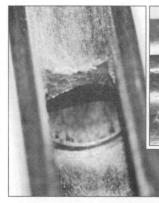

Firearm manufacturers recognized the problem of forearm damage on the Browning long recoil shotguns and tried to strengthen the wood using laminate inserts.

If you look carefully you can see several cracks at the rear of the top tang on this Model 11 Remington shotgun. The stock will fail eventually at this point.

The inner shoulder in the Remington Model 11 forearm is often damaged by repeated blows from the barrel lug, and cracks appear near the forearm tip.

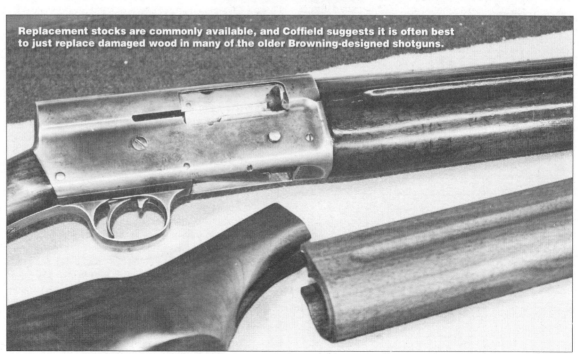

Replacement stocks are commonly available, and Coffield suggests it is often best to just replace damaged wood in many of the older Browning-designed shotguns.

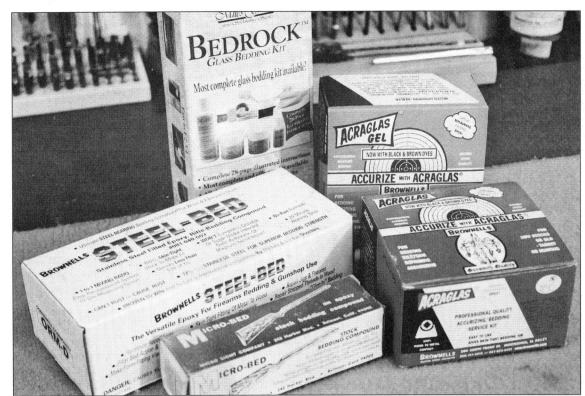

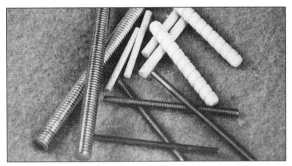

Coffield regularly uses a variety of pins, wood dowels, and threaded rods to repair and strengthen stocks. These add additional rigidity to the repair.

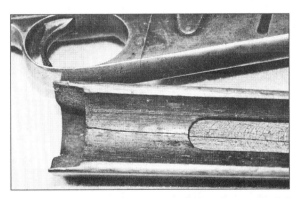

Note the crack on the forearm of this Remington Model 8 semiauto rifle. Today's synthetics and modern design mean you'll never see something like this on an AR.

Sometimes it's just not possible to drill from the inletting into the wrist. On a couple of occasions I've had to remove a pistol grip cap and drill up from under the cap into the wrist. Once the repair has been made, the cap was replaced and the repair was hidden.

I have yet to drill from the rear end of the buttstock for a job like this. While that's theoretically possible, it could be darn hard to do. You always run the risk of having the drill bit wander or move when you drill a really deep hole like that. The thought of having the drill pop through the side of the wrist is truly awful, so I've avoided doing this thus far. I may some day have to do it, but I sure don't look forward to doing so.

Most of us think in terms of bolt-actions when thinking of bedding compounds, but all of the common types will do a good job in repairing two-piece stocks.

Within the gunsmithing community there is some disagreement over whether it's better to use a metal pin or a wooden dowel as a stock reinforcer. I normally tend to make more frequent use of metal pins than wooden dowels. Some gunsmiths are concerned about metal pins rusting or corroding and causing damage. I've never had that happen thus far, though I suppose it's technically possible. However, once you fully coat a pin with epoxy, I think the risk of rusting is really small.

I've made use of wood dowels several times because of the necessity to later drill through the dowel. I remember once when I had to place a reinforcing dowel through the rear guard screw hole on a rifle stock. Once the repair was made and the epoxy had cured, I used a drill to come down through the guard screw hole and drill through the dowel where it was blocking the guard screw hole. I would not have been able to do that (certainly not easily!) if I had used a metal pin in the same spot.

One other point to keep in mind when bedding a two-piece buttstock has to do with the removal of wood for the bedding. Just as with bedding a one-piece stock, you seldom can or should just throw bedding on the wood surface.

To get a reasonable thickness and to maximize the strength of the bedding, you'll frequently need to remove some wood. I almost always use a variety of small round cutters in my Dremel to route out a few grooves in the wood surface to provide space for the bedding. In addition, this ensures that the bedding will have reasonably fresh, clean wood to which it can bond. I think this is generally more important with two-piece stocks than with the typical one-piece rifle stock. Here again it's good to keep in mind that the bedding is almost always stronger than the wood, so the more bedding you can use, the stronger your stock.

Now don't go overboard with that last comment. I've seen bedding jobs on stocks where the wood was basically just a shell to hold the bedding compound. I swear to goodness on one stock I ran across years ago there was more bedding than wood!

There are basically two schools of thought relative to bedding the forearm on a two-piece rifle stock. Some folks

contend that the forearm should never touch or place any pressure on the barrel. In essence, the barrel should be free-floated. The other group contends that the forearm should be firmly mated with the barrel. In one sense, both groups are right. It just depends on the circumstances and the design of the gun.

For example, in my experience with the Ruger No. 1, which has the forearm attached to a hanger extending from the front of the receiver, I'll get the best performance and accuracy when the barrel doesn't contact the inside of the forearm. On the other hand, with a rifle such as the Marlin 336 which already has all sorts of parts such as the magazine tube, magazine tube band, and forearm band hanging off the barrel, I want the forearm firmly bedded against the barrel and receiver.

With the Marlin 336, Winchester 94, or even the M1 Garand you have so many components contacting the barrel that you might as well make the contact as secure and consistent as possible. If the pressure is going to be there, make sure it doesn't vary because of the movement or shifting of the parts as the gun is used. It's kind of like the old saying, if you can't beat 'em, join 'em!

That was the reason I bedded the rear of the forearm on this Marlin. I wanted to make sure that the forearm would not shift or move as the rifle was used. If there had to be pressure on the barrel I wanted it to be as consistent as possible.

How far can you go with this? Well, I have seen some very accurate Garands where the handguards were epoxied to the barrel. The only way you could remove 'em was to literally cut 'em off! For the competitive shooters using these rifles, that was not an issue. They fully expected to replace the barrels at the end of one or two shooting seasons anyway and the cost of a couple of handguards was of no consequence. Accuracy and performance was all that mattered.

As for repairing forearms, with some guns it's frankly seldom worth the effort. A great example is the forearm on the Browning designed long recoil shotguns such as the Remington Model 11, the Browning A-5, or the Savage/Springfield 720, 745, etc. The design of these guns has the barrel ring or hanger slamming into the inside of the forearm as it returns to the forward position.

This continued battering virtually ensures that the forearm will sooner or later crack. If you have an undamaged forearm you can reinforce the contact point with bedding, but if it's already cracked or battered you might as well go ahead and replace the forearm with new wood. Fortunately, replacement forearms are readily available from folks like Boyds, Numrich, or Brownells.

One other point about these Browning-designed shotguns; most of these guns are fairly old and the forearms have seen a lot of service. Even though you could theoretically fix cracks in the rear of the forearm, the wood is frequently oil soaked and can make getting a good epoxy to adhere extremely difficult, if not impossible. Again, it's often best to just junk the old forearm and replace it.

Forearms on other shotguns such as the Winchester Model 97 and Model 12 are often in just as bad a shape, but these can frequently be repaired. The difference is that these forearms are not subject to the same stress and constant battering as those on the old automatics.

Still, if given the opportunity I'd replace the wood if possible with a new forearm. That's one of those situations where you have to make a judgment call based upon the individual gun, the condition of the forearm, and the desire of the owner.

As you can see from just this brief look at two-piece stocks, there are a lot of things to consider when repairing or bedding for accuracy. In many respects, working on a two-piece stock can be much more challenging than bedding an ol' Mauser or that new Remington 700. One thing you can absolutely count on is that you'll see lots of rifles and shotgun with two-piece stocks that need some help!

Until next time, good luck and good gunsmithing! ◉

Upgrading AK Furniture

By George Spafford

AK purists may cringe, but Spafford says a collapsible stock makes the Kalashnikov a much more useful rifle, especially for shooters of varied statures.

Tired of that East European mystery wood and runny finish? There are many ways to improve the buttstock and fore-end of your AK, but keep in mind the need for U.S. parts!

I read Steve Matthews' great article on how to build an AK rifle in Shotgun News (9/20/05) and for reasons not entirely clear even to me, that's when I caught the AK bug and became actively involved in an absolutely huge industry that has built up around the AK series of rifles.

You can spend $500-1,500 on the rifle and then thousands on aftermarket accessories. Entrepreneurs are recognizing that many gun stores you go in to have at least one AK for sale–usually a WASR from Romania, an Arsenal made in the USA using Bulgarian and U.S. parts or a Russian Saiga.

For owners looking to customize their rifles there is a huge selection of various types of "furniture"–the buttstock, pistol grip and front hand grips–available ranging from surplus to new and imported to U.S.-made. It is that last part of that sentence that we need to review for a moment due to a particular BATFE regulation.

The BATFE ruled that a non-sporting firearm cannot be assembled with more than 10 foreign parts. This matters because the AK-47, AK-74 and other variants need U.S.-made parts added. The exact combination can vary depending on how the rifle was classified depending on type of stock, magazine design and so on.

For the owner of an AK, this isn't just an academic issue. If you want to change the parts on your AK it is important to understand what impact that will have on the parts count and thus the legality of the rifle.

For example, removing all the current furniture and replacing it with a Russian set or an Israeli set may result in a rifle that has more than 10 foreign parts, rendering it illegal. The buttstock counts as one part, the pistol grip as one and the front handguard set (both upper and lower) count for one. That means the furniture accounts for three potential compliance parts either for, or against, your 10-part maximum.

It's vital to understand what parts in your AK are American-made and which are foreign made. If you replace the current parts with U.S. parts of the same configuration you are generally okay. If you replace a part with a foreign part, then compliance with the 922r parts count regulation needs to be factored in.

If you are in law enforcement or some other position that requires high-reliability, there are stocks you should consider and ones you should frankly avoid. The AKfiles.com gun board has many posts about what furniture is more for the casual user than for professionals. At the same time, the materials used and, more often than not, pricing are giveaways.

When speaking of AK furniture, there are two broad categories–traditional style that follow the original Russian design, and non-traditional designs that blend features from other rifles, such as the U.S. M4.

If you have a wood stocked AK, one approach is to refinish what you have. This is actually a very straightforward and rewarding option. The first step is to remove the furniture and liberally coat the wood with a wood stripper such as Bix.

Follow the instructions and repeat this two or three times or until you are satisfied. Then rinse with water and make sure all of the chemical is out of the wood. Some builders will actually dunk the stock a few times in a solution of bleach and water to get the wood as light as possible. As for myself, I just rinse the stock and let it dry completely for a few days.

The next step is to sand the stock to get rid of any dings and then use finer and finer sandpaper to get a nice smooth surface. Alternatively, you can use steaming to raise dents.

Once the wood is ready to apply a finish you have a number of options. There are commercial formulations and home-grown recipes to duplicate the dark "Russian Red" you see on stocks and then seal them in a shellac. While that gives a good traditional look, I used a variety of Minwax stains rubbed in by hand and then buffed with 000 steel wool to make sure the finish stays smooth.

After the stain has dried, I apply polyurethane finish and buff with steel wool after the first one or two coats. I'll apply five or six coats of the sealer. This not only makes for a great-looking, if inauthentic, stock, but the polyurethane

The original furniture for AKs varies wildly in appearance, given the country and time of manufacture. One thing it usually is not seen to be is especially attractive.

The ACE M4 stock with the module stock block doesn't require any modifications to the receiver's rear trunnion, making it easy to switch back to the original stock.

really helps protect it. Given all the colors of stains available, you certainly have plenty of choices.

In the case that your stock is damaged or you want a longer buttstock, you can buy new wood furniture. Other than purely custom stock makers there is one firm, Ironwood Designs, that is making brand new U.S. bare wood stocks for many of the different AK variants. They are very well-made and give you a great foundation to then finish how you want. Moreover, they are truly U.S.-made, so you get three compliance parts.

Another approach is to remove the wood stock and replacing it with a synthetic unit. The big benefit is that synthetics are impervious to the elements. AK wood stocks are sturdy and and resistant to warping, but they can delaminate if exposed to harsh weather.

For example, the synthetic stocks made for Bulgarian AK-74s will fit just fine on a Romanian G model AK-47. K-VAR offers some great deals on high-quality furniture that is both new and made in the USA as well as both new and used furniture from Bulgaria. They have very good prices and usually some interesting variations to choose from.

K-VAR also has both the traditional short Warsaw Pact-length stocks and longer NATO-length stocks that taller shooters find much more comfortable. Again, it pays to do some checking to see just what options you have.

In addition to new furniture, there is a large variety of surplus stocks out there. Before you buy one you need to understand what receiver it was made for and if it will work with your particular rear trunnion. The trunnion is the forged metal block in the back of the receiver that the stock attaches to, and can vary from country to country as well as model to model.

The design of the rear receiver and the thickness of the receiver mean there are some stocks that can't be substituted. For example, a Hungarian AMD-65 has a rear folding stock that has a dedicated rear trunnion. Given that the trunnion is riveted in place, not only would it need to be removed and holes welded shut, but the new rivet hole pattern would need to be drilled and cutouts made in the receiver for the folder mechanism and lock release.

For someone who doesn't mind welding and cutting an AKM receiver, that level of involved swap may be an option. Most will be better served to look at one of the side folders that can work with the standard rear trunnion.

The same is true for the pistol grip and front handguards—you will want to make sure that what you are looking at will accommodate your class of rifle whether it is from Yugoslavia, Romania, China or some other nation.

One thing to bear in mind is that the pistol grip is often a compliance part. There are lots of U.S.-made pistol grips

that have a traditional design so unless you know you can use a foreign grip, you are well advised to replace the pistol grip with a U.S.-made grip.

There are also furniture options for pretty much each piece of the furniture depending on the type of AK you own.

An increasingly common approach is to replace the AK's traditional rear stock with a telescoping stock like you have on the M4. This makes the AK purists cringe and snarl, but the truth is that the result is very maneuverable rifle that has a comfortable length of pull.

I've always been impressed how the Soviet design teams developed rifles with very mild recoil–even the 7.62x39 chambered AK-47 has mild recoil. One trick you can do with the Ace stock, or any stock for that matter, is to insert a C&H mercury buffer in the stock tube to further manage the recoil. C&H makes different lengths and diameters to accommodate different stocks and levels of recoil. They can help you spec out what will work in your situation.

Having a collapsing stock can be handy for professionals who need to accommodate different thicknesses of clothes and body armor, but the design also allows civilians of different sizes to share a rifle and quickly change the length of pull for each person.

For example, Ace Stocks, which is now part of J&T Distributing, makes some great military-grade modular stocks for the AK and have both skeleton and M4-style collapsing buttstocks. Moreover, either model can use their very strong folder mechanism.

The Ace system starts with one of two styles of modular aluminum blocks. One can go in an AKM with the existing rear trunnion's "tang" in place. This is very handy if you ever want to remove the stock and try something else but, there's always a but, the modular block sticks out of the end of the rifle. The other option is to use their internal block that requires you cut off the tang. This results in a cleaner look, but your options are cut off in terms of going back to

The Bulgarian AK-74 stock from K-VAR is one of the best-looking alternatives for any AK, provided you have enough American-made compliance parts included in the gun.

They're putting rails on everything these days, and the AK is no exception. This is a UTG quad rail system mounted on an AMD-65. Filling them all makes for a heavy gun.

This started out as a Romanian G parts kit and Spafford refinished the wood using Minwax products. The Tipton vise is helpful when doing gunsmithing jobs on rifles.

You may find that a sloppily applied finish has the buttstock glued to the receiver. A carefully applied heat gun can warm the receiver and help loosen finish.

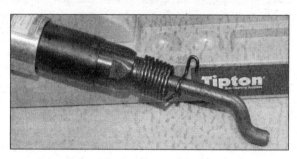

This pneumatic offset rivet set makes short work of removing a stuck stock from a receiver. The alternative for those without air tools is a hammer and wood dowel.

a traditional stock–you could, but the rear supporting tang would be conspicuously absent.

From there you can select one of their stocks or buy the "hog nose" adapter to screw in a M4 carbine buffer tube and use the stock of your choice. The Ace components are all high-grade aluminum for the block and key stock parts plus plastics used where it makes sense without compromising strength. There are other makers that only use plastic and users who need high-strength buttstocks should note the differences.

Command Arms' M4 stock with optional cheek piece creates some very clean lines. The Ergo AK pistol grip makes for a nice feel and adds one US 922R compliance part in this instance, offsetting the Command Arms foreign part count.

I also have an AK with the Israeli-made Command Arms rear M4 style stock with the optional adjustable cheekpiece. It has both an aluminum stock adapter and aluminum tube that has an integral adapter for mounting to AKMs with fixed stock rear trunnions. Since it is foreign-made, ensure the foreign parts count does not go over 10 by having sufficient American-made parts elsewhere.

If the parts count sounds worrisome just bear in mind that it gets easier with time and searching on www.ak-files.com in the gunsmithing and legal sections will turn up lots of questions, answers and examples.

There are also non-standard options on the pistol grips. Ergo Grip offers US-made grips, while Command Arms grips are made in Israel. Both are big improvements over the traditional AK grip in terms of fit and are both very well made.

The photo of the Command Arms buttstock also shows an Ergo AK pistol grip installed. The combination makes for an ergonomically friendly rifle.

The front gas guard is where there are some big opportunities for customization. The same way that rail integrated systems (RIS) have come to ARs, they have come to AKs.

There are Russian polymer units that are very nice but then there are also aluminum systems ranging from a high-end Surefire to the low-end but functional UTG rails.

None of the rails free-float the barrel like you'd find with some AR rail systems but then again the need isn't really there either. A tuned AK can give 3-4" accuracy at 100 yards and most are anywhere from 6-12" at a 100 yards. For a stock AK there really isn't a point in trying to free-float the barrel.

On an AK, as with other rifles, the RIS comes in handy for accessories. For example, on a couple I have mounted a red-dot on the top rail and it makes for a very easy to shoot gun. Does it hold a perfect zero? No, but we are talking about an AK.

A lot of AK owners, including me, initially went overboard and added an optic, laser and flashlight. You know what? All that stuff makes for a front-heavy rifle. Swinging the rifle around to engage is like spinning and stopping a 8-pound sledgehammer in motion! At this point, I still use rails with their rubber covers in place but I only keep one accessory, an optic, if anything at all

You might wonder why I said "if anything at all". If not used for accessories then why have a RIS at all, you might ask. My answer is easy–I have a fondness for the AMD-65. It has an unwieldy folding wire stock and a unique metal handguard. This looks slick, but it doesn't protect your fingers from the hot gas tube at all. The same is true for the full length AMD-63 rifle.

Some guys really like the look and leave it alone. I use a standard AKM rear trunnion so I can use a regular stock, a fixed barrel extension to get to the required 18" barrel length and then I use a UTG quad rail handguard to protect my fingers.

On one AMD-65 I have a red dot and on the other I didn't put anything. The balance is so much better with just the handguard that I only use iron sights with it. Best of all, I don't have to worry about batteries or the on/off switch for the iron sights!

You can remove the furniture from many AKs with just a blade screwdriver. I like to use a Tipton gun vise to hold on to my rifles when I am doing light work. If you ever do heavier work and need to use a true vise, remember that an AK's receiver is sheet metal and can be crushed if you aren't careful. Only the areas on each side of the front and

rear trunnions have much strength and I prefer to use the front trunnion area surrounded by leather to protect it.

To remove the buttstock, make absolutely sure the rifle is unloaded and remove the recoil spring assembly, bolt and carrier to get them out of the way. There will be one or two slotted screws located on top of the trunnion that secure the stock in place. Some AKs may have a metal strap/tang on the bottom of the stock that will also have one or two screws to remove.

After identifying the screws, use a screwdriver that fills the screw slot to turn and remove the screws. This can sometimes require a fair amount of torque, so you need the big screwdriver to engage as much of the screw slot as possible. Here's where a set of gunsmith screwdrivers comes in handy.

The sides of a gunsmith screwdriver blade are straight and the front and back are hollow-ground and not tapered the way most household and general-purpose screwdrivers are. This design makes for a very solid mechanical fit between the bit and the slot of the screw.

Thus, with a Romanian AK, an 8mm straight blade screwdriver bit provides the best fit to remove the two stock screws. I keep several types of 1/4" bit screwdriver handles around and several large assortments of bits to handle different fasteners.

If you're lucky, you can wiggle the buttstock up and down and it will come out. But the shellac may have adhered to the receiver and you may need a mallet and dowel to knock it backwards. It can even be so stuck that you need to use a heat gun to get the finish to release the parts. Before you hit the stock, one tip–make sure all of the screws out. If you're tired or in a rush, it is all too easy to overlook one oddball screw somewhere.

My secret weapon is a 4x air riveter with an offset rivet set that I bought surplus off of eBay. It makes a graceful curve like a letter "S," but the top and bottom are straight.

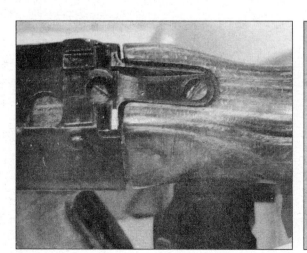

This top-down view shows the two wood screws that hold the buttstock in position. Original screws can be rusted in and may require a lot of torque to remove.

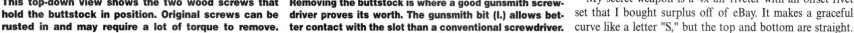

Removing the buttstock is where a good gunsmith screwdriver proves its worth. The gunsmith bit (l.) allows better contact with the slot than a conventional screwdriver.

Secure the machined end of the gas tube in a vise and then rotate the wood either clockwise or counterclockwise to remove it. The steel clip inside will pop off.

It lets me get the face of the rivet set right square against the buttstock and hammer it backward. That has always worked for me but I didn't have it when I first started. Maybe it'll give you a few ideas.

The pistol grip is retained by a throughbolt that engages a square angled block. It usually comes out very easily. Just take a second to note how the receiver block is oriented. There is a front and back due to the angle it needs to match up to the screw. If you get it in backwards the angle will be reversed and very obvious, just pull it out and start over.

The front lower handguard comes right off as well. First, make sure the cleaning rod has been removed. Next, rotate the little lever in the front right corner up and forward. Depending on how tight it is, you may need a screwdriver to pry it up. Once the lever is turned 180°, the retainer will slide forward and then the handguard will slide straight forward out of the receiver and come free.

It's the gas tube cover, or the upper handguard portion, that drives people nuts. It is shaped like a half tube and is held in place by friction. Put something in your vise's jaws to keep them from chewing up the machined portion of the tube that goes in the rear sight block.

To be clear, this is the forged section with straight sides and definitely not the thin walled metal tube itself. At any rate, secure the gas tube, firmly grasp the cover and rotate it. It may turn easier to the right or left and either direction will work. Rotate it 180° and pull the cover off the gas tube.

If the gas tube cover simply will not budge, its finish may have adhered to the retaining portions of the gas tube. Use a heat gun and warm those portions and try again. Bear in mind that the gas tube cover is thin. If it's wood, be careful and rotate it by applying pressure to its edges and don't crush it.

There are tons of options that you can read about on the Internet and see what meets your needs. My personal favorite is www.akfiles.com. There are a lot of how-to articles and people that share their knowledge. ◎

ADDITIONAL RESOURCES

There are many resources on the WWW that readers can use to learn more about AKs and the many different furniture options. They include:

* Ace Stocks   http://www.aceltdusa.com/
* Apex Gun Parts   http://www.apexgunparts.com/
* Command Arms   http://www.commandarms.com/
* Copes Distributing   http://www.copesdistributing.net/
* DPH Arms   http://dpharms.com/
* Ergo Grips   http://www.ergogrips.net/
* Ironwood Designs   http://www.ironwooddesigns.com/
* K-VAR   http://www.k-var.com/
* The AK Files   http://www.akfiles.com/
* Tick Bite Supply   http://www.tickbitesupply.com/
* Surefire   http://www.surefire.com/
* UTG / Leapers   http://www.leapers.com/

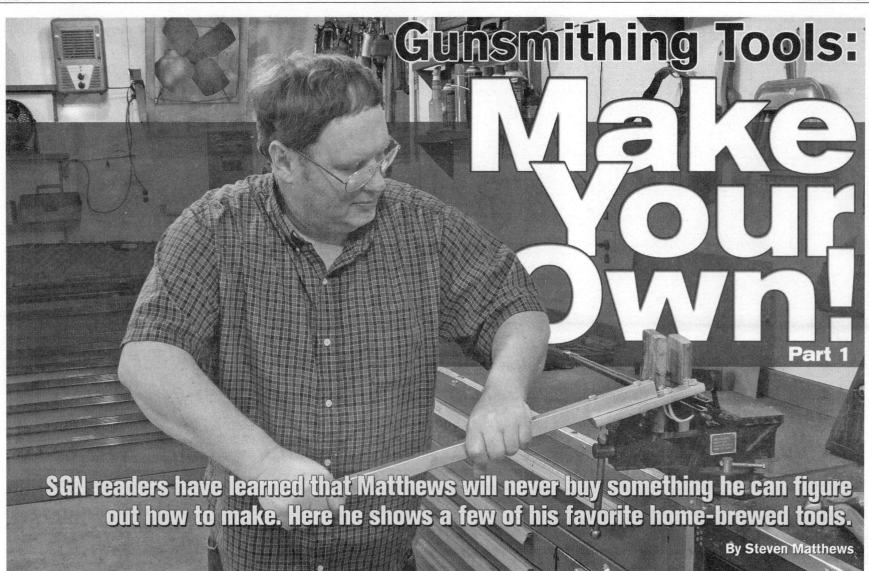

Gunsmithing Tools: Make Your Own!

Part 1

SGN readers have learned that Matthews will never buy something he can figure out how to make. Here he shows a few of his favorite home-brewed tools.

By Steven Matthews

It is interesting how the printed word can set your path in life. In the mid-1970s I was just beginning my earliest efforts at firearms collecting. At this time in my life I had little money for gun collecting and even less for customizing guns or paying for repairs on broken guns.

It was at this time when I read an article in one of the major gun magazines that started me on a lifelong hobby. The article was about "improvised gunsmithing" by members of the mountain tribes of Afghanistan and Pakistan.

They were poor, uneducated and oppressed by one political power or another for decades. To obtain arms to fight against their oppressors, they had to make them themselves since they couldn't buy them on the open market. Using the crudest of materials and techniques they duplicated the weapons that were common in their part of the world.

They hand shaped SMLE receivers and various other gun parts out of railroad rails with files and hand drills. Barrels were made from concrete rebar. Any piece of scrap steel was used

While Matthews is perfectly capable of calling on a lathe or milling machine when need be, he takes pleasure in improvising tools from scrap metals and spare parts.

wherever it could be used. While the materials were substandard, the workmanship was amazing.

They would take weeks or months to build just one gun by hand, but they did accomplish their goal. I had always wanted to do some gunsmithing but I couldn't afford the high-priced tools of the trade. What I saw in this article was that you didn't have to have the best tools if you had the desire, skill, and imagination to figure out an improvised method to do gunsmithing work.

"Improvised" in this instance means using the most basic and inexpensive tools and to complete a project with little concern for the time involved. Since I had little money and a lot of time, I thought if these poor uneducated tribesmen could do gunsmithing, then I could, too.

I had an advantage over these tribesmen; I had access to good materials and gunsmithing information. With this incentive, I began

You can buy specialized tools for gouging the barrel channel in a wood stock, but Matthews finds a piece of Surform rasp soldered to an old screwdriver works well.

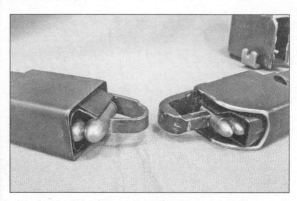

You can buy a plastic mag loader, but where's the fun in that? Matthews has made them from sheet metal and even from scrap magazine wells. Soldering skill is required.

Use a ball peen hammer to form sheet metal around a steel bar that approximates the size of the magazine. Cut the ends so they meet at the back of the loader box.

The result looks a little crude before smoothing, deburring and finishing, but when painted, the $1 homemade unit looks as good as the store-bought $15 mag loader.

Make the plunger that inserts the cartridges by hammering a strip of steel over a rod or big bolt clamped into a vise. Use one large enough to take the stress of forming.

cost of paying someone else to do it. With the proper skills and a generous amount of time the semi-skilled amateur can produce quality work. The goal is to do quality work but at minimal expense.

If you think like I do you may be interested in some of the tools, techniques, and small projects I have improvised over the years. Some of these methods are extremely crude and I only recommend them when you have no other options. Today I have a full hobby gunsmithing machine shop in my garage, but in years gone by these methods allowed me to achieve some good results when I had no other way to do the job.

Surform Bar Channel Tool

I picked this idea up from an amateur stockmaker, so I can't claim it as my idea, but it really works well. This tool makes short work of opening up a barrel channel, thanks to its aggressive cutting nature. The Stanley Tool Co. makes a flat woodworking tool that looks like a cheese grater. It's known as a Surform rasp.

It aggressively removes wood with its many sharp cutting edges. They also make it in a round form much like a large round file. It comes as a tool about 8-10 inches long, which is too long for stock

While these methods have worked for me, you should not consider them carved in stone.

a lifelong hobby of improvised gunsmithing. My early projects were amateurish, but as time went by, I developed the skills to achieve professional-grade results without professional grade expense.

Over the last 30 years I have used many improvised tools and techniques to complete many projects at a fraction of the

While these methods have worked for me, you should not consider them carved in stone. Part of improvised gunsmithing is being creative. You may think of a better, easier, or less expensive way of doing your project. Here are a few ideas for your consideration.

work. For stock work, cut off a section about 1½ to 2 inches long and solder or braze it to the shank of an old screwdriver.

The Surform blade is very hard and will have to be cut with an abrasive cutoff wheel. Putting an offset in the screwdriver shank will allow for easier use. Before attaching the blade to

Once the plunger is formed, you can solder it to the body of the loader. Locate it right over the seam, then clamp it in position so that it doesn't move during soldering.

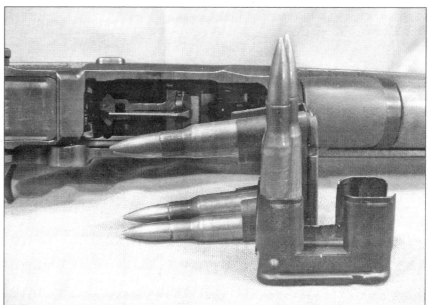

A two-round M1 clip comes in handy when shooting high power rifle matches where "two and eight" loading is standard for the Garand. Other capacities are easy to make, too.

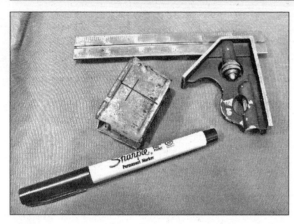

Start the process by measuring and marking the cutting points. Then use an abrasive cutoff wheel in the Dremel tool. This is required for cutting the hard steel.

the screwdriver shank, orient the cutter so that it cuts on the pull stroke to allow for easier control. This tool only cost a few dollars and with all the left over blade material you will have years' worth of "refills".

Magazine Loaders

If you are a fan of military arms, you are probably familiar with high-capacity magazines. Many of these magazines have one negative feature, they are hard to load due to the high spring tension required to move the many rounds up in the magazine. Some can be real thumb-busters. Loading can be made much easier with the help of a magazine loader.

These loaders can be purchased but they can also be easily made for just a few cents worth of scrap steel. All that is needed is a housing to slide over the magazine body and a plunger to depress the top round low enough to insert the next round without any spring tension on it. Once the new round is under the magazine lips the spring and follower can be released and all that is needed is to slide the round to the rear of the magazine. This makes loading high capacity magazines a lot easier.

The loader made for this article is for a MAC-10 or M3 grease gun magazine, but you can adapt them to just about any magazine. The housing can be fabricated by forming 16-gauge sheet steel. If you are making a loader for a common military gun, you can also purchase a surplus magazine housing such as the Sten housing that was used to make the other loader shown along with the scratch-made M3 loader.

I formed the housing over a heavy steel bar by hammering out a rectangle and then soldering the seam together. The plunger was made from a piece of 1/8x1/2-inch flat stock. It was formed over a 5/8" bolt.

Once a correct position for the plunger was determined, it was soldered onto the rear of the housing. After a little finishing work it was painted. If you do a good job, it will work and look almost as good as a purchased one. This loader only took about an hour to make, which makes it an easy project

M1 Garand Low Capacity Clips

The M1 Garand eight-round en bloc clip is fine for a military gun, but for some recreational uses a smaller size is desired. Some state laws restrict magazine size for hunting and some competitive M1 shooting matches require an eight-round and a two-round clip.

Breaking a barrel loose from the action can be a relatively easy task if you have the right tool for the job, in this case, an action wrench made from scrap steel.

Smaller sized M1 clips can be purchased for under $10 but they can be made by the hobbyist for only about 50¢. Garand clips can be bought for about 30¢ to a dollar each. In about a half-hour you can modify an eight-round clip to any smaller size.

Since Garand clips are so inexpensive, you're not out much if it takes some trial and error to get it right. The clip shown was modified for two rounds, but any size can be made by changing location of your cuts on the clip before reforming the lips.

Part of improvised gunsmithing is being creative.

You start by cutting a slot from the front of the clip to about a half-inch from the rear. The best tool for cutting these hardened spring steel clips is a Dremel Moto-Tool with abrasive cutoff

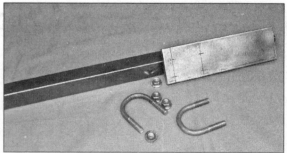

Use a torch to heat the cut area red hot. This anneals it enough to allow it to be bent into the proper shape for reduced capacity. Heat, then slowly withdraw the flame.

Carefully mark the flat base of the wrench to allow proper position of the U-bolts. Grind the interior of the U-bolts flat so that clamping force is evenly distributed.

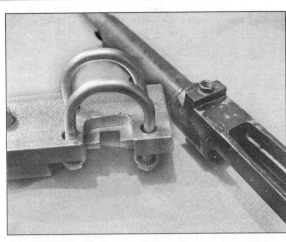

Some action types may require cutting a recess for the recoil lug. A milling machine comes in handy here, but Matthews says the job can be done with hand tools.

A case separation leaves the forward part of a bottle-neck case stuck in the chamber while the head is withdrawn and ejected. You need a special tool for removal.

An old fine-cut round file can be made into an effective stuck case remover. Bend the handle 90° and add metal to allow a piece of pipe to slide on for leverage.

wheels. These are quite fragile, but will cut through almost any hard steel.

You also cut an up-and-down groove at the rear of the previous cut to allow for bending new magazine lips. If you place your cuts correctly, you can make your clips "doubles" such as two rounds on each end or if desired, you can have more rounds on one side than the other. A little experimenting can result in some unique sizes.

Since this is heat-treated spring steel, you will have to anneal the clip where you are going to bend new magazine lips. Heating it red hot with a propane torch and then slowly withdrawing the flame to allow slow cooling will soften the steel enough that you can bend it with a pair of needle nose pliers or vise grips. After forming the lips, deburr the edges and then touch up the finish with paint or cold bluing.

First, place the gun safety in the "on" position. Place the number of rounds needed, plus one, in a convenient location. Hold the butt of the gun against your hip or leg with the left hand under the forearm. Use your right hand to retract the bolt handle. One round will eject.

Continue to hold the bolt open and support the rifle with your right hand. Use your left hand to retrieve the rounds needed to top off the magazine. With the action open you can now insert the rounds just as any other blind magazine and fill the clip to its full capacity. Once full, the bolt can be released to strip off the first round in the clip. This is easier than it sounds once you have done it. This method also has the side benefit of allowing you to fill the magazine before it is ejected out onto the dirty ground.

dered rosin, but powdered rosin isn't easily found. I have found that a good substitute was to wrap a layer of 320-400 grit emery cloth around the barrel to increase grip.

A lot of force can be needed to break loose some barrels and the vise shown here is too small except for very light duty jobs, it was just used for photographic purposes. I have used this improvised method to change several barrels and it has worked well for me and cost very little.

Stuck Case Remover

If you shoot military surplus rifles and like to feed them budget-priced surplus ammo, eventually you will have a case separation. This is especially true if you are a user of the cheapest, most rock-bottom priced variety of unknown quality that often exceeds a half century in age.

When some of this old ammo is fired, the age-hardened cases crack and separate just ahead of the cartridge base. When the round is ejected, all you get is the base and the rest is stuck in the chamber. The problem now becomes how to get the remainder of the case out of the chamber.

The usual method is to use a tool known as a stuck case remover. These can be purchased, but what if you don't have one and you don't want to wait a couple weeks to mail-order one? A tool can easily be made at home for just a couple bucks. A fine-cut tapered rat tail file can be modified to remove a stuck case.

For a .30 cal. case, a 5/16- or 3/8-inch file works fine. Start by sliding a good case over the end till the mouth contacts the file. Mark the file here and then cut it off with an abrasive cut-off wheel at this point so that no cutting edges extend into the chamber when in use. You can leave it a little longer if you want, but be sure to grind the cutting edges smooth so it won't damage the chamber.

Now you will have to guess how much length you need to allow the file to reach into the old case and grip it. The length needed will vary depending on action length and how deep the barrel sits in the action. Once you have a good guess, add a few inches to that length to allow for a handle to be bent on the end.

If you want to have a removable handle, only add a couple inches, to which a piece of pipe can be added to make a handle. Once the correct length is cut, use a torch to heat the file red hot where you want to bend it and bend it 90°. The tool is inserted into the stuck case and twisted to get the file teeth to bite into the brass case neck. Usually this twisting and gripping breaks the case loose and the case remnants can be removed.

This tool does look crude, but I have used it many times with excellent results when I was using very poor quality ammo in my belt fed Browning 1919A4 gun. ◎

M1 Garand Magazine Top Off

One myth concerning the fine M1 Garand rifle of World War II fame is that its en bloc clip can't be "topped off". Myth has it that you have to shoot till it's empty or eject the partial clip to refill it to its eight-round capacity. I believe the proponents of this myth simply pass on the myth rather than think about whether or not it's true. The M1 en-bloc clip can be refilled in the gun just as any other blind magazine; it just requires a little more work. To refill a partial clip to its full capacity just follow this easy procedure.

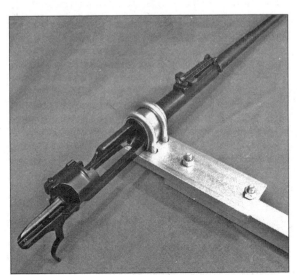

Put a thin aluminum or brass shim between the clamps and the action to prevent marring the finish. Then turn the clamp screws down tight to avoid any clamp slippage.

Improvised Action Wrenches

Many times the hobbyist gunsmith wants to change a worn-out barrel on a military surplus gun with an inexpensive surplus barrel, but is hindered by the high cost of the tools needed for the job. An action wrench and barrel vise can easily exceed the cost of the gun.

Fortunately an action wrench can be made for less than $10 and a barrel vise can be easily improvised. Many rifles feature a round receiver with a flat bottom. An improvised action wrench can be easily made for this type of receiver from a piece of 5/8x2 flat stock steel, two muffler clamps, and a 3-foot piece of 1x1 square steel. For the 98 Mauser action wrench featured here, 1 3/8-inch heavy duty muffler clamps were used to clamp the action to a strong piece of flat stock. I cut a recess into the flat stock to allow clearance of the recoil shoulder on the 98 action.

This recess can be cut by drilling, grinding, filing, etc. Some action types will not even require a cut out, so they can be very easy to make. Once the clamp holes are drilled and any relief cuts made, a handle can be attached by welding or bolting it in place.

The insides of the clamps should be ground flat, to distribute the clamping force more evenly. When in use, a piece of brass or aluminum sheet stock should be placed between the clamps and action to prevent marring the finish. Before the action wrench can be used, the barrel must be secured. For decades, the improvised method of choice has been to clamp the barrel in a conventional heavy duty vise with hard wood blocks against the barrel.

The wood blocks need to be oriented with the grain perpendicular to the barrel to prevent splitting the blocks. When the wood blocks are tightened down the barrel will sink into the wood somewhat and increase the gripping surface.

Sometimes, however, the barrel will still slip in the vise. The old-time method to increase grip was to sprinkle on some pow-

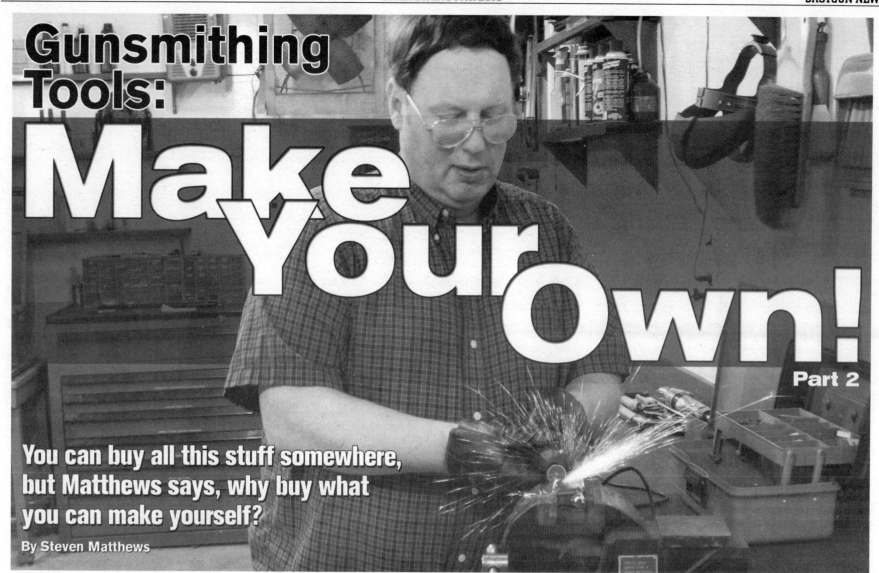

Gunsmithing Tools: Make Your Own!

Part 2

You can buy all this stuff somewhere, but Matthews says, why buy what you can make yourself?

By Steven Matthews

M1 Garand Gas Plug Wrench

One of the tools a M1 Garand owner needs to care and maintain his rifle is a gas plug wrench. A small combination tool was originally supplied with the gun but the screwdriver type attachment was very small and didn't offer much leverage on very tight gas plugs.

Several commercially made wrenches are available for about $20 but it's easy to make your own for less than a dollar's worth of steel and less than an hour of effort. What is needed is basically a stubby offset screwdriver. A file, hacksaw, and a 5/8" x 6" Grade 5 bolt are all you need for this project.

Start by cutting off the threads on the bolt and then cut off about half the thickness of the bolt head. Cut off four of the flats (two on opposite sides) even with the shank of the bolt. This will leave two opposing flats that can be filed to fit the slots in the gas plug. Filing a little relief on the shank will allow for a little more tool engagement.

After you have filed the head to what is basically a double screwdriver blade, smooth up and deburr everything and apply a coat of paint. With its 3 to 4-inch length, you will be able to loosen even the most stubborn gas plug.

High Capacity Magazine Size Reduction

It seams these days everyone wants large-capacity magazines in their military guns. 20-, 30-, and 40-round magazines are common sizes. Sometimes, though, you just don't want or need 30-plus rounds sticking out of your gun. Suppose you want a smaller one?

Smaller sizes are available but usually cost considerably more than the common military-issue sizes. It's easy to reduce the larger sizes by cutting off the bottom of the magazine at the appropriate place and reforming the floor plate tabs.

You can buy most all the tools and accessories you need right here in SGN, but there are those, like Matthews, who like to go the old-fashioned route and make their own.

The Sten magazine featured in this article was reduced from its normal 32-round capacity to a more-handy 20-round size. I removed the floorplate, spring and follower, leaving only the magazine body. The body was then saw cut to reduce its length. Once squarely cut, I filed down the front and rear potion a little more to allow for material to extend past the end to form new floorplate tabs.

I formed the tabs by bending over with vise grips or needle-nose pliers. After the new tabs were formed, everything was deburred. Since the magazine body is now considerably shorter, the spring needs to be shortened also. Spring length is determined by guesswork (start long) and depends on the size you have made the body.

Assemble the magazine and if spring tension is too tight, shorten the spring till it's correct. This modification can be

Removing the gas plug on an M1 requires a proper tool. Matthews made this X-shaped version that supports all four surfaces, but says you can make a simpler model.

Get a Grade 5 bolt at any hardware store, cut off the threaded part, trim and thin the head to make it fit the plug, and you have a handy tool at almost no cost.

The first step in making a shortened magazine is accurately marking the cut. Needless to say, both sides of the box must be the same length for everything to fit.

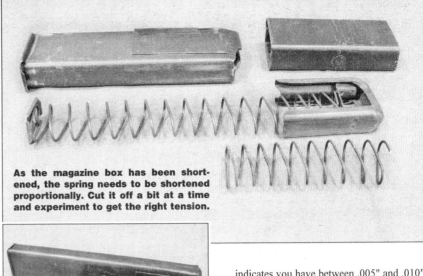

As the magazine box has been shortened, the spring needs to be shortened proportionally. Cut it off a bit at a time and experiment to get the right tension.

Next, sever the bottom of the magazine box. This requires a fresh hacksaw blade, secure clamping and smooth, careful strokes with the saw to keep the cut exactly square.

made on just about any magazine. If you have a magazine with floorplate tabs that face inward, they can be formed by similar methods. Use a steel block inside the magazine body and form the tabs inward by bending over with a small hammer. This project only takes about 30 minutes per magazine, so you can make a series of specially sized magazines in a very short time.

Improvised Headspace Check

Headspace in its most general definition is the amount of space between the face of the closed bolt in a firearm and the rear of the chambered cartridge. Too much or too little space here can cause problems and in some cases even be unsafe. This amount of space is only a few thousandths of an inch.

Special headspace gauges known as go and no go gauges are used to measure this dimension. These gauges cost between $40 and $50 each, which really discourages the hobbyist from checking his guns.

There is, however, an improvised method to check headspace which will give you a rough idea of the headspace condition of your gun. This method is *not* a substitute for a professional check, but rather a general indicator of whether you should have your gun checked by a professional gunsmith.

Using a selection of new cartridges and several precision-sized discs, a general reading can be obtained. Obtain several examples of cartridges for your firearm from different makers. Several are needed due to size variations among brands.

Obtain some precision shim stock in the sizes of .005", 010", 015". This can be purchased from gunsmithing suppliers, tool and die suppliers or simply by buying a set of automotive type feeler gauges. Out of each size of this material, cut out round discs just slightly smaller than the base of the cartridge. Use aviation tin snips to cut this very thin material. Deburr all cut edges and verify that they are uniform in size with a micrometer.

Before using this method, remove the firing pin and extractor (and spring-loaded ejector if it has one) from the bolt. This is for safety and accuracy reasons. Place the .005" disc on the front of the bolt. A bit of grease will hold the disc on the bolt face.

With the firearm pointed in a safe direction, insert each cartridge in the chamber and see if the bolt will easily close on the round. With this .005" disc the bolt should close on all rounds unless headspace is too tight.

A cleaning rod can be used to push the cartridges back out of the chamber. Next, go to the .010" disc and repeat the test. With this size disc, some rounds may not allow the bolt to close easily. Do not force the bolt closed, because there is enough camming force to crush the cases and make the reading inaccurate. This

indicates you have between .005" and .010" clearance between the bolt face and the chambered cartridge.

This is acceptable but if most rounds allow the bolt to close, you are getting close to the limit of acceptable tolerance. If all rounds allow the bolt to close, you need to go to the .015" disc. If the bolt closes on the .015" disc and several of your cartridges, the gun may have excessive headspace and you should have it checked by a professional gunsmith.

It should be noted, though, that many foreign-made military guns exhibit very generous headspace, since they are intended to function under very dirty conditions. These guns may fail a SAAMI specification headspace check but be considered adequate for combat use by foreign armorers.

A Local Source for Project Steel

Not all steel is created equal. The strength varies depending on the chemical composition of the steel. One type of steel can be several times stronger than another. Firearms generally require good high strength steels rather than common low strength mild steel.

Unfortunately, if you need some raw material for a gunsmithing project, you can't go down to your local hardware store and say "I want to buy some good steel." Well, maybe you can if you need round stock under an inch in diameter and only a few inches long.

High quality bolts, those rated as Grade 5, 8 or 9 are made from good steel. While common mild steel has a tensile strength of about 50,000 psi (pounds per square inch) the steel in Grade 5 bolts is rated at 120,000 psi. Grade 8 bolt steel is rated at 150,000 psi and Grade 9 is 180,000 psi.

So how do you know what grade of bolt steel you are getting? High quality Grade 5 and 8 bolts will be marked with a series

Next, form the floorplate retaining tabs on the bottom of the magazine box and then use Vise-Grips to bend them out to the proper angle. Then file to fit the floorplate.

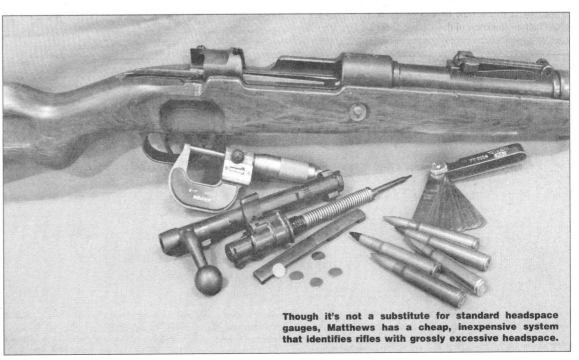

Though it's not a substitute for standard headspace gauges, Matthews has a cheap, inexpensive system that identifies rifles with grossly excessive headspace.

Use a dab of grease on the bolt face to retain a precision shim disk. The disk will establish clearance between the bolt face and cartridge base when the bolt is closed.

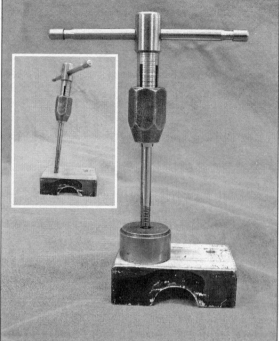

It takes a sharp eye to keep a tap aligned when turning by hand. A steel tapping block makes the job a lot easier by supporting the tap as it bites into the workpiece.

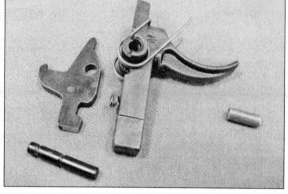

Holding a lot of hammer and trigger parts together while installing is almost impossible without a slave pin that keeps them aligned. The real pin drives it out.

of radial lines on the heads. Grade 5 bolts will have three radial lines on the heads while Grade 8 bolts will feature six.

Bolts with no markings usually are Grade 2 or lower and are very weak and should not be used for gunsmithing projects.

Grade 9 bolts are usually of the Allen head type with a black oxide finish and are not marked individually, but the packaging should indicate the grade. If no grade is specified, assume they are soft, low-quality steel. Grade 5 bolts are relatively easy to work with metal cutting tools (saws, drills, files, etc.). Grade 8 bolts are considerably harder to work. Grade 9 bolts are very hard, and very sharp tooling is required to work them.

Tapping a Straight Hole

Tapping a hole is a common gunsmithing chore. Unless you have very "straight" eyes, it can be difficult to align the tap exactly perpendicular to your work. Aligning the tap properly will help prevent breaking it and also produce a better tapped hole. One easy method to align the tap properly is to use a tapping block or tapping guide. These can be bought but they also can be made for just pennies.

Lockwork Helper

It seams when installing triggers and disconnectors in AR-15 and FAL type rifles you could use a third hand to hold and align all the pieces before you insert the pins. The parts need to be held and lined up under spring tension, all the while trying to align it to install the pin through the receiver.

A simple "third hand" can be easily made to help with the job. A small piece of pin diameter rod can be cut and inserted through the trigger and spring-loaded disconnector to hold them together as a sub-assembly rather than loose parts. Once the sub-assembly is placed in the receiver and the trigger pin installed, it will push out the small pin as it is pushed into place. This "third hand" allows your other two hands to more easily install the parts.

ing punches can be easily made by forming a rounded depression in the end of a flat point punch.

These punches can be bought or made at home out of high-quality drill rod. Pre-hardened punches will have to have the faces annealed prior to cutting the recess. A tool for cutting the recess can be made by grinding a round profile on the end of a common drill bit; just be sure you sharpen the new shape correctly. The size is determined according to the size head you wish to form.

Partially drill the recess with a standard bit to almost the correct depth and then switch to the rounded bit to final form the hole to the rounded profile. After the recess is formed, re-harden the tool's

Not all steel is created equal. The strength varies depending on the chemical composition of the steel.

The easiest method to make a tapping guide is to cut off some 1-inch round stock and then precisely square the ends. Once the ends are squared up, drill a hole a few thousandths larger than the tap all the way though the ends. This hole needs to be almost exactly perpendicular to the ends, so it should be drilled on a lathe, milling machine or at the very least, a drill press. Do not try to do this with a hand drill, because hardly anyone can drill that straight by hand. Placing these guides over the hole to be tapped and securely holding them in place while tapping will ensure a correctly tapped hole.

Rivet Head Forming Punches

Many modern military arms often feature riveted construction. Although this may look primitive to some, it is a proven method. They are quick and easy to install in the factory environment. They are somewhat slow to install at home without special tools.

A rivet head forming tool can be easily made for home setting rivets. This tool will allow the user to form that round head on the rivet when it is set. Manufactured head forming punches are available but they can also be made "on the cheap." Head form-

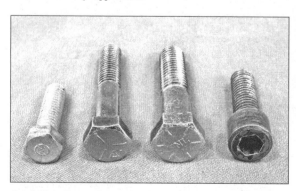

Graded bolts can provide a source of high-strength steel for gunsmithing projects. Avoid ungraded bolts like the one on the left; look for Grades 5, 8 and 9.

The tapping guide is made with relative ease if you have a sturdy drill press and can get the ends square for proper alignment. The tap will need a bit of clearance.

Punches needed to form rivet heads are easily made by drilling a recess in the face of a flat-point punch. Use a standard drill to start, then one with a round tip.

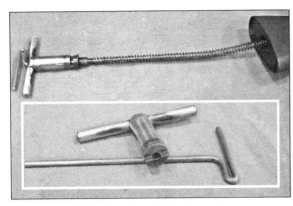

Replacing the FAL recoil spring by hand can be a nightmare. This special tool, combining a stubby screwdriver and a guide rod, will make the job a whole lot easier.

face by heating red hot and then quenching in oil. When rivets are solidly supported and the punch used to form the head, the shank will expand in the recess and form the classic round head form.

FAL Buffer Spring Tools

Installing the buffer/recoil spring in a FAL without special tools can be like trying to stuff a wiggling snake into a deep hole. The spring is so long and stiff that when you compress it enough to get it into the tube it wants to kink and shoot out of your hand long before it is held captive by the buffer tube.

The solution to keep the spring from kinking is to install a long, small-diameter rod through the spring and retaining nut. The rod will pass through the hole in the nut. Since the buffer tube nut needs to be tightened with the rod still in place, a simple stubby screwdriver with a hole in the center to allow for passage of the rod can be made for the job.

This tool can be made by filing a short, wide screwdriver blade on the end of a piece of 1-inch diameter material. A handle can be welded on to allow for easy use. Once the tool is made, drilling a hole all the way though will allow the tool to pass over the rod. This tool really simplifies the installation of this spring and nut.

Improvised Milling Machine

There is no good substitute for a milling machine, but sometimes you need something better than cutting steel by hand with

No lathe? Small parts like pins can be fabricated using a drill press or even a hand drill, files and measuring tools. It's not the fastest way, just the cheapest.

files and saws. While this solution leaves a lot to be desired it is better than no milling machine at all.

In a pinch, a drill press and a compound cross feed vise can be an improvised milling machine. It requires a drill press with good tight bearings and a cross feed vise with all slop removed from its travel. The vise needs to be very securely clamped and squarely aligned on the drill press table and the table also needs to be tightly locked in place.

Since drill chucks are not made to hold double end mills, a single end mill will have to be used. Very light cuts at slow feed rates will help keep the tool from chattering. Setting depth of cut is tricky but can be done if you are careful. Before I had my milling machine, I used this method on many occasions to do good work; you just have to go slow to get a good cut.

Improvised Lathe

Sometimes the hobbyist gunsmith needs to turn a small part but with no metal cutting lathe what can he do? If you are good at hand-making parts a crude lathe can be improvised that will allow you to make some small parts. A lathe in its simplest form is just a machine spinning a piece of steel while it's being cut with a tool.

You can use a drill press or a hand drill clamped in a vise to spin the material and a file to form it. In the example shown, an AR-15 hammer pin is being made with this improvised method. The part was made by marking the location for the grooves and then using a file to cut the grooves in the spinning steel. After the grooves are cut, the pin can be cut to the correct overall length.

In a pinch, a drill press and a compound cross feed vise can be an improvised milling machine.

This pin only took a few minutes to make. While this pin is a very simple example, more complex types of parts can be made, it just depends on the skill level of the user. If you take your time and accurately measure your parts while fabricating them, pretty decent results can be obtained with this improvised method.

5¢ "Peep" Sight

Many shooters prefer the aperture or peep sight. One famous military gun, the AK-47, doesn't have such a sight. The hobbyist gunsmith can add a peep sight to this or several other types of gun for the grand total cost of 5¢. To make a peep type sight for this gun I just soldered on a small washer to the existing rear sight.

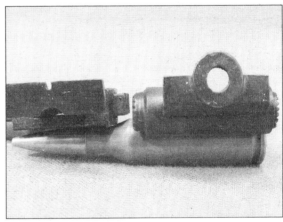

Prefer a peep sight to the old V-notch? Just solder a washer onto the sight leaf, clean it up a bit and then finish with a spray-on finish like Lauer Dura-Coat.

A round groove slightly larger than the hole in the washer was filed in the rear notch. All metal finish was removed from the place where the washer was to be soldered in place. The surface was roughed up with a file to increase the adhesion the solder. Once the washer was soldered in place, the sight was painted with flat black paint

In the preceding segments the most basic of tools and improvised methods were used to achieve the goals at the expense of time. While this is fine for those on a limited budget there are those who wish to use more professional tools and methods. For those, I can recommend two excellent sources for gunsmithing tools, supplies and information: Brownells and MidwayUSA. Brownells is the traditional source for the gunsmithing professional. They carry just about any tools and materials plus all the information you would ever need to do any gunsmithing project. I have used Brownells products for years with total satisfaction.

Midway for years was known as a source for firearms accessories and ammo and they have in recent years added gunsmithing tools, supplies and informational material to their catalog.

Whether you use the best tools and techniques or improvised at every opportunity, gunsmithing can be an enjoyable hobby. Give it a try and you may find yourself a lifelong hobby just as I have.

It's no substitute for a milling machine, but some minor milling jobs can be performed with the combination of a solid drill press and compound cross feed vise.

Ever wanted to do those big gunsmithing projects like Steven Matthews? There's no substitute for machine tools when there's a lot of metal to move, Cramer says.

MACHINING *for* BEGINNERS
INTRODUCTION

Got the bug to make some of the projects you see here in SGN?
Cramer takes a break from politics to help get you started.

By Clayton E. Cramer | Additional photography by Steven Matthews

I suspect that some of you have read the articles here in SHOTGUN NEWS about machining gun parts and found yourself saying, "Gee, I wish that I knew enough to use a lathe, a vertical mill, and some of those other cool machine tools." Many community colleges offer a range of machine shop classes that teach everything from the basics to advanced machining. That's one route to getting that level of knowledge—but you may not have such a school nearby. Or perhaps your schedule is too busy for something that regular. This article series is for you!

I have been fascinated for a number of years by our industrial civilization—how we can, in repeatable fashion, make astonishingly precise gadgets. When I was working on my M.A. in history, I was startled to see how recently inventors created many of the machine tools that make industrial civilization possible. While researching my last book, *Armed America*, this fascination increased, as I learned how the U.S. government intentionally created our modern industrial base, through the granting of musket contracts starting in the 1790s.

I started a sideline business a few years ago making telescope accessories. At first, I subcontracted out the machining side of it, but eventually, my desire to improve profits and be in control of quality and schedules meant that I needed to start machining parts myself—so I bought a small lathe, a small vertical mill, a drill press, and started learning.

Owning machine tools doesn't make you a machinist anymore than owning a National Match M1A makes you a marksman. I would say that after a bit more than three years of part-time use, I have worked my way up to

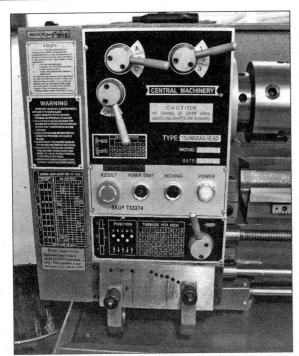

For big projects involving barrels and other long parts, there's no substitute for a big engine lathe. For smaller jobs, table-top units can get the work done.

You might think of the milling machine as a very accurate power file; it can shape a wide variety of parts using cutters in many different sizes and shapes.

a beginning machinist—knowledgeable enough to show you the ropes, but still with memories of how much I didn't know at the start!

WHAT ARE THESE TOOLS? AND WHAT DO YOU USE THEM FOR?

What is popularly called a lathe is actually properly termed an "engine lathe," because these were first used for making perfectly round steam engine pistons and cylinders. (Think about how you would make anything perfectly round with a file, and you will see why this was so important an invention.)

Many people have at least some idea what an engine lathe is, and how to use it, because a wood turning lathe works on the same basic principle: you spin a piece of wood between two supports, and then use cutting tools to shape the wood. The precision engine lathes for machining metal use the same principle, with some additional advantages that let you make parts that are accurate to one-thousandth of an inch (or better!). In general, if you are making a part that is cylindrical, you use a lathe.

The vertical mill looks a lot like a weird kind of drill press—and you could use it as a clumsy kind of drill press—but that's not its purpose. Think of a vertical mill as a precise way to file parts to fit. In the early days, if you needed to make a replacement part for a gunlock, you would file the edges of a flat piece of steel until your replacement part matched the original. Pioneering American gun manufacturers such as Simeon North and Eli Whitney came up with a way to make that filing process very repeatable, very fast, and very accurate.

A vertical mill lets you move a cutting tool in three axes: X (left and right); Y (in and out), and Z (up and down). If you are one of those people who asked your high school geometry teacher, "When am I ever going to use this?"—here's your teacher's revenge.

A properly set up vertical mill lets you position that cutting tool in all three directions within one-thousandth of an inch. Then, it lets you cut through metal in all three directions with similar accuracy. If you need to machine something that isn't round—for example, a block or sheet of steel or aluminum with precisely located holes, or slots, or particular angles—a vertical mill is usually the right tool.

You could use a vertical mill to do everything that a drill press does—but it would be slow and clumsy. This doesn't work in reverse; a drill press is not a low accuracy

vertical mill. A drill press makes holes in one direction (the Z axis). When you want to make a hole with a vertical mill, you turn a wheel that moves the drill bit in the Z direction very slowly—unlike the drill press, where you pull down on a spring-loaded handle, and the drill bit cuts down until you release it.

It is possible to use a drill press with vise that has a similar, although slightly less accurate X and Y axis movement system.

If you try to move an object in the X or Y axes with a cutting tool spinning in the drill press, the drill bit chuck will pop loose, and if you are lucky, it will fly in some direction that doesn't cause blood spatter and screaming. You should only use a device like this for positioning a workpiece (the material you are machining) to a particular location, then turn on the drill press. I repeat: do not try to move the workpiece while cutting. It may work briefly, but a drill press does not have the bearings to handle the side loads; a vertical mill does.

There are machine tools that combine vertical mill and drill press into a single assembly—and some that combine a lathe as well—but these strike me as being rather like a Swiss Army knife, which has a bunch of adequate tools in a single highly portable package. I carry a Swiss Army knife, but if I need serious versions of any of these tools, I pull out a lockback knife, my good set of gunsmithing screwdrivers, my needlenose pliers, or an awl—all of which are serious tools for one purpose.

A drill press isn't a precision machine tool, like the lathe or the vertical mill—but it lets you do some steps that would otherwise take far longer on the vertical mill. Best of all, because drill presses don't work at thousandths of an inch accuracy, even a floor model drill press, in dollars per pound, is dirt cheap compared to the lathe or vertical mill.

HOW DO PRECISION MACHINE TOOLS MAKE STUFF SO ACCURATELY?

At the heart of every precision machine tool are very accurate screw threads. For machine tools calibrated in inches, the screw has 20 threads per inch (TPI). A little arithmetic will tell you that for every complete rotation of a 20 tpi screw, any part riding on that screw will move .050". When you put a hand wheel with 50 evenly spaced

lines on the end of that screw, each line represents .001" of movement. Depending on how accurately the thread was cut, and how large the wheel is, you may be able to position a cutting tool to an accuracy of .0005".

Really big, expensive machine tools (the kind neither of us can afford, and that take a forklift to move) will have positioning accuracy of .00001"! (For metric machine tools, the screw usually has threads 3mm apart, and 30 lines on the wheel—so positioning accuracy of 0.1mm.)

The drill press can do a few other jobs, but its reason for being is to drill holes with speed and accuracy. A drill press vise is an essential accessory.

Cut neither too quickly or too slowly for clean results and longer tool life. Moving belts among various pulleys adjusts the drill press or a small lathe.

Of course, just because the tool is this accurate, doesn't mean that you will start off making parts that precise. A Remington 700 Police Sniper Special may be capable of quarter-minute accuracy, but it will take a lot of practice before most owners will consistently get half-minute groups, and some never will. Remember that as with most work in the shop: measure twice (or even thrice), cut once.

You also need to be realistic about how accurate your work needs to be. I am gratified that I can make 10 parts for my telescope accessory business that are within .001" of each other in diameter and length. But .005" is as accurate as these parts really need to be. Getting parts accurate to .010" is trivial; .005" is a bit more effort; and .001" is more effort than my customers can afford.

You may well find yourself as a matter of pride making high precision parts where it isn't really required—just don't forget why you are doing so, especially if you figure out how to turn what you are doing into a business. I recently made a part to anchor a Harris bipod inside a Springfield Armory M1A fiberglass stock—and I thoroughly enjoyed getting carried away, making the part far more precisely than it needed to be!

To give you some idea how accurate .005" is: if you put two cylinders side by side by a flat surface, most people can feel a length difference of .005" by running their fingers across the tops, but can't feel a length difference of .001".

CUTTING SPEEDS

Regardless of whether you are using a small desktop machine tool, or one of the massive monsters, you will need to understand cutting speeds. Cutting speed is how fast either the workpiece (on a lathe) or the cutting tool (on a vertical mill or a drill press) is spinning—usually expressed as inches per second (IPS).

The tougher the material, generally, the slower the cutting speed needs to be. If your cutting speed is too high, the cutting tool will overheat and lose its sharpness. Dull cutting tools work about as well as dull steak knives and dull scissors, with the added excitement that they sometimes pull the workpiece out of the chuck or mill vise, and propel it across the garage. (Good rule for the beginning machinist: Stand out of the likely trajectory, and don't put any of your wife's good china in the way.)

There are formulas for calculating cutting speed, depending on the diameter of the workpiece and the material—but generally, start slow, and work your way up. In my experience, it is pretty darn obvious when your cutting speed is too high. The worst that happens if you run too slow is you waste time. (Well, okay, with some carbide tools, running too slow actually wears out the tool.) If you have to make a living at this, spend the time learning the formulas for cutting speed.

Associated with cutting speed is cutting depth. Changing the cutting depth can compensate for changes in speed. If you start to hear what is called "chatter," this means the tool is bouncing off the workpiece, producing an uneven and ugly finish, and wearing the cutting tool prematurely.

In this case, reduce the speed, or increase the cutting depth, or both. The chattering is because the cutting tool is not making solid contact with the workpiece, perhaps because the tool is bouncing off high points. It may be counterintuitive, but increasing the cutting depth reduces chatter because you are forcing the cutting tool into the metal, and it has less chance to bounce.

A tool that is properly cutting produces a very high-pitched sound that could almost be mistaken for an otherworldly voice. The first mechanical voice synthesis devices were developed as a result of a chance discovery at the Federal Screw Works (no, it's not in Washington, D.C., in spite of the name), back in the 1930s. Whine is fine; chatter does matter.

Cutting produces a lot of friction—and that means a lot of heat. If you are cutting metal, you should plan on cooling the workpiece with oil or water. Your cutting tools will last longer without resharpening, and your workpiece's dimensions won't change because of thermal expansion. (If that seems impossible—remember, we're trying to make parts accurate to .001". Even a 0.05% expansion of a 2.000" long piece means it is now 2.001" long.) The workpiece may be very hot when you remove it, even if you have been cooling it.

One of the materials that I machine is acetal, a plastic that is almost as hard as aluminum. One of acetal's advantages is that it is self-lubricating. When I machine it, a very fine layer of it actually turns to gas, carrying away heat, and letting me avoid the nuisance and mess of having to use cooling sprays. Obviously, if you are making gun parts, you are going to be using steel or aluminum—not acetal!

USING THE RIGHT TOOL

If you need to make a steel part that is 2.453" long, you could start with a 3" workpiece, and use the vertical mill or lathe to trim the excess—but it would be a very slow and inefficient way to do so. A bandsaw or a chop saw will cut your workpiece far more quickly than a machine tool. Measure carefully, and you can cut the workpiece to within 1/8" of the dimensions that you want.

That sounds like a pretty precise measurement—but remember, that's still .125" longer than you need—and if your workpiece is made of some tough material like stainless steel, you may be slicing off .020" at a time—so the closer you can get to the right length with the powerful, brute force tools, the better.

Next month: The Engine Lathe, Part 1.   ◉

—

Clayton E. Cramer is a software engineer and historian. His sixth book, *Armed America: The Remarkable Story of How and Why Guns Became as American as Apple Pie* (Nelson Current, 2006), is available in bookstores. His web site is http://www.claytoncramer.com.

Get the workpiece as close as possible to final dimensions using tools like a power hacksaw or chop saw. You want to cut only the last bit with precision tools.

Floor model lathes have geared drives that are regulated by levers. This is a lot quicker and easier than having to change belts, but comes at a dollar cost.

Ask the Gunsmith

By Reid Coffield

M14 MAUSER SIGHT

Q *I have an old VZ-24 Mauser that I like to shoot occasionally. The problem I have with it is the military front sight. I just cannot get use to or use that darn inverted "V" front sight. Any suggestions?*

A On a number of Mausers I have installed an M14 front sight. It makes for a nice military type conversion and provides a square post front sight. I would not encourage you to do this to a "collectable" or nice Mauser but if you have one that's pretty rough or just a shooter, it can make it a lot more usable.

With careful file work, you can mount an M14 front sight on many Mauser rifles for a better sight picture and a really cool look. Coffield covered this in greater detail in the 10/10/02 issue.

P.38 BARREL

Q *I have a World War II German P.38 9mm pistol. The gun is in pretty rough shape and has evidently seen a lot of use. My main problem is the barrel. It is heavily pitted and does not shoot well even with jacketed bullets. Shooting lead bullets accurately is just simply impossible. Would it be possible to use one of the newer postwar P.38 or P1 barrels in my old pistol? I, of course, would keep the original barrel to preserve the gun as a collectable but I really would like to have a barrel with a decent bore for the times when I want to shoot it. I also need to replace a number of smaller parts as well. Any suggestions for where I can get them?*

A Yes, you can fit one of the newer barrels to your older P.38. However, when you do that there is more involved than just slappin' it into the slide. You'll need to check the lockup and headspace before you fire it. More than likely, you won't have any problems. I've done this with a couple of P.38s and it has worked out quite well.

As for a parts source, there are a number of advertisers here in SHOTGUN NEWS that can supply just about anything you might need. I recently discovered and picked up a heck of a deal in P1/P.38 parts from Numrich Gun Parts, P. O. Box 299, Dept. SGN, West Hurley, N.Y. 12491, telephone 866-686-7424. Currently they're offering packets of parts from P1s that include everything except the barrel, slide, and front sight for only $136.45. If you need multiple items and you can use P1 parts, this is definitely the way to go!

In one of my projects I needed a magazine latch, grips, and a new magazine. If purchased separately, the cost of these three components would have been darn close to the cost of this packet of parts from Numrich. It was a no brainer; I ordered the packet! I got what I needed and ended up with some spares that are always handy to have in the shop. ◉

Often you can find great bargains on parts by buying parts kits such as this one offered by Numrich Gun Parts for the Walther P1/P.38. You'll wind up with some left over, but they can be used later.

A big lathe lets you take on big projects, though a table-top model will perform a surprising number of gunsmithing jobs if you have the patience for using it.

MACHINING for BEGINNERS
THE ENGINE LATHE — PART 1

This is the machine that started the Industrial Revolution, and mastering it makes big gunsmithing projects possible.

By Clayton E. Cramer | Additional photography by Steven Matthews

If you are familiar with a wood turning lathe, the engine lathe won't be a surprise—but it has a few little additions to it that help it make such accurate parts. It consists of a motor, a headstock, a tailstock, a bed, a cross-slide, a tool holder and a cutting tool.

The motor turns the headstock, which usually uses a three or four-jaw chuck to hold the piece of raw material that you are going to machine, also known as the workpiece. (There are a few other, less common ways to hold a workpiece.)

My lathe uses a variable speed motor controller to change the speed that the headstock turns; other lathes have a range of speeds that you set by picking particular gear combinations from the transmission. (And yes, it is a transmission much like a car has—converting an electric motor's fixed speed output into many different combinations of speed and torque.)

The bed holds the cross-slide and tailstock. The cross-slide (which holds the tool holder, which in turn holds cutting tools) is attached to the lead screw, so that when you

turn the hand wheel at the right end of the bed, it moves the cutting tool back and forth .050" for every rotation.

The tailstock can hold a drill bit chuck, which holds a drill, for making very precisely centered holes in the workpiece, or a tap (for cutting interior threads). Alternatively, the tailstock can hold a "center."

There are both "dead centers" and "live centers." Both of these are gadgets that hold the workpiece steady and centered while it is spinning, letting you turn the workpiece faster and take deeper cuts. A dead center doesn't

A big free-standing lathe is a very capable machine tool that can accept a wide variety of tools and accessories and can shape materials from plastic to steel.

Whether it's a table top lathe or a big unit in a factory, the basic assemblies are the same: motor, headstock, tailstock, tool holder, cross-slide and bed.

turn, so it will need lubrication between it and the workpiece. A live center spins as the workpiece spins and doesn't require lubrication.

The cross-slide, as the name implies, moves across the axis of rotation of the workpiece. It is positioned on a screw thread that moves it (very precisely) in and out, just like the one that moves the cross-slide left and right. This allows you to cut the workpiece to a particular diameter—again, within .001" if you are patient enough.

The tool holder is adjustable, so that you can set different angles for the tool to meet the workpiece. Sometimes, you want the point to be at a 90° angle, such as when you are turning a cylinder to a particular diameter.

Sometimes, you want the point to be at an angle because you are making the end of the cylinder perfectly square or you are cutting a shoulder into a cylinder.

CENTERING THE WORKPIECE

You may be wondering: can you just put a cylinder in the lathe and start turning it, or is there something special that you have to do to get everything properly positioned? Well, you can almost just put a cylinder in the chuck and start turning it.

The most common method of holding a workpiece in a lathe is with a three or four-jaw chuck, which screws onto the headstock. Most three-jaw chucks are called "self-centering," which means that if you put something round in the chuck that is close to square at the end that goes into the chuck and tighten the chuck, the workpiece will be very close to perfectly centered.

In some ideal world, the jaws would always tighten on the presumably parallel sides of the workpiece and the workpiece would be perfectly centered. But depending on how much force you use when tightening the jaws, if the end isn't perfectly square, the workpiece might be off-center.

How close? The three-jaw self-centering chuck for my Sherline lathe generally puts the workpiece within .010" to .030" of center

without really trying. That may sound pretty accurate, but depending on what you are going to do, that may not be close enough for your needs.

How far off center is it? If you start the lathe turning slowly and you can see the end of the workpiece wobbling, you are not adequately centered. Here's an example where I am using a dial caliper to measure how much variation there is in the end as I turn it (by hand) in the chuck.

Centering the workpiece is important, not just to make sure that you end up with a perfectly square end, but because you need the workpiece centered if you want to put a hole exactly in the center. Why would you care about perfectly centering a hole in the end of the workpiece?

Remember the live center we discussed earlier? It has to go into a hole so that the workpiece is suspended if we want to turn the exterior diameter to a particular size. If the workpiece isn't perfectly centered, or very close to centered, your workpiece will be off-center, and will wobble.

When you try to turn it to a particular diameter, the ends will be moving more than the center, and you may end up with 2.365 inches diameter at one end, 2.355

inches in the middle and 2.362 inches at the other end—which for machining, is pretty sloppy.

One way to improve centering is to turn the jaws just barely tight enough to hold the workpiece in place, set the lathe turning very slowly and lightly tap the end. If the end in the chuck is very close to square, this may be enough to center the workpiece. But if not, you may find that you have to keep moving the workpiece in the jaws until you can't see any wobble.

SQUARING THE WORKPIECE

Once you have your workpiece as close to center as you can manage, you square one end by turning the cross-slide until the cutting tool cuts across the end of the workpiece, until it reaches the center. It may take a couple of passes until you have the end perfectly square—and you will immediately be able to tell which parts you have sliced away and which you have not.

Once you have squared one end, you can turn the workpiece around and the end that you just squared is now much closer to square than the end that was in the chuck. It may take a couple of tries of squaring one end, then reversing the workpiece and squaring the other

"[The engine lathe] consists of a motor, a headstock, a tailstock, a bed, a cross-slide, a tool holder and a cutting tool."

The live center spins as the workpiece does, meaning no lubrication is required between center and workpiece. It keeps the work correctly aligned while cutting.

The cutting tool may meet the workpiece at different angles, depending on whether you are reducing the diameter of the piece or cutting a shoulder in it.

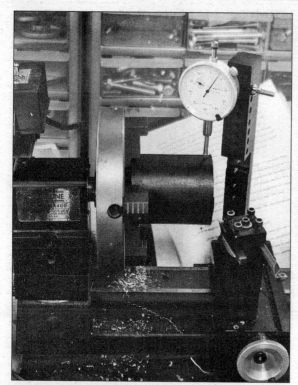

It'd be nice if the work were always centered in the jaws, but that rarely happens. Use a dial indicator to measure runout and adjust the workpiece.

A light tap with a mallet may be required to square up a round workpiece in the three-jaw chuck. You don't want to bang it; just move it over a few thousandths.

approach to get the workpiece centered. Instead, you leave the jaw not quite tight, tap with a little hammer until the dial indicator's variation as you turn the workpiece is small enough to make you happy, then carefully tighten the chuck.

TRIMMING TO LENGTH

You are almost certainly going to want to cut your workpiece to a particular, rather exact length. You use a caliper to measure the length of what you have and see how much you need to trim.

Let's say you are building a cylindrical part that needs to be 2.453 inches long and .400" in diameter. You started with a 1/2" diameter steel rod. You used a bandsaw to cut your workpiece to 2⅝ inches long. When you measured it with a caliper, it was 2.678 inches. After squaring both ends in the lathe, it is now 2.620 inches long.

Now we get to the precision part of using a lathe. We adjust the cutting tool so that it is at an angle to the end of the workpiece.

Advance the lead screw by turning the hand wheel until the cutting tool is in contact with the end of the workpiece. On some lathes, you can adjust the dial on the hand wheel so that the dial reads zero. On others, you will have to remember what the dial shows.

Dial the cross-slide out so that the cutting tool isn't touching the workpiece. Turn on the motor, and then advance the cross-slide until the cutting tool makes contact.

Because you squared the end of the tube, you should have only a very small amount of metal being removed, if any. Advance the cross-slide to the center of the workpiece, back out again, then advance the lead screw

end, but eventually, you will have a cylinder that is very close to perfectly square.

If you are patient enough and willing to waste enough material, this can even work with a poorly centered workpiece. (It is better to get the workpiece more precisely centered, however—it's faster and wastes less material.)

THE FOUR-JAW CHUCK

I earlier mentioned that there were both three-jaw and four-jaw chucks. Why would you want a four-jaw chuck? You can hold a round workpiece in a three-jaw chuck, but with other shapes the jaws won't all be touching—and if all the jaws aren't solidly gripping the workpiece, it won't be held securely enough to machine.

The reason for the four-jaw chuck is to hold square, rectangular, octagonal or even irregularly shaped workpieces. A four-jaw chuck is this flexible because the jaws move independently of each other, so each jaw can be adjusted very precisely to center a workpiece.

I recently purchased a non-self-centering, four-jaw chuck from Sears. This is intended for their wood lathes, but it uses the same 3/4"-16 threads as my Sherline lathe, and it is big—so I can turn workpieces that Sherline's lawyers would probably prefer not to know about. It is a bit more work to get something centered—but you can easily (if tediously) adjust the jaws until the workpiece is centered to within .004"—maybe better.

The trick to this is to use a dial indicator that measures how much the workpiece wobbles as you turn it by hand. When you find the point where the right end of the workpiece (the far most distant from the chuck)

> "The reason for the four-jaw chuck is to hold square, rectangular, octagonal or even irregularly shaped workpieces."

is lowest, you loosen the jaw on top and tighten the jaw on the bottom. It can take several tries, but you will end up with something that is very, very precisely centered.

You can use the dial indicator approach with a self-centering chuck as well, although you can't use the same

by a few thousandths and advance the cross-slide again. This time, you will be removing material from your workpiece.

For very tough materials, you are going to be advancing the lead screw perhaps as little as .010" each time—and you can even advance the lead screw a few thousandths when the cutting tool is in the middle of the workpiece, before you crank the cross-slide back out.

For softer materials, such as aluminum, brass, or some plastics, you can take off .020", .025" or even .030" at a time, depending on how sharp the cutting tool is and how securely the chuck is holding your workpiece.

Assuming that you did everything correctly, you should not need to measure the workpiece again. You started with a 2.620-inch length workpiece; advancing the lead screw by .167" should get you a 2.453-inch long workpiece. Of course, it might end up as 2.451 inches or 2.455 inches because that dial is marked in thousandths of an inch. If getting the length that precise matters, you might stop after advancing the lead screw .160", remeasure the workpiece and resume trimming, to get it exactly right.

Next month: The Engine Lathe, Part 2.

Clayton E. Cramer is a software engineer and historian. His sixth book, *Armed America: The Remarkable Story of How and Why Guns Became as American as Apple Pie* (Nelson Current, 2006), is available in bookstores. His web site is http://www.claytoncramer.com.

Once the workpiece is centered in the chuck, you can square the end by cutting in at a right angle. This also precisely sets the overall length of the piece.

The four-jaw chuck is the way to go for irregularly shaped workpieces. Each jaw can be adjusted independently to provide a firm grip on all sides of the piece.

The lathe can perform an amazing number of metal-working chores, provided you have the know-how, the patience and the tooling that are required for the job.

MACHINING *for* BEGINNERS
THE ENGINE LATHE — PART 2

Now that you have a lathe and accessories, what are the basic jobs the machine can do?

By Clayton E. Cramer | Additional photography by Steven Matthews

Previously, we discussed the basics of the engine lathe, how to center a workpiece in the chuck, how to square a workpiece and how to trim it to a specific length—within a thousandth of an inch. In this article, we'll discuss the other beginning machinist actions with the lathe.

CENTER DRILLING THE WORKPIECE

I mentioned in the previous article the importance of a perfectly centered hole for holding the workpiece between the chuck and the live center. That's not the only reason that you want a perfectly centered hole. In some cases, you may need to bore a hole into or through a workpiece—and you almost certainly want that hole perfectly centered.

What most people think of as a "drill bit" is actually a very specific type of bit called a "twist drill." Twist drill bits, in spite of being made of steel, are actually slightly flexible. This is both a disadvantage and an advantage, depending on how you are using it.

When you want a very precisely centered hole, the flexibility of a twist drill bit means that it may not make a hole exactly where it hits the workpiece, especially if there are any imperfections in the material. This is why you use a center drill, which is short and stiff: it makes a hole exactly where the point hits the workpiece.

A center drill is very short, so it won't make a very deep hole—but once you have a pilot hole in place, the flexibility of the twist drill bit is actually an advantage because it will follow the pilot hole.

Center drills come in a variety of sizes; if you are going to use a .25" twist drill, you probably want your starter hole to be .25" diameter or a little smaller, so use that size of center drill to make the pilot hole. Remember, unlike a drill press or a power drill, when you use a lathe to center a hole in the end of a workpiece, the drill is stationary and the workpiece is turning.

You will notice that the tailstock has a little hand wheel on it, too. You use this to advance the drill chuck

forward, and then back again. Be aware that if your workpiece is not very solidly held by the chuck, when you back out the drill chuck mounted on the tailstock, it may pull the workpiece with it!

TURNING A DIAMETER

You are almost certainly going to want to turn at least part of your cylinder to a particular outside diameter. There are two ways to do this—either holding the workpiece at one end in the chuck or holding it with the chuck at one end and a live center at the other.

If you can use the live center, it reduces wobble and lets you take deeper cuts. If you have a long or heavy workpiece, you will probably want to use a live center as well.

If you can't have the hole for the live center in the final product, you might find that it makes the most sense to machine the workpiece a little too long, then trim off the end with the hole where the live center was holding it.

When starting a hole, you want to use the short, stiff center drill to locate and start the hole. Then you can use a twist drill to open and deepen the hole.

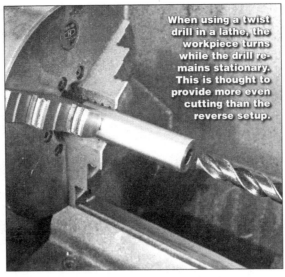

When using a twist drill in a lathe, the workpiece turns while the drill remains stationary. This is thought to provide more even cutting than the reverse setup.

If you have to bore a hole to accommodate a live center, you can make the workpiece overlong and then trim and square the end for a smooth surface.

Position the cutting tool so that it is at a 90° angle to the axis of rotation, and start the motor. Now, slowly move the cross-slide in until the cutting tool just makes contact with the workpiece. Advance the lead screw.

Because your workpiece may not be perfectly round, the first couple of passes are just making it consistent. You don't want to try to remove too much material on these first passes since heavy cuts at high speeds on an uneven surface will cause "chattering" of the cutting tool, which is hard on the sharp end.

Once the surface is a consistent diameter, stop the motor and measure the diameter using your calipers. (Do not try to measure the workpiece while it is turning; if you are lucky, it will only throw the calipers across the garage.)

If the diameter of the workpiece is .512" and .400" is your goal, the cross-slide is going to need to go in .056". (That's .512"—.400" divided by two—because you are cutting from one side of the cylinder. Some lathes have the cross-slide dial measuring diameter, not radius, so you won't need to divide by two.)

Again, how much material you remove at each pass is going to depend how tough the material is. Stainless steel? Plan to take a very, very small amount on each cut. Tool steel is softer; aluminum is softer still. Depending on the material, you will probably want the last pass to be a very light cut of only .001" or .002" deep. This gives you a very smooth finish. Another pass at the final diameter will also remove chips and debris from the surface.

Making a shoulder (like a firing pin) is much like turning a diameter, except that the cutting tool will be at an angle.

How do you get a consistent diameter in a workpiece if one end is in the chuck? The answer is you can't. You could turn most of the workpiece, turn it around in the

chuck and then turn the part that wasn't in the chuck, but no matter how hard I try, I have never ended up with a satisfactory result.

You aren't likely to have the workpiece exactly centered in the chuck both times (unless you use a 4-jaw chuck), and you will be able to feel and see where you started turning the other end.

The easy way to do this, if you are going to need a 2.453" long finished part, is to start with a 2.75" long workpiece so that one end is strictly used for holding it in the chuck. After you have turned the 2.453" long part of your workpiece to the correct diameter, use a chop saw or bandsaw to remove the "holder" section, put the finished end in the chuck and trim the workpiece length down to 2.453".

BORING HOLES

At some point, you are almost certainly going to need to bore holes either into or through a workpiece. If this hole is a standard twist drill bit size, lucky you. But if you need a hole that is 2.268" diameter, or some other odd or large size, you will use a boring bit.

A boring bit is a cutting tool that mounts in the tool holder. You turn the tool holder so that it is parallel to the axis of rotation. You don't need to be exactly aligned—but you do want to be close.

You should start with a hole already present, big enough for the boring tool to enter. This is for the same reason that you use a bandsaw to do the rough sizing of the workpiece—it's a lot faster!

If you have a drill bit that is just a bit smaller than your intended hole, that's a good choice, especially if you use the lathe to center-drill the hole. If you want a bore that is 1.45" deep, you want the rough hole to be 1.45" deep or you are going to be working a lot harder with that boring

tool for the last fraction of an inch. Remember also that a twist drill bit, because it is pointed, will cut a deeper hole at the center than at the edge.

You may find that it makes sense to use an end mill to make the rough hole, because an end mill makes flat bottomed holes. You may be able to mount an end mill in the drill chuck, and have enough power in your lathe to make the rough hole, or use a vertical mill for that purpose.

But there is another way, too. As we have discussed in a previous article, you should never use an end mill in a drill press to make a cheap, low accuracy vertical mill. It won't work going to the sides. But if you need a flat bottom hole, and you are going straight down, putting an end mill in the chuck of a drill press works well. Just make sure that you don't run it at too high a speed; a drill press has a lot of power and you don't want to break an end mill.

Just as when you make the first couple of passes on turning the outside diameter of the workpiece, the first pass or two with a boring tool is to get a consistent diameter. You want the tool just barely to touch the walls, and at a pretty low speed.

Then you can start taking deeper cuts, turning the cross-slide out before you start each pass. Like we did on squaring the ends, you can turn the cross-slide out a little when the boring tool is at the bottom of the bore to enlarge the bore on the way out.

While boring bits usually produce a very nice finish, the same rule applies to boring as it does to turning—make the last cut quite shallow to produce a smoother finish. Run the boring bit back and forth with no change in diameter at all to clean up any burrs and make a nicer finish.

ACCESSORIZING

As with every other cool piece of gadgetry, accessorizing is everything! You can buy die holders that go into the tailstock that let you apply external threads to a part. Because there is no reverse on most lathes, you advance the tailstock while turning the chuck that is holding your workpiece by hand.

You can buy threading devices that let you cut either internal or external threads in all sorts of odd sizes and thread profiles. This could be useful if you are restoring or reproducing antiques that use non-standard threads. Some lathes (such as the Sherline) have ways built in to let you make tapered cylinders; others require attachments to let you do this.

Next month: The Vertical Mill.

Clayton E. Cramer is a software engineer and historian. His sixth book, *Armed America: The Remarkable Story of How and Why Guns Became as American as Apple Pie* (Nelson Current, 2006), is available in bookstores. His web site is http://www.claytoncramer.com.

Cutting a shoulder is much like cutting a diameter, except the tool is placed at an angle. Careful measuring and sharp tooling with make this task an easy one.

Need to bore a big, smooth hole? Start with a twist drill close to the final size, then finish the hole with a boring bit that will leave a smooth finish.

The vertical mill is the king of bench machine tools; with it you can shape flat surfaces, cut slots and keyways and use a huge variety of tools and accessories.

MACHINING *for* BEGINNERS
THE VERTICAL MILL

You know you've arrived when you add one of these to your shop. With the right tooling, you can do just about any job with a milling machine.

By Clayton E. Cramer | Additional photography by Steven Matthews

The vertical mill is the most versatile of machine tools. Theoretically, a vertical mill can make a lathe, or another vertical mill, but a lathe can't make a vertical mill, or another lathe.

A vertical mill consists of a table, a spindle, a motor, a base and a column.

The table has a lead screw that moves the table left and right (the X axis), and a cross-slide screw that moves the table in and out (the Y axis). The spindle accepts one of several tools, including an end mill holder, a fly cutter or a drill chuck. The spindle and motor sit on a vertical

column which can be raised or lowered by yet another screw, giving the Z axis of motion. Like the lathe, each axis of motion has a hand wheel with .001" marked lines.

Usually, there is a mill vise mounted on the mill table—but for very oddly shaped or sized objects, there are other ways to clamp an object into position. (For a basic introduction, we'll stick to the mill vise.)

The mill vise is a high precision form of the vise that you use to hold objects in place on the workbench. The sides are very parallel so that if you have a rectangular workpiece in the mill vise and the mill vise is square to

the table, the workpiece will be square to the table. The table, of course, must be very square to the rest of the vertical mill to get high accuracy cuts.

Now that you are familiar with the lathe, most of the operations of the vertical mill will be pretty obvious. The cutting tools in the spindle spin and the workpiece is stationary. You use the X and Y axes to move the workpiece relative to the cutting tools; you use the Z axis to move the cutting tools relative to the workpiece.

The three cutting tools that we are going to focus on in this introduction are the end mill, the fly cutter and

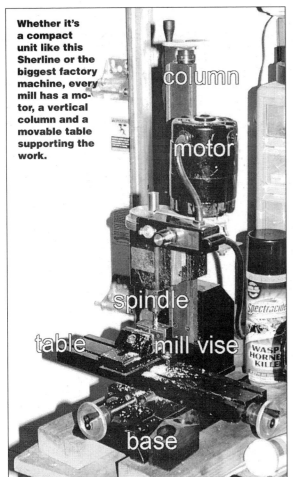

Whether it's a compact unit like this Sherline or the biggest factory machine, every mill has a motor, a vertical column and a movable table supporting the work.

column
motor
spindle
table
mill vise
base

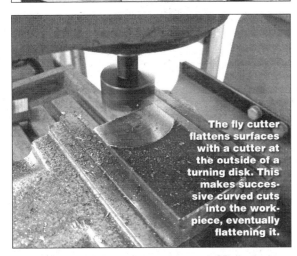

The fly cutter flattens surfaces with a cutter at the outside of a turning disk. This makes successive curved cuts into the workpiece, eventually flattening it.

the drill chuck. The drill chuck is familiar to you: you put a drill bit in it, and you can then make very precisely located holes in the workpiece.

As we did with the lathe when center drilling holes, we use a center drill bit to make a starter hole and a twist drill bit to make it deeper or wider. But using a vertical mill as a drill press doesn't make a lot of sense. Use the vertical mill precisely to position holes in your workpiece; use the power and speed of the drill press to enlarge or deepen those holes.

The fly cutter is a single-purpose tool, but a very useful one: it removes a thin layer of material from a large area, producing a very flat surface. It is a blade that spins over a large area.

Let me reemphasize the word "thin" in the paragraph above; if you try to remove .050" of aluminum with a fly cutter with anything but a powerful vertical mill (the forklift delivery kind), you are going to be disappointed at what happens. But within its limitations, a fly cutter does a great job of evening out a large area.

I've saved the end mill for last because this is really what vertical mills are about (as the name of the cut-

ting tool implies). An end mill looks like a stubby kind of drill—except that it is flat on the bottom, not pointed.

End mills are attached to the spindle with something called an end mill holder. It uses a set screw to lock the end mill into position. The end mill holder is threaded to screw onto the spindle. Here's a useful trick that I have learned: end mill holders can be round, or they can be hexagonal.

Sometimes, you discover that the vertical mill has tightened the end mill holder onto the spindle so effectively that you can't remove it by just grabbing hold and giving it a manly turn with your hand! And that's where it is nice to have an end mill holder that is hexagonal, so you can put a wrench on it, and apply some leverage. A2Z Corporation (http://www.a2zcorp.us) makes a very nice set of hexagonal end mill holders that I use for exactly this reason.

An end mill cuts on the face (the end) and on the sides. You can go straight down into the workpiece with an end mill (called "plunge milling" for obvious reasons). The face of the mill is doing the cutting here, and as long as you don't plunge too quickly, you can keep going until the spindle hits the top of the workpiece.

You can cut with the edge of the mill along the top of the workpiece as well. The same rules that you learned about cutting with the lathe apply here: very tough materials require low speeds, lots of coolant and small slices: say, .010" for stainless steel.

You can cut with the edge of the mill on the sides of the workpiece, too.

This is called peripheral milling, and has two variants: up (or conventional) milling and down (or climb) milling. Up milling means the end mill is rotating into the material.

Down milling means the end mill is rotating away from the material. Down milling puts a lot more force on the workpiece, so the mill vise needs to be holding it very tightly or the forces involved will jerk the workpiece loose.

Up milling puts much less force on the workpiece, and you can take deeper cuts. Up milling usually produces a nicer finish, too. You will almost immediately notice the difference when you start to mill.

If you are going to make several passes, removing say, .020" at a time, my experience is that you should use up milling to do the cutting and make no change in the depth of cut on the down milling pass. At worst, you waste time. At best, you don't end up chewing up the edge when the down milling pass jerks your workpiece loose from the mill vise.

Holding the workpiece in place has been the most frustrating part of the learning process for me. As a general rule, if the workpiece is more than four times higher than the jaws of the mill vise, and especially if it is a slippery material (such as plastic or a highly polished metal surface), the mill vise will have a hard time holding it in place.

You can still mill—but you are going to have to take very shallow cuts, and it will take a very long time. If you were going to do peripheral milling, it may make more sense to turn the workpiece 90° and do face milling instead, or vice versa. If this means that the part is too large to fit in the mill vise, you may need a larger mill vise, or find some other way to clamp the part to the table.

Milling machines were once for professional shops, but imports like these from Grizzly and Harbor Freight have put them within reach for the home gunsmith.

There are more end mill types than you might at first imagine. There are different sizes of shank (the diameter of the metal that goes into the adapter that turns onto the spindle), and of cutting face. Big cutting faces let you mill big areas; little cutting faces let you do more delicate work, or if you need to cut an interior right angle.

If you spend a little time with an end mill, you will quickly see that right angles have to be cut with the face—and because end mills are round, to make a right angle by plunge milling requires a very fine end mill for the corners.

End mills have two, three, four or even six "flutes," which refers to the number of cutting surfaces on the face and edges. A two flute end mill is usually the best choice for aluminum, plastics and other materials that produce chewy, gooey strings. A four flute end mill works well for steel, which doesn't have the chewy, gooey problem, lasts longer and produces a nicer finish.

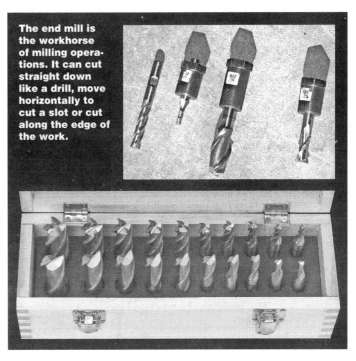

The end mill is the workhorse of milling operations. It can cut straight down like a drill, move horizontally to cut a slot or cut along the edge of the work.

There are roughing end mills and finish end mills and you can really waste a lot of time using the wrong one. I tried to use a finish end mill to remove big chunks of acetal and all it did was grab the workpiece and pull it loose from the mill vise. A roughing end mill did what it was supposed to do: remove the big chunks without fighting.

MACHINING FOR BEGINNERS
WHERE TO BUY

Where to buy? From SHOTGUN NEWS advertisers, of course!

Generally speaking, machine tools fall into the factory production category and the hobbyist category. Unless you find a used (sometimes well used) production machine tool, you are going to spend five figures, you are going to need a forklift to move it and you may find that your garage doesn't have the power to run it (Many require three-phase 220 volt power—which is not what your electric dryer uses, and which few houses have—but there are generators that convert single-phase power to three-phase).

Down from the production machine tool level are what are often called minilathes or minimills—which are going to run in the $500–$8,000 range, depending on exactly how mini they are. A number of companies sell them here, including Grizzly Manufacturing, Harbor Freight Tools and several others. These are made in China. I have no experience with any of them. They are heavy, but not forklift heavy. I suspect that once you get most of these positioned in your garage, you are not going to want to move them without a very good reason.

The next size down are commonly called microlathes or micromills, like the Sherline products that appear in these articles, or the similarly sized Taig and Proxxon machine tools. They are so small as to fit into the "cute" category and light enough that I can pick up the lathe or the vertical mill and carry it anywhere I need it. When lecturing about early American industrial development, I have brought my microlathe and micromill to the classroom as visual aids.

While I would not recommend it (because it will get metal shavings everywhere), you could set up any of these micro machine tools on the kitchen table. Your wife might not approve!

Taig is made in Arizona. Proxxon is made in Austria. Sherline is made in California and as you can see from the pictures, Sherline's lathe and vertical mill is what I have used to move into the ranks of amateur machinist.

In my experience, Sherline's products are very precisely made and they provide excellent customer support. This isn't a criticism of Taig or Proxxon. I have no experience with their products, nor have I seen no substantial criticism of their products, either. To the extent that I have heard anything about either Taig or Proxxon, both have good reputations. ◎

There are end mills with weird shapes for rounding edges. There are end mills for cutting U-shaped slots, T-slots and dovetails. End mills are made in high-speed steel, in carbide and with diamond coatings. Each has its purpose for particular materials. Generally, the more durable the end mill, the more expensive it is.

SQUARING THE WORKPIECE

Much like we did with the lathe, you will usually want to square the workpiece before you do anything else. Cut the workpiece as close to right angles as you can; the closer you can get to square with the coarse tools, the less time you will spend using the fine tools to square those corners.

Unlike the lathe, where you can do some adjustment to get a workpiece exactly centered in the chuck, there's not much you can do with the mill vise. But fortunately, there is not much that needs to be done, either.

Once you get the workpiece clamped into the mill vise, use the fly cutter to produce an even surface on the top. Because the mill vise jaws are exactly perpendicular to the spindle, now that the fly cutter has made a pass across the top of the workpiece, the top is now perpendicular to the spindle.

Turn the workpiece upside down and you now have a perfectly flat surface against the bottom of the mill vise. Now run the fly cutter again across the top; you now have two absolutely parallel surfaces.

Now turn the workpiece to the side. The two parallel surfaces you created with the fly cutter are clamped by the mill vise's jaws. When you run the fly cutter across the top of the workpiece, you have now created another surface that is a right angle to the first two surfaces you fly cut. Flip it again, run the fly cutter again and now four of the six faces are right angles. To square the ends of the workpiece, use peripheral milling.

FINDING EDGES

One of the really necessary tools is called an edge finder. This is a little piece of metal with a spring-loaded end, usually .200" in diameter. The edge finder goes into an end mill holder, which you then screw onto the spindle. Start the motor at a slow speed and bring the spring-loaded end into contact with the edge. When the end actually touches the edge, it will very noticeably move and it usually makes a clicking sound.

You now know that the center of the spindle is .100" (half the diameter of the edge finder) away from the edge. Remove the edge finder assembly from the spindle and turn the hand wheel .100" in the direction of the workpiece. For that axis, the spindle is now exactly centered on the edge of the workpiece.

You can also find the edge of the workpiece by just moving the end mill into the material. When you hit the edge, you will hear and see it. While not quite as precise as

using an edge finder, it is faster to set up. If you are milling a slot that only needs to be accurate to .010", this is generally sufficient.

ARITHMETIC IS YOUR FRIEND

You are going to be doing a lot of arithmetic if you want to use a vertical mill. It isn't very complex arithmetic, but unless you want to throw away a lot of pieces of steel, plan to do arithmetic and check your calculations before you start milling. Here's an example:

1. You want to make a 1.5-inch long slot in the workpiece.
2. You are using a .375" diameter end mill.
3. You have positioned the spindle over the edge of the workpiece.
4. The radius of the end mill is .375"/2, or .1875".
5. If the end mill starts centered over the edge of the workpiece, then when you start cutting, it will be already be .1875" into the slot.
6. You need to advance the table by 1.5 inches—.1875" to the left—or 1.3125 inches.
7. Since it is .050" advancement per hand wheel turn, you will make 26 rotations and then another .025" beyond that.

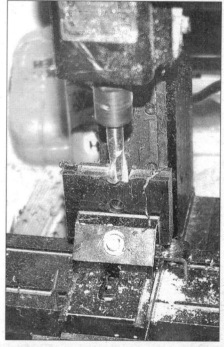

A plunge cut is when you press the face of the end mill down into the work. Secure clamping of the workpiece is vital if you are to hold close tolerances.

The edge finder pops out of line with an audible click when it encounters the edge of the workpiece. You then can align the tool for accurate edge milling.

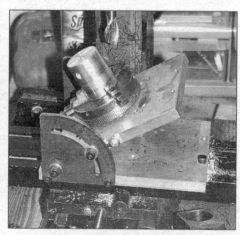

When milling a cylindrical workpiece, you use a chuck much like the one you'd use on a lathe to secure it for milling. It's vital to get it square and tight.

If you need to mill at an angle, you can use a tilting table that will orient the workpiece at a desired angle to the tooling. Measure very carefully here!

ACCESSORIES

Vertical mills seem to be even more accessory-rich than engine lathes. You probably noticed when we were discussing the mill vise that it holds rectangular objects. What if you need to mill something round? You use a chuck, very much like the one on the lathe, and attach it to the mill table with an adapter. Tighten the chuck and the workpiece won't be going anywhere.

What if you need to mill at an angle? There are tilting tables to which you can attach either a chuck or a mill vise and then tilt the entire assembly to a variety of angles.

There are rotating tables, which let you turn the workpiece by very precise .1" increments, for making very precise lines. (How do you think the .001" lines on the handwheels were made?) And you can combine all of these gadgets in really odd ways to do all sorts of odd tasks.

Part of what makes these accessories is that they really aren't required to get started machining. You may find that machining isn't your thing—but you can get a pretty good idea of whether you really want to invest the time and money required to become competent at this without spending many thousands of dollars.

With the proper mill, you can work on even the tiniest projects. This miniature shotgun was made using a Sherline mill. The quarter at right gives the scale.

Clayton E. Cramer is a software engineer and historian. His sixth book, *Armed America: The Remarkable Story of How and Why Guns Became as American as Apple Pie* (Nelson Current, 2006), is available in bookstores. His web site is http://www.claytoncramer.com.

MACHINING FOR BEGINNERS: *THE VERTICAL MILL*

Ask the Gunsmith

By Reid Coffield

CARBINE PISTON NUT

Q *What is the thread size used on the gas piston nut on the M1 Carbine?*

A The gas piston nut is threaded 1/2"- 32NS threads per inch. Note that the threads are cut to full depth down to the lip of the gas piston chamber. If you recut or clean these threads, you'll need to modify your tap so it is a true bottoming tap and cut right up to the lip of this chamber. Don't attempt to use a taper or plug tap, which because of the tapered nose would cut into the lip or end of the gas chamber.

The piston nut, shown here, is threaded 1/2"-32NS. Coffield says to use a true bottoming tap when recutting or cleaning the piston chamber; a tapered or plug tap will cut into the lip.

FLUX APPLICATION

Q *I have problems soldering. Specifically, whenever I use a liquid flux, I end up with a hell of a mess. The flux runs all over everything and if I have something that is blued, it takes off the finish. I want to use a liquid flux as it works well and my soldered joints are always good. It is just the darn mess that is causing problems. How can I deal with this?*

A I had the same problem for many years. If you looked at the floor near my bench you would always find the paint on the floor had been eaten away by spilled and dropped flux. Also, my poor vise was always getting splashed with flux and then rusting. It was a mess!

I wish I could claim that I came up with an answer to this, but I didn't. Years ago, a good friend was watching me work with solder one day and noticed the mess I was making with the flux. He suggested I just take a piece of welding rod or any other type of heavy wire, even a piece of stripped coat hanger, and use it to apply the flux. All you do is grind a point on the wire and then dip it in the flux. You'll pick up just one or two drops and you can then place these drops of flux exactly where you need 'em. You no longer have excess flux running all over your work piece or your bench. It makes for much cleaner, nicer looking soldering.

Coffield uses a piece of welding rod ground to a sharp point to apply just a drop or two of soldering flux exactly where it's needed. This saves the workbench and vise from flux dribbles.

TIG WELDING

Q *When you are TIG welding, what do you use for your filler rod?*

A Generally for most jobs I will just use standard .035" MIG welding wire. This is small enough to easily flow on small parts where I need to be especially careful to avoid melting the part! If I get into situations where I need higher amperage as in building stands or tools, I'll use heavier, thicker TIG welding rods.

POLICE
Automatics:
Are They a Bargain?

Yes, says Coffield, if you know how to inspect and select one. Here are a few tips that will help.

By Reid Coffield

When growing up in North Carolina there was one thing you could absolutely count on with the local law enforcement folks. It didn't matter whether you were talking about the county sheriff, the town police, or the state highway patrol. No matter who the officer was, for whom he worked or how long he had been on the job; if you looked at his holster you'd see a revolver.

More often than not back in the '50s and early '60s it would be a Colt revolver in either .38 Spl. or for the some of the younger, more firearms savvy guys, .357 Mag. A few carried Smith and Wessons but my recollection was that "real guys" carried Colts.

That has certainly changed over the years. Now it's rare to find a peace officer carrying anything other than an automatic of some sort. This change took place over a period of many years starting back around 1980 or so. There were a variety of reasons ranging from giving the officer more firepower to the idea that it was easier to train a person to use an auto than it was to use a revolver. Needless to say, the debate on some of the justifications for the switch still rage on and it's not one you or I will never settle.

The first automatics to be adopted were pistols such as the Smith & Wesson Model 39. A few agencies even adopted the Colt 1911 Government Model. Others picked up the Beretta 92 or variations of it. While calibers ranged from 9mm to .40 to .45 ACP, there was one common aspect of these first-generation police automatics; they were all metal. The frames might be steel or aluminum with steel slides but they were made entirely of metal.

As years passed and firearms technology developed, newer designs and materials were incorporated in police handguns. The Glock is an excellent example of a firearm with a polymer frame that replaced many of these first-generation police handguns. That transition is still in progress as police agencies and departments replace handguns that in some cases have been in their inventory for almost 30 years. As

firearms technology continually evolves and develops, new handguns will constantly be replacing older models.

When replacing their sidearms, many organizations trade in their older guns to get a better deal on new firearms. These older guns are showing up on the commercial market in significant numbers. Several large dealers and distributors that advertise here in SHOTGUN NEWS such as Century Arms International are offering a variety of these used police automatics at very attractive prices.

Are these guns good deals for the civilian shooter who is looking for a general purpose handgun? Aside from the price, what should you look for when considering the purchase of one of these used handguns? Is the caliber a problem? These are just a few of the questions you and I might want to consider as we look at these guns.

I had noticed the increase in ads here in SHOTGUN NEWS as well as seeing more ex-police and agency handguns at various gun shows. Like a lot of guys, I have to watch my spending, and especially for discretionary items like firearms. I just don't have as many dollars to spend as I did in the past. If I'm going to buy a "new" used handgun, it's got to be worth the money.

With that in mind, I recently traded for a well-used police trade-in Beretta 92FS from a local. I'd been wanting one for some time. The military version of this handgun, the M9, has been the service pistol since 1985. While I have always been partial to the 1911, which was the service pistol when I was in the military, my oldest son used the Beretta when he was in service. He thinks highly of the pistol and had been urging me to add one to my accumulation.

I also picked up a few other typical police automatics. The pistols I accumulated were a SIG P6, a Smith and Wesson Model 4046, and a Smith and Wesson Model SW99. All were police or government trade-ins. The Smiths had originally come from Century. As I understand, Century is very aggressively purchasing police trade-ins both

Your local gun shop is the first place you'll look for a used police auto. More often than not they already deal with many of the distributors that advertise in SGN.

here and in Europe. Consequently, from time to time they offer some pretty amazing deals. Be sure to check 'em out if you're at all interested in acquiring a good used auto pistol.

Three of these pistols, the Beretta, the SIG and the Smith and Wesson SW99, were in 9mm. The 9mm cartridge is characterized by some as ineffective when compared to other car-

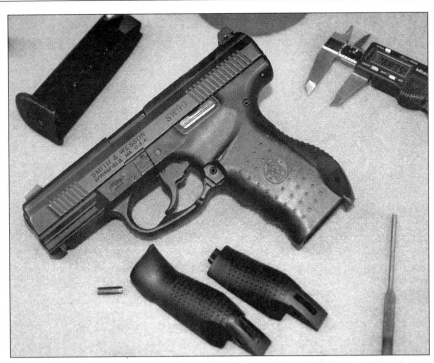

Newer police pistols, like this S&W Model SW99, are available with options like light or laser rails or interchangeable backstraps to allow fitting to the user's hand.

Later police pistols like this S&W SW99 will have plastic frames. Since the Glock, that's the style that has come to dominate the law enforcement pistol market.

tridges such as the .45 ACP. There's an element of truth in that, but a lot of this criticism is based on the type of bullet used.

For years, the only 9mm ammunition you could get was ball ammo with full metal-jacketed bullets. Nothing could be worse for expansion or transferring energy to a target than ball ammo. Back then about the only thing ball ammo had going for it was that it was readily available, very cheap, and it fed reliably from almost any magazine.

That's no longer the case. We now have a variety of new, well-designed bullets in various brands of commercial ammo that will feed through your gun and expand reliably and effectively in the target. Because of this, I honestly believe that a 9mm can be more than adequate for the vast majority of civilian shooters.

The fourth pistol police trade-in, the Smith and Wesson Model 4046, is in .40 S&W. Compared to the 9mm or the .45 ACP, this is the new kid on the block. The cartridge was

developed in the late 1980s and introduced to the public in 1990. It has since become one of the most popular handgun cartridges in the U.S.

It's midway between the 9mm and the .45 and appeals to a lot of folks for just that reason. Like the 9mm, it is available from virtually every ammunition manufacturer with a variety of very effective bullets.

My experience in unpleasant places where people shoot at you is fairly limited and I have no desire to "visit" those places again. However, I learned quickly that when you're getting shot at or are facing the possibility of being a target, no one I know of including myself has ever questioned or even cared what caliber gun was being used by the opposition. I don't care whether it's a .22 Short or a .44 Mag., it can do serious damage and I'm gettin' out of there if at all possible. I believe even folks who would like to take my wallet, my truck, or harm my family probably feel the same way.

What is more important than the type of gun or the caliber is just having a gun!

Because of this, I think that for 99% of gun owners concern about the suitability of the specific caliber when purchasing a used police handgun is not really all that important. Whether it's a 9mm or a .40 Smith and Wesson or a .45 ACP, it doesn't really matter. All will be quite adequate if the shooter does his part.

By the way, when it comes to ammo, more is not necessarily better. More in this case refers to pressure and velocity. Some manufacturers of these police handguns do not recommend or encourage the use of +P or +P+ ammo. Beretta, for example, is quite specific about discouraging the use of this ammo in their handguns.

I don't use these hotter loads myself and really can't see that there is all that much benefit to using 'em. Standard pressure loads with good bullets properly placed will take

The first wave of police autoloaders tended to be fairly large, like the Beretta 92FS (top) and the Smith and Wesson 4046. They also had steel or aluminum frames.

The SIG P6 has been imported in large numbers from Germany, where it was used extensively by various government agencies. It's a very well made and durable pistol.

The Smith & Wesson 4046 in .40 S&W has a stainless steel frame and is an extremely rugged and durable handgun if you happen to like double-action-only operation.

Police trade-ins like this Beretta 92FS will tend to show lots of holster wear to the finish. Coffield says this can generally be disregarded, as it's just cosmetic.

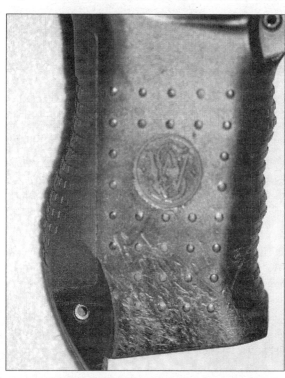

On most police handguns the right side of the grip will have the most wear in the form of nicks and scratches, as this is the side right-handers have on the outside.

care of virtually any problem you or I might encounter. On top of that, these standard pressure loads won't overstress our handguns and will give longer life and fewer mechanical problems. Also, they're a lot more pleasant to shoot and you will normally have better control for any quick follow up shots.

Let's say you've decided to buy one of these older police trade-ins. It may be used as your primary personal and home defense handgun or it may just be a spare. You've seen some of these police guns at the local gun shop and at some gun shows and the prices are pretty darn good. In many cases you'll find them selling for about half the cost of similar new models.

As you shop around what should you look for? How can you determine if a handgun is mechanically sound and reliable? How can you tell if one is worn out? What are some things to look for? You want to buy a pistol that'll give you good service. You definitely don't want a lemon!

First, if at all possible it's best to buy from a local dealer who'll guarantee what he sells and back it up. Yeah, you might pay a few dollars more, but to me it's worth it to get the reassurance of knowing I can take the gun back if there's a major problem. My local shop here in Columbia, Mo., the Powder Horn, is like that. They've been in business for a lot of years and they want to stay in business for many

more. Because of that, they'll take care of their customers. Most good shops are like the Powder Horn. Besides, as consumers we need to support our local shops. It's darn hard to be a shooter without having a gun shop in town!

With gun shows you'll often have the advantage of greater selection and maybe, lower prices. However, if something goes wrong with the gun you may have a darn hard time ever hooking back up with the dealer that sold it to you. Also, your opportunity to really examine the gun closely may be very limited. While the local shop will let me take a gun apart on the counter, at most gun shows that isn't really an option!

So–let's look at a few guns! First, check the overall condition and finish. Most police guns are carried a lot and fired very little. For that reason I'm normally not too concerned about the wear on the finish. Holsters will eventually wear through almost any type of blued or parkerized finish. Just because a gun has some bear metal showing, I won't automatically write it off. Some of the first generation police automatics such as the Beretta 92 had aluminum frames that can look especially bad as the anodizing wears. Keep in mind it's strictly cosmetic and won't necessarily relate to the mechanical condition of the pistol.

Grips can and do take a beating as police officers get in and out of cars, move through tight spots, etc. You can often tell whether the officer carrying the gun was right- or left-handed. If the gun has the right grip panel pretty beat up but the left panel is fine, you can figure the officer carrying it was probably right-handed. The right panel would be the one away from his body and most

exposed to wear and tear. More often than not, grips can be replaced. Because of this, I won't worry too much about chips, cracks, or wear on the grips.

Examine the sights to check if they're bent or broken. Years ago I knew a cop who carried a Smith & Wesson revolver for years with the entire rear sight leaf missing! Yeah, he was sure gonna be a threat if he ever had to fire his handgun. On these pistols you're more likely to find sights loose or damaged from being dropped rather than missing.

Sights can be replaced but this is often a job for a gunsmith. You might want to keep this in mind and figure that into the cost. If you are gonna have to take the gun to a gunsmith for repair, you might want to consider another gun.

Check the fit of the slide to the frame. The slide has to move freely back and forth on the frame but you sure don't want to see much if any side-to-side play. If there's a lot of side-to-side or up-and-down movement, that can be an indication of a lot of wear or an improperly fit slide. If you see this, it's best to keep on looking!

Look closely at the muzzle for signs of damage or wear. With some pistols you can easily have the barrel recrowned and remove up to an eighth of an inch or so of the barrel length. Other handguns have the barrel flush with the end of the slide and recrowning is a bit more problematic.

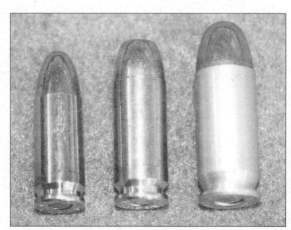

The two most commonly encountered police calibers are the 9mm on the left and the .40 S&W in the center. A .45 ACP cartridge is shown on the right for comparison.

Be sure to check the sights for wear or damage. Rear sights are especially exposed to unexpected impacts in police service. Replacement sights can be expensive!

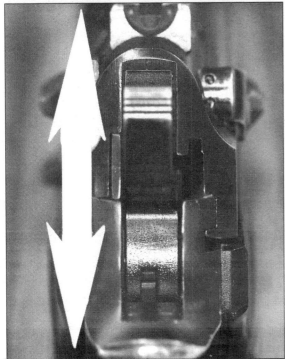

The slide should have very little side-to-side or up-and-down movement of the slide on the frame. A loose slide can mean poor accuracy or poor function or both.

One easy way to check for burrs at the end of the rifling is to insert a Q-tip into the barrel, press it against the rifling and then pull it out of the barrel. If there are any burrs they'll snag bits of cotton which you can easily spot.

An easy way to check for accuracy-destroying burrs or nicks at the muzzle is to use a cotton swab. Any projecting metal will snag some cotton fiber and be easily seen.

You can find many high quality aftermarket magazines for pistols like the Beretta 92. If you buy a used pistol, always make sure you can obtain extra magazines.

Check the bore for pits or signs of corrosion. With modern ammunition, this is seldom a problem and the vast majority of police handguns I've looked at had very good to excellent bores. In fact, it would be very unusual to run across one with a rough bore.

Check the magazine body for dents or cracks. Give special attention to the top portion of the magazine around the lips. That's the area of greatest stress and wear. While magazines can sometimes be repaired, it's often best just to replace one that's defective.

One of the points you'll want to consider is the availability and cost of replacement magazines. If you're like me, you'll want a fair number of extra mags and if you're paying $50 or so each, that can get darn expensive really quick.

Some guns have magazines that are more readily available than others. I just bought some used S&W factory magazines from Numrich for the Smith 4046 at just a hair over $15 each. That's not bad; in fact, it's one heck of a bargain! That alone can make the Smith look very attractive.

Another gun where magazines are readily available is the Beretta 92. Gunsmith suppliers such as Brownells and other large retailers carry a variety of aftermarket magazines for the Beretta. In addition, you can often find surplus military magazines. At a recent gun show I bought two for $20 each.

When buying military surplus magazines, I always try to make sure they are made by Beretta. They'll be stamped with the makers name so they're easy to spot. Thus far I've not had any problems with these Beretta military surplus magazines.

By the way, Brownells sells a gauge specifically for measuring the spacing between the feed lips of the Beretta mags. It is a simple, double ended "Go", "No

Go" type gauge. It's easy to use and something you can have in your pocket as you look for bargains at the local gun shop or gun show. It sells for $39.95. If you have a Beretta, you might want to contact Brownells for one of these handy little gauges. By the way, Brownells offers a lot more stuff for the Beretta, up to and including an armorer's kit.

Magazine springs do weaken with age and use. You may find the last round or two will not feed consistently if the mag spring is defective. Replacement springs are available for many popular handguns. Wolff Spring Company offers an amazing variety of replacement magazine springs and these are available through most major parts and gunsmithing suppliers.

Aside from the magazine lips and body, check the baseplate. When a magazine is dropped, that's where it usually lands. Plastic baseplates can and will break so don't be sur-

When buying surplus military magazines for the Beretta 92, Coffield prefers those made by Beretta itself. They will be clearly marked with a "PB" as shown here.

The Brownell Beretta magazine lip gauge is an excellent tool to help locate good used magazines. It operates much like a chamber gauge, with go and no go surfaces.

The KleenBore magazine brush is available in a variety of sizes to fit most popular pistol magazines. Cleaning the magazine interior is an often overlooked task.

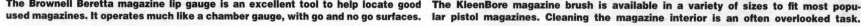

prised if you find a damaged one. Again, keep this in mind when looking at the costs of replacement magazines.

Pull the slide back and inspect the face of the slide around the firing pin hole. The surface should be smooth and free of pits, corrosion, or heavy machine marks. If there's an eroded ring around the firing pin hole, that's a darn good indication the gun has seen extensive use. While this is rare, I would pass on a pistol if I found evidence of this. Remember the ideal is a pistol that was carried a lot and used very little.

While you have the slide back, check the extractor and ejector. The hook of the extractor should not be worn or chipped and there should be good spring pressure on the extractor. The tip of the ejector should not be bent, worn or damaged.

Lower the slide and check the safety if the pistol has one. Some pistols like the Beretta 92 or the SIG 226 (P6) will have one; others like the Smith and Wesson 4046 or Model 99 won't. It's a good idea to read up on the specific make and model of handgun you're interested in so you'll be familiar with the various safety features. By knowing this you will be able to check the functioning of those features as you examine the gun.

Dry fire the gun (with the owner's permission, of course!) to check the trigger pull. Don't be surprised if the pull's a bit heavier than you might expect. Remember these are police or agency guns and because of liability issues, the trigger pulls are often heavier than you and I as civilians would want. More often than not, this can be corrected by a knowledgeable, competent gunsmith. However, if you do need to have a trigger job, keep in mind it'll add to the overall cost of the gun.

Some guns, such as the Smith and Wesson 4046, are designed for double-action-only firing. If you're used to thumbin' back the hammer of a revolver and pulling off the shot single-action, this can take a bit getting used to. You can do some darn good shooting with guns like these, but you have to learn to use 'em and that, of course, is true with all guns.

If the pistol passes your inspection, the odds are you'll have found a pretty darn good gun. While it may have a bit of exterior finish wear, it should be mechanically sound. Once you get it home, the first thing you should do is take it apart for a through cleaning.

Having served as an armorer for several police agencies, I can assure you that some officers seldom, if ever cleaned, their guns. If their handgun was occasionally wiped down with an oily rag, that was as good as it got! Don't be surprised if you find a lot of crud and junk inside the gun.

Clean it thoroughly and use a good solvent to dissolve any hardened grease or oil. Reassemble the pistol and apply fresh lubricants. Remember that more is not necessarily better! A little oil or grease at the various friction points is all that's needed.

Take the magazine apart as well. Clean the inside of the body or tube using a brush. For years I used an old toothbrush for this. Brownells now carries a series of magazine bushes made by KleenBore designed specifically for this job. This uniquely shaped brush can also be used to clean out the magazine well in the pistol frame. It's slicker than sliced bread and a great addition to your cleaning gear.

If you're gonna replace the magazine spring, now's a great time to do it. Before you reassemble the magazine, be sure to wipe down the spring and the inside of the mag tube with an oily patch. While most gun owners will clean their guns, many overlook the importance of cleaning and maintaining their magazines. That's really

Coffield believes that police trade-ins can frequently provide excellent bargains for the cash strapped consumer.

short-sighted, as without a properly functioning magazine all you have is a very slow loading single-shot!

With your new gun cleaned, the next stop is the range! Don't just put the gun away in your vault, use it! The more rounds you run through it, the more comfortable and skilled you'll become with it.

These older police guns have a lot of life left in 'em. They'll typically outlast you or me or any average shooter. In my opinion, they represent some of the best bargains in guns and in today's economy, who would want to pass up a bargain! And yes, I've bought several. They were great buys.

Until next time, good luck and good gunsmithing!

When compared to the new Brownell magazine spring (l.) it's easy to see how the old magazine spring has compressed with age and use. It should definitely be replaced!

Coffield's spent a lot of time on surplus Mausers and Mosins, but don't think he's forgotten sidearms. This time he upgrades a former rent-a-cop revolver.

RECLAIMING A RENT-A-COP REVOLVER

PART 1

BY REID COFFIELD

Coffield applies some wheelgun wizardry to a popularly-priced Smith Model 64 from J&G Sales, turning it into something new.

OK, I know what you're thinkin', "What the heck is a 'project' revolver?" Admittedly, that's an unusual term. By project revolver, I'm referring to a revolver you would use as a platform to try various gunsmithing tasks. Its sole function is to provide the user with experience and training or even just opportunities for experimentation.

This is in contrast to most guns I've written about here in SHOTGUN NEWS. Generally, I'm working on a gun for a specific purpose and the owner or I definitely plan on using it after the work is completed. A project revolver or rifle or shotgun for that matter, may not be used at all. In fact, some project guns are simply collections of parts or are so old, beat-up or worn that they couldn't be used. Ideally, a project gun can be used for many different jobs or projects for many years. It's basically just a learning tool that you can use many times.

A good example of a project gun is a Mauser barreled action used over and over again by gunsmithing students to practice inletting or stockmaking. The actual work the student does or the stock he builds is of no consequence. What is of value is the knowledge and skill developed as the student uses the barreled action. The barreled action itself or the piece of birch or beech used for the stock is just practice material. Nothing more, nothing less.

It's pretty easy to find project rifles or shotguns, but handguns can be a different story. Most folks seldom want to do anything to 'em other than to make 'em better shooters or better lookin'. The idea of altering a handgun just for the sake of learning a bit of gunsmithing is not something many folks would want to do. However, if you're reading this, you just might find the idea interesting.

One of the biggest obstacles to locating a project revolver is cost. Let's face it; especially in today's market,

the cost of most handguns is pretty high. You don't run across $50 revolvers at your typical gun show nowadays.

However, there are still bargains available and not too long ago I found one! A few weeks ago I noticed the folks at J&G Sales, 440 Miller Valley Rd., Dept. SGN, Prescott, AZ 86301, telephone 928-445-9650, were offering some S&W Model 64 revolvers for only $249.95. These were stainless steel, 4-inch barrel, .38 Spl. caliber, double-action-only models that had been used by a security company.

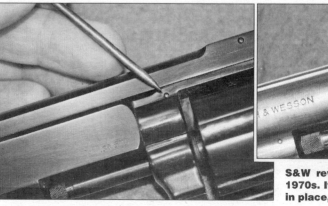

S&W revolvers came with barrel pins up until the 1970s. If you try to screw out the barrel with the pin in place, you can ruin the barrel, pin and frame alike.

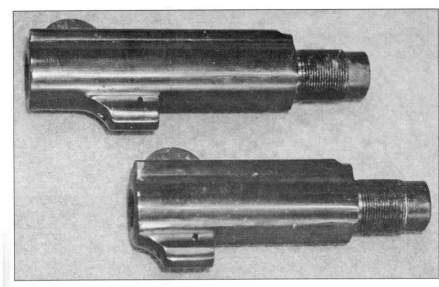

Coffield picked up these short S&W barrels from Numrich Gun Parts, a valuable source for parts for almost any gunsmithing project. He found the price was right.

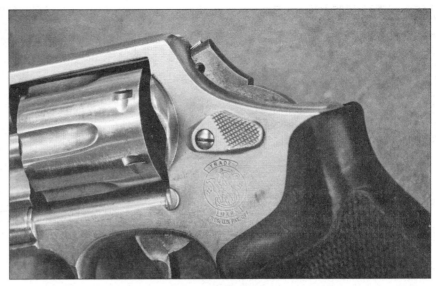

The Model 64 S&W revolver Coffield got from J&G Sales was originally intended for double-action-only use, but that configuration can easily be changed!

Needless to say, the guns had been carried a lot but shot very little. Once I noticed the ad here in SGN, it didn't take long at all to give the good folks at J&G a call to order one. When it arrived promptly a few days later, I was very pleased. It was in nice shape and just the gun I was looking for! Based on this experience, you can bet that I'll surely be watching the J&G ads for future bargains, and they do have 'em!

While I wouldn't deliberately ruin a nice Smith like this, I'll definitely not hesitate to use it for a variety of gunsmithing projects or experiments. In doing any work, I'll just make sure nothing I do will permanently alter the gun or disable it. I'll still have a shootable gun and can always return it to its original condition. All things considered, this Smith is just about perfect for a variety of revolver gunsmithing projects.

Admittedly, that's a bit different from my take on some of the rifles and shotguns I've picked up for project guns over the years. Many of those were truly $50 guns and I'd not hesitate to use them and then break 'em up for parts.

Before doing anything with this Model 64, I took it out to the range for a bit of shooting. It was a bright, sunny day and those conditions pointed out one of the problems with this handgun, as well as with other stainless steel revolvers.

It's stainless steel with fixed stainless steel sights. While that makes it just about as tough and durable as any revolver can be, stainless steel sights do have drawbacks. The integral front sight blade and the integral fixed rear notch in the stainless frame picked up a lot of light. In fact, the glare off the stainless steel was such that it was just about impossible to see the sights clearly.

As usual, I had a can of Birchwood Casey Sight Black in my range kit. I used this fast drying aerosol spray to blacken the sights and this made my shooting much more accurate and enjoyable. However, I definitely wanted to do something about the sights.

I had noticed the good folks at Numrich Gun Parts Corp., Box 299, Dept. SGN, West Hurley, NY 12491, telephone 866-686-7424 were offering some blued .38 Spl. K-frame barrels that had been shortened to anywhere from 3–3½ inches. The barrels had apparently never been used and were priced at only about $20. It didn't take long to order a couple for experimentation.

I was interested in just how my Smith would shoot with a shorter barrel, as well as the look and appeal of a blued barrel on a stainless frame. I've had stainless slides on blued frames on 1911s and that always looked kinda sharp, but I've never even seen a similar combination on a revolver. I was just plain curious and this revolver was the ideal platform to check it out.

Also, I wanted to swap out the double-action-only hammer and replace it with a standard double-action/single-action hammer. While there is a lot to be said for having a revolver with a bobbed hammer, especially one used for personal defense, I do like to have the option of being able to cock the hammer for single-action shooting. This is especially so for casual shooting at the local range.

Again, the folks at Numrich had just what I needed. In fact, if you need revolver parts for Smith and Wessons or almost any make of handgun for that matter, you really ought to get a copy of their latest #32 catalog. It has literally millions of parts both new and used. If they don't have it, you're probably not going to find it anywhere!

The first step in the process was to strip the handgun. As I removed the parts, it became even more evident that the revolver was actually fired very little. There were burrs around the locking notches on the cylinder from a lot of dry firing, but that was just about it.

The interior face of the frame around the firing pin hole showed virtually no wear or distortion as you often find on revolvers that have been shot a lot. Also, the sideplate screws were not buggered up. The screw slots were still sharp and crisp, indicating that no ham-handed owner had been inside it.

If you plan on replacing a barrel on a Smith and Wesson, be sure to check for a barrel retaining pin. For many years, Smith used a transverse pin to help secure the barrel in the frame. This pin *must* be removed before the barrel can be turned out of the frame. I have seen a number of Smiths where folks failed to drive out this pin before removing the barrel. The results were always disastrous!

The barrel pin will, under enough pressure, shear off and then as the barrel is turned out of the frame, the remnants of the pin will destroy the barrel threads inside the frame. The threads on the barrel will also be mutilated. In just a matter of minutes, both the frame and barrel can be ruined beyond repair for all practical purposes.

One of my first encounters with a "real" gunsmith took place when I was about 16 years old. I drove a buddy to a nearby town to pick up a 1917 Smith and Wesson belonging to his dad. His father had dropped the gun off with "the gunsmith" to have the barrel changed.

They had been shooting some old ammo and had stuck a bullet in the barrel. Unfortunately, they fired another round and bulged the barrel near the muzzle. Anyway, when we got to the gunsmith shop, the gunsmith gave my buddy his revolver in a paper bag and told him that he couldn't fix it. As I recall, he said barrels weren't available anymore.

This was back in the early 1960s and 1917 parts were cheap and readily available! Even a 16-year-old knew that. When we got home, my friend took the gun out of the bag and we discovered the gunsmith had pulled the barrel but failed to remove the barrel pin. An otherwise beautiful 1917 Smith was ruined because of ignorance and incompetence. By the way, years later when I had my gunsmith shop, I repaired a number of guns this fellow had worked on. Bottom line; make sure you remove the barrel pin if one was used.

Smith and Wesson used the barrel pin up until the late 1970s. On the revolvers built before then, it's normally pretty easy to spot. The only time I've had any problem in doing so was years ago with a revolver that had been reblued. The guy doing the work had ground the ends of the pin flush with the frame and without looking closely, the pin could have been missed.

Though there were several small nicks and dings on the frame from use, the undamaged screw slots were a good indication the internal parts were untouched.

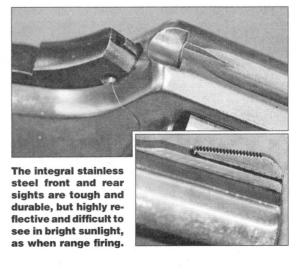

The integral stainless steel front and rear sights are tough and durable, but highly reflective and difficult to see in bright sunlight, as when range firing.

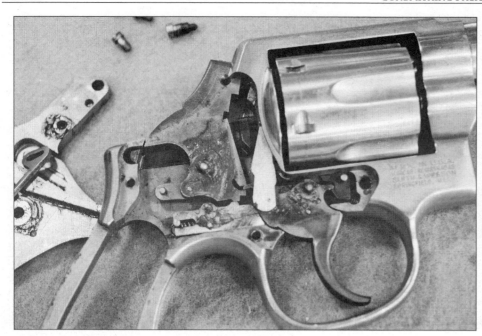

The internal components were in excellent condition as you would expect with a former security service handgun. It was carried a lot but shot very little.

If you have a pin, it's normally easy to drive it out with a punch. The ends of the pin are rounded, so don't use a standard flat-faced punch. If you do, you'll flatten or distort the end of the pin, which definitely detracts from the gun's appearance. Brownells offers some cup tipped punches specifically for dealing with rounded-end pins. They are well worth the price, but for goodness sakes don't ever use 'em for anything else! The cupped tips are easily ruined if used on standard flat end pins.

Taking the barrel off the frame is simple, and rarely will it require much pressure. The problem you'll face is ensuring the frame is not twisted or bent as the barrel is removed or later when it's put back.

If you look at the front of the frame from the muzzle end with the crane removed, you'll be impressed at just how thin the frame is under the barrel. The thinnest point on my Model 64 frame was less than .200" thick! My friends, that's not much metal and the frame can be easily bent at this point when installing or removing barrels.

By the way, the danger of bending the frame is not limited to Smith and Wessons. This is something you want to watch for with just about all revolvers. Single-action revolvers, both Colts and Colt clones, as well as Rugers, are also subject to frame distortion or bending.

Frame damage can be avoided by using the proper tools and techniques. The point to keep in mind is that you want to support the frame as pressure is applied when removing or installing the barrel. The easiest way to do this is to use a properly designed frame wrench, and fortunately several are available commercially. I have two different ones I got from Brownells I've used for years and I like 'em both. One is produced by Maryland Gun Works and the other is made by Brownells. Each has its advantages.

The Maryland Gun Works wrench uses hard nylon inserts, precision machined to fit the contour of the front of the revolver frame. These two part inserts are held inside a massive machined aluminum head. The wrench has a 3/4" steel handle that extends about 12 inches from the revolver frame so you have plenty of leverage.

Of course, you could always put a piece of pipe or cheater bar over the handle if you needed to, but I've never had to do that. One of the really great features of the Maryland Gun Works wrench is that because of the use of the nylon inserts, you never have to worry about marring or scratching the finish of your revolver.

The only downside of this wrench is a limited number of available frame inserts, though the most popular guns such as the Smith K, L, and N frames are covered.

My other wrench is made by Brownells. It consists of a set of 3/4x3/4x5½-inch inch long bars of machined aluminum that are designed to be used with the massive steel Brownell Action Wrench head. The Brownell tool, unlike the Maryland Gun Works wrench, is designed to be used with the revolver crane in place to help support the frame.

Even though it's made of aluminum, I always put a strip or two of masking tape on the inside of the aluminum blocks to prevent any

Coffield used a Maryland Gun Works frame wrench to remove the original barrel. Its two-piece nylon insert fits around the frame, providing full support.

With the shorter blued Numrich barrel installed, Coffield will need to fit the barrel/cylinder gap next. This is actually good, as he can regulate the gap.

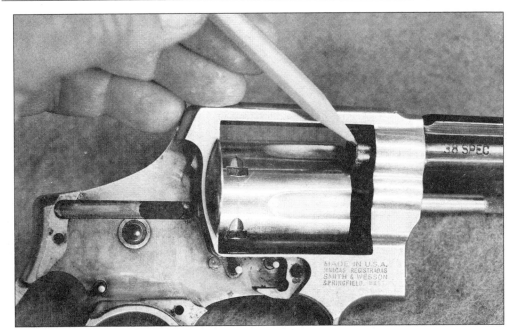

As installed, the barrel shank is too long and does not allow the cylinder to close and lock into the frame. He could file it shorter, but has a better idea.

There's no need for expensive specialized tooling to check the barrel/cylinder gap. A regular cheap automotive multi-leaf feeler gauge will do the trick.

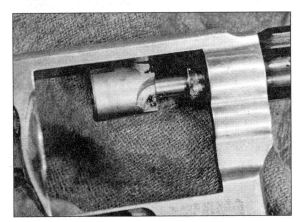

The Brownells barrel facing cutter easily adjusts the length of the barrel shank to very close tolerances, with no chance of making the cylinder gap lopsided.

possibility of marring or scratching the guns finish. What is both an asset and liability for the Brownell tool is its weight. It is one massive tool!

If you have a revolver with a really tight barrel, the Brownell tool does the trick, no doubt about it. While the integral handle of the wrench is only 10 inches long, it's 1¼ inches in diameter! It's *massive!* If you put a pipe on the handle, *something* is gonna turn! Keep in mind this tool was originally designed for rifle work, where you often have extremely tight barrels to be removed. It's a heck of a good tool.

Once you have your frame wrench on the revolver, your next step is to firmly secure the barrel. I generally just clamp the barrel between two oak blocks in which I have drilled a hole to match the diameter of the barrel. I also dust the hole in the blocks with a bit of rosin to help keep the barrel from slipping or turning. The oak barrel blocks are then clamped between the jaws of my bench vise or, if the barrel is long enough, in my barrel vise.

One of the problems you'll encounter with revolver barrel work is dealing with very short barrels. It's often difficult to get a grip on 'em; there just isn't much to work with! I often have to make my barrel blocks relatively thin because of this.

When setting your barrel up, make sure your barrel block does not contact the front sight or, if it's a Smith, the barrel lug that houses the ejector rod locking bolt. If you do overlook this and the barrel turns inside the blocks, you could bend or shear off the front sight blade or damage the barrel lug. I've seen both happen and it's a horrible way to ruin a good barrel.

If you plan on putting your take-off barrel back on the revolver, make darn sure you have either an index mark on the barrel and frame or some other point of reference so you can tighten it back up to the same point. In my case, I'll probably put the stainless barrel back on this gun some day. Fortunately, I have a ready made index mark in the form of the integral top rib on the barrel. When the barrel is properly aligned with the frame, the barrel rib is aligned with a matching flat on the top strap of the frame.

Once the old barrel was removed, I cleaned the frame to remove any gunk, carbon and dirt. I also checked the threads of my shorter barrel to make certain they were not damaged. I then applied some grease to the barrel threads and turned it into the frame by hand. The Maryland Gun Works wrench was again used to do the final tightening.

If you're like me, getting the new barrel properly positioned will take a bit of time. I did not want to overtighten it and have the front sight positioned beyond 12 o'clock. Because of this, I would apply just enough pressure on the wrench to turn the frame just a tiny bit and then I would remove the barrel blocks and wrench to check my work.

It took about a half-dozen tries to get the front sight where I wanted it. It's very darn easy to have the front sight blade slightly canted, so take your time and check your work frequently. Believe me; eventually you'll get the front sight aligned just the way you want it.

With the new barrel in place, I next checked the fit of my cylinder. Sure enough, the rear of the barrel contacted the cylinder and would not allow it to fit into the frame. This is not unusual, and is really a good thing. The extra length of the barrel shank will allow me to fit the barrel so there's a minimal gap between the barrel and the face of the cylinder.

Generally you want to have a gap of about .004" to .010" between the end of the barrel and the face of the cylinder. If you have too much more than this, you'll be losing a lot of gas when a cartridge is fired. Also, a large barrel-to-cylinder gap can often lead to the gun "spitting" bits of carbon or bullet material to the side. These can often hit the shooter and even cause injuries.

Fortunately, fitting the rear of the barrel shank is not difficult. While I've seen guys in gun factories do it with nothing more than a file, I wouldn't recommend or encourage that technique. I use a Brownell barrel facing tool.

This has a multi-bladed cutter turned by a rod extending through the barrel. This ensures the newly cut face of the barrel is perfectly flat and uniform. Since barrel shanks vary in size, Brownells offers these cutters in several different diameters. The cutter I used had a diameter of .560".

Two things to keep in mind when using the Brownell barrel facing tool: always use a bit of cutting oil and never turn the cutter backwards or counter clockwise. Turning the cutter backwards will roll the edge of the cutting blades and make it dull. If it's dull, it won't cut nearly as smoothly and evenly.

As you cut, stop frequently, remove the tool and install the cylinder. Like me, you can use a simple feeler gauge to measure the clearance between the front of the cylinder and the rear face of the barrel. Once you reach your desired gap; stop!

Coffield installed Miculek grips. These have an integral filler or spacer behind the trigger guard. He found these positioned his hand for maximum comfort.

It does look a bit strange! It's not every day you see a stainless steel revolver with a blued barrel! Collectors call these "pinto" revolvers.

Some folks think the smallest possible gap is best. I don't go along with that, because you have to have enough clearance to allow the cylinder to rotate without dragging on the barrel. Keep in mind that as you shoot the revolver, carbon will build up on the face of the cylinder. Your barrel cylinder gap has to be large enough to allow for this fouling buildup. If it doesn't, you're gonna be in real trouble after firing a few rounds!

By the way, be sure to clean the face of your cylinder *before* you start fitting the barrel shank. As you cut back the rear end of the barrel and measure the gap between the barrel and cylinder face with a feeler gauge, you definitely don't want to get a false measurement because of cylinder fouling.

In cutting back the barrel, I would generally rotate the cutter only two or three complete turns before removing it, cleaning the chips away, and then installing the cylinder. I then used my feeler gauge to check my progress. It's easy to get impatient and cut too much, so I had to make myself go slow. I stopped cutting when I could insert a .005" feeler gauge into the gap between the barrel and cylinder.

I noticed that I had a bit of chatter on the face of the barrel where I had been cutting, so I used a 1/2" inch square India stone to polish out the chatter marks. I was careful to keep my stone level so as to not angle the barrel face. The chatter was very shallow; in fact, it was more cosmetic than anything. By the time it was polished out, the barrel cylinder gap was only .006".

The only work left was to use an 11° cutter to chamfer the inside of the forcing cone or taper leading into the rifling. An 11° cutter is thought to provide a nice gentle transition for the bullet from the cylinder into the rifled bore of the barrel. Also, there is a contention by some, and I agree, that this gentle taper will help provide optimum accuracy for lead bullets.

Once that was cut, I used an 82° cutter to break the edge of the inside of the barrel at the barrel face. After doing all that cutting, you end up with a sharp edge on the inside of the barrel and it's best to remove it. All these cutters are available in the Brownell Revolver Barrel Chamfering Tool Kits, or as separate items.

I then reassembled the revolver. I was not particularly happy with the old rubber grips, so I went ahead and installed some Jerry Miculek Competition Grips. These are really nice smooth, slender Pau Ferro wood grips I got from Brownells.

One reason I like 'em so much is they provide a filler behind the trigger bow and the smooth wood grips won't snag or catch on clothing. I wanted to try 'em out and this project gun is just the ticket to do that. Once they were installed, I headed for the range. I was anxious to check the results of my experiment and see how my hybrid revolver shot.

At the range, the Smith shot quite well. It was a lot easier for me to pick up the front sight of the shorter blued steel barrel. I no longer had the glare from a stainless steel sight blade. Also, the sight blade was significantly narrower and for me, it's just easier and faster to use. I don't mind at all having a nice easily seen space in the rear sight notch on either side of the front sight blade. On too many newer guns, the front sight blade is so thick I can hardly determine when it's centered in the rear sight notch.

What did surprise me was the fact that the front sight blade on my replacement barrel was far too high. I thought it might be a bit tall but in shooting the revolver, I saw just how much I had underestimated this. At 25 yards I had to hold about 18 inches above my target to hit it! The gun was shooting very low.

I have to admit, I failed to think about the issue of front sight height. Fortunately, with this barrel the blade readily lends itself to reshaping. Once I got back to my shop, it took only a few minutes to file the sight blade down.

Remember when working with the front sight, you move the opposite direction of where you want the bullet to hit. If you want the bullet impact to come up; you lower the front sight. If you want the bullet impact to go down; you raise the front sight. It's just the opposite of what you do with the rear sight.

I made sure the final shape was both pleasing to the eye and would not snag on clothing or a holster. It ended up being a shallow ramp. While out at the range, I had done some experimentation, aligning the rear sight at different points on the front sight blade so I knew that I basically had to reduce the height of the blade by half.

However, just to be safe, I only cut the sight down about 25%. It was originally .212" high so I initially cut it to about .150" or so. You can always cut more later, but you've got a heck of a mess if you cut off too much the first time around!

I didn't serrate the face of the front sight ramp. You can easily do this with a checkering file. However, I wanted to make at least one more trip to the range to make certain I had the proper front sight height before I did that. I can always serrate the front sight ramp at a later date.

The next time we get together, I'll change the hammer and convert the revolver back to where it has both a single- and double-action capability. I'll also show you a trick that's virtually guaranteed to smooth up any Smith K-frame action.

Until next time, good luck and good gunsmithing! ◎

With the new short barrel at 10 yards, the revolver shot almost 6" below the point of aim at the top of the target. Yes, the front sight was way too tall!

A few minutes work with a file reshaped and shortened the front sight blade to regulate impact point. The masking tape helps to protect the barrel finish.

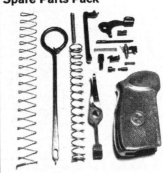
Ask the Gunsmith

By Reid Coffield

03A3 REAR SIGHT

Q *What is the value of the windage clicks on my 1903A3 Springfield rear sight?*

A The windage knob on the 1903A3 is designed to provide 1 minute of an angle or approximately 1 inch of horizontal movement for each click or increment of adjustment.

The windage knob on the 1903A3 moves the sight approximately 1 minute of angle per click. This sight is generally thought to be one of the design's best features and is easier for most users than the original 1903 sight.

GUNSMITH CHECK SHEET

Q *I have been gunsmithing for many years and have gradually built up my business to the point that I have hired two additional gunsmiths. These are good men that do good work. My problem is that I find that each of the three of us does things a bit differently. In most instances that's no problem. However, we run into problems when doing initial checks or inspections of guns. Everybody does it differently and each of us sees as well as misses different problems or defects in a gun. Do you have any thoughts as to how we could make our inspection process more through as well as uniform?*

A Let me begin by stating right up front that I hate paperwork. It's a pain in the rear and something I hate to deal with, but in this case I believe the solution to your problem is a check sheet. Check sheets are simply lists of items or points to check as a gun is inspected or repaired. The check sheets will serve a number of functions. First, they'll help to ensure that everyone in your shop looks at or for the same things. Second, they'll provide a record or document showing what you've done and how long it took to do it. This alone can make it worth while.

On more than one occasion I've spent time on a gun and then forgot to add that time into the bill. With a check sheet where you can make notes of what you've done, that won't happen. Also, the notes you make on the check sheet can be helpful when describing to the owner exactly what you did when working on the gun. I was first exposed to check sheets at the Colorado School of Trades and over the years, I've become a believer in them. Get with your fellows and design an initial one- or two-page check sheet. After about a month of using it, you'll all see points that need to be changed, expanded or eliminated. Try to keep in mind that this is just another tool in your shop to help you do better work in a more efficient manner.

TURK MAUSER BARREL THREAD

Q *I have a large ring Turkish Mauser that I plan on sporterizing, including rebarreling with a pre-threaded, short chambered commercial barrel. My question has to do with the barrel thread size. How can I tell if my Mauser has a large ring or small ring thread?*

A Based on my admittedly limited experience with Turkish Mausers, the only way I can be certain as to the thread size on a Turkish Mauser is to pull the existing barrel. Just a few days ago a couple of fellows I know were involved in a project similar to yours. They both had seemingly identical large ring Turkish Mausers. When they pulled their barrels, one had an action that took a standard large ring thread while the other had an action that took a small ring barrel thread. Again, the rifles looked to be identical.◉

Coffield uses his mill/drill and the Power Custom fixture to drill the crane for the ball detent lock. Removing the ejector rod lock improves double-action pull.

RECLAIMING A RENT-A-COP REVOLVER

PART 2

BY REID COFFIELD

Coffield saw this bargain-priced S&W from J&G Sales as the perfect test bed for some of his ideas on revolver gunsmithing, and he says you can do the same.

Gunsmiths, both amateur and professional, often have trouble getting experience doing certain jobs. Sure, you'll repair screw heads, install recoil pads or mount scopes every day, and get pretty darn good and relatively fast at it. But some jobs just won't show up at all, and you'll often be faced with doing things for customers or yourself you've never done before.

This hardly builds self-confidence. It doesn't have to be that way. You can broaden your base of experience and try various tasks in a planned, deliberate manner rather than just waiting for chance or fate to send those unusual jobs your way.

Project guns help you practice your skills and develop your techniques. They're guns obtained specifically for learning and practice. They are often well worn, missing parts, or in pretty rough shape. As long as the parts or assemblies you need to work on for a specific task are there, that's all that matters.

For example, if you want to practice inletting and bedding a stock, all you need is a barreled action and a stock or stock blank. Of course, if you're like me, cost is also an important factor. You seldom want to invest a lot of money in a gun on which you'll be practicing. After all, you just might screw it up! Learning entails making mistakes and everyone makes 'em, even gunsmiths! Sometimes you find no matter how hard you try, you still just don't have the touch or right technique to do a specific job.

I remember watching a tyro try to solder the ribs on a double-barrel shotgun, a very difficult task that requires a lot of practice. His first attempt was a disaster. Fortunately, he was working on an old junker side-by-side, and the fact that it didn't work out was no problem. He started with junk and ended up with junk! He didn't ruin a good gun. Actually, the exercise was a success in the sense that he gained valuable experience that helped him later.

Finding affordable project guns, especially handguns, can be a problem. The day of the military surplus Smith & Wesson or Colt selling for $35 is long gone. However, there are still bargains out there and some of 'em are ideal for project guns.

Not too long ago, I found an ad here in SGN from J&G Sales, Dept. SG, 440 Miller Valley Rd., Prescott, AZ 86301, telephone 928-445-9650, for a Smith & Wesson Model 64 revolver. These stainless steel 64s had 4-inch barrels, fixed sights, and were double-action-only. These revolvers, which were in good to very good condition, had been used by a security company. They were offered for only $249.95.

Now don't get me wrong, I'm not so flush with cash I could deliberately ruin a nice Smith. However, I wouldn't hesitate to use one like this for a number of gunsmithing tasks and experiments. This is especially true if I made sure I could always return the gun to its original condition. This

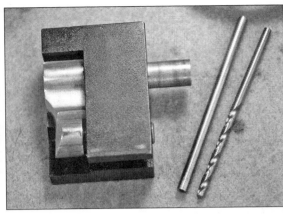

The Power Custom Crane Ball Detent Drilling Fixture is shown with the S&W crane in place. This enables you to drill the detent hole in exactly the right spot.

Use a #30 drill to drill the hole for the spring-loaded ball detent. Then carefully stake the detent in position. Don't overdo it, or it'll be too low.

When I started gunsmithing almost 35 years ago, you always had to hand-fit almost any replacement part to an S&W or Colt revolver. In fact, those guns were all basically handmade, and parts would seldom interchange without fitting.

That's not the case today. With the use of CNC and various forms of investment casting or metal injection molding to produce parts, today's revolvers do not require anywhere near the same amount of handwork and fitting of individual parts.

As I mentioned earlier, I did fit one part of the new hammer assembly, the double-action sear. I had to shorten it a bit so it would engage the top surface of the trigger. While I was at it, I also polished the bottom of the double-action sear to make the double-action pull a bit smoother.

It doesn't take much effort to do this, and I have to admit, it was almost done from habit having learned to do so years ago when working on competitive modifications to S&W K-frame guns.

Every gun is different, and with every gunsmithing task you'll probably run into something unique. Sure enough,

still left me with plenty of options, so I didn't hesitate to order this S&W from the good folks at J&G Sales.

When I got the handgun I was delighted with it. After a little shooting, I was soon involved in a number of experiments and tasks. In Part 1 of this series, I replaced the 4-inch stainless steel barrel with a 3-inch blued chrome-moly barrel.

I had wondered what a blued barrel would look like on a stainless steel revolver frame and this was a chance to find out! Actually, it looks pretty neat and the folks that have seen it seem to like it as well.

I also wanted to have a blued front sight to make shooting easier with less glare. Additionally, the blued barrel itself also reflects less light and helps cut down on glare. By the way, I picked up my "experimental" blued barrel from Numrich Gun Parts Corp, Box 299, Dept. SGN, West Hurley, NY 12491. Numrich, which also advertises here in SGN, is a treasure chest of parts for the gunsmith and experimenter. I found these K-frame .38 barrels for only $20 each. You can't get much cheaper than that!

In fitting the barrel, I shortened the barrel shank and recut the forcing cone. The front sight was reshaped and a set of Jerry Miculek competition grips from Brownells were installed. I had never used grips like this so I wanted to try 'em out and my project gun was the ideal platform to do so.

I thought perhaps these smooth grips would be a bit hard to hold under recoil, but that was not the case at all. The design of the grips provides for an integral filler behind the trigger bow. This kept my hand from slipping up on the grip frame as the gun was fired. All in all, these grips worked out just great for this revolver.

While this Model 64 was sent from the factory in a double-action-only mode, I wanted to see just what would be involved in converting it back to the standard configuration that allows for both double-action and single-action use. Fortunately that is relatively simple and easy. All that's required is to replace the double-action hammer assembly with a standard spurred hammer.

In test-firing the Model 64, I had used some old U.S. military .38 Spl. ammo dating from the early 1970s. It had pretty hard primers and occasionally I would get a misfire. However, each time I allowed the primer to be struck a second time, the round would fire.

I attributed this both to a hard primer and the fact that when firing double-action, the hammer does not move as far back in the frame as it does when firing single-action. Because it has less overall travel, there is less energy transferred to the primer.

Another equally important factor is the weight of the hammer. The double-action hammer weighs only about 514.2 grains, while a standard single/double-action hammer weighs in at approximately 557 grains. A heavier hammer moving over a longer distance or throw should have more energy or force. With all of

this in mind I was anxious to install a standard hammer to see if that would resolve the misfire problem.

As always, Numrich Gun Parts had just what I needed in the way of S&W parts. I ordered a standard stainless steel hammer assembly. Once I had it, it didn't take long at all to install it. In fact, it was pretty darn close to a "drop in" fit.

The only "fitting" I had to do was to take a bit of material off the bottom of the sear or, as the folks at Ruger call it, the hammer dog.

This was not always the case with S&W parts. Before CNC machining techniques were used to produce parts, they were basically produced one at a time on milling machines. The result was parts with much greater variations in specs or dimensions.

Individual operators working on different machines simply could not hold tolerances as tight as a computer controlled mill. Sure, you can still get junk parts if the CNC machine is not set up properly or if the computer program contains errors. However, if everything is working properly, you just can't beat CNC produced parts when it comes to precision.

The ball detent leaves a mark in the Dykem machinist layout fluid to show where the detent seat should be cut. Cut toward the end of the mark to start out.

After spotting with Dykem, Cofield cut the seat for the crane ball detent in the frame beneath the barrel shank. This helps keep the crane secured in the frame.

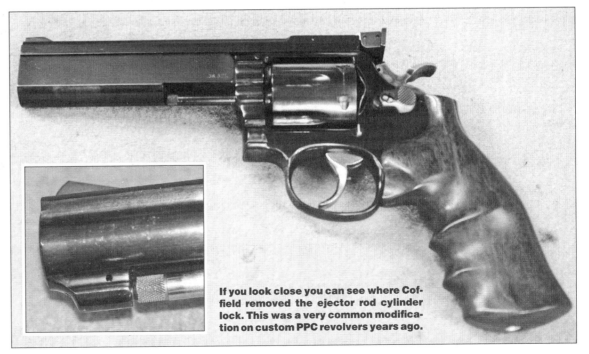

If you look close you can see where Cofield removed the ejector rod cylinder lock. This was a very common modification on custom PPC revolvers years ago.

The military surplus .38 cartridge case on the right shows a much more positive strike on the primer as a result of a heavier hammer and a longer hammer throw.

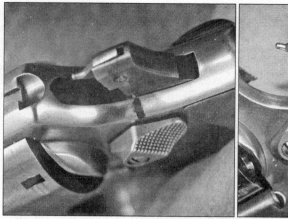

The front mark shows where the DAO hammer is positioned at full cock. The rear one shows the same position for the conventional spurred, heavier hammer.

When working on S&W revolvers you'll need cup tipped punches like this.

with this Smith & Wesson I encountered a rather unusual situation regarding the firing pin or firing pin nose.

The diameter of the tip of the firing pin nose was just a bit larger than needed. So when the hammer dropped forward, the firing pin nose would stick in its bushing in the frame.

I honestly can't remember when, if ever, I've encountered this. It wasn't a real problem; all it took was just a minute with a small strip of 400-grit cloth-backed abrasive to polish the sides of the firing pin tip.

I doubt that I removed more than a thousandth from the diameter of the tip, if that. It was just one of those odd little things you often encounter when working on guns.

By the way, when removing the small pin that holds the sear and the sear spring in place in the hammer, be sure to use the proper size and shape punch. Like most Smith & Wesson pins, the ends of the sear pin are rounded, not flat. Consequently, you'll want to use a punch that is shaped to match this rounded surface.

Fortunately, Brownells offers punches designed specifically for this task. You'll find 'em listed in their latest #63 catalog. If you do a lot of Smith & Wesson work, you'll definitely want to get a set of these special punches.

In addition to being heavier, the new hammer, when used in the single-action mode, had a longer throw or distance to travel. In fact, it moved about .150" further than the lighter double-action only hammer.

As I mentioned earlier, with the greater weight and longer distance to travel, the hammer should have more energy or force when it strikes the primer. That should be very helpful when dealing with the harder primers on my old military .38 Spl. ammo.

With the new hammer installed, there was one more modification I wanted to make to this revolver. What makes a revolver's action heavy or stiff is usually a combination of friction and spring weight.

In the case of my revolver, the weight or strength of the trigger return spring and the mainspring play a major role in just how much resistance you feel when you pull the trigger. However, you can easily modify or lighten this resistance by installing lighter or less powerful springs. Wolff Springs, which are sold through most gunsmith supply houses such as Brownells and MidwayUSA, offers a wide selection of trigger return and mainsprings in various reduce weights. These are excellent springs and I've used 'em for years.

The other factor, friction, is generally a lot more difficult to handle. Sure, you can use a good lubricant and polish the internal components. The problem is deter-

mining just which parts to polish and even what portions of those parts to polish.

Keep in mind that the parts of a revolver are often precisely fit with minimal tolerances. If you take off steel from those parts, and in polishing you do remove material, you can easily make a drastic change in how those parts fit and function.

Over the years, I've had more than one revolver brought into my shop that no longer cycled properly. The cylinder did not lock up or turn into position when it was supposed to when the trigger was pulled or the hammer fell forward too soon, etc.

More often than not, the reason for this was that someone had "slicked up" the action by inappropriate polishing. Don't get me wrong, in order to do a good action job on a revolver, you will have to polish and smooth the contact surfaces of some of the internal parts. The problem is in knowing which ones to polish, where and how!

But friction can also be overcome by modifying or changing the design of the gun. An example of this is the lockup of the cylinder on this Smith & Wesson. As with most Smith & Wesson revolvers, the cylinder is locked or secured in the frame at three places.

It is locked at the rear by the bolt that protrudes through the frame. It is also locked by the cylinder stop that engages a milled notch cut into the side of the cylinder. And lastly, it's secured at the front by the locking bolt that seats into the front end of the ejector rod.

All three points of contact help to secure and immobilize the cylinder so the revolver can be safely fired. That's good. The downside is that all three points add a certain amount of friction to the cycling of the handgun.

It doesn't necessarily have to be that way. In fact, you can actually safely eliminate one of these locking points

and substitute a locking point that adds absolutely no friction to the cycling of the gun.

Before you give up on me as a crazy old coot, let me point out that years ago gunsmiths did just that when building competitive PPC revolvers on Smith & Wesson K-frame guns. The elimination of the ejector rod locking bolt would dramatically reduce the drag on the cylinder when firing double-action. That was very important to competitive PPC shooters years ago.

While you could just remove this locking bolt and use the gun without it, I think it's a darn good idea to install a crane ball lock to help secure the crane in the frame.

The crane ball lock is nothing more than a small spring loaded steel ball detent installed in the top of the crane. With this in place and the crane pushed into the frame, the ball detent engages a matching seat in the frame, helping to lock the crane in place.

The beauty of this is that it places absolutely no drag or friction on the cylinder. The only negative is that the cylinder will not just fall open if the cylinder release or thumbpiece is pushed forward. You'll have to apply a bit of pressure to the cylinder from the right side to depress the ball detent and free the crane.

Installation of a crane ball detent is pretty simple thanks to Ron Power, the noted pistolsmith and inventor. Ron developed a fixture specifically to aid in the drilling of the crane. This fixture is available from either Ron at Power Custom, Inc., 29739 Hwy. J, Gravois Mills, MO 65037-9802 or from Brownells Inc., 200 South Front St., Montezuma, IA 50171, telephone 800-741-0015.

The fixture sells for $60 and it's well worth it. Keep in mind that's less than the price of just one crane or yoke if you happen to ruin one by drilling too deep or in the wrong place.

The Ron Power fixture holds the crane and precisely locates the #30 drill you'll use to drill the hole for the detent ball and spring. By setting up the fixture in my mill/drill, I was able to control the depth of the #30 hole.

Ron recommends a hole depth of .250" or 1/4". I followed this recommendation and consequently the spring and detent ball fit perfectly. I then used a hollow base punch supplied with the fixture to stake the ball detent in the crane.

It doesn't take much force to move enough metal around the hole to secure the ball detent. Don't overdo it! If you try to swage over too much metal you'll cause the ball to be depressed further into the hole and limit its ability to hold in the frame.

When Coffield was a young gunsmith, working on revolvers required lots of skilled hand-fitting, but today's parts often fit with very little modification.

When installing the DA/SA hammer, Coffield needed to fit the bottom of the double-action sear so it would properly engage the top of the trigger.

Coffield's "project gun" shows a number of unusual modifications and experiments, but he could restore it to original condition if needed.

The next step is to use a small 1/8" Dremel carbide ball cutter to make a seat for the crane ball detent in the frame. To properly locate this seat, I initially coated the frame under the barrel with Dykem machinist layout blue. Once that was dry, I installed the crane and closed it several times.

The ball detent left a small track in the Dykem and let me know exactly where it would be located when the crane was in the fully locked position.

I then took my Dremel and made a very small divot or indentation in the frame. This divot or seat was purposely located about .010" or so on the frame side of the end of the track left by the ball detent. The crane was then installed so I could see, or rather feel, whether or not the ball detent was seating. It wasn't.

I used the Dremel again very slightly to deepen and extend the seat forward towards the end of the track in the Dykem. Again, I checked the fit by installing the crane to verify whether or not the ball detent was entering the seat. This I repeated about four or five times until the ball detent was seating in the divot. Don't worry, you can feel and actually hear the little ball pop into place when it's right.

You should go very slowly when fitting the ball detent. You definitely don't want to cut too much towards the outside of the frame, as the ball would not have a locking surface that would pull the crane closed as it seated. Once you get it right, stop! The big danger here is in overcutting the seat for the ball detent.

With that completed, the revolver was reassembled and set to take out to the range. I was especially interested in whether or not my modifications had any effect on the ignition of my old 1970s vintage U.S. military .38 Spl. ammo.

I fired more than 50 rounds, both single- and double-action, and did not have a single misfire. Before, I would have had at least three or so out of every box. The indentation of the firing pin in the primer was noticeably deeper and more pronounced.

Keep in mind that I did not install a more powerful mainspring. The only significant change was the use of a heavier hammer and when firing single-action, having longer hammer travel. Very interesting!

Of course, this revolver is not "completed" and it never will be! It's my "project revolver" and I suspect there'll be more ideas to try out and more experiments to do. If and when I finally decide that enough is enough and I want to return the Smith to a more normal role as a working handgun, I can always simply install the original parts. Other than the presence of the crane ball detent, there'll be no indication that I've done anything to the gun.

I hope you'll also consider picking up a project revolver or rifle or shotgun. There are lots of 'em available, just check the ads here in SGN from suppliers like J&G Sales.

Having something like this on hand will allow you the freedom to experiment and practice in a way you would never experience if you're just working on customer guns or on guns you own that may have a special use or special meaning for you.

Until next time, good luck and good gunsmithing!

RECLAIMING A RENT-A-COP REVOLVER PART 2

Ask the Gunsmith

By Reid Coffield

CIVILIAN VS. MILITARY ARMS

Q *I recently retired after 30 years in the U.S. Army. I am just getting started in setting up my hobby shop where I will be doing some gunsmithing. My problem is that I just don't want to work on military firearms right now, no matter what their age or what army used them. I guess I am just burned out when it comes to military arms. I have noticed that in many of your articles you have focused on repairs and modifications to older military arms. Why is there such an emphasis on military arms? Will you be working on any civilian arms?*

A I have done a lot of work on older military arms over the years. The primary reason for that is the fact that they are and historically have been darn cheap! For the hobbyist, surplus military arms have always been just about the cheapest guns around for experimentation and developing their skills. The "golden age" for this type of work was definitely the late 1950s through the early 1970s, when surplus Mausers, Springfields, etc. were flooding the market.

Since then, there have been periods when some of the major importers brought in large shipments that temporarily dropped the prices of some arms. Right now,

Civilian firearms such as this well used and slightly abused 12 gauge Model 12 Winchester can often be purchased relatively cheaply and can be great projects for the gunsmith hobbyist.

the cheapest bolt-actions are the Russian Mosin Nagant rifles. Eventually even these rifles will be sold out and I frankly don't expect to see anything like that again.

However, what I am seeing is that many older, well used and non-collectable sporting firearms are showing up in larger numbers on the market. Very often these guns can offer some darn good opportunities for the hobbyist. I recently picked up an old Model 12 Winchester 12-gauge pump for a very modest price. By the way, the ideal time to buy used sporting firearms is right at or after the end of hunting season. Most shops

want to get rid of those guns and that's the time to buy 'em!

As for future articles dealing with the repair or modification of sporting arms; I definitely have some of those planned. So…keep an eye on the gunsmithing section of SHOTGUN NEWS for new and different projects. By the way, if you have some suggestions for projects you would specifically like to see covered; please don't hesitate to write to me in care of SHOTGUN NEWS. I'd love to hear from you!

WILDCATS

Q *I am thinking about having a rifle built for a wildcat cartridge that a friend of mine developed. Before I do that, I was wondering how you felt about wildcats.*

A In general, I'm less than impressed with the vast majority of wildcat cartridges. More often than not, you can find a standard commercial cartridge that will do basically the same thing. That's especially true if you handload and can tailor loads to your specific needs. I honestly think that many wildcats have been developed just so the person that developed it will have something with his name on it. It's more a function of ego than ballistics.

That said; if you want it, go for it! Lots of folks enjoy and find it very satisfying to work with a wildcat forming the cases, working up loads, etc. This is especially true for folks that are pretty hardcore handloaders. If, on the other hand, you enjoy shooting a lot more than you enjoy spending time at the reloading bench, you might want to reconsider and stick with a standard cartridge.

The BASIC BLACK RIFLE
Making "tactical" practical again

By Jeremy D. Clough

Enough with the rails and gizmos, already! Here's an AR that is modern, but not overdone. It's practical and it really shoots.

The Basic Black Rifle concept focuses on the three things that make a great combat rifle: sight, trigger and ergonomics, with reliability being a foregone conclusion.

For starters, the Picatinny rail thing has gotten way out of hand. Flattop receivers with rails, front sight bases with rails, rail-mounted auxiliary rails, forends with rails on all four sides, and now covers that fit on the rail to make the forend round once again.

Let me go quickly on the record to say that there's absolutely nothing wrong with having a rail on your AR15, or mounting whatever accessory you please on that rail. But we've hit the point where, in the AR world, the word "tactical" means that you spend more on batteries than you do on ammunition.

The current wars in Iraq and elsewhere have brought a whole world of new accessories to the M16/AR15 rifle, and these have begun the inevitable filtering down from military users to civilian purchasers.

In the process they've transformed what was once a light, fairly handy rifle into a huge black weapon bristling with lights, lasers, optics, redundant iron sights, and coffeemakers. There's a certain irony to the fact that the original three-prong M16 flash hider was canned because it was believed prone to snagging, and now no AR seems complete without a vertical foregrip.

Thus the point of this article: to sift the current tactical upgrades for the M16/AR15 class of rifles in order to select those modifications that give us a good, practical rifle, without the unnecessary stuff. The first step in this project should be the first step in any gun buildup: evaluate your needs, and of those needs, which ones you expect this gun to fill.

While there is a very real need for the multiple-rail carbine in military use, where an extended deployment may require a variety of mission-specific items to be added, this was not my need. In my case, I was looking for a fairly compact carbine that could serve primarily as a vehicle and home defense gun.

Since I spend plenty of time in wide open spaces, the gun would need to be accurate at least to 100 yards (200, ideally), but still be short enough to be handled ("deployed," if you speak the tactical dialect) easily inside a car. With these rough parameters in mind, I decided on a carbine-length AR, and started with a Stag Arms flattop upper/lower receiver set.

Although Stag Arms is just now coming onto the AR scene under its own name, they've long served as an OEM manufacturer for other, far-better known manufacturers. Because I intended to use optics on this rifle, instead of the traditional carry-handle sights, I selected a flattop receiver.

While the stock iron sights are just about at the right height to line up naturally under the eye, and allow you to get a good cheek weld on the stock, bolting a scope on top of the carry handle makes this virtually impossible.

Not only do you have to have a cheek pad to keep your eye consistently lined up with the scope, the higher your sights are above the axis of the bore, the shorter the range at which your sights will be accurate: it's a simple matter of parallax. We'll get back to sights later: first, let's start at the back of the rifle and work more or less forward.

With my Stag Arms receiver in one hand and my Brownell's catalog in the other, it was time to select the parts that would complete my defensive carbine. While there are other sources for gun parts and gunsmithing supplies, in the decade or so I've been dealing with them, I've almost never found any need to look further than Brownell's. Not only do they have an excellent selection, their customer service has proved itself second to none.

Instead of the traditional AR plastic-and-foam buttstock, I selected a Rock River Arms CAR15-style collapsible stock, which slides forwards and backwards on the rifle's buffer tube, locking into one of six different positions.

The two classic drawbacks to this stock are that it's not as stable as a fixed stock (they all rattle around a little bit), and they don't save a tremendous amount of length compared to, say, a folding stock. "You sure you want to do that for just 4 inches?" a gunsmith friend asked me skeptically.

In a word, yes: if you want a rifle that can be swung around inside the confines of a car, every little bit of length matters. Federal law proscribes certain barrel lengths for long guns (16 inches is the minimum for a rifle), so there's only so much you can take off of that end, and 4 inches is the best you can do on the tail end. It ain't much, but it's all you got.

For those who do entry-type SWAT work, the collapsible stock also allows you to adjust the rifle's length of pull to compensate for body armor. This particular handling characteristic didn't concern me as much as making the gun short, however.

One area where fit'n'feel did matter to me is the pistol grip; the stock AR15 grip is notoriously uncomfortable. Several

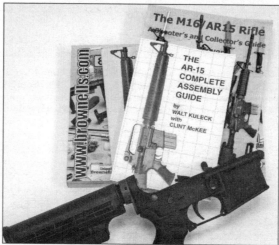

Know what you're doing before you build. Reading up on the topic is a great place to start. Poyer and Kuleck's books provide excellent technical info and tips.

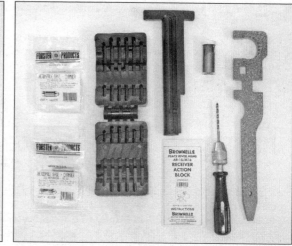

You'll need go/no-go headspace gauges, a vise block for the receiver, drill bit used to ream trigger pin holes, and DPMS combo tool. A torque wrench is also required.

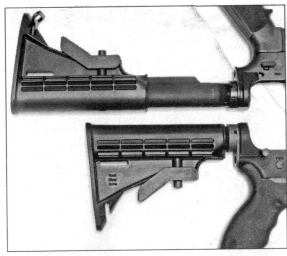

Because an AR has to have a buffer tube in order to function, a collapsible stock can only save you so much room—about 4 inches. Still, it's better than nothing.

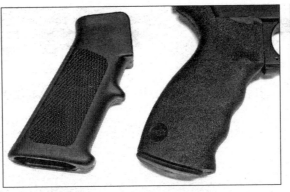

Falcon Industries' Ergo grip (on rifle) compared to a stock AR15 grip. The Ergo grip is slightly flatter in cross-section, and does a better job of filling the hand.

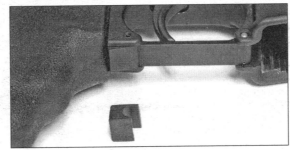

The Falcon Industries "Gapper," fills the gap between the bottom of the trigger guard and the pistol grip, making the gun significantly more comfortable to shoot.

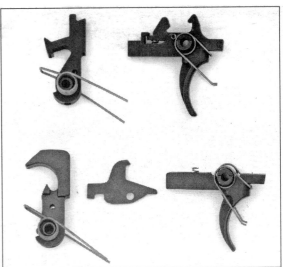

Rock River Arms' National Match trigger (top) is easier to assemble than a stock AR trigger, and Clough much prefers its two-stage pull to the usual single-stage unit.

months ago, a friend of mine showed me the custom-built AR he had shot at Gunsite, and it was equipped with a much more comfortable Ergo Grip.

Falcon Industries' Ergo grip package consists of an ergonomically shaped pebbled pistol grip, a rubber plug for the bottom of the grip, and a nifty little piece of rubber called "the Gapper." Aside from the shape, the most irritating thing about the grip of an AR15 is the gap between the bottom of the trigger guard and the pistol grip.

While it's never bothered me, this has the potential to become seriously uncomfortable during long strings of fire. The "Gapper" is a U-shaped piece of black rubber that fills the gap. 'Nuff said.

For most of the internals, mil-spec DPMS parts were used, with the exception of the two-stage Rock River National Match trigger. Although there are single-stage triggers available for the AR, I shoot an M1911 more than anything else, and I've grown quite accustomed to having that little bit of takeup in the trigger just before things start happening very fast.

Especially in a rifle that may be used in a defensive mode, there's a lot of wisdom in having that extra bit of slack; no one in their right mind wants to shoot someone else, and you really don't want to do it accidentally.

The Rock River trigger, which requires pins barely larger than the stock .154" diameter, broke cleanly, with virtually no creep or overtravel, and felt like it broke nearly a pound lighter than the 4½- to 5-pound pull Rock River advertises. Installation is simple, even simpler than the stock trigger assembly (the disconnector stays assembled in the trigger) but requires opening up the stock .154" trigger/hammer pin holes to .156". I reamed mine by hand, using a 5/32" Cobalt drill bit (do the math, it works out).

The rest of the controls were essentially left stock: there are no extended, ambidextrous safeties, charging handles, or bolt stops. Remember, simplicity is the goal: while I frequently shoot pistols both-handed, I don't do that with rifles, making an ambi just one more thing to break.

Instead, I used the stock controls that came with the DPMS upper- and lower-receiver parts completion kits supplied by Brownell's.

Unfortunately, each of the completion kits was missing one minor, but indispensable, part (the pivot pin retaining plunger for the lower, and the C-clip for the ejection port cover for the upper). Replacement parts were provided by Brownell's, posthaste and free of charge. New-production Brownell's magazines were also used, both in 20- and 30-round configuration.

Inside the receiver, I added two other seemingly minor parts: the Accu-wedge and the D-Fender, both small pieces of rubber. The Accu-wedge is a compressible wedge of rubber that fits in the rear of the lower receiver, and is compressed by the upper receiver when the two are assembled together.

While most upper and-lower receivers are loose and start to rattle with time, the Accu-wedge does away with that play. It won't give you any significant increase in accuracy, but folks, no one likes a gun that rattles. It's $5 that'll make you feel better about your gun.

Three pieces of rubber you should think about having in your AR: Accu-wedge, Gapper, and D-fender. All are quite inexpensive and add to comfort and reliability.

The D-fender, however, is a much more serious piece of equipment. One of the classic weak spots of the AR is in its extractor; frequently, the extractor spring isn't powerful enough to do its job of pulling the spent case out of the chamber, and when this happens, the gun double feeds, and you're in big trouble.

The D-fender is a wee little "D"-shaped piece of rubber that fits around the extractor spring, and serves to add tension to the extractor to ensure positive extraction.

Which brings us to the public-service portion of this article. I happen to have had extensive gunsmithing training prior to taking on an AR buildup, and if you are not a gunsmith, this is a project you should leave to a qualified professional. The operating pressure of the .223 is around 52,000 PSI, and that's not the sort of thing you want cutting loose next to your face.

In the course of selecting parts and assembling the carbine, I relied heavily on Joe Poyer's *The M16/AR15 Rifle* and Walt Kuleck's *AR-15 Guide Volumes 1 and 2. Volume 2, the The AR-15 Complete Assembly Guide*, was especially helpful. All three books are available from Brownells, and I ordered them along with the assembly tools, which consisted of the Brownell's action block, a DPMS combo wrench, and Forster go/no go headspace gauges.

Being well-prepared, however, doesn't mean you're immune to mistakes; I burred up the charge handle badly by dropping the bolt while the barrel was not installed on the otherwise-completed rifle. It was a stupid mistake, and I knew better.

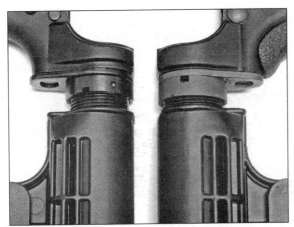

Here's a tip; screw in the lock nut on the buttstock with the notches facing forward (right) as opposed to rearward. Clough asserts this makes it more snag-free.

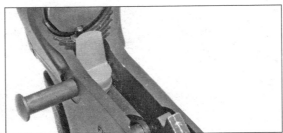

The bright red Accu-wedge takes up slop between the upper and lower receivers. It's not a huge functional upgrade, but it'll make you feel better about your rifle.

A rail on a rail on a rail? Clough argues the rail thing has gone way too far: know when to say when. Unless you're patrolling Al Anbar, you probably don't need it.

SureFire's X200 LED Weaponlight fit in front of the ACOG scope on the flattop receiver, and didn't appear in the field of view, making it ideal for this rifle.

Picking optics gets harder every day, with the Aimpoint, the EOTech and the Trijicon ACOG all competing to be the top combat sight. While the Aimpoint and the EOTech are excellent sights, especially in close-quarters work, I was looking for a sight more suited for longer-range shooting.

Trijicon, which is perhaps best known for its self-luminous tritium night-sight inserts (virtually all of my defensive pistols have Trijicon inserts), also produces the ACOG (Advanced Combat Optical Gunsight) line of optics, which, if you watch the news long enough, you'll see perched on any variety of rifles being used in the Big Sandbox.

The variant I selected is the RCO (Rifle Combat Optic) model currently in service with the United States Marine Corps, and has a range-marked reticle calibrated for the bullet drop of the M4 carbine in .223.

Instead of the familiar zero-magnification and mobile red dot of the conventional red-dot scopes, the rubber-armored ACOG has 4X magnification, and a self-luminous red chevron-shaped reticle.

While the reticle doesn't move around in the field of view, the sharp-pointed triangle makes finer accuracy possible than

Trijicon's ACOG RCO scope features rugged, forged aluminum construction, and a red self-luminous chevron reticle that requires no batteries. It's popular in Iraq.

the multiple-moa dots on other combat sights. Slightly slower on target, but higher accuracy potential at long range: such are the tradeoffs of life.

Not to say that it's slow, though, because it's not: due to something called the Bindon Aiming Concept, that, frankly, I don't understand, the ACOG can be used with both eyes open, which also helps—and we're speaking tactical again here—maximize situation awareness.

The little red chevron also doesn't have to be turned on. It's illuminated by a top-mounted fiber optic during daylight (making it self-adjustable to the amount of ambient light), or by tritium at night. No batteries are required, and the compact ACOG bolted neatly in place on my flattop upper receiver.

Even with my aversion to rails, there's one rail-mounted accessory that's virtually a requirement on a tactical carbine: a light. While it's not always practical (and seldom wise) to identify your target by pointing a rifle at it, if it gets down to the pointing stage, you need know exactly where your bullets are going.

A handheld light is generally the best option for identifying whatever has just gone bump in the night, but when the time comes to bring a weapon to bear, nothing works as well as having one on the gun.

On my AR, it just so happens that the eye relief on the ACOG caused it to be mounted all the way at the back of the flattop receiver, leaving a good couple of inches worth of rail exposed in front of it. Through some strange mixture of dumb luck and curiosity, I discovered that a SureFire X200A Weaponlight would fit, upside-down, on the rail just forward of the scope, without appearing in its field of view.

While the LED-powered X200 isn't a flamethrower like SureFire's dedicated rifle lights (it's intended for pistols) it's bright enough to ID a target out to a good 75 yards or so, and compact enough to fit unobtrusively on the rifle. Additionally, mounted on the flattop, it's neither near the muzzle nor hanging off the bottom of the rifle, which makes it that much less likely to get knocked off on a doorway. If you hold the rifle by the front of the mag well, it's a short reach to hit the on/off toggle switch.

And now to the heart of the rifle: the barrel, which in this case was made of stainless steel, with a versatile 1:9 twist that's capable of shooting almost any grain weight bullet with reasonable accuracy. While there are a number of aftermarket AR barrels available, in dozens of different profiles, I chose to have a custom profile turned by Lothar Walther.

Founded by the son of Carl Walther, Lothar Walther Precision Tools is primarily an OEM manufacturer, making barrels for many big name gunmakers, and their quality is well-known.

The 16.1-inch tube began life as a heavy barrel, with a nominal diameter of nearly an inch under the handguard, stepping down to .750" for the gas block, and then tapering down to .732" near the muzzle. Although I toyed with the idea of omitting the flash hider, I decided to have the muzzle threaded at 1/2 x 28 TPI to fit a Vortex flash hider.

Initially, there was some concern about the effect that would have on accuracy (reducing a barrel from .732" to a major diameter of .500" plays havoc with barrel harmonics), but this proved not to be the case.[1]

The rest of the barrel contour was driven by my choice of a full-length free-float handguard, which, when placed on a short 16-inch barrel, mimics the look of the Bushmaster Dissipator rifle.

While the design improves heat dissipation over a standard shorty handguard (hence the name), there are several other

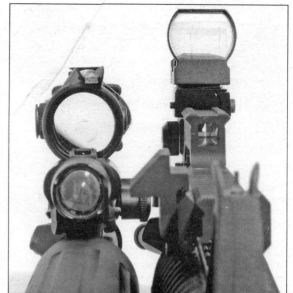

There's no substitute for a flattop if you're planning on mounting optics. Note how much higher the red-dot sight rides on a traditional carry-handle receiver (r.).

reasons to consider this option. If you're using iron sights, the full-length tube gives you a longer sight radius, which takes a lot of the human error out of shooting a carbine.

Even with a scope, the float tube protects the barrel from coming into contact with anything that could interfere with the barrel harmonics and shift the rifle's point of impact. And, of course, it gives your hands added protection against a hot barrel during long strings of fire.

While the dissipator look appears to have a full-length gas system, it doesn't; the front sight is a dummy gas block, while the real block is under the handguard in the traditional carbine location.

In order to function reliably, a gas system has to have a specific amount of both gas pressure and volume, and on an AR15, that means the gas port in the barrel needs to be a certain distance from the muzzle. As a rule, you can't just use a full-length gas tube on a short barrel.

I used a low-profile steel gas block from Yankee Hill Machine that was specifically designed for this sort of application, and it fits neatly under AR handguards. While Brownell's supplied blocks in both aluminum and steel, I went with the steel block, for longevity reasons.

A steel front sight base, with the usual Dick Swan-designed 1913/Picatinny rail, was fixed on the barrel at the end of the handguard, should I ever have the need for a front sight. Other than the flattop, this is the only rail on the gun. Both the sight base and the gas block were held in place by set screws.

Since this profile was a new one at Lothar Walther, they assembled and test-fired the barrel on my upper receiver assembly, and, after the appropriate wait, I drove down to pick it up. "It likes heavy bullets," I was told, after I unzipped the black cloth case and pulled out the assembled upper.

And it did: shooting from prone, I managed to shrink one of my first test groups to 1 inch at 100 yards with Hornady's

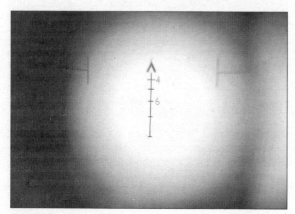

The red chevron reticle of the ACOG is marked for bullet drop, and is available calibrated for either the full-size M16/AR15 rifle, or for the shorter M4 variant.

Using a full-length handguard on a 16-inch barrel gives the rifle a deceptively long appearance. Its primary virtue is that it leaves less of the barrel exposed.

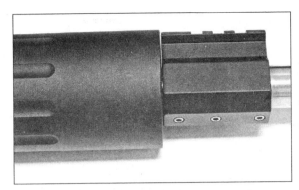

That's not a gas block—the rifle's gas system is fully concealed beneath the handguard—but a front sight base, should redundant iron sights ever become necessary.

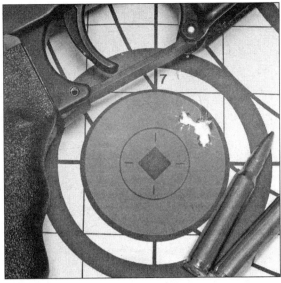

Yes, Virginia, there is such a thing as a one-hole AR carbine. This very satisfying 100-yard group was fired with handloads using 40-grain Sierra bullets.

Spyderco's Manix folder is a big handful of knife. The broad, heavy blade is well-designed for large cutting chores, and Clough says the knife fits well in the hand.

60-grain TAP FPD ammo: Greek surplus SS109s (green tip) did about 1½ – 2 moa. The folks at Lothar Walther were unimpressed: "We were getting quarter- and half-inch groups when we tested it," they told me when I called. "Why don't you try again, and let us know how you do."

In order to ensure that I was getting the maximum performance out of the rifle, the T&E manager of Lothar Walther accompanied me to the 100-yard range at Riverbend Gun Club, where we took off the combat-oriented ACOG and torqued on a serious Night Force target scope with a huge objective lens and 30-something-X magnification.

While pistols are best judged by their average accuracy, it may be that rifles are more fairly judged by their finest accuracy: concentrating intently with the sandbagged rifle, I was able to shoot groups that went down to a quarter-inch at 100 yards. While factory ammo shot quite well, we got that kind of accuracy out of carefully-prepared handloads using Sierra bullets. Average accuracy results obtained using the ACOG are shown in the accompanying table.

Throughout testing, which included firing 500 rounds, give-or-take, the only malfunctions resulted either from poor ammo (remember, there's a reason that stuff was surplused out), or from overloaded mags.

One of the cardinal rules of the AR—really of all hi-caps—is that you download your mags by 10% in order to ensure perfect reliability.

My rifle suffered from a couple of no-feeds with fully-loaded mags, but once they were reduced (to 27 rounds for 30-round mags, 18 for 20s) there were no more malfunctions. Think downloading is a silly idea? The SAS does it. And let's face it—as a civilian, if you're in a position where the difference between 27 and 30 bullets is going to cost you your life, you're probably already in over your head.

Whatever you plan to do with a rifle, it's no good if it's not there when you need it, or it's been beat to death bouncing

around in your trunk. It's got to be protected (especially if there's any sort of optic involved), and the time-honored way of protecting an AR is what we affectionately know as the "Grab'n'go" bag, shown here as manufactured by Brownell's. A little ballistic black nylon, a lot of foam, and several mag pouches on the side, and you've got everything you need, which includes a functional, still-zeroed rifle. Mine also has a sling and a Spyderco folder.

For article purposes, I paired the basic black rifle with Spyderco's C95 Manix. With a broad 3¾" blade made of CPM-S30V steel, and weighing in a couple ounces shy of a half-pound, the Manix is a large knife.

Despite its size—and the weight of its blade—it has a smooth, light action, and handles very well. While there's a smaller version available, the large Manix clipped neatly into one of the mag pouches on my grab'n'go bag, where its large size isn't a problem. In fact, in the field, it's an asset.

When all was bolted together, the gun came out like I'd planned: as short as the law allows, fairly uncomplicated, and superbly accurate. It may not fit everyone's idea of what an AR should look like...but it sure fit mine.

1 For those interested, this barrel, in any number of calibers, is now a standard profile, and is available from Lothar Walther as the WM-01.

SOURCES

Brownells
www.brownells.com
200 S. Front Street
Montezuma, Iowa 50171
(800) 741-0015
(641) 623-3896 (fax)

Lothar Walther
www.lothar-walther.com
3425 Hutchinson Road
Cumming, Ga. 30040
(770) 889-9998
(770) 889-4919 (fax)

Stag Arms
www.stagarms.com
515 John Downey Dr.
New Britain, Conn. 06051
(860) 229-9994
(860) 229-3738 (fax)

D.P.M.S., Inc./Panther Arms
www.dpmsinc.com
3312 12th St. SE
St. Cloud, Minn. 56304
(800) 578-3767
(320) 258-4449 (fax)

Sierra Bullets
www.sierrabullets.com
1400 West Henry St.
Sedalia, Mo. 65301
(888) 223-3006
(660) 827-4999 (fax)

SureFire, LLC
www.surefire.com
18300 Mt. Baldy Circle
Fountain Valley, Calif. 92708
(800) 828-8809
(714) 545-9537 (fax)

Hornady
www.hornady.com
PO Box 1848
Grand Island, Nebr. 68803
(308) 382-1390
(308) 382-5761 (fax)

Spyderco
www.spyderco.com
820 Spyderco Way
Golden, Colo. 80403
(800) 525-7770
(303) 278-2229 (fax)

Trijicon, Inc.
www.trijicon.com
49385 Shafer Ave.
Wixom, Mich. 48393
(800) 338-0563
(248) 960-7725 (fax)

Hornady's defense-oriented 75-grain TAP hollow-point ammo proved capable of excellent accuracy; this 100-yard group came in just a hair over an inch, edge-to-edge.

ACCURACY RESULTS

While the basic black rifle proved capable of match-grade accuracy when fired with a target scope, for article purposes, I chose to test it with the scope it was paired with, which is the combat-oriented 4x32 ACOG. Groups shown were fired from prone position at 100 yards. Two five-shot groups were fired with each load; the better of the two groups is shown, measured center-to-center. Velocities shown are in feet per second (fps) and are the average of ten rounds, measured with a ProChrono chronograph placed 10 feet from the muzzle.

Load	Group Average Size (ins.)	Extreme Velocity (fps)	Standard Spread	Deviation
Olympic Ammunition 62-gr. SS109 (Green Tip)	1.34	2925	225	67
Hornady 75-gr. TAP FPD	.92	2509	75	25
Hornady 60-gr. TAP FPD	1.39	2824	54	14
Winchester Ranger 55-gr. Ballistic Silvertip	2.00	2876	74	20
Hornady Custom 55-gr.	1.35	2975	206	61
53-gr. Sierra (handload)	1.15	2963	172	55
55-gr. Sierra (handload)	1.65	2825	176	57

Average accuracy: 1.39"

Why Retro?

Jeremy D. Clough

A forward-thinking look at the backwards-focused M1911

There's a current craze for throwback 1911s; what modern touches are just nice and which ones do you really need? Clough explores.

Why retro? Built with only a minimal number of new parts, this retro Springfield M1911 proved itself quite capable of match-grade accuracy and outstanding reliability.

We are living in the golden age of the M1911. Today's factory pistols look hopelessly exotic compared to what was available a mere two decades ago, and the ready availability of CNC machines–even to fairly modest custom pistol shops–has made precision more precise and custom–well, more custom.

Accessory rails, beavertails, exotic materials and a dazzling array of sizes make selecting an M1911–especially a custom one–an impossibly complex task. So, in the midst of all this exotica, why are retro pistols so popular? From Colt's erstwhile as-issued M1911 (not M1911A1, mind you) .45, to U.S. Firearms' 1910-styled .45 and the heavily retroed pistols from Yost-Bonitz custom, old is the newest thing. To find out why, let's look first to the history of the custom M1911.

In the beginning were the service pistols, and the service armorers–highly-skilled 'smiths whose stock in trade was making the guns more suitable for service-based competitions. Accurizing was the key here, and while there were custom sights, grips, and grip textures, accuracy was king.

Then, in the '70s, when practical shooting came to us, courtesy of Jeff Cooper and others, accuracy was less the focus than making the spurhammer beast more comfortable to shoot.

Men like Charlie Kelsey of Devel silver-soldered up beavertail safeties, one at a time, and Safari Arms mass-produced their upward-curled grip safety that kept the .45's long-tailed hammer from leaving its bloody track mark in the web of the hand.

Armand Swenson and others brazed longer contact pads on the thumb safety to make it faster to hit. Checkering became popular, as did custom sight installations like the Smith & Wesson K-frame revolver sight, and then dedicated M1911 sights like the Bo-Mar adjustable.

By the '90's, virtually all of these things were commonplace on custom pistols, and began to trickle into production lines as "factory custom" pistols, a market which exploded when Kimber hit the scene in 1996.

In these beavertailed, night-sighted, speed-safetied pistols, however, one thing was lacking: hand fitting and attention to detail. While they were leaps and bounds ahead of other production guns, they were still assembly-line guns, and therefore didn't have the individual attention that makes a custom gun superior to a factory one.

In some ways, the retro craze is a reaction–a decision to make pistols that are distinctive simply because they don't look the way we're now told a custom M1911 should look. Far more than simple aesthetics, though, it also provides the minimalist pistolsmith with a chance to burn the fat off of the M1911 and make it into a truly distinctive, high-performance pistol, minus the unnecessary fluff.

And it's okay if there's less there, as long as what's there is done right. As for what must be done, usable sights, a good trigger and unquestionable reliability are the three baseline attributes that you must demand of any pistol, with ergonomics serving as a lesser light to guide the gunsmith's hand.

With these things in mind, and a recently-purchased Springfield Mil-Spec M1911 in hand, I made my semi-annual pilgrimage up to Novak's .45 Shop in Parkersburg, W. Va., to build my first retro .45.

I had been inspired on a previous trip by a concept gun Novak had built some years ago to explore the idea of modernizing M1911A1 service pistols: other than sights, a speed safety, and a good barrel, all the gun's improvements were in the work.

In keeping with this, and with the grand minimalist tradition of making do, as many early 'smiths had to, I planned to use as few custom parts as possible. I also intended for the gun to wind up looking so plain that, at first glance, it could pass for a pistol made 20, 30, or even 50 years ago.

Here's Clough's basic boondocking gear: a Springfield .45 carried in a Blackhawk SERPA holster, along with Cold Steel's Recon Tanto and SureFire's U2 LED flashlight.

The lanyard loop, long a trademark of the service M1911s, has seen a resurgence, partly due to recent combat experience overseas. This Mil-Spec Springfield came with one.

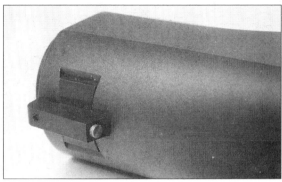

The Novak dovetail front sight is retained with a roll pin. The gold dot–and yes, that's real gold–serves to collect light, making it an old-school night sight.

The Springfield was a perfect starting point for such a project. Shot very little–probably less than 100 rounds–I had picked it up very reasonably from a friend. Simply put, the gun didn't run; the barrel would catch going into battery. Lapping the barrel had not helped, nor did a simple swap with a take-off Colt barrel. More serious surgery was in order; as usual, we'll take it from the top of the slide down.

Since the stock barrel kept the pistol from functioning, the first order of business was installing a Kart National Match .45 barrel. Although a custom barrel is not strictly necessary on a "basic" .45, one of the great strengths of the M1911 platform is its inherent accuracy, and to make the most of it, you pretty much need a hand-fit barrel.

While there are several other excellent barrel makers out there, Kart gets credit for being the manufacturer of the 7791414-marked National Match barrels used by the Marksmanship Training Unit. Karts also have a brilliant, glass-smooth bore, and are among the easier barrels to fit.

While early pistolsmiths were constrained to weld up the fitting areas on a .45 barrel prior to fitting, the ready availability of barrels with oversized lugs and hoods has made that one part of .45 lore that's best left in the past. In the actual fitting process, I followed the hard-fit technique as taught by John Miller.

First, the hood is narrowed with a file until it will fit in the slide, then shortened until the barrel begins to go into lockup. Once you're there, it's a tedious Dykem-and-try operation as you shorten the hood and lower the depth of the rear locking lug with a "safe" lug file.

When the barrel goes fully into battery–you use a range rod to check lockup height–it's lapped in place until it comes gently out of battery with light finger pressure. Then, it's time to fixture the barrel in place in the slide and cut the lugs on the bottom of the barrel so that the barrel will ride up the slide stop crosspin and be perfectly supported by it once it's fully in battery.

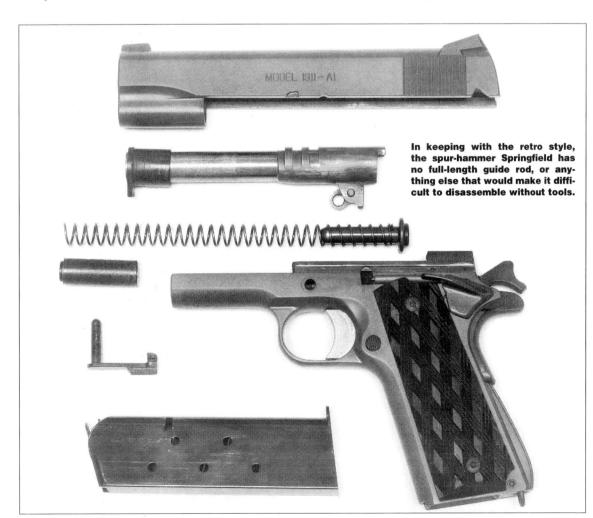

In keeping with the retro style, the spur-hammer Springfield has no full-length guide rod, or anything else that would make it difficult to disassemble without tools.

In order to ensure good support by the slide stop, the factory one was replaced with a World War II-era fully-machined one that had been measured and found to have a dimensionally-correct .200" crosspin.

A little more lapping, and it was time to fit the bushing. While many shops recommend a break-in period for a freshly-built M1911, proper lapping should allow the parts to wear in before it ever leaves the bench. Even so, proving the gun before relying on it is still the best course of action.

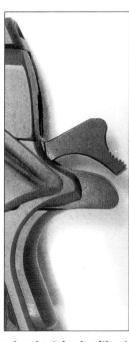

The spur hammer was shortened and retained, without the addition of a beavertail grip safety. It didn't bite, but it didn't spread out recoil like a beavertail, either.

Stock Springfield hammer (bottom) with modified Colt hammer, The shorter, rounded spur is still easy to cock manually, but much less likely to bite the shooter.

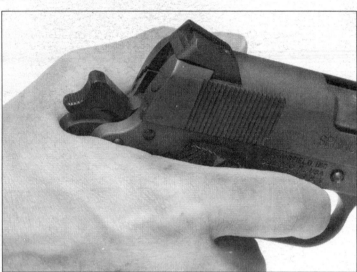

The higher your grip on an M1911, the better the recoil control–and the greater the likelihood of hammer bite if the pistol is equipped with "rat tail" grip safety.

Since this gun was intended to be a hard-use gun that may need to be taken down in the field, the bushing was fit just loose enough to be installed and removed with finger pressure alone; no bushing wrench is required.

Similarly, the slide-to-frame fit was not adjusted in any way. The parts had only minimal play, and tightening the fit adds little to accuracy, while making the gun more dependent on lubrication.

While I love a tight .45, it's not required to shoot well, nor is it ideal for a gun that may be out in the great outdoors for days at a time. While it's still an important feature on a full-house custom gun, in the grand scheme of things, barrel fit is far more critical.

With the Kart barrel in place, the only thing left to make the gun a more accurate shooter was a good set of sights. Even from the early days, factory hump-and-a-bump sights have been weighed in the balance and found wanting. They're small and

The ejection port was lowered and beveled at the rear, in place of the now-customary scallop. Kart's National Match barrel proved capable of exceptional accuracy.

thin, tough to line up precisely, and virtually impossible to pick up fast.

These days, most M1911s come with high-visibility sights somewhere in the neighborhood of .125" wide, in place of the original .058" width. The slide was machined for a Novak LoMount fixed rear sight, arguably the most practical–and most copied–rear sight ever put on a pistol, and for a pinned-in-place dovetail mount front sight, which does away with the nasty tendency of peened-in sights to cut loose of the slide and head south unexpectedly.

While self-luminous tritium sights are now commonplace, defensive pistols have been around for hundreds of years without them. Perhaps the definitive old-school night sight (other than the ivory dot found on African rifles) is the gold bead popularized by revolver shooter Ed McGivern, and that's what I opted to install on this pistol.

The brightly-polished dot set into the front sight does a good job of collecting ambient light, making it easy to pick up in semidarkness, and since gold doesn't tarnish, it has no half-life to worry about.

With the sights/accuracy part of the equation complete, it was time to move on to the gun's lockwork. While there was nothing wrong with the stock Springfield parts, I wanted a fully-machined hammer and sear in place of the factory parts. Rummaging through some take-off parts, I came up with a Colt spur hammer and sear that fit the bill.

After installing a long, solid Videki trigger (no three holes here, folks!), the Colt parts came together with a light, fairly crisp trigger pull that had only a touch of discernable creep as it broke. While I could have stoned the hammer hooks to remove it, because this gun might very well spend its weekends banging against rocks (that's how it spent the last one), I decided to leave the extra bearing surface for extra security. While the M1911 is one of the safest pistols there is, over-engineering never hurts anything.

Even leaving the hammer hooks alone, though, there was still cutting to be done. The action job had been completed, and all the appropriate chamfering and polishing had been done to make the gun reliable (check the chamber dimensions and the extractor, refine the breechface, polish the feedramps), and I had replaced all the stock springs with extra-power Wolff springs. With that, the threshold sights/trigger/reliability requirements had been met, and it was time to focus, ever-so-briefly, on handling characteristics.

First on the list was shortening the hammer spur to keep it from biting. On an unmodified spur-hammer .45, the tail of the hammer hangs over the top of the grip safety, and pinches the web of your hand every time you fire. This is the "hammer bite" of yore, the excitement of which the younger generation of M1911 shooters has largely been deprived. If you take a high grip on the gun (which I do), it can get ugly fast. A little grinding to shorten the hammer, and all that remained was to recut the serrations with a triangle file and de-horn the finished part.

Next, all the sharp edges on the rest of the gun were removed, to make it easier on both hands and holster, and the mag well was beveled to speed up reloads. Also in the interest of speed, I replaced the factory thumb safety, with its little nubbin of a thumb pad, with a King's speed safety that was well-rounded to make it snag-free.

I also bolted on a pair of Herrett's skip-line checkered stocks. Long since fallen out of favor, Herrett's distinctive Argyle-like American walnut stocks were once common currency on custom M1911s (they were on the first custom .45

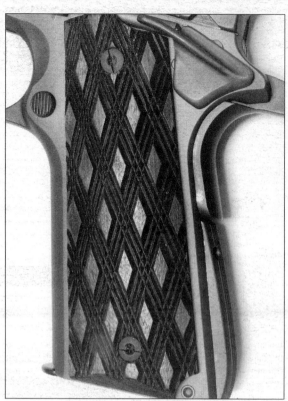

Herrett's skip-line checkered walnut stocks are an old standby, and are still readily available. With the retro look so en vogue, skip-lines are also made by Ahrends.

I remember seeing), and the look is returning in a small way, with other companies–such as Ahrends–now offering skip-line stocks. Herrett's, of course, were the originals.

While add-on mag wells are quite popular, on this gun, a simple bevel is all that was required. Also note the lanyard loop on the stock Springfield mainspring housing.

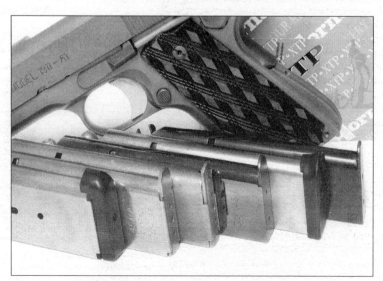

Magazines are still crucial. The article gun worked with all mags used, including these from Wilson, Kimber, Detonics, Novak, Para-Ordnance, and Springfield.

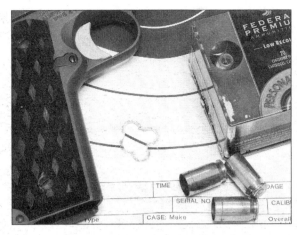

Fitted with a Kart NM barrel, the Springfield proved capable of exceptional accuracy–including this .547" group. It averaged about 1.7" with all rounds tested.

Custom spur-hammer Springfield with some of the rounds used in testing. In 500 rounds, one magazine failed to lock the slide back. There were no other malfunctions.

As a final throwback to the early days, I left in place the lanyard loop that had come installed on the pistol's mainspring housing. Although the lanyard loop is dated, since it hails back to the days when many .45s were retired service pistols, the current military action in the Middle East has pointed up the importance of being tethered to your pistol; thus, many of the most high-speed fighting .45's made right now have them.

Even if you're not currently serving in the military, if you spend time around water or great heights, a lanyard is still an excellent idea. As a more-or-less random aside, Hallock's .45 Auto Handbook, still a classic of the M1911 trade, has a photo illustrating how a lanyard loop can be used as a bottle opener.

The only thing required to make my pistol's lanyard loop practical was the addition of a lanyard, which I obtained from Bowen Classic Arms in Louisville, Tenn. Looking as though it would be every bit as comfortable on a break-barrel Webley as on my M1911, the braided cord came with a snap link at one end, and had the other end formed into an adjustable loop that is intended to be pulled snug across the top of the arm to allow for both security and freedom of movement.

When it came time to refinish the gun, I went with Parkerizing, and not the modern black version, either– I mean the dull, greenish-gray finish of yesteryear. Nominally more corrosion-resistant than bluing, and light years behind the Teflon-based finishes, it simply seemed like the right thing to do.

Completing the buildup, however, is never the end of a project. With the gun freshly Parkerized, oiled, and assembled, it remained to be seen how well it would run. In this case, I also wanted to see what it told me about the viability of the retro approach.

In the course of testing the gun (including accuracy testing), it consumed exactly 500 rounds: 100 rounds of Winchester "White Box" ball, 300 rounds of handloads using Hornady's excellent 200-grain XTP jacketed hollow-point (which has shown excellent accuracy in other tests I've done), and 100 rounds of mixed JHPs.

All of them went in and came out without a bobble; the only irregularity was when one magazine failed to lock the slide back. In addition to the factory Springfield magazine, I used mags from Novak, Wilson, Kimber, Detonics, and Para-Ordnance, all of which fed flawlessly.

From the very first sight-in session at Novak's, it became clear that this was going to be a very accurate pistol; hits at 25 yards were a given, and accurate shots could be made out to 100 yards. In the Ransom Rest, it averaged about 1.74" at 25 yards,

and fired one group that measured an astounding .547". For complete accuracy results, see the accompanying table.

In the course of firing those 500 rounds, I learned one very important thing: the M1911 needs a beavertail grip safety. While I'm all for minimalism on a working gun, this is where I've got to part ways with the retro crowd.

One of the greatest advantages of the beavertail is the way it spreads out recoil across the hand. Although the shortened hammer on my Springfield never bit me, the narrow rat-tail safety dug into my hand during firing. In long strings of fire, it was so uncomfortable that one shooting buddy of mine actually thought he was experiencing hammer bite. While nostalgia and aesthetics are on the side of the spur hammer, the retro look might be better served by marrying a shortened spur hammer with a beavertail.

Although I have a great appreciation for fine craftsmanship, expensive parts and sophisticated machine work are simply not required to make an accurate, serviceable pistol. When I reviewed Yost's retro-style 1* pistol last year, I was struck by the fact that what used to work so well, still does. Hamilton Bowen, the custom revolver maker, commented to me recently that the biggest change he'd seen in the industry was the availability of custom parts, and he may very well be right; other than the looks, what makes a good gun really hasn't changed. ◉

Why Retro? TEST RESULTS

LOAD	Group Size (ins.)	Velocity (fps)	Extreme Spread	Standard Deviation
Winchester 230 FMJ	2.38	845	19	8
Black Hills 185 JHP	1.42	969	—	—
Federal Personal Defense 165 JHP Hydra Shok	.836	1103	12	7
Speer 230 Gold Dot JHP	1.80	900*	—	—
Winchester 230 SXT JHP	2.65	861	19	7
Remington 185 Golden Saber	1.33	1013	48	18
Average: 1.74				

*only 6 rounds chronographed.

Groups were fired from the Ransom Rest at 25 yards, with velocities measured by a Competition Electronics ProChrono chronograph placed 10 feet from the muzzle. Groups shown are the average of two five-shot groups, measured center-to-center.

Contact

Bowen Classic Arms Corp.
www.bowenclassicarms.com
P.O. Box 67, Dept. SGN,
Louisville, Tenn. 37777
(865) 984-3583

Herrett's Stocks, Inc.
www.herrett-stocks.com
P.O. Box 741/169 Madrona St., Dept. SGN,
Twin Falls, Idaho 83303-0741
(208) 733-1498 (208) 733-1632 (fax)

Kart Precision Barrel Corp.
3975 Garner St SW, Dept. SGN,
Shallotte, N.C. 28470
(910) 754-5212 (910) 754-5210 (fax)

Novak's .45 Shop
www.novaksights.com
1206 1/2 30th St., Dept. SGN,
Parkersburg, W. Va. 26101
(304) 485-9295 (304) 428-2676 (fax)

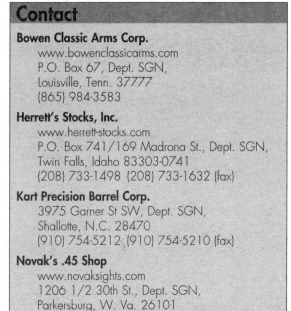

Back to the 60s
Building the "classic" AR-15

While more modern ARs make better target guns, Matthews likes the light weight and fast handling of the Vietnam-era M16A1.

By Steven Matthews

Matthews has assembled more than a dozen ARs over the years and thinks building one is an ideal project for the hobby gunsmith as parts are widely and cheaply available.

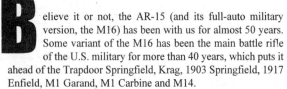

Believe it or not, the AR-15 (and its full-auto military version, the M16) has been with us for almost 50 years. Some variant of the M16 has been the main battle rifle of the U.S. military for more than 40 years, which puts it ahead of the Trapdoor Springfield, Krag, 1903 Springfield, 1917 Enfield, M1 Garand, M1 Carbine and M14.

Of course, today's M16A2 and M4 carbine are a far cry from the earliest AR-15/M16 rifles. As originally designed in the late 1950s it was a basic lightweight rifle with superior handling qualities. I personally think the AR-15 is hands down the best "feeling" rifle ever made, even though many have issues with the caliber.

In these early days there were no red dot sights, Ergo Grips, Picatinny rails, lasers, night vision, etc. The early guns were lighter and a little shorter than today's versions. To old-timers like me, the "classic" AR-15/M16 is the version that served our troops during the later years of the Vietnam conflict. From the mid-'60s until the last U.S. forces left in 1975, it was featured almost nightly on the network news reporting of the conflict.

My first AR-15 was obtained in the late '70s, and other than lacking the forward assist feature and the full-auto capability of the M16, it was pretty much the same as the one fielded during the war years. Eventually this was traded off for one of the newer models, since I too fell into the newer-is-better mentality.

The original model was known as the A1 model and the newer updated type came to be known as the A2 version. Now many years later, I find myself longing for an A1 to complement my A2 models. I guess it's a "first love" thing older people get as we age!

I have had more than 15 ARs over the years, but at the moment, I have only a NFA full-auto M16 shorty and a semi-auto HBAR type with compensator and scope set up for target shooting. I thought it was about time to add a classic version to my collection.

I've owned several Colts, but the majority I built myself from parts from the smaller manufacturers. Building them myself saved money and allowed me to customize them my way. Add to that the satisfaction of knowing I "made it myself" and the building option was my preferred method of obtaining AR-15s.

This classic version differs from today's version in several ways. The early A1 versions featured a 3-prong flash suppressor that was later replaced with today's birdcage style when it was found to catch on vegetation in the field.

This flash suppressor was also attached to a lighter barrel with a slower rifling twist (1:12 versus today's 1:9). Over this

lighter barrel were smooth triangular handguards that I find very comfortable. The handguards have a unique feel unlike anything previously fielded on military rifles.

Early versions featured a smooth-sided receiver without the raised "fence" around the magazine catch. This raised area was incorporated into military models early on but remained missing on civilian AR-15 A1s until the advent of the A2 models in the 1980s.

While early Air Force M16s had no forward assist, the Army insisted on it in the M16A1. Colt used the M16 configuration for civilian ARs until A2 versions were offered in the 1980s. Many purists disdain the forward assist on grounds it only encourages the shooter to shove a stuck cartridge in harder, but it has persisted through the years. The triangular case deflector was added to commercial and military models both in the 80s, making life better for left-handers.

Early ARs had a straight-sided handguard retaining ring. It was hard to grasp when pulling against spring pressure, so it was changed to a delta shape for easier disassembly. The A1 buttstock was about 3/4" shorter than the A2 style, and had a more rounded butt.

The most noticeable difference between the A1 and A2 models is the sights. While the front sights are both adjustable for elevation, the A1 post is rounded on top, as opposed to the flat-topped A2

The rear sights were the big news, and are a big part of the reason the A2 is considered more of a shooter's rifle than the A1. While both are aperture designs housed in the carry handle, they are radically different in operation.

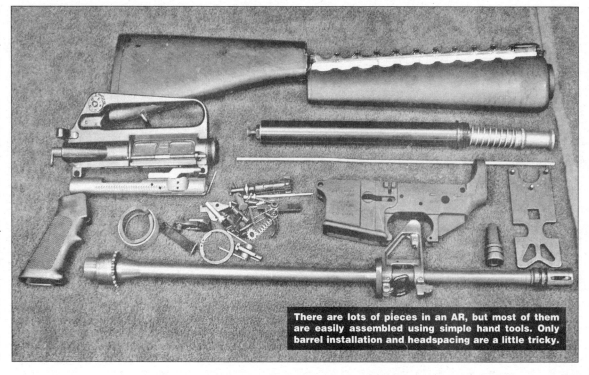

There are lots of pieces in an AR, but most of them are easily assembled using simple hand tools. Only barrel installation and headspacing are a little tricky.

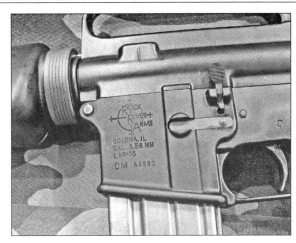

Matthews likes Rock River's lower receiver, and he found one at the right price for this project. The lower carries the serial number, so requires an FFL for purchase.

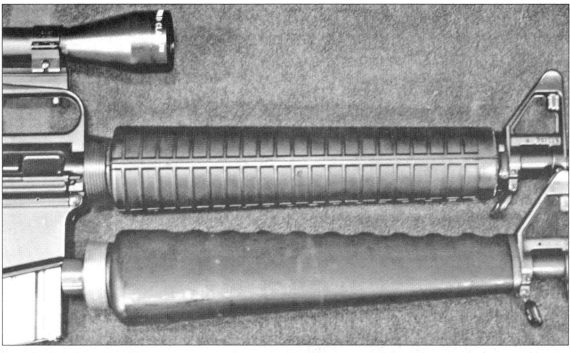

Triangular handguards were a visible feature of the A1 model. Note how the snap ring that retains them is cylindrical, in contrast to the delta shape of the A2 ring.

The early A1 style sights feature a two-position folding aperture adjustable for windage. Making the adjustment required using a bullet point to rotate the windage adjustment disk. Elevation was adjusted by turning the front sight up or down. This was and still is a very simple, rugged and foolproof design for combat, but is hardly satisfactory for target shooting.

Later A2 models feature easy-to-grasp knobs for adjusting windage and elevation. These sights could be best described as "semi target sights" as they feature much finer adjustment than the A1 sights. Ironically, the A2 sights appeared just as red dots and sights like the Elcan and Trijicon ACOG came on the market, and troops in Iraq and Afghanistan are commonly seen with various optical sights.

So if you want a "classic" AR-15, where do you find the "classic" parts? The parts common to both A1 and A2 versions parts are widely available from the many AR-15 parts vendors featured in SHOTGUN NEWS. The "classic" parts are harder to find, since they have been out of production for years.

Consumer demand for the latest styles means vendors don't advertise the older parts, even if they still have them lying around in a dusty corner of the warehouse. These parts are out there but you have to search them out. I found my classic parts at the larger gun shows. Some were slightly used while others were new old stock.

I found some dealers consider these old parts to be rare antiques and price them accordingly, while others consider them undesirable and hard to sell. I easily found unissued Colt chrome-lined A1 barrels: some dealers wanted over $225 while others wanted only $100. Guess which dealer got my money!

For my Vietnam era "classic" AR-15 I choose the three-prong flash suppressor, triangular handguards, 20-inch Colt chrome-lined A1 style barrel, Colt M16A1 style upper receiver with forward assist, straight handguard ring and A1 style buttstock.

Once I had all the parts rounded up, it was time to assemble them. The AR-15 is one of the easiest guns for the hobbyist gunsmith to build. There are no parts to make, there is little

hand-fitting, the parts are easy to install, and only one specialty tool is needed. In this article I will cover the basics of the build process for this classic AR-15 but it is also applicable to the later versions.

The specialty tool you will need it a AR-15 /M16 barrel wrench. There are several styles available, but I choose the combination type that has provisions for the buffer tube and flash suppressor installation as well as the barrel. It is widely available for less than $20. A good vise and basic hand tools will be needed to complete the build.

Assembling the lower receiever

Let's start by assembling the lower receiver assembly. I choose a Rock River Arms AR-15 lower receiver, as I have had excellent results with them on past build projects. I have found them to be extremely well made and priced reasonably. While most parts are available by mail order, the lower receiver is the serial-numbered part, so it must be sold just like a completed gun with the associated paperwork and background check.

Most larger gun shows have several dealers selling various brands of receivers. The prices in my area run from $100-$150 depending on brand and dealer. For the internal parts for the receiver I bought a lower receiver parts set from J+T Distributors since I have had good results with them in the past. I first assemble the buffer tube by simply screwing it into the rear of the receiver.

A drop or two of removable threadlocker applied to the threads will help hold it together. Before you screw it down all the way, insert the buffer detent and spring into the hole just ahead of the threads. Press it down and hold it in place to allow the tube to

extend over the top of the detent when screwed down all the way. Using a wrench or the combo tool, snug up the tube to the receiver.

Don't go nuts on tightening it down; you are working with aluminum and you will strip threads if you tighten excessively. One little tip I will give here is to be careful when installing this and any other spring-loaded detents in this gun. If you slip and release the detent and spring before it's secured it will shoot off into parts unknown and be lost forever! I speak from years of experience in losing parts!

Do NOT use a pipe wrench, pliers, etc. for this job, as you will ruin the nut.

Next, move on to the front takedown/pivot pin. This is held in place with a spring and detent that has to be in place before you slide in the takedown pin. Place the spring and detent plunger in the hole on the right side of the receiver and depress it with a thin screwdriver or knife. While holding it in place, take the takedown/pivot pin and insert it into the hole with the head on the right side. Release the detent and it will now hold the takedown pin in place.

The swing-down trigger guard can be easily installed now. Put it in place with the through holes located at the rear where

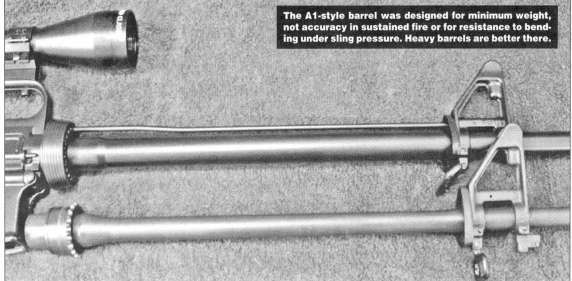

The A1-style barrel was designed for minimum weight, not accuracy in sustained fire or for resistance to bending under sling pressure. Heavy barrels are better there.

The A1 stock was about 3/4" shorter than the A2, and early versions had a rounded butt. Curiously, the M4 with adjustable buttstock has now become the dominant type.

The prong flash suppressor was replaced by the "bird-cage" configuration after the former caught underbrush in Vietnam. Now the pronged Vortex style is popular.

Next, install the spring and detent for the front pivot pin and the swing-down trigger guard. Padded pliers are the right tool for installing the roll pin there.

the holes are located in the receiver trigger guard area. Press in the appropriate roll pin to retain it. The single hole in the front will retain the trigger guard detent and lock it in place. The magazine catch looks tricky to install but isn't once you know how it's done.

Insert the spring into the hole on the right side of the receiver, followed by the catch button. Press it in all the way till it stops. When it's in all the way, the bottom will be about 3/8" below the edge of the receiver. While holding this in place, insert the magazine catch shaft into the hole on the left side of the receiver and screw it into the magazine catch button that you are holding in.

Screw the catch in until you can feel the shaft even with the top of the button. Align the magazine catch with the slot in the receiver and gently release it. The bolt hold-open lever, spring, plunger and pin can now be installed in the left side of the gun. This allows the bolt to remain open when the magazine runs dry.

...when the nut is tightened properly, the grooves may not line up.

Insert the spring and plunger into the hole and then place the hold-open lever in place. Align the holes in the receiver and the hold-open lever, then insert the roll pin to hold it. This pin can be inserted with pliers or by a small hammer and punch. If using the pliers method, place some cardboard under the jaws so you don't mar the receiver finish.

Once it's installed, check for free movement of the part. It must move freely; if it binds, it will cause malfunctions. If it drags a little, remove it and smooth up the edges of the catch or

receiver. Finish the lower assembly by installing the buffer and spring in the buffer tube.

Installation of the lockwork is next on the list. It must be installed in the proper order. The first part to go in is the trigger/disconnector assembly. Place the trigger return spring onto the trigger as shown in the picture. Place the disconnector spring, fat end down, into the recess in the trigger. Place the disconnector over the spring and between the edges of the trigger.

Slide this assembly into the receiver, position it so that you can slide the trigger pin through the edge of the receiver and into the trigger. As you are holding this in place, push the pin in and adjust the disconnector to allow the pin to slide through it also. Once aligned, push the pin all the way through. This does require a little bit of patience, since you are holding everything under spring tension and trying to align it at the same time.

The next piece to go in is the safety. This will slide through from the left side of the receiver and will be retained by a spring-loaded detent at the rear of the receiver on the right side above the pistol grip. Insert the safety, then place the detent in the hole followed by the spring. Slide the pistol grip onto the receiver and press the spring up into the hole with the grip. Be careful not to kink the spring when installing the grip.

Once in place, hold it tight while you install the grip screw to hold everything in place. The last lockwork pieces that need to be installed are the hammer, spring and pin. Place the spring on the hammer as shown. Insert the hammer and spring into the receiver with the spring legs on top of the trigger pin. Press the hammer down and forward to align the hammer with the pin hole in the receiver.

The hammer spring will place a lot of tension on the hammer and you will have to hold it under tension while you install the hammer pin through the sides of the receiver and through the hammer. Once installed, the legs of the hammer spring will interlock with the trigger pin and hold it in place. A spring in the hammer that was installed at manufacture will hold the hammer pin in place.

Two final items need to be installed to complete the lower receiver assembly. Place the rear takedown pin in the receiver with the head on the right side. This pin is retained by a spring and plunger that inserts from the back of the receiver on the right side.

Place the plunger and spring into the hole and then slide the buttstock onto the buffer tube. When the stock is in place, it will hold the spring and plunger in place. Be careful not to kink the spring when sliding on the stock. Once in place, the stock is retained on the buffer tube with a screw though the buttplate.

At this time, it's a good idea to check to see if everything works smoothly. Both takedown pins should slide freely in the receiver, but it's not uncommon for them to be rather hard to get

Start lower receiver assembly by installing the buffer tube. It's pretty soft, so don't overtighten. A few drops of removable threadlocker will keep it in place.

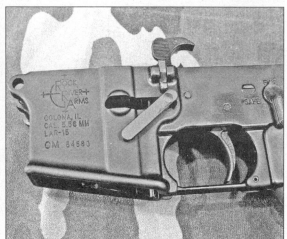

The magazine catch is easily installed by screwing it into the button on the other side of the receiver. Then install the bolt hold-open lever, spring, plunger and pin.

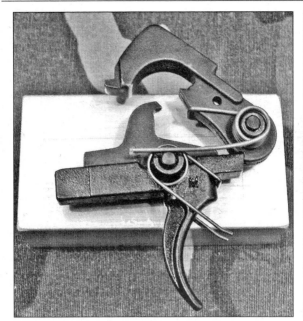

Assemble the lock parts outside the receiver so you understand their relationship and the order in which they must be inserted in the receiver.

The recoil spring and buffer are installed in the buffer tube and retained there by a detent and spring at the mouth of the tube. These are the last parts installed.

moving till there is some wear on them. Check your lockwork to be sure it works properly. Make sure the safety turns and locks in both positions. If things don't work smoothly and properly, a little hand-fitting may be required, but most times everything goes together without any hand fitting.

Upper receiver and barrel assembly

Now our attention is directed to the upper receiver/barrel assembly. If your barrel assembly is not completely assembled now is the time to complete it. The flash suppressor screws on to the front of the barrel and a lock washer prevents loosening. The combo tool has a notch cut out the size of the wrench flat on the birdcage-style suppressor.

It also has cutouts that will engage the prongs on the older three-prong type, since this type has no wrench flat. Your front sight base should already be installed, but you may have to install the sight post in the base. It screws into the base and a spring and detent prevent it from rotating unless pressed down with a tool or bullet point.

The safety lever and rear takedown pin are retained by detents that in turn are locked in position by the pistol grip and buttstock, respectively. Don't kink springs!

Place the spring and detent in their hole and then screw in the sight post. When the sight begins to contact the detent, push it down and out of the way with a small screwdriver or punch. The height of the sight post will have to be set when you sight in the gun, so just screw it in until its detents are about even with the sight base.

Your barrel nut should already have been installed by the manufacturer, but the handguard ring will have to be installed. Slide the handguard ring onto the barrel nut with the shallow side towards the front and follow that with the wafer type spring. Slide on the large snap ring and position in the groove to lock in place.

Install the ejection port door before the barrel. The door pivots on a long pin and is tensioned by a torsion spring to hold the door open after the first shot has been fired. Put the door in place and insert the pin with the C-clip towards the front and slide it about halfway in place.

When the pin reaches the center cutout in the door, insert the torsion spring and twist it so that it places tension on the door (tension so that it holds door open). Then slide the rod the rest of the way through till it is stopped by the small C-clip on the pin.

Your barrel is now ready to install on the upper receiver. Slide the barrel assembly into the upper receiver with the peg on the top of the barrel extension sliding into the groove in the top of the upper receiver. Before hand-tightening the barrel nut to the receiver, place a bit of grease on the threads to prevent galling when tightening.

Place the barrel in a padded vise. I use wood blocks for padding, so that the finish is not marred. Clamp it as close to the receiver as possible, not out on the end or you may bend the barrel when tightening. You will now need that special barrel wrench to tighten down the barrel. It has pegs on it to engage the notches in the barrel nut.

Do *not* use a pipe wrench, pliers, etc. for this job, as you will ruin the nut. Using the barrel wrench, tighten the nut down to about 15 foot-pounds of torque: this is just a preliminary tightening.

Now comes the "interesting" part. As you have probably noticed, the barrel nut has grooves or notches in it and these must be aligned with the hole in the front of the upper receiver to allow the gas tube to pass through.

Barrel installation starts by placing the handguard ring, spring and snap ring on the barrel nut. Then use the combination tool to tighten the nut and align slots.

Aligning the barrel nut groove with the receiver is critical for proper gas tube clearance. A No. 16 drill perfectly fits the carrier key for checking alignment.

The problem here is that when the nut is tightened properly, the grooves may not line up. You will have to either tighten a little more or a little less to get the grooves to allow passage of the gas tube. Obviously a little too loose is not acceptable and a little too tight could strip the threads and ruin the upper receiver.

If you are extremely close, a little more or less may be acceptable but if off much more than about a half groove, then you have to do something to get it to line up. I find that I am usually off about 1/4 to 1/2 groove off. My solution to this problem is to face off the front of the receiver *slightly* with a wide fine-cut file. A few passes will remove enough metal to allow tightening that extra 1/4 notch or so.

This facing has to be done squarely or you will ruin your receiver. If you don't think you can do it straight, take it to a gunsmith. I usually tighten the barrel nut down to about 25 ft-lbs of torque. Getting this proper alignment/clearance is made easier if you have some sort of alignment tool.

A simple improvised tool can be made by inserting a No. 16 drill into the hole in the carrier key on the bolt carrier. Simply slide the drill into the gas hole in the front of the carrier key and install the bolt carrier into the receiver. Align the wafer spring and handguard ring to allow passage of the drill. Push it through the hole in the front of the receiver and see if the grooves are aligned to allow passage of the gas tube. This will make it pretty easy to get proper alignment.

You don't want the nut to contact the gas tube since it will push it out of alignment. Once you have your barrel nut tight-

ened and aligned properly, the gas tube can be installed. The end with the holes drilled into it goes into the sight base with the gas hole facing down towards the barrel.

Slide the receiver end of the tube into the hole in the front of the upper receiver and rotate it to allow the front to clear the front sight base. Pull it forward and slide the front into the sight base, being sure to have it oriented properly (gas hole down).

Align the crosspin holes in the sight base with the holes in the gas tube and insert the small roll pin to hold it in place. It is not uncommon for the gas tube to need some adjustment. You can't see it from the outside, but the gas tube must freely enter the hole in the carrier key when the bolt slides forward.

Place your completed carrier into the receiver and slide it forward and see if the gas tube enters freely into the carrier key. If it doesn't slide together smoothly, you will have to bend the gas tube *carefully* to obtain proper alignment. When checking for alignment, be sure the handguard ring, snap ring or spring is not pressing on the gas tube.

You don't want the nut to contact the gas tube since it will push it out of alignment.

Once the tube is properly installed, you can install the handguards. The handguards are held in place at the front by the flange on the rear of the sight base and at the rear by the spring loaded handguard ring. Install each half.

The extremely stiff springs mean it can sometimes be very hard to install the second half of the handguards. Pulling the ring down enough to allow the handguard to slide in can be really difficult, especially with the older smooth ring.

If you have chosen the forward assist upper receiver, you will have to install the forward assist plunger, spring and pin. To install, just slide the spring over the plunger and slide it into the hole in the receiver with the little finger on the plunger facing towards the bolt carrier. Press it in all the way and then while holding it in. insert the retaining roll pin.

The last thing to be installed to complete the upper assembly is the sights. Start by placing the flat sight spring in the pocket with the hump facing up. Lay the flip-up sight on the spring and insert the sight screw in from the left side and thread it through the sight.

When the screw gets to the right side of the handle, press it down to enter the hole and then push it the rest of the way through, being sure the head of the screw fully enters the recess in the handle. Insert the spring and detent into the hole in the side of the receiver and then place the adjusting disc on the end of the shaft. Rotate it until the holes in the shaft and disc line up, then insert the small roll pin to hold it in place.

You often will find that the gas tube needs some careful bending to align with the carrier key. A very small roll pin retains it in the front sight base/gas block.

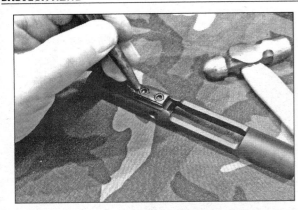

The carrier key screws need to be staked firmly to prevent them turning out. Inserting the firing pin and its retaining pin complete the bolt carrier assembly.

Bolt Carrier Assembly

Now that your upper receiver is assembled you need something to put in it; the bolt carrier assembly. The AR-15 features a small bolt head in a larger bolt carrier. This carrier also features a cam pin, firing pin and a carrier key. The carrier key is the part that directs high pressure gas into the carrier to unlock the bolt; it also serves to prevent the bolt carrier from turning out of alignment.

This carrier key is a rectangular piece with a small tube on the front that attaches to the top of the carrier with two Allen screws. Place the key on top of the carrier with gas tube hole facing forward and insert the two Allen screws. Tighten the screws down snugly.

To prevent the screws from coming loose, they need to be staked in place. Use a center punch to dimple the edge of the hole. The idea here is to displace a small amount of steel, causing it to press tightly against the screws to prevent them from turning out. My carrier key was not staked properly so I had to restake it.

The photo shows four dimples on each screw, but only two are needed. The bolt now needs to be installed. Every bolt I have ever bought was completely assembled so I won't go into how to install the extractor, ejector or gas rings. Install the bolt into the front of the carrier with the extractor on the right side. I always place a drop of oil on the gas rings to ease installation.

Once the bolt's in the hole, you will see the cam pin hole in the bolt through the cam pin groove in the carrier. Rotate this hole all the way to the left and insert the cam pin. This pin can only clear the carrier key in one direction. After the pin is in all the way, pull the bolt all the way forward (rotate the bolt to the right). Once the

cam pin is rotated and in its forward position, rotate it 90° to align the hole in the cam pin to allow passage of the firing pin.

Insert the firing pin into the rear of the bolt carrier and push it all the way forward. Once it is in all the way, the pin that looks like a cotter key can be inserted through the side of the carrier to retain the firing pin. Even though it looks like a cotter pin it is not, do not bend the ends over; this pin will be retained by the wall of the upper receiver. Once everything is in place, you can see how all the parts interlock, the cam pin holds in the bolt, the firing pin holds in the cam pin and the little cotter key type pin holds in the firing pin.

Installing the Bolt Carrier and Charging Handle

Install the charging handle in through the bolt carrier passage in the upper receiver. Once it is in part way, there is a notch in the top of the passageway under the handle that will allow the charging handle to slide up and out of the passage. Once it is in the charging handle groove, pull it all the way to the rear.

Pull the bolt into the forward position in the bolt carrier then place the completely assembled carrier into the rear of the upper receiver. The rounded forward part of the carrier key will fit in a recess in the charging handle. Slide the handle/ carrier assembly into the receiver.

If your gas tube is aligned properly, the bolt carrier will slide all the way forward and the handle will snap into its forward position. You can't see it from the outside, but as the carrier assembly slides forward it will cause the bolt to enter the barrel extension and rotate to lock the bolt and barrel together.

The Headspacing Issue

No barrel installation is complete without discussing the issue of headspace. In very broad terms, headspace is the amount of space remaining between the closed bolt and the chambered cartridge. A certain amount of space is required for proper operation, however too much space will cause problems. This amount of space is only a few thousandths of an inch.

In many firearm designs this headspace is set during barrel and receiver assembly. The AR-15/M16 design has no provisions to adjust this dimension. In theory the AR-15 design is supposed to be made to high enough tolerances that it doesn't need adjustment. Unfortunately what works on paper doesn't always work in the real world.

Tolerance "stacking" of several parts can cause excessive headspace. If you have a half-dozen dimensions that are only off a thousandth of an inch or so, it can add up to an out of spec assembly. The only option to correct improper headspace in an AR-15 is parts replacement with parts made closer to the design dimensions.

Of the 15 or so ARs that I have built, most have been OK on the issue of headspace. I have had two that were right up there at the very limits of acceptable headspace, not necessarily unsafe but still more than I would like. With this in mind, I will recommend that any time you build an AR-15 (or any other homemade gun for that matter) that you have the headspace checked by a qualified gunsmith.

Final Assembly

All that remains is to assemble the upper and lower receivers together. Simply push out the takedown and pivot pins and fit the two halves together. This is best done with the hammer

in the cocked position so that the hammer doesn't catch on the carrier or firing pin. With the halves together press the pins back in. Cycle the action to see if everything moves freely and functions properly.

Be sure the disconnector works properly. Cock the gun, then pull the trigger (unloaded gun, of course!), keep the trigger pulled all the way to the rear and cycle the action. The hammer should not follow the bolt forward, the trigger should have to be released in order to fire the gun again. If things do not appear to be right, correct the problems *before* proceeding to test firing. If you are unsure if you have done everything right have it checked out by a professional gunsmith.

The AR-15 is a very simple design and a qualified person should have no problem in determining if it is assembled correctly. If everything checks out, you can proceed to test firing. Most ARs that I have made worked OK as assembled, but occasionally they need to be fired a couple hundred rounds to get broken in.

If you have minor problems, it may require a little "tweaking or tuning." The AR-15 is a pretty simple design and easy to troubleshoot if you have problems. The best place to find info on troubleshooting a AR-15 is one of the many gun forums and AR15 websites on the internet. I dislike computers in general but have to admit that the internet is a wealth of information when it comes to working on guns. If you have problems there is someone out there in cyberspace that is willing to help.

If you have done everything right you should now have a fine example of the gun that gave birth to all the many variations of AR-15s that we have today. I believe the "classic" version deserves a place in every military arms collection. Although many in the military arms field may debate the virtues of the AR-15/M16 weapon system, it has served our military forces for more than 40 years and will probably serve on for years to come. ◎

Approximate Costs

Approximate cost to build the "Classic" AR-15 (your price will vary according to your negotiating skills with vendors!)

New Rock River Arms AR-15 lower receiver	$100
Old stock/unissued Colt AR-15 A1 chrome-lined 20-inch barrel assembly	$125
New J+T Distributors Complete AR-15 lower receiver parts set	$60
Used complete Colt M16 type upper receiver (sights, charging handle, FA plunger, door)	$65
New bolt carrier assembly (bolt, carrier, extractor, ejector, key, screws, etc.)	$115
Used A1-style triangular handguards and A1 buttstock	$20
New buffer tube, buffer, spring	$30
Old stock/unissued 3 prong flash suppressor	$10
Total	$525

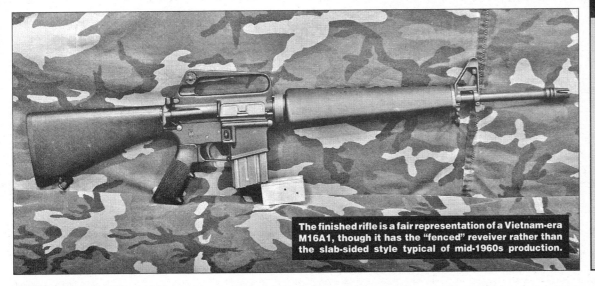

The finished rifle is a fair representation of a Vietnam-era M16A1, though it has the "fenced" receiver rather than the slab-sided style typical of mid-1960s production.

Sources

Rock River Arms, 1042 Cleveland Ave., Dept. SGN, Colona, Ill., 61241 309-792-5780 www.rockriverarms.com

J+T Distributing, Box 430, Dept. SGN, Winchester, Ky., 40392, 888-736-7725, www.jtdistributing.com

Sherluk Marketing, P.O. Box 156, Dept. SGN, Delta, Ohio, 43515, 888-M-16PART, www.sherluk.com

Lauer Custom Weaponry, 3601 129th St, Dept. SGN, Chippewa Falls, Wis., 54729, 800-830-6677, www.lauerweaponry.com

DPMS, 3312 12th St. SE, Dept. SGN, St Cloud, Minn., 56304, 320-258-4448, www.dpmsinc.com

Model 1 Sales, P.O. Box 569, Dept. SGN, Whitewright, Texas, 903-546-2087, www.model1sales.com

An Accurate AR for Less than a Grand?

If you're willing to do a little work yourself, yes! And this isn't a monster Matthews project; you can do it in an afternoon.

By Steven Matthews

I've had a variety of AR-15s over the years, but one type that always fascinated me was the heavy-barrel target rifle. I'd love to have one from Les Baer or Wilson Combat, but there's no way one of those fits in my budget.

I decided to see just how much accurate rifle you can buy for less than $1,000, and I think the answer will surprise you.

When I start thinking about a project, my first stop is always right here in the pages of SGN. If you've been reading for long, you know there are dozens of advertisers offering upper receivers and other assemblies for ARs that you can buy direct.

The lower receiver is the serial-numbered part, meaning you have to order one though a federally licensed dealer.

I have defensive and hunting ARs; this time I wanted one just for shooting good groups from the bench. Most every manufacturer offers an upper receiver in what could be called a basic heavy barrel target gun configuration. These feature flattop upper receivers, free-floated handguards and heavy barrels.

J&T Distributing (Box 430, Dept. SGN, Winchester, Ky., 40392, 888-736-7725, www.jtdistributing.com) is a longtime SGN advertiser and offers this sort of rifle. They claim it will shoot sub 1-inch groups at 100 yards with the right ammo. At the price, I was skeptical of that, but since I had built several AR-15 rifles using their components over the years, my friend and I decided to purchase their Bull Barrel AR-15 rifle kits.

Tight budget? No patience for those big Matthews projects? Here's an easy, quick one. The J&T Bull Barrel kit took less than one hour to build, and no special tools.

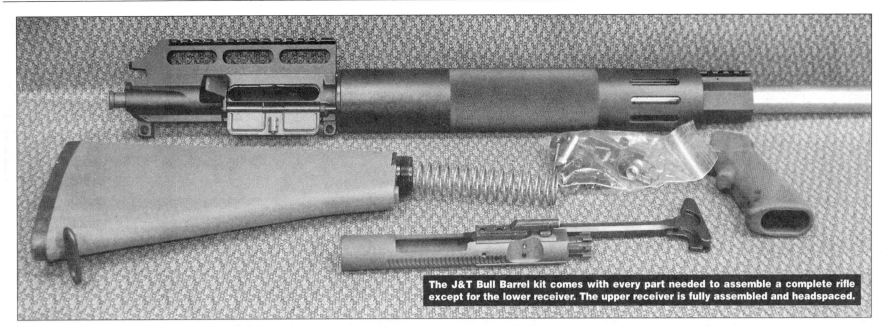

The J&T Bull Barrel kit comes with every part needed to assemble a complete rifle except for the lower receiver. The upper receiver is fully assembled and headspaced.

You can choose a standard flattop upper receiver or a high rise upper for an additional $10. The higher upper allows for better eye location for some shooters.

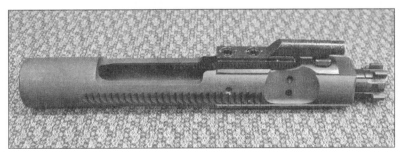

The bolt carrier assembly is pre-assembled with the carrier key screws staked in place. The bolts are headspaced to the barrel, so there's no need for headspace gauges.

My friend mail-ordered his kit from J&T. He selected the basic bull barrel kit with the $10 option of a high-rise upper receiver that brings the scope up to a more comfortable position. The price for this kit was $564.99. This "kit" isn't all that much of a kit, since the upper receiver assembly is completely assembled by J&T.

Unlike many kit sellers who sell you a box of individual parts that must be assembled, J&T assembles and headspaces their upper assemblies. This basic target gun kit featured a 24-inch barrel (1:8 twist) made from 416-series stainless steel and had a recessed crown.

It was .937" diameter in front of the gas block and 1.050 inches behind, which would be considered a *very heavy* barrel compared to the .750" heavy barrels found on some kits. Handguards were free-floated aluminum, with ventilation slots cut in the front. A 1913 rail gas block was installed on the barrel.

The upper receiver featured a case deflector and forward assist. All parts were very well finished. This kit configuration (excluding the $10 high rise option) was the cheapest of the several bull barrel kits offered.

I wanted the same configuration, but I decided to purchase my kit in person at the J&T display table at the Indy 1500 gun show in Indianapolis. This would assure that the kit I received for evaluation was not specially selected for a gun magazine article; I would be getting the same kit as anyone who bought from them at the show.

By the time I got to the show, they were out of the standard barrel flattops and had only the more expensive fluted barrels. These are the same diameter as the standard bull barrels, but feature flutes that reduce barrel weight and allow for slightly faster cooling due to the greater surface area.

This increased the cost about $75 over the smooth barrel kits, making my total $625. I really wanted the high rise upper option, and my friend indicated to me that for a few bucks he would be willing to swap his high rise upper receiver for my standard flattop receiver, so I bought the standard flattop kit with the more expensive fluted barrel .

Then I needed the parts to complete the lower receiver: the internal parts and a buttstock assembly. These parts also looked to be very well made. Assembling them to a lower should take less than one hour.

For this project, I chose a Double Star AR-15 lower receiver that I obtained at a gun show for approximately $85. The choice of this receiver was for more than just the low price. J&T has been selling AR-15 parts kits for many years. Several years ago they began offering complete guns utilizing their parts and newly made receivers.

To distinguish the parts kit business from the completed firearms business, they created Double Star Corp. Today complete guns come from Double Star Corp. and kits come

from J&T Distributing. J&T parts and Double Star receivers mate perfectly.

If you combine a Double Star lower receiver with a J&T upper, the gun will look just like a Double Star gun, since Double Star guns are built with J&T components. You will not have a parts gun with mismatched parts, but rather a complete Double Star gun that you assembled yourself.

The Double Star AR-15 lower receiver is conventional, utilizing standard M16-style push pins. It is made from 7075 T6 aluminum alloy. It is forged, then CNC machined to exacting tolerances. Since it is made to fit the J&T parts, upper to lower fit is tight; looseness can affect accuracy.

Finish is anodized hard coat that matches very well with the finish on the J&T upper assembly. The receiver looks to be very well made.

The fluted J&T bull barrel features a concave crown, while the smooth barrel features a stepped/recessed crown. Both are made from 416 series stainless steel.

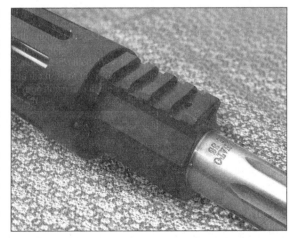

The J&T bull barrel features a large gas block with 1913 rails for mounting folding front sights. The gas block/sight base is retained with three set screws.

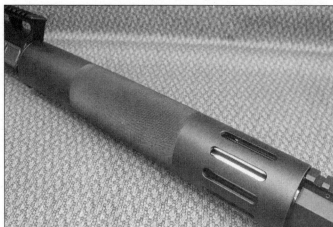

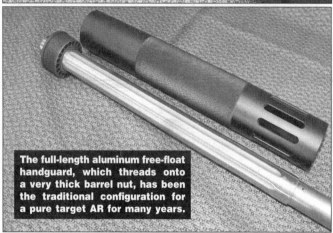

The full-length aluminum free-float handguard, which threads onto a very thick barrel nut, has been the traditional configuration for a pure target AR for many years.

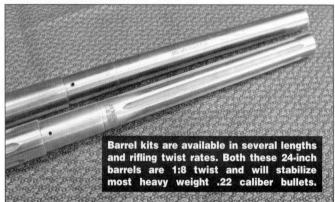

Barrel kits are available in several lengths and rifling twist rates. Both these 24-inch barrels are 1:8 twist and will stabilize most heavy weight .22 caliber bullets.

The J&T kit came with a standard AR-15 grip, but I wanted something more hand-filling. I purchased and installed an ambidextrous Ergo Tactical Grip with no palm shelf on this project.

The only thing that needs to be done to "build" this kit is to assemble the lower receiver and install it onto the upper receiver. This assembly is very easy. Anyone with basic mechanical knowledge should be able to do it in less than one hour. Only basic home workshop hand tools are required. I will briefly cover the assembly process for those who've never assembled an AR. There are a lot of ways to do it, but this is how I do it.

1. Install front takedown/pivot pin. This slides into the front of the receiver and is retained by a spring detent. Install the detent spring and detent into its hole in the receiver. Depress the detent with a thin screwdriver or knife blade to allow the takedown pin to pass over.

2. Install the magazine catch by first inserting the magazine catch button and its spring into its hole in the right side of the receiver. Push it in as far as it will go. Insert the catch into its recess on the left side and screw the shaft into the depressed button till the shaft end is flush with the top of the button.

3. The bolt catch/bolt hold-open device installs next. Drop the bolt catch spring and plunger into its recess in the side

of the receiver with the plunger on top. Start the crosspin into its hole from the rear side. Use a pair of pliers to push the pin into the hole partway. Use a piece of cardboard between the pliers and receiver to prevent marring the finish. Place the bolt catch into its recess and then push the pin the rest of the way through the hole in the bolt catch.

4. Screw the buffer tube partially in place. Before screwing it all the way down, install the buffer detent and spring in the bottom of the buffer tube hole. Press the buffer detent down and then screw the buffer tube on the rest of the way. Use a wrench on the flat on the end of the tube to tighten it. Be aware that the tube is aluminum and you can't tighten excessively or you may damage the tube. Once tight, install the buffer spring, followed by the buffer.

5. The trigger guard is held in place with a crosspin at the rear and a detent at the front. Just drive the pin through receiver and trigger guard with a small hammer.

6. Install the trigger spring on the trigger. Place the disconnector spring in its pocket with the widest end of the spring in the pocket. Place the disconnector into the trigger. To hold these parts together and ease installation into the narrow receiver, an assembly aid can be made from a 3/8" long piece of 5/32" rod. Insert this short pin into the trigger and disconnector to hold them together.

When the parts are installed in the receiver they will be partly aligned by the short pin and it will be easier to install the trigger pin since it is difficult to hold everything in alignment under spring tension. When the trigger pin is installed, it will just push the short pin out of the side of the receiver. Install the trigger in the receiver.

7. Next, install the safety lever. It will be retained by a spring detent that is installed in the lower receiver and grip. Place the detent into the lower receiver then place the spring into the grip. Slide the grip into place on the receiver being careful not to kink the spring as you push the grip into place. Once the grip is against the receiver, install the grip screw.

8. The hammer can now be installed. Install the hammer spring on the hammer, making sure you have it oriented correctly. Slide the hammer into the receiver, with the legs

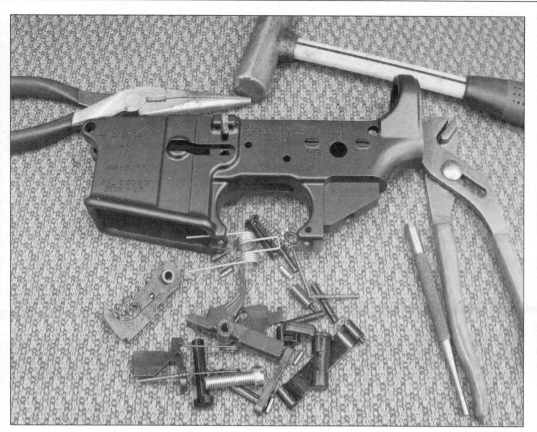

If you have thought other Matthews projects were too ambitious, you'll love this one. The lower receiver can be assembled in about a half-hour with simple hand tools.

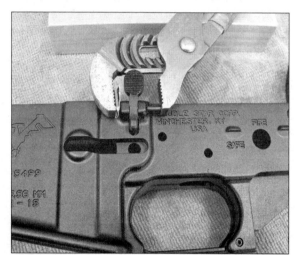

The hold-open is installed by pinning in place after installing its plunger and spring in the receiver. Use some heavy cardboard on the plier's jaws to prevent marring.

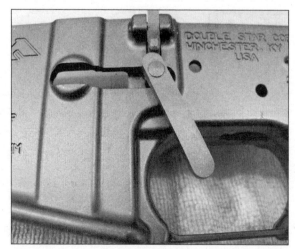

Install the magazine release by pressing the button and spring into the receiver. Then insert the catch through the left side and screw the shaft into the button.

When installing the buffer tube to the lower receiver, be sure to depress the buffer detent before the tube is fully seated to prevent damaging the tube or receiver.

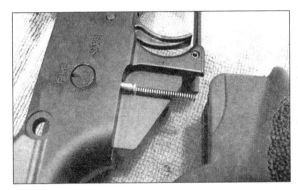

The safety lever is retained by a detent and spring that is inserted though the bottom of the receiver. The detent and spring are retained by the grip when installed.

Before installing the buttstock, place the rear takedown detent and spring in their hole. Be careful not to kink the spring when installing the stock, which retains it.

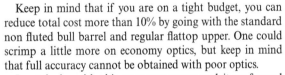

If using the A2 length stock, be sure to install the buffer tube spacer before you slide the stock onto the tube. Buffer tubes are still sized for the short A1 stock.

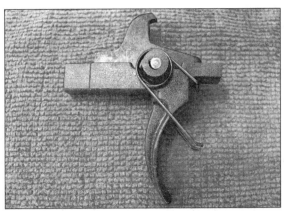

The trigger, disconnector and springs are pre-assembled before installing in the receiver to ease assembly. The slave pin will push out when the trigger pin is installed.

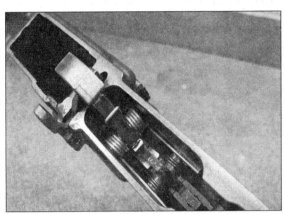

The AR-15 fire control group is now installed. Manually work the fire control group to verify the safety, disconnector, hammer, and trigger all function properly.

of the hammer spring resting on the pin that passes through the trigger. Align the holes and insert the hammer pin. Once installed, the hammer pin will be retained by a small spring that is pre-installed in the hammer and the hammer spring legs will retain the trigger pin.

9. The rear takedown pin slides into the receiver with the head on the right side. It is retained by a spring detent that installs from the rear of the receiver. The spring and detent are installed in the hole in the rear. The buttstock retains and tensions the detent when the stock is installed on the buffer tube.

Before sliding the buttstock onto the buffer tube, drop the buttstock spacer down into the hole in the stock. Slide the stock onto the buffer and be careful not to kink the takedown detent spring as you push the stock up tight against the receiver. Install the stock screw through the buttplate to secure the stock.

Other than mating the upper and lower together, the assembly of this kit is complete.

I wanted a decent but low-cost scope to keep this a budget-priced project for the working class Joe. Today almost all new made low cost scopes, regardless of name brand, contain inexpensive Chinese optics. Chinese optics don't perform like high-cost American or European optics, but at their low cost they do offer an attractive alternative for budget-conscious shooters. I purchased a Target Sports 10x42mm with 30mm tube tactical scope (#TAR31) from CDNN Sports (www.cdnnsports.com) for about $65. In keeping with the budget theme, the scope was mounted with low cost imported high rise rings that were also obtained from CDNN Sports for the low cost of $7.99.

The assembled AR-15 Bull Barrel project looked pretty good. My friend had reported to me that his gun was surprisingly accurate, so I was eager to test mine. My total cost was about $800, which is quite the bargain considering what AR-15s go for these days.

Keep in mind that if you are on a tight budget, you can reduce total cost more than 10% by going with the standard non fluted bull barrel and regular flattop upper. One could scrimp a little more on economy optics, but keep in mind that full accuracy cannot be obtained with poor optics.

I got lucky with this economy scope and it preformed as well as vastly more expensive optics, but I have bought economy optics that preformed less acceptably. While low cost is fine, it means nothing without performance.

It was time to do some accuracy shooting and find out if this bargain-priced target gun was really a bargain. As this article is being written in late 2009, the ammo market is still in the midst of the Obama administration induced buying panic. .223 Rem./5.56 NATO ammo is scarce and expensive, with prices two or three times normal. I had to do a lot of searching to find ammo for testing.

Fortunately my friends at The Ammo Store, Inc. (Box 292353, Dept. SGN, Kettering, Ohio, 45429,937-684-7916, www.ammoninc.com) had several varieties in stock. Nine types of ammo supplied by them and out of my personal supply were used for testing. While accuracy testing is usually done with premium match ammo, I also wanted to test economy grade ammo, since this project is aimed at budget shooters. That was a good choice, since some results were pleasantly surprising.

I fired all groups with the aid of a CTK Precision AR-15 rifle rest. This adjustable rest will allow for the most secure gun hold and produce the best group size.

Keep in mind, however, that groups sighted in with and shot with a mechanical rest will be slightly different than

The lower receiver assembly required less than 20 minutes for Matthews to assemble. Even a novice should be able to assemble this project in less than one hour.

In keeping with the budget theme, Matthews chose a Target Sports/NcStar 10x42mm Tactical scope with 30mm tube. Performance was great for the low cost of about $65.

As you might guess, Federal Gold Medal 69-grain match rifle cartridges printed the most accurate group, but the ever-thrifty Matthews found some cheaper loads that did surprisingly well.

groups shot off of a simple sandbag rest. When sighting in for varmint hunting, I use sandbags, since they more accurately duplicate a field hold.

I ran a couple dozen rounds through the new gun to loosen it up. There were no failures to function at any time through the testing. Every round functioned just as if the gun was well worn in, all rounds fed and ejected smoothly.

After sighting in, I fired five-round 100-yard groups with each ammo type. Unsurprisingly, Federal Gold Medal Match 69-grain ammo produced the best groups. This ammo is generally considered the gold standard in factory match ammo. Group size was an unbelievable .36". This is amazingly good performance out of an "economy grade" target gun.

The next group was shot with one of my generic handloads consisting of a Sierra 52-grain MatchKing bullets over 25.5 grs of Winchester 748 powder in mixed G.I. cases. This load was assembled for common plinking use with no special accuracy preparations or materials other than the bullet. This ammo produced a .46" group, still pretty impressive!

I tried two types of Russian Wolf .223 FMJ ammo, the 55-grain version and the 62-grain. These performed as one would expect for economy grade ammo with groups running from 1.6" to 2.3".

I then tried some Russian Silver Bear 62-grain hollow-point boattail loads. This is another economy-grade import ammo, so I expected similar results to the Wolf ammo. To my surprise, this ammo shot a .80" group. Considering its low cost, its performance was exceptional.

I then tried one more economically priced import .223 ammo, the Prvi-Partizan 62-grain FMJBT load. This gun definitely did not like this load at all! Group size was a disappointing 2.7". The two U.S.-made economy grades tested, Winchester USA .223 and Remington-UMC .223, performed at 1.5" to 2" which was expected since these are really intended for informal target shooting or plinking.

One U.S. made load that I had high hopes for was the Hornady TAP 60-grain offering. While the 1.1"

group size wasn't what I would call bad, I had hoped this higher priced ammo ($17.95 per box) would have preformed better than the economy grade Silver Bear ($6 per box) ammo.

I guess this just goes to show you that rifles don't necessarily pay any attention to the price tags, they just shoot whatever they like best!

This budget priced AR-15 .223 cal. target rifle, with the best shooting loads, performed as well as rifles costing vastly more. With better optics, a match grade trigger, and several other accuracy-enhancing products that the builder could add when funds become available, its performance could be even better.

I find that the J&T Bull Barrel AR-15 kit to be an excellent starting point for a budget priced AR-15 target rifle. If your budget is tight then one of these kits may be right for you. Its low cost and high accuracy make it a "keeper" for me. ◉

J&T Distributing AR-15 .223 Bull Barrel Kit
Accuracy Results

Load	Group (ins.)
Federal Gold Medal Match: 69-grain HP #GM223M	.36"
Handload—Sierra #1410 .22 cal.: 52-grain HP Match, 25.5 grain Winchester 748	.46"
Silver Bear: 62-grain HP Boattail	.80"
Hornady Tap: 60-grain	1.12"
Winchester USA: 55-grain FMJ	.54"
Wolf: 62-grain FMJ	1.63"
Remington-UMC: 55-grain FMJ	.95"
Wolf: 55-grain FMJ Military Classic	2.36"
Prvi-Partizan: 62-grain FMJBT	2.75"

Testing conditions: Temp 55 degrees, Variable cross winds 0-5 mph. All 100 yard 5-round groups fired with a CTK adjustable rifle rest. Group sizes measured center to center.

The cost of around $800 was hundreds of dollars less than some factory assembled AR-15 target guns. Don't think you can't afford an accurate AR; just do it yourself!

M14 Maintenance & Inspection

By Gus Norcross
Photography by Emily Fortier

They're all more than 40 years old, but M14s are serving in Iraq and Afghanistan, and armorers are bringing back tricks from the past.

A rifleman in Iraq scans for insurgents using the 10X scope on his M14. These rifles are almost always older than their users, but are still serving. (U.S. Army)

For a rifle that hasn't been produced since 1964, the M14 displays surprising longevity. Although it was officially replaced by the M16 as the standard service rifle 40 years ago, it soldiers on in specialized roles. Accurized National Match M14s were standard equipment for civilian and military rifle teams until the mid-1990s. The Army has used the M14 as a sniper rifle or "designated marksman rifle" from Vietnam to the present Iraq conflict and demand for 7.62mm precision rifles in combat zones remains strong.

Few of our present-day military or civilian marksmen have had detailed instruction in cleaning or maintaining this decades-

old weapon system. The paragraphs that follow are intended to provide the new M14 owner/operator with the knowledge he needs to keep his rifle in top form.

These instructions assume the rifle operator is familiar with M14 rifle parts and disassembly procedures. The term "M14" will denote both actual military rifles and civilian clones, such as the Springfield M1A.

If you are dealing with an unfamiliar rifle with an unknown maintenance history, a detailed cleaning and inspection will be necessary to determine its serviceability. Keep a log book of rounds fired, repairs, zero data and scores. Establish a good

relationship with your armorer. He has the specialized tools and knowledge needed for proper maintenance. Armorers who were actually trained in the nuances of the M14 rifle by military marksmanship units are no longer numerous but there are still some around.

Let's start by removing the rifle from the stock. On bedded rifles, the action will not drop out freely and a few taps on the underside of the receiver heel with a brass drift may be necessary. If the action falls freely from the stock, it is time for the bedding to be renewed. Normally, we would only remove a bedded action from its stock at the end of our annual shooting season

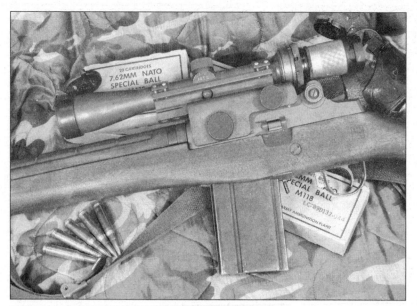

Here's an M21 sniper rifle with a 1980s vintage ARTII scope. While considered obsolete by some, these 1960s-vintage rifles still serve with front-line units in Iraq.

for a detailed cleaning prior to storage or if the rifle has been subjected to severe environmental conditions such as heavy rain or blowing sand. Frequent removal of the action from a glass-bedded stock may result in premature loosening of the bedding and is discouraged.

Remove the operating rod spring and spring guide. Remove the operating rod and bolt. Now would be a good time to record throat erosion and headspace readings in your log book if you have access to the proper gauges. At this point a padded vise would be helpful. Remove the gas cylinder plug and piston. These components are hollow and the carbon must be removed from inside them every few hundred rounds.

Get yourself a letter "P" drill. Holding the gas cylinder plug in one hand, twist the drill into the rear of the plug with finger pressure and carbon dust will be reamed loose. Dump out the carbon. Repeat this procedure with the same drill bit and the large end of the gas piston.

To clean inside the piston tail, use a long #15 drill. A set of these drills with handles installed is available from commercial vendors. Clean the gas piston with solvent and polish with crocus cloth but avoid abrasives. We don't want to reduce the piston diameter.

Gas piston minimum diameter is .497". Check it with a micrometer. Brush out the gas cylinder with solvent and a .45

cal. brush. Patch it dry. Do not use lubricants in the gas system.

Check the gas cylinder for looseness on the barrel splines. If you can remove it by hand, it's too loose. The barrel splines may be lightly tapped to roll the edges with a small hammer.

On match or sniper rifles the front band, gas cylinder and spindle valve should be screwed or welded into one solid assembly. The cost of this modification is minimal and special tooling is required. See your armorer.

When reinstalling the gas cylinder, make sure it is aligned properly with the barrel gas port. You should keep a 1/16" Allen wrench in your basic cleaning kit. It can be used as a gauge to align the gas cylinder with the gas port and to loosen or tighten the gas cylinder lock set screw.

Badger Ordnance makes a nice gas cylinder alignment gauge. The gas cylinder lock should stop at the 6 o'clock position bearing solidly against the face of the gas cylinder with the gas cylinder only a few thousandths of an inch from the barrel shoulder.

Some gunsmiths use shims behind the gas cylinder to position it on the barrel. I prefer to leave a very slight gap between the barrel shoulder and the cylinder for heat expansion. Install the piston. Put a smear of grease on the gas cylinder plug threads and snug it down to 115-125 in/lb with the barrel and gas cylinder held solidly in a padded vise. The gas cylinder should not be removed for routine maintenance.

The flash suppressor should also be tight. Back out the set screw with your 1/16" Allen wrench and loosen the nut with G.I. flash suppressor nut pliers. If you can move the flash suppressor, it is too loose. Lightly tap the edges of the mounting splines on the barrel with the smooth face of a small ball peen hammer.

National Match modified flash suppressors are reamed out on a lathe with a taper pin reamer to avoid misalignment with the barrel. GI flash suppressors are only very slightly larger than the bore. Bore/suppressor alignment is checked with a precision plug gauge. Since you most likely won't have access to one of these gauges, have your armorer ream your flash suppressor to NM specs.

The exit hole should measure about .406" when this is properly done. Many commercial flash suppressors are manufactured to NM specs and don't require modification. Wipe the carbon from the slots in the suppressor and scrub the bore with a .45 cal. bore brush.

Holding the barrel end of the suppressor in your hand, tap the forward end against your vise. You should hear a ringing sound. If you hear a thunk, your flash suppressor may be cracked. Check

Armorer tools. Bolt assembly tool, flash suppressor alignment gauge, headspace gauges, throat erosion gauge, firing pin hole gauge, log book and bolt roller pliers.

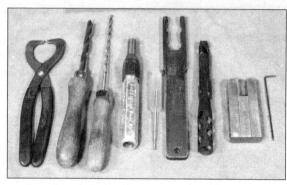

Gas system tools: Castle nut pliers, drills with handles, cylinder gauge, Badger alignment tool, holding and combination tools, gas piston gauge, 1/16 inch Allen wrench.

the front sight screw for tightness. The flash suppressor will not normally be removed for routine maintenance.

Check the handguard. On a match or sniper rifle, the tabs on the front band should be annealed and bent upwards to tighten the front of the handguard to the unitized front band/gas cylinder assembly. Check the fit of the handguard. There should be a slight clearance between the rear of the handguard and the receiver.

The bottom edges of the handguard should not touch the fore-end. We want the handguard to touch the rifle only at the front band. Glue the front end of the handguard into the front band with Devcon 5-minute epoxy. Stake the barrel grooves just behind the handguard clip as a final touch. The handguard should not rattle.

Check the op rod guide. Make sure it is tight. It is driven onto a knurled portion of the barrel and secured with a roll pin. A loose op rod guide is not acceptable.

Unlike the M16, M14 barrels must be cleaned from the muzzle end. Use a muzzle guide to avoid damage to the muzzle. Do not use the issue segmented military cleaning rod. Get a 24-inch

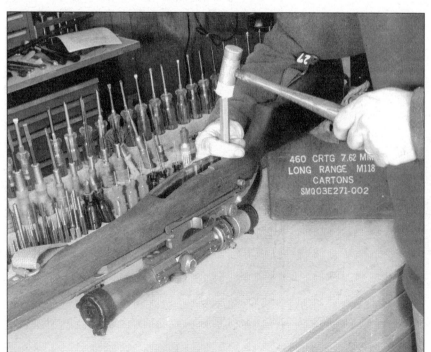

To remove the action from a stock that has been glass bedded, invert the rifle, pull out the trigger group and tap the receiver heel with a brass drift or wood dowel.

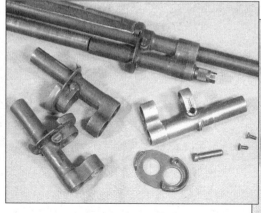

These are unitized gas cylinders on the left, component parts (cylinder, front band and spindle valve) on the right. They can be "screwed and glued" or else welded.

Keep a 1/16-inch Allen wrench in your kit as a gauge for aligning the gas cylinder with the gas port and to loosen or tighten the gas cylinder lock nut set screw.

Check the op rod guide. Make sure it is tight. It is driven onto a knurled portion of the barrel and secured with a roll pin. A loose op rod guide is not acceptable.

Check the tightness of the elevation knob screw by grasping it with a padded pair of pliers and trying to tighten the screw with a proper size flat tip screwdriver.

one-piece stainless steel or plastic coated cleaning rod from a commercial vendor.

Clean the barrel with the rifle sights-down in a padded vise or rifle cradle. Keeping the rifle inverted will prevent solvent from dripping into the gas cylinder and the bedding. Use a commercial cleaning solvent that will attack copper. Hoppe's Benchrest, Shooter's Choice and many other brands will all work fine if you give them time.

Saturate the bore with solvent. Loosen carbon with several passes with a brass core bronze bristle bore brush. Patch out the fouling. Wet the bore again with solvent and let the rifle sit overnight. In the morning patch out the bore. Note the green copper residue on your patches.

There is a way to avoid all this mechanical cleaning. Buy a can of Wipe-Out. This cleaner looks similar to shaving cream when squirted out of the aerosol can. A short length of drinking straw is necessary when squirting this cleaner into the bore on an M14 through the flash suppressor. Remove the gas cylinder plug and piston.

Stuff a couple patches into the gas cylinder to block the gas port. Put your finger over the chamber end of the barrel without sealing it completely. Fire a short squirt of Wipe-Out through the straw into the bore. The foam will fill the barrel. Let it sit for a couple hours or overnight if the barrel hasn't been decoppered in a while.

Run a couple patches through the bore to clean out the residue. The patches will be bright blue in color and the bore will be very clean. No brushing necessary. Be advised that this squeaky clean bore will affect your zero. If possible, fire a few rounds through the rifle before the next big match to "season" the bore.

Clean the chamber. A military ratcheting chamber brush is available but I've always used the M3A1 combination tool issued for the Garand. Wrap a wet patch around the brush on the combination tool and twist it back and forth in the chamber. Follow with a dry patch. Actual brushing of the chamber is usually not necessary. A tight patch will clean it. If you have used Wipe-Out to clean the barrel the carbon in the chamber patches out easily.

Scrub out the receiver with solvent and a toothbrush to remove old grease and grit. This loosened residue can then be blown out with a quick-drying aerosol solvent. Wipe the grease and fouling off the bolt including the bolt face. Wipe the old grease off the op rod. Check the trigger group and clean as necessary.

Check the tightness of the elevation knob screw by grasping it with a padded pair of pliers and trying to tighten the screw with a proper size flat tip screwdriver. These will shoot loose over a period of time. Run the sight up 20 clicks and put downward thumb pressure on the rear aperture. The aperture should not move. If it drops a few clicks, tighten the center screw on the windage knob one click and try again. If the rear sight is disassembled, put a bit of grease on the rails of the rear aperture where it fits into the rear sight base.

While the stock is off the rifle, check it for cracks. If the rifle is to be stored, a light coat of oil may be rubbed over all parts at this time.

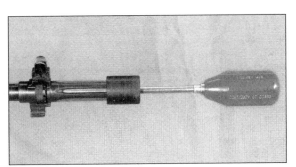

Like the Garand and unlike the M16, the M14 must be cleaned from the muzzle. Be sure to use a bore guide to protect the muzzle and select a one-piece 24 inch rod.

Begin reassembly by greasing the boltways and op rod rail of the receiver using a Q-tip or acid brush dabbed in grease. Acceptable lubricants include military issue rifle grease, Plastilube, Lubriplate and similar greases. No oil is necessary for lubrication. In extreme cold or sandy conditions, use only a bare minimum of lubricant or none at all. The M14 will function dry when necessary.

After greasing the wear points of the receiver, move on to the bolt. Grease must be forced into the roller bearing. Badger Ordnance makes a small, inexpensive tool for this purpose. Dab grease on the bolt lugs. Install the lubricated bolt in the receiver. Grease the camming surface of the op rod where the bolt roller rides.

Put a dab of grease on the underside of the barrel at the breech end where the op rod rubs. Also, lubricate the cylindrical portion of the op rod where it rides in the op rod guide. Assemble the op rod to the receiver. Make sure the op rod and bolt move freely.

Lightly grease the op rod spring guide and put a few dabs on the spring and rub it into the coils and assemble them to the rifle. Put a smear of grease on the underside of the bolt. When you assemble the rifle to the stock, put a bit of grease on the stock ferrule where the tab on the front band touches it (center bottom).

The trigger guard should lock with some resistance. If the trigger guard fits loosely and locks without resistance the stock may have to be bedded. Also, don't forget to periodically clean your magazines. ◉

Commercial flash suppressors won't need it, but a standard military suppressor should be reamed to NM specifications. A modified #7 taper pin reamer is used for this.

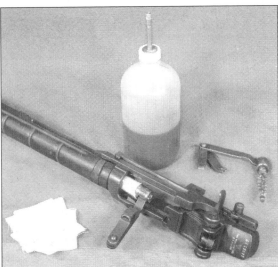

Norcross prefers the M3A1 combination tool issued for the Garand to the ratcheting chamber brush. Wrap the brush in a wet patch and twist it back and forth.

The Weekend Garand

By Reid Coffield

Coffield already had an M1 glass-bedded for competition, but wanted a rack-grade Garand for John Garand matches, While he was at it, he put together a replica M1D.

Coffield has written about some ambitious projects lately; here's one that you can put together in short order and then head for the range!

I've owned and shot quite a few U.S. military rifles over the years, starting back when I was a kid in a small town in the foothills of North Carolina. When I was 18 my dad and I helped organize a gun club, the Piedmont Rifle and Pistol Club, which is still going strong almost 50 years later. After getting established, the club linked up with the NRA and the Director of Civilian Marksmanship (now known as the Civilian Marksmanship Program). One of the benefits at the time was the loan of some rifles and handguns and a yearly ammo allotment.

In return, each year the club members had to shoot and send in their scores to DCM. Some of the guys shot .22 rifles, others the 1911 .45 handguns, and a few, including yours truly, shot the Garands we'd been issued. Each year on a specified date we would get together and shoot. It was a blast!

Many of the members were middle-aged World War II and Korean War vets who had seen plenty of shooting in other circumstances. When we got together, a lot of those guys were more than content to hang out in the clubhouse and "let the kid shoot my score." Since I was "the kid", I thought that was a great idea!

I have absolutely no idea how many rounds I fired through those Garands shooting targets for older club members but it was a lot. At the end of the day, I would come dragging into the clubhouse with a very sore shoulder and a grin on my face. I was the luckiest kid in the world!

Partly because of that experience and the fact so many men I looked up to and admired had carried a Garand, I've always had a special feeling for this rifle. Over the years I've owned several. Currently the only one I have is one I set up for competitive shooting many years ago. I bedded it, installed a match grade .308 barrel, added match sights; the whole nine yards. It was and is a great shooter. In fact, I shot it for a number of years at Camp Perry and the stock still has a sticker on it indicating the trigger had been weighed and checked by the line officials.

Still, I wanted a plain old standard, rack-grade Garand. I wanted a rifle like those carried by so many of my friends from years past who have gone on to their reward. I didn't want a match rifle. I wanted just a plain, ordinary G.I. M1 Garand of the type used in combat all over the world. Besides, one of the local gun clubs started having John Garand Matches during the summer.

Some years ago CMP and the NRA got together to sponsor a special rifle match at Camp Perry during the National Matches. This match was limited to standard, unmodified Garands. If your rifle had been bedded, had match sights added, or was otherwise "tricked out," it couldn't be used in this match.

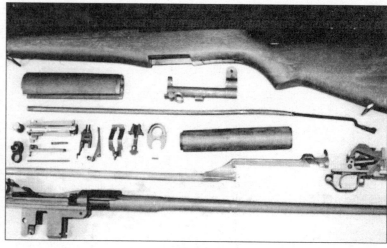

Before you begin putting together your M1 Garand rifle, make sure you have all the necessary parts. SGN advertisers like Numrich Gun Parts are your ideal sources.

Coffield's "mystery" receiver was made by Australian Defense Industries at the arsenal at Lithgow. These were imported by a firm in Sacramento, Calif., in the 1990s.

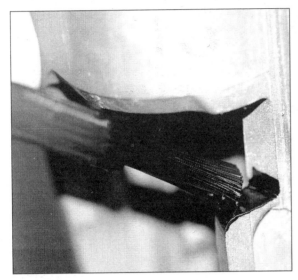

Coffield brushed on Dykem to coat the receiver bolt lug seats to help determine the amount of contact with the bolt lugs. It's important to get maximum lug contact.

The idea was to encourage average guys who owned ordinary Garands to shoot 'em. What a great idea! Additionally, it was a special tribute to John Garand, the firearms genius who designed the M1 Garand. It was a great idea and has actually drawn more shooters than any other event at the National Matches. Just this last year, there were more than 1,100 shooters participating in this one match!

Since my upgraded Garand was not "legal" for these matches, I decided to put together a rifle I could use. Sure, I could have gone down to the local gun shop and bought one. There is almost always a Garand or two in the used gun rack. However, I wanted to put together my own rifle. Not only would this be a fun project, but it would allow me to use up a bunch of parts and pieces I've accumulated over the years.

Since I'm no longer actively gunsmithing for the public, I've had little need to keep an extensive parts supply. In addition, this would be a rifle that might mean a little more to one of my kids or grandkids since "the old man" put it together.

Also, I have to admit that as an old competitive shooter, I greatly value a good barrel. Many of the used Garands I've seen for sale have bores that have definitely seen better days. By putting together my own rifle, I could be sure I'd have a bore that was nice and smooth with no pits or throat erosion.

I've noticed too that stocks on many used Garands are pretty beat up and often loose due to the wear and normal shrinkage you encounter in stocks that are 60+ years old. Since I would use new wood, that problem would also be eliminated.

Fortunately the good folks at Numrich Gun Parts Corp., 226 Williams Lane, Dept. SGN, West Hurley, N.Y. 12491, telephone 866-686-7424, could supply the items I needed. In

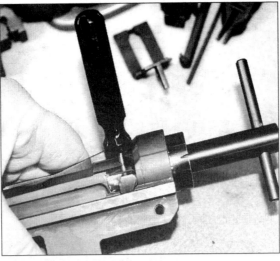

The Brownell lug lapping fixture makes it easy to lap in the bolt lugs and ensure even, solid contact. It pushes the bolt back against the locking recesses.

fact, while I was talking about the project, one of the fellows there suggested I consider making the rifle into an M1D sniper version.

This Garand sniper rifle was first built in late 1952 and was used for many years. Some were even used in Vietnam. It's basically just a standard, ordinary Garand with a special barrel incorporating a scope base. The only other modifications are a shortened rear handguard and a strap-on leather cheekpiece. The M84 scope was a simple 2.2X with a plain post crosshair.

The more I thought about it, the more I liked the idea. At 63, I no longer have the vision of that 18-year-old kid back in North Carolina. Having a scope mounted would sure make shooting, especially when working with handloads and trying to get the smallest possible groups, a lot easier. And besides, I could always pop the scope off when I wanted to participate in a John Garand Match which is limited to rifles with the standard issue iron sights.

Numrich offers a complete, brand new stock set for the Garand that does not include any of the metal hardware for only $159.95. This stock is made to standard G.I. specs from beech that's been given a very dark, walnut-like stain. Most importantly, it's not oversize like many aftermarket target or competitive stocks for the Garand. Of course, they also have used G.I. stocks for considerably less.

The action wrench Coffield used is contoured to match the top of the Garand receiver and well taped to prevent scratching. This is essential for barrel installation.

Also, they have new, unused .30-'06 barrels at only $225 that come with the M1D scope mount base. Numrich offers a copy of the M84 scope for $399. That's a lot less than you would pay for an original M84 scope in new condition. Of course Numrich also has G.I. type quick-detachable rings, as well.

For a very modest outlay, I was able to pick up the parts I needed to complete my rifle. If you want a set like this or need any Garand parts, I would definitely encourage you to give the folks at Numrich a call. Odds are they'll have anything you might need. Whether it's for a regular Garand in .30-'06 or some variation like my M1D, Numrich has anything you might want or need to put it together.

By the way, from time to time I've seen ads here in SHOTGUN NEWS for Garand parts kits. That's a great way to get all the bits and pieces you'll need if you don't already have 'em. Then again, if you have a really well used and worn Garand, you might just want to consider rebarreling or restocking it or even converting it into an M1D.

If you've never put together a Garand, it's really not all that difficult. There are lots of good books available to guide you thru the process. The best gunsmithing guide for the Garand is the book by Jerry Kuhnhausen, *The U.S. .30 Cal. Gas Operated Service Rifles, Vol. 1 and 2*. This book which is available from Heritage Gun Books, P. O. Drawer #887, Dept. SGN, McCall, ID 83638, telephone 1-888-634-4104.

Don't even think of turning a barrel into a receiver without first coating the threads with grease. The barrel can gall and become permanently attached in the receiver.

Place a machinist level on the receiver flat behind the rear sight housing and another on the front sight base quickly and easily to index the barrel to the receiver.

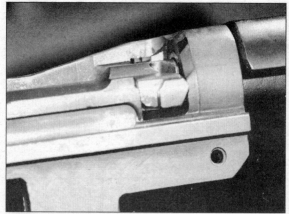

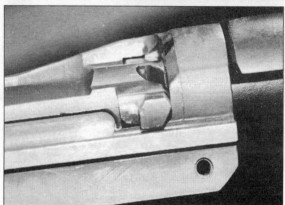

Note that the bolt will not fully close with a "No Go" headspace gauge in the chamber. With the "Go" headspace gauge in the chamber, the bolt will fully lock down.

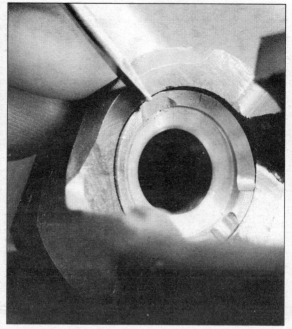

In order to get the bolt to close, Coffield had to extend the relief cut on the lip of the rear of the barrel. This was quickly done without removing the barrel.

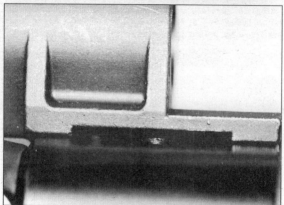

By filing down this pad, Coffield was able to zero at 100 yards. From the right side, you can see the two pads on the scope ring and how they contact the scope base.

It will answer *any* possible question you might have about the M1 Garand or the later M1A/M14. It's an excellent book and a great addition to any gun owner's library. It sells for about $45.

Another excellent book is *The M1 Garand Complete Assembly Guide* by Walt Kuleck with Clint McKee, published by Scott Duff. This book sells for only $22.95 and is available from Scott A. Duff, Box 414, Dept. SGN, Export, PA 15632, telephone 724-327-8246. Any of these books can be purchased from the publisher or from dealers in firearms books that advertise here in SHOTGUN NEWS.

The first step in the process was to lay out all the parts. Not only did this give me a chance to inspect each item to make sure that it would be suitable, it also helped me to make sure that I hadn't overlooked anything.

The Garand contains numerous individual parts and assemblies and it's easy to miss something unless you're pretty systematic and careful. It's always better to make sure you have everything *before* you get started than to be halfway through the project and realize you have to wait while you order a missing component. An easy way to do this is to just lay out your parts and check them against the schematic in your Numrich catalog.

You might think putting together a rack grade Garand is a pretty complex and time consuming project. Actually, it's not. In fact, unless you run into a major problem, you can easily complete this whole project in one weekend! You can without a lot of effort assemble the rifle on Saturday and be out at the range on Sunday! In fact, that's exactly what I intend to do!

The receiver I used for this project is a commercial copy of the Garand. I know very little about it other than it's a casting and is marked "Lithgow." I couldn't spot any defects or problems with it so I decided to use it for this project. Again, this was a good way to use up some odds and ends of Garand parts I had in my shop.

I began the assembly process on a nice Saturday morning by first checking the fit of my bolt to the receiver. I was especially concerned about in the amount of contact between the bolt locking lugs and the lug seats in the receiver.

I wanted a lot of good, solid contact between both of the lugs and the receiver. On most rifles this isn't a problem, but I've seen a number of situations where the lugs did not bear evenly. In fact, I've seen several rifles where only one lug was actually in contact with the receiver!

To check this, I began with a stripped bolt body. The bolt lugs and the lug seats in the receiver were cleaned with alcohol. I then coated the rear face of the lugs and the lug seats with Dykem machinist layout fluid. I next installed the bolt and fitted a Brownells lug lapping tool.

This tool has been available from Brownells for many years, and is set up so that with different threaded "sleeves" it can be used on a wide variety of rifles. It applies spring pressure to the face of the bolt and forces the lugs firmly back against the lug seats. By the way, if you don't have the latest #61 edition of the Brownell gunsmithing catalog, now is the time to get it! The address is Brownells Inc., 200 S. Front St., Dept. SGN, Montezuma, IA 50171, telephone 800-741-0015.

Once the bolt was in place in the receiver, I used a handle supplied with the Brownell tool carefully to rotate the bolt just a few degrees. I didn't move it much, and you definitely don't want it to unlock. Just a tiny bit of movement is all that's necessary. After a few minutes of moving the lugs against the lug seats, I removed the Brownell tool and pulled the bolt from the receiver.

By checking the amount of wear on the Dykem on the lugs and lug seats I could tell where I was getting contact. In my case, the right lug gave me lots of contact but the left lug showed only about 15% contact. Since I was using a new receiver and an old, well-worn bolt, that was not unexpected.

If you find your lugs do not bear evenly, all you have to do is apply a bit of 320-grit lapping compound between the lugs and lug seats. The bolt is then opened and closed just enough to allow minimal movement of the lugs. The abrasive compound laps the lugs and lug seats to a uniform mating surface.

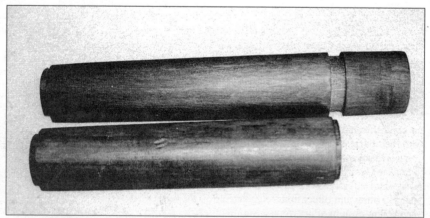

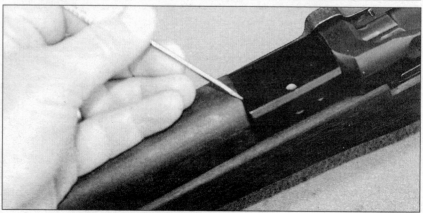

The standard rear handguard is shown above the shorter M1D handguard. The short guard leaves space for the M1D scope base that is mounted on the barrel just ahead of the receiver.

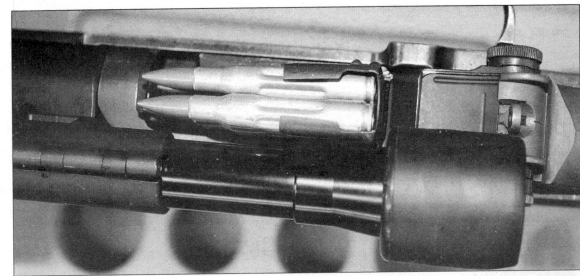

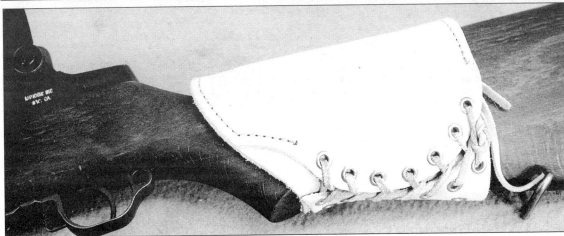

The M1D scope must be offset to the left to allow for loading and ejection of the eight-round clip. A lace-on cheekpiece provides facial support for the shooter.

While the Brownell tool makes this task fast and easy, you can do all of this simply by sticking your finger through the front of the receiver and applying constant pressure to the face of the bolt. It's a bit slower and certainly not as easy but it works!

Once my bolt was fitted to the receiver, the next step was to install the barrel. While the barrel was chambered, the chambering was just a bit short to allow for proper head-spacing. Keep in mind the folks at Numrich have absolutely no control over the receivers and bolts which will be used with their barrels.

If you have a worn receiver or bolt that was made to maximum dimensions, your chamber length would have to be different than on a barrel fitted to a new receiver and a bolt made to minimum dimensions. Having a short chambered barrel allows you to adjust your chamber and headspace to match your bolt and receiver.

The barrel threads were coated with Sentry Solutions Hi-Slip Grease to prevent galling. I learned long ago *never* to turn a barrel into a receiver unless it has some grease on the threads. To turn in a barrel "dry" is to court disaster! A little grease can prevent a lot of problems.

The barrel was held in my barrel vise while the receiver was secured with a Brownell action wrench. This wrench is machined to match and support the contours of the front of the receiver so pressure can be applied with little or no risk of damage. I also placed the gas cylinder on the barrel. The barrel was positioned so that the top of the gas cylinder where the front sight is located was level. I used a small machinist level to check this as I worked.

With the barrel secure, the receiver was turned on to the barrel shank. Once it seated, I checked the receiver to see if it was also level. There is a flat milled area right behind the rear sight that is ideal for positioning a level. Once this

level matches the level on the gas cylinder, the barrel should be properly positioned and seated in the receiver. Also, you shouldn't have any problems later with either the front or rear sight being canted. A small machinist level is all it takes!

Now that the barrel was fit to the receiver, I could determine whether or not my chamber would need to be length-

ened or extended. A "Go" headspace gauge was installed in the chamber and the stripped bolt was carefully moved into position. My chamber turned out to be so short that I could not even begin to lock the bolt. The chamber would have to be lengthened.

While you could pull the barrel off the receiver to cut or extend the chamber, I used a Clymer pull through reamer. This type of reamer, which is a copy of an old U.S. military reamer, is positioned in the chamber. A threaded rod is then inserted in the barrel from the muzzle and screwed into the front end of the reamer.

The stripped bolt is held against the rear of the reamer as it's slowly turned by hand. Once the bolt drops into the locked position, the chamber is complete. It's dirt simple and very easy to use. This type of reamer is still available from Clymer as well as Manson Precision Reamers.

Once the chamber was reamed, I checked it with my Forster headspace gauges to be sure there had been no slip ups. The bolt would close on my "Go" gauge but it would not come even close to closing on my "No Go" gauge. It was right on the money.

The extractor, ejector, and firing pin were then added to the bolt and it was once again checked to make sure it would lock up. That's when I got a little surprise! The bolt would not lock up! I was getting a bit of interference between the outside edge of the extractor and the lip on the face of the barrel. Part of this lip had been beveled, but not quite enough.

It didn't take but a minute or so with a carbide cutter to extend this bevel about .200". I didn't even need to take the barrel out of the receiver.

I also checked the firing pin protrusion. The minimum acceptable protrusion is about .044" while the maximum is .060". My firing pin measured right at .052". That should give me consistent ignition without any danger of a pierced primer.

I continued on assembling the rifle. Initially I didn't lubricate any of the parts. I just wanted to make sure everything was there and that it fit. I had one more surprise, as the op rod I had picked to use was bent. I had not noticed this initially until I did this "dry" assembly. Fortunately, I had a couple of others I could use and found one that while pretty doggy lookin' was not bent or damaged.

Finished and ready for the range! Coffield added a Brownells Competitor Plus sling, which duplicates the classic M1907 leather sling originally used on the M1.

The extra weight of the scope, base, and ring brings total the weight close to 14 pounds, which Coffield found makes the rifle very stable when shooting offhand.

By the way, when you install the op rod you should check the clearance with the bottom of the chamber area of the barrel when the op rod is in its rearmost position. If there is any contact with the barrel) or the underside of the scope base if you have an M1D barrel), you may need to do a bit of polishing. I had just the slightest amount of contact but a few minutes on the belt sander took care of that.

Once the "dry" assembly was completed, I disassembled the rifle. I then reassembled the rifle using plenty of lubricant in the appropriate places. The Garand is a rifle that runs best "wet." It's not a rifle that works well with little or no lube. I made extensive use of Sentry Solutions Hi-Slip Grease in lubricating the bolt, the op rod, and other points of friction.

I prefer grease to oil on this rifle as there is less chance of the grease running off the parts and soaking into the wood stock. I also made darn sure the threads in the rear sight were well lubricated. The rear sight assembly is often overlooked but a good lubricant will help to eliminate wear and make sight adjustments a lot easier.

Once this final assembly was completed, I checked functioning with a clip of eight rounds of dummy ammunition. I wanted to make sure the rifle would feed, chamber and eject the rounds. It appeared to work just fine and threw the dummy rounds about half way across my shop. The ol' Garand always did have a very healthy and robust ejector!

With the rifle completed, I then mounted the Numrich M84 scope. The ring was initially installed on the barrel scope base. Once this was in place, the scope was positioned in this clamp type ring. The scope is furnished with a rubber sun shield on the eyepiece. It looks a little odd as it's partly cut away. This cut is deliberate to provide clearance for access to the rear sight elevation knob.

My sun shield was initially not positioned properly but this was easily corrected. You just push the sun shield forward on the scope and then rotate it to the correct position.

Once you have it where you want it, you just slide it back on to the eye piece.

Keep in mind that this scope was designed to be zeroed at about 300 yards. If you're like me, most recreational shooting is at the local range and is limited to 100 yards. Because of this, I expected that I might have to adjust the mounting of the scope to lower the crosshairs.

After installing the scope, I attached the cheekpiece. Since the scope is offset and mounted to the left of the receiver, you need something to provide support for your face when using the scope. The leather covered cheekpiece acts as a spacer or extension of the stock.

It is initially held in place by a leather lace. Once you have it drawn up nice and tight, two brass wood screws are employed to secure it to the stock. By the way, I used a #40 drill to drill pilot holes for the wood screws. I also made sure that I rubbed a bit of beeswax on the threads of the wood screws before I turned then into the stock. Wax will "lubricate" the screw threads and make it much easier to seat the screws.

If you're not familiar with the Garand, you might wonder why the scope is offset to the left. I admit that it sure looks odd. It has to be done this way as you load the rifle from the top of the receiver with eight-round clips. Also, once you have fired all the rounds, the clip is ejected straight up. If the scope were mounted over the center of the receiver as it is normally on most rifles, you couldn't load the gun or eject the empty clip.

The last component to be added to the rifle was a good leather sling. I used a Brownells Competitor Plus, which is a copy of the old U.S. military 1907 sling. It's a well made, heavy duty sling I've used for years and years. Unlike many other slings, this one is very appropriate for a Garand, a Springfield, or a 1917 Enfield.

All in all, it didn't take very long to put the rifle together. I started on Saturday morning and was finished up by about 2:00 or so. Just in time to take care of some chores for my wife.

The next morning I met a buddy at the range to see how my Garand would shoot. I had some old .30-'06 military

ammo that needed to be used. Just like you and I, ammo will deteriorate with age. I try not to keep ammo around that's more than 15 years old. I never had any real problems with this but then I do make an effort to shoot up the old stuff from time to time.

I started off by firing about 10 rounds or so in single-shot mode to see how the rifle functioned and to get on target. By the way, I was using the iron sights for this initial shooting. I had no problems with the rifle and was basically on target within three rounds.

I then loaded an eight-round clip. The rifle functioned flawlessly and after the eighth round, the clip was automatically ejected. As with many Garands, this rifle threw the empty cases into a nice little group about four feet to the right and a foot or so ahead of the muzzle. It was really easy to collect the empties!

The group size was not terribly impressive by match rifle standards, and that was to be expected. I could put 5 rounds into about 2½ to 3 inches at 100 yards. This is pretty typical of standard Garands with old military ammo. I'm certain I can cut the group size down quite a bit by using handloads and I'll definitely plan on doing that.

Once the rifle was sighted in, I figured all I would have to do was hold the rifle steady in the sandbags and move the scope crosshairs on to the group. Simple. Unfortunately, the scope was designed for a minimum range of 300 yards, so it was far too high for my 100-yard target. I was afraid that might happen and it sure did. However, I figured I could adjust the position of the scope on the mount to compensate for this shorter range.

On the underside of the mount where it contacts the top of the scope base, there are two raised pads. By filing down the front pad and lowering it by about .040", I was able to change the angle of the scope just a bit. This lowered the crosshairs and made it match my iron sights at 100 yards. I fully understand this is not something you would want to do if you were planning on shooting at 300 yards or more. I don't! As I indicated earlier, my shooting will most likely be limited to 100 to 200 yards at most.

If I ever need or want to zero the scope at 300 yards, all I have to do is drill and tap this front pad and install a set screw. I could then adjust the protrusion of the screw through the pad on the mount and return it to the 300 yards zero. No big deal.

With the scope now lined up with my iron sights, I returned to the range for another shooting session. This time I concentrated on using the scope. The Numrich copy of the M84 scope is a replica of the original right down to the markings. You should keep in mind that this is a 1950-vintage design and it doesn't have the power, clarity or optics of the commercial scopes we commonly use today.

By some standards, it's almost primitive. However, it can give you a great appreciation of what countless G.I.s experienced using a rig like this.

For my purposes, it was great and worked just fine. The adjustments for both windage and elevation were simple, positive, and easy to manipulate. It's a small thing, but I really appreciated the hinged turret covers. Just flip 'em up and you can make the needed adjustments and then you just snap 'em back in place. You never have to hassle with unscrewin' 'em and then dropping or misplacing 'em.

The reticle is a simple post with a horizontal line. You can zero the rifle to shoot either to the top of the post or at the intersection of the horizontal line. I opted for having my point of impact at the top of the post as this gave me a better view of the target.

Even with my old military ammo, I was able to get five-shot groups that ran just under two inches. Again, not bad at all, given the age of the ammo and the fact that the rifle was not bedded.

I'm very pleased with my rack-grade Garand. I can't help but think of those old vets I shot for years ago when I use this rifle. While they never thought of themselves as special or unique, I sure did back then and still do to this very day.

Until next time, good luck and good gunsmithing! ◉

"How-To" Build An AR-15

We teach you how step-by-step ON VIDEO!

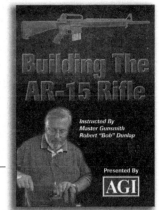

Want to build a Legal AR-15 from a Kit? Learn the easy way without making common, costly mistakes. Once again AGI shows you how step-by-step. Using parts from several of the top AR-15 manufacturers, Robert Dunlap takes you through the entire process of building up a rifle from parts. Includes parts identification, installing and fitting all the parts, headspacing the barrel, final assembly, test firing, and tuning. A number of after-market accessories are covered along with examples and demonstrations of the tools required to make the job easy. Plan on getting started on your project today by ordering this course. It will save you time and money by avoiding common mistakes. 120 min. **DVD#3234** $39.95 ($7 S/H)

Building The AR-15 Rifle — Instructed By Master Gunsmith Robert "Bob" Dunlap — Presented By AGI

OTHER AR VIDEOS AVAILABLE FROM AGI:

AR-15 Rifle Armorer's Course

Own An AR-15? This AGI Armorer's Course will teach you how to repair most common failures and keep it operating. Understand step-by-step how the AR-15 and its clones function, including how the unique gas system works.

Complete disassembly and reassembly, lubrication, maintenance, feeding, trouble shooting, solutions, and repairs are all explained and shown in eye-opening detail, along with what critical spare parts are needed to keep on hand.

Concludes with installation of a .22 LR conversion kit and a target shredding live fire full auto demonstration. Instructed by Robert Dunlap. 108 min. *(Does not cover barreling and headspacing - see Course #3234 above.)* **DVD#1034** $39.95 ($7 S/H)

Get All 3 AR DVDs Shown Here For ONLY $97!
Reg s/h is $21 but you save $12 on shipping when you order all 3! **Product # ARX3DVD** SAVE Over $34!

AR-15 Trigger Job Course
Learn how step–by-step!

The AR-15 rifle is now used extensively in both shooting matches and competitions around the country. The heavy barrel flat-top models also make excellent varmint rifles. Whether you are shooting in formal competitions or just plinking, you want a good, clean, safe trigger pull. This course will show you how to accomplish this goal. 60 min. **DVD#3354** $39.95 ($7 S/H)

Make Money part-time, full-time, or as a retirement income Doing What You Love!
Become A Certified Gunsmith!

Free Gun Repair Introductory DVD Lesson & Special Report:

"How To Get Started In Gunsmithing"

Professional Gunsmithing Course Introductory Lesson — Become A Certified Gunsmith In As Little As 3 Months - GUARANTEED!

FREE DVD*

Order your complete information package which includes a one hour introductory video lesson and complete information on how to get started in gunsmithing part-time, full-time or as a retirement income. **ALL FREE!*** *We just ask that you pay $3.97 for priority mail shipping and handling and *that's totally refundable!*

IN THIS INTRODUCTORY VIDEO LESSON YOU WILL LEARN:
- How to insure reliable auto-pistol feeding and prevent jams
- Understanding and timing Remington 870 cartridge stops
- Checking and adjusting "range" on Smith & Wesson revolvers
- Trouble shooting ejection problems on the Browning A-5 shotguns
- How a gas system works on a Colt AR-15
- AR-7 trigger repairs and much more . . .

Master Gunsmith Robert "Bob" Dunlap reveals secrets of fast and easy gun repair! Exclusive teaching method demonstrated in proven video format that makes learning a snap!

Call 1-800-797-0867 for your FREE DVD!

---

2 Months FREE TRIAL Membership In The GUN CLUB OF AMERICA*

AS AN ADDED BONUS with your order you will automatically receive a **2 Month FREE* Trial Membership** in the Gun Club Of America which includes: the monthly GCA Newsletters and the monthly GunTech DVD Video Magazines *(each GunTech DVD contains 2 hours of insider firearms information and a disassembly/reassembly course on a unique, rare, or commonly owned firearm)* • Access to the Members Only Website • Tech Support from Qualified Gunsmiths • Manufacturer & Industry Discounts • 20% OFF all AGI videos *with the exception of already discounted courses, certified, and professional courses.* **A $60 value!** *Only $9.97 to cover the shipping and handling for both free issues with option to continue membership. Offer available with credit card orders only.*

THE GCA CONNECTION — GunTech DVD MAGAZINE — Disassembly/Reassembly Course: Winchester Model 88 — In The Classroom: Blue Steel vs Stainless Steel

Get 2 FREE DVD Magazines and Newsletters!!!→

Ad Code# SGNbook2

 1-800-797-0867 www.AmericanGunsmith.com

Mail your written order to:
AGI, 351 Second Street, Napa, CA 94559
or fax your order to 707-253-7149
CA residents add 8.75% sales tax

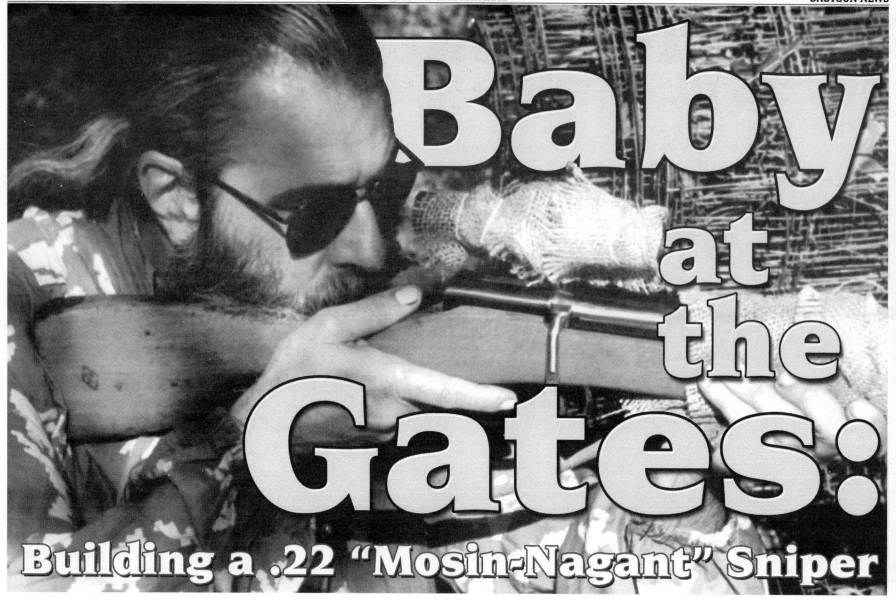

Baby at the Gates:

Building a .22 "Mosin-Nagant" Sniper

If the Warsaw Pact had ever taken up smallbore silhouette shooting, the rifle might have looked like this.

By R. W. Parker/Photos by Heidi A. Parker

Remember your first "real" gun? Where you grew up and how your parents felt about guns probably had a lot to do with what it was. Denied a rural upbringing by a cruel snub of fate, I was raised in a loving but "gun-free" suburban home located in the socialist paradise of New Jersey.

However, despite this unfortunate circumstance, my first "real" gun was actually a hatchet-sporterized Type 38 Arisaka carbine! While some of you are probably saying "Big whoop!", I should mention that only the most fortunate of my peers at the time were permitted to own even a BB gun—and they only got to touch it under strict parental supervision.

I, however, not only conned my Mom into purchasing that $35 beauty for me, but soon managed to get my hands on a 6.5 Jap Lee Loader, a few Norma cases, and some components as well.

From time to time, I'd clandestinely spirit the rifle and some home-made ammo out of the house and into a small patch of local woods, where I'd blast the bejeebers out of some poor tree. Reflecting back on those days, I can honestly say that few things since have given me a bigger thrill than I got from sneaking that old Jap rifle out of the house.

As some allege, I'm now an adult. As such, I can play with just about anything in the way of guns, but I still love the old military stuff—and it probably has a lot to do with that Arisaka carbine. While I build fine custom guns for my customers, my personal collection looks more like a bargain rack at Sarco.

So, when a few distributors began advertising surplus "Polish Mosin-Nagant .22 Training Rifles" awhile back, my interest was quickly aroused. I'm a pushover for .22 rifles, especially military trainers with "genuine cultural significance."

The "Wz48" (correct nomenclature for these Polish trainers), is an enigma that showed up in the flood of surplus arms brought in after import restrictions were relaxed. Virtually unknown in the west prior to being imported, there still isn't a great deal of historical information available on this little rifle.

The .22 cal. Wz48 trainer closely mimics the Soviet M44 carbine (above), especially in the stock lines, with the exception of the 48's longer 24.75-inch barrel.

Distributed by a number of surplus gun dealers, the Wz48 was made by Zaklady Metalowe Lucznik, (or "Lucznik Metal Works") located in Radom, Poland. The literal translation of Lucznik is "archer", and a stylized archer logo was stamped on firearms made there up until early 1940. After this, the logo

Big boys like to play army, too. The author takes a bead on plastic "army men" with the Wz/PU sniper. Burlap camouflage makes the short-range sport all the more fun.

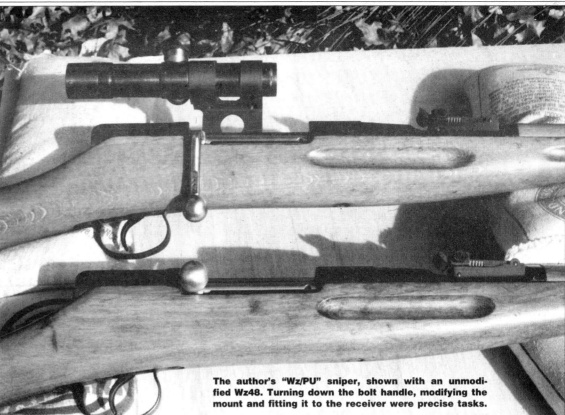

The author's "Wz/PU" sniper, shown with an unmodified Wz48. Turning down the bolt handle, modifying the mount and fitting it to the receiver were precise tasks.

became a numeral "11" in an oval—a change mandated by the communist government.

Superficially, the Wz48 bears a strong resemblance to the Russian service rifle, but the mechanism of this rifle has little in common with the Mosin-Nagant. Nonetheless, it is a well made and extremely robust rimfire rifle. As most distributors were selling these for around a hundred bucks, I knew right away that I had to have one.

Although few "minty" examples of the Wz48 were apparently imported, it's still obvious that the quality of their manufacture is excellent. Some of my friends were fortunate enough to obtain rifles in very nice shape but, since I've yet to run across any "mint-unfired" examples (like some of the Lucznik-produced M44 carbines imported in the past), I'd say it's a safe bet that most of these rifles saw extensive use rather than being warehoused. One story has it that they were a favorite for "police competition" in Poland.

As ordering a sight-unseen surplus firearm is often "luck of the draw", the first Wz48 that I received was a bit ratty and had a mismatched bolt. I returned it to the distributor, asking if they might be able to swap it for one in somewhat better condition.

The replacement they sent had about 60% finish remaining on the metal, the stock was a bit beat up and oil soaked—but it did have matching numbers, all the way down to the buttplate. However, every brand of ammo that I shot through the rifle produced groups no smaller than 6 inches at 25 yards.

Slugging the bore revealed the trouble—quite a bit of wear in the last inch or so of the barrel. Cleaning these rifles from the muzzle with an unguided steel rod must have been popular with their previous owners, as I've examined other Wz48's that have had their muzzle counterbored to remove the worn portion of the rifling.

Rather than counterboring the muzzle of my rifle, I decided to ship the barreled action to Randall Redman (Redman's Rifling and Reboring, 189 Nichols, Dept. SGN, Omak, Wash. 98841 509-826-5512) and have him re-line the bore.

I've installed quite a few of Randall's .22 caliber liners in the past with excellent results, but now I just ship re-lining jobs directly to him. His work is top quality, fairly priced, and having him do this work saves me valuable time in my shop. When I received the re-lined Wz48, I was pleased to see that it could now keep its shots in tiny clusters at 25 yards.

Some time later, a friend sent me a Soviet "PU" telescopic sight outfit. The successor to the earlier PT, VP and PE telescopic sights, the PU was perhaps the most prolific of World War II-vintage Soviet telescopic sights.

While a slight variant of this scope was made for use with the semi-automatic SVT rifle, the PU telescopic sight was primarily employed on the M91/30 Mosin-Nagant sniper rifle. It features 3.5X magnification with a 4 degree 30 minute field of view. The overall length of the sight is 6.59 inches, and the eye relief is approximately 71mm.

It's an extremely rugged sight, and the example that I obtained actually bears a manufacture date of 1970! Though the PU doesn't incorporate a focus adjustment, the optics on the sight that I acquired are crystal clear as-is.

The reticle is the "picket and post" type, and is heavy enough to allow accurate shooting in low-light conditions. Adjusting the windage or elevation knobs moves the entire reticle. The windage knob is graduated in Russian mils, plus or minus 10, and elevation adjustment is provided for ranges of 100 to 1300m. The adjustment knobs do not have click detents.

The rig that I received came complete with leather lens caps, canvas cover, mount, base, mounting screws and dowel pins. As I examined the outfit, I started to think that it would be a neat item to mount on my Wz48 rifle. Sort of like a "baby" M91/30 sniper rifle, it'd be just the ticket for "Enemy at The Gates"-style rifle practice on those green plastic army men that they sell by the bagful at the dollar store.

While the dimensions of the Wz48's stock are nearly identical to the M38 and M44 Mosin-Nagant carbines, its barrel is nearly 5 inches longer at 24.75 inches. The most noticeable difference between the '48 and its 7.62x54R caliber brethren is its lack of the distinctive triangular magazine, as this rifle is a single-shot.

The bolt is quite massive for a rimfire rifle, and its design is unlike that of the service rifle. The sliding "half-moon"-style extractor/ejector is also behemoth, its style similar to that used on some older U.S.-made single-shot .22 rifles.

Stuck cases are a thing of the past with this extractor, even when shooting steel-cased Russian rimfire ammo. Ejection of the spent cases is a howl—the empties are tossed straight up, from 2 to 5 feet in the air! The barrel shank is pressed into the receiver and cross-pinned, and the outer dimensions of the receiver, bolt and barrel are very similar to their centerfire counterparts.

The Wz48 bolt modified to "sniper" configuration (l.), shown with an unmodified example. Preserving the machined "flat" and serial number complicated the job somewhat.

Adapting the PU telescope outfit to the Wz48 meant reshaping the inside radius of the mount, carefully adjusting it to align scope and bore and inletting the stock.

Overall length is similar to other military trainers at 44.5 inches. With a heft in the 8-pound range, this is a .22 rifle that's built like a Soviet KV-1B heavy tank.

The trigger pull on these rifles is smooth but rather heavy, primarily due to a stiff helical spring that rests in a pocket in the stock and bears upward against the trigger bar. Oddly, the rifle's designer didn't incorporate a provision on the trigger bar to capture the end of this spring.

As a result, the alignment of the unguided spring can possibly become skewed—allowing the side of the spring to bear on the trigger bar, rather than the end. Though not a particularly common occurrence, it can be potentially hazardous. If this spring isn't bearing on the trigger bar properly, the trigger can let off with barely any pressure applied.

Further, the cocking piece could jump the sear and fire the rifle when the safety is pushed off. Home gunsmiths who replace this spring with a lighter one in hopes of effecting a "trigger job" on the Wz48 only enhance the potential for trouble.

If you come across a Wz48 that has an extremely light trigger, you'd be well advised to pull the stock off and check the condition of this spring.

Turning the Wz48 into an authentic looking PU sniper variation involved three steps: modifying the rifle's straight bolt handle, correctly mounting the sighting apparatus, and fabricating a new elevation turret for the scope, calibrated for .22LR ammunition.

To obtain the lengthened and turned-down "sniper" configuration bolt handle, I incorporated the knob and stem of the original straight bolt handle. I cut off the existing bolt handle near the root. Next, I machined flat surfaces on the stub of the bolt body and the end of the cut-off handle, perpendicular to their axis.

Each end was then drilled and reamed for two diametrically opposed 1/16" dowel pins. I then fabricated a steel elbow section with corresponding reamed holes in either end, and the three pieces were press-fit together.

The pins held everything in absolute alignment while the new bolt handle was TIG-welded together. The whole process was a bit involved, but was necessary to preserve the machined flat and serial number on the existing handle.

These handles could also be modified in a style that simply replicates those on M91/30 sniper rifles (without the "flat" and serial number). This would require less work, and would certainly appeal to owners of rifles with mismatched bolts.

Next was the installation of the PU base and mount. Its design means properly installing this outfit on a M91/30 sniper rifle isn't nearly as straightforward as scoping a modern bolt-action rifle.

Adapting this apparatus to fit the Wz48 involves still more work, because the smallbore rifle's receiver diameter is actually larger than the 91/30's. So the inside radius of the PU base must be machined to match the Wz48's receiver.

After machining the new radius, the base is fixtured to the receiver at the proper location. Since the holes for the mounting screws and dowel pins on these bases are rarely located on a common centerline, the true position of each hole must be individually located at assembly before adding the corresponding holes to the receiver.

After drilling, tapping, and reaming for the dowel pins, the heads of the base mounting screws are installed and spot faced for their locking screws. It should be noted that utilizing a PU outfit never previously mounted to a rifle will substantially simplify the mounting procedure.

These are supplied with two "virgin" 6x.75mm base mounting screws, lock screws, and two base dowel pins. The unused mount, base, and hardware set makes the job easier for two reasons. First, the tabs on the mount that control windage zero have the necessary amount of material to be machined for proper alignment.

Second, since the base mounting screws haven't been previously machined for the locking screws, welding the heads and re-spot facing them is eliminated.

	Velocity (fps)	ES	Best group (ins.)	Worst group (ins.)
Wolf Match Extra S.V. 40-grain solid	1046	68	0.60	0.75
Aguila Super Extra S.V. 40-grain solid	1039	60	0.315	0.42
Federal Lightning H.V. 40-grain solid	1248	56	0.47	0.55

After the base is installed, the procedure for establishing windage zero can begin. PU mounts are corrected for windage zero by machining two integral pads that bear against the base. However, the design of the PU mount (like some other side-

Integral pads (arrow) bear against the base when installed and allow fine windage adjustment. Parker says it's best to start with an unissued mount if possible.

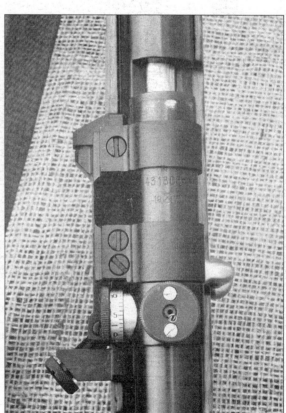

Parker's Wz48 sniper conversion incorporates a 1970-vintage 3.5X Soviet sight. His careful installation meant its reticle could be centered in the field of view.

The finishing touch: Parker made a new adjusting ring for the PU's elevation turret, calibrated for the trajectory of Federal Lightning ammo at 50, 75 and 100m.

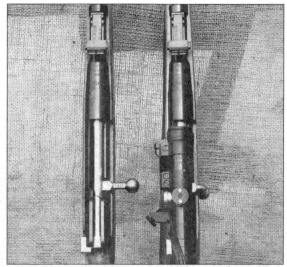

The Wz48 has an unusually large bolt for a .22; turning down the handle enables scope installation. Note the circled 11 that signifies maker Zaklady Metalowe Lucznik.

mounting systems) makes it tricky to get the axis of the scope directly over that of the bore.

Even the most carefully assembled M91/30 sniper rifles will sometimes exhibit some alignment error. Examination of several original M91/30 sniper rifles revealed that Soviet armorers corrected this error by two methods: they either canted the scope (which rotates the bore axis until it's directly under the reticle), or they set the zero on scope's windage turret to compensate for the error (resulting in the frequently seen "off center" reticle).

Considering the circumstances under which these sniper rifles might have been assembled, makeshifts such as these are perfectly understandable. However, since I wasn't hampered by Comrade Stalin's production quotas or MG-42 fire intermittently blazing through my shop window, I had the luxury of machining the various components to remove as much error as the system would allow.

After installing the base, mount, and scope on the barreled receiver, I measured the actual error between the bore and scope axis. I then removed the mount and machined its integral pads to achieve the required correction.

I then recessed the stock to accept the mount base, and assembled the rifle in the stock and test fired it with scope installed. I measured the actual deviation between center of impact and the point of aim, and machined the mount pads again for the final windage zero correction.

The canvas cover supplied with the PU outfit protects both scope and action. Parker found the steep drop of the buttstock required a "chin weld" with the scope.

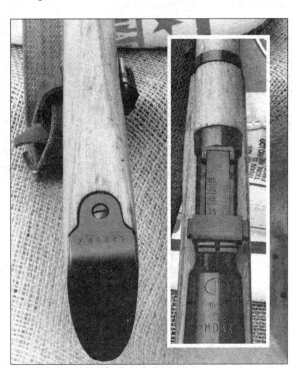

The author's Wz48 had matching numbers, even down to the buttplate. The Wz48 open rear sights are typical Mosin-Nagant, but are calibrated from 25 to 100 meters.

It's essential to correct as much alignment error as possible by machining the mount, as you want to have the scope reticle as closely centered in the sight picture as possible. In the end, all of this work paid off—groups fired at ranges from 25 to 100 meters showed no horizontal displacement, and the scope's reticle was properly centered.

The "coop-dee-gracie" for the "Wz/PU" sniper outfit is making a new graduated ring for the scope's elevation turret—one that tracks the ballistic path of .22 Long Rifle ammunition, rather than 7.62x54R.

Accuracy tests with iron sights revealed that my Wz48 shot various brands of high velocity ammunition almost as well as standard velocity (with a slight nod going to Federal Lightning), so I chose to calibrate the ring for that ammunition. I thought the slight accuracy advantage of standard velocity ammo wasn't worth trading for the increased power of high velocity ammo at longer ranges.

Since the Wz48's rear sight is graduated from 25 to 100m, I graduated the new ring for three ranges: 50, 75, and 100 meters. Of course, I could have used the existing 7.62x54R ring and simply noted the graduations that corresponded with the .22 trajectory—but I thought that would be a bit crude.

And certainly, some would rather not go to the trouble of making up the replacement turret ring, as its fabrication involves considerable time. It sure is a nifty addition to the little rifle, though.

Like the 91/30 sniper, the PU telescope sits about 2 inches above the axis of the Wz48's bore. Combined with ancient styling of the rifle's stock, it's impossible to achieve anything that resembles a cheek weld with this outfit.

However, I found that the "chin weld" required for accurate shooting with the PU was very quick to master and, needless to say, iron sights are immediately accessible. While it's not a rifle I'd bring to a bench-rest match, my "Wz/PU" sniper will keep all of its shots in a quarter at 50 meters, and in the base of a soda can at 100. And it will do this all day long.

Even without click detents on the windage and elevation knobs, the PU scope demonstrated outstanding repeatability, provided the slack was taken out of the screw by turning the knob back to the stop prior to changing the setting.

I was delighted that the new elevation ring tracked the trajectory of Federal Lightning .22LR with uncanny precision. Even the PU's mount surprised me, its ability to return to zero after removal and replacement is flawless.

After all was said and done, I gave the stock a good steaming and sanding, being careful to preserve the cartouches. This was followed by a rubbed linseed oil finish to fill up the fairly porous wood.

As the rifle's metal only exhibited finish wear with no real rust or pitting, these parts were given a quick "shoe-shine" with a Scotch Brite strip, and then dipped in a Du-Lite black oxide bath to restore the original black color.

Building the "Wz/PU" sniper outfit was, start to finish, a very gratifying experience. The procedures involved are well within the ability of any good gunsmith or toolmaker. While some of the tasks are a bit involved, everything should go smoothly, provided each operation is properly thought out and executed.

And, if you're as crazy about World War II military iron as I am, I've got to tell you this: zapping green plastic "army men" with the "Wz/PU" sniper is more fun than you could possibly imagine! ◎

SOURCES

Gulf Coast Ammunition www.gulfcoastammunition.com (800) 725-6578. Wolf and Aguila Ammunition.

Redman's Rifling and Reboring (509) 826-5512 Quality reboring, re-rifling and relining services.

BUDGET BUILDING the Model 1911

Want to get a "retro" .45 at minimum cost and learn your pistol inside and out? Think about building one from scratch.

By Steven Matthews

Can you build a .45 on a kitchen table? It can be done, Matthews says, if you have the right tools, the right parts and, most importantly, the right information.

Most products invented more than a century ago are antiquated by today's standards. Some firearms, however, have stood the test of time, none more so than the Model 1911 pistol. Though it has been modernized and accessorized, the original design still holds up well. While lightweight polymer-framed wonder guns may feel right to the younger generation there is something about the old heavy all-steel 1911 that feels right to us older shooters.

Apparently the older shooters aren't alone, because the 1911 is even more popular today than it was in its early years, with dozens of makers cranking them out, and even more making parts.

Competition among parts makers has made 1911 parts widely available and inexpensive enough that you can build a 1911 from scratch very economically. With a box full of parts, some basic tools and gunsmithing information, the mechanically inclined hobby gunsmith can build a 1911 himself.

Here I will cover the basic building process. I won't cover every detail, but will hit the high points so you can decide if you would like to take on a 1911 build project. Full 1911 building tutorials can be found online for free and several SGN advertisers sell excellent books and videos on building and customizing the 1911. Since it was the U.S. service pistol for more than 70 years, there's probably more information about working in the 1911 than any other gun.

Here I will cover the basic military Model 1911, a simpler design than the Colt Series 70 and 80 Government Model variations, which makes it easier for the novice to build.

You can purchase a complete parts kit or you can buy your parts "piecemeal" when you find bargain-priced parts. If you are in no great hurry, the piecemeal method can be the most economical. By scrounging up bargain-priced parts at gun shows over time you can obtain almost all the parts you need. Be aware, however, that no-name parts can require a lot of hand-fitting and will not be as easy to use as custom parts from SGN advertisers like Ed Brown, Chip McCormick, Wilson Combat or many others.

If, however, you want to get right to building your pistol, the parts kit option may be for you. SGN advertisers offer a multitude of options. Slide kits, frame kits, and complete kits are plentiful.

My friend Phil took the complete parts kit option and obtained a basic 1911 kit. Phil is a Viet Nam-era veteran and like many veterans, has a certain fondness for the arms issued him during his time of service. Phil is not a gunsmith, so I offered to help him build his 1911 and document the build process for this article.

He got a complete 1911 kit from Numrich Gun Parts Corp. (item #485240, priced at $378). All parts were blued, the majority matte finished with a polished frame. I was expecting many unfinished "in the white" parts, but was pleasantly surprised that everything was completely finished.

The frame was exceptionally well finished, and I found that Phil lucked out there. The standard frame was out of stock and rather than just saying "sorry, out of stock," Numrich substituted a higher quality frame. It's nice when a vendor gives a little more to satisfy the customer.

All you need to build a 1911 kit are basic hand tools: files, punches, hammer, a vise, pliers, etc. A Dremel Moto-Tool is helpful for polishing parts but not required, as polishing can be done by hand. In a bit I will show how to make the one required specialty tool.

The most essential "tool" is information. An exploded view diagram will help in determining parts fit and interaction. Books on pistolsmithing are also valuable resources. I have been doing hobby gunsmithing for more than 25 years and I still review diagrams and books before and as I work on a project. You can never know too much about a project but it is very easy to not know enough, so study reference materials every time you do a project.

Manufactured 1911 parts are supposed to be interchangeable. Unfortunately this is more true on paper than in the real world. Manufacturing tolerances among dozens of parts makers mean a certain amount of hand fitting will probably be required. A few strokes of the file and some polishing may be required to get parts to fit and operate smoothly.

This should not discourage the potential builder, as many times it's obvious what needs to be fitted. This kit did require a fair amount of hand work because the frame was a "match" frame made for hand fitting to get tight tolerances. One point I should make is that any time you file a part to hand fit it, follow it up with polishing. A good polish job goes along way in promoting smooth operation.

The starting point for this build was checking slide-to-frame fit. The frame and slide should fit together with little or no hand fitting. If the slide is a little too tight, filing the rails or grooves may be required. Small needle files are good choices for this chore. Just be sure of where and how much material needs to be removed. Once the metal is filed off it can't be put back on.

Since this was a match frame, the slide-to-frame fit was very tight and a lot of filing was required. This is not necessarily a negative, since a very loose slide is easier to fit but can be detrimental to accuracy. Pistolsmiths use a variety of special tools and procedures to tighten slide fit where it's loose, so starting tight lets you work toward a rattle-free fit. Follow it up with a good

Before you start it, read about it. There's no substitute for getting familiarized with the work, and there are plenty of books and videos for the job.

Matthews' buddy Phil got a kit from Numrich Gun Parts Corp. that contained all the parts required to build a 1911. He got lucky with a bonus finished match frame.

The Dremel Moto-Tool is the king for polishing feed ramps, but remember you're polishing steel, not removing it. You don't want to chance changing the ramp angle.

Fitting the slide to the frame is the first step in building a kit gun. Match-grade parts meant lots of hand fitting for Matthews; rack-grade parts fit easier.

polishing of the rails. If fitted and polished very well, the slide can feel like it's riding on ball bearings!

This is a good time to polish the feed ramp on the barrel and the frame. Just polish and don't grind any different angles. A mirror-smooth feed ramp will help all sorts of bullet shapes to feed reliably.

After we had the slide fitted, it was time to assemble the rest of the slide parts, including the firing pin and spring, extractor, firing pin stop and sights. The rear sight is fixed and fits in a dovetail in the slide. It is tapped in with a soft punch till it is about centered.

The front sight is a little harder to install, since it needs to be staked in place. A small tang on the bottom of the sight extends though a slot in the slide. This tang is peened down into

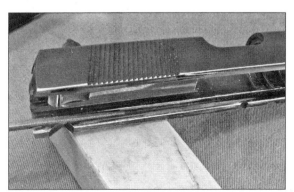

Fine files, wielded with care, remove the small amounts of metal required to make the slide ride smoothly on the pistol's frame rails. Slow and careful needed here.

a small depression on the inside of the frame. It's basically just riveting. If your slide doesn't have a small semi-circular depression for setting this "rivet" simply grind it in with a small grinder.

Insert the tang into the groove and press it down tight. Place the sight against a solid surface (a soft metal block such as brass or aluminum is ideal) and then, using a long punch, hammer the tang into the depression just like a flat-head rivet. As you are setting it, check often to be sure it is still tight against the slide. Once it is tight, grind off any excess that extends past the surface.

The extractor, firing pin and its spring install through the rear of the slide and are held in place by the firing pin stop. Slide the parts into the rear of the slide and line up the groove in the extractor with the grooves in the slide. Slide the firing pin stop into the grooves in the slide. Depress the firing pin to allow the stop to go all the way into place.

Once in place, the firing pin will pop back through the hole in the stop and hold the stop and extractor in place. Check for free movement of the firing pin; if its binds it will cause problems. The slide is now complete.

Now its time to turn your attention to the frame, starting with the plunger tube that houses the slide stop and safety plungers and their spring. This plunger needs to be staked in place, and just as with the front sight, it's essentially a riveting operation.

On the back of the plunger tube are two small stubs with hollow ends. These stubs function as tubular rivets. These stubs extend through the side of the frame and are flared out into small depressions on the inside of the frame to hold the plunger in place.

If your frame doesn't have a slight counterbore on the holes on the inside just grind out a small depression with a Dremel tool. A special tool is required to set these rivets. It can be purchased from gunsmithing supply dealers but for a one-time job an improvised tool can be easily made.

Take a piece of 1/2 x 1/4 x 4-inch steel and grind a taper on the end so it can get into the tight space inside the frame. Near the point of this taper drill a 3/32" hole about 2/3 of the way through. In this hole place a short piece of 3/32" drill bit with a 60° point ground on the end. This point will be used to flare out the ends of the tubular rivets on the plunger.

Install the plunger tube fully into the frame and be sure it's oriented correctly. Place the frame on a solid surface (a block of brass, steel, aluminum, etc.) and rag under it to prevent marring

the finish. Place the point of the tool in the holes in the end of the plunger rivets.

Support the other end of the tool with another solid piece of material so that the tool is square to the work. With the plunger solidly backed up, strike the tool close to the frame to drive the point down into the rivets and flare them out. Pay particular attention to keeping the plunger tight against the frame.

You don't have to hit very hard to flare out the plunger tube legs. After you have set them, grind off any extra material that extends above the frame.

The trigger simply slides through the rear of the frame and will be held in place by the magazine catch when it is installed. Be sure the trigger slides easily and doesn't bind. Also be sure it is right side up. If the magazine catch isn't already assembled, insert the spring and magazine catch lock into the hole in the catch. Press it in and rotate it to lock it in place in the magazine catch.

With the trigger all the way forward, insert the magazine catch into the frame and rotate the catch lock to release it. This will retain the magazine catch in the frame. You may have to move the catch a little to get the lock to drop into its recess in the frame.

Now comes what I consider the most difficult part of the build process, installing the lockwork. The hammer, sear, disconnector, trigger, grip safety, safety lever, sear spring and main spring all have to interact with each other to operate properly. The reason it is somewhat difficult is that if you don't put the parts in right and place the spring in place when all the other parts are located correctly it won't work.

Its easy to jiggle the parts out of alignment during installation. If they go together wrong they won't work right. Various sources list

You might think that 1911 parts are standardized, but a certain amount of fitting is required for any "gun in a box." Here the firing pin stop needs attention.

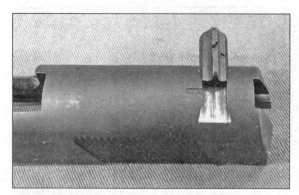

The rear sight fits into a dovetail at the rear of the pistol's slide. Tap it in place with a brass or nylon punch until it is correctly centered up in the slot.

The front sight is staked into its cut in the slide. Staking is essentially like riveting. More recent 1911 variants have tended to have dovetails for the front sight.

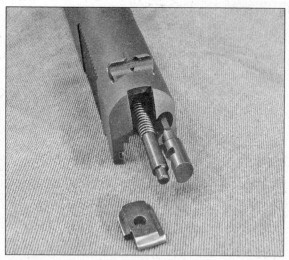

The firing pin assembly and the extractor are retained by the firing pin stop, which in turn is positioned by the head of the firing pin, which must move freely.

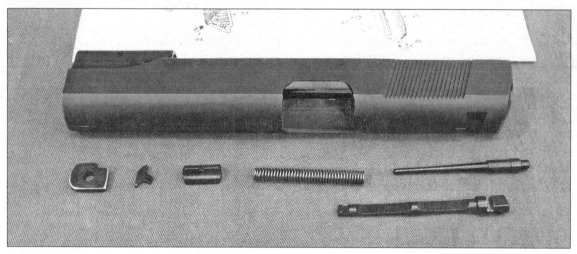

The slide of the standard 1911, which is not equipped with a firing pin safety, is quick and easy to assemble; only staking the front sight requires much attention.

different procedures for assembling these parts, but this is what has worked for me. Start by installing the disconnector and sear into the frame. It's a real tight space down in the frame and a pair of tweezers or needle-nose pliers will help getting the parts in place.

The plunger at the top of the disconnector goes up through the hole in the frame and the sear slides over the disconnector. Refer to your parts diagram to get the proper orientation of these parts, because they have to be right. Install the disconnector/sear pin once the two parts are aligned. Be sure the disconnector slides easily up and down in the frame and be sure the sear rotates freely on the pin. Binding parts will cause problems.

The hammer assembly can now be installed. If it isn't already put together, assemble the strut to the hammer with the small strut pin. Pay particular attention to the proper orientation of the strut. Place the assembly into the frame and install the hammer pin into the frame to hold it in place.

Assemble your mainspring housing by inserting the mainspring housing pin retainer (pointed end down) into the housing, followed by the spring. The mainspring cap is placed on the top of the spring. This spring and cap will have to be compressed down into the housing to install the mainspring cap pin. A vise will help with this job as the spring is very strong and difficult to compress by hand.

Place a small bolt or pin on the cap and compress the spring with the vise. Once the cap is low enough in the housing install the pin that will retain the cap. Be careful when doing this as if things slip parts will shoot off into places unknown! Set this assembly aside till you need it later.

Take the slide stop plunger, spring and safety lock plunger and install them into the plunger tube. Kinking the spring lightly will help hold the parts in place. Be sure the plunger is installed in the right direction.

Next to go in is the sear spring. This is the three-fingered flat spring in your kit. These fingers press on the sear, disconnector, trigger and grip safety (when installed later). These parts need to be in the proper position when the spring is installed. The left finger presses on the sear and the middle presses on the disconnector and the right finger presses on the grip safety when it is installed.

With the hammer in the cocked position, place the spring in place. The small tab at the bottom of the spring fits into the small slot in the frame. Slide the mainspring housing into its groove in the frame just far enough to hold the three-fingered spring in place.

Slide the grip safety into place in the frame. The grip safety has a slot machined into it for the hammer strut. The pin on the back of the safety lock is used to hold the grip safety in place. Slide the pin into place. It won't go all the way in until the stub on the back of the safety lock enters the frame.

Look through the hole in the frame and make sure the sear and hammer are in the right place to allow the stub to enter the frame. It also has to be in the right position to slip into place. It will only go in when the safety lock is down slightly from its fully up position.

Besides all this, the plunger for the safety lock needs to be depressed when the safety lock is pressed all the way home. This all sounds very complicated and it is the first few times you try it, but is much easier once you have done it a few times. Once all these parts are in place, release the hammer to allow it to go all the way forward.

Slide the mainspring housing in the rest of the way, making sure the hammer strut sits on top of the mainspring cap. Before it is all the way up, depress the grip safety so that the mainspring housing slides over the tabs on the grip safety. Once it's all the way up, insert the mainspring housing pin to hold it in place.

If you have done everything right, your lock work should function properly. Cock the hammer and see if the trigger and sear engage it. See if the safety lever operates. Gripping the frame properly to depress the grip safety see if the trigger will release the hammer (with the safety off). Do *not* drop the hammer on the frame; damage can result from allowing the hammer to hit the frame hard.

Hold it with your thumb and allow it to go down easily. At this point, the disconnector function will not work because the slide has to be cycled to make it work, this will be checked later. If you have problems and things don't work right refer to your diagrams, books or building tutorials. There are a variety of checks you can use to be sure lockwork fit is correct.

Install your grip screw bushings. They just screw into place. A little thread locker will help keep them tight. Install the grips and grip screws to complete the job.

The barrel link and pin can also be installed. The small end of the link goes into the hole in the bottom of the barrel and the barrel link pin is just pressed in to the holes.

The slide/barrel assembly can now be installed. With the slide upside down, place the barrel into the front of the slide and slide it all the way to the rear and let it drop down into the locking lugs

The front sight stem protrudes inside the slide. With the sight supported securely, stake it into its recess. Use a grinder to remove any excess material inside.

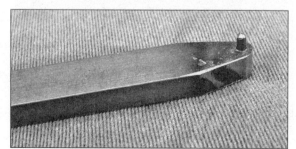

You can buy a plunger tube staking tool from Brownells or MidwayUSA, but Matthews found it easy to improvise one with a small steel bar and a piece of drill rod.

Position the plunger tube in the frame and support it from the bottom. Support the back end of the staking tool and place its point on the leg. Tap to flatten it.

It looks really great, but be sure to test all safety mechanisms and feeding, using dummy ammunition, before loading any live ammo into your finished kit 1911.

in the slide. Insert the barrel bushing into the front of the slide, rotating it to allow it to drop in place. Once it's in place rotate it out of the way so that the recoil spring can pass through.

Place the recoil spring over the recoil spring guide. Slide the open end through the front of the slide. Lay the recoil spring guide on top of the barrel with the concave section against the barrel. Slide it all the way to the rear. Flip the link straight up to allow the guide to go all the way back.

Slide the barrel/slide assembly onto the frame until you can see the hole in the link through the hole in the frame where the slide stop will install. When the holes line up, insert the pin on the slide stop. To get it in all the way you have to line up a small cut out in the slide to allow passage of the slide stop.

You also may have to depress the slide stop plunger to get it in, some drop right in and others need a little tension taken off the plunger to get it to pass by. After the slide stop is in place, return the slide to the forward position. Place the recoil

spring plug over the spring and press it down into the slide. Once it is in the slide all the way rotate the barrel bushing to lock it in place.

At this point you should have a complete and properly functioning gun. Cycle the action to see if it works properly. Cock the hammer and pull the trigger, keep the trigger pulled. Cycle the slide with your hand. The hammer should recock and you should have to release the trigger to reset it. Check both safeties. The gun should not drop the hammer unless the grip safety is depressed and it also shouldn't drop the hammer if the safety lever is in the safe position.

If there are any faults, correct them before you attempt to fire the gun. If everything appears to function correctly, you can advance to testing with dummy rounds. Using the dummy rounds in a high-quality magazine, check feeding and ejection. If you have problems with feeding the feed ramp may need some extra work.

Conventional 1911s have a two-piece feed ramp (part on the frame and part on the barrel) and if they don't align right, the round may catch and cause feeding problems. If you do have to do some work on the ramps, do so with caution; once you remove metal to reshape the ramps it can't be put back on!

If you have ejection problems there may be a burr on the extractor or it may not be tensioned correctly. There are many small things that can cause problems and if you do have problems, refer to the troubleshooting procedures in your build tutorial.

This is one of the reasons I recommend the books and videos, nobody is perfect and if you have trouble its nice to have some info to help figure out what's wrong. Many times I have problems and have to refer to reference materials to figure out what I did wrong. I'm the first to admit I don't know everything! Keep in mind that the original 1911 was designed to use full metal-jacketed ball ammo for proper functioning. They can be made to operate well with hollow-points and wadcutter target ammo but that is beyond the scope of this article.

This gun kit from Numrich Gun Parts Corp. worked well. Some polishing of parts and a couple hundred rounds of break-in were required to get to acceptable reliability, but this was expected from a "box of parts" project. The cost of this project was very reasonable.

One side benefit from building a gun from parts is that once done, you are intimately familiar with how it functions. A good price, learning something about your gun and the satisfaction of knowing you built it yourself all make this a worthy project for the hobbyist gunsmith. ◎

The staking tool will flatten the plunger tube legs into the frame, firmly retaining it. If any excess material protrudes, grind it off to leave a smooth surface.

The sear and disconnector are retained in the frame by a headed pin. A light polish will smooth their operation, but resist the temptation to remove any metal.

The ejector fits into the top of the frame and is held in place with a crosspin. Be sure the latter does not protrude into the slide grooves in the pistol's frame.

The safety and slide stop plungers and spring fit into the plunger tube. A little kink carefully made on the coil spring helps hold it in position in the tube.

Fixing a "Non-Repairable" Pistol

Someone may give you one as a parts gun or a partial trade on something newer. Coffield says don't assume it's shot; with the proper parts and techniques, it'll fire again.

By Reid Coffield

There are lots of Spanish and Italian pocket pistols from the 1950s and '60s floating around the marketplace. Many are broken, but Coffield says they are fixable.

The 1950s and '60s saw a tremendous influx of relatively inexpensive European handguns. While some were revolvers, most of these were .25, .32, and .380 semiautomatics. Many were new production, though thousands of older, used handguns were also imported. At that time, it seemed like you couldn't open a gun magazine or walk into a gun shop without seeing lots of examples of these guns.

While I, like many others, had little regard for these handguns, they were fairly popular with the general public. They were cheap and they appealed to folks who wanted an inexpensive personal defense handgun. I will admit that I too, being on a very limited budget, ended up owning a few of these guns at the time.

When I later opened a gunsmith shop, I saw a number of these guns brought in for various problems. Because these were personal defense handguns and more often than not

owned by non-shooters, they seldom had seen a lot of use. My partner often commented that few if any of these guns fired more than a couple of hundred rounds during their lifetime. Most lived out their existence in purses or dresser drawers. Eventually they were passed on to another family member or given away.

The importation of handguns of this type was pretty much ended with the passage of the 1968 Gun Control Act. It wasn't until many years later after a change in the law that we would again see small handguns imported in large numbers.

Not too long ago I was given just such a handgun. It's a Spanish made .380 semiauto pistol produced by Echasa-Echave y Arizmendi y Cia SA. The model of this particular pistol is stamped on the slide as the Basque. The word Basque is also molded into the side of the grips.

The gun was probably made back in the late '50s or early '60s, and the manufacturer has long since gone out of business. I believe the company was actually liquidated back in 1979. The pistol is basically a Spanish copy of a handgun produced by a French company known as MAB.

It's a simple blowback design with an aluminum alloy frame and steel slide. It features an exposed hammer along with a seven-shot magazine.

Echave y Arizmendi was one of many small makers of pocket pistols in the Basque region of Spain. The logo's similarity to the AyA logo was probably not an accident.

Like many other small handguns, it is a single-action. You can have the hammer down on a chambered round and to fire it you must first pull the exposed hammer back to the full cock position. The pistol can then be fired. On subsequent shots the hammer will be in the full cock position due to the movement of the slide.

It's a fairly compact little handgun and is a bit unusual because of the caliber. Most of handguns like this are in .32 ACP while this one is in the larger .380 Auto round. At the time it was made, the .32 ACP cartridge was extremely popular in Europe. In fact, it was considered to be a very suitable police round.

The reason I was given the handgun was pretty simple; it didn't work! The owner had tried to fix it and had failed. As far as he was concerned, it was just a piece of scrap with little or no value. It was just one more junk gun that was cluttering up his gun safe.

When I got the pistol, I took it apart and could immediately see a number of problems. First and foremost was the trigger bar spring. I could tell it was not original to the gun. It did not fit the recess in the frame and the ends of the spring gave evidence of having been cut with a wire cutter.

Most importantly, it was simply too long, the diameter was too large, and it did not fit the trigger bar properly. There was a machined groove on the front end of the trigger bar that appeared to be the seat for the spring. However, this homemade spring did not come even close to fitting in this slot.

My guess is that the person doing the work may not have realized the significance of this slot and how it related to the spring. I have often found that you can get valuable clues as to the shape and dimensions of missing components simply by the careful study of adjoining parts. In addition, there were scratches and dings where the spring was seated in the frame indicating that someone had installed and removed it a number of times.

This pistol is a bit unusual as it is chambered for .380 Auto rather than the more common .32 ACP cartridge. The Walther PPK-inspired lines are not a big surprise.

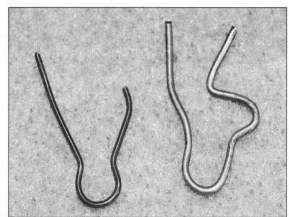

The homemade trigger bar spring (r.) did not even come close to functioning properly. Poor gunsmithing techniques just made the problems this gun had even worse.

Coffield's pistol had been subjected to some gun butchery: the original ejector had been modified with an extension. This is an excellent example of a bad repair!

Some unnamed gun plumber had at some point in the past brazed an extended tip on the ejector (l.). Though it needed some fitting, the replacement worked much better.

I also noticed the ejector had been modified. An extension had been brazed on to the ejector tip. This may have been done to make the ejector a bit longer than standard and later I found that this was indeed the case. I had seen repairs like this before in an attempt to solve ejection problems.

The feed ramp in the frame was very rough. This was not too unusual as the feed ramp is aluminum like the rest of the frame. Unlike a steel feed ramp, this feed ramp would have been subject to impact and possible distortion whenever the slide slammed the nose of a bullet into it as the round was stripped from the magazine and fed into the chamber.

Finally, one of the grip panels had been cracked and repaired with what appeared to be JB Weld. While the grips could still be used I was concerned as to just how long this repair would last.

I learned long ago that while it's possible to make missing or damaged parts, it's seldom economical to do so. Sure, if you have a lot of time you can do it but I had other things on my plate and I just wanted to get this puppy up and running as soon as possible.

Back in the '50s and '60s there was one shop that was *the* place to go when you needed parts for inexpensive imported handguns. That was Bob's Gun Shop, Box 200, Dept. SGN, Royal, Ark. 71968, telephone 501-767-1970. Over the years I've ordered parts from Bob Brown many times. When I saw this handgun, the first thing I did was check an old copy of his catalog. Sure enough, Bob had parts listed for this Spanish .380.

Since the catalog was at least five years old, I also checked his web site, www.gun-parts.com. This gave me up to date prices and let me know which items were still in stock.

I called Bob and sure enough he had the parts I needed. In talking with him I found that these were all original parts. He even had original magazines so I took advantage of that and ordered one more for this pistol. Nothing is worse than having just one magazine! Well, maybe not having any is worse!

A few days latter a package arrived with the needed parts. By the way, I decided to go ahead and order a new set of grips as well. That old repair might hold forever and then again it might break tomorrow. Since Bob had grips, I decided I better get them while I could. When you are dealing with an obsolete firearm that's no longer in production, if you have a chance to pick up parts you know you'll use, it's always best to buy them. The next time you need parts; they may well have all been sold or are no longer available.

Installation of the trigger bar spring was pretty straightforward. The only fitting I had to do was to use an India stone to slightly round the ends of the new spring. One end fitted against the trigger bar while the other bore against the magazine latch. Rounding the ends of the spring ensured that it would not catch on these parts and function smoothly.

In working with European guns like this, it is not at all unusual to have to hand-fit parts. This is es-

A properly fitted trigger bar spring bears at the front on the safety lever shaft and at the rear on the trigger bar. This is effective and economical design.

pecially true of Spanish made firearms. Normally it is just a matter of noting how the new part fits and then making a few minor adjustments. Occasionally you'll run into something a bit more involved. That happened to me with the ejector.

In examining the new ejector, I noticed that it was numbered. That to me indicated that it probably had been fitted to another gun at some point. That's not say that this was a used part. The fact is that the Spanish would often disassemble guns that were never completed or with which there were problems and sell those components as parts. Certainly, that's not the ideal situation for the guy that is making a repair but it sure helped the manufacturer to get rid of inventory!

My problem with the ejector was that the base was a bit larger front to back than the slot in the frame. That could easily be resolved with a few strokes of the file, but there was a complicating factor and that was the through hole for the pin securing it to the frame. The darn hole was in a slightly different location than that on my original ejector!

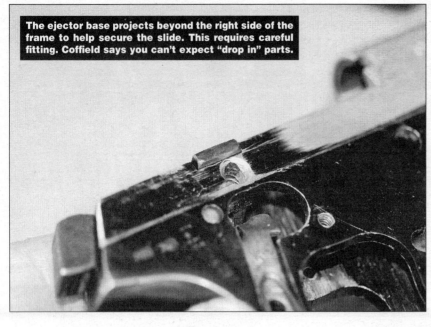

The ejector base projects beyond the right side of the frame to help secure the slide. This requires careful fitting. Coffield says you can't expect "drop in" parts.

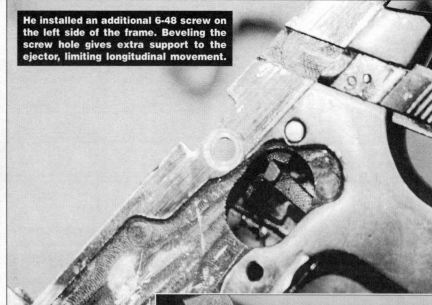

He installed an additional 6-48 screw on the left side of the frame. Beveling the screw hole gives extra support to the ejector, limiting longitudinal movement.

In fitting the ejector to the frame I tried to place the hole for the pin as close to the pinhole in the frame as possible. Since I had to remove material from the front as well as the back of the ejector base, I had some leeway here in how I positioned the ejector. I made a point of checking the fit to the frame frequently. I definitely did not want to take off too much and have a poor, sloppy fit.

Once the ejector was in place in the frame, I could tell that the pinhole was still misaligned. I could not just re-drill the hole in the part or in the frame. However, before dealing with that problem, I wanted to check the fit of another component, the magazine.

The reason I needed to check the magazine fit is that the rear of the magazine bears against the front of the ejector base. Sure enough, the original magazine was a tight fit against the ejector. I could see from the file marks on the original ejector that some metal had been removed to accommodate the magazine. All I had to do was take off the ejector and file away a few thousandths from the front of the ejector base.

I had to be very careful to not change the fit of the ejector to the frame as I did this. Once the original magazine was fitted and could be easily inserted and removed, I tried my other new magazine. Unfortunately, it stuck tight against the ejector base! Once again I had to do some additional fitting.

You never want to assume that *anything* on a handgun of this type will "drop in!" Always be prepared to do some fit-

ting. It may be minor as with this trigger bar spring or it can be fairly involved as with the ejector. With the magazines fitted, I could then finish fitting the ejector to the frame.

In measuring the pinhole in the ejector base, I found that it was just slightly smaller than the drill size for a standard 6-48 screw. It occurred to me that I could use two Weaver-style 6-48 screws to hold the ejector in place. Since the Weaver screw has a fairly large diameter head, this would allow me to move the holes in the frame to match the hole in the ejector base.

Once I did that, when I used a taper reamer to countersink the frame for the underside of the V-shaped heads of the Weaver screws. The seats for these screw heads would also eliminate the misalignment of the frame pin holes.

Use of two 6-48 screws rather than a single pin would actually provide more and stronger support for the ejector base. Not only was the diameter of the screw shank larger, I also had the holding power of the vastly larger screw head. In addition, the taper of the V-shaped Weaver screws helped to provide more support for the ejector base. I had absolutely no worries about the ejector block pulling out during use.

The tops of the Weaver screws were slightly curved or rounded. In order to be sure the top of the screws did not interfere with the slide, I ground down the screw heads and polished them. This removed only a few thousandths and did not compromise the strength or holding power of the screws.

I checked clearance between the inside of the slide and the screw heads by coating them with Dykem and installing the slide. The first time I did this. I found I had some contact on the screw heads which made movement of the slide very stiff. The height of the screw heads was adjusted and this problem was quickly resolved. The slide then moved easily back and forth on the frame.

Once the ejector base was in place, the only thing left to do was polish the feed ramp. This is one of those simple jobs that could easily lead to more problems. When working with aluminum, you have to keep in mind that it is much softer than steel and you can quickly take off too much if you're not careful.

When Coffield went to install a new ejector provided by Bob's Gun Shop, he discovered the pinholes were misaligned. So he replaced the pin with a 6-48 screw.

The magazine safety is a pivoting sear block that prevents firing until a magazine is inserted in the gun. These are common on European autoloading pistols.

I used a fine Cratex polishing point along with my Dremel tool. All I wanted to do was smooth out the surface. There was no need for a super high polish. Also by using this rubberized fine polishing point I lessened the chance of taking off too much metal.

With the ramp polished, the repair part of the project was basically completed. I did a bit more work cleaning up the odd burr or rough surface, applied Sentry Solutions lubricating grease to the inside of the slide and around the barrel under the recoil spring. The gun was then reassembled for the final feeding check.

Many years ago in my shop I did a very foolish and stupid thing. I was working on a little American made .25 ACP pistol. I had completed the repair and needed to check to make sure it fed properly. I had a test fire room in the back of the shop but I was too busy to go back there, or so I thought.

Also, I didn't have any dummy ammo so I figured that I could use some live rounds. All I needed to do was just keep my finger off the trigger. I bet you know where this is going!

Sure enough, when I pulled the slide back and released it on that live round, the gun fired. Fortunately I had the pistol pointed at the wall behind my bench, which was concrete. Unfortunately the bullet hit a bottle of Birchwood Casey Stock Stain before it hit the concrete. Do you have any idea how much damage a little .25ACP bullet will do to a small plastic bottle filled with a liquid at a range of about 10 inches? Let me tell you; a lot.

I blew stock stain all over my bench, my tools, and myself. My partner, Wayne Spears, heard the shot and came running back into the shop. He saw me standing there with a gun in my hand and a red liquid dripping off my face. He just knew I had shot myself.

When I finally got Wayne calmed down, he started laughing. My partner, my good buddy couldn't stop laughing! Nope, there was no sympathy shown that day or for many days thereafter. Anybody that came into the shop was treated to a greatly exaggerated version of this minor incident, complete with a tour of the shop and my bench. To say that it was embarrassing would be a gross understatement.

I'm now a lot older and maybe a little smarter. I do not check the functioning of a firearm with live ammo! *Never!* In this case I contacted Brownells Inc., and ordered some .380 Auto action proving dummies. These are cartridges with no primer or powder designed specifically to function through the action of a firearm. They are made just like a regular round with the same weight, length, and materials but cannot be fired.

Most European pocket pistols chamber the .32 ACP cartridge (l.), but this autoloader chambered the somewhat larger .380 Auto cartridge with a 95-grain FMJ bullet.

Some consider the .380 Auto to be at the bottom of the list of acceptable personal defense cartridges. Coffield says that FMJ bullets are the way to go here.

Brownells offers a wide selection of action proving dummies. In fact, I think they offer more different calibers than any one else. If you need action proving dummies, contact Brownells Inc., 200 South Front St., Dept. SGN, Montezuma, IA 50171, telephone 800-741-0015. They'll take care of you.

The action proving dummies cycled perfectly through the gun without a hitch. That left only a quick trip to the range to test the gun with live ammo.

There are all sorts of different types of .380 ammo on the market. If I were going to put this gun to serious use, I would spend a lot of time testing various types of hollowpoint ammo. I would be looking not only for performance but also, most importantly, for feeding reliability.

In this case, I picked up a box of standard Winchester .380 ball ammo from my local gun shop. I just wanted to make darn sure the gun functioned safely and reliably. As I expected, it did exactly that at the range. It emptied both magazines without any problems. While it would never by my first choice for a concealed carry or house gun, it would work in a pinch.

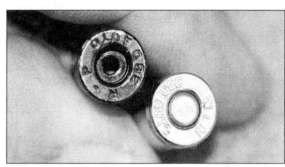

The action proving dummy (l.) has no powder or primer and has a dark color to make it easy to spot. The shinier live round has a primer that's readily visible.

It was an interesting project and there are a lot of guns of this general type still out there. Don't be surprised if you run into one from time to time. Most of the time, they can be fixed. It just takes a little patience, a little planning, and knowing where you can find the right parts.

It only took a couple of hours of work and modest investment in parts. In return I ended up with a fairly decent handgun. All in all, it's not too bad for a gun that was "unrepairable"!   ◉

The aluminum feed ramp was battered from years of use. Coffield had to polish it lightly with a Cratex point to remove roughness which had caused feeding malfunctions.

When you put a pocket pistol like this one back into operation, you're not looking to win Camp Perry. If it shoots to the sights at 15 feet, you're doing fine.

Dummy Up!
Part I
The Sten Mk. 2

In the first of a four-part series; Matthews shows how to turn a parts kit and some scrap steel into a display piece you'll be proud to show off.

By Steven Matthews

Matthews says a Sten dummy is the perfect place to start gunsmithing military-style guns, as the original gun was made using relatively crude manufacturing methods.

I f you've been reading SGN for the last couple years, you have probably read some of my articles on building many of the more popular semi-auto military firearms available to the hobbyist today.

There is another type of military collectible that can be also economically built: dummy or display guns. These are non-functional items not legally classified as firearms. They are non-guns.

Why would anyone want one? For some cost is an issue: real guns are expensive. Others live in localities that restrict ownership of military-style firearms, especially full-autos. Some just don't want the responsibility.

Unfortunately there are also some who have spouses who proclaim "we aren't going to have one of those things in our home." For those who would still like a little piece of military history, dummy guns can be an option. They do have their advantages. They are considerably cheaper than the real thing. They are pretty much unrestricted if built correctly.

Since they are non functional, you don't have to worry about who will suffer from their misuse if lost or stolen. For those who like to display their "toys" openly, it makes more sense to display an inexpensive replica than a very expensive original. For those just getting started in hobby gunsmithing, they offer good practice before advancing to building real guns.

Since they are non-functional, they are easy to build. They don't have to be finely fitted to function right because they don't function at all! All they have to do is look like the real thing. While I have a nice collection of real guns, I also have several

dummy guns. I look as them as "knickknacks" for firearms collectors. They fit right in with my model warplanes, inert artillery shells, and other displayed military items.

This article starts a series that will cover building dummy guns using widely available surplus parts kits. Since they will have some real gun parts, I will look at the legal requirements to keep them classified as non-firearms. I will use construction methods and tools available to the average home workshop owner. A few items may have to be hired out but they will be procedures that can be done cheaply.

The easiest dummy to build is the British Sten Mk 2 of World War II fame, thanks to its extremely simple design. The Sten gun was the most crudely assembled and finished gun widely fielded by a major military power. This crudeness

means even those with limited skills can make a reasonable representation.

It is also very inexpensive to make. The dummy Sten featured in this article cost a grand total of $45 (excluding finishing sup-

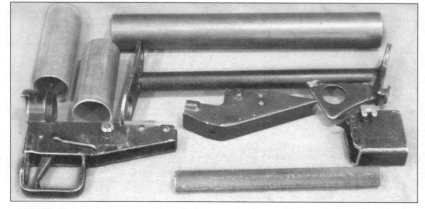

Some readily-available Sten Mk 3 parts, some steel round stock and tubing are most of what's required to make this project. Simple hand and power tools are needed.

For realism, an ejection port and magazine opening are formed in the solid receiver. Drilling holes to remove material will leave less to file or grind by hand.

The dummy receiver features an ejection port opening, a hole for a dummy barrel and a relief cut for the barrel shroud. The rear needs drilling for the stock plunger.

plies). I found an incomplete Sten Mk 3 parts set at a gun show for $30. The Mk 3 parts sets are less expensive than the Mk 2 sets and can be adapted to look like a Mk 2.

That was perfect for this project, since very few of the original gun parts will be used. If you don't buy a complete parts set, you can get by with the following Mk 3 parts—trigger housing with cover, trigger, trigger pin, buttstock, magazine housing, magazine, safety/selector button and charging handle.

You have no need for anything in the bolt group or fire control group except for the trigger. Add to this a 12-inch piece of 1½-inch diameter steel round stock, an 8-inch piece of 3/4-inch steel round stock, a 3½-inch piece of 1½-inch internal diameter tubing, a 4½-inch piece of 1½-inch O.D. tubing and you have most of the parts you will need to make a dummy Sten.

The first part to make is the dummy receiver. You cannot make a duplicate of the original submachine gun receiver. To do so would be creating an unregistered machine gun under BATFE rules. The penalties for possessing an unregistered machine gun are *severe*, so don't even think about making a close copy of the original.

The receiver for this dummy gun must not be "readily restorable" to machine gun configuration. In fact since we are making a dummy gun it must not even be readily restorable to any form that would allow it to fire even a single round.

Although there are several methods to achieve this goal, the simplest and cheapest is to use a solid piece of round steel stock to form a solid receiver. This does make it rather heavy, but it certainly makes it not readily restorable to firearm status.

Receiver Fabrication

Making the receiver is the most difficult part of the project. To make it realistic, put an oval hole all the way through the round stock to replicate an ejection port and magazine opening.

At a point centered on the round stock and 1¼ inches back from the front, draw a rectangle 1⅞x7/8 inches. The inside of this rectangle will be removed. A milling machine is great for this job, but it can be done with a drill press and files.

Solidly secure your parts in a strong drill press vise before drilling. At each end of the rectangle, drill 3/4" holes all the way through. Drill in several size steps to prevent overworking a small drill press. Between these large holes, drill a series of closely spaced small holes across the top and bottom.

Drill with progressively larger size bits until the hole edges meet and then knock out the center. Drilling many small holes like this is like sawing with a drill press; it's just being done one small hole at a time. Smooth up the edges with a file or hand grinder.

Now you need a hole drilled all the way through to the opening in the front of the round stock for your dummy barrel. For this project, the hole needs to be 3/4". A lathe, mill or drill press can be used to do this job. Whichever method you use, be sure the hole is drilled squarely.

A piece of 3/4" round steel stock will serve for the dummy barrel. Drill 3/8" holes in either end to make it look more realistic. Nothing "readily restorable" here!

A relief cut or groove needs to be formed on the front of the receiver to allow a shroud to slide over it. A lathe is best for this job, but since most don't have lathes, it can be ground with a bench grinder or filed by hand.

Draw a line all the way around the receiver 3/4" back from the front and grind down the material in front of the line so that your tubing will slide over the front of the receiver. It doesn't have to look very good, since it will be covered later by the magazine housing.

Now is the time to turn our attention to the rear of the receiver. The Sten buttstock is retained by a spring-loaded plunger. Drill a 3/4" hole into the center of the receiver for this plunger. You only have to drill in about 2 inches, but since I wanted to remove some of the material to reduce weight, I drilled in about 6 inches.

Now it's time to add a hole for the fake bolt handle. The handle in my parts kit was 1/2" so that's the size hole I drilled. The hole can be drilled wherever it looks good to you; placement is not important. One other feature I added at this point to increase realism was a fake bolt handle slot in front of the handle.

I milled a shallow half-inch slot about 4 inches in front of the handle. If you want this feature and don't have a milling

machine, it can be added by rough grinding with a hand grinder and then finished up with a Dremel type grinder. This finishes the receiver work.

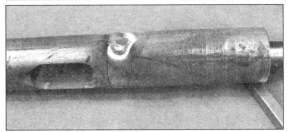

Slide the barrel into the front of the dummy receiver and weld it into place, making sure it is straight. The barrel shroud then can be plug welded into position.

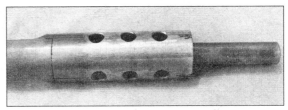

Drill ventilation holes into the barrel shroud. This can be done before or after installation. Nine ventilation holes are evenly spaced 120° apart around the shroud.

The ejector is an integral part of the magazine housing on a Mk3 Sten gun. Since it has no function on a dummy gun, it can be cut off to allow easier installation.

The magazine housing collar can be made from a piece of 1½-inch I.D. tubing. The opening cut in it needs to correspond with the appropriate cutouts in the dummy receiver.

Use a magazine in the housing to align it with the cutouts in the receiver. Then place the housing on the collar at 90°. Make sure it is straight before welding.

Dummy Barrel Fabrication

Since this is a dummy gun with a dummy receiver, it might as well have a dummy barrel. The barrel material was an 8-inch piece of 3/4" rod. For realism, 3/8" holes were drilled into each end to make it look more like a barrel. That's all there was to making a dummy barrel.

Remove the remnants of the original receiver by grinding out the spot welds. Once these are removed, the trigger housing will slide right onto the dummy receiver.

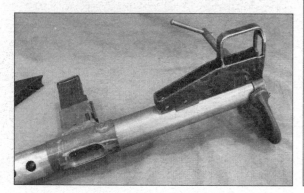

Locate the trigger housing on the dummy receiver perpendicular to the magazine housing. Once it is located correctly, make three spot welds to hold it in position.

Once you're sure the housing is properly positioned on the collar, tack weld the pieces together. Finish welding can wait until the assembly is attached to the receiver.

Once the magazine housing is completely welded to the collar, use a single plug weld at the bottom to lock the assembly onto the receiver. Be sure the angle is right.

Magazine Housing Fabrication

Since a Mk 2 magazine housing is much more expensive than a Mk 3 housing, I used the cheaper one to duplicate the look of the Mk 2 housing. Use the 3½-inch piece of 1½-inch I.D. tubing (it must slide over the 1½-inch O.D. receiver) to make a collar for the housing. Cut out sections on each side to duplicate the cutouts on the receiver for the ejection port and magazine opening. Cut them a little undersize and then slide it on the receiver to match them to the receiver cutouts for final sizing.

Take your magazine housing and butt it up against the collar. Use a magazine in the housing and through the cutout in the receiver to get things aligned correctly. Place a few small tack welds between the collar and housing to locate the parts. Do not completely weld the assembly at this point.

The Sten's buttstock is retained by a plunger in the rear of the receiver. That part is easily made using a piece of 3/4" round steel stock with a 5/8" diameter stub.

Barrel Shroud Fabrication

The barrel shroud is made from a piece of 1½-inch O.D. tubing 4½ inches long. Nine ventilation holes are drilled in the shroud, are spaced 120° apart. The first of each group is located 1 inch back (to the center, not the edge) from the front. The rest are spaced at 1 inch center to center.

Buttstock Plunger Fabrication

The plunger that retains the buttstock can be made on a lathe or ground by hand. It can even be filed by hand. It is simply a piece of 3/4" round stock with a 5/8" diameter stub formed on the rear. This stub needs to be about 1/4" in length.

Assembly

Now that all the pieces are made, it's time to assemble them. The preferred method is by arc welding, either MIG or stick. If you don't have a welder, the parts could be attached by brazing or soldering. Take your dummy barrel and insert it into the receiver so that it is flush with the inside of the ejection port opening.

Place a couple small welds on each side to lock it in place. Be sure before welding that it is aligned properly, so that when the shroud is installed, the barrel will be centered. Attach the barrel shroud by sliding it into place on the front of the receiver.

Before welding, make sure one set of holes it straight up. Align it so that the barrel is centered. Weld it in place and then grind off the welds so that the magazine housing can slide over the seam. Take your partially completed magazine housing and slide it over the receiver and align the cutout in the housing and receiver.

Use a magazine locked in place to align the assembly, and then remove the magazine before welding. Once it's aligned, finish welding the housing to the collar. Place a small spot weld between the housing and receiver to lock it in place.

The trigger housing can now be attached to the receiver. If all remnants of the old receiver have been previously removed, the housing should slide right over the rear of the receiver. Slide it on until the rear of the housing is flush with the receiver.

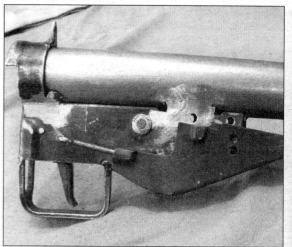

The Sten's trigger is retained by the trigger pin, which in turn is retained by the trigger housing cover. The safety/selector button is retained by a cotter pin.

Locate it perpendicular to the magazine housing and clamp it in place.

View it from several angles to get it exactly right. Once located, weld it in place with a couple small welds on the remaining housing tabs on each side. A small weld at the top in front of the sight can also be made. This will duplicate the original construction.

The bolt handle can be inserted into its hole and welded in place. I welded from the inside for a good appearance. The trigger is inserted into the housing and held in place with the trigger pin. Since the trigger is non-functional it was simply tack welded inside the housing in a convenient position.

You now can slide the trigger housing cover into place. The buttstock plunger installs in the hole in the rear of the receiver. A 3/4" spring will tension it. Size the length of your spring for your particular hole depth.

Press the plunger in behind the spring and slide the buttstock up into place. Once the stock is fully seated in the housing, the plunger will snap into the hole in the buttstock and lock it in place. The safety /selector button is installed in the trigger housing and is retained by a common cotter pin. It does look crude but it is the way it was originally done.

The last thing to be done on this dummy gun is attaching a sight. The original Sten sight was simply a "V" dovetailed into the top of the receiver. Once in position it was tack welded in place. I fabricated a sight from scrap steel and welded it in place.

Dummy Magazine Fabrication

For this gun I wanted a realistic dummy magazine. Since Sten magazines can be had for less than $5, I used a surplus magazine. To make the magazine a "dummy" I removed the spring. I welded the follower in place through the body to allow about four dummy rounds to fit tightly in place. The floorplate was then welded on.

Final Finishing

After all parts were assembled, all the welds were ground down and deep scratches ground smooth. The Sten featured a very crude finish, so you don't want to smooth things up too much. This is one gun that needs to look rather rough to look original.

Original Stens featured several finishes over their production lives. They were blued, Parkerized, and crudely painted. To duplicate a Parkerized finish *easily*, I finished the dummy gun with Brownells Aluma-Hyde II.

This is an aerosol spray epoxy finish available in several colors. It can be applied to metals, wood and plastics. Brownells conveniently had a color called "Parkerizing gray," so that's what I ordered. I also ordered some matte black Aluma-Hyde II to add some highlights to the gun.

Before applying the finish, I abrasive blasted the gun to increase adhesion. This is not required for this dummy gun project, but it will result in a more durable finish if you are using it on a real firearm.

Aluma-Hyde applies just like any spray paint, so it can be applied by almost anyone. After spraying according to the instructions, it needs to be left for several days for a full cure. I sped the process up some by gently baking it after it air dried. I baked it at 120° for three to four hours. This is not in the instructions, so bake at your own risk!

Once assembled, the gun looked better than most original Stens. For originality, you want it to look rather crude because that was one of the gun's most noticeable characteristics. Stens were made under the most grueling wartime conditions and were meant to work, not look, good. This project came out as a very reasonable replica of the full-auto Sten submachine gun and was very inexpensive to make. Display guns like this can be fine companions to your collection of real firearms.

Firearms Finishing Supplies
Brownells, 200 S. Front St., Dept. SGN, Montezuma, Iowa, 50171, 1-800-741-0015, www.brownells.com

Disclaimer

Under federal firearms regulations a firearm is defined as any weapon which is designed or may be readily converted to expel a projectile by the action of an explosive. The frame or receiver of any such device is also considered to be a firearm.

A solid piece of material only externally shaped as a firearm would not be considered a firearm under this definition. A non-functioning firearm with only minor modifications such as having the bolt welded shut would, however, still be considered a firearm since it would be readily restorable.

Dummy guns, while containing many real gun parts, must not be readily restorable. This is why so many modifications must be made when utilizing real gun parts to make a dummy. The frame or receiver must be made or modified so that it is not readily convertible to firearm status. Many internal parts must also be modified to prevent them from performing their original function. Various methods are used to accomplish these goals.

The methods used in this article series are the author's best attempt to comply with these regulations and create items that are considered non-firearms. These methods should not be considered legal advice. Neither the author or SHOTGUN NEWS assume any responsibility for the legal classification of these projects. Before building any dummy/display only/non functional/ non-firearms the builder should verify that the project complies with all federal, state and local regulations.

Due to ever changing rules and regulations the definition of what constitutes a firearm may change. It is in the builder's best interest to verify the latest rules on making non-firearms. The builder should verify that the particular project and build procedures result in a non-firearm classification. For federal firearms regulations contact the BATFE.

Contact info: Bureau of Alcohol, Tobacco, Firearms, and Explosives, Firearms Technology Branch, 244 Needy Rd., Martinsburg, W. Va., 25401, www.atf.gov

Ask the Gunsmith

By Reid Coffield

COLT JR. EJECTION

Q *I have an old Colt Junior .25ACP handgun. In looking at it I could not find an ejector yet when I fire it, it ejects the fired cases quite well. Am I missing something or more to the point, is my gun missing something?*

A Like a number of handguns, the Colt Junior did not have a separate ejector. Instead, the firing pin tip protruded through the face of the slide and acted as the ejector as the slide was moved to the rear of the frame. It was a simple and effective design. The only problem with this for me is the idea of the firing pin contacting a live primer if you needed to eject a live round. For that reason, I would much prefer a design that utilized an independent ejector.

Like many pistols, especially .25s, the Colt Junior did not have a separate ejector. The firing pin protruded through the face of the slide and acted as the ejector.

INDEX MARK

Q *In your articles you some times mention an index mark. Just what is an index mark?*

A When you have two parts that go together, you will often have marks on the individual pieces. These marks when aligned are used to indicate the optimal positioning of the two components. For example, it is very common to have a small line on both the barrel and receiver of a rifle that are positioned opposite one another and often actually touch. If the barrel is removed and then reinstalled, it is easy to make sure it is properly positioned or "indexed" by checking the position of these two index marks. If they are aligned with one another, the barrel and receiver are assembled correctly.

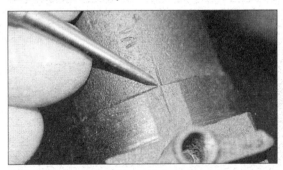

If you look closely at the tip of the pointer, you can see the index or witness marks used to align the barrel and receiver on this 1917 Enfield. These are especially important at the factory.

18-INCH .30-'06

Q *I have an older used Remington Model 700 rifle in .30-'06 that I am thinking of converting to a carbine. If I cut the barrel back to 18 inches, I know I will lose a bit of velocity. Are there any other negative consequences that I should know about?*

A If you cut the barrel back to 18 inches, the most noticeable negative effect will be a major increase in muzzle blast. With a short barrel, the .30-'06 cartridge can be very uncomfortable to shoot or even be around when someone else is firing it.

Dummy Up!
Part II

Last month, Matthews got this series started with the crude, but easy-to-build, Sten. Here he tries something with racy Italian styling.

Beretta 38A Submachine Gun

By Steven Matthews

Last month (11/20 issue) I showed how to make a dummy Sten gun in the first of a four-part series on building dummies. I started with the Sten because it is the simplest, and crude construction actually makes it more realistic. This month we will move on to something a little more elegant, the Beretta Model 1938 SMG.

The Model 1938 or 38A is well known in other parts of the world but obscure here. It was a very successful design used extensively by both the Italians and Germans in World War II. It was made into the early 1950s. As is the case with most well-made guns, they were sold to less affluent countries after they have been removed from front-line service so the Beretta 38A may be encountered just about anywhere.

It was made with old-world craftsmanship using finely machined parts and excellent fit and finish. It featured closed-bolt operation and selective fire with an unusual two-trigger configuration, one for semi-auto and the other for full auto. By today's standards it was very long and heavy for a 9mm subgun, but in its time it was considered a first-class modern weapon. It was modernized and simplified and evolved into later models that were made well into the '60s and '70s.

Federally registered and transferable examples of this gun are rare and very expensive, which places it out of reach of most. There is however a way you can have an inexpensive representation of this gun, build a dummy/display version.

IO, Inc., of Monroe, N.C., has very reasonably priced parts kits available that can be combined with a solid receiver to make a dummy. I thought I would like a display model, so I ordered a parts set from them. The parts kit received was in typical military surplus condition, well used but not all that bad for a 50-year-old military gun that may have seen decades of use.

Very little finish remained, but the parts were in decent mechanical condition. The kit came with the torch-cut receiver sections and a deactivated barrel. The barrel was deactivated by welding the chamber shut and drilling holes in the bore. With the parts kit, self-made dummy receiver and some parts fabrication, you can make a nice display gun.

Last month, Matthews showed how to make a dummy gun from a Sten parts kit. This time he takes on something a bit more challenging; the Beretta 38A submachine gun.

Dummy Receiver Fabrication

At a glance, the Beretta 38A looks to be a "tube" gun like a Sten or M3, but its receiver is not simply a tube spot-welded to a frame. The receiver does feature a tubular shape above the wood line, but it is actually a finely machined one-piece part that extends well down into the stock.

The lower unexposed portion houses the fire control group and magazine housing. Fortunately, since we are building a non-functional dummy gun, we do not need this and can get by with a solid piece of round steel for a dummy receiver. A piece of 1⅜x11¼" cold-rolled round stock will work fine.

This piece of steel will create a solid receiver that cannot readily be converted to firearm status. Being solid, though, it is very heavy. To lighten it somewhat I drilled a 3/4" hole in the rear about 6 inches deep. This removed considerable weight.

This drilling can be done on a lathe, milling machine or drill press. If you don't mind the weight, this procedure can be bypassed. To mount the dummy receiver to the stock, drill and thread holes in the bottom of the round stock. Install the trigger guard in the stock.

Lay the round stock in the receiver channel. Leave about 1/4" space at the front for the barrel, which will be installed later.

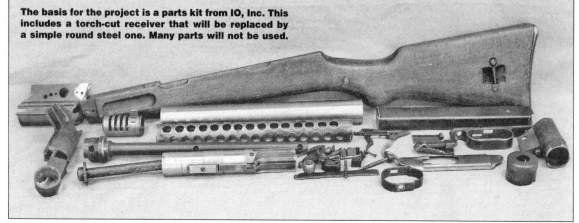

The basis for the project is a parts kit from IO, Inc. This includes a torch-cut receiver that will be replaced by a simple round steel one. Many parts will not be used.

First mark the location for the ejection port, using the stock as a guide. The port can then be milled out or, if you are patient, ground out with hand power tools.

Saw off the barrel threads and then square and bevel the stub. Bevel the front of the dummy receiver to provide a weld groove. Weld the two parts, then grind clean.

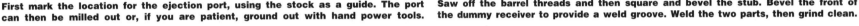

Clamp the dummy receiver to the stock so it won't move. Use long transfer punches through the holes in the trigger guard to mark hole locations for the mounting screws. Be sure your punches are straight with the stock so you get the holes in the proper place on the receiver.

Once the holes are marked, remove the round stock and drill the holes 13/64" and then tap them 1/4"-20. Obtain some 1/4"-20

machine screws and cut them to the correct length to use for mounting the solid receiver to the stock.

Then a false ejection port can be drawn out on the round stock. On the Beretta 38A this port is on the left side, opposite where you might expect to find it. About 3/4" back from the front of the receiver, draw a rectangle about 7/8x2". Use the ejection port cut out on the stock as a guide to help get it where it looks right.

Either machine or grind out this rectangle about 1/8" deep to simulate an opening in the receiver. This feature does add a lot of work but it really adds to the realistic look when the gun is done.

The Beretta 38A receiver features a charging handle on the right side of the receiver just above the wood line. This handle rides in a raised protrusion or rib and is about 9 inches long. There is an easy way to make this part, though it's not especially authentic.

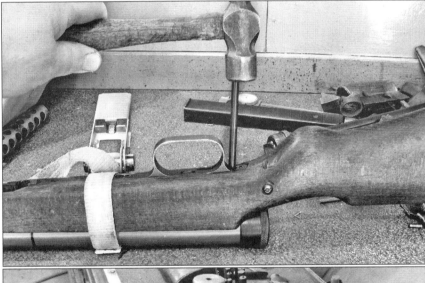

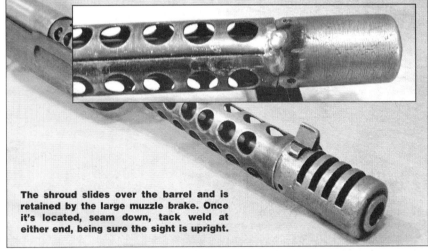

The shroud slides over the barrel and is retained by the large muzzle brake. Once it's located, seam down, tack weld at either end, being sure the sight is upright.

Clamp the trigger guard to the stock and use transfer punches to mark the spots for the guard screws. Then drill and tap 1/4-20 holes, ensuring they are square to the work.

The rear of the dummy receiver is closed off with a cap and plug. Drill the rear of the receiver to reduce weight, then tack weld the cap in place; no need to thread.

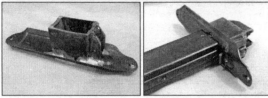

The magazine housing is torch cut and has to be welded back into one piece. Then cut it off and use a magazine to align it with the guard plate. Then weld it in place.

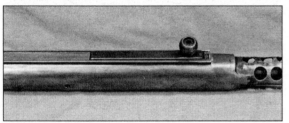

The charging handle rides on a rib on the right side of the receiver. It then can be bolted in position. Make the rib more realistic by milling down its center.

Take a piece of 5/8x1/8x9" piece of flat steel and simply solder it to the side of the receiver using a propane torch. Use the cut out in the stock as a locating guide. A more realistic looking part can be made by using a piece of 5/8x3/16x9-inch steel flat stock and either filing or milling a shallow 3/8" groove centered along its length.

Matthews used a Brownells set to tap holes for the 6-48 screws that hold down the rear sight. Getting these properly located is vital to building a realistic dummy.

Since there's no fire control assembly, Matthew just spot-welded the safety lever to the dummy receiver. The stock covers the welds, making it look as it should.

After the groove is cut, solder it to the receiver. Whichever type you use, be sure to roughen up the solder joint area with sandpaper to help the solder to adhere better. After either rib is attached, drill and tap a 1/4"-20 hole about an inch back from the front and centered on the rib.

Remove the bolt from the charging handle (if installed) and drill the hole in the handle to 1/4". Thin along the length of this handle to 3/8" by filing off the protrusions on the sides. Use a 1/4" machine screw through this hole to attach the handle to the raised rib.

If you used the rib with the groove, one bolt will hold the handle since it is in a groove. If you went with the flat rib you will have to add a small screw, rivet or pin to the other end to lock the handle in place.

To complete the receiver, install the original end cap. Grind out the protrusions inside the cap so that it will slide over the

The lack of a fire control assembly also means there's nothing for the triggers to engage, so Matthews just welded them into position for a realistic appearance.

end of the receiver. Before welding the cap in place, cut off the plunger on the end of the recoil spring assembly.

Grind it flat and place it inside to fill in the hole in the cap. Slide the cap onto the receiver tightly and weld it in place. A small weld on the bottom of the receiver at the small notch on the cap will be sufficient. This finishes the dummy receiver portion of the project.

Barrel, Barrel Shroud, and Muzzle Brake Installation

The barrel of the Beretta 38A screws into the front of the receiver on a real gun but I found an easier method since the receiver is solid. Saw off the barrel threads. Face off the end so it is square. Be sure the face of your dummy receiver is square also. Grind a small bevel on each piece to form a weld groove. Align the barrel and receiver evenly and squarely and then weld them together.

Grind off any excess weld flush with the receiver. The barrel shroud slides over the barrel and is retained by the muzzle brake, which screws onto the front of the barrel. Orient the shroud so the seam is on the bottom. You may have to trim the shroud some to get the sight on the muzzle brake pointed straight up when it's tight. Once everything is aligned, place a small tack weld on each end of the shroud to lock it in place.

Rear Sight Installation

The rear sight is attached to the receiver with two 6-48 screws. It is located about 4 inches back from the front of the receiver. Disassemble the base from the sight by pushing down and rearward on the sight to get it to pop out of its groove. I simply

Since the dummy receiver has no opening for the magazine, that part must be shortened to lock in place. Mathews reshaped the feed lips to accept dummy rounds.

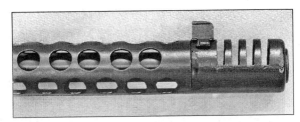

The impressively large muzzle brake is one of the Model 38A's interesting and unusual features. Whether a 9mm really needed a unit like this is debatable, of course.

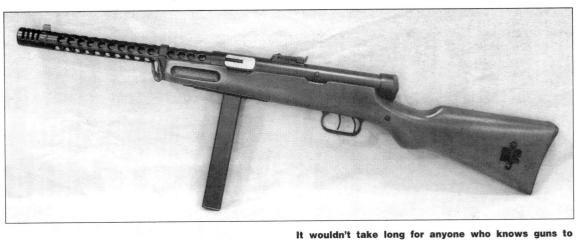

It wouldn't take long for anyone who knows guns to figure out it's non-functional, but the dummy Beretta is an attractive display piece and fun project.

laid the sight base on the top of the receiver and aligned it so it looked good and then marked the hole location.

The holes were then drilled and tapped for 6-48 scope base screws with my Brownells drill and tap set. This drill and tap set is especially designed for small gun-sized screws. Once the base was installed, the sight was re-installed.

Trigger Assembly

The dual Beretta 38A triggers are part of the original fire control group that was housed in the full-auto receiver. Since this is a dummy gun, the receiver has no provisions for it. The triggers are there simply for looks and do not function in any way. I simply tack welded them to the trigger guard and then cut off the top halves.

Magazine Housing

The magazine housing on this gun is part of the torch-cut receiver. As a result of BATFE cutting specifications, the housing featured a cut right down through the housing. There is, however, enough material left to fabricate an improvised housing. Cut off the magazine housing pieces flush with the round part of the cut receiver. Grind off any slag or melted metal so the pieces are smooth. Lay the pieces out on a flat surface and clamp them in place.

Use a 38A magazine between the pieces to space the pieces where they should be. Do not fit the pieces too close as welding will shrink the assembly somewhat. Once the pieces are spaced, you will weld the pieces together to form a new housing. Place a piece of copper or aluminum under the gap between the pieces and weld in the gaps. The weld will not stick to the copper or aluminum and will allow you to fill in the gaps without a lot of excess weld running into the inside of the housing. Grind off any excess weld when done.

Take this assembly and place it flush against the inside of the sheet metal cover that surrounds the magazine opening in the stock. Use a magazine to align the two pieces and when aligned clamp them in place. Once aligned, solder the two pieces togeth-

er. After the pieces are soldered together, install the magazine latch and spring. This assembly will attach to the stock with two wood screws just as the original.

Since our dummy receiver is solid there is no opening for the magazine in the receiver and the magazine must be shortened to lock in place. Cut off the top 3/4" of the magazine and reform the lips to hold in dummy cartridges. It doesn't have to work, it just has to look good.

Safety Lever

The Beretta 38A has a small safety lever on the left side. Since there is no lower section of original receiver, this lever can just be welded onto the round dummy receiver. A couple small spot welds below the wood line will work fine.

Finishing the Project

The original finish on the gun was bluing. Due to the fact that parts were soldered on and bluing won't take on solder, it was unsuitable for this project. The same goes for Parkerizing. I still wanted a black finish, so I decided to go with a spray and baked-on finish. I chose Brownells Teflon/Moly Oven Cure Gun Finish (part No. 083-049-016).

This high-quality finish is extremely durable. It greatly exceeds the need for a dummy gun but I am a big fan of these high tech sprayed and baked finishes, so that's what I decided to use. Brownells Teflon/Moly finish is easy to apply. You just abrasive blast, clean, spray and bake. If you want to take the cheapie route you can just spray paint the project.

For the wood I just sanded out the dents and dings and stained it. A coat of satin lacquer sealed things up. Lacquer is especially useful on oily military gunstocks since it dries so fast that the

underlying oil doesn't get into the finish as it does with slow-drying finishes that seam to draw out the oil.

Once everything was refinished the project was re-assembled. While close examination by a knowledgeable person will reveal it to be a dummy, it does look very realistic. I even cut out a small piece of aluminum and placed it in the false ejection port to simulate a bolt inside the gun. Total cost to build this project should be about $125 excluding finishing supplies. Some people build model cars or airplanes but firearms enthusiast can build display guns. It is good practice for making real guns and a rewarding experience, so give it a try. ◉

Disclaimer

Under federal firearms regulations a firearm is defined as any weapon which is designed or may be readily converted to expel a projectile by the action of an explosive. The frame or receiver of any such device is also considered to be a firearm.

A solid piece of material only externally shaped as a firearm would not be considered a firearm under this definition. A non-functioning firearm with only minor modifications such as having the bolt welded shut would, however, still be considered a firearm since it would be readily restorable.

Dummy guns, while containing many real gun parts, must not be readily restorable. This is why so many modifications must be made when utilizing real gun parts to make a dummy. The frame or receiver must be made or modified so that it is not readily convertible to firearm status. Many internal parts must also be modified to prevent them from performing their original function. Various methods are used to accomplish these goals.

The methods used in this article series are the author's best attempt to comply with these regulations and create items that are considered non-firearms. These methods should not be considered legal advice. Neither the author or SHOTGUN NEWS assume any responsibility for the legal classification of these projects. Before building any dummy/display only/non functional/ non-firearms the builder should verify that the project complies with all federal, state and local regulations.

Due to ever changing rules and regulations the definition of what constitutes a firearm may change. It is in the builder's best interest to verify the latest rules on making non-firearms. The builder should verify that the particular project and build procedures result in a non-firearm classification. For federal firearms regulations contact the BATFE.

Contact info: Bureau of Alcohol, Tobacco, Firearms, and Explosives, Firearms Technology Branch, 244 Needy Rd., Martinsburg, W. Va., 25401, www.atf.gov

Matthews used an airbrush to apply Brownells' Teflon/Moly Gun Finish. After air drying and baking at 300° it is very durable, and is an easy alternative to bluing.

Dummy Up!
Part III
Finnish Suomi m/31

He's assembled a couple of easy projects; now Matthews shows you something a bit more challenging in building a dummy gun.

By Steven Matthews

I started this series of stories about building dummy guns with the Sten Mk 2 (11/20/07), as it's a relatively easy build and if it comes out a bit crude, that just means it's true to the original. I followed that with the Beretta 38A (12/20/07), which was a bit more elegant in appearance and required a bit more building skill.

This month, I'm going to take on the m/31 Suomi submachine gun from Finland. Peter Kokalis covered its history and design in the last issue (1/10), so I'll get quickly to the building.

Registered and transferable examples of this fine gun are few and far between and priced accordingly, which puts it out of reach for most working-class military gun collectors. So building a dummy is an attractive option for those who would like to have one.

Parts Kit

One of the best parts of building a Suomi is that parts kits are very inexpensive: about $60. I found excellent condition Suomi parts kits being offered by Cope's Distributing of Pitsburg, Ohio for $59.95. As soon as I saw that number, I decided this would make a good prospect for a dummy gun project. I called and ordered a kit from Cope's and am pleased to report that the kit I got was in the advertised excellent condition. It must have been

obtained from a new or little-used gun. Metal finish was about 95%, and the wood was excellent, too.

In a business where product is commonly overrated, it's nice to deal with people that honestly rate their offerings. Combining

The Finnish m/31 Suomi is a relatively uncommon, but influential submachine gun. Parts kits are cheap right now, making it the perfect basis for making a dummy gun.

this excellent kit with a well-made dummy receiver was going to result in a nice-looking wall hanger.

Dummy Receiver Fabrication

The Suomi appears to be a common "tube gun" but really is much more than that. The receiver is finely machined and extends well down into the stock. The upper tube part is just what is exposed above the wood line. The lower portion contains the fire control group, charging handle and magazine housing. To duplicate this lower portion would be difficult and isn't really needed on a dummy gun, since our version will have no need for a fire control group.

By using a piece of solid steel round stock and salvaging some parts off of the BATFE-mandated demilled receiver that comes with the kit, you can duplicate an acceptable dummy receiver. We will also delete a few other real gun features to ease the building of this display gun.

Start with a piece of steel rod 1½ inches in diameter and 11½ inches long. This is actually a little over diameter for a Suomi receiver. The original was sized at 1.460 inches. If you have a lathe, you can remove the extra .040", but you really don't

Combine a Suomi parts kit with a 1½-inch steel cylinder, the right tools and lots of patience and you have everything you need to make a dummy gun for home display.

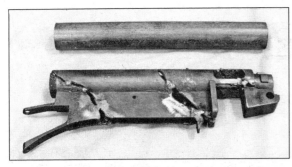

The parts kit receiver is torch-cut in three places to satisfy import regulations. Its rounded top means a steel cylinder makes a realistic dummy receiver.

have to. If you leave it on you will just have a very small step between the receiver and barrel shroud and will have to open up your stock slightly. Since I have a lathe, I went ahead and removed it.

Next, to lighten this heavy piece of steel, I drilled a 3/4" hole about 6 inches deep into the rear to remove a lot of material. At this point you may ask "why don't you just use tubing for the receiver?" The BATFE frowns on tubular receivers for dummy guns since they think it makes them too easy to convert back to firearms status.

Just to be on the safe side, I went with a solid receiver, which has been the standard for non-gun receivers. Many display gun makers use plastic, but I like steel for a more realistic feel and look.

In the front of this round stock I drilled a 3/4" hole centered and about an inch deep that will accept the dummy barrel later. I then machined a stub about an inch long and sized it to allow the barrel shroud to slide over it. My stub was about 1.044 inches, but yours may vary.

These machining jobs took me about an hour, so if you don't have a lathe, you should be able to hire them out for about an hour's worth of shop labor at your local machine shop.

If you have a good-sized drill press, you can do the hole drilling without the need for a lathe. If you are good at hand-crafting parts, you can probably even hand-shape the stub on the front for the barrel shroud; it doesn't have to look good since it will be covered with the shroud. It just has to allow the barrel shroud to be located evenly before you weld it on.

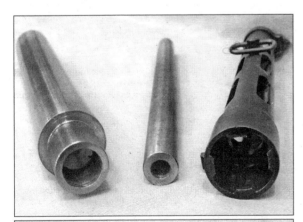

A stub and hole machined into the front of the receiver will accept the barrel and shroud. The shroud will slide over the receiver stub and barrel to be welded.

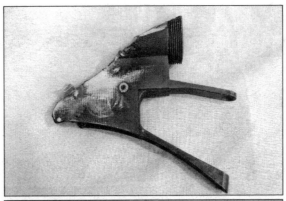

The tang of the demilled receiver must be salvaged. Shape the top to fit the dummy receiver and weld it in place, being sure the welds don't interfere with assembly.

One more little item I did was to add a false ejection port to the receiver to add some realism. I used a combination method of milling and grinding by hand to get it done. I made it about 1/8" deep and sized it about 1x1½ inches. You don't have to have this item but it sure improves the looks of the project when done.

Now we have to salvage some pieces from the demilled torch-cut receiver that came with this parts set. You need the rear section that has the stock tangs, the front section of the magazine housing and the section that retains the receiver in the stock and also contains the rear portion of the magazine housing.

Cut these pieces out with a saw or grinder and shape them to fit the new dummy receiver. Take the tang section and weld it to the new receiver. Extend the receiver about 1/2" past the end to allow for the installation of the end cap later. Before welding, be sure the part is sized right so that when installed, the new receiver will fit into the stock correctly.

Also, be sure you weld it on in the right place for the ejection port to be located properly. Once the tang section is welded in place and everything fits right, you can locate the front stock cap/rear magazine housing and weld it in place. Be sure the receiver is solidly in the stock before you locate and weld this item in place because this is what holds the stock and receiver together.

I just applied a couple small tack welds to the sides to locate it and then removed it from the stock and welded it from the rear where it wouldn't show. Once these two pieces of salvaged receiver are attached to the new dummy receiver, the trigger housing that was originally installed between them needs to be welded in place.

The Suomi magazine is supported at front and rear rather than by a magazine well. The supports need to be removed from the scrap receiver with a saw or grinder.

The trigger housing is welded between the tangs and stock cap/magazine retainer. Be sure to align it evenly before welding, so it will slide into its slot in the stock.

Before you install this piece, remove the sear from the housing so that it will lie flush against the receiver. You will probably have to do some filing or grinding to get this part to fit between the front and rear pieces .

Once you have it so it will slip into place, weld it to the rear tang section. The front needs to be welded to the cap/rear magazine housing but needs to be properly centered before welding in place. Be sure when you weld it in that you don't weld over the hole for the magazine catch pin.

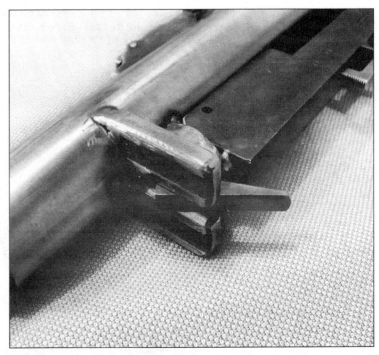

The magazine catch lever is mounted in the rear magazine support. Use the magazine itself to locate the front support correctly before welding it into position.

The Suomi features a charging handle below the end cap that looks like a small bolt-action rifle. It passes through the tang piece, which retains the stock at the rear.

Make a fake ejection port on the right side of the receiver above the magazine. This is a quick job with a milling machine, a tedious but possible one with a grinder.

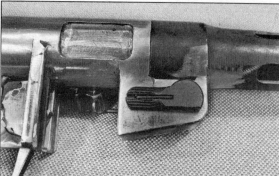

The takedown lever is non-functional, so it can be welded in position with plug welds from the opposite side of the front magazine support. Then grind them smooth.

Once this assembly is welded in place, re-install the receiver into the stock. You will notice that there is a gap between the stock and trigger housing. Make appropriate sized spacer strips and weld then to the housing to fill in the gap.

Unlike most firearms that have a magazine housing that completely surrounds the magazine, the Suomi only supports the magazine at the front and rear. Small grooves on the front and rear of the magazine housing interlock with tabs formed on the Suomi magazine.

The rear portion of the magazine housing has already been attached, so now we must correctly locate the front section. This is best done with a Suomi magazine as a guide. If you haven't done so already, shape the salvaged portion so that it fits up against the new dummy receiver yet leaves enough room to allow the barrel shroud to slide into place on the stub .

Place the magazine into the grooves in the rear section and place the forward section of magazine housing over the magazine tabs in the front. You want this piece located so that the magazine is held snugly but not so tight that removal is difficult. Once things are located, weld the front magazine housing to the receiver.

If you have your shroud installed to help locate things, be sure you don't weld into the shroud. Once all your welding is done you can install the original magazine catch in the housing.

Magazine Modifications

As long as we are working on the magazine housing, we might as well modify the magazine. Since the dummy receiver is solid, it has no opening into which the magazine extends. To get the magazine to lock in place, it needs to be shortened.

After removing the follower and spring, I cut off the top of the magazine and reshaped the top to fit flush against the dummy receiver. A fair amount of trial-and-error fitting is required to get it to fit up snugly against the receiver and to lock in place. Once you get a good fit, reinstall the magazine floorplate.

Dummy Barrel Fabrication and Installation

A dummy gun project needs a dummy barrel. Although you could use a functional barrel, it will help maintain dummy status if you use a non-functional barrel. You have two options here: demil the barrel that came with the kit or make a solid dummy barrel. The accepted method to demil a barrel is to weld the chamber shut and drill cross holes into the bore. The barrel that came with my kit was just like new so I didn't want to destroy it since I could use it for a later project.

Since the original Suomi barrel diameter was 3/4" (.750") it would be a simple matter to make a solid dummy barrel from a piece of 3/4" round stock. I took a piece of 3/4" rod about 12 inches long and drilled a 3/8" hole 1 inch deep in the end to simulate the bore. It was then inserted into the 3/4" hole previously drilled in the front of the dummy receiver and welded in place. Be sure when installing and welding in the barrel it is aligned straight so that the shroud will fit properly when installed.

Rear Sight Installation

The large rear sight on the Suomi attaches to the receiver with screws. A protrusion under the sight fits into a slot in the original Suomi receiver and must be ground off to fit our solid dummy receiver. Once removed, the sight will lie flat on the receiver.

Locate it about 3 inches from the rear of the receiver, making sure that it is aligned straight up so that it looks right. Mark the hole locations through the mounting holes. Drill and tap the holes. I drilled them 6–48 (scope base screw size) with my Brownells tap set. This high quality tap set is sized for the small screws commonly found in firearms. Common machine screw sizes can be used if you don't have gunsmithing sized taps.

End Cap and Charging Handle

The end cap on the original receiver was threaded on, but to avoid that machining operation, I simply used a small hand grinder with a grinding stone to remove the threads so it would

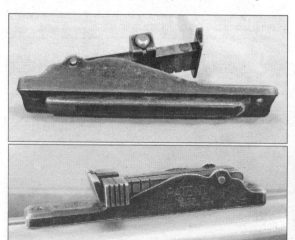

The protrusion on the bottom of the Suomi sight needs to be ground off before mounting the sight on the receiver. Drill and tap the dummy receiver for 6-28 screws.

The front magazine support is welded to the receiver. Be careful to locate it properly and to weld carefully, so that the barrel shroud can slide into position.

As the dummy receiver has no opening for the magazine, the latter must be shortened to fit flush against the bottom of the receiver until it will latch in place.

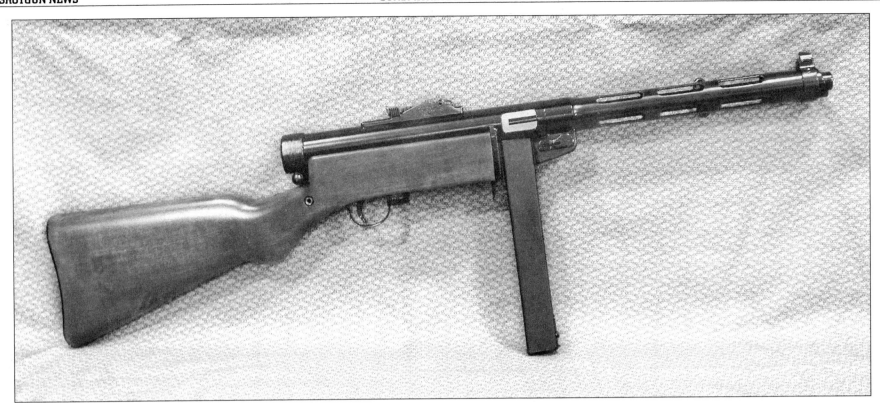

slip over the rear of the receiver. If you have a lathe, you can also use that to remove the threads.

Whichever method you use, be sure to fit it snugly to the receiver. A small screw or pin through the end cap and receiver can be used to secure the cap to the receiver when it is assembled later.

The Suomi features a rather odd charging handle directly below the end cap. It resembles the handle of a bolt-action rifle. On the original gun, this handle extended into the receiver and allowed cocking. Since this dummy gun doesn't have a bolt, this handle is just there for looks and won't do anything. To make installation easy, I just cut off the handle and welded it to the end cap.

Barrel Shroud Installation

If you attached your forward magazine housing correctly, your barrel shroud should still slide into place on the stub on the front of the receiver. The original Suomi barrel and shroud were retained with a takedown lever on the right side of the forward magazine housing.

Since this is a dummy gun, I decided to delete the takedown feature. Slide on the barrel shroud so that it is tightly against the receiver and align it so that the front sight is straight up. You will probably have to do some hand fitting to get things to fit up right.

Once aligned, a couple small welds in discreet locations will lock everything in place. Your takedown lever needs to be installed with the handle on the right side. Insert it into its hole and plug weld it from the opposite side to lock it in place.

Final Finishing

To make this project look good, it needs to be nicely finished, since the Suomi was finished to very high standards for a military arm. While hot tank bluing would be the most original finish, most don't have the capability to do this at home, and hiring it done would make the project pricey.

To give it a semi shiny black finish, I choose to use Brownells Aluma-Hyde II spray on epoxy finish. I choose the semi-gloss black version since I felt gloss black was just too shiny. This aerosol spray finish is easy to apply by anyone who can paint with a spray can.

It does dry slowly, so you will have to wait a few days after spraying before re-assembly. Before spraying on Aluma-Hyde II, I ground all welds down flush and removed all scratches and gouges. Although not absolutely required I also abrasive blasted the metal parts for better adhesion.

With a few weekends' work and about $75 worth of materials, Matthews was able to build a dummy that nicely recreates the distinctive angular lines of the Suomi SMG.

After a good cleaning and degreasing, the parts were sprayed and left to air dry for a few days. The wood stock in this kit was in such good condition that all I needed to do to it was a light sanding followed by staining. A quick coat of spray lacquer followed to give it a satin finish.

The Completed Project

Once everything was refinished and re-assembled, this project really looked good. The total cost excluding finishing supplies was only $75. With such a low cost and a good looking display piece this project deserves your consideration. ◉

Brownells Aluma-Hyde II finish is easy to apply without harsh chemicals, and yields a smooth, shiny finish appropriate for an Old World piece like the Suomi m/31.

Disclaimer

Dummy Up!
Part IV
Building an AK-47

If you've successfully built the three submachine gun dummies covered in previous issues, you're ready to tackle this challenging project.

By Steven Matthews

The AK-47 is seen almost daily on the television news, and even those who know little about firearms can usually identify it. It has been made by the millions over the last 60 years. As such an important historical arm, it certainly qualifies as a candidate for a dummy/display gun build project. In this last article of a four-part series, I will show how to build a nonfirearm AK-47. If you've been following this series (11/20/07, 12/20/07 and 1/20/08), some of the techniques will be familiar.

The basis of this project will be one of the widely available Romanian AK-47 parts kits. It will have a dummy receiver made by using a frame flat and a flat bending jig. The frame/receiver will also be modified for non-gun status.

AK parts kits are widely available, but I went with DPH Arms because they have an excellent reputation on several AK building internet discussion forums. The parts kit arrived by the big brown truck and it exceeded my expectations. The parts were a little scratched up from the disassembly process but were in otherwise excellent condition. The metal finish was about 95% and the wood was very good also. Apparently these were from little used guns. The kit was well worth the $120 asking price.

Two other items were also obtained from DPH Arms. The first was a Tapco semi-auto AK-47 frame flat. This flat is an unbent and incomplete receiver blank that is used by home builders to build semi-automatic AK-47 receivers. It is made from 4130 steel. It is *not* classified as a firearm in this condition.

Riveted construction makes some parts of this dummy project simple, but there's a fair amount of welding required to make a non-gun that satisfies BATFE requirements.

Completing the receiver requires it to be precisely bent and have frame rails welded in place. Since this is a dummy gun, I won't be installing the frame rails.

The other item from DPH was the AK frame bending jig. This easy-to-use fixture allows the home builder to bend a frame flat precisely. Anyone who has tried the crude hammer and vise method to bend a frame flat will attest to how much better a job you can do with a jig. The jig was a simple design and well made.

Parts Modification

To start this project I first removed the old pieces of demilitarized frame from the front and rear trunnions. The rivet heads were ground off and the old rivets were drilled or punched out. The next thing I did was to throw away a couple parts. The kit came with the full-auto sear and spring and since there is no need for them on a semi auto or dummy build, they were immediately discarded.

The trigger was modified to non-functional condition by grinding off the hook at the top that engages the hammer. In fact the only fire control parts will be the modified trigger and the safety lever. The bolt carrier will be retained, but we don't want it to be able to accept a bolt. We want this bolt carrier to be absolutely non-functional and not readily restorable to operational status.

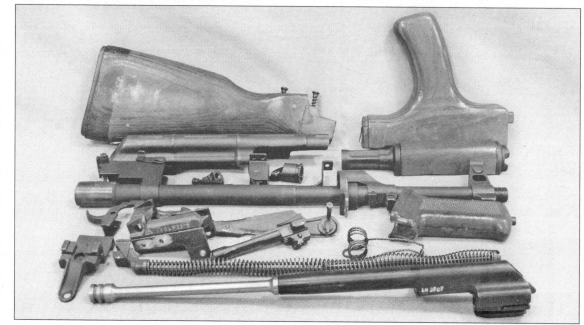

A Romanian AK parts kit from DPH Arms was the basis for Matthews' dummy project. Some parts were used as-is, but many others were modified, some quite extensively.

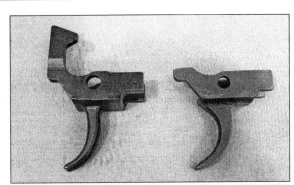

To make the trigger non-functional, remove the hook that engages the hammer. Saw off the bolt carrier extension that retains the bolt to demilitarize the carrier.

Using a solid barrel saves welding the muzzle and chamber shut and cross-drilling the barrel. It also preserves a good barrel for potential future projects.

To prevent the carrier from ever being able to accept a bolt, it was modified by grinding off the bottom. It was ground down until all that was left was just enough material for the frame rail grooves.

The next part to be modified to non-functional status was the barrel. The traditional method for deactivating a barrel is closing off the chamber and muzzle by arc welding and then drilling a hole in the chamber and also in the rifled section of the barrel.

When you demilitarize your barrel, be sure to drill your holes in an inconspicuous location under the handguards. The barrel in this kit was just about perfect, so I decided to save it for another project. I made a solid barrel on my lathe. I just duplicated the outside contour on a solid steel rod. I also made it shorter and added a large muzzle brake/flash suppressor for looks.

After I installed my dummy barrel, I welded it to the front trunnion, and I recommend you do the same if you use a deactivated barrel. You do not need to remove your barrel from the trunnion as you would if you were building a real gun, so this will make it a lot easier.

Dummy Receiver Fabrication

I will use the Tapco semi-auto frame flat as a starting point for the dummy receiver. The first operation is to bend it with the DPH Arms bending jig. I will just cover the basic procedure, since DPH supplies instructions with the jig. It has an angle iron base that functions as a "die" and a three-piece "punch" that presses the flat into the die to form it.

The frame flat is aligned on the punch with locator pins. Once located over the die, the punch is pressed down into the die with

a hydraulic press that bends the flat to the correct size and shape. My 12-ton arbor press easily formed the flat, so I believe even a smaller press could be utilized.

When I removed the flat from the die and examined it, I saw that it was bent neatly and relatively accurately. The only fault I could find was that the sides weren't quite 90° due to spring-back. A little massaging with a hammer and steel block brought the sides to roughly 90°.

Barrel/Trunnion Installation.

Since a dummy gun doesn't require much in the way of strength, I used an easy method to attach the barrel and trunnion assembly to the formed frame. The assembly slides onto the frame through grooves in the trunnion and is riveted in place (three rivets on each side) on functional guns, but I substituted screw construction to ease the job.

Screws will also remove the need to remove the barrel from the trunnion as you would if riveting. Before installing the trunnion, drill out the rivets and holes with a No. 21 drill and tap the holes 10-32. You can drill right into the barrel to make the holes deeper and easier to tap.

Drill the corresponding holes in the frame 3/16" to allow the 10-32 screws to pass through. Slide the trunnion/barrel assembly onto the receiver and use 10-32 screws to attach it. These screws will not look like rivets, so modify them by grinding the heads down to remove the screw slots.

Once the slots are gone, they will look like rivets. Just be sure you have everything right before you grind down the heads.

Rear Trunnion Installation

The rear trunnion slides into the rear of the receiver and is retained by two rivets extending all the way through the trunnion

and receiver. You can use original metric size rivets available from AK parts dealers or drill them out a little to use fractional size rivets available from hardware suppliers.

You may also use the screw method if you choose, but I went with rivets since they are easier to install than screws in this location. To install the rivets, you just insert them through the tightly clamped parts with about 3/16" extension and then form the heads by hammering .

They can be flat or you can form them rounded by tapping around the edges with a small punch. Be sure to support the rivet heads solidly; you want your hammer force going into the rivets, not the frame.

Trigger Guard / Magazine Release Assembly

The trigger guard assembly is installed on the bottom of the receiver. Four rivets on the front and one in the back are all that's required. 5/32" rivets are about right here if you don't have original AK metric rivets. A spacer/safety lever stop is placed between the frame and trigger guard. Install the rivets with about 1/8" extension (trim to length).

Use the preformed heads on the outside. With the parts pressed tightly together and the heads solidly supported with steel blocks, flatten the heads on the inside with a hammer and punch. They don't show, so they don't even have to look good. Once the assembly is riveted in place, check magazine fit and do any hand fitting required.

Receiver Blocking

At this point we want to weld steel blocks into the receiver to prevent the installation of a hammer or an operational bolt carrier. I know this may seam silly since the gun has non-operational barrel, but it must be done to maintain non-firearm status of the dummy receiver.

I slid a steel block 1¼ x 1¼ x 5/8" in from the back and welded it in place 1/16" back from the magazine opening. I then welded

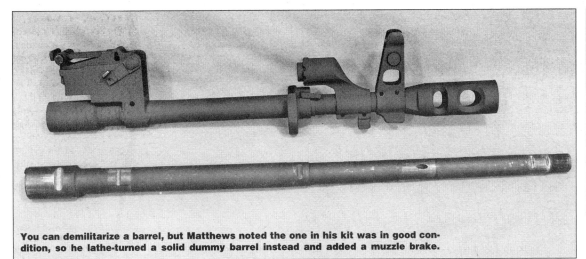

You can demilitarize a barrel, but Matthews noted the one in his kit was in good condition, so he lathe-turned a solid dummy barrel instead and added a muzzle brake.

The Tapco frame flat is intended for making semi-auto AKs, but is, with the proper modifications, just the thing for making a dummy, using the DPH bending jig.

Matthews chose to attach the front trunnion to the frame with machine screws. He then used a grinder to remove the screw slots and round the heads to look like rivets.

The frame flat locates on the punch with locating pins. The punch self-aligns with the die. Matthews found his 12-ton arbor press was more than adequate for the job.

For the rear trunnion that supports the buttstock, Matthews stuck with the original riveted construction. Riveting is easy if you have the proper tools for it.

another small block on top of the large block to fill in the remaining space under the modified bolt carrier.

At this time I also welded shut the hammer pin holes. The receiver is very thin and it is easy to burn through. Placing a block of copper or aluminum behind where you are welding will help prevent burn-through.

Gas Piston Modification

The dummy bolt carrier is going to be permanently installed, so the gas piston needs to be shortened so it can be withdrawn far enough out of the gas tube to allow the latter to be installed or removed. Insert the carrier into the receiver. Position the rear of the carrier just a little in front of the carrier installation cut outs on the top of the receiver.

At the front of the sight base where the gas piston enters the gas tube, mark the piston and cut it off at that point. On this stub you can weld on a 3/8" nut and grind it round the same size as the front of the cut off piston. This will help align the carrier in

the gas tube and keep the dummy carrier operating smoothly. This is a lot of work for a minor detail. You may find that your carrier with the cut off piston moves smoothly enough with out this modification; it's your call.

Locking in the Bolt Carrier

Once you are sure your gas piston is short enough to allow removal of the gas tube, it is time to lock the dummy carrier in place. Take a 1¼ x 3/16" piece of steel high enough to reach the top of the receiver and weld it into the carrier installation cut out notches. Grind it flush with the top of the receiver.

This is a lot of welding and blocking, but to keep this dummy receiver classified as a non-firearm it must be permanently modified to prevent easy restoration to a functional firearm. If the blocks were not welded in place you would still have a semi-

auto firearm receiver. The whole idea of a dummy gun is to have a non-firearm; you only want it to look like a firearm.

Trigger Installation

Install the non-functional trigger and spring into the receiver. The trigger pin needs to be retained with a spring clip or e-type snap ring, available at hardware stores.

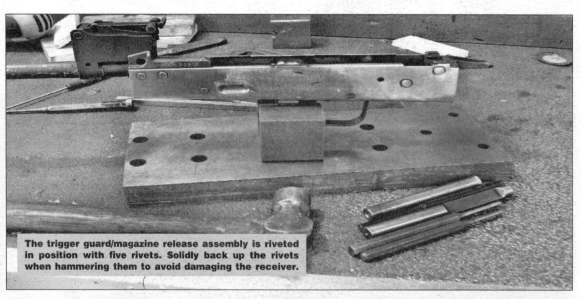

The trigger guard/magazine release assembly is riveted in position with five rivets. Solidly back up the rivets when hammering them to avoid damaging the receiver.

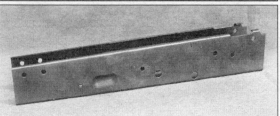

Once pressed into the die, the flat is precisely formed. Matthews found there was a little spring-back that was easily corrected with a few taps from the hammer.

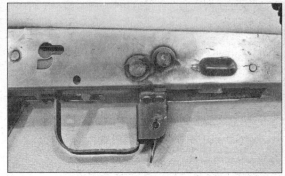

Matthews welded blocks into the receiver that prevent installation of an operational hammer or bolt carrier. While at it, he welded shut the hammer pin holes.

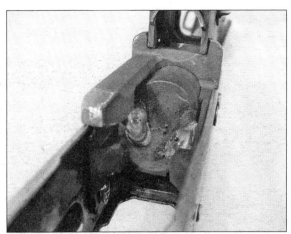

The solid dummy barrel was welded into the trunnion. Matthews chose to make a 12-inch barrel and install the muzzle brake, front sight and gas cylinder by welding.

Top Cover Installation

You will now need to check your top cover fit, since it is dependant on how the receiver and trunnions were fitted. The cover slides down over the rear of the receiver. The front engages a groove in the sight base and the rear is retained by the plunger on the end of the recoil spring. A little hand fitting is usually required to get it to drop in place easily.

Stock Installation

The stocks may need to be fitted to your new receiver, since the front handguards and rear buttstock extend into the dummy receiver. A little filing may be needed to get the parts to slide in to full depth. If, on the other hand, the fit is too loose, you may have to glue on some thin shims to thicken the stock tangs.

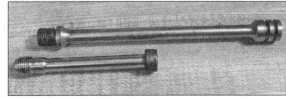

As the carrier's travel is reduced, the gas piston must be shortened to allow installation or removal of the gas tube. Matthews added a new end for smooth operation.

Finishing

Once everything fits right, it's time to refinish the metal and possibly the wood. The original metal finish on this gun was a very dark, almost black, Parkerizing. I decided to keep the black color but didn't want to set up my Parkerizing system just to do one gun. I choose to finish the metal parts with Brownells Aluma-Hyde II in semi-gloss black.

This is an aerosol spray epoxy firearms finish that is easily applied. It sprays very much like spray paint, so almost anyone can apply it. It is available in several colors. It can be applied to metal, plastics and wood. It air dries and cures in a few days but can be gently heated after air drying to speed up cure time. I heated the parts to about 120° for about three hours to speed up curing. This procedure is not in Brownells' instructions so take it with a grain of salt! While it's not mandatory, I abrasive blasted the parts before spraying to provide greater adhesion.

The wood on this kit was in very good condition, but was covered in a very thick and shiny layer of ugly varnish. I stripped this off and then sanded and stained the wood. I then applied some satin spray lacquer for a less shiny finish.

After all the finishes were dried and cured, I assembled the dummy gun. The gun looked better than most as-issued AKs.

Welding a block in the carrier removal notches at the rear of the receiver prevents the carrier from being removed. Install the trigger with pin and spring clip.

After finishing with Brownells' Aluma-Hyde II, the dummy AK looks better than most real ones. They won't be able to tell it's a dummy without close examination.

Most original AKs are not finely finished so you really don't want it to look too good if you want an original look. This dummy gun makes a very interesting knickknack to display on your wall. It also gives the novice home gunsmith a little insight into real gun building without the pressure to get it exactly right. It is a worthy project for the hobbyist who likes to build things himself.   ◉

Disclaimer

Under federal firearms regulations a firearm is defined as any weapon which is designed or may be readily converted to expel a projectile by the action of an explosive. The frame or receiver of any such device is also considered to be a firearm.

A solid piece of material only externally shaped as a firearm would not be considered a firearm under this definition. A non-functioning firearm with only minor modifications such as having the bolt welded shut would, however, still be considered a firearm since it would be readily restorable.

Dummy guns, while containing many real gun parts, must not be readily restorable. This is why so many modifications must be made when utilizing real gun parts to make a dummy. The frame or receiver must be made or modified so that it is not readily convertible to firearm status. Many internal parts must also be modified to prevent them from performing their original function. Various methods are used to accomplish these goals.

The methods used in this article series are the author's best attempt to comply with these regulations and create items that are considered non-firearms. These methods should not be considered legal advice. Neither the author or SHOTGUN NEWS assume any responsibility for the legal classification of these projects. Before building any dummy/display only/non-functional/ non-firearms the builder should verify that the project complies with all federal, state and local regulations.

Due to ever changing rules and regulations the definition of what constitutes a firearm may change. It is in the builder's best interest to verify the latest rules on making non-firearms. The builder should verify that the particular project and build procedures result in a non-firearm classification. For federal firearms regulations contact the BATFE.

Contact info: Bureau of Alcohol, Tobacco, Firearms, and Explosives, Firearms Technology Branch, 244 Needy Rd., Martinsburg, W. Va., 25401, www.atf.gov

Dummy guns built from parts kits are fun, but the kits just keep getting more expensive. What if you could build a dummy from commonly available commercial steel?

A Scratch-Made Dummy M1919

Part 1

By Steven Matthews

It's one thing to make a dummy gun from a parts kit. It's another to make one from raw steel pieces. Matthews shows how in this two-part series.

In recent years I have written several articles for SGN on building dummy versions of famous military full-auto firearms. Display guns offer a low cost way of owning representations of your favorite machine guns without the cost, paperwork and responsibilities of owning registered full-auto firearms.

Whether you own the real versions or not, non-functional display guns are the responsible way of displaying ordnance. Compared to real guns, display guns are very inexpensive. While commercially-made display guns can be pretty pricey, home-built versions can cost a fraction of the price of manufactured display guns.

I have eight dummies guns hanging on my wall that if real would represent tens of thousands of dollars spent. I have

less than $500 in the whole lot. I usually purchase a surplus parts set and use a dummy receiver to build the project. On many hand-held guns this is usually very inexpensive.

The problem is that when you move up to belt-fed guns, the cost can really escalate. An example of this the Czech ZB-37 heavy machine gun I wrote about in 9/20/08 and 10/20/08. Parts kits for this rare gun can easily exceed $1000, and a tripod will drive the cost up even more. The only way I got to do this project was that I scored a parts set for an incredibly low price.

I recently decided that I needed a display version of the Browning 1919A4 belt-fed machine gun. Since I have a semi-auto version of this historic gun, I thought a display version would be a nice complement to the real one. I also wanted

to do an article on the build process. Deciding I wanted one and making it a financial possibility are two different things! I'm sure that in these tough economic times there are many readers in the same situation.

The usual method of buying a surplus parts set (about $450) and a dummy sideplate (about $125) would be too costly on my restricted budget. I needed to find a less expensive option if I was going to have a 1919A4 hanging on my wall.

My semi auto 1919 was self-built from a Ohio Ordnance Works semi auto kit, plus I had built a NFA-registered full auto many years ago, so I was familiar with the gun. I had my semi-auto sitting on the work bench trying to figure out how to build an inexpensive display gun when I noticed something.

In its most basic form a Browning 1919A4 is simply a rectangular box with a round extension extending out the front. To this basic rectangle several sub-assemblies are attached. These sub-assemblies are also very basic shapes and would not be too difficult to roughly replicate in the home workshop.

The raw materials for this project are common steel pieces available from any steel supplier. If you have access to a good scrap pile, the price can be even lower.

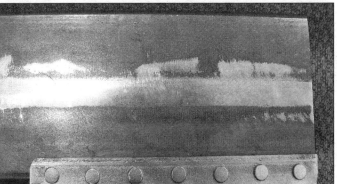

Matthews doesn't mind riveting himself, but knows there are those who don't, so he cooked up a way to use screws and make them look like rivets. Just grind the heads down.

I also figured that materials to make these parts would be inexpensive. A quick trip to the local steel retailer/recycling center confirmed that material cost to replicate these parts would be less than $30. This $30 figure included both new and recycled steel. All new steel would push the cost up to about $50, but that would still be a bargain.

With such a low cost for the gun I got to thinking that a replica M2 tripod might be nice, too. I had previously writ-ten an article for SGN on building a functional replica of the M2 Tripod for less than $50. Since I was familiar with the construction of a functioning tripod I figured I could simplify that design into a display version.

By using lighter materials and deleting functional features, I figured a display version could be made for less than $20 worth of materials. The low cost of the gun and tripod projects convinced me to start the project. In fact I built three versions, one for me and a couple for other friends.

Total time to build one 1919A4 replica was about 15 hours and one M2 tripod took about 10 hours. 25 hours of your time can result in your having a nice display gun and tripod.

Before we get into the building of this project, I want to address a couple issues. These two projects will only be rough replicas, not exact copies. Only the exterior features will be duplicated. No internal parts will be made and no real gun parts will be used. Exact copies could be hand made but the work would run into hundreds of hours.

If you want an extremely detailed replica, then spend the $600 and buy a parts set and dummy sideplate. This article and project are intended for those who want a reasonable approximation of a Browning 1919A4 and M2 tripod with a minimal amount of time and money expended.

This project is not dimensionally precise. Many dimensions were altered from the original gun and tripod to ease the build process and allow common materials to be used. Also please note this story does not contain all the information you need to complete the project. You will have to supplement the information here with you own fabricating skills and knowledge.

Tools required for the project are basic home workshop tools, however the more tools you have, the easier the project will be. An arc welder is absolutely required for this project, with the MIG type preferred over a stick welder. Power tools such as bench mounted disc sander, band saw, drill press, and small hand held angle grinder will greatly ease the build but are not absolutely required.

The receiver of the Browning 1919A4 is a rectangle. I used a 14-inch piece of 2x4x1/8" wall rectangular tubing. I would have preferred thinner wall material but that was all that was available where I bought it. Thinner wall tubing will have a sharper corners, which would look better.

To this basic rectangle all subassemblies will be attached and from it some cutouts will be made. These assemblies will include the barrel and shroud, front and rear sights, top cover, spade grips, charging handle, top cover latch, and several small frame components. The builder can choose the build order he prefers; the order described here is what worked for me.

Once the 2x4-inch tubing was squarely cut and deburred, I decided to make the cutouts. A slot for the charging handle

Cut the slot in the receiver sideplate for the operating handle by drilling a hole at either end and then using a Dremel tool and cutting disk to cut the sides.

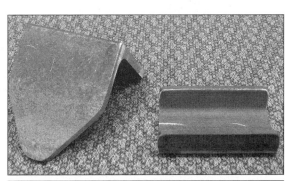

The cast rear sight base of the Browning was recreated with a piece of angle iron and a section of square tubing, welded together and affixed to the dummy receiver.

To keep the dummy gun from looking hollow, Mathews welded a steel bar behind the receiver slot to resemble the original gun's bolt. The operating handle is a common bolt.

A real M1919 rear sight would have been costly, so Matthews substituted an inexpensive surplus rifle sight and made a dummy windage knob from a piece of 1/2" rod.

A C-shaped bracket around the cartridge belt openings replicates the feed tray. Screws with the heads ground off replicate the look of the small rivets that hold it.

needs to be cut in the right side of the receiver. This slot is 1/2" wide and 4½ inches long. It is located 5½ inches back from the front and 1½ inches down (to the center of the slot) from the top.

The ends should be left round. This slot can be cut out by drilling a 1/2" hole at both ends, then cutting the remainder out with a cutoff wheel in a hand-held grinder. Cut slightly under size and file the remainder flat to finish size. An opening for the ammo belt and cartridges also needs to be made.

You have two options here. The standard 1919A4 features left-hand feeding and has an opening on the left side large enough to allow the loaded cartridge belts to pass though.

On the right side, the opening is only large enough to allow the empty belt (or metallic links) to exit the gun. There is however a variation known as the M37 that features right and left feed options and features a large opening on both sides.

I choose to use the dual-feed M37 pattern on my project to allow the belt to extend out of either side, depending on how the gun was displayed. I sized the openings 17/32" wide by 3⅜ inches long. These openings were 1 inch back from the front and 1/2" down from the top and were cut out with the same method as the handle slot, but the ends were filed square.

Once these openings were cut, I could see into the receiver and the project looked hollow. To give the appearance of a bolt in the receiver, I welded a piece of 3/16x1-inch flat stock behind the handle slot. I added a piece of steel on the inside between the openings in the receiver for the cartridge belt. This gives the appearance of the feed tray on the front trunnion.

One of the most distinctive features of the M1919 is its riveted construction. The 1919 featured two sideplates connected by upper and lower frame components. These parts, as well as other internal parts, were connected with exposed

head rivets. All these exposed rivet heads (about 24) give the gun a very distinctive and solid "old time" appearance.

For a reasonable replica, these rivet heads need to be duplicated. While riveting is a very easy process, it seems to intimidate novice builders. With that in mind, I used a procedure that will give the appearance of rivets without actually having to rivet.

All the small 3/16" shank (about 3/8" head) rivets were actually 10-32 screws with the heads ground partially off to simulate rivet heads. The rivet holes were drilled and tapped, the screws installed and then the heads were partially removed. Quick, easy and they looked like rivets!

The first parts to be "riveted" on were the lower frame components. On original guns this is a large single-piece casting that connects the two sideplates at the bottom rear. This part would be very hard to duplicate. To easily duplicate its outward appearance, I attached a 7-inch piece of 3/4"x1/8" angle iron to each side.

The angle was drilled with seven 3/16" holes centered on the angle. Once the holes were drilled, the angle was clamped to the receiver and tack welded to hold it in place.

I drilled tap holes (#25 drill) through the existing holes and into the receiver wall. The holes were then tapped and the screws installed. The slots in the screw heads were then ground off. Be sure when selecting your screws that you get screws that have some head remaining under the slots so that you have enough head left to give the appearance of a rivet head. Phillips screws cannot be used since the slots are too deep.

With the angles installed, you can fabricate and install the tabs on the bottom that secure the gun to the T+E assembly. These tabs were made from 1x1x1/4-inch flat stock. A hole was drilled near the bottom and the bottom end was rounded off before they were welded to the angle. These tabs were located about 2½ inches from the rear of the receiver.

Several more false rivets need to be installed on each side of the receiver. The right side has four more of these small rivets. One each is installed on the front and rear corners, which are located about 1/2" in and down from the edges. One is installed about 3/4" below the receiver top and 5/8" behind the cartridge opening. The last small one is installed 4⅞ inches from the rear of the receiver and 1/2" down from the top.

One large "trunnion" rivet needs to be installed in both sides of the receiver. This one is 2 inches back from the front and 2½ inches down from the top. This rivet head is made from the head of a 1/4" carriage bolt. A hole is just drilled in the receiver and the rivet is set in place followed by spot welding from the back side. Be sure it is tight and flush before welding.

Six of the small rivets need to be installed in the left side of the receiver. The left side gets one in each corner just like the other side and the one that is 4⅞ inches from the back also needs installed at the top just like the right side. Two are installed 3/4" down from the top at 6 and 8 inches from the rear of the receiver. The last one is installed 1¼ inches down and 9 inches from the rear.

The Browning 1919A4 features brackets or protrusions around the lower portion of the openings for the cartridge belt. This bracket houses the belt holding pawl and is also an attachment point for an optional feed chute. Since this bracket doesn't function on a display gun and features a lot of notches that would be hard to duplicate without a milling machine, it will only be roughly copied.

I fabricated a bracket from a piece of 1x1/4-inch flat steel. I just cut out a piece 4¼ inches long and cut a notch in it the size of the

cartridge belt opening. Since my project featured right or left feeding, I made one for each side. It was secured to the receiver with small 8-32 screws using the same fake riveting method as before.

The next assembly to be made was the rear sight. The 1919A4 features a large ladder type sight. It is attached to receiver with a heavy cast angle bracket which extends over

A light sheet metal cover will substitute for the original heavy machined original. A carriage bolt and spring substitute for the original pivot pin group.

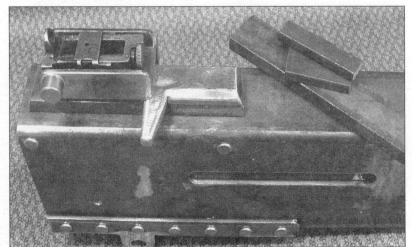

The top latch is represented by three steel flats welded and shaped to look like the latch and handle of the original. This part takes a little bit of artistic skill.

the top of the receiver. This original part would be hard to duplicate, so I found an improvised solution in the form of a shaped angle iron bracket.

Material is 2½x3/16-inch angle iron that is 2⅜ inches long. One leg (the top portion) of the angle is narrowed to 1¾ inches. The side leg is shaped by angling the lower sides inward to create a tapered profile. This taper begins about halfway down the side and is rounded on the end.

To attach the bracket to the receiver, two holes were drilled in the side for plug welds. This bracket should be located 3/4" in from the rear of the receiver and a 5/8"-3/4" gap should be left between the top of the receiver and the bottom of the bracket.

Weld the bracket on, then grind the welds smooth. The original sight featured protective sides cast right into the base/bracket. To duplicate this feature, weld a 2⅜" long section of 1¼x1/8-inch square tube to the top of the bracket. This piece of material should be 9/16" tall.

The square tube section is welded to the bracket and then all welds are ground smooth so that the sides look to be one piece with the base. Between these protective sides a ladder type sight was installed. Original 1919A4 sights can be pretty pricey, so I just picked up a military surplus bolt action rifle sight at a gun show that looked very similar for $5.

I installed it by drilling a hole through the sides of the sight base and installing a pivot pin so it could be flipped up or down. After the ladder sight was installed a 1/2" long piece of 1/2" rod was soldered to the side to simulate the looks of a sight adjustment knob.

The next assembly to be made was the top cover latch. The original 1919A4 latch is a single piece casting. To duplicate the looks of this part I welded three pieces of flat stock and shaped the weldment to resemble a latch.

The first piece was a 1x3/8-inch flat 5 inches long. I welded a piece of 1x1/4x1¾-inch flat to the top of it. Right behind this piece a section of 1/4"x1/2" stock 2" long was welded on to form a handle. This handle part was beveled to resemble the original handle shape.

Once all the pieces were welded together, the assembly was contoured to duplicate roughly the original top cover latch. To attach this latch to the receiver without any noticeable welds, I drilled 1/4" holes in each end of the latch. I then located the latch on the receiver top so it was about 1/4" from

 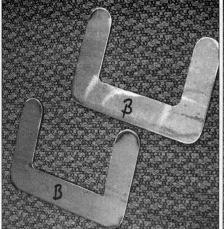 

Spade grip brackets are made from rounded, contoured C-shaped pieces of 1/8" flat stock. Bolt them together to space them properly before welding them to the backplate.

the rear of the receiver and marked two hole locations on the receiver top.

Then I drilled holes and installed short pieces of 1/4" bolts from underneath to act as studs. Once everything was aligned and clamped in place, the holes in the top where the studs where located were welded shut and ground smooth. The heads on the inside of the receiver were also spot welded so they were tight.

The next part to be duplicated was the top cover. The original top cover and associated machining would be very hard for the hobbyist to duplicate, so the top cover featured here can be best described as a "representatation" of the top cover. This was made from 1/16" flat steel sheet.

My cover was made from a piece 8¼ inches long and 3 inches wide, but yours may vary depending on your specific build dimensions. I bent 1/2" sides on the material so that I had a channel that had a 2-inch inside width. To this piece a 1/2"x1/2" stub was attached to appear to be a feed lever pivot.

It was located 3½ inches from the rear and 5/8" from the right side. A piece of 3/4"x3/4"x1/8" flat stock was attached to the rear center to look like a catch for the top cover latch. Both were plug welded from the underside of the cover so no welds showed.

Two 3/8" holes were drilled in the sheet metal top cover to allow it to be plug welded to the top of the receiver. After welding in place, I ground these welds smooth so there were no obvious welds showing.

The original 1919 top cover featured a pivot pin at the front with a spring between the head and the top cover. To duplicate this feature, I installed a 1/4" carriage bolt with a spring under the head. The bolt was installed through a drilled hole and the bolt was tack welded on the inside of the receiver.

The open end at the rear of the receiver can now be filled in. To replicate the 1919 backplate and buffer assembly, I cut a filler plate from a piece of 1/8" flat stock. For the buffer I chose to use a representation of the short buffer assembly, which looks better with spade grips.

This was made with a piece of 1¼-inch diameter rod 1½ inches long.

This rod was contoured by forming a step at about the halfway point. The rod was attached to the backplate by plug welding it from the rear of the plate. It was centered and about 1¾ inches down from the top. Once the buffer was welded to the backplate, the assembly was welded to the rear of the receiver tube.

While original Browning 1919A4s featured a single pistol grip, aftermarket spade grips are a popular option for 1919 shooters. While not original equipment, spade grips do look more "machine gunny" and are more user-friendly. This style of grip is also very easy to make for a display gun, since it doesn't need to function.

Simple grip brackets are made from 1/8" flat stock. These brackets look like a large "C". To make the brackets, cut

Use 1⅛-inch hardwood dowels for the spade grips, drilled with 1/4" holes all the way through. These are inauthentic, but make the dummy look more "machine gunny."

out a piece of flat stock that is 4½x3 inches and remove the center of the "C". I made the width of the "C" portion 7/8" wide.

Once the "C" parts were cut out, I rounded the ends. These "C" pieces had holes drilled in the ends for 1/4" carriage bolts that will extend though the wooden grips. These two "C" pieces were then welded to the rear of the receiver at a 3⅞-inch spacing. To maintain this spacing and the better to hold the brackets, I used carriage bolts and nuts to secure the parts in the right location.

After the "C" brackets were installed, grips were made from 3⅞-inch sections of 1⅛-inch hardwood dowel.

Since this is a non-functional item, the thumb trigger of the spade grips was replicated with 3/4" flat stock and welded to the top bracket. Locate it to your preference. This doesn't look original, but then you don't have to replicate all the complicated linkage found on functional spade grips.

One more thing needs done to the receiver before moving on to the shroud construction. The filler plate that was welded in behind the handle slot needs to have a 1/2"-13 hole drilled and tapped at the front for the cocking handle. A handle can be made from a short 1/2" bolt. Length of the handle can be to your preference. I rounded the head so that it didn't look like a bolt head and had about 1 inch of unthreaded shank extending out of the receiver.

Next month (12/20 issue) building the barrel and tripod. ◉

The receiver rear is fitted with a steel backplate, welded in place. A 1¼-inch rod, stepped down in diameter, represents the buffer tube of the original machine gun.

Matthews put together the dummy gun's receiver last month; now he takes on the barrel, shroud and tripod. Like a lot of Matthews projects, there's more work than cost.

A Scratch-Made Dummy M1919

Part 2

By Steven Matthews

In Part 1 (11/20 issue), Matthews showed how to make the receiver of this inexpensive dummy. Now he turns to the barrel and tripod.

Now its time to move on to the Browning 1919's other distinctive feature, its full-length ventilated barrel shroud. The 1919A4 features a very heavy weight 24-inch barrel surrounded by a heavily ventilated shroud that features something called a booster on the end. The booster also houses a front barrel bushing.

For barrel shroud fabrication, we will use 1½-inch EMT, which is also sometimes called 1½-inch electrical conduit. This material has an outside diameter of roughly 1.675 inches, which is about 1/4" under original shroud size. It is lightweight and inexpensive so that's what was used for this project.

You will need a piece about 18 inches long. This is about an inch and a half shorter than the real gun, but I decided that since the diameter was smaller, the length should be re-

duced proportionally. The original shroud is perforated by eight rows of holes with approximately 100 5/8" holes and looks like a long piece of Swiss cheese.

To ease the build I cut this back to four rows of holes, two with 11 holes and two with 10. This really reduces the work, because 100 holes is a *lot* of locating, drilling and deburring.

Four rows look pretty good, but if you really want all the holes then go ahead and do them. The holes were spaced at 1½-inch centers. The top and bottom rows started 1½ inches from the front and the side rows started 2¼ inches from the front. This was so that the holes were offset evenly.

When drilling your holes, solidly secure your parts in a vise. Drilling holes in round stock can be troublesome unless the parts are solidly supported.

To simulate the appearance of a heavy barrel within the shroud, I installed a 17⅞-inch long piece of 3/4" black iron pipe (actual O.D. about 1.035) centrally in the shroud. To locate it centrally in the shroud, I welded washers to the end and then ground them down to fit inside the shroud.

Then I tack-welded it in the shroud. Just as the rear of the receiver was closed up with a 1/8" piece of flat stock, the front is also. Before it can be welded in place, this plate needs to have the shroud welded to it. You can simply butt the shroud up against the plate and weld the outside but this doesn't look the best.

I choose to put a shroud-sized hole in the center of the plate and set the shroud into the hole so that the welding could be done on the back side of the plate where the weld would not show. This gives a much better appearance, but it is more work.

Whichever method you use, be sure the plate is square with the shroud, so when installed you barrel extends out straight. Before you install the shroud into the receiver, the booster on the front needs to be fabricated and installed. Two styles of

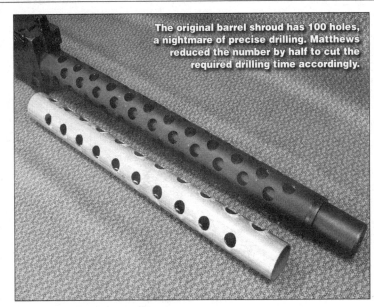

The original barrel shroud has 100 holes, a nightmare of precise drilling. Matthews reduced the number by half to cut the required drilling time accordingly.

It's vital to locate the ventilating holes accurately to make a realistic barrel shroud. Use a rod in the previous pair of holes to align the shroud squarely in the vise.

There's no need to buy a huge drill bit to drill the hole in the front receiver plate. Just drill a series of small holes, cut between them and file to final shape.

One of the most important welds is the shroud to the front receiver plate. It must be square. You can weld front or back, but the weld behind the plate is neater.

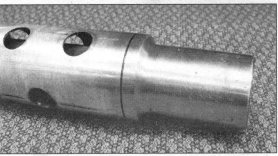

Weld a half-inch washer to a piece of iron pipe to make the booster. A short stub of "barrel" will center it on the shroud. Contour it and scribe a false seam.

boosters are found on 1919s, one is a tapered cone shape and the other is a straight sided reduced diameter style.

I used the reduced diameter style, since it is easier to replicate. This booster will be made from a 2½-inch long piece of 1-inch (actual size about 1⁵⁄₁₆ inches O.D.) black iron pipe. The front end of this booster was capped with a 1/2" flat washer welded in place. The washer was then ground down flush with the pipe.

The rear of the booster was placed up against the front of the shroud and welded in place. Be sure that the booster is located squarely and centered on the shroud. Having it run off crooked will really detract from the realistic look of the project.

Once it's welded in place, grind off the excess weld so that the booster looks to be one piece with the shroud. You don't want any weld seams to show here. To make the booster look like an item that attaches to the shroud just like the real one, a shallow groove was cut in the shroud about 1/4" back from the booster. This gives the appearance of a seam. It can be cut with a thin cut off wheel in a hand grinder.

The shroud can now be welded to the front of the receiver. For good looks, it must be straight with the receiver. Use a straightedge to verify it is located straight before and during welding. If it moves while welding, reposition it before continuing the weld. Nothing looks worse on a display gun than having the barrel running off at some skewed angle!! Once it is welded on straight, grind off any excess weld so no seams show.

A front sight can now be made and installed. Rather than build a functional sight for a non-functional gun, I just copied the outside contour of the real sight. A 2⅜-inch long piece of 1¼x3/8-inch flat steel was used for the sight material.

The sight looks something like an up side down "P". The post portion was a half-inch wide and 1⅜ inches tall. The last quarter-inch of the post was filed down to the shape of a sight blade.

The remaining 1x1¼ inches at the bottom was drilled in the center with a 7/16" drill so that it could be plug-welded to the front of the receiver. After welding, the excess was ground smooth.

Once all these parts have been installed, the project can be final-finished. All rough spots, scratches, bumps, excess welds need to smoothed up. If one wishes more details they can be included in the previously made parts before finishing.

I wanted to duplicate the appearance of a typical Parkerized finish found on real 1919s without the cost and effort of a real Parkerizing job. Unfortunately one can't just go to the store and tell the clerk you want some paint to match the finish on a 1919, you will just get a blank look!

There is however a place you *can* get a color match for a Parkerized finish, Brownells. Brownells offers an epoxy-based firearms finish known as Aluma-Hyde 2. It is available in aerosol cans or liquid form for those with spray equipment.

Brownells offers two Parkerizing color options: light and dark Parkerizing gray. The light version duplicates the color of zinc phosphate Parkerizing and the dark option matches the color of manganese phosphate Parkerizing.

I tried both color options on this project and found only a slight color difference. You had to look very closely in bright light to see the difference. I preferred the dark version but either looked right.

I was using the liquid form and perhaps there is more color difference in the aerosols. One thing I do know is that for large projects such as this, the liquids are much better options over the aerosols.

Conventional spray equipment such as a small paint gun (air brushes are too small for this project) can apply a much better finish than spray cans, because they can apply more material, atomize it better, and the pattern can be adjusted for your needs.

For best adhesion, I abrasive-blasted the parts prior to spraying the Aluma-Hyde 2. Blasting is not absolutely required, but it will give a more durable finish. Aluma-Hyde 2 will dry to the touch in a few hours but full cure will take many days.

Gentle heating (about 140º) for a few hours will help speed the curing, but not as much as you might think. After initial drying, Aluma-Hyde cures by a slow chemical reaction, not solvent drying out of the finish. I have yet to figure out how to speed up the process. Once cured, the finish is very hard and durable, but you should be prepared to wait some time for a full cure.

After a few days of curing time, I checked the parts. The color was what I wanted, but the flat finish looked a little caulky for my taste. The project also looked a little too monochromatic (single-colored).

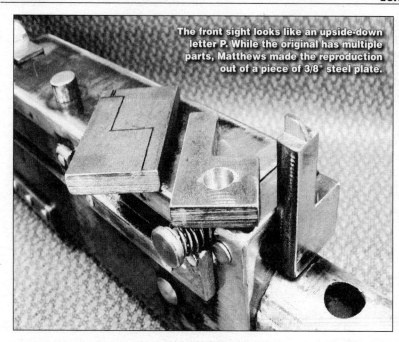

The front sight looks like an upside-down letter P. While the original has multiple parts, Matthews made the reproduction out of a piece of 3/8" steel plate.

Brownells Aluma-Hyde 2 epoxy finish duplicated the color of manganese phosphate Parkerizing. Matthews highlighted the rivet heads by the expedient of a Sharpie pen.

To break up the color, I decided to highlight some of the small details with a darker color. I darkened the rivet heads and a few other features. These parts, once highlighted, really made the project look just right.

You may choose to paint the heads and small items but I used an extremely crude method that worked surprisingly and exceptionally well. I used a black Sharpie pen to color in the rivet heads and used a soft rag to wipe off the excess ink.

This resulted in a subdued darkening effect that looked just right to my eyes. The ink seemed to stain the heads just enough for the effect I wanted. A later application of oil did not affect the colored heads.

To remove the slight chalkiness that is sometimes found in flat finishes I used a soft rag to apply a *very light* coat of oil. The oil seemed to make the finish look like a lightly oiled Parkerized finish, just what I wanted. Once the sprayed finish was complete, I installed the previously stained and lacquered wood grips.

The completed Browning 1919A4 looked very much like a real 1919 at a distance of a few feet. You needed to get pretty close and be familiar with this type of gun to tell it was a fake. While not a precise replica, it was a pretty reasonable facsimile, especially considering its low cost of $30. A $600+ replica made from real gun parts may be fine for people with money, but for us poor folks, this $30 replica works fine.

M2 Tripod Fabrication.

Now that the gun portion of this project is complete it's time to make a mount. While the Browning 1919A4 was mounted on several mounts over its career, the most common was the M2 tripod. It featured a central head with three folding steel tubing legs. The gun was attached at the front to a swivel known as a pintle and the rear was attached to an assembly known as a traversing and elevation mechanism, also referred to as a T+E.

An original M2 tripod can easily exceed $600 for a well-used example, so this do-it-yourself option is the way to go for an inexpensive display mount. I had previously written a piece for SGN (11/20/06) on building a inexpensive (about $50) functional replica for owners of 1919A4 semi auto guns, so I just simplified that design for this non-functional display mount.

I went with thinner steel materials, deleted the folding leg function, and made the T+E out of very light material and deleted any functionality. This resulted in a M2 tripod that looked very much like a real tripod yet weighed one third as much, could be built in one day, and only cost about $10. The end result looked pretty good for the $10 investment.

The display tripod can be built with common home workshop tools. I used a power band saw to cut materials but there is no reason a hacksaw won't work; it's just slower. I made the bends in the head with a self-made bending die in an arbor press but the bends can be made with nothing more than a large vise, steel blocks, and large hammer.

I used a drill press for drilling holes, but a hand drill can be used if you are skilled at hand drilling. An arc welder is needed for this project. A MIG type is preferred, since they more easily weld light gauge materials, but a stick welder can be used with small electrodes.

Materials can be new or used/recycled. New materials will push the price up to perhaps $25, but that's still cheap. If you use salvaged/recycled materials, you should have no trouble

Matthews cut tabs out of steel plate to connect the T+E mechanism at the rear of the receiver and to reinforce the front where the gun is attached to the tripod pintle.

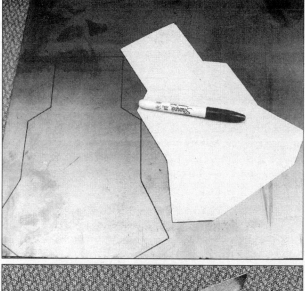

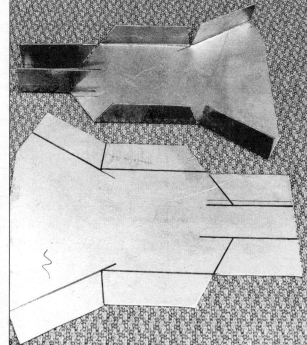

Matthews made a cardboard template for the tripod head and used it to mark cutting lines on the steel. Then it's a matter of cutting the steel and bending it.

point on each side of the large rectangle 3⅛ inches up from the bottom.

Draw a line from this point to the end of the 1¾-inch line to form a triangle. The lower points of these triangles now need to be removed. Use a square and draw a 2-inch line from the outside edge of the triangle until it intersects with the bottom edge of the rectangle.

Now that the blank is drawn out, cut the material with a saw or tin snips, followed by deburring all edges. Since the sides of the tripod head will be 1 inch tall, bend lines need drawn on the blank. Draw the bend lines on the angled portion and the sides of the 5¾-inch wide rectangle only.

On the front of the 3¾-inch wide rectangle, the bend lines need to be drawn 1⅜ inches in from the edges so that when bent, the channel formed will be 1 inch wide. Once all the bend lines are marked, relief cuts need to be made between the segments to allow each part to bend independently.

The blank can now be bent. I used a self-made bending die set in an arbor press to make my bends, but simply placing the blank in a large vise and bending the sides with a large hammer works alright also.

Some steel blocks will aid in hand-bending the material and give a smooth professional look to your bends. If you are unsure of how to work sheet steel, study up on the process by reading metal fabrication books. Folding sheet metal is very easy if you know the techniques.

The most important part is getting nice smooth precise bends. Once all the sides are formed, the rear angled part of the head needs to be bent to 23°. You may need to make some small relief cuts in the sides to allow for a full bend.

The front leg support needs to be bent to a different angle, 45°. When making both of these bends, be sure you don't twist the parts out of alignment; they need to remain parallel. A twisted head will result in legs that run off at odd angles and look bad.

The rear sides can now be welded together. The front sides also need to be welded together, but first the front edge will need to be trimmed off at an angle and a filler plate made to fill the gap.

Draw a line back from the front leg support back to the main body of the head. The exact angle isn't important, just

If you have a press, a bending die set is just the thing for shaping the head. If not, you can use a sturdy bench vise and a dead-blow hammer to accomplish the job.

staying under the $10 mark. Be aware that this tripod is being made from very light materials.

This tripod is only suitable for display purposes and should *never* have a functional gun fired on it. If you want a display tripod that will work for functional guns, then build the functional replica version in the previous article.

The first part to be made will be the tripod head. While this head when completed will look like a real head, it will be made out of easily-worked 16-gauge steel. You will need a couple square feet of material. Cut a blank of sheet stock and then bent it to form the head.

I used a template so I had a re-usable pattern, but you can just draw the dimensions out on the sheet steel. Start by drawing a 3¾-inch wide by 10-inch tall rectangle on the steel. Centered over one end of this rectangle, draw another rectangle that is 5¾ inches wide and 7 inches tall.

Please note that on my template and blank the upper ends are angled, but this is not required on yours. I found this feature unnecessary for this lightweight head but just didn't alter my template from my previous tripod project.

What you should have now is a large rectangle with a smaller one over the top. On each side of the bottom of the large rectangle, extend a line out 1¾ inches. Now mark a

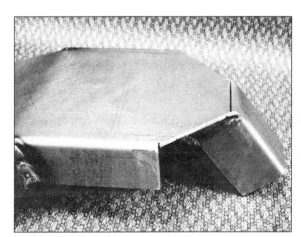

The front edge of the head is angled to duplicate the shape of the original tripod head where the front leg enters. A filler piece is welded in to fill the gap.

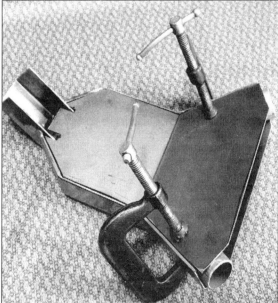

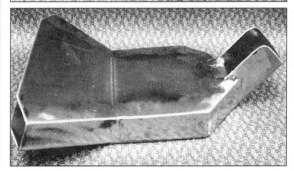

Matthews used cut-off stubs of the legs to space the head top and bottom plates for welding. Be sure not to weld the stubs in place when finishing the head assembly!

The pintle is a simple U-shape made from 1/2x1/4" flat steel and a 1/2" bolt. The half-inch bolt is plenty for a display gun; never use this tripod with a real firearm.

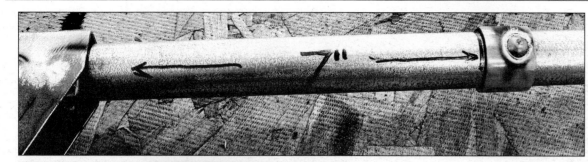

After welding a collar 7 inches from the top of each rear leg, Matthews installed a traversing bar made from lightweight and inexpensive 1/2" electrical conduit.

whatever looks right to you. Just be sure the sides are equal for good looks.

Once the angled front is cut, weld in a filler section made from 1x1/8" flat stock. After welding in the filler piece, grind the welds smooth so that the filler piece looks to be one with the head body. The open bottom of the head now needs to be filled in with a 16-gauge plate.

To size this part, I simply laid a piece of thin cardboard on the head and traced around it and then trimmed it to fit between the sides of the head. This bottom plate will need to

be bent to follow the contour of the top and have a couple relief cuts made at the front for the leg support sides.

To maintain correct spacing of the upper and lower pieces before welding, short sections of leg material were clamped between them. This leg material is 3/4" EMT, also known as 3/4" electrical conduit.

Although referred to as 3/4", exterior size is really about .925". Once they were spaced correctly, all sides were arc welded followed by grinding smooth.

Once all welding was done, the rear edges of the upper and lower sections were trimmed even with each other and the angled ends were verified to be close to 1 inch wide. The front edges of the front leg support were also rounded over. Except for drilling holes, the head forming and fabrication is done.

The next item to be made was the pintle. The original M2 tripod pintle was a heavy casting with a machined tapered extension on the bottom that fit in a tapered socket in the head.

For a display tripod there is no use duplicating this difficult-to-make part. The pintle for our display model is made from 1/4x1½-inch flat stock, a 1/2" bolt, and a 9/16" bolt.

Start by cutting two pieces of 1½-inch stock 2¼ inches long. Cut another piece 2⅜ inches long. Be sure all ends are square. Verify that your 2⅜-inch piece is at least 2.370 inches long. If you made your 2⅜-inch cut a few thousandths short, you gun may not fit the pintle, since a real 1919 is about 2.350 inches wide.

Squarely clamp the two sides to the outside of the 2⅜-inch center piece and weld them together. Grind a weld groove on the bottom seam so that the welds can be ground smooth.

After welding, measure the part to be sure the sides are still parallel and you have at least 2.370" between the sides.

In the center of the bottom piece drill a 1/2" hole all the way through. A 9/16" hole needs to be drilled in both sides near the top for a gun mounting/pivot pin. This hole should be centered and about 1⅝ inches up from the outside bottom. This pin can be made from the smooth shank of a long 9/16" bolt. I rounded the head so it wouldn't look like a bolt.

A hairpin clip can be used to retain the pin. A 1/2" stud welded into the pintle secures the pintle to the head. Use a bolt shank for this part. Drill a 1/2" hole in the head for the pintle stud. Locate it centered and about 2½ inches back from the bend point on the front leg support.

Place a 1/2" washer between the pintle and head to prevent the pintle from scraping on the top of the head when it swivels. Use a flat washer and lock nut to secure the pintle to the head. The sides of the pintle can be contoured. The original pintle featured sides that tapered inward at the top, but I just rounded mine over at the top.

Next comes leg construction. The two rear legs are made from 24-inch long pieces of 3/4" electrical conduit and the front is made from a 12-inch piece of the same material. Both these legs are overlong to allow for cutting the bevels on the ends for the foot pads later.

To fit the legs to the head, you need a large flat and level work surface, some "C" clamps, a tape measure, level, and a selection of blocks or shims. Insert the front leg into the front leg support until it is against the bottom of the head and clamp in place.

A 2x4 makes a handy gauge for trimming off the legs. The spiked feet of the original tripod here are replaced with large washers welded to touch the floor evenly.

The T+E mechanism required only about $5 worth of parts, the important one being a beam clamp. When assembled and finished, it does a good job of imitating the original.

When Matthews brought the finished dummy to the Knob Creek Machine Gun Shoot, visitors by the dozen stopped by to look. Many assumed that it was a miniature M1919.

Insert the rear legs into the head about 2½ inches and clamp in place. Set the tripod up on a level and flat surface. Place a level on the head and shim all legs till the head is level in all directions. Once level all the way around, use a block as a height gage and scribe a line on the legs to mark the cutting location.

Remove the legs, cut to length, then re-install. If you marked and cut your legs accurately, your angled cuts should be flush against the work surface. If your cuts aren't even, remove each leg and trim until they are. The cuts must be right so that when the foot pads are installed later, they will be flat on the surface.

Crooked cuts with gaps will look bad. Once all legs are correct, they can be spot-welded to the head, since the folding leg feature was deleted on this display tripod. Place your spot welds on the inside of the head where they won't show. Once the legs are welded on, holes for bolts need to be drilled in the head and legs to simulate the look of a real M2 tripod head.

For the rear legs, 5/16" holes need to be drilled 9/16" in from the side and about 2 inches up from the bottom. Once bolts are installed, this will give the look of pivot bolts in the head.

Two folding leg stop bolts need to be placed in the lower part of the head. These bolts will be 1/4" diameter. Locate these holes and bolts about 1/2" up from the bottom and about 2 inches in from the sides. Trim all bolts so they are flush with the installed nuts. A 5/16" bolt also needs to be installed in the front leg support. Locate it centered and about 1 inch up from the bottom.

Before foot pads can be installed, two collars need to be installed lid over the legs. The traversing bar/brace will be welded to these collars to prevent warping the legs and to also give the appearance of the real collars.

Since the legs are made from 3/4" EMT, a steel 3/4" EMT coupler was used for collar material. All you have to do is cut the coupler in half and you then have two collars. The screw hole in each half of the collar was enlarged so a plug weld could secure the collar to the leg.

The collars were slid over the legs and located 7 inches from the head and plug welded in place. A fake traversing

bar brace was made from a section of 1/2" EMT (1/2" conduit). The ends of this brace were flattened to about 3/8" thick and then the ends were cut at an angle to align with the collars. Once the length and angles were right, the brace was welded in place and the weld ground smooth.

The foot pads were installed next. The original M2 tripod featured foot pads, about 2¾ inches in diameter with cleats on the bottom to dig into the ground. Our display tripod doesn't need cleats, so they were deleted. To give the rough appearance of the foot pads, 2¼-inch diameter steel washers were welded to the ends of the legs.

To support the rear of the gun and allow precise aiming the original M2 tripod featured a device known as a traversing and elevation mechanism, also referred to as a T+E.

This original T+E featured more than 50 machined parts and it is way too difficult for home builders to duplicate. To ease the build of this project I made a simple "representative" T+E. While non-functional, this T+E will look something like the original and allow the builder to point the display gun in any reasonable direction.

The materials needed to make this part are one beam clamp (used to hang pipe or conduit), a 5/16" bolt, a 1/4" nut and thumbscrew, 3 inches of 1/2" conduit, a 2x3/4" disc (steel, aluminum, brass, plastic, etc), a 6½-inch piece of 5/8" rod, 1½ inches of 3/8" black iron pipe, a 5 to 6-inch long 7/16" bolt, and one retaining clip.

I started by attaching the beam clamp to the top end of the 1/2" conduit. I brazed it on, but it can be welded on or soldered. On the opposite side, I drilled a 9/32" hole and brazed a 1/4" nut over the hole for a thumbscrew. The assembly was then ground smooth.

The interior of the conduit was drilled out to 5/8" so it would slide over the rod. Check to verify that the opening in your beam clamp is wide enough to easily slide over the 1/2" conduit, if not, file to size. For a clamping screw, I bent the end of a bolt 90° and removed the head.

An elevation rod was made from a 6½-inch piece of 5/8" rod. At the top of this rod a 1½-inch long piece of 3/8" pipe was welded on as a cross piece. A pin to secure the gun and T+E together was made from a long 9/16" bolt shank.

The head was ground round and a hole was drilled for a retaining clip. The real T+E assembly featured a large adjusting knob so one was made for the display tripod.

I used a disc of aluminum with a 5/8" hole drilled in the center, but about any kind of metal material would be fine. A set screw in the side secured it to the rod. To add some realism to the project you may choose to mark numbers or graduations on the knob.

When the T+E is installed, you should have a full range of movement. Elevation can be set by loosening the thumbscrew and adjusting the rod up and down. Side-to-side movement can be done by loosening the clamp and sliding the assembly right or left on the traversing bar.

This should allow you to set up your display in any direction that an original tripod could be set. Granted this doesn't look exactly like the original but then it doesn't cost much either. An original T+E runs about $200 and this one cost about $2, good enough for display purposes!

At this point your tripod fabrication should be complete except for finishing. Before finishing, smooth up any rough spots. Good finishing can be the difference between something that looks professional or cobbled together.

Finish options are many. You can choose common inexpensive paint, Parkerizing, high-tech sprayed finishes or anything in between. For the tripod part, I chose inexpensive common oil-based olive drab paint since I already had a gallon of it and I had three tripods to finish.

I abrasive blasted the parts for best adhesion and then sprayed the paint. I chose a different finish for the T+E portion. Since the elevation rod slid in a tight-fitting tube I wanted something that was thin, hard and durable, so I used Brownells Teflon-Moly Over Cured Gun Finish in the color of matte black. This finish is very durable and once baked and cooled, it's at full hardness, no need to wait for days for a full cure.

Once all the parts were finished, I mounted the display gun on the display tripod and inserted a loaded belt of ammo into the gun. I was quite pleased with the results. Compared to my semi auto 1919A4, the display version looked pretty respectable. From a distance of 10-15 feet the display version was almost indistinguishable from the functional gun.

Only when you got close could you notice the lack of small details that would tip one off that it wasn't real. People who don't know guns probably wouldn't even realize it wasn't a real gun.

A display gun built from real Browning 1919A4 parts would cost more than $600 and a real tripod would add another $600, fine for rich people. My sub-$50 project looked nearly as good for more than $1,000 less. For those less affluent gun collectors who want a display version of the Browning 1919A4, this project is an attractive economic option. If this sounds like your kind of project, why not give it a try? ◉

Build Your Own AK?

Build your own AK-47? Sounds hard, but Matthews demonstrates how it can be done with patience, careful measuring, persistence and common hand tools you already have.

Yes, You Can!

By Steven Matthews

With a little patience and common hand tools, you can save hundreds by assembling your own AK-47. Here's how.

If you look through the pages of SGN, you have probably noticed that there are an abundance of ads for AK-47 parts kits, accessories and receivers. You may be surprised to know that these ads are not entirely directed towards manufacturers that build AK series semi-auto rifles.

In fact the main target of these ads is the hobby gunsmith or do-it-yourself gunbuilder. There are large numbers of people who enjoy building their own firearms. If done according to BATFE regulations, which allow individuals to make guns for their own use, it is completely legal.

There are dozens of model variations of the AK series, and depending on the model chosen, the cost savings can be substantial. You don't have to be a real mechanical wizard to make one of these guns. If you are reasonably competent with tools,

can read and follow instructions and have a basic understanding of how firearms operate, it is "doable" for the average gun hobbyist.

I have been occasionally building guns from kits for more than 20 years and have a fair amount of skill, so I decided it was about time for me to build an AK rifle (or pistol!). I have built several AR-15s, an FN-FAL, single-shot .50 BMG rifle, semi-auto Browning 1919A4, NFA M16, NFA MAC-10, NFA Browning 1919A4, NFA suppressed Ruger MK1, and too many others to mention.

Based on my past experiences, if an AR-15 build would rate a 1 on a 1-10 scale and a Browning 1919A4 a 10, I would rate an AK-47 build about a 5. I will say that gunbuilding is one of those things that is not all that hard, but you have to pay attention

to what you are doing and have the knowledge required to build a project safely.

You don't want to just slap together some parts when you don't really understand what they do, then expect things to work, especially when you are discharging a cartridge developing 40,000+ psi just inches from your face.

The first job is to decide what model variation of the AK series you want to build. The AK-47 series of guns is well known to anyone even vaguely familiar with military firearms. If you've ever watched the network news, you've seen one!

Designed by Mikhail Kalashnikov and adopted by the Soviet military in 1947, it was the official battle rifle of the communist world for more than a half-century. Early AK-47s featured a machined steel receiver that was time-consuming and expensive

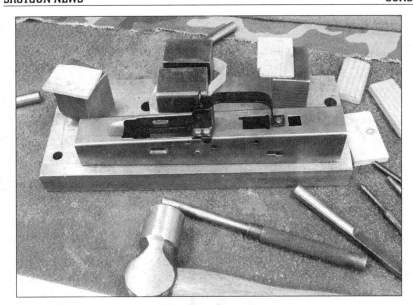

Building the AK receiver requires precise riveting, which is best accomplished with a sturdy steel bench plate, steel backing blocks, ball-peen hammers and punches.

to manufacture. The AKM series was designed in the 1950s to use a sheet metal receiver reduced raw materials requirements and machine time.

This sheet-metal receiver is what really makes this build project so desirable. Because they're easy to make, they are inexpensive, usually in the $50-$80 range. Combine one with a surplus parts kit for $100-300, and you have a very cost-effective project.

Things got a little more complicated as of July 13, when BATFE issued a letter to importers stating it would no longer issue import permits for frames, receivers and barrels. In the case of AKs, this means barrels, since full-auto receivers were unimportable anyway. There are still lots of imported barrels on hand, and this ruling will spur U.S. production of AK barrels, but prices may go up for a while.

Before we go any further, I should address the legal issues involved in building an AK-47 style semi-auto rifle or pistol. While it is completely legal for an individual to build a semi-auto AK type rifle (or pistol), it does have to be done according to the rules.

You are allowed to build these guns for your own personal use, not to manufacture for resale. First off it does have to be *semi-auto* only! Full-auto guns are highly regulated and require prior BATFE approval and are beyond the scope of this article.

The second biggest issue in building these guns is the fact that you will be using a lot of imported parts to make an AK and the BATFE has a limit on just how many imported parts can be used in the construction of a semi-auto rifle.

This 10-part rule is commonly referred to as the Section 922r ruling. According to the rules, you may use no more than 10 specified parts out of a list of 20 (see box). You can use any combination as long as it is not more than 10 imported parts; the rest have to be U.S. made. The U.S.-made parts may be identical to the imported parts. It's kinda dumb to replace good foreign parts with the same U.S.-made parts, but those are the rules. You have to do it that way to be legal!

Only the parts on the list are regulated, if it's not on the list, you can use it. Small parts such as pins, springs and hardware are not on the list, so they can be used without restriction.

I recommend you use a U.S. made semi-auto fire control group (hammer, trigger, disconnector). This counts as three U.S.-made parts and is what most people use for an AK rifle build.

Just to make things more interesting, there's an important exception. The 10 parts rule only applies to semi-auto rifles, not pistols! A pistol version of the AK can have as many imported parts as you care to use, as long as they are in semi-auto configuration.

Thanks to this regulatory quirk, it is very inexpensive to make an AK pistol, since it only requires a kit and a U.S.-made receiver. As far as receivers go, it is not mandatory to use a U.S.-made receiver, but it is recommended since they are the type readily available and they do count as a U.S. part in the 10 parts rule.

Since I am going to be making a rifle and a pistol for this article, it's important to address just what the technical difference is between a rifle and pistol. The BATFE requirements for a rifle state that it must have a minimum barrel length of 16 inches and a minimum overall length of 26 inches.

A pistol may have a barrel of any length but must not have a buttstock or forward pistol grip or the means to attach either.

In addition to the length requirements, the pistol has to have a receiver that is classified as a pistol receiver and the rifle has to have one classified as a rifle receiver.

If you are using a "virgin" receiver, this classification can be specified at the time of purchase. When you buy it, have it listed on the BATFE form 4473 as one or the other and also have a receipt that specifies which it is. At this point its identity as a rifle or pistol is set. You cannot legally change it once it is papered.

For more info on the legal issues of home gun building, check out the BATFE website at www.atf.treas.gov/firearms/faq/index.htm

The internet is a wealth of information on building AK rifles or pistols. One of the best internet sources for AK building is the "Gunsmithing and Build It Yourself" section of the akfiles. com. It is a discussion forum that is frequented by multitude of experienced AK builders with first-hand knowledge that can be especially useful to the novice builder.

If you aren't into computers, there are many advertisers in SGN that offer books, DVDs, and tapes that take you through the building process step by step. A complete step-by-step tutorial would be too large for this article, so I will just cover some of the more important aspects of building. If you are knowledgeable on how guns work, you can fill in the gaps. If you aren't, you can research on the internet or buy one of the instructional videos or books.

Knowing rules and regulations is vital when building your own. For example, a pistol can't have a front pistol grip or place to mount one, so the handguard was modified.

Once you have the info on how to build you need the parts and the best source of parts, SGN, is in your hands right now. After researching this project, I decide I wanted to build two AKs. I decided to build an AK-74 rifle, which is the 5.45x39mm version of the older 7.62x39mm AK-47. It is almost identical to the older 7.62 gun other than caliber.

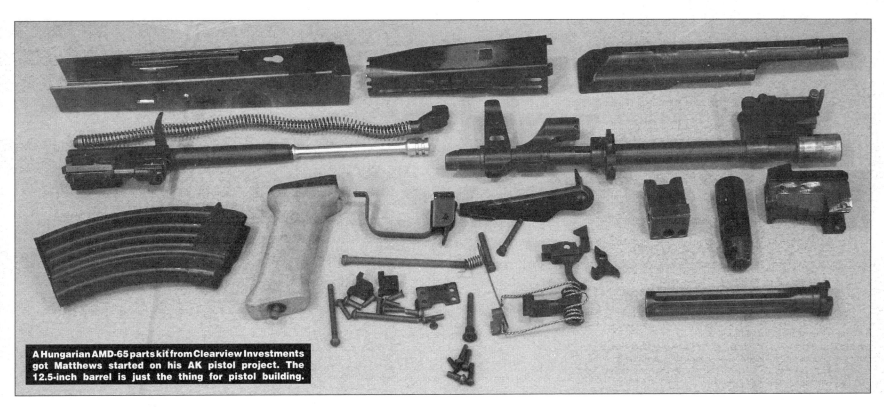

A pistol can't have a buttstock or mounting point for one, either, so the Hungarian rear trunnion had to be welded to prevent future installation of a buttstock.

I also decided to build an AK pistol in the original 7.62x39mm. The pistol version is just a short-barreled AK-47 without a buttstock or forward pistol grip. For the rifle, I ordered a Bulgarian AK-74 kit from Akron Armory. This kit was advertised as in excellent condition and was priced at $199.

When received, it was in the stated condition. In a business where conditions are generally over-hyped, it was nice to get one that was as advertised! For the pistol build I ordered a Hungarian AMD-65 kit from Clearview Investments that was advertised as in unissued condition and was priced at $129. It also was as advertised.

What makes the AMD-65 kit so desirable for a pistol build is that it comes with a 12.5-inch barrel, which is just right for this type of pistol. It also has a wire stock that is easy to delete for the pistol legal requirement. Both of these kits were also advertised as "all matching numbers," which indicates that the bolts are already properly headspaced to the trunnions.

This makes the building a lot easier and less costly. One thing I might mention about the condition of these kits is that they were in excellent condition for Com-Block military guns. Don't expect them to have the fit and finish of an American made commercial gun. They were made for functionality, not good looks!

I chose Ohio Ordnance Works AK-74 and AK-47 receivers; there are slight differences between the two. I obtained one from a gun show vendor for about $85, which I thought was a bit high, so I looked for a better price on line. I found that Ohio Rapidfire in Troy, Ohio, sold them for $65, and since they were only about an hour or so away from where I live I drove down to buy one.

I was surprised when I got to Ohio Rapidfire to find they carry many parts and accessories for the AK builder. Most shops don't carry anything for home builders and it was nice to find a place that catered to my hobby interest. The OOW receivers are U.S. made and are generally considered to be one of the better receivers on the market.

An interesting side note on these receivers is that they are known as Ohio Ordnance Works receivers, but are marked as being made by "ITM." I contacted OOW about this and was told that ITM is their manufacturing source. Since the rifle required several U.S.-made parts for legality, I bought a U.S.-made gas piston and fire contol group (hammer, trigger, disconnector) from TAPCO for $50.

I also bought a U.S.-made pistol grip($10) and U.S. muzzle brake($25) at local gun shows. These parts brought the U.S.-made parts count up to the legal requirement. I also bought several $8 military surplus(new) magazines for both guns.

Now that I had the parts, receivers and info on how to build, what about tools? I built both kits with basic hand tools that you would find in any well-equipped home workshop. These included include a small die grinder or Dremel Moto-Tool, hammers, punches, files, dial calipers, marking fluid or black marker, a large strong vise, screwdrivers, clamps, blocks of steel for backing up rivets, etc.

To keep costs down, I chose to use basic tools even though there are specialty tools available for AK building. Riveting tools and an arbor press are somewhat expensive, and since I was only building two guns, I traded off ease of building for cost savings.

Installing parts in a U.S.-made receiver boils down to riveting in the front and rear trunnions and a trigger guard/mag release assembly.

The trigger guard/mag release assembly location is already drilled and located on the OOW receivers. The trunnions have to be located and drilled by the builder. This is to accommodate the multitude of AK kits that may come from several manufacturers and countries. Locating and installing these trunnions (and also the barrel) is the most difficult part of AK building.

You need to choose at this point whether to use rivets or screws.

The truninons and trigger guard assemblies are riveted in place on factory-built AK-47s and AK 74s. This was and is the fast and easy way to assemble them in a factory setting. For the home builder with nothing but basic hand tools, this riveting method is doable but rather slow and somewhat difficult, but I traded ease of build for reduced cost. If you want your AK to look original, the rivet method is the way to go.

One downside of rivet builds is that it also requires the barrel to be removed from the trunnion to install the new rivets. Screw builds don't require barrel removal,

Steel backing blocks support the rivet heads as the trigger guard assembly is riveted in place. Holes are pre-drilled here, so it's a good place to start assembly.

but do require drilling and tapping several holes and using screws and some nuts instead of rivets. The shallow depth of some of the holes can make tapping difficult. Screw builds are a proven method of home building AKs, but in my opinion, screws make the gun look cheap and amateurish.

I started one of these guns as a screw build but soon abandoned it when it became apparent to me that a screw build was not that much easier than a rivet build. For more about riveting, see the sidebar.

The first part to be installed on the new receiver is the trigger guard/ mag release assembly. This is not a random choice, as this location is set by the receiver manufacturer and this location also determines where the front trunnion will locate.

To install the trigger guard on a rivet build, you obviously need rivets. You can buy the correct metric rivets at a rather high cost($10-15 for a dozen or so rivets) or do as I did and replace them with standard size rivets that are available at hardware stores for a few cents each.

The trigger guard holes are sized just about right for common 5/32"x 1/2" round head steel rivets. They will need to be shortened so that only about 1/8" extends through the trigger guard/ mag release assembly, selector stop plate and receiver. This will be enough to form a head on the inside or the receiver.

Assemble the parts (be sure you get the selector stop on the correct side!) and insert the rivets with the round heads on the outside and the unformed shanks extending into the receiver. Use a couple blocks of steel under the round heads to back up the rivets. Also support the receiver so that it doesn't fall over when you are working on it.

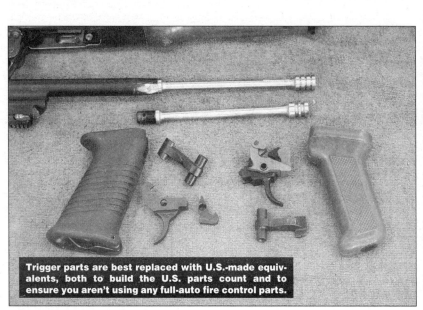

Trigger parts are best replaced with U.S.-made equivalents, both to build the U.S. parts count and to ensure you aren't using any full-auto fire control parts.

Slide the front trunnion into the receiver and use a magazine to set the proper location. Use a dial caliper to measure hole positions and transfer to the receiver.

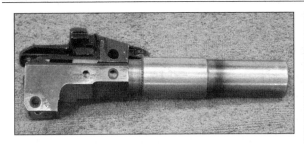

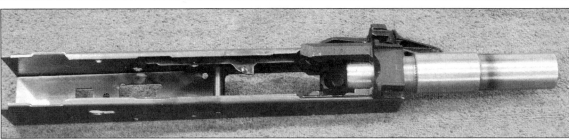

A steel backing bar takes the place of the barrel in the trunnion, supporting it and the receiver as the rivets are flattened. This is the toughest part of the job.

Use a large hammer and punch to flatten the ends of the rivets. You don't need to form round heads, since this is on the inside where it is not visible. Make sure you have the rivets backed up solidly; you want your hammering force to be transferred to the rivets, not the parts.

If you don't have the rivets supported well, you will bend your parts! Also, make sure that the parts are staying tightly together while riveting. You may want to do one rivet at a time to make it easier, but don't fully tighten the rivets till all are in place. Once the rivets are tight, it is hard to reposition any parts that may have moved while you were hammer-forming the previous rivet.

The two forward rivets are hard to reach, but if you angle in your punch, you can form a head that is adequate for the inside where it won't show.

Now comes what most builders consider to be the most difficult part of AK building, locating and installing the front trunnion. Before you can install the front trunnion, you must remove the barrel from the trunnion since the old rivets are under the barrel and the new ones will go in their place.

Place your trunnion assembly *securely* in a vise and use a large hammer and appropriate-sized punch to drive out the barrel-retaining crosspin. These pins are sometimes very hard to remove, so make sure you have everything clamped securely. You may really have to bang on it, so be careful you are not bending anything when trying to remove it.

Once the pin is out, you can remove the barrel from the trunnion; this may also require a lot of force. The method I used was to wrap the barrel in a rag and lightly clamp it in the vise and butt the trunnion up against the side of the vise jaws. The idea here is to allow the barrel to slide through the vise jaws but have the trunnion stopped by the jaws.

Place a couple of soft copper coins or soft washers against the rear of the barrel and use a punch slightly smaller than the barrel shank to drive out the barrel. An alternative method I saw on the Internet was to use an automotive-style gear puller to press out the barrel.

I didn't try it but I don't see why it wouldn't work. If you have a hydraulic arbor press, it works a lot easier for barrel removal than the hammer method. On the pistol build that I did first I pressed the barrel out with a hydraulic arbor press at my workplace.

Total time to set it up and press it out was only about 15 minutes, so if you have to take yours to a machine shop you should only have to pay about $15-20 (shop rates in my area are about $50-60/hour) For the rifle build, I used the "big hammer" method which worked well and didn't cost anything other than effort.

It's up to you to decide if you can handle it yourself or you want to hire it done. If you take it to a machine shop, be sure it's "gun friendly" and even then don't even mention the words

AK-47. We know this build is completely legal, but the general public only believes what the media tells them about those "evil AK-47s!"

Some barrels may be so hard to remove that you may have no choice but to take it somewhere and have it pressed out for a few bucks. Mine came out fine with the hammer method. Once the barrel is out, use some emery cloth to polish up the barrel shank, crosspin, crosspin hole and the trunnion hole to remove any burrs that will make reinstallation difficult.

Now the bare trunnion needs to be fitted to the new receiver. Slide it into the receiver with the upper receiver edges sliding into the groove in the trunnion. Some hand fitting may be required to get the parts to fit properly.

The rear trunnion is installed in much the same way. Measure the rivet locations, transfer them to the receiver, center punch and then drill, carefully.

You locate the trunnion in the receiver with a magazine, since the front magazine catch is machined into the rear of the trunnion. You slide the trunnion in until you get a good fit of the magazine. The magazines need to be held securely but not so tight as to make removal difficult. Try several magazines to make sure they fit correctly.

Once a good location is found, use a c-clamp to clamp the trunnion in place and then trim the edges of the receiver flush with the trunnion. Some receivers will not require trimming. Having this trimmed up evenly will aid you in locating the holes you'll need to drill for the front trunnion rivets.

Remove your trunnion and, using dial calipers, measure how far back from the front and how far down from the top your new holes need to be drilled. Measure to the edge of the holes and add 1/2 a rivet diameter to get the center point for your hole location. Measure both sides, as there may be some difference between the two.

Transfer these dimensions to the receiver and center punch them before drilling. Drill the holes several sizes undersize and slide the receiver and trunnion together to verify they are where they are supposed to be. If you have made a mistake, you may have to move the holes by filing on one side or the other to correct it. If they are exactly where they are supposed to be, go ahead and drill them full size.

After I drilled the correct metric-sized holes and verified that they were right, I clamped the two pieces together and re-drilled them to accept the next size larger standard rivets, 3/16". These are only a few thousandths larger and a lot easier to find.

Once you've located and drilled your holes, it's time to install the rivets. I installed the four front rivets with the round heads on the inside of the trunnion and also trimmed them to conform to its inside radius.

They extended about 3/16" past the outside of the receiver to leave enough material to form a round head. I did one rivet at a time. Clamp a piece of steel just a little smaller than the hole in the trunnion in your vise to back up the rivet heads and slide the trunnion receiver assembly on to it. You will probably have to trim the round rivet head to allow you to slide the assembly onto the back up piece.

Once you have the rivet head supported, begin hammering the shank that extends through the receiver. I hammered them flat about halfway, then began to hammer around the edges of the rivet to form a round head. By tapping the edges with a small hammer, you can get a pretty decent looking rivet head without the need to buy rivet-forming punches.

Continue forming the head till you are sure it is tight, then proceed to the next rivet and repeat the process. Remember you want all your hammering force going into forming the rivet, not deforming your trunnion or receiver, so be sure your backing bar is supporting the rivet head.

The two lower rivets will need to be installed next, using the same technique. After your rivets are set, be sure to check that

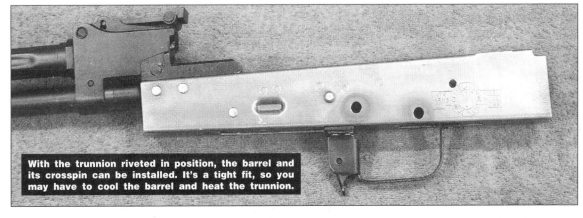

With the trunnion riveted in position, the barrel and its crosspin can be installed. It's a tight fit, so you may have to cool the barrel and heat the trunnion.

Install the fire control group. Matthews suggests ditching the "shepherd's crook" spring and retaining parts with easily available and installable steel clips.

the heads on the inside of the trunnion hole are below its edge. If they are too high, file or grind the heads below the edge of the trunnion hole so that they won't interfere with re-installing the barrel

To locate your rear trunnion, you use the top cover to find a location that allows it to fit properly. Use the same methods that you used to locate the front trunnion to locate the rear. Locate holes, drill and rivet in place.

While on the subject of the rear trunnion, I should mention one of the legal issues on building an AK pistol. A pistol must not have a buttstock or a means to attach one, so before installing your rear trunnion, modify the one you got in your rifle parts kit so that it cannot accept a buttstock. This may require cutting off the stock tang on some models or filling in any stock recesses in the trunnion on other models. I welded in the recesses for the folding stock hardware on my AMD-65 kit and ground it down flat.

Now that both the trunnions are installed, its time to get the barrel back in place. Although a hydraulic press is the easiest

way of reinstalling the barrel, I did it the old-fashioned way with the trusty big hammer method You ain't a gunsmith if you don't have a *big* hammer!

There are two hammer methods and either will work; I tried both and got equal results. The first is to clamp the barrel in a vise and slide the trunnion/receiver assembly on to the barrel stub and use a soft piece of material as a punch and tap the trunnion/receiver onto the barrel till the crosspin hole lines up exactly. Hammer on the trunnion only as the receiver is too thin to hammer on.

The other method is kind of a reverse of the first. Clamp trunnion/receiver assembly in a vise (be careful to clamp down only where the receiver is supported by the trunnion so you don't crush it). I also recommend that you use some wood blocks between the vise jaws and the receiver to prevent marring the receiver.

Then insert the barrel into the trunnion and tap into place. Place a piece of soft material over the muzzle so that you don't mar the end of the barrel, I used an old muzzle brake that was

basically scrap material to protect the muzzle. I recommend small taps when you get close to lining up the crosspin so you don't go too far.

The crosspin hole needs to be lined up almost perfectly. The barrel requires an interference fit, so I recommend the following procedure to make it easier to install. First lightly oil both the trunnion hole and barrel shank. Then place your barrel in your kitchen freezer; the cold will shrink the diameter slightly.

With a propane torch, gently heat the trunnion to expand the trunnion hole; only heat it to 200-300°. An alternative to guessing on the temperature would be to place your trunnion and receiver in your kitchen oven set to the proper temperature for about 30 minutes. Expanding the hole and shrinking the shank will make the two slide together a lot easier.

Once you start sliding the hot trunnion and cold barrel together, don't piddle around, as the two will immediately begin to equalize their temperatures and again be very hard to slide together. Have a large wrench at hand so that if the barrel needs to be rotated to align the crosspin hole, it is there where you can get to it quickly.

Once the crosspin hole is lined up perfectly, clamp the trunnion in your vise and reinstall the barrel crosspin. Lubing both the pin and the hole will make installation easier. I might add at this point that even though you are hammering things together, you just don't beat things together with large hammer blows, you want to apply the force precisely where it needs to be applied and not to the surrounding parts.

If you aren't confident reinstalling your barrel yourself I recommend taking it to the machine shop that removed it for you and having them reinstall it. Just make sure they understand how precisely the parts have to be assembled and make sure they don't damage anything during reassembly.

Now that your trigger guard/mag release assembly, front trunnion, rear trunnion and barrel are installed, the hardest part is done. All that remains is to install the rest of your parts.

Riveting: A Skill You Can Master

One of the biggest concerns of the novice AK builder is the issue of riveting the gun together. Some think that this is difficult and requires some great skill; nothing could be further than the truth. Some even question how a firearm can be safely built using those crude-looking old-fashioned rivets.

Rivets are one of the oldest and well-proven methods of fastening items together. The industrial age was based on rivets!

Rivets have stood the test of time as fasteners. This Port Huron steam tractor, made early in the last century, still stands up to high pressure with riveted construction.

Screws, nuts and bolts were only cheaply and readily available since the mid 1800s when high volume screw-making machinery became available.

Before that, screws were basically hand-made and too expensive for most applications. Even into the mid 20th century, rivets were the most common fastener in applications like as shipbuilding, skyscraper construction and locomotives.

When the AK-47 was redesigned in the 1950s to use the sheet metal receiver the manufacturers wanted a strong, permanent fastener and choose rivets! Although rivets are made from soft steel because they need to be malleable, they are more than adequate for the job.

In a factory setting, the receiver and other parts are held in alignment by precision fixtures and fastened using pneumatic rivet squeezers. It's fast and can be done by semi-skilled assemblers, a vital consideration in wartime when labor is scarce.

The rivets in an AK are not under a great deal of stress. They only serve to hold the receiver and components together and in alignment. The barrel, front trunnion and bolt are the parts under stress at the time of firing. All forces of firing are contained within these parts.

The receiver and riveted in components are there to allow the internal parts to reciprocate in the receiver for functioning and to provide a place to hang the magazine. The only stresses that are involved are the forces from recoil and the spring-driven bolt carrier assembly returning to battery.

Select rivets long enough to provide enough shank material to form an effective head. Too long means a lot of grinding, too short means a joint that might not hold.

Rivets also hold together some of the worlds most durable machine guns, most notably the Browning 1919 MG and the more recent FN-MAG (M240). These guns have a design life rated in the hundreds of thousands of rounds.

Let's look at some *extremely* basic hand riveting methods. I did my rivet setting by hand with nothing more than a hammer, punches, and backup blocks. You can choose from a multitude of riveting tools and methods that range from basic rivet forming punches to hand held forming tools to hydraulically operated setting tools.

Since hand riveting is so easy and there are only 15 rivets in an AK type firearm I could not justify the cost for the specialty tools.

Rivets have to be soft enough so that the head will form without breaking or cracking, and long enough to extend through the parts to be assembled. Heads can be round, flat, short, tall, countersunk, etc., and each type will require a different amount of extra material to form the heads.

Manufacturing tolerances mean some minor hand-fitting of the remaining parts may be required.

The fire control group needs to be installed in the receiver, but not just any fire control group, it needs to be a semi-auto fire control group. While the hammer and triggers are basically the same on the full auto and semi-auto, the semi-auto has a different disconnector.

Either use a manufactured semi disconnector or modify the full auto disconnector by grinding off the tail so that it cannot be contacted by the safety/selector.

The safety lever is installed by orienting it straight up, sliding through the hole in the receiver and then rotating it down into place. You will have to push the disconnector forward to allow it to be put into position.

The fire control group in a semi AK consist of a hammer, trigger, disconnector, safety lever, hammer spring, disconnector spring, two pins and a pin retainer spring. If your kit comes with any of the full-auto fire control parts, I recommend that you throw them away just to stay legal. You don't need them and possession of them can be construed by law enforcement as "intent" to make an unregistered full-auto gun.

One thing that has caused a lot of frustration to AK builders is installing the "shepherds hook" spring that holds in the hammer and trigger pins, it's just flat out difficult to install. The simplest solution to this is to just throw it away and use E-clips or pin retaining clips that are available at hardware stores.

After your fire control group is installed, attach your pistol grip with the long screw and the angled nut that fits into the inside of the receiver. The lower handguard fits into the recess under the front trunnion at the rear.

A lever on it rotates a cam that allows it to slide forward to allow handguard installation. The gas tube/upper handguard is installed between the gas port block and the sight base. It also has a lever and cam for removing and locking in place.

Install the bolt into the bolt carrier and install it into the receiver followed by the recoil spring assembly. The spring end goes into the back of the bolt carrier and the lug on the rear of the spring assembly engages into the groove in the rear trunnion.

Slide the front of the top cover into the groove in the rear sight base and the rear in the groove that is machined into the rear trunnion and is held by the square spring loaded lug on the rear of the recoil spring.

If you are doing a rifle build, this is the point at which you install the buttstock. That part is usually held in place by fitting into the rear of the receiver and by two additional screws. If you have a flash suppressor or muzzle brake, screw it onto the barrel. It will lock in place by the spring-loaded pin in the front sight base.

Since one of the more popular U.S.-made parts to be replaced is the gas piston, I need to mention that not all gas pistons are the same. Model variations with different length barrels sometimes have different length gas pistons. For example, the 12.5-inch barreled AMD-65 doesn't have the same piston as the 16-inch standard models.

Also the AK-74 and the AK-47 have slightly different piston lengths, but you can modify the bolt carrier in the AK-74 by shortening it to use a standard AK-47 piston. If you use the wrong piston, your gun may not function properly, so be sure to use one that is compatible with your parts kit.

Riveting: A Skill You Can Master

Simply flattening the head about halfway is the first step in hand-forming a rivet. To get a rounded profile, you just start tapping the edges against the workpiece.

For this AK project I didn't want a large head protruding from the sides of my receiver and about 3/16" extra was all that was needed for forming my heads. As shown in the picture, you start with a rivet protruding from your work. With a hammer (or hammer and punch if you prefer) hammer the solidly supported head down about 1/2 its length.

To form the traditional round shape on the rivet head, just begin tapping around the edges of the rivet to round it over, work your way around the head till you have a nicely rounded head that is tight on your work. This forming is done with many light taps, not heavy hammer blows.

After you have properly formed the head, smooth it up with a small file or grinder. Make sure that your rivet is always well supported so that all your hammering force is going into the rivet and not deforming your parts. If it's not properly supported, all you will do is push your rivet out of your parts!

For backing blocks I used flat blocks of steel (except for the backing block in the barrel hole). Flat blocks will cause the opposite heads to flatten somewhat when forming the head but since I didn't want protruding heads, this was fine with me. If you want to retain the round heads on the opposite ends you will have to have a backing block with a head shape machined into the block.

Although the hammer method will work fine, you can also use a rivet head forming punch, which will allow you to form the head in one operation. This is simply a punch with a recess formed in the end that will allow the rivet shank to form a head as it is struck.

It will still take many hits to form the head but it does make a nice looking head that requires no finish work. This punch can be bought or made. To make one, just grind a depression in the end of a large punch in the shape of a rivet head with a small stone in a Dremel Moto-tool. Just remember to make it large enough to form a head that is large enough not to pull though your work pieces.

As with any project, there are some tips that may make the job easier or give better results. Here are a few. Always keep your parts firmly clamped together when riveting; you don't want to get your head all formed only to find out that the parts are loosely fitted. A lot of small hits work better when hand setting rivets that a few large hits, the hammer is easier to control and you will make fewer mistakes.

When forming the heads, the rivet shanks in your work will expand and be very difficult to remove if you screw up and want to redo them (don't ask how I know this!), it's best to get them

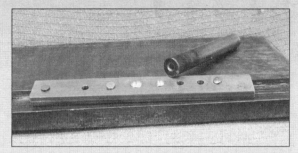

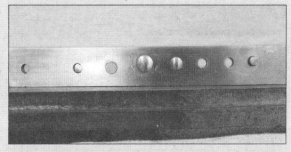

Grind a recess into the end of a large punch and you've made a rivet head punch. It will give a nicely rounded head (r.) without a lot of grinding and finishing needed.

right the first time. If you choose to use "generic" rivets rather than ones already sized for your project like I did you will have to experiment to get the right length for proper head forming. If you are uncertain on using the generic rivets, by all means spend the extra money for the ready-made ones for your own peace of mind.

You can find a variety of sources for rivets on the Internet, and the sites make for interesting reading.

Don't be intimidated by riveting. Remember medieval blacksmiths were riveting hundreds of years ago, it's not high tech! Whether you use basic hand tools or the expensive rivet setting tools, you are just squashing a soft piece of metal

Matthews chose KG GunKote finish for the rifle, hot tank bluing for the pistol. These guns aren't going to have a shiny commercial look, but can stand on their own.

Once all your parts are installed, I recommend you do a final check of all your parts and how they function and then test fire before you proceed to final finishing. You may find some minor fitting problems that need correction before you apply the finish.

There are a multitude of finish options ranging from simple spray paint to traditional or high tech finishes. For the AMD-65 pistol build I went with a traditional hot tank bluing job that I did myself.

For the AK-74 rifle build I went with KG GunKote in charcoal gray that I also applied in my workshop. KG GunKote is a sprayed-on phenolic resin finish that is baked on to form a hard and durable finish and is an excellent finish for military firearms.

These two finishing methods have been covered in previous articles that I have written for SGN if you are interested in the process of applying them. Another popular finish is Lauer Custom Weaponry's DuraCoat, which has also been covered in a previous article.

I suppose the final test of how well you built your guns is how well they work. I guess I got lucky because both of mine worked extremely well. Both functioned fine and the AK-74 was especially surprising in how accurately it shot.

Most AKs in 7.62x39mm will generally only shoot 6-inch groups at 100 yards. This rifle shoots 3-4" groups, even with the crude AK sights. I can't help but wonder how well it would do with a scope. I compared this AK-74 to a Polytech AK -47 7.62 sidefolder I have had for about 15 years and the AK-74 shot considerably better.

The AK-47 pistol was something of a surprise also but not for 100-yard accuracy. I was skeptical about how a pistol this large would handle. Although it was very heavy by pistol standards, I found that from a sandbag rest (with small magazines) I could shoot it as well as any long barrel pistol.

It was a bit like a big semi-auto T-C Contender. Recoil was nowhere near as heavy as a 44 Mag. handgun yet the ballistic tables would indicate similar muzzle energies. At 100 yards I could shoot the AK pistol somewhat better than my S&W 629 44 Mag. with 8⅜-inch barrel.

One of the big incentives of building yourself is the cost savings. For the AMD-65 pistol build I had $130 in the parts, $85 in the receiver and about $20 in finishing cost for a total of $235, which is about $200 under the wholesale price of a factory-built AK pistol. This was a huge cost savings and well worth the work involved.

The need for U.S.-made parts and the higher kit price meant the AK-74 rifle cost more. The kit cost $200, the receiver cost me $65, the U.S. made parts were about $85 and the KG GunKote was about $25 for a total of $375. This is also about $200 under wholesale price for factory-built AK-74 rifles. Add on dealer mark up and the cost savings are even greater.

The large cost savings plus the satisfaction of knowing that you built it yourself make this a very attractive project. If you are willing to put in some work and study the project this may be one for you. I enjoyed the project and saved money so it doesn't get much better for me! ◉

These are the 20 parts that are regulated by the BATFE for the construction of semi-auto rifles.

No more than 10 of these parts can be imported and used to construct a semi-auto rifle.

Note: Not all rifles have all the parts on the list.

1 Frames, receivers, receiver castings, forgings or stampings
2 Barrels
3 Barrel extensions
4 Mounting blocks (trunnions), receivers and trunnions may be counted as one part if in one piece
5 Muzzle attachments
6 Bolts
7 Bolt carriers
8 Operating rods
9 Gas pistons
10 Trigger housings
11 Triggers
12 Hammers
13 Sears
14 Disconnectors
15 Buttstocks
16 Pistol grips
17 Forearms, Handguards
18 Magazine bodies
19 Magazine followers
20 Magazine floorplates

Any combination of these parts can be used as long as no more than 10 imported parts are used, however certain parts are more commonly used by builders. The most popular U.S. parts to use are hammers, triggers, disconnectors, receivers, gas pistons, pistol grips, stocks, muzzle attachments (flash suppressors, muzzle brakes), magazine bodies, followers and floorplates.

Semi-auto AK-47(74) Resource List

Information on building

http://www.akfiles.com

American Gunsmithing Institute, 1325 Imola Ave. W., Suite 504, Dept. SGN, Napa, Calif., 94559, www.americangunsmith.com

Parts, acessories and receivers

Tapco, P.O. Box 2408, Dept. SGN, Kennesaw, Ga., 30144 www.Tapco.com

Inter Ordnance, 3305 Westwood Industrial Drive, Dept. SGN, Monroe, N.C. 28110 www.interordnance.com

Ohio Ordnance Works, P.O. Box 687, Dept. SGN, Chardon, Ohio, 44024 www.ohioordnance.com

K-VAR, 5015 W. Sahara Ave., #125 PMB-136, Dept. SGN, Las Vegas, Nev. 89146-3407 www.K-VAR.com

Clearview Investments Inc., 102 Fieldview Dr., Suite 300, Dept. SGN, Versailles, Ky. 40383 www.clearviewinvest.com

Akron Armory, 2419 Front St., Dept. SGN, Cuyahoga Falls, Ohio, 44221 www.akronarmory.com email: AkronArmory@aol.com

Ohio Rapidfire, 537 N. Elm St., Dept. SGN, Troy, Ohio, 45373 www.ohiorapidfire.com

"How-to" Video Technical Manuals for Your Guns!

BUY 1 GET 1 FREE

Completely Disassemble, Maintain, Repair, and Reassemble ANY of these 50 guns, Fast and Easily with Total Confidence using these Video Manuals

Limited Time Offer Buy 1 of these DVDs:

Get 1 of these DVDs FREE:

These Videos are Packed with Exclusive Information and Equal to a Complete Factory Armorer's Course!

Why it is critical for you to own these AGI Armorer's Courses NOW! We believe you can't fix firearms unless you truly understand HOW the gun is intended to work. We use an exclusive cutaway gun to explain in detail the design of the feeding and locking mechanisms, the trigger system, proper ejection, and every other function of that specific model of firearm with views of the intricate internal workings not normally visible. After you have a complete understanding of the design and function we show, step-by-step, complete disassembly and reassembly, then teach you basic trouble shooting and repairs at an Armorer's level. *Plus, AGI keeps you out of trouble by telling you what parts you should never remove!* These really are technical manuals on video! **Each DVD includes a FREE printable schematic!** DVDs run 90 min. to 2 hours in length. $39.95 and $7 s/h each.

Protect your rights, fix your own guns and save a pile of money!

Offer cannot be combined with any other promotional offers or discounts. Cannot be applied to any previous sales. Limit 3 free with 3 purchased.

AGI

1-800-797-0867 • www.AmericanGunsmith.com

Ad Code# SGNbook3

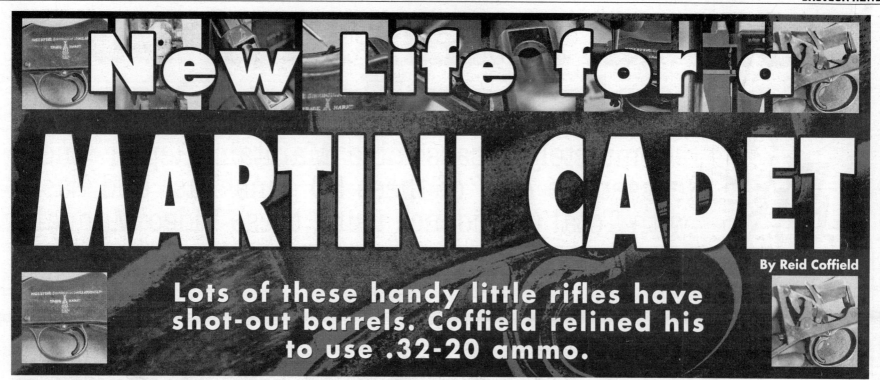

New Life for a MARTINI CADET

By Reid Coffield

Lots of these handy little rifles have shot-out barrels. Coffield relined his to use .32-20 ammo.

Several years ago I was cleanin' my shop and gettin' rid of extra equipment. A buddy offered to trade for one of the items and I ended up with a very tired and well used Martini Cadet rifle with a less than perfect bore.

For those that might not be familiar with the Martini Cadet, it's a small action, single-shot, falling-block rifle. They were for the most part produced prior to World War I in England. The Martinis were used extensively for smallbore shooting and for military training in what would be the equivalent to our high schools in England, New Zealand and Australia.

Within the last year or so some importers have been bringing quite a few .22 caliber Martinis into the States. I have seen a number of 'em at gun shows. Most were in pretty good shape, but a few did have rough bores. While my lining project involves a centerfire Martin, the same basic procedure can be applied to a .22 as well.

The rifle I received had been used in Australia and was in the original .310 caliber. This is a fairly mild little round. It normally fired a 120-grain lead bullet and was quite adequate for its intended purpose of teaching basic marksmanship. The only

problem as far as I was concerned is that ammo is hard to get and expensive when you can find it.

About 30 years ago I had another Martini that had also been "rode hard and put away wet". Back then I was able to find a virtually unfired barrel and a new stock and proceeded to rework the little rifle. It ended up looking just great. It was cute as a button and was a nice little shooter to boot. Unfortunately a fast talkin' rifle collector used his talents of persuasion and talked me out of it. The little Aussie departed for a new home.

I wanted to rebarrel this particular rifle, but new barrels are a thing of the past. However there's a way around that. What I really wanted was a shiny new bore in a rifle that would be a good, fun shooter. I also wanted it in a readily available caliber that I could afford.

The outside of the barrel was not that big an issue as I could always refinish it along with the rest of the metal. The solution to this problem was to line the barrel and convert it to another caliber.

Lining a barrel is basically just installing a new barrel *inside* the old one! It may sound a bit strange, but it's not all that hard and well within the capabilities of the average hobbyist. In lining a barrel, you first drill out the old barrel, removing all the rifling and the original chamber. You then install a new barrel or liner inside the old barrel in this newly bored hole. The liner is just a very thin barrel. It's rifled but not chambered.

Most of the rifles I have lined in the past have been .22 rimfires, but as long as you are dealing with relatively low pressure cartridges, a lined barrel will seldom give you any trouble. In fact, I have seen numbers of cases where lined barrels provided excellent to absolutely superior accuracy.

When it comes to liners it is very important to understand that there is a "front end" and a "rear end". I know that sounds kinda strange but it's true. When a liner is made, the tool to form the rifling is pulled through the metal tube. You always want the

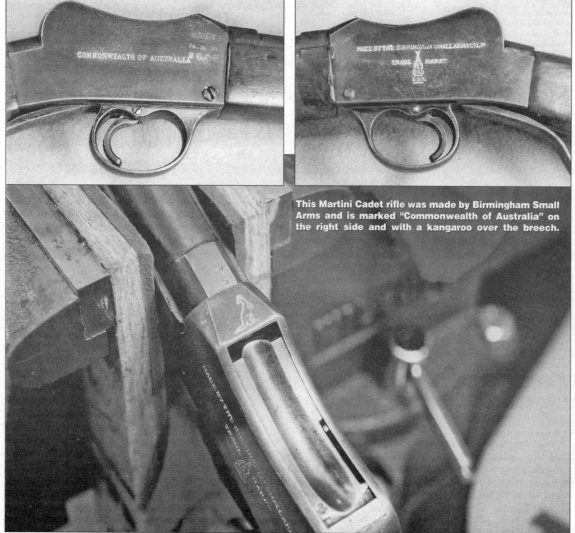

This Martini Cadet rifle was made by Birmingham Small Arms and is marked "Commonwealth of Australia" on the right side and with a kangaroo over the breech.

A neat feature of this Martini is this projection which indicates that the rifle is cocked and ready to fire. These rifles were used to train high school-age students.

The rear sight is adjustable for windage and elevation. It is also graduated up to an amazingly optimistic 600 yards! Target shooting was important in the early 1900s.

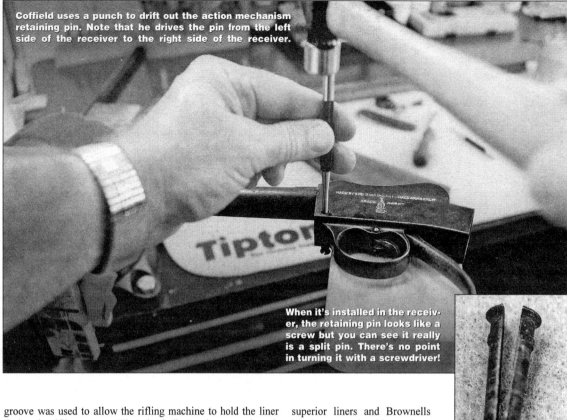

Coffield uses a punch to drift out the action mechanism retaining pin. Note that he drives the pin from the left side of the receiver to the right side of the receiver.

When it's installed in the receiver, the retaining pin looks like a screw but you can see it really is a split pin. There's no point in turning it with a screwdriver!

end where the tool started to be the breech end. By doing this the bullet will be going in the same direction as the rifling tool.

Why? As the tool moves down the tube or barrel, it either cuts or presses down the steel to form the lands and grooves. In doing this, it leaves a surface that looks smooth, but really is fairly rough when viewed under a microscope. You can see little teeth or ridges caused by the cutting or compressing of the metal ahead of the rifling tool. It's almost like the grain of a piece of wood.

If the bullet travels against the "grain" it will leave tiny bits of lead or bullet jacket material in the bore. The barrel will foul quickly and will never deliver the optimal accuracy. If the bullet travels with the "grain," there is always less fouling.

You can normally determine which is the breech or rear end of a liner. On most button-rifled liners, there will be a machined groove cut around the outside of the liner near one end. This

groove was used to allow the rifling machine to hold the liner during the rifling process. That also indicates the rear or breech end of the liner. Sometimes this holding groove is obvious and other times you will have to look for it.

Some liner makers will mark the breech end of their liners, some don't. The important thing is that you determine the breech end *before* you install the liner. Redman liners, which I really like, have the holding groove visible at the breech end.

I have always admired the little .32-20 round. When I was a kid, a friend had an old Winchester 92 in .32-20 and it was just a delight to shoot. It's a mild little cartridge with very little recoil or report. And as an added benefit, the .32-20 is a great cartridge for the handloader and bullet caster. The cartridge was designed originally for lead bullets. Also, for a lazy guy like me, commercial ammo is readily available and not all that expensive.

The first order of business was locating a suitable liner. That was no problem at all. I just checked my #58 Brownell catalog (200 South Front St., Dept. SGN, Montezuma, Iowa 50171, telephone 800-741-0015) and sure enough the good folks there were offering just the liner I needed. For less than $96 you can purchase a 25-inch liner made by Randall Redman.

Redman, a longtime advertiser here in SGN (Redman's Rifling and Reboring, 189 Nichols St., Dept. SGN, Omak, Wash. 98841) has a well-deserved reputation of producing

superior liners and Brownells has been carrying his products for many years. He also rebores Broomhandle Mausers to 9mm.

The liner I got was actually 26¾ inches long and rifled with a 1:18 twist. As I understand, these liners have been very popular for reworking old shot-out Winchester 92s for cowboy action shooting. While my liner was a bit longer than listed in the catalog, you have to keep in mind that you will be cutting off about an inch from both the breech and muzzle ends.

The rifling tools will not cut or form a perfect bore when they first start in the barrel and as they exit the bore. By cutting the liner off you eliminate these areas. If you have an unusually long barrel, you need to be aware of this when ordering a liner.

While I was at it, I also picked up from Brownells a 13mm drill specifically designed to drill out the barrel for this liner. The diameter of the liner is .503" and the drill will cut a hole that is .511" to .512" in diameter. This will provide enough clearance for the liner to fit inside the bore easily. In addition, the drill is piloted so it will not "wander" as it cuts its way down the bore.

The breechblock is hinged at the rear and tilts down to expose the chamber for loading. Dual extractors pull the empty cartridge out from the chamber after firing.

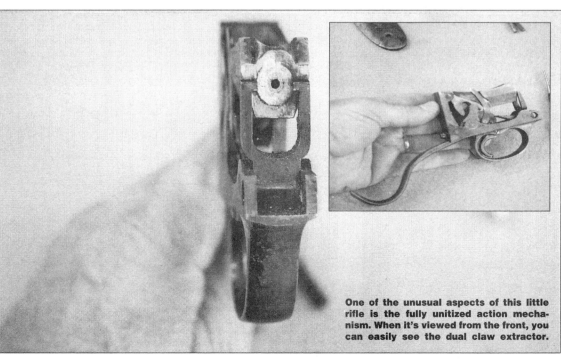

One of the unusual aspects of this little rifle is the fully unitized action mechanism. When it's viewed from the front, you can easily see the dual claw extractor.

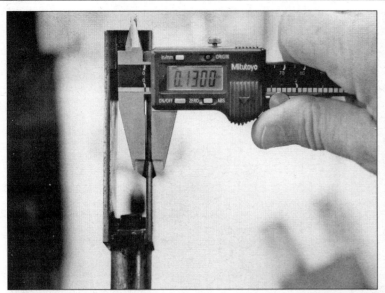

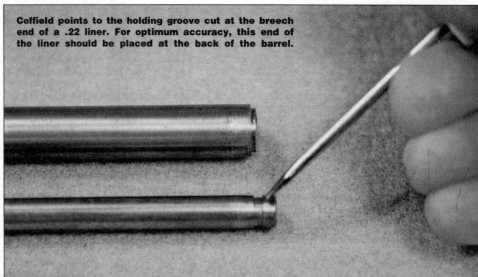

Coffield points to the holding groove cut at the breech end of a .22 liner. For optimum accuracy, this end of the liner should be placed at the back of the barrel.

The sides of this little receiver are very thin at only .130".and are easily bent. It is absolutely essential to support the receiver when using an action wrench.

The pilot is really just a projection or stud on the end of the drill that follows the existing bore. The cost of the drill was about $89. Needless to say, you want to take real good care of that drill. I have other liner drills in other sizes that I have used for over 25 years. If you take care of 'em, they'll outlast you!

The drill is only about 11 inches long and my barrel is just a shade over 25 inches long so I had to add an extension to the drill shank. That can be done a number of different ways. I simply welded a two foot section of 3/8" diameter steel rod to the end of the drill shank.

Some might silver-solder the extension to the drill shank, but I find it easier and less hassle just to weld the darn thing. Besides, since the drill is so short, I will always need an extension, so I might as well just go ahead and make it permanent.

There are two things to keep in mind when welding on an extension like this. First, you need to grind a nice point or taper on the end of both the drill shank and the extension rod. This will ensure that your weld is not just on the surface of the drill shank and extension rod.

Next, you want to make sure the drill shank and the extension rod are as straight as possible. It wouldn't do to have the extension runnin' off at an angle from the drill. This could cause the extension to rub against the inside of the barrel and even prevent the drill from moving into the barrel if it were bad enough. Perfect alignment is more critical if you use it in a hand drill. If like me you use this drill in a lathe, the drill will be steady and the barrel will be turning. Because of this absolute perfect alignment is not quite as important.

A dirt simple way of aligning these two rods is to use a piece of angle iron as a holding fixture. Lay the two rods down in the "V" of the angle iron. If like me your extension rod is a smaller diameter than the drill, you have to account for this in your set up. Be sure to cut a good size hole directly under the point where the two rods come together. This will allow flame and heat from the torch to go on past the rod and not be deflected back in your face!

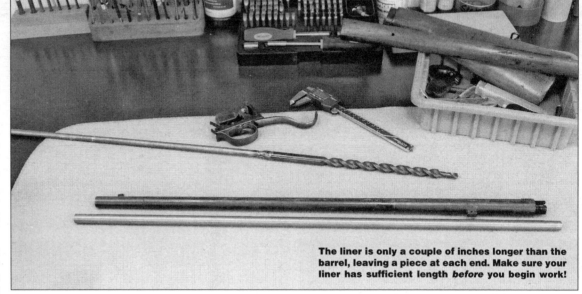

The liner is only a couple of inches longer than the barrel, leaving a piece at each end. Make sure your liner has sufficient length *before* you begin work!

Your weld doesn't have to be a work of art; it just has to hold. Build the weld up above the surface of the drill shank so you can file or grind it down for a nice smooth surface. This is not nearly as critical as, say, welding on a bolt handle so it's a good practice project if you are not an experienced welder.

If you don't have a welding outfit, any welding shop or friend who has a welding set up should be able to knock this out in a matter of minutes.

The next order of business is disassembling the rifle. With this Martini Cadet rifle, you begin by pulling the trigger assembly from the receiver. It is one single unitized assembly and is really quite a nice piece of engineering. There is a large pin that runs through the front of the receiver. One end looks like a slotted screw but it's *not*! You can turn this until the cows come home but it will never unscrew. Instead get a 5/32" diameter punch and carefully strike the *left* or solid end of the pin. You should be driving the pin out of the receiver from the left to the right.

Once the pin is out, you can drop the lever and pull the trigger assembly out. Nothin' to it!

Now remove the buttplate and use a large flat-bladed screwdriver to loosen the slotted buttstock screw. With the buttstock off the receiver, the next step is to remove the forearm. There is a pin that runs through the front barrel band. Drift this out with a punch. By the way, I have seen a number of these pins staked in place. Evidently they tended to come out over time so some folks upset the pin head to keep 'em in place.

Fortunately mine came right out with no hassle. That left just a single crosspin in the forearm back near the receiver. This again was drifted out and the forearm was then lifted off

the barrel. That's it! I told you these were simple little rifles and their design is a marvel of simplicity.

In order to line the barrel and then chamber the liner, we need to pull the barrel from the receiver. It is screwed into the receiver and generally will come off with very little pressure. However, there is a problem in pulling or unscrewing the barrel. Like so many thin, flat-sided receivers it is possible to bend or collapse the sides of the receiver with an action wrench. The side walls of this receiver are only about .130" thick and my friends, that's not all that much.

Some folks like to leave the bolt or other internal components in place to act as supports for the receiver sidewalls. That can work but you have to be darn careful that there are no compo-

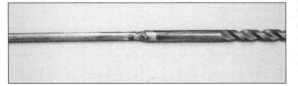

The smaller diameter pilot on the front of the liner drill helps guide the assembly during drilling. Coffield welded on an extension so the drill would reach.

Looking inside the breech end of the liner, you can see the step where the rifling button was first engaged. This part needs to be outside the barrel and cut off.

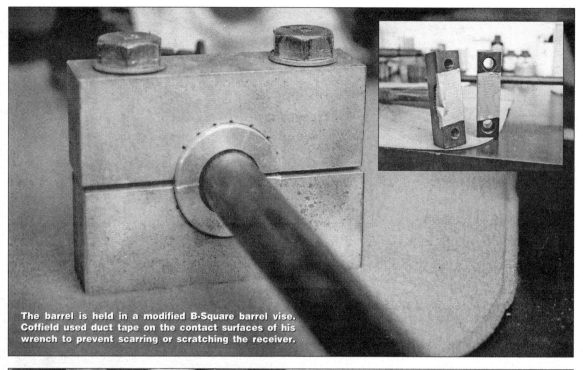

The barrel is held in a modified B-Square barrel vise. Coffield used duct tape on the contact surfaces of his wrench to prevent scarring or scratching the receiver.

To make a jack to support the receiver, remove any raised marks on the head of the bolt, then cut the bolt to the proper length. Adjust the nut to give full contact.

With jack bolts in place and the receiver wrench secured to the front end of the receiver, Coffield applied pressure with a cheater bar to break the barrel loose.

nents that interfere with the rotation of the barrel. For example, if the extractor were left in place in the slotted seats in the breech of the barrel you would quickly snap off the extractor hooks and probably scar up the breech end of the barrel in the process.

I don't want to even have to think about that so I make it a practice normally to remove all internal components. To replace these and to provide support for the receiver walls I have some adjustable supports or jacks. These are simply machine bolts with nuts that have been cut to length. The threaded shank is cut just a hair short of the internal width of the receiver.

I also am darn careful to polish off any raised markings on the head of the bolt. If you don't, these letters or marks may scar the inside of the receiver.

Once the jack has been prepared, I thread the nut on to the shank and slide the jack inside the receiver. I make sure I position it where it will support my action or receiver wrench. With

this Cadet rifle I made up three jacks. I might have gotten away with just one or two but there is no sense in taking any chances and besides the jacks are cheap and easy to build.

Once you have finished with the project, keep 'em around. You'll use 'em if you ever pull the barrel on a Winchester, Marlin or some other flat-sided lever gun.

Even though I will eventually refinish the metal, I placed some tape on the contact surfaces of my action or receiver wrench. Virtually any type of tape can be used. I ended up using some duct tape simply because it nice and thick and it happened to be near my bench. You can apply the tape to the receiver or the wrench. I prefer putting it on the wrench.

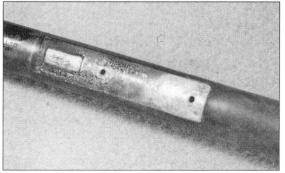

The rear sight base was secured with soft or lead solder. This melted easily with a hot air gun, allowing the rear sight to be pulled off the barrel with pliers.

I secured the barrel of the rifle in my barrel vise, and then clamped the action wrench over the receiver. I was very careful to make sure the wrench was positioned on the forward portion of the receiver over the barrel shank. I also checked to make darn sure my jacks were positioned properly to support the thin walls of the receiver.

Once all this checked out, I tightened the bolts on my action wrench. The wrench needs to be tight enough so it will not slip or move on the receiver. No need for more pressure than that.

With the wrench tight and the barrel secured in the barrel vise, I applied a steady pressure to the action wrench handle to turn the receiver counterclockwise. Unfortunately, nothin' happened! This barrel was *tight*! After a couple of tries, I added a 3-foot pipe cheater bar to my action wrench handle. With this added leverage, the receiver broke loose and turned off the barrel shank with only moderate pressure.

Now that I had the barrel off the receiver, I still had a bit of work to do, namely removing the rear sight. I removed the sight leaf but the base was secured by a small screw as well as solder. I removed the screw, which had been used to help position the sight base as it was secured with solder.

I didn't really want to crank up my welding outfit, so I just got out my hot air gun. Since this gun was made around 1900 or so, I was pretty confident soft lead solder had been used originally and I figured I could melt it with the air gun.

Though it took a bit longer than I planned, my hot air gun when set on high did generate enough heat to melt the solder. Once it liquefied, I was able to lift off the sight base with pliers.

The barrel is now basically ready to be set up in my lathe and drilled. Next time we'll drill out the barrel, install the liner, chamber it and then refit it to the receiver.

Until next time, good luck and good gunsmithing!

Installing a Barrel Liner in a MARTINI Part II

By Reid Coffield

Getting the chamber cut and the extractor grooves filed require careful hand work that pays off at the range.

There're a lot of older rifles sitting in gun racks or hiding in the back of closets that are great potential shooters. The primary problem with many of these older guns is the bore. Because of rust, neglect, corrosive ammo or just plain wear, the bores are no longer capable of providing decent accuracy. Because of that these older guns have been pushed aside and virtually forgotten.

However, that doesn't have to be the case. It's well within the capabilities of most hobbyists to repair many of these barrels and get some of these fine old guns back into the field and on the range. One simple and effective method of repairing these rifles is to install a liner inside the barrel. A liner is nothing more than a rifled tube. You can also think of it as a very thin gun barrel.

Basically, the bore of the original barrel is drilled out and the liner fitted inside the barrel in the new, larger hole. The liner provides fresh, clean, sharp rifling with no pits or irregularities. It is a great way to restore a rifle and, most importantly, it's not all that difficult and often can be less expensive than having a gunsmith install a new barrel.

While most lining projects involve .22 rimfire rifles, I'm currently working on an Australian Martini Cadet rifle that was probably made around 1900. It's .310 cal. and suffers from a very, very bad bore. It's so bad I decided to line the barrel and convert it to .32-20. The .32-20 cartridge, unlike the .310 round, is readily available and will make a darn nice little plinker. Keep in mind that while this is a centerfire cartridge, the basic procedure is the same you would use on a .22 rifle.

If you do decide to try lining a barrel, I would strongly encourage you to start with a .22 rifle. That will be the least costly in

terms of expense for a liner, chamber reamer, and barrel drill.

I've already pulled the barrel on the Martini and prepared my barrel drill. This special drill was obtained from the good folks at Brownells Inc., 200 S. Front St., Dept. SGN, Montezuma, Iowa 50171, telephone 1-800-741-0015. It's a special 13mm piloted drill designed specifically for this task and sells for $88.75.

The cutting end of the drill has an integral pilot that projects forward about one inch. This pilot ensures that the drill can not "wander" away from the center of the bore. When doin' this job, you sure don't want to drill out the *side* of your barrel!

Before you begin, it's *imperative* that you check the pilot to be certain it fits your bore. It shouldn't be loose or undersize. Ideally, it'll be a sliding fit and there'll be virtually no side-to-side movement.

I also picked up a 1:18 twist 26-inch long liner from Brownells made by Randal Redman. It was designed primarily for use on old Winchester Model 92 .32-20s with bad bores. However, it was just the ticket for this Martini project. This liner currently sells for about $95.50.

The only modification necessary to the liner drill was to weld on an extension to the drill shank. The drill was only 11 inches long yet our barrel is over 25 inches in length. The extension was just a 19-inch piece of 3/8" round rod welded to the drill shank.

I set the barrel up in my 13 x 40 Jet lathe for drilling. The barrel was wrapped with some duct tape to prevent scarring and then placed in the three-jaw chuck. The breech end of the barrel extended about 6-8 inches from the face of the chuck. The back end of the liner drill extension was secured in a Jacobs chuck in the lathe tailstock.

There's a minor problem in starting the liner drill at the breech end of the barrel. The chamber is a larger diameter than the bore of the barrel and consequently, the drill pilot is a bit too small and loose. The pilot can and will move side to side and up or down in the larger diameter chamber. One way to deal with this when using a fixed pilot drill is to take an empty or fired .32-20

Coffield's Martini Cadet Carbine looked nice, but testing showed the bore was shot. Relining it and rechambering to .32-20 gave him a trim, accurate little plinker.

Always check the fit of the chamber reamer pilot in the bore of your liner before you begin work, Coffield says. If it's loose, the reamer will usually tend to chatter.

The pilot was much smaller than the chamber though it fit the bore perfectly. The pilot keeps the drill centered in the barrel, preventing it from wandering off line.

Before Coffield started installing the liner, he turned in the sight base screws to prevent epoxy from getting into the threads in the barrel and clogging them up.

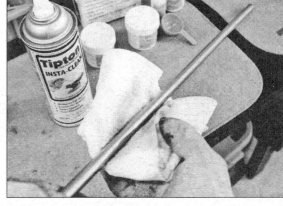

Carefully clean the liner with a solvent to remove all traces of oil or grease, then use a liberal amount of solvent to clean the newly drilled hole in the barrel.

Coffield used a cartridge case to center the pilot in the chamber. You can just start the lathe with it in place and allow it to be chewed up as the drill advances.

Miles Gilbert Bedrock available from MidwayUSA was used to secure the liner in the barrel. It's primarily a glass bedding compound, but will work fine for this job.

cartridge case and cut off the head of the case. Then slide the forward section of the case over the pilot. The case acts as a spacer sleeve and provides the needed support for the pilot while it's in the chamber.

As the drill advances, the pilot moves into the bore of the barrel and is then properly supported. I've seen folks gradually trim back the case support as the drill advances into the chamber and I've also seen folks just let the drill cut into the case support as it advances. I've done both and both ways work. With this barrel I just let the drill cut away the case support.

The lathe was set up to turn the barrel at a moderate speed, approximately 580 rpm. The drill was advanced with the tailstock about .375 or 3/8" then it was removed and the chips cleared from the drill flutes. It is important to clear the flutes frequently as packed chips generate friction and cause the drill to heat up. This heat can ruin your drill or at least cut into its useful life.

Also, lots of cutting oil was used. It really doesn't matter what type of oil you use, as long as you use lots of it! Remember, cutting oil is considerably cheaper than barrel liner drills!

When starting at the breech end, you have to cut through the two machined slots for the extractor. These "gaps" can be a bit hard on your drill so go especially slow making very shallow cuts until you have drilled beyond them.

The Martini barrel is 25 inches long, so I continued drilling from the breech end until I was approximately halfway through the bore. At that point I reversed the position of the barrel in the lathe and began drilling from the muzzle end.

The primary reason for this was that by having a shorter distance to remove the drill it made the work a bit faster. Although

I wasn't keeping track of the time, I think it took about an hour to drill out the entire barrel.

While I used a lathe, it's possible to drill out a barrel by hand using an electric drill and over the years I've done it that way a couple of times. The only problem with using an electric drill is you don't have as much control over the drill bit. It may tend to grab or cut too deeply too quickly. This can jam the drill in the barrel or cause your extension to break off the drill shaft.

I've modified the angle of the cutting faces of the drill to make it much shallower and less aggressive when using a hand drill. By the way, it's just as important to use lots of cutting oil and continually clear chips as when using a lathe.

Once the barrel had been drilled, it was removed from the lathe. I used my favorite solvent, Insta-Clean, available from MidwayUSA, 5875 W. Van Horn Tavern Road, Dept. SGN, Columbia, Mo. 65203, telephone 1-800-243-3220, to thoroughly clean both the barrel bore and the exterior of the liner to remove all traces of oil or grease. I then checked the fit of the liner in the barrel. It's important that the liner slide smoothly into the full length of the barrel. Be sure to check this *before* you begin to bond the liner permanently into the barrel!

I had already cut about a half-inch off the breech end of the liner, which was identified by the remnants of a groove cut around its exterior. This groove had been used to hold the tubing while a carbide button was pulled though it to form the liner rifling.

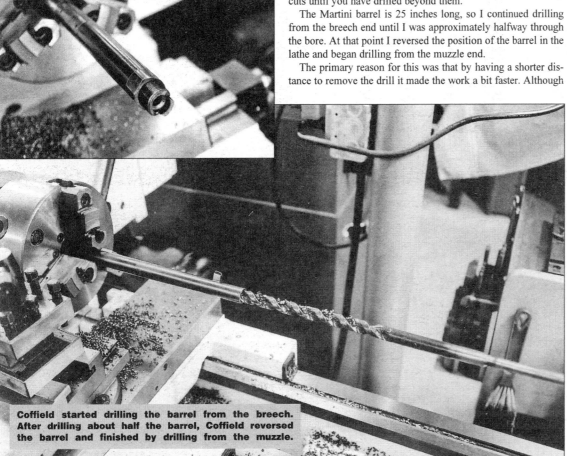

Coffield started drilling the barrel from the breech. After drilling about half the barrel, Coffield reversed the barrel and finished by drilling from the muzzle.

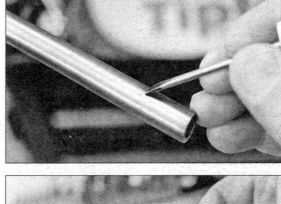

Mark the breech end of the liner so it is not accidentally reversed when it's installed in the barrel. Use a simple wooden plug to keep epoxy out of the liner bore.

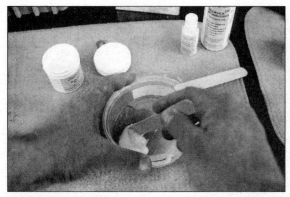

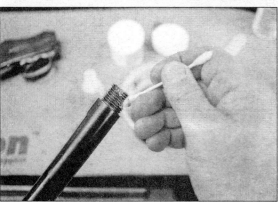

Bedrock is a two-part epoxy of equal parts resin and hardener. A release agent is liberally applied to the exterior of the barrel threads to make cleanup easier.

You always want the breech end of the liner to be located at the breech end of the barrel. Don't ever reverse the liner, as this will lead to a barrel that will quickly foul. I marked the breech end of the liner with two small file marks just to be sure that I kept the liner properly oriented.

Traditionally liners have been secured with solder. I did it that way for years, but let me tell you, I won't do it anymore! I am now a firm believer in epoxy as the best way to anchor a liner in a barrel. It's faster, easier, and just as strong as the solder I use to use.

With the Martini I used Bedrock, the epoxy bedding compound sold by MidwayUSA. It's a two part epoxy mixed one part hardener to one part resin. This mixing ratio makes it very

When fully seated, about a half-inch of liner protrudes from either end of the barrel. The extra epoxy around the liner prevents gaps between the liner and barrel.

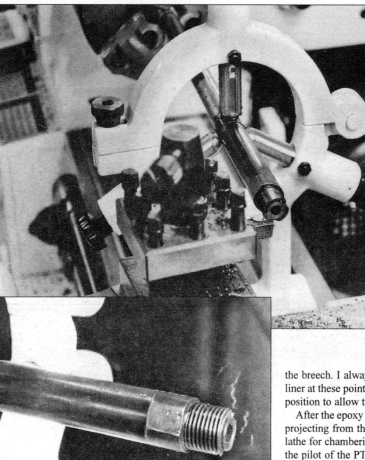

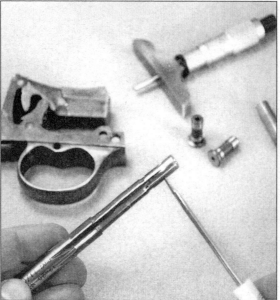

The barrel was placed in Coffield's lathe and the liner faced back to within about .050" of the breech face. Once it was faced off, it was ready to be chambered.

easy to use. It also has a liquid like consistency that is helpful in coating both the liner and the inside of the barrel.

Bedrock can be thickened when used as a bedding compound but for gluing jobs like this, you want your epoxy to be very thin. When mixing it I also went ahead and used a black dye included in the bedding kit to color the epoxy. Later when the gun is blued, the black epoxy visible at the muzzle of the barrel will be virtually unnoticeable.

The barrel was placed in a vertical position in my bench vise with the breech end up. The jaws of the vise were padded to prevent marring the barrel.

I cut a small wooden plug and sealed the muzzle end of the liner to keep epoxy out of the bore as it was pushed through the

When chambering the liner, it's essential that you have a depth mike, headspace gauges, and chamber reamer. Be sure the reamer pilot is a perfect fit for the bore.

barrel. I then coated the first 3 or 4 inches of the liner with epoxy.

Next, I placed a nice big "glob" of epoxy in the breech end of the barrel and started feeding the liner down the barrel. A wooden mixing stick was used to spread epoxy along the exterior of the liner as I carefully pushed it down into the barrel.

It's important to make sure the surface of the liner is fully coated as it enters the barrel. Excess epoxy will of course build up at the breech as it's scraped off the liner. Just use the mixing stick to continually spread this epoxy along the outside of the liner.

Work quickly, as you want the liner in place before the epoxy sets up. You should have about an inch or so of liner protruding from the muzzle and from the breech. You'll also want to make sure there are no visible gaps in the epoxy between the liner and the barrel at both the muzzle and the breech. I always leave a bit of a "pile" of epoxy around the liner at these points. The barrel was then set aside in a horizontal position to allow the epoxy to cure for 24 hours.

After the epoxy cured, I cut away all but about 1/8" of the liner projecting from the breech. The barrel was then put back in the lathe for chambering. Before I began this project, I had checked the pilot of the PTG .32-20 finish reamer to make sure it fit the bore of my liner. It was just a matter of sliding the pilot into the end of the liner.

It always amazes me how many people fail to make this simple check and then have *major* problems when their reamer will *not* enter the bore. *Always* check your reamer pilot *before* you begin your project. This can save a lot of trouble and frustration.

My PTG reamer is sold by Midway and sells for $89.99. A good reamer like the PTG will provide many years of service, but you have to take care of it. As with the liner drill, you want to use *lots* of cutting oil and clear your chips frequently. Most importantly, never allow the reamer to be turned counter clockwise as this will roll or dull the cutting edges.

I cut the chamber to almost full depth in the lathe. I was about .050" short. I then removed the barrel from the lathe to finish chambering by hand.

I used a depth micrometer to measure from the face of the receiver to the face of the breechbolt in its locked position. This was right at .657".

With a Go headspace gauge in the chamber of the barrel, I again used the depth micrometer to measure from the rear face of the headspace gauge to the shoulder of the barrel. This was about .720". Now it was just a matter of slowly and carefully using the PTG reamer to cut the chamber and move the rim recess forward.

I continually checked the distance from the rear face of the headspace gauge to the shoulder of the barrel. My goal was to

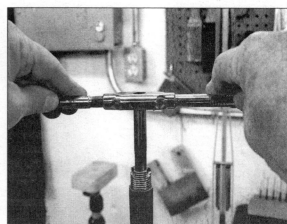

The new .32-20 chamber was cut to approximately half to three-quarters depth in the lathe, then Coffield finished it to full depth by hand, using a large tap handle.

Coffield measures the distance from the face of the receiver to the face of the closed breechbolt using a depth micrometer, then inserts the Go gauge in the chamber.

Coffield used a countersink to break the liner edge around the rim cut. This is important for smooth feeding and ejection. Then he checked with a magnifying glass.

have the distance from the back of the Go gauge to the shoulder of the barrel to be right at .655". By taking my time and checking with my depth micrometer frequently I was able to hit that mark.

By the way, as I deepened the chamber, I occasionally had to use a file to lower the rear face of the liner that extended around the outside of the rim cut. That always had to be slightly below the rear face of the headspace gauge, otherwise it would be impossible for the breech face to properly support the cartridge case.

As soon as I had reached a distance of .655" from the barrel shoulder to the face of the headspace gauge, I was ready to check for fit using the action. I stripped the bolt of the striker or firing pin and striker spring. The barrel was then screwed back into the receiver, a Go gauge placed in the chamber, and the breechblock *carefully* and slowly pivoted into the locked or battery position.

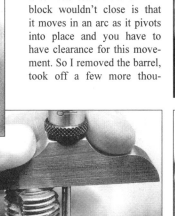

While theoretically everything should have fit, it didn't! The breechblock would not close. Actually, I didn't expect it to. The reason the breechblock wouldn't close is that it moves in an arc as it pivots into place and you have to have clearance for this movement. So I removed the barrel, took off a few more thousandths, replaced the barrel, and tried it again. At that point the breechblock closed on the Go gauge. I then removed the Go gauge, inserted the No Go gauge and carefully moved the breechblock into the closed and locked position. It wouldn't go! Now my headspace was correct.

With the headspace set, the next step was to fit the extractor. The Martini uses a double hook extractor that engages the case rim at 3 and 6 o'clock. It's well designed and provides very positive extraction and ejection. Fitting the extractor can be a bit touchy, but if you use the extractor and the remnants of the original extractor cuts, it's not all that difficult.

If you're ever faced with a project like this and you don't have another barrel available to look at as you work, make a photograph or drawing of the face of the barrel with emphasis on the extractor cuts before you drill your barrel. This can later help as you slowly and carefully file in the extractor cuts.

I used some photographs, another Martini barrel I happened to have, and the remaining parts of the cuts on my existing barrel. Following these guides I used some needle files to carefully begin making the extractor cuts. Using the extractor, I checked for fit frequently and worked very slowly. I probably spent as long fitting the extractor as I did drilling out the barrel.

It's important to remember that like the breechbolt, the extractor moves in an arc; it doesn't move straight back. Consequently I had to taper or angle the lower sides of the cuts to accommodate this curving movement. When I thought I had it right, I fit the barrel to the receiver, installed the trigger mechanism with the breechbolt and extractor in place, and tried the extractor.

I wish I could say I got it right the first time. Or even the second or third time. It took about six trips over to the barrel vise before I had the extractor operating to my satisfaction and really kickin' out an empty case with vigor and authority.

During this process it was mandatory that I worked slowly and never allowed myself to get in a hurry or feel rushed. Whenever that happens in gun work, I *always* screw up!

Once the extractor fit properly, I used an angled countersink to break the sharp edge of the rim cut in the liner. This is not the

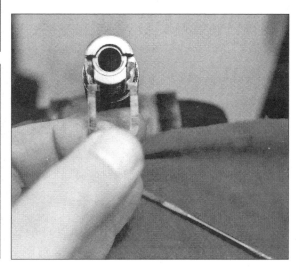

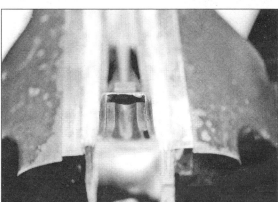

At this point the back of the gauge is quite high above the breech face. Coffield measures the distance from the end of the Go gauge to the barrel shoulder.

Initially, the breechbolt would not close on the Go gauge. The chamber had to be cut a bit deeper. Finally, the chamber was cut deep enough to close on the Go gauge.

Fitting the extractor is perhaps the most difficult part of the project, but you can do it if you go slowly and constantly check the fit of the extractor as you work.

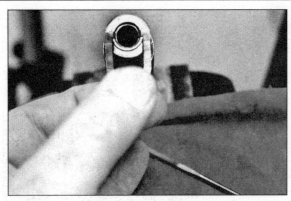

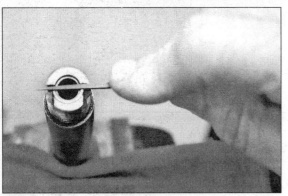

Check the extractor fit often. Several small needle files are the choice to fit it. It's good to have an additional barrel to which to compare the new extractor cuts.

rim seat, but the portion of the liner that extends above the rim. If you don't break this edge, it will definitely cause you trouble with scratched cases and may even cause some chambering problems when you load a round.

With the barrel chambered, headspaced, and the extractor fit, it was now time to turn to the muzzle. I bet you had forgotten about that! Years ago I learned when installing a liner, *always* cut and crown the liner at the muzzle *last*. The reason for this is simple.

What if in setting the headspace I had cut too deeply? If we still had some liner sticking out the muzzle, we could theoreti-

Lots of different types of ammo and a good quality bench rest; there is no substitute for these when you want to determine the true accuracy potential of a rifle.

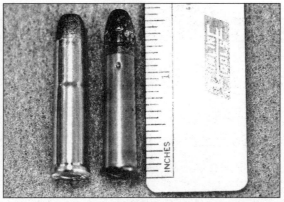

The .32-20 cartridge is shown on the left and the .310 cartridge on the right. The two rounds are in the very same class so far as accuracy and power are concerned.

cally heat the barrel until the epoxy softened and then tap the liner back toward the breech a few thousandths and correct our headspace problem. We could even do this if we had messed up the extractor cuts.

Leaving an inch or so of liner protruding from the muzzle until the last step is cheap insurance.

I cut the excess liner with a hacksaw, then put the barrel back in the lathe. I faced off the end of the muzzle with a simple 90° flat cut. This duplicated the original barrel crown. I also made a very light angular cut on the outside edge of the barrel to remove the sharp edge.

I still had a bit of work to do where the bore of the liner joined the face of the muzzle. For this, I placed the barrel muzzle up in a padded vise. I took a slotted round-headed brass screw and dipped the head in 600-grit lapping compound.

The threaded shank of the screw was chucked in my electric hand drill and the head of the screw placed in the muzzle. As the drill was turned on I rotated the hand drill in a figure-8 motion. Periodically, I would remove the screw and check the muzzle. As soon as I could see a faint angular line 360° around the end of the rifling in the liner, I stopped.

A cotton swab was inserted in the muzzle, pressed against the side of the bore and pulled out. If there were no strands of cotton caught by tiny burrs at the muzzle, I was done.

With this completed, the rifle was reassembled and I headed for the range. I had previously checked the MidwayUSA catalog for .32-20 ammo. As far as I know, no one else offers as large a variety of factory .32-20 ammo as Midway. I order a good selection, as I wanted to determine what would shoot best in my little rifle.

At the range two things became very evident. The rifle preferred the heavier 115-grain bullets, particularly those used by the folks that produce Ultramax ammunition. I was able to get some very nice sub 1½-inch groups at 50 yards.

The other point brought out at the range was that the rifle shot about 8 inches high. The original factory front sight was far too low.

Back in the shop, this was quickly resolved. I used a 1903A3 Springfield front sight blade to

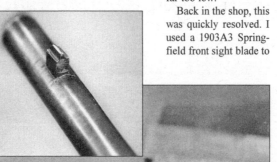

From the initial range session, it was quite evident that the Martini's barleycorn front sight was far too low. Coffield filed it away even with the sight base.

An 03A3 Springfield sight blade is just the thing to correct the sight picture. Coffield fit it into a slot in the sight base, trimmed and filed it to correct height.

make up a higher blade for the Martini. I filed away the original barleycorn blade, leaving the sight base. Since the Springfield blade was already drilled for a holding pin, I placed the sight against the side of the base and marked the location of the hole for the pin. This was then drilled.

After that, I used my hacksaw and some needle files to cut a vertical slot for the blade. Once the blade was pinned in place, I took a file and cut away the excess material on the sight blade that extended from the front and rear of the base.

I had to wait a few days before I could get back to the range. When I went out, I took a file with me as I knew the Springfield blade was way too high. It was just a matter of doing some shooting and slowly filing down the blade until my point of impact was where I wanted it on my target. Then a touch of cold blue and the job was almost done.

Again back in the shop I used my number stamps to stamp the new caliber, .32-20, on the left side of the barrel just ahead of the receiver. It is especially important to designate the true caliber when you have made so little change in the exterior appearance of the rifle.

Since it still looks pretty much original, a new owner might assume it was still .310 cal. While a .310 cartridge could probably be safely fired in this particular rifle, it's just not worth the liability risk and besides, it's just the right thing to do.

By the way, as the politicians all say now days, I misspoke in the previous article on the Martini. At that time I said that new stocks were just about impossible to find. I was wrong!

The good folks at Boyds Gunstock Industries, Inc., 25376 403rd Ave., Dept. SGN, Mitchell, S.Dak. 57301-5402, telephone 605-996-5011, offer a semi-finished butt stock as well as a sporter forend for the Martini.

The sample I received is of good solid American walnut that would be a perfect replacement for a sporter or you could just use the butt stock if you needed a longer length of pull on a military piece. If you need some good wood for a gunsmithing project for a Martini or any other rifle or shotgun, contact the folks at Boyds, they offer a great selection and probably have just what you need.

While you might not have a Martini, I do hope this piece will give you a better idea of what is involved in lining a barrel. It's not all that hard and it can be a lot of fun to make an old rifle with a ruined bore shoot well. If you're thinking about lining a barrel, I would encourage you to do a .22 rimfire first. Once you have a couple of those jobs under your belt, you might then consider a low pressure centerfire cartridge.

Until next time, good luck and good gunsmithing!

Restoring a Veteran Firearm for a Returning Veteran

Matthews usually keeps to military arms, but when a neighbor asked if he could bring a .22 pump back to life for his son, he showed some flair for the sporting side.

By Steven Matthews

Matthews' neighbor brought him a project a bit off his usual specialty of military arms. Could he rescue an old pump .22 rifle and turn it into a presentation piece?

I live in a rural location and am about a quarter-mile from the road. My driveway is more than 1200 feet long, so I spend some time mowing along its sides. Recently while making one of my slow passes down the 1200 foot side I saw my neighbor standing at the head of my drive 1200 feet away. From that distance, it appeared that he was holding a long stick or garden tool in his hand.

As I slowly got closer, I could make out the shape of a firearm in his hand. As I got even closer, I could see he was holding a very rough condition rifle. As I shut off the tractor, he showed me an extremely used and abused Remington pump .22 rifle. The wood was scratched and gouged, and it featured some user-applied varnish of the stock.

One feature stuck out like the proverbial sore thumb. Apparently sometime over its hard life, the buttplate had been damaged and someone smeared some caulking putty on the butt and tried to crudely form a new buttplate with a putty knife.

The metal finish was speckled with rust with some deep pitting. Little original bluing remained under the rust. This gun had apparently seen hard use and abuse over the years. It was a "veteran" of many hunts, plinking sessions, and appeared to have fought many battles with other items rolling around in a truck or trunk of a car, judging from all the dents and dings in the wood and metal.

This was one hard used and battle damaged gun that had had 75 years or more of hard time. My neighbor went on to explain that this gun had previously belonged to his deceased father. The neighbor's son was presently serving in the U.S. Marine Corps in Iraq and was scheduled to return home in couple months.

Upon his return my neighbor wanted to present his father's gun to his son as a welcome home gift and a memento of the son's grandfather. My neighbor recognized the gun was in very poor condition and wanted to know if I could do anything to make it look presentable. He also said the gun didn't work very well and wanted to know if I could repair it.

My interest is military guns and gunsmithing, not old .22s, but since this was for his returning veteran son I said I would look it over and see what could be done. When I got it home and examined it in more depth, the reason it didn't work well was obvious. The bore and chamber were *extremely* corroded. In fact the rust was so bad in the bore that it didn't even look like a .22 hole.

It was one of the worst "sewer pipe" barrels I have ever seen. There was no trace of rifling to be seen. The rusty chamber was causing the fired cases to stick and fail to extract. This was compounded by the excessively caked up and rusted bore, which appeared to be driving pressures up when the lead of the soft .22 slugs was scraped off the bullets and applied to the rough bore as they exited the gun.

I returned to my neighbor's house and explained the situation to him. Due to the extremely poor condition the cost to return this gun to a shooter and to professionally refinish the gun would vastly exceed its value. He understood this but wanted to know if I could make it look better so that it at least could be displayed as a "wall hanger" for his son.

He also wanted to know if something could be done to allow at least a few shots to be fired in it for "old times sake". I told him that I would refinish the wood, replace the caulking putty buttplate, remove the rust, give it an "economy grade" blue job and get enough rust and lead fouling out of the bore to fire a few rounds for nostalgia's sake. He said to do what I could and he would be very grateful.

I realize that some readers may think the gun should have been left as is in "relic" condition, but the neighbor really wanted something that looked half-decent to present to his returning son. I know that there are other readers who also have some beat up old gun that they would like to return to some semblance of decent condition. This article will give a simple and easy method to do this for very little expense.

I do want to warn people to verify that their intended project is not some rare and valuable collector piece. Some firearms even if in "relic" condition are still highly collectable and valuable if left as is. Any attempts at refinishing these guns can destroy their value. Only refurbish firearms that are run of the mill items with no collector value.

The procedures in this article will allow the hobbyist to return an old beat-up gun to something that looks half-decent for as little as $35. It won't turn a sow's ear into a silk purse but it will greatly improve the looks of that old gun.

The old Remington pump had obviously beaten around the cab of a pickup for years, with little or no lubrication or maintenance. Fixing it would be no easy job.

The first thing I did was to disassemble the gun and clean it. There was even rust on the inside of the action and the gun showed no signs of being lubricated for decades. I then turned my attention to the barrel. I pushed a stiff bronze bush down the bore and this resulted in a small pile of rust and lead coming out. Even with part of the rust and lead removed, there was only the slightest hint of rifling remaining between the deep pits and scale.

Since the bore was a lost cause at this point, I decided to take drastic measures. I took a tight-fitting patch and coated it with automotive valve grinding compound and scrubbed the bore, which actually did improve it. I could now see some rifling.

The majority of the rust was gone, but the excessive deep pitting remained. To smooth up the rough chamber, I wrapped some fine sandpaper (400 grit) around a cleaning jag and spun it in the chamber to polish it. Even though some pitting was still evident, this did smooth up the chamber considerably. I lubricated the gun and reassembled it then I took it outside to see if it would fire and eject.

I could get about 10-15 rounds out before barrel and chamber fouling got so bad that the cases began sticking in the chamber again. A quick cleaning allowed a few more rounds to be fired before malfunctions returned. This certainly wouldn't be considered a fix, but it would allow a few rounds to be fired in the gun for nostalgia's sake.

I then turned my attention to the wood. I have done a lot of stock refinishing and know some pretty beat up wood can be saved and turned into a decent stock. Fortunately the scratches and gouges in this gun were not too deep and could be removed by careful sanding. When I say "careful sanding," I really mean "careful".

Someone had replaced the original buttplate with a form-less glob of wood putty. It didn't look realistic, but at least had the virtue of keeping water out of the stock.

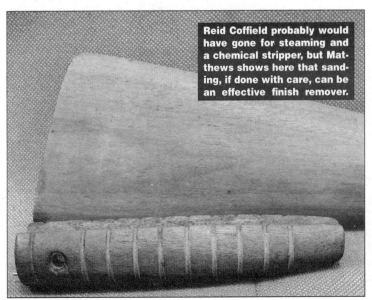

Reid Coffield probably would have gone for steaming and a chemical stripper, but Matthews shows here that sanding, if done with care, can be an effective finish remover.

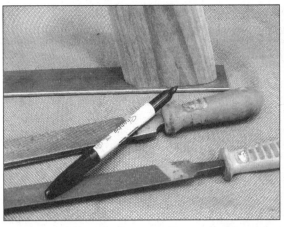

Matthews will always find the thrifty method, and here he made a new buttplate for the rifle by cutting one out of 3/16" steel bar. He used the butt as his template.

Guns made back in the early years featured wood that was closely fitted to the metal parts. Unlike inexpensive guns made today that may have 1/16" of wood extending over or under the metal, even .22s made back in the day featured wood that was flush and even with the metal parts.

Any excessive sanding where wood meets metal on these old guns will result in a poor wood-to-metal fit. At these points, you only want to remove minimal amounts of material to maintain the good fit. Before sanding, I removed the old varnish with a soaking in lacquer thinner; paint remover could also be used here if you wish.

Once the old varnish was removed, I used 100-grit sandpaper to remove most of the scratches, scrapes and dents. This was followed by sanding with 150- and 220-grit sandpaper. Remember not to excessively sand the wood where it meets metal. After sanding the wood looked pretty good.

In the "old days," even inexpensive .22s featured good walnut stocks.

With the wood cleaned up and smooth, it was time to see what could be done to replace the previously removed caulking putty buttplate. Parts for 75-year-old .22s can be hard to find and expensive. I found some used ones for sale in a catalog for about $20.

To keep cost down I decided on a 50¢ alternative. Many old guns featured steel buttplates, so I decided to make a new steel replacement out of 50¢ worth of 3/16"x1½-inch flat steel. I placed the buttstock on the steel and traced the approximate shape around the stock with a felt-tip pen. This shape was then sawn out of the steel with plenty of extra material for final shaping.

Before final shaping, I located the buttplate screw holes drilled them in the steel part. The oversize buttplate was then attached to the buttstock.

To prevent marring the stock while working the buttplate, I wrapped a couple layers of masking tape around the stock. Material can be removed from the rough buttplate till it is flush with the tape. This will get you to within about .010" (10 thousandths of an inch) from finished size. Material can be removed with a file or by careful use of small power tools.

I used 2-inch diameter sanding discs on an air powered angle grinder. When I just started to scuff the first layer of masking tape, I knew it was time to stop. Once the plate was shaped all the way around to within the .010" thick tape layers it was removed for final shaping.

The additional .010" was carefully removed so the plate would be flush with the wood buttstock. Occasionally re-installing the buttplate will tell you if you need to remove more for a flush fit. Removing material and checking often will keep you from going undersize.

Once he'd rough-cut the buttplate with a hacksaw and files, he drilled holes for the screws and attached to the stock. Then he finish-sized it with careful filing.

Remember that you can always remove more material if the edges don't meet but you can't put more back on if you go too far. Once the outside shape was right, I contoured the sharp edges over on the back to duplicate the appearance of a manufactured buttplate.

Matthews finished the buttplate in Brownells Gun-Kote, a sprayed and baked aerosol. He then stamped it with the initials of its new owner and the completion date.

A $5 can of spray lacquer was a quick, inexpensive choice for finishing the wood. Tung oil would be an alternative, but would require many coats for best results.

If you can do good work, the self-made buttplate will look just as good as a factory unit. The metal buttplate will also be much more durable than the original plastic version. Since the gun was going to be presented to a returning veteran, I personalized the buttplate by stamping in the new owner's initials and date with a set of inexpensive ($5-$10) metal hand stamps.

To keep letters and numbers aligned while stamping, apply a few layers of tape straight across the buttplate. This will give an even ledge to locate the stamps. Initially, tap the stamp lightly to see a faint mark on the steel. If the figure is out of alignment it can be slightly repositioned before stamping to full depth.

Once the plate was completely shaped and stamped, I roughed it up with some sandpaper in preparation for applying a finish. Since most buttplates are black, I wanted a durable black finish on this one. I could have used spray paint, but I wanted something a little better. I chose to use Brownells GunKote spray-on gun finish.

It's a sprayed and baked polymer that is extremely durable and maintenance free. It is available in liquid form or in aerosol cans for those who don't have spray equipment. I only needed about $2 worth of a full can to finish the buttplate.

The buttplate was cleaned, sprayed and baked at 300° for a half-hour. Once cooled the part was complete and could be installed after the wood finish was applied.

Since the wood was no longer being used to size the buttplate, it could have its final finish applied. The wood was light-colored walnut, so I applied some stain to darken it. This was followed by spraying on a couple coats of satin finish aerosol lacquer. At this point the cost for wood finishing was about $5 for a can of spray lacquer, $3.50 for sandpaper, $3.50 for a small can of wood stain, and $2 worth of lacquer thinner for finish removal.

For a total of $14, the beat up wood was returned to a nice attractive gunstock. The buttplate cost about 50¢ to make and about $2 worth of GunKote was used to finish it. For a grand total of $16.50 and a few hours work the wooden stock and buttplate looked almost like new.

With the stock returned to some semblance of its former glory it was time to turn my attention to the metal finish. Originally my neighbor inquired about a complete refinish job with hot tank bluing. This was cost prohibitive since even a standard reblue job could easily exceed $100. Add to this the fact that the gun had severe pitting that would require extensive polishing and metal removal and it become apparent that this was not an economical option.

When a gun's finish gets this bad there are few inexpensive options. I presented two low cost options for this project and showed him samples of each. The first option was to remove all rust by abrasive blasting and then apply Brownells GunKote firearms finish in the color of "gun blue." This would fill in the pits and return the gun's finish to a smooth texture that roughly duplicated an original finish.

The other option was to sand off all the rust and most of the original finish and then give the gun a complete cold blue job with Brownells Oxpho-Blue. Oxpho-Blue is one of the best cold bluing solutions available to hobbyist. It doesn't duplicate the look of a professional hot bluing job, but it doesn't look half bad and is relatively inexpensive to apply at home by the gun owner.

While I liked the GunKote option, the owner liked the Oxpho-Blue finish. He thought that the Oxpho-Blue looked more like a slightly worn original finish, and so looked more appropriate on a 75-year-old gun. Therefore Oxpho-Blue was going to be the finish.

Oxpho-Blue is available in several sizes and I used 4-6 ounces for this project. Four ounces cost about $10 and 8 ounces cost about $20 but if you're not wasteful, you may be able to get by with the 4-ounce ($10) size. I tend to really lay it on, so I use more than some would.

Possible finishes included everything from conventional spray paint to modern compounds like Brownells Aluma-Hyde and Lauer DuraCoat. Each of these has strong points.

Over the last 20 plus years I have been using Oxpho-Blue, I have found several application techniques that seem to give good results for the best possible finish. These methods will be discussed when we get to the application.

The first thing that needed to be done was to remove the rust and most of the remaining original bluing. Not every bit of original bluing needs to be removed such as in hard to access places since Oxpho-Blue will blend in somewhat with the original finish. I used 220-grit sandpaper to remove the majority of the rust and old bluing. This was followed by going over it again with 400-grit sandpaper.

I used the black automotive refinishing type of sand paper known as wet or dry sandpaper. This type of paper seems to be more durable when sanding metal than the common wood use types of sandpaper. This sanding was followed by heavy rubdown with a purple "Scotch-Brite" abrasive pad. Although this did not remove all the pitting, the metal was at least cleaned up enough to apply Oxpho-Blue.

Pitting as bad as found on this gun cannot be easily removed by hand methods, and you just have to live with a few pits for economy's sake. I started the bluing by cleaning with lacquer thinner to remove all oil and leave a clean surface. This solvent cleaning method works well most of the time, but I have found that sometimes it needs to be supplemented.

Occasionally the bluing solution beads up on the metal surface and doesn't blue evenly. I have found that a cleaning with hot water and dish soap after solvent cleaning allows the solution to spread out better over the steel better and not bead up.

Apply Oxpho-Blue according to the instructions on the bottle. I have an alternative procedure that has worked well for me for more than 20 years of using this solution. You need a small bowl for the solution, a degreased/cleaned #0000 steel wool pad, some soft textured rags, and some spray oil. For the

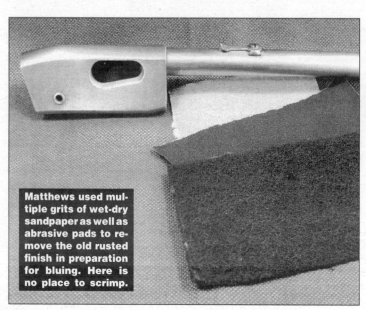

Matthews used multiple grits of wet-dry sandpaper as well as abrasive pads to remove the old rusted finish in preparation for bluing. Here is no place to scrimp.

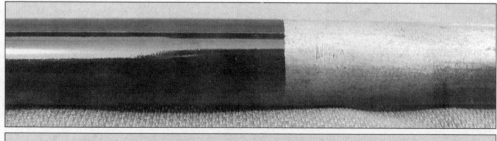

Matthews recommended Brownells Gun-Kote, but his neighbor thought that finish too shiny for an old gun. So Matthews used Oxpho-Blue, which looked more authentic.

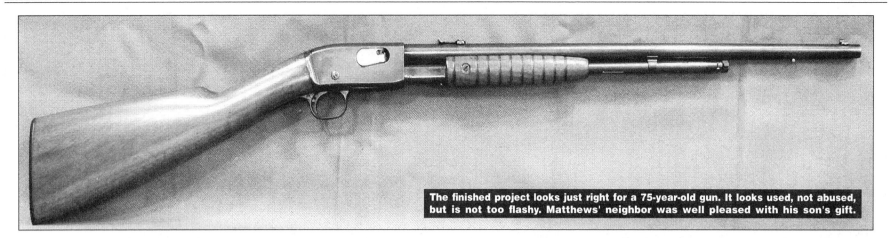

The finished project looks just right for a 75-year-old gun. It looks used, not abused, but is not too flashy. Matthews' neighbor was well pleased with his son's gift.

spray oil I recommend CRC Power-Lube that is available from auto parts suppliers. Other oils may also work well but Power-Lube is my favorite. I absolutely do not recommend WD-40 which tends to dry up over time and leave little oil for surface protection.

I take a small piece of the clean steel wool and dab it in the bluing solution. The solution will blue the steel wool but don't worry about that. I use the solution soaked steel wool to spread the solution on the steel. It seems that the solution on the pad only blues so much before its potency is depleted even though it is still wet with solution.

When the solution doesn't blue well, replenish the solution on the pad with fresh solution. Observe the color of the steel and if darker and lighter colors are observed, lightly rub the soaked steel wool over the metal to evenly blend them.

After the steel is evenly colored, I leave the surfaces soaking wet with bluing solution for a couple more minutes before wiping off the excess with a soft rag. I then drench the blued parts with spray oil. If you do the project in sections be careful not to get oil on the remaining bare metal that hasn't been blued as oil will affect later bluing of the bare steel.

I leave the newly blued surface soaking wet with the spray oil till the rest of the metal is blued. I then wipe off the excess oil with a soft rag, but leave a slight film for protection.

Any blued finish, whether professional hot blue or home applied cold blue, needs a thin coating of oil for protection. Dry un-oiled bluing offers only marginal protection to the steel. This is why bluing has been replaced by more durable and better protecting modern finishes on sporting and military arms that are subjected to severe conditions. Bluing is a traditional finish that is appropriate for old guns, but it really isn't very durable.

Once the cold blue was applied and the parts oiled up, the resulting finish looked vastly better than the old rusty finish. While some pitting was still evident because of the original poor condition of the metal, there was no remaining rust and the steel was evenly colored a dark gray/light black color. This finish looked appropriate for a 75-year-old gun.

The finish looked somewhat used, without that flashy new finish appearance.

With the wood and metal work done the gun was lubed and re-assembled. The completed gun did look used but it no longer looked abused and beat to death. This gun will never be a shooter again. It will, however be a fine presentation gift for the neighbor's returning veteran son to display and maybe shoot just a couple rounds for old times' sake.

When my neighbor picked up the gun, he was very pleased and thought it looked just right: slightly used without looking newly refinished. If you have an old, worn out and abused gun that you would like to display, try these methods to make old beater something you'll be proud to display. Returning your old veteran firearm to display condition economically can be a rewarding experience so why not give it a try?

FIREARMS REFINISHING SUPPLIES

Brownells, 200 S. Front St., Dept. SGN, Montezuma, Iowa, 50171, 1800-741-0015, www.brownells.com ◉

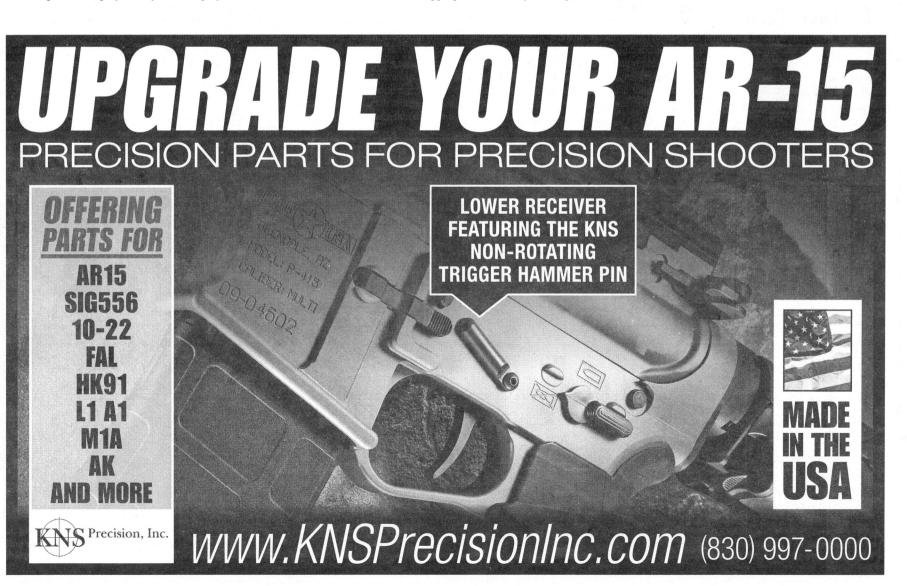

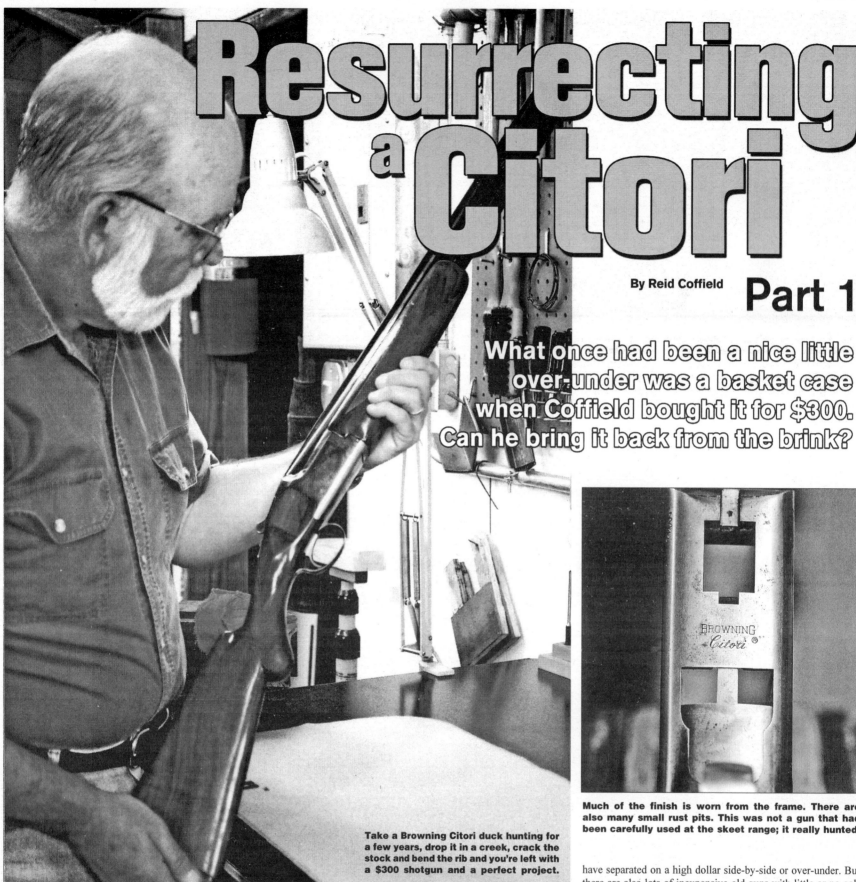

Resurrecting a Citori

By Reid Coffield

Part 1

What once had been a nice little over-under was a basket case when Coffield bought it for $300. Can he bring it back from the brink?

Much of the finish is worn from the frame. There are also many small rust pits. This was not a gun that had been carefully used at the skeet range; it really hunted!

Take a Browning Citori duck hunting for a few years, drop it in a creek, crack the stock and bend the rib and you're left with a $300 shotgun and a perfect project.

W hen reading various gun magazines over the years, it has always struck me as odd how gunsmithing articles almost always deal with rifles or handguns. To me it's odd, because there are so darn many shotguns. In fact, I would go so far as to bet that more shooters go into the field each year with shotguns than with centerfire rifles.

In addition, there're a lot more "games" such as trap, skeet, sporting clays, etc. you can play with shotguns than with rifles. In my old shop back in western North Carolina I always had more shotguns sitting in the rack awaiting repair than centerfire rifles.

Shotguns offer a lot of potential as various gunsmithing projects for the hobbyist. Equally important, project guns can often be picked up at gun shows or gun shops at relatively modest prices and are frequently a lot cheaper than centerfire rifles or handguns.

Many of these guns offer lots of opportunities for stock and metal work. Often the techniques and skills developed working on shotguns can easily and readily be transferred to rifles or handguns. For example, the procedures used in refinishing the stock of a shotgun are the same as used on a rifle. There's really no difference in fitting a recoil pad to a shotgun than it is when fitting a rifle pad.

Now I'd be remiss if I didn't acknowledge that there are some shotgun jobs that are darn difficult to master and should be left to specialist. A good example would be resoldering barrels that have separated on a high dollar side-by-side or over-under. But there are also lots of inexpensive old guns with little or no collector value that you and I can work on and develop our skills.

Not too long ago I had a chance to pick up a shotgun that had been "rode hard and put away wet" many times and it showed! It was a Japanese made Browning Citori 12-gauge over-under. To give you an idea of just how rough this old gun was, I only paid $300 for it. Brownings are darn fine guns and to encounter one that was this cheap you just have to figure there's something wrong with it. And boy, are you right! There are *lots* of things wrong with this gun!

So I bought the gun with the idea that in repairing it we could look at a lot of different repair techniques and procedures. Because there is so much to be done it will take about four or five separate installments. By the time it's finished, I should have a good, serviceable over-under that I won't be embarrassed to take to the field or have in my gun rack.

The rear face of the barrels shows evidence of rusting. The breech face of the frame looks a lot worse than it really is. Fortunately, there is no deep pitting.

The checkering is well worn, especially on the left side of the stock. This will have to be recut. The curving patterns on the pistol grip knob will be interesting.

The first step in a project such as this is to determine just what's wrong with the gun and make a list of the problem areas. Once that is done, you can then make a plan for systematically attacking them. It's important to be very logical in terms of what is done and when it's done. A list helps to plan the sequence of repair work for maximum efficiency. Unfortunately, or fortunately depending upon your outlook, the work list for this shotgun is pretty darn long.

One of the first problem areas is a very noticeable dent in the rib about six inches from the muzzle. In addition, the stock is cracked at the wrist. There's also a small crack in the fore-end. The stock has numerous dents, scratches, and other damage to the finish. The checkering is well worn and needs to be recut.

The recoil pad has hardened with age and is no longer offering the recoil protection it once did. Over the years, the recoil pad has also been removed from the stock several times with ill fitting screwdrivers and the face of the recoil pad is torn around the screw access slits.

At some point while the forearm assembly was off the gun, it was dropped. This bent part of the forearm bracket, leaving a slight gap when the gun is completely assembled. By the way, Browning uses the term "forearm" where I normally use "fore-end". Since this is a Browning Citori, I'll try to use the Browning terms but don't be too surprised if I slip up now and again.

The metal finish is extremely worn with lots of pits from rust. Fortunately, most of these pits are relatively shallow. However, there is some engraving on the Citori, so that poses a challenge as to how it will be best to handle the removal of these pits without obliterating the engraving.

Just as the outside of the shotgun has seen a lot of wear and some rusting, the chambers and bores also show signs of very light pitting. There are also scratches in the bores

that are primarily cosmetic but such that you and I would want to remove 'em for both the sake of appearance and to cut down on fouling. The chambers have the original Browning forcing cones which are fairly short and abrupt. I'll want to recut the forcing cones making them longer with a shallower angle. I believe this will help with a bit less felt recoil and it will normally help make patterns a bit more uniform.

As I initially mentioned, the rib is dented. I suspect that the gun was dropped or perhaps the owner fell with it. Unfortunately, someone tried to raise the damaged portion of the rib by jamming a tapered screwdriver in the rib vent and prying the rib up. All they accomplished was to damage both sides of the rib. In addition to properly raising the rib, this damage definitely must be repaired.

Before you decide this gun is a total waste of time, there are some bright spots! Unlike many older shotguns, there are absolutely no dents in the barrels. The basic mechanism functions flawlessly. In fact, I've shot maybe 500 plus rounds through it without a glitch of any type. And, something I noticed right away, none of the slots in the screws were distorted or mangled. Generally if you see damaged screw slots they're a darn good indication someone who didn't know what he was doing had been inside the gun. In this case, the screws showed no evidence of damage. In all, it's just a nice old gun that needs some TLC.

So…I've got quite a "to do" list! Now before I jump into the project, I need to give some careful thought to the sequence of the work. I will be the first to admit that on more than one occasion I've made a repair to a gun and then later had to redo part of that work because I failed to plan my project properly. Believe me; you definitely don't want to make that mistake!

For example, this shotgun has a noticeable crack running from the frame inletting back along the wrist. I can repair this but I need to do so *before* I strip the finish from the stock. The reason for this is that chemical finish removers often contain wax or other agents that would inhibit the adhesion of any epoxy or glue used to repair the crack.

Also, if I have a crack extending from the frame inletting, I need to consider the possibility that the frame may not be bearing evenly against the stock. After all, what caused the crack in the first place? I really think I ought to glass-bed the frame. This will provide a perfect fit between the wood and steel and reinforce and strengthen the stock. *But* I should do the bedding *before* I refinish the stock. By doing that I eliminate any possibility of damaging a nice new finish with any bedding that might run out and contact the finish.

I'm sure you see what I mean by the importance of planning the sequence of the work. Any time you have a repair project that involves more than one step or action, make darn sure you fully understand and appreciate the effects of each repair on the

The barrels are fitted for screw-in choke tubes. Coffield was very pleased to find that there was no damage around the muzzle from improper use of choke wrenches.

The stock has a multitude of dents, dings and scratches. The wood will definitely have to be refinished, but damage is mostly limited to the wood surface.

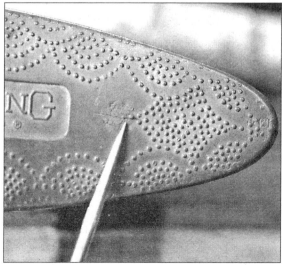

The screw slots in the face of the recoil pad show someone didn't bother with the lubricant or special bit. The pad will be replaced with a soft new Pachmayr pad.

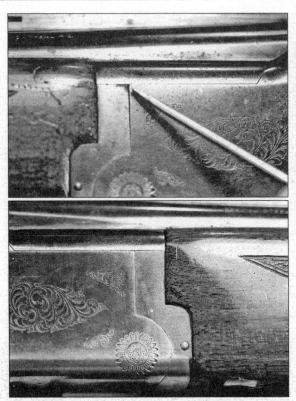

Note the gap between the forearm bracket and the front of the left side of the frame. Unlike its mate, the right side shows no damage and fits the frame perfectly.

sequence of your other work. If you don't, I'll guarantee that like me you'll end up wasting time and energy redoing work you've already done. My friends, that can put a real damper on the party.

Of course there are some parts of this project that could be done at any time. For example, the bores and chambers need to be polished. This could be done right away or I could wait until the very last thing before I reassemble the shotgun. It really doesn't matter as this will have little or no impact on any other step in the repair and refinishing process.

Here's my list of projects and the sequence in which I intend on doin' 'em.

1. raise the dented rib
2. repair the damage to the sides of the rib
3. repair dent in forearm bracket
4. repair gap on left side of forearm bracket
5. repair the crack in the buttstock
6. bed the frame in the buttstock
7. repair the crack in the forearm
8. fit new recoil pad
9. strip old finish from buttstock and forearm
10. refinish buttstock and forearm
11. prepare metal prior to refinishing
12. refinish metal
13. cut long forcing cones in barrels
14. polish chambers and bores

That's the plan! However, the sequence of some steps may be changed as the work progresses.

There is a serious crack in the buttstock on the right side behind the frame. A crack at the wrist is a common fault and one that definitely needs to be corrected.

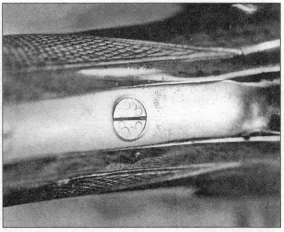

Coffield liked the fact that the Citori's screw slots were in great shape. That meant no amateur gunsmith had helped himself to a look at the shotgun's interior.

OK, time to get started! The first item on the list is the dented rib. As I mentioned earlier, someone tried to "repair" the dent by inserting a screwdriver in the vent and prying up on the top of the rib. Not only did they fail to raise the rib properly, they also left a good many little "dings" and "divots" along the bottom and top of the vent.

As far as I'm concerned, there is currently only one way safely and correctly to raise a dented rib like this and that's with a Murray's Vent Rib Tool. The tool consists of a rectangular brass bar about 2¾ inches long, a half-inch high and a quarter-inch thick. The bar is partly relieved on one edge, which is placed on the top of the rib above the dent.

A pair of claws extends down on either side of the brass bar from a steel elevating pad that is positioned on the top edge of the bar. A threaded screw runs down from the elevating pad and contacts the top of the bar. A rubber band is used to keep the two claws in place against the elevating pad as well as to hold the ends of the claws under the rib.

The tool is really a neat little job! Once you hook the claws in place, you just turn the elevating screw in with an Allen wrench. This lifts the elevating pad, which in turn lifts the claws, which then lift the dented rib. Since there is a clearance cut on the bottom of the rectangular bar, you raise the rib a bit above level. Most ribs will have a bit of "spring" to 'em so you raise it a bit higher than needed, then let it settle back into place.

Someone tried to pry up a dented rib, with damage to the sides the result. Fortunately there is little damage to the top. The right tool is needed for this job!

The Murray's Vent Rib Tool is used carefully to raise the dented rib. It operates like a gear puller, putting even lifting force on either side of the dented rib.

If you have a severe dent you will want to set the lifting claws up slightly ahead of the dent first and raise it just a bit. Then set the claws up behind the dent and raise it a bit more. Finally you can set the claws up directly under the lowest part of the dent and raise it.

Fortunately the dent in the Citori was not severe. I was able to raise it without the necessity of using the Murray Tool at more than one spot. After initially using the tool I checked my work by looking down the side of the rib. Even if there is only a hint of irregularity in the top of the rib, you'll quickly spot it. Oddly enough, sometimes when looking along the top of the rib as when you're shooting, you won't see minor irregularities in the top of a rib. But, if you'll just look along the side of the rib, it'll stand out like a sore thumb!

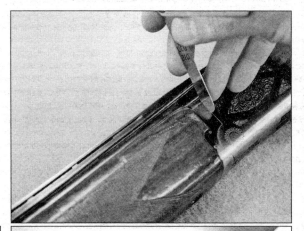

The gap between forearm bracket and frame was .012". When the forearm was dropped, the bracket was bent. Repair left little gap between frame and bracket.

The gap between the bracket and the forearm was caused by the compression of the wood when the bracket was damaged. The only way to repair this is glass bedding.

If you accidentally raise the rib too much and you now have a "hill" rather than a "dip" in the rib, don't worry. All you need to do is take a plastic faced hammer and carefully tap the raised portion of the rib down. Go just a tad below level and then use the Murray Tool to carefully raise the dent. The Murray Tool is simple to use and it'll do a great job.

You can get one of these little jewels from Ben Murray, Murray's Gunsmithing, 12696 FM 2127, Dept. SGN, Bowie, Texas 76230, telephone 940-928-0002. I believe the current price for the Murray Tool is $35.

With the rib raised, the next order of business was to repair the many little divots on the bottom and top of the vent. The metal from the divots was still there; it had just been pushed out or upset by a screwdriver blade. If I were to just file these divots or metal projections off, there would still be little depressions or voids. The trick to making a good repair is to first drive that displaced metal back into place where it was originally.

This was done by having a buddy hold the barrel with the side of the rib firmly against the flat of my vise anvil. While he held it, I used a flat faced punch to swage each individual divot back into place. Generally it didn't take but just a tap or two with the punch.

Once these dings were smoothed out, I then took some 180-grit cloth-backed abrasive and wrapped it around the end of a flat file. This was then used to smooth up both sides of the rib where the damage had occurred. Because of the work with the punch, the surface was relatively flat and didn't really require much in the way of polishing to remove all traces of the damage.

The next order of business was to repair the left side of the forearm bracket. I measured the gap between the forearm bracket and the front of the frame with a feeler gauge. The gap was an incredible .012"! That's a heck of a big gap and certainly indicates that the metal was pushed back quite a ways. This also explains why there is a small crack in the forearm behind the left side of the forearm bracket. When it was dropped, the metal was shoved into the wood and something had to give.

Once the bracket was off the forearm wood and the left ejector hammer removed from the bracket, I first used a small 4-ounce

The buttstock is removed by taking out the buttstock bolt. The bottom of the crack on the right side of the stock is much more severe. However, this can be repaired.

hammer carefully to swage back the burr on the top edge of the bracket. Just as with the rib; I wanted to put that metal back in its original position. I definitely don't want to file or sand it off as this would leave a gap.

Next, I clamped the bracket in my vise and, using a nylon-faced hammer, I carefully tapped on the front left side of the forearm bracket to move it back into its original position. I wish I could say I got it fixed right away, but I didn't. It took several attempts until I had it right. The metal of the forearm bracket is relatively thin and soft, so it didn't take much pressure to bend it. If you ever encounter something like this, be darn careful and don't get in a hurry or heavy handed. It's just a matter of adjusting or slightly bending the bracket, trying it on the gun, and then making additional corrections. Go slow and check your work frequently.

After completing the work and reassembling the forearm, I checked my work with the feeler gauge. After the repair, I was unable to get even a .003" gauge in the joint between the bracket and the frame. Quite an improvement over .012"! This simple repair made a significant difference in the appearance of the gun. To me it looked a lot less "tired and worn!"

The next project was to deal with the crack in the buttstock. I removed the screws from the trigger guard and lifted the guard out of the buttstock. Next I took the recoil pad off the stock and loosened the stock bolt that holds the buttstock to the frame.

I was a little surprised when I first saw the inside of the frame. This gun had obviously taken a bath in a stream or pond. There was a fine coat of rust over some of the internal parts and also some mud deposits in the frame. It had definitely been used as a duck gun!

With the buttstock off I was able more closely to examine the crack on the right side of the stock. It wasn't all that bad. Since I plan on refinishing the stock, I didn't hesitate to use a liberal amount of Insta-Clean to flush out the cracks and remove any oil or crud that might be present.

Be very careful if you use a solvent to clean the wood; make darn sure it won't harm your finish. Of course, if like me you'll be refinishing the stock, then there's nothing to worry about. I get my Insta-Clean from MidwayUSA, 5875 W. Van Horn Tavern Road, Dept. SGN, Columbia, Mo. 65203, telephone 800-243-3220. I've found it to be about the best darn aerosol solvent I've used. I especially like it as it cleans without leaving any residue.

Once the cracks had been cleaned, I carefully spread the cracks and put in a few drops of Hot Stuff glue. This is a very

Not only was the wood in the forearm compressed, the forearm itself was also cracked. This will have to be repaired as well, using a very thin glue to bind the wood.

Coffield applied a thin glue to the crack and then wrapped the stock in surgical tubing to hold it closed while the glue cured. Tubing is ideal for this.

thin liquid glue that will penetrate deep into a crack. I have used it for years to make stock repairs. It's available from Satellite City, Box 836, Dept. SGN, Simi, Calif. 93062, telephone 805-522-0062. A number of suppliers carry it and you might even run across it in your local hardware store.

As soon as the glue was in place. I wrapped the stock with a piece of surgical tubing. This is the greatest stuff in the world for holding odd-shaped pieces of wood together while they bond. I then let the stock set for several hours and then removed the tubing. With the crack repaired, the next step will be to glass-bed the frame. This will further reinforce the stock repair and ensure that the frame is uniformly supported by the stock.

That's about it for now. Until next time, good luck and good gunsmithing!

Repairing & Refinishing a Citori

Part 2

By Reid Coffield

Stock Bedding Repair

Coffield's old Citori was rode hard and put up wet, but with the proper materials and techniques, its stock will be good as new.

In this installment, Coffield shows how to repair the stock bedding and how to install a fresh recoil pad, using his well-traveled Browning Citori as the test subject.

Well-used older shotguns often provide excellent opportunities for the hobbyist to develop his gunsmithing skills as well as increase his knowledge and experience. As an added benefit since shotguns are probably the most common type of firearm after .22 rifles, the cost of project guns can be darn reasonable.

The Browning Citori I am using for this series was picked up for just a few hundred dollars. It has a number of problems ranging from numerous cracks in the stock, to a damaged and hardened recoil pad as well as a worn and rusted metal finish. These plus other "problems" have made it into an ideal project gun. Admittedly it'll take quite a bit of time and elbow grease to fix all the problems but once it's finished, I hope to have a darn nice

shooter that I'll be happy to take to the field or set in my gun rack.

As you follow this series, keep in mind that many if not most of the operations performed on this shotgun can be applied to other types of firearm. Techniques for removing rust pits are generally the same whether it's done on a rifle, pistol or shotgun. The same goes for repairing and refinishing stocks, installing recoil pads, disassembly and assembly procedures, etc.

In the first installment, I repaired a major dent to the ventilated rib, a large crack on the right side of the buttstock behind the frame and damage to the left side of the forearm bracket. In making these repairs I was following a list that I made for all

the work that was to be done. Not only will that list help keep me on track, it will ensure that the various repair tasks are done in a logical and systematic manner.

You definitely don't want to complete a major repair only to have to undo and later redo part of the work because of the effects of some other necessary work. For example, I definitely want to repair the cracks *before* I bed or refinish the stock.

If you missed the first part of the series, the following is a list of the various steps in the repair and refinishing process.

#1. Raise the dented rib—done
#2. Repair the damage to the sides of the rib—done
#3. Repair dent in forearm bracket—done

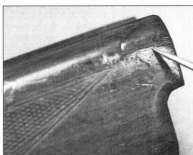

Straightening the forearm bracket left a gap between the bracket and forearm; the latter was cracked. Hot Stuff instant glue penetrates the cracks for a firm seal.

#4. Repair gap on left side forearm bracket—done
#5. Repair crack in the buttstock—done
#6. Bed the frame in the buttstock
#7. Repair the crack in the forearm
#8. Fit new recoil pad
#9. Strip old finish from buttstock and forearm
#10. Refinish buttstock and forearm
#11. Prepare metal prior to refinishing
#12. Refinish metal
#13. Cut long forcing cones in barrels
#14. Polish chambers and bores

That's quite a list and a lot of work! But, like so many lengthy and complex projects, if you just take it one step at a time and stick with it, you'll eventually get it done. You don't have to do a lot at any one time to make real progress. Given enough small steps taken on a regular basis, even the biggest project will eventually be completed.

Many hobbyists get discouraged with projects that seem to take forever. They just can't maintain the energy or interest to finish it up. I've had more than one partly completed project gun brought into my shop for me to finish. One way to avoid this problem is to divide the project up into smaller segments and then take 'em one at a time.

If you have a part of the project that's time consuming and maybe even boring such as hand polishing the entire gun, do

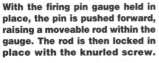

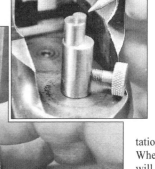

only one part at a time. For example, don't even touch the barrel until after the trigger guard is done. By taking a big project in small "bites" you get the mental reinforcement of completing something and in seeing more and more of the total project done. With this positive reinforcement it's a lot easier to stay interested and committed to the project.

So much for that! While the cracks in the buttstock were repaired in the first session, there are still cracks in the forearm that have to be repaired. As with the buttstock, I used Tipton Insta-Clean, an aerosol degreaser, to clean thoroughly the cracks and remove all possible traces of oil, gunk and grease. As you know by now, Insta-Clean is one of my favorite solvents and is available from MidwayUSA, 5875 W. Van Horn Tavern Road, Dept. SGN, Columbia, Mo. 65203, telephone 800-243-3220.

Once the cracks were cleaned, I used a very thin, water like glue called Hot Stuff to repair the crack. Hot Stuff has amazing penetrating qualities and will flow into the smallest cracks. In my experience it is far superior to standard thick epoxy glues. Hot Stuff is available from Satellite City, Box 836, Dept. SGN, Simi, Calif. 93062, telephone 805-522-0062. Once the Hot Stuff was applied I used a number of ordinary rubber bands to help clamp the crack together. When working on a thin forearm such as the one on this Citori, you have to be very careful that you do not accidentally break the forearm as you try to repair it!

Now let's get back to work on the buttstock. With the major crack repaired, we now need to bed the frame in the stock. Synthetic bedding will do a couple of things. First, it will strengthen the wood and help prevent future cracks. It will also help to prolong the life of the stock by sealing the wood, so any oil or solvents used on the frame can not penetrate into the wood and thereby weaken it.

Finally, it will absolutely ensure that we have a perfect mating of the wood and metal. There is a darn good possibility that the original crack was caused at least in part by the metal not bearing evenly against the wood. Synthetic bedding applied to the wood will mold itself to the contact surfaces of the metal with a precision that no human being could duplicate.

The first step in bedding the frame is to strip out the internal parts. This will make it easier to fill the openings in the frame with modeling clay. The clay helps to keep the bedding out of screw and pin holes as well as other open recesses. If the bedding were to get into those areas and harden, it could easily lock the frame into the stock. Attempting to remove a stuck frame can often result in major damage to the stock.

Also, we need to take the Citori completely apart simply to clean it. Every individual part should be thoroughly cleaned. Remember when the buttstock was removed I found evidence of mud and rust on the internal parts. This old shotgun may well have gone for a swim more than once!

In addition to cleaning the various internal parts, this will also be a chance to check for wear or damage. I am especially concerned about the firing pins and the hammer springs. Citori shotguns have a bit of a reputation for developing ignition problems with the lower barrel. When the firing mechanism for the lower barrel is removed, it will be given extra attention.

OK, let's get to work! If you are working on a gun you are not familiar with, by all means, get a disassembly manual. If that's not available; then try to find an exploded drawing of the gun to help with the disassembly. An exploded drawing can

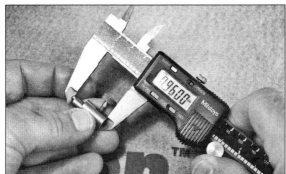

Then measure the gauge with the extended rod. Subtract the length of the gauge. Coffield determined that the firing pin was protruding only .060", well within spec.

If you don't have a disassembly manual or an exploded drawing, a photograph or a drawing showing the relationship of the parts can be invaluable when reassembling.

also be worth its weight in gold when you later have to put the gun back together. If you cannot locate any drawings or exploded views, then definitely make some rough sketches to show the relationship of any parts you think you even *might* have problems putting back together. This is *especially important* if a project like this might stretch over a period of weeks or months.

Coffield will also label parts with notes to help in later reassembly. This is especially important when completing a project that may extend over weeks or even months.

Coffield used a brass punch to remove this round-end pin. A standard flat-point steel punch would have scarred the end of the pin, but the soft brass won't mar it.

Coffield said the Citori was dirty! An amazing amount of dirt and foreign matter was found inside. The cocking lever was also coated with dirt, oily grime, and carbon.

If you are like me, you can easily forget just how that little spring was attached or positioned or how that odd-shaped lever was installed. By the way, a lot of folks are using digital cameras to take a few quick shots during disassembly to record the position and location of internal components.

Fortunately, I have some darn good resource material for this project. I have a copy of a Browning factory exploded parts drawing for the Citori that identifies each individual component and shows their relationship. This can be especially helpful when reassembling the gun. In addition, I have a copy of a neat little book titled *Gunsmithing the Shotgun: Tips and Techniques*. This book is a collection of articles from the *American Gunsmith Magazine* relating to shotguns.

There are two articles in this book written by an old and dear friend, Chick Blood, which are invaluable for anyone working on a Citori. The first is "Servicing the Browning Citori" and the other is "Repairing Ejectors on the Browning Citori." Both are *extremely* detailed and well-illustrated. If you don't have this book and you are interested in the Citori, *get it*!

I think this book may still be in print and available from the publishers of the *American Gunsmith Magazine*. If you're interested just give the AGA folks a call at 1-800-241-7484. They can also give you info on their monthly magazine that is packed with gunsmithing articles. I've subscribed for years and have found it to be a very useful tool for my shop.

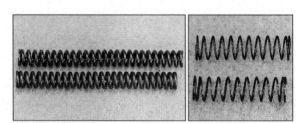

The old firing pin return spring on the bottom is slightly shorter due to compression over time, while the difference is more noticeable with the hammer spring.

Coffield removed just enough wood to allow for a bead of bedding to strengthen and reinforce the end of the buttstock. Use the Dremel tool judiciously in this job.

When disassembling a shotgun, either an over and under or a side by side, that has two sets of firing and/or ejecting mechanisms, it is *critical* that you keep the components separate. If you accidentally try to install the upper barrel hammer in position for the lower barrel you'll have trouble. The idea of throwing all the parts in a cigar box is an invitation to disaster or at least a headache or two.

I avoid the problem of mixing parts by simply using labeled plastic bags. I have one bag that I label "Over Barrel" into which I put all components that relate to that barrel. This includes the hammer, firing pin, firing pin retaining pin, hammer strut, hammer spring, etc. Another bag is labeled "Under Barrel" and contains parts relating to that barrel. However you handle it, the important thing is to keep track of your parts and don't let them get mixed.

Oh yes, I also keep separate plastic bags for the right and left ejector mechanism housed in the forearm. The basic point which took me longer than I want to admit to learn, is that you need to store parts in a systematic manner to make reassembly easier and faster. 'Nough said about that.

As I removed the internal parts, I was particularly concerned about the firing pins, the hammer springs, and the bottom barrel firing pin return spring. Remember that this old gun had been well used and is probably in the neighborhood of 20 years old or more. Those parts and especially the coil springs probably spent a lot of time compressed. I believe that it's just prudent to replace inexpensive coil springs periodically to maintain maximum reliability. Also, when you're going to have the gun totally apart, it's darn easy to do.

As for the firing pins, the Browning Citori has a reputation for being hard on the lower barrel firing pin. Often the firing pin tip will wear or erode due to gas leakage from the primer. The firing pin return spring can also wear and weaken with age and use. If you are going to replace the parts, now is the time!

Before removing the old firing pins, I used a firing pin protrusion gauge I made years ago while I was a gunsmithing student at the Colorado School of Trades. A very similar gauge is currently available from Brownells Inc., 200 South Front St., Dept. SGN, Montezuma, Iowa 50171, telephone 800-741-0015. According to my gauge, the top barrel firing pin would extend .060" when fully depressed. The bottom firing pin extended a bit more at .064". This was well within the specs I have of a minimum of .047" and maximum of .070". I made a note of these figures to keep in mind when fitting the new firing pins.

The original hammer springs were shorter than the new replacement springs. Over time, they had taken a "set" or collapsed a bit. The hammer spring for the lower barrel showed the greatest degree of compression, as I expected. Both of these springs will be replaced when the gun is reassembled.

As I disassembled the frame I had to remove the pin on which the cocking lever rotates. Both ends of the pin are flush with the sides of the receiver. That wouldn't be so bad, but the sides of the receiver are curved and the ends of the pin are also curved. Using a standard flat steel punch would damage or scar the ends of the pin.

For this reason I had to rummage through my tools until I found a brass punch. Brass, being softer than the steel in the pin, will not damage the end of the pin. Whenever you are faced with removal of a pin that has a curved or shaped end, *always* use an appropriate punch. Nothing looks worse than a dinged up pin in the side of a receiver.

In addition to disassembling the frame, I also took apart the forearm iron, which contains the ejector mechanism. Again, I was very careful to keep the parts separate and appropriately labeled. You can avoid so many problems by simply using nothing more than zip-lock sandwich bags and a marking pen!

After stripping the frame and forearm iron, I cleaned these two components with Insta-Clean. I blasted out an incredible amount of carbon, dirt, mud, bits of weeds, and shavings of brass and plastic. As I looked at the pile of crud on my bench and floor I was just amazed that the old girl had continued to function.

Don't economize on the modeling clay used to fill milled slots and pin holes. If you go short with it, bedding compound can lock the forearm iron permanently to the wood.

Next I used two very small burrs or cutters in my Dremel tool *carefully* to rout in grooves where the frame contacted the stock. Two important points about these grooves; first, they were necessary to provide space for the bedding, and secondly, they had to be located so they did not extend beyond the sides of the frame.

These grooves would hold the bedding, which in turn would strengthen the stock to prevent further cracking, ensure that there was 100% contact between the frame and stock, and help to seal the grain of the wood to prevent damage from oil or solvents leaking from the frame.

The burrs I used were quite small. The round burr I used was only .081" in diameter. The other burr had a straight cutting shaft that was only .051" in diameter. Even then, I worked very slowly and carefully so I could fully control my cuts. You definitely don't want these cuts to be visible when the stock is in on the gun.

I also did the same thing on the forearm. Part of the forearm iron, which Browning calls the forearm bracket, had been bent. Once that was repaired, a sizeable

Note how the bedding has filled the grooves Coffield routed into the end of the buttstock and around the recoil shoulder. Excess bedding will need to be trimmed away.

A razor sharp bench knife will make short work of removing excess bedding. Just always be sure to cut only the excess bedding compound, not into the stock wood itself.

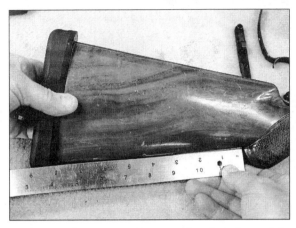

When choosing a new rubber recoil pad, make certain that it is large enough for your stock. Check to ensure that the line of the toe will continue through the pad.

gap was present between the wood of the forearm and the bracket. Bedding will fill this gap, strengthen the forearm, and again seal the wood to prevent oil and solvent damage.

Once the stock and forearm were prepared, I carefully examined the forearm bracket and frame to determine what holes and milled cuts needed to be filled with modeling clay. Since I

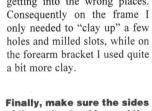

would be using a very small amount of bedding, there was very little chance of any bedding getting into the wrong places. Consequently on the frame I only needed to "clay up" a few holes and milled slots, while on the forearm bracket I used quite a bit more clay.

Finally, make sure the sides of the pad extend beyond the sides of the stock. You need enough clearance on all sides to be able to sand even with the buttstock.

Coffield uses a straightedge to check the butt, which must be absolutely flat for proper pad installation. A sanding block and paper will true it if it's out of square.

If you are doing bedding and especially if this is one of your first projects, don't hesitate to use *lots* of clay! You could literally fill every slot and hole in the frame and not go wrong. The only downside would be the extra time you would take later cleaning up the clay. On the other hand, you would know darn well that you would not be allowing bedding to get into locations that would later cause you trouble. If in doubt, fill it with clay! The frame and forearm bracket were then liberally coated with release agent supplied with the bedding kit.

After preparing the frame and bracket, I mixed my bedding. I used a Miles Gilbert Bedrock Kit which I obtained from MidwayUSA. It's very good synthetic bedding and I like it. It's a two part epoxy that can be thickened to just about any consistency you want by adding Microballons as filler. Also, it comes with a dye to enable you to color it.

After applying the Bedrock to the stock, I installed the frame and secured it with the stock bolt. By the way, I also coated the threaded end of the stock bolt *just in case* it came into contact with any bedding. As with the clay, don't hesitate to coat any and all parts that even *might* come in contact with bedding. Release agent is cheap! As the frame seated in the stock, there was a bit of excess bedding that pushed out. Once the frame was secure I wiped away this excess bedding with a clean cotton cloth. It's always a lot easier to remove bedding while it's soft than later when it hardens.

This procedure was duplicated with the forearm and then both the forearm and buttstock were set aside to allow the bedding to cure for 24 hours. The next day, I loosened the stock bolt, but had a bit of trouble pulling the stock off the frame. A bit of careful tapping on the frame with a plastic hammer was sufficient to jar it loose. I was concerned that I had allowed some bedding to get into one or more recesses in the frame but this was not the case. It was just a very close and tight fit. The forearm bracket came off with no difficulty.

Once the metal was removed, I used a sharp bench knife to trim away all excess bedding. I wanted to make sure that I did not have any bedding that would later cause problems with the functioning of the parts in the frame or forearm bracket. It's important when doing this cleanup work that you do not damage the bedding that actually supports your frame or forearm bracket. Be very careful and make sure you are only cutting away excessive bedding.

I then cleaned the frame and forearm bracket to remove the clay and release agent.

With the buttstock bedded, the next step is to install a new recoil pad. The old pad is brittle and hard with age and no longer provides the recoil reduction I want. Also, it's an old style red open-sided ribbed pad and I prefer a softer, solid black pad. I chose a Pachmayr solid black Old English style Decelerator pad. It has an inner core of soft recoil absorbing material that is much more effective than the old original Browning pad.

When choosing a recoil pad, it's important that the new pad be large enough. Aside from being wide enough, it must extend far enough above the heel of the stock and below the toe of the stock to allow for proper fitting. The lines of the toe and the comb need to run straight on through the pad.

You don't want the end of the pad to form a compound angle. Be sure to check your pad by placing it on the buttstock and then place a straightedge along the toe and comb. The straightedge should extend right on through the pad. If it does, you'll have enough pad material to grind down during fitting.

It is quite easy to sand down the toe of the stock, and that will leave a gap. Coffield urges caution when sanding near the toe; try to avoid this spot if you can.

Just as the end of the buttstock must be flat, the contact surface of the new recoil pad must also be flat. This new pad will definitely need a bit of attention.

Be sure to check the hole spacing for your attaching screws. In most instances it seems that my new pads *never* have hole spacing that matches the original screw holes. With this project I got lucky! The hole spacing on the new pad matched the old pad perfectly. If it had not, I would have needed to drill out the old holes, glue in some wooden dowel rod, and then drill new pilot holes for the attaching screws.

Another point to watch when fitting a pad is surface of the end of the buttstock. You need this surface to be *absolutely flat* if you want your pad to fit properly. Nothing looks worse than a pad installation where you have a big gap between stock and the pad. You can make sure the end of the buttstock is flat by checking it with a straightedge.

If there is a dip or low spot, you'll spot it. You can then take some sandpaper backed by a block of wood and flatten the butt. When you do this, be very careful that you don't sand down the very end of the toe. It's easy to do this, so stay away from the toe as much as possible.

After flattening the butt, you will also want to flatten the contact face of the recoil pad. I placed a sheet of sandpaper on a piece of plate glass and then worked the recoil pad back and forth over the abrasive. It didn't take long until the bottom of the pad was flat and true. This doesn't take much time, but it will help significantly in making the installation look so much better and more professional.

Next time, we'll install the new recoil pad and shape it to fit the stock. We'll also get started on refinishing the wood as well as the metal. Right now I'm still considering just how we'll handle the metal refinishing since this Citori has some engraving and we definitely want to preserve that.

Until next time, good luck and good gunsmithing! ◉

Repairing & Refinishing a Citori

Part 3
By Reid Coffield

Fitting a Recoil Pad and Stripping Stock Finish

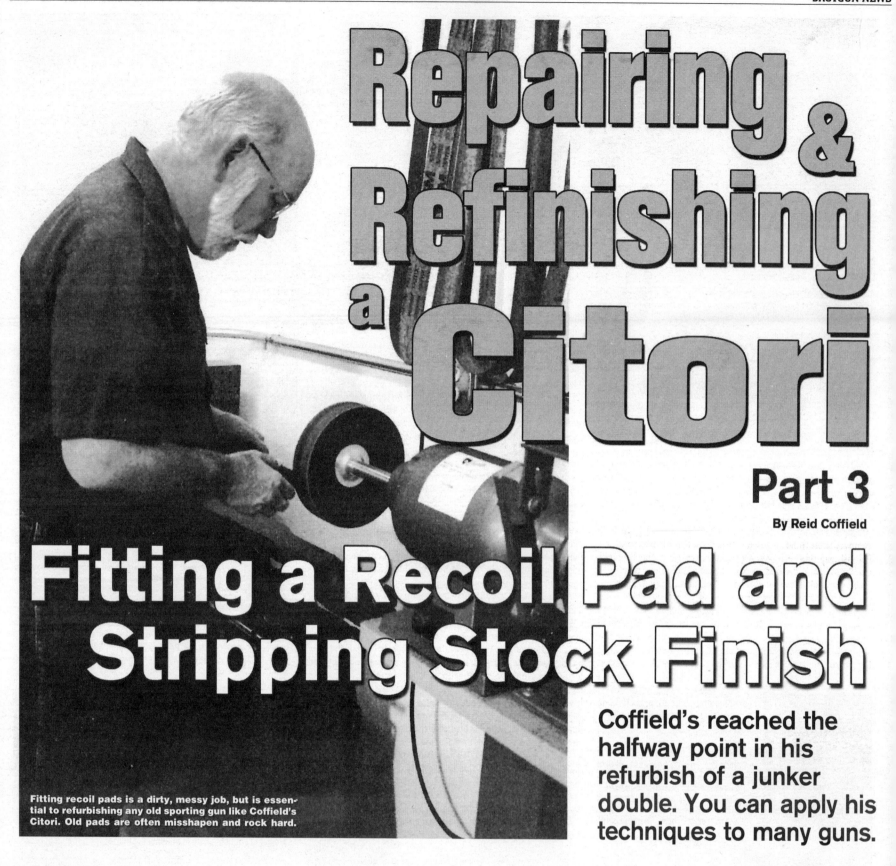

Fitting recoil pads is a dirty, messy job, but is essential to refurbishing any old sporting gun like Coffield's Citori. Old pads are often misshapen and rock hard.

Coffield's reached the halfway point in his refurbish of a junker double. You can apply his techniques to many guns.

Traditionally the basis for most home gunsmithing projects has been a rifle. Lord knows how many millions of 98 Mausers, Enfields and Springfields have been converted, modified or rebuilt by hobbyists over the years.

As sources for military surplus bolt actions become more limited, other firearms are beginning to be used by the hobbyists to develop their gunsmithing skills and knowledge. The most common and readily available commercial firearms are .22 rifles and shotguns. Either of these can provide excellent opportunities for learning and experimentation.

Keep in mind that many, if not most, of the skills involved in working on a shotgun or .22 rifle can also be applied to centerfire rifles or even handguns.

In this project I am working with an old Browning Citori 12-gauge over-under shotgun that I picked up not long ago. It had a lot of problems due to use and abuse but it was basically sound mechanically and had a lot more years of shooting left in it.

When I started this project, I made a list of the various steps required to repair and refinish this Citori. The list serves a couple of functions. First, it helps me to keep track of what needs to be done and most importantly, the proper sequence of the repairs. I definitely don't want to make a repair and then have to do it over because of the effects of some other necessary repair.

It also helps me to stay on track. As each task is completed I can see that I am getting closer to the finish. This can be

darn important when you are working on a project that literally might take months to complete. All too often, folks will become discouraged and give up on a project. A list where you can cross off the steps as you complete them can be an important and sometimes essential motivating tool. If you don't currently make a work list when attacking an involved or long term project like this Citori, I would sure urge you to do so.

My list thus far has quite a few items completed.

    #1. Raise the dented rib—done
    #2. Repair the damage to the sides of the rib—done
    #3. Repair dent in forearm bracket—done
    #4. Repair gap on left side forearm bracket—done
    #5. Repair crack in the buttstock—done

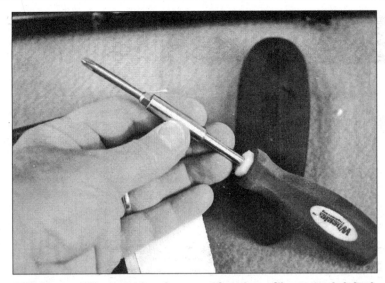

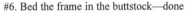

Coffield uses a Wheeler Engineering screwdriver along with an extended shank Philips head bit to install the new pad. The right tool pays off in doing this job.

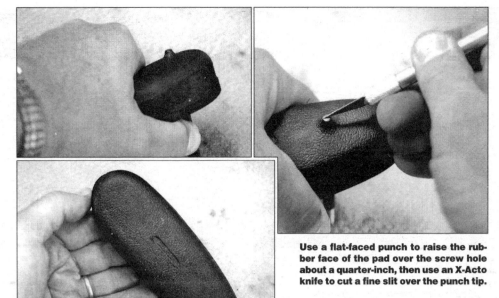

Use a flat-faced punch to raise the rubber face of the pad over the screw hole about a quarter-inch, then use an X-Acto knife to cut a fine slit over the punch tip.

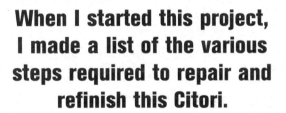

#6. Bed the frame in the buttstock—done
#7. Repair crack in the forearm—done
#8. Fit new recoil pad
#9. Strip old finish from buttstock and forearm
#10. Refinish buttstock and forearm
#11. Prepare metal prior to refinishing
#12. Refinish metal
#13. Cut long forcing cones in barrel
#14. Polish chambers and bores.

At this point I'm actually about halfway done and in this installment, I'll get a couple of more items out of the way and a few others started.

Last month I began fitting a new recoil pad. The original pad was just about as hard as a brick and the face of the pad had been damaged and torn as the attaching screws were installed and removed from time to time. A new solid black Pachmayr Old English pad was selected as a replacement. To me a solid color pad, either black or red, is much preferred.

I began by making sure my new pad was the appropriate size for this stock. In order to fit it properly it needed to overhang the stock, especially at the heel and toe. This allows for later grinding of the pad to perfectly match the lines of the stock. I also made sure that the rear face or end of the buttstock was absolutely flat as well as the corresponding contact surface of the pad. If these two surfaces are not flat, you can almost count on a gap when the two are joined together.

The next time you are at a gun show or in a shop with lots of used guns, check the fit of recoil pads on older shotguns. I'm willing to bet that you will quickly find lots of examples of poorly or improperly fitted pads.

When I started this project, I made a list of the various steps required to repair and refinish this Citori.

Even though the stock is to be refinished, I carefully wrapped the sides of the buttstock with masking tape to protect the wood as I ground the pad to shape. Some folks would not do this reasoning that since the wood is to be refinished; it won't hurt if the stock is scratched or nicked a bit as the pad is ground to shape.

I disagree with this line of reasoning. If you do scratch the stock you may have to do quite a bit of sanding to remove those scratch marks. That can be a *lot* of work! To me, it's better to spend just a few moments applying some masking tape and save yourself a lot of possible work later on.

Also, this is darn good practice for fitting a pad to a finished stock. After all, this is a project gun on which to practice and develop skills so you can later use those skills on other guns.

With the pad and the buttstock flattened and tape applied to the stock, the next step is to attach the pad to the stock. Two Philips head screws are used for this. But there's a problem…there are no screw holes in the rear face of the pad. Most pads are cast with solid rear faces. In order to install the screws it's necessary to make two tiny slots in the pad. The trick is to make these slots virtually invisible.

That's not all that hard to do and it always amazes me when I see pads where the slots for the screws look like they were chewed out by starving beavers. You can easily avoid this with just a little care. First use a 5/32" punch inserted from the bottom or contact surface of the pad to raise the rubber membrane of the rear face of the pad. Don't push the punch all the way through! Just raise the rubber of the rear face about 1/4". Now take a sharp razor knife and slit the thin rubber on top of the tip of the punch. Repeat this at the other screw hole location.

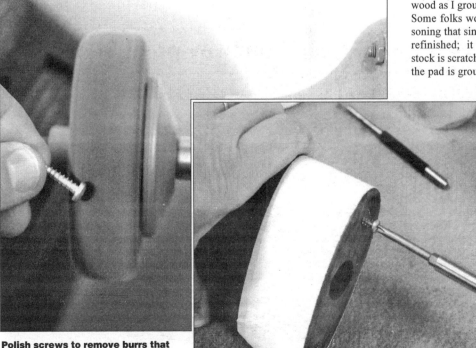

Polish screws to remove burrs that might tear the pad, and run them into stock holes before installing. This helps ensure they will fully seat and hold the pad securely.

A trick Coffield uses to help eliminate tearing of the face of the recoil pad as the screws are inserted is to use a bit of liquid soap around the screw slots to lube.

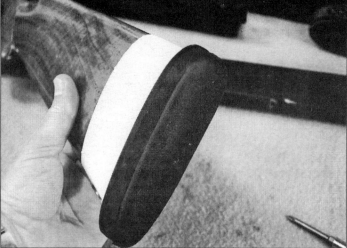

The new recoil pad must extend beyond the sides of the stock. The pad has been attached to the stock and is ready to be ground to shape, with masking tape for protection.

Next take both screws and polish the underside and sides of the screw heads. This is to remove any small burrs or irregularities that might tear the rubber of the pad. While I used a buffing wheel, you could just as easily use a Dremel tool with a felt or cotton polishing bob.

A trick I learned long ago was to apply a bit of liquid soap, wax or Vaseline to the rubber around the two slots. This will further prevent any tearing of the rubber as the screws are inserted.

When inserting the screws, don't just push them into the pad. Instead, open up the slot and carefully *thread* the screw in until the head is flush with the face of the pad. Now take a good smooth shanked Allen screwdriver and push the head on through the pad with one quick motion.

Don't pull the screwdriver out of the pad just yet! Position the pad on the buttstock and turn the screw until the pad is held tightly against the stock. With this particular shotgun, I was fortunate in that the screw holes for the new pad lined up perfectly with the original holes. I think in more than 30 years of gunsmithing, this has occurred only a few times!

Now remove the screwdriver and do the same to the remaining screw. If you do it right, the slits in the face of the pad will come together and be virtually invisible. To me it has always been a point of pride to have my customers look at a pad and then ask me how I attached it to their stock as they could see no signs of a screw hole. All it takes is a bit of practice.

With the pad on the stock, the next step is to grind it to shape. Before I do that, I take a ruler and a white grease pencil

and draw a guide line through the pad that matches the line of the stock at the toe and at the heel. These lines are purely to help guide me as I grind down the pad. I definitely don't want to have the toe or heel of the pad at an angle to the line of the stock. Again, when you're checking older guns with aftermarket pads, note how many don't have a nice smooth continuous line with the pad and the stock.

There are many ways of grinding down a pad. I learned to install pads using a nice big 12-inch disk sander. For me that is still the ideal tool for this job. However, 12-inch disk sanders are darn expensive and I don't have one! In fact, right now I don't even have a disk sander in my shop.

Instead I'm using a Scott Murray drum. This is an 8-inch diameter, 2-inch wide rubber-covered aluminum wheel that is mounted on a shaft on one side of a Grizzly belt sander. As the Scott Murray drum spins, the rubber covering expands and holds the 2-inch wide sanding belt quite securely. When the drum stops, the rubber contracts and the belt is easily changed.

That's one of the great features of this tool that I really like. You can change belts in a heartbeat. I keep an assortment of belts with various grits ranging from a very coarse 60 to an extremely fine 400 grit. It makes grinding and polishing much faster and easier. If you don't have a Scott Murray drum you might want to consider picking one up. Many tool suppliers have 'em. MidwayUSA, 5875 W. Van Horn Tavern Road, Dept. SGN, Columbia, Mo. 65203, telephone 800-243-3220, carries them along with a wide selection of other gunsmithing tools and supplies.

I used an 80 grit belt to grind down the recoil pad. With the motor running, I held the stock firmly with both hands in a horizontal position and carefully brought the toe of the pad into contact with the surface of the wheel. I made sure that the toe line of

the stock was parallel with a line across the face of the Scott Murray drum. This helps to ensure that I keep the toe line straight and not angled. The mark that I made earlier also helped me properly orient the stock.

As I ground the pad, I did not attempt to take a lot off at any one time. I would take a little off then rotate the stock a bit and then grind a little more from the pad. By taking small "bites" I was never in danger of making big mistakes or grinding away too much.

This process was repeated with the heel of the pad as well as with the sides. I continually checked the pad as I worked. Not only would I look down the side of the stock and pad, I would also look at the pad from the rear. I wanted to make sure that the shape of the pad was uniform and symmetrical as I worked and that I did not have any flat spots on the sides of the pad. I took extra care to blend the sides of the pad into one continuous smooth surface.

Did I mention that grinding a pad is absolutely filthy work? You'll get bits of rubber everywhere! I strongly encourage anyone doing this to wear protective glasses and ideally, wear some type of air filter. Since I have a beard, I seldom can get one of those things to fit properly so I end up with a lot of rubber dust in my nose and mouth. I doubt it's life-threatening, but it sure is nasty!

A list where you can cross off the steps as you complete them can be an important and sometimes essential motivating tool.

The grinding is continued until the belt begins to rub against the masking tape. Here again a light touch is important as you don't want to grind through the tape and into the stock. Once the edge of the pad is even with the tape all around the stock then this task is complete.

I then removed the tape from the stock. Even though I ground the pad down even with the tape, there is still a very slight "ledge" between the stock and the side of the pad. This "ledge" corresponds to the thickness of the tape, which was about .006" or less. On a finished stock I would wrap some abrasive paper around a flat file and oh so carefully file the side

A white grease pencil line indicates the proper angle of the toe. This is a continuation of the toe line of the stock and it is vital to get it aligned properly.

A similar line is drawn on the heel of the recoil pad to serve as a guide. Again, this line is simply a continuation of the comb line of the top of the stock.

Coffield used JASCO stripper to remove the polyurethane finish on the Citori. The stripper is applied with a brush over the entire stock including the checkering.

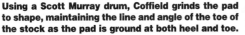

Using a Scott Murray drum, Coffield grinds the pad to shape, maintaining the line and angle of the toe of the stock as the pad is ground at both heel and toe.

of the pad down flush with the stock. With this Citori I will be refinishing the wood and doing a modest amount of sanding so I will take the last bit of the pad down with sandpaper when working on the wood. This will absolutely ensure that the pad is a perfect match to the stock.

Now that the pad has been fitted and then removed from the stock, the next step is to strip the old finish from the wood. As with most gunsmithing tasks, this can be done a number of different ways. I prefer to remove old finishes chemically rather than using sandpaper or scrapers.

There are a couple of reasons for this. By using a chemical stripper, I will not remove any wood from the stock. This is especially important when you have a stock that was precisely fitted to the action. If you sand away wood where it joined the metal, then there is a darn good chance that the metal and wood will no longer be even. The metal will stand above the wood. That's something that definitely should be avoided.

Another good reason for using a chemical stripper is that it will often help to pull oil and even dents out of the wood. And finally, for me chemical strippers are just plain faster and easier to use than traditional sanding.

This Citori had a polyurethane finish which was factory original. It was a tough finish and withstood a lot of abuse. That's the good part. The bad part is that a polyurethane finish can be a real bear to remove. Some chemical strippers won't even touch 'em. I used a product called Jasco Premium Paint and Epoxy Remover that I picked up at Lowe's in the paint department. It works darn well and is fairly fast.

It is hazardous, as you would expect from anything that will strip polyurethane. If you get it on your skin it will burn, so be sure to wear protective gloves and glasses to protect your eyes.

I prefer to remove old finishes chemically rather than using sandpaper or scrapers.

I spread some old newspaper on my bench and then applied a coating of the stripper to the stock with a cheap, throwaway 1 inch wide brush. This was allowed to work for about five to 10 minutes. By then, the finish had started to "bubble" in places. I used an old plastic hotel key or credit card to scrape as much of the finish and stripper off the stock as possible.

Once that was done, I took the stock over to my sink and rinsed the rest off with hot water. The stock was then dried with a soft cotton towel. This process was repeated about four or five times until all the original finish was removed.

It seemed to me that the stripper would dissolve some of the finish while it just made some of the remainder quite brittle. The edge of the credit card would fairly easily scrape off and break up the brittle finish. All in all, it took no more than about half or three quarters of an hour to strip both the buttstock and forearm.

The areas of checkering were also given a liberal coating of stock stripper. Over the years a lot of gunk and grime had built up in the checkering and the stripper actually helped to remove some of this. When I rinsed the stock to remove the stripper, I used a soft brush to clean out the checkering. This caused no damage to the checkering and will later make it easier to recut.

The stock and forearm were then hung in my drying cabinet to allow any last trace of moisture to evaporate.

As I work on refinishing the wood, I will also be working on the metal. With the metal, I am faced with a problem. The receiver is engraved. If I were to simply polish the metal to remove the old finish and any pits or scratches, I would also remove some of the engraving. Ideally, the metal would be hand polished and the engraving would then be recut. That's a great idea in theory but it's about as practical as a screen door in a submarine, especially on a $300 shotgun. It's just doesn't make economic sense, so I have to look at other alternatives.

I could simply polish off all the engraving. That would be one way of doing it. However, I like the modest amount of engraving that's on this old Browning. Another option would be strip the metal chemically and then use a fine wire wheel to go over all the metal surfaces. That can produce a very nice brushed appearance on the metal and it will seldom have any negative effect on the engraving. Unfortunately, this technique will seldom hide any of the surface irregularities such as pits or scratches.

After quite a bit of consideration, I have decided to bead blast the gun and then have it hot-blued. In bead blasting, tiny glass beads are blown against the steel surface with an air gun. The beads will hit the steel with such force that they leave thousands of tiny peening marks. These peening marks can remove or hide many of the smaller surface blemishes. The aggressiveness of glass beading can be controlled by both the size of the glass beads, the amount of air pressure used, and the angle and distance between the work surface and the air gun.

When combined with caustic salt or hot dip bluing, glass beading can often give a gun the appearance of traditional rust blue. Rather than a high gloss finish, you have a more subtle satin finish. That, combined with the fact that this technique will allow me to avoid removal of the engraving, makes it a very attractive option.

In the next installment, the metal will be prepped, beaded and blued, and the stock will be sanded and refinished. Once that is done, the project is just about completed. If all goes well, this old Citori should be lookin' good for the fall hunting season.

Until next time, good luck and good gunsmithing!

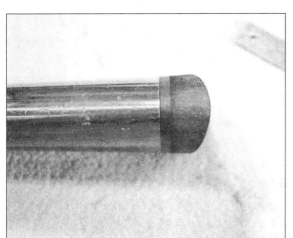

When viewed from the toe, the sides of the pad also continue the lines of the stock. Slow, patient work will pay dividends here; hurrying can led to a botched job.

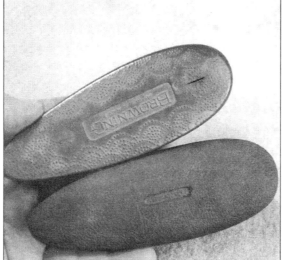

Unlike the old "ventilated" pad, the new solid black recoil pad shows no evidence of the location of the screw slots and it has the same angle of the toe and heel.

Repairing & Refinishing a Citori

Part 4
By Reid Coffield

Wood Finishing and Metal Preparation

Coffield has fixed the functional problems, now he's ready to start making his shotgun look like new.

After stripping the original finish Coffield examines the stock for dents and gouges. Due to the protective polyurethane finish, the wood was in pretty good shape.

One of the most satisfying moments in gunsmithing is when you've finally completed the repair and refinishing of a "basket case." You look at the finished gun and realize that not only do you have a darn nice firearm in your hands, you've probably saved a good gun from being destroyed or broken up for parts.

It doesn't really matter whether it's a high dollar sporting firearm or a common inexpensive old military bolt-action. What's important is the sense of accomplishment in transforming a beat-up collection of parts into something that will provide many years of pleasure and enjoyment.

What a great feeling! How often in our regular day jobs or in life in general do we have the chance to feel this way? For most folks, it's not very often. That special feeling is one of the most

important aspects of gunsmithing for me and you know I bet it is for you too!

The Citori shotgun I've been working on may not have quite qualified as a "basket case" but it was darn close! In the first three parts of this series, I made a number of major and minor repairs. A damaged and dented top rib was repaired. The forearm bracket was straightened and refitted. Several cracks in the buttstock and forearm were repaired, a new recoil pad was partially fitted to the stock, and the original, well-worn stock finish was stripped from the wood.

At this point the project is well over halfway completed and I can begin to see the light at the end of the tunnel. Once this project is finished I fully expect to have a darn nice 12-gauge over-under that will provide many years of service for hunting, skeet

shooting, and the occasional round of sporting clays. While it'll still show some effects of past use and abuse, it'll be a nice attractive shotgun that I'll be proud to own and use.

Last month, I fitted a new recoil pad to the gun. Even though I plan on refinishing the stock, I took extra care in fitting this recoil pad. In fact, I treated the stock as though it had a perfect finish that absolutely could not be scratched or damaged while installing the pad. There were a couple of reasons for doing this.

While I've installed a *lot* of recoil pads, it's always good practice and it helps me to continually improve my skills and technique. Let's face it; you never get *too good* at any gunsmithing task. You can always improve even if you've been at it for 30 years or so.

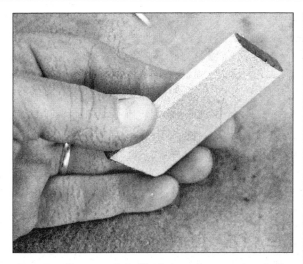

When sanding a stock Coffield strongly recommends the use of a sanding block to achieve a smooth, even wood finish. Using bare hands will inevitably lead to ripples.

In addition, I wanted to avoid making any sanding or grinding marks on the stock. These marks would later have to be removed. Not only do I avoid extra sanding, I'm also able to leave the maximum amount of wood on the stock. One of the "secrets" of good refinishing is to avoid removal of any more wood than is absolutely necessary.

How often have you seen older guns with excessively sanded stocks? Lots of times, right? When you examine the inletting, the metal is often much higher than the wood. It looks like the wood shrunk. In other cases, all the sharp edges of the stock have been rounded. That's especially the case at the butt where the sides of the buttplate or recoil pad don't come anywhere close to matching the sides of the stock. These mistakes can easily be avoided with a few simple techniques that we'll cover.

When installing the new recoil pad, the sides of the pad were ground flush with a layer of masking tape wrapped around the buttstock. In doing this I made sure the heel and toe lines as well as the sides of the stock were properly extended and matched the sides of the recoil pad. The goal was to make the pad look like an integral extension of the stock rather than some poorly fitted attachment.

The pad and masking tape were then removed. A commercial wood finish stripper was applied to the stock and the original polyurethane finish removed. Again, a common mistake in refinishing is simply to sand off the old finish. While that will certainly work, you'll also remove a heck of a lot of wood. As indicated earlier, it's always best to remove as little wood as possible. Removing the original finish chemically rather than by sanding is faster, easier, cleaner, and it preserves the wood.

The recoil pad was reinstalled and the interface between the pad and the stock was hand sanded for a perfect level transition. You should feel no gap in this area.

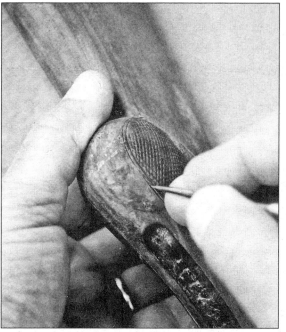

Prior to applying masking tape to protect the checkering, Coffield uses a scribe to clean the border groove around the checkered panels. This cleans the groove out.

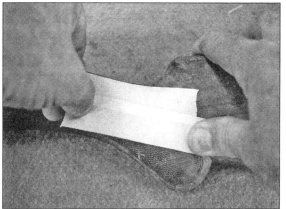

Overlapping strips of masking tape are applied over the checkered panel. Each panel is completely covered. Note how the tape extends beyond the edges of the panel.

By the way, with the old finish off the stock, I was pleasantly surprised to discover very little damage to the wood. There were almost no dents, gouges, or scratches. All things considered, the wood was in darn good shape.

The original Browning polyurethane finish, though pretty rough lookin' by the time I got the gun, had done an excellent job of protecting the wood. While a lot of gunsmiths and gun owners don't like polyurethane finishes, I have to admit that it's a tough, durable protective coating.

If you have a gun that's going to see a lot of rough use, polyurethane may be your best choice in wood finishes. Because of the protection polyurethane provided for this stock, I would only need to do some light sanding with 180- to 280-grit sandpaper.

Before doing that, I still had just a bit of work to do on the recoil pad. It was reattached to the buttstock and the fit to the stock was again examined. Remember how I'd wrapped the stock with masking tape and ground the sides of the pad flush with the

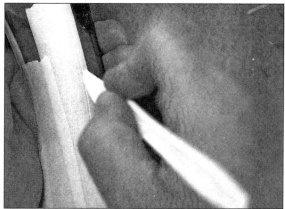

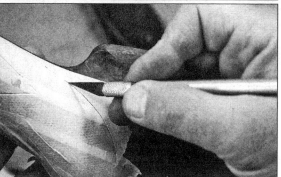

Coffield uses a modified plastic picnic knife to help define and locate the border of the panel by tracing around the pattern, then cuts it out with a razor knife.

tape? Now that the tape was removed, the pad extended beyond the sides of the stock by a distance equal to the thickness of the tape. We're only talkin' maybe .004" or .006" or so but you can see it and feel it. We don't want that.

The sides of the pad should be absolutely flush with the wood. When you run your finger across the stock and on to the pad, you shouldn't feel a step or ledge. That can be easily achieved with a bit of judicious sanding.

But before we do any sanding, we need to protect the checkering. Think back on those refinished guns you've seen and how often the checkering was ruined by sanding. I'll never understand what a person is thinking as he blissfully sands away the checkering on his stock! It happens frequently. We can easily avoid that by simply protecting the checkering with a layer of masking tape.

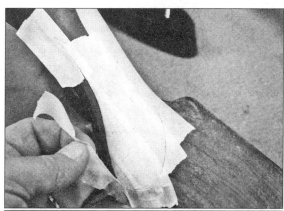

The excess tape is pulled off after it has been cut away from the panel with the razor knife. This protects checkering from accidental damage when sanding the stock.

Coffield uses a systematic approach to his sanding. He always begins by first sanding the comb or top of the stock, followed by sanding the toe line or bottom side.

It'll also later protect the checkering from being filled in with stock finish.

The first step is to use a scribe to trace around the border of the checkered panels. This removes crud in the border groove and helps to make the border a bit more pronounced and easily visible under the tape. I normally lay a number of slightly overlapping strips of 1" wide masking tape over the checkering. The tape extends well beyond the border of the checkering and totally covers the checkering panel.

Once that's done, I go over the tape with my thumb to press it into the checkering. I should be able to see the impression of the checkered panel through the tape. A plastic picnic knife with a rounded, dulled blade is used to trace around the checkering panel in the border groove. A modest amount of pressure on the blade is usually enough to depress the tape into the groove and make the location of the border readily apparent.

A razor knife is now used to carefully trace around the edge of the panel border in the border groove cutting away all excess tape. Go slow and easy when doing this! If you get in a hurry or heavy handed you can easily cut into the stock outside the panel border.

With all the checkering panels protected with masking tape, the final fitting of the recoil pad and sanding of the stock can begin.

I'm a firm believer in using a sanding block. A sanding block is simply a rigid backing for the sandpaper. The sanding block I most often use is just a simple 1½- by 3-inch piece of quarter-inch thick wood. Using a sanding block ensures that my sanded surface is as flat as possible.

A stock naturally has areas that are harder or softer than others. Without a sanding block to bridge these hard and soft areas, sandpaper held in your hand will remove more wood in soft spots than in hard spots. This results in ripples and dips that will show up once the finish is applied.

Another area where folks run into trouble is around the inletting. You will often see so much wood removed that the receiver and especially the receiver tang is actually higher than the surrounding wood. This can sometimes be avoided by simply leaving the metal in place and sanding up and on to the metal. Of course you then have to refinish the metal as well to remove those sanding scratches.

But what if the metal is engraved or you don't want to refinish the metal? What if the wood is already dead level

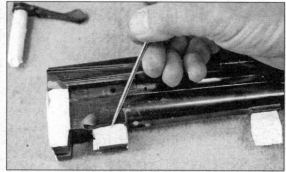

Note how Coffield uses masking tape to protect critical areas on the barrels when blasting; the locking lug recess, the hinge pin pivot, and the forearm hanger.

with the metal and you simply can't remove any by sanding?

I deal with these situations by sanding only to within about 1/8" or so of the inletting. I just stop before I get to the edge of the inletting. Only on my last sanding, using my finest grit, will I make one, just one, very light pass over this narrow 1/8" strip of wood.

If on the other hand, the wood is "proud" or higher than the metal, then I can be a little more aggressive in my sanding and sand right up to the inletting. I still have to be darn careful.

With this old Citori I had both situations. The wood was even with the receiver top tang and consequently I could not remove any wood there at all. Along the sides of the receiver, the wood was considerably higher than the metal. There I could afford to sand up to the inletting.

In sanding it's important to be systematic. You don't want to just grab some sandpaper and rub aimlessly on the stock. If you do some areas will be sanded a lot more than others. My technique is to sand specific areas of the stock in a certain sequence or pattern.

I begin by sanding the top of the comb from the pistol grip to the recoil pad. I then sand along the toe line or bottom edge of the stock from the behind the pistol grip to the recoil pad. Next I sand the right side of the stock behind the pistol grip followed by the left side. I then sand the top, sides, and then the bottom of the pistol grip.

With the forearm, I will sand the right side, left side, and then the bottom. By following this routine I make darn sure that I cover every part of the stock evenly. It may seem like overkill, but it actually saves time. Since I began using this systematic approach I seldom every later find little scratches or sanding marks that I've overlooked and have to resand.

In addition to using a systematic approach to sanding, it's also important to always sand *with* the wood grain. Fortunately on virtually all stocks, the grain runs lengthwise from the tip of the forearm to the stock butt. Make every effort to avoid sanding across the grain. If you do you'll invariably leave sanding marks or scratches that can be difficult to remove. In fact, you can almost count on finding some of the cross grain sanding marks *after* you apply your finish!

Because the stock is in such good shape I began by using 180-grit sandpaper. This was followed by 220-grit and then finished with 280-grit. At that point I had a darn nice smooth stock. As I finished sanding, I was a bit surprised in that the pores in the grain were not open but appeared to be filled.

When the stock is shaped, the cellulose fibers on the surface are cut open by the various woodworking tools. This results in the openings or pores which we see as little black dots or elongated channels in the surface of the wood. A primary requirement for a good stock finish is to fill these pores.

Though this surprised me a bit, I continued on and wiped the stock down with a damp cloth to raise any tiny bits of wood or "whiskers" that might have been generated by my sanding. As the water evaporates, any "whiskers" would stand up from the surface. After waiting a bit I examined the stock and forearm and found no whiskers!

Apparently the original polyurethane finish had penetrated the surface of the wood. While my chemical stripper removed the surface finish, neither that nor the later sanding had evidently removed the polyurethane that penetrated the wood and filled the pores. This to me is another darn good reason to limit sanding when refinishing a stock!

With no need for further sanding to remove whiskers and with the pores almost completely filled, I was able to immediately apply my first coat of finish. For this stock I'm using the Miles Gilbert Classic American Gunstock Oil Finish available from MidwayUSA, 5875 W. Van Horn Tavern Rd., Dept. SGN, Columbia, Mo. 65203, telephone 800-243-3220. This is an oil-modified polyurethane. I chose it because of the polyurethane base and the fact that it should adhere or bond with any residual original finish.

Coffield uses both a dust mask and hearing protection when working with his bead blasting cabinet. Coffield's bead blasting outfit is neither expensive or high tech.

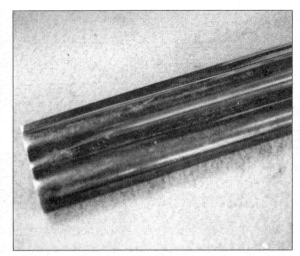

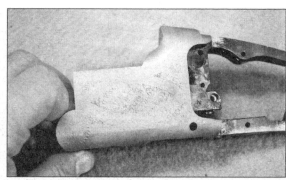

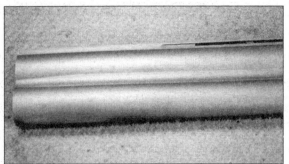

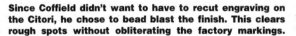

Since Coffield didn't want to have to recut engraving on the Citori, he chose to bead blast the finish. This clears rough spots without obliterating the factory markings.

Application of the first coat was simple and easy. I just poured a bit into a plastic lid and then dipped my fingers into the liquid. This was then rubbed on to the stock. I made sure I had total coverage of the stock yet not so much that I had runs.

Once the forearm and buttstock were coated, I hung them in my stock drying cabinet to dry for at least 8 hours. Any finish I had left in the plastic lid was discarded. Once finish is taken from a bottle, I think it's best to discard it rather than putting in back in the bottle and risking contamination of the rest of the finish.

By the way, there is a great clean up tip on the Miles Gilbert stock finish bottle. To make getting the finish off your hands easier, first rub your hands with a vegetable based cooking oil. The oil seems to lift the polyurethane off the skin so all that's required for clean up is just plain ol' soap and water. That's a lot easier and less hassle than using all sorts of flammable solvents.

As far as the stock is concerned it's now just a matter of applying additional coats of finish. Once the finish builds up to a nice smooth even layer over the surface of the stock we'll be done. In between applying coats of finish I can begin to concentrate on refinishing the metal.

The metal is more of a problem than the stock. While there are some scratches and some minor pitting, all in all, it's not too bad. The problem is the engraving. How do you refinish steel without disturbing or polishing away engraving?

That question had bothered me for years and I just couldn't figure out a good answer. That is until I had a chance to visit the Browning repair facility in Arnold, Mo., years ago. I asked the fellows there how they did it and they told me it was real simple. They just polished the gun as though there wasn't any engraving. If engraving was polished away, no big deal! I was shocked when I heard this but the fellows just grinned and told me that they would then give the gun to their in-house engraver to restore or completely recut the engraving! While the mystery was solved, it still didn't help me much as I sure couldn't engrave.

Many, many years ago while in gunsmithing school, I had a chance to take some engraving lessons from Ralph Bone, a great guy, a true master gunsmith and an extremely talented engraver. At the conclusion of one of the classes, Ralph carefully examined my work and then asked me what I planned on doing after graduation. I replied that I wanted to do general repair work. Ralph looked at me then back at my engraving. After just a moment or two of looking at my work Ralph replied, "Yeah Reid, you definitely should go into general repair." Thus ended my engraving career.

So recutting the engraving on this Citori is not an option for me nor is removal of the engraving. On this old field grade gun there's not much engraving but I do like it.

My solution, though not an ideal one, is to glass bead blast all the exterior metal surfaces. Glass beading is simply using a high pressure air gun to bombard the metal with millions of tiny glass balls or beads. These tiny glass balls will tend to peen the surface resulting in millions of small overlapping depressions. Normally you remove little or no metal and that's one of the great advantages of glass beading. Also, when the surface is then hot blued, the resulting finish will often look like a tradi-tional rust blue.

The metal was prepared by again using masking tape to pro-tect all critical areas such as the chambers, the locking lug notch, the hinge pin, etc. Any place where you don't want to alter the surface should be taped.

Because bead blasting creates a dust of microscopic glass par-ticles, it absolutely has to be done in an enclosed cabinet. Mine is an inexpensive imported unit I bought at the local hardware store. The dust filter, an absolutely essential component was purchased from Enco, a major tool distributor. My used air com-pressor came originally from Sears.

Keep in mind that you can vary the effect of your bead blast-ing by the size of the glass beads, the amount of air pressure, and the distance and angle the work piece is held from the air gun. When you first use a bead blasting outfit you should do some experimentation to see how you can alter these individual vari-ables for different effects or degrees of coarseness.

Even though you are using an enclosed cabinet and have a dust collector, you should also wear a respirator or dust mask. The dust generated by the break up of those glass beads can and will do serious damage to your lungs. Think of it this way; you're breathing powdered glass!

After bead blasting, each part was carefully cleaned with Insta-Clean, available from MidwayUSA, to remove all traces of the beads. When cleaning away the beads and glass dust, you can not be too thorough. That glass dust can work into even the smallest cracks and seams. If not removed, it could later cause wear to critical components.

Once the parts were cleaned, they were oiled to prevent rust-ing prior to bluing. The gun will be given a caustic salt or hot dip blue. This is how the gun was originally finished. Unlike many older side-by-side or over-under shotguns, the Citori barrels are not soft-soldered together. Caustic salts will dissolve or "eat" soft lead solder and can easily cause barrels and ribs on older

double barrel guns to separate. No need to worry about this with the Citori.

Since moving to my new shop, I've not yet been able to set up my bluing outfit. Because of that I'm sending the metal to anoth-er gunsmith for the bluing. The gunsmith I'm using is an old friend with whom I've worked for many, many years, John Treakle.

John now runs Hi-Caliber Gunsmithing, 2720 E. Hwy. 101, Dept. SGN, Port Angeles, Wash. 98362, telephone 360-417-6847. John is an excellent craftsman and does exceptional work. He is especially good in all phases of metal work, from rebarrel-ing and chambering to refinishing.

I often hear from folks who are having difficulty locating a gunsmith. The reality is that there are not as many gunsmiths as there once were. This just means that like me, you may have to use the services of a gunsmith in another state. To find that gun-smith you could begin by checking the ads here in SHOTGUN NEWS.

If you find a fellow that offers the services you need, be sure to give him a call *before* you send him your gun! Talk with him about what you want done and make sure he can do it. Also, talk about what the cost will be. You definitely don't want to be sur-prised by the bill! You should know ahead of time about what it will cost.

Don't hesitate to ask the gunsmith about his experience and training. Also, ask about any guarantee that he may offer. Ask for references. Ask if he test fires each gun and how he does this. Any reputable gunsmith will not hesitate to answer your ques-tions. He will understand your concern about sending a gun to someone they have never met or even seen.

If you send in parts to be blued, be sure to include a complete list of each and every part. That way the gunsmith will know what he is receiving. Keep a copy of this to use as a check list when the parts are returned. If you send in a complete gun, remove the scope, receiver sight, or sling. Make sure you pack-age the parts securely. You can't blame the gunsmith if your flimsy box breaks open in transit and you loose some parts.

When it comes to packaging; think *overkill!* Individually labeled plastic bags are ideal for the smaller parts. Talk with the gunsmith about shipping. He may have a preference because of service in his area. Also, don't forget to insure your package.

That's about it. Next time we'll recut the checkering on the refinished stock, polish the insides of the barrels, and reassemble the Citori completing this project.

Until next time, good luck and good gunsmithing!

Repairing & Refinishing a Citori

Part 5
By Reid Coffield

Stock Finishing and Checkering

It's taken a lot of work, but Coffield has finally taken his Citori from junker to a piece he can carry with pride.

The heavy lifting is completed, and Coffield is ready to do the checkering and finishing work that will make his Citori not a junker but a source of true pride.

There are many satisfying moments in gunsmithing. For me, one of the best is when I finally finish a project. The moment is even sweeter if the gun was in really rough shape. Not only do you have the satisfaction of completing the work, you also realize you've possibly saved the gun from being junked or broken up for parts and you've most likely extended its life by many years. As my grandfather used to say, "Boy, that's somethin'!"

The Citori is just about at this point. I completed most of the metal work and had shipped the parts to be blued to my good friend of many years, John Treakle. John runs Hi-Caliber Gunsmithing, 2720 E. Hwy. 101, Dept. SGN, Port Angeles, Wash. 98362, telephone 360-417-6847. He is a master at refinishing; both wood and metal.

Since I don't have a hot or caustic salt bluing setup in my shop at this time, John is the man I turned to for bluing. It was just a matter of packaging the parts up and shipping them out via UPS. John had 'em in a few days, blued 'em and then had 'em back in my hands very quickly. Again, his work was excellent and very reasonably priced.

While the metal parts were out of the shop, I used the opportunity to finish the woodwork. The stock had been stripped and sanded. Originally it had the standard Browning polyurethane finish. While the original finish was in pretty rough shape, I was surprised and pleased to find the wood under the finish had suffered very little if any damage.

The scratches and dings were mostly in the finish rather than in the wood. That was absolutely great news as it cut down considerably on the work required. All I needed to do was a bit of sanding. I started with 180-grit sandpaper and worked my way up to 280-grit. When I finished sanding there were no visible sanding marks or scratches left from the sandpaper.

The grain of the wood appeared to be filled with very few open pores. Wood is simply a large bundle of hollow cellulose fibers. Where these fibers are cut open as the stock is shaped and sanded, there are small holes or pores. The pattern of these pores is often referred to as the grain of the wood.

In order to properly finish a stock, these pores should be filled before the finish is applied. It looked to me as though the pores of my Citori stock were still filled even after stripping the finish and lightly sanding. I was delighted as this would save time and work.

I was wrong! Most of the pores were still filled but a number were not. I didn't realize this until I had already applied some finish to the wood. At that point it was too late to use a filler. Because of this I had to put a lot more finish on the wood and sand it down a couple of times to fill these open pores. I basically used the finish as a filler. Ultimately it would not cause any problems with the finish but it did take more time than planned.

When sending any gun out for bluing or other finishing work, always check against a copy of your packing list to ensure that all your parts have been returned.

This pin could easily be reversed if you failed to notice the detent for the Allen screw that holds it in place. Always reassemble with care, don't rush the job.

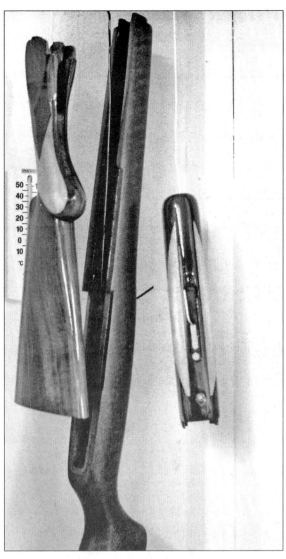

Coffield not only used his drying cabinet to cure the finish, he also used it store the buttstock and fore-end while awaiting the return of the parts to be blued.

I chose to use the Miles Gilbert Classic American Gunstock Oil Finish available from MidwayUSA, 5875 W. Van Horn Tavern Road, Dept. SGN, Columbia, Mo. 65203, telephone 800-243-3220. This is an oil-modified polyurethane finish I've used on several other stocks with good results.

Also, since polyurethane from the original finish that had penetrated the wood, I felt this finish would bond chemically with the original to make a tough, durable coating. While some folks don't like the appearance of polyurethane, even they will have to admit it's probably the toughest, most durable and protective finish you can put on wood.

Application of this finish is simplicity itself. A small amount is poured out of the bottle into a container. You then take your finger, dip it into the finish and wipe it on the stock. You put as much as you can on the stock without getting runs. I generally start at the fore-end and work my way back to the butt. Long, even strokes are used to apply the finish. Again, you have to be darn careful that you don't get runs.

Unlike some finishes where you rub and rub and rub, with this finish you just wipe it on as quickly as possible and then set the stock aside to dry for a minimum of eight hours. Normally I let my stocks sit for about 24 hours between coats.

By the way, more often than not, I can't find an appropriate container in which to pour the finish. A small plastic food container of the type you get with dips is ideal but I never seem to have 'em when I need 'em. I got around this by just buying a roll of heavy duty aluminum foil to keep in the shop. I tear off a section about 8 inches long and then fold it in half a couple of times.

I bend up four sides about an inch or so high and there I have a nice flat-bottomed container for my finish or stain or filler. It's really handy and it saves a lot of hassle lookin' for containers I never seem to be able to find. By the way, a pad of aluminum foil is also darn nice for mixing bedding compound. And of course, once you are done with it, just throw it in the trash can. Quick, easy, and always available.

As I mentioned earlier, because I didn't see some open pores it took quite a few more coats of finish than I planned. In fact, it took 17 coats of finish. When I'm applying finish to a stock, I keep a record of when I apply each coat. This includes the number of the application, the date and time. This helps to keep track of where I am with the project.

It's especially important if I'm working on more than one stock at a time. The note is thumb tacked to the door of my drying cabinet. Each time I pull the stock out to apply a coat, I just

If you are not sure of exactly how to reassemble your gun, use a factory manual or aftermarket assembly guide. This can save time, frustration, and damaged parts.

add that info to the running record of what I've done. Again, it's simple and easy to do and it helps to have this reminder of where I am on a project.

Once the last coat of finish had been applied, I allowed it to cure for about a week. This ensured that the finish was totally dry. I then used 800-grit sandpaper and water to go over the finish. This removed any surface irregularities or dust nibs.

This was then followed by rubbing out with soft cotton pads and pumice. This resulted in a dull finish rather than the original high-gloss finish used by Browning. I might add that when rubbing out the finish with rottenstone, you need to repeatedly clean the stock with a soft cloth or cotton pads and check for shiny spots. These indicate areas you missed with the rottenstone. Just keep at it. It'll take a while but eventually you'll have a nice uniform finish over the entire stock.

Since I bead-blasted the metal for a dull, blued finish, the stock should also have a dull finish. This gun will be used primarily for hunting and occasionally for sporting clays or a round of skeet or trap from time to time. It will definitely not be a "show gun." It's gonna be a workhorse!

A dull, utilitarian finish on both the metal and wood will help to hide the inevitable scratches, dings and nicks that'll come it's way. Also, I firmly believe that wood and metal finishes should be consistent and complimentary. Having a high gloss on one while the other is dull, just looks odd to me.

For those who might be offended by this choice of finishes, keep in mind that all of this can be redone. The metal can be

The finish used for this project was the Miles Gilbert Classic American Gunstock Oil Finish. Coffield likes to use it because it is easily applied using a finger.

polished to a high gloss and the stock can be refinished as well. Nothing was done to the gun that could not be altered at some point in the future by the next owner.

After rubbing out the stock, it was time to remove the masking tape used to protect the checkering. A major mistake some folks make is to just pull it off. If you do, I'll almost guarantee that you'll "lift" or damage the finish next to the checkered panels.

To avoid this, take a sharp razor knife and carefully cut around the tape on each panel. This will break the bond between the finish which has gotten on the tape and the stock. It takes a few minutes but it can save you hours of trying to repair the finish.

With the tape removed, the next step is to recut the checkering. However, before doing that, the gun will be reassembled. John had completed the bluing and the parts had returned.

Upon receipt of the parts, I checked them against a copy of my original packing list to make sure everything was there. If you ever send a gun or parts off to have work done, you should *always* keep a packing list so you can keep track of what you have or should have. As expected, all the parts were present.

I then broke out my assembly manuals or guides. The older I get the less I want to rely on my memory, especially about a complex mechanism and how it's assembled. I used *Firearms Assembly/Disassembly Part V: Shotguns Second Edition* by J. B. Woods as well as the American Gunsmith Library's *Gunsmithing the Shotgun: Tips and Techniques*. The latter book has two articles by Chick Blood on the Citori that are absolutely outstanding.

The forearm mechanism was assembled first. I put all the other parts away and had only those parts used on that assembly on the bench mat. This is helpful as it keeps from getting parts confused. A pin used in the receiver might look awful similar to one used in the forearm bracket but be just a tad different. If used it could lead to a damaged part or make some other component inoperable.

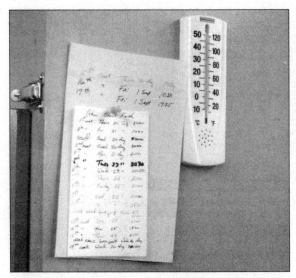

Coffield suggests keeping a simple log listing when each coat of finish is applied. This helps to avoid confusion especially when working on multiple stocks.

Holes in the grip panel on the buttstock are filled with wood putty prior to recutting the checkering. Fine checking like this is prone to damage in hunting use.

To recut the Citori's checkering, Coffield used 60° cutters as shown on the left. He normally uses a 90° cutter when checkering standard grade American walnut.

Remember those zip-lock sandwich bags I put the parts in as I took the gun apart? The bags were labeled at the time. Now it's just a matter of getting the appropriate bags. This simple but systematic approach not only saves time and confusion but it helps to prevent lost or misplaced parts.

In addition to using manuals and assembly guides, I used the parts as guides as well. If you look closely at individual parts, you'll often find clues as to where and how they fit into the mechanism. Take the cocking lever crosspin for example. Near one end of the pin on the side of the shank there's a small indentation. This is the seat for a set screw to hold it in place.

It would be possible to reverse the pin but if you notice this indentation, you know immediately which end of the pin is located under the set screw located on the left side of the receiver. Any gun has lots of "clues" about how and where parts fit together. It's just a matter of looking for those clues and understanding 'em.

This was also the point at which I installed some new parts in the receiver. I fitted new firing pins, new lower firing pin return springs, and two new hammer springs. All of these Browning parts were obtained from Brownells Inc., 200 South Front St., Dept. SGN, Montezuma, Iowa 50171, telephone 800-741-0015. These folks have an extensive inventory of Browning Citori parts and ship super quickly.

Before the metal components could be joined with the wood, I had to use a razor knife to carefully scrape away a bit of finish that had gotten into the inletting. Were this not done, the metal

would not fit or in the worst case, it might cause the wood to be damaged as the metal was forced into the inletting.

After completing the fore-end assembly and placing it on the barrel and attaching the completed receiver to the buttstock, I could then recut the checkering. The thinness of the fore-end means it should be supported by the barrel while checkering to avoid cracking the wood.

Also, it's just a pain in the tush to rig up some type of holding device for the forearm when the barrel is right there. The same holds for the buttstock. The receiver helps to support it at the front.

I used my regular checkering cradle, clamped in my bench vise. When working on the buttstock, I often just laid it on some soft clean rags on top of my bench. The checkered panels on the buttstock are really fairly small and easy to get to so it was not always necessary to use the cradle.

Before beginning the recutting, I examined the checkering with a magnifying glass. While most of it was worn smooth, it was evident that it was fairly fine. As best I could measure, it ran about 22 lines per inch. Also, the individual diamonds were thin and had narrow bases. When I checker regular American walnut, I normally use 90° cutters. These make diamonds with a broad base. That's important when dealing with porous, open-grained wood. Smaller diamonds tend to break off more easily.

This Browning had checkering that looked like it had been cut with a narrower cutter. I chose 60° cutters to match it. These will cut deep, narrow grooves and produce sharp, thin diamonds.

It was, as best I could tell, what was probably used during manufacture.

When recutting checkering, you do not normally use any multiple-line cutting tools. I only use single-line tools that cut just one groove at a time. If you try to use a multiple-line cutter, you'll probably get into trouble. Think of it this way. You have a nice set of Gunline or Dembart checkering tools that are 22 lines per inch.

However the multiple line tool used to originally cut the checkering had spacing between the cutting teeth that was .005" different than your tooling. No big problem right? After all it's only .005" (five thousandths of an inch) which is just a bit larger than the thickness of a sheet of paper.

On one or two lines you're right; it probably wouldn't make any difference. But what happens when you are say 10 or 20 lines over? If it's 10 lines that means that your tooling is cutting a groove that is now .050" off from the original line. If it's 20 lines over you are now .100" off from the original line. My friends, that is a big difference and you would notice it.

The easiest way to handle the problem is to stick with single-line cutters when recutting checkering. It also saves some money on tooling as well.

Recutting checkering, especially on a worn and damaged stock such as this, is not always easy. I ran into several problems. The first was rocks! At some point the previous owner had dropped the gun in sand or had mud on his hands while shooting and had ground this into the checkering. I literally had to pick a couple of grains of embedded sand out of the wood with dental picks. These little rocks sure don't do your cutters any good either!

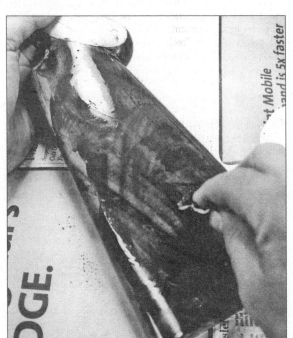

Once the finish has cured, it is wet-sanded to remove any stray dust nibs. Any sanding marks left from the wet sanding are removed by polishing with water and rottenstone.

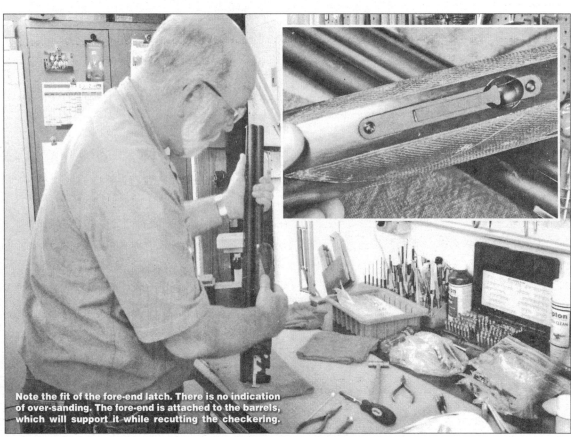

Note the fit of the fore-end latch. There is no indication of over-sanding. The fore-end is attached to the barrels, which will support it while recutting the checkering.

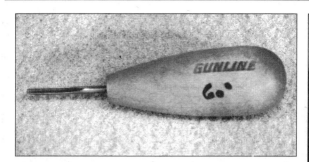

The Gunline 60° veiner, a very small, sharp chisel, was used extensively to point up diamonds in the corners of the checkering panels. This is truly exacting work.

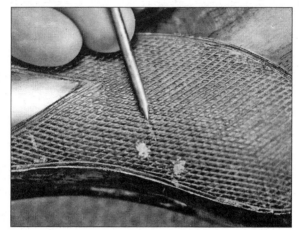

Coffield found lots of damage to the Citori's checkering. Here he has already filled two holes with wood putty, and points out a gouge that will need some repair.

Aside from the "rocks," the grit built up in the grooves was really hard on the cutters. I had to replace a couple of the cutters about three quarters of the way through the job as they were simply worn out and too dull to cut effectively. When checkering new stocks, more often than not I can complete several stocks before having to replace cutters.

Another major problem had to do with damage to the checkering. There were numerous places where entire diamonds had been broken off or there were small gouges in the checkering panel. Most of this simply was not practical to repair. As I deepened the new lines in recutting the checkering, some of these blemishes were eliminated or minimized.

This panel is about complete. Many of the damaged areas were eliminated as the checkering was recut. The last step with checkering was to brush in a coat of finish.

Finally, the wood in the checkering had been subject to body oils, dirt and grease for years. This weakened the wood fibers. Consequently as I used my cutters every now and then a diamond would simply break off. It was unavoidable. I might have been able to use some type of thin epoxy to reinforce or strengthen the wood but the fact that the checkering had been exposed to oil and grease might have made it difficult for a strengthening agent to be effective.

I did find a couple of places where the manufacturer had originally made repairs to the wood before checkering. A wood putty of some sort had been applied to some cracks or voids in the wood before or during checkering. Some of this had come out of the stock. I replaced this with some new wood putty I found in the local hardware I wanted to try. When working on your own gun as I am, this is the time to experiment with new materials and procedures. Only after you've determined that it's the way to go, should you even consider using it on someone else's gun.

Once the checkering had been recut, a few drops of the Miles Gilbert Classic American Gunstock Oil Finish were brushed in with an old toothbrush. The idea here is to seal the wood that was exposed when the checkering was recut. You definitely don't want to use so much you begin to fill those grooves that took so darn long to recut.

By the way, I think it took me about eight hours total time to recut all four panels. Part of that was definitely due to the poor condition of the original checkering. The fore-end and buttstock were then set aside to dry.

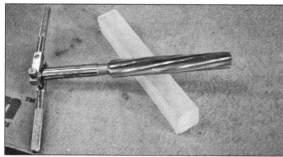

This Manson Precision spiral fluted reamer was used to recut the short, steep factory forcing cones. Coffield prefers to turn it by hand for maximum precision.

A modification that I believe is very helpful for a field gun such as this old Citori is to lengthen the chamber forcing cone. The forcing cone is located immediately ahead of the chamber and serves as a transition between the chamber and the bore. Traditionally factory forcing cones have been rather short with a steep, abrupt angle.

By recutting and lengthening the forcing cone with a more gradual angle or taper, there is less deformation to the shot. You can also make the case that it helps to reduce pressure and felt recoil. It's a simple operation and one that can be accomplished with very little equipment.

I used a Manson Precision spiral fluted long forcing cone reamer I picked up years ago. Dave Manson, who produces these as well as many other high quality precision cutting tools, is without a doubt one of the most knowledgeable and innovative men in the firearms business. If you need a cutting tool, he probably has it or can make it for you! If you need a reamer of any sort, contact the good folks at Dave Manson Precision Reamers,

Coffield uses his checkering cradle with the fore-end mounted on the barrel. He advises using a single-line tool when recutting old checkering to avoid mismatches.

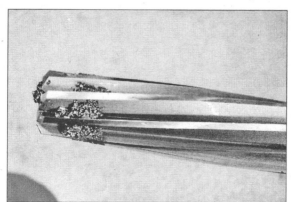

Here's the mark of a well-made reamer. The "chips" are more like fine dust. When you see this, you know that your cut will be smooth. Never turn it counterclockwise.

The nodules of honing abrasive on the Flexhone are attached to nylon bristles. Note also that the shaft has a rubber coating to protect the inside of the barrel.

The day after the Citori was completed, Coffield had it out on the skeet range. It was a great shooter! He says this is the best part of any project; using the gun.

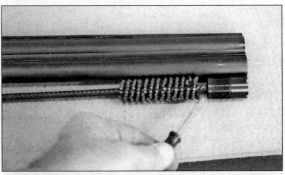

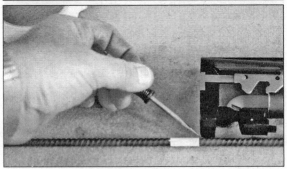

Coffield determined the location of the internal seat for the choke tube skirt and fixed a piece of tape to the Flexhone shaft to mark the limit for inserting it.

8200 Embury Road, Dept. SGN, Grand Blanc, Mich. 48439, telephone 810-953-0732.

Cutting a new long forcing cone is simple. Before you start, clean the barrel, and while holding it up to a light, look through the bore. As you look through it, you'll notice several distinctive planes of light. Starting at the muzzle, you'll see a short parallel section that's the choke. Behind this there's a short tapered sec-

tion which is the lead or forcing cone that is the transition from the bore to the choke. Behind this is the longer parallel section of the bore. Between the bore and the chamber is the original chamber forcing cone.

To recut the chamber forcing cone, position the barrel vertically in your padded vise with the muzzle over a bucket or trash can. By placing the barrel vertically, the reamer will not tend to push off to one side. Instead it will be pulled straight down into the barrel. Also the cutting oil will flow through the barrel and help wash away the chips.

Apply a generous amount of cutting oil to the inside of the chamber and to the reamer. The reamer should be held in a tap handle. Insert the reamer into the chamber and allow it to move down until it contacts the existing forcing cone. Now just turn the tap handle in a clockwise direction for half a dozen or so rotations. Carefully remove the reamer and clean all chips from the blades. By the way, don't allow the reamer to turn counter clockwise, as this will roll the sharp edges of the cutting blades and dull the reamer. The reamer must always be turned clockwise; don't back it up like a tap.

After removing the reamer, run several patches through the barrel, removing chips and cutting oil. Now hold the barrel up to a light and look through the barrel again. In addition to those five original and distinctive planes of light, you will notice a new plane between the old chamber forcing cone and the bore. That's the beginning of the new forcing cone you're cutting.

Each time you reinstall the long forcing cone reamer and cut a bit more, that new band of light will grow. It'll appear to only be moving back towards the chamber. In reality, it's moving towards the muzzle as well. Just keep cutting until the new forcing cone merges with the end of the chamber.

Be sure to cut away all of the original forcing cone. If you don't, you'll have a forcing cone with a compound angle and that's not good for a smooth transition of the shot from the chamber to the bore. There's no specially gauge or measuring tool needed to determine when you've finished. Just look through your barrel and you can easily see when the forcing cone is completed.

The last operation was to polish the bore and chamber. The bore was not especially rough, but it could stand a bit of polish. There were a few scratches and minor pits that needed to be removed. Also as the bore was polished, the new forcing cones and the chambers could also be smoothed up.

The tool I used was a Flexhone which is available from MidwayUSA. This is an abrasive brush mounted on a long, rubber-coated flexible steel shaft. The business end of the brush consists of numerous nylon bristles mounted at 90° to the shaft. On the end of each bristle is a small nodule or ball of abrasive. The other end of the shaft is locked into the chuck of an electric drill.

Before you begin, you will want to lay the Flexhone alongside the barrel. Since this barrel has screw-in chokes it's important that the Flexhone not extend up into the choke or even to the seat for the choke tube skirt. The seat is a small ledge inside the barrel. The rear end of the choke tube bears against this seat or ledge.

You definitely don't want to round over this seat, as that could allow bits of the plastic shot cup or lead to work their way under the choke tube. In the worst case, this could result in the choke tube being split or blown out the barrel!

With the front end of the Flexhone positioned behind the choke tube seat, wrap a bit of tape around the shaft where it's even with the breech. Now you know not to push the Flexhone into the barrel beyond that bit of tape. As long as that piece of tape is outside the breech, you're in good shape!

A special oil is supplied for use with the Flexhone. This oil helps to keep the abrasive nodules free of metal and working effectively. In fact, it also helps to prolong the life of the tool so it's a darn good idea to use the oil and lots of it!

Place the barrel horizontally in your padded vise with the bucket or trash can under the muzzle so any oil that runs out will not get on your floor. It's a messy job but it sure works. A few minutes with the Flexhone and you can see a world of difference in an old barrel. It won't take out deep pits, but it sure will help with smaller blemishes and the normal scratches and scars a barrel can pick up over the years.

Once the barrels and chambers had been polished the job was over! It was just a matter of reassembling the Citori and it was ready to shoot. In fact, the day after I finished this shotgun, some friends and I headed out to our local gun club for some informal skeet shooting. The old Citori shot like a champ! It was a delightful gun to shoot and there was a special feeling in knowing that I had taken a gun that had been used and abused and had made it once again into an attractive and functional firearm.

I hope you'll also consider the possibilities of reworking some of the older well-used shotguns we all see at gun shows and gun shops. As with this old Citori, many of these guns have lots of good years left in 'em. All it takes is just time, a bit of TLC, and some basic gunsmithing.

Until next time, good luck and good gunsmithing!

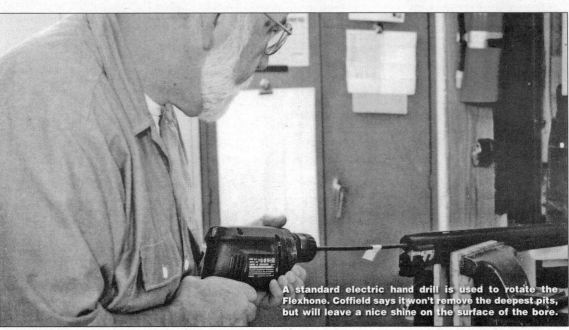

A standard electric hand drill is used to rotate the Flexhone. Coffield says it won't remove the deepest pits, but will leave a nice shine on the surface of the bore.

GUNSMITHING AND SHOP PROJECTS
YOU CAN ACCOMPLISH!

Get out into the shop, have some fun, and achieve the personal satisfaction of completing some useful gunsmithing projects! You could build a gorgeous Custom Mauser rifle, an AKS rifle from a kit, a tack-driving hunting or varmint rifle, or totally trick out your Glock pistols, all by following these simple step-by-step video courses from the American Gunsmithing Institute!

Vol 1 - Master Gunsmith Gene Shuey reveals the four areas you can greatly improve on this excellent pistol!

These are the sights, the barrel, the grip frame, and the trigger pull. To get the most out of your Glock you really need to know how to address each of these areas. Mr. Shuey has developed a simple step-by-step system that will enable you to customize your Glock the way **YOU** want it. In addition, Gene also covers how to tune the overall pistol to improve fit, feel, and function, plus a whole lot more.

Over three hours in length!
DVD#3424 $79.95 ($7 S/H)

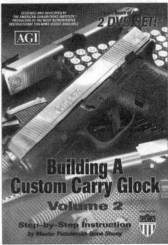
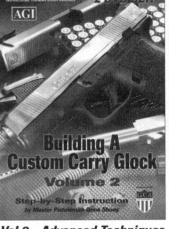

Vol 2 - Advanced Techniques

Discover and perform advanced techniques Gene Shuey has developed that were previously closely guarded gunsmithing secrets. This course is applicable to all models of Glocks. Learn how to modify your Glock into a custom carry-gun using detailed step-by-step instruction. By following these methods you can build a truly custom Glock that combines stunning looks and exceptional performance! These are the operations and techniques that will enable you to build the ULTIMATE, one of a kind Glock carry-gun.

Over six hours in length!
DVD#3434 $79.95 ($7 s/h)

Master Gunsmith Gene Shuey will show you each step, from removing old parts, to installing and headspacing a new barrel. In this epic production you will see a solid old military 98 transformed into a classic hunting rifle. We start with two identical guns and then go through every single conversion step in detail. Actions, triggers, barrels, stocks, mounts, slings, sights and custom accessories are covered in extensive detail.

Over 7 Hours!
DVD#3064 $79.95 ($9 S/H)

Save Hundreds of Dollars!

Before you go out and spend hundreds, or possibly thousands of dollars on a new custom rifle, squeeze all the potential performance out of the rifles you already own! Darrell Holland will show you how to cut your group sizes in half or more by improving the rifles function using existing parts and by employing the tricks of custom gun makers that you can do yourself.

OVER 3 1/2 HOURS!
DVD#3254 $49.95 ($7 S/H)

Master Armorer John D. Bush shows and demonstrates step-by-step: identifying, sorting and selecting parts and receivers, checking parts for wear and fit, and a clear demonstration of the barreling and headspacing process. Along with total assembly and final fitting is a discussion on how to identify parts by manufacturer, interesting facts and bits of history. This is the only complete course detailing everything you need to know to assemble an M-1 Garand from a parts kit. 109 min.

DVD#3144 $39.95 ($7 S/H)

BUILDING THE AKS RIFLE FROM A PARTS KIT

Build From A Flat or Pre-formed Receiver!

Parts Selection
Parts Identification
How To Rivet
Bending Flats
Receiver Selection
Barrel Installation
Fitting A Trunnion
Tooling Blueprints
Construction
Techniques
Much More!

Build This Gun Legally!

Printable Tooling Blueprints Included!

DVD#3294 $59.95 (s/h $7) *NOTE: Knowledge of complete disassembly and reassembly is a prerequisite for this course. Order the AKS Armorer Course #1054 for this important information.*

You Still Can Build A Semi-Auto AK From A Parts Kit Legally!

Because of our thorough research and painstaking experiments, YOU can build an AK from a kit with ease and guaranteed success. We have eliminated all the guesswork and shown you a foolproof method for building up a Semi-Auto AK from a receiver or from a flat. Follow the procedures we show you, use the tooling we give you prints for, and you simply can't miss. Every step in the process is covered in detail along with the proper safety checks. Then it's off to the range to test fire. You'll be impressed at how well the gun operates. *3+ hours!*

Building The Ultimate Tactical Or Varmint Rifle

Build A Custom Rifle Capable Of Putting ALL The Bullets Through The Same Hole!

EVERYTHING IS COVERED from cartridge and caliber selection for tactical and varmint applications, all the way through the fitting and assembly of a custom rifle capable of putting all the bullets through the same hole! Master Rifle Builder Darrell Holland covers ALL the options so you can select the style and features that suit your own tastes. NOTHING is left out! Darrell shows you the different features and styles you can choose from and explains the advantages and disadvantages of each. Darrell actually reveals his exclusive, patented, V-block bedding system, giving you an inside look at one of the most repeatedly accurate mounting systems ever invented.

Darrell covers proper procedures for barrel break-in and sighting-in so you can preserve the accuracy potential of your newly built rifle. Darrell then shows you proper cleaning techniques and methods in order to maintain that accuracy! Whether you want to take out varmints at 500 yards with uncanny accuracy or you need a tactical rifle that can perform when it's needed, this is the course for you. 120 min. **DVD#3124** $49.95 ($7 S/H)

SGN BONUS: With your order you will automatically receive a **2 Month FREE* Trial Membership** in the Gun Club of America! **This is a $60 value!**
*Only $9.97 to cover the shipping and handling for both free issues with option to continue membership. **Get 2 FREE DVD Magazines & Newsletters** →

1-800-797-0867 Ad Code# SGNbook5 **www.AmericanGunsmith.com**

Mail your written order to: AGI, 351 Second Street, Napa, CA 94559 or fax your order to 707-253-7149 CA residents add 8.75% sales tax

KATHMANDU to COLUMBIA

Reviving a Nepalese Martini

By Reid Coffield

Part 1

Importer IMA says these rare Martini variants are "untouched," and Coffield says that's the truth. Cleaning off more than a century of grime is a big job.

I've always been fascinated by 19th century single-shot military rifles. I guess part of this is because when I started getting interested in firearms as a teenager in the late 1950s, these were the only ones I could afford! There weren't as many collectors then and these old guns were just that; old guns. For the most part, few folks were interested in 'em and they were often pretty darn cheap. This was especially true of the military single-shots

Single-shots were popular with the military for a relatively short period between about 1865 and 1885 when armies all over the world changed over from muzzleloaders to cartridge arms. Single-shots were the first step in this conversion.

It wasn't that those in charge were always totally opposed to adopting repeating arms. But many of the early repeaters were simply not strong enough to withstand the pressures of the cartridges in use at the time. I once read it was considered essential that a proper military rifle round should be powerful enough to kill a horse at 100-200 yards. If that seems crazy, keep in mind for an infantryman facing a cavalry charge it was a darned important and a very practical consideration!

You also had problems with ammunition. Fixed ammo was still in its infancy: cartridge cases were made from everything from strips of brass soldered together to paper. Various types of primers, powder and bullets were tried. The bottom line is that ammo used at that time was not nearly as good or as reliable as what we use today.

Consequently, the guns had to be simple and strong enough to deal with ammo that was often less than perfect. If you had a bad round, the mechanism had to allow it to be easily cleared. Many early repeating rifles were pretty complex and this often made dealing with bad ammo problematic.

Finally, one other human factor was involved. Soldiers at that time were often not as mechanically inclined as to-day's recruits. Few had any experience at all with complex mechanical devices and were neither trained nor equipped to deal with 'em. For an army, that's a problem. You simply can't give soldiers complex firearms they can't maintain. If you do, in very short order you'll soon have soldiers walkin' around with inoperable firearms.

So, most of the major military powers, including the USA, opted initially for simple, inexpensive, easy to maintain and use single-shot rifles chambered for reasonably powerful cartridges. The Remington Rolling Block is perhaps the most basic and perhaps the simplest design that achieved widespread acceptance. Another outstanding design, which also originated in the USA, was the Martini as used by the British.

Over the years I've owned a number of Martini rifles in various calibers. I've always liked 'em. They're everything you would want in a military single-shot. It's a simple design with few parts, easy to maintain, and rugged as the devil. These rifles served the British well all over the world until the adoption of the bolt-action .303 cal. Enfield.

As I'm always on the lookout for rifles like this, I was pleased to note that International Military Antiques, 1000 Valley Road, Dept. SGN, Gillette, NJ 07933, telephone 908-903-1200, one of the regular advertisers here in SHOTGUN NEWS, was offering a variety of Martini rifles. These rifles had come from the last large collection of military arms that will probably ever be offered to the American public. In 2000 IMA owner Christian Cranmer purchased about 430 tons of antique arms from the government of Nepal and in 2003 brought almost all of it here.

Included in this collection were hundreds if not thousands of Martinis. Many were British made while some were made in Nepal. It seems that after a short war around 1813, the British gained a great deal of influence and control over the government and army of Nepal. Since this country was on the northern border of India, the most prized colonial possession of the British, the strength of the Nepalese army was of major importance. The British wanted the Nepalese to be strong enough to deter any aggressors from the north but

To avoid loss, you should always store parts in a designated container such as this parts tray.

When IMA calls its Nepalese Martini rifles "untouched," it's not kidding! Coffield soaked his gun in many coats of turpentine to remove the dust of 125 years.

not so strong as to pose a threat to India. (for more on this, see the 11/20/04 SGN)

One of the ways the British tried to keep the military power of the Nepalese in check was to control the types of arms they used. In general, the British attempted to keep the Nepalese one generation of arms behind the British. When the British were using percussion rifles, the Nepalese were theoretically limited to flintlocks; when the British had single-shot cartridge guns, the Nepalese had percussion muzzleloaders.

However, the Nepalese were pretty smart. They fully understood the importance of having arms as advanced and up-to-date as possible. So when the British adopted the Martini in .577/450, the Nepalese realized they needed them, too. Since the Brits would not allow them to have British-made Martinis, the Nepalese simply made their own!

All they needed were a few "sample" guns and they shortly thereafter began producing their own version. And they didn't just make straight copies. Instead, they opted to produce an interesting and unique variation of the British rifle. In many respects, the Nepalese Martini might well be considered to be an improvement!

The British Martini has all the internal action parts held by various screws and pins in the inside of the receiver. This could make assembly or disassembly a bit of a challenge if you were not familiar with the rifle. The Nepalese opted to utilize a concept developed by the Belgian arms maker Francotte and later used by Westley Richards.

Francotte designed a small-action Martini like rifle in which all the internal action components were attached to the trigger guard housing. In effect, the internal components were unitized. To disassemble the gun all you needed to do was drop out the trigger guard and all the internal parts came along with it! The other major difference in the Francotte design was that there was no cocking indicator on the right side of the receiver.

The Francotte concept was adopted and used by the Nepalese with their large military action. To a casual observer, the Nepalese Martini is identical to the British rifles. Other than lacking the cocking indicator on the right side of the action, the guns are outwardly identical.

These locally-made rifles were used in large numbers. Later British-made Martinis were also obtained and used. I would not be surprised if both Nepalese and British made guns were employed within the same units. According to what I have read, these guns saw some degree of use up until World War II.

In any event, they are interesting and unusual artifacts of a time long past. When I saw that International Military Antiques was offering these rifles for only $275, I was hooked! When I called to place an order, Alex Cranmer went to great lengths to make sure that I understood that these were Nepalese-made rifles and that they were "untouched."

OK, you're thinking "untouched" means 100% mint, unused, right? If so, boy have you missed the mark! "Untouched" simply means the rifles are being sold in the same condition they are in when they were pulled from the storage in Kathmandu. I.M.A. goes to great pains to clean many of the other guns they are currently selling but these are being sold in the same "untouched" condition as they were found.

Does this mean that they have a bit of dust or rust on 'em? Nope, they are far beyond that! These rifles are *filthy*! They are covered with 100+ years' worth of dirt and crud. In fact, these are among the dirtiest firearms I have worked on in 30+ years of gunsmithing and I've worked on a lot of dirty guns!

When I pulled the rifle out of the shipping box, I was shocked at the condition. It was definitely going to need a lot of work. At the same time, I was thrilled. This was a historic firearm from a remote and exotic place. This was going to be a project that would truly be a labor of love.

The first order of business was to decide just what I wanted to do with this rifle. When dealing with an antique, you have three active options; restoration, repair, and refinishing; and one inactive option; don't do a thing, just leave the gun just as you found it. Each of these is very different and each poses some challenges.

With this rifle, my basic goal was to ensure its preservation. After all, the darn thing is more than 100 years old and is a piece of history. Not only is it a piece of the history of the British Empire

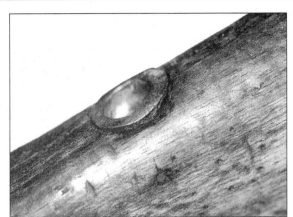

The retaining cup for the lever was poorly inletted when the rifle was built. Coffield decided not to correct this, as he wanted the finished gun to reflect history.

but also of Nepal and, in a way, of gunmaking. I wanted to preserve this in years to come, others would have a chance to study it and enjoy it just as I have.

Given that I wanted to preserve the rifle, I could attempt to restore it. However, keep in mind there is no one universally accepted understanding of exactly what restoration involves. For example, to many people restoration of a gun is to return it to the condition it was in when it was originally manufactured.

To others, restoration might mean just returning the rifle to the condition it was in at some time in the past. More often than not, good restoration procedures entail using the same tools, techniques, and materials used when the gun was made. Well-done restoration is difficult and challenging. Very few people can do it well and I am certainly not one of those gifted few.

Repair generally entails just fixing any broken or damaged parts. The techniques used may or may not be period appropriate. For example, if you have a crack in a stock, you might use a modern epoxy rather than a glue of a type commonly used when the gun was in service. Quite often with antique firearms, no work other than the needed repair is done.

The rear sight was slightly bent but this was not a big job to fix. The left side of the receiver was heavily pitted, as the rifle was stored in an old palace.

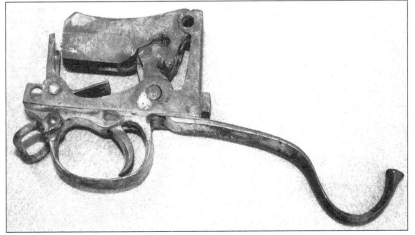

The Francotte design modified the Martini by unitizing the internal action parts. Removing just one pin allowed the receiver quickly and easily to be disassembled.

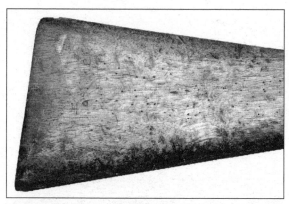

After much of the black coating of crud was removed, you can actually see the wood! Some might well argue to leave a wallhanger like this in as-found condition.

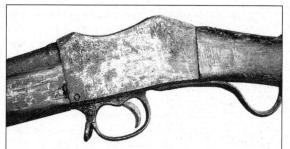

Note the pitting on the receiver as well as the damage to the forearm. Guns stored in stacks in Third World countries will tend to have this level of damage.

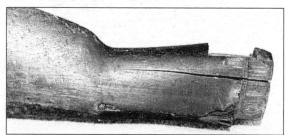

The extra "practice" stock shows signs of an early repair. Coffield says getting spare parts and testing techniques and materials on them is a smart idea with old guns.

At the top of the buttstock where it joins the receiver, a lot of wood has been chipped away and lost over the years. There will be the chance for some skilled woodworking.

Refinishing, as generally understood, entails removal of any remaining original finish on the stock or the metal and replacing it. The new finish might or might not be correct for the period. This is a subject and practice that can cause a lot of controversy.

Some folks see refinishing an old gun using a modern metal or wood finish as acceptable, while others think it absolutely ruins the firearm. People can get really hot under the collar on the subject, and I've seen more than a couple of guys come close to throwin' punches over this.

I basically don't want to do anything to damage the gun or its history. It's an old gun that has seen a lot of use and a bit of abuse along the way. I definitely don't want to even try to make it look "new". Part of the history of this gun is contained in the scars and dings of use.

I just want to make enough repairs so it'll properly function and be preserved for future generations. I also want it to be clean and attractive to the point that it'll be considered a desirable collectable. After all, like all the guns that you and I own, every one of 'em will someday be owned by someone else. In the case of this old antique rifle, if it's an attractive, interesting collectable, it's much more likely to survive and not be broken up for parts or made into a lamp!

Since this is my goal, I'll be doing a bit of repair and a lot of cleaning. It won't be "pure" restoration but I don't think too many folks will find a lot to criticize.

The first step in the process was to carefully examine the rifle and determine what was wrong and get a general feel of what needed to be done. I was a bit limited due to the incredible buildup of 100 years' worth of dust, dirt and crud. I also got the impression that this rifle had not been all that well taken care of before it was turned in for storage.

I could tell that the buttstock had been damaged where it joined the receiver. It was very loose, and a good bit of wood had been chipped away on the top of the stock where it bore against the receiver. From what I could tell at that time, that damage was very old.

There was also a lot of rust and deep pitting on the left side of the receiver. The forearm was in much better condition, with only one major area of damage. This was at the back of the forearm on the right side where it joined the receiver.

Having worked on a number of older guns in the past, I expected problems like this. When I ordered the rifle I also

obtained a spare broken buttstock. I didn't plan on using it on the gun but as a source for wood to make repairs to the stock if needed. I had no idea what type of wood was used on this rifle and the chances of finding a match was pretty slim. Having a junk buttstock solved that problem. It also gave me a piece of wood to experiment with in trying to find the best cleaner and cleaning technique.

I first used turpentine applied with a soft fiber brush to clean the spare stock. Turpentine is a natural solvent make of pine resin. It took me almost an hour to clean about 1½ inches of the buttstock! The dirt and crud had created an incredibly thick, black mud-like coating that was extremely difficult to remove.

The next day, I again worked on this same spare buttstock. It was soon apparent that just gentle washing with the brush and turpentine was not very effective on this particular stock. On the right side, I then tried using 4/0 steel wool in combination with the turpentine with virtually no hand pressure on the steel wool.

On the left side I used 4/0 with maximum pressure. The left side showed more crud removal and there was no evidence of wood being removed or worn down. The only negative consequence of this was the deposition of small fragments of steel wood in some of the holes in the stock and I wanted to avoid that.

I next tried using a green Scotch-Brite Pad along with the turpentine. The results were much better. I was initially worried that it would remove or sand away wood. Luckily, it did not do this. It was very effective, though I still had to spend hours of work on the built-up crud.

I actually spent an hour a day for six days to clean this spare buttstock, but it was worth it. By the way, I also tried a couple of "green" cleaners on the wood that were labeled as safer and biodegradable. The ones I tried were Citristrip and Simple Green. Simple Green seemed to be the most effective in removing oil from the wood after the surface crud had been eliminated.

It may seem like a waste to spend so much time experimenting on this junk buttstock but that's the best way I knew of to find out what works without any possibility of damage to the Nepalese gun. I learned long ago that experimentation should always be done on scrap, so if something doesn't work or it causes unexpected damage, no harm is done.

Once I had finished with the junk buttstock, I started on the rifle. The first order of business was simply to wash it down with turpentine to remove as much dirt and gunk as possible. There was no attempt to disassemble the rifle. The wood and metal were repeatedly swabbed or washed with turpentine.

I used a long metal cleaning tank, though I could have used a bucket or almost any large container. The old

bluing tank was ideal and made it a bit easier to handle the rifle. Again, I used a paintbrush to apply the turpentine and allow it to float away the crud.

I did this several times, and each time I strained the dirty turpentine through a filter of paper towels before returning it to the one-gallon container. If you do this, you can reuse the turpentine for cleaning many times. You'll also get a good idea from the residue in the filter as to just what you're taking off the stock. You'll be shocked!

When I finally had the rifle cleaned to a reasonable degree with most of the dirt and surface crud removed, I began the disassembly process. In working with older guns like this you need to be very careful during disassembly. Even with the best of intentions and extreme care, you can often inadvertently damage your gun. A good example of this occurred with this rifle.

In order to remove the buttstock which was held to the receiver with a throughbolt, I first had to remove the buttplate. It was attached with two large screws; one at the top and one at the bottom. The bottom screw came out in a normal fashion. Unfortunately the top buttplate screw was swaged into the screw hole in the buttplate and could not be turned!

The poor condition of the Nepalese Martini will make this a very, very challenging project! Coffield will make no attempt ever to shoot it; it's a decor item.

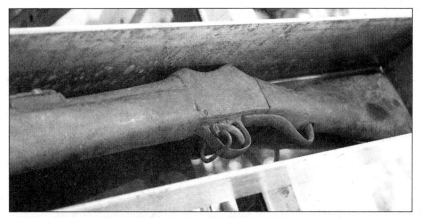

Coffield uses an old bluing tank for especially tough cleaning jobs, and this rifle certainly qualified. Cleaning it was an exceptionally tough and messy task.

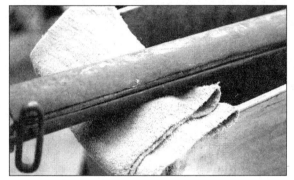

Even though the stock was in poor condition, Coffield used a cloth pad made of old rags to prevent additional damage from the sharp edge of the steel cleaning tank.

I was forced to pull the buttplate off the stock. In doing this I found that the top screw was wrapped in an old piece of cloth and jammed into the stripped screw hole. It had probably been that way long before the rifle was turned in for storage.

The heel of the buttstock had a crack extending forward from this top buttplate screw hole. This was caused in part when I pulled the buttplate off. I inadvertently made a bad situation a bit worse and that happens from time to time. There is always a danger of damaging the gun as you work on it. This is much more of a problem with an old gun than it generally is with a newer one.

As I disassembled the rifle, I chose to leave a transverse pin that helps to secure the lower barrel band in place in the forearm. In looking closely at the ends of the pin which project above the wood on either side of the forearm and at the surrounding wood, I could tell that the pin was rusted.

The problem is that as rust forms and creates scale, this scale tends to expand and dig into the wood. This makes removal of the pin or any rusted part much more difficult. It will almost always cause the wood to chip out or break. In many instances I have found it is better to just leave the

part in place and forget about removing it.

However, even leaving parts in place can pose problems. For example, the end of the lever is secured by a circular cupped metal housing in the buttstock. The inletting job around this part was probably not the best even when the gun was new. Wear and rust have taken their toll and now it looks even worse. Also, the spring loaded plunger in the cap that engages the end of the lever is not functioning. I would like to take it apart and repair it if possible.

The problem is that the cap is held in the wood with a transverse pin. In removing that pin, I could possibly damage the stock further. Is a possible repair to the lever retainer worth the risk? Questions and situations like this constantly arise when working on an older gun. Is there a "correct" answer? No, there's not. Many will have opinions and some will be very strongly held and expressed. The bottom line is there is no universally accepted rule or procedure. It is purely a judgment call on your part.

The lever retainer also brings up the issue of whether or not it's proper or correct to "fix" work that was originally done poorly. I could make a strong case that the workmanship shown on the rifle, good or bad, is a valuable part of the history of the gun. Again, this is a judgment call and no matter what you decide you can be absolutely certain that someone will disagree with you!

If you do opt to make repairs they should be either so well executed that they are invisible or, if you are a mere mortal like me, make them look like they are period appropriate for the gun. The ideal from my perspective is to make the repair look like it was done while the gun was still in service. The repair should look just as old as the rifle.

Once the stock was removed I then disassembled the action. Here I found several more surprises! When I took the trigger guard assembly out of the receiver along with the breechbolt and other action components I found that someone long ago had lost a couple of the major pins. The individual had then whittled out wooden replacements! These certainly would not have held up if the gun had been fired but they were just fine for keeping everything together so he could turn this gun in for storage!

Keep in mind that guns work their way down the food chain. The best guns go to the most important units or organizations. Those in turn pass their old guns on down to the next level. The guys at the second level then pass their old guns on down to a lower level and so on. Eventually, sooner or later every gun ends up at the bottom level.

The firing pin tip was severely damaged as well as the face of the breechblock. By the time this rifle was stored, it already had very little real fighting potential.

The bottom of the barrel was also severely pitted. That's just one more reason Coffield believes this rifle is unsafe to fire. It's an interesting historical artifact.

In this case, I would think that the Nepalese probably had some form of rural constabulary or police. By the time these guys got these Nepalese-made Martinis, the rest of the armed forces were probably long since using bolt-action .303 Enfields.

Like so many organizations, they probably carried their guns a lot more than they ever shot them. This was confirmed when I finally cleaned and checked the bore. It was almost perfect! The rifle had obviously been carried a lot but seldom ever fired. I suspect that it was more of a badge of office than a tool.

With the rifle disassembled I was able to make an evaluation as to whether or not it could or should be fired. International Military Antiques does not encourage firing any of the antique arms they sell and this is understandable. In examining this rifle, I found there was extensive and extremely deep pitting on the bottom of the barrel as well as along the left side of the receiver. Since I have no way of knowing precisely how deep these pits are, I must assume that they would compromise the safety of the rifle.

I also found that the internal action parts were not all that well fitted or made. Keep in mind that these rifles were made almost 125 years ago, virtually by hand. That, coupled with the use of unknown steels and heat treatment, would make the safety of the rifles suspect. I may well be too conservative about safety issues but keep in mind that you are seldom ever sued for an accident that doesn't happen!

The bottom line is that I do not believe that this rifle should ever be fired. It is a wall hanger! It's a wonderful artifact, a piece of history from a remote and exotic place and a bygone era. It's a great collectable but definitely not a shooter.

The next time we get together I'll finish cleaning the metal and stock, make a few wood repairs, replace the wooden action pins, make various metal repairs, and deal with an important safety issue. If all goes well, we should end up with an interesting and unique collectable from the heart of the Himalayas.

Until then, good luck and good gunsmithing!

If you look closely you can see the cracks extending from the buttplate screw hole. Old military arms took a beating from endless parade-ground drill practice.

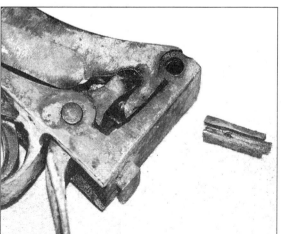

Coffield discovered that the breechblock pivot pin was just a wooden peg! IMA warns against firing these rifles, and this is a good example of why you shouldn't.

KATHMANDU to COLUMBIA

Reviving a Nepalese Martini

By Reid Coffield

Part 2

Now that he's got the grime and crud of more than a century cleaned off his rifle, Coffield's ready to repair the wood and do some metalworking.

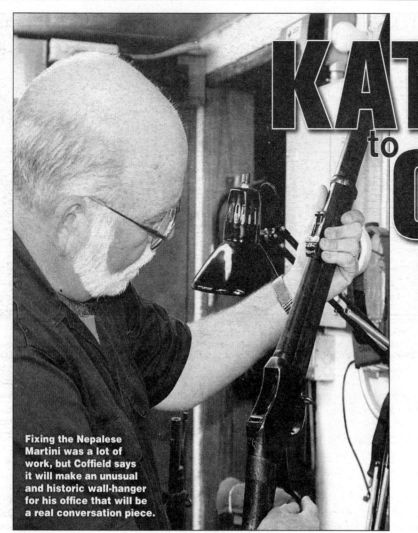

Fixing the Nepalese Martini was a lot of work, but Coffield says it will make an unusual and historic wall-hanger for his office that will be a real conversation piece.

"Why bother?"

That was the question a buddy asked after looking at my newly acquired Nepalese Martini. I could definitely understand his comment. The rifle was a mess. Even though I spent many hours just cleaning it, it still looked like a fugitive from the junkyard.

The wood was in rough shape and needed a number of repairs. The receiver was pitted and didn't have even a trace of original finish. The barrel was also suffering from terminal rust. In addition, there were parts missing and the gun simply didn't function. Yeah, it was a mess.

But, why bother? I guess I'm just an incurable romantic. The idea of some young Gurkha soldier having carried this rifle in pursuit of bandits or renegades high in the Himalayas, at the roof of the world made it special. Also that it was made in the late 1800s by the Nepalese was an incredible achievement in and of itself. Add to that, the fact it was built under the very nose of the British while the Brits were doing their best to restrict and limit the Nepalese access to modern arms was also a great story. This rifle was truly a unique piece of history and an artifact of a bygone era.

I admit it; I find guns like this incredibly interesting, no matter what their condition. And, if I don't miss my guess, I bet you share some of the same feelings. So, my friend's question was really easy to answer. I wanted to save this gun because of its past and I wanted to do all I could to make sure that in the future someone else would have the opportunity to look at this rifle with the same amazement and interest that it stirred in me. That's why!

This project started when I learned that Christian Cranmer at International Military Antiques, 1000 Valley Road, Dept. SGN, Gillette, N.J. 07933, telephone 908-903-1200, whose ads I'm sure you've seen here in SHOTGUN NEWS, had a bunch of antique Martini rifles. I've always been fascinated by single-shot military rifles made during the last half of the 19th century.

Most of these were made during the transition from muzzleloading to cartridge firearms. They saw extensive use for only 15 or 20 years or so before they were obsolete and replaced by bolt-action repeaters. But they played an important role at the time and took part in many famous military actions as well as thousands of little known or forgotten battles and skirmishes.

Perhaps the best-known battle we Americans are aware of in which the Martini played a major role was that of Isandlwana in January of 1879. Even if the name doesn't ring a bell, I'll bet you've probably seen the film *Zulu* which was based on this incident. This battle took place in southern Africa between a group of about 1,400 British soldiers and close to 20,000 Zulu warriors. The end result was the total defeat of the British with a loss of almost 1,300 men.

Within a day, another battle took place not too far away at Rorke's Drift. Here a small unit of a little over 100 British soldiers armed with their Martini rifles stood off an estimated 4,000 Zulu warriors. It was a gallant stand resulting in the award of 11 Victoria Crosses to the soldiers of that unit. No other single action saw so many VCs awarded to one small

group. And through it all, in defeat and victory, the Martini rifle was right there.

While the Martini rifle I got from I.M.A. was not used during the Zulu wars, it was very much like the rifles used during that conflict. To me, it was worth the work to save it and make sure it survived to be enjoyed by future collectors and history buffs.

And it would take a lot of work! One of the biggest problems was the fit of the buttstock to the receiver. While the gun was being used, the stock bolt had loosened. This allowed the stock to twist up and down and bear unevenly against the rear of the receiver. Consequently, a fairly good-sized chip of wood was broken from the top of the wrist right behind the receiver. Evidently this happened early on and the problem just kept getting worse over time because of two factors.

The thin sharp edges of the rear of the receiver were a poor design feature that led inevitably to chipping and cracking at the forward end of the old rifle's buttstock.

Coffield got a scrap buttstock along with his rifle as a source for spare wood and used this old repair on it as a guide in making the repair to his Martini stock.

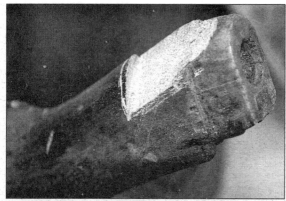

The initial cut has been made, but more wood will need to be removed. It is imperative that chisels be as sharp as you can possibly make 'em for clean, even cuts.

In the first part of this series, I did some major cleaning and disassembled the rifle. In cleaning the stock I used turpentine extensively. Turpentine is a natural wood product made from pine resin. To the best of my knowledge, unlike many of the harsher chemical cleaners, it has no negative effect on the wood or wood fibers. Using turpentine, I was able to clean off most of the black crust of dried grease and dirt coating the stock and metal. Once that was done, I was then able to begin the first of the major wood repairs.

When I ordered the rifle, I also obtained a scrap piece of a broken buttstock. I thought I would probably need some wood to splice in for repairs. Since this rifle was made in Nepal, the chance of me getting a piece of local wood that would match was somewhere between slim and none. Having this scrap stock would be helpful.

Even if it wasn't a perfect match, at least the case could be made that a wood of that type would be historically appropriate for the repair. From what I've seen of repairs made in third world countries, there is often little or no effort made to use the same specific type of wood used in the stock. That would definitely be the case with this repair. My Martini stock and my scrap stock appear to be of different woods.

Since I could not make my repair invisible, the next best thing for me to do was to make the repair look like it was correct for the period and for the users of the rifle. As an added bonus, the scrap stock had at one time been repaired and this old repair gave me a good idea of what I needed to do.

When making a repair, you definitely don't want it to be technically inappropriate. A great example of a bad repair of this nature is the visible use of modern bedding compound as filler for cracks or missing wood. This stands out like a sore thumb and will normally make the gun much less desirable as a collectable.

I spent a lot of time making sure I located the repair to maximize the benefit of adding wood to the stock. I wanted to make darn sure I removed as much of the damaged area of the stock as possible. In laying out the repair, I used a white grease pencil to locate my cuts on the stock.

In making an angular cut to support the rear of the wood splice, I used a Japanese-style pull saw. This hand saw works on the pull stroke rather than as a traditional American saw, on the push stroke. I found this gives me a bit more control as I cut with the saw. Once I made this cut, I used my bandsaw to make a cut parallel to the axis of the wrist. Again, I was very careful to make sure my new cut matched the bottom of the angular cut.

I used a number of chisels and files to flatten and smooth the cut made in the wrist. I took the time quickly to touch up the edges of my chisels before I used 'em. You simply cannot have your cutting tools too sharp! Ultimately, a sharp chisel will enable you to do quicker and more accurate work.

Next I cut a segment of wood from my scrap stock just a bit larger than needed to repair the top of the wrist. I made an angular surface on the rear of my repair wood to match the angular cut on my stock. A lot of this work was done using a disk sander.

I did my best to make sure that the two pieces of wood fit together as closely as possible with no gaps. Once I had a good fit, I used a two-part epoxy to bond the wood. Purists may find this use of epoxy objectionable. One school of thought among traditionalists is that you should only use glues that would be period correct.

Well, I appreciate that in a true restoration, but I'm not attempting to do that, nor am I claiming that I am. This is not, as far as I'm concerned, a true restoration. I think of it basically as a repair to stabilize and ensure the survival of this rifle.

Once the wood was glued in place, I used surgical tubing to wrap around the wrist. Surgical tubing makes a great clamp, as it can be applied over odd shapes and it will not dent or damage the wood. More than once I've seen scars or dents left by clamps used when repairing stocks.

First, whoever built the receiver made its rear edges where it contacted the stock extremely narrow. In fact, these edges are almost sharp! As you can imagine these thin, sharp edges tended to dig into the wood when the rifle was fired. These sharp edges then lead to more splintering and chipping at the head of the stock.

Also, the buttplate could not be removed, since the top buttplate screw was swaged into place. Since you had to remove the buttplate to get to the stock bolt to tighten it, the stock bolt was probably never tightened! This just meant the loose buttstock stayed loose and the damage to the front of the stock just kept getting worse. It didn't help that the inletting between the buttstock and the receiver was not all that good to begin with.

While this sort of situation would be totally unacceptable in a modern army, you have to keep in mind how these rifles ultimately ended up being used. While it may have been issued to the best unit in the Nepalese army at one point, as time passed and other better made and more modern and up-to-date arms were acquired, this rifle made its way down the food chain.

Eventually I would be willing to bet that it was issued to the equivalent of a local sheriff or policeman. It was carried as much as a badge of office and authority as a tool or firearm. In fact, based on the fact that the bore is in fantastic condition, I would bet that it was seldom ever fired in its last years of use.

Since the final user was not shooting it, the fact that the stock was a bit loose probably didn't matter to him. I'd bet he was a lot more concerned with just keeping track of the darn thing and making sure he could account for it during inspections. Eventually it was turned in and lay for decades in a dusty old building in Kathmandu.

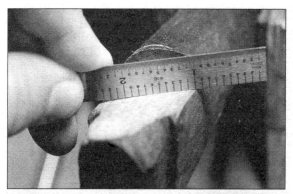

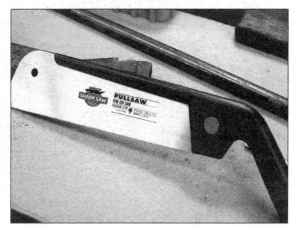

A Japanese-style pull saw is favored by Coffield for making precise, accurate cuts. Because these cut on the pull stroke, they can be much thinner than U.S. saws.

Coffield checked the bottom of the repair cut often to make sure it was flat. This is essential if he is to get a good close fit with the block serving as a patch.

Coffield believes that surgical tubing is one of the strongest and best wood clamps you can use. It conforms to most any shape, and won't dent wood as clamps may.

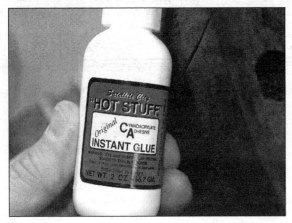

To repair thin cracks, Coffield uses Hot Stuff glue as it penetrates deep into even the smallest cracks. It's a very thin cyanoacrylate that will flow most anywhere.

While waiting for the epoxy to cure on the wrist repair, I went ahead and took care of the crack at the heel. When removing the buttplate, cracks developed extending from the upper buttplate screw hole to the heel. These two cracks were fairly small and I didn't want to open them up to try and force in epoxy.

Again Coffield uses surgical tubing to secure the stock while repairing the crack at the heel. Heel cracks are very common in old military rifles from drill use.

Coffield used plenty of masking tape to protect the stock when using files and sandpaper. The wrist repair is 80% complete. A bit more inletting and it'll be done.

Instead, I used some very thin, high strength glue I obtained from Brownells, the gunsmith supply house. This glue, sold as Hot Stuff, is extremely thin and will penetrate deep into the smallest crack. I applied the glue and then wrapped the wood with surgical tubing to hold everything together. I let it set for 24 hours while the epoxy and glue cured.

The next day I used a 3/8" drill to clean out the buttplate screw holes. I then epoxied in a piece of 3/8" diameter wooden dowel rod. When prepping the wooden dowel I used a small rat tail rasp to cut a spiral groove around the length of the dowel. This groove allowed any air and epoxy trapped under the dowel to escape as the dowel was inserted into the stock.

Without this groove you can sometimes either further crack the stock because of the hydraulic pressure or the trapped air will often push the dowel out before the epoxy or glue sets up. By the way, I left the surgical tubing in place to further support the stock and as insurance to prevent cracking.

Once the epoxy was cured, I trimmed the excess dowel from the buttstock with my pull saw. I cut the dowel about 1/8" above the face of the buttstock so I wouldn't accidentally cut or scar the stock with my saw. After that I used a carbide burr with a Dremel tool to cut the stub of the dowel down to the stock face.

The next step was to locate my new screw holes using the buttplate. I drilled two pilot holes for the buttplate screws using a special tapered drill. The buttplate screws were coated with a bit of beeswax and then turned into the wood. Once that was done, the buttplate was installed and the fit checked. It looked good.

I removed the surgical tubing from the wrist and roughly shaped the new wood to match the lines of the wrist. The patch extended forward beyond the point where the rear edges of the receiver would be located. This was done deliberately. I wanted to make darn sure the receiver was properly supported. During the next hundred years I didn't want the buttstock to start rocking back and forth again and lead to more wood damage.

To ensure the inletting was done properly, I coated the rear of the receiver with Jarrows Inletting Black. This is a black oil-like paste. You simply brush it on to the metal and then carefully bring the metal into contact with the wood. Where there's contact at the high points you'll find a trace of the inletting black. It's then just a matter of cutting away the wood where you have contact. Eventually you should get close to 100% contact between the rear of the receiver and the head of the stock.

It's slow, messy work and it can be especially challenging when you're working on the end grain of a piece of wood. I used a variety of small chisels that were as sharp as I could make 'em. If there was ever a situation where you absolutely had to have sharp tools, this is it!

As you repeatedly check the wood to receiver fit, be sure to keep the position of the buttstock the same each and every time. If you allow the angle to change, you will get a false reading with the inletting black. Admittedly this is kinda hard to do especially when you're really only inletting one part or portion of the stock head. Just go slow, be careful, and you'll get it done!

Once the receiver was fully inletted, I finished shaping the new wood. The stock bolt was installed and the buttstock was pulled tightly against the receiver. I initially used a number of small coarse files. I had to be careful that I didn't strike the receiver or the rest of the stock. At various times I used pieces of masking tape to protect the receiver and the stock.

When I finished with the files I moved on to sandpaper. I started out with 120 grit and worked my way up to 220. Again, the emphasis was on avoiding sanding the metal or the rest of the stock. To help with this I again used masking tape to protect these surfaces. I always used a sanding block of some sort to keep my surfaces flat and true.

Once the sanding was completed, I dampened the wood with a wet cloth and then dried it with a hot air gun. I did this to raise the grain. The wood was then sanded again with the fine 220-grit sandpaper. I didn't raise the grain as often

Coffield cut a spiral groove around the dowel to allow air and excess glue to escape, then used a pull saw to cut it off almost flush with the face of the butt.

as when working on a new stock. Keep in mind the objective is to have the new wood splice match the general color and texture of the buttstock.

The next step was to make sure the "new" wood looked old and matched the rest of the stock. I had a variety of wood stains I picked up from the folks at Brownells. However, before applying any stains I once again washed the buttstock down with turpentine. I not only cleaned the stock a bit more but this washing also helped to stain the new wood patch with some of the residue lifted from the rest of the stock.

I then used the Simple Green biodegradable cleaner after the initial washing with turpentine. Frankly I just wanted to experiment further with this product. It worked and it helped to pull out additional grease and gunk from the stock.

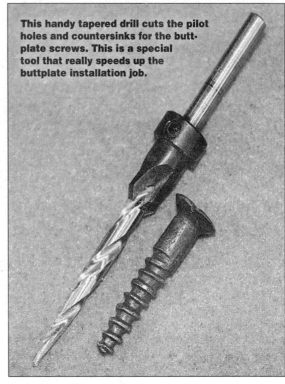

This handy tapered drill cuts the pilot holes and countersinks for the buttplate screws. This is a special tool that really speeds up the buttplate installation job.

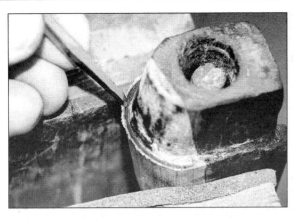

Almost done! Inletting black lets Coffield know precisely where he needs to remove wood for a perfect wood-to-metal fit. He wants a clean line for this spot.

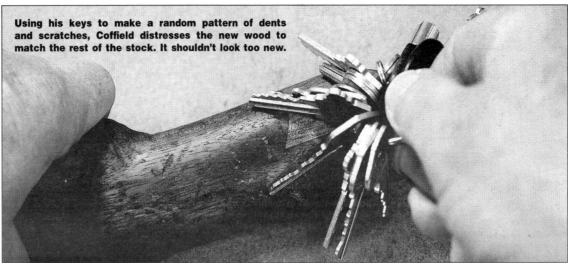

Using his keys to make a random pattern of dents and scratches, Coffield distresses the new wood to match the rest of the stock. It shouldn't look too new.

Judicious use of files and sandpaper, secured to sanding blocks, left a smooth, tight fit between the stock and the new wood that will be invisible after finishing.

The wood of the repair is much lighter than the stock so I wanted to stain it a bit. I will eventually use tung oil on the stock and this will darken it, but it has been my experience that it's best to get the color of the two woods as close as possible before applying any finish. Also, many finishes will make it almost impossible for some water and alcohol based stains to effectively color the wood.

So I first gathered my stains. I had about a dozen different types, all of them from Brownells. They have a great selection of stains and I don't know of anyone that offers more different types. I tested the stains on a part of the repair that would be hidden by the receiver.

After testing about six different stains, I found my best match with the Birchwood Casey walnut stock stain. I applied this to the repair and then wiped it down with a paper towel to remove any excess. Once this was allowed to dry overnight, I applied a coat of tung oil.

After the initial coat of tung oil was applied to the entire buttstock, I "distressed" the repair. Keep in mind that the rest of the stock shows about 125 years worth of scratches, dents, dings and gouges while the repaired area is perfectly smooth. That's just not natural!

Using my keys like a flail, I worked over the repair. You don't want to overdo it, but in general you want the surface to have about the same amount of dings and scars as the rest of the stock. The two biggest dangers in distressing wood are overdoing it or not making the marks in a random pattern. One trick to help with this is to find a scar in the stock next to the repair and continue the scar into the new wood. This helps to visually blend the two pieces of wood together.

After scarring the wood, I used a bit more dark stain to simulate the natural collection of gunk and crud down in the new scratches and dents. I just applied the stain with a Q-tip and wiped off the excess with a paper towel.

At this point, I started working on the metal. The major task was just cleaning off the accumulated rust and crud. For the most part, I used a brass toothbrush. You have to be darn careful that you don't use a cleaning tool that is so tough and abrasive that it removes the patina of age from the metal. You definitely don't want a bright raw metal finish showing.

There is a tendency to use a wire wheel for work like this. If you have a wire wheel with very fine wire teeth, you can sometimes do this and it can sure save time. However, if all you have is a standard hardware store medium or coarse wire wheel, I will almost guarantee that you'll do more damage than good.

While you can still spot the repair, the casual observer might think it is as old as the rest of the rifle. Military guns almost always will have period repairs.

If you're in doubt about the suitability of your wire wheel or if you're not sure of your technique using it, don't! If you stick to the less abrasive brass brushes, you shouldn't have any problems. By the way, I picked up my brass brushes at the local Harbor Freight store. They're cheap and they work!

As I cleaned the breechblock, I found that it had been cracked and later repaired by brazing. It was an interesting repair and it definitely reinforced my decision to make sure this rifle could not be fired in the future. It is a fascinating artifact but it is, in my opinion, not safe to fire. Because of liability

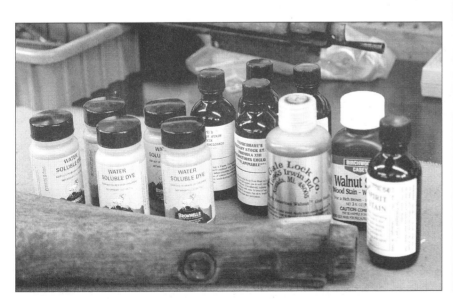

Coffield experimented with a lot of different wood stains and water-soluble dyes to find the best match for coloring the new wood. Matching can be an exacting process.

Coffield found the rifle's trigger return spring was broken. He used its stub to scribe lines in a piece of hardware-store mild steel that would serve as a replacement.

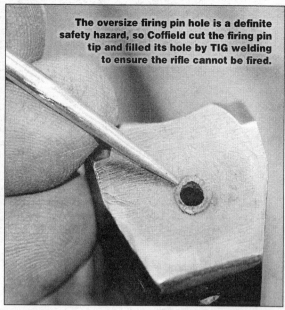

The oversize firing pin hole is a definite safety hazard, so Coffield cut the firing pin tip and filled its hole by TIG welding to ensure the rifle cannot be fired.

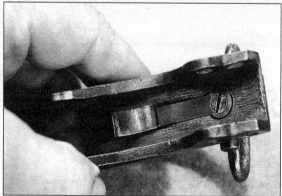

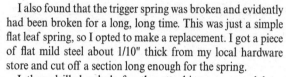

After proper shaping, the spring needed only to be heat-treated and trimmed to the proper length before Coffield screwed it back into the bottom of the rifle's receiver.

concerns I definitely want to make it extremely difficult if not impossible for anyone that later owns this rifle to fire it.

Many years ago when I was a teenager I found an old shotgun in my grandfather's workshop. I, of course, tinkered with the gun until I could get it to fire and I eventually shot it. That was a mistake! It had some safety problems I was not aware of and I almost got hurt. The folks that put it there knew it was unsafe but I didn't! I've never forgotten that experience and it has tended to make me very conservative about this issue of demilling unsafe guns.

To deactivate this rifle I first cut the tip off the firing pin. By the way, the firing pin was far too big and improperly shaped. It would probably have pierced a primer if it had been used. I also welded up firing pin hole in the face of the breechblock. This will still allow the action to cycle so you can see how the rifle works but it should keep most folks from ever firing it. If someone does fire it someday, he will have to do a *lot* of work!

I also found that the trigger spring was broken and evidently had been broken for a long, long time. This was just a simple flat leaf spring, so I opted to make a replacement. I got a piece of flat mild steel about 1/10" thick from my local hardware store and cut off a section long enough for the spring.

I then drilled a hole for the attaching screw and later used that hole as the central point to draw the outline of the rest of the spring. The excess steel was cut away using a hacksaw and files. The original spring was about .070" thick at the screw hole. I made mine just a tad thicker.

Once this was done, I polished the spring to remove any scratches or file marks. If you leave marks or scratches in the surface, these can later become stress points and the spring will break.

There was one pin and one screw missing from the action. The screw held the action assembly in the receiver and the pin served as the pivot for the breechblock. Both of these had been replaced with bits of wood! I initially thought that both were pins until I found threads in the receiver for the screw. It was a simple matter to just turn down some mild steel rod to replace the pin. I certainly didn't try to do anything fancy. I just wanted to have something to hold the various parts in place and allow the gun to cycle properly. Fortunately I got lucky and found a screw that I

could modify to replace the missing screw. You don't get that lucky very often!

After that, it was just a matter of a bit more cleaning and oiling down all the components. The rifle was then reassembled. I left a couple of "problem areas" as I found them. The most noticeable was the lever retainer located in the buttstock. This part was not properly inletted when the rifle was built, so I felt that correcting the problem was not appropriate as it would change part of the history and character of the gun.

You could, of course, make the same claim about the fit of the buttstock to the receiver. However, the buttstock repair was done to prevent further damage which I believe would have occurred. Also, that repair made the gun a bit more attractive and helped, I hope, to ensure its survival. The lever retainer, on the other hand, is a fairly minor component and would have little effect on the appearance and survivability of the gun.

It certainly isn't a high dollar collectable but it's an interesting piece of history. I'm happy to own it and it'll find a place on the wall in my office. Whenever I look at it, I'll always have visions of Gurkha troops high in the Himalayas or outnumbered British soldiers standing shoulder to shoulder facing native armies. It's the romance of history and this old rifle is definitely a part of that.

Until next time, good luck and good gunsmithing! ◉

It's definitely an old warhorse that's seen extensive use but it'll make a great wall-hanger for Reid's office, and compared to a "before" version, it looks great.

If you look closely, you can see a crack in the breechblock that some forgotten smith closed up by brazing, just one more reason why this rifle should never be fired.

Ask the Gunsmith

By Reid Coffield

BUFFING VS. POLISHING

Q *I am confused by the terms "buffing" and "polishing." In talking with various gunsmiths I hear the terms used interchangeably. Do they really have the same meaning? Is there a difference between "buffing" and "polishing?"*

A I am not sure if this is technically correct but years ago at the Colorado School of Trades where I got my gunsmithing training, I was taught that polishing entailed the removal of surface metal on the workpiece. By removing metal you were able to get down below pits, scratches, and other imperfections. This resulted in a smooth, uniform surface.

Buffing, on the other hand, entails little or no metal removal. The only objective in buffing is normally the removal of tiny hair line scratches left by the final polishing process resulting in a perfectly smooth, high gloss finish.

The compounds used on muslin, felt, or sisal wheels for polishing are normally coarser than the compounds used for buffing. However, some polishing compounds can be extremely fine and produce very high gloss finishes. My experience has been similar to yours in that I find that most folks do tend to use the terms interchangeably.

LATHE LEARNING

Q *I have been doing some hobby gunsmithing for quite a few years. Up until now I have only used basic hand tools. I have been thinking about buying a lathe, but I want to be able to learn to use one before I make the purchase. Is there anyplace I could go to take a course on using a lathe before I buy one?*

Metal lathes like this one from Grizzly Industrial are well within the means of today's hobby gunsmith, but it's not a tool on which to learn by doing. Get some qualified instruction before trying it.

A Check with the folks at Murray State College, One Murray Campus, Dept. SGN, Tishomingo, Okla. 73460. Murray State offers a series of NRA Summer Gunsmithing Courses, including a one-week course on basic lathe operation. I think this would be just what you are looking for. Call Dean Arnold, the NRA Coordinator at the college, at 580-371-2371, ext. 235. He can get you all set up. By the way, Murray State offers a variety of other NRA summer courses ranging from stockmaking to engraving to color-casehardening. It's a great program and well worth checking out.

7.62x51MM HEADSPACE GAUGES

Q *I know that the 7.62mm NATO cartridge is dimensionally different from the .308 Win. My problem is finding 7.62mm headspace gauges. Where can I get a set?*

Forster offers both 7.62x51mm and .308 Win. headspace gauges. The difference between the two is small, but for precision work, the correct gauge is well worth having.

A That's easy! Check with the good folks at Forster Products, 310 E. Lanark Ave., Dept. SGN, Lanark, IL 61046, telephone 815-493-6360. They offer the 7.62mm NATO gauges, along with sets of .308 Win. headspace gauges in increments of one thousandth. Their gauges are first rate and I've been using them for years and years.

Gunsmithing the Russian Nagant Revolver

Part 1
By Reid Coffield

Although he has been gunsmithing for many years, Coffield had not worked on the Russian Nagant revolvers which are now quite commonly available at most gun shows.

Every gun show has a few of these unusual revolvers, but few have tried to gunsmith them. Here Coffield shows a few tricks for upgrading the old warhorse.

My grandmother was an amazing woman. As a kid, her father took the family from their home in western North Carolina to Oklahoma and Texas in search of a fortune he never quite found. During those years in the latter part of the 19th century, Grandma had quite an adventure. She traveled by horse and by wagon, she came face to face with the famous Comanche Quanah Parker, and she saw cattle drives, cowboys, and outlaws.

It was a remarkable experience for a young woman from the foothills of Carolina. In her later years her adventures would keep one particular grandson spellbound for hours as she told story after story of her time in the west.

Like many women of her age and time, she called upon a vast array of folksy sayings to instruct the young. No matter what the situation, Grandma could always be counted on to share a pearl of wisdom such as "waste not, want not" or "a stitch in time saves nine" and so on. I have to admit that at the time many of those sayings meant absolutely nothin' to me... .I couldn't figure 'em out! But they must've been important since Grandma set such store by 'em.

There was one that she was particularly fond of and any time I would voice a judgment about someone or something, she would trot out this old horse. It's been over 40 years since she passed on but I can still hear her saying as only an elderly Southern lady can, "Don't judge a book by its cover."

I have to admit that many times I have done just that, not only with people but with guns as well. The Nagant revolver is a prime example of my forming an opinion based just on looks.

Nagant revolvers have been around for quite a while and we've recently seen a lot of 'em imported by the good folks at Century Arms International from Russia and other countries formerly under Soviet control. It's not a thing of beauty to say the least. The revolver was basically designed by the Nagant brothers, Emile and Henri-Leon, who owned an arms manufacturing plant in Belgium. The Nagant brothers produced a variety of firearms and sold a substantial number to the smaller countries that could not afford their own armsmaking facilities.

Eventually they landed a contract with the Imperial Russian government for about 20,000 revolvers. These were unique in that the design and cartridge were such that the gap between the cylinder

and the rear of the barrel was sealed when the cartridge was fired. This was a unique feature that most other revolvers didn't have.

Upon firing a standard Colt or Smith and Wesson there is a gap between the cylinder and barrel. This permits the escape of some of the gas created by the burning powder. Theoretically this would lead to a reduction in pressure behind the bullet and a loss of velocity. Years ago I remember reading an article in the *American Rifleman* by Pete Dickey about the Nagant in which he determined through testing that there was about a 15 to 20% increase in velocity due to the lack of a gap between the barrel and cylinder.

That's certainly not much, but if you were a firearms salesman back in the 1890s, you could sure go to town with somethin' like that. Evidently the Nagant boys did just that and made a darn good deal with the Russians.

Not only did they sell the revolvers, they also sold the Russians the tooling and gauges necessary for them to set up their own production in the Tula Arsenal. The Russians were evidently pleased with the handgun and it stayed in production through World War II.

I can not ever remember having one of these revolvers come into my shop but I did see them at gun shows from time to time. No matter how you slice it or dice it, they are just plain ugly. To me it seems too angular or disjointed. There are no smooth lines or curves. Instead there are short abrupt lines that seem to change direction every half inch. Also, it just looks like it was made up of spare parts. It's a hard gun to love! Besides having grown up in the '50s and '60s, it was a Communist gun and no red-blooded American boy would have one.

Times change, you get older and anyway, I ultimately ended up with one a few years ago that was produced in 1913. I got it because of my interest in World War I firearms. I never shot it and since then it's been consigned to the vault. I hadn't thought much about it until I was at a small gun show and ran across a Nagant cylinder in .32 ACP. The Nagant is normally chambered for a 7.62 x 39 mm rimmed cartridge that can be a bit hard to find.

Currently Fiocchi produces this ammo and it's available through MidwayUSA, 5875 West Van Horn Tavern Road, Dept. SGN, Columbia, Mo. 65203, telephone 800-243-3220. While it's great ammo, the cost is pretty steep. At this time, a box of 50 rounds of the Fiocchi ammo sells for $35.99. Some Russian and eastern European ammo is occasionally available through suppliers advertising in SHOTGUN NEWS. However, the idea of a cylinder that would allow me to fire the inexpensive and readily available .32 ACP round seemed like a really neat idea so I bought it.

Not long after that I was talking with one of the fellows at Century Arms and he mentioned that they had had some .32 cylinders made for the Nagant. Since my cylinder was unmarked and came off a table piled with all sorts of odds and ends, I had no idea who produced it. By the time we finished talking I found myself not only the proud possessor of another cylinder, but I also ended up with *another* Nagant.

This second revolver was a target model with a heavier barrel and adjustable sights. It was originally produced in 1944 and then converted to a target configuration at some later date. By the way if you're in the market for one of these revolvers or for almost any other military surplus firearm, contact the folks at Century Arms, 430 South Congress Dr., Suite 1, Dept. SGN, Del Ray Beach, Fla. 33445, telephone 800-527-1252. They are by far and away the largest importer of military firearms in the U.S. and offer some amazing items.

Later I was talking to a buddy and he produced another Nagant! His was a standard revolver produced in 1945. It was in excellent condition. He purchased it several years ago just as a curio. He loaned it to me so I could compare it to the other Nagants.

With three revolvers and two spare cylinders I decided that it was time to get serious about this unusual handgun. One of the first things I discovered was that the two cylinders did not necessarily fit the handguns. The cylinder I got from Century Arms fit both the target revolver and my old 1913 gun. My gun show cylinder fit the target revolver but not the 1913 piece. Neither cylinder fit my friend's 1945 revolver.

Start disassembly by turning out the takedown screw on the right side of the frame. Then tap on the left side of the trigger guard to pop loose the sideplate.

I was puzzled and decided that I was going to fit these cylinders to my old 1913 revolver as well as the target model. By the way, the folks at Century told me that it had been their experience that there were often dimensional variations in the Nagants and the cylinders did not always drop in. It was a challenge, and by golly, I was going to figure it out.

The first thing I did was to mark each cylinder so I could keep track of what fit and what didn't fit. Anytime you're trying to fit extra parts to a firearm, always be sure to mark the parts so you won't get them confused. It doesn't matter whether it's an oddball handgun like these Nagants or a common Model 10 Smith and Wesson or Ruger Security Six, failure to mark your parts and keep track of them can make your task virtually impossible.

The trigger pull on the 1945 revolver as well as my two was poor at best and all of them needed some trigger work. The target revolver also had a pretty rough barrel crown and needed to be recrowned before it was to be shot. Generally other than tuning triggers and perhaps fitting one of the new .32 ACP cylinders, there is darn little work that you will probably ever have to perform on the Nagants. From what I have read these revolvers were well regarded in Russia for their durability and reliability. The darn things seldom broke!

...these revolvers were well regarded in Russia for their durability and reliability. The darn things seldom broke!

The first order of business was to take care of the terrible triggers. By the way, the Nagants were initially produced in both single- and double-action. According to most sources, the single-actions were for enlisted soldiers while the double-actions were issued to officers. My 1913 is a single-action.

The target revolver was originally produced in 1944 as a double-action. However when it was converted for target shooting the double-action mechanism was modified and it was useable

Note the hole in the frame above the top of the "V" spring and in the notch of the hammer. The takedown screw can be threaded into the hole to further aid disassembly.

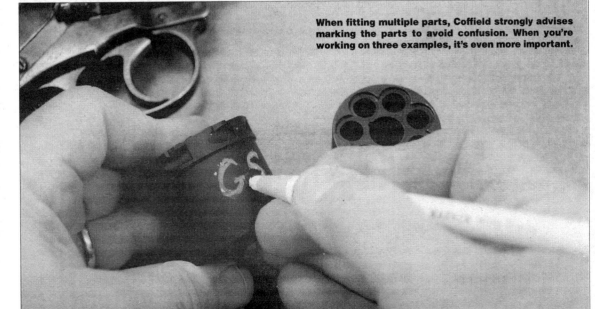

When fitting multiple parts, Coffield strongly advises marking the parts to avoid confusion. When you're working on three examples, it's even more important.

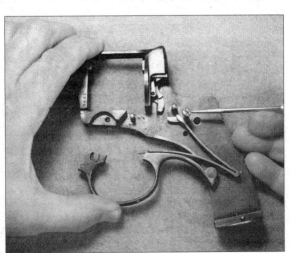

The takedown screw helps to capture the "V" mainspring as the trigger guard is pivoted down after removal of the hammer, trigger and other moving parts of the frame.

only as a single-action. The only difference between the double-action model and the single-action model is a different hammer assembly with a double-action hammer pawl and a slightly modified sliding wedge. My friend's revolver, produced in 1945, was still double-action.

Working on the trigger pull of a Nagant is not at all like working on a K-frame Smith. You can pretty well forget getting a smooth, light double-action pull. The design of the Nagant simply has the trigger doing too many things during double-action to allow for a reasonable pull.

As the trigger is drawn back during double-action operation, the hammer is pivoted back, the sliding wedge is pushed up, the cylinder is rotated, and at the same time the cylinder is pushed forward. Also, the moveable breechblock that supports the cartridge head is also pushed forward and locked in place by the sliding wedge. That is a lot of motion and friction.

The Russians considered it a lost cause and made their target revolvers single-action only. Realistically, I believe that it is best to work just on getting a light, crisp single-action pull. If you can do that, you've done a great job!

The first course of action was to measure the weight of pull of each revolver using a Lyman electronic trigger pull gauge. The 1913 revolver had a 10 pound, 13.5 ounce pull; the target revolver had a 7 pound pull; and the 1945 revolver was right at 10 pounds, 6 ounces. All obviously need some major TLC. Just to put this in perspective, a Smith and Wesson Model 17 that I happen to have in the shop had a single-action pull of just 3 pounds, 7 ounces and that was just as it came from the factory.

The fact that the "target" revolver had such as heavy pull just amazed me as I would have thought that for competitive work the pull would have been much lighter.

After weighing the trigger pulls, the next step was to determine just what the major mechanical factors were that caused the pull to be so darn bad. As you might expect, the angle and width of the engaging surfaces between the trigger and hammer were important factors.

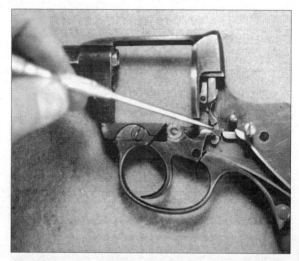

The tail of the trigger is positioned in a cut out in the sliding wedge that moves and locks the breechblock in place. The Nagant lockwork is unusually complex.

Note the engagement between the hammer and the trigger of Coffield's 1913-manufactured single-action Nagant. Single-actions were issued to enlisted personnel.

The double-action revolvers have a slightly different hammer assembly that incorporates a pawl for trigger cocking. The sliding wedge is also slightly modified.

However, the most significant element affecting the trigger pull was not the hammer or the trigger; it was the lower leg of the "V" mainspring. As you pull the trigger you are compressing this robust spring. By simply lightening this spring, you can significantly alter the trigger pull.

That's all well and good, but how the heck do you lighten this "V" spring? Glad you asked. All you need to do is carefully thin the lower leg of the spring. This is done using an abrasive sanding drum on a Dremel hand grinder. This was then followed by careful polishing on an 8-inch diameter polishing wheel to remove any grinding marks left by the Dremel tool. When you are using the small sanding drums you absolutely must grind lengthwise along the leg of the spring. Do not under any circumstances grind across the spring.

Be careful that you do not get the spring hot, as this could easily ruin it and give you nothing but a "V" shaped piece of soft scrap. A good rule of thumb is to cool the spring by quenching in a cup of water whenever it becomes warm to the touch. Yeah, it makes for a long job but you won't ruin your spring. Just take your time and *always* quench frequently.

On the 1913 revolver, the spring measured about .040" thick at the end of the leg and .057" thick 1.750 inches back. The target revolver measured .035" thick at the end of the leg and tapered back to .045" thick at the 1.750-inch mark. By careful grinding and then polishing, the 1913 revolver spring was reduced to .0335" thickness at the end of the leg and .039" thick at the 1.750 mark.

When reinstalled in the revolver, this gave a trigger pull weight of 4 pounds, 8 ounces. That's a pretty significant change. In fact, it was so light that I was worried as to whether or not I had taken it down too far. To test this I installed the Century Arms .32 ACP cylinder and then pulled the bullet on a Winchester .32 ACP cartridge with an inertia bullet puller.

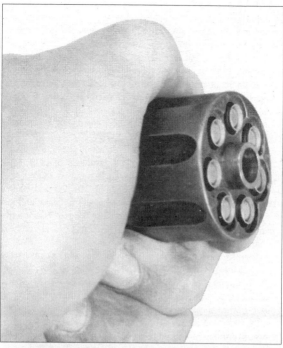

The 7.62 Nagant cartridge extends beyond the face of the cylinder to form a gas seal between the cylinder and the barrel when the former slides forward in the frame.

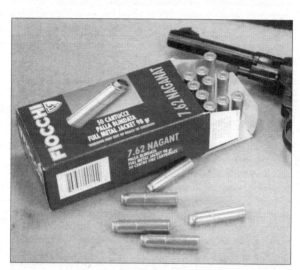

Currently Italian made Fiocchi ammunition is available from MidwayUSA. It is very reliable, well-made ammo, but the price is pretty brutal for any extended firing.

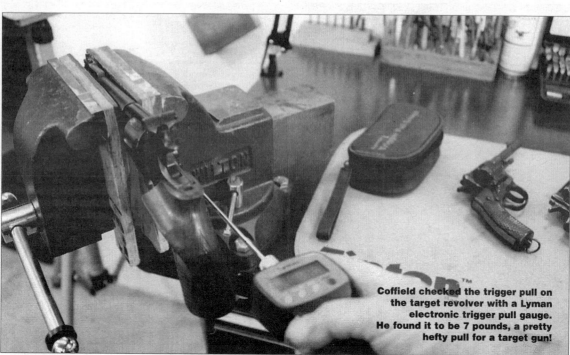

Coffield checked the trigger pull on the target revolver with a Lyman electronic trigger pull gauge. He found it to be 7 pounds, a pretty hefty pull for a target gun!

An adjustable rear sight base was welded to the frame of a standard 1944 production Nagant during the conversion. This sight is only adjustable for windage.

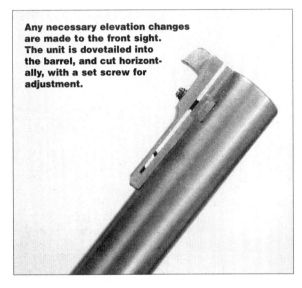

Any necessary elevation changes are made to the front sight. The unit is dovetailed into the barrel, and cut horizontally, with a set screw for adjustment.

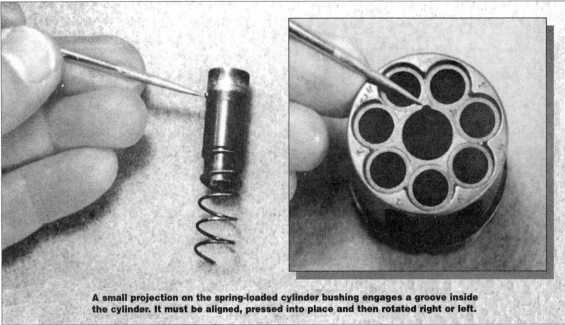

A small projection on the spring-loaded cylinder bushing engages a groove inside the cylinder. It must be aligned, pressed into place and then rotated right or left.

Also, if you check the inside of the frame, you may find wear or drag marks made by the spring. Narrowing the width of the spring is often the best way to eliminate this contact. This will make the spring more efficient as the energy will be totally transferred to the hammer rather than wasted against the sides of the frame.

With the weight of pull on the 1913 taken care of, I was still not completely pleased with the trigger. I could feel creep or movement of the trigger before the hammer fell. This was due to the fact that the sear surface on the hammer was a bit too wide. All it would take would be to carefully stone back the tip or end of the hammer sear notch. The trick is to do that without canting it.

The empty primed case was then installed in the cylinder and rotated until it was under the hammer. When the hammer fell, the primer ignited so I believe we are OK. Remember that these springs had to be strong enough originally to ensure functioning under the worst conditions of cold, dirt, mud, etc. In that sense they are "overpowered" for the conditions under which you or I will typically use these revolvers.

As you work on the mainspring, keep in mind that you can also do a bit of polishing and reshaping to the sides of the spring to lighten it a bit. As always, you will grind and polish lengthwise to the spring. You can carefully add a bit of taper to the spring if you wish.

Unfortunately there are no commercially available jigs or holding fixtures for this unusual revolver. However, as my old grandmother would say, "Where there's a will, there's a way"!

All you need is a small vise with parallel jaws whose tops are even. Just place the hammer between the jaws with just a thousandth or so of the tip of the hammer protruding above the jaws. Now take an India stone and carefully stone down

However, as my old grandmother would say, "Where there's a will, there's a way"!

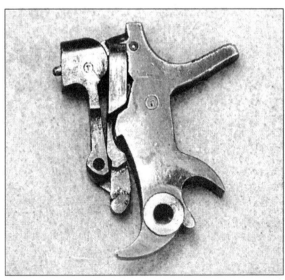

The hammer, wedge, and breechblock are shown in their proper positions at the moment of firing. You can appreciate why this revolver has such a long firing pin!

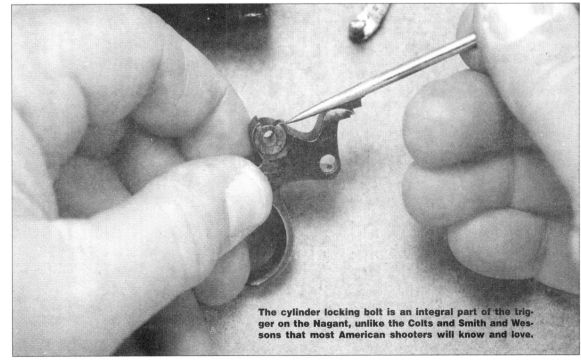

The cylinder locking bolt is an integral part of the trigger on the Nagant, unlike the Colts and Smith and Wessons that most American shooters will know and love.

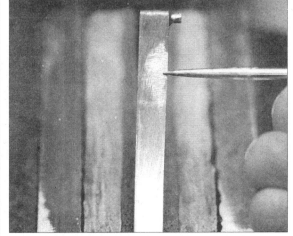

The target revolver had a "V" mainspring that had been improperly ground. Note the grind marks that run across the spring rather than lengthwise. Never do this!

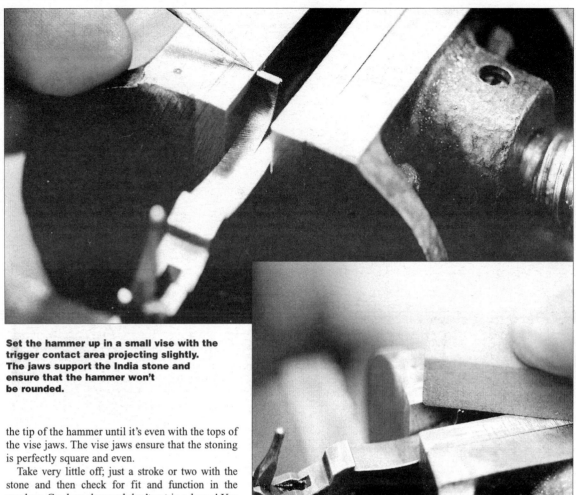

Set the hammer up in a small vise with the trigger contact area projecting slightly. The jaws support the India stone and ensure that the hammer won't be rounded.

the tip of the hammer until it's even with the tops of the vise jaws. The vise jaws ensure that the stoning is perfectly square and even.

Take very little off; just a stroke or two with the stone and then check for fit and function in the revolver. Go darn slow and don't get in a hurry! You can always take off more metal but puttin' it back is a bear!

With the trigger work completed on both the target revolver and the 1913, my next job was to try and determine why one of the .32 ACP cylinders would not work in the 1913. Both cylinders would fit just fine in the target revolver but only the Century Arms cylinder would work properly in the 1913. I initially installed the gun show cylinder in the 1913 and carefully checked to determine if there was any interference with the rear end of the barrel. There was none.

I then looked at how the hand moved the cylinder. With the sideplate off the revolver, I could see that the trigger was not cycling completely because the hand was binding on the cylinder ratchet. The cylinder was properly aligned with the bore, but the ratchet was bearing against the hand and not allowing the hand to move far enough to permit the hammer to be fully cocked.

Just to be sure that I was on the right track, I took the original cylinder and the good Century Arms cylinder and compared the angle of the ratchet cuts. It was most revealing. My gun show cylinder had a much shallower angle. This was made evident by laying a straightedge along the engaging surface of the ratchet and extending it over the chamber. The straight edge on the "good" cylinders extended noticeably further over the chambers. It was readily evident.

No sweat, or so I thought. I pulled out my Barrett file which I normally use to recut ratchets. To my surprise the file would not even scratch the surface of the ratchet. It was harder than woodpecker lips! Next I tried some diamond-coated needle files. These did move some metal, but it was obvious that it would take far longer than I wanted to invest in this job.

The crown on the target revolver is rough and uneven. If you look closely you can see a rough taper into the bore. Obviously "target" can be a very relative term!

Ideally you would use a precision grinder to reshape the ratchet but I don't have one. Consequently I had to re-evaluate my objective. While it would be nice to have both .32 ACP cylinders work with either revolver, this just wasn't gonna happen. Instead I marked the cylinders to ensure that I could tell them apart and put the gun show cylinder with the target revolver and the good Century Arms cylinder with the 1913 revolver.

As I mentioned earlier, the muzzle crown on the target revolver was a bit rough and pitted. Evidently at some point the bore had rusted. Someone probably fired corrosive ammo and then failed to clean properly. Fortunately, I just happened to have the best hand crowning tool currently manufactured available for testing.

This patented tool is produced by Dave Manson of Manson Precision Reamers in Grand Blanc, Mich., telephone 810-953-0732. Unlike other currently available traditional hand crowning tools that use standard fixed blade cutters, Dave's tool uses tiny replaceable carbide blades that closely resemble and act like fine files. This virtually eliminates any possibility of chatter which is so common with other tools.

Another great feature of the Manson crowing tool is the utilization of precision ground expandable pilots that perfectly fit the bore. Other tools may use pilots but these seldom are a perfect fit for the bore. After all, a .30 pilot must fit all .30 bores even though bores will often vary larger or smaller by several thousandths. It doesn't sound like much but even a tiny bit of

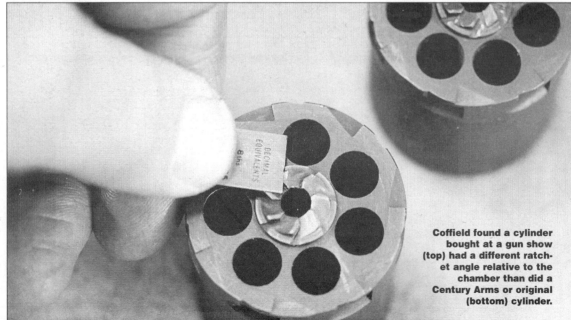

Coffield found a cylinder bought at a gun show (top) had a different ratchet angle relative to the chamber than did a Century Arms or original (bottom) cylinder.

The Manson crowning tool has three small, precisely fitted carbide files in the cutting head, which is supported and guided by an adjustable expanding bore pilot.

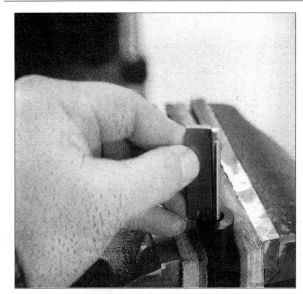

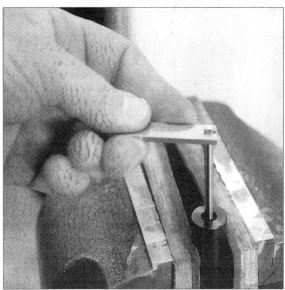

The pilot wrench serves as a gauge to position the bore pilot, and then to expand it in the bore. Precise fit of the pilot and cutter head means no chatter.

looseness will lead to chatter. Manson effectively solved this problem with his precision adjustable pilots.

In use, the pilot is inserted into the bore and expanded with a special wrench until it is a snug, firm fit. The cutter assembly is then placed over the shank of the pilot that extends out the barrel. After lubricating with cutting oil, the cutter is turned clockwise by hand as it is held against the face of the muzzle. Simple and easy.

Coffield finds the Manson Crowning Tool the best hand operated crowning tool available. A good tool means good work. This crown was cut by hand in about 15 minutes.

Manson supplies both a 90° facing cutter, an 11° target crown cutter, and an outside chamfering cutter to taper the outside edge of the barrel. Using first the 90° cutter followed by the 11° target crown cutter, it took less than 15 minutes to remove the original damaged crown completely. The new crown is clean, sharp, and chatter free.

It is an absolutely amazing tool. No, it's not cheap but quality tools like these never are. The tool kit with two cutters, the driving mechanism, wrench, setup gauge, case, manual, and two pilots of your choice will run $295, and in my humble opinion, it's worth every penny. The complete, master kit with 10 pilots and the outside deburring/chamfering cutter sells for $650. I would encourage anyone serious about gunsmithing to consider this fine tool.

With the trigger pulls reduced and a new crown on the target revolver, the next step will be to see just how these puppies shoot. In the next and final installment I'll use a new handgun machine rest to test these handguns. I am especially interested to see how the guns shoot with the .32 ACP cylinders.

As I have worked on these Nagants I've developed a much greater appreciation and respect for them. While the machine work, especially on those produced during World War II, is rough

or even crude by American standards, the mechanism is unique and fascinating. It was a transitional design developed in the late 19th century when so many designs and ideas about firearms were being developed and tested.

What is remarkable is that it stayed in production and served well into the 20th century. Even though it looks cheap and fragile, it soldiered on through quite a few wars and revolutions in some of the toughest and most brutal environments in the world. It's really an amazing handgun. As my old grandmother would quickly point out, "Don't judge a book by its cover" or a firearm by it appearance!

Until next time, good luck and good gunsmithing!

Note how the cutting head produces fine, hair-like metal chips, leading to an incredibly smooth cut surface. There's no substitute for the right tool for the job.

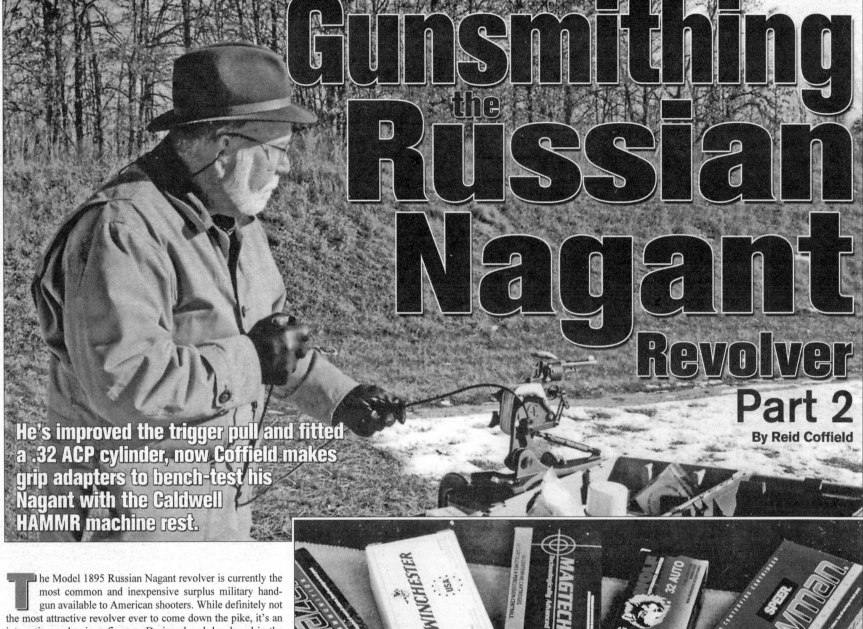

Gunsmithing the Russian Nagant Revolver
Part 2
By Reid Coffield

He's improved the trigger pull and fitted a .32 ACP cylinder, now Coffield makes grip adapters to bench-test his Nagant with the Caldwell HAMMR machine rest.

Coffield modified his Nagant revolver for a better trigger pull and to accept a .32 ACP cylinder for cheaper shooting. Now it was time to bench-test it for accuracy.

The Model 1895 Russian Nagant revolver is currently the most common and inexpensive surplus military handgun available to American shooters. While definitely not the most attractive revolver ever to come down the pike, it's an interesting and unique firearm. Designed and developed in the late 19th century by the Belgian arms producers, Leon and Emile Nagant, it was adopted by the Russian Imperial government in 1895 and continued to serve the Russian military until well after World War II.

Though it's fragile looking, it's actually a pretty tough old bird that developed a reputation in Russia for reliability and durability. Keep in mind that during its 50+ years of service, it saw use in every conceivable type of climate and under extreme conditions. From jungles to deserts, from sea service with naval troops to arming aircraft crewmen, the Nagant revolver has truly "been there and done that" as much, if not more than many other better known military firearms.

The only "fly in the buttermilk" with the Nagant is the caliber. Not only was the original military 7.62mm round loaded with a little 108-grain bullet propelled at a very modest 1000 feet per second velocity, modern commercial ammo for the 1895 can be expensive and hard to find.

Probably the best commercial ammo is that loaded by Fiocchi. This ammo is available here in the U.S. from MidwayUSA, 5875 W. Van Horn Tavern Rd., Dept. SGN, Columbia, Mo. 65203, telephone 1-800-243-3220. The ammo is not cheap at $40.99 per box of 50 but it's darn good quality ammo and if all you want is one or two boxes, that's the place to get it. By the way, the Fiocchi ammo is loaded with a slightly lighter 92-grain bullet than the original military ammo.

I like to shoot my Nagant but I definitely could not afford to shoot a lot of this ammo, it's just too expensive for me. Consequently I jumped at the chance to pick up a .32 ACP cylinder for my old 1913-dated Russian revolver. This was found at a local gun show and goodness knows where it came from or who made it.

I later got another one from the good folks at Century International Arms, Inc., 430 South Congress Dr., Suite 1, Dept. SGN, DelRay Beach, Fla. 33445, telephone 800-527-1252, website www.centuryarms.com Not only do the folks at Century offer these .32 ACP cylinders but they also offer some great deals on Nagant revolvers including some rather unusual target models. As the largest importer of surplus military arms in the U.S., Century offers some amazing items at very attractive prices.

In fact, when I called Century I initially was just looking for another .32 ACP cylinder. By the time I got off the telephone I'd also picked up one of the Nagant target conversions. Yep, they have some real fine salesmen there as well!

One of the characteristics of all the Model 1895 Nagants I have worked with is an almost universally heavy trigger pull. The hammer is propelled by a very powerful and rugged "V" spring. It was designed with sufficient strength to ensure ignition under extreme conditions and it did just that. However, you and I will not be using our Nagant in a combat situation in the middle of a Russian winter. At most we will probably just be punchin' paper or plinking tin cans with 'em when the weather is nice. In the first article I described the procedure for lightening the trigger pull to a more manageable and comfortable weight.

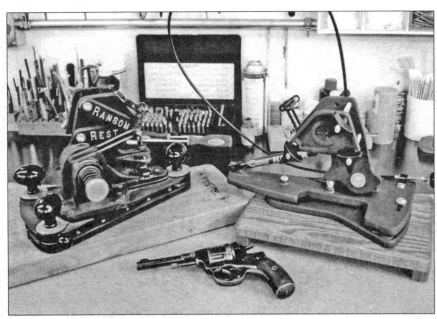

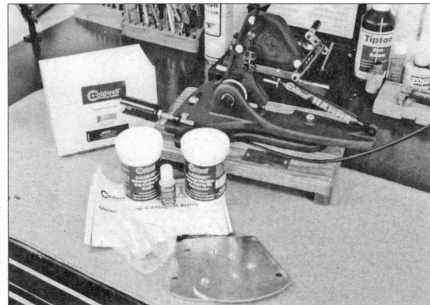

Coffield took advantage of this Nagant test to try the Caldwell HAMMR machine rest (r.), a new and much more economical competitor to the well-proven Ransom Rest.

Ransom offers hundreds of grip adapters for pistols common and obscure. Caldwell is countering with a kit that lets you mold a set of adapters to your own pistol.

This basically involved the careful thinning of the legs of the "V" spring. A word of caution here, if you thin the spring too much, you may get misfires. I would strongly encourage anyone who plans on altering this spring to have a spare on hand just in case you go a bit too far.

Extra mainsprings along with a variety of other parts can be obtained from Mark Kubes Firearms, 8440 Ulmerton Road, Suite 500, Dept. SGN, Largo, Fla. 33771, www.buymilsurp.com. Mark sells the mainsprings for $16 each.

I also covered the fitting of the .32 ACP cylinders. While my two cylinders looked to be identical, there was a very slight

The Caldwell machine rest accepts standard Ransom Rest pistol inserts as well as Caldwell inserts, which are currently made for pistols like the K-frame Smith & Wesson.

difference in how the ratchet on the end of the cylinders was machined. This ratchet is what is engaged by the hand or pawl as the hammer is pulled to the fully cocked position. The hand pushes up and turns the cylinder placing a loaded chamber in front of the firing pin and in alignment with the barrel.

I found that my "gun show" cylinder would only fit my target Nagant, while the Century Arms cylinder fit both the target as well as the older 1913 Nagant. While it would have been nice to have the cylinders fit in both revolvers, the ratchet on the "gun show" cylinder was harder than woodpecker lips. There was no way it could be cut and fit with a file.

Since it would work on one revolver, I decided it was best to accept that and not try to push my luck. Recutting a super hard ratchet like this could only be done properly with much more sophisticated equipment than I had and I didn't want to ruin the cylinder.

With the cylinders fitted and the trigger pulls reduced to manageable proportions, it was time to head to the range. While I appreciated the fact that the .32 ACP cylinders would allow me to shoot inexpensive ammo, I was concerned as to just how well the revolvers would shoot with this conversion. The conversions might deliver accuracy that was in keeping with what I would get with the Fiocchi 7.62mm Nagant ammo or it could be a lot worse. I had no idea as to how it would work out.

In handgun articles one of my pet peeves is reading about folks that go to the range, do a bit of shooting, make excuses about their vision, age, poor shooting, etc. and then state that the

gun shoots groups of a certain size. I am always left wondering just how the heck the darn gun shoots! For that reason, in testing a handgun I always try to use a machine rest.

For years I have used a Ransom Rest for testing handguns. This is a device designed by the late Chuck Ransom back in the 1960s or so. It was the first machine rest made for the consumer. Virtually every serious pistolsmith and upper level competitive pistol shooter I know had one.

In use the handgun is held by the Ransom Rest as it is fired. The only contact the shooter has with it is to reset the device after each shot, load the gun, and depress the trigger activation bar. It is a darn good, well made tool and one that has served me for years.

The only problem with the Ransom Rest is the price. Currently the standard Ransom Rest with the adjustable windage base and one insert to hold a handgun will sell for well in excess of $600. That's not small change! Until recently that was just the price of doin' business if you needed a machine rest.

However, not long ago the folks at Caldwell Shooting Supplies sent me a sample of their new handgun machine rest. It's called the HAMMR and is available from a number of suppliers such as MidwayUSA. It's similar to the Ransom in many ways. In fact, it will use Ransom made inserts to hold the handgun. Unlike the Ransom, the Caldwell HAMMR employs a hydraulic cylinder to help deal with the recoil forces when the handgun is fired and to reset the machine rest after firing. With the Ransom you have to

The HAMMR uses a cable-activated lever mechanism to trip the trigger. The integral windage base allows impact point to be moved left or right on the target.

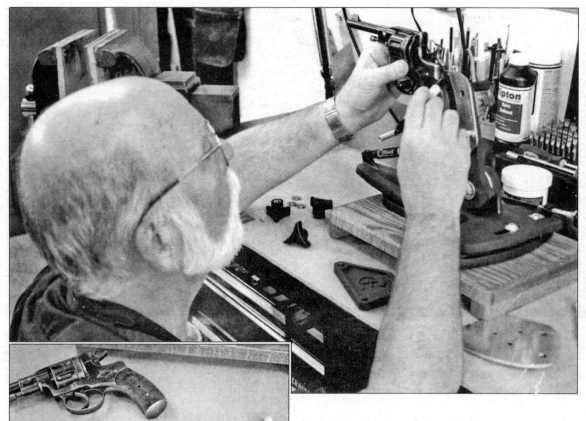

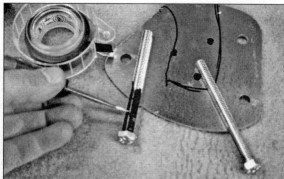

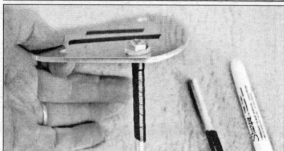

The attaching bolts are wrapped with electrical tape and a clay washer placed between the bolt head and the insert base to prevent leakage of the casting material.

Position the pistol on the rest and mark the location of the grip frame on the aluminum insert base. The barrel should basically be parallel to the base of the rest.

manually push the machine rest forward to set it up for the next shot.

In addition, the Caldwell machine rest incorporates a windage adjusting capability as standard equipment. It's not a $200+ option as with the Ransom. And finally, the Caldwell machine rest offers the user the ability to use a three foot cable release to trigger the handgun. Not only can this provide a nice margin of safety for the user, it allows the user to stand away from the gun as it's fired. You are able to watch the gun and observe its functioning as it fires. This could be very useful under some conditions.

The best news is the price. The Caldwell HAMMR machine rest sells for right at $180. Caldwell brand inserts for many popular handguns are available for $34.99 each. That's quite a difference compared to the Ransom! Because of this I was anxious to get a chance to try out the machine.

That was the good news. The bad news was that neither Ransom nor Caldwell offered inserts for the Nagant revolver. The folks at Caldwell must have been thinking about guys like me who like to work with weird and strange handguns so they offer a Casting Kit to enable you to make up your own inserts. The Casting Kit sells for the same amount as a standard insert, $34.99. It consist of all the materials you will need for this project including two aluminum plates on which you can mount the casting.

Actually you can permanently attach the casting to the plates (as they are with a Ransom Rest adapter) or you can coat the plates with release agent and reuse the plates as needed. I know I will want to have a permanent set of inserts for the Nagant, so I allowed the casting material to bond to the aluminum plates. This makes for a stronger, more durable insert.

The first step in making your set of inserts is to position one of the plates on the machine rest. Next, hold the handgun against the plate so you can determine the angle of the barrel relative to the base of the machine rest. You want to make sure when you cast the insert you don't have the pistol pointing down into the ground or way up into the air! Yes, you do have an elevation

adjustment in the machine rest but you don't want to have to use it all up or worse, have to shim the base just getting the pistol on the target. Generally having the barrel level and parallel to the base of the machine rest will do the trick.

Once you have the handgun set up with the barrel level, use a marker to draw the outline of the grip on the aluminum plate. That will serve as a reference mark when you are positioning the handgun against the plate as you pour in the casting material.

One other thing you'll want to check is the position of the trigger relative to the trigger release bar. Different makes and models of handguns put the trigger in different positions so you'll have to experiment a bit to ensure that you have the trigger positioned to allow it to work properly.

With the position of the handgun relative to the aluminum plate established and marked, the next step is to take the plate off the machine rest along with the three mounting bolts. Wrap a bit of plastic electrical tape around the threaded section of the bolts and then coat the bolts with release agent and insert them through the holes in the plate. This will ensure that the bolts can pass through the casting material when the insert plates are mounted on the machine rest.

Be sure to make three little washers of the modeling clay supplied with the kit to go under the heads of the bolts. The clay will compress when the bolts are seated and provide a seal to keep the casting material from leaking through the bolt holes.

Next a clay dam is constructed around the edge of the plate to contain the casting material. The dam has to be high enough to allow a bit of casting material between the pistol and the plate and yet still cover about one third to three eighths of the width of the frame. Later you'll make another casting to cover the other third to three eighths of the frame. The two can then be used to clamp the frame and securely support the handgun in the machine rest.

You will almost always remove grips from a gun when placing it in a machine rest. Both the Caldwell and Ransom Rest inserts normally are designed to clamp on to the metal frame of the handgun. Generally this ensures that the inserts are clamping against a flat metal surface for maximum rigidity. With the Model 1895 Nagant I did and I didn't! I removed the grips on either side of the frame but I left the spacer that fits between the side plate and the grip portion of the frame.

Pieces of plastic electrical tape were used to cover several open screw holes in the frame. You definitely don't want the casting epoxy flowing into the pistol and permanently attaching it to the insert plates. The frame and the tape were then coated with release agent. This is one time you don't want to be stingy. Make darn sure you coat any part of the handgun that even *might* come in contact with the casting epoxy.

Once the modeling clay dam was constructed around the edge of the insert plate, the casting material was mixed. It's about as simple a mix as you could ask for; one part resin to one part

Coffield says never go cheap with the release agent supplied with the casting kit. You don't want the pistol frame to become a permanent part of the grip adapter.

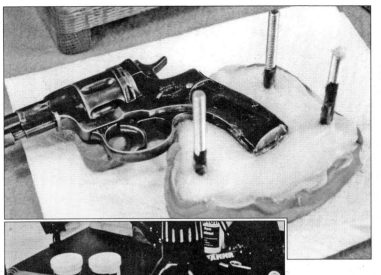

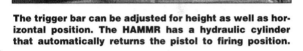

Coffield used a clay support to keep the handgun level as the casting material set up. A bit of extra heat supplied by the bench light helped speed up the process.

The trigger bar can be adjusted for height as well as horizontal position. The HAMMR has a hydraulic cylinder that automatically returns the pistol to firing position.

hardener. I initially started out with five tablespoons of resin and five of hardener. Unfortunately, this did not give me the depth that I wanted, so I mixed an additional three tablespoons of hardener and resin.

Due to the amount of casting material I used, it was necessary to use an additional casting kit. One kit just didn't have enough material to make the insert as large and as deep as I wanted. Also, the frame of the Nagant is relatively small and that just means more casting material is required. When I had a depth of about 3/8 inch, I positioned the pistol so the grip frame extended over the modeling clay dam and supported the front of the pistol with a block of clay.

I wanted to make sure that there was casting material between the pistol grip frame and the insert plate. The inserts must be able to compress around the grip frame. If the frame is contacting either or both of the insert plates, the compression needed will not take place and the pistol will not be held as securely as necessary.

The casting material should not extend to the midpoint of the frame. Ideally I would want it to cover approximately one third the width of the frame. I actually ended up getting the level of the casting material a bit high but that was easily corrected with a quick trip to the disk sander! Later when casting the grip frame insert for the other side of the handgun, I tried to cover approximately one third of the width of the frame. This left the center one third uncovered. By leaving this gap, there would be room for the inserts to compress around the grip frame. The insert material, even when fully cured, is slightly flexible and will compress a bit. It will not set up "rock hard" as will many bedding materials.

In making my grip insert, I cast one half one day and the other half the next. I gave the insert material a good 24 hours to cure before pulling out the pistol frame. Once it was out, it was just a matter of cleaning the insert up, trimming off any excess, and removing all traces of release agent from the grip insert as well as the pistol frame.

With the insert completed, the next stop was one of the local pistol ranges. I chose this particular range because it offered some wonderfully sturdy concrete benches. I wanted to make sure that the machine rest was firmly supported. Any machine rest is only as good as the base on which it's mounted. The bench or table you use must be rock steady with absolutely no movement. If the bench moves at all, this will show up as enlarged groups on the target. The machine rest was attached to an oak board which was in turn secured to the bench with several large

"C" clamps. There was little chance that it would shift or move during use.

I should point out that the day I chose to go to the range was bitterly cold. I think it was about 8° with a light wind. In fact I began to worry about the fact that I had weakened the main spring. I was afraid that the cold would cause the lubrication to stiffen up and cause misfires. Fortunately, that didn't happen but it was incredibly cold and that could not have helped. It sure didn't inspire me to spend any extra hours on the range!

Targets were set up at 25 yards. In my opinion 25 yards is the best distance to test for accuracy with a handgun. If the gun will group well at 25 yards, it will normally shoot well at just about any distance. Now keep in mind that it is highly unlikely that anyone opting for a .32 ACP cylinder for a Nagant is going to do anything more than fairly close range plinking. I would suspect that 50 feet is probably the maximum range for a .32 ACP Nagant. I know that is certainly my plan!

I first secured the older 1913 vintage Model 1895 revolver in the rest and fired several groups with the Fiocchi 7.62 Nagant ammunition. I fired five groups and got an average group size of about 3 inches. The best group I got was seven shots in 2½ inches.

I then fit the .32 ACP cylinder and fired three seven-shot groups with each of five different brands of ammo. The best groups I got were seven shots in 5½ inches with Winchester 71-grain full metal-jacketed ammo. The worst groups were seven shots in 8 inches with some CCI Blazer ammo. The Wolf,

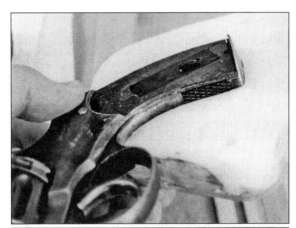

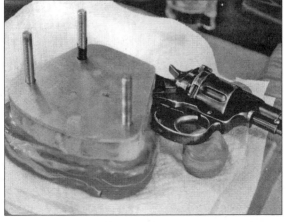

Note that the insert extends to only about 1/3 the width of the pistol grip frame. This gives room for the inserts to compress a bit as they are clamped in the rest.

Magtech, and Speer Lawman generally ran just a little over 6 inches or so. Certainly not inspiring but for plinking at close range it's not too bad.

I then duplicated this testing with the target Nagant. The groups were smaller as was expected. The Fiocchi ammo gave me groups of just over an inch. Not bad at all! The .32 ammo performed a bit better with the average groups of about 4 inches.

My guess is that accuracy could be significantly improved in the .32 ACP with a good cast lead bullet on the order of 100 grains or so. I just don't believe that the bullets we normally find used in most .32 ammo is optimal. This is definitely something to be researched further but when it's a *lot* warmer!

The Caldwell HAMMR machine rest performed flawlessly. The hydraulic cylinder reset the handgun automatically after each shot. There was no need for me to touch the machine during the testing cycle. This alone eliminated one possible variable that could have affected the accuracy results. I only had to thumb back the hammer on the Nagants since these revolvers were single-action only.

The HAMMR provides excellent value for the price. At $179.99 it is the most affordable handgun machine rest on the market that I know of. At that price I would think a lot of pistol shooters and gunsmiths will want to take a closer look at it.

Based on the results of these test groups, I believe that the .32 ACP cylinder is a good accessory for the Nagant. While it certainly will not deliver "target grade" accuracy, with a bit of tweaking and perhaps trying a few more different brands of commercial ammo, I think accuracy could be further improved. Even if you don't want to do that, at close "tin can plinkin' range" the .32 ACP cylinder makes the Model 1895 Nagant a much less expensive gun to shoot and enjoy.

Next we will take a look at another Nagant, the Mosin-Nagant rifle. Currently thousands of these rifles have been imported into the U.S. and are without a doubt the least expensive centerfire military surplus bolt-action rifle available to the U.S. shooter. While most folks probably use and shoot them as issued, we're going to take a look at what can be done to sporterize this rifle.

Yep, you heard me right; we're going to sporterize the Mosin-Nagant rifle. I'll be right up front; I've never done a conversion of one of these rifles so it will be a learning experience for me as well.

Until next time, good luck and good gunsmithing!

Building a 10/22 Garand

By Reid Coffield

Coffield gives his playful side some rope with a project that will mystify and amaze your friends.

A Ruger 10/22 receiver on an M1 barrel? Why? Coffield says "why not?" and shows you how to do it in a project that will yield a gun you won't find just anywhere.

I guess it all goes back to one of my many bad habits. I have a weakness for practical jokes and more than once (like a *lot* of times) I have gotten in trouble with my jokes but it has never seemed to stop me. There's just something about messin' with people's minds that appeals to my dark side.

This has naturally bled over into my gun work. While I seldom have ever played one of my practical jokes on a customer, I have had lots of fun over the years building or modifying guns just for the fun of confusing or fooling folks.

Now don't get me wrong; I won't put together fakes or counterfeit copies of desirable collectables. I won't do that but I sure will build guns that never existed and are just figments of my warped imagination.

A good example is a .45 ACP bolt action Mauser carbine I put together a couple of years ago here in SGN. It was "The Carbine That Never Was" (3/10/05). As I recall, I used parts from at least six different rifles in that project. It was a lot of fun and the folks that have seen it seem to think it's kinda neat.

Before that, I'd made a M1 carbine look-alike out of a Ruger 10/22. This project started one afternoon when I happened to have an M1 carbine and a Ruger 10/22 lying side-by-side on my workbench. I couldn't help but notice the similarities in the outlines of the guns. One thing leads to another, and pretty soon I found myself seeing just how far I could go in making that 10/22 look like an M1 carbine.

The end result was a nice little carbine if I do say so myself. In fact, not too long ago I was at a meeting with some folks from Ruger and showed them the 10/22 M1 carbine. They seemed to be interested in it and took a lot of photographs. Later, they asked if I could make any other 10/22 look-alikes. That started me thinking.

The more I thought about it, the more I decided that it just might be possible to make a 10/22 M1 Garand. So with that thought in mind I began to gather the necessary components.

One of the things I learned when doing the carbine project was that this is an ideal opportunity to use "bad" or defective parts. There is seldom any need to use good parts. Save those for making repairs on good guns. Besides, defective parts can often be had just for the asking or at a very reasonable price.

The first item to obtain was a stock. Fortunately my good friend John Teachey is a competitive service rifle shooter who has used Garands extensively in the past. He had an old Garand stock that had been used on a number of rifles over the years. During the course of its use on competitive rifles it had been refinished countless times.

Needless to say, there was not a single stamping or cartouche remaining on the stock. The stocks value as a collectable was virtually nil. This would be an ideal stock for this project.

Modifying a standard Ruger 10/22 to look like a M1 Garand is one of Coffield's wildest and wackiest ideas. With the right tools and techniques, you can do it, too.

Believe it or not, the carbine on top is a 10/22 that Coffield converted into a M1 carbine look-alike several years ago. Ruger executives were amazed when he showed it.

The rear sight from Tech-SIGHTS will help give the 10/22 Garand a suitable military look, even though it more accurately duplicates the M16A1 rear sight unit.

Note the difference in the shank of the Garand barrel on top and the Ruger 10/22 barrel below. While the M1 barrel threads in, the 10/22 is a slip fit secured by a wedge.

Coffield made extensive use of worn, damaged, or otherwise useless parts for the 10/22 Garand. A project like this is no fun if you have to pay much for the parts!

The next major item was a barrel. With the carbine I purchased the cheapest aftermarket .22 caliber bull barrel I could find at a local gun show. It was a used barrel and the price was right. With the Garand the problem is a bit more complex. A lot of parts are attached to the barrel such as the gas cylinder, gas cylinder lock nut, the handguards, etc.

Using a regular .22 rimfire barrel would necessitate some major mill and lathe work in order to attach those components. My idea was to use a modified Garand barrel. By doing this I would have the proper length barrel and it would already be machined for the handguards, the gas cylinder, and gas cylinder lock nut.

Coffield lathe turns the Garand barrel shank to match the Ruger 10/22 barrel shank. There's not much chance of doing this project if you don't have access to a lathe.

Finding a Garand barrel was actually very easy. The good folks at Numrich Gun Parts Corp., 226 Williams Lane, Dept. SGN, West Hurley, N.Y. 12491, telephone 866-686-7424, provided just what I needed. They currently have some newly-made Garand barrels that are defective. The chambers are too large, so Numrich is selling them to be used in "non-guns", drill rifles, or display pieces. They are ideal for that purpose. At only $39.95, the use of this barrel saved me an incredible amount of work and machine time.

In using a full size Garand barrel, it'll be necessary to modify the manner in which the Ruger receiver supports the barrel. The 10/22 receiver is fairly small and made of aluminum. It just wouldn't have the size or mass necessary to support the weight of the full-length Garand barrel.

Because of this, my plan is to attach the receiver to the barrel and then full-length bed the barrel in the stock. The receiver will not be bedded. In effect, the barrel will support the receiver instead of the receiver supporting the barrel. This is basically the same technique that many gunsmiths use when attaching a heavy bull barrel to the Ruger 10/22.

As for the other parts, they came from a variety of sources including my shop "junk box!" Again, the important thing is to use ruined or worn-out parts. Since these are often non-functioning, there is absolutely no need to use good components. The parts are basically just for looks.

The final component I needed was a .22 liner. It will be necessary to modify the defective Garand barrel, since it was produced with a .30-'06 chamber and .30 bore. This has to be modified to .22 rimfire. For this I am using a Redman liner I obtained from Brownells Inc., 200 South Front St., Dept. SGN, Montezuma, IA 50171, telephone 800-741-0015. I don't know of any other company that offers more in the way of gunsmithing supplies than Brownells. If you don't have their latest #60 catalog, give 'em a call and ask for one. You'll be glad you did! It's an essential resource for anyone doing gunsmithing work either as a full time professional or as a hobbyist.

The first step in the project was to disassemble the Ruger 10/22 and lay

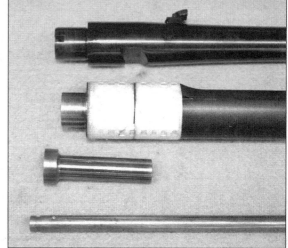

A 15/32" drill is used to bore out the .30-'06 chamber. Then the turned chamber plug and extension as well as the .22 rimfire liner can be installed in it.

it out on the bench along with the Garand parts. I needed to determine the relationship between the length of the 10/22 receiver, the Garand barrel, and the Garand stock. My initial impression was that the stock would have to be shortened a bit due to the shorter length of the Ruger receiver. Because the barrel will be a standard, full-length Garand barrel; I shouldn't cut the stock anywhere under the barrel. The shortening will have to take place under the receiver.

One of the most important aspects of a conversion like this is the sight system. The front sight will be a standard G.I. sight mounted on the gas cylinder. The rear sight is a bit more challenging. It needed to be a receiver sight and at the same time have the general outline of the original Garand rear sight.

I looked at a number of possibilities including modifying the rear of a demilled Garand receiver to fit over or on the 10/22 receiver. I really couldn't come up with a practical solution to this problem until I noticed an ad here in SGN.

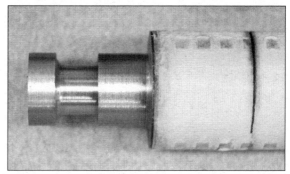

The chamber plug and extension is shown partly seated in the bored out Garand chamber. These will support the barrel liner and align the chamber and bolt face.

This drill gauge confirms that the 15/32" drill has a 58° point. Coffield points out the plug doesn't have to be a perfect fit; epoxy will fill any small gaps remaining.

An outfit called Tech-SIGHTS, LLC, offers a number of military type sights for a variety of firearms including the SKS and Ruger 10/22. The photograph in the ad looked promising so I contacted the folks at Tech-SIGHTS. After speaking with Larry Nesseth, who started the company, I ordered a 10/22 rear sight. These sights sell for only $50 plus $5 shipping and are really neat.

The front of the chamber plug is coated with Dykem to check contact inside the Garand chamber. The drill gauge is also used to check the angle of the front of the plug.

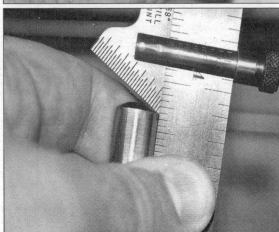

There are two models; the TSR100 and the TSR200. The 200 has an elevation adjustment in the rear while the 100 does not. These sights are basically an adaptation of the old M16 rear sight. If you are interested in these sights, give Larry a call. The address is Tech-SIGHTS, LLC, 2242 18¾ Ave., Dept. SGN, Rice Lake, Wis. 54868, telephone 715-234-1793. It looks like it will be fine though I may need to put a small spacer under the rear of the sight base. That can be dealt with later in the project.

With the 10/22 disassembled, the original barrel was set aside to use as a guide in altering the breech end of the Garand barrel. Keep in mind that the Garand barrel is threaded into the receiver while the Ruger barrel is a slip fit and secured with a clamp.

It will be necessary to reduce the diameter of the Garand barrel shank to .686". The length of the shank should be .746" to match that of the Ruger. The Ruger has a small but longer barrel shank than the Garand so it will be necessary to extend the shank of the Garand as the work is done.

In turning down the Garand barrel shank I, of course, removed all the original threads. I also removed the "collar" or recess at the end of the barrel shank that normally partly enclosed the head of the bolt. One of the reasons for this was to make it easier to fit a liner for the chamber but more on that in just a bit.

Installing a .22 liner in the bore of the Garand barrel is really no big deal. However, there is a major problem with the chamber. Because the chamber is so large, there would be nothing to support the liner. The way I dealt with this was to install a special liner or plug in the chamber to support the .22 liner. This is the same technique I've used on a number of occasions when converting other centerfire rifles to .22 rimfire.

I first measured the chamber and determined that a 15/32" drill would clean out the chamber. Long ago I found that it's a LOT easier to make a chamber liner with straight, parallel sides than to attempt to duplicate the taper and angles found in many centerfire chambers. When drilling out the chamber, I went in just far enough to cut into the original shoulder of the chamber with my 15/32" drill.

I then rummaged through my scrap box and found a section of an old .22 barrel. This was put in the lathe and a plug or liner was made for the drilled out chamber. This ended up lookin' like a fat nail. The front section was turned to .468" with a length of just over 2 inches.

The rear of the plug had a diameter of .686" for a length of about .300". The reason for the head or larger diameter portion is that it will be necessary to extend the shank of the Garand barrel. Remember that the Garand barrel had a shorter shank than the Ruger 10/22 barrel and this difference must be made up.

This "head" matches the outside diameter of the modified Garand barrel shank. As for the length or thickness of the head, at this point it doesn't have to be exact. Once it is mounted in the chamber and the liner installed, I will face off the liner and the end of the chamber plug to match exactly the length of the original Ruger 10/22 barrel shank.

When I drilled out the chamber, I used a standard 15/32" drill, the end of which is tapered. This left a matching taper or angled shoulder inside the modified chamber. The point of my drill has a standard 58° taper.

While I could have set up my lathe to duplicate this on the front of the chamber plug, it was really easier and faster to do it by hand using an abrasive belt on one of my buffers. I used a standard 58° drill point gauge to check my work as I duplicated this angle on the end of the chamber plug.

As I worked I would from time to time put some Dykem machinist layout fluid on the front of the plug and on the underside of the head of the plug. I then put the chamber plug in the Garand barrel and rotated it. By rotating it I would get a mark on the Dykem which let me know when and where I had contact. Ideally, I would like to have contact at the front of the plug and under the head of the plug at the same time.

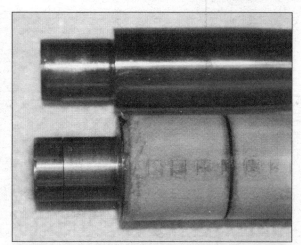

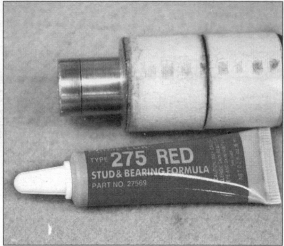

With the chamber plug secured with a high strength adhesive, the shank of the Garand barrel is longer than the Ruger barrel shank. This will eventually be cut back.

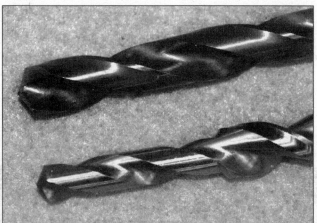

A Brownell liner drill, with a reduced diameter pilot at the point, is used to open up the chamber plug and barrel bore. Not much material is actually removed here.

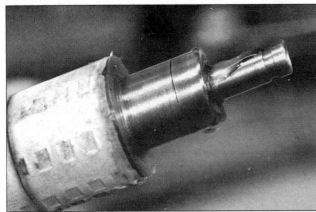

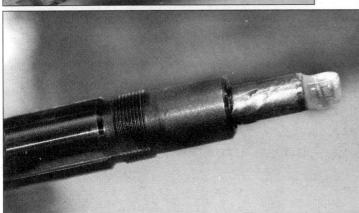

The liner extends from the Garand barrel and muzzle. Coffield says to keep some protruding in case you make a mistake and need to readjust the liner in the bore.

It was just a matter of carefully grinding back the front of the plug at the appropriate angle and monitoring the points of contact. This is just basic parts fitting. Now when you do this, don't get too carried away or fixated on this. The reality is that the front of the plug doesn't actually have to fit perfectly. After all, there will be a pretty good sized liner going across any tiny gap between the chamber plug and the bore. Also, the epoxy used to secure the chamber plug will fill any opening.

With the plug completed, I cleaned the barrel chamber with a solvent to remove oil or other contaminants. I also carefully cleaned the outside of the chamber plug. I then coated the inside of the chamber and the outside of the plug with Prime Lok Stud and Bearing Formula 275 Red.

This material is rated as having a holding strength of 3000 psi when fully cured. That will be more than enough to hold the chamber plug in place. Keep in mind that the liner will also be epoxied in place to add additional holding strength to the chamber plug.

The Garand barrel was then set aside to allow the Prime Lok to cure for 24 hours. Although you can handle the parts in about 15 minutes, I wanted the chamber plug fully secured before the next step which was drilling out the plug and bore for the liner.

The next day I was back at the lathe to complete installation of the liner. Once the barrel was secured in the three-jaw chuck of my lathe, I placed a piloted liner drill in a chuck in the lathe tailstock. This drill, sold by Brownells, has an integral projection or pilot.

This reduced diameter pilot is designed to follow the bore and keep the drill from wandering. The pilot is sized to slide inside most .22 rimfire bores. While I will start off in a .22 barrel, as soon as the drill passes through the chamber plug, the pilot will be inside a .30 bore. If you're thinking that it won't be fully supported, you're absolutely correct.

However, it really won't matter. The liner drill is only 8mm or about .315" diameter. Since I am cutting through a .308" bore, I will only be removing about .003" or .004" on a side. That combined, with the length of the drill itself, keeps it from wandering excessively. There really isn't much stress on the drill when going through the Garand bore.

In using the liner drill, I first drilled from the breech end of the barrel to a point approximately half the length of the barrel. I then repositioned the barrel and drilled in from the muzzle, completing the hole.

One of the typical problems encountered when drilling out a barrel for a liner is having the drill "grab" or go in a bit too deep. This throws up two burrs that are sometimes pretty large. You'll know right away when this happens as the drill bit will generally start spinning in the tail stock chuck.

This actually happens more often when an electric hand drill is being used to power the liner drill, as you have less control over the feed of the drill bit. Anyway, this is more of an irritant than anything else. Some times you can solve the problem by just drilling from the other end of the barrel and cut out the burr from the other side. If that's not possible, you can take a steel rod just about bore size, run it down the bore from the other end of the barrel and break off or flatten the burrs.

If this is a continual problem for you, it's also some times helpful to reduce the cutting angle of the liner drill bit. You can make it a little less aggressive, reducing its tendency to cut too deeply.

With the drilling completed, the barrel bore was washed out with solvent to remove all traces of oil. The outside of the liner was also cleaned. A two-part five-minute epoxy was mixed up and used to coat the outside of the liner. A modest amount was also placed inside the bore.

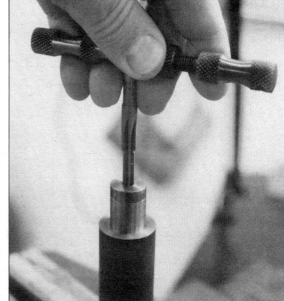

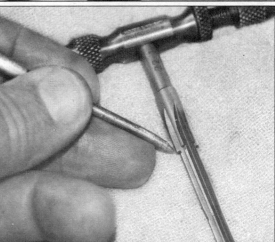

Coffield likes to chamber .22s by hand. This step or rim cutter on the chambering reamer will indicate how deeply the chamber should be cut on this barrel.

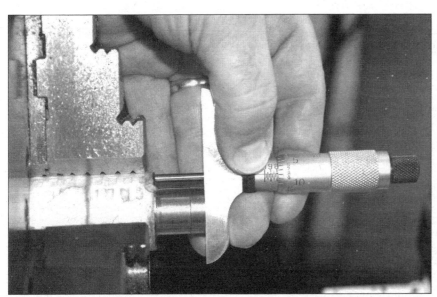

Once the epoxy holding the liner has hardened and it been trimmed flush with the barrel extension, the extension will be shortened to match the 10/22 barrel shank.

A clearance cut must be made on the bottom of the barrel for the receiver extension. To save time, Coffield used a hacksaw to remove as much metal as possible.

Once the clearance cut for the receiver extension was completed, the standard Ruger slotted takedown screw was used to clamp the barrel securely into the receiver.

I put a small wooden plug in the muzzle end of the liner to keep out epoxy. The liner was then inserted into the Garand barrel from the breech end. As it was pushed into the barrel, I continually added a bit of epoxy to the surface of the liner. I wanted to make sure that it was as fully coated as possible. Once it was in place, I made sure I had an equal amount of liner extending out of both ends of the barrel.

The liner was also obtained from Brownells. It's made by Randal Redman and is one of the best liners I've used. When using a

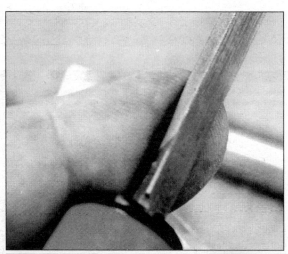

Coffield used a safe-sided triangular file to cut the angled engagement surface for the barrel clamp. A safe sided file will not deepen the barrel clamp cut.

Redman liner you can always tell which end is the breech end by a small groove cut into the outside of the liner about a quarter inch from the end. This is where Redman's machine held the liner while a carbide plug was pulled or pushed through it. If you reverse a liner, you'll often get excessive fouling or leading, so always make sure the breech end of the liner is placed at the breech end of your barrel. The grooved end is the breech end.

Once the epoxy had cured, I used a hacksaw to remove the excess liner extending from the barrel breech. I then checked my measurement of the Ruger 10/22 barrel shank, which was right at .749". I then placed the Garand barrel back in my lathe and faced off the barrel shank until it matched the Ruger barrel.

You might have wondered why I didn't cut off the liner at the muzzle. The reason I didn't is basically CYA. If by some strange set of circumstances in cutting the chamber I make a mistake and end up with excessive headspace, I will be able to correct it. I can do this by simply heating up the barrel and tapping the muzzle end of the liner, driving it back towards the breech.

This would or could take care of any excess headspace. Always leave cutting of the liner at the muzzle until the very last step. Yep, I once screwed up chambering a .22 liner after I had cut and crowned the liner and barrel. There wasn't a darn thing I could do except pull out the liner and start all over again. What a waste of time!

With the barrel breech faced off, I then chambered the barrel. This was done at my bench. Since so little metal is removed when chambering a .22 rimfire, I seldom do the work in my lathe. When using a chamber reamer, there are just two important points to keep in mind. First, use lots of cutting fluid. Cutting fluid is cheap; reamers are not. Cutting fluid will help keep your reamers in good shape for a much longer time. Also, cutting fluid will help to ensure that the chamber is smooth and free of scratches and machine marks.

Secondly, when using a reamer *always* turn it clockwise. *Never*, never reverse a reamer and turn it counterclockwise. If you do, you will roll the cutting edges of the reamer. This will dull it and make it less effective.

The chamber of the Ruger is set up so the rim seat is flush with the face of the breech end of the barrel. In using the reamer just watch the reamer and as soon as the rim cutting portion of the reamer touches the face of the barrel; stop! The chamber is complete.

The next step in fitting the Garand barrel is making a clearance cut under the chamber for the extension on the front of the receiver. This extension or lug is designed to accept the two screws that pull the barrel back into the receiver using a "V" block barrel retainer as a clamp.

The Garand barrel is now firmly attached to the Ruger receiver. Note the clearance cut for the barrel clamp screw heads. Tighten them down and the barrel is installed.

Using a file along with a Dremel tool and a sanding band, the necessary metal was removed from the barrel shank. In doing this, I had to be very careful and frequently check my work. It was important to remove no more metal than absolutely necessary.

At the same time I wanted to make sure that the barrel was properly oriented so the front sight would be at 12 o'clock. This was checked by installing the gas cylinder and front sight on the barrel and simply looking at it from the rear of the receiver. If the sight is canted, it's readily noticeable. Once the barrel was fitted into the receiver, the Ruger stock screw was used to temporarily secure the barrel to the receiver. This screw extended through the lug and pressed against the underside of the barrel; effectively holding it in place.

The final aspect of attaching the barrel is cutting a seat for the "V" block barrel retainer. This is actually not too hard. I first filed a flat on the underside of the barrel that would allow the "V" block to be properly positioned in front of the lug. I then used a safe-sided triangular file to make an angled cut in the barrel under the lug. This would match the angled surface of the "V" block retainer.

Once that was completed, I then had to make a flat on the barrel ahead of the "V" block retainer to allow clearance for the heads of the two attaching screws. Again, this was just a matter of a bit of filing and frequently checking my work. Once that was completed, the "V" block barrel retainer was attached to the receiver securing the barrel.

All that remains is to make the extractor cuts on the face of the barrel and then cut the liner at the muzzle and crown the barrel. However, we'll hold off on that until next time. We'll also fit the stock, install the rear sight, and finish this little project up.

So...if you've got a 10/22, some junk Garand parts, and a sense of humor, consider making your own 10/22 Garand. It's a fun project and guaranteed to attract attention the next time you go to the range.

Until next time, good luck and good gunsmithing!

Ask the Gunsmith

By Reid Coffield

SURPLUS PISTOLS?

Q *I love to tinker and work on guns as a hobby, with primary emphasis on handguns. My problem is finding project guns. Unlike rifles, you don't see many military surplus handguns for sale. Have you got any suggestions for where to look and what to look for?*

The S&W SW99, Beretta 92FS, and S&W Model 4046 are typical of the many police trade-in pistols that are currently available from a number of dealers here in SHOTGUN NEWS.

A Absolutely! Sure, the day of the $35 Colt or Remington Rand 1911 is long gone and you won't find too many $40 to $50 Lugers or Browning Hi-Powers. In fact, you probably won't find any! Even more so than long guns, it seems that military handguns have for the most part achieved collector status along with collector pricing.

But that doesn't mean that you can't find relatively inexpensive handguns for your projects. First of all, don't necessarily look just at or for military surplus handguns. I would strongly encourage you to look at police trade-ins. There are huge numbers of police organizations both here in the U.S. and in other parts of the world that are regularly trading in or upgrading their handguns. Century International Arms, Inc., 430 South Congress Ave., Dept. SGN, Delray Beach, FL 33445, 561-265-4500, which advertises here in SHOTGUN NEWS, is a major buyer and importer of surplus police handguns. I have gotten a number of darn nice used police handguns from these folks over the years. Not too long ago I picked up a nice used S&W99 in 9mm and later a S&W Model 4046. Both handguns were evidently carried a lot but shot very little.

J&G Sales, another SGN advertiser, has had large quantities of S&W Model 64 revolvers taken in from a large security company. Again, these were clearly carried a lot more than shot.

Guns like this are great for experimentation and various gunsmithing projects and best of all, the prices were very, very reasonable. In fact, when compared with the price of new handguns or even the run-of-the-mill used handguns you typically see in most gun shops, they were bargains.

So check the ads here in SGN and you'll see a number of outfits that offer police trade-ins. If you don't see what you want, give the advertisers a call. Often police trade-ins are in such small quantities that the dealers won't run a big ad. Sometimes also, they have guns that are missing parts, sights, etc. that can be purchased with quite a discount. Century often has listed on their website guns that need some TLC and a bit of repair work.

MAKING PLUG SCREWS

Q *Where can I get 4x48 plug screws? I need them to plug the screw holes for a front sight ramp in an old Remington .22 rifle barrel.*

A I don't know of any commercial source for anything other than standard 3x56, 6x48, and 10x32 plug screws. However, that doesn't mean you cannot get the plug screws you need. All you have to do is find an appropriate threaded screw and make one. Just file the threaded end of the screw flat and cut or file a slot in the center of this flat. That's now the head of your plug screw. All that's left is to cut the threaded shank above the new head to depth or length you need. Simple, cheap, and fast!

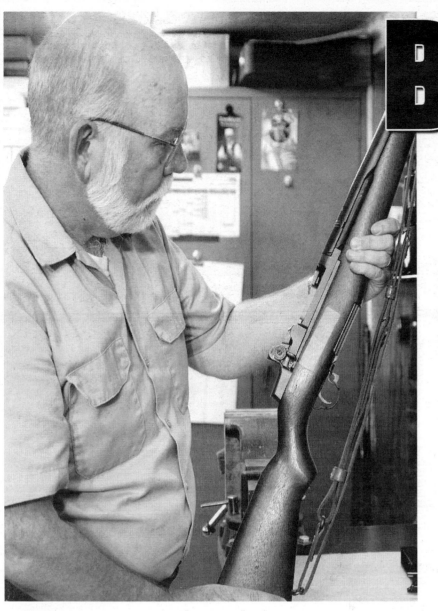

Building a 10/22 Garand

Part 2

Continuing a project started in the 9/10 issue, Coffield shows how to combine a 10/22 action with scrap M1 parts into a very unusual plinker.

The Ruger 10/22 has to be one of the greatest .22 rimfire rifles ever produced. Whether you measure "great" in terms of numbers made, popularity, value for the dollar, or durability; the Ruger 10/22 has to be on that very exclusive list. One of the features the 10/22 has that also makes it so popular is its unique capacity for modifications.

I don't know of any other rifle that can and has been modified in so many ways for so many different applications. Part of this is the simple, yet very sophisticated modular design. The barrel, for example, is held in the receiver with an incredibly strong yet simple clamping mechanism that allows the barrel to be easily changed. The design of the receiver also lends itself to easy fitting to different stocks. It's amazing just how attractive and popular this rifle is with the hobbyist or shooter who wants something "different".

If you want a real eye-opener, check out the latest Brownells #61 catalog, the current MidwayUSA catalog, the internet, or this issue of SHOTGUN NEWS for aftermarket parts and items related to the Ruger 10/22. From barrels to stocks to triggers; the variety is just mind-boggling. This is obviously a very versatile and extremely popular rifle for aftermarket modifications.

As I mentioned in Part 1 of this series, several years ago I modified a 10/22 into an M1 carbine lookalike. It was a fun project and generated a lot of comment among folks that have seen it. Last year I had a chance to show it to some folks from Ruger and during the course of the conversation one of them asked if I could use the 10/22 as the basis for any other military rifle look-alike. I thought about it and replied that I thought it might be possible to come up with a 10/22 Garand. That idea set on the shelf for several months until I finally decided to give it a shot.

In the last installment, I bored out a defective M1 Garand barrel, obtained from Numrich Gun Parts, 226 Williams Lane, Dept. SGN, West Hurley, N.Y. 12491, telephone 866-686-7424. Next, a Redman .22 rimfire liner from Brownells, 200 South Front St., Dept. SGN, Montezuma, Iowa 50171, telephone 800-741-0015 was installed. I chambered the barrel and fitted it to a Ruger 10/22 receiver. Use of this barrel allowed me to easily attach standard GI handguards, a gas cylinder, gas cylinder nut, and front sight.

By the way, all of the Garand parts I'm using on this project are defective in one way or another. Projects like this are ideal for using items that would otherwise end up in the garbage.

Before getting into the nuts and bolts of putting this rifle together, I had best say a word or two about the order in which the work is done. Some folks like to do all the metal work first; others like to do the wood work first. I tend to bounce back and forth between the two. In some cases it's necessary because one will depend upon or affect the other or I just have some down time while waiting for bedding to cure, etc.

In other cases I have to admit it's just because I want a break from what I've been doing. When you do your rifle you can certainly vary the sequence of your work. Nothing I do with this project is carved in stone and I definitely don't believe that my approach is the only or even necessarily the best approach. This just happens

to be the way I did this job. If and when I do it again, I'll probably do it a bit differently.

With the barrel fitted to the receiver, the next step was to fit the stock. I started out with an old U.S. GI Garand stock that my friend John Teachcy had given to me. It had been used for years on a number of Garands for competitive shooting and it was ready to be discarded. There were a lot of dings and nicks and it had been refinished many times. All markings had long since been sanded off and it was of no value to any collector.

After studying the relationship of the stock to the barreled receiver, I initially cut a section about 2 inches long out of the rear of the receiver area of the stock. I thought that I could make this one cut and shorten the stock enough to compensate for the shorter 10/22 receiver. I was wrong!

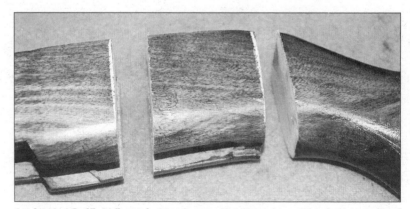

A mistake! Coffield first tried to shorten the stock by cutting just one piece out of it. As he discovered, it won't work—the wrist is left at a peculiar angle.

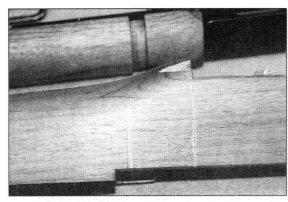

To position the trigger unit and magazine properly in the Garand stock, Coffield had to make two cuts: one near the front and one at the rear of the receiver inlet.

Coffield used a 2x4 to align the stock parts when gluing them together. Wax paper keeps glued squeezed out of the joints from securely sticking the stock to the 2x4.

After removing a section, Coffield glued the stock together. He says you should glue the sections one at a time; trying to glue two at once can lead to a crooked stock.

The wood was pretty decent but it had several chips. Also, the importer had stamped the stock with cartouches to give the impression that it was a genuine U.S. G. I. stock. In other words, it was a fake. I don't mind reproductions of guns or components but they shouldn't be marked in such a way that they can or will be confused with original items. Because of this, that stock had lived for years in my junk box. By the way, that importer went out of business many years ago.

Aside from making the cuts in the stock in the right spots, one of the hardest aspects of this was coming up with a way of clamping the pieces together so they were properly aligned. I ended up using a 2x4 clamped in my vise as a jig. That, combined with a couple of clamps, did the trick. To keep from gluing the stock to the 2x4, I placed a sheet of wax paper under the stock at those points where epoxy was applied. You can also use aluminum foil in the same way.

The stock pieces were glued together with a standard two-part epoxy. I also used some dyes that I got from Brownells to color the epoxy. By coloring the epoxy, I hoped to help hide or at least make the seams between the different sections of the stock a little less obvious.

By the way, I cut and glued the front section of the stock first. Once that was cured, I then cut and glued the rear section of the stock. Don't even think of making both cuts at the same time. It would be a nightmare trying to glue all the sections of the stock together and still keep everything aligned.

While the epoxy was curing, I went back to work on the metal components. Like the wood, all the GI metal parts I used were garbage. The gas cylinder, for example, was worn oversize from extensive use. Other parts were extensively rusted or damaged in one way or another. As I pointed out earlier, projects like this are great opportunities to use worn-out or defective parts.

For most of these parts, I first bead-blasted to remove the rust and give the base metal a decent finish. I then used a number of different

By using Brownell epoxy dyes, Coffield was able to color the epoxy used to join the stock components. He selected a relatively dark shade to coordinate with the handguard.

In order to fit the receiver and have the trigger unit and magazine properly positioned within the stock, I discovered I would have to make two cuts. It was necessary to shorten the stock at two different points; one near the front and one at the rear of the receiver inlet. The length of wood taken out at the rear of the receiver area was about 1.36 inches long, while the section removed from the front of the receiver was much shorter; only about .630".

This was a little frustrating as I hated to waste a good "bad" stock but that sort of thing happens when you're working on something unique like this project. Fortunately, I had another "bad" stock I could use. This stock was an early import from a company in Italy.

types of finish on the parts. If you look at almost any Garand, and especially one that has seen a bit of use, you'll note that the various parts aren't completely uniform in terms of finish or color. This is due to a number of factors, including the replacement of parts during the service life of that gun.

Many years ago I had an opportunity to talk with a couple of fellows who had worked at Springfield Armory during the 1940s and '50s in the metal finishing shop. I asked them both what the "true color" was of military Parkerizing. The response was a lot of laughter as well as a question to me. The question was basically, what day of the week are you asking about?

It seems that color was not an issue at Springfield and anything from light gray to black was acceptable. Also, the type of metal being Parkerized, the age of the bath, the amount of contamination in the bath, and who was doing the work all affected color. So... variations in color are the norm rather than the exception.

Because of this, I decided to use a number of different finish colors on the parts. For the gas cylinder, which was very rough, I bead blasted, cleaned, and then coated it with Brownells Teflon/Moly Oven Cure Gun Finish. This aerosol finish is available in a variety of colors so I opted for "dark Parkerizing gray" for the gas cylinder as well as a number of other small parts.

The finish is easy to use. Just spray it on and let it dry for 30 minutes. If you need to add another coat, you can do so after the 30-minute drying period. Once you have the finish you want, bake the part in an oven for 30 minutes at 300°. That's all there is to it.

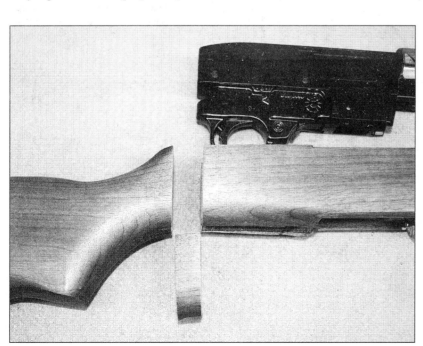

Coffield removed about 1.36 inches at the front of the receiver inlet; just a much smaller section was removed from the rear of the inlet area, measuring .63".

A medium cut wood rasp was used to help shape the shortened M1 stock. Remove material very carefully here to help avoid leaving a wavy surface to the stock wood.

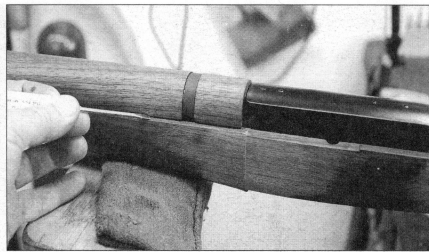

The underside of the rear handguard is level with and almost touching the stock when the receiver is fully seated. This makes a convenient gauge for the inletting.

An old toaster oven was used to bake the Brownell metal finish. Coffield says to avoid using the kitchen stove; your wife won't like the smell that persists after baking.

Oh yes, there is one more thing. If you don't want to get in trouble with the better half, *don't* use her oven (unless she's out of the house for a couple of days). There is an odor and to preserve peace in the family it's best just to buy a toaster oven and an oven thermometer and do it outside or in the garage. What's even better, offer to buy her a new toaster oven and you take the old one. You get an oven and you score some points. Never a bad thing!

With the stock shortened, Coffield began inletting the Ruger receiver. As it has a flat bottom surface, this is not an especially complicated wood removal process.

After the epoxy had cured, it was time to modify the inletting of the stock for the Ruger 10/22. Fortunately the 10/22 has one of the easiest receivers you can imagine to inlet. First, remove the trigger guard if you haven't done so already. Now take a look at the barreled receiver. It's basically just a long rectangle with straight sides. The trick is to inlet the receiver first and make sure it is fully seated in the stock.

Once that's done, attach the trigger guard. Now, you inlet the receiver and trigger guard as a unit. Use plenty of inletting black as you work so you can see where you have contact and make darn sure your chisels and gouges are sharp.

Initially you can use the lower band, which should be attached to the barrel, as a pivot to help guide the receiver into the stock. Just like with a regular M1 Garand, you slide the lower band over the projection on the front of the stock ferrule and lower the receiver into the stock. The receiver will move in an arc.

You could try dropping the receiver straight down into the stock as you would with a Mauser 98 or Remington 700 action but it's easier to use the stock ferrule and lower band as a means of keeping the action properly aligned. It'll be very unlikely that you'll shift the receiver to the right or left if you do this.

It's a slow process. Just take your time and you'll eventually get there! Inletting is like that. When you first start you think that you'll never get the darn metal deep enough into the wood. But you do get there!

When the rear of the receiver had been inlet about a quarter of an inch into the stock, I installed the rear handguard on the barrel. This had two functions. First, it helped to keep the action square and prevent tilting to the right or left. In addition, it served as an indicator of when I had dropped the receiver deep enough into the stock. Once the flats on the left side of the bottom of the handguard were parallel with the top of the stock, I knew I had inlet the receiver as deep as necessary.

Just to make things look a bit nicer and to ensure as much support for the receiver as possible, I opted to bed the receiver. For this I used Brownells Acraglas Gel. This is a one-to-one, nylon-based bedding material. It's easy to work with and can be readily dyed. I used the brown dye supplied with the bedding kit to help match the color of the wood. It's not a perfect match but that's OK. Remember this is a "military" rifle!

The next day, after the bedding set up, I removed the barreled action and cleaned up the excess bedding. Once that was done I attached the stripped trigger guard and continued inletting.

One of the things to keep in mind is that unlike the original 10/22 where you assemble the rifle by installing the rear of the receiver into the stock first and then pivot the barrel down into the stock, with this gun you have to do just the opposite. The barrel ferrule is attached to the stock first and then the receiver is pivoted down into the stock. The receiver moves into place in a shallow arc and this affects just how close the inletting can be at the back of the receiver.

Once the metal was finally fully seated, I began shaping the stock. The 10/22 action is a bit thin measured from top to bottom for this stock so wood had to be removed. I first made a mark on the stock inside the trigger guard. This served as a guide to prevent removing too much wood as I rasped the stock down. I continued to check my progress as I worked by installing the metal and noting the relationship between the bottom of the stock and the trigger guard. Keep in mind that the wood has to be low enough to allow the safety to function.

As I removed wood from the bottom of the stock, I realized I would soon cut into the inletting forward of the magazine well. To deal with this, I cut away the stock and installed a block of walnut in this area. This block served two func-

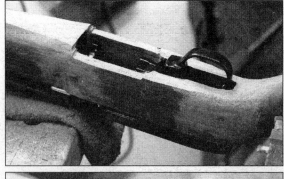

Once the receiver and trigger housing had been inletted, Coffield was able to begin modifying the bottom of the stock. Note the flat on the stock ahead of the magazine well.

Coffield used a hacksaw to cut the floorplate from the trigger and hammer support. He wanted to retain the floorplate to give the rifle an authentic look.

The finger opening in the floorplate begins to take shape by drilling and joining the holes. It's required for access to the magazine release and the bolt stop.

The stock is insufficiently deep at this point, leaving too much receiver protruding. Wood must be added to the top of the stock to get the right proportions.

tions. First, it filled in a void that would have been opened as the stock was thinned. Secondly, it served as a pillar under the rear of the 10/22 barrel directly below the barrel clamp.

I also went ahead and actually bedded the barrel at that point using Brownells Acraglas Gel. By making a bedding pillar, the barrel was supported at two points; under the stock ferrule and under the clamping block. This removed all stress on the receiver from the heavy Garand barrel.

I should point out that the receiver was also bedded so the entire barreled action turned out to be very well supported. Initially in planning this project I didn't think I'd be able to bed the receiver but it turned out that I could. In projects like this, you often end up modifying your initial ideas or plans as you work. That's both a blessing and a curse!

This walnut block was used both as a filler in the stock and as a support for the barreled action. Note that it extends forward into the barrel channel about 2 inches.

After a bit of stock shaping, I took time out to modify the Garand magazine floorplate. This is one of the distinctive design elements of the rifle and one I felt I had to include in this conversion to ensure the 10/22 had the right appearance. I began by cutting away the floorplate extension that housed the hammer and trigger, as this would not be needed.

I then made an oval opening in the floorplate ahead of the trigger guard. The 10/22 has a magazine release tab and a bolt hold open lever directly ahead of the guard which you have to be able to access. My idea was to make a cut out in the Garand floorplate to permit this.

I also planned on eventually attaching the floorplate to the bottom of the 10/22 magazine. The magazine would provide a mounting surface for the floorplate. In making the finger access cut out, there is no "correct" size. I made mine just big enough to allow my fat finger to operate the mag release and bolt hold open.

With that completed, I continued with shaping the stock. The more I worked at it, the more I realized I was going to have to add wood to the stock! The 10/22 has such a shallow action, measured from top to bottom, that the Garand stock when modified to accept this action just looked strange. It was too thin ahead of the pistol grip.

A way around this was to add about a quarter-inch of wood to the top of the stock around the 10/22 receiver. This would give the visual impression of a thicker, more "normal" size Garand stock.

I started with a quarter inch thick slab of walnut on which I had drawn the outline of the bottom of the receiver. This was then cut out, creating a large "U". I then filled the ejection port of the receiver with clay and gave the receiver a good coating of Brownells Aerosol Release Agent. Some Acraglas Gel was mixed up, dyed brown, and applied to the top of the stock around the receiver. The walnut "U" was then clamped in place and the Gel allowed to harden.

Once the Gel cured, the receiver was removed and the excess wood on the outside of the "U" was taken off with a rasp. I was careful to avoid cutting into the stock, as I wanted to maintain the lines and overall shape of the Garand stock. By the way, in using this quarter-inch slab of walnut the top of the stock is now high enough to keep the bolt stop pin in place in the receiver.

In working with the receiver, I discovered the metal finish was being degraded by the solvents I used to clean away the release agent. Originally the older receivers were anodized but this newer receiver appears to be painted. Because of this I'll have to use the Brownell baking lacquer to color it. I have no problem with this, as it's a very tough finish and much more resistant to solvents and wear than this Ruger factory finish. Just as with the gas cylinder, I'll bead blast the receiver, clean it, apply the finish, and bake it. Simple and easy.

Originally I had hoped to use a ruined op rod to fill the gap in the right side of the stock. Unfortunately I was unable to locate one when I needed it so I decided instead to fill the gap with walnut. It was just a matter of cutting a piece of wood to fit the opening and using some colored epoxy to secure it in place. Now that I've done it, I think that might actually be the best way of dealing with the opening in the stock.

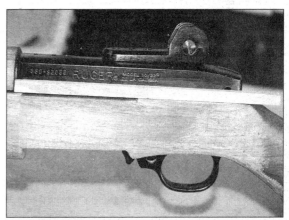

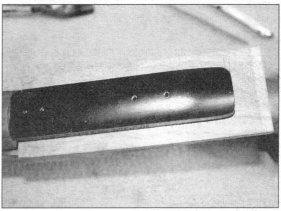

Adding a quarter-inch thick piece of walnut that extends around the receiver in a large "U" to the top surface of the stock makes it more closely resemble the M1.

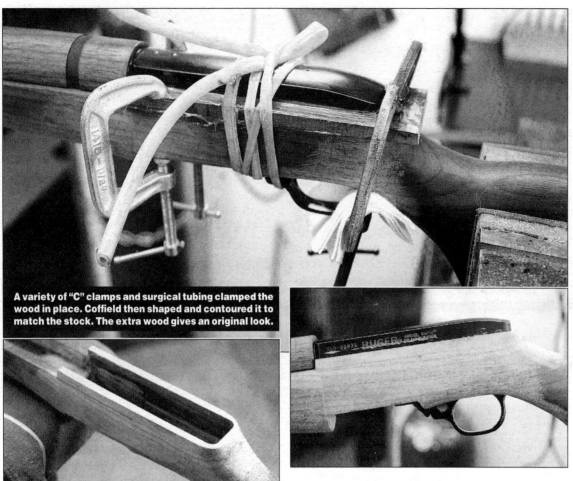
A variety of "C" clamps and surgical tubing clamped the wood in place. Coffield then shaped and contoured it to match the stock. The extra wood gives an original look.

barrel. To crown the barrel, I used the absolute best hand crowning tool available. Dave Manson, Manson Precision Reamers, 8200 Embury Road, Dept. SGN, Grand Blanc, Mich., 48439, telephone 810-953-0732, makes the best hand crowning tool of anyone I know.

Unlike other hand tools that use cutters with fixed blades, Manson's tool uses three small, adjustable carbide files set into a holder to cut away the metal. It provides a fast, clean, and smooth surface. In the three years I've been using this tool, I've *never* had any chatter on any crown I've cut with it. It's a remarkable tool.

Also, it's piloted off the bore, so your crown is always concentric with the axis of the bore. It's not cheap and prices range from $295 on up, but then again, really good tools have never been cheap. As the old saying goes, you get what you pay for!

The takedown screw was then installed by drilling a hole in the stock under the receiver extension. To ensure the proper location of the hole, I first marked the location of the hole inside the stock. To do this, I used an old 12-24 tap with a sharpened point.

The tap was inserted in the receiver extension with the point projecting so it would make a mark when the receiver was placed in the stock. Once that was done, it was a simple matter to use a #1 drill on this mark to properly locate the hole. With the hole drilled, the stock was reversed and the hole countersunk for the takedown screw head using a modified 5/16" drill bit.

The last major step in the process was to sand the stock. In the course of all this work, I had rasped away a lot of wood and had added additional pieces of wood in various places. I started with 80-grit sand paper and worked my way up to 150-grit. Once that was done, I stained the wood using a dark walnut color. This helps to blend in and hide the various additional pieces of wood. Also, the forward handguard is pretty dark, so making the stock darker makes it a better match.

The last major bit of work relating to the stock inletting was to put a bit of bedding compound around the bottom of the trigger guard where it came through the stock. Depending upon your inletting, you may not have to do this. I admit it, I had to!

After completing this wood work, I looked at my Tech-SIGHT rear sight. It's a darn good sight but it sets a bit too far back on the receiver for the Garand look I needed. As manufactured, you really can't move the sight forward be-

cause of the bottom contour of the sight base. However, this is easily corrected by just doing a bit of metal removal on the bottom of the sight base with a Dremel tool and a sanding drum. When doing, this you have to be careful as the hole for the windage detent is darn close to the bottom of the base. You sure don't want to grind into it.

I moved the sight forward to second rear sight base hole in the receiver and drilled and tapped another hole for the front attaching screw. This gave the sight a much better position and it looked a lot more like the Garand rear sight.

One other "problem" was an angular cut on the rear of the sight base. This cut just looked out of place, so I mixed up a bit more Brownells Steel-Bed, dyed it black to match the sight, and used it as filler for this gap. Release agent was applied to the receiver but not to the sight base. When the Steel-Bed set up, it was securely attached to the sight and filled the unsightly gap. This was just cosmetic but it does help with the over-all look of the 10/22 Garand.

The next order of business was to cut an extractor slot in the barrel. I think that it's best to begin by looking at the extractor cut in the Ruger factory barrel. You'll note that it's not at exactly 3:00 on the right side of the barrel breech. In fact, it's slightly lower.

With this in mind, I applied some Dykem to the breech face of my new barrel, inserted the breech bolt, and marked the location of the extractor. The barrel was then removed from the receiver and placed in my vise.

While you could cut the extractor slot with a milling machine, it's faster and easier simply to use a Dremel tool with a couple of cut-off wheels stacked together. Mark the location of the extractor and *carefully* cut away the metal. As you do this, measure the width of the slot. It's approximately .120" wide so you don't want to be much larger than that.

Also, make sure you don't cut into the chamber. You'll be close, so be careful. Once the extractor cut had been completed, I installed the barrel in the receiver and checked functioning with dummy cartridges.

With the breech work completed, I could finally cut away the excess liner projecting from the muzzle and crown the

Coffield hoped to find a junk op rod, but when he didn't, chose to add a filler. The op rod opening is no longer an unsightly gap between the handguard and the stock.

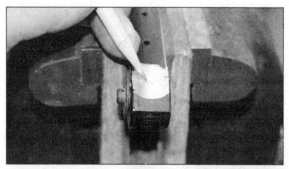

Coffield contoured the underside of the TECH-Sights rear sight and filled the gap at the rear of the sight base. The altered sight has more of a realistic "M1" look.

When shaping the bottom of the stock you must remove enough wood to allow the safety button to function, yet the stock must still be kept as thick as possible.

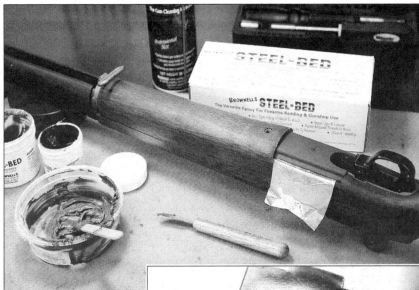

After staining the stock, I gave it a coat of tung oil. The tung oil was applied by hand and rubbed in with the heel of my palm. This is very similar to the old military linseed oil finish but it has the advantage of drying much quicker. The stock was then allowed to dry for about 24 hours. After that, the rifle was assembled.

The last item to be addressed was the magazine. In order to fit it properly to the floorplate, the rifle was first assembled. The fit and functioning of the magazine was checked. It was especially important to make sure the magazine ejected properly. Once that was done, the bottom of the magazine, which is made of plastic, was prepared using a Dremel tool and a small ball-shaped cutter or burr.

One of the last steps was cutting a groove in the breech face of the barrel for the extractor. Coffield says stacked cutoff wheels in a Dremel tool will do the job.

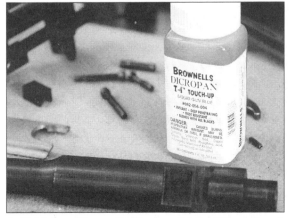

Coffield chose Brownells Dicropan T-4 cold blue to touch up the bare metal in the slot made for the barrel clamp. This is important to prevent rusting down the line.

I used the burr to under cut the lip of the magazine base. This would provide a holding surface or mechanical lock for the epoxy that would join it to the Garand floorplate. I used Brownells Steel-Bed for this job.

I mixed a small amount of Steel-Bed and pressed it into the magazine floorplate, which had already been inserted in the rifle. I had previously used some modeling clay to help determine just how much Steel-Bed I would need. The Garand floorplate was then cleaned and positioned in the stock over the magazine. I made sure I used enough Steel-Bed so it would compress between the magazine and the floorplate.

To prevent any overflow of bedding from contacting the stock, I used several small pieces of aluminum foil to shield the wood. The bedding was then allowed to set up, forming a bond between the two parts.

With the magazine completed, the only task left was to range test the rifle. After getting this far, I was really anxious to see how it shot. Unfortunately the outdoor range where I normally shoot was closed, so instead, I went to a local gunshop and indoor range.

The rifle performed beautifully, as you would expect with a Ruger. What was amazing was the reaction of other shooters and folks at the gunshop. I can absolutely assure you that if you build a 10/22 Garand it *will* be the center of attention at any range, gunshop or gathering of gun people! Folks love it!

Coffield undercut and roughened the magazine to ensure adhesion of the Steel-Bed, then carefully masked off the wood with aluminum foil to prevent it sticking.

This has definitely been one of the most interesting and enjoyable projects I've done for SHOTGUN NEWS. It's a unique rifle that's a lot of fun to shoot and one that brings a smile to anyone who sees it. If you're a fan of the ol' M1 Garand and are looking for an interesting project, I highly recommend building a 10/22 Garand. It's a hoot!

The next time we get together we'll take a look at working on another old warhorse. We'll be cleaning up and repairing a Nepalese Martini type rifle I got from the folks at International Military Antiques. The rifle is more than 125 years old and poses some unique challenges.

Until next time, good luck and good gunsmithing! ◉

You won't meet yourself on the street with this one! A bonus was that the Garand replica turned out to be an excellent shooter in addition to being very distinctive.

Enfield? Martini? or Both?

Part 1

When Coffield found he could simply screw an Enfield barrel into a Martini action, an idea was born.

By Reid Coffield

It's a Martini in the middle, but an Enfield at either end. Coffield has combined two classic British rifles into one to make a fun, if inauthentic, shooter.

A few months ago I made a trade with an old friend. I had a Mauser carbine he wanted and he had a .303 cal. single-shot Martini rifle that I just had to have. It didn't take long, and we quickly swapped rifles. As is so often the case when tradin' with an old buddy, neither of us was concerned about who got the best deal or making a profit on the transaction. We were both just glad to see the other guy with a rifle he wanted and would enjoy.

The Martini I got had been built in 1888. Originally it was chambered for the .450/577 cartridge. Later, in 1899, the rifle was rebarreled and converted to .303. These converted rifles were then used by militia groups in various parts of the British Empire. My rifle had seen use in Canada at one time. Other similar rifles were also sometimes issued to native troops in India and Africa.

My .303 Martini had seen a good bit of service and was certainly not a pristine collectable. The bore, for example, shows the wear and pitting associated with the use of corrosive ammunition. It's definitely less than perfect. However, it's one hell of a fine shooter. With cast bullets and the standard military iron sights, even an old guy like me can punch out five-shot groups of less than an inch at 50 yards. On top of that, it's just a wonderfully pleasant and fun old rifle to shoot.

As I worked with this rifle, I wondered just what it would be like to have a .303 Martini with a perfect, unpitted bore. If this old 1899 rifle shot so well, what would one in even better condition do?

Unfortunately, there was just no way I would ever find out! A mint or near-mint Martini in .303 is pretty darn rare and far beyond my budget. There was no way I could ever even begin to afford a nice rifle like that.

A few days later I was in my shop and ran across a virtually mint condition No. 1 Lee-Enfield barrel. It had been pulled from an action but the bore was just about as perfect as you would ever find. As an accumulator of British arms, I've picked up a fair number of parts and pieces over the years, and this barrel had somehow found its way into my parts supply.

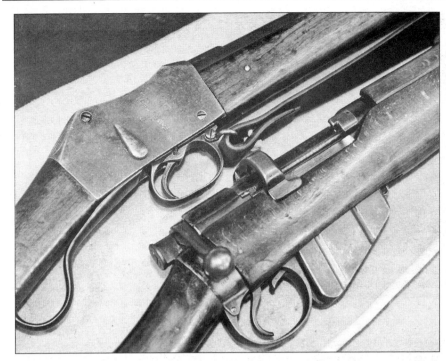

A Martini-Henry on the left is shown beside a British Lee-Enfield. Two very different rifles yet Coffield will combine them to make a unique .303 cal. single-shot.

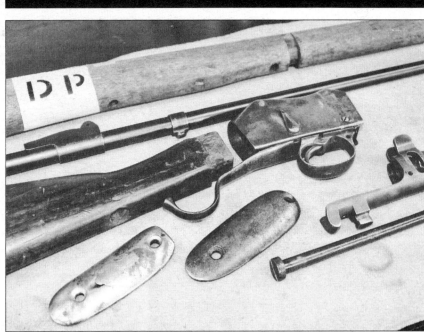

Most of the parts used in building this unusual rifle were ruined and had been accumulated while working on other projects. The "DP" marking is for Drill Purpose.

In looking at this barrel, I noticed that the threaded shank looked darn similar to that of a Martini barrel. I immediately went back to my library and pulled some reference books and sure enough, the thread was the same. Both rifles had a barrel shank threaded with 14 "V" threads per inch and a major diameter of right at 1 inch. Well now, that was interesting!

Would it be possible to fit this barrel to a Martini action? I did some more research and this included talking with a number of friends in Canada. It seems that Enfield barrels have been used on Martini actions in the past. One of my friends reported seeing some Martinis years ago that had been hastily barreled up for the Home Guard in England during World War II using discarded or old No. 1 Enfield barrels.

Another source told me that in Australia, this was a fairly common conversion both before World War II and into the early '50s. In addition, I ran across a couple of Martini collectors who had made just such a conversion.

All this was music to my ears! At that point I decided I would build an Enfield/Martini utilizing SMLE parts and a Martini action. This would be my chance to build a single-shot military type rifle with a perfect bore for cast bullets. The more I thought about it, the more excited I became.

Now the only problem was locating a suitable action. Fortunately, with the influx of Martinis from Nepal sold by International Military Antiques, Inc., 1000 Valley Road, Dept. SGN, Gillette, NJ 07933, telephone 908-903-1200, there have been a few that were, shall we say, distressed.

Another friend made me a heck of a deal on just the action from one of these rifles. At some point in the past it had been refinished, perhaps multiple times, and there were virtually no original markings left on it. I could barely make out the word "Enfield" on the right side of the receiver. No other markings or dates were visible. A few proofmarks remained on the left side of the receiver but that was about it.

This was a short-lever Martini so it was probably built in the 1870s or 1880s. The action was still very tight and all the components were there. While there was no original finish left on the action, there was minor pitting along with the usual dings and nicks you normally find on a rifle action of this age.

All in all, this seemed to be a perfect action for my project. It was definitely not a collectable. Besides, most collectors would have little interest in it due to its condition and especially so since it was not a complete rifle. I would caution anyone who is considering a project like mine to avoid modifying or using a good, collectable rifle. Those rifles are far too desirable to modify or alter. They should be left as original and preserved as historic military artifacts.

Ruined rifles or actions alone are available. It just takes time to find 'em. They can turn up anywhere; gun shows, local gun shops, or even a good buddy might have what you want. The point is to keep looking; sooner or later you'll find one.

While I had already decided to use a SMLE forearm and handguards, I was still not quite sure what to do about the buttstock. Fortunately I ran across a large action Martini buttstock. It was in much worse condition than the action and would require quite a bit of work before it could be used.

There were several major cracks, and a good bit of wood was missing from right behind the receiver shoulder. However, it was basically good, sound walnut and would meet my needs for this project.

Some of the damage to the buttstock was due to the use of an iron buttplate. This had rusted and the wood next to the buttplate had been damaged. As I looked at it, I thought it might have been a lot better to use a brass buttplate. There would have been no rust damage to the wood if that had been done. With that in mind, I decided to fit a brass buttplate to my hybrid rifle. Besides being functional, it'll look nice!

The buttstock was missing the small retainer cup for the end of the finger lever. This cup is inletted into the buttstock and contains a spring latch to keep the finger lever from dropping down when the breechblock is closed. From the condition of the stock, it appeared that the cup had been extensively rusted.

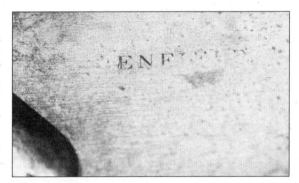

Since it had been refinished, perhaps multiple times, there were virtually no original markings left on the British-made Martini receiver for a collector to enjoy.

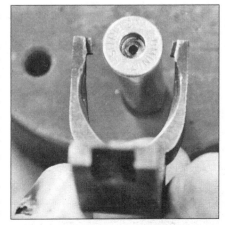

Yes, the original extractor will require extensive modification and hand fitting to work with the smaller .303 cartridge. Coffield will extend either side by about .1".

The extractor is shown with a spacer bar that will be welded between the two hooks. The modified extractor then can be cut at the center for the .303 case head.

Conveniently, for this project, the Enfield barrel has the same thread form and spacing as the Martini barrel. Coffield found it screwed right into the Martini receiver.

The firing pin tip was turned down to fit the modified Martini breechblock. It is important it be the right size to prevent the primer cup from flowing into the gap.

The pin that retained the cup was still in the stock and had rusted to the point that it could not be driven out. Also, there was quite a lot of rusted metal from the cup fused to the wood. It was a mess!

I initially thought I would just have to make another cup. However, I got lucky! While looking in the large trash can where I store discarded stocks and bits of wood, I found part of a Martini buttstock I had saved from an earlier project. The gunsmithing gods were smiling on me as it contained a finger lever cup. What a break!

It was in surprisingly good condition. Needless to say, I pulled it off the scrap stock for use with this project. Once again, it just proves you should *never* throw away old gun parts. Chances are, sooner or latter you'll use 'em!

After taking the action apart and cleaning it, I checked the fit of the barrel. Sure enough, it turned in just fine. However, before going any further, I needed to do something about the extractor slot cut in the face of the barrel. All I needed to do was to cut and file a piece of steel to act as a filler. Once this was made, I soldered it into place using Brownells Hi-Force 44 solder.

This is a fairly low temperature solder that flows at 650°, yet it has a tensile strength comparable with many silver solders. Also, it's not affected by bluing salts. If I were ever limited to just one solder in my shop, this would be the one I would have. I've used it for more than 30 years and I really like it.

Once the filler was installed, I filed it down even with the face of the barrel. A note of caution; do not under any circumstances take any metal off the face of the barrel. Later we'll have to fit the barrel and breechblock and we'll need as much steel here as possible to obtain proper headspace. You definitely don't want the face of the barrel to be too short!

On the side or threaded shank of the barrel, I made sure the filler block was slightly below the threads so it would not contact or damage the receiver threads. This was not all that difficult as most of the filler block was not in line with the threads.

Enfield? Martini? or Both? | Part 1

Coffield had to lathe-turn a special tool to drill out the welded up firing pin hole in the Martini breechblock. This rod passed through the rear of the breechblock.

While I was working on the barrel, I had the buttstock soaking in a bath of turpentine. This is a solvent made from pine rosin and as far as I can tell, it won't damage the wood as will so many petroleum-based solvents. I initially had the buttstock soak for 24 hours.

During that period, I occasionally wiped down the stock with a very soft brush to help remove the surface crud. It was amazing how this helped to clean the stock. It looked like a different piece of wood when I brought it out of the tank.

I dried it off and then looked closely at the location of the finger lever cup. It was a bit cleaner and I could see more clearly the condition of the two remaining parts of the retaining pin. There was no way these could be driven out without further damage to the stock.

Instead, I opted to drill them out with a #40 drill. There was no problem with this, as the pins had rusted to an extreme degree. As I drilled them out, there were no metal chips or shards; it was all an oxide dust! This also took out a tiny bit of wood, but that was OK. The wood next to the pin was rotted and would have had to be replaced in any event.

After removal of the pins I placed the buttstock back in the turpentine bath and let it soak for several days. I wanted to remove as much oil as possible, since I

would be gluing several pieces of wood to the buttstock during the repair process. The less oil you have in the wood, the better the glue or epoxy used in any repair will hold.

Getting back to the barrel, I applied some anti-seize compound to the threads and turned the barrel into the receiver. In order to hold the barrel I used a special barrel block in my barrel vise. Enfield and Martini barrels have what is called a Knox form over the chamber. This is a flat projection on the top of the barrel.

I don't know the history of this or exactly why the Brits used it. If you have a special fixture designed for it, it can make barrel changing pretty easy. If you don't, you may have some problems!

Years ago when I was involved in quite a bit of Lee-Enfield work, a friend made up a block for the Knox form. It's a two-piece affair. One part has a tapered hole to secure the rounded part of the chamber area of the barrel while the second part is designed to fit the flat of the Knox form. The two parts are held together and aligned with two large pins. It was a true pain in the tush to make but it has been handy.

You can still, of course, secure the barrel by just clamping it in your barrel vise further out beyond the Knox form. That's not ideal as you generally want to hold the barrel as close to the receiver as possible but

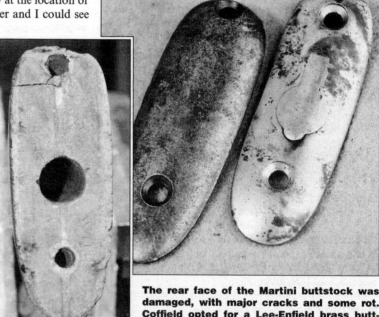

The rear face of the Martini buttstock was damaged, with major cracks and some rot. Coffield opted for a Lee-Enfield brass buttplate rather than the Martini steel unit.

The buttstock was damaged at the wrist where it contacts the receiver. The SMLE stock had been damaged when someone tried to remove it before taking off the forearm.

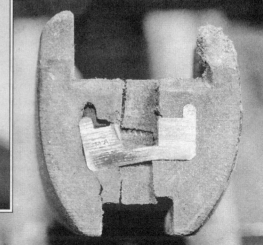

Once the barrel was properly seated in the receiver, Coffield placed an index mark on both the barrel and receiver to make it easy to retighten the barrel exactly.

The face of the breechblock has been welded up, drilled, and the smaller diameter firing pin tip fitted. Coffield had to shorten the firing pin tip a bit.

it'll work. For years prior to getting my Knox form barrel clamp I did it that way.

When placing an action wrench on the Martini action, you have to be very careful that you do not crush or bend in the sides of the receiver. It's very thin and this can happen easily. You can avoid this by making sure the action wrench is far enough forward to be supported by the internal web at the front of the receiver.

Another option is to place supports inside the receiver. These supports or jacks are nothing more than flat-headed machine bolts. With this receiver I used some 3/4"x1/4" machine bolts. The nuts were threaded on the shank of the bolt, which was placed inside the receiver.

The nuts were then turned to bring pressure to bear against the opposite side of the receiver. They were in effect "jammed" in place. Using these "jacks", there was very little possibility of the sides of the receiver being crushed or bent inward. This same technique can also be used on many other actions.

The barrel was initially turned in as far as possible by hand so I didn't have very far to go. In fact, I only needed to go about 1/8th of a full turn to have it seated and the Knox form at 12 o'clock. The Knox form and the fact that the sight bases are already installed on the barrel helped to make sure it was properly aligned.

Once this was done, I also made a witness mark on the barrel and on the receiver. The barrel will, by necessity, be pulled back off the receiver for chambering and then later for fitting the extractor. With the witness marks I'll have no problem at all in turning the barrel back to exactly the same point time after time.

With the barrel in place, I checked the fit of the breechblock. It locked in place, which was somewhat of a surprise. I thought I would have to file down the face of the barrel but that was not necessary. However, before doing any chambering and headspacing, I needed to do a bit of work on the face of the breechblock.

The problem was the firing pin. It was too large a diameter for a modern smokeless powder cartridge like the .303. At a diameter of almost .092", it was fine for the blackpowder .450/577 cartridge where the chamber pressure is very low. If I did not reduce the diameter of the firing pin I might experience problems with the primer flowing back into the breechblock when firing .303 cartridges even with modest handloads. Note that I said "I might". It's possible that I wouldn't, but I didn't want to take the chance.

I could not just turn down the firing pin tip as recommended by Frank de Haas, a noted authority on single-shot rifles and the author of *Mr. Single-shot's Gunsmithing Idea Book*. I would also have to reduce the diameter of the firing pin hole in the face of the breechblock. By the way, this book by de Haas is just

Enfield? Martini? or Both? | Part 1

loaded with great information for anyone working on the Martini. As far as I know it's still in print and can be obtained from most suppliers of firearms books.

While turning down the tip of the firing pin is pretty straightforward, dealing with the breechblock is a bit more involved. I could bush or reduce the diameter of the firing pin hole a number of different ways. The British cut a dovetail across the face of the breechblock, fitted a metal plate in this dovetail, and then drilled the plate for the smaller firing pin. That certainly worked, but it might entail annealing the front of the breechblock.

I could also spot anneal the area around the firing pin hole and then drill and tap it for a plug screw. The plug screw would then be faced off even with the breech face and drilled for the firing pin tip.

Another option was to TIG weld the firing pin hole in the breechblock. This would entail closing up the existing firing pin hole and then drilling it out for the smaller firing pin. I decided to try that first. If it didn't work out, I could always fall back and use one of the other two options.

Besides, as is so often the case with these one-of-a-kind gunsmithing projects, this is something I've never done before. To learn, you simply have to experiment and try new procedures and techniques. Even if this doesn't work, I'll learn from it.

I used my bead blasting set up to thoroughly clean the face and inside of the breechblock. When TIG welding, you don't want to have any rust or contamination, as this will affect the quality of the weld. While I was at it, I also cleaned the hooks on the extractor.

The .577/450 has a large diameter rim that measures about .745". The .303 cartridge has a much smaller diameter rim that typically measures about .522". Because of this the extractor hooks had to be extended by approximately .100" on each side to engage the smaller cartridge case.

Rather than just building up the two hooks, I welded a small piece of steel between the hooks and then cut out the excess material in the center. I felt this would give me a stronger, more durable extractor.

In drilling out the welded up firing pin hole, it's best if it's drilled from inside the breechblock. In order to do this, I first had to turn down a piece of steel rod to a diameter of .555" so it was a sliding fit inside my breechblock. This piece of rod would serve as a holder for my drill as I drilled out the firing pin hole.

One end of the rod was center drilled and then drilled to a depth of approximately 3/4" with a #49 drill. The shank of this same drill was then shortened and inserted in the newly drilled hole. I didn't want much of the business end of the drill to protrude from the front of the rod. The less drill I had protruding, the "stiffer" and less likely it would be to bend or flex when used to drill the firing pin hole.

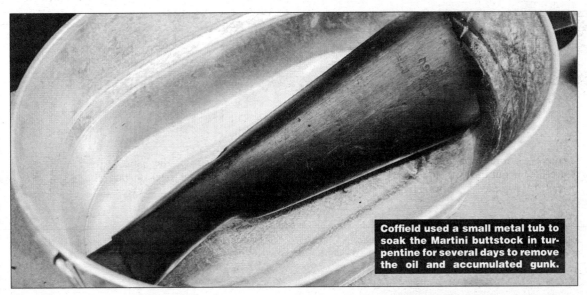

Coffield used a small metal tub to soak the Martini buttstock in turpentine for several days to remove the oil and accumulated gunk.

The filler for the old extractor slot was cut from a piece of mild steel. Then Coffield fitted it and soldered it in place, being sure it fit with the existing thread.

The special barrel holding fixture Coffield used to secure the Lee-Enfield barrel. Note how the top block of the fixture fits over the Lee-Enfield barrel Knox form.

Coffield used two "jacks" as supports for the thin-walled Martini receiver when installing the new barrel. Without these in place, the receiver walls can bend and twist.

The #49 drill will theoretically cut a .073" hole, but in most cases a drill will tend to cut a hole a bit larger due to either imperfections in the drill or run-out due to the machine used for drilling. If my firing pin hole is a bit small, I can always open it up with a broach when fitting the firing pin.

To secure the cut off drill in my holder, I used some red Permatex Threadlocker. This makes for a virtually permanent installation. You could, of course, use solder, but this was faster and I only needed to drill one hole that was only about 1/16" of an inch or less deep.

Once you finish drilling out the firing pin hole, be sure to mark or in some way have some sort of identification on this drill extension. This is especially important if you ever work on another Martini. Nothin' is worse than having to make up another tool when you know you already have one; you just can't find the darn thing.

Enfield? Martini? or Both? | Part 1

And yes, I have far too many "special use" tools I didn't mark and now for the life of me, I can't identify what the darn things are for!

After drilling out the breechblock, I used a fine India stone to smooth off any burrs on the breech face. Once that's done, the old firing pin tip was turned down to fit the new breechblock hole. When doing this, you don't want to have the diameter of the firing pin tip to be more than two or three thousandths smaller than the diameter of the hole.

If you have more than this, you may have problems with the primer flowing back around the firing pin. I opted to turn my Martini firing pin tip down to .075", which is the diameter of the firing pin tip of the U.S. 1903 Springfield and it's also just a tad smaller than the new firing pin hole in the breechblock. This was just a little smaller than recommended by de Haas. Keep in mind that this was done *after* completing work on the breechblock.

With the firing pin turned down and fitted to the breechblock, I installed the firing pin spring and the retainer. I could now check the firing pin protrusion. Generally, it should run about .055" to .058". Also the tip of the firing pin should be a nice smooth radius. You definitely don't want it flat or with sharp edges that could lead to a pierced primer. Initially my firing pin protrusion was about .095"! I had to cut it back quite a bit to get it to an acceptable .058". Once I had it shaped and polished, that part of the job was done.

The next time we get together (5/10 issue) I'll fit the extractor, lengthen the chamber a bit, and cut the cartridge rim recess in the face of the barrel. After that, it'll be mostly wood work as the forearm is modified and fitted and the buttstock repaired.

Until next time, good luck and good gunsmithing!

Ask the Gunsmith

By Reid Coffield

ELGIN SHOTGUN

Q *I have a double-barrel, side hammer shotgun made by Elgin that belonged to my grandfather. He bought it back in the 1920s. I shoot all kinds of loads in the gun, which is in excellent condition. Can you tell me anything about the history of the gun and if it is safe to fire?*

A Your shotgun was probably made by Crescent Firearms Company in Norwich, Conn. This company was founded in 1892 and produced a tremendous number of inexpensive shotguns for the hardware trade. These guns were sold in great numbers by companies such as Sears, Straus and Schram, and Fred Biffar and Company of Chicago, Ill. In 1893 the company was purchased by H. & D. Folsom Arms Company but continued operating under its own name until 1930, when it was merged with the Davis Warner Corporation. The company was finally bought by Stevens Arms & Tool Company in 1932 when it basically ceased to exist.

As for shooting this shotgun with "all kinds of loads," I would not encourage that! This is an old, basically blackpowder-era gun that does not have the strength to withstand modern, high pressure loads. I would encourage you to immediately have the gun inspected by a knowledgeable, competent gunsmith.

If, and only if, he considers the gun safe should you consider any further use of it and then only with blackpowder loads. Keep in mind that this shotgun is close to 100 years old and was not of the highest quality when it was manufactured. It was an economical, low-priced gun designed for moderate use.

One of the most common questions any gunsmith gets is "can I shoot Grandpa's gun?" If it's an old hammer shotgun, especially with Damascus barrels, the answer is usually no.

CARBINE BOLT CRACKS

Q *I have a couple of M1 carbines I have had for years and use for both recreational shooting and personal protection. I realize these guns are not in the same class as the newer AR's but my wife and I both like them a lot. I have put away some spare parts for emergency repairs; extractors, firing pins, etc. I was told I should also have a couple of bolts. Have you ever seen a bolt break? I can not believe I would ever have to replace a bolt body!*

As you can see, the extractor hole removes a lot of steel from the M1 Carbine bolt at the base of the right locking lug and the lug can break off under the right conditions.

A Actually you've gotten some good advice! The M1 carbine bolt is subject to breakage and I've seen several where the right locking lug has broken off from the bolt body. The holes that are machined in the bolt for the extractor, extractor spring and plunger remove quite a bit of material from the base of the right lug. Given quite a bit of use and age, the right locking lug can and will break off from the bolt body. It is unusual but it can happen.

Enfield? Martini? or Both?

Part 2

In Part 1 (4/10 issue), Coffield modified the breechblock and extractor. This time he fits the barrel and reworks the stock.

By Reid Coffield

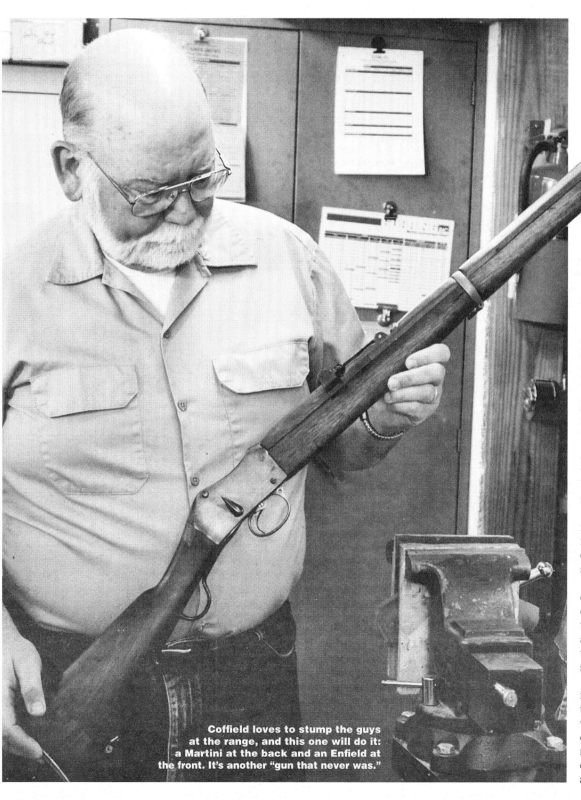

Coffield loves to stump the guys at the range, and this one will do it: a Martini at the back and an Enfield at the front. It's another "gun that never was."

Over the years I've put together a number of guns using parts and pieces from a variety of different firearms. A few years ago I made up a .45 ACP Mauser carbine that had parts from, as best I can recall, about seven different rifles. It was a lot of fun and I've always enjoyed projects like that.

Maybe it relates back to the fact that years ago I had the opportunity to see some Bannerman rifles. These were military type rifles made up by Francis Bannerman, a major civilian dealer in surplus military arms who started his business during the later part of the 19th century. His company, located in New York, was still in business until after World War II (see 7/20/08 issue).

In the early part of the 20th century, Bannerman offered a number of bolt-action rifles that were made up of parts from various firearms. I remember one 7mm bolt-action that had a 1917 Enfield action and Krag sights! It was quite a rifle.

My current project is putting together a single-shot rifle using a .450/577 Martini action and the barrel and forearm furniture of a No. 1 Lee-Enfield. I wanted a .303 carbine with a good barrel I could use for recreational shooting with cast lead bullets.

Also, I have to admit, I wanted something unique and different. Some of you who have followed my articles over the years know that one of my greatest pleasures is to show up at the local range and have folks look over at my rifle or whatever it is I'm shooting and ask, "What the hell is that?" It's always a lot of fun and leads to some great conversations at the range.

I should say something about the caliber designation for the Martini as there is a lot of controversy about this. Should it be .577/450 or .450/577? Many shooters go with .577/450 as the later Martinis used a .45 cal. bullet on a necked-down .577 case. The British military just referred to it as a .450 Long. I'm comfortable with any of the three designations. I know what you're talking about no matter which label you use!

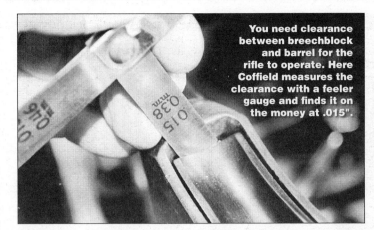

You need clearance between breechblock and barrel for the rifle to operate. Here Coffield measures the clearance with a feeler gauge and finds it on the money at .015".

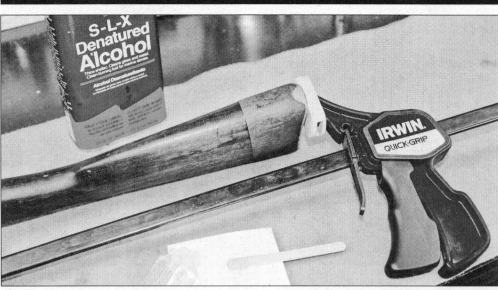

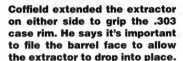

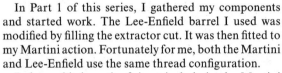

Coffield extended the extractor on either side to grip the .303 case rim. He says it's important to file the barrel face to allow the extractor to drop into place.

Next, cut the rim recess to .049". When combined with the .015" clearance, there's room for the breechblock to close over the .064" Go gauge. The filler fell out.

Coffield cut the last couple inches off a scrap Enfield stock and glued it to the shortened Martini stock, using a couple of cut-off brads to align the two parts.

In Part 1 of this series, I gathered my components and started work. The Lee-Enfield barrel I used was modified by filling the extractor cut. It was then fitted to my Martini action. Fortunately for me, both the Martini and Lee-Enfield use the same thread configuration.

I also welded up the firing pin hole in the Martini breechblock, reduced the diameter of the Martini firing pin, and fitted the modified firing pin to the breechblock. The .450/577 Martini extractor was also modified for the smaller diameter .303 cartridges by welding in a steel bar and then recutting the extractor hooks.

I found an original Martini buttstock, but it was in very poor condition with lots of damage. This was soaked for several days in turpentine to remove most of the gunk and crud. Before attempting any wood repairs or modifications, I wanted to get the wood as clean as possible. The less oil you have in the wood, the better epoxies and glues will hold.

The last and most challenging part of the metal work is the fitting of the extractor for the smaller .303 cartridge. The .303 cartridge has a rim diameter of around .525" while the .450/577 measures about .743". That is quite a difference. As I mentioned earlier, I opted to modify my extractor by welding in a bar between the two hooks. I then planned on later cutting this bar when I fit the new hooks to the .303 cartridge rim.

The first step in doing this was to fit the extractor to the breech face of the Enfield barrel. I turned the barrel into the receiver after having coated the breech face with machinist layout fluid. I then installed the trigger guard and the extractor, using the guard screw and the cocking indicator to hold everything in place.

I held the extractor against the breech face and used a sharp scribe to trace along the extractor. This helped me determine where I need to remove metal from the breech face to allow the extractor to be fully seated.

I then removed the barrel from the receiver and clamped it securely in my vise. I cheated a bit and used a couple of cutoff wheels in my Dremel tool to remove most of the metal from the barrel face for the extractor cuts. If you do this, be darn careful! You can easily cut or grind away too much metal very quickly. Once a good

portion of the metal was ground away, I used a variety of needle files to remove the remaining portion of the metal for the extractor cuts.

This is basic gunsmithing where you're hand fitting two metal parts. It's not all that hard, but you just have to go slow and be darn careful with your work. You need to know also that you'll have to put the barrel back on the receiver several times to check the progress of your work and to make sure everything is properly fitted.

Keep in mind that you're basically just wanting to fit the modified extractor so it's flush with the face of the barrel. I also had to make sure the extractor would pivot properly into and out of the slots in the face of the barrel. This entailed putting the barrel back on the receiver, installing the trigger guard as well as the extractor.

Don't make the mistake of skipping this step! The extractor has to move into and out of the recesses in the barrel freely *before* you even think about the final fitting and cutting the rim recess. Other than that, that's all you need to do at this point.

As always, when putting an action wrench on the Martini receiver, be sure to use a support or brace for the inside of the action. I use a couple of "jacks" that are nothing more than machine screws with nuts. By unscrewing the nuts inside the action, these "jacks" effectively prevent any compression or bending of the sides of the Martini action. Supports like this can often be used in other thin or easily deformed receivers.

Once the extractor was flush with the face of the barrel and I had checked to make sure the breechblock would move freely, I cut away the center section of the bar I had welded between the extractor hooks. I then used my Dremel and needle files to make sure the hooks were flush with the inside of the chamber wall. You might be tempted to try to fit the ends of the hooks with the chamber reamer, but I would not encourage you to do so. It's just a lot easier to do it with files and a Dremel.

Having trouble leveling up the buttstock at the bandsaw? Use ordinary playing cards to shim it up; you can adjust to a very fine tolerance by using the cards.

Note how Coffield cut through the Enfield stock swivel base inletting. The portion that remains will be helpful when installing the base into the Martini stock.

The next job was to headspace the chamber. The first step was to install the barrel once again in the receiver along with the breechblock. You lift the breechblock into the closed position and use a feeler gauge to measure the distance from the face of the barrel to the face of the breechblock. With my rifle, that measurement was .015". The rim thickness of the Manson Precision "Go" headspace gauge measures .064".

Consequently, I'll need to use my chamber reamer to cut the rim recess to a depth of only .049" to ensure I have proper headspace. (.064" minus .015" equals .049", the depth of the rim cut). I definitely don't want to go beyond a depth of .056", as that would allow the "No Go" gauge with a rim thickness of .071" to fully seat with the breechblock in place.

By the way, the headspace gauges used for the .303 British cartridges are the same ones used for the .30-40 Krag cartridge. These two cartridges have the same rim thickness and the gauges are interchangeable.

The barrel was removed from the receiver and positioned vertically in my vise. The extractor was held in place in the barrel breech face and the reamer with lots of cutting oil was inserted into the chamber. I'm using a Manson Precision reamer I got from Brownells. Dave Manson produces some of the finest reamers you can buy. I've used his reamers for years and have never been disappointed. His reamers, as well as his other gunsmithing products, are absolutely top notch. If you're not familiar with his line, go to his web site at www.mansonreamers.com or just give him a call at 810-953-0732. Brownells also stocks most of his line and can provide these reamers and headspace gauges as well as virtually any other item you might need for any gunsmithing projects.

As I cut into the barrel for the rim recess, I would frequently stop, install the "Go" gauge and measure from the end of the headspace gauge base to the face of the barrel with a depth micrometer. Here again, you want to go darn slow and check your work frequently.

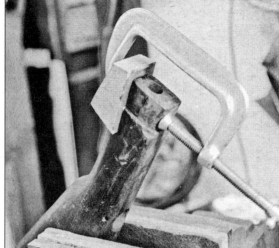

Coffield sawed out a section of damaged wood from the front of the buttstock behind the receiver, then shaped, fitted, and epoxied a walnut plug into the buttstock.

You can cut an awful lot very quickly! Once I reached the point where the distance from the face of the barrel to the end of the "Go" gauge was right at .015", I stopped.

While cutting the rim recess, I ran into a problem I had hoped to avoid. The filler I had so carefully made and soldered into the Number 1 Lee-Enfield barrel extractor cut popped out! I wasn't a happy camper when this happened and I admit my language reflected that unhappiness. Fortunately, I was alone in my shop.

The bottom line is simply that my solder joint was not as strong or as well done as I thought. Don't get me wrong; the fault was mine, not the materials I used. I just did not get as strong a joint as I thought I had.

I could have tried to resolder the filler, but as I looked at the extractor cut, I realized this was not absolutely necessary. The rim cut from the chamber reamer runs a full 360° around the chamber and fully supports the cartridge. The only advantage to having the filler was cosmetic; it looks nicer. On the other hand, leaving the original extractor cut demonstrates this is a No. 1 Lee-Enfield barrel.

So, take your choice; you can do it either way. I decided to go ahead and leave the filler block out since it was nonfunctional and just cosmetic. However, if I do another one of these rifles I will still make a filler block and try to do a better job of soldering.

The barrel was then put back into the receiver, the breechblock installed, and the headspace checked. First the "Go" gauge was inserted in the chamber and the breechblock pushed into the locked position. Next, the "No Go" gauge was placed in the chamber and the breechblock raised into the locked position.

If you have not run the rim cut too deep, the breechblock should *not* close on the "No Go" gauge. That was the case with my rifle. If it had closed, I would have had excessive headspace and would have had to set the barrel back and refit the breechblock. Fortunately, that didn't happen!

With this completed, I turned to the buttstock for a bit of woodwork. The end of the buttstock had been damaged over the years. There was a major crack at the heel and there was extensive rot or wood damage caused by the rusting of the cast steel buttplate. I opted to repair this by cutting about 1¾ inches off the butt, removing all the damaged area.

I then cut about 2 inches off an old No. 1 Lee-Enfield buttstock. This section was then epoxied to the Martini buttstock. This also allowed me to utilize an Enfield brass buttplate. For the life of me, I don't understand why the Brits used steel on the Martini that would rust and ruin the wood. Keep in mind they used brass on the rifles that proceeded and followed the Martini! Maybe it was just an experiment that failed!

By the way, if you cut a stock on a bandsaw and you're having problems keeping it level so your saw cut is perpendicular to the centerline of the stock, you might want to try a trick I learned years ago. I use ordinary playing cards I keep in the shop just for this reason.

Each card is only about .011" thick, so I can make adjustments easily and in very small increments. Also, the plastic coated cards slide smoothly over the bandsaw table. From time to time I also use cards as shims when working with my mill or even with my drill press.

Since the joint between the Martini stock and the Enfield stock extension was flat, I needed something to help hold the two pieces of wood together as the epoxy cured. To do this, I drove two small nails into the rear face of the stock and then cut them off with a wire cutter almost flush with the wood. This left two small steel posts sticking up. The epoxy was applied and then the Enfield wood pressed into place. The steel posts acted as anchors and prevented any slippage.

I let the epoxy cure for 24 hours, and then removed the adjustable clamp I had used on the buttstock. I then started work on repairing some of the wood damage on the other end, where it joined the receiver. I had an especially bad section right on the top of the stock so I first had to splice in a piece of wood there.

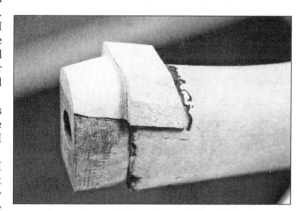

Once the epoxy was set up, Coffield inlet the buttstock into the receiver, then shaped the rest of the plug to the stock. At this point, the work is about 80% complete.

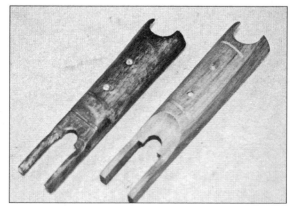

The rear handguard (left) was in extremely poor condition and would have required extensive repair. Coffield was able to order a new one from Numrich Gun Parts.

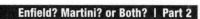

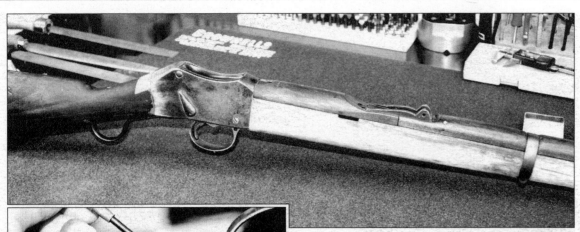

The Enfield forearm extends well below the Martini receiver and will require more wood to be removed to fit properly. Some wood needs to come off the sides, too.

buttstock. This was especially important for the top or comb and the bottom or toe line.

With that done, the stock was then sanded to 180 grit. When sanding the stock, I wanted to keep a military look and with that you seldom have the wood finished to as smooth a finish as you would in a civilian sporting arm. I purposely left some minor scratches and dents as you typically find on arsenal refinished arms.

After working on the buttstock, I turned my attention to the forearm. My first action was to cut the No. 1 Enfield forearm about 3/8" back from the end of the barrel channel. This turned out to be just ahead of the front guard screw.

After the stock was cut, I coated the front of the receiver with inletting black and began inletting the stock into the receiver. There is a slight recess ahead of the trigger guard, and the forearm wood needs to fill this recess. This projection of the forearm keeps it from rotating on the barrel.

It was a slow process, but not all that difficult. Most of the work was done with some flat files and small chisels. By the way, towards the end of the process I installed the nose cap on the forearm and used a leather mallet to help tap the forearm back against the receiver.

Once the forearm was fully inlet and installed on the barreled action, I used a fine rasp and a half-round cabinetmaker's rasp to shape the forearm. The Martini action is rather thin and has a deep rectangular cross section while the Enfield forearm is pretty thick and round. I needed to remove enough wood to have the forearm blend into the receiver. This was actually a good thing in that it allowed me to remove a lot of damaged and dented wood from the forearm.

After shaping the forearm, I went ahead and sanded it. As with the buttstock, I only went to 180 grit, as this was a military stock. Once the sanding was completed, I installed the two handguards and the nosepiece just to get a feel for how the completed rifle would look. I have to admit, I was very pleased.

The last bit of metal work I needed to do was to install and bed a recoil shoulder on the underside of the barrel. While the forearm is held to the barrel with a screw attached to a barrel band, I thought there was still a need to have something more substantial.

Keep in mind that when the rifle is fired, the inertia will cause the forearm to more forward. I wanted to make sure that did not happen and that the forearm would not be damaged. The type of recoil shoulder I had in mind was simply a small block attached to the barrel with the rear face or side at 90° to the bottom of the barrel. It would be very simple and basic.

There wasn't anything really unusual involved in making the repairs at the front of the stock. It was just a matter of cutting away the damaged wood, fitting a piece of good wood, and gluing it in place. After the epoxy cured, I initially used my bandsaw to cut away the excess wood used for the repair. Long ago my old partner Wayne Spears taught me to cut away as much wood as possible with a saw prior to using rasps, files, or chisels. You save a tremendous amount of time by doing so.

I then refitted the receiver to the buttstock. In doing this, I did not remove any more wood than absolutely necessary. Overall shaping of the buttstock would come only after two final stock repairs were made. In this case, that was to fit the replacement finger lever cap in the buttstock and install a sling swivel base. By the way, I will definitely glass bed the buttstock to the receiver. This will be done when the finger lever cap is installed and bedded.

In working with older military rifles utilizing a two-piece stock, I often find the hole for the buttstock bolt has shrunk as the wood has expanded over the years from the absorption of moisture. My salvaged buttstock had a slightly undersize bolt hole and this required a bit of work.

I used a couple of round rasps to remove some wood from the buttstock hole until the stock bolt would slide freely into and out of the buttstock. If you encounter something like this, don't ignore it. Sooner or later the stock will split as it swells around the stock bolt or the stock bolt seat extension in the receiver.

The original finger lever cap was missing from the buttstock but fortunately I found one on a junk stock that was in pretty good shape. This was removed and cleaned. I also modified it so it could be attached with a wood screw rather than the original transverse pin. This would allow much easier removal for cleaning and maintenance.

All I had to do was file away the original square tenon on the bottom of the cap and then drill and countersink the cap for a No. 8x5/8" wood screw. I then inlet the cap into my buttstock, fit the wood screw, and then to make everything even more secure, glass bedded the cap for the best possible fit.

It was a lot of work for a small part but absolutely necessary. While I had bedding mixed, I went ahead and applied some to the front end of the buttstock where it seated against the receiver. The bedding here would protect the wood from any oil that might leak from the receiver and provide a perfect, tight fit with the metal.

When I cut off the rear of the No. 1 buttstock, I cut through the inletting for the rear sling swivel. That was fine, as I needed to install a sling swivel on the buttstock and that provided about half the inletting as well as the exact location for the sling loop base.

It was just a matter of tracing around the base with a pencil to help determine where the wood needed to be removed and then cutting away most of the wood with a series of small chisels and gouges. Once most of the wood was cut away, I coated the sling base with inletting black to get a more precise reading on where additional wood needed to be removed. It was then just a matter of making an impression with the inletting black and cutting away the points of contact until the base was fully seated in the buttstock.

Once that was done, I used a series of fine rasps and files to shape the buttstock. The new wood I added had to be taken down to the point where it matched the lines of the original

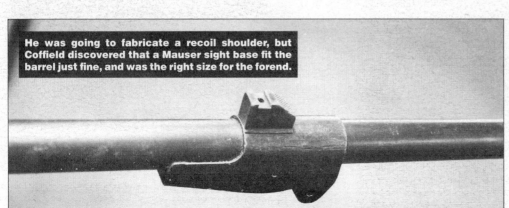

He was going to fabricate a recoil shoulder, but Coffield discovered that a Mauser sight base fit the barrel just fine, and was the right size for the forend.

The recoil block has been attached to the barrel with two screws and the area where it will be inletted into the forearm has been marked in preparation for cutting.

Coffield uses an old British military front sight mover to adjust the position of the front sight blade. This is a lot faster than tapping the sight back and forth.

Coffield stashed several windage adjustable Enfield rear sights years ago, and finally got the chance to use one. Fine adjustments will come in handy in range firing.

I initially cut a piece of round cold-rolled steel about 1/2" thick with the intention of cutting the recoil block out of it. However, as I had this piece of steel lying on my bench I realized I already had a recoil block!

As I have mentioned a number of times, you *never* throw away a gun part. Some day, you'll need it! Sure enough, I pulled out my Mauser parts and there were several front sight bases I had removed from junk barrels. It was just a matter of cutting off the band and then doing a little file work and my recoil block was virtually complete.

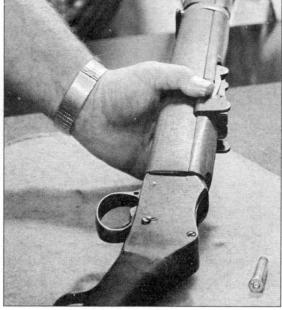

The Enfield forearm and handguards started out pretty bulbous, but with some judicious hand-shaping by Coffield, they look like they were made for the Martini.

I did drill out the existing hole for the original indexing screw as I planned on using an 8x40 fillister head screw as the main attaching screw. Once that was done, I positioned the recoil block on the underside of the rear sight base and then drilled and tapped it for the 8x40 screw.

Just to be on the safe side, I went ahead and drilled the recoil block for an additional 8x40 screw and then drilled and tapped the barrel for this second screw as well. One screw might have been just fine but it only took a few minutes for this extra insurance.

After installing the recoil block, I inletted the forearm and then bedded it for a nice tight fit. I also bedded the rear of the forearm where it fit into the front of the receiver. By doing this, I made sure that the rear of the forearm would not tend to pull down or away from the barrel.

With all the metal work and bedding completed, I then used a dark walnut alcohol-based stain on the buttstock and forearm. I have American walnut, European walnut and Australian coach wood in

And yes, you can fit a bayonet to the Enfield Martini! If you insist. The result of Coffield's conversion is a rifle that is a lot easier and less expensive to shoot.

my stock, and consequently I have quite a range of color. Using a dark walnut type stain gave me a little more uniformity.

After allowing the stain to dry, I then went over the stock with a couple of coats of tung oil. Tung oil will give the appearance of the traditional military linseed oil finish but will dry much, much faster.

While the stock was drying, I assembled the metal components of the rifle. The only unusual feature I added to my hybrid Martini was the use of an early windage-adjustable Enfield rear sight. Most No. 1 Enfields were built with non-windage adjustable rear sights. Since I will be doing quite a bit of bench shooting with various handloads I wanted the most easily adjustable military sights I could find.

Years ago I picked up a dozen or so windage adjustable Enfield sights. This was the ideal opportunity to use one of 'em. This will really help out when punchin' paper at the local range.

I should mention that the one part I had to get for this project was the rear handguard. The only one I had was just terrible and not worth the effort of trying to fix it. Instead I made a call to Numrich Gun Parts Corp., telephone 866-686-7424, and ordered one from those good folks. The one I got was literally brand new and in perfect condition. By the way, Numrich has tons of Enfield parts. I know as I visited Numrich last summer and saw 'em! Pallet after pallet after pallet piled high with boxes and boxes of Enfield parts. If you need an Enfield part, they've got it!

Reassembly of the rifle was pretty simple with no unexpected problems. Once that was done, I cleaned the barrel to make sure any dust or grime that might have settled there during the project was removed. I then headed out to the range to do some test firing. There was snow on the ground, it was cold as the devil, and no one else was at the range and honestly, I didn't want to be there either! Yeah, the older I get the more of a fair weather shooter I become!

I first fired some military ball ammo to check for extraction and the location of the firing pin. When you alter the face of the breechblock you sometimes make a minor change in where the firing pin strikes. With this rifle, the firing pin was not hitting in the very center of the primer but, it was still well within an acceptable range.

I also used some older handloads with jacketed bullets and these more moderate loads fired and ejected with no problems. I did notice that the rifle was shooting a bit high at 50 yards. Because of this when I got back to the shop and after warming up, I replaced the front sight blade with one that was a bit higher. This will lower the relative position of the barrel and cause the point of impact to drop down a bit.

The one thing I planned but did not do was to rust blue the metal. I'll admit I simply wimped out! As I write this we've had snow on the ground for the last three weeks and the high yesterday was about 15°. It's just been too darn cold to work outside and do any bluing. At some point later in the year when the weather is nicer I'll pull this rifle out and take care of the bluing.

The process I use is very simple, pretty easy, and definitely one you can use at home. In fact, the last gun I rust blued, I did it using our barbecue grill! So, that'll be the subject for another time. To make the rifle more presentable for the time being, I used my old standby cold, Brownells Oxpho-Blue, to touch up the receiver. This will be just fine, it looks good and it'll be a good repair until I'm later able to do a more professional rust blue.

If you decide to make one of these hybrid Martinis, I hope you'll enjoy the project as much as I did. It was a lot of fun and the end result is a truly unique and unusual rifle.

Until next time, good luck and good gunsmithing! ◉

The .22 Caliber
Nº4 Lee Enfield

THE ULTIMATE ECONOMICAL MILITARY SNIPER RIFLE, PART 1

Coffield has cooked up another way to put a junker British rifle to good use; this time it's making a .22 cal. sniper rifle from a variety of No. 4 parts.

A stroll through the Numrich Gun Parts catalog got Coffield to thinking about a way to put some old Enfield parts to use. Here's an economical project that will yield a fun-to-shoot rifle.

By Reid Coffield

When I was about 14 years old I was both blessed and cursed. I had inherited a well-used and slightly abused Winchester Model 67 from my maternal grandfather when I was 11 years old. I loved that rifle and it served me well back then and still does today. Most importantly, it got me hooked into firearms.

It wasn't long until I was chafing at the bit for a "real" rifle…a large bore military rifle. At that time, back around 1960, you could pick up good Mausers, Springfields, or Enfields for $35 or less. I well remember walking into a Sears store and seeing several garbage cans filled with No. 1 Lee Enfields which were being sold for $20 or so.

I had the hots for an Enfield, specifically a No. 1. I had seen an old World War II film with Victor McLaglen in which he played a British army sergeant in charge of a squad of soldiers trapped in the desert. The film wasn't all that memorable, but I was absolutely taken with the No. 1 Lee Enfields the troops were carrying. What a rifle! I had to have one.

Unfortunately I had no money or way I could ever take advantage of those $20 Enfields at Sears. I was stuck. But then the gun gods smiled upon me, if only for a moment. My mother worked in a textile mill and was approached by a fellow worker to take a chance on a punch board for

a rifle. It only cost a quarter a chance, so Mom bought a chance and got lucky. She won the rifle! It turned out to be a No. 4 Lee Enfield sniper rifle, complete with original mount and scope including the metal scope carrying case.

She brought it home and gave it to me. I was blessed! I was the happiest kid in western North Carolina. I finally had a *real* rifle. No more .22 kid stuff. But then the curse came into play. Remember, I was constantly busted with no money and the only .303 ammo I had available was Remington commercial ammo.

Sure, back then you could go into just about any hardware store and buy just one or two rounds. They were

Never throw anything away, Coffield says, and he shows why by using a selection of parts from his scrap pile and others obtained from Numrich for this project.

I HAVE TO ADMIT, I MISS THAT FIRST ENFIELD AND WISH I HAD IT BACK."

always willing to break a box and sell individual rounds but at 25–27¢ each. However, that was expensive stuff. I was seldom ever able to buy more than four rounds at a time.

So while I loved my Enfield, I had some problems with it. There was the cost of the ammo and the fact that the headspace was excessive. Every now and again I would have a case separate when it was fired. That's not a good thing and even at the tender age of 14 I knew that needed to be corrected.

The problem was there were no gunsmiths in the area and I was stuck. Also, I discovered that the scope, while it looked really cool, was busted! You couldn't make any corrections to the point of impact. Needless to say, that was a bummer.

And finally, it wasn't a No. 1. The skinny little piece of barrel sticking out beyond the front sight on the No. 4 just looked ugly. Eventually I traded it off for some other rifle, beginning a long history of trades and purchases of various military arms.

I have to admit, I miss that first Enfield and wish I had it back. However, if you've noticed the price of original World War II sniper rifles lately, you'll know there is virtually no chance of that happening! A nice complete No. 4 Enfield sniper will easily run over $2,000 nowadays if you can even find one for sale. No, I won't ever have another one, or so I thought.

A couple of weeks ago I was looking through the Numrich Gun Parts website and ran across a listing for a replica No. 4 sniper scope mount and bases. The mount was selling for only $133.85 and appeared to be a very close reproduction of the original mount. There were

also bases for the mount at $43.23 and even the distinctive wooden cheekpiece for $37.80.

Compared to the cost of an original mount and bases, the price wasn't bad at all. In fact, you could make the case that it was a bargain! The more I thought about it, the more it only made sense to order these items and use them along with my existing parts. A few taps of the computer keys and the order was placed for the components I needed.

Over the years I've picked up a fair number of parts and pieces for the No. 4. As I looked over my pile, I realized I probably had enough of the components to put together a rifle. I decided to do that rather than modify an existing rifle. Besides, I could use some of those junk parts you would never want to use on a good rifle.

However, I didn't want to put together a "fake" sniper. There are too many folks who are putting together copies of World War II sniper rifles and tricking unsuspecting buyers. I wanted a rifle but I didn't want to be responsible for some poor guy shelling out big bucks only to find his Enfield sniper was a fake.

The initial answer for me was to build my rifle in .22 rimfire. That was the Enfield I should have had 50 years ago! I would be able to shoot it frequently and inexpensively. Now there is one problem with this solution. In researching this project I ran across some very interesting information.

According to Peter Laidler in his excellent book *An Armourer's Perspective: .303 No. 4 (T) Sniper Rifle and the Holland and Holland Connection* there were a few .22 training rifles made up like the No. 4 sniper rifle. Laidler actually saw some while he was in the British military, so it's not just a figment of the imagination.

Because of this, I'll have to be very careful to make sure my rifle is not mistaken for one of those authentic British military variations. I will definitely mark the rifle in several obvious places with my name and date. I'll do my best to make sure to

identify it so only a complete idiot would mistake it for anything other than just another one of Coffield's crazy gun projects.

I also discovered in the Ian Skennerton book, *The Lee-Enfield Story*, that there were some regular No. 4s converted or made up in .22 rimfire. I've never seen one of these rifles, but Skennerton mentions them and indicates that quite a few were made. These are No. 7 Enfields and there were Canadian and British versions, with a total of about 25,000 made. Again, this is an important point to keep in mind and it definitely makes it imperative to mark your rifle to ensure that it's never mistaken for an original.

With this thought in mind, I placed another order to Numrich for a couple of extra items. The first was a .22 cal. No. 4 extractor and the other was for an additional bolt head. Since I'll have to convert the bolt head from a centerfire to a rimfire I figured I ought to have at least one extra bolt head in case I made a mess of the first one. I've never converted a No. 4 bolt head, so I want to make sure I have a backup in case something goes wrong.

If you want to join me in putting together a backyard British sniper rifle, you can still get No. 4 Enfields from Century International Arms, 430 South Congress Ave., Suite 1, Dept. SGN, Delray Beach, Fla. 33445, telephone 1-800-527-1252. The last time I checked they had quite a few at very reasonable prices. You can also often run across good No. 4 project rifles at local gun shows. I've recently seen several that had been cobbled up and would not be at all appealing to collectors or even shooters. Often these rifles can be picked up fairly inexpensively.

In a factory setting, rifle barrels are straightened by a very skilled and experienced craftsman using a large capstan-handled press like this one.

Not only did the scrap Enfield barrel have worn-out rifling, it was severely bent. A B-Square barrel press was the ticket for getting it back into line.

The .22 liner is much smaller than the .303 chamber, so Coffield will have to drill out and sleeve the chamber. He chose a 31/64" drill to open the chamber.

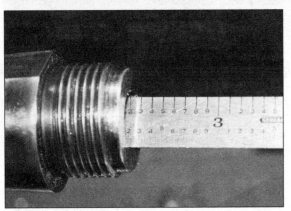

By drilling to 2.3", Coffield removed virtually all of the original chamber, making it easier to install a cylindrical bushing to support the barrel liner.

By all means, *do not* even consider altering a good collectable rifle. Nice Enfields should be preserved in their original military configuration. With each passing day, there are fewer and fewer good original rifles and these artifacts of a bygone time deserve to be preserved for future collectors and shooters. Also, as I mentioned earlier, there were a few .22 sniper training rifles built, so it's only ethical and proper to properly mark your rifle to ensure it's never mistaken for an original British military conversion.

One other item I needed was a good .22 liner. The .303 barrel I selected for this project had a very bad bore. There was quite a bit of pitting, but it was just perfect for lining. Fortunately I had a nice Redman .22 liner from Brownells, the gunsmith supply house in Montezuma, Iowa. Brownells has been selling Redman liners for years and I've used 'em for a great many lining projects. I've never had a problem with 'em. If you need a liner, just give the good folks at Brownells a call at 800-741-0015 and they'll fix you up.

The first step in this project is the installation of the Redman liner in the Enfield barrel. This is not as straight-forward as an installation in an existing .22 rimfire barrel where all you basically have to do is drill out the bore and insert the liner. With a centerfire barrel, you have to first drill out and bush the chamber; otherwise the liner would not be supported, as the chamber is much larger than the diameter of the liner. The breech end of the chamber measures about .455", which is quite a bit larger than the liner, which measures only about .309".

I set the barrel up in my lathe and used a 31/64ths or .484" drill to open up the chamber. When drilling out the chamber, it's very important to have the barrel properly centered in the lathe. I initially used a four-jaw chuck and a dial indicator to try to make my set up as accurate as possible.

I ran into a number of problems getting the barrel centered and initially couldn't figure out what was going on. If I got the breech end of the barrel centered, the muzzle end was way off!

Finally I pulled the barrel out of the lathe and checked it closely. Sure enough, the barrel was bent! I hadn't noticed. So I changed out the four-jaw chuck and installed the three-jaw chuck. I also allowed the muzzle end of the barrel to float rather than try to set it up and center it.

This set up allowed the chamber to be centered and in line with the drill in the tail stock. So take your time and make your setups as accurate as possible. A little extra time spent now could save a lot of time and hassle latter and don't let a bent barrel fool you like it did me!

I drilled the chamber to a depth of about 2.3 inches to ensure my drill reached the bore. This gave me a nice uniform cylindrical hole instead of the original tapered chamber. That made it much easier to fit a bushing.

After removing the barrel from the lathe, I pulled out my old B-Square barrel press to straighten the barrel or at least try to remove as much of the bend as possible. This barrel press is, like so many B-Square tools, really very simple. It consists of a square aluminum tube with two adjustable loops to hold the barrel and a massive threaded screw mounted between the loops used to press against the bend in the barrel.

Traditionally barrel presses are suspended from the ceiling or held in a fixture above the operators head. This ol' tool is small and light enough to be used while clamped in my vise, which is darn handy for a small shop like mine. Basically you just place the barrel in the press with the high point of the bend under the threaded screw.

You then just turn in the barrel press screw, which pushes down on the bend and straightens the barrel. It takes a bit of practice and since the barrel is somewhat flexible you often have to press in a bit beyond the point where the barrel is straight to allow for spring back. Eventually I got most of the bend out of the barrel.

I then took a piece of scrap .303 barrel and turned it down for a nice sliding fit in the 31/64" hole. One end was cut at a 115° angle to match the point angle of the drill I had used to make the chamber. The chamber bushing I purposely left longer than necessary. At this point, mine extended out from the barrel breech by about 3/8". Later, I'll cut the bushing extension to the proper length.

The new hole in the breech end of the barrel and my bushing were cleaned with alcohol to remove all traces of cutting oil. Any residual oil would make it very difficult, if not impossible, for an epoxy to take hold and bond the bushing in the barrel. I cannot be too emphatic about the importance of making sure all metal surfaces that will be coated with epoxy are as clean and free of oil and grease as possible. The cleaner you have the surfaces, the stronger the resulting epoxy bond.

I mixed a two-part epoxy made by Loctite and applied it to the outside of the bushing, which was then inserted in the breech end of the barrel. While the epoxy was still soft, I ran a patch or two through the barrel to remove any epoxy that had worked its way into the bore.

Once this was done, I let everything set up for 24 hours. I wanted to make sure the epoxy was fully cured and holding the chamber insert with maximum strength as the next step involved drilling into the insert for the liner. According to the manufacturer, this Loctite epoxy will theoretically provide up to 2729 psi of holding strength when cured. That should be more than enough to hold the bushing and liner in place.

The liner has a diameter of about .309". Since the barrel bore is only .303", it will have to be opened up a bit. Again Brownells offers a nice piloted barrel lining drill of just the right diameter. Unfortunately, the pilot is a

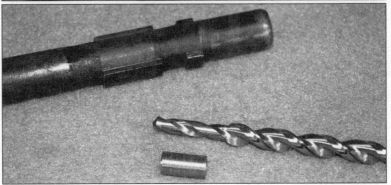

Coffield turns a .30 cal. pilot bushing from a piece of standard cold-rolled 3/8" steel rod. This fit over the original integral .22 cal. liner drill pilot.

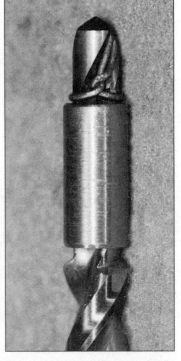

The .30 cal. bushing is shown mounted on the liner drill pilot and secured with a single wrap of steel wire. Sometimes the simple technique proves the best.

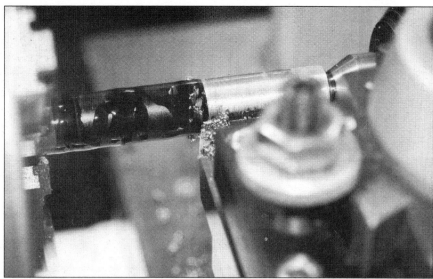

The chamber sleeve was turned from a piece of cut-off .303 barrel and secured with Loctite 5 minute epoxy. Be sure to leave some extending from the barrel.

bit small, since it was intended for drilling out .22 rimfire barrels. I didn't want to have the liner drill unsupported with a non-functioning pilot. Without a pilot, the drill may not follow the bore as precisely as I would like.

However, this problem was easily corrected. Using a piece of plain cold-rolled 3/8" diameter steel rod, I made a bushing for my liner drill pilot. The bushing has a diameter of .302", which is a nice slip fit into the bore. The bushing was drilled out to a diameter of .219", which allowed it to fit over the liner drill pilot.

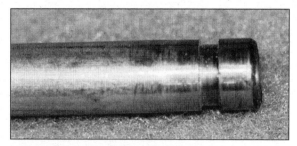

The breech or chamber end of the Redman barrel liner is clearly indicated by a groove cut into the outside. Be sure this is at the chamber end of the barrel.

A small wooden plug helps keep epoxy out of the bore of the .22 liner. Be sure to leave plenty of liner extending from either end in case you make a mistake.

In order to keep this bushing from coming off the pilot while the drill was being used, I had to have some means of holding it in place. To do this, I simply cut a groove around the pilot with a Dremel tool cutoff wheel and used a small piece of wire wrapped around the end of the pilot in this groove.

This loop of wire will keep the bushing from coming off inside the barrel. Admittedly, it's not the most sophisticated fix, but it works! By the way, be sure to hang on to your pilot bushing and keep it with the liner drill. Eventually, if you're like me, you'll end up with a pretty good assortment of bushings of various sizes.

The barrel with the chamber bushing was placed in the lathe. The liner drill was secured in the lathe tailstock. It was then just a matter of drilling out the bore. Actually, this was just about the easiest part of the project. There is very little stress on the liner drill, as I'm not taking out all that much metal. It's almost as if I'm just cutting out the rifling. It didn't take long at all; less than half an hour. And that was going slow and clearing the chips from the drill frequently.

As always, even though there was little stress or load on the drill, I used plenty of cutting oil. Compared to the price of drills, cutting oil is darn cheap and using it will make your drills last longer and cut more efficiently.

Once the barrel was drilled out, I took it out of the lathe and cleaned it thoroughly with alcohol. I wanted to remove all traces of oil or any other material that would inhibit or compromise the strength of the epoxy. I also cleaned the exterior of the liner to remove any grease or oil.

When working with liners, keep in mind there is a breech end and a muzzle end. On the Brownell liner, the breech end is marked with a circular groove around the circumference of the liner. This groove was machined in the liner to allow it to be held in the rifling machine. In the case of this liner, a carbide button was inserted in the secured end of the liner and pulled or pushed to the other end.

When shooting, you'll want the bullet to move in the same direction as that carbide button. As the button was passed through the liner, it swaged the lands and grooves into the steel tube and as it did it pushed metal ahead of the button to a slight degree. This created a subtle roughness that is all but invisible.

Keep in mind these tiny "waves" or, as it was once described to me, the grain of the steel, have their crests pointed towards the muzzle. If the bullet follows the direction of the carbide button, it is not affected by this. However, if you

reverse the liner, the bullet will be moving against the peaks of the waves. This will more often than not result in excessive fouling as lead is stripped from the bullet.

The bottom line is to make sure your liner is marked as to the breech end and don't, for goodness sakes, install it with the breech end at the muzzle! By the way, this also applies to cut rifled barrels. If you inadvertently reverse a barrel blank, you'll end up with the bullet running against the direction in which the rifling cutters were moving, resulting in excessive fouling. The bottom line is to always make sure you properly position a barrel or liner.

One other important point to keep in mind when installing a liner is to make darn sure you have liner extending out from both the muzzle and breech end of the barrel. There'll be a need for extra liner at the breech end when the chamber is cut and headspaced.

"...GET YOURSELF A JUNKER NO. 4 ENFIELD AND JOIN ME IN THIS PROJECT.

Also, just in case there is a mistake, by having extra liner extending from the muzzle I could theoretically heat the epoxy and move the liner back a bit to correct excessive headspace. In either case, don't make the mistake of cutting away the excess liner until a bit further along in the project.

To prevent epoxy from entering the liner bore, I simply plugged the liner's muzzle end with a small wooden dowel. Once the end of the liner was clear of the barrel, I removed it. Again, I used the Loctite 5-minute epoxy and allowed it to cure fully for 24 hours.

After setting aside the barrel, I took the bolt head for the No. 4 and began work on it. One of the great aspects of this project is that the Enfield uses a two-piece bolt. Unlike the 1903 Springfield I converted to .22 rimfire in SGN last year, I won't have to cut the original bolt and make a new bolt head.

Still, there's quite a bit to do as the bolt head is set up for a centerfire cartridge and I need to convert it to a rimfire. After disassembling the bolt head and removing the extractor and extractor spring, I checked the hardness with a file. Sure enough, the bolt head is harder than woodpecker lips. Since I'll have to drill it for a new rimfire firing pin, I'll have to soften or anneal it first. Also I'll need to fill the centerfire firing pin hole.

We'll take care of all that the next time we get together. So, if you're interested in putting together a really unique and interesting replica of a great World War II sniper rifle, get yourself a junker No. 4 Enfield and join me in this project. I'll guarantee it'll be fun to build, to own, and to shoot.

Until next time, good luck and good gunsmithing!

The .22 Caliber
Nº4 Lee Enfield
THE ULTIMATE ECONOMICAL MILITARY SNIPER RIFLE, PART 2

Last month he worked on the barrel; now he takes on modifying the .303 bolt to operate with rimfire ammunition.

By Reid Coffield

The heart of the bolt work is modifying the bolt head to accept a firing pin that will strike the cartridge case rim rather than a centrally located primer.

In the 6/10 issue, I began construction of a .22 rimfire No. 4 Lee Enfield sniper rifle. Many years ago when I was just a kid, I was given a World War II-vintage No. 4 sniper rifle. It was a fantastic rifle, but it had a few mechanical problems and most of all, for a kid with virtually no money, it was just too darn expensive to shoot. Eventually I traded it off for another rifle but I always regretted letting it slip through my hands.

Not too long ago, I noticed Numrich Gun Parts was offering replicas of the No. 4 sniper scope mount along with the scope bases and the unique cheekpiece the Enfield used. The prices were reasonable and it wasn't long until I placed an order for these items.

My plan was to build an affordable replica of the old No. 4 sniper rifle. With prices for an original running into the thousands of dollars, there was just no way that I could ever afford to replace the rifle I had as a kid. However, I could definitely build one.

The only problem with this is that no ethical person wants to fake a collectable firearm or even to mislead someone years from now with a gun they had built. In order to avoid doing this, I planned on making this sniper rifle in .22 rimfire. Not only will it be cheap to shoot and a lot of fun to use, not too many folks will confuse a .22 with an original .303.

I should point out that I later found references to a .22 No. 4 trainer that was set up as a sniper rifle. To avoid confusion with these very rare rifles, I'll make a couple of design changes in my rifle and will also mark mine in several locations to indicate who made it and when. If someone still mistakes it for an original British military rifle, they'll really have to work at being both dumb and blind!

To avoid ruining a nice collectable No. 4, I'm putting my rifle together using a variety of parts and pieces I've collected over the years. If I had not had these parts I would have picked up a butchered or sporterized Enfield at a local gun show. Thousands of these military rifles were modified or converted to inexpensive sporters back in the 1960s and '70s. Today these rifles have little or no value to collectors or shooters and they can often be picked up very inexpensively.

I should also point out that many of the suppliers of surplus arms that advertise here in SHOTGUN NEWS, such as Century Arms International, offer Enfields that are not necessarily collector grade. It can often be worthwhile to check with these outfits if you're looking for a project gun.

In Part 1, I assembled all my components and started work on the barrel. It was drilled out and a .22 cal. Redman liner from Brownells installed. The liner was bonded to the barrel with 5-minute Loctite epoxy. This will be more than adequate to provide a safe, secure bond between the liner and the barrel.

The next part of the process is perhaps the most difficult and that's modifying the bolt head. The Enfield uses a two-piece bolt and the detachable head is set up for a centerfire cartridge. It'll have to be altered for a rimfire, and this entails filling the original firing pin hole, drilling an offset rimfire firing pin hole, making and then fitting a rimfire firing pin. The first step will be to anneal the bolt head, as it is

Coffield drilled the annealed bolt head for the centerfire firing pin plug, which retains a nib Coffield will use to help locate the rimfire firing pin hole.

The original .303 firing pin will need to be cut at the front of the firing pin collar. This effectively changes its function from a firing pin to a striker.

IN PART 1, I ASSEMBLED ALL MY COMPONENTS AND STARTED WORK ON THE BARREL."

extremely hard and would be virtually impossible to drill or modify with standard tooling.

To anneal the bolt head, I will need to heat it to about 1000° and then allow it to air cool. Ideally I would use a heat treating furnace, but frankly, I just don't have one. They are wonderful tools to have in your shop but they tend to be darn expensive and I just don't have the space or the money! Because of this I'll use a standard oxyacetylene gas welding torch. While I have used a standard propane torch to anneal smaller items, on an Enfield bolt head I've had to go to a hotter heat source to get consistent results.

By the way, years ago I made up a couple of No. 1 Mark III Lee Enfields in .22 rimfire. To anneal those bolt heads, I just wrapped the bolt head in aluminum foil and placed it in the charcoal of my barbeque grill when I started the fire. I left it in the coals all during the cooking and didn't take it out until late the next day. When I did, the bolt head was beautifully annealed and soft enough to drill easily. The object of this is just to point out that where there's a will, there's a way!

In annealing this bolt head, I used a firebrick soldering platform. This consists of a couple of fire bricks or furnace bricks mounted on a wood base I can clamp in my vise. The firebricks, unlike regular bricks, are made to withstand extremely high temperatures without damage.

You've probably seen firebrick; it's the light-colored brick often used to line fireplaces. Most brickyards can supply 'em. I picked mine up locally and only paid about a buck and a half each. By the way, my soldering platform has aluminum sides to hold the brick in place. I used aluminum "L" channel rather than wood since I know I'd eventually burn any wood sides with my torch. It was a little more work initially but well worth it.

In using a torch to heat metal to a specific temperature, you have to be able to see and judge the color. If you try doing this in a brightly lit room, you're going to have problems. The regular light will keep you from seeing the color as the metal heats. For this reason, once you get the torch going and have everything in place, cut off your room lights. The torch will provide enough light to see the bolt head.

I positioned the bolt head on my firebrick platform and placed two additional firebricks behind it, forming an "L". One other brick was placed over the other two, forming a small covered area into which I positioned the bolt head.

Then I lit the torch and heated the entire bolt head until it got up to a nice bright red color. I held it at that point for a few minutes. I then took one more firebrick and covered the opening to my makeshift furnace. This would trap the heat in place and make the cooling process a bit longer. Generally, the longer it takes to cool the metal, the more effective the annealing.

After the bolt head had cooled, I placed it in my drill press vise with the rear end up and drilled it out with a #13 drill. This was followed by a standard #13 drill.

It's important to center the bolt head under the drills to ensure that the larger hole is precisely located in the center of the bolt. This will aid in locating the new firing pin hole.

Once the bolt head had been drilled out, I turned a plug for it in my lathe. I used a piece of mild cold-rolled steel for this plug, as I wanted to make sure I could easily drill it for the new firing pin. Keep in mind you'll be drilling a small but long hole and you'll want to make it as easy as possible. Also, if the plug is too hard your drill could easily wander or move off to the side.

One other thing about the plug; I left a small nib at the center of the breech face end of the plug. This nib will later be removed, but it will definitely help to position the rimfire firing pin hole properly. The center of the rim-fire firing pin should be located about .110" from the center of the bolt face. Also, the breech face end of the plug was made with a slight lip to help cover the joint between the plug and the bolt head. It's not much but I figured it wouldn't hurt and it has to help a bit in holding the plug in place.

As to the solder, I used Brownells Hi-Temp Hi-Force 44. This is a very strong solder that is rated at about 38,000 psi. When using this solder, you'll also want to use the Brownells Copper Bond Flux, which is specifically formulated for the Hi-Temp Hi-Force 44.

I admit that I'm probably one of the world's sloppiest users of solder. I tend to get solder and flux all over everything. I have long envied those guys that can put just a dab of solder in one spot and have it flow exactly where they want it. My parts end up looking like they have been dipped

in liquid silver after I'm finished. The only consolation I have as I spend time cleaning up my messy parts is that I normally do get the solder in the places I need it to be.

After cleaning up the bolt head, the next step was to drill the hole for the firing pin tip. This hole will be started at the face of the bolt and will extend all the way to the rear of the bolt. I located and marked a spot approximately .110" from the center of the bolt face.

I used that little nib in the middle of the bolt face plug to help me find this point. Also, I drilled the hole at the 3 o'clock position. My extractor hook will be almost directly across at the 9 o'clock position.

Coffield uses an Enfield firing pin tool to install the firing pin in the bolt body. Tabs on the firing pin tool fit into the notches in the firing pin collar.

The .22 liner has been cut and crowned to match the muzzle of the .303 military barrel. The crown helps protect the rifling from damage if the gun is dropped.

Coffield is just starting to cut off the excess chamber insert and barrel liner with a hacksaw. Don't make the mistake of making the cut flush with the barrel!

Coffield indicates where he removed metal from the rear of the .22 extractor in order to fit it into the modified bolt head. Good extraction requires a good fit.

Note how the tip of the extractor extends a bit more than a third of the width of the bolt face. There's no doubt that it will engage the rim of the .22 case.

"DUMMY ROUNDS ARE THE *ONLY* WAY TO GO AT THIS STAGE OF THE GAME.

Once I drilled the initial hole all the way through the length of the bolt head, I then opened up this hole from the rear of the bolt head for the bolt body. The tip of my firing pin measured .084", while the body of the pin was .169" in diameter. The hole for the firing pin tip was drilled with a #44 drill for a diameter of .086".

I needed it to be a few thousandths larger so I would have a good slip fit. As for the body of the firing pin, I reversed the bolt head in my drill and starting with a #43 drill, gradually worked my way up to an 11/64" drill. Remember that with number drills, they get larger in diameter as the number gets smaller.

This took a bit of time, but it ensured that my larger hole was concentric with the smaller hole. I then removed the bolt head and did the final fitting by polishing the fir-

ing pin on a polishing wheel. Again, I wanted to make darn sure the firing pin would move easily and freely in the bolt head.

There is nothing unique or special about the dimensions of my firing pin. You can definitely make your firing pin to different dimensions. Just make sure that it will fit your bolt head and move freely back and forth.

The overall length of the firing pin was adjusted so its rear end was even with the rear of the bolt head and the tip protruded through only about .035". The design of the Enfield bolt means there'll be no need for any pin or screw to hold the firing pin in place. Basically, it has no place to go and is "captured" by the bolt head and the original Enfield .303 firing pin, which will be modified a bit as the project progresses.

Once the bolt head was completed, I cut off the excess liner and chamber insert from the breech end of the barrel. I made sure to leave about .100" extending from the breech face. Remember that the Enfield is set up for a .303 rimmed cartridge that seats on the face of the breech. You have to make allowances for this normal gap between the breechface and the bolt face.

Then I screwed the barrel back into the receiver, making sure that it was indexed properly so that the front sight was at exactly 12 o'clock. When working with Enfields, don't make the mistake of assuming that the flat on the top of the barrel over the chamber is always the perfect indexing point. Sometimes it is and sometimes it isn't! I always prefer to use my front sight as the final authority. If it's straight and the barrel is locked up, I'm good to go!

By the way, once you have the barrel turned into the receiver and positioned properly, take a small punch or chisel and make two adjacent witness marks; one on the receiver and one on the barrel. You'll be taking the barrel off and then replacing it several times, and these indexing marks will make it so much easier and faster to properly and consistently align the barrel and receiver.

I then used a Clymer .22 Long Rifle chamber reamer to cut the chamber and rim recess. In using the reamer, I used an extension handle so I could cut the chamber by hand while the barrel was fitted to the receiver. This allowed me to continually check headspace with my Forster headspace gauges as the work progressed.

The object of the exercise was to cut the chamber and rim recess deep enough that the bolt would close on the Go gauge but would not close fully on the thicker-rimmed No Go gauge. There's also a third Field gauge that has rim even thicker than the No Go gauge, but you don't want to even think about getting into a situation where you need to use that one!

Just make sure you don't cut so deeply that you end up allowing the bolt to close on the No Go gauge. It's not difficult. Just go slow and check the headspace frequently. Also, be darn sure to use plenty of cutting oil and clean away the metal chips often as you work.

Once the chamber had been completed and the rifle headspaced, I cut away the portion of the liner that extended from the muzzle. I used a hacksaw initially and then faced off the stub of the liner with a file. After that, I used a Manson Precision crowning tool first to face the muzzle off flat at 90° to the axis of the liner.

I then used a special cutter supplied with the Manson tool to cut an 11° crown around the bore. This is somewhat like a shallow countersink that'll protect the edge of the bore. Finally, I used a cup-shaped cutter to chamfer the outside of the muzzle. Oddly enough, this tool seemed to pretty well match the original chamfer on the old military Enfield barrel.

I then pulled the barrel off the receiver to allow cutting of the extractor slot in the chamber extension and liner at the breech. Fortunately, there is a lot of the original extractor slot left in the .303 barrel, and this serves as a perfect guide for what needs to be done. I used a variety of needle files to remove the excess metal.

You have to be careful as you file close to the chamber that you don't cut into the chamber. You have to leave enough of the chamber rim to support the cartridge case rim, yet it also has to be cut back or tapered enough to allow the extractor to hook on to the rim. Once this was done, the barrel was placed back in the receiver.

Numrich had also offered a .22 extractor for the No. 4, so I had ordered one at the same time I ordered the scope base and mount. This extractor is just a bit different than the standard No. 4 extractor, with a thinner hook that extends a bit further onto the face of the bolt. You could modify a standard No. 4 extractor but it would be a lot easier to just use the Numrich extractor. Even with this extractor I needed to alter the back side of it a bit by grinding it down to facilitate the use of the No. 4 extractor spring.

I also took a bit of material off the underside of the extractor to allow the hook to reach a bit further onto the face of the bolt. It might have been fine the way it was, but I wanted the extraction to be as positive as possible. All this entailed was a bit of file work with my needle files,

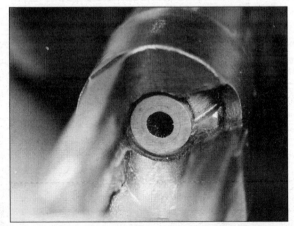

The breech of the lined barrel is seen through the receiver. The extractor slot for the original bolt head makes it easy to see where to slot the .22 barrel.

The chamber reamer first cuts inside the bore, then cuts outside to form the cartridge rim recess. It's an easy process if you proceed slowly and carefully.

A .22 action proving dummy along side a set of Forster Go, No Go, and Field .22 headspace gauges. These are essential tools for setting the rifle's headspace.

With the No Go headspace gauge in the chamber, the rifle bolt will not fully close. If it does, headspace is excessive and the barrel will have to be moved.

Note how Coffield extended the existing extractor cut into the chamber insert and .22 liner. It's important to leave the cartridge case supported all around.

so there wasn't much to this but it's something you might want to keep in mind as you work on your rifle.

I installed the modified extractor in the bolt head, which then was placed in the bolt and extraction checked with a .22 rimfire dummy round. For goodness sake, when checking the functioning of a firearm at your bench, don't use live rounds! If you do, sooner or later you'll put a bullet hole in your bench or the wall of your shop or worse. Dummy rounds are the *only* way to go at this stage of the game.

My extraction looked good, so the next step was to alter the original .303 firing pin. This is super simple. All you need to do is take your Dremel cutoff wheel and cut away the firing pin from right in front of the firing pin

collar. In doing this, you'll have changed the original firing pin into a striker. The face of the collar, which you'll want to clean up and polish, will impact against the rear of the rimfire firing pin.

If you check the length of the modified Enfield firing pin against the bolt and bolt head, you'll see that the new rimfire firing pin is effectively captured in the bolt head. It can slide back, but it can't fall out of the bolt head. Because of this, you don't need to use any screws or pins to hold the rimfire firing pin in place in the modified bolt head.

After assembling the complete bolt and rimfire bolt head, I took a standard .22 cartridge and pulled the bullet and dumped the powder. The empty case was then in-

serted in the chamber. The bolt was placed in the receiver and the barrel pointed towards the floor of my shop. I pulled back the cocking piece by hand and then released it. This fired the rifle with a nice little pop. I wanted to check to see exactly where my new firing pin was hitting in relationship to the cartridge rim.

Fortunately, my firing pin was just about where I wanted it. It struck the rear of the cartridge case just to the inside of the edge of the rim. I doubt that I'll have any problems in the future with misfires, based on this test.

By the way, unlike some modern .22 rifles and handguns, you'll not want to allow anyone to dry fire your .22 Enfield. There is a good possibility that the tip of the firing pin will strike the edge of the chamber or the rear of the barrel. If this happens you could damage either the firing pin or the chamber. So don't ever fire this rifle unless you have a round in the chamber or a fired cartridge case which would act as a cushion for the firing pin.

The next step will be to mount the scope. This will entail drilling and tapping the side of the receiver. Also, we may need to modify the scope mount bases to ensure that the scope is properly aligned. Some folks don't do that and as a consequence, they use all of their windage adjustment in the scope to compensate for this oversight.

I want to have the maximum amount of potential adjustment in my scope, so I'll want to make any necessary corrections to the scope mount. I'll get into that in more detail when we get together to finish this up this project.

Until next time, good luck and good gunsmithing! ◎

Next month (8/10 issue): Finishing the No. 4 .22 sniper.

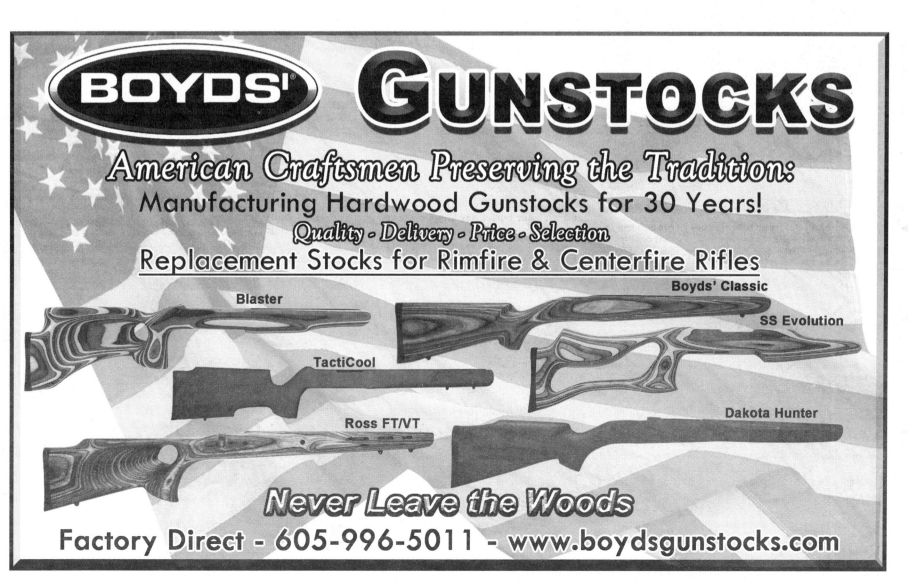

The .22 Caliber
Nº4 Lee Enfield
THE ULTIMATE ECONOMICAL MILITARY SNIPER RIFLE, PART 3

With a Weaver Classic installed in a Numrich mount and a proper cheekpiece on the comb, Coffield found the .22 Enfield sniper a pleasure to shoot on the range.

In the first two parts (6/10, 7/10), Coffield relined the barrel and modified the bolt. Now he's ready to finish this junior-sized sniper.

By Reid Coffield

In gunsmithing, nothing is quite as exciting as starting a new project and nothing is quite as satisfying as finishing one! In this third and last part of the series on building a .22 replica of a World War II No. 4 Lee Enfield sniper rifle, we'll wrap this project up.

In the previous two parts, I drilled out the .303 barrel and lined it with a Redman .22 barrel liner. After that, I modified the existing centerfire bolt head. The original firing pin hole was plugged and a new rimfire firing pin was made and installed. Following that, the .22 chamber was cut and the proper headspace established. Finally, I installed a modified extractor with a longer hook.

Keep in mind that with this project I'm not trying nor do I want to duplicate an original British sniper rifle. Those rifles are fairly rare and very valuable. To try to build one and pass it off as an original is definitely unethical and probably even illegal. I want to make sure my rifle is never mistaken for an original. My goal is simply to build a military-looking rifle in .22 rimfire I can use for plinking and perhaps occasionally for squirrel. It's nothing more than a fun rifle to be shot and enjoyed.

I might add that my particular rifle is basically a parts gun. Over the years I collected a lot of parts and pieces for No. 4 Lee Enfields, including a couple of stripped

receivers. This was a chance to use a ruined barrel along with a lot of other odds and ends.

In fact, I needed only a few other parts; primarily stock components. A call to Numrich Gun Parts was all it took to get the wood I needed. Numrich has tons of parts for Enfields as well as other obsolete military arms. If you need parts just give 'em a call.

If on the other hand you need a complete rifle, you might want to check with the folks at Century International Arms, Inc., 430 South Congress Ave., Dept. SGN, Delray Beach, FL 33445, telephone 561-265-4500. Century often has Enfields whose condition

Coffield thought the new Weaver Classic 1x3.5 variable was a good fit for his No. 4 sniper. It's about the same size as the original scope, but more useful.

The essential first step in mounting this scope or any other scope is to center up the crosshairs so you have plenty of available adjustment in any direction.

would not make them prime candidates for collectors, but would be very suitable for a conversion like this.

The next step in this project is to drill and tap the receiver and install the scope mount. The mount I am using is one I obtained from the good folks at Numrich. The mount is a very close copy of the original British military mount and will be perfect for this project. Currently this mount sells for about $133.

On the original British sniper rifles, the scope bases or "pads" were both screwed and soldered to the receiver. That was necessary to resist .303 recoil and the weight of the old #32 scope. The hefty scope placed tremendous stress on the scope bases as the rifle recoiled.

However, since I am making this rifle up as a .22, recoil stress is not an issue. Because of this, I can dispense with the soldering. It's not needed and the lack of solder on the bases will help to identify this rifle as a latter-day conversion.

Also I will not be using the same #4 screws the British used to anchor the scope bases. Instead, I'll just use some standard Weaver 6-48 scope base screws. In addition, I'll not stake the screws in place.

The British staked their screws into the mounts to keep them from loosening under recoil. Again, lacking these stake marks and using Weaver screws will be just additional indications that this is not a British military firearm.

I'll be using a new Weaver V-series scope. This current production scope is very similar to the old #32 British scope in general outline or silhouette. However, it's different in a number of important ways. First, it's a variable; 1-3.5X. Secondly, it has standard civilian type dual X cross hairs. You don't have the more complex reticle used on the #32 scope, but for plinking and maybe an occasional squirrel, that's not important.

When installing the scope bases, I want to do so in such a way that the Weaver scope will be properly centered. I definitely don't want to have to use up all or even a major portion of the internal windage or elevation adjustment in my scope to get on target.

The way to do that is to first make sure the crosshairs in the scope are centered in the middle of the range of adjustments both up and down and left to right. All you need to do is first turn the windage adjustment clockwise until you come to the built-in stop.

Now turn the windage knob in the opposite direction, counting the clicks or turns until you come to the other stop. Take the total number of clicks or turns, divide by two, and turn the windage knob back by that number. At that point you'll have the crosshairs mechanically centered. All of this takes a little time but it's worth the effort and essential for properly centering and mounting the scope.

Once the scope was adjusted, my next task was to install the two scope mount bases. Since the spacing of the two bases is critical, I'll install the rear base first.

That way if it's necessary to make an adjustment in the location of the front base, I can do so without any problem and since the front base would be attached to the mount, it's just easier.

To help with proper spacing, I initially placed the bases on the mount and positioned the whole assembly on the left side of the receiver. I had previously used some machinist layout fluid to coat the side of the receiver where the bases would be located.

I then scribed a line on the receiver by the front and rear sides of the rear base to help properly locate it once the scope mount was removed. I then set the scope mount aside and positioned the rear base on the receiver between the two scribed marks.

While holding the rear base in place, I used a transfer punch to locate the center of the rearmost screw hole of the base on the receiver.

The transfer punch I used is a perfect slip fit in the base screw hole, so my center punch mark was right on the money. If you don't have a set of transfer punches, I strongly urge you to get a set. They are inexpensive, yet they can save you a lot of time and help make your work more accurate.

Once I located the rear screw hole, I drilled and tapped it for a 6-48 screw. The base was then attached to the rifle and the front hole located, drilled and tapped. So much for attaching the base to the receiver.

The scope mount does not, however, screw into this base. The rear mount screw is actually threaded directly into the receiver. The larger hole in the base between the two holes for the 6-48 screws is a clearance hole for the large knurled hand screw.

I initially thought that this screw had a 1/4-28 thread but in checking with my thread pitch gauge, I found that it was 1/4-27. Unfortunately there are no standard taps available for this oddball size.

The reality though is that the difference in the spacing of individual threads between a 27 and a 28 thread is only about .002". Coupled with the fact that the actual amount of thread engagement will be only about 1/10" or less, I decided I could use the more common 1/4-28 tap. In this situation I'll get plenty of purchase and there'll be no danger of stripping or damaging the threads on the thumbscrew.

Once all the holes were drilled and tapped, the bases were installed. I did not nor do I intend on later applying any Loc-Tite or similar product to the screw threads. Since this is just a .22 rimfire, there's very little or no danger of the screws working loose under recoil.

Besides, I still may have to fit the bases to the mount to ensure proper alignment of the scope. If that's necessary, I want to be able easily and quickly to remove the base mounts or pads.

Because the forearm will be in contact with the barrel and may affect the point of impact, I reassembled the

The Numrich mount is a massive, rugged unit mount ready to have the Weaver scope installed. Coffield found no need to solder bases as was done on the original.

Coffield drills the side of the Enfield receiver for the rear base mounting screws. The rear base should be mounted first; there's more room at the front.

The center hole on the rear base is a clearance hole for the thumbscrew on the scope mount. The rear of the mount actually attaches directly to the receiver.

The front mount or pad is secured to the receiver with three 6-48 screws. Coffield thinks this many screws will easily hold up to recoil without solder.

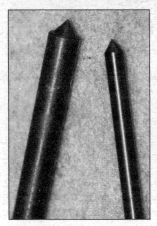

Coffield made frequent use of transfer punches like these while working on this project. The shaft fits the hole in the workpiece, centering the point to mark.

Instead of removing metal from scope mount bases or pads, Coffield used a mill to remove .040" from this contact point on the mount to center the scope.

scope. After that, I used some Brownells T-4 touch up bluing to cover the raw metal on the scope mount. It was then oiled and everything reassembled. The final adjustments were made on the scope to center the crosshairs in the center of the collimator grid.

The buttstock had been left off the receiver so I could have easier access to the scope while setting up the scope mount and aligning the scope with the collimator. Once that was done I attached the buttstock. I also installed the buttplate and rear sling swivel base and loop.

The final step in the assembly of my .22 sniper was to install a replica of the detachable cheekpiece the British used on their rifles. The comb of a standard Enfield is far too low for use with a scope, so they would add a cheekpiece to the issue buttstock. The cheekpiece I had was from Numrich. It's a nice piece of walnut and attaches with two large wood screws. The British used large blued steel screws but I'll be using brass screws instead. Again, this is to help make sure no one thinks that this is an original or British made rifle.

The cheekpiece required a modest amount of inletting to make sure the radius on its bottom matched the curvature of the comb. In order to modify the inletting on the cheekpiece properly, I first wrapped the buttstock with a piece of aluminum foil and made sure it was pressed tightly against the comb. I then coated the thin aluminum foil with inletting black.

It was just a simple matter of pressing the cheekpiece against the coated foil to determine where I was getting contact on the bottom of the cheekpiece. These contact points would show where the inletting black contacted the wood. I used a variety of gouges and scrapers to remove these contact or high points. Gradually the cheekpiece settled more and more onto the comb with a nice even fit.

If you don't fit the cheekpiece properly to the buttstock, you run the risk of cracking or splitting it when you attach it to the comb with wood screws. It's got to be a good solid even fit to avoid damage to the cheekpiece. Take your time when you do this. It's not hard, just kinda slow!

Once I had the cheekpiece fitted, I used an adjustable clamp to hold it in place on the buttstock. I then took a

transfer punch that fit through the cheekpiece to center-punch the stock. A #32 drill was used to drill pilot holes for my attaching screws. Then I coated the threads of the wood screws with beeswax and turned them into the stock. Once that was done, the adjustable clamp was removed.

I should point out that the British used steel wood screws to secure the cheekpiece. To differentiate my rifle, I used brass screws. Besides, they'll never rust and it adds a bit of contrast to the wood. Finally, after all of this was done, I removed the cheekpiece and on the underside I put my name, date, and other data to indicate the maker of this unique .22 rifle. I will also have appropriate identifying markings on other parts of the rifle. If you make one of these rifles, and I sure hope you do, please go the extra mile in marking it to avoid any misunderstanding as to its origin.

With that done, I cleaned the bore one more time to remove any dust or grit that might have gotten into it during the project. I started to put a standard Enfield web sling on the rifle but then I remembered I still had the original sling that had been on the Enfield sniper I had almost 50 years ago as a kid.

That original rifle had a 1907 U.S. pattern military sling on it. How it got there, I have no idea. When I traded the rifle for some reason or other I kept the sling. It has since seen use on a variety of U.S. military rifles. It most currently lived on a 1903 Springfield. It didn't take me long to pull the sling off the Springfield and put it on my "new" .22 Enfield sniper.

In a way, everything had now come full circle. I started out with an Enfield sniper when I was just a kid and here I am half a century later with another Enfield sniper. This time I have one that is cheap to shoot, has a great fully functioning scope, and it doesn't have any headspace problems.

Now it was time to head to the range for an initial test firing. I wanted to check the firing mechanism, extraction, and basic alignment of the scope. The weather was threatening rain so I didn't fire more than 10 rounds at 25 yards but that told me a lot.

First of all, the rifle was 100% reliable in terms of ignition. There were no failures to fire or hangfires. Second, the scope lined up right on the money. The point of impact was a bit low but the windage was right on. I was very happy to say the least.

The only fly in the soup was extraction. My extractor hook was not catching reliably on the case rim. So it was back to the shop and more work on the extractor. Ultimately I ended up reshaping the top of the hook where it contacted the angled ramp I had filed on the barrel for the extractor. Evidently the angle of the top of the extractor was not matching the angle of the ramp, and the extractor hook was actually being pushed out away from the cartridge rim.

I also found that the hook was extending too far in towards the cartridge case. This was putting stress on the case and making it more difficult to pull the case

rifle before going any further. I'll be using a collimator to align the scope and the collimator is positioned in a spud in the muzzle.

Consequently if there's any pressure on the barrel from the forearm, it will reflect in the alignment of the scope and collimator. Once I had the collimator in place, I discovered that the crosshairs were just a bit to the left and a tad low.

The British would resolve this by removing metal from the scope mount pads or bases. Once that was done, the pads were unique to that rifle and barrel. You normally could not remove those pads and install them on another rifle.

That was fine for the British military, and it made sense with their scopes, which had a limited range of adjustment for windage and elevation. Our modern scopes are much more sophisticated and typically have a much greater range of internal adjustment.

I opted for removing a bit of metal from the inside of the mounting bracket on the scope mount. By doing it this way I could use a standard 1/2" end mill in my mill/drill. It was faster and it allowed me a lot of control over just how much material I removed.

I ended up taking off right at .040". This moved the crosshair to the right just on the right hand side of the centerline of the collimator. Once the metal was removed, I checked it by mounting the

After careful shaping of its bottom, the cheekpiece was held on the buttstock with an adjustable clamp when locating and drilling holes for the wood screws.

Coffield chose two brass wood screws to attach the cheekpiece to the buttstock; he wanted to use something different than the British-specified steel screws.

Coffield loves to stump 'em at the range with this sort of setup, a No. 4 sniper rifle, but in .22 and with a modern Weaver scope. It's a fun, practical rifle.

all the way out of the chamber. The bottom line was I had to do an hour or so worth of tweaking to get the extractor to function properly.

Ideally I would prefer to have an extractor similar to the one I made for the 1903 Springfield .22 conversion (4/10/09). That extractor is a lot more reliable. However, I just didn't think I had enough thickness in the barrel shank to make something similar on this No. 4 Enfield. However, when I have more time I may revisit that, pull the barrel, and look again at adding another extractor. I would have one on the barrel and a hook on the bolt.

Over the years in working with a number of .22 conversions of the old No. 1 Lee Enfield, I've found that extraction has always been less than optimal. Using a single hook on the Enfield bolt has worked for the most part but you still occasionally have a case stuck in the chamber that needs some extra help.

Two days later I was back out at the range with my shooting partner and fellow SGN contributor Paul Mazan. This time the rifle worked much better. The only problem was the weather. The wind was extremely strong. Since I was firing at 50 yards, it was quite noticeable in terms of the grouping.

By the way, this rifle tended to prefer standard Winchester high velocity ammo. I also shot some Remington and Federal match ammo but neither gave me as tight a group. It may just have been the wind. While I know the rifle will shoot better, I was able to get one group of just over 1" for five shots with the Winchester ammo. Not too bad for a first effort.

In the future I'll try some other brands of ammo to see if I can shrink my groups a bit more. One thing I've found over the years is that .22 rifles are sensitive to ammo. To get the best accuracy, you'll often have to experiment a bit with various brands and types of .22 ammo.

I also checked the movement of the scope when it was taken off the rifle and then reinstalled. While my mount sure looks like it would be a perfect return to zero, that was not the case with this rifle. I found upon remounting the scope, the rifle shot just a tad, maybe 1/2" or so, to the right. Because of this I would leave the scope on the rifle once it was sighted in, which I had planned on doing anyway.

By the way, the Weaver Classic 1x3.5 scope is just ideal for this rifle. Not only does it look a lot like the old British #32 scope, the clarity, wide range of adjustment, and ease of use makes it a real winner. It really impressed me and made me very glad that I had chosen this scope. I would definitely encourage you to consider a Weaver Classic 1x3.5 as well.

There is still some minor tweaking to do; the trigger pull is way too heavy. It's great for a military rifle but considerably less than ideal for a .22. All in all, I'm really happy with this rifle. It's truly the rifle I should have had back when I was just a kid and my mother won that original .303 No. 4 on a punch board. This rifle is cheap to shoot, has a great scope that functions flawlessly, and it has no headspace problems! It's just perfect for a kid, even one who's 64 years old!

Until next time, good luck and good gunsmithing! ◉

Ask the Gunsmith

By Reid Coffield

IVER JOHNSON EJECTION

Q *I have an Iver Johnson Model 66 .22 revolver. A friend told me that when I break open the gun it should automatically eject the fired cartridge cases. Mine will not do that. Is my gun broken?*

The Iver Johnson Model 66 (top) has a manual ejector rod, while the Harrington & Richardson Model 999 has automatic ejection. They are otherwise similar inexpensive top-break revolvers.

A Nope, your friend is just mistaken. The Iver Johnson Model 66 has a manual extractor. The ejector rod that projects forward from the cylinder under the barrel must be depressed manually to activate the extractor. I'd almost be willing to bet that your friend has it confused with the Harrington and Richardson Model 999, which looks very similar. The Model 999 did have an automatic ejector that was activated when the action was opened.

TACK RAGS

Q *I am very careful to sand stocks with progressive grits, always use a sanding block, and employ a tack rag to remove sanding dust. My problem comes when I apply the stock stain. I prefer a water-based stain as they are easy to work with and readily available. The problem is that my staining is never even. It seems like something is on the wood but for the life of me I can not figure out what it is. Can you help?*

A Right off hand I would tend to think that your problem may be caused by the tack rag. Tack rags generally are nothing more than pieces of

cloth that have been soaked with a varnish like material. Chances are some of this varnish or the chemical in your tack rag is being transferred to the surface of your stock as you wipe it down. This in turn is inhibiting the water-based stain.

My experience has been that there is less of an effect from tack rags if an alcohol-based stain is used. I have begun to try to get away from using tack rags after many years of messing around with 'em. Instead, I use a nice clean, new paint brush to remove dust from the stock. I also use my shop vacuum with a brush attachment. Either of these methods seems to work well for me and you might want to try 'em.

LEE-NAVY SEAR

Q *A good customer brought in a U.S. Lee Navy rifle in 6mm. It is in fairly good shape. The problem is that the sear is missing. Now I have the rifle and do not even have the old part to go by in trying to make a new one. Can you help?*

A Contact the folks at S&S Firearms, 74-11 Myrtle Ave., Dept. SGN, Glendale, N.Y. 11385, telephone 718-497-1100. They list this part in their catalog and even include a photograph. Believe me; you don't even want to think about making this part! It's extremely complex. It'll be far cheaper and less hassle to just buy it and the cost is very reasonable. And, this will make you look like a hero! S&S Firearms has been around for many years and is a good source for original and reproduction 19th and early 20th century U.S. military arms parts. Over the years I've bought a number of items from 'em. ◉

Building the STEN Mk 2.5
Semi-Auto Carbine
Part 1

By Steven Matthews

This isn't a one-weekend project, but Matthews says if you have the eye, the skills and the ambition, you can make a realistic semi-auto Sten for a price that will leave you some ammo money.

Building your own gun is a big project, but Matthews says you can do it with planning, patience and the right tools and materials. A commitment to the job is needed.

The Sten series of British submachine guns needs no introduction to fans of World War II arms. It was made by the millions and issued to almost all of the armies of the former British Empire. The British military had bought thousands of Thompsons, but needed millions more submachine guns that were cheap and easy to produce.

With these design parameters paramount, Reginald Shepard and Harold Turpin submitted a design that became known as the Sten Mk 1. This design featured basic blowback operation, a steel tube receiver, a horizontal magazine, fixed sights, sheet-metal construction, low cost, and an absolute minimum number of parts.

This design was later simplified somewhat and designated the Sten Mk 2. Only the barrel, barrel bushing, bolt, and a few other small parts were machined. The rest were easy-to-produce steel stampings that were spot- or arc-welded together. Simple-to-make parts could be subcontracted to many small producers, helping prevent one air strike from wiping out Sten production.

The approximate cost for the Sten Mk 2 was $5 each. With Germany poised to invade and conquer, the British immediately adopted it and placed it into production. Efforts were made to reduce cost and manufacturing time even further. A simplified version known as the Mk 3 replaced the steel tube receiver with two pieces of flat steel shaped into half-round sections that were welded together.

The rotatable magazine housing was fixed into position and simply welded to tabs formed in the receiver. The machined barrel bushing was replaced with stamped steel spacers which were arc welded to a simplified barrel and then riveted into the receiver.

These and a few other small changes sped up production and lowered cost, even if it did make the gun look even cruder than ever. There were several variations of the Sten design (Mk 1, 2, 3, 4, 5, 6) over the years but the Mk 2 and Mk 3 were the most common and are the ones that concern us here.

I have discussed the Mk 2 and Mk 3, but what is a Mk 2.5? I made up the name for a semi-auto carbine hybrid of the Sten Mk 2 and Mk 3 submachine guns. I designed it to replicate the Sten Mk 2 by using a spare parts set for the Sten Mk 3.

I collect military firearms and I wanted a semi-auto replica of the Sten Mk 2 for my collection. The *ultra* inflated prices of the registered machine gun market meant a semi Sten was about my only option.

The going rate for a registered full-auto Sten Mk 2 is about $3,500, and I absolutely refuse to pay $3,500 for a $5 gun! Although I have other NFA items, I bought them before the market went nuts (my M16 was about $450 and my MAC 10 was about $150 compared to $7–8,000 now for the M16 and about $3,000 for the MAC), I am priced out of the legal full-auto market.

Add to that the full-auto paperwork hassles and a semi-auto carbine looks pretty attractive. You may ask why I don't just buy a semi Sten. Unlike the widely available semi-auto copies of the M16, Uzi, AK-47, etc., there are simply no widely available mass-produced semi Stens on the market.

There are some specialty gun makers making small numbers of them, but they are relatively costly. This caused me to look at the DIY build option, since I do have a certain amount of hobby gunsmithing skill.

I did find a manufacturer who made a semi conversion kit for the Mk 2, but it was about $250 plus another $250 for a parts set. This was still more than I wanted to invest in that $5 gun.

Unlike the Mk 2 kits which cost about $250 and are getting scarce, the Mk 3 kits are widely available and priced in the $40–$60 range. I decided that I could figure out a way of duplicating the appearance of the Mk 2 with a Mk 3 kit. In this project I planned to use only a few original parts, so I thought the Mk 3 option was the way to go to keep cost reasonable.

Deciding I wanted a semi-auto carbine was the easy part. I had to figure out a way to duplicate the appearance of the Mk 2 all on my own. There was no information available for this type of project and I was starting with the proverbial "blank sheet of paper."

I bought a couple of Mk 3 parts sets and set about trying to figure something out. BATFE regulations meant it had to be converted to fire from a closed bolt. It also had to be "not readily convertible" to the previous full-auto configuration or be able to accept full-auto parts.

It also could not use more than 10 imported parts on a list specified by the BATFE. Use fewer than 10 parts and you have a plain old semi-auto American-made gun with a few imported parts; more than 10 makes it a prohibited "imported semi-auto assault weapon."

What I came up with would satisfy all the rules and still be relatively inexpensive and easy (depends on how you define easy) to build. I decided that I could use eight of the parts on the list which would get me in under the 10-part rule.

I could use several parts out of the kit that weren't restricted. I could add a U.S.-made fire control group made from modified AR15/M16 parts which are plentiful and relatively inexpensive. The remaining parts I could either make or purchase. Since it is completely legal for individuals to make firearms for their own use (not for resale!), I figured I had it all figured out at this point.

Little did I realize just how much engineering and trial and error work it would require to get a safe and reliable firearm! I had to decide how to modify the existing parts, how and what kind of new parts to make, and how to fit them all together into a functional firearm.

After a lot of head scratching and experimenting, I came up with something that would work. I will explain how I built this project and you can use it for a general guide if you should decide to build one as I have.

Matthews says you can do it with hand tools, but the proper bench tools make it a lot easier. This import lathe and mill combo cost him about $1,200 and came in handy.

Sten Mk 2.5 Material List

1-2 Sten Mk 3 Parts Sets

2 feet 4130 seamless chrome-moly steel tubing 1.5-inch diameter x .083" wall thickness

1 foot 4130 seamless chrome-moly steel tubing 1.625" diameter x .058" wall thickness

1 16-inch or longer 9mm Luger barrel. (barrel blank or prechambered barrel from some existing firearm)

1 foot 1.5-inch diameter cold-rolled round stock for bushing and end cap

2 feet 7/32" diameter cold-rolled rod for the recoil spring guide

1 12.75-inch x .041–.045" wire size compression spring for the recoil spring (may be cut out of bulk spring stock)

1⅝" diameter x 6-inch Grade 5 bolt for raw material for bolt handle

1¼" diameter Grade 8 socket head cap screw for raw material for firing pin

1 Extra long (need about 2 inches of shank) 5/64" (.078") high quality drill bit

1 each M16 hammer with spring and pin, AR-15 trigger with spring and pin, AR-15 disconnector and spring,

Approximate cost for these items is $150.

This *should not* be considered a step-by-step process on building this gun. There are just too many variables. The dimensions that I will supply will only be rough guides. Sten parts that were produced by hundreds of manufacturers, and varying tolerances and design changes mean considerable variance in dimensions can occur.

What worked for me may not be exactly right for you. I would consider this an advanced hobby gunsmithing project and you will have to use skill, knowledge and judgment in the building of this project. Test carefully at every stage of construction; don't just put it together, shove in a magazine and pull the trigger.

Much hand-fitting of parts will be needed, and you need to understand how the parts function when you are fitting them. You will need to do some simple metal lathe work and basic milling machine work. Some of the lathe and mill work can be done by improvised hand methods if you don't mind the extra labor, or you can farm it out to a gunsmith or machinist with the proper gear.

A good drill press can be used for some of the drilling operations if you are especially skilled in its use, but a milling machine will be more accurate. Some of the small turned parts can be made by improvised methods (the poor man's lathe, a spinning drill chuck and a file) if you are skilled in hand-making parts.

I have a fairly well equipped hobby gunsmithing workshop with lathes, milling machines, grinders, welders, hand tools, precision measuring tools, etc., so I used power tools as much as possible but the project can be done without a full machine shop, it just takes longer to work things with hand tools.

Before you can start this project, you need your parts. Listed below are many of the parts I used for the project. I might add that buying more parts than you need is a good idea.

I bought 2 Sten Mk 3 kits and picked out the best parts for the project and saved the extra parts for spares in case I messed up the best parts. I bought more tubing than required in case I screwed up something and had to do it over.

It's real easy to make a simple mistake that will ruin a part (I know this from experience!). It's nice to have a spare handy to avoid the inconvenience and delays in obtaining new parts.

Besides the previously mentioned power tools (if you choose power over hand work) you will need basic hand tools such as saws, files, hammers, punches, tape measure, drill bits, pliers, vises, etc. The more tools you have, the easier the project, the right tool for the job makes it a lot easier!

One other *must have* item is a pair of dial calipers graduated in .001". Even though a Sten is very loosely fitted, you will have to make parts that are accurate to a few thousandths of an inch. High-dollar calipers are fine if you have them but some of the cheap ($20) imported ones will probably get you by on this project.

Reworking the bolt

We are going to start with the most difficult part first, modifying the old Sten full-auto bolt to semi-auto configuration. This modification is the heart of this project. If you can't get this part right, there is no use in making any of the other parts.

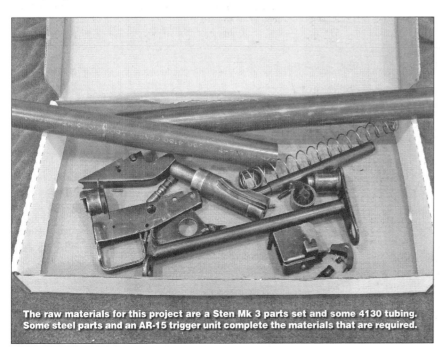

The raw materials for this project are a Sten Mk 3 parts set and some 4130 tubing. Some steel parts and an AR-15 trigger unit complete the materials that are required.

BATFE requires the new receiver not accept full-auto parts. Matthews used tubing with heavier walls, requiring that the bolt be lathe-turned to a smaller outside diameter.

The original bolt (r.) shows the fixed firing pin typical of Stens. Matthews needed to replace this with a moving firing pin that would be driven forward by a hammer.

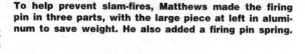

To help prevent slam-fires, Matthews made the firing pin in three parts, with the large piece at left in aluminum to save weight. He also added a firing pin spring.

BATFE regulations mean this gun cannot use the original "open bolt" firing system, which incorporated a fixed firing pin in the front of the bolt. It must be converted to a "closed bolt" firing system that features a conventional firing pin. When originally designed in the 1940s, no thought was given to some amateur gunsmith reworking the design 50 years later.

There is barely enough room to fit this modification into the bolt. If you get everything right on the mark, there is just enough room, but not much room for error. As shown in the diagram, we are going to be drilling several holes in the bolt for a firing pin system and a recoil rod and spring setup.

The bolt is soft enough for drilling, but is hardened somewhat so it won't drill as easily as common steel. I started by first filing a flat on the front of the fixed firing pin about the size of the hole I would be drilling (5/64"). I center-punched the exact center of this flat in preparation for drilling.

This location needs to be exactly in the center, so you will have to measure it with your dial calipers. There are only a few thousandths of an inch leeway here, so be sure it is right.

Now it has to be set up in the milling machine or drill press exactly in the line of travel of the quill. If it's not perfectly in line it will start out where you want it but then be off-center at the bottom after you have drilled in an inch or two.

In machinist's terms, it has to be set up in a drilling or milling vise and "indicated in." This indicating procedure is a "machine shop 101" procedure. It is a basic setup process that is taught to anyone learning the machining trade.

I will only briefly explain it; if you don't understand how to do it, get yourself a basic machine shop text book and study the process. Use a dial indicator held in the drill chuck or milling machine collet with a holder. Place it against a straight side of the part (front, back or sides).

As you lower the quill, you align the part so that there is no movement of the dial. This indicates the quill is staying straight in reference to the starting point.

If you start exactly in the center of a properly indicated part, then the finish point will also be exactly in the center. Do this on both the X and Y axes (front-to-back movement and side-to-side movement).

Once the part is indicated-in precisely, reposition it so that the center-punched starting point is exactly centered under the drill or mill quill.

This is also a basic machine shop procedure that you can learn from a machine shop manual. Once everything is located, clamp it down (make sure nothing moves when clamping) and spot drill the punched hole location with a center drill.

Be sure to spot drill only a small spot that is smaller than the final drill size. You don't want to spot drill a hole that is bigger than the hole you will be drilling!

Drill the hole with a 5/64" (.078") drill about 1½ inches deep (see print for depth). Run your drill fast and use a light feed to prevent walking off center, also use plenty of oil to get a smooth finish.

Once this hole is drilled, file off any remaining material on the bolt face so that it is smooth on the front. Now turn the bolt over and a drill a larger hole exactly in the center from the rear to meet the smaller hole.

You have to go through the whole "indicating in" procedure again to get the two holes to meet. Once set up, drill the larger hole as detailed on the bolt drawing. This centered passageway will be where the firing pin will be installed after it is made.

When I drilled the larger hole I used a 1/4" (.250") drill, which was slightly larger than I should have used. This resulted in me having an opening on one side of the passageway where the bolt was at its thinnest. It still worked OK but you may want to reduce the hole size by 1/64" to leave some material for a sidewall.

If you do reduce the size, you will have to adjust your firing pin diameter accordingly.

Before I could drill the recoil spring hole on the top rear of the bolt, I had to mill some material off of the extension on the rear of the bolt. I used a milling machine but it could also be ground or filed off. I machined it to the listed dimensions.

To avoid double the work setting up, you may want to have this machining done first so that you can drill the spring hole when drilling the center holes. I did it several days after I did the center holes, since I didn't have that part of the project figured out yet.

Mark your drilling point as per the bolt print. This is going to be a very deep hole, so you will need a standard drill and an extra long drill. Use the standard length drill to begin, then switch to the longer one. The setup for this hole will also have to be "indicated" as the other holes were to keep the drilling exactly straight.

It's not as critical as the other holes, but you need to make it fairly straight. You need to keep it from drilling though the upper side of the bolt after a few inches.

Once you have drilled the proper sized hole to the depth described on the bolt print, you will then finish drilling though the bolt with a smaller drill to allow for passage of the recoil rod.

Pay particular attention to the depth of the spring hole, as it will be getting very close to the extractor pin hole and you don't want to drill into it. After both holes are drilled, chamfer the ends to ensure smooth operation.

After the holes were drilled, I had to machine off the bottom of the bolt as indicated on the bolt print. This can be done by hand if you don't have a mill. I machined off the full-auto sear catch and also the bottom front of the bolt for hammer clearance.

Some more machining of the bolt bottom may be required later to fine-tune the bolt-to-hammer relationship (in other words, to get things to work). There is one final machining procedure that needs to be completed per BATFE regulations. The new receiver cannot be the same size as the original full-auto receiver. The receiver has to be smaller in internal diameter to prevent the use of the original full-auto parts. The original full-auto Sten receiver was 1.5 inches x .062".

Our new semi-auto receiver will be 1.5 inches x .083". The thicker sidewalls mean the bolt has to be machined to a smaller

Modifying the bolt is the most exacting stage of the job. Drilling the hole for the firing pin requires the bolt be very carefully aligned with the drill press quill.

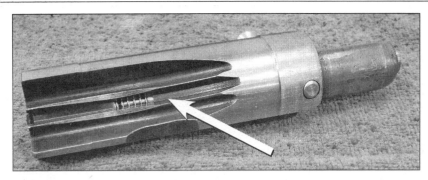

When Matthews says there's just enough room in the bolt, he's not kidding. His drill was oversized and made this cut through the side (arrow). It didn't affect function.

diameter to fit the new receiver. I chucked up the tail of the bolt in the lathe and used a live center in the firing pin hole in the front of the bolt and removed the material.

Be sure to use a "live center" for this operation since a "dead center" will wear the firing pin hole. Take light cuts, since the odd-shaped bolt may cause the cutter to dig in after passing open space on the bolt.

The bolt is the hardest part of this project and tends to be where mistakes will be made. Before starting, I had a couple extra bolts in case I messed up. I got it right on the first try, but I highly recommend having extra bolts on hand unless you are highly skilled and confident that you will not make mistakes.

The next section, firing pin assembly, while still needing to be made precisely will be much easier and not as easy to mess up. Later sections of this project will be very easy, so if you have made it this far, things will be getting much easier.

Firing Pin Assembly

With the bolt properly modified, it's time to make the appropriate parts to go in it. I needed a firing pin assembly and

previous experimenting had indicated that a solid one-piece steel pin would be too heavy and also be difficult to fabricate. Keep in mind that a too-heavy firing pin invites slam-fires with commercial ammunition, and can cause doubling that might invite scrutiny from law enforcement. You want this gun to go off only once with each trigger pull!

Something in two pieces would be lighter and easy to build. I decided to make a short two-piece steel firing pin and a longer three-piece aluminum and steel extension.

I chose aluminum to reduce weight. I made the firing pin to the dimensions specified on the firing pin drawing and press-fitted a .078" pin to the end. The larger part would ride in the 1/4" passage and the .078" pin would extend though to the bolt face.

I used a 1/4" Grade 8 screw for the main part. Grade 8 steel is more than twice as strong as common mild steel and this grade is commonly available at hardware stores.

For the small .078" pin I used the shank of an extra-long high quality drill bit. These are made from a steel known as M-2; it is strong and hard, yet still somewhat flexible.

I turned the body section on the lathe and drilled the .078" hole with a drill bit that due to manufacturing tolerances was about .001" under the .078" size of the piece I was going to use for the pin.

The undersized hole would expand when lightly heated, allow the .001" larger pin to be inserted and then grip it tight when it cooled. The firing pin body also features a return spring to help prevent slam-firing.

Since the rear of this extension would be struck by the hammer, I installed a steel insert made from a Grade 5 bolt to prevent peening after multiple hammer hits. I bored out the aluminum rod and threaded it for the bolt. I then used permanent

thread locker and assembled it. I then turned the head off in the lathe in a rounded profile.

On the opposite end I used the same method to form a hard extension on the front to impact the firing pin. Once completed, there may be some hand fitting required to get things to operate smoothly due to size variations between the holes and newly made parts. Once the pieces are assembled and installed in the bolt, the long .078" pin will have to be cut to length to provide for proper firing pin extension.

When pushed all the way forward, the pin needs to extend past the front of the bolt face by .065"–.075". The rear needs to extend past the rear of the bolt extension about .100" when in the retracted position to allow the hammer to drive it forward before contacting and being stopped by the extension.

The overall lengths listed on the firing pin drawing should give you enough extra length to hand-fit these pieces. After you have these pieces fitted, you need to pause here and fabricate the bolt handle if you have not done it already. The bolt handle will lock the firing pin and firing pin extension into the bolt.

An oval hole in the firing pin extension will allow the bolt handle to lock the pieces into the bolt but allow for forward and back movement needed for firing pin functioning. After you have made your bolt handle to the drawing specifications, assemble the bolt and firing pin assembly. Press the firing pin assembly all the way forward and use a transfer punch in the bolt handle recess to mark the firing pin extension.

Drill the proper size hole in the firing pin extension. After drilling, file this round hole into an oval shape to allow proper forward and back movement for the firing pin assembly. The firing pin should retract into the face of the bolt about .030" to .050".

The fitting of this assembly is where good hand fitting skills will be needed. The lengths I have listed are oversize to allow you to fit your parts to individual pieces that you made. These figures worked for me, but if you varied too much from the specifications, you may have to alter things to get them to work. If you have got this far successfully, then the rest of this project will be "a piece of cake."

Ask the Gunsmith

By Reid Coffield

FINDING SCRATHCES

Q *How do you check a stock for scratches prior to applying the sealer or stain? I almost always find some scratches after I have applied the stain, and then I have to sand the stock all over again. It is very frustrating and I waste a lot of time.*

A Before applying your stain or sealer, wipe the stock down with a clean rag soaked with alcohol. If you have any scratches, they'll show up. Also, as an added benefit, the alcohol will help to clean any dirt, dust or lint off the stock.

BACK BORE REAMER DEPTH

Q *How much can or should I cut out of a shotgun barrel with each reamer when I back bore it?*

A I will not attempt to cut out more than .003" if I am turning the reamers by hand. If I am doing the work on my lathe, I can increase that to .005" or so.

SADDLE RING INSTALLATION

Q *I have a Winchester 94 in .30-30. I have already put on a large lever loop with no trouble. Now I want to put on a saddle ring I got from Numrich Gun Parts that is threaded for 10-32. My question is do I have to remove any internal part before I drill and tap the receiver. I know the exact place to drill.*

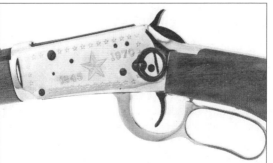

Adding a saddle ring gives and Old West look, but Coffield says it's important to remove internal parts before drilling and tapping to avoid getting chips inside the mechanism.

I strongly urge you to strip your receiver completely when installing the saddle ring stud. In drilling and tapping the receiver, you will definitely get small chips and pieces of metal from the hole you drilled inside the receiver. In addition, if you lubricate the drill and tap properly, you'll get some cutting oil inside the receiver as well. All of this should be removed to ensure that nothing interferes with the proper functioning of the rifle mechanism. Even the smallest metal chip can under the right circumstances prevent the rifle from working properly. Also, there's a good chance that there will be a burr at the end of the hole on the inside of the receiver. This burr will most likely need to be removed so it will not contact any of the internal parts. Besides, when doing a job like this you have the perfect opportunity to completely strip the gun and give each and every part a good cleaning.

1905 WINCHESTER BOLT LOCK

Q *I have an old Winchester Model 1905 .35 caliber rifle that I inherited from my grandfather. My question is this, is there any way of getting the bolt to stay back so the gun can be cleaned?*

A There certainly is! First, remove the magazine and push back on the operating sleeve tip to open the bolt and make sure the chamber is empty. To lock the bolt open, while the operating sleeve is fully depressed, turn the tip either to the right or left. This will engage an internal lug on the sleeve and lock it in the open or rearmost position. To close the bolt, just turn the sleeve tip back to the original position and allow it to spring forward.

Building the STEN Mk 2.5 Carbine

Part 2

By Steven Matthews

If you've made it this far, the rest is easy. Soon you'll have a 9mm carbine you won't see everywhere!

Careful design and construction meant Matthews' Sten worked 100% from the start. You may not be so lucky; be prepared for some hand-fitting to accommodate varied tolerances.

In the first installment, Matthews gathered parts, modified the bolt and fabricated a firing pin assembly for his semi-auto Sten gun. Now he's ready to finish the job.

Trigger Housing

The next segment of this project was the trigger housing and fire control group. I wanted to use commonly available parts to avoid having to make them by hand. I got lucky on this one when I found that the Sten trigger housing was just about wide enough to contain AR-15/M16 components.

The AR-15/M16 fire control system is inexpensive and well proven, so it was perfect for this application. Start by preparing the Sten trigger housing. The Sten trigger housing was originally welded onto the receiver tube. When the parts were demilled for sale, the restricted full-auto receiver was crudely sawn out and many pieces were still attached to the trigger housing.

Matthews found that an AR-15 trigger would just fit in the front of the Sten trigger housing. He installed it and made a transfer bar back to the original trigger.

These remaining pieces need to be removed by grinding, sawing or filing. Once the trigger housing is cleaned up, two holes need to be drilled through the housing in the appropriate positions to hold the trigger and hammer pins.

The dimensions shown on the trigger housing diagram need to be very close to ensure proper functioning. If they vary much, the parts will have to be hand-fitted to work properly. Even if they are positioned correctly, some minor hand-fitting will probably be required due to the variations in the other parts.

After the holes are drilled, the following parts need to be installed in the housing: a modified M16 hammer, hammer pin and spring, an AR-15 trigger, trigger spring and pin, AR-15 disconnector and spring.

These parts need to slide into the housing and are retained with pins. If the trigger housing is a little narrow, it can be spread slightly to allow for insertion and free movement. Before you insert the M16 hammer, it needs to be modified by grinding it roughly to the shape shown in the drawing. Fine tuning the shape may be required for proper functioning after assembly.

This reshaping will allow for smoother operation, since the M16 hammer is a little too tall when pushed down by the reciprocating bolt. Place the hammer (with spring correctly installed) in the front holes and push the legs of the springs up and out of the way, I used some pre-existing holes in the housing and an Allen wrench to hold them up.

These legs will later rest on the trigger assembly to tension the hammer. The next parts to be put in are the trigger and disconnector assembly, along with their springs. This requires great manipulation and about three hands!

First, get a small piece (about 3/8") of trigger pin size rod and assemble the disconnector and spring to the trigger and insert the short pin to hold everything together. This will give you one less thing to position when trying to install this difficult-to-insert part.

If your trigger spring legs have a small bend on the ends, straighten them out to make fitting easier. What makes this hard to install is that the trigger spring legs must be held high

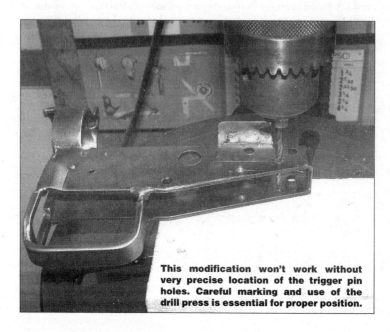

This modification won't work without very precise location of the trigger pin holes. Careful marking and use of the drill press is essential for proper position.

To work with the highly modified Sten bolt, the M16 hammer needs to very carefully be rounded off to this shape. Matthews says you may need some cut and try.

enough to go over the hammer spring coils but the sear needs to be placed under the trigger.

I used a set of needle-nosed vise grips to clamp the springs up high on the trigger. Then I slid it in and inserted the pin all the way through the trigger. The short pin holding the disconnector will be pushed out as the full-sized pin is inserted.

Once both hammer and trigger are in place, release both springs. The hammer spring legs will rest on the trigger spring coils and the trigger spring legs will rest on the hammer spring coils, resulting in everything being tensioned properly.

You should now have a functioning fire control group. If the parts don't work properly, some hand-fitting may be required. Be sure the disconnector works properly; the trigger should have to be released after recocking to reset the hammer for firing.

I certainly didn't want my trigger located this far forward on my gun, so I cut off part of the trigger and fabricated a transfer bar that connected the original Sten trigger to the new one. The rear trigger simply pulls the front trigger.

I thinned down a stub on the AR-15 trigger and drilled a hole in it for a pin. There was a little finger pressed out to hold a spring on the original Sten trigger. I removed this finger, leaving a slot in the trigger that I slid the transfer bar through.

I placed a small roll pin in the transfer bar to keep it from slipping out of the trigger.

The other end of the transfer bar is connected to the stub of the AR-15 trigger and the hole is located and drilled at assembly rather than ahead of time to get it just right. You can use a small screw for testing purposes but I made a small pin and cotter key for final assembly.

Once you have these parts in place and working right, you can insert the old Sten safety/selector to function as a trigger stop. I didn't make a safety for my gun, but one can be easily made and installed. Simply lathe turn a thin collar that will be installed on the safety/selector that can slide under the trigger and block trigger movement when the selector is moved back and forth.

One final thing I added was an additional trigger return spring. With the addition of a secondary trigger and transfer bar, the single return spring was a little lighter than I wanted. I just drilled a hole in the upper rear of the trigger housing, placed a roll pin in the hole and attached a spring between the pin and the top of the Sten trigger.

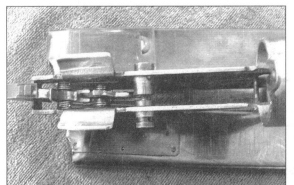

The Sten housing is just wide enough for the modified AR-15 and M16 parts. Matthews says a bit of judicious stretching may be required to get everything in position.

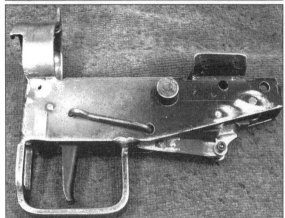

The housing looks odd with the AR trigger dangling at the front, but it soon was trimmed to a stub and connected to the original Sten trigger in the trigger guard.

It's important that the gun not fire if it's accidentally dropped and lands on its butt. After installing the additional spring, I dropped the piece repeatedly and the hammer never fell. Always think safety when you are making your own gun design!

Receiver Tube
After all this hand fitting and fine measuring, it's time for something a little less demanding. One of the Sten's design features was the simple steel tube receiver. I made my receiver of 1.5-inch x .083" chrome-moly seamless tubing. This is much stronger than common steel tubing.

Cutting the tube squarely to length and making the various openings shown in the receiver diagram are the only work that needs to be done to make the receiver. The bolt handle slot should not be cut to full width until its precise location can be determined at assembly after the magazine housing has been welded in place. This is because any variation in the location of the mag housing will affect where this slot is to be cut.

I recommend making a small starter slot in the beginning and then later opening it up to full size after the mag housing location has been finalized. I used a milling machine to make all my cutouts, but a Dremel tool with a cutoff wheel could be used if you prefer.

Charging/Bolt Handle
The bolt handle of my redesigned gun performs several functions. As well as cocking the gun, it also precisely locates the bolt face between the magazine lips when a magazine is inserted into the housing.

The handle also retains the firing pin extension in the bolt. I lathe-turned the handle to the dimensions listed on the handle drawing. The form outside the receiver is not really important; I just made it that shape to resemble the original handle.

The dimensions of the handle inside the receiver, however, do need to be very close since they are fitting and aligning other parts.

Barrel Bushing and Barrel
For the barrel, I wanted something commonly available, inexpensive and pre-chambered. I choose the Uzi 16-inch semi-auto carbine barrel. I have found several at gun shows priced under $60; I got mine for $45.

A mill is the right tool for making the various openings in the receiver tube. Matthews says not to make the bolt handle slot full-sized to start; make a pilot slot.

You can use a barrel blank if you don't mind the extra effort and cost of chambering and turning to size. I made a barrel bushing out of common cold-rolled steel. Before I turned the outside diameter, I drilled a hole in the bushing sized to create a light press fit on the barrel.

This size will probably vary, depending on the barrel you buy. I then pressed in the barrel so that it was flush with the end and secured it with a tight-fitting 3/16" crosspin I ground flush after installing. To ensure the best alignment, I placed the barrel in the lathe and then turned the bushing to the proper size.

The finished size of the bushing should be about .001" over the inside diameter of the receiver tube. This is so the receiver will have to be gently expanded with heat to securely grip and align the bushing when it cools. One last thing that needs to be done is to cut an extractor relief cut in the edge of the bushing and barrel.

A modified bolt handle retains the firing pin and also correctly locates the bolt in relation to the magazine feed lips. It needs to fit its slot in the receiver.

Matthews press-fit a surplus Uzi barrel into a steel bushing, then installed a 3/16" crosspin to retain it. Then he lathe-turned the assembly for proper alignment.

A parts-kit magazine housing and the appropriate size tube are all you need to make a Mk 2 style housing. This is also a part that requires careful welding technique.

I just placed the bolt and barrel/barrel bushing assembly together and noted where the extractor contacted and made a cut for clearance. Make this relief cut no deeper than you have to, since too much metal removal may cause bulged cases due to poor support of the chamber.

Magazine Housing Assembly

Although the Sten Mk 3 kit used for this project featured a magazine housing rather crudely welded onto flanges that protruded from the receiver, I wanted a reasonable duplicate of the Sten Mk 2 magazine housing. The Sten Mk 2 featured a housing welded onto a tube that slipped over the receiver tube. This housing also rotated to cover the openings when not in use. but I deleted this feature and made it stationary to greatly simplify things.

Once you have removed all the old pieces of receiver welded onto the mag housing, you can use it and some tubing to make an acceptable duplicate of the Mk 2 housing. Remove the ejector on the magazine housing before starting; it will be reinstalled after you have made this part and welded it to the receiver.

I used a piece of 1.625" x .058" 4130 seamless tubing with a clearance cut the size of the housing and welded it together. Make the rear curved section of the mag housing flush with the inside of the tubing and tack weld it in a few places, making sure it is square and positioned correctly.

A small piece of scrap 1.5" x .083" tubing inside the larger piece will help in locating everything, just be sure not to weld through the thin tubing and weld the two pieces together (don't ask how I know this little tidbit!). After you have the assembly

tack-welded together, finish welding the rest.

Use no more weld heat than necessary, as it will probably warp if heated too much. If it does warp, you will have to grind and file the inside of the tubing to make it fit. Check to see if it will slide over your receiver, if it does cut out for the ejection port and then you are done with this part.

End Cap / Recoil Spring Rod Assembly

One of the design features of the Sten was its economical use of parts. Nothing exemplifies this better than the end cap, recoil spring housing and buttstock interaction. The cap and housing retain the bolt and recoil spring in the receiver, and are in turn retained by the buttstock. The buttstock is retained by a stub on the back of the end cap.

Each part retains something else. I wanted to adhere to this principle in my modified Sten design, but that requires some redesigned parts to accommodate closed-bolt operation. I made a new style end cap that features a recoil spring guide rod.

The cap is made from cold-rolled steel. It has a clearance hole in the center for the extension on the rear of the bolt, a groove machined in the top for spring clearance, and a hole for attaching a guide rod.

Besides holding everything in place, the end cap limits rearward bolt travel so the bolt handle cannot reach its removal cutout. The end cap should be just a few thousandths of an inch smaller than the tubing inside diameter to allow for easy insertion, but needs to be large enough so that the buttstock is held tightly. The stub on the back of the end cap should fit the hole in the buttstock with little clearance to ensure tight fit.

Barrel Shroud/Handguard

The original Sten SMG used a 7.75-inch barrel surrounded partially by a ventilated barrel shroud. Since this semi carbine is using a 16-inch barrel as required by BATFE regulations, I lengthened the shroud to make it proportional to the longer barrel. It also gives a little more room for the hand. The shroud will be welded to the exposed portion of the barrel bushing at the front of the receiver tube.

Front Sight

One last part needs to be made, the front sight. The original Sten SMG featured a rather crude blade dovetailed into the receiver

which was then welded in place. I wanted a little adjustment on my redesign, so I fabricated a simple screw-on adjustable sight. I used a piece of the 1.625-inch tubing for a base, to which I brazed on a simple blade.

I put slotted screw holes in it and mounted it on the barrel shroud with screws. I drilled the holes 6-40 size and used short screws to hold it on. This allows for some windage adjustment. I made the blade tall so that I could file it down for proper elevation setting.

This adjustable sight is not original but doesn't look out of character for this crudely made gun, if you want something more original, just delete the slotted screw holes and weld it in place. I determined an approximate mounting location for the sight by bore sighting though the barrel and receiver.

Drilling through the receiver and barrel shroud tubes into the barrel bushing allows the three parts to be "plug welded" together. Three or four welds will do it.

A stub machined on the end cap will interlock with the buttstock and retain it. The end cap also needs a recess milled in to allow clearance for the bolt extension.

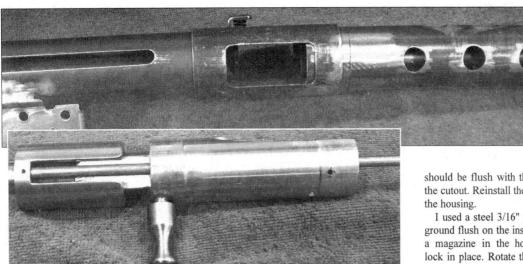

The bolt and end cap assembly shows how the end cap is hollowed out to allow the extension at the rear of the bolt to move rearward during the recoil stroke.

Assembly Procedure

Now that all the parts are made its time to assemble and hand fit everything together. I started by installing the barrel/barrel bushing assembly in the receiver. I warmed the front of the receiver to expand it slightly and slid the assembly in until it was a quarter-inch from the edge of the cutouts for the mag housing and ejection port.

Be sure it is indexed so that the extractor relief cut is at the 90° location so that the extractor has clearance when the bolt is installed later. As the receiver tube cools, it will tighten up on the bushing. If you don't have it aligned properly, you will have to reheat and reposition.

Using the same method, install the barrel shroud with the holes lined up on the tops and sides. After these parts are assembled, use a straightedge on the assembled tubes and verify everything is straight.

Once everything is aligned, drill three or four 5/16" holes about 3/8" deep equally spaced around both the receiver and shroud into the bushing. Do not drill too deep and drill into the barrel! These holes are then plug-welded with a MIG welder (a stick welder can be used, but it is much more difficult) to attach the assembly permanently.

Allow cooling time between welds to prevent overheating the barrel and receiver. After welding, grind the welds flush with the receiver.

Magazine Housing

With the ejector removed from the magazine housing assembly, slide it over the receiver tube and locate it over the cutout for the magazine. The inside front of the magazine housing

Level with yourself about your welding skills here. Getting the receiver tube too hot can warp it or result in a burn-through. Careful MIG welding is needed here.

should be flush with the edge of the cutout. Reinstall the ejector to the housing.

I used a steel 3/16" pop rivet I ground flush on the inside. Install a magazine in the housing and lock in place. Rotate the housing so that the magazine is centered in the cutout. Be sure the magazine is almost flush with the front edge of the cutout. This is the proper position and you now want to mark the assembly so that you can verify that it hasn't moved when you weld it.

At the front of the magazine housing on the tubing, drill one hole 5/16" dia. and 1/4" deep into the housing tube, receiver tube and barrel bushing. Be sure that you are over the bushing. Verify that nothing has moved and plug weld in this hole to permanently locate the housing assembly. Grind smooth after welding.

Completing the Bolt Handle Slot

Locating and cutting the bolt handle slot to its proper size and location is critical to proper functioning. The final location of this slot is dependent on the alignment of the bolt face between the magazine lips when a magazine is in the mag housing. Insert a magazine into the housing and lock in place.

Slide the bolt into the rear of the receiver and slide it forward. The bolt face should be centered between the feed lips of the magazine. The ejector should also be roughly centered in the ejector groove that is machined into the bolt.

Some hand fitting of the ejector may be required. When things are lined up, this is the proper location of the bolt in the receiver.

Observe where the bolt handle hole in the bolt is in reference to the starter slot in the receiver and then machine the slot to its proper width where needed to maintain the proper alignment. This is best done in small increments with repeated checking to be sure you are keeping things properly aligned.

If you take off too much metal on one side, it cannot be put back on, so be sure you are removing steel only where needed. Since the handle slot aligns the bolt, it needs to be a very good fit. Too loose and it won't hold things in proper alignment and too tight will cause it to bind.

Once you are getting close, insert the bolt handle through the handle removal cutout and hand fit the slot to the handle for proper fit.

Attaching the Trigger Housing

The trigger housing now needs to be located and welded in place. This is best done with the trigger components removed. Slide the housing onto the receiver and align it so that it is perpendicular (90°) to the mag housing. Slide it on until the rear of the receiver tube is even with the lower rear edge of the housing.

Be sure the hammer clearance cutout in the receiver is between the housing sides and not extending past the edges.

The hammer cutout does not have to be centered, since it can be hand-filed later if clearance for the hammer is needed. The important part is that the housing is perpendicular to the magazine and mag housing.

Once it is located, it needs to be lightly clamped in place and then welded in five places. Weld both of the front tabs, once on

each side at the rear, and one on the top right in front of the rear sight. No more welding than necessary should be done, since excessive heat will warp the receiver and cause the bolt to bind when installed.

MIG welding with small welds is the preferred method.

Some minor filing or grinding inside the receiver may be required after welding to clean up the weld area. When complete, re-install the fire control group.

Front Sight

If you made the same style of front sight as I did, you will have to mount it on the barrel shroud. I determined its location by bore sighting and drilled holes in the center of both screw slots and tapped them for 6-40 screws.

Final Assembly and Hand-Fitting

Depending to the varying dimensions and locations of your parts, both the ones you made and your kit parts, little or considerable hand fitting will be required to get everything to work properly. You may have to remove some more material from the bottom of the bolt or the hammer to get the fire control group to function properly; it all depends on how all your parts fit.

Insert the bolt and bolt handle and check to see if it slides over the hammer (you may have to reach inside the receiver and press down the hammer). The bolt should slide over the hammer and re-cock the hammer after it has been tripped by the trigger.

If everything appears to be right, then it's time to install the end cap with guide rod and the spring. Slide the 12.75-inch spring over the guide rod and insert the other end into the spring hole in the bolt. Press in the end cap until the stub on the back is past the end of the housing and then slide the buttstock up into place.

Matthews says five welds are needed to retain the trigger housing. Once they are smoothed, install the front cover, which hides the modified trigger and retains its pins.

Releasing the end cap will allow the stub to interlock with the hole in the buttstock and lock the stock in place. Using *dummy rounds, not live ammo* partially load a magazine (10 rounds or so) and operate the action by hand to see if it functions properly. If there are problems make modifications and corrections.

Believe it or not, mine functioned immediately with dummy rounds. If the dummy rounds work OK, then it's time to try test-firing with live ammo. Always, especially when test firing a new gun, wear the proper safety equipment. Safety glasses and ear plugs are mandatory and I even wear gloves when I'm testing a new design.

The Sten looked like something of a mongrel before finishing, but a treatment with KG GunKote did wonders for its appearance. Lauer DuraCoat would be an alternative.

Matthews' home-brewed replacement for the front sight may be inauthentic, but allows for windage adjustment and does have a rough wartime sort of appearance about it.

I also recommend firing from the hip to keep everything away from your face and eyes till you are sure it's working correctly. Load only single rounds to start with, then a couple, then five. You don't want to find out you have a trigger problem by firing off a whole magazine!

When I test fired mine I had one minor problem, occasionally an empty case would bounce back into the action after hitting the edge of the ejection port. I simply opened up the rear of the port a little further and then functioning was 100%. Once I had

completed test-firing and had a good working gun, I proceeded to final finishing.

I smoothed up all the rough edges and dressed the welds down and removed scratches. I didn't take this to extremes though. Original Stens were very crudely made and little effort was put into finishing. With this in mind I left in a lot of the "crudeness" to duplicate the original appearance.

Marking

Although federal law doesn't require marking a makers name, address or serial number on a home-built gun, it could change in the future, since so many people are building their own guns. I would highly recommend marking your gun. Marking this info on the gun may prevent future problems, especially if you have contacts with law enforcement when shooting this gun.

Over the years I have had many "contacts" with law enforcement (game wardens, sheriff deputies, etc.) while shooting, even on my own property. Cops aren't necessarily up on minor paragraphs of federal gun law, and may assume someone illegally removed the serial number to make your gun untraceable.

Rather than explain the rules to them and try to convince them you made it, why not mark it as made by you? A serial number also comes in handy if the gun is stolen.

I also find it's an ego boost when you show your shooting buddies your latest creation! A metal stamp kit can be bought for under $10, so buy one and mark your project. I stamped mine with my business name and made up a serial number.

Finishing

There are many options for a finish on this project. Original Sten SMGs, depending on when and by whom they were manufactured, had several different finishes. They were Parkerized, blued or painted. The most common finish was a crude paint job, but I wanted something just a little better wearing.

What I chose was vastly superior to the painted finish, but still duplicated the look. I finished my Sten with KG GunKote in a self-mixed color of charcoal grey that looks very much like manganese phosphate Parkerizing. KG GunKote is a sprayed and baked-on polymer finish that is incredibly durable. I sprayed mine with an airbrush but KG GunKote is available from Brownells in spray cans for those who don't have spray equipment.

Another alternative is Lauer Custom Weaponry's DuraCoat. I have previously done articles for SGN on applying both these finishes along with Parkerizing and hot bluing. If you are interested in the processes for them, refer to those back issues.

I now have a reasonable replica of the Sten Mk 2 for my military arms collection. The cost was less than $150, although the cost in time was big, especially the design work. But if you're like me, you have more time than money. Since I built it myself, I knew it was built to my quality standards and I was quite happy with the results.

I spent a month or so of my free time designing and building this gun, but since I have done a lot of the design work it should only take a skilled hobbyist gunsmith 20-30 hours to build. In a couple of weekends and a few evenings, you can also make a semi-auto Sten for your collection at a bargain price. ◉

Matthews recommends using steel stamps to identify the gun with a serial number. It's not required, but try explaining that to a skeptical cop in the middle of the night.

Save money with the #1 source of firearms!

SHOTGUN◉NEWS

The trading post for anything that shoots.

More
than just ads!

Every issue has a unique blend of fascinating feature stories and information-packed columns. Here's where you'll read about the guns you see advertised in SHOTGUN NEWS!

Three times a month, Senior Editor Peter Kokalis brings his tart, scrupulous brand of commentary to the world of tactical arms. With features in the first and third issues of the month and his popular "Mostly Machine Guns" column in the second, you'll get a healthy dose of Kokalis every 10 days.

The first issue of the month adds Clayton E. Cramer's scholarly take on gun politics and a historical look at ammunition from Paul Scarlata.

David Fortier looks at some of the newest developments in ammunition, firearms and optics in the second issue, along with Reid Coffield's folksy insights on gunsmithing. Frank James offers his hand-gunning expertise, while Vin Suprynowicz applies his blowtorch wit and insight to the struggle for the right to bear arms. The SHOTGUN NEWS New Products column gives you a look at the newest arms, ammo and accessories—well before the monthly firearms magazines get to them.

A jackpot package of features comes your way in the third issue of the month, along with Tom Gaylord's "Airgun" column.

Every issue of SHOTGUN NEWS features Neal Knox's pointed and pungent political commentary.

Firearms & accessories
SUPERSTORE!

SHOTGUN NEWS is loaded with exciting bargains on rifles, shotguns, revolvers, and pistols. Save on all kinds, makes, models, manufacturers, and vintages. Plus discover your best buys on ammo, optics, gun parts, and many more accessories, supplies, & services.

New issue every 10 days!

Constantly revolving inventory gives you more to choose from. And as a subscriber, you'll never miss an issue – so you never miss out on a great deal!

SUBSCRIBE TODAY
1-800-345-6923
Visa/MasterCard/Discover users

- -

HOME BUILDING THE FN/FAL

PART 1:

Selecting a parts kit and installing the barrel

Matthews likes to get his guns the most inexpensive way possible, so when a friend asked about an FAL, do-it-yourself was the way he recommended.

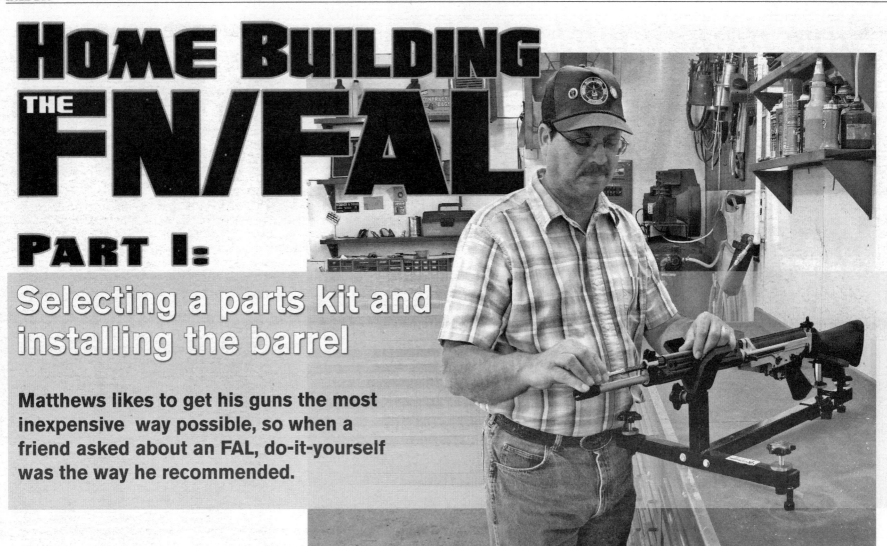

By Steven Matthews

Matthews' friend Kent wanted to expand his horizons from blackpowder shooting to military arms. Matthews pointed out the advantages of home building an FAL rifle.

Home building the FN/FAL rifle can be an enjoyable experience and maybe even allow you to have one of the world's most respected battle rifles at a bargain price.

In the decades following World War II, the armies of the world almost universally abandoned the bolt-action rifles that had served for the previous half-century.

In the mid 1950s, Fabrique Nationale of Belgium was one of the first to offer a truly modern battle rifle in the form of the now-famous FN FAL. It featured high capacity, semi-auto or full-auto fire, quality construction and fired the new 7.62x51mm cartridge.

Collectors of modern military rifles find the semi-auto FAL is a "must-have" item. There are several brands of factory built guns. These range from commercial grade copies to true military-specification rifles. The quality can also range from poor to military grade excellence.

One way to get a military grade FAL is to build it yourself using quality components. Building a semi-auto FAL at home can be relatively easy if you have some basic hobby gunsmithing skill and a few tools.

Home building can also save you some money if you are a smart shopper. My friend Kent is mainly a blackpowder shooter, but he's interested in modern military firearms. Price has stopped him from buying one, so I suggested building an FAL might be a good way to get into the hobby.

Since I've built FALs before, I offered to help him find some bargain-priced parts and help him build this gun.

I will cover the high points of the build process. This article in no way should be considered a step-by-step build tutorial; it's just a brief overview of the build process. If you think it's within your abilities, there are several sources with detailed instructions that will cover the process in much greater detail. A couple good ones are listed at the end of this article.

The first thing needed for a build project is good parts. I ordered a parts kit from SGN advertiser Inter Ordnance of Monroe, N.C. This kit was made by Imbel in Brazil. They are an

FN licensed manufacturer; the word is that the kits were excellent quality.

The kits include all parts except an upper receiver, which has been demilitarized prior to importation. These kits are in "used" condition and have been obtained by demilling used/surplus rifles from some South American countries. Rumor has it that this kit was from Chilean military sources. The kit received was advertised as "excellent" condition.

Excellent military surplus condition is somewhat different than excellent commercial condition. Any parts kit obtained from disassembling used military arms is going to show considerable finish wear, especially arms coming from "third world" countries.

This kit was in excellent mechanical condition but showed a lot of finish wear, indicating it was carried a lot but shot little. The barrel gauged as almost new. Since the gun was going to receive a complete refinish job, the worn finish was of no concern.

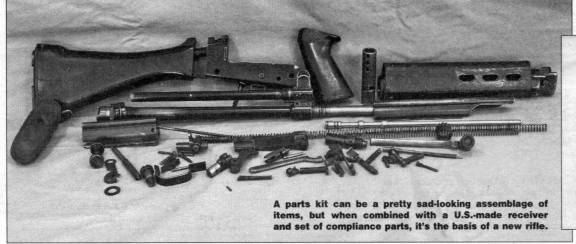

A parts kit can be a pretty sad-looking assemblage of items, but when combined with a U.S.-made receiver and set of compliance parts, it's the basis of a new rifle.

BUILDING THE FN/FAL Part 1

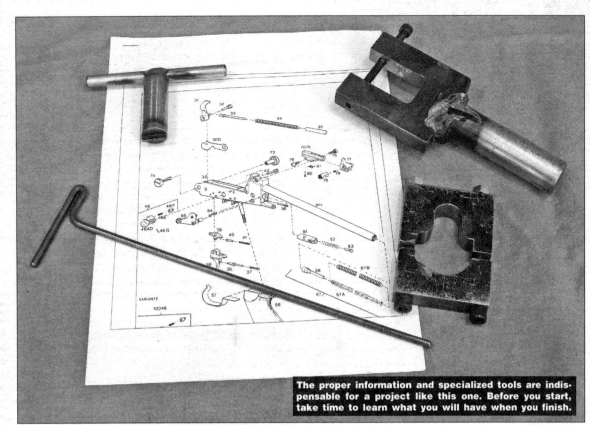

The proper information and specialized tools are indispensable for a project like this one. Before you start, take time to learn what you will have when you finish.

DSA will provide you a nicely finished action wrench for about $60, but for the tightwad, there's nothing like making your own with some scrap steel and a Moto-Tool.

view diagrams can be found in many FAL parts catalogs such as DSA's catalogs or the Numrich Gun Parts Corp. catalog. There's even an online version on Inter Ordnance's site: http://www.interordnance.com/library/FN%20FAL%20manual.pdf

Once everything is ready, it's time to start the project. The parts kit as received was covered in grease and oil. As bad as it looks, this grease is your friend! It protects the metal from rust and corrosion. The more the better! Even though this kit had little finish left on it, there was absolutely no rust anywhere.

I have found the best way to remove this heavy grease is to soak everything in mineral spirits (paint thinner) for a couple hours, then scrub away what didn't dissolve. After the first cleaning, dump your dirty solvent and then use clean solvent and clean again.

When everything is clean, dry off the parts and apply a light coat of thin oil on all operating parts. Most FAL kits I have seen were not disassembled into individual parts, but just broken down into the major assemblies of upper and lower receiver sections. If you aren't going to do a complete refinish job and go with it as-received, total disassembly isn't required.

For this project I wanted to completely refinish all external parts so everything was removed and refinished. If you do disassemble everything, pay attention to how things come apart and take notes. It will make putting it back together easier if you know where the parts came from!

Most upper receiver assemblies will have a small chunk of the old receiver still attached to the barrel shank and it will have to be removed. This removal and later installation of the barrel is where your barrel wrench and action wrench/vise will be worth their weight.

If you have the right tools, removing the barrel will only take a couple minutes. The proper tools will allow the parts to be held tightly yet not stress the parts. If you don't have the right tools, it could take a long time and result in damage to your project.

This kit also included a new U.S.-made buttstock, forearm, and pistol grip. These U.S.-made parts are a couple of the parts we were going to have to replace due to BATFE regulations. See the sidebar about the legal requirement for building semi-auto rifle from foreign parts.

I got a U.S.-made gas piston and charging handle from Tapco. I had a couple U.S.-made fire control group parts in my personal inventory. I made a flash suppressor so it was "U.S." made, too, as was the magazine floorplate.

All these parts need to be assembled into an upper receiver. DSA Inc. has the reputation of building the finest U.S.-made FAL receiver. Many think they are equal in quality to FNs. As it's made in this country, it counts towards the U.S. parts count.

At one time DSA receivers were considered pricey, but since parts kits are getting hard to find, DSA receivers are now competitively priced. It may cost a little more but you won't have any "building issues" with a DSA receiver as you sometimes have with other brands. The high quality means the demand for the DSA receiver is high and availability is limited. There is usually a waiting list for a bare receiver, so if you are going to do a FAL project, get your order in as soon as possible.

Besides parts and basic hand tools you will need to buy or make a few specialized tools. You will need an action wrench/vise and a barrel wrench. I made both mine from pieces of steel I had lying around so my cost was $0. These tools are available from many sources if you aren't into the make-it-yourself mode.

For an action wrench/vise I took a piece of half-inch steel and cut out a profile of the front of the receiver with drills, saws, files and a Dremel Moto-Tool. This was then drilled for clamp bolts and then cut in half. This did take a few hours but it did save about $60 compared to buying one from DSA.

When clamped onto the receiver, it securely holds it without marring or stressing the receiver. Welding on a handle makes it a wrench or you can leave it square and clamp it in a vise as I did.

For a barrel wrench I took a piece of steel and cut out a section the size of the barrel flats. I added a clamp bolt to help secure it to the barrel. Some people use an open end wrench rather than buy or make a specialized tool. If you do this, be sure to get a wrench that fits very tight. The barrel flats are small and the tool will slip and round off the flats if it's loose. I *do not* recommend any adjustable wrench for this job since the jaws tend to flex under high torque and will slip and mar your barrel.

A couple more items may be needed. If you wish to set the headspace on your rifle yourself, you will need a set of headspace gages. Brownells charges $30 each for .308 Go and No Go gauges, so many builders will simply hire this procedure out to a qualified gunsmith.

One thing that isn't a tool but will greatly help the home builder is information. A set of exploded view diagrams and an operator's manual will greatly assist the home builder. Exploded

Former military arms can vary widely in condition. Matthews gauged the barrel and found that it must have been shot very little during its years of military service.

No, you don't want to use that big Chinese crescent wrench for this job! Specialized tools can be bought, or if you are thrifty like Matthews, made at home.

BUILDING THE FN/FAL Part 1

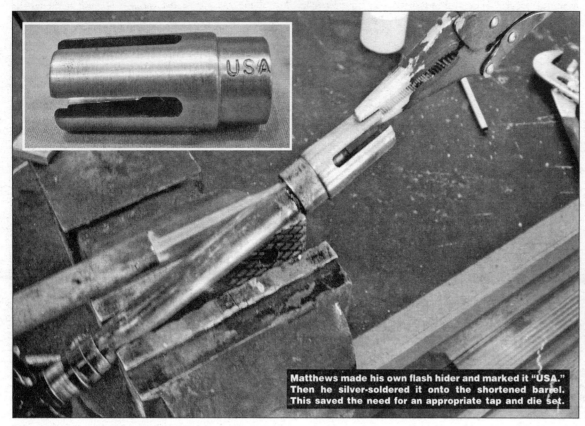

Matthews made his own flash hider and marked it "USA." Then he silver-soldered it onto the shortened barrel. This saved the need for an appropriate tap and die set.

Using the barrel and action vise, Matthews tightened the two parts together. It's important not to force the issue: the receiver can be bent if you crank too hard.

Some try to just clamp the old action remnant in a vise and go to work with a crescent wrench. Unfortunately as you clamp down tight on the old receiver, the vise exerts extreme pressure on the threads, making the removal even harder. The extra effort needed makes it easy to round off the barrel flats with the flexing jaws of an adjustable wrench. I'm all for improvising, but only if the methods are good!

First remove the gas tube assembly. This is done by removing the handguards, which are held on with one screw through the gas block. Then remove the gas plug by depressing the detent button and rotating it till it pops out and then remove the gas piston and spring.

Turn the regulator nut all the way off and let it slide down the tube. The tube is threaded into the gas block and it held in place with a small crosspin that needs to be removed. Once it is unscrewed all the way, you can unscrew the gas tube nut that screws into the front of the receiver. The proper tool for removing this nut is a spanner that engages the notches, but if you don't have one you can carefully use a punch in the notches to loosen it enough to turn by hand. Once it is loose, slide it up on the gas tube and you should have enough room to remove the tube.

Once these parts are removed you can attach your barrel tools and quickly and easily remove the barrel from the receiver stub. Since the barrel was installed with about 100 foot-pounds of torque, it will take considerable force to remove. The threads are right-hand so be sure you turn the right way.

Your kit may or may not come with a center section of the old receiver that contains several parts that need to be salvaged for later use. The locking shoulder, magazine release, bolt hold-open assembly and associated pins and springs will be needed in the new receiver.

It may also have the old ejector block in it, but that's not needed since the semi auto receiver will have a semi ejector block already installed. You can save it if you want in case you ever need an ejector. Once you have salvaged any usable parts, take the old receiver sections and throw them away along with the auto sear if it was included in your kit.

There is no need for any auto parts or old receiver sections when building a semi-auto FAL. Over the years the BATFE has repeatedly approved demilitarized parts and later changed its mind and declared old pieces of receiver as restricted machine gun parts. Just pitch them and avoid future problems.

Kent and I decided to incorporate a non-standard barrel length in this project. The standard FAL barrel was 21 inches, with a long flash hider adding about 2 more inches to that. To reduce the length and make a handier gun, I shortened the barrel to 17¾ inches and made a shorter flash hider (about 1¼ inches long) in my shop.

I turned it out on my lathe and milling machine in about an hour. Since I made it here in Ohio, it counts as a U.S.-part. This resulted in barrel length of about 19 inches rather than the previous 23. Since I didn't have the correct taps and dies for the barrel and flash hider, I made it a slip fit on the barrel and silver-soldered it in place.

The barrel can now be installed on the new receiver. The new barrel will have to be "indexed" to the correct position when installed. This means that when torqued down to the proper tightness, the front sight will be almost exactly straight up in the 12 o'clock position.

Having it properly aligned will allow your sight to be centered correctly. If not almost exactly straight up, your rear sight will have to be moved off to one side to obtain proper sight alignment. Some barrel/receiver combinations will align properly when tightened; others may require adjustment.

Generally if you can hand-tighten it and it goes to about the 11 o'clock position, it will probably index right when torqued down. If it goes past the 11 o'clock position to say for example 12 or 1–2 o'clock, then a thin shim washer will be required to compensate. Some peen the barrel shoulder with a hammer, but I

don't approve of that. If, on the other hand, it won't get to the 11 o'clock position when hand tightened then some barrel shoulder will have to be removed.

This was the case in this build project. When hand tightened, the barrel only made it to about 10 o'clock. Trying to force it into position by overtightening may damage the barrel or receiver, so material had to be removed. The barrel needed to go about 1 more "hour" of rotation.

How much material to be removed is easily calculated. The barrel threads are 16 threads per inch, which means that each pair of threads are .062" apart. One full turn of the barrel would move it in .062". Using the clock method, the barrel needs to rotate in about 1 hour or 1/12 turn; that equals about .005" (.062" divided by 12).

I chucked up the barrel in a lathe and removed .005". If you are real good with tools, you might be able to do this with files, but be warned; few have the skill required for such fine hand

Matthews "eyeballed" alignment by placing straight-edges on the receiver and front sight and ensuring they were parallel. You can buy gauges for this process, too.

BUILDING THE FN/FAL Part 1

work. When I reinstalled the barrel by hand, it went almost to 11 o'clock.

Then I attached the action wrench/vise and placed the assembly in a secure bench vise. I used the barrel wrench to torque it down. To bring it up to the 12 o'clock position requires about 100 foot-pounds of torque. A couple methods can be used to get it "just right".

A fixture is available that consists of a rod in a flat base that sits in the receiver and another rod that is screwed into the sight base. Aligning these two rods gets it pretty close. This tool is fine if you want to buy one, but as my readers have probably guessed, I improvised a decent method.

My method is the old "eyeball" method with the aid of a couple straightedges (rulers or scales). I tighten up the barrel till it looks about right then place straightedges on the receiver and sight base. When you sight down these two and they are parallel, it is about right. Just a little more got them aligned right.

I also observe the location of the barrel flats and notches (gas tube nut and extractor cut) in the barrel to indicate that is pretty close. I have used this method on a couple builds and it has worked well. The sights were pretty well centered when sighted in. I always try to view things from several angles to insure that I am

When the barrel is properly indexed, the gas tube bushing will slide right into position, clearing its notch in the barrel. Careful work will pay off at this point.

as seeing "straight." The eyeball method will work if you have the skill to see "straightness" but the tools will help those who don't.

Once the barrel is torqued and indexed, the gas system can be re-installed by reversing the disassembly procedure.

Put in the gas piston and spring and push it though its movement range to be sure it is not binding when it passes through the new receiver. Once checked, remove it for later assembly. ◎

10 PARTS
Why They're Important

When you are looking for FAL parts, you may see some advertised as U.S. Compliance Parts or 922(r) Compliant. This is because under BATFE regulations no more than 10 parts out of a list of 20 specified imported parts can be used to build a semi-auto rifle. This is due to the law restricting the importation of semi-auto rifles that are considered by BATFE to be "semi-automatic assault rifles." If the gun contains 10 or fewer of the parts on the list, it is considered to be U.S.-made and therefore legal.

If it contains more than 10 of the parts, it is considered to be an "imported semi-automatic assault rifle" and thus illegal. Several manufacturers make U.S.-made replacement parts that can be used to get the legal parts count. The only difference in the U.S. made parts is country of origin.

It may seem stupid to replace perfectly good foreign parts with U.S.-made parts, but that's the law the politicians have saddled us with. The 20 regulated parts are as follows:

1. Frames and Receivers
2. Barrels
3. Barrel Extensions
4. Mounting Blocks (trunnions)
5. Muzzle Attachments (muzzle brakes and flash suppressors)
6. Bolts
7. Bolt Carriers
8. Operating Rods
9. Gas Pistons
10. Trigger Housings
11. Triggers
12. Hammers
13. Sears
14. Disconnectors
15. Buttstocks
16. Pistol Grips
17. Forearms or Hand Guards
18. Magazine Bodies
19. Magazine Followers
20. Magazine Floor Plates

Not all rifles have all the parts listed. What matters is that you have no more than 10 imported parts that are on the list. Parts not on the list are unregulated and don't count for or against the parts count. Price considerations make several of the listed parts popular for builders, but any combination can be used as long as the parts count is right.

It should be noted that these are Federal regulations and state or local regulations may affect the legality of your gun. It is the builder's responsibility to verify legality in his location. ◎

Ask the Gunsmith

By Reid Coffield

always nice to know I can go back to my instruction binder and quickly and easily find the appropriate instructions. With this binder the instructions never get lost, mislaid or discarded. They're right there when you need 'em.

FINDING GOOD TOOLS

Q *I have been following your gunsmithing articles for a number of years now and I am gradually trying a few projects on my own. As I do this I find that I occasionally need some specialized gunsmithing tools and equipment. I have noticed that there is often a considerable range of quality for such equipment. My question is this; how do you tell the difference between good equipment and no so good? Often the descriptions in the catalogs look pretty much the same.*

Coffield has been using this Forster Universal Sight Mounting Fixture for almost 35 years, and it's still going strong. When precise results are essential, you don't necessarily want to economize.

A This can certainly be a problem and I'll be the first to admit that I've been burned on more than one occasion myself. In general, I find I can avoid most disappointment if I make my purchases from a reputable, established company. I also try to deal only with outfits that really push a guarantee of total customer satisfaction. You're either happy with the product or they'll give you your money back with no hassles and no questions asked.

I also expect to pay good money for good tools. There's no free lunch and good tools are seldom ever cheap. Those Chinese-made drill sets or tap and die sets that sell for less than $20 are generally just about useless. You will have to pay for good tools, but good tools give good service and last for years. An example of this is a Forster Universal Sight Mounting Fixture I have. I bought that fixture when I first opened my very first shop. I well remember the pain of paying for that thing but you know what? I'm still using it almost 35 years later! When I look back at the initial cost and how long I've used it, it really wasn't all that expensive.

By the way, when you buy a good tool you'll almost always get good instructions with it. I find that it's been very helpful to save those instructions in a dedicated binder. Some tools don't get used frequently and it's

FACTORY BARREL INSTALLATION

Q *How are barrels installed in gun factories*

Century International Arms uses this large machine to install barrels on FN FAL receivers. The big wheel, coupled with the use of multiple gears, gives it tremendous leverage.

A More often than not, in large commercial and military manufacturing facilities, the receiver of a rifle is turned on to the barrel using a geared machine rather than a simple action wrench as used by most gunsmiths. The machine is faster, easier to use in a production situation, and can safely apply more pressure to the action. ◎

THE HOME-BUILT FAL

PART II:

Headspacing, Finishing, Assembly

In Part I, Matthews selected a parts kit and installed a barrel. This month, he completes a personally-built FAL.

By Steven Matthews

Next comes the most difficult and to some the most confusing aspect of building a FAL rifle, setting headspace. This is where a lot of potential builders balk. If you are familiar with firearms headspacing, the FN/FAL is one of the easiest guns to set up. In fact it was designed for easy headspacing, that's why it has a removable locking shoulder that allows for easy setting without machining as is common on bolt-action rifles.

Many builders do not feel comfortable doing this procedure and hire it out to a qualified gunsmith. If you have any doubts, I highly recommend that you do that. Since it is a very easy job, the costs should not be great.

Headspace, for those unfamiliar with firearms, is the clearance between the breechface and rear surface of the barrel. It may be measured at the rim, as in .22 Long Rifle cartridges, at the case mouth, as in a .45 ACP, or on the belt, as for magnum rifle cartridges. For a 7.62 mm rifle, it is measured from the base to a specified point on the cartridge shoulder.

Too little or too much space here can result in an unsafe condition. There are several methods for setting headspace in this rifle. The *correct* methods involve using two (sometimes three) cartridge-shaped headspace gauges. These are machined to very specific dimensions. One is called a Go gauge and the other is called a No Go gauge. There is also a third gauge called a Field gauge, but it is seldom used in a new installation. There is a dimensional difference of a few thousandths of an inch between the Go and No Go gauges.

These are inserted into the gun's chamber using a stripped bolt (no extractor or ejector). As the names imply, the bolt should close on the Go gauge and not close on the No Go. By alternately checking with these gauges and making adjustments to the gun, a proper headspace setting can be obtained.

You can get a lot more information on this topic from build tutorials such as the FAL video (item No. 1224) offered by AGI (American Gunsmithing Institute) and build tutorials available free on the internet.

Having an FAL is fun, but it's even more fun if you made it yourself. With a DSA lower receiver, a parts kit and some homemade items, it's a simple task to build one.

One of the best internet sources for FAL building info is the FAL discussion forum at www.falfiles.com. It has a gunsmithing and build-it-yourself section that is frequented by amateur and professional FAL builders. There is a wealth of info there by knowledgeable people that can explain in great detail the headspacing procedures. They are a great bunch of guys and will offer any help they can.

On an FAL rifle, the bolt rides in a bolt carrier that reciprocates in the receiver. As it reaches its forwardmost position, the rear of the bolt is cammed down into a recess in the receiver to lock the bolt in place.

In this notch there is a piece called a locking shoulder that is inserted just above the hinge pin. It can be had in several sizes to compensate for receiver and barrel differences and also for

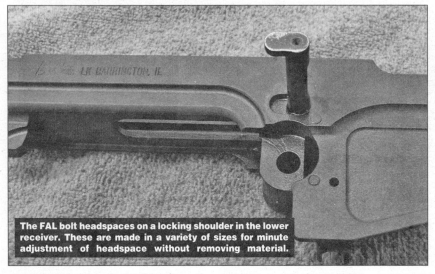
The FAL bolt headspaces on a locking shoulder in the lower receiver. These are made in a variety of sizes for minute adjustment of headspace without removing material.

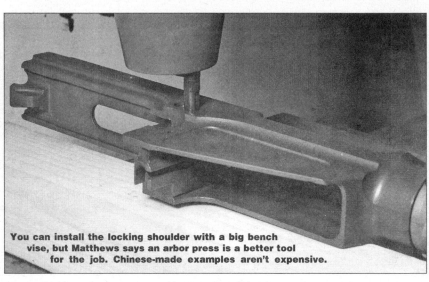
You can install the locking shoulder with a big bench vise, but Matthews says an arbor press is a better tool for the job. Chinese-made examples aren't expensive.

BUILDING THE FN/FAL Part 2

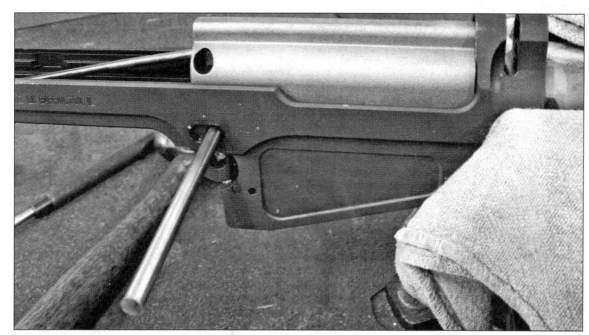

Headspace must be set with a stripped bolt; no extractor in place. If the extractor is installed, the headspace gauges won't work as intended, giving false data.

The supplied shoulder wasn't the right size, so Matthews used a series of precision pins to determine the proper dimension. Brownells offers a tool made for this.

compensating for wear on the parts. It may be as small as .240" or as large as .270". Most are in the .255"–.265" range.

When you buy a kit, one locking shoulder is usually included, but in most cases it will not be the correct size for your project. The building tutorials previously mentioned explain how to determine the correct size to use. Sometimes the one supplied will work since the tolerance range is a few thousands of an inch.

Brownells offers a stepped rod with diameters from .256" to .272" for determining the proper locking shoulder. If you plan to build a lot of FALs, it's a useful tool, but at $89, it's a bit high for one build.

Since they sometimes work, I went ahead and installed the one that came with the kit. The supplied locking shoulder was sized at .257". The locking shoulder is pressed into the recess in the receiver. Be careful to keep it aligned properly. A hydraulic press is best used but some press it in with a bench vise. Hammering it in is not recommended due to the risk of damaging the part.

Once it's installed, place the barreled action in a padded vise. Remember to strip the firing pin and extractor. This is necessary to get an accurate reading.

If the bolt is still in the carrier, pressing the firing pin in a little will allow enough room to slide the bolt down and out of the carrier. A crosspin holds the firing pin and spring in place. Removing the extractor is somewhat difficult due to the strong spring on the extractor plunger. Take a pointed punch and place it in the dimple in the plunger and press it all the way back. Once

all the way back the extractor can slide rearward slightly and be removed.

This is a three-handed job, so place the bolt in a vise to securely hold it. If you slip, the plunger and spring may shoot off to areas unknown, so be careful. DSA offers an extractor tool for $25 that makes this procedure a lot easier.

Place the bolt back in the carrier and insert the assembly into the bolt grooves in the receiver.

Because there can be a lot of size variation among U.S. commercial ammo and the surplus military stuff most of us like to use in a gun of this sort, I supplemented the headspace gauge test with live ammo of various types. The bolt would close on some rounds with a shove, but would not close at all on others.

This indicated that the .257" locking shoulder was just a little too large, so I removed it. It's relatively easy to determine the correct size by using pins of specific sizes in the locking shoulder recess. I inserted a .250" pin in the recess and all cartridges were tried again. This time all rounds chambered easily.

This indicated that the proper size was between .250" and .257". I decided that .252" should be about right. You can get locking shoulders for about $25 from FAL parts suppliers, but since I had a .257" shoulder and also a precision surface grinder, I reground the old shoulder to .252".

Be advised that the fine tolerances required mean you can't do this job with hand tools, so if you don't happen to have a surface grinder and the knowledge to use it, just buy the replacement part.

I reinstalled the .252" locking shoulder and rechecked with the gauges and my sample rounds. All passed the test this time. This

Measurement showed the shoulder needed to be reduced by about .005" for proper fit. Matthews used a precision surface grinder for the job; most will just buy a new one.

With the proper locking shoulder installed, the bolt will close easily on the Go gauge, not on the No Go. Matthews recommends checking with a variety of sample cartridges.

BUILDING THE FN/FAL Part 2

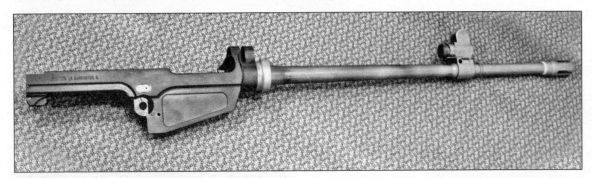

With the barrel installed, indexed and headspaced to the DSA receiver unit, Matthews was ready to apply an appropriate finish to the upper receiver assembly.

resulted in a gun with about .005"–.003" tolerance between the bolt face and cartridge.

This was verified by using precision shim stock in disc form between the bolt face and cartridge. This is a little tight for a military gun, but since Kent won't be doing any full-auto firing in the mud, it should be fine.

Before I refinished the lower receiver, I added a stop to prevent the safety/selector lever from rotating past the fire position to the old auto position. On a semi-auto, this allows the hammer to follow the bolt down, which causes a malfunction.

At the bottom of the receiver I drilled and tapped a 6-40 hole and installed a screw as a stop. If you don't have a tap and die set, a round head rivet could be substituted.

When the stop is located at the bottom of the receiver, a relief will have to be filed into the safety lever to allow it to rotate far enough to engage the detent. Location isn't critical as long as it's high enough to clear the inside bottom of the receiver and low enough that you don't have to file away too much safety lever.

The screw should be only about 1/8" long and locked in place with thread locker and also by staking the couple threads that extend into the receiver.

I wanted a low-maintenance finish on this project, so I chose KG GunKote. It's a sprayed on and baked finish that is extremely durable. It is easy to apply, and even the hobbyist gunsmith can apply a professional-grade finish. It is sprayed on a lightly sandblasted surface with an airbrush and baked at 325°.

If you have a forgiving wife it can be baked in your kitchen oven. For those without spray equipment it is available from Brownells in spray can form. The colors chosen were "brushed stainless steel" for the receivers and barrel and "satin black" for the controls and a few other parts.

For those who don't want to use a baked-on type of finish Lauer Custom Weaponry offers the fine DuraCoat finish. I've covered the application of both of these products in past SGN articles.

Once the parts were refinished it was time to begin assembly. Reassembly is fairly easy, due to the FAL's uncomplicated design. Anyone with basic hobby gunsmithing skills can do it. A simple exploded view diagram is all most people need to figure it out, but if you have bought a build video, it will walk you though it. I'll just hit the high points here.

Start with the lower receiver. First install the locking catch lever and locking catch. The catch is inserted through the rear of the receiver along with the spring and plunger. They are retained by a crosspin in the receiver. The lever inserts through the side of the receiver with the stub on the lever in the groove in the catch. The lever is retained by a screw in the rear of the receiver.

The rear sight slides into the dovetail in the top of the receiver. Two screws retain the sight and allow for adjustment. Loosening one and tightening the other moves the sight.

Now install the trigger, sear, sear spring and plunger. Insert a 5/32" slave pin into the assembly to hold the trigger and sear assembly together. When you insert the trigger pin through the receiver, it will push out the slave pin.

Place the trigger /sear assembly into the receiver and push it back against the trigger spring under the receiver and line up the holes. Then insert the trigger pin from the side. The hammer is next to go in. This is easy since there is no spring tension on the hammer yet. Line up the hole and slide in the hammer pin.

After it's in, you can slide in the hammer/trigger pin retaining plate. The groove in the front of the plate engages a groove in the hammer pin. Rotating it down will allow the center groove to slide into a groove in the trigger pin. Once pushed down into position, it will be held in place by the safety lever when it is installed through the hole in the plate.

To install the safety lever, place it in the 12 o'clock position and slide it into the receiver, making sure it goes through the hole in the locking plate. Once it's in place, rotate it down into the fire position. If your hammer is in the cocked position, pull the trigger and move it to the forwardmost position.

Then install the hammer spring, spring housing and plunger. The strong spring makes this a job. Place the end of the spring housing in the dimple in the receiver. Grasp the front of the

plunger with a pair of needle-nose pliers or vise grips and depress it so that it can be inserted into the recess in the hammer.

The tab on the front of the trigger guard can now be slipped into the slot in the receiver. Rotate it into position and slide on the pistol grip, which will retain the guard when installed. Place the grip nut on the screw and tighten it up.

After assembling the fire control group, work it by hand and verify that it functions properly. Make sure it cocks and holds the hammer in place, disconnects the trigger when cycled and that the safety works.

All that remains is to install the buttstock and recoil spring assembly. Slide the buttstock onto the recoil spring tube. With the buttstock pointed up, slide in the spring plunger and spring. The buttstock and spring will be retained by the large round nut that threads onto the end of the tube.

A piece of rod through the spring and nut will help keep the spring from kinking when it's compressed into the tube. Compressing the spring and starting the nut all at the same time can be difficult, so be sure you have the receiver held in place solidly. Once the nut is started, screw it in the rest of the way and tighten it up with a large screwdriver or other improvised tool.

DSA offers a special tool for this job at $9.95 that also accepts a cleaning brush for cleaning the gas tube. If you intend regular detail disassembly of FALs, it's well worth the price.

The buttplate is held in place with a screw through it and into the buttstock nut. A small screw in the tang at the bottom of the receiver screws into the buttstock. Your lower assembly is now complete.

Now the upper receiver can be completed. Both the bolt hold-open device and magazine release are inserted though the bottom of the receiver and held in place with a common pin/screw.

Slide the bolt hold-open into its hole and insert the pin in the side of the receiver, being sure that the pin enters the bolt hold-open above the internal spring. Before pushing the pin all the way through, slide the magazine catch and spring up into its recess.

Align the hole and push the pin the rest of the way through. Once it's properly through the bolt hold-open and the magazine catch, screw the threaded part down and tighten it up.

The charging handle can be inserted into its groove in the side of the receiver. Before it can be inserted the pin or screw (some have pins, some have screws) needs to be removed to allow the handle to slide into the groove. Once the handle is in place the pin or screw can be reinstalled.

Slide the regulator sleeve and gas tube bushing onto the gas tube. Screw the assembly into the gas block on the barrel. Tighten all the way and then back it out slightly to align the two gas vent holes in the down position.

The front edge of the threaded portion of the tube is beveled on the side for a crosspin that keeps it from turning out. Once it's aligned, insert the crosspin.

You then can screw the rear bushing nut into the front of the receiver. If you are using a carry handle, insert the handle before you screw in the bushing, since it holds the handle in place.

Slide the regulator nut onto the gas block and screw it in place. Screw it all the way on, then back it up till the vent hole is open

There are lots of small parts for finishing, and Matthews says the easy way is to hang them with small wires, allowing convenient 360° application of the finish.

In contrast to bluing, which requires boiling caustic chemicals, modern finishes like KG Gun-Kote or Lauer DuraCoat are easy for the hobbyist to apply in the garage.

BUILDING THE FN/FAL Part 2

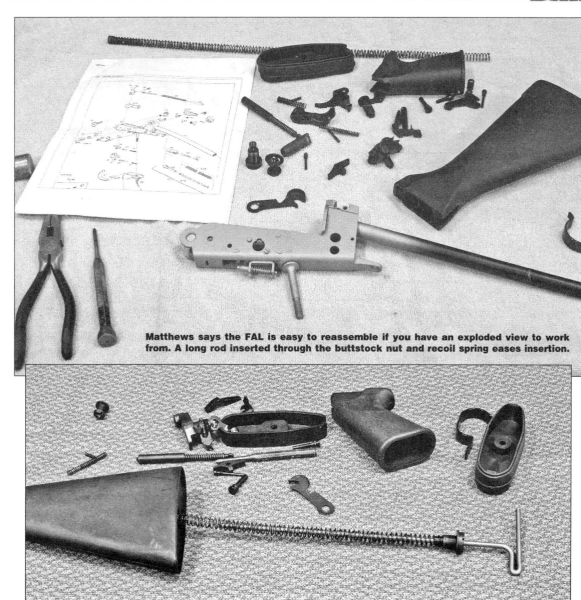

Matthews says the FAL is easy to reassemble if you have an exploded view to work from. A long rod inserted through the buttstock nut and recoil spring eases insertion.

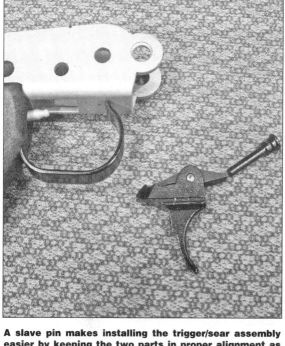

A slave pin makes installing the trigger/sear assembly easier by keeping the two parts in proper alignment as they are installed. The trigger pin pushes the slave out.

since this is where you start when setting the regulator later. The regulator nut spring will hold it in place and keep it from turning loose during use.

The gas piston and spring insert through the front of the gas block and are held in place by the gas plug assembly. The gas plug has a hole in one side and this hole must be oriented down towards the gas port for normal operation. Put the plug into the gas block and push the button on the plug to allow the plug to be turned into its proper position.

The notches in the gas block will allow the protrusions on the plug to enter the block, and when turned into place it will hold in the plug just like a bolt in a bolt-action rifle.

All that remains is to install the handguards. The tabs on the rear of the handguards fit into the handguard ring. The guards are retained in the front by a screw though them and the gas block.

The bolt and carrier assembly that was taken apart for the headspacing procedure must be reassembled before it can be put into the upper receiver.

The firing pin and spring are inserted though the rear of the bolt and a crosspin holds them in place. Be sure the pin is aligned so that crosspin clearance cut out on the firing pin allows passage of the crosspin.

The extractor spring and plunger are inserted into the bolt. The plunger is pressed all the way to the rear with a punch point in the dimple in the plunger. This will allow room for the extractor to be placed in the bolt.

Releasing the plunger will hold the extractor in place due to its interlocking design. Solidly supporting the bolt in a padded vise will help prevent slipping when holding the plunger against its strong spring!

Place a little grease on the camming surfaces of the bolt and install it in the bolt carrier. The bolt slides in at an angle and the

firing pin will have to be depressed slightly to allow it to drop in place. The bolt and carrier can now be installed in the receiver.

Before installing the bolt and carrier, place a little grease on the locking shoulder in the receiver. With the bolt forward in

the bolt carrier, slide the assembly into the carrier grooves in the receiver. Push it all the way forward and then install the top cover, which slides into the thinner grooves in the receiver.

The upper and lower assemblies can now be mated together. Align the pivot holes in the upper and lower assemblies and insert the large pivot pin.

Once that's in place, insert the spring half of the pin and screw it together. It only needs to be hand tight; the spring tension will keep it from unscrewing. Before trying to close the two halves, be sure the hammer is in the cocked position, as it will make closing easier.

As you close the two halves, be sure the "rat tail" on the bolt carrier enters the socket in the recoil spring plunger in the recoil assembly in the buttstock. The two halves should lock together when closed. If they don't, you may have to do some hand fitting of the upper and lower assemblies to get the locking catch to engage.

If the gun is a little stiff, you may have to push down on the locking lever some to allow it to close and lock.

If you have done everything right you should now be able to cycle the action and check for proper functioning. Pull the bolt

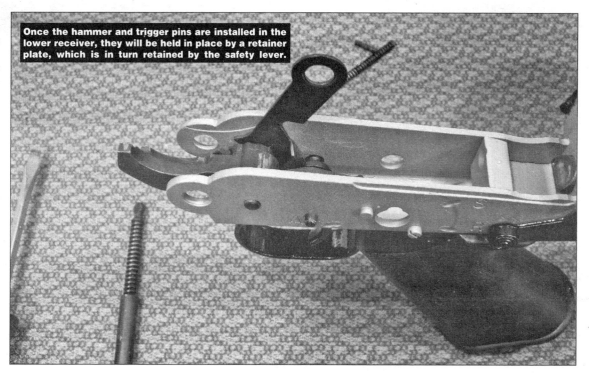

Once the hammer and trigger pins are installed in the lower receiver, they will be held in place by a retainer plate, which is in turn retained by the safety lever.

BUILDING THE FN/FAL Part 2

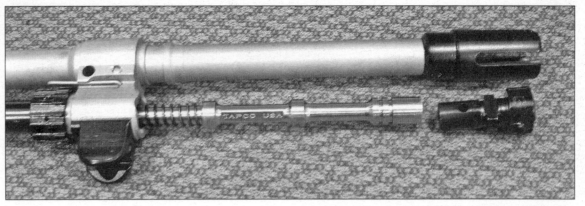

The gas piston, another Tapco part, and its spring are installed through the front of the gas block. The gas plug holds everything in place when screwed in the block.

The bolt hold-open device and magazine release are installed in the bottom of the rifle's upper receiver. They are both retained there by a common pin or screw.

to the rear with the charging handle and let it go forward under spring pressure. It should lock the bolt in battery and cock the hammer.

Place the selector in fire position, pull the trigger and see if it drops the hammer and works properly.

Keep the trigger pulled and cycle the action again. The hammer should cock and you should have to release the trigger to reset it. With the gun cocked, place the safety "on" and pull the trigger; the hammer should not be released.

Lock an empty magazine in place to check that it seats properly. The bolt hold-open device can be checked with the empty magazine in place.

Pull the bolt back with the handle. The empty magazine should activate the bolt hold-open and keep the bolt open.

If everything looks like it's working correctly, you can advance to test firing and setting the gas regulator.

The FAL gas system uses only enough gas to cycle the action; the rest is vented off through a vent hole. This venting is regulated by an angled surface on the regulator nut covering more or less of the vent hole. It's adjustable to compensate for different conditions and ammo types, and can be shut off entirely for firing rifle grenades.

If the vent is completely open, the rifle probably won't have enough gas to cycle the action, if completely closed it may cycle the action too hard and subject the rifle to excessive stress.

The method I use to set the regulator is one I found on the internet, I don't know if it's the "official" method but it has worked well for me.

Start with the gas vent port completely open. Point the rifle in a safe direction, load a magazine with a few rounds of the ammo you will be using most in it, hold the gun at hip level so that it is free to recoil. Cycle the action with the charging handle to chamber a round.

Fire the round. It shouldn't have enough gas to cycle the action. Turn the regulator nut in further (1-2 notches) to reduce the amount of gas vented and increase the amount available for cycling the action.

Continue this fire and adjust procedure until the gun will cycle properly (fire, eject, and rechamber a live round). Once it will cycle reliably from the hip, increase the regulator setting in two more notches and then it should be set correctly.

On this particular build, shortening the barrel reduced the amount of gas available for cycling and the regulator nut had to be adjusted to completely close off the vent port to achieve good functioning.

Barrel length changes greatly affect the amount of gas available and also the time it has to work on the system, so be careful making any drastic barrel length changes.

After the regulator was set, the gun was rough sighted in and checked for functioning.

This gun had a minor problem. Every 20–30 rounds, it would double. This was traced to a defective sear. It was only barely engaging the hammer notch, and when the bolt slammed shut, it would knock it out of engagement and drop the hammer, causing the malfunction.

Replacing the sear, sear spring and sear spring plunger corrected the problem. Parts for the FAL are widely available and inexpensive, so it wasn't a big deal. Now that the bugs are worked out, the rifle features the usual FAL reliability.

Now that Kent's rifle is complete, the next question is how much does it cost to build one? The constantly changing availability of parts kits and receivers mean prices can vary a lot.

Two years ago, I built a FAL for myself and at that time receivers were plentiful and inexpensive. Prices ranged from $125 to $400, depending on which manufacturer's product you bought. Parts kits, on the other hand, were hard to come by and priced at about $300.

The cheapest U.S. parts combination runs about $150. Today, several months before you are reading this article due to publishing lag time, the situation is reversed. Receivers are scarce and somewhat pricey. The DSA receivers are $375–$450, depending on where you get it (but well worth

it for their high quality). Imported Imbels are no longer importable and if you can find one, they are priced at about $300–$350.

Even the lowest quality models that used to be around $125 now command more than $200. Parts kits, on the other hand, are very inexpensive, some as low as $129. The kit used in this article obtained from Inter Ordnance was in the mid-$200 range since it was a matching number kit with excellent bore and also included a U.S. buttstock, handguards, and pistol grip.

Inter Ordnance, at writing time, had kits priced from $139 to $299 depending on options and condition. U.S. compliance parts are still priced about the same.

Finishing supplies can be as little as $5 for a can of auto spray paint to about $50-$75 for a self-applied finish such as KG GunKote or LCW DuraCoat.

If you are a frugal shopper and search for bargains at gun shows and from vendors here in SGN you may get by for less than $550. Getting a world-class battle rifle for $550 is pretty good and the satisfaction of building it your self just makes it all the more fun. ◉

PARTS & INFORMATION
Sources

FAL Parts and Accessories
Inter Ordnance
3305 Westwood Industrial Dr., Dept. SGN, Monroe, N.C. 28110, 866-882-1479, www.interordnance.com

Tapco
Box 2408, Dept. SGN, Kennesaw, Ga. 30156, 800-554-1445, www.tapco.com

DSA Inc.
Box 370, Dept. SGN, Barrington, Ill. 60011, 847-277-7258, www.dsarms.com

Gunsmithing Supplies and FAL Building Information
Brownells
200 S. Front St., Dept. SGN, Montezuma, Iowa, 50171, 800-741-0015, www.brownells.com

American Gunsmithing Institute
800-797-0867, www.americangunsmith.com

FAL Discussion Forum
www.falfiles.com

KG Industries
Box 939, Dept. SGN, Haywood, Wis. 54843, 800-348-9558, www.kgcoatings.com

Lauer Custom Weaponry
3601 129th St., Chippewa Falls, Wis. 54729, 800-830-6677, www.lauerweaponry.com

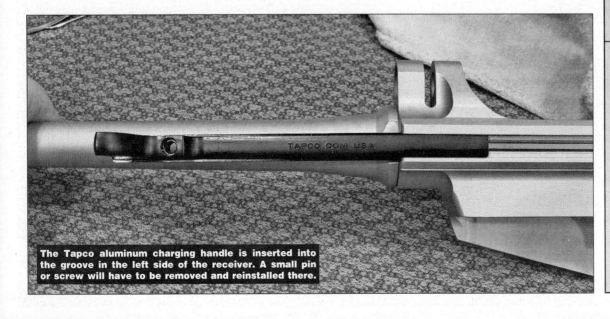

The Tapco aluminum charging handle is inserted into the groove in the left side of the receiver. A small pin or screw will have to be removed and reinstalled there.

Ask the Gunsmith

By Reid Coffield

BENCH-RESTING NO. 1

Q *I have a Ruger No. 1 in .223. It has a heavy barrel and is fitted with a nice Leupold varmint scope. My problem with the rifle is that my best friend consistently outshoots me with my own rifle! Under normal circumstances that would not be a problem, but I know for a fact that I can always shoot better than my buddy and do so frequently with any rifle we shoot except my Ruger No. 1. I am at a loss as to what is causing this and, of course, my buddy finds the situation extremely amusing. Do you have any ideas as to what is going on with this rifle? By the way, when we have our regular "matches" we shoot from a solid bench with an adjustable rest for the forearm and a sandbag supporting the rear of the stock.*

For best accuracy with the Ruger No. 1, always rest the forearm at the same spot for each shot. Coffield says this single-shot design is very sensitive to pressure against the fore-end.

A I would be willing to bet that the difference is how you and your buddy position the No. 1 on the front rest. The No. 1 can be very, very sensitive to pressure on the forearm. The next time you shoot with your buddy watch where he places the forearm over the front rest. When it's your turn, make sure the forearm is supported at the same point. I wouldn't be at all surprised if your shooting improves dramatically.

MODEL 37A RIFLE CONVERSION

Q *What is your take on fitting a Winchester Model 37A break-open single-barrel shotgun with a rifle barrel chambered for .243?*

A I would not encourage such a conversion, considering the high pressure of the .243 cartridge. The .243 typically has a maximum breech pressure of about 52,000 p.s.i. On the other hand, the 12 gauge shotshell on average has a maximum breech pressure of only about 12,000 p.s.i. The .243 has a pressure well over four times greater than the shotshell for which the receiver was designed.

Keep in mind the pressures and metallurgy of the time the gun was produced when considering a new chambering. Coffield advises against converting a Model 37A Winchester to .243.

DON'T LOSE YOUR PLACE

Q *How do you keep track of what line you are cutting when checkering? This is especially difficult for me when I am deepening lines and I cannot easily see the difference in the lines I have cut and those that I have not yet deepened.*

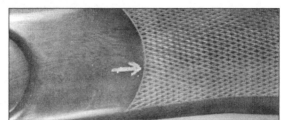

Coffield keeps track of the last line he cut by marking the stock at the end of the line with a grease pencil. The arrow indicates both the last line cut and the direction he is cutting.

A I have the same problem! My solution is to take a standard grease pencil and make a small mark on the stock outside the checkering pattern opposite both ends of the last line I have deepened when I stop work. I also draw an arrow to indicate the direction in which I am deepening the lines. This is pretty simple but it has worked quite well for me.

.22 RF ACCURACY

Q *I have a very accurate factory stock .22 hunting rifle that I love to shoot. What would you suggest I do to make it even more accurate?*

A This is a bit unusual in that most folks start out with a gun that won't shoot all that well! Starting with a rifle that is a tack driver puts you a leg up right away. There are three areas that normally can be addressed and will show some positive results.

First, bed your rifle. Seldom will most factory .22 rifles be bedded properly. A glass bedding job generally will help in ensuring that your rifle will group more consistently as you see changes in temperature and humidity.

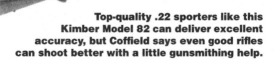

Top-quality .22 sporters like this Kimber Model 82 can deliver excellent accuracy, but Coffield says even good rifles can shoot better with a little gunsmithing help.

Next, put a good scope on your rifle. Don't even think of putting one of the many inexpensive ".22" scopes. Instead, at a minimum choose a scope that you would be comfortable putting on a high powered rifle. You will get better optics and that will immediately translate into better accuracy.

Finally, if your trigger pull is at all typical for factory rifles, have a competent gunsmith do a trigger job on your rifle. While it won't make your rifle more accurate, it will enable you to shoot it more accurately.

CENTER PUNCHING

Q *I always and I really mean always, seem to have a problem getting my center punch to be located exactly where I want it. No matter what I do, my punch mark seems to be off ever so slightly. Can you help?*

A There are a number of things you can do to more precisely locate your center punch marks. First, always use an appropriate size center punch. Center punches come in a variety of sizes and some folks often use one that is too large for the drill they'll be using. I tend to use a punch that is just a bit larger than the tip of the drill. If you look closely at the point of a drill bit you'll notice there is a web where the two flutes meet. I always use a center punch that's just a bit larger than this web. Also, when you use a center punch that's too large, it's more difficult to position it properly.

Second, make sure the center punch is sharp. Many folks just keep using a center punch and never pay much attention to it. The point will gradually dull and become rounded. This makes it harder to position accurately. If your center punch is dull, take a few minutes and sharpen it.

Finally, when you place the point of the center punch on your mark, don't try to come straight down on the mark. Instead, approach the mark with your punch at about a 45° angle. By coming in at an angle, you can see the tip of the point of the center punch and place it precisely on your mark. Once the point of the center punch is where you want it, raise the center punch to a vertical position. Now you can strike it and be pretty darn certain of having the punch mark where you want it.

One other trick is to use a magnifying glass when placing the point of the center punch on your mark. This definitely helps me in making sure my punch point is in the center of my mark. The more precise I am in locating my center punch point, the more accurate my center punch.

HIGH STANDARD EJECTOR SPRING

Q *I have an old High Standard Double Nine .22 revolver. When I depress the ejector rod to kick out the fired cases, it does not automatically return or move back into the cylinder. There are lots of scratches along the left side of the frame where the ejector has been left out and the cylinder closed. That seems like a bad design or is something missing or broken on my revolver?*

The High Standard Double Nine was a .22 revolver that looked like a single-action, but had double-action lockwork. It was made 1958–70 with an aluminum frame, then 1971–84 with a steel frame.

A Evidently the ejector return spring in the cylinder is either missing or broken. The ejector should be pulled back into the cylinder by this spring once the fired cases have been expelled from the cylinder chambers. Replacement springs, as well as other parts for the old High Standard Double Nine revolvers, can be obtained from Numrich Gun Parts, 226 Williams Lane, West Hurley, NY 12491, telephone 866-686-7424. ◎

VZ-58: A really easy Wallhanger

BY STEVEN MATTHEWS

Have you been scared off by some of Matthews' more ambitious parts kit projects? Here's one you can finish in an afternoon, and it looks great!

If some of Matthews' more epic projects have thrown you off, here's one that requires no welding and just a little big of grinding. It will take just a few hours.

For the last several years, SGN advertiser Ohio Ordnance of Chardon, Ohio has offered a U.S.-made semi-automatic version of the Czech VZ-58. The original is a select-fire rifle that uses the 7.62x39mm cartridge. It looks somewhat like an AK-47, but is a completely different design and has no parts in common.

Rather than having a rotating bolt like the AK, it features a bolt and carrier that cams down into the receiver. It looks very similar to the locking system on the P-38 pistol. It also is striker-fired rather using the more common hammer-fired system.

One unusual feature of the VZ-58 is its stock material. Rather than being wood or plastic as is common on most military guns the VZ-58 features both! The VZ-58 wood is a mixture of wood chips and plastic resin. It looks very much like construction grade OSB (Oriented Strand Board). It is durable and works well but it sure looks odd.

The semi-automatic version of the VZ-58 rifle is marketed as the VZ-2000. By all accounts it is a fine firearm but it is pricey for those of us on a blue collar worker's income.

Since it is rather different I thought I would like to have a VZ-58 in my collection. A less costly option for home gun builders like me is to purchase a BATFE-approved semi-auto receiver and some sec. 922 compliant U.S. made parts and combine them with a surplus parts set. This is a project that I may take on later and write up as a build article but at the present time other projects and financial constraints make it a no go right now.

A while back while researching this idea on the internet I was viewing Centerfire Systems' website and came across their ad for VZ-58 parts kit on sale for $49.95. The ad also had a notation that if you bought a VZ-58 parts kit during this sale they would sell you a VZ-58 dummy receiver for the sale price of $9.95.

For only $60 plus shipping, I could have a display version of the VZ-58 until I could afford a real one. I like display guns, so my order went in for the parts and receiver. One thing I really like about display guns is that you can hang them on the wall and not worry about someone stealing

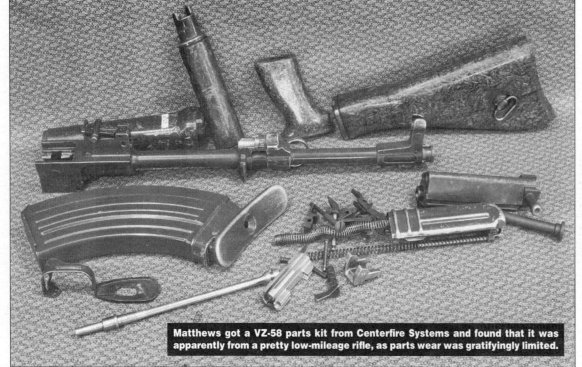

Matthews got a VZ-58 parts kit from Centerfire Systems and found that it was apparently from a pretty low-mileage rifle, as parts wear was gratifyingly limited.

The Advanced Technology dummy receiver is BATFE approved, and easily replaces the original. As it's made of plastic, there's no danger of making an illegal restoration.

thousands of dollars' worth of ordnance if you suffer a break-in. Some people like to hang pictures and knick-knacks on their walls but I like to display firearms.

When the UPS truck delivered my package, I was impressed with what I got. The parts set contained all the parts of a VZ-58 except for the receiver. The painted finish on the parts was pretty good and there was no rust on any part. There was very little wear on the parts, indicating that the parts were obtained from little-used firearms.

The Advanced Technology replica receiver was a very realistic copy of the original VZ-58 receiver. It was made from black plastic and workmanship appeared good. An instruction sheet was also included. A quick look through the instructions revealed that this project was going to be very easy.

If you've thought some of my past display gun projects required too much in the way of gunsmithing skills, this project is for you. If you can use basic hand tools you can easily complete this project. It is so easy that from beginning to end it only took about an hour and a half to complete it into a completely assembled display gun (excluding finishing work). It takes longer than that to build a model car!

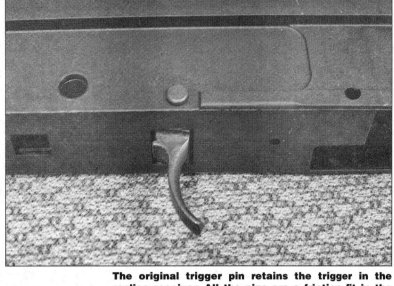

When installing the selector lever, the trigger legs go under the selector shaft. Since the selector doesn't function, it can be in any authentic-looking position.

The original trigger pin retains the trigger in the replica receiver. All the pins are a friction fit in the plastic, as they won't be doing a lot of rotating.

Before starting the project, I decided that since the parts were a little scratched up and the receiver color was different I would refinish the completed project. I wanted to duplicate the original sprayed-on dark gray finish. I decided to go with Lauer Custom Weaponry's DuraCoat gun finish. DuraCoat is a sprayed on polymer finish that is very easy for the home gunsmith to apply.

I placed an order with LCW and included a note that I had chosen a standard color I thought was close to original but to substitute if they had a closer color match. When I got my DuraCoat I was pleased to find that they had substituted an exact match in a color that was marked as VZ-2000. I found it pleasing to deal with a supplier who would take the time to send just what you needed rather than just quickly fill your order with what was close to your needs.

With the parts set, replica receiver and finishing supplies at hand, it was time to get started. While the Advanced Technology replica receiver comes with instructions, I will briefly cover the build process for those who would like to see how it's done before buying the project.

First, you lay out all the needed parts from the VZ-58 parts set. The instructions specify the parts needed by pictures. You also lay out the replica receiver and its parts.

The first part to be installed is the trigger. It just drops into place in the receiver and is retained with the original trigger pin. The next part that goes in is the selector lever. When this

is installed, the shaft of the lever goes above the legs of the trigger. The trigger guard is then installed with two small sheet metal screws. The pistol grip is installed just as on the real thing by a long screw through the grip. It threads into an angled nut that you place in the receiver.

Since this is a display gun there is no need for a bolt. Only the bolt carrier is used, and it is locked into the receiver. The firing pin assembly that slides into the rear of the carrier is removed by pulling it all the way to the rear and then rotating it until a groove and pin align, at which time it can be withdrawn.

The stock furniture is made of wood chips impregnated with a plastic resin. This was high-tech for the 1950s, though it's a bit peculiar looking to our modern tastes.

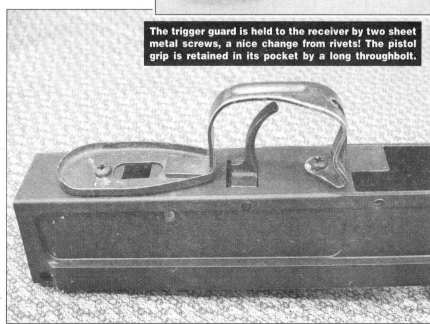

The trigger guard is held to the receiver by two sheet metal screws, a nice change from rivets! The pistol grip is retained in its pocket by a long throughbolt.

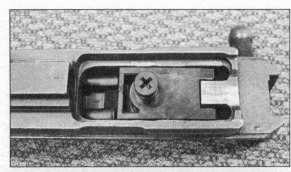

A plastic block wedged into the bolt carrier will allow it to be installed in the dummy receiver. A screw through the receiver and block will hold the carrier in place.

The bolt carrier will be installed in the display receiver but needs a way to securely retain it. A rectangular piece of plastic is inserted into the bolt recess in the receiver and two plastic wedges are inserted from the rear of the carrier to lock it in place. The bolt carrier is then placed all the way forward in the receiver and held in place with a small screw through the receiver and into the plate in the carrier.

Be sure to drive out the crosspin before attempting to remove the barrel. The pin will be tight and require a strong punch and a heavy vise on a sturdy workbench.

To release tension on the barrel, slice the receiver down to the shank using a hacksaw or cutting wheel. Then use a heavy chisel to spread the cut receiver apart.

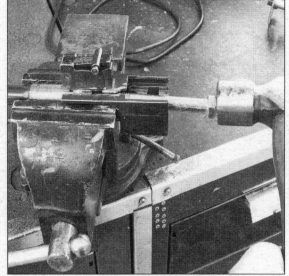

With the receiver cut to release its grip on the barrel, use a large punch to drive the barrel out. Use a soft-faced punch or place washers between punch and barrel.

The original magazine latch is installed by placing the catch and spring into the receiver and installing the original crosspin to hold it in place.

If there is one difficult part of this project, it is the barrel installation. Well, actually, it's the removal of the old barrel from the demilled receiver section. The VZ-58 barrel is tightly pressed in place, than crosspinned. The instructions recommend driving out the crosspin and then pressing the barrel out with a press.

Most people don't have hydraulic presses, so I will give an easier method for removal. First drive out the crosspin with a punch. It will probably be very tight, so you will need to have the assembly solidly secured in a vise.

After the crosspin is out, use a hacksaw or hand grinder with a cutoff wheel to cut lengthwise along the receiver above the barrel shank. Cut till you are right up to the barrel shank. Once you have a groove almost to the barrel, drive in a chisel to wedge apart the receiver to release the tension on the barrel.

You can then use a large wood dowel or soft faced punch to drive the barrel out the front of the old receiver. If you use a hard punch, place something between the rear of the barrel and the punch to keep from damaging the barrel in case you need the original barrel for a later real gun build.

Once the barrel is out, it will just slide into the replica receiver. It will be retained by a small set screw. You will set the barrel seating depth when you install the gas tube next so don't tighten the set screw now.

The VZ-58 barrel simply slides into the replica receiver. It will be retained by a set screw after adjusting for proper position. Replacing is a lot easier than removing!

Tightening the hex socket set screw will lock the barrel into the dummy receiver. The screw needs to be flush to allow the handguard to go all the way into position.

Install the gas tube by sliding the front under the ledge on the gas block on the barrel. Push the barrel in until the hole in the rear of the gas tube is even with the pinhole in the replica receiver. The crosspin can be pushed in to lock the gas tube in place.

Before you tighten the set screw, be sure the barrel is straight and not canted off to one side. The set screw needs

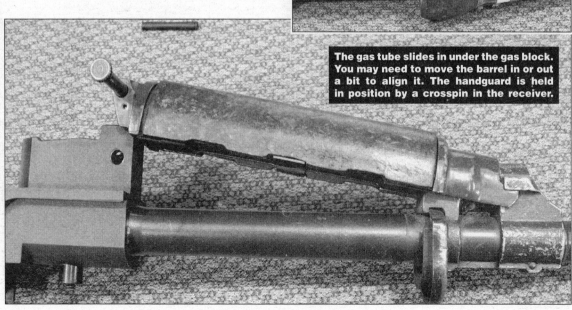

The gas tube slides in under the gas block. You may need to move the barrel in or out a bit to align it. The handguard is held in position by a crosspin in the receiver.

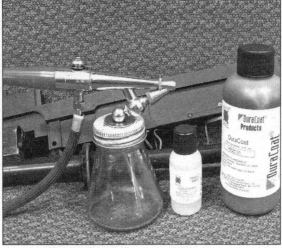

The buttstock is retained shotgun-style by a long through-bolt and tightened with a hex nut supplied with the dummy receiver. This requires a very long screwdriver.

Lauer Custom Weaponry cooked up a spray-on finish that nicely duplicated the original Czech paint job on the VZ-58. DuraCoat is easy to apply with an airbrush.

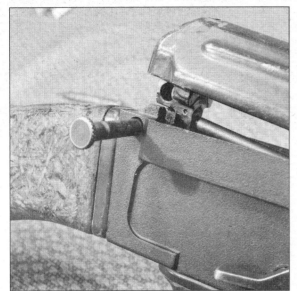

A crosspin through a hole at the rear of the receiver holds down the top cover. Springs inside the cover need to be removed before it can be assembled to the receiver.

One last thing needs to be removed from the old receiver stub, the rear sight. To remove the sight, use a punch and hammer to drive it out. Place the punch over the pivot point and angle it slightly rearward. When you strike the punch with a hammer, it will compress the sight spring which will press the sight down and out of the groove in the sight base. Once the sight is removed, it just presses down into the slot in the new receiver's sight base.

Your project is now completely assembled. To make your VZ-58 display gun more visually pleasing you may want to partially or completely refinish it. This will require partial or complete disassembly depending on how you refinish the project. I chose to refinish the project just as I would a real gun so I disassembled everything and prepared it for applying LCW DuraCoat.

Since this was only going to be a display gun and not subjected to rigorous use, I really scrimped on surface preparation. Better surface prep will result in a more durable finish but a wall hanger won't see much handling.

To prepare the metal parts I used a wire wheel on a bench grinder to remove most of the original paint. I then cleaned with LCW's degreaser/cleaner. I used a small airbrush to apply the DuraCoat. The LCW color, VZ-2000, was an exact match to the remaining original finish color.

I let the parts cure for a couple days before reassembly. The plastic dummy receiver was roughed up a little with a Scotch-Brite pad, and then cleaned with a lint-free rag. I spayed the DuraCoat and left it to dry for a couple days also. The plastic/wood chip stock, pistol grip and handguards were a little scuffed up, so I gave them a quick sanding with 400-grit sandpaper followed by a couple spray coats of satin lacquer.

I reassembled after the finishes were hard, and the project looked better than a new gun. One nice thing about this dummy gun build is that none of the original parts were changed in any way. If I later decide to build a legal semi-auto VZ-58, I already have a source for parts.

It's a pain to disassemble a gun you've just laboriously put together, but Matthews says it's worth it if you want to get the best possible surface treatment.

Semi-auto U.S.-made receivers and some U.S. compliance parts are available. For those of you who want to try a gun building project that's easy, this project is worthy of your consideration. The Centerfire Systems replica receiver and parts set are very inexpensive and the project is easy to build so why not give it a try? ◎

SOURCES for the VZ-58 DISPLAY GUN PROJECT

Lauer Custom Weaponry
3601 129th St, Dept. SGN, Chippewa Falls, WI 54729
800-830-6677 http://www.lauerweaponry.com

Centerfire Systems
102 Fieldview Dr., Versailles, KY
800-950-1231 http://www.centerfiresystems.com

to be flush with the stub on the replica receiver because the handguard won't go on all the way if the screw sticks up. If it sticks up, use a shorter screw or grind it down.

The forearm installs under the barrel and gas tube. The front slides up into a collar on the gas block and the rear slides up into the front of the receiver. It is retained by a crosspin. The buttstock is held to the receiver by a large screw through the inside of the stock. A common nut on the inside of the receiver secures it.

The top cover closes up the top of the receiver. Before installing, the springs that are attached to it need to be removed. One spring simply slides off the rod that it's on. The recoil spring is retained by a retainer on the end of the wire guide. Press the spring back and pull the retainer out of the wire guide. Remove the spring and wire guide. Once the springs and guide are removed, the top cover is slid on the rear of the receiver and retained by the crosspin on the rear of the cover.

If you like an authentic well-used look, you can stop right here, but Matthews likes his dummies to have an as-new finish, so he broke the piece down for refinishing.

With DuraCoat applied to the metal and the synthetic stock and handguards sanded and coated with clear lacquer, the dummy looks better than an original and cost about $80.

Dummy Up a PPSh41

By Steven Matthews

He had a box of parts left over from making a semi-auto, so Matthews put them to good use building a dummy gun for safe display.

In an upcoming series that will appear next year, I will build a semi-automatic rifle version of the famous World War II Russian PPSh41 submachine gun. As in most of my build articles, I recommend that the potential builder purchase extra parts in case he makes mistakes on the build and needs more parts to replace the messed up parts.

Fortunately, I took my own advice on the semi-auto PPSh41 project. I had obtained two complete Polish PPSh41 parts sets since the parts sets offered by Class Three Supply of Hermitage Pennsylvania were in such good condition and priced right.

I picked out the best parts for the project and began the job of recreating the I.O., Inc. SR-41 semi-auto copy of the PPSh41. Unfortunately, as is common with many of my engineering projects, not everything went well on the first try. My first attempt at modifying the bolt for semi-auto operation resulted in an off-center firing pin hole in the rear of the bolt that turned it into scrap metal.

Inattention to detail and watching the wrong line while machining out the bottom of the lower receiver resulted in another scrap part. Making a design change in midstream on the TAPCO semi-auto fire control group rendered another previously made trigger part useless.

I'm my own engineering department, which means there will be mistakes! I tend not to dwell on the foul-ups and report the good news, but believe me, I foul up on a regular basis. If you have problems on projects, it may comfort you to know even experienced tinkerers have their share of problems.

While the PPSh41 project did result in a fine working example of the semi-auto PPSh41 it also resulted in a leftover box of de-militarized receiver sections, good unused parts and the botched parts. I like to display unusual firearms, but I prefer to keep the "real things" safely and responsibly secured in a gun vault.

I see no reason to openly display thousands of dollars worth of potentially dangerous firearms where any criminal with a window opening tool (this is a common rock!) can access them at will. For safe and responsible display, I have built several dummy guns. I decided to use the PPSh41 leftovers to build a display version.

Display guns are very easy to build, since they only have to look good and do not need fine fitting to function properly. This one will use a few of the remaining real gun parts but be completely non-functional. I made a dummy receiver from the remnants of the two BATFE-mandated demilled and torch-cut multi-piece receiver sections.

You will need to make the dummy receiver in a certain way for it to be legal. Once completed, the display PPSh41 will look every bit as good as an original gun when it's hanging on the wall. Close examination by the firearms enthusiast will reveal it to be non-functional, but most will not be able to distinguish it from an original firearm at a distance.

This project is very easy to build, and all that is needed beyond common hand tools is an arc welder and power (air or electric) hand grinder.

The PPSh41 parts needed for this project are as follows: stock assembly, trigger housing assembly, lower receiver assembly, bolt handle, magazine, pivot pin and retainer, trigger and the demilled receiver sections from both of the PPSh41 parts sets.

You need the demilled receiver sections from two parts sets because the BATFE-mandated demilling procedures mean a few inches of original receiver is missing on each parts set. On the parts sets I had, about 2-3 inches of receiver on both sides of the trunnion/pivot block were missing.

Hand tools, a grinder and an arc welder will let you build a good-looking PPSh41 dummy gun. Matthews had lots of spare parts left from an upcoming semi-auto project.

BATFE requires torch cutting of machine gun receivers, so it takes two parts kits to make one new receiver. A good welder can combine two for a realistic look.

The two receiver sections must be carefully sawn square and then aligned and clamped for welding. A piece of scrap angle iron keeps the sections perfectly square.

"Readily restorable" can't apply when you've welded in a 3/4" steel rod in place of the barrel. You then can drill a hole in the muzzle end for a realistic appearance.

The rest of the barrel shroud and rear receiver remained. These remaining portions will be used to replace the missing sections. You'll also need some locally available round and flat steel stock.

Before we get into the fabrication of the dummy receiver, some legal issues need to be addressed. Under BATFE regulations you *cannot* re-weld the remaining pieces into a duplicate of the original machine gun receiver.

Doing so would be creating an unregistered machine gun receiver. This would be a federal felony, punishable by fines and imprisonment (up to 10 years!). You can use the previously destroyed receiver sections to fabricate a dummy/non-firearm receiver, but it must not be "readily restorable" to machine gun or firearm status.

Also under BATFE regulations, it must not contain features common to machine guns or firearms. The easiest way to meet these requirements is to make the dummy receiver solid and incapable of accepting a barrel, bolt or fire control group.

Some commercially available BATFE-approved dummy guns and receivers do have several working parts incorporated in their construction, but these have been evaluated by the BATFE and have been issued an "Approval Letter" for the design.

The more working parts you incorporate, the closer you get to "readily restorable status" and therefore closer to illegality. For the hobbyist and home builder, it is best to go with the solid receiver, no bolt, no fire control group and no real barrel option to stay well within the non-firearms classification.

You want your homemade project as inert as possible. Even without these parts you can make a very realistic dummy gun, so why take chances?

Barrel Shroud Fabrication

The barrel shroud on the PPSh41 is formed in one piece along with the rear upper receiver section from heavy-gauge sheet steel. The shroud is a rounded edge square section about 11 inches long with four oblong ventilation holes on each side and three round holes on each side and the top.

The three round holes function as a crude muzzle brake. The demilled barrel shroud sections included in each parts set had the front muzzle brake section and about 5 inches of the shroud, including the front sight. The remaining 4-5 inches that extended over the trunnion/pivot block were missing due to the BATFE-mandated demilling procedure.

This missing section will be made from the piece of barrel shroud from the second parts set. I started with the front muzzle brake section and the portion that contained the front sight. The torch-cut sections were saw-cut straight and trimmed to length so that the front round holes were close to size.

The cut edges were beveled and then arc welded together. A simple alignment fixture can be made from a piece of 1½-inch angle iron. Clamping the pieces in the "V" section will align the sides and hold the assembly in place while you weld two of the exposed sides.

After welding those sides, you can remove the part and weld the other two sides. Once they're welded, use a hand grinder to smooth the welds down flush. A file or round grinding stone in the grinder can be used to shape the round holes to size.

The rest of the barrel shroud will be made from the other piece of barrel shroud that also featured a front sight. Remove the sight and weld in the holes and then grind it smooth with the rest of the shroud.

The previously made section of shroud featured about 2½ oval holes, so the next section needed about 1½ oval holes to look right. I oriented the piece so that the barrel spacer in the rear shroud section would be at the rear and could be used to support a dummy barrel. I cut the two shroud sections so the remaining pieces matched the hole pattern and then welded them together, followed by grinding smooth.

Just behind the last (fourth) oval hole, you'll need to fabricate a new pivot block. Before it is installed, install a dummy barrel to make it look authentic. I used a piece of solid 3/4" round steel stock. I drilled out the rear barrel spacer in the shroud to allow the dummy barrel to be inserted through the rear.

I drilled the muzzle end about 1 inch deep with a 5/16" drill bit to give the illusion of a real barrel. I ground down the muzzle end so that it would extend a little way through the front spacer and into the muzzle brake section.

The dummy barrel was inserted into the shroud and then marked and cut to length prior to welding it permanently in place. The dummy barrel needs to be permanently installed by arc welding so that a real barrel cannot ever be installed in the dummy receiver. This will help maintain the "not readily restorable" status.

Now you can make the trunnion/pivot block. The original was demilled and removed per BATFE regulations. You do not want to make a new trunnion/pivot block to the original style. You want it to be solid and incapable of accepting a barrel. Ours will be no

A solid steel bar welded in place "solidifies" the dummy receiver and prevents installation of a working bolt, making it impossible to restore the dummy to function.

more than a block that will allow the upper and lower receivers to be mated.

Do not even consider drilling a barrel hole in it. To do so could be interpreted by BATFE as attempts to reconstruct a functional machine gun trunnion that could accept a short machine gun barrel. This will also help maintain non-firearm status.

The barrel shroud was cut about 1/2" behind the fourth oval hole to duplicate the trunnion position and look of the original receiver. I selected a steel block 1⅜x1⅜x1. I rounded the top to fit the inside of the shroud/receiver and then welded it in place. It should be located so that about half the shroud covers the block; the remainder will be covered by the rear receiver sections. The pivot hole will be drilled later.

The PPSh41 receiver latch allows the gun's upper receiver to pivot. Matthews simply welded the latch in position from the inside for a better outside appearance.

The rear portion of the PPSh41 receiver is simply a flattened half round section of sheet steel that was formed along with the barrel shroud. BATFE demilling specifications required a few inches of the rear receiver to be removed along with the trunnion.

What remains is about the last 7 inches or so of the original receiver. I further cut this last section in two pieces, one forward piece about 5 inches long that contained the rear sight, and the very end of the receiver which was about 2 inches long.

Take one section with the sights and remove them and then weld in the rivet holes followed by smoothing up the top surface. Cut the ends square and butt it up against the barrel shroud over the pivot block. You can hold it in alignment with your angle iron fixture.

Weld it to the barrel shroud and the pivot block and then smooth up the welds. Before you can weld on the next piece, you must weld in a solid steel bar to "permanently solidify" the receiver. This blocking bar must be welded in place with deep penetrating welds to lock it in place permanently. Bolts or screws would not meet BATFE requirements.

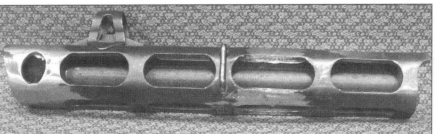

The combined demilled barrel shroud sections duplicate the front part of the receiver. Next, you need a trunnion/mounting block to connect the upper and lower receivers.

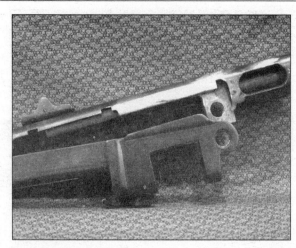

The PPSh41's receiver halves are held together by a pin. Carefully locate its hole in the trunnion to be sure it aligns precisely with the lower receiver hole.

Do this before fabricating the rest of the receiver so that at no time do you have a receiver that can accept the original machine gun bolt. Failure to "solidify" the receiver at this point could be construed as making an original machine gun receiver, which would be illegal.

You do not want the dummy receiver to be able to accept any original machine gun parts. I used a piece of 3/8x1x5½-inch flat steel stock to fill in the receiver cavity. It was located so that it was slightly above the lower edge of the receiver section.

After this block is permanently installed, you can continue the dummy receiver construction. Take your receiver section that features the rear sight and smooth up any slag on the rear where it was torch cut. Use a saw and cut the front even and squarely. Cut it as long as you can. You will use the receiver catch from the original receiver to complete the rear of the receiver.

There is no need to use the last rounded end portion of the old receiver to finish off the back of the dummy. The receiver catch slides over that portion and it can't be seen. Slide the catch over rear of the sight section until it is about a half-inch from the rear of the sight base and then place a small tack weld on the top to lock it in place.

Be sure to align it straight with the other piece. Once it is located properly, turn it over and weld the pieces together. Welding from the underside will make for a better appearance. We now need to install the partially completed upper receiver to the lower receiver and drill the pivot pin hole.

The upper and lower parts need to be mated so you can determine the correct length for the last section of receiver. Align the upper and lower, mark the hole location and then drill it. Drill the hole undersized and then check to see if it is aligned correctly before drilling to finish size in case you need to move it slightly.

Once your pivot pin hole is located and the upper and lower are mated together, you can size your last pieces. The receiver catch stub fits in a square hole in the lower receiver tang. What you

want to do now is to squarely cut the ends of your barrel shroud/receiver and your end piece with the sight and receiver catch to a length that results in the correct overall length.

Once a proper length has been determined, you can fit the pieces together and weld them. The bar that was welded into the forward section can be used to help align the two sections. Weld the seam between the two pieces on the outside.

Separate the upper and lower receivers and then turn the upper over and weld the bar inside the rear portion of the receiver. You want the receiver sections and the bar to be one solid assembly. Be sure that all parts are aligned correctly before welding and that they don't move while welding.

Keeping everything aligned, square and flat is vital for a good appearance. For a more authentic look, I removed the bolt handle from the bolt and welded it into the receiver. This handle looks to be formed with the bolt body, but it is really just very tightly press fitted to the bolt body, and it can be removed with a hydraulic press or very large hammer and punch.

After all your pieces are welded together, you can do some finish work to make your receiver look better. If the receiver is warped or bowed from welding, you can straighten it. Any misaligned parts can be blended together by grinding or filing.

Any unwanted holes or voids can be filled in. All welds can be smoothed up to your satisfaction. The amount of work put into finishing will be the deciding factor in how good your project looks when completed.

Lower Receiver Modifications

To prevent an original machine gun bolt from ever being installed in the lower receiver, weld in a steel block. I welded in a piece of 3/8x1x6-inch flat steel. Use several small deep penetrating welds to lock it in place.

Do not weld all the way along the sides as this will warp the lower receiver and make later fitting difficult. Once this lower receiver is permanently blocked, the upper and lower receivers can be mated together. After you have verified that all parts fit correctly, I recommend welding the upper and lower together to form one inert chunk of steel that cannot accept any functioning machine gun parts.

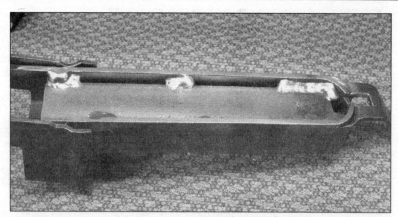

Matthews welded a steel block into the lower receiver to prevent installation of a bolt. He tacked it in several spots to keep from warping the lower receiver.

After removing the full-auto fire control parts, Matthews welded a steel plate into position in the trigger housing to prevent any future reinstallation of the parts.

Trigger Housing Modifications

The PPSh41 featured a fire control group in the trigger housing that allowed for fully automatic and semi-automatic fire. What appears to be a safety in the trigger guard is actually the selector switch. For appearances we want to retain this selector and the trigger but no other automatic parts.

To remove the automatic parts, drive out the small pin in the front side of the trigger housing and remove the parts that were retained by the pin. The selector has a spring-loaded pin that extends through it on the outside and into a couple internal parts.

This pin holds the selector together with the housing. To remove the remainder of the auto parts, press down on the pin from the inside while keeping the selector pressed against the housing.

This will allow access to a crosspin on the outside that will release the pin. Drive out the crosspin and remove the remainder of

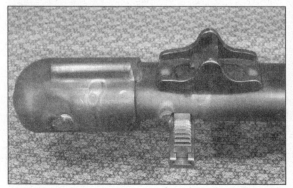

There's no bolt, so Matthews recommends just removing the original bolt handle and installing it by welding into the dummy receiver to give an authentic appearance.

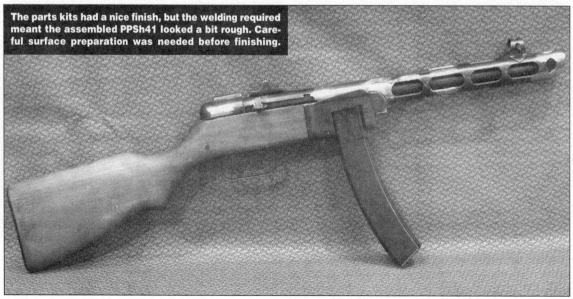

The parts kits had a nice finish, but the welding required meant the assembled PPSh41 looked a bit rough. Careful surface preparation was needed before finishing.

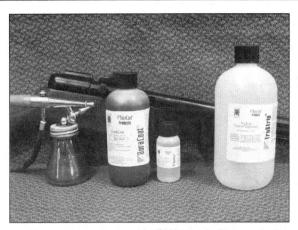

Matthews chose Lauer DuraCoat to duplicate the original blued finish. While he has hot bluing equipment, DuraCoat is a lot easier to use and yields a durable finish.

If you connect and shape the sections carefully, the dummy receiver will look as good as the original. No seams are visible even though it was made from six pieces.

fore going to final finishing. The wood stocks on both the kits I received were in very good condition and only needed some minor cleanup.

I stained the stock to give it a darker color; then I applied a coat of lacquer to seal in the stain. The metal finish, while very good as received, got pretty beat up in the build procedure. All the welding and grinding really took its toll.

The original finish was hot tank bluing and that's the color (black) I wanted to retain. I have an improvised hot tank system, but it's a mild weather operation since part of it is done outside. It was 20° out with a brisk wind when I did this project, so bluing was out.

I wanted a finish that could hang on the wall for years with no maintenance and would be easy for the readers to apply. Common spray paint would work for those on a budget, but I wanted something a little better for my project. I decided to use one of the modern spray-on gun finishes to duplicate the original black color.

I chose Lauer Custom Weaponry's DuraCoat finish. DuraCoat is a sprayed-on finish that can be easily applied by the hobbyist with little more than an inexpensive air brush and a compressed air supply. DuraCoat is a very durable firearms finish and is available in a multitude of colors. It is also inexpensive.

For a one-gun project you can get by for about $25. If you have enough skill to paint a model car, you can probably apply Dura-Coat. I roughed up the metal with a wire wheel on a bench grinder, degreased and then sprayed the DuraCoat. For a real gun project you would probably put in more effort in surface preparation, but for a dummy gun this was all that was required to get a decent finish.

After drying for a couple days, the project was assembled. The only negative about the finishing process was that it looked too good! Original PPSh41 guns were crudely finished, and mine really wasn't crude enough, but I guess I will have to live with that.

The completed PPSh41 dummy gun project looks pretty good hanging on the wall with my other display guns. Total cost was about $125, and it was fairly easy to make. Total build time was about eight hours. Low cost, ease of building and great results makes this project worthy of your consideration. ◎

the parts. Re-install the pin, spring and crosspin and selector switch.

Since all the automatic parts have been removed, the trigger will be loose. Place the trigger in a pleasing position and place a small tack weld on the inside between the trigger and housing to lock the trigger in place.

To prevent any full auto parts from ever being installed in the trigger housing, weld an appropriately-sized steel block into the top of the housing. To prevent warping the housing, weld it only on the front and back and then only put a small weld on each side.

Final Finishing

This pretty much completes the build procedure. Assemble all your parts together to be sure everything fits and looks good be-

Thousands of dollars' worth of full-autos? Nope, just inexpensive and easy-to-make dummy guns. You can keep the real guns in the safe and display these for visitors.

Legal Disclaimer

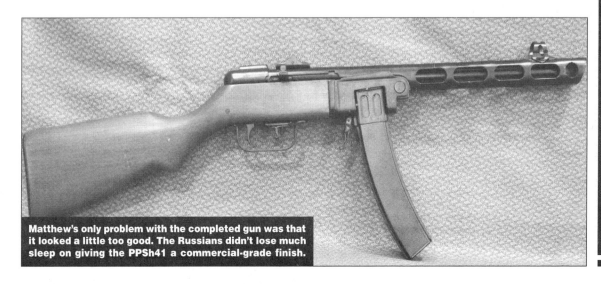

Matthew's only problem with the completed gun was that it looked a little too good. The Russians didn't lose much sleep on giving the PPSh41 a commercial-grade finish.

BUILDING
A Semi-Automatic
PPSh-41
Part 1

BY STEVEN MATTHEWS

Combining a Polish parts kit with a I.O., Inc., receiver yields a street-legal shooting version of the classic Soviet burp gun.

Matthews says a milling machine always makes these projects easier, but he's designed this semi-auto PPSh-41 project to be possible using hand tools and drill press.

A lot of us older collectors grew up in the 1960s and documentaries about World War II flourished on television even before the History Channel. A staple of shows like "The 20th Century" and "World at War" was the mass attack by Soviet solders carrying PPSh-41 submachineguns with their large distinctive drum magazines.

While many today would scoff at the idea of a 7.62 x 25mm battle rifle, anyone defending a position being attacked by hundreds of soldiers emptying 71-round magazines would probably disagree. What was lost in bullet power was more than made up with high volume.

The PPSh-41 was designed by Georgiy Semenovich Shpagin in the fall of 1940 and adopted just before the new year of 1941.

The PPSh-41 featured sheet metal construction and was designed for fast production. Workmanship was crude, but the situation demanded huge numbers of guns in the shortest amount of time due to the very real threat of Nazi domination.

The Soviets produced more than 5 million PPSh-41 guns, but they are rare in the United States. There are some transferable examples available, largely Korean War bringbacks, but one will set you back several months of blue collar wages.

There are a few semi-automatic U.S.-made versions but they are rather pricey at about $700. "Poor folk" like me need a cheaper alternative to have any kind of PPSh-41 in a collection. The less expensive alternative was to build a semi-automatic version myself.

The first thing I needed was a parts set minus receiver. While they're not as common as some parts sets, you can find them if you search them out. While attending the Knob Creek Machine Gun Shoot and Gun Show, I found several for sale priced from $150 to $225.

I was almost ready to buy one for $179.95 when I decided to look through the large gun show one more time. I passed the Class Three Supply of Hermitage, Pa. table and out of the corner of my eye saw a small hand written sign laying on the table that said "Polish PPSh-41 parts sets minus barrels $100–ask to sec".

Well, I had to ask! What was being offered were unissued Polish PPSh-41 parts sets without barrels. They looked like they had just come off the production line. Needless to say, I jumped on this offer. In fact, after I got home and looked the set over, I decided the set was so good I needed another one and phoned in an order for one more kit.

After I completed this project I was still very impressed with what I had got and decided to buy yet another one for a future 9mm PPSh-41 project. I guess I just can't pass up a good deal.

The next thing I needed was a BATFE-approved semi-automatic U.S.-made receiver. I couldn't find any at the gun show so as soon as I got home I got out my old issues of SGN and began searching the pages for a bargain receiver. I found one advertised at $349 but that was getting towards the high end of what I could spend.

When I was looking through the I.O. Inc. (InterOrdnance) ad I saw a small ad that said "SR-41 receivers complete with barrels and sights $249, Stripped (no barrels, sights, or trunnion) $149–BATFE Approved". This was more in line with my price considerations so I phoned in an order for one of each.

I suppose at this point I should explain what a SR-41 receiver has to do with a PPSh-41 semi-auto project. Back in the late 1990s. InterOrdnance of Monroe, N.C. announced plans to offer a BATFE-approved semi-automatic version of the PPSh-41 they called the SR-41.

The Polish PPSh-41 parts kit from Class III Supply appeared unissued to Matthews. It came without a barrel, but with many other useful parts for the build.

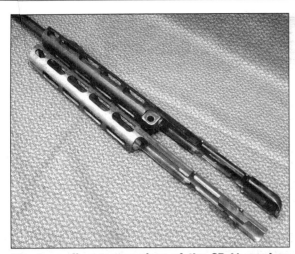

I.O., Inc., offers two versions of the SR-41 receiver. One of them is stripped, while the other is sold complete with the sights, barrel and trunnion installed.

The bolt handle needs to be permanently welded in place so it cannot move in the slightest, since machining processes will be done on the interior of the bolt.

They had imported large numbers of PPSh-41 parts sets from eastern European sources and had arraigned for a North Carolina firearms maker to make the rifle with some of the surplus parts, new U.S.-made semi-automatic parts and a BATFE-approved U.S. made semi-automatic receiver.

There were delays and examples were not on dealer shelves till early 2000. When it did make it to the hands of the shooting press and public, reviews were mixed. Some reviews praised its workmanship and reliability and others complained of the lack thereof.

Apparently the manufacturer's quality control was rather erratic. Prices were also kind of high for a gun that was based on a crudely built military sub-machine gun. Prices were lowered but the early bad press, quality control problems and low demand eventually lead to the SR-41 being discontinued.

The fixed firing pin of the full-auto PPSh-41 bolt has to be removed and replaced with a conventional moving firing pin. BATFE frowns on fixed firing pins.

This left InterOrdnance will a lot of SR-41 parts to liquidate. In mid 2006 the company, now called I.O., Inc., received approval from the BATFE to offer the SR-41 semi-auto receivers as a stand-alone item. The previous approval had been for the complete rifle. From doing research on the internet on the old SR-41 rifle and reviewing problems reported by owners, I thought there were no problems directly attributable to the receivers.

Just as the SR-41 receiver was classified a semi-automatic, the rest of the operating parts also had to be of a semi-automatic design. The original SR-41 rifle featured a PPSh-41 bolt remanufactured to semi-automatic configuration. The fixed firing pin was removed and replaced with a conventional spring-loaded moving firing pin.

The bolt was also modified to fit in the SR-41 semi-auto receiver, since the SR-41 receiver was made to prevent a full auto bolt from being installed. The fire control group was a modified U.S.-made semi-automatic AK-47 system. If implemented correctly this system would seem to work well.

Some of the recent PPSh-41 semi-auto clones feature a striker-fired system but rather than re-inventing the wheel, I decided to use the SR-41 system. The SR-41 system was BATFE approved when the gun was on the market, so to keep this project legal, I just roughly copied the SR-41 format.

I chose to get the receivers and to keep cost down, to duplicate the rest of the SR-41 parts. The duplicated design is not dimensionally exact to the SR-41 parts but is functionally the same system and should be just as legal as the original SR-41.

The complete receiver featured sights and the U.S.-legal 7.62x25 16-inch barrel installed in the trunnion. The barrel was a shorter version that was brought up to 16 inches by welding on an extension. The stripped version was basically just the formed sheet metal without any barrel, sights, or trunnion.

For reasons unknown, the two receivers were somewhat different. Both featured a restriction or protrusion on the side of the receiver to prevent an original full-auto PPSh-41 bolt from being installed in the SR-41 receiver. On the completed receiver this protrusion was made by folding part of the receiver wall into the interior of the receiver.

Drilling the firing pin hole requires a very exacting setup. If the bolt body is at an angle to the drill, the hole will drift across the bolt body and ruin it.

On the stripped version, the protrusion was a block welded to the side of the receiver. Both preformed the same function but were implemented differently. I guess there was some design change somewhere during the manufacturing life of the SR-41.

Both receivers were made from 1/8" sheet steel. They were somewhat crude but this isn't necessarily a negative. The original PPSh-41 was crudely manufactured and to be appropriate to the design a certain amount of crudeness is acceptable.

These receivers require a certain amount of finishing. The only fault I found was that the completed receiver was slightly bent just behind where the bolt restriction was formed. It was easily straightened, but this indicated a definite weakness at this point.

To strengthen the receiver I welded on a reinforcement plate at the weak point. I also marked the makers' name on this plate, since the original markings on the side of the receiver were so light that I was afraid they wouldn't show after final finishing.

Although the PPSh-41 parts set was absolutely great, only a few of the parts will be used in the semi-auto project. Out of the parts set we will use the stock, lower receiver, trigger housing, trigger, selector assembly, bolt, front sight hood, pivot pin and retainer plus various small pins.

Threading the firing pin bushing hole must be done squarely for a straight bushing installation. If the bushing is cocked, the firing pin will bind against it.

The bushing is easily made from a hex socket screw, but the firing pin hole must be drilled exactly through its center. Then it's ground flush with the bolt face.

For the fire control group we will use the U.S. made TAPCO G2 semi-automatic AK-47 trigger group. This trigger group is available in a single hook version and a double hook version, I used the double hook version. You will also need two AK-47 hammer/trigger pins.

This trigger group is available from many sources, but I got mine through Brownells since I was ordering other items for the project from them. Their prices are competitive with other sources so it saved time to get it with my other Brownells items.

You will need an AR-15 firing pin, and I also obtained it from Brownells. Various small pins will be needed for the project and some can be salvaged from the PPSh parts set. You will need several springs for this project and they need to be high quality springs. These were also obtained from Brownells in the form of their gunsmithing spring assortments.

Beyond basic hand tools you will need a couple machine tools to ease the build project. A small lathe, drill press and milling machine will greatly ease making the parts. If you don't mind a lot of tedious hand work and have the skill, you can make many of the parts with nothing more than a drill press and Dremel tool. The milling machine and lathe do make it easier but it is possible to do the project without them.

Be realistic though, if you can't drill a shallow hole straight you certainly can't accurately drill a small diameter hole 3 inches deep and get it within a few thousandths of where it's supposed to be.

I reverse engineered this project from internet pictures of the discontinued SR-41 rifle. I had no actual design specifications for the old SR-41. This is only my interpretation of the BATFE-approved SR-41 design. The SR-41 design was

not perfect by any means but it was BATFE approved. The design, methods and procedures used here were chosen to accommodate home gunsmiths with greatly varying degrees of skill, ranging from those with complete machine shops and developed machining skills to those with only basic hand tools and limited abilities.

I have chosen methods to accommodate those at the lower end of the skill range. If your skills and equipment let you modify this design, feel to do so, but keep in mind you should stay very close to the original SR-41 design to stay legal. If you stray very far from the SR-41 design, may be wise to submit your design to the BATFE for approval.

Every gun design doesn't have to be BATFE-approved, but when you are making something derived from a machine gun, small issues can be the difference between a legal or illegal gun. Also please note that this article should only be considered a rough guide. It does not contain all the information you need to make this project. You will have to supplement this information with your own gunsmithing skills and knowledge.

This is advanced hobby gunsmithing and you are solely responsible for building a safe and legal semi-automatic firearm. Neither SHOTGUN NEWS nor the author assume any responsibility for the construction, safety or legality of this project.

The heart of any semi-automatic firearm is the bolt and firing system. Our semi-auto will feature a bolt with a conventional spring-loaded moving firing pin. This is required by BATFE regulations. More than 20 years ago, BATFE issued an opinion that no future fixed-firing pin designs would be legal even if they were semi-automatic.

Fixed firing pin operation has been determined by the BATFE to be solely a full-auto feature and cannot be used on a semi-automatic firearm. The original PPSh-41 bolt would not be legal, so several modifications will be made to it to create a legal semi-automatic bolt.

The original bolt will simply be raw material for making a new bolt. The fixed firing pin will be removed and the bolt will be machined to accept a spring-loaded AR-15 firing pin. The centrally mounted single recoil spring assembly will be discarded and replaced with a dual recoil spring system.

The sear catch on the bottom of the bolt will be machined away. The bolt will also be machined to fit the SR-41 semi-automatic receiver, since that will not accept an unmodified PPSh-41 bolt. Other than the change to dual springs, this will more or less duplicate the semi-automatic SR-41 bolt design.

These modifications are not difficult in principle but are easy to mess up during implementation. Attention to detail and thinking things through *before* doing any machining

will go a long ways towards success. Take this advice to heart! I made mistakes on my first bolt that resulted in a scrapped bolt simply from not following my own advice. Fortunately, I had an extra bolt from another parts kit. I highly recommend that you have extra parts on hand in case you make mistakes and have to scrap parts.

The first thing that needs to be done is to remove the fixed firing pin. Fortunately the PPSh-41 fixed firing pin was made to be removed by driving out a crosspin in the side of the bolt and pushing the pin out the front.

You can access the rear of the firing pin by removing the extractor and its spring. Lift the front edge of the spring and push it forward over the extractor and remove it. The extractor can then be removed. A pocket or small groove is machined into the bolt body right behind the firing pin.

Now comes the most difficult part of this build project, precisely drilling several holes in the center of the bolt. These holes must be centered all the way through the bolt. The exit hole must be precisely in line with the entrance hole. You can be off a few thousandths (.010"-.015") but not much more than that or your bolt will be unusable.

The procedures to drill deep small diameter holes are basic machine shop knowledge and are beyond the scope of this article. I will briefly explain how I modified the bolt but this article is not a machine shop course. If you are unsure of your skills you may want to study up on machining procedures or hire this part out to a skilled machinist.

A return spring and an extension will be added to the AR-15 firing pin. It will need to be turned down to 1/4" and the edges beveled to fit the new firing pin hole.

After drilling a firing pin hole entirely through the bolt body, you'll need to drill the other direction to accommodate the firing pin rear. Use a piloted drill.

Before we drill any holes the pressed-in bolt handle needs to be permanently secured to the bolt body so it cannot move during building or while in use. We will be drilling the firing pin hole right through the bolt body where the handle passes through and we want it never to move.

The bolt handle needs to be arc-welded in place. You can weld it where you wish, but note that this bolt is alloy steel and wherever you weld the bolt, it will be very hard due to weld heat-treating the area.

After you have secured the handle with a deep penetrating weld, grind off the excess weld flush with the bolt body. The existing firing pin hole in my bolt was .153". This roughly equates to a #23 drill. We will use the existing hole as a guide to drill a #23 size hole into the bolt body as deep as the bit will allow.

At the bottom of the existing hole in the pocket there is a small ridge that needs to be removed by grinding or milling so the bit will not be deflected when it passes past it. Since the bit was being guided by the existing hole, I thought I could just push right past the ridge when I drilled. Well I was wrong and ruined my first bolt.

The ridge deflected the small bit just enough to alter its course so that the exit hole was over 1/8" off course. On the next attempt, I smoothed out the ridge and this time my exit hole was pretty close to where it was supposed to be.

Set your bolt up in a sturdy vise and precisely align the bolt with the downward travel of your drill or mill quill. This is known as "indicating in" your part and also is a basic machine

shop procedure. The alignment has to be very precise so that when you start in the center of the bolt face, the exit hole 3-4 inches away will still be centered in the bolt body. Failure to set up this procedure accurately will result in ruined parts, so be sure it's right before you drill.

Once you start drilling, you won't know if it's right until the bit comes through the rear of the bolt and at that point it's too late if it wasn't right to begin with. Start by drilling as deep as you can go with the standard #23 drill. Drill with a very light feed and use plenty of lubricant. The standard #23 drill won't reach as deep as it needs to, so you will have to switch to a longer drill bit.

I didn't have a long #23 bit so I jumped up a few thousandths and went with a long 5/32" drill. When you switch bits, be sure that your parts are still aligned before you begin drilling again.

If you have to move your part to get the bit in the drill chuck, it must be returned to the very same location or the long bit will wander off course for the rest of the drilling. Once you have a 5/32" hole precisely drilled and centered through the bolt body, you will need to drill both ends to other sizes.

The hole in the face of the bolt will need to be drilled and tapped to a standard bolt size so that a firing pin bushing can be made and fitted. The closest size that I found could be used was a #12 machine screw. I used a 12-28 screw, so I drilled the hole with a #14 drill. You could also use a 12-24 screw, so then you would drill the hole with a #16 drill. Drill to a depth of about 5/8".

Once you have your hole drilled, tap your hole for the size you choose. When you tap this hole it must be precisely aligned or the hole will be tapped at a slight angle and the bushing will be off-center when installed. Any misalignment may cause binding when the firing pin is installed later.

Next, a 1/4" hole needs to be drilled in the rear of the bolt. This will allow the reduced-diameter AR-15 firing pin to be installed later. Drill this hole about 3 inches deep. This hole is located in a position that will not allow a standard drill bit to be used.

The edge of the 1/4" hole would extend beyond the material since the 5/32" hole is very close to the ledge on the rear of the bolt. To drill the 1/4" hole precisely along the path of the 5/32" hole, you will need a 1/4" drill with a 5/32" pilot. The pilot will keep the bit on course.

You can purchase these bits from tooling suppliers or you can make your own. To make one, just grind down the last 1/4"-1/2" on a standard bit to form a smooth pilot and then re-sharpen the sides that extend past the edges of the 5/32" pilot. This pilot needs to be smooth and round so it doesn't damage the existing hole when it drills.

After you have the hole drilled to depth, polish the inside of the hole with a piece of

sandpaper on a spinning dowel or use a honing stone. This will help the firing pin and its spring to slide smoothly in the hole.

If you have got the holes drilled in the bolt precisely, you have made it through the hardest past of the project and following procedures will not be so easy to mess up. The firing pin bushing can now be made to fill in the hole in the face of the bolt.

I used a 13/16" long piece of the threaded portion of a #12-28 machine screw to make my bushing. This part should be turned on a lathe to maintain precision. Face off both ends square. Use a small center drill with a point under 1/16" to spot drill the face of one end.

Be absolutely sure your drill chuck is aligned on the lathe's centerline for accurate drilling. A 1/16" hole needs to be drilled all the way through the center of the bushing. This small and fragile 1/16" bit must be fed in very lightly to keep the bit from running off course due to deflection. Use plenty of lube and take your time.

Once you have your hole through the bushing, check to verify that it is centered on both ends because small bits can easily run off course. If it's not, make another one until you get it right. Now turn your part over and drill a larger hole in the other end. Drill a #37 (.104") hole into the 1/16" hole. Drill to a depth that leaves 3/16" (.187") of the 1/16" hole.

The remaining 3/16" will allow the .060" wide point of the modified AR-15 firing pin to extend past the face of the bolt when the 1/8" flats are ground off. On the last 1/8" of this bushing. file flats on opposite sides. These flats will allow you to grip the bushing with a very small wrench or needle-nose vise grips when you are screwing it in place.

Install a crosspin at the rear of the bolt and grind a groove in the firing pin extension to retain it and to set firing pin travel. It should retract about 1/16".

The bushing can now be installed in the bolt face. Before you install the bushing, lightly flatten a few threads so the bushing will screw in tightly. Also use some high strength thread locker. Screw the bushing in until the flats are just slightly above the face of the bolt. Use a small grinder or file to work the bushing down even with the bolt face.

One item that needs to be addressed before we go on concerns the feed lips on the front of the bolt face. These lips protrude out from the bottom of the bolt face and are required on fixed firing pin bolts to keep the fixed firing pin from catching the base of the cartridge when it slides up into place on the bolt face.

Many semi-automatic bolts also feature bolt faces with these bottom lips extending forward. This allows the cartridge to be solidly held on the face of the bolt. One of the general "recommendations" by the BATFE when converting full auto guns to semi-automatic is to remove these lips on the front of the bolt face so that it is smooth on the bottom.

The original SR-41 that was BAFTE approved retained these feed lips. The bolt face of the SR-41, other than the removal of the fixed firing pin, was identical to the full auto version. I therefore did not remove the feed lips. Due to the design of the gun and bolt I do not know if the gun would operate correctly with the feed lips removed and that may be why the SR-41 designer retained them.

The AR-15 firing pin now needs to be modified to fit our new bolt. The rear of the firing pin needs to be turned down to 1/4" (.250") so it will fit the hole. The point on the front also needs to be turned back further so the .060" point is .125" to .140" long.

This will allow the pin to pass through the 1/16" hole in the face of the bolt and extend about .050" and still have a little for clearance so the point doesn't bottom out in the interior of the bolt. Install your firing pin and check for smooth operation. It must slide back and forth with no binding. Binding will especially be noticeable when the point extends past the bolt face.

This is where the accuracy of your drilling, polishing and straight tapping is noticed. If any of your holes were off-center or angled, then your close tolerance firing pin will bind. You can't get a straight pin to slide easily though crooked holes. If you have any binding, you will have to do whatever is required to get it to operate smoothly.

If it binds during use, it could create a slam-fire condition and run away full auto firing. Besides being dangerous it would also create an illegal full auto gun. You now need to install a firing pin spring. This spring is *absolutely required* to keep the firing pin from impacting the primer when the bolt reciprocates. This could also cause slam-fires.

Firing pin springs are installed in many semi-auto guns for just this reason. There are some guns on the market that don't have firing pin springs in them and they sometimes have slam-fires when using ammo with soft primers. We do not want this on our project!

My spring was just slightly under 1/4" diameter and 1¼" inches long. Wire size was .025" with 12 coils per inch. The spring needs to be strong enough to keep the firing pin from significantly striking the primer on the cartridge when the bolt reciprocates but not so strong as to cause light primer hits.

You may have to experiment a little to get the spring tension just right. I obtained my spring stock for this spring and the other springs used for this project from Brownells. Common hardware store springs are usually not up to the standards required for gunsmithing.

Brownells offer several assorted sets of bulk gunsmithing coil springs. I have several of their sets to cover my gunsmithing needs. If you are going to be doing much hobby gunsmithing you might as well "spring" for these assortments. I recommend the following coil spring kits, (# 080-950) - 325AA, 350AA, 125AA and 150AA and possibly set #025-069-000AA.

Since the AR-15 firing pin and spring are buried in the interior of the bolt, an extension needs to be fabricated so the hammer can impact the firing pin. This extension will be initially made over length and later hand fitted to our project. This extension is just slightly under 1/4" (.250" or less) and 1¾ inches long. This extension pin needs to be made from high quality steel since it will be repeatedly struck with the hammer. It must be hard but not brittle.

A good easy-to-obtain raw material source for this extension is a piece of high quality 1/4" drill bit shank. This is a steel known as M2 and it is adequate for this use. Bevel the ends of this extension and polish it up smooth. This pin needs to be retained in the correct position in the bolt. A crosspin installed in the bolt body will retain and position the pin. I used a piece of 1/8" drill bit shank for a crosspin.

Its hole was located about 5/8" from the rear of the bolt. It was further located so that the hole intersected the top 1/3" of the firing pin hole. This will allow a wide groove in the extension pin to retain the pin in the bolt body and to also allow for proper firing pin travel.

The groove needs to be ground in the extension so that the firing pin spring retracts the firing pin from the bolt face by about 1/16". It also needs to be ground to allow for about .050" of firing pin extension out of the bolt face when it is hit by the hammer.

Making this pin can take a fair amount of trial and error fitting, so use a piece of common steel rod as an experimental piece. Once you have the right size groove to allow for proper extension and retraction you can then use the experimental piece as a pattern for the piece made from high quality steel.

Since we will be repeatedly removing and installing this piece during the build project, we won't permanently install it at this time. At the end of the project when everything is just right you can stake the hole edges to retain the crosspin. ◉

Next month (1/20 issue): Finishing the PPSh-41 semi-auto

Ask the Gunsmith

By Reid Coffield

SAUER 38 FIRING PIN

Q *How can I get the firing pin out of an old Sauer Model 38 pistol that my grandfather brought back from Germany after World War II?*

A The Sauer Model 38 has an independent breechblock that is pinned inside the slide. To access the firing pin, you must first remove the breechblock retainer pin. There is a small transverse hole near the top of the slide between the rear sight and the ejection port. Use a small punch to drive the pin out. The punch should be inserted in this hole on the right side of the slide and the pin driven out the left side. Once the pin is removed, the breechblock will drop out of the slide.

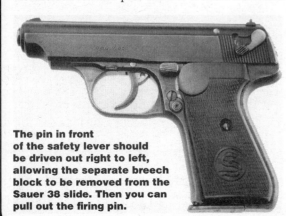

The pin in front of the safety lever should be driven out right to left, allowing the separate breech block to be removed from the Sauer 38 slide. Then you can pull out the firing pin.

COMPETITION AR-15

Q *I plan on building a target rifle based on the AR-15. I used the M16 while I was in the Army and now work as a machinist. I believe that I can build just about anything I need to make a good rifle. My problem is information. I can find lots of stuff on putting together ARs and little bits and pieces about making them shoot. I want information and ideas on a much more sophisticated across the course rifle. Do you know where I could find some or all of what I am looking for? Any help would be most appreciated.*

A I would strongly encourage you to pick up a copy of the David Tubb DVD, *The Art and Technique of the Modern Match Rifle.* Tubb, who is without a doubt one of the finest competitive high power shooters in the world, provides lots of great information on shooting the modern match rifle. While the rifle he uses is the T2K, a bolt action which shows strong influence from the AR15/M16, there are many design elements of this rifle that you will find interesting. I believe you can pick up some great ideas and insights into modifications that you might want to incorporate into your rifle.

For example, you might want to consider utilization of David's sight set up or the manner in which he designed the fully adjustable buttstock and how he literally fits the rifle to the shooter. While this DVD set wasn't designed to instruct a person in building his own rifle, the innovative and unique ideas are right there for anyone to see and possibly incorporate in their own rifle. David also has another DVD on the Tubb 2000 (T2K) rifle. This is both an "owners manual" for his rifle as well as providing some great information on shooting. Either of these DVDs retail for $49.95 each and are available directly from David Tubb, Superior Shooting Systems, 800 North Second, Dept. SGN, Canadian, Texas 79014, telephone 806-323-9488, www.DavidTubb.com.

ARISAKA BARREL THREAD

Q *I was given a junker 6.5 Jap sporter by a neighbor. The barrel is in pretty bad shape so I thought I might try rebarreling it. Do you know what thread was used on this action?*

A According to the info I have, the Type 38 Arisaka barrel has a major diameter of 1.025" with 14 "V" type threads per inch. ◉

BUILDING
A Semi-Automatic
PPSh-41
Part 2

BY STEVEN MATTHEWS

In Part 1 (12-20-08),
Matthews modified the bolt for
semi-auto operation. In this story,
he finishes the revamped burp gun.

If you got through the first half of this project, Matthews says the rest will be easy. There's lots of parts fabricating, but with patience, you can get it done.

The SR-41 receiver features a blocking protrusion on the side to prevent a full auto PPSh-41 bolt from being installed in the receiver. The semi-automatic bolt will have to be modified to fit in the SR-41 receiver. You need to machine or grind a clearance groove down the side of the bolt to clear the protrusion.

The size and location of this groove will vary depending on which type of receiver you have. Only machine this groove as deep as you need for clearance. The bolt needs to remain as heavy as possible and we don't want to remove any more material than absolutely necessary.

To allow for passage of the hammer on the bottom of the bolt we need to machine or grind a groove in the bottom. We also need to remove the full auto sear notch. One groove will do both jobs.

I machined a groove .675" wide and .125" deep, centered on the bottom of the bolt. The forward section of this groove was machined to the same depth as the original surface of the bolt bottom. This leaves a small ledge at the rear of the bolt. This ledge was left on to allow it to push the hammer down far enough to catch when the bolt reciprocates. The front and rear edges were beveled to allow the hammer to slide over the ledge easily.

The original PPSh-41 bolt featured a centrally mounted recoil spring. Since the SR-41 features a centrally mounted hammer, this spring must be relocated. On the original SR-41, this spring was moved all the way to one side and part of the hammer and trigger was removed for clearance.

From references I found on the internet this arrangement caused some minor problems. With all the recoil spring force applied to one side of the bolt it caused some misalignment of the very loose-fitting bolt. This misalignment also caused some dragging of the bolt in the receiver.

To correct this, I decided to go with a dual recoil spring setup. Rather than one large central spring, I would use two smaller springs on each side of the bolt. This would reduce drag and misalignment. I machined spring grooves on each side of the bolt. The grooves were .210" wide by .200" deep (from the side of the bolt, not the recess) and run the full length of the lower bolt.

The bottom of the grooves were located .480" up from the bottom of the bolt. Once spring grooves were cut, I fabricated spring stops to allow the guide rods to pass through but retain the springs. I machined notches in the side of the bolt to help hold them in place before welding, but this was probably unnecessary.

It would probably be easier to just weld on the retainers flat against the bolt. I also drilled pockets in these retainers but I don't think that was necessary either. I did it this way to get as much spring length as I could, since space for the recoil springs was tight.

The spring retainers were ground down flush with the sides of the bolt after they were welded in place. I then drilled 9/64" holes in the retainers to allow the 1/8" guide

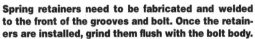

Spring retainers need to be fabricated and welded to the front of the grooves and bolt. Once the retainers are installed, grind them flush with the bolt body.

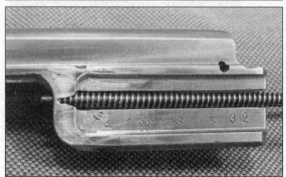

Grooves must be wide enough to allow easy passage of the springs. Use a drill that fits the groove to drill a spring pocket, then drill through for the guide rod.

rods to pass through easily. Since so much material had been removed during the modification procedure, the semi-auto bolt was lighter than the original PPSh-41 bolt.

Blowback firearms need to have bolts in a certain weight range for proper function. To replace some of this lost weight, I filled the now-unused central recoil spring hole with lead. I dropped in a plug to fill the front hole and followed it with molten lead to within 1/4" of the top. I placed a steel plug over the lead and welded it in place to lock the weight in position.

The change to two using small-diameter recoil springs meant I needed to fabricate two guide rods and attach them to a backing plate. The springs chosen were 7 inches long by .195" diameter with a wire size of .028". Coil spacing was 16 per inch.

These springs were obtained from the previously recommended Brownells Gunsmithing Spring Assortments. You need these high quality gunsmith grade springs since common hardware store variety springs will deform when fully compressed and not return to full length when released.

For the guide rods I used pieces of heat-treated music wire 1/8" diameter by 6¼ inches long. Common steel rod probably wouldn't last long so that's why I used high-strength music wire.

I made the backing plate from a piece of 1/8" flat steel stock shaped the same as the PPSh-41 recoil buffer. This very hard buffer was ground flat so that the plate would bear on it evenly. Holes were located and drilled in the back plate so the guide rods would be centered in the spring grooves in the bolt. The guide rods were then brazed in place since they need to be secured to the back plate.

The bolt in the PPSh-41 is moved rearward at a pretty high speed after firing since the 7.62 x 25mm is a fairly hot round. Early Soviet PPSh-41s suffered from premature buffer failure due to the high impact force. Eventually they got the material right and got one that would hold up.

This buffer is very hard and doesn't "cushion" very much. Since our bolt is even lighter than the original and will hit even harder, I decided to make a soft buffer to place between the rear of the bolt and the recoil plate. This buffer will soften the impact and also allow for more room for the springs so they don't bottom out when the bolt is all the way rearward.

I fabricated it out of 3/4" thick rubber that was just a little softer than common tire rubber. It was shaped like the backing plate and had clearance grooves for the guide rods and springs. I drilled a hole in it for firing pin extension clearance. This hole also was used for a mounting screw so the buffer would stay attached to the backing plate.

Be sure your screw is very deep in the hole or the firing pin extension will strike the screw when the bolt compresses the buffer. Failure to keep this screw from impacting the firing pin extension will result in bolt and firing pin damage. I know this from personal experience!

The fire control group on the SR-41 was a modified U.S.-made semi-automatic AK-47 design and I roughly duplicated it for this project. The first job is to remove all the full-auto parts from the PPSh-41 trigger housing. Save the housing, trigger and its pin, selector button or lever, selector stud, pin and spring. Discard all the full auto parts.

I used the TAPCO Double Hook G2 U.S.-made semi-auto AK-47 trigger assembly. This trigger group was obtained from Brownells and was priced competitively with other AK parts sources. The assembly will be held in the trigger housing with cutoff sections of AK-47 hammer/trigger pins that can be obtained from AK parts suppliers.

Before doing any trigger parts fitting, make a simple fixture to learn how the AK trigger group operates. A full understanding of hammer, trigger and disconnector function is *absolutely necessary* for modifying and fitting this fire control group.

A flat plate with two holes is all that's needed. Drill one hammer pin hole and then drill a trigger pin hole 1.550" behind and .280" below the first. By installing your parts on this plate, you can study how all the parts interact. The pin holes in the housing need to be located and drilled precisely for proper function. The hole size is .196", which is roughly a #9 drill.

The center of the hammer pin hole is located 2.10" back from the front of the hous-

To replace weight lost during machining, fill the now-unused recoil spring hole with lead and cap it with a welded steel plug. This maintains the proper bolt mass.

ing and .265" down from the top. This hole must be drilled squarely, so I recommend marking and drilling from both sides rather than marking one side and drilling through from one side, which can lead to misalignment.

The center of the trigger pin hole is located .280" below and 1.550" behind the center of the hammer pin hole. This translates to about 3.650" from the front of the housing and about .545" down from the top.

The hammer needs to be modified to fit in the PPSh-41 housing, since it is too wide. It is also too large to accept the hammer spring we will be using. The shoulders for the pin need to be shortened equally for an overall width of .590" to fit. The diameter of these shoulders also need to be reduced in size to about .300".

It's easy to make this little fixture that allows you to study the trigger group function. Matthews recommends making one before you drill the trigger housing.

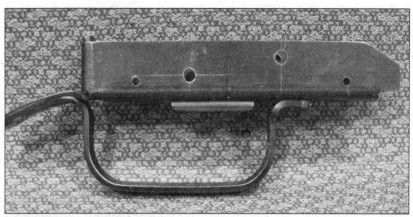

It's absolutely essential that the hammer and trigger pin holes be drilled with great precision in the trigger housing. Drill from both sides rather than through.

The lower portion of the central body of the hammer needs to be thinned to about .165" thick. This is so an AR-15 hammer spring can be utilized to operate the AK hammer. A standard AK hammer spring is way too wide for this application.

Machining this hammer to size is easily done on a metal lathe but you could possibly do it by hand grinding if you don't have a lathe. A stock AR-15 hammer spring is too wide to fit the housing and hammer, so one coil on each side was unwound from the spring to make it narrower.

The unwound leg was then cut to the former length. Some AR-15 springs will not work when one coil is removed, they don't have enough "spring power" remaining. The springs I used were Brownells standard strength (these springs were red in color) AR-15 hammer springs.

The TAPCO AK hammer needs to be thinned to allow installation of a modified AR-15 hammer spring. Experimentation with spring shape and tension may be required.

These springs didn't deform and lose much of their strength when compressed to their elastic limit. I tried the extra strength springs and while stronger initially, they would not keep from deforming when compressed to their limit.

You may want to try several types or brands of springs to find the one that works the best. Once you have the hammer and spring modified, install it in the trigger housing with a shortened AK hammer pin.

The trigger now needs to be modified to operate the hammer. Because of the positions of the trigger housing, bolt and fire control group, the G2 trigger cannot be used as the primary trigger.

The G2 trigger can be used to trip the hammer, but it must in turn be tripped by another trigger. The G2 trigger needs to have the trigger blade cut off the bottom. Once it is cut off, an extension needs to be made and welded that allows a modified stock PPSh-41 trigger to operate it.

I used a piece of 1/8 x 1/2 x 1 flat steel to fabricate the extension. The end was shaped to allow it to fit between the rear sides of the G2 trigger. I installed it flush with the top of the G2 trigger and then welded it in place and smoothed it up.

When this modified G2 trigger is installed, a modified PPSh-41 trigger will push up on this extension and trip the G2 trigger. Due to all the variations from home making parts there is no use in giving you any dimensions for the modified PPSh trigger. Just grind off the top portion so it looks close to the pictured example and experiment until it works.

Start oversize and work your way down. Be sure, though, that you don't grind into the hole for the pivot pin. You want the PPSh trigger to be sized so that it will cause the G2 trigger to release the hammer when it is pulled and also to allow the G2 trigger to return to its at-rest position.

This is where your test fixture will come in handy. You can test fit all the parts together outside the trigger housing where you can see what needs to be done. Once you get a working trigger set up, you need to make a return spring for the triggers. One homemade spring will operate both triggers.

I made this spring from music wire stock that was obtained from Brownells. They offer a spring wire kit (part # 025-150-000AA) that has 100 pieces of assorted size spring wire. Each spring wire only cost pennies when bought in a kit, and you can make hundreds of springs and pins from the material in this kit.

I used a piece of .040" wire to make the torsion spring. I formed it around a 1/8" pin with the top legs about 1¼ inches long and the bottom legs about 7/8" long. You may take several tries to get it shaped right and set for the right amount of tension, but at only a few cents for each spring you can afford to experiment.

You want this torsion spring to press down on the top of the extension, which in turn will press down on the modified PPSh trigger. It will be held in place by roll pins installed in the side of the trigger housing. You want the tension to be strong enough to return both triggers to their at-rest positions when you release the trigger.

Saw the blade off the TAPCO G2 trigger and weld onto it an extension that will allow the modified PPSh-41 trigger to push up on it, thereby releasing the hammer.

My homemade spring placed just the right amount of tension on the triggers so that it felt just like a typical AK-47 trigger, a long and easy pull. When everything is installed and hand-fitted, you should have a working trigger assembly.

Verify proper functioning. The trigger needs to catch the hammer when it is pushed back by the bolt. It needs to release the hammer when pulled. The disconnector needs to catch the hammer when the hammer is cocked and hold it until the trigger is released, at which time the trigger should catch the hammer.

You should have to release the trigger for every cycle of the bolt (this is semi-automatic operation) before you can drop the hammer again. Making and fitting all these parts together is rather time-consuming. I took the better part of a day to figure it out from scratch, since all I had were pictures of the SR-41 fire control group.

The dimensions and parts are somewhat different but it duplicates the original semi-automatic fire control system. One more thing should be done to the trigger housing. To prevent any full auto parts from ever being installed in the trigger housing, a block should be welded in front of the hammer and the holes in the side of the housing that located full auto parts should be welded shut. Be sure to locate your block far enough away from the hammer to avoid interfering with its movement.

One last thing that can be added to your trigger housing is a safety, if you want one. A very easy-to-make safety can be added to this project without having to make a lot of complicated parts.

The PPSh-41 features a selector lever or button in the front of the trigger guard. This selector consist of a sliding button and a stud that extends into the trigger housing through an oval opening. The rear of this opening for this stud is right under the front edge of the G2 trigger.

You can install the stud so that it slides under the G2 trigger and blocks its downward travel. By sliding the stud and button forward, it will slide out from under the G2 trigger and allow the trigger to move normally.

The stud can be fitted to the button with a spring and crosspin and will slide in the original selector groove. You may have to bevel the edges of the groove for smooth operation.

A modified PPSh-41 trigger under the extension (the shiny part at left), will push up on the latter, actuating the G2 trigger. This allows semi-automatic firing.

The clearance cuts in the lower receiver allow full hammer movement. They can be made by hand, but a milling machine sure makes cutting them a whole lot easier!

Before fitting the trigger housing to the PPSh lower receiver, make an opening in the lower receiver to allow the hammer to access the bolt. This opening only needs to be wide enough to allow the hammer to pass through with adequate clearance.

There are already openings in the lower receiver so there will be more openings than required. I made two rectangular openings in the bottom of the lower receiver. The first was 1⁵⁄₈ x 5/8" wide and was centered 1 inch forward of the notch in the receiver that retains the trigger housing. The next opening was centered in front of the first and was sized 9/16" wide by 1¹⁄₈ inches long. This should give plenty of clearance, but you should check to verify that the hammer doesn't hit the edges when it operates.

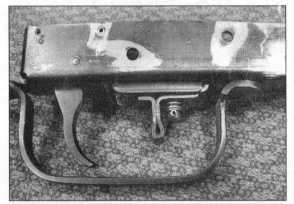

The PPSh-41 selector in front of the trigger handily becomes a trigger-blocking safety when the AK trigger assembly is modified and installed in the semi-auto gun.

While you are working on the lower receiver, you will need to machine a notch in the side to allow a stub on the semi-automatic SR-41 receiver to fit in the lower. This stub or protrusion was added to the SR-41 receiver to prevent full-auto lower receivers from being attached to the SR-41. Since our receiver is now a semi auto we will modify it to fit.

Fit the upper and lower receivers together to note the notch location and then use a milling machine or hand grinder to remove the material for clearance.

Now that all the parts are made, assemble and final-fit them. Assemble your fire control group in the trigger housing and attach it to the lower receiver. It doesn't have to be in the stock for initial fitting. Assemble your bolt assembly and install it into the lower receiver along with the buffer unit. *Do not* install the firing pin assembly at this time.

Manually cycle the bolt to verify that it cocks the hammer. Verify that you have proper trigger and disconnector function. If you have any problems with the fire control components or the bolt, correct them now before doing the final fitting of the firing pin.

If everything is OK, you can final fit the firing pin extension. To determine proper fit of the firing pin assembly you need to have the upper and lower receivers connected and the bolt installed.

Unlike the original PPSh-41 that pivots at the front on a large pin and then tilts down to latch into a recess in the tang of the lower receiver, you place the catch at the rear of the upper receiver into the notch in the tang of the lower receiver and then pull the front down to insert the large crosspin.

Once the upper and lower are assembled with the bolt in the forward position, mark the position of the bolt in the lower receiver. I drew a line along the side even with the handle to know where the bolt will be located when the upper is removed. Remove the upper and install the firing pin assembly into the bolt.

Reinstall the bolt in the lower and place it in the same position that it would be in if the gun was assembled and the bolt was all the way forward on a chambered round. Clamp it securely so it doesn't move. The firing pin extension needs to be fitted with the bolt in this position.

It needs to be trimmed so that no more than absolutely necessary extends out of the rear of the bolt. You want the hammer to strike the firing pin extension and drive it forward only enough to get the required .045"-.050" protrusion out of the bolt face before the hammer comes to rest on the rear of the bolt body.

This will direct the excess hammer force into the bolt body rather than into the firing pin. If the hammer bottoms out the firing pin in the bolt body, it will lead to early firing pin failure. Forcing the firing pin into the bolt could also deform the firing pin and cause it to bind in the bolt in the extended position and cause slam-fires, a very dangerous situation.

When you are trimming and fitting the firing pin extension, form the rear of the extension in a rounded shape so that it doesn't dig into the hammer.

Weld a block into the front of the trigger housing and weld in any holes to prevent installation of any full-auto parts. Seems like overkill, but it's wise.

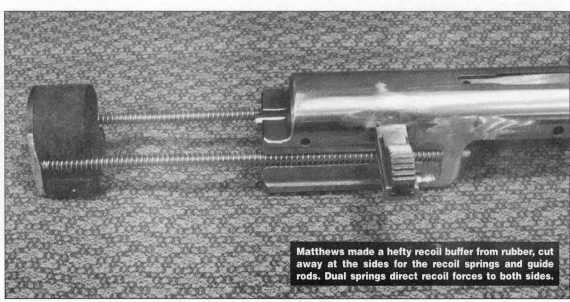

Matthews made a hefty recoil buffer from rubber, cut away at the sides for the recoil springs and guide rods. Dual springs direct recoil forces to both sides.

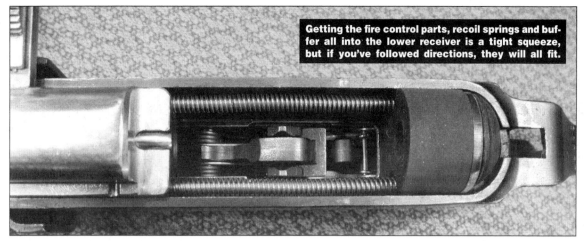

Getting the fire control parts, recoil springs and buffer all into the lower receiver is a tight squeeze, but if you've followed directions, they will all fit.

If everything appears to be working correctly, you can now advance to function testing with *dummy* rounds. Make up 15-20 dummy rounds and load them into a magazine and attempt to cycle them through the action.

When checking function, pull the bolt handle all the way to the rear and then release it so that it goes forward under full force. Observe the primers on the dummy rounds. There should not be any significant indenting of the primer by the firing pin. If there is anything more than a faint mark, you will need to install a stronger firing pin spring.

On my gun all the rounds chambered and ejected correctly and there were no excessive firing pin impacts on the primers. If you have any problems, correct them now. Adding 35,000 psi of firing pressure to the test won't make things work better, so get it to work right with inert rounds before going to live fire.

If everything is working correctly, you can advance to live fire testing. When testing a new self-made gun I recommend wearing safety glasses or even a full face shield, gloves and hearing protection. I usually test fire from the hip to keep the gun away from my face.

Begin testing by loading one round in the magazine and firing it to see if everything is alright. If one works right, go ahead and load two rounds and fire two rounds. If things are good you can increase the rounds for each succeeding test. The reasons for testing this way is to keep things under control if your gun would malfunction and go into full-auto.

Runaways are a common malfunction on semi-automatic arms and have to be especially watched for on a homemade gun. You don't want to find out you made something wrong

by having a full magazine dumped with a single pull of the trigger.

Besides that, this malfunction is an "illegal" malfunction. Believe it or not, the BATFE has ruled that a malfunctioning semi-automatic gun firing more than one round with a single pull of the trigger is an illegal machine gun. Doesn't matter if it is an unintentional malfunction, they still consider it an illegal machine gun.

Take this into consideration when you decide where you are going to do your live fire testing. If you have any problems with feeding, ejecting or firing, correct them before doing any more testing.

Also check the condition of your fired cases. There should be no excessive bulging of the cases or blown primers. The PPSh-41 is a military design and no consideration was given to how it treats the ejected cases, so they probably will get beat up; just watch for anything abnormal.

Cases will be ejected quite sharply and straight up in front of your eyes and over your head. It's very disconcerting, but normal for this firearm. Unbelievably, my project worked almost perfectly. I was surprised, since most projects require some fine tuning, but I wasn't going to complain. All rounds chambered, fired and ejected correctly.

I only had one misfire with the 50-year-old Bulgarian 7.62 ammo I was using. This was the ammo's fault, because it was hit hard enough, it just didn't go off from old age. If things work right, you can move on to final finishing.

For the finish on this project I wanted something that looked original yet required no maintenance. I choose Brownells GunKote firearms finish in the color of "matte gray." This color is almost an exact match for manganese

phosphate Parkerizing. Brownells GunKote is a sprayed and baked-on finish that is extremely durable and easy to apply. It is virtually maintenance-free and can even be used on internal parts.

Unlike some sprayed on finishes it is ready for use as soon as it comes out of the oven and cools. To apply the finish, you abrasive blast, clean and then spray on the GunKote, followed by baking in an oven at 300° for one hour. Due to the excellent finish on the parts set and the new GunKote finish the project looked better than a new gun.

This project was labor-intensive, but the cost was low. By building it myself, I saved a couple hundred dollars or more. Building project guns yourself also gives you an intimate knowledge of your firearm, you will never have to take your project to a gunsmith because you were the gunsmith who made it!

You can build to your own meticulous standards rather than high speed assembly line standards. Building an interesting firearm and saving money in the process makes this project worthy of your consideration. If this looks like your kind of project give it a try. ◉

SOURCES

SR-41 Receivers –
I.O., INC.
Box 847, Dept. SGN, Monroe, NC 28111
866-882-1479, www.ioinc.us

Gunsmithing Supplies –
BROWNELLS
200 S. Front St., Dept. SGN, Montezuma, IA 50171
800-741-0015, www.brownells.com

Polish PPSh-41 Parts Sets –
CLASS THREE SUPPLY
1400 N. Hermitage Ave., Dept. SGN, Hermitage, PA 16148
742-962-1890, www.classthreesupply.com

ANOTHER LEGAL SIDE OF THE PPSH-41 SEMI-AUTO PROJECT

While this project features a BATFE-approved semi-automatic receiver, there is still another issue that needs to be addressed, since several of the parts used to build the project are imported.

Under Federal law you cannot build a semi-automatic rifle with more than 10 imported parts out of a specified list of 20 parts. This is generally called being "922r compliant".

Not all firearms have all the parts on the list and parts not on the list are unregulated. These parts are as follows.

1. Frames or receivers.	11. Triggers.
2. Barrels.	12. Hammers.
3. Barrel Extensions.	13. Sears.
4. Mounting Blocks or Trunnions.	14. Disconnectors.
5. Muzzle Attachments.	15. Buttstocks.
6. Bolts.	16. Pistol Grips.
7. Bolt Carriers.	17. Forearms or Hand Guards.
8. Operating Rods.	18. Magazine Bodies.
9. Gas Pistons.	19. Magazine Followers.
10. Trigger housings.	20. Magazine Floor Plates.

Out of this list the semi-auto PPSh-41 project featured here has 14 of the listed parts. The U.S.-made parts on this project were the hammer, trigger, disconnector, trunnion, receiver, barrel extension, and handguards, which are part of the receiver. These seven parts leave only seven imported parts and therefore this firearm is considered to be a U.S.-made semi-automatic rifle and not a prohibited imported semi-automatic rifle.

Although this firearm meets Federal requirements, state and local restrictions may affect the legality in your area. You should verify the firearms laws in you specific location before constructing any firearms.

After final finishing with Brownells GunKote, the project gun looks better than it did from the factory. It will accept 35-round stick or 71-round drum magazines.

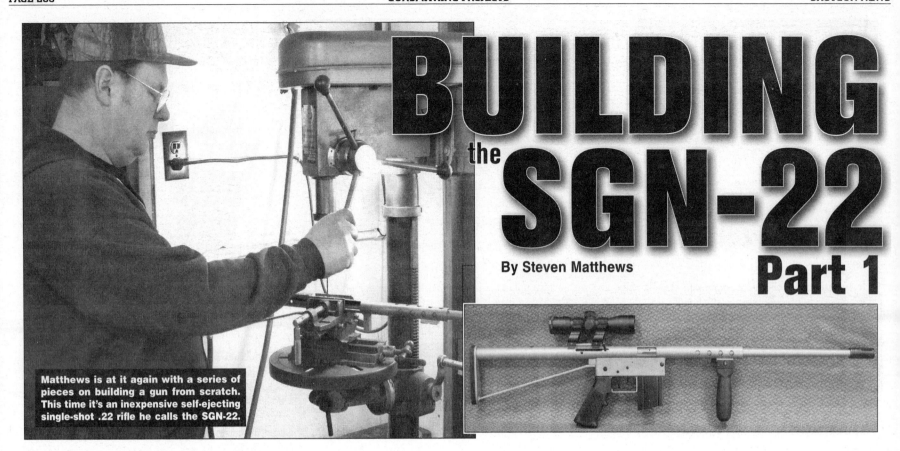

BUILDING the SGN-22 Part 1

By Steven Matthews

Matthews is at it again with a series of pieces on building a gun from scratch. This time it's an inexpensive self-ejecting single-shot .22 rifle he calls the SGN-22.

Ready to try building a gun largely from scratch? Here's a simple self-ejecting single-shot that's easy and cheap to build.

If you have been a regular reader of SGN for the last three years or so, you have probably read some of my gun build articles. If you've built some of them, you have learned a lot about firearms fabrication. You may have thought about going a little deeper into firearms building by actually building a gun from homemade parts rather than using a collection of manufactured components.

With that in mind, I recently wrote an article series on building a 9mm semi-auto carbine known as the SGN-9 (4/20/08, 5/20/08, 6/20/08, 7/20/08). The SGN-9 was a blow-back-operated semi-auto 9mm Luger chambered rifle that featured tubular construction and many self-made parts along with some purchased parts.

The skills and tools needed to build it went far beyond what was needed to do a simple kit building project. I thought of it as a good beginning project for those who wanted to advance to actually making their own guns rather than just assembling parts made by others.

The SGN-9 project required the use of a lathe, milling machine, welder and a multitude of hand tools. It also required extensive hand fitting of parts. While it didn't seem all that hard for me, since I have been doing hobby gunsmithing for more than 25 years, it may have been intimidating to first-time builders.

So I decided I should try a slightly easier project.

Design Parameters

I decided to retain the basic look of the SGN-9, since its tubular construction made it easy to build. I would just scale down the size. I also felt this would make it appealing as a "baby brother" to the SGN-9.

I decided to scale the project down to .22 Long Rifle. By utilizing the low pressure .22 Long Rifle round, it would make building easier and be more forgiving on issues of strength. I wanted the action to be easy to build and at first thought a bolt-action would be the way to go. The more I thought about designing a locked breech and rotating bolt action, the more I realized that a straight blowback action would be easier to make.

Magazine feed, however, would make it harder to make, and the original idea was to make it as easy to build as possible. That's when I got the idea to make it a straight blowback type like an autoloader, but to leave off the magazine to ease the build process.

The added benefit would be self-ejection of the fired case. The unlocked breeching system would be very forgiving and the home builder wouldn't have to worry about the action giving way when the bolt was locked in place and fired if they didn't build it just right.

This is not an original idea. If you read Tom Gaylord's article on the Wham-O guns (9/20/08 issue), they, along with the H&R Sahara, were self-ejecting single-shots.

For the fire control system I decided to use the AR-15 fire control group since it had worked well on the SGN-9 project. I would just scale it down to fit in the smaller trigger housing of the new project. Using a manufactured fire control group would ease the build for those not ready to make hammers and triggers from scratch.

This project would require a specialized bolt I'd design myself. This, along with the receiver and trigger housing, would be the main self-made components of the project. The self-made bolt could be made from about $10 worth of materials and would be as easy to build as I could make it.

I wanted a readily available barrel that was inexpensive and I found one that fit the bill perfectly. The SGN-9 project cost about $175-$250 to make and I wanted this project to be less expensive. What I came up with could be built from $75 to $175 depending on how frugal the builder was in obtaining the necessary materials.

If the builder had a few of the parts lying around, as many hobbyists do (we all have that drawer full of gun parts!) and really scrimped on finishing, the cost could be very low. If, however, you had to buy everything, the cost would be at the high end of the price range. I had some of the parts so this project cost me about $125.

Once I had the basic design and parts selection figured out, I had to figure the easiest way to build the project. I have a well-equipped hobby machine shop, so I can make just about anything, but I wanted this project to be able to be made with the minimum of specialized tools.

The methods and tools are what I consider the bare minimum. Many operations and procedures are highly improvised gunsmithing. If you have better tooling and methods, by all means use them. The more tools you have, the easier the project will be.

Some may look at features of this project and say there is a better way to do it and they may be right, but I designed this project for those minimum of tools and skill. As far as equipment goes, the minimum needed is a small drill press, arc welder (MIG type preferred), basic home workshop hand tools, a small powered hand grinder like an air grinder or Dremel tool, a good set of dial calipers, and a small hobby lathe.

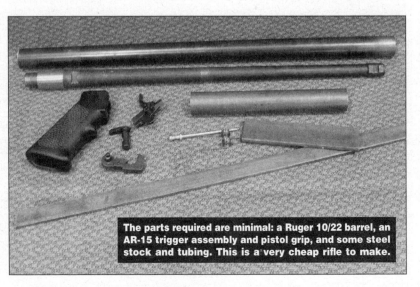

The parts required are minimal: a Ruger 10/22 barrel, an AR-15 trigger assembly and pistol grip, and some steel stock and tubing. This is a very cheap rifle to make.

This job is easier with a milling machine, but Matthews says a cutoff wheel and a Dremel tool will cut the ejection port into the steel tubing that will be the receiver.

The barrel shroud is made from 4130 thin wall tubing. The hole size and spacing is up to you, but use a drill press and vise to keep the holes aligned and spaced.

Small table-top metalworking lathes adequate for this project are available from suppliers like Grizzly Tools or Harbor Freight for as little as $350, so this project may be the incentive to buy this versatile machine tool. For those who don't have a lathe and don't want to buy one, there is an option.

A couple of the lathe operations can be hired out and the remainder can be done on the "poor man's lathe." You can shape many small items with nothing more than a drill press to spin the parts and some files to shape them. This improvised turning method is a lot of work, but you can get quality results if you have the skill and are patient.

I have made many small round parts over the years before I had a lathe with nothing more than files and a drill press to spin them. Since this project would look like a scaled down version of the SGN-9, I decided to name it the SGN-22.

Parts Acquisition

The first part needed for this project is a barrel. There is one common and readily available barrel that is perfect for this project. The large numbers of hobbyists customizing the Ruger 10/22 with special barrels mean there are many take off/used surplus barrels for sale. At the last gun show I attended before I started this project, there were a half-dozen used barrels to choose from. Prices ranged from $10 to $35.

I found one with a poor exterior finish that was excellent inside for $10. Since I was going to be doing a finish job on this project, the $10 barrel was perfect. The Ruger 10/22 barrel is 18.5 inches long and features a 3/4" smooth shank sized at . 685-.687" diameter.

This shank will fit in a 1-inch diameter by .156" wall piece of 4130 chrome-moly seamless tubing quite well. I decided to use this size for the receiver just for that reason. This type of high strength tubing is available from many steel suppliers and also from aircraft suppliers such as Wicks Aircraft.

You will need a couple feet of this tubing for this project, but you really should buy extra in case you make mistakes and have to make a part over. It is priced at about $6.50 per foot. For a barrel shroud, I was going to use the same outside diameter, but didn't want it to be that heavy.

The widest part of the 10/22 barrel is .930-.935" diameter and I found that 1-inch by .035" wall chrome-moly tubing would be just about right for the purpose. It would slide right over the barrel at the breech end. About one foot would be right for the project, but luckily I took my own advice and ordered extra. I made a couple mistakes and needed the extra material. This size tubing runs about $3 per foot.

For bolt fabrication, I bought a couple feet of 3/4" 4130 chrome-moly rod, also available where you find the tubing. I especially recommend buying extra bolt raw material since the bolt is very easy to screw up and it may take more than one attempt to get it right. You only need a foot for the project but you never know! This rod is about $3 per foot.

A faux flash suppressor will be made from a 2½-inch piece of 7/8" x .120" wall chrome-moly tubing, but any type of steel would be fine if you can find this size. The trigger housing for the SGN-22 will be made from a 6-inch piece of 3/4 x 1½ x 3/32 (approximate thickness) wall rectangular mild steel tubing that should be available from local structural steel suppliers. A foot or two of this material should only run you a couple bucks.

A couple feet of 1/2 x 3/16" flat steel will be used to make part of our stock. It should run you less than $1. The buttplate can be fabricated out of a 6-inch piece of

Plug weld the shroud to the barrel itself, then weld it to the receiver tube to fill the joint. Use several small welds with cooling time between them to avoid overheating.

1½ x 3/16" flat steel, also priced under a dollar. I used a couple pieces (one piece of 3/4" rod and one piece of 1/2" flat stock) of scrap aluminum that I bought at the scrap yard for a couple dollars to make the faux magazine and the recoil spring plunger.

Since the magazine is fake, you could make it out of anything you want-wood or plastic or even steel if you don't mind the weight. You will also need a couple more miscellaneous pieces of steel and some screws and pins.

To ease the build process, I used several factory-made parts. I got several DPMS-made AR-15 parts from Brownells, an excellent source for gun parts, both original equipment and custom. You need these AR-15 parts for this project: hammer, trigger, disconnector, the springs for these parts, safety/selector lever, firing pin, pistol grip and two hammer/trigger pins.

These parts can be bought individually, but it's usually cheaper to by one of the sub-assembly parts kits and save the leftover parts for future projects. A few of the other parts can also be obtained from Brownells. I used a Weaver #81 scope base to attach a scope and vertical foregrip.

Since this rifle features a straight-line stock, I used tall extension scope rings to raise the scope high enough. I also selected a Pachmayr RP250 black recoil pad.

Since my eyes aren't what they used to be (getting old stinks!) I ordered a compact 4X scope from SGN advertiser CDNN . This imported scope was only $18.

Disclaimer

Before we get into the actual building of this project, it's time for the customary legal disclaimer since I am just a hobbyist gunsmith and am simply documenting my own amateur efforts. This article is *not* a step-by-step build tutorial. It

The Ruger 10/22 barrel should be a tight fit in the receiver tube. You may need to heat the tube for a shrink fit or ream it slightly on the inside. Then pin the barrel.

Drill rows of holes in a length of tubing, then file out the remainder to make a muzzle brake. It then can be silver-soldered to the barrel after removing the finish.

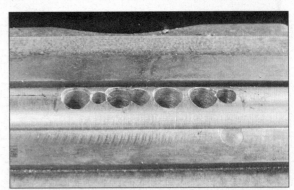

A milling machine makes cutting the hammer slot in the bolt a lot easier, but you can do it by drilling a series of holes and filing out the spaces between them.

This should not discourage potential builders, it's all part of learning gunsmithing. One learns very little by just reading an instruction sheet that says place part B into slot C followed by part A. That is simply "assembling," not building a gun.

When you make, fit and modify your own parts you become intimately familiar with your project and are learning gunsmithing skills far beyond a simple assembly job. This learning process has inherent dangers associated with it since firearms are sometimes dangerous items.

You must accept and understand the hazards involved in building and using firearms. If you do not understand what you are doing you will be putting yourself at risk and you should not do this project. Neither SGN/ Intermedia or the author assume any responsibility for the construction, use, legality or safety of your self-made project. It's your project and you, the builder, assume full responsibility for your own project.

Receiver Fabrication and Barrel Installation

The receiver of the SGN-22 will be made from 1-inch by .156" wall 4130 seamless chrome-moly tubing. You will need a piece about 20 inches long. This is slightly overlong, so that when the project nears completion, you can cut the receiver/stock to the preferred length of pull. Be sure to square the ends after cutting, since you will be measuring from the ends.

While the specifications for this tube would indicate an internal diameter of .688", there are manufacturing tolerances to consider. Your actual size may vary a couple thousandths from the stated size and this will need to be compensated for during building.

The first step is to cut an ejection/loading port in the receiver tube. This cutout needs to be large enough for the user to comfortably insert a cartridge. Since I have fat fingers, I made this port roughly 1¾ inches long by 11/16" wide. I located it about 3/4" back from the front of the tube. This will result in the rear of the barrel being just about even with the front edge of the port.

This port can be cut out with a milling machine or by hand with a Dremel type tool with cutting disc. Once cut, smooth up all edges. The barrel can now be installed in the front of the receiver tube. The shank of the barrel needs to fit snugly into the tube.

Manufacturing tolerances in the barrel and tubing mean your barrel may fit just right or be too loose or too tight. Mine was a little loose, since my tubing measured .687" and my barrel shank was .685". To get a snug fit, I had two options: either shim the shank with .001" shim stock or shrink the tube.

I chose to shrink the tube diameter a couple thousandths. This is easily done by placing the end of the tube in a vise and *lightly* clamping it in place. One side of the last 3/4" of the clamped tube was heated red hot with a torch. This heating expands the tube wall and since it is clamped, it can't expand and therefore swells slightly and thickens.

When the tube cools, the wall contracts, and since it is now slightly thicker, the diameter is slightly reduced when cool. This is only a few thousandths of an inch but that is all that is needed on this project. This brought mine to a good snug fit.

This isn't a real precise method, but it does work. If it shrinks too much, file, ream, grind or sand it to the right size. If, on the other hand, yours is too tight to begin with, you will just have to file your barrel shank a little smaller or open up the tube diameter a little by grinding, filing, etc.

You can also just lightly heat the tube with a torch to expand it,

then insert the barrel while the tube is hot, When you insert the barrel into the receiver tube, you will need to index the barrel to locate the extractor groove in the right place. Install your barrel so that the extractor notch in the face of the barrel is about 1/8" above the bottom edge of the ejection port. This should leave adequate clearance to keep the ejected case from striking the receiver when being ejected from the gun.

Once the barrel is in the correct position, the barrel needs to be locked in place. I pinned my barrel in place by drilling a 5/16" hole through the receiver wall and about .100" into the barrel shank. Be sure you don't drill too deep and drill into the chamber.

I tapped in a tight-fitting pin and then cut it flush with the receiver and welded over it to permanently lock it in place. I then ground it flush to the receiver tube.

I also used the barrel shroud installation the further to lock the barrel in place. I made a ventilated barrel shroud out of a 7-inch piece of 1-inch by .035" wall tubing. The hole size and spacing can be to your preference. My tubing was a little undersized, so I had to reduce the barrel diameter slightly to get the shroud to slide over the barrel.

At the rear of the shroud, I drilled two 5/16" holes on opposite sides so I could plug weld the shroud to the barrel. The shroud was slid over the barrel till it was about 1/8" from the front of the receiver. This thin groove will be a weld groove. Before doing any welding, be sure your shroud is oriented correctly so the holes look good.

Also be sure the barrel is centered in the shroud. You don't want your holes to be running off at odd angles or have uneven gaps between the barrel and shroud. Plug weld the two holes to secure the shroud to the barrel. Use only enough weld heat to lightly penetrate the barrel and allow it to cool before you do the other hole to keep heat down.

Now weld the shroud to the front of the receiver tube. Weld in the groove and use enough weld heat only lightly to penetrate the barrel surface. Only weld about a half-inch at a time and allow for cooling before doing more welding. After welding, grind down all the welds smooth with the receiver and shroud.

The shroud is now attached to the barrel and to the receiver, so this is further locking the barrel to the receiver tube. This, along with the pressed-in pin, is more than adequate for a rimfire.

Next month (4/20 issue): Building the bolt.

will only cover the high points of the build process. I will give some general dimensions and procedures, but the builder will have to supplement the project with his own gunsmithing skills and knowledge.

As in any self-built project there will be builder-induced variations or mistakes that will have to be compensated for. If one part is made slightly out of spec. another part may have to be heavily modified to make the project work correctly. This is part of the "art" of gunsmithing. Hand-made parts by their very nature generally need to be hand-fitted for proper function.

The recess for the cartridge head must be precisely located in the bolt face. A lathe is best, but a drill press will do. Drilling to the proper depth is critical.

Ask the Gunsmith

By Reid Coffield

CRACK REPAIR

Q *I am trying to repair a stock, and there are a number of cracks that I cannot get to hold together no matter what type of glue I use. I get some degree of adhesion but once I apply any significant pressure the break will separate. Any suggestions? By the way, due to the location of the cracks I can not use pins or dowels as the wood is too thin!*

A This is not all that uncommon a problem. One of the techniques I use to help deal with cracks that will not stay together is to use a U- shaped metal inlay. I'll take a small nail, cut off the head, and bend it into a U shape. The dimensions of this clamp will be contingent upon the size and location of the crack.

I then use my Dremel tool with a small ball cutter to rout a matching U-shaped groove in the wood. This groove has to extend across the crack. Ideally, the two legs of the U will be parallel to the crack. The depth of the groove is generally determined by both the thickness of the wood where I am working and the diameter of the metal used to form the U clamp.

Once the groove is completed, I clean the U with alcohol, place it in the groove, and then cover it with bedding compound. Later when the bedding has hardened, I smooth it down to match the surface of the wood. Needless to say, this technique is normally used only inside the stock inletting, under a grip cap, or beneath the buttplate or recoil pad. Once it's done, you have both the strength of the bedding compound as well as the metal clamp to help hold the crack together.

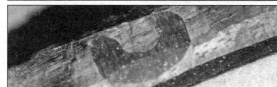

Coffield uses a small Dremel ball cutter to rout out a seat for a metal stock support. Note how the bedding applied over the U support has been cut down to match the inside surface of the stock.

ROSS BARREL THREAD

Q *I have an old junk Ross rifle that I am taking apart. I have not been able to get the barrel to turn off the receiver. There was a small screw that ran into the barrel threads but I removed that. Have you had any experience with these guns? Any idea as to why the barrel is so hard to remove?*

A I would be willing to bet that you are turning the action in the wrong direction! The Ross, unlike almost all other rifles, has a left-hand thread on the barrel. You have to turn the action in the opposite direction as you would a Mauser, Remington or Winchester centerfire rifle.

ORBITAL SANDER FOR STOCKS?

Q *Can you sand a stock with a hand-held orbital sander? My local gunsmith says you absolutely cannot do that. What is your opinion?*

A I hate to disagree with your gunsmith but you can sand a stock with an orbital sander. I have done it and I've seen others do it as well. With that said, there are some things you need to do in order to get a good sanding job with a hand-held orbital sander. First and most importantly you have to move the sander slower than molasses on a cold day. If you move the sander over the surface too fast you will get tiny little loops or swirl marks from the sanding grit. Again you need to move very, very slowly. An inch of movement per second is about right.

I've also found that no matter what type of orbital sander I use, I still end up needing to do some hand sanding to get into the nooks and crannies that I just can't reach with an electrical hand sander.

SHORTENING SCREWS

Q *O.K., I give up! How the heck do you cut a screw to shorten it without messing up the threads? Every time, and I mean every darn time I try to shorten a screw I end up with the threads at the end of the screw folded over, uneven, you name it! I need help!*

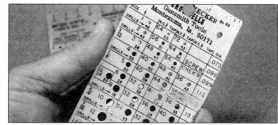

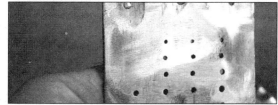

The Brownell Screw Chek'r has many uses aside from simply identifying screw thread sizes. After the initial trimming of the screw shank, the shank is ground down even with the Screw Chek'r plate, which protects the tip.

A It's actually pretty easy. The first thing you'll need to purchase is a Brownells Screw Chek'r. This is a metal plate with a number of threaded holes corresponding to the most commonly used screws.

All you'll need to do is run your screw through the plate in the appropriate hole. Extend the shank of the screw out far enough so you have the finished length you need when measured from the face of the rear of the Screw Chek'r to the underside of the screw head.

Now shorten the screw using a wire cutter, hacksaw, whatever. Following this, go over to your belt grinder or use a Dremel tool with an abrasive grinding point to smooth the cut end of the screw down to match the rear surface of the Screw Chek'r. Now turn the screw out of the Screw Chek'r and you'll find that the threads on the end of the shortened screw are perfect since they were protected by the Screw Chek'r.

By the way, the Screw Chek'r is available from Brownells for both U.S. and metric screw threads. It's a great way to quickly determine the thread size of a screw. It also has printed on it the tap size and clearance size for each screw thread. It's a handy little tool and one that I've had on my bench for over 30 years.

"DARRA" GUNS

Q *Do you have any idea what a Darra gun is? I thought I was fairly knowledgeable about firearms but I have never even heard of such a thing. What is it? I heard a fellow at a gun show mention this but before I could ask him about it he moved on and I lost him. At the time he was talking to another fellow he was holding a British Webley revolver.*

A Darra gun usually refers to a handmade copy of a firearm, generally British, made in northern Pakistan. More often than not guns like this are described as Khyber Pass guns. They are certainly interesting and are a testament to what you can do with simple hand tools and *a lot* of time! I would consider these as purely curios and would *never* even consider firing any of 'em.

H&R FRONT SIGHT

Q *How do I make an elevation adjustment on an old H&R Model 999 .22 revolver? I can adjust the rear sight for windage but I cannot for the life of me figure out how to handle elevation changes.*

A The rear sight on the H&R 999 is not adjustable for elevation. Elevation adjustments must be made to the front sight. Check the gun to make sure that it's empty, then look at the end of the muzzle. If you look carefully you will see a small slotted screw in a hole on the face of the barrel rib directly under the front sight. By turning this screw in or out you can raise or lower the front sight blade. Remember when adjusting the front sight that to raise the point of impact on your target you lower the sight. To lower the point of impact, you raise the front sight. This is just the opposite of what you do with a rear sight. ◉

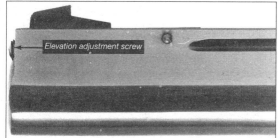

Elevation adjustments on the H&R Model 999 must be made by regulating the front sight. Remember to move the front sight blade in the opposite direction you want hits to appear on target.

BUILDING the SGN-22

By Steven Matthews

Part 2

The receiver is made and the barrel installed, now it's time to build the bolt.

With the receiver made, Matthews is ready to move on to the most challenging part of the project, the bolt. It will require very precise work for proper function.

In Part 1, (3/20 issue), Matthews acquired the parts, fabricated the receiver and installed the barrel. Now he moves on to the bolt.

False Flash Suppressor Fabrication and Installation

To make this project look more interesting, I decided to make a fake flash suppressor. Obviously a .22 Long Rifle doesn't need one, but it just makes the gun look better. Since it is non-functional, I just took a 2½-inch piece of 7/8" x 1/8" wall tubing and cut four slots and some grooves in to replicate the looks of a flash suppressor.

To install it, I removed the front sight and filed the sight base down so it was smooth with the rest of the ring on the barrel. It fit a little loose, so I stippled the barrel to tighten up the fit.

I then soldered the flash suppressor to the barrel with Brownells High Force 44 silver solder. High Force 44 is 96% tin and 4% silver and is much stronger than common lead/tin solders. When soldering it in place, I first tinned both parts and then slipped them together while the solder was still melted and then oriented the slots for proper looks.

Be sure to use good soldering techniques for a strong joint. The parts need to be clean and slightly roughened with sandpaper or files to expose bare steel; you can't solder on scale or any surface finishes. Also use the proper flux for good results. Be sure to remove any flux when done because many solder fluxes are corrosive and will cause rust if left on bare steel.

Bolt Fabrication

Now comes what many will consider the most difficult part of the project, making the bolt. Since I used a modified AR-15 fire control group, the SGN-22 bolt looks much like a scaled down AR-15 bolt carrier. This bolt will be made from a 4.8-inch piece of 3/4" 4130 rod.

While 4.8 inches is the finished size, make the piece about a half-inch longer to ease the building process and trim to length at the end of the build process. Making the bolt requires it be turned to the correct diameter, slotted for the hammer, a bolt face formed, a handle fitted, holes for the firing pin and spring type ejector formed and an extractor made and fitted.

This sounds like a lot of work, but it really isn't that bad if you take it slow and pay attention to what you are doing. The most important thing will be accurately setting up your work before doing any machining operations.

A small drill press and small lathe are required to make the bolt. You may be able to get by without the lathe if you hire out some of the lathe work and hand-make the small pins and parts. The first thing that needs to be done is to turn the bolt material to the correct size to fit the receiver. My receiver was .687", so I turned my bolt to .682" to have .005" running clearance.

If your tube size is different, then adjust your dimensions to maintain .005" to .007" running clearance. Be sure to face the ends squarely. You now need to make a recess in the bolt face to support the base of a .22 cal. cartridge. This recess will be .275" to .278" in diameter and .045" deep.

There are two ways to make this recess. The easiest is to form it on a lathe. If you don't have a lathe, there is a way you can do it on a drill press. Just to be sure it worked, I did it the drill press way and it worked fine, although it was not as accurate as the lathe method.

The drill press method was why I recommended starting with an overlong piece, since it is somewhat imprecise in getting the right recess depth. Start by center-punching a drill location in the very center of the bolt face. Set your bolt up in a drill press vise and align it precisely square with the table and quill travel.

Make sure it is tightly clamped in the vise so it doesn't move during drilling. At the drilling point, use a series of drills to drill the face to 17/64" (.265"). Start with a small drill and then

jump up a few sizes at a time to keep the hole centered. Large bits tend to wander if started in a small center-punched hole. Drill about 5/16" to 3/8" deep at the point.

Now you need to make this hole flat on the bottom. To do this you use a flat point 17/64" drill which you will make. You make this bit by grinding the point flat and then grinding a slight relief on the flutes of the drill so it will cut on the end. This drill bit will look like a two-flute mill with very large flutes.

Remove the barrel finish, then make a muzzle brake by drilling rows of holes in a length of tubing and filing out the remainder. Then silver-solder it to the barrel.

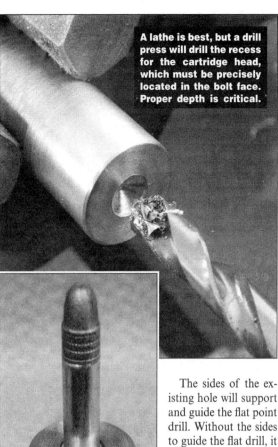

A lathe is best, but a drill press will drill the recess for the cartridge head, which must be precisely located in the bolt face. Proper depth is critical.

The sides of the existing hole will support and guide the flat point drill. Without the sides to guide the flat drill, it would run all over the place. Drill the hole so that all angled edges are gone and the bottom of the hole is flat and square. At this point you are probably wondering why I said to use a 17/64" (.265") drill to make a .275"-.278" hole. It is because this method is rather imprecise.

The flat bit, even though it is guided by the edges of the existing hole, may wander and cut a little oversize. When I did this job to verify that it worked, my bit cut about .010" oversize. If you started at full size (.275") and it runs oversize, then your finished hole would be about .285" and too large.

You can cut the hammer slot in the bolt by drilling a series of holes and filing out the spaces between them, but a milling machine makes the job a lot easier.

If you get lucky and your hole is still under the desired size, you can grind a slightly larger flat point drill to get up to the correct size. Drills known as letter sizes are available in many small increments between common fractional sizes. "I" and "J" drills are just a little larger than a 17/64 drill.

Get yourself a drill chart if you want to know all the decimal sizes of fractional, number and letter drills. Once you have the proper size hole in the bolt face, work the front down until you have a .045" deep recess. Be sure to keep the face square. Lightly chamfer the edges of the hole and the bolt.

The lathe method is way easier, but this method does work for those without a lathe. Once you have the recess in the bolt face to the correct depth, you can go ahead and trim the bolt to the finished length of 4.8 inches. This length is not critical and you can go slightly longer if you wish; just don't go any shorter.

Cut a slot in the bolt for hammer access to the firing pin. It will be about 3/8" wide by 2¼ inches long, starting at a point 1.970 inches from the front of the bolt face. This slot can be easily cut with a milling machine, but can also be cut with a drill press and hand tools.

This hand method can be done by drawing the outline of the slot on the bolt body and then drilling a series of holes through the bolt body to remove as much material as possible with the drill press. The remainder can then be removed with files or grinders. A Dremel tool with thin cutoff wheels works well for this job.

The rear of the slot can be left rounded, but the front needs to be square and flat. Once you have your bolt to length, the rear needs to be drilled out to 3/8" to allow access for drilling some holes later. Drill out the rear till the hole meets the 3/8" slot.

The holes for the firing pin and plunger-type ejector can now be drilled into the bolt face. In these operations it is vital that your workpiece is set up perfectly square to the drill quill travel. If it's not, you may be drilling in the right location, but as the bit drills 2" deep into the bolt, it will stray off line and your parts will be ruined.

Both these holes will be drilled from the front at one size and then counterbored from the rear to another size. The first hole that will be drilled is the firing pin hole. This hole will be at the top or 12 o'clock position in the recess and hammer slot in the bolt. Be sure you orient this hole correctly in reference to the hammer slot.

You want this hole to exit centered in the slot. The hole will be located right at the edge of the recess so that the firing pin will contact the rim of the .22 cartridge.

This hole will be sized at 5/64" (.078"). Drill this hole all the way through the bolt until it exits in the slot. Drill the hole with a very light feed, as small bits will deflect and run off course if pushed too hard.

If your hole is a little off-center in the slot, the bolt can still be used, but if it's off much more than about .015", you will have to make a new bolt, because there isn't much room to spare in the small .22 cal. bolt face. The holes for the firing pin and ejector are very close together, and you have to be sure they don't run into each other.

Next you will need to drill for the plunger-type ejector. This hole will be located at about the 4:30 location (as viewed from the front) in the bolt face recess. This hole will also be drilled right at the edge of the recess. It will be sized at .100" (#39 drill). Just like the firing pin hole, it will be drilled all the way through the bolt and must exit in the hammer slot in the same location as where it started.

Be sure your setup hasn't moved and you are still square with the quill travel. Correctly locating this hole is very important. Drill with a very light feed and use plenty of lubricant when drilling to keep the holes smooth inside.

Once these holes are drilled, the bolt must be turned over so we can enlarge the back side of the holes. Be sure to set it up squarely before doing any drilling, or the counterbore my run off course. Both holes will be drilled .125" (1/8"), but to different depths. You will need to use a very long bit for this operation. The firing pin hole needs to be drilled to a depth of 1.86". This will leave 1/16" of the .078" hole remaining for the firing pin point to extend through.

Drill a little and check depth often to prevent drilling all the way through and ruining your part. The ejector hole needs to be drilled to a depth of 1.6 inches, which will leave about 3/8" of the .100" hole. Once you have your holes to depth, polish the hole interiors for smooth operation (use lapping compound, sandpaper, small fine-cut file, etc).

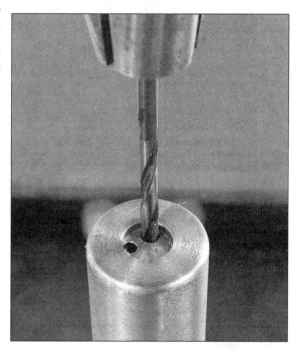

First drill the firing pin hole in the bolt face, then add the ejector hole. It is vital that the workpiece be held rigidly square to the drill before you start.

Then drill back the other direction to counterbore the holes. You'll need a very long, sharp bit for the job, and also carefully to modulate the drill feed rate.

Just modify an AR-15 firing pin, a much easier job than making one from scratch. It should protrude about .040", so shorten it to get that amount of protrusion.

Firing Pin and Ejector Fabrication

Now it's time to make the spring-loaded plunger-type ejector. This part needs to be made from good steel. Music wire, drill bit shanks, or high-quality Allen screws are good sources for improvised material. Overall length will be about 5/8".

To begin, turn this piece down to .122" so it will slide easily in the .125" hole. The front section now needs to be turned down to .098" so it will easily pass through the .100" hole.

This smaller diameter front section needs to be about .450" long. Once completed, this will result in about .075" extension out of the bolt face when it is installed. Once it's completed, chamfer the edges of the ejector and polish it up smooth. A small plug can be made from the same materials. It is simply a piece .120" diameter by 1/2" long.

A small spring passes between the front ejector and the rear plug. The spring I used was .115" diameter by 1⅛ inches long. Wire size was .018". This spring-loaded ejector assembly will be retained by the head of the firing pin when installed later. This assembly will also function as a firing pin return spring.

An AR-15 firing pin provides raw material for the firing pin. The first thing you need to do is to thin the shaft down to .120"-.122" so it will slide easily in the .125" firing pin hole. Now cut off the stub on the rear of the firing pin so that the collar that remains can be used as the new firing pin head.

Round this head so it looks like a round-head screw. If your hole in the bolt is centered correctly, you can leave the head full size but if your hole is off, you may have to reduce the diameter so it doesn't rub on the sides of the hammer slot.

At a point about 1.780" from the front of the firing pin head, thin the remainder of the shaft down to .075" so it will slide through the .078" firing pin hole in the bolt.

Once you have this thinned, install the pin in the bolt and push it all the way forward. You want about .040"-.045" protrusion for the firing pin. Trim the pin to obtain this amount. After you have the pin to length, round the point to duplicate the original firing pin profile. You don't want the pin to extend past the front of the bolt or it will strike the rear of the barrel and deform.

To retain the firing pin and set its travel, you will file a flat on the side of the pin. The width of this flat will determine how far the pin can extend and retract. A flat point 8-32 Allen screw through the bolt body and into this flat will be used to retain the pin. It will be threaded in just far enough to clear the flat on the pin and be retained by the edges.

File the flat so that the pin will extend fully and retract back into the bolt face about 1/32". The Allen set screw will be staked in place to keep it from loosening during use. Do not stake it in until the project is complete. Once all your parts are made, the bolt can be assembled and checked for smooth operation.

The ejector is installed in its hole, followed by the spring and plug. The firing pin is installed in its hole and the set screw will be tightened until it's just above the flat. Once installed, the head of the firing pin will retain the plug of the ejector assembly and the set screw will retain the firing pin. All parts need to operate smoothly and the spring tension should return all parts to their correct positions after being compressed.

Extractor Fabrication and Assembly

The groove for the extractor must be cut in the correct location and this will be determined by the position of the bolt in the receiver. Place your receiver solidly in a vise and orient the project with the top up.

Draw a line on the rear of the bolt straight up and down in reference to the slot in the bolt. This will allow you to see that the hammer slot is oriented top to bottom when the bolt is deep inside the receiver. Slide the bolt into the receiver until it is almost against the rear of the barrel.

Look into the rear of the receiver and align the mark so it is straight up and down, indicating the hammer slot is oriented correctly. Observe the location of the extractor relief cut in the face of the barrel and transfer that location to the bolt.

After the precise location is marked on the bolt, it can be removed and the slot can be formed in the bolt. Precisely locating this position is important because if the hammer slot is angled off to one side rather than being straight, the hammer will not clear the bolt when it operates.

Form a slot .125" wide and 1.25 inches long in the side of the bolt. This can be cut with a milling machine or by hand with a small hand grinder. Cut the slot to a depth even with the recess in the bolt face.

You now need to fabricate and fit an extractor. The steel for this part needs to be of high quality and capable of being heat-treated. Many types of tool steel are fine for this part. Two of the most common are known as 0-1 and 0-2.

These oil quenching steels are available from tool steel suppliers. If you live close to a tool and die shop you may be

able to buy a small piece of scrap tool steel from them for a couple bucks. This steel can be easily shaped while soft and then heat-treated to make it very hard. I used a 1¼ x 1/4 x 1/8 piece of 0-1 tool steel to make my extractor.

I made this part with nothing more than a hacksaw and some files. First, shape this material so that it will fit in the extractor slot. Shape the outside so the surface is just below the edge of the bolt.

Now mark the inside of this piece at a point that corresponds with the bottom of the recess in the bolt and then add another .045". Thin the portion of the extractor behind this line about .035" thinner than the front. This will form a hook that will be the front of the extractor.

A stub about 1/8" long can be left on the front to form the front edge of the extractor. Bevel this little stub so that it will slide over the cartridge rim. This extractor will have to pivot, so you will have to drill a hole at its center point to match a hole in the bolt body.

To drill this hole, you solidly clamp the extractor in its slot and drill through both the side of the bolt and the extractor at once. You will need to grind a flat spot on the side of the bolt for a starting point for the drill or it will walk off the side. The hole needs to be centered lengthwise and crosswise so that the hole will be centered on the extractor and not off to one side.

I drilled this hole with a #52 (.0635") drill so my pivot pin could be made from a shank of a 1/16" (.062") drill bit. Once the pin is installed, the extractor will not be able to pivot, since it is tight against the bolt body. You want to file its rear portion, behind the pivot point, to allow for adequate movement. Once you have the rear beveled and it moves far enough for the front to slide over the rim of a cartridge, you need to drill a shallow spring pocket for an extractor spring.

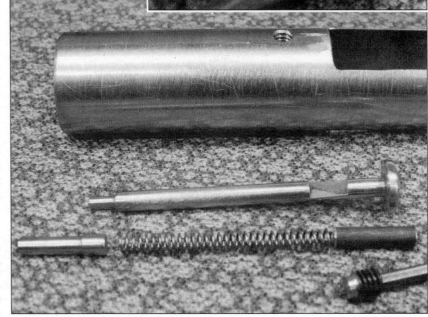

Firing pin and ejector assembly run parallel to each other so closely that the firing pin head can retain the ejector spring, which in turn returns the firing pin.

The extractor can be formed with nothing more than a hacksaw, files and a drill. The material should be tool steel for durability, and properly heat-treated.

Be sure you do not drill too deep into the firing pin passage. I used a short piece of .115" x .018" wire spring for this part. Cut it to a length that gives enough tension to solidly grip a .22 rim. Since you now have the extractor roughly formed, you can heat-treat it by heating red hot and quenching in oil. This is a very imprecise method, but is adequate for this project.

After quenching, clean off any scale and then place it in a 550° oven for one hour to temper the steel. After heat-treating, any additional shaping will have to be done with small grinding wheels. Final shaping will be done after the bolt is aligned in the receiver by the bolt handle.

Locating the Bolt Handle and Handle Slot

The position of the bolt handle, handle slot and extractor all interact and need to be precisely located to work correctly. The bolt handle for the SGN-22 will be 7/32" (.218") in diameter. You need to cut a 3-inch long by .220" wide slot in the side of the receiver. This slot will be overlong for clearance on both ends. The width needs to be very close to the handle size, since the handle will be the only thing aligning the bolt in the receiver.

Cut this slot in the side of the receiver starting 2½ inches back from the rear edge of the ejection port. The exact location of this slot around the circumference of the tube can be to your preference, but I recommend about 90° from top. I went about 60° and my handle barely cleared my scope base.

Once you have the slot cut and deburred, install the bolt and push it all the way forward. The angled extractor tip should enter into the extractor relief cut in the rear of the barrel. If it doesn't slide in easily, reshape the end so it does. With the bolt now aligned in its correct position, you can mark the rear of the bolt body for the handle hole.

The 7/32" hole for the handle must be precisely centered in the slot to maintain the correct positioning of the extractor when it is all the way forward. If the handle location is off, the extractor will not align with the relief slot in the barrel and smash into the barrel and probably break.

Remove the bolt and drill the hole, making sure that it is drilled squarely so that when it extends out the other side it is centered. After you have this hole drilled, you can use the shank of a 7/32" drill as a temporary handle and install the bolt and check for proper alignment. You will be setting bolt stroke length later.

Bolt Handle Fabrication and Fitting

We want a bolt handle that is easy to make and also easy to install and remove. We will fabricate a handle with a 7/32" shank and a 1/4" head. This will look something like a fat nail. A recess in the bolt body will allow the head to be flush.

The extractor will pivot on a pin in the side of the bolt. A small coil spring at the rear will tension it to retain the cartridge rim. Drill through bolt and extractor.

Use a 1/4" grade 5 bolt shank for raw material for this part. I made my handle 2⅛" long but you can make yours to your liking. Turn the bolt shank down to 7/32"(.218") but leave about 3/32" of 1/4" material for the head. Bevel the sides of the head. On the bolt body counterbore the left side of the 7/32" hole to allow the head of the handle to be below the edges of the bolt. This will allow the handle to fit in the bolt with no fasteners since it will be retained in place by the receiver wall. To allow the handle to be removed, a 5/16" hole will be drilled into the left side of the receiver at the end of the handle travel. In use, the bolt will not go far enough back to reach this hole and fall out. The only time the hole will align with the handle will be during disassembly.

Next month (5/20): Building the fire control assembly and stock. ◉

Ask the Gunsmith

By Reid Coffield

CONTROLLING SHOP DIRT

Q *My shop is pretty small at this point. My problem has to do with dirt and dust. My buffers, grinders, saws, etc., generate a lot of mess and this gets into and on everything. I know it is beginning to turn away some customers. Have you had this problem and how did you handle it?*

A One of the problems inherent in a small shop is dirt and dust. Any time you use a buffer, a saw, or sand a piece of wood, you'll get dust everywhere. Ideally, you would want to have a "dirty room." This is a separate room in which you have all the equipment that generates major messes.

I've been fortunate in a couple of shops where I've worked in the past where there was a designated dirty room that housed all the buffers, grinders, and saws. This helped eliminate most dust and dirt problems.

On the other hand, I've also worked in several very small shops. Currently, my shop is only about 20x18 and, as you can imagine, crammed with equipment. In order to contain dust and dirt, I make extensive use of my shop vac by attaching it directly to machines that generate dust, like my disk sander or bandsaw when they are in use.

Admittedly, this does take time, but it helps to control dust and dirt. Also, I make it a point to sweep and dust my shop daily and not allow dirt and crud to build up.

Finally, I try to avoid having any open storage shelves. Open shelving just collects dirt and makes it harder to clean. Instead, I make extensive use of closed cabinets, both floor and wall mounted. These provide needed storage space and help to keep the contents clean and dust free.

SAVAGE 99 BARREL THREADS

Q *I have a Savage Model 99 rifle that I want to have rebarreled. The local gunsmith says that the barrel threads are such that he cannot cut them. Is there something special about the Savage 99 barrel threads?*

A Nope. The Savage 99 uses a thread that is 12 square threads per inch with a major diameter of .896". I bet the problem is the gunsmith rather than the gun. Lots of folks don't like to cut square threads. It's a bit more challenging and it'll require a special threading tool. My advice would be to find a different gunsmith.

RAISING RIB DENTS

Q *I am having problems raising dents in shotgun ribs. No matter what I do, I still end up with either a wavy rib or dents in the sides or edges of the rib. How do you do it?*

Coffield has used this Murray Vent Rib Tool for years quickly and easily to straighten dented or crushed vented shotgun ribs without twisting the rib or leaving it wavy.

A While you didn't describe the technique you are using, I would be willing to bet that you're trying to use wedges or the tip of a screwdriver to bend up or raise the dented rib. I tried doing it that way for years and, like you, I never had the results I wanted. Now days I use a Murray's Vent Rib Tool made by Murray Gunsmithing, 12696 FM 2127, Dept. SGN, Bowie, TX 76230, telephone 940-928-0002. This tool, which sells for about $40, uses a screw attached to two hooks to raise the rib. The hooks extend under the sides of the rib at the point of the dent. As the screw is turned in, it raises the hooks and pulls out the dent. It's simple, effective and so much easier to use than anything else I've ever tried. ◉

BUILDING the SGN-22

By Steven Matthews

Part 3

The receiver, barrel and bolt are ready to go. Now Matthews builds the fire control unit.

A milling machine makes a project like the SGN-22 a lot easier, but Matthews says you can build it with simple tools if you have patience and a very steady hand.

In Part 2, (4/20 issue), Matthews made the bolt and fitted it to the receiver tube. This time, he puts together the fire control assembly.

Bolt Handle Fabrication and Fitting

The bolt handle is easy to make and also easy to install and remove. It has a 7/32" shank and a 1/4" head. This will look something like a fat nail. A recess in the bolt body will allow the head to be flush. Use a 1/4" Grade 5 bolt shank for raw material for this part. I made my handle 2⅛" long but you can make yours to your liking.

Turn the bolt shank down to 7/32" (.218") but leave about 3/32" of 1/4" material for the head. Bevel the sides of the head. On the bolt body, counterbore the left side of the 7/32" hole to allow the head of the handle to be below the edges of the bolt. This will allow the handle to fit in the bolt with no fasteners, since it will be retained in place by the receiver wall.

To allow handle removal, drill a 5/16" hole into the left side of the receiver at the end of the handle travel. In use, the bolt will not go far enough back to reach this hole and fall out. The only time the hole will align with the handle will be during disassembly.

Trigger Housing Fabrication and Fire Control Group Fitting

Our SGN-22 will feature a modified AR-15 fire control group fitted in a self-made housing. The trigger housing will be made from a piece of common 3/4 x 1½ x 1/16 or 3/32" wall mild steel rectangular tubing that is available from structural steel suppliers. Start with a piece 6 inches long.

Cut off one of the 3/4" sides to form a channel, but leave as much of the long sides on as possible. File the edges straight, flat and square, so it will fit up against the receiver tube with no gaps. Also, be sure the ends are cut square. If the sides bow in after removing the top, bend them out until they are straight.

Now locate the trigger pin, hammer pin and safety lever holes. For testing purposes, I used stock AR-15 hammer and trigger pins, but once the gun is complete, a set of shorter pins will need to be made to fit the narrow SGN-22 trigger housing.

The exact location of these holes is vital for proper trigger group function. You also must completely understand how all these parts interact. I recommend making a simple test fixture that will allow you to study the function of the parts. Just take a thick piece of 3x3 material and drill two 5/32" holes on the proper locations. Drill one hole about 1 inch in and 1 inch up from the bottom. This will be the trigger pin hole.

At a point (center to center) .843" in front and .314" above the trigger pin hole, drill another 5/32" hole for a hammer pin location.

Once the fixture is made, you can place your hammer and trigger (with disconnector installed) on the pins in the fixture and observe how the parts interact. You will see why the holes need to be precisely located for proper functioning.

The first 5/32" pin hole to be drilled in the trigger housing will be the trigger pin. It will be located .325" up from the outside bottom of the housing and 4³⁄₁₆ inches back from the front. When you locate these locations, do so on both sides and drill from each side. If you drill through from one side, the

small bit may wander off location when it contacts the other side since the inside is not center-punched for a starting point.

These holes need to be squarely drilled so the pins and parts are not installed at slight angles. Always center-punch your hole locations. The 5/32" hammer pin hole will be located .314" above and .843" (center to center) in front of the trigger pin.

A safety lever hole can also be located and drilled. It is .375" in diameter. It is located 1.125 inches behind and .220" above the trigger pin hole (center to center). Cut an opening for the trigger in the bottom of the housing. After determining the location, just drill two holes and file out the remainder.

The bolt handle will fit in the rear of the bolt. Its head will fit in a recess and the inside wall of the receiver tube will retain the handle in place in the bolt.

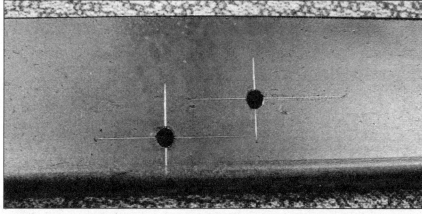

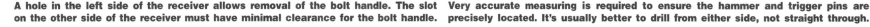

A hole in the left side of the receiver allows removal of the bolt handle. The slot on the other side of the receiver must have minimal clearance for the bolt handle.

Very accurate measuring is required to ensure the hammer and trigger pins are precisely located. It's usually better to drill from either side, not straight through.

Since the internal width of the SGN-22 is narrower than an AR-15 receiver, the hammer, trigger and safety will need to be narrowed. Thin the hammer and trigger down evenly on both sides until they fit into the housing. The safety lever must be shortened on the round end so it is flush with the outside of the housing.

This will require that the groove in the center of the safety that blocks or releases the trigger be widened as well. The safety lever will also need a thin groove cut in the shank to allow an e-clip to retain the lever in the housing.

Cut this groove even with the inside edge of the housing. A slight bend on the e-clip will tension the lever enough to allow it to remain in the proper position during use. Install the trigger, trigger spring, disconnector and spring into the housing.

The safety can be installed next. Lock it in place with an e-clip. Check to verify that the safety blocks the trigger when applied (safety horizontal) and releases the trigger when on fire (vertical).

Before installing the hammer, the hammer spring must be modified. To reduce the width, unwind one coil on each side of the spring and then cut the excess off to the original length. The hammer will need to be shortened to fit the SGN-22 receiver, but this will be done later.

Install the hammer and its spring. The legs of the hammer spring will rest on the edges of the trigger. After the parts are installed, check to see that they function correctly. The hammer should cock and be held by the trigger. The disconnector should catch the hammer when it recocks if the trigger is kept pulled. When you release the trigger, the disconnector should let the hammer go and it should then be caught by the trigger.

Check the safety to see if it works right. Note that on the AR-15 trigger design, depending on the tolerances and fit of your parts, you may not be able to apply the safety if the hammer is not cocked. This is normal. Depending on how you fit your parts, some hand fitting or tuning may be required to get things working right.

Once you have this part done, you can fit an AR-15 grip to the housing. You need to fabricate a 3/8" wide steel block with an angled bottom to fit in the grip and then weld the block to the housing. The angle on the bottom of the block is 30° or 60°, depending on which direction you measure.

A 1/4 x 20 hole needs to be tapped in the bottom to attach the grip. After the grip is attached, you will need to fill in the open back of the trigger housing. I welded in a piece of 1/4" pipe to fill in the gap and then contoured it smooth with the housing. It was trimmed to length and contoured to fit evenly against the 1-inch receiver.

To make this project look more interesting, I made a false magazine out of a block of aluminum and attached it to the front of the housing with screws. The shape and material can be whatever you like, since it is just for looks. Just be sure that any attaching screws don't interfere with the lug that will later be installed at the front of the housing. You can also fabricate a trigger guard and attach it between the magazine and grip. I formed mine out of 1/4 x 1/8" flat stock and welded in place.

A piece of quarter-inch pipe welded into the rear of the trigger housing and properly contoured makes a secure mounting point for the plastic AR-15 pistol grip.

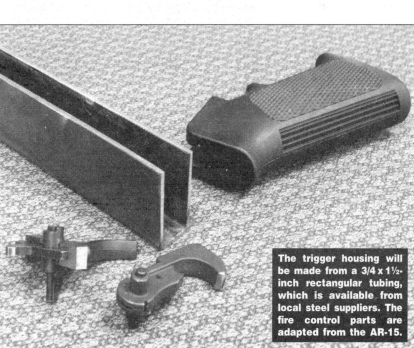

The trigger housing will be made from a 3/4 x 1½-inch rectangular tubing, which is available from local steel suppliers. The fire control parts are adapted from the AR-15.

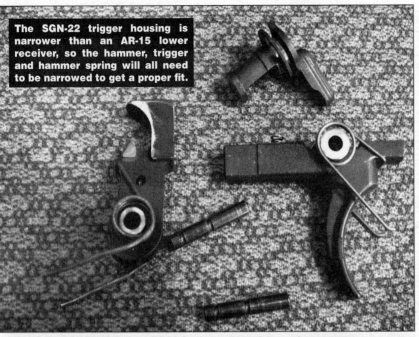

The SGN-22 trigger housing is narrower than an AR-15 lower receiver, so the hammer, trigger and hammer spring will all need to be narrowed to get a proper fit.

Small slotted screws make satisfactory stops for the safety lever. A modified e-clip will tension the lever enough to hold it in position inside the trigger housing.

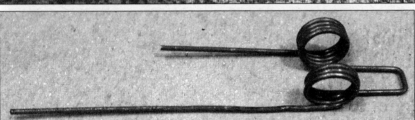

Trigger Housing Locating and Mounting

The partially completed trigger housing must now be fitted to the receiver. The hammer must also be shortened to fit the 1-inch receiver tube. Properly locating the housing is critical for proper functioning. An opening for the hammer to access the bolt and firing pin must be cut in the bottom of the receiver. It must be aligned with the hammer slot in the bolt when it is in the closed position.

I made my opening 1/2" wide and 2½ inches long. The front-to-back location can be determined by transferring measurements from bolt to receiver. The edges of this opening should extend a little past the edges of the slot in the bolt. The location around the circumference of the receiver tube can best be determined by cutting a small starter slot in the approximate location and then opening up the slot to keep it centered with the hammer slot in the bolt.

The location of this opening is important because if it's wrong, the hammer won't be able to access the slot in the bolt without rubbing on the edges. The opening must also be positioned so that when the trigger housing is mounted, it is straight on the receiver and not running off at some odd angle.

To secure the trigger housing to the receiver, fabricate a square lug and weld it to the receiver. The width of this lug should be sized for a snug fit in the housing and the top should be contoured to fit the round receiver. Initially, make it overlong so it can trimmed for a good fit. This lug cannot be welded in place until you determine the correct position for the trigger housing.

An easy-to-make fitting fixture will aid in hand-fitting the housing and trimming the hammer. Just take a piece of receiver tube material and cut two openings sized like the opening that was cut in the bottom of the receiver. Cut one on the bottom and the other on the top. With the openings, you will be able to see inside the tube and determine proper fit.

The first thing is to shorten the AR-15 hammer so it is short enough not to hit the inside of the receiver tube when it moves. You want to shorten it just enough that when it is in the 90° position (straight up), it just clears the receiver tube. Once you have it shortened, round the top over so that it the bolt can slide over it easily.

By using this test fixture, you will be able to see how the hammer is cocked by the reciprocating bolt. The hammer and trigger housing has to be sized so that the hammer cocks when pushed back by the bolt. It must also allow the hammer to go past the front edge of the hammer slot in the bolt without binding because the front part of the bolt will be over the hammer when the bolt is at its rearmost position.

It also has to push the hammer far enough to be caught by the disconnector when the trigger is still being pulled. To obtain the right fit, you may have to shorten the height of the housing or hammer. Considerable hand-fitting will be required to get everything just right. Once you get the trigger housing sized right for proper functioning on the test fixture, the housing can be transferred to the actual receiver.

When the housing is being located, the bolt needs to be completely assembled and installed all the way forward in the receiver. To determine the correct front-to-back positioning of the housing on the receiver, the hammer must be in the straight up (90°) position, just as it would be when the hammer strikes the firing pin.

The narrowed trigger and hammer need correspondingly shorter pins that won't stick out the sides of the trigger housing in unsightly fashion. These you can make.

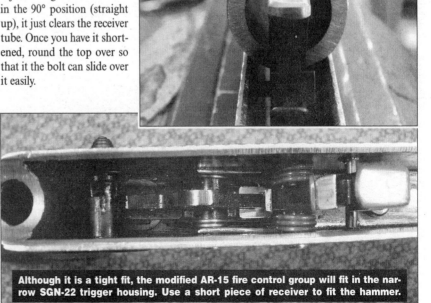

Although it is a tight fit, the modified AR-15 fire control group will fit in the narrow SGN-22 trigger housing. Use a short piece of receiver to fit the hammer.

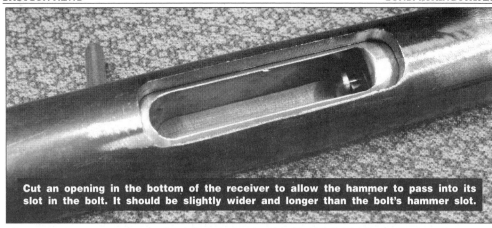

Cut an opening in the bottom of the receiver to allow the hammer to pass into its slot in the bolt. It should be slightly wider and longer than the bolt's hammer slot.

As the magazine box is only for looks, you can make it out of anything you like. An aluminum block is fine, as is plastic or even wood. You can use your imagination.

Lock the hammer in this position any way you want. I clamped the side of housing with a C-clamp to make the hammer tight. With the hammer locked in position, you want the housing to be located so that the straight hammer just contacts the firing pin head. Mark this location on the receiver tube. The square lug can now be fitted and welded in place on the tube.

On my project the lug went just below the barrel shank. Install the lug to maintain the proper housing location. Weld it to the receiver with as little weld heat as possible to prevent warping but still make a good weld.

After welding in place, smooth up the welds and trim the height of the lug to allow the housing to slide over it. The housing will be attached to this lug with 10-32 button head screws, but do not install them until all fitting is done.

With the trigger housing secured in place with C-clamps, check for proper functioning. The bolt should cock the hammer without binding as it is pulled rearward, it needs to be pushed back far enough to catch both the trigger and disconnector and not bind.

The part in front of the bolt slot also has to be able to pass over the hammer about 1/2" without binding. If things don't work right, correct them now before going any further. If you get everything fitted right, you can then drill and tap the 10-32 holes in the lug to attach the housing. Be sure to locate the mounting holes so the housing stays tight against the receiver.

A small lug will need to be made and attached to the rear of the trigger housing. Contour the top to the shape of the receiver tube. Drill a hole through the lug and thread a 10-32 button head screw into the receiver tube to secure the rear of the housing. The screw will have to be sized so that it doesn't extend past the inner wall of the receiver. A piece of the stock assembly will also attach here, so you may want to wait until that part is made before you cut a screw to length.

Trigger and Hammer Pin Fabrication

While the stock hammer and trigger pins were used for testing purposes they are too long for the narrow SGN-22 trigger housing. Once you have all the fire control group work complete, you need to make some pins for the project. Raw material for these pins can be the shanks of small high grade Allen screws.

The hammer pin is very easy to make. Just make a pin the correct diameter and length and form a shallow groove in the center. This groove will interlock with a small spring that is inside the hammer to keep it from coming out.

The trigger pin needs to have a head on one end and a small groove on the other end for an e-clip that will retain the pin in the receiver. They are easily made on a lathe or even on a drill press with a file.

Stock, Buttplate and Recoil Pad Fabrication and Assembly

A buttplate can now be fabricated for the skeletonized stock. A 1½ x 5 x 3/16" piece of steel flat stock will be used to form a buttplate. The top needs to have a 1-inch hole drilled in it so it will slide over the 1-inch receiver tube. The shape of the buttplate can be whatever suits you. I made mine somewhat like a tapered oval. If you want a rubber recoil pad, obtain one and form it to fit the buttplate.

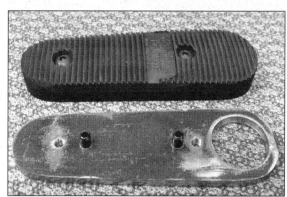

Matthews selected a Pachmayr RP-250 recoil pad and shaped the steel buttplate to fit it. A 1-inch hole in the top lets it slide over the receiver tube for welding.

Grind it to match the buttplate before you install the buttplate to the receiver. The recoil pad will need to be removable since the bolt passes through the rear of the receiver tube. Before you weld the buttplate to the tube, the latter will need to be trimmed to the length you prefer. I went with a length of pull (distance from the trigger to the rear of the recoil pad) of 13½ inches.

Be sure your buttplate is oriented correctly before welding in place. You don't want the buttplate to look crooked compared to the rest of the gun. I welded my plate on from the rear so I wouldn't have weld showing. To create the skeletonized buttstock, I installed a 1/2 x 3/16 piece of flat steel stock between the buttplate and the rear of the trigger housing. It was welded on at the buttplate and attached at the front with the screw through the lug on the rear of the housing.

Next month (6/20 issue): finishing the SGN-22

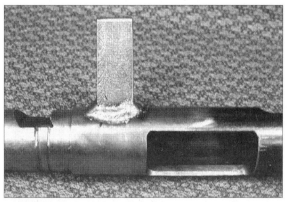

Weld a rectangular lug to the bottom of the receiver for attaching the trigger housing. When welding on the receiver tube, use methods that reduce heat distortion.

Weld a small lug to the back of the trigger housing so that it can be fixed to the receiver using a 10-32 hex socket screw. The front will be fixed by a cross screw.

There's no legal requirement for it, but the BATFE recommends stamping homemade firearms with a serial number and the maker's address. It might save you some trouble.

BUILDING the SGN-22

By Steven Matthews

Part 4

The receiver, bolt and fire control are complete; now Matthews finishes this economical self-ejecting rimfire.

Matthews shows the SGN-22 and a scale Model 1917 machine gun to an appreciative crowd at the Knob Creek Machine Gun Shoot. The SGN-22 actually got more attention!

In Part 3, (5/20 issue), Matthews fabricated the fire control assembly. Now he puts on the finishing touches.

RECOIL/BUFFER ASSEMBLY FABRICATION AND FITTING

This assembly will allow the bolt to cycle and also set the bolt stroke length. I started by making a plunger that would rest against the rear of the bolt. A reduced diameter section of this plunger will allow a spring to slide over it. It will also be sized to prevent the recoil spring from being completely compressed during recoil.

I made the plunger out of a piece of 3/4" 6061 aluminum. This common grade of aluminum should be available locally. I bought a piece of scrap at the recyclers for a buck or so.

The head of the plunger was sized at .680" and the thinner shank was sized at .550". Overall length was 3 1/4 inches and the head was 3/4" long. Both ends were slightly beveled to prevent binding.

A spring slightly smaller than 11/16" (.687") outside diameter will be needed. Length should be about 6 inches with a wire size of about .045"-.047". Coil spacing should be 3-4 coils per inch. I couldn't find one locally and didn't want to order a single spring from a hardware supplier, so I made my own.

It's easy to make a spring on a lathe if you have a good-sized lathe with thread cutting abilities. For spring material I used a 36-inch piece of .047" music wire (sometime called spring wire by hobbyists) that was available at a local hobby shop. I set my lathe up for four threads per inch at the lowest speed (about 50-60 rpm). I then installed a 5/16" square of steel with a 1/16" hole in it to serve as a guide in the tool holder.

I wrapped the wire around a rod with the lathe to get a four coil-per-inch spring. Drill a small hole in the rod to

secure the end of the wire. Spring-back means the size rod needed to get the correct diameter spring will vary depending on how tight you pull on the wire while it is winding and the temper and diameter of your wire stock.

I used a 7/16" rod and pulled very hard on the end of the wire while it was winding. I ended up with a spring a little over 6 inches long and about .650" diameter, which was just right for this project. The ends were then squared up.

To relieve stresses and set this shape, the spring was baked in a 550° oven for one hour. One end of the spring will slide over the end of the plunger and the other will bear against a 11/16" diameter neoprene disc that will serve as a buffer.

This disc can be made from a piece of 1/4" neoprene shoe sole available at shoe repair shops. Make and insert a plug into the receiver. This plug will be locked in place with a bolt and will set the length of bolt travel.

This plug will be made from common steel and will be sized at .685" x 1½ inches. With the bolt, plunger, spring, and neoprene disc in the receiver, install the plug and set it at a distance that will allow for 2 inches of bolt travel before the plunger bottoms out.

Measure in from the back of the receiver to get a dimension for the plug depth. At the halfway point on the plug (plug depth plus 3/4")

and centered on the receiver, drill a 1/8" hole through the receiver wall and plug. Be sure the plug stays in position while you are drilling.

Next, increase the drill size to a #3 drill bit and drill through again. Drilling in steps will help keep the hole locations right while drilling. Now remove the plug and increase the hole size in the plug to 1/4", making sure the larger hole follows the path of the original hole.

The hole in the top of the receiver wall needs to be increased in size also. The top hole needs to be sized and drilled for the head diameter of the 1/4"-28 Allen head screw that will be used for a locking screw. The #3 sized bottom hole needs to be tapped with a 1/4"-28 tap.

When selecting a bolt for this part, use a bolt with as much smooth shank as possible. Trim the bolt so that it doesn't extend too far out of the bottom of the receiver when installed.

A plunger, spring, neoprene buffer disc and end plug with screw comprise the recoil assembly of the SGN-22. The spring can be purchased or homemade on a lathe.

A hex socket screw holds the end cap in position in the receiver tube. Countersink its head into the tube to transfer recoil force to a larger area of the receiver.

After making this plug, reinstall all the parts (bolt, plunger, spring, neoprene disc and plug) and lock the plug in place with the screw. You should be able to cycle the bolt under spring tension. It must move smoothly and if it doesn't, correct any problems.

Pull the bolt all the way to the rear, which should be about 2 inches of travel. At the maximum travel point under or above the handle, cut a small vertical slot for a bolt hold-open feature. This small slot needs to be sized for the handle diameter and angled slightly forward. This feature will allow the user to keep the bolt open for easy loading.

SIGHTS

Sights for the SGN-22 can be open sights, scopes or one of the modern dot types. To keep costs down, I decided to use one of the inexpensive compact scopes with extension rings to raise the scope to a comfortable height. By using the Weaver scope base specification sheet available on the Brownells website, I found that a #81 one-piece base was the closest I could get for a 1-inch receiver.

This base is actually sized for a .946" receiver, but was close enough for this project. This base has a taper; one end is about .020" higher than the other. This causes the scope to point slightly higher or lower than if it was completely flat. It needs to be installed in the right direction to get the scope as close to point of impact as possible before adjusting the scope.

Since I was using a very short scope, I only needed about 2/3 of the base, so I cut it to length. The rings and scope were then mounted on the base and lightly tightened. I secured the rifle in a vise for a solid hold and bore-sighted the gun at a distant (about 100 yards away) object.

I placed the scope assembly on the receiver about where it was going to be mounted and I looked through the scope to see how far from the bore-sight view the scope was pointed. I then reversed the base and checked again. I chose the direction that resulted in the closest match.

I found that welding the lug to the receiver tube may have warped the receiver tube a bit and actually caused the barrel to point slightly down. This angled/tapered base can help compensate for this misalignment. The receiver wall of the SGN-22 is sufficiently thick to allow #6-48 scope mounting screws. You may have to add a screw hole in the base if you cut down the base like I did. Decide where you want your base and locate the holes for the screws.

Drill to the correct size (#31) for a #6-48 screws. #6-48 screws are pretty much the industry standard for scope mounting. If you don't have a #6-48 tap, they are available from Brownells. In fact Brownells offers a very useful tapping set (Brownells Tap and Drill Set #2) that is especially useful for the hobbyist gunsmith. I bought mine years ago and have used it on dozens of jobs.

Trim the screws so they don't enter the interior of the receiver. I used the remaining piece of the #81 base to add a mounting point on the bottom of the barrel shroud for a Falcon Ergo-Grip brand vertical fore grip that I found in my parts drawer. Since the shroud tube has thin walls, I riveted it in place with four steel pop rivets rather than using screws.

FINAL FUNCTION TESTING

Since this is a single-shot firearm, final testing should be easy. Even though you should have verified that all subassemblies worked correctly as they were made, there may still be some minor issues to be resolved when they are combined.

For final testing you need a few empty .22 Long Rifle cases. Just take a few and pull out the bullets with a pair of pliers and dump the powder, being careful not to deform the cases. Completely assemble the gun and then open the action and insert an *empty* case. Close the bolt. The extractor should easily slide over the cartridge rim.

If it doesn't, the point of the extractor may need to be reshaped slightly or polished. If this part works OK, then pull the bolt to the rear. The cartridge should pull out of the chamber and be held securely on the bolt face until the front edge of the case clears the barrel, at which time the spring-loaded ejector should flip the case out of the firearm.

If the extractor doesn't pull the case out, you may need to reshape it or change spring tension. Rimfire extractors are notoriously finicky because of the small rim and its rounded shape, so don't be surprised if you need to do some fine-tuning.

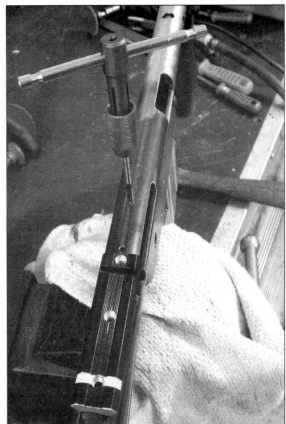

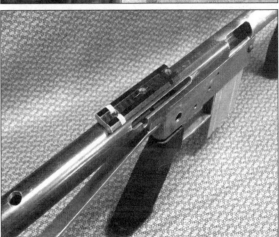

The receiver tube is plenty thick enough for tapping. Matthews found a shortened Weaver No. 81 base was the right size; it needed an extra slot cut for the rear scope ring.

When I made mine, it worked OK on some brands, but not others. It took a couple hours of fine tuning to get it just right for all brands of .22 ammo. When you get things right, you can check firing pin operation. Load an *empty* case in the chamber and close the bolt.

There is still priming compound in the cases so point the gun in a safe direction and pull the trigger. The hammer should strike the firing pin with enough force to set off the primer and you should get a little pop as it goes off.

If it doesn't, check for dragging parts or sluggish operation of fire control parts. If you did things right, you should get a good firing pin strike on the cartridge rim and be able to move on to live-fire testing.

I rounded up several brands of ammo and headed off to my home range. I opened the action and inserted a round in the chamber. I closed the bolt, and when I pulled the trigger it went "bang" just like it was supposed to. The empty was ejected a couple feet out of the gun.

I had no live-fire failures of any kind. I attributed this to the fact that as I built each assembly I verified that it worked correctly before going on to other parts of the project. When building guns, attention to small details goes a long way towards a successful project.

Cutting a bolt hold-open notch in the receiver tube will make it a lot easier to load the SGN-22. It can be located on the top or bottom of the operating handle groove.

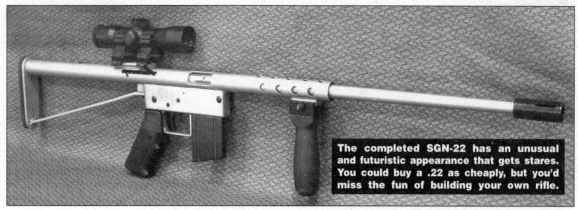

The completed SGN-22 has an unusual and futuristic appearance that gets stares. You could buy a .22 as cheaply, but you'd miss the fun of building your own rifle.

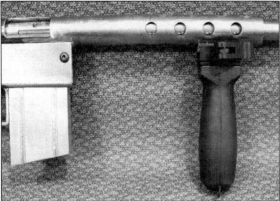

The cut-off piece of Weaver base was perfect for attaching to the front end of the receiver tube as a support for a vertical foregrip. Matthews riveted it in place.

OPTIONAL FEATURES AND PROCEDURES

Before advancing to final finishing, I want to throw a couple ideas out to builders. To make this project as easy as possible I deleted several things that some may want to incorporate into the project. One thing that I added was a crosspin in the trigger housing to limit hammer overtravel. This pin will keep the hammer from dropping down into the trigger housing when the trigger housing is separated from the receiver if the trigger is pulled.

Due to the small size of the receiver, the hammer is hard to reach if it drops into it. I located this pin so the hammer could only go past 90° by about another 30°.

Another feature I did not add but you may choose to add is an automatic bolt hold-open device so that you don't have to re-open the bolt for loading after the round has fired and ejected.

A simple spring-loaded pin extending up from the trigger housing and through the receiver wall in front of the bolt face after it moves all the way rearward would make using the gun more convenient.

A small lever on the pin assembly could be made to release the bolt. I would, however, highly recommend not allowing the bolt to slam shut on a loaded round. I would recommend closing the bolt slowly just as one would on a bolt-action rifle for safety concerns.

I didn't heat-treat the bolt. Although 4130 steel is not as hardenable as some steels, it can be hardened somewhat. Heat-treating the bolt would increase durability but I was concerned that novice builders would put extensive amounts of work into making the bolt and then possibly ruin it while heat treating it.

If you want to attempt heat treating the bolt, get a machinist book and study the procedure. One could pay a tool and die shop to do this but it wouldn't be cheap and would drive up project cost.

FINAL FINISHING

After you get everything functioning correctly, you can apply the finish of your choice. Smooth up all scratches, welds or any other undesirable features. It's your project, and you have the option of making it look like some barnyard blacksmith cobbled it together or making it look like a skilled craftsman built it.

A wide range of finishing options are available for the home gunsmith. On the low end of the cost scale is common spray paint. It is cheap and can be made to look good but it won't be very durable. There are some more expensive "spray paint" type finishes such as Brownells Aluma-Hyde II that can be applied straight out of an aerosol can that are very good options to common spray paint.

If you did an especially good job you may go for bluing, but be warned this traditional finish will not hide any surface defects. Parkerizing would be another option. Bluing and Parkerizing, however, are not inexpensive unless you have the equipment to do the process yourself.

One popular option for home gunsmiths is Lauer Custom Weaponry's DuraCoat sprayed-on finish. It is a relatively inexpensive product and is easily applied by those with a small air compressor and an airbrush. I however chose to apply my favorite finish, Brownells GunKote. Brownells GunKote is a sprayed-on polymer finish that is baked on at 300°.

The finish is *extremely* durable and it can easily be applied with an airbrush or small automotive spray gun. GunKote is available in many colors and even available in aerosol cans, but the aerosol version has a reputation of not being as durable or as easy to use as the conventionally sprayed version according to internet "experts."

I have always used the conventional liquid sprayed-on version and have never been disappointed in its performance. GunKote can be textured from a rough finish like coarse Parkerizing or sprayed as smooth as any paint depending on your application methods.

To apply Brownells GunKote, you abrasive blast, clean, spray and bake. When it comes out of the oven and cools, it's ready to go; no wait for a full cure like some finishes. The SGN -22 featured in the pictures was coated with the color of "brushed stainless steel" with "matte black" highlights.

When the project was complete, I was very impressed with the results. It looked very good and was a perfect companion to the larger SGN-9. With today's high ammo prices .22s are a lot more economical to shoot. Although .22 Long Rifle cartridges are the least expensive, this project will also handle .22 CB, .22 BB, .22 Short, and .22 Long.

While the cost to make this project is comparable to buying a used .22, there is a certain amount of pride in knowing you made you own unique gun. If this sounds like your kind of project why not give it a try? ◎

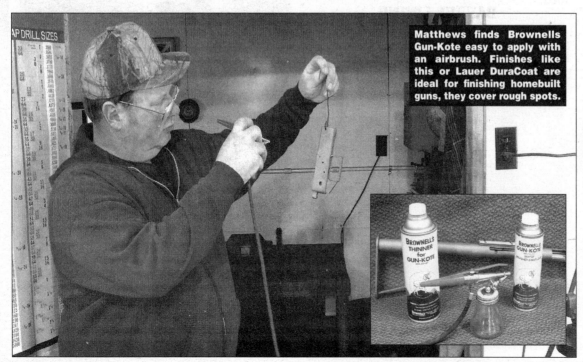

Matthews finds Brownells Gun-Kote easy to apply with an airbrush. Finishes like this or Lauer DuraCoat are ideal for finishing homebuilt guns, they cover rough spots.

PROJECT SOURCES

**Gunsmithing Supplies and Quality Gun Parts–
BROWNELLS**
200 S. Front St, Dept. SGN, Montezuma, IA, 50171,
1-800-741-0015 • www.brownells.com

**Budget Priced Compact Rifle Scopes–
CDNN**
Box 6514, Dept. SGN, Abilene, TX, 79608,
1-800-588-9500 • www.cdnnsports.com

**4130 Steel Tubing and Rod–
WICKS AIRCRAFT SUPPLY**
410 Pine St., Dept. SGN, Highland, IL, 62249,
1-800-221-9424 • www.wicksaircraft.com

Ask the Gunsmith

By Reid Coffield

AUXILIARY CHAMBERS

Q *I was looking at some old magazines and saw an ad for auxiliary chambers for centerfire rifles. As I understand, these would allow the user to shoot lower-cost pistol ammo in centerfire rifles. It looked like a good idea to me. Before I start trying to find some of these things, have you had any experience with them and if so, what was your impression? Are they worth the money?*

Note how the steel auxiliary chamber insert or adapter is chambered for, in this case, the .32 ACP pistol cartridge. Auxiliary cartridges were once popular for indoor target shooting with military rifles.

In testing the auxiliary chamber inserts, one of the rifles Coffield used was this very accurate No. 4 Enfield which had been set up for match shooting. He found .32 ACP tended to string vertically.

A Auxiliary chambers or chamber inserts as they are sometimes called have been around for a long time. At one time the U.S. Army used a form of auxiliary chamber with the Krag and the 1903 Springfield for indoor training.

My impression is that the "golden age" of these devices was in the period between the World Wars. Evidently a lot of folks liked to shoot indoors in their homes during the winter months with large caliber rifles and handguns. These devices allowed them to do so.

There were a number of advantages to the auxiliary chambers. First, your ammunition was a lot less expensive. In addition, the muzzle blast and report when firing a small handgun cartridge like a .32 ACP in a rifle such as a .303 Enfield was minimal.

Some time ago I purchased two auxiliary chambers; one in .30-'06 and one in .303 British. Both were chambered for the .32 ACP handgun round. Like you, I was curious as to just how good (or bad!) these things might be.

Shortly after getting them I grabbed two rifles and headed for the local range. Due to the crowds there, I was not able to get on the pistol range, which had a 25-yard firing line. Instead I had to do my shooting on one of the rifle ranges where the targets were set up at 50 yards which would certainly be a stretch for a .32 ACP.

The No. 4 Lee Enfield rifle I used was set up as a competitive target rifle and it has always shot extremely well for me. The ammo that I used was standard commercial Winchester .32 ACP with ball or fully jacketed bullets.

At 50 yards the accuracy was disappointing, but probably all that you could expect from a .32 ACP at this distance.

I could hit a standard 12 inch bullseye target but that's all! The shots were vertically strung almost the entire width of the target. Oddly enough, the horizontal dispersion was not too bad at all.

The real surprise came with the 1903A3 Springfield that I used next. This is a rifle I've had for years and is also a darn good shooter. Again, the auxiliary chamber was set up for .32ACP cartridges. I knew that I had problems after the first shot.

The sound was distinctly different and there was no hole on the target! I pulled the bolt and sure enough, the bullet was stuck in the barrel about 4 inches from the muzzle. Fortunately, I always take a cleaning rod with me to the range, and it was easy to push the bullet on out.

The next shot cleared the muzzle but fell to earth about three feet ahead of the shooting bench. That was when I decided that my "test" was ended! I was not about to risk damaging a good barrel.

Auxiliary chambers might be OK when shooting at 50 feet or less. However, at ranges greater than that you may well be disappointed. Also, I am very concerned that as I experienced, you could stick a bullet in your barrel. If you don't catch this and then fire an additional round, you could easily ring or damage your barrel.

Bottom line; I doubt that I'll be buying any more auxiliary chambers. If I want to do some indoor shooting I'll just use a .22 rimfire or make up some reduced power handloads. I think I can get better accuracy and have less risk of damage to my rifles. If you decide to use an auxiliary chamber just be very careful that your bullet always clears the barrel before your next shot.

BARREL LINING

Q *I have a small Remington Rolling Block in .32 rimfire with an absolutely awful bore. The exterior finish is also not all that good and the gun is definitely not a collectable. I would like to make it into a shooter but I am not sure how to do this. Any suggestions?*

A If the rifle were mine, I would consider lining the bore and converting the rifle to .22 rimfire. The action is definitely strong enough for the .22 and the cartridge is cheap and readily available. The only challenging part of the job would be moving the firing pin, but any good gunsmith should be able to handle that job.

Coffield says converting any of the 19th century rimfires to .22 Long Rifle is the way to go if there's no collector interest in the gun. Lining the bore and moving the firing pin get it done.

THROAT EROSION

Q *What is the best way to determine when the barrel throat on an M1 Garand is shot out? I think using a throat gauge is best while my buddy contends that making a chamber casting is better. What do you think?*

A The only reliable way for me to determine if a barrel has throat erosion to the point that it affects accuracy is to take the rifle to the range and do some shooting. If the rifle still prints nice tight groups, it's fine no matter how much or little throat erosion is present. I've seen Garands where the throat erosion gauge indicated absolute maximum wear yet would still shoot beautiful groups. On the other hand, I have seen rifles with "perfect" throats that would not shoot accurately. An old armorer who worked for years at Camp Perry once commented that he probably pulled off hundreds of good barrels simply because the owners looked at a throat erosion gauge and decided their barrels were worn out rather than testing them on a target.

At Colt I was once shown test targets for HBARs. Some of the rifles had throat erosion a third the length of the barrel after firing tens of thousands of rounds yet still shot beautiful groups. The bottom line is that only a serious range session will tell you if a barrel needs to be replaced. If it still shoots, no matter what the throat looks like, leave it alone!

1911 GRIP BUSHINGS

Q *The little studs that my grip screws go into on my Colt .45 pistol are stuck. I tried to remove them but they won't budge. What type of penetrating oil would you recommend to loosen them?*

A The grip screw bushings on the 1911 Colt are not rusted in place. The bushing are threaded into the receiver and then staked in place. In order to remove them you will have to overcome this staking which is normally visible on the inside of the magazine well. Once a bushing is removed, it is normally ruined. I seldom ever reuse a bushing.

M1911 grip screw bushings are staked into the frame. Twisting them out hard enough to iron out the staking generally ruins them. Replacements are widely available and easy to install.

LOCATING TOUCH HOLE

Q *Where should the touch hole on a flintlock be located relative to the pan?*

A The touch hole, which leads from the lock to the bore, should be located slightly above the bottom of the pan. If it is located at the bottom of the pan, the priming powder must burn down until it reaches the opening of the touch hole before you will have ignition. This leads to slow ignition, which can make shooting a flintlock even more of a challenge. A properly located touch hole can make ignition much faster. ◉

Building the SGN-9

BY STEVEN MATTHEWS

Part 1
Selecting Parts, Making the Bolt

A lot of Matthews' previous projects could largely be accomplished with hand tools, but this one is a bit more advanced and requires some pieces be made on a lathe.

Have you wanted to build a gun that's truly your own? Here Matthews shows how to take some steel and a handful of parts and turn it into a gun. It takes the right tools and techniques, but if you've followed his other stories, you can do it.

At some point every hobbyist gunsmith wonders if he could build his own gun. Many advance into this segment of their hobby by "building" a gun from a parts kit. Kits like the AR-15 are very easy to build with factory-made parts. The skilled hobbyist gunsmith can assemble a box of AR-15 parts into a functional firearm in a couple hours or less.

One may however question if this is building or just assembling, which does not require much gunsmithing skill or knowledge. Someone completely unfamiliar with firearms could do it, which is exactly the point with modern military firearms. The less skilled labor required, the better. A lot of those in our mostly male firearms fraternity would be surprised to know that guns are mainly assembled in the factory setting by women.

Someone else has done all the engineering work. They have decided what parts to make and how to make them, what material will be used to make them, and how all the parts interact to perform the intended function. The other extreme of "building" your own gun would be to design and fabricate all the parts needed to create a functioning firearm. This extreme is not really practical for the hobbyist. The amount of design work, technical knowledge, and tooling to create every single part would be cost and labor prohibitive.

Even custom gun makers use many parts manufactured by others to keep manufacturing cost reasonable. For the hobbyist gunsmith the "build it yourself" option should fall somewhere between these two extremes.

A couple years ago I decided to design and build a gun project for an SGN article. I created a design and built and documented the project but other article projects always seemed to push this project to the back burner. I have done more than 20 articles for SGN over the last two or three years and my article idea list was getting pretty low, so I figured I better get this project out of mothballs.

I wanted to use some factory-made parts to keep the project doable for the hobbyist. If it was too difficult or required too

much machining, it would discourage potential builders. A simple single-shot firearm would be the easiest project for the hobbyist, but interest would probably be minimal. Semi-autos are the most popular today, so that's what I decided to design and make.

I decided to use the simplest operating system, straight blowback. This dictated the use of a low powered pistol cartridge such as .380 ACP, 9mm Luger or .45 ACP. I chose 9mm Luger

because ammo is cheap and many inexpensive military surplus gun parts could be used to ease the build.

To keep fabrication relatively easy, I decided to make the receiver from high-quality 4130 tubing. Fire control parts require considerable engineering, so I decided that AR-15 fire control parts, which are well-designed, easy to understand, inexpensive and widely available, would be the way to go.

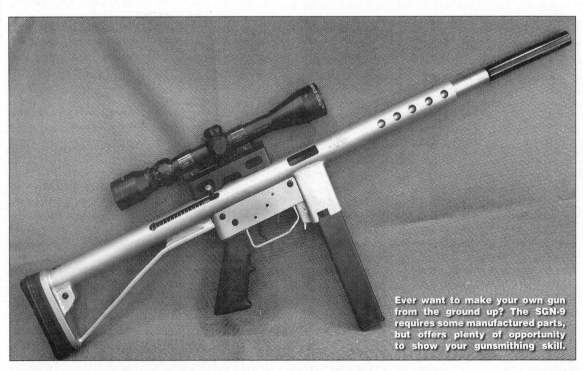

Ever want to make your own gun from the ground up? The SGN-9 requires some manufactured parts, but offers plenty of opportunity to show your gunsmithing skill.

Combining Soumi M31 and AR-15 parts with some steel tubing and common steel stock gives you the raw materials for a 9mm carbine. You'll have to supply the labor.

Every semi-auto firearm requires a bolt, and these can be very difficult for the hobbyist to make from scratch. What I needed was an inexpensive surplus bolt that could be the "raw material" for making a semi-automatic bolt. A barrel for this project could be made from a commercially available 9mm barrel blank but these could be expensive ($50-100).

The Soumi bolt is heat treated, and Matthews found drills and cutters barely scratched it. Careful annealing is required to make it soft enough for easy cutting.

The bolt will need to be reduced to 1.00-inch outside diameter to fit inside the new tubular receiver, and there's really no substitute for a lathe for doing that.

A less expensive option is to use a military surplus barrel. Most military surplus 9mm barrels are from submachine guns and are under the BATFE mandated 16-inch overall length needed for a semi-automatic rifle. These barrels can, however, be modified by permanently installing an extension to bring them up to the required length.

I wanted magazines that were very inexpensive and were single-feed. Double-feed magazines are more reliable, but pose some design difficulties for the home builder. A design that is far from perfect in the theoretical sense, but that was perfect for this project, is the Sten magazine.

Sten magazines can be found for less than $10 each, I have gotten them for as little as $3 each on occasion. What I ended up with was a design that used many factory-made parts but would contain enough hand made parts to be far beyond an "assembly job" gun project.

Since this project was going to be the basis of a SHOTGUN NEWS article, I decided to call it the SGN-9 Semi-Auto Carbine. In this project the builder would have to make the receiver, trigger housing, magazine housing, barrel shroud, stock, sight mount, and various small parts.

The bolt will be "made" by heavily modifying an SMG bolt to semi-auto configuration. Purchased parts will include the bolt, barrel, fire control group, firing pin, grip, recoil spring, recoil pad, and various small parts and hardware. All these parts will have to be hand fitted together into a functional and safe firearm.

Before we get into the specifics of this project several issues need addressing. This article is not going to be a step-by-step build article. I will give some general details of how to make and fit the parts but the builder is going to be totally responsible for the fit, function, and safety of all parts.

Given the variables associated with home-made parts, considerable hand fitting and modifying of parts may be needed to ensure proper functioning. A minor size variation of one part may result in some other part not functioning correctly. This project is *advanced gunsmithing* and the builder *must* know how each and every part is made and how it functions.

If you do not completely understand how this firearm functions, *do not* build it! The builder is the gunsmith/manufacturer on this project and has the final say on what is correct and safe. Neither SHOTGUN NEWS nor the author are responsible for the construction, use and safety of this firearm.

It is also the builder's responsibility to ensure that this firearm is legal to build and possess in his location. Although this firearm is designed as a legal semi-automatic rifle, some locations may restrict ownership of certain types of firearms. I have no

professional firearms engineering experience and this project is presented solely as an amateur's attempt at firearms design.

Parts Selection

The first step is to obtain the needed parts. When I decided to start this project, the first thing I did was to look through my pile of gun parts to see if there was anything I could utilize. I found that I had many parts that could be used.

I had a full (minus receiver) parts set for a Soumi M31 submachine gun, designed and built in Finland in the 1930s (see 1/10 and 1/20/08 issues). The barrel was 3/4" in diameter and was 12 inches long, which would work very well and meet BATFE guidelines when a 4½-inch extension was permanently installed.

The original full-auto bolt featured a fixed firing pin and would be prohibited under BATFE regulations, since the agency considers a fixed firing pin a machine gun feature. The fixed firing pin is, however, removable and the bolt can easily be modified to use a conventional firing pin, making it a semi-automatic system.

The Suomi kit also contained a magazine release and spring that could be used. The best part of using Suomi M31 parts is cost. Suomi M31 parts sets are advertised in SGN for as little as $60. This is a great price for a high quality barrel, bolt and magazine lever.

The AR-15 hammer, trigger, safety, disconnector, and associated pins and springs would be used for the fire control system. AR-15 parts are widely available from SGN advertisers. I got mine from Brownells, since I was going to obtain finishing supplies from them as well. You might associate Brownells solely with gunsmithing supplies, but they are an excellent source for gun parts, both standard and custom.

You could order parts individually, but I found that they offered a complete DPMS AR-15 lower receiver parts set for the price of just a few individual parts. The unused parts can be saved for future projects. Their prices were also competitive with other AR-15 parts suppliers.

I ordered an AR-15 firing pin and standard length recoil spring, along with a 9mm Luger chambering reamer to adjust chamber depth and headspace after assembly. This reamer may or may not be needed depending on how precisely you assemble your project.

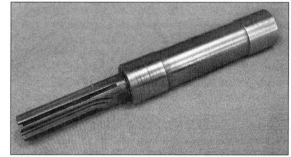

Although it's reduced in diameter, the bolt needs to retain the original outside contour, with a reduced center section between two larger ends. This will reduce binding.

A milling machine is sure a lot easier, but Matthews experimented and found that the large slot in the bolt can be made by drilling multiple holes and filing out the rest.

The 7.16" slot in the bolt allows conversion to an AR-15 hammer and other fire control components. Matthews picked AR-15 parts because they are cheap and available.

PART 1 | BUILDING THE SGN-9

The Soumi firing pin is pressed in place and then cross-pinned with a small pin that is about 3/4" back from the front of the bolt. Driving it out allows pin removal.

The receiver of the SGN-9 will be made from 1¼"x.120" wall seamless 4130 chrome-moly tubing. This material is available from aircraft supply dealers. I recommend about 4-5 feet of this just in case you make a mistake and need to make a new piece. A barrel shroud will be made from 1¼"x.062" chrome-moly tubing. A couple feet will be plenty.

I chose this thinner size to keep weight down, but you could use the heavier receiver tubing if you want, you will just have to adjust your barrel shroud bushing size to compensate for the size difference. A foot of 7/8"x.120" wall chrome-moly tubing will make a barrel extension.

The trigger housing/lower receiver and magazine housing will be made from common 1"x 2"x3/32" rectangular steel tube. This is available at well equipped steel dealers. A couple feet will be more than enough.

A foot or two of solid 1¼" solid chrome-moly rod will be used to make the barrel bushing, bolt stop, and end cap. This is also available from aircraft suppliers.

A common grade 5¾"x6" bolt can be used to fabricate the bolt extension that will be attached to the rear of the bolt.

A foot each of 3/4"x3/4" and 1"x1" square steel stock will be used to make some small parts.

The buttplate will be made from a piece of 1/4"x2" flat steel stock. Get a couple feet in case of a foul-up.

A 2-foot piece of 3/16"x1/2" flat stock will be needed for the stock construction if you choose to make a skeltonized buttstock.

I wanted a rubber buttplate and I used a buttplate and spacer from an FN/FAL rifle. These are available for a few bucks from gun parts dealers. If you don't mind a solid steel buttplate, you can delete this item.

Various small pieces of steel, pins, and screws will be used and discussed in the fabrication text. Total parts cost for this project excluding finishing supplies will be about $175, but this figure can be reduced considerably if you are a frugal shopper and search out bargains.

Tools Required

Parts are readily available for this project but nothing can be done unless you have the right tools. You'll need basic home workshop tools such as a vise, files, drills, taps, hammers, saws, punches, etc. The more tools you have, the better; more tools usually make the job easier.

A metal turning lathe is absolutely needed for this project since many of the parts are turned to precise sizes. The lathe work is not very difficult and you don't have to be a master machinist, but you just can't do this project without a lathe and the skill needed to operate it.

A milling machine will greatly help on this project but is not an absolute necessity. Many of the milling machine made parts can be made by hand with saws, files, drills and grinders. It just takes longer and requires more skill to make them by hand.

I made gun parts by hand for more than 20 years before I could afford a milling machine. Hand making parts is slow and tedious, but it does work and you don't have to spend hundreds on a mill. Hand making parts will really help you hone your fabrication skills, too.

A drill press with a vise is just about a must-have tool for this job since most (the author included) can't drill accurately and squarely with a hand drill. A Dremel Moto -Tool or small air angle grinder will really help keep hand filing to a minimum.

One power tool that I find especially useful in parts fabricating is a bench type disc sander. This tool is great for shaping steel that needs to be flat without dips and gouges.

Of course, you need accurate measuring tools such as a scale or ruler graduated in 32nds and 64ths. A set of dial calipers is needed for making measurements more precise than can be done with a ruler. One other must-have tool is an arc welder, since many of the parts are welded in place. I recommend a MIG welder since, they are better for small fabrication projects.

A common stick welder can be used, but you must use very small electrodes and use welding methods that control heat distortion since stick welders generally generate much more heat and distortion in the workpiece than a MIG welder.

Bolt Fabrication/Modification

The first part that needs to be made is the bolt. This is the hardest part of the project and everything else depends on getting the bolt right. If you can't get the bolt fabricated correctly, there is no use doing the rest of the project. Making the semi-automatic bolt is the absolute heart of this project.

The "raw material" for this part is the Suomi M31 submachine gun bolt. Modifying this fixed firing pin bolt to conventional firing pin operation is much easier than fabricating a new bolt from scratch.

The bolt will be modified by removing the fixed firing pin and then "bushing" the hole, machining the interior of the bolt to accept an AR-15 firing pin, and cutting a hammer slot in the bolt to allow use of the semi-automatic AR-15 hammer and other fire control parts.

The bolt will also be reduced in diameter so that it will fit the new SGN-9 receiver. A bolt handle will be added to the new semi-automatic bolt but it will be done later since its location will be affected by the location of other parts not yet made.

A bolt extension will be added to the rear of the bolt to increase its mass since so much weight was removed when it was modified for the

Once the bushing is installed, a 1/16" hole needs to be drilled in the center of the bolt face for the firing pin. Then face off the bushing flush with the bolt face.

new receiver. Firearms operating by the blowback principle must have bolts that have enough mass to keep the bolt closed until chamber pressures have dropped to safe levels. If blowback bolts are too light, functioning and safety problems will arise.

To begin the bolt work, you need to remove the extractor by using a small screwdriver to pry up at the front of the bolt face and then slide it forward and off. Before doing any machining work, you may have to soften the bolt by annealing it with heat. It may be too hard to machine easily.

This bolt is a high quality item and was heat treated for maximum wear resistance. The bolt I used in this project was so hard that drills and lathe cutters would barely cut the steel. To anneal the bolt, use a propane or oxy-acetylene torch to heat the bolt till it just begins to turn dark red. Heat it very evenly and do not overheat it since it will make it too soft and it will wear out easily.

Once you have the whole bolt a dull red color, slowly remove the heat source and allow it to cool slowly. When it's cool, you can check to see if you softened it enough by using a file to test hardness. If the file easily cuts the steel, it has been softened. If the file doesn't cut easily, it probably needs to be reheated a little hotter for a little longer.

The Suomi bolt features a fixed but removable firing pin. This firing pin is pressed in place and then crosspinned with a small

The former firing pin hole is tapped for a 12-28 bushing. Threading the hole must be done precisely; using the lathe chuck and tailstock will help keep it straight.

Any slam-fires must be avoided, both for safety and for legal reasons. A firing pin return spring helps prevent them by keeping the firing pin from flying forward.

PART 1 | BUILDING THE SGN-9

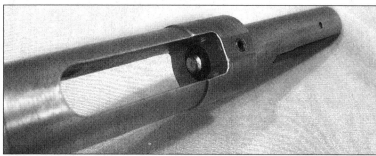

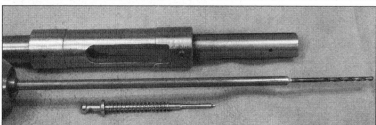

Extra-long tooling is required to drill through the length of the bolt for the firing pin. The pin and its spring are retained in the bolt body by a hex socket screw.

pin that is about 3/4" back from the front of the bolt. It is located straight up and down and sometimes is hard to see, so keep looking if you can't find it right away.

My bolt was so finely finished that the pin was almost invisible. Once the crosspin is driven out with a small punch, the firing pin can be driven out. It will come out the front of the bolt and a long pin punch can be used to drive it out. This is one of those procedures that looks good on paper!

On my bolt, the crosspin wouldn't budge and neither would the firing pin. After bending a couple pin punches, I decided that the parts must have been extremely tightly pressed in place at manufacture. I had to partially drill out both pins to relieve tension before they would move. Even after annealing the bolt, these pins were still pretty hard, so be sure to use sharp drills if you have to drill them out.

The receiver of the SGN-9 will be made from 1¼"x.120" wall thickness 4130 chrome-moly tubing. This leaves an internal diameter of 1.010". A running clearance of .010" will mean the bolt will need to be machined to 1.00". You can vary this a little, but if the bolt is too large, it will bind and if too small it will be a sloppy fit.

Place your bolt in your lathe and turn it down to this size. Profile it just like the original. The wide ends should be the

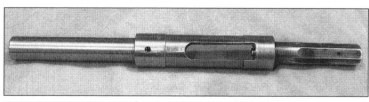

specified size of 1.00" and the reduced part in the center should be .020-.030" smaller. This is especially important for smooth functioning. If the bolt body was the same size all the way any distortion in the receiver could cause binding. After it is turned to size, chamfer the ends on both sides for smooth operation when it slides in the receiver.

The next procedure will be to cut a slot in the bolt body for the AR-15 hammer. This slot will allow the hammer to contact the firing pin and also allow the bolt to cock the hammer when it reciprocates.

This 7/16" slot needs to be oriented from top to bottom so be sure it is located correctly before you start removing material. The front will be squared up and fitted by hand, but the rear can remain rounded. The slot will extend from roughly .600" from the front of the bolt body and extend to within about 1½" from the rear of the bolt body.

The rear dimension is not too critical, but the front needs to be fairly close, because the front edge will also stop the hammer when it strikes the firing pin. Give yourself plenty of room here, since you will be hand fitting the bolt and hammer later.

You can mill out this slot with a milling machine but if you don't have a mill, it can be done with a drill press and file method. Draw out your slot on the bolt and then drill several holes within the slot area and then use files to remove the remainder of the material.

Hand work like this is slow but it doesn't cost a thing! Once the slot is cut out it's time to start on the firing pin segment.

That nice round hole where the fixed firing pin used to be now needs to be filled back in. This procedure is a variation of the old-time procedure of "bushing" a worn firing pin hole. Many old-time guns wore out the firing pin holes and a new hole had to be made by drilling out the bolt face and then installing a threaded insert and then drilling a new firing pin hole.

The hole in the front of the Suomi bolt was sized just right as a tap hole for a 12-28 tap and bolt. A 12-28 tap was simply used to thread the hole. How deep to thread and how long the insert should be is up to you. The longer and deeper is better, since what is not needed will be drilled out anyway. If memory serves me correctly (it been a couple years ago) I believe I went about 1" deep.

A 12-28 Grade 5 screw was used for a bushing. Once it was threaded in all the way, I cut it off then faced it off even with the bolt face. Install it very tight and use permanent thread locker before cutting it off. A quick note here about the 12-28 tap and bolt. This size was common in years gone by, but has fell out of favor in modern times since it is only slightly smaller than common 1/4" tap and bolt sizes.

Bolts and taps in this size are still available, but you will have to get them from places that carry a large selection of taps and bolts, you won't find them at hardware stores. Brownells catalogs this size and many large industrial suppliers also have them.

Once the insert has been installed and faced off, drill a new firing pin hole from the front and drill the rear to accept the AR-15 firing pin. A fair amount of skill is needed for this procedure. It's not all that hard, but it's easy to mess up if you are not paying attention to small details.

Start by chucking up the bolt in your lathe with the front of the bolt on the working side. Be absolutely sure it is centered and running "true." If it's not correct, your holes will run off-center. Also be sure your tailstock and drill chuck are running on the centerline. If the tailstock is off more than a thousandth or two, things can get off-center also.

Start by using a very small center drill and just put a small dimple on the bolt face for a starting point. The very tip of an AR-15 firing pin is about .060" so we will use a 1/16" (.0625")

To compensate for the weight of material removed, Matthews added an extension to the rear of the bolt that conveniently became the guide rod for the recoil spring.

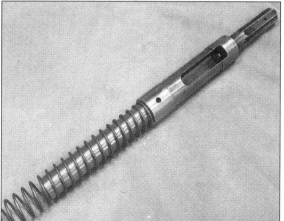

drill to drill a hole in the bushing. Drill all the way through the bushing you installed. These small bits are very flexible, so drill with a very light feed to keep it from walking off center.

Later holes will track off of this hole when they are drilled from the rear, so it has to be right. Once your hole is complete, you can turn the bolt over because all the rest of the holes will be drilled from behind. Now you will have to drill out a profile of the firing pin in the center of the bolt and insert. This is where your gunsmithing/machining skill is going to be important.

I will give the diameters of the holes that will need to be drilled, but depth is going to be a matter of your own judgment. You want the exact shape of an AR-15 firing pin in the bolt with a few thousandths for clearance.

Your drills will have to be very long to reach the full drilling depths. You will have to obtain long drills or weld/solder/braze small bits to an extension. Drill all holes with shorter, more rigid, bits before moving on to the more flexible long bits to keep your holes from running off center.

The tip of the firing pin is .060" and will fit through the 1/16" hole you drilled in the bolt face, but the section behind the tip is about .100"-.102". You need to drill a hole big enough for this section of pin and a couple thousandths for clearance. I recommend about .104" which is a No. 37 drill. You *do not*, however, drill all the way through the bushing.

This is going to be drilled in two steps, one to the approximate depth and then it will be final drilled to the finish depth after you have enough holes drilled to install the firing pin and hand fit it just right. Drill with the #37 drill till the tip is about 3/32" from the front of the bushing. Use whatever method you like to determine this drilling depth, but do not drill through the front of your bushing.

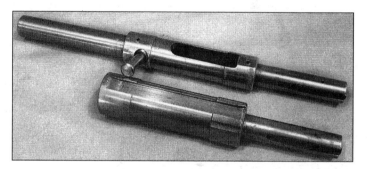

The modified bolt (top) is far removed from the original Soumi bolt. Changing it is a lot of work, but is certainly a lot easier than making a bolt from whole cloth.

The next wider portion of the firing pin is about 5/32" (.156"). You need to drill a clearance hole for this portion of the pin. A No. 21(.157") or No. 22 (.159") drill bit is about right for this hole. This hole will be drilled to about 3/4" from the bolt face. This dimension is not critical, but try to keep it close to this depth. The large head of the firing pin is about .335" and an "R" drill (.339") may be needed for clearance in the bolt body. The existing hole in my bolt was just a little under this size and I only had to drill very little to get the head to fit in the bolt body.

To prevent slam-fires and a runaway full auto malfunction a firing pin return spring *must* be used. The spring will prevent the firing pin from striking the cartridge primers when the bolt reciprocates. This is a necessary feature found on most semi-automatic firearms. *Do not* delete this feature!

Failure to incorporate this feature could result in a malfunction that causes automatic fire and authorities have in the past ruled that a malfunctioning firearm is actually an illegal full-auto firearm. You don't want to have to convince them that your malfunction isn't really a prohibited firearm. The penalties are severe for unregistered full auto guns!

For a firing pin return spring I used a 7/32"x1½" spring that would easily slide over the .156" part of the firing pin, and drilled a recess for this spring in the bolt. Drill the recess to a depth that allows the spring to keep the pin in the rearward position. The spring should be strong enough to keep the firing pin from moving under recoil.

Once all your holes are drilled, you must verify that the firing pin moves freely in its recess in the bolt. A pin that binds can cause the same full auto malfunction mentioned previously, so be sure it moves freely.

PART 1 | BUILDING THE SGN-9

At this point your firing pin must be hand-fitted to your particular bolt. The clearance hole for the .100" section of the firing pin now needs to be carefully drilled to allow about .035" to .040" of the firing pin tip to extend out of the bolt face. You want as much material as possible to remain around the firing pin tip to support the rear of the cartridge. Some of your other hole depths may need to be adjusted to allow the tip to reach this amount of extension. I used a hand drill with a long bit to do this final drilling. Drill a little, then check the fit.

Once you have the firing pin fitted to the bolt, it's time to square up the front of the hammer slot. The goal here is to have the square edge of the slot flush with the head of the firing pin when it is all the way forward. This is to ensure that when the hammer strikes the firing pin and drives it forward and pushes it to its full extension (.035"-.040") that the hammer comes to rest on the bolt and not the firing pin.

You want the hammer to "bottom out" on the bolt, not the firing pin, reducing stress on the latter. Place your firing pin in the bolt without the spring in place and note how much material needs to be removed from the front of the slot to make it flush with the pin head. Hand-file the rounded slot to a square shape. Check your progress often and be sure you do not remove too much material. Remember you can always take off more to get it to the right size but you can't put it back on if you take off too much.

After your firing pin is fitted and moves smoothly, a firing pin retainer set screw need to be installed in the bolt. I used a 8-32 set screw. This set screw will function just like the cotter key type of retainer used on an AR-15 bolt carrier. Locate it so it allows full travel of the pin but doesn't allow the pin to extend too far out of the rear of the bolt.

The screw needs to extend into the recess in the firing pin head but not to deep to contact the pin's shank. Locating the set screw so that the pin extends about .100" rearward of the edge of the squared-out slot is about right. When you tap this hole, tap it a little shallow so that the last few threads are very tight; this will help keep the screw tight. A little removable thread locker should also be used.

Adapting the firing pin to this bolt does require a lot of hand fitting to get right. I highly recommend that you proceed with great caution when drilling all these holes and shaping the bolt. Due to variations on your hand-made and -fitted parts (plus the manufacturing tolerances in the bolt and firing pin) your actual dimensions may be different than the ones I used. Since one little mistake can ruin the bolt, be absolutely sure of anything you do. Remember, part of gunsmithing is making decisions concerning how to do any operation the correct way.

Since I'd reduced the diameter of the SGN-9 bolt for the new size receiver and machined a slot in it, a lot of weight was lost and needed to be replaced to maintain an acceptable bolt weight. I added an extension to the rear of the bolt that brought bolt weight back to within a couple ounces of the original.

This extension needs to be about 3/4" in diameter and extend out of the back of the bolt by 4 inches. It also needs to extend into the interior of the bolt till it is even with the hammer slot. I used a common 3/4" Grade 5 bolt for this part. You may drill out the rear of the bolt and tap it for this extension or you may machine the extension to fit the existing hole in the rear of the bolt .and then press fit the stub into the rear of the bolt.

The existing hole in the rear of the bolt is rather small and an odd size so you may want to drill it to a standard size such as 5/8", and then fit your extension to that size. Weather you thread the hole or use the press-fit method drill a hole for a crosspin to keep it from working loose.

Roll or spring pins work well for this. After this extension is installed I recommend chucking the bolt up in a lathe and truing up the extension so it is exactly in line with the bolt body. If you installed it half ways straight removing .020"-.030" will probably be enough.

The hammer must slide easily over the bottom of the bolt. A shallow flat groove the same width of the hammer slot needs to be cut in the bottom. This groove has to be cut to a depth that is only slightly higher than the diameter of the front section of the bolt. It has to be shaped so that the hammer will slide over easily on both the forward and rearward strokes.

A generously sized radius will be formed on the back of the groove, but the front will need a more gradual taper so the hammer will slide back over easily. The hammer will be cocked when the bolt moves to the rear and the hammer will have to slide back over this part when it moves forward.

This shaping to provide smooth operation is going to be totally dependent on the shape of the modified AR-15 hammer that will be made later. The location of your lower receiver and fire control group will also affect the operation of these parts. Considerable hand fitting and shaping of these two surfaces will be required to get a smooth operating bolt and hammer. You might as well wait till you have these parts made before you cut this groove. Just don't forget it later.

Similarly, you will need to make a bolt handle and fit it to the bolt. You'll drill a two-diameter hole in the bolt and the handle will interlock with the bolt and help align the bolt in the receiver. This hole cannot be located until the receiver is made.

If you have made it this far on this project without major problems, the rest of the project will be much easier. I can't overemphasize the importance of fabricating the bolt correctly. All other gun functions depend on the bolt working properly. It may seem hard to make, but if you take your time and think things through, it's not all that difficult.

I spent about six to eight hours working on the bolt, but that included all the design work. Your time may be more or less, it just depends on how skilled you are. I'm no genius; if I could do it so can you! ◉

Ask the Gunsmith

By Reid Coffield

WELD BARREL PITS?

Q *Is it possible to weld up the pits on the outside of a rifle barrel? I have a nice old pre-war Winchester Model 70 in .30-'06 with extensive deep pitting on the underside of the barrel beginning just ahead of the receiver. I was told by some fellows at a gun show that welding could save the original barrel. My local gunsmith will not do it and won't even discuss the matter with me. What is your opinion?*

A While it is technically possible to weld up the pits on your barrel I would not be at all comfortable with doing so. I would be very concerned as to the safety implications of applying the heat necessary to weld up "extensive deep pitting" on a barrel for a high pressure cartridge such as the .30-'06. Also keep in mind that whoever would do the welding would be assuming the legal liability for that barrel.

It sounds like you local gunsmith is very much aware, as he should be, of these safety and liability issues. Over the years I have found that it is very darn easy for someone who will not be doing the work or who will not be liable for the consequences to say that you can or should do something. After all, it's no skin off their teeth if

something goes amiss. I would always encourage you to first seek feedback from the guy that will be doing the work rather than the "experts" at a gun show.

There are a few limited situations where I would not hesitate at all to weld on a barrel but this is certainly not one of them! I would strongly advise you to simply have the barrel replaced.

WET OR DRY CHAMBER?

Q *Is it better for functioning to have the chamber dry or slightly oily?*

A Your chamber and barrel should be completely oil-free when you fire the gun. Oil in the chamber will not allow the case to expand and hold on the sides of the chamber as the cartridge is fired. This means that the reward thrust of the case is exaggerated and extra pressure is placed on the bolt and bolt locking lugs. In some cases that pressure could be excessive and lead to damage or an unsafe condition. Oil in the bore could in some cases act as an obstruction and lead to a bulge in the barrel. It's always best to shoot with a dry bore and chamber.

S&W MAINSPRING ADJUSTING

Q *How do you adjust the mainspring strain screw on a Smith and Wesson double-action revolver?*

A I was taught that the strain screw should be fully seated in the frame. In fact, it needs to be turned in nice and snug so it does not work loose. As far as "adjusting it", I have shortened the end of the strain screw where it contacts the mainspring and thus reduced the tension on the mainspring. If you do that, you should always make sure that the point of the screw where it bears against the mainspring has a nice smooth, round tip. ◉

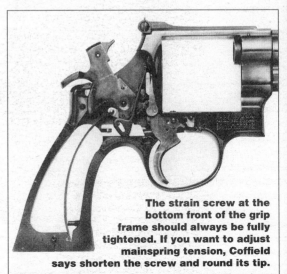

The strain screw at the bottom front of the grip frame should always be fully tightened. If you want to adjust mainspring tension, Coffield says shorten the screw and round its tip.

Ask the Gunsmith

By Reid Coffield

BUFFING WHEELS

Q *I do some hobby gunsmithing for myself, friends and family. Very soon I will finish putting together a hot bluing set up. My question concerns the polishing wheels for metal prep. How do you set up the buffing wheels? I have tried to get my polish, which I got from Brownells, to go on the wheels but most of it is thrown off. I am using 10" stitched muslin wheels on a homemade buffer that turns about 3,200 rpm.*

A Setting up a caustic or hot bluing system is something very few hobbyists are able to do, so you are one of a fortunate few! Way to go! Having a hot bluing system available will allow you to do a lot of interesting and enjoyable work.

Getting polish to adhere to a wheel reminds me of an experience I had years ago. I was just getting started in gunsmithing and was really working hard at impressing an old guy I was working with. I wanted him to know that I knew my stuff.

One day he told me to get the 33% polish and put it on the wheel. I looked and looked but other than the normal polish, I couldn't for the life of me find the "33%" polish. Finally in desperation I admitted to him that I couldn't find the "33%" polish and in fact, didn't even know what it was.

He laughed and told me that any polish used on a motorized wheel was "33%" polish. You get one third on the wheel, one third on the floor and walls, and one third on yourself! He wasn't that far off! Putting polish on a wheel or "heading up" wheels can be a frustrating, messy business. However, there are a number of things you can do to make it easier, less of a mess, and get more polish on the wheels rather than on you and the rest of your shop.

First, cut down the speed of your buffer. I don't like to have my buffing wheels turning over about 1750 rpm The faster your buffer turns, the more centrifugal force comes into play to throw the polish off the surface of the wheel.

Next, make sure your wheels are true. The surface of the wheels should be concentric with the axis of your buffer shaft. If the wheels are out of round even a bit it will make polishing more difficult and applying polish to the spinning wheel.

The surface of your wheels should be clean, smooth, and even for the first application of the polish. Any grease, dirt, or loose cotton fiber will make it more difficult for the polish to adhere.

Finally, don't try to apply your first coat of polish to a spinning or running wheel. I know these polishes are sold and promoted with the idea that you can head up the wheels while they're running, but it's a very wasteful use of the polish. Instead, remove the outer plastic or cardboard wrapper and cut off a 2-inch long section of the polish. Take this piece of polishing compound and cut it up into smaller chunks. Now place those chunks in a small metal container with some water and heat it to melt the polish. This will give you a paste.

Just dip your fingers into the melted polish after it cools enough so it doesn't burn you, and apply the paste to the face of your wheel. The buffer should not be running! Make your coating as smooth as possible and then let it dry for about 24 hours.

The next day, take an old piece of a junk barrel and do a bit of polishing on it first. This will further smooth the surface of your wheel. Now it's ready to be used.

You can apply additional polish by holding the stick of polish against the spinning wheel and will get more of a deposit much faster with less being slung off. However, I have gotten away from that and now always apply polish with my fingers. If I do this after each polishing session, my wheels are always ready to go the next day so it doesn't slow me down.

It's a lot less mess and it saves me a lot of money on polish. I'm not paying for polish that just ends up on the walls, the floor and me!

SHOTGUN CHAMBER MEASURE

Q *What's the best way to measure a shotgun chamber?*

Coffield often uses this BoreMaster digital gauge for shotgun work. He finds it to be easy to read, versatile, and compact. It will measure chokes, forcing cones and bore diameter down to 6 inches.

A There is no one "best" way to measure shotgun chambers. You can obtain good, accurate measurements using a variety of different tools and techniques. Years ago when I first started gunsmithing I measured a *lot* of shotgun chambers with a simple Barrel Caliper from Brownells along with a standard 1-inch micrometer. I also made castings of chambers with Cerrosafe and then measured the castings. This was more accurate than the Barrel Caliper but, as you can imagine, it was more time consuming.

Lately I've been using the BoreMaster digital gauge from the Robert Louis Company, Inc., 31 Shepard Hill Rd., Dept. SGN, Newtown, Conn. 06470, telephone 1-800-979-9156. I like this gauge for a number of reasons. First, it's very versatile and with one tool, I can measure a lot of different things. I can measure chambers, forcing cones, chokes, and bores down to a distance of about 6 inches from the muzzle or 6 inches from the breech end of the barrel. In addition to this, it's very fast and easy to read, since it uses a digital screen to display the measurements.

There is no lining up marks on a micrometer or setting the dial. However, like all measuring tools, you have to practice with it and learn to use it properly. There is no measuring tool made that you can't use improperly! Yeah, I've seen people screw up with a yardstick!

The point to keep in mind is that every tool offers some type of advantage. It may be less costly, more versatile, easier to read, or faster to use. You have to decide on what features you want in a particular tool and then once you have the tool, *learn* to use it! Many folks make the mistake of not giving a tool a real chance by never learning to use it properly. Once you learn to use the tool you've chosen, you'll probably be OK no matter what tool or technique you've selected.

TRANSFER PUNCH

Q *When I have to drill a pilot hole for a wood screw in a specific spot, in a buttplate for example, I almost always end up with the screw too far to the right or left, up or down. It will not be off much but it will be off enough to effect the positioning of the buttplate or other part. I am getting really frustrated and cannot seem to ever get it right. Can you help?*

A I believe I can! To center your new hole properly, you must first accurately locate the center of that hole. Simply scribing a line inside the buttplate screw hole will seldom do that as you still have to find the center of that scribed circle. A better technique is to use a transfer punch. These are sometimes also called locating or spotting punches.

Transfer punches look like ordinary punches except they have a precision machined point in the face or end of the punch. The transfer punches are normally produced in diameters equal to the various number, letter, fractional, and metric drills so you can more often than not find one that will perfectly match the hole in the part you are attaching to your stock. You just take the proper size punch that is a snug fit in the hole in your part, place it in the hole, and give it a tap with a hammer. The projection on the end of the punch will leave a mark that is perfectly centered.

A transfer punch is shown to the left of a regular, flat faced punch. It is designed to fit an existing hole and be punched through it to transfer a dimple to a workpiece located underneath.

BABY HAMMERLESS REVOLVER

Q *I have a small gunsmith shop and recently a very good customer brought in a Baby Hammerless revolver for repair. I have never worked on one, don't know anything about them, and don't know where to get information on them. That's the problem. Where can I get good information as well as some drawings or photographs of the internal components?*

A You are in luck! There is, to my knowledge, only one book on the Baby Hammerless revolvers. It was written by Frank Sellers just a few years ago. The title is *Baby Hammerless Revolvers* and it's available from Andrew Mowbray Publishers, 54 East School St., Dept. SGN, Woonsocket, RI 02895, telephone 401-597-5055. It's a softcover book and sells for about $25. A lot of good info and the only source I know of for help on the Baby Hammerless. ◉

Building the SGN-9

BY STEVEN MATTHEWS

Part 2
Receiver and Magazine

With the tough bolt modifications behind, Matthews turns to the receiver and magazine housing. The gun is starting to take shape.

Matthews used a milling machine for some processes, but having built many guns with hand tools, he says that large machine tools aren't required for this project.

In Part 1 we covered the most difficult part of the build process, making the bolt. The Suomi M31 9mm SMG bolt was modified to a semi-automatic hammer-fired design. It was also reduced in diameter to fit the new SGN-9 receiver.

Fortunately, this part will be much easier, focusing on receiver fabrication and barrel work. As before, you'll have to make decisions on how the parts will fit together and function. This will only be a rough guide to building the project. Because there are so many variables in hand-building a firearm many of the dimensions listed will be over- or undersized to allow the builder to hand fit the parts.

Receiver Fabrication

The receiver of the SGN-9 carbine is 1¼-inch diameter by .120" wall thickness chrome-moly seamless tubing. While the 1¼-inch diameter may not seem unusual, some may question the thick wall size. Many "tube" guns feature receivers with tube thickness of .060" to .080".

I chose this size for the benefit of builders who lack strong welding skills. Welding on steel tubing (or any piece of steel) induces stress in the material. This stress causes warping and distortion in the workpiece. Heavier materials resist these stresses better than thinner ones. I chose this size to keep distortion at a minimum.

To start your receiver, cutout a piece of tubing at least 26 inches long. Since the receiver is also the stock, we'll later cut the tube to fit the builder. Before you fit the buttplate, you can decide what length feels good. Once you have the tube squarely cut, deburr the ends so that parts will slide in easily. Also check the tube for dents or out of roundness that could interfere with later parts installation. You don't want to work for hours only to find that a big dent or smashed spot on the receiver renders the piece unusable.

Cut out an opening for the magazine; this can be done with a milling machine, Dremel tool or by hand with a drill, saw and file. A rectangle sized about 3/4x1½ inches will be a good start. The hole will be opened up later, once it is determined to be aligned correctly. It must be aligned so that it is centered in the tube and that it is parallel to the length of the tube.

Locate the front of the rectangular hole about 2 inches back from the front of the receiver tube. Once you have the starter hole made use a Sten magazine as a guide and hand-file the hole so that the magazine extends far enough into the receiver for proper depth.

It needs to extend into the receiver far enough that the feed lips of the magazine just clear the feed lip relief cuts on the bottom of the bolt. Also notice that the magazine is not a true rectangle, the front is narrower than the rear and the cutout needs to follow that shape.

The next cut that needs to be made is for the ejection port. The size for a starter hole should be roughly 7/16x1⁵⁄₁₆ inches. This

cut should start about 2 inches back from the front edge of the receiver tube. This starter hole is considerably smaller than finish size to allow for final locating the hole. This cutout must be correctly located around the outside of the receiver.

Rather than give a complex mathematical dimension to locate the cutout we will just use the bolt in the receiver as a guide. Slide your bolt into the receiver with the bottom of the bolt parallel to the magazine cutout. Observe the location of the extractor and at the centerline of the extractor, draw a line along the side of the receiver.

Center your starter cutout here and once you have it, observe if you got it centered on the extractor. If it's not, remove metal from whichever side you need to get it centered. When it's centered, file the sides equally till you get to a finish size of 17/32". This should give adequate clearance for ejection. If you find that cases hit the ejection port, open it up for extra clearance. Port size isn't really very critical on this item.

Now you can cut the hammer slot on the bottom of the receiver. The front of the slot will be located about 1⅛ inches behind the rear of the magazine cutout. It should also be centered with the magazine cutout. It will be 3/8" wide by 3 inches long. The slot ends can be squared or left round, it's your call.

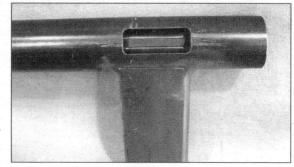

The ejection port should be cut in the side of the receiver. It should be centered over the ejector on the bolt and above the cutout for the magazine housing.

The first opening to be made in the receiver tube is for the magazine. If you don't have a handy milling machine, Matthews says it can be done with a Dremel tool.

The gun's magazine housing will be made from common 1x2-inch rectangular steel tubing. Cutting, shaping and welding will match it to the proper size Sten magazine.

Magazine Housing Fabrication

Next, you will need to fabricate a magazine housing and fit it to the receiver. This will be made from a 3-inch piece of 1x2x3/32" wall mild steel rectangular tubing. The Sten magazines are trapezoidal in shape, two parallel ends with inward angling sides. To obtain this shape, you will need to cut the rectangular tubing lengthwise, remove or reshape material and then weld it back together.

Depending on which contractor made them, Sten magazines can vary widely in size. The size can vary a 1/32" or more. If you make your housing to the larger size, smaller magazines will be loose. If you make them for the smaller size, some may not fit at all. Look for several magazines the same size and fit the housing to that size.

For test fitting, take one magazine and grind off the stop tabs on the sides. This will allow you to slip the magazine all the way through your housing when you are making and sizing it. Before you start the fabrication process, file out the weld seam on the inside of your tubing so the interior is smooth and flat.

A Sten magazine is just a little over 1/12" long. Cut off the back of the tube to slightly over this size. Spread the sides of

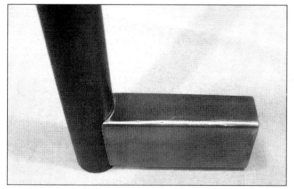

The top of the magazine housing needs to be contoured to fit flush against the receiver tube. Be absolutely sure it is square and centered on the tube before welding.

Matthews advises welding only at the front and back of the housing. This helps minimize distortion of the housing or tube caused by excessive absorption of heat.

the remaining tube out so the magazine will fit between them. Depending on the size of your tubing, the front may be about right or it may have to be widened or narrowed to allow the magazine to fit. Once you have the housing sized right, cut a small piece of steel and weld it in place to close up the back.

To maintain proper clearances you may want to place a .010" shim on one side and the front or back before clamping and welding it back together. Once the assembly is welded back together, dress down all your welds and check for proper fit. If it distorted or shrank due to welding, it is easier to work it now than after it's installed on the receiver.

You need to form a radius in the top of the housing to allow it to fit tightly up against the receiver. It is especially important to get this recess centered and squared correctly so that the magazine will be oriented correctly when it is installed.

I shaped this recess with a file and round grinding stones on a hand-held air angle grinder. Considerable hand fitting will be required to get this just right, it's not hard but is time-consuming.

This squaring and centering is vital so that the rounds in the magazine are centered in the receiver and feed straight out of the magazine and into the barrel. You want the magazine lips to be aligned correctly with the magazine relief grooves in the bolt.

When you get the proper fit, the housing can be welded to the receiver. To minimize warping of the receiver tube, weld it only on the front and back. With good welds, this will be more than adequate. If welded all the way along the sides it would warp excessively.

A MIG welder is best for welding on this project thanks to its lower heat. If you only have a stick welder, be sure to use very small electrodes and use welding techniques that minimize warping. Be sure that your parts are securely clamped and aligned exactly before you weld them in place. A "do over" will add extra distortion to an already touchy procedure. The gaps along the edges can be filled in with low temp solder at final finishing if the gaps are objectionable to you.

Barrel Work

It's now time to do some of the barrel work. You will need to turn a bushing on a lathe to install the barrel in the receiver tube. You also will fabricate and permanently install a barrel extension.

If you have chosen to use a barrel blank rather than the Suomi M31 barrel, you will have to pre-chamber your barrel and con-

A lathe-turned bushing mates the Suomi barrel to the tubular receiver. Matthews beveled it to form a short feed ramp. It should extend about .100" past the barrel.

tour it to whatever size suits you. Chambering is relatively easy and can be done without overly expensive tools. For a simple pistol barrel a chambering reamer and a tap handle is about all that's needed.

Reamers are pricey but will last for dozens of jobs if used correctly. If you choose the chamber-it-yourself method, I recommend "short chambering" the barrel before installation and then finishing the chambering job after the barrel is permanently installed. If you are unfamiliar with the chambering process, I recommend you get a basic gunsmithing book to review the process. Since we used a chambered barrel for this project, I won't go into detail on using a barrel blank for this project but it is an option for those who don't want to use the Suomi barrel.

For this project I used the Suomi M31 barrel, which is a high quality item and a bargain for the price of a parts kit. The Suomi barrel is "roughly" 3/4" in diameter. The chamber end is a little over that size and the muzzle is a little under. It also tapers from a few inches in front of the chamber to the muzzle.

Begin by chucking up the barrel in the lathe so you have more than 3 inches of working area on the chamber end. Be sure to chuck it up on the straight portion of the barrel and not the taper so that it runs true. Turn the last 3 inches of the barrel to exactly .750". This .750" will be the internal size of the barrel bushing that you will be making next. Place a piece of 1¼-inch diameter chrome-moly round stock in the lathe with at least 3 inches of workable material extending out of the chuck. Face off the end square.

Center drill the face and then begin drilling a series of holes all the way through the work piece. Start with a 3/8" bit then move up to 1/2", followed by 5/8" and then finish the rough drilling with a 23/32" or 47/64" bit. Drilling in steps is much easier than trying to shove a large bit through all at once and usually results in a more precisely centered hole.

Finish the hole to exactly .750" by using a precision reamer. If you don't have a precision reamer you can use a small boring bar on your lathe to finish the hole to size. You also may be able to final drill with a slightly under size 3/4" bit and them hand file and polish to the final size. Whichever method you use, you will need a very tight fit. A tight slip fit or a light press fit is about right.

The outside of the bushing now needs to be turned to size. The internal size of my tubing was 1.010 inches so this was the size for the bushing. Turn the last 2 inches of the chamber end to this size or just slightly larger. You want a very tight fit here, so approach the final size slowly to insure not going undersize.

Use a small section of your tubing as a test piece to get a good snug fit. The 2-inch part will go in the receiver tube but the front unturned 1-inch section now needs to be turned to the barrel shroud size. On my project, the barrel shroud material had a thinner wall thickness so this part was turned to an appropriate size for a tight fit. The barrel shroud will only be attached at the end and will free float so be sure it fits very tight.

The bushing can now be installed on the barrel. Install it so that about 3/32" to 1/8" extends past the end of the chamber. This extension will be chamfered later to help promote smooth feeding. To help hold the bushing and barrel tightly together prior to drilling the crosspins, I soldered them together with low temp silver solder (Brownells Hi-Force 44). Tin both the barrel shank and the bushing, then slide them together while the solder is liquid.

Matthews permanently joined the barrel and the bushing by soldering and crosspinning. Then he polished the chamber and feed ramps before installing the unit.

BUILDING THE SGN-9 | PART 2

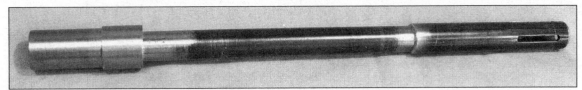

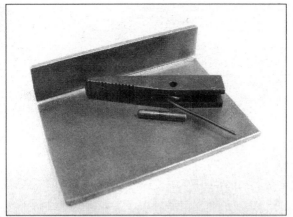

The 12-inch Soumi barrel must be lengthened to the legal minimum 16 inches. Matthews soldered and cross-pinned an extension that he styled like a muzzle brake.

Be advised that soldering these parts together is just for holding them in place while drilling, they still must be pinned to properly secure the barrel and bushing together.

Install the barrel permanently in the bushing by crosspinning with 3/16" pins. The pins can be made from hardened dowel pins, drill bit shanks or music wire. Do not use common soft rod stock as this material will deform under use and cause the barrel to work loose.

Drill your crosspin holes exactly on the seam between the bushing and barrel. This will result in a pin that is half in the bushing and half in the barrel. These pins need to be very tight, so size your hole appropriately. To get the drill to drill accurately and not wonder off course you will need to machine a flat spot where the drill will start. If you don't the bit may move off course and drill into the bore.

I recommend at least two crosspins, and four wouldn't be too many, since they are small. Offset them so they aren't across from each other. Also locate them away from the chamber. To get a tight fit, drill the holes one size under (#13 .185") on the first drill through then go to the full 3/16" size. If the holes come out oversized you can use a #12 (.189") drill for pin material. Be warned that drill bits are not really intended for precision holes and will drill slightly over or under the specified size, so be sure of the hole size before you drill.

Install your pins, then grind the excess off even with the bushing so that it will slide into the receiver. Now that the pins are in place, you can chamfer the part of the bushing that extends past the end of the barrel. Chamfer it at the same angle as the feed ramp in the barrel. You can do it on a lathe and chamfer it all the way around or just use a file to chamfer it just at the feed ramp area.

Barrel Extension

As the 12-inch Suomi SMG barrel is too short to be legal, it must be lengthened by adding a barrel extension to bring it up

the BATFE mandated minimum of 16 inches. I made it 16.5 inches just to be on the safe side. Use a 6-inch piece of 7/8"x1/8" wall chrome-moly tubing. This size will leave 4½ inches for the extension after you slide it 1½ inches over the barrel. This extension must be "permanently" installed according to BATFE regulations. It cannot just be soldered in place or retained with screws.

The method we will use is blind pinning after it is silver soldered in place. Once you have a 6-inch piece of tubing cut and squared up, you need to decide if you want any particular look for your extension. I decided to duplicate the rough appearance of a flash suppressor by machining in four slots 3/32" wide and 1½ inches long. You can stylize yours as a muzzle brake or any other design that suits your fancy, as long as it makes the barrel longer than 16 inches.

The internal diameter of the tubing is about 5/8" and the barrel at the muzzle is just a little under 3/4". To bring both these dimensions together, I drilled the rear of the extension to 11/16" and 1½ inches deep. The last 1½ inches of the barrel was turned down to the same 11/16". A nice tight fit is needed, so carefully size the parts.

Once the machining is done, tin both pieces and slide them together while still hot. Be sure you pay attention to the orientation of the extension compared to the barrel, you don't want your slots installed at odd looking angles. This operation is best done muzzle down so that excess solder doesn't run down into the barrel.

Also remove any excess flux, since many acid-based solder fluxes are mildly corrosive. Your extension now needs to be permanently installed by blind pinning with a 3/32" pin in the same way you pinned the the barrel bushing. Drill a hole right on the seam between the barrel and extension.

Make a flat spot at the starting point to prevent the drill from walking off the rounded extension. Don't drill quite all the way through, stop about 1/16" from the edge. Cut a short piece of pin and tap it into the hole so it is just under the edge of the extension. Place a small weld over the hole and grind off the excess weld.

Barrel Shroud

The SGN-9 features a ventilated barrel shroud that also functions as a forearm. It can be as long as you like, but I made mine about 6 inches. I used 1¼ x .062" wall tubing to keep weight down. I also drilled four rows of 7/16" holes along the sides. Two opposing rows featured five holes and two featured four. These were staggered at the halfway mark between the other holes. I used holes but you could use slots or even leave it solid. In the rear of the shroud I drilled three 3/8" holes so it could be plug welded to the barrel bushing after barrel installation.

Buttplate

A buttplate can be fabricated from quarter-inch mild steel flat stock. The shape can be whatever you want as long as there is room for a 1¼-inch hole near the top so it can slide over the receiver tube and be welded in place. Since I was going to be using a FN/FAL rubber recoil pad and spacer I just laid the spacer on a piece of steel and traced it out.

I cut it out and sanded it even with a disc sander. A 1¼-inch hole was drilled near the top so it would fit snugly over the receiver tube. To lock the spacer on the flat plate, I installed several roll pins flush with the plate and spacer. It will be welded in place later.

Magazine Catch Housing

Rather than hand-making a new magazine catch, I just used the Suomi catch and its torsion spring. It will be hand shaped to fit in the square notch in the rear of the Sten magazines, and will need some type of housing to retain and locate it.

Since the Suomi catch is about 5/16" wide, I just took a piece of 5/16" flat stock and used it as a mandrel and hammer-formed

Making the magazine catch housing meant forming a steel sheet over a steel block, oversized for later shaping. The catch is installed in it with a crosspin.

a piece of 1/16"or 3/32" sheet steel over the mandrel. The rough size of this housing was 1⅛ inches long by 9/16" deep. This piece will require hand fitting, so be sure to make it plenty oversize. I'm not going to give any dimensions for the location of the catch in the housing due to variations that are sure to occur by builders locating all of the other parts. This is one of those things that will be placed wherever it works best.

In the next part of this series we will be making a lower receiver to house the AR-15 semi-auto fire control group, do some more receiver work and several other small parts. Until then take your time making these items and enjoy the building process. ◉

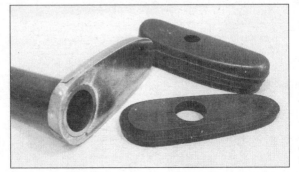

Matthews made a buttplate assembly using a flat steel plate, combined with a FN-FAL spacer and recoil pad. Drill a 1-inch hole in the top for mounting the assembly.

Building the SGN-9

BY STEVEN MATTHEWS

Part 3
Fire Control Mechanism

Getting the parts is easy enough, but some careful hand-fitting is required to adapt an AR-15 trigger assembly to this 9mm carbine.

While Matthews says much of the SGN-9 project can be made with hand tools, a lathe and drill press, a milling machine certainly makes some operations a lot easier.

One of the key elements of any semi-automatic firearm is the fire control system. Rather than design and fabricate fire control parts for the SGN-9 project, I decided to use the widely available AR-15 fire control group.

This system is well-designed and uses a minimum number of parts to provide reliable semi-automatic fire. In this part, I will show how to make a trigger housing or lower receiver to house the AR-15 fire control group. The lower receiver will also incorporate the grip assembly and trigger guard. It will be made slightly oversize and then hand fitted to the tubular receiver of the SGN-9.

The first step in this process will be making a simple fixture that will allow the builder to study how the components interact and function to give semi-automatic fire. Completely understanding how the parts work is vital for the safe building and fitting of the parts. This project is more than just a build project,

it is a learning experience that will help you understand firearms functioning principles that can be used for future projects.

This fixture only requires accurately drilling two holes. Start by obtaining a 3x3-inch piece of 3/4" to 3/8" steel or aluminum plate. Drill one 5/32" hole about 1 inch up from the bottom and about 2⅜ inches from the left side. Now you will have to accurately locate one more 5/23" hole .314" above and .843" to the left of the first hole.

Please note that these dimensions are center to center, not to the edges. This hole spacing is the same that will be used on your trigger housing when it is made later. This hole spacing needs to be within a few thousandths of an inch for proper functioning. Install your pins in the holes and place your trigger (with disconnector and spring installed) over the lower pin.

The hammer is placed over the upper pin. You can install the hammer and trigger springs if you wish but the action of the parts is easier to observe without them in the way. Once you have the fixture built, operate the parts and observe how they interact.

You need to understand how the trigger holds the hammer and how the hammer is retained by the disconnector until it is reset. You also need to understand how the bolt will push back

the hammer and how far back it needs to be pushed to operate correctly. It is imperative that you fully understand the principles involved here because you will be determining the proper fit and functioning when you fabricate and fit the parts.

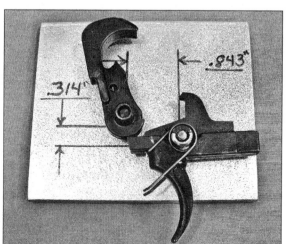

The gun just can't work if the hammer and trigger aren't located very precisely. Matthews recommends making this simple fixture to study fire control parts orientation.

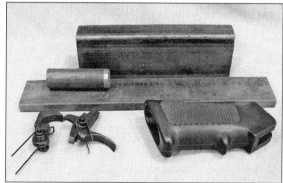

Matthews made the lower receiver from common rectangular steel tubing, flat steel stock and easily obtainable AR-15 parts. Lots of trial and error was required.

The steel tubing was cut lengthwise and rewelded to the right inside dimensions for the trigger parts. Then Matthews added a lug to support the AR-15 pistol grip.

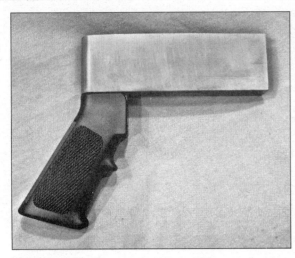

Matthews closed in the rear of the lower receiver box with a steel block and radiused it to match the contour of the grip. Be sure to remove the grip before welding.

The trigger guard can look however you want it to, but keep in mind that there must be plenty of clearance for the shooter's thumb to contact the magazine release.

Lathe-turn a bolt handle to fit the socket in the side of the bolt. When it is pushed through the access hole in the receiver, the handle will be held in position.

You will be fitting the parts to allow the hammer to be cocked, engage the disconnector to provide semi-automatic fire, and also to locate the parts so that the bolt will slide over the hammer without binding. I will not give specific locations for the fitting of the lower receiver to the SGN-9 tubular receiver because parts and skill in fitting them may vary. Hand-fitting this assembly will give you an intimate understanding of how fire control groups operate.

To begin building the lower receiver you will need a 6-inch piece of 1x2x3/32" wall rectangular tubing. You will also need a couple other small pieces of steel, sizes of which the builder can determine. You will need two AR-15 hammer/trigger pins, one AR-15 trigger with disconnector and its spring, one AR-15 hammer and hammer spring, AR-15 selector/safety with detent pin and spring, and an AR-15 grip.

Start by cutting off one of the 1-inch sides of the rectangular tube so that what remains is a deep "C" section. Cut this "C" section down through the middle of the remaining 1" side so that you have two L-shaped pieces. Take the two L-shaped pieces and thin the short legs down so that when they are placed back together the housing is about .700" wide.

Once you have the .700" width, the two pieces will be welded back together to form a "C" section with the desired width for the AR-15 fire control group. Arc weld these two pieces together. Improvise a fixture to keep the parts located and square while welding. Weld from the outside. Use a deep penetrating weld so that when you grind off the excess weld to make the seam smooth, the pieces are still solidly welded together. If your weld penetrated through to the inside, smooth it up also.

You can now drill your 5/32" hammer/trigger pin holes in your housing. The trigger pin hole will be located 2⅜ inches from the end that will be the rear of the housing and 3/8" up from the outside bottom. The hammer pin hole will need to be drilled .314" above and .843" in front of the trigger pin hole. Accurate placement of these holes is mandatory for proper functioning.

Tolerance for this hole spacing should be kept to .005" or less.

Failure to properly locate these holes can result in insufficient trigger engagement on the hammer, binding or unsafe or unreliable operation. Before the trigger can be installed, make an oval hole in the bottom of the housing. Start with a simple 3/4" hole directly below the trigger pin and elongate the hole front and back to allow the trigger to fit and allow full movement.

After the oval hole is cut, the trigger can be installed along with the disconnector and spring. The hammer and its spring can be installed next. At this point, you need to check for proper function. The top portion of the trigger should be roughly parallel to the bottom of the housing when it is holding back the hammer.

There should be adequate clearance under the front of the trigger to allow the trigger to drop low enough to release the hammer when it is pulled. The disconnector should hold the hammer until the trigger is released, at which time it should allow the trigger again to catch the hammer. If parts don't operate correctly, hand fit them to get proper function.

You may have to add a trigger stop (a spot of weld works well for this) under the front of the trigger to prevent overtravel or possibly grind a little here or there to get things right. Whether you have to do anything to get it working right depends on how well you located your parts.

Once you have the hammer and trigger located and working properly, you need to remove the hammer for a minor modification. To allow for smooth movement of the bolt when it reciprocates, you need to radius the top of the hammer and remove the notch in the face of the hammer. A pretty generous radius is required and you will have to experiment to get it right.

Fit an AR-15 grip to the housing by use of a mounting block. This part is simply a piece of 3/8" x 1¾-inch steel flat stock with a bevel formed on one side to match the bevel on the grip. Add a 3/4"-20 hole in the face of the bevel will be added to attach

the grip. The attachment location can be adjusted to suit the builder's preference for trigger reach.

To attach the grip, cut out a slot in the housing and weld the block to the housing so that it is flush on the inside. Dress down any weld on the inside so that it doesn't interfere with trigger movement. With the grip mounted, the rear of the housing can be shortened and the end can be filled in with a piece of steel welded in place (remove grip to prevent melting it when welding!). Radius the end to match the contour of the grip.

Next, I wanted to add a safety to the fire control group. Many home builders delete safeties to ease building but I think that's a mistake. Drill a 3/8" hole to allow installation of the safety lever. This hole is located 1⅛ inches behind the trigger pin hole and .220" above it. If you don't get it right, the safety is large enough that you can remove some material on the surfaces to get it operating correctly.

The AR-15 safety/selector is retained in AR-15 rifles by a spring and detent that is located in a hole in the bottom of the lower receiver and grip. This is the method I used but there is not much room on the housing, so it can be touchy getting it located right. You may improvise a different method for locating and retaining the safety lever if you choose. Just be sure it retains the lever and it will lock into the safe and fire positions solidly.

For a trigger guard I used a piece of 1/8x1/2" flat steel. The shape can be what ever pleases you as long as it protects the trigger and doesn't interfere with any other parts. I ran mine up to the magazine housing and added clearance for operating the magazine release lever. You may want to leave fabricating this part until you have the lower receiver fitted to the tubular receiver and have fabricated the magazine latch.

One item I added to the lower receiver was a hammer over travel stop. This prevents the hammer from moving to far forward and striking the bottom of the trigger housing when it's not installed on the receiver. The stop should allow the hammer to go about 20–30° past top but then stop it from any further rotation. A small piece of steel welded in at the proper location will be adequate. This part will also help stiffen up the housing.

The lower receiver/trigger housing at this point will be considerably oversize and will have to be hand-fitted to the tubular receiver to get a correct hammer-to-bolt relationship. The height will have to be reduced so that when the bolt reciprocates, it cocks the hammer. It will also have to allow the bolt to slide over the hammer smoothly without binding.

Add to this that it must be positioned so that the flat face of hammer contacts the firing pin at the proper position. Fortunately, one position will satisfy all needs. I found this fitting is best done by trail and error.

A very easy-to-make fixture will greatly ease the fitting of this part. Take an 8-inch piece of receiver tubing and cut out a hammer slot just as you did on the SGN-9 receiver. On the opposite side of the fixture, cut out a larger version

Precisely locating the hammer and trigger pin holes is absolutely vital to making the SGN-9 work. You need to hold a tolerance of ±.005" for reliable function.

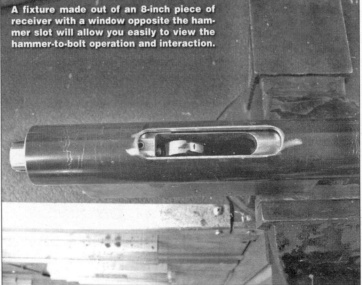

A fixture made out of an 8-inch piece of receiver with a window opposite the hammer slot will allow you easily to view the hammer-to-bolt operation and interaction.

BUILDING THE SGN-9 | PART 3

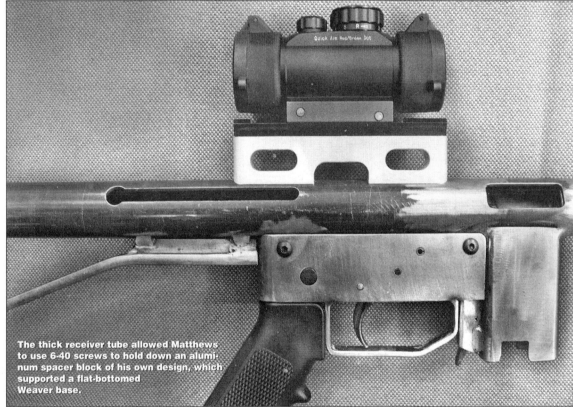

The thick receiver tube allowed Matthews to use 6-40 screws to hold down an aluminum spacer block of his own design, which supported a flat-bottomed Weaver base.

Now you can make some less complex parts. After the lower receiver is fitted correctly, it will be attached to the SGN-9 receiver with screws into blocks that are welded to the receiver tube. These blocks can be made from pieces of 3/8" thick x 3/4" wide x 7/8" long steel flat stock. Thin the 3/4" side down to the lower receiver's width of .690" to .700".

Radius one end to match the 1¼-inch receiver tube. These blocks will be installed in the next part of this article series.

The recoil spring and buffer assembly will be retained by a plug or cap in the receiver tube. This part needs to be sized just a little under the receiver's internal diameter.

A piece of 1.0-inch diameter chrome-moly rod was used for this part. About 1½ inches is about right, but size is not critical. A 1/2" pin through this plug and the receiver will lock it into the receiver tube. This pin hole will be drilled later.

The 1/2" pin will transfer recoil forces from the reciprocating bolt to the receiver. To allow this force to be spread out over a larger area and not deform the receiver wall, a block will be added below the receiver tube. This block can be made out of a piece of 1x1x1-inch piece of steel. Contour it to match the receiver.

You could reduce this part to 3/4" all the way around to reduce weight if you choose. After I used the larger size, I thought the smaller would be better but didn't want to cut it out after I welded it in place. This block will be located at final assembly.

To reduce wear and tear on the gun I made a recoil buffer out of a piece of 1-inch thick neoprene rubber. I used a hole saw with an internal size of just under 1 inch and cut out a 1-inch plug. This will be placed between the rear of the recoil spring and the end plug at assembly.

A bolt handle can now be made, but it too will be fitted at assembly. This handle will be turned on a lathe. If you don't have a lathe or you hired out the previous lathe work and didn't have the handle made at that time it can be hand made by turning in a drill and hand filing to shape.

Material for this part can be improvised from the shank of a Grade 5 or higher 7/16" (or larger) x4-inch bolt. This handle will feature a 5/16" shank with a ridge or protrusion that is 7/16". This ridge will retain the handle in the receiver. The grasping end of the handle can be whatever shape that pleases you.

Turn a section to 5/16" diameter for the first 1/2" and then turn a section 7/16" in diameter for the next 3/4". The sides of this wide section should be beveled at about 45° degrees. After the 7/16" section is formed, an additional 3/16" of 5/16" diameter shank should be formed to allow the handle to extend through the receiver wall when it is installed later. The remainder can be as long and whatever shape you want.

One last item can be made before we go on to assembly. You need to fabricate some type of sight mount. I chose to use a scope or red dot sight on the SGN-9, so I machined a spacer block and mounted it to the receiver.

Since the receiver wall is fairly thick, this base can be installed with #6–40 screws. I shaped a block out of 1x3/4x43/4-inch aluminum. The bottom was shaped to match the contour of the receiver tube.

Once it was shaped, a flat-bottomed Weaver base was screwed to the top. After locating all screws and holes, the base was contoured to a more pleasing shape. The straight-line design of the stock/receiver means any sights need to be raised well above the stock line just as in the AR-15 type of rifle.

In the next and last segment, we will make a few more parts and assemble and final fit all the parts into a functioning semi-automatic rifle. At this point you should be getting very familiar with this project and that is just the way it should be. When it's completed, you will almost be an expert on the SGN-9 Carbine and you should be! You will have made almost every part and fitted them together. That's what real gunsmithing is all about! ◉

of the hammer slot. This will allow you easily to view the hammer-to-bolt operation and interaction. The lower receiver needs to be contoured at the rear to allow the sides to fit flush against the tubular receiver. This can be contoured with files or a hand grinder.

After you have the rear shaped, you can do your first test fit with the fixture. With the trigger housing pressed tight against the fixture and the hammer in the hammer slot in the bolt, push the bolt rearward to cock the hammer. At this early stage, the hammer will probably not be pushed far enough back to be caught by the trigger. What you need to do is to continue reducing the side and rear heights till you get it sized correctly to cock the hammer.

Once you get the hammer to catch, you also need to check to see if it is being pushed back far enough that the disconnector holds the hammer after firing until the trigger is released and reset.

Proper disconnector function is absolutely necessary for reliable semi-automatic fire. Failure to properly fit these parts could result in a firearm that fires more than one shot per trigger pull which would fit the BATFE definition of a machine gun.

Penalties for possession of an unregistered machine gun are *severe*, so be sure your fire control group operates in the correct semi-automatic only mode.

You want to build a completely legal semi-automatic rifle, not an unregistered illegal machine gun. At this point, you just have a preliminary fit. You must verify that the bolt slides easily over the hammer. If it doesn't, you may need to adjust the radius on the top of the hammer or slightly rework the groove on the bottom of the bolt.

The face of the hammer must also contact the base of the firing pin on a flat section of the hammer and not on the radius. If you have to adjust these parts for smooth operation you will have to recheck the fit of the lower to the SGN-9 receiver, since all parts fitting and function are inter-related.

At this point you are probably thinking that this is a lot of difficult hand fitting and adjusting of parts. You're right, it is! This project is a learning experience and learning to properly fit fire control parts is a vital gunsmithing skill that must be mastered. Simply assembling part "A" at location "B" is just that, assembling, which any unskilled person can do on an assembly line. You are learning gunsmithing skills here!

Building the SGN-9

BY STEVEN MATTHEWS

Part 4
Final Assembly

Hours of cutting, filing, welding and grinding pay off as Matthews puts together his project carbine. The results: worth the effort!

If you have been following Matthews' series on building the SGN-9, you may by now be thoroughly sick of filing, but in this installment the job is finally finished.

The first parts of this article series involved making many of the SGN-9 individual parts and now we will fit many of those parts together. The first part to be fitted to the receiver will be the bolt. The bolt will be properly aligned in the receiver by the position of the bolt handle and its slot in the receiver.

This slot will be initially cut undersize to allow for errors that the home builder may have made and later brought up to full size once it is determined to be aligned correctly. The handle slot will be located at about the same angle around the receiver tube as the ejection port.

I lined my handle slot just about even with the center of the ejection port. This would be approximately 45° from the top of the receiver. The exact location can however be where ever the builder likes it, remember it's your project. At my chosen location I scribed a straight line parallel along the receiver tube. Start about 4 inches behind the ejection port and extend the line rearward about 4¼ inches.

Either mill or hand cut a quarter-inch slot along the line. Once you have this starter slot cut, temporarily install your barrel and bushing into the front of the receiver. Align it so that the extractor

relief cut in the rear face of the barrel is centered in the ejection port.

Place your bolt in the receiver and slide it all the way forward. Slide a magazine into the housing and align the bolt so that the magazine lips are aligned evenly with the magazine relief cuts in the bolt. With the bolt properly aligned with the magazine, mark a bolt handle hole location on the rear full size section of the bolt through the handle slot.

Remove the bolt and drill a quarter-inch hole at this location. Be sure the location for this hole does not interfere with the pin you previously installed to lock in the bolt extension. Also, be sure to drill the hole squarely so that the handle will be extending at the correct angle.

Reinstall your bolt and use a quarter-inch pin or bolt as a test handle. Observe if the bolt is still properly aligned. The slot and handle will be the only thing keeping the bolt properly aligned with all internal components so it must be correct.

If it is still aligned, you can proceed to opening up the slot to its finished size of 5/16". Be sure to keep the slot centered by removing equal amounts from each side. If your alignment is not right you will have to remove more on one side than the other to bring the bolt into alignment when you bring it up to finish size.

Once your slot is up to full size you can drill your starter quarter-inch bolt handle hole in the bolt up to a full 5/16". You'll need to drill a 7/16" counterbore in the bolt handle hole to allow the 7/16" protrusion on the handle to fit flush with the side of the bolt.

Drill this hole only deep enough to contain the protrusion. This 7/16" section of the handle will allow the 5/16" slot to retain the bolt in the receiver.

At the rear of your handle slot cut a half-inch diameter hole for a disassembly notch. This will allow you to remove the handle when the bolt is all the way to the rear during disassembly. When the bolt operates during use the bolt handle will not reach the notch, since it will be stopped by the buffer.

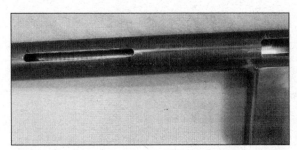

A quarter-inch starter slot will allow the builder to begin fitting the bolt to the receiver. Starting the slot a bit undersize will allow for careful fine-tuning of the fit.

A recess in the bolt body will allow a protrusion on the handle to lock the latter in place. The 5/16" handle slot will keep the handle positioned in the bolt.

A quarter-inch bolt can be used to check alignment of the bolt before opening the slot to full size. Remove the proper amount from each side to maintain alignment.

A takedown hole at the end of the slot will allow the handle to be removed from the bolt during disassembly. The protrusion on the handle will lock it into the bolt.

Now that the bolt is fitted to the receiver, you can install the barrel and barrel bushing. With the bolt installed and aligned, slide the barrel assembly into the front of the receiver. Slide it in until the rear of the bushing is even with the rear of the ejection port.

Locate the barrel assembly so that the extractor relief cut in the rear of the barrel is aligned with the extractor on the bolt. Drill three or four 3/8" holes through the receiver wall and slightly into the bushing. Plug weld these holes to attach the barrel assembly to the receiver securely and permanently.

Be sure to have adequate penetration into the bushing, but don't over-penetrate. Weld only one hole at a time and allow for cooling between welds to prevent overheating the barrel. Also, be absolutely sure everything stays aligned while you are welding.

Once your barrel assembly is installed, you can install the barrel shroud using the same method. Be sure to align it correctly so that the barrel is centered in the shroud and the holes are where they look good. After your welds are complete, dress off the excess weld smooth with the receiver tube.

One item that knowledgeable builders will notice that has been missing is an ejector. We have previously made an ejection port but now we need to make the ejector that will push the empties out of the gun. This part is extremely simple in design and function.

On many firearms the ejector is simply a fixed protrusion that impacts the rear of the cartridge as the bolt moves rearward. This protrusion stops rearward movement on one side but the extractor continues to pull cartridge rearward on the other side. This causes the empty to be sharply thrown from the gun.

The barrel and bushing are installed in the receiver by plug welding in place. Weld only one hole at a time and allow it to cool thoroughly before doing the next weld.

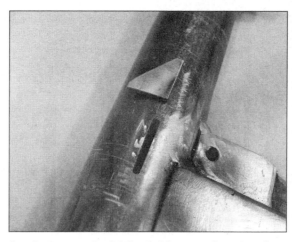

An ejector can be fabricated from a triangular piece of tool steel. A slot in the receiver wall will allow the ejector to be welded into the side of the receiver.

The ejector is welded in position from the outside. It must be properly aligned with the ejector slot in the bolt. This is a critical dimension, so measure carefully!

The Suomi bolt used in the SGN-9 features a slot machined in the side of the bolt to allow for passage of a fixed ejector. All that is needed is a small piece of metal to be attached to the receiver and have it ride in the ejector groove in the bolt.

I fabricated an ejector out of a 1/2"x1/2"x 5/64" (.078") right triangle-shaped piece of 0-1 type tool steel. I chose tool steel so that the face could be hardened after shaping for wear resistance.

The sharp point on the face was squared off on the cartridge end to increase its strength. At a point about 1/8" behind the rear magazine housing edge, I cut a thin slot in the side of the receiver tube to allow the ejector to be inserted. The ejector is inserted through the side of the receiver and located in the bolt's ejector groove so that it almost touches the bolt.

Once positioned, it can be welded in place. You can shorten the ejector on the receiver side so that it is just below the receiver tube wall and then weld it flush. If you don't mind the part showing on the outside, you can let it extend out the side and then weld it in place.

A collar that slides over the front of the bolt will be installed in the receiver and function as a bolt stop. Its other function will be to set headspace.

When the magazine is in place, its lips should just clear relief cuts in the bolt. The face of the bolt should engage the cartridge with plenty of contact area.

Whatever method you use, be sure that it stays aligned as you are welding it in place. If it moves when you are welding it, you will have to adjust it by bending or filing so that it doesn't drag on the bolt.

When building any type of firearm the subject of headspace must be addressed. Headspace is the amount of space between the base of the cartridge and the face of the locked bolt. On locked-breech designs this space is determined by the location of the fixed bolt and chamber depth. On an unlocked blowback action, this distance can "self adjust" somewhat and can be very forgiving.

If headspace is too tight (no space between the bolt face and cartridge base) the bolt simply will just be back a little further when the round is fired. As long as this is within reasonable limits, all is fine. What is of concern in the case of this SGN-9 project is that there is enough space but not too much space.

To get an acceptable headspace setting on this project we will use an improvised method that will not be exactly perfect but it will work and you won't have to buy expensive headspace gauges. The method here is crude but it does work on a blowback gun.

The tabs on the sides of the Sten magazine and the sides of the magazine housing will determine seating depth. Notches can be cut in the sides or the side shortened.

BUILDING THE SGN-9 | PART 4

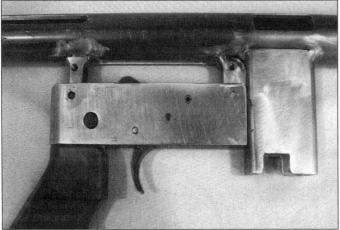

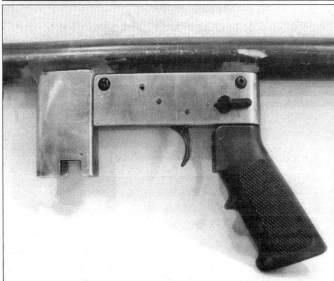

After final fitting of the lower receiver, it is attached to the lugs with 1/4"-20 button-head Allen screws. The button head screws will give the receiver a smooth look.

will hold the shim in place. Insert your bolt stop ring into the receiver, followed by the bolt. Slide the bolt all the way forward so the bolt is tight against the gauge and shim.

With the bolt tight against the gauge and the bolt stop ring tight against the bolt, mark a location for a couple holes that can be drilled through the receiver directly over the ring. Two 3/8" holes opposite each other should be enough.

Remove the parts, then drill the holes. Reinstall your parts, making sure everything is still tight, and then you can plug weld the ring in place in the receiver. When welded in place, this should give you a clearance of .005" between the bolt face and the cartridge when using SAAMI specification ammo.

The previously installed magazine housing can now be sized for proper magazine seating depth since it was made oversized. The tabs on the side of the Sten magazine and the sides of the magazine housing will determine seating depth. I filed notches in the sides of the magazine housing wall to keep the sides as long as possible for good support, but you could file the sides even if you wish.

You want to size the sides of the housing so that the lips of the magazine are just slightly below the bolt. The relief cuts in the bolt will allow the bolt face to extend down between the magazine lips to strip a round out of the magazine. You want the magazine as close as you can get it to the bolt without it binding or dragging. Once you have the proper depth, chamfer the edges of the housing to allow for easy magazine insertion. The magazine catch will be fitted later.

The lower receiver/trigger housing can now be fitted and attached to the receiver tube. Before welding on the lower receiver, you need to trim and fit the attaching blocks to allow the hammer to be at about a 90° angle when the hammer strikes the firing pin. Install the bolt into the receiver and slide it all the way forward.

With the hammer in the forward position, slide the trigger housing up to the receiver and slip the hammer through its slots in the receiver and bolt. With the housing pushed all the way forward, observe the angle of the hammer. You want to trim the front of the trigger housing so that when it is pushed all the way forward against the magazine housing and the hammer is resting on the firing pin, the hammer is at about 90°.

This is to insure that when the hammer strikes the firing pin, it is doing it squarely and not pushing the pin off to one side. Once

Matthews cut a square clearance notch in the front of the trigger housing for the magazine catch assembly. Note the extra coil spring he installed for the catch.

you have the housing sized and fitted, you can attach the mounting blocks to the receiver. Locate the mounting blocks so that they hold the housing square and centered on the receiver tube.

Also be sure to locate them so that when the housing is installed the blocks don't interfere with any internal parts. Weld the front and rear blocks in place using welding techniques to minimize receiver distortion. After the lugs are welded in place, install the trigger housing tightly against the receiver tube and then drill #7 size holes through the sides of the housing and through the blocks.

Remove the housing and drill out the #7 holes in the sides of the housing to 1/4". Tap the #7 holes in the mounting blocks with a 1/4"-20 tap. This will allow the housing to be attached with 3/8" long button-head Allen screws.

Now that the trigger housing/lower receiver is attached, we can finish up the magazine housing work. A magazine catch needs to be fabricated and fitted into a housing to lock the magazines in place. The Sten magazines feature a square notch in their back side and this will be used to lock the magazines in the housing.

Cut a square hole in the back of the magazine housing to allow access to this hole. The previously made magazine catch housing

Do not use this method on locked breech guns. Obtain or make a dummy/non-live 9mm Luger (9x19mm) round that has a case length (case only, not overall length) close to the SAAMI specification length of .754".

This dummy round will be our improvised headspace gauge. Get a piece of .005" shim stock and cut out a disc slightly under the size of the 9mm round's base. Deburr the edges and measure to verify that the disc is .005".

We will need to make a bolt stop that can be installed in the receiver. I simply made a doughnut-shaped ring that would fit snugly in the receiver tube. This ring featured a hole in the center that would allow the round forward portion of the bolt to extend through it and seat flush against the bolt body.

Insert your improvised headspace gauge into the chamber of the SGN-9 with the .005" shim disc on the base. A dab of grease

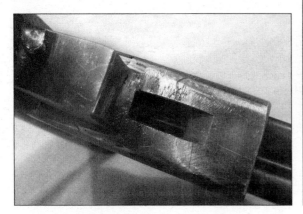

A square hole cut in the back of the magazine housing will allow the magazine catch to engage the square notch on the magazine. Careful measuring is required here.

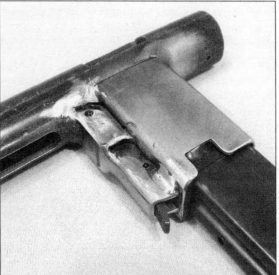

The magazine catch housing is welded into position after final fitting. The pivot pin should be staked in place to retain it securely in the magazine housing.

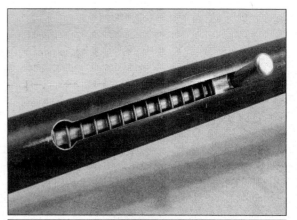

Weld the buttplate to the receiver tube and then install a reinforcing block under the tube to spread out recoil forces that will be transferred through the end plug.

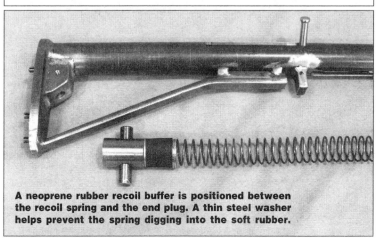

A hard half-inch pin is installed down through the receiver, end plug and reinforcement block. The pin should fit tightly to lock the parts together securely.

will be fitted over this hole and a salvaged Suomi magazine catch and spring will be modified to work on the SGN-9.

Fitting these parts will require a fair amount of trial-and-error fitting, but this is the best way to get a good snug fit. You need to reshape the tip of the Suomi catch to allow it to extend through the hole in the back of the magazine housing and engage the notch in the back of the Sten magazines.

The tip needs to be shaped so that as it moves rearward when operated, it releases the magazine without pushing the latter upward. The pivot pin hole in the catch housing needs to be located so that when the catch is pushed, it will allow for enough movement to release the magazine.

Locate the catch and pivot pin in the catch housing, then hand-trim the assembly so that it locks the magazine in place and will release it easily. The Suomi catch features a torsion return spring that I used in the SGN-9, but this seemed a little light, so I added a small coil spring pressing against the catch on the front bottom side. A shallow pocket drilled on the face of the catch locked the spring in place.

It's now time to determine pull length before you weld on the buttplate. Everyone has their own personal preference for the distance from the trigger to the buttplate. On my SGN-9 I chose a length of 13½ inches. Since I was using a recoil pad and spacer that was about an inch thick, I cut my stock/receiver at a point about 12½ inches behind the trigger.

When you determine what length you want, the buttplate can be welded in place on the tube. Be sure it is aligned with the trigger housing so it looks straight and be sure it is square with the receiver tube before welding in place.

After welding on the buttplate, I added a reinforcement block under the receiver tube. This block was added to help distribute the recoil forces to the stock when the bolt reciprocates under recoil. The block was made from a piece of 7/8"x7/8"x1" steel. It was contoured to fit flush against the receiver tube and buttplate.

I inserted a 1x1½" end plug flush with the end of the receiver tube and clamped it securely in place. Then I drilled a 3/8" hole from the top all the way through the receiver tube, end plug and reinforcing block.

Then I drilled a half-inch hole through the same point but this time stopped it before it went all the way through the reinforcing block so that there was a restriction in the hole to keep the half-inch pin that will be installed later from coming out the bottom. This 1/2" hole needs to be a snug fit so the 1/2" pin isn't loose when installed.

It also needs to be drilled very straight so that it doesn't run out the side of the reinforcing block. After your hole is drilled, cut yourself a half-inch diameter steel takedown pin that is just long enough to extend slightly out of the top of the receiver tube. I recommend some type of hardened steel such as a dowel pin or drill bit shank. On the side of your reinforcing block, drill and tap a hole for a #8-32 set screw to retain the pin.

I wanted a skeletonized buttstock, so I added a 1/4"x1/2" piece of flat steel between the buttplate and the receiver tube. I ran it up to the trigger housing and added a spacer to offset it from the receiver tube. This is where you can get creative if you want. Since this feature is basically just for looks, you can use whatever design you like.

For an action or recoil spring I chose the standard length AR-15 buffer/recoil spring. Depending on how long you made your stock, the spring may be the correct length or it may need to be shortened. I simply guessed on my project after all the other parts were installed in the receiver. After installing the bolt, spring, rubber buffer, spacers and end plug I decided mine was a little tight so I cut off a few coils, but your situation may be different. Remember this project is about making some of your own decisions and this is where you will have to use your own judgment.

Install your bolt followed by the action spring. At this point I added a rubber recoil buffer behind the spring. I simply used a hole saw and cut a 1-inch diameter by 1-inch long rubber plug out of a piece of neoprene rubber. To keep the spring from digging into the soft rubber, I added a 1-inch diameter steel washer between the spring and neoprene plug.

At this point, the length of bolt travel must be set so that the bolt stops before the

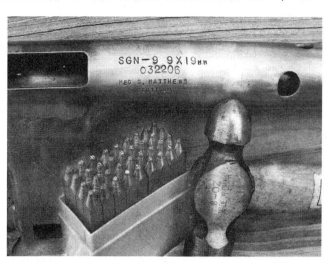

Serial numbers are not required for homemade guns, but Matthews advises one just in case you are stopped by a policeman who doesn't know the details of federal law.

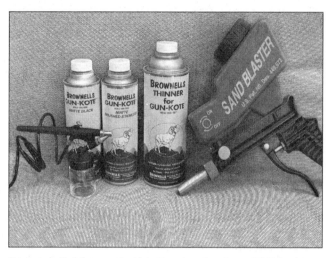

Spray-on finishes make it easy to give your SGN-9 a professional look. Matthews used a hand sandblaster to even up the surface, then an airbrush with Brownells GunKote.

handle gets to the takedown cut out on the slot. Install your end plug and operate the bolt. If the handle goes back far enough to reach the takedown notch, you will need to add a spacer between the rubber recoil buffer and the end cap to limit the travel. I set mine up so that the handle stopped about a half-inch in front of the takedown notch.

At this point it is time to start checking for proper function. Make or purchase several dummy/non-live rounds for testing. These will be used to check for proper chambering and ejection. Do not ever use live rounds for preliminary function testing!.

It is extremely dangerous to use live rounds on an unproven firearm. Load several dummy rounds into a magazine and seat the magazine in the gun. Pull the bolt to the rear and release it. The rounds should strip out of the magazine and chamber. When you pull the bolt back it should eject the round.

Next, check for proper fire control group function. When you pull the trigger, the hammer should fall. While keeping the trigger pulled, cycle the action. The hammer should re-cock and the trigger should have to be released before the hammer can be released again.

If there are problems, correct them before you advance to live-fire testing. If there are problems, you want to correct them when you are using non-firing dummy rounds! When I tested my project it worked well with non-live rounds so I could advance to live fire testing. When doing live fire testing be sure to use safety glasses, gloves and hearing protection.

Start by single loading; then move on to two rounds and only after firing successfully, try more rounds in the magazine. This is a prudent precaution for testing any semi-auto, even factory guns, as guns can double on you.

When I tested my project with live ammo, it worked perfectly, which was quite a surprise. I find many of my projects

Matthews shaped a quarter-inch by half-inch bar of flat stock to reinforce the buttplate. This as an area you can style as you see fit when you make your own SGN-9.

A neoprene rubber recoil buffer is positioned between the recoil spring and the end plug. A thin steel washer helps prevent the spring digging into the soft rubber.

BUILDING THE SGN-9 | PART 4

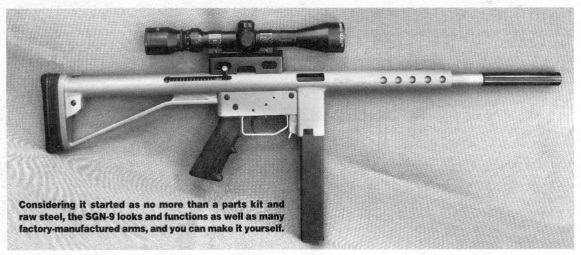

Considering it started as no more than a parts kit and raw steel, the SGN-9 looks and functions as well as many factory-manufactured arms, and you can make it yourself.

require a certain amount of fine tuning. I guess sometimes you get lucky.

Final finishing can determine if your project looks professionally built or crudely assembled. Finishing can also determine if your firearm looks to be a commercial sporting arm or utilitarian military arm. I prefer the rather crude all-business look of military firearms, so this is how I finished mine.

I went through and smoothed up all welds and removed any weld splatter and deep scratches. One last thing I did before finishing was to add firearms identification information. Although Federal law does not require this information on home-built guns, it is a good idea to add it. If you ever have "contacts" with law enforcement while possessing this gun they may consider it to be a gun that has been altered to obscure its identity.

Most law enforcement personnel are not familiar with the specifics of home firearms making and don't know the guns don't have to be marked. Rather than trying to explain the laws to them (they won't believe you anyway!) just go ahead and mark your creation. I stamped in my name and address along with a serial number. For a serial number I just used the date it was made and finished.

Since you made it you can serial number it how ever you want. Finishing on this project can be whatever you choose. Bluing, Parkerizing, high tech finishes such as LCW DuraCoat or Brownells GunKote are all good options. You can even use spray paint if you choose.

For the SGN-9, I chose one of my favorite low maintenance firearms finishes, Brownells GunKote. This is a spray and baked-

on finish that is extremely durable and is a great finish for military or sporting firearms. It is available in many colors and for this project I chose the "brushed stainless steel" color for most of the gun and "satin black" for highlights.

Before applying this finish I abrasive blasted and degreased the parts. The GunKote was sprayed on with a small spray gun. It is also available in spray cans for those without spray equipment. After baking for one hour at 325°, it was left to cool. After cooling, the parts can be reassembled immediately; no need to wait weeks for a full cure.

After reassembly, I tried both a scope sight and a red dot sight on the self-made sight base. Both worked well but I am partial to items that don't have batteries that can go dead so I went with the scope. I started with a full size scope but later I changed to a compact scope that looked more appropriate on this type of firearm.

All in all I was quite pleased with the results of this project. It was relatively easy to build since it used some manufactured parts, but also had enough self-made parts to make it far beyond a simple assembly project. If you have that desire to "make your own" this project may be for you. ◎

Ask the Gunsmith

By Reid Coffield

NO MARTINI SAFETY?

Q *At a recent gun show I saw a British Martini .22 target rifle. It looked like a nice rifle but I was struck by the fact that it evidently did not have a safety. Is this normal?*

A Yes, it is. The Martini target rifles were basically designed for use on a range where you did not load until you were ready to fire. Consequently there was little practical need for a safety.

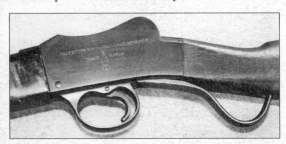

There's no real function for a safety in target firearms where loading only takes place just before firing. So no safety was specified for this Martini smallbore target rifle.

RIMFIRE M1

Q *I know this sounds really strange but I have to ask. Would it be possible to convert a .30-'06 Garand to .22 rimfire? I have seen AR-15s converted to .22.*

A Yes, it can be done! In fact, I have seen both an M1 Garand and an M1A converted to .22 rimfire. In both cases extensive work was done to the bolts to convert them to rimfire. Also, the barrels were bored out and lined with a .22 liner. In each case the conversions were single-shots. I have never seen or heard of a conversion that would permit autoloading.

TRIGGER SHOES

Q *Where can I get trigger shoes? I used to see them everywhere but none of my local shops have them nor do they know where to get them.*

A Contact the folks at Tyler Manufacturing, Box 94845, Dept. SGN, Oklahoma City, Okla. 73143, telephone 800-654-8415.

MAUSER COCKING NOTCH

Q *For years, I have noticed a notch cut on the side of the cocking piece of various Mausers I have owned. I have never seen anything that indicated the purpose for this notch. Do you know?*

The milled groove in the cocking piece allowed cocking without opening the bolt. A cartridge rim will fit into the groove and allow the cocking piece to be easily pulled to the rear.

A As I understand this notch was cut into the cocking piece to allow the shooter to cock the rifle using the rim of a cartridge case. This would allow you to cock the rifle without opening the bolt. In normal situations that would seem to be of little value, but in the case of a hang fire, it could be quite helpful. Recall that guns like the 1903 Springfield had knurled knobs to let the shooter recock the rifle. ◎

Ask the Gunsmith

By Reid Coffield

AR .22 CONVERSIONS

Q *I am thinking about buying a .22 rimfire conversion unit for my AR-15. With the high cost of .223 ammo, the idea of practice with the cheaper .22 ammo is a major factor. My primary concern has to do with lead fouling. I am worried that lead fouling will gum up the gas port and cause problems when I switch to .223. Also, I am a bit concerned about the faster twist in my .223 barrel as to whether or not it will allow me to shoot the rimfire ammo with reasonable accuracy. Can you help?*

Conversion units in .22 rimfire such as this one made by Colt are popular accessories for ARs. While continuous firing with them can cause fouling, Coffield says it's easily removed.

A Not too long ago, a friend asked about this same issue. Fortunately I had an old AR-15 that had been used extensively for .22 rimfire that I could check out. The rifle is kinda interesting in that I put it together many years ago. When I assembled it, I fired maybe five to 10 rounds of .223 to make sure it functioned properly. After that, I immediately installed a Colt .22 rimfire conversion unit and its never been used for anything else since that time. Over the years my sons, who are now grown, and I fired literally thousands of rounds of .22 rimfire through this old AR. During that time maintenance of the rifle was minimal at best. At no point had I ever attempted to clean the gas port or gas system.

When I pulled the rifle out to check it I used a Hawkeye Bore Scope made by the Gradient Lens Corp., 207 Tremont St., Dept. SGN, Rochester, N.Y. 14608, telephone 800-536-0790. This let me look at the gas port under magnification from inside the barrel. I found that there was very little lead or fouling buildup in the gas port.

I then cleaned the bore and chamber but did not do anything with the gas system. The rifle was taken to a local range and fired with 20 rounds of standard military .223 ammo. I wanted to see if this would blow out the small amount of fouling that I had seen and how the rifle would function.

When I fired the first round, the rifle failed to eject. The bolt came back but the case did not extract. I cleared the rifle and closely examined the case. There was evidence of fouling along the case body. I then reloaded and fired the remaining 19 rounds without incident. The rifle functioned perfectly.

Later back in the shop I checked it again with the Hawkeye Bore Scope and sure enough the fouling in the gas port had been eliminated. Based on this experience with my .22 conversion unit, I would say go for it!

By the way, I initially had some concerns relating to accuracy. Keep in mind that most rimfire barrels have a 1:16 twist rate while centerfire barrels are much faster. My AR has a 1:9 twist. However, for plinking and general recreational shooting I have never had any accuracy issues. The gun shoots quite well and neither I nor anyone else that has used it has had any complaints.

Coffield found that extensive use of the .22 rimfire conversion unit did not cause any problems when converting back to .223. His first round failed to eject, but subsequent shots worked fine.

NAGANT TARGET REVOLVER

Q *This weekend I saw a fellow at the local range with a strange revolver. I walked over and asked him about it and it turns out that it was a target model Russian Nagant. It looked really different. Have you ever worked on one of these guns? What was your impression? Where could I get one?*

While it does look weird, the Nagant target revolver is an interesting, unique handgun that can be a lot of fun to shoot. They were made for international center-fire pistol shooting.

A Yep, those revolvers are indeed strange when compared to standard Colts, Smith and Wessons or Rugers. The most unusual feature is the manner in which the cylinder is moved forward and surrounds the rear portion of the barrel when it is fired. At the same time, the cartridge case bridges the gap between the cylinder and the barrel. This is to prevent the loss of any gas and make the gun more efficient and powerful.

One very positive feature that I've never seen mentioned is that by closing off this gap, you really do cut down on the fouling on the front of the cylinder and around the cylinder pin and cylinder pin sleeve.

Like a lot of Russian firearms, the later ones made during World War II are often pretty rough with lots of machine marks and very little emphasis on the quality of the exterior finish. However, they are deceptively rugged and served in some of the worst environments in the world. They are an interesting collectable and a lot of fun to shoot.

The target versions, like the standard handguns, often look rather crude but the ones I've used have shot quite well. I own one of these target models and have used it from time to time for about two years or so. It's a lot of fun and they definitely will attract attention at the range! If you want one of these handguns, just give the good folks at Century International Arms, Inc., 430 South Congress Dr., Suite 1, Dept. SGN, DelRay Beach, Fla. 33445, telephone 800-527-1252 a call. They've got bunches of 'em. Or, you can probably just go to your local dealer and have him order one for you from Century. Either way, they'll fix you up!

6.5 VETTERLI

Q *have a rifle as pictured. Can you tell me where these rifles were made and if they were rebarreled for service use and if so, in what caliber? Do these rifles have any value?*

A You have an Italian Vetterli rifle, Model 1870/87/15. Your rifle was built at the Torino arsenal under license from the Swiss. Originally it was a chambered for a blackpowder cartridge and was a single-shot. Late in the late 1880s these rifles were converted to a magazine feeding system. Shortly thereafter these rifles were replaced by the 1891 Carcano which used a 6.5mm cartridge.

The older Vetterlis were either sold off as surplus or stored. During World War I, the Italian army couldn't obtain enough rifles, so these old Model 1870/87 rifles were pulled from storage and converted to 6.5mm. The barrels were lined, a new magazine was fitted and the bolt modified.

These are very interesting and unusual conversions. Unfortunately, as far as I am concerned, they are not safe to fire. The Vetterli was originally chambered for a blackpowder round and the 6.5mm Carcano cartridge generates far more pressure than this rifle was designed to contain back in 1870.

Also, I have seen a number of these rifles with various problems including one in which the 6.5mm barrel liner was split about halfway down the bore! As for value, the ones I have seen for sale in the last year or so were priced around $100.

The Vetterli, converted to 6.5mm, was one of the most unusual rifles used during World War I, and probably the worst. Coffield says never, ever try to shoot one with 6.5mm ammo.

GRIT NOMENCLATURE

Q *You have probably answered this before but I am confused by sanding grits. What is "coarse", what is "medium", and what is "fine"? I see gunsmiths and woodworkers referring to sandpapers with these terms but they often do not define them.*

A There is nothing written in stone about this or is there any "official" grit designation as far as I know. I define coarse as 50 grit, medium as 80 grit, fine as 120 grit, and extra fine as 240 grit and higher. This is just the system or scale I use but it works for me and I believe it would be compatible with a good many other woodworkers. I'm sure some folks would disagree but there it is!

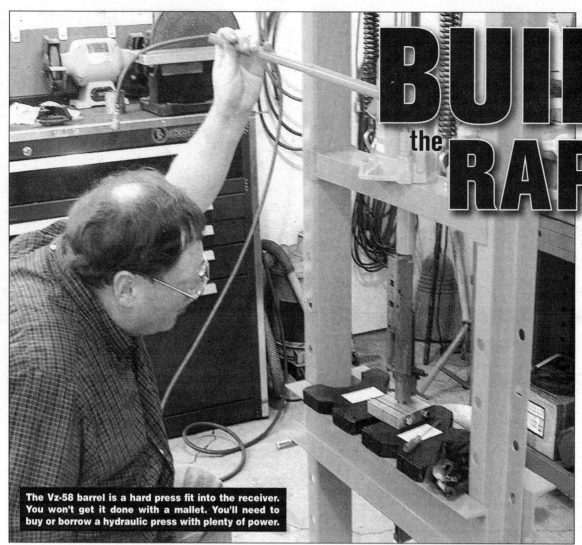

The Vz-58 barrel is a hard press fit into the receiver. You won't get it done with a mallet. You'll need to buy or borrow a hydraulic press with plenty of power.

BUILDING the RAPID FIRE Vz-58

By Steven Matthews

Part 1

He's already made a Vz-58 dummy, a very easy project. Now Matthews takes on the more complicated task of putting together a semi-auto rifle.

I've always been intrigued by the Czech Vz-58. Authentic examples are very rare and way out of my budget, but the arrival of parts kits in recent years made it easy to put together a dummy, a project I wrote about here (11/20/08). The completed project looked very good but I did long for a real version.

Since then, Rapid Fire of Troy, Ohio began producing a BATFE-approved semi-automatic receiver. They were also offering a U.S.-made semi-auto "922(r) U.S. compliance package". This would allow home builders like me to build an inexpensive semi-auto Vz-58.

The first thing you need for this project is a Vz-58 military surplus parts set. These contain all the parts for a Vz-58 rifle except for the receiver. These parts sets are obtained from Vz-58 rifles that were taken out of service. Since the Vz-58 wasn't used in any major conflicts, most of the parts sets are in pretty good mechanical condition. They appear to have been carried a lot but shot little, the finishes are worn but the parts aren't.

When I did my dummy Vz-58 article, I bought my parts set from Centerfire Systems at the on-sale price of $49.95. For this project, I salvaged my parts from that previous project rather than buy another set. As this article is written, prices for Vz-58 parts sets have risen to $100-$150 from several military parts suppliers that advertise in SHOTGUN NEWS.

Even at these higher prices, this is still a bargain. Obtain your parts set *before* you purchase a receiver, since there are some legal issues that need to be addressed before you get a receiver.

A U.S. made semi-auto "922(r) compliance" parts package will also need to be purchased. I purchased mine from Rapid Fire, and at the time, the price was $150. This semi-auto parts package contains a gas piston, trigger, sear, disconnector and various small parts.

Rapid Fire also offers a U.S.-made muzzle brake that can be purchased for $40, since an extension needs to be added to the original Vz-58 barrel. This is a fine part, but I made my own extension for about $10 since I am a notorious cheapskate and can't bear to spend money on parts I can inexpensively make myself.

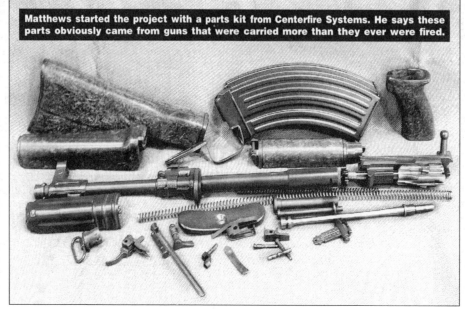

Matthews started the project with a parts kit from Centerfire Systems. He says these parts obviously came from guns that were carried more than they ever were fired.

You will need a U.S.-made semiautomatic receiver for this project and Rapid Fire offers one for about $350 (the price for this part has also fluctuated over the last year or so). It is reasonably well-made from 4140 steel, but some hand fitting will be required to assemble the project, since it is made to the low end of the tolerance ranges and some parts will need to be hand-fitted.

This is preferable to having sloppily fitted and loose parts. Since the receiver is the firearm as defined by the BATFE, you will have to obtain it through a local FFL holder. You can personally order it from Rapid Fire but it must be shipped to a FFL holder where you will sign for it just as a complete firearm.

Don't consider this to be a complete step-by-step build tutorial. I will only cover the high points, and builders will have to supplement this information with their own firearms building skills and knowledge.

I am not a professional gunsmith and this article only documents my experiences with this project. There are several internet resources for the hobbyist gunsmith on the building of the Vz-58 rifle and they are well worth reading. Remember you are the gunsmith on this project and you are supposed to be knowledgeable so do your pre-project research! Neither SHOTGUN NEWS/InterMedia Outdoors or the author assume any responsibility for the safe and legal construction of this project. You are the builder, you are responsible for your own work. Be aware that while this project was legal in the author's locality, state and local laws vary widely.

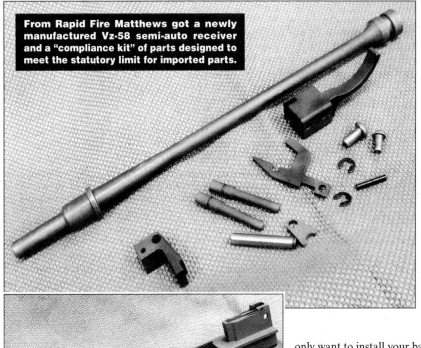

From Rapid Fire Matthews got a newly manufactured Vz-58 semi-auto receiver and a "compliance kit" of parts designed to meet the statutory limit for imported parts.

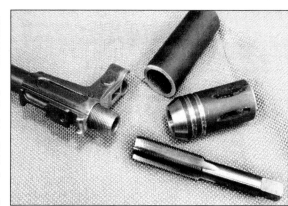

Matthews sawed off and reshaped an AR-15 muzzle brake, then threaded it. He didn't want to spring for an oddball 14mm tap, so he used the common 9/16" instead.

With the extension, the barrel now measures a legal 17 inches. Matthews says it's essential to weld the extension to the front sight to make installation permanent.

Let's start with parts kit preparation. Your parts kit should contain all the parts from a functional Vz-58 rifle except for the original fully automatic receiver. You may have one or more destroyed pieces of the old receiver that will have parts in them that need to be salvaged.

All parts are easily removed except for the barrel. The barrel of the Vz-58 is pressed tight into place at manufacture and can be difficult to remove. To remove the barrel from the destroyed section of receiver, you drive out the barrel crosspin and then press out the barrel with a hydraulic press.

If you use this method, be sure to protect the barrel face when you press it out. Vz-58 barrels are not readily available, so you don't want to ruin yours. An easier method is what I used since at the time I had not purchased my press that would be needed for barrel installation.

First, I drove out the cross-pin. These crosspins can be very hard to get out. I then used a thin cutoff wheel in an air-powered grinder to slice what was left of the receiver apart. I just cut a slot through a thin section of receiver until the depth was right at the barrel shank. Be especially careful not to cut into the barrel shank if you use this method.

Once the slot was cut, I drove a cold chisel into the slot to spread the receiver apart. Once spread out, the receiver stub simply slid off the barrel stub.

Whichever method you use, there is a small part inside the barrel hole that needs to be saved. It is a crescent-shaped piece of steel called a gas piston stop. This part must be saved and installed in the new receiver before you install the barrel.

It extends up through the top of the receiver into the gas piston/sight base and prevents gas piston overtravel. It is a small and easy-to-overlook part but it must be installed in the new receiver before you press in the barrel.

If you forget it before you install the barrel, your only option will be to take out your barrel and reinstall it. Believe me, you only want to install your barrel once on this project.

Once the barrel is removed and before you take possession of your new receiver, the barrel must be modified to meet BATFE regulations that specify a rifle barrel must have an overall length of at least 16 inches. Since the original Vz-58 barrel is only 15½ inches long, it must be modified to be legal.

The BATFE opinion is that possession of a receiver, parts set and short barrel is illegal, since the authorities regard you as having a complete short-barreled rifle in your possession, even if it is unassembled. The penalties are severe for possession of an unregistered short-barreled rifle. The Federal registration procedure for short-barreled rifles is complex and beyond the scope of this article and will not be covered since we are building an unrestricted rifle for this article.

To be legal, you must *permanently* attach a muzzle extension to bring the overall length to 16 inches or more. The most popular method to increase the length to minimum standards is permanently to attach an extension in the form of a flash suppressor or muzzle brake.

Rapid Fire offers a part for this purpose but I chose to make my own for a few dollars. I decided to use a "slip over barrel" type made for the AR-15. The AR-15 flash suppressor is threaded for 1/2"-28 threads so it will not fit the Vz-58 threads, which are 14mm by 1 thread per millimeter right-hand pitch.

This long slip over type was chosen for raw material since it has a larger minimum diameter than the standard short birdcage type. The AR-15 suppressor was cut just behind the beginning of the internal threads. The old threads were then drilled out and tapped to fit the Vz-58 barrel.

This is where a small cost problem arose. 14mm x 1 taps are pricey; $25 where I could find them. Since my build was on a tight budget, I began to look for a lower cost standard-size tap.

Ignoring metric standards, I measured the barrel threads and found them to be .560" by 25 threads per inch. This .560" size is 9/16" and 9/16" taps are available. The 25 threads per inch size was, however, not available. The closest size available was 9/16"-24, which was priced at about $8.

Since the threaded portion of barrel and flash suppressor was only about 1/2" long I decided to try the 9/16"-24 tap to see if it would work before the mismatch in thread pitch caused it to bind.

I drilled and tapped the AR-15 flash suppressor and installed it on the Vz-58 barrel. To my delight, it threaded on smoothly and only started to bind from

thread pitch differences when it was about 1/8" from being fully seated. A slight beveling of the front threads on the Vz-58 barrel allowed it to go on all the way.

I do not generally recommend mismatching threads like this, but since the parts are not under any great stress and will be secured in place, I figured it was OK in this case.

Once installed, the flash suppressor needs to be permanently attached to meet regulations. The BATFE-approved methods for attaching barrel extensions are blind pinning, high temperature silver soldering/brazing or welding (arc or fusion).

I chose to arc-weld my flash suppressor in place by placing two small welds between the suppressor and the sight base. This is, however, not a permanent method, since the sight base can easily be removed by driving out two pins. Once the pins are out, the whole assembly could just be screwed off as if the flash suppressor was just screwed on the end of the barrel.

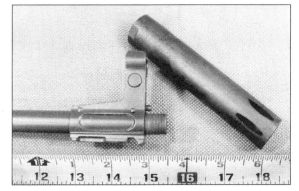

The original Vz-58 barrel is only 15½ inches long. A permanently-attached extension needs to be added to bring it up to the U.S.-legal length of 16 inches.

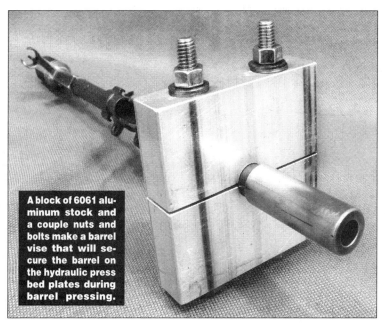

A block of 6061 aluminum stock and a couple nuts and bolts make a barrel vise that will secure the barrel on the hydraulic press bed plates during barrel pressing.

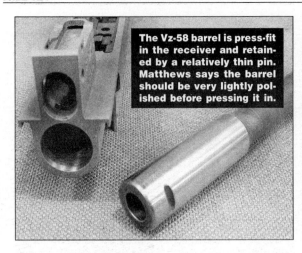

The Vz-58 barrel is press-fit in the receiver and retained by a relatively thin pin. Matthews says the barrel should be very lightly polished before pressing it in.

Headspace gauges are essential for inserting the barrel to the proper depth in the Vz-58 receiver. The bolt must close on the Go gauge and not close on the No Go.

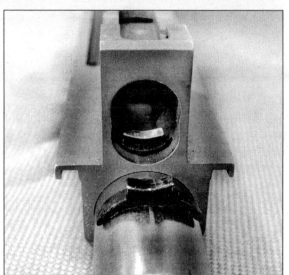

The gas piston stop absolutely must be in position in the receiver before you start the barrel. A spare stop shows the crescent shape that rides the top of the barrel.

With the Go gauge chambered and the bolt closed, slowly and carefully press the barrel into the receiver. Stop when the locking piece lugs contact the receiver lugs.

Matthews made the mistake of overpolishing his barrel, so he extensively stippled the area for more grip before pressing. It's better just not to overpolish.

To make this setup permanent, I arc-welded the sight base to the barrel so that neither part could be removed by unscrewing the assembly. Once you have your barrel modified to meet BATFE guidelines, you can then take possession of a receiver without any concerns about possessing an unregistered short-barreled rifle.

Before ordering your receiver, you should precisely measure (down to .0001") your barrel to verify its exact shank diameter. From what I gather from internet discussion forums, there can be a couple thousandths difference between barrel sizes encountered in Vz-58 parts kits.

Rapid Fire has sized the barrel hole in their receiver to fit most barrels, but some barrels may be over or under the optimal size. Contact Rapid Fire to see if your barrel is within acceptable size limits. If your barrel is undersized, it will not fit tight enough to be secured properly, since this gun requires a very tight press fit on the barrel.

The receiver hole is supposed to be about .0002" to .0005" under barrel shank size, so that it creates an "interference" fit. When the barrel is pressed in place, the receiver will actually expand slightly and securely grip the barrel.

Although the barrel is crosspinned in place, the crosspin is very small and does not fully secure the barrel to the receiver. The tight fit is required on this design to secure the barrel fully. When the gun is fired, there are 3-4 tons of back force trying to separate the barrel and receiver; the tight fitting barrel and the crosspin both function to secure it. If your barrel size is oversize by too much, it will have to be machined to the correct size.

The Rapid Fire receiver is made to semiautomatic specifications, so the original full-auto fire control group cannot be used. The fire control group must function in semiautomatic mode only and not be readily convertible to automatic operation.

The U.S.-made fire control group offered by Rapid Fire meets this requirement. It is also U.S. compliant or some times referred to as 922(r) Compliant. This package consists of the trigger, sear, disconnector and several other small fire control group parts. A U.S-made gas piston is also in the U.S. compliance package.

The parts looked to be very well made and were Parkerized in a nice dark gray color. The gas piston was not finished in

any way since it is stainless steel. It did, however, have a slight golden tint to it from the heat treating process.

When the receiver arrived at my local FFL, I eagerly opened the box and inspected it. Preliminary examination revealed it to be well-made and finished. The receiver is made from a block of 4140 chrome-moly steel that is machined by CNC machining centers on site at Rapid Fire.

The receiver has reproductions of some of the original Czech markings. The receiver is "in the white" so it can be finished to the builder's preference. The receiver is very close to an original Czech receiver minus the full auto features. With all the parts in hand, I got started.

The first procedure in the build is also the hardest, installing the barrel. The barrel will be pressed into place with a hydraulic press. A press with a 6-8 ton capacity should suffice. If you don't have a press and are going to buy one for this project, be aware that many inexpensive press capacities are vastly overrated.

Many cheap presses are rated at a certain tonnage, but it's just about at the unit's breaking point. It's better to buy a slightly larger press than to get one that doesn't live up to its advertised maximum capacity.

I made a barrel vise to hold the barrel securely on the bed plates while it would be pressed in place. You will also need a set of 7.62 x 39mm headspace gauges. This set will consist of a "go" gauge and a "no go" gauge. These will be used to determine the proper pressing depth when the barrel is installed. I obtained my gauges from Brownells of Montezuma, Iowa. Brownells has been supplying gunsmiths, both professional and amateur, with quality gunsmithing supplies for decades.

Before you can press the barrel in place, fabricate an easy-to-make barrel vise from a 4 x 4 x 1 piece of 6061 aluminum flat stock. Simply drill a hole in the center of the block the exact size (plus or minus a couple thousandths) of the barrel just in front of the large barrel shank. Then drill two 3/8" diameter holes through the sides for clamp bolts.

Cut the block through the center of the hole with a saw. File the cut on each half block smooth so that when the blocks are placed around the barrel, there is a 1/16" to 3/32" gap between the two halves. Install a 3/8" Grade 5 or better bolt in each hole and use the bolts to tighten the blocks evenly on the barrel.

Before installing the barrel, polish up the barrel shank and the hole in the receiver to remove any burrs. Do not over-polish! There is only about .0005" difference in size between barrel and receiver, and over-polishing can make the fit too loose. Lightly chamfer the first 1/4" or so of the shank so it can easily enter the barrel hole before it gets tight.

If you can install the barrel past the first 1/4" or so by hand or with a large mallet, the fit is too loose. If your barrel is too loose for a proper tight press fit, you have relatively undesirable options. You can replace the barrel with a slightly larger one or increase the barrel shank diameter by knurling the shank on a lathe or by extensively hand-stippling the shank.

I found my barrel entered the hole almost halfway before it encountered much resistance. This indicated that my barrel hole was slightly larger for the first portion. To tighten the fit, I extensively stippled the last half of the barrel shank. This made the fit tight enough.

The procedure I will describe here to install the barrel and set headspace is what worked well for me but it certainly is not the only method available. The first thing you must do is to install the small crescent-shaped gas piston stop in the groove in the barrel hole.

You may have to do some hand fitting to get it in place. Also be sure that the bottom edge is flush with the edge of the barrel hole and not extending into the barrel hole. If it extends into the barrel hole, it will ether stop the pressing process or possibly damage the barrel or receiver when installing the barrel. Do not, I repeat do not, forget to install this part before you begin installing the barrel.

I began by installing my barrel vise just in front of the barrel shank and tightened it down very tight so the barrel wouldn't slip in the vise while pressing. The barrel and vise were set on the press with the vise setting on the bed plates and the muzzle extending down between the plates.

I applied a light coating of grease to the barrel shank and inside the barrel hole in the receiver. The receiver was placed over the barrel shank, roughly oriented and was *very lightly* pressed on about a quarter-inch. With the barrel lightly installed a little way into the receiver, I removed the assembly from the press to index the barrel before continuing the pressing. The barrel must be indexed correctly before pressing so that the sights are aligned when the barrel is fully installed.

There are tools and fixtures to help in this operation, but I used an improvised method that cost nothing and worked well. I set the barrel/receiver assembly up on some blocks and bore-sighted through the barrel at an object about 300 yards away.

I then looked through the sights to see how far they were off from the bore sight. I rotated the lightly installed barrel so that the right to left alignment of the sights matched the bore sight view. Elevation alignment is not important here, just the left to right alignment.

I used this method to check alignment several times as I pressed the barrel in place. It is important to keep the sights aligned from the very beginning because after the barrel enters the receiver and begins to tighten, you will no longer be able to rotate the barrel to get the correct alignment.

Once the barrel is indexed correctly, you will begin the hard pressing of the assembly. Use some blocks with shims between

the press ram and the receiver to evenly support the rear of the receiver, After the barrel was pressed on about an inch or so, the "go" gauge was dropped into the chamber, which must be clean to get an accurate reading.

The bolt, bolt carrier with striker, and locking piece will be installed in the receiver during the rest of the pressing operation. To get an accurate headspace reading, the extractor and firing pin should be removed before installing the assembly into the receiver.

To remove the extractor and firing pin, you depress the plunger behind the extractor with a small punch. This will allow the extractor to slide rearward so that it disengages grooves cut in the bolt body. Once rearward, it can be removed from the bolt body.

Once the extractor is removed, the firing pin will simply slide out, since it was retained by protrusions on the rear of the extractor. This job seems to require three hands and can be difficult.

You also want to be careful to keep the extractor plunger spring under control or it will launch off into areas unknown once the extractor is removed. I do know this from personal experience!

With the barrel started and indexed and the "go" headspace gauge installed, you can install the bolt carrier, bolt and locking piece into the receiver. Slide the assembly all the way forward until the locking piece is cammed into the locking lug recesses in the receiver.

With the bolt locked in the closed position and all the way forward, there will be a few thousandths clearance between the rear of the locking piece and the lugs in the receiver. The receiver is slowly pressed on until the bolt face just contacts the headspace gauge.

When the bolt starts to contact the headspace gauge, it will begin to push the rear of the locking piece towards the locking

The manufacturer marks the spot for drilling the barrel pin hole. Drill carefully so as not to make the hole oversize, then press the 4 mm crosspin into place.

STEEL + RAPID FIRE = Vz-58 RECEIVER

At a time when U.S. manufacturing jobs seem to be disappearing every day, the gun industry is a happy exception. While the Rapid Fire receiver is based on a 50-year-old Czech design, it is totally made in the USA, providing jobs for American workers. There are foreign-made semiautomatic Vz-58 receivers, but these days, I prefer to buy American.

Rapid Fire receivers are machined onsite at Rapid Fire's facility in Troy, Ohio. Several Rapid Fire employees set up and operate large CNC machining centers to fabricate their Vz-58 receivers.

Operators set eight blocks of 4140 steel into machining fixtures in the machining centers. These computer-controlled machining centers then begin the long process of carving a Vz-58 receiver out of a block of steel.

Each machining center performs several operations on the receiver blanks. Other than loading and unloading, the CNC machines run without human assistance. Controlled by complex computer programs, they decide what tool is needed to do each operation and automatically change tools for the next operation.

Each machining station performs several operations and then the part is indexed to the next position for continuing machining. These machines can even self diagnose many problems such as a broken or dull tooling. As each operation is completed, the computer program instructs the machine to change to the next needed tool.

If a major problem arises, the machine can alert the human operator for assistance. I have watched many machining centers operate and it's just amazing to see the machine quickly and accurately machine materials. As all operations are completed on each machining center it shuts down and waits to be unloaded and reloaded by the operator.

The partially machined receivers are moved to another machining center for more precise machining. Since these CNC machines run without human operators, one worker can "supervise" several machines as they run more or less unattended.

Between machining centers the parts are randomly gauged. It would take days to make a Vz-58 receiver the old fashioned way with single-purpose machines. After the process is completed, the receiver does have some minor machining marks. These are removed by a surface finishing process after heat treating.

The Rapid Fire Vz-58 receiver when completed features a nice matte steel finish. This nice finish means that little surface preparation is required for final finish application. The Rapid Fire Vz-58 semi-auto receiver is well made but it will need some hand fitting of parts thanks to the tolerances encountered in the 50-year-old parts sets.

Every manufactured part is made to a tolerance range and one cannot make a mating part that will fit several sizes of parts perfectly. Rapid Fire has done a good job of duplicating the Vz-58 receiver. Many parts will need to be hand fitted but this is preferable to the receiver being made so oversized that many parts fit sloppily.

The receiver featured in this article was the 349th in the Rapid Fire's first production run and did have some issues. With the exception of the feed ramp issue, the problems were easy to overcome. Any new product will have some glitches that have to be worked out and I'm sure Rapid Fire will address any issues that

arise. All in all, the Rapid Fire semiautomatic receiver is a pretty decent product for the home firearms builder.

Rapid Fire's facility in Troy, Ohio, includes a factory and a retail store. The emphasis is on military firearms, and they manufacture for both foreign and domestic markets. ◉

Rapid Fire's facility in Troy, Ohio, includes a factory and a retail store. The emphasis is on military firearms, and they manufacture for both foreign and domestic markets.

The receiver starts life as a solid block of 4140 steel and everything that's not a Vz-58 is milled away. This requires a couple hours of cutting on CNC machines.

A table of partially machined receivers waits its turn in the next machining center. They go through dozens of operations in several machines before they are finished.

lugs in the receiver. Continue to slowly press until the clearance between the locking piece and receiver lugs is eliminated. Press only until the clearance is gone and no more.

If you press too hard, the bolt will be very tight against the headspace gauge and it will be too tight and very hard to open. Once all clearance is eliminated, headspace should be set at minimum specifications.

Remove the receiver and barrel assembly from the press and open the bolt. It should open easily if you didn't press too tight. It may be pretty tight and require a stiff tug, but as long as it opens without having to pull too hard, it will be fine. Cartridges are a few thousandths smaller than the headspace gauge and things won't be as tight with cartridges.

Also as the components wear in, another thousandth or two will be created to loosen things up slightly. As long as you can close the bolt on a "go" gauge, you can now check with the "no go" gauge. Install the "no go" gauge into the chamber and attempt to close the bolt.

If things are right, you should not be able to close the bolt on the "no go" gauge. If you can, you did something wrong and must find the problem. In its most simple form, headspace gauges are just setting a minimum and maximum distance from the bolt face to the rear of a chambered cartridge. The "go" gauge tells you there is enough space and the "no go" gauge tells you if there is too much space.

If your headspace gauges tell you that the barrel is installed correctly and your sights are properly indexed, you can now crosspin the barrel. The Rapid Fire receiver has a dimple machined in the side to locate the new crosspin right at the interior seam of the barrel shank and receiver hole.

This location is offset from the original pin location so you don't drill into the old crosspin hole. A new 4mm crosspin is included in the Rapid Fire compliance package. My 4mm pin was sized at .1575".

Compared to other pressed and pinned barrel firearms, this pin is very small. The pin on an AK-47 is twice the size and

is part of the reason those barrels don't have to be as tightly pressed in place. I really think a larger pin should have been used so the press fit isn't so difficult, but this gun wasn't designed in Czechoslovakia for home builds!

Drill the crosspin hole for a tight press fit when the 4mm pin is installed. The pin must be very tightly pressed in place so it doesn't come out during use. To get this tight fit, I first drilled with a #23 (.154") drill and then followed up with a 5/32"(.156") bit. Drilling all at once with a 5/32" bit may result in a hole that is oversize and the pin will not be tight enough when installed.

The hole as drilled with my 5/32" bit was about .1570", which was just right for press fitting a 4mm (.1575") pin. Be aware that drill bits are not designed for drilling holes to precise sizes and most bits vary a few thousandths from the specified size. Before drilling, measure your bits to determine their precise size and remember that drill bits commonly drill slightly over size.

Once your hole is drilled, install your crosspin. Depending on fit, you may be able to drive it into place with a hammer but a press is better since there is less risk of breaking off the pin from off-center hammering. At this point I'm going to tell you what I did but I don't necessarily recommend this to others.

Due to over-polishing the barrel hole and barrel shank my barrel did not fit as tight as I would have preferred. This is why I warned you earlier not to over-polish these parts prior to installation. This was totally my mistake and I had to find a solution to correct the problem.

While it was tight, I thought it should have been tighter, since a big part of the breeching strength on this design is from the extremely tight press fit. To strengthen this barrel installation, I installed two more 1/8" barrel crosspins in the forward portion of the receiver on each side of the sight base/gas piston block. These pins were tightly pressed into place just as the metric pin was.

Unless you are skilled in machining, I don't recommend you do this, since you have to locate the holes precisely to prevent

VZ-58 BUILD ARTICLE SOURCES

Gunsmithing Supplies and Finishing Materials–
BROWNELLS
200 S. Front St., Dept. SGN, Montezuma, Iowa, 50171, 1-800-741-0015, www.brownells.com

DuraCoat Firearms Finish–
LAUER CUSTOM WEAPONRY
3601 129th St., Dept. SGN, Chippewa Falls, Wis., 1-800-830-6677, www.lauerweaponry.com

Vz-58 Parts Kit–
CENTERFIRE SYSTEMS INC.
102 Fieldview Dr., Dept. SGN, Versailles, Ky., 40383, 1-800-950-1231, www.centerfiresystems.com

U.S. Made Vz-58 Semi-automatic Receivers and Fire Control Parts–
RAPID FIRE
1285 Archer Ave., Dept. SGN, Troy Ohio, 45373, 1-937-332-0833, www.ohiorapidfire.com

Information on Legal Aspects of Gun Building BATFE Contact Information–
BATFE/FIREARMS TECHNOLOGY BRANCH
244 Needy Rd, Martinsburg, WV, 25401.

drilling out through the side of the receiver. I mention this just to let readers know that even gun writers have problems on build projects and that you don't need to be discouraged if they make some mistakes. Everyone makes mistakes on projects and fixing your mistakes is all part of the process.

At this point your barrel installation is complete and the hardest part of the project is done. If you found this part of the build stressful then sit back for a while, relax and wait for Part 2 of this project in next month's issue of SGN. In Part 2 (8/20 issue) we will complete the project and apply a nice finish to the project.   ◎

Ask the Gunsmith

By Reid Coffield

1911 ACCURIZING DEAD

Q *Years ago I used to see lots of articles on accurizing or match conditioning the .45 auto. Nowadays I seldom if ever see anything like that. Any idea why?*

The golden age of 1911 accurizing was the 1960s and '70s when gunsmiths heavily modified stock Colt Government Models for use in conventional pistol shooting with weights and target sights.

A I think there are several reasons for this. First, there has been a significant drop in competitive bullseye pistol shooting. A lot fewer people are doing it and consequently fewer guns with the necessary accuracy are needed. In addition, with modern manufacturing techniques, especially computer controlled metal working and cutting machines, gun manufacturers can produce guns with much closer tolerances than in years past and there is less need to have a gunsmith rebuild or tighten up the handguns. Many years ago, most folks were starting with some pretty sloppy old G.I. surplus 1911s and that was absolutely essential. Today you can turn to SGN and get a gun from a maker like Les Baer or the Springfield Custom Shop and take it straight to Camp Perry.   ◎

CHECKERING MEASURE?

Q *What is the best number of lines per inch to use when checkering a stock?*

A Unfortunately, there is no "best" number of lines per inch to use when doing stock checkering. The number of lines per inch that you use should be contingent upon a number of factors. First and foremost, is the porosity of the wood that you are using for your stock. If the wood is quite porous, as found on lower- to medium-grade factory walnut stocks, then you will want to go to a fairly coarse pattern with 16 to 20 lines per inch. This will make your diamonds fairly large and that in turn will make the bases of the diamonds quite strong.

If, on the other hand, your wood is very dense with very small pores, then you can use much finer checkering ranging from 24 to 28 lines per inch. The greater the number of lines per inch, the smaller the individual diamonds. And of course, the smaller the individual diamonds, the smaller and weaker the base of each diamond.

The other factor that you also have to consider is how the gun will be used. If the rifle is a showpiece and

realistically will have little if any actual wear, then a very fine checkering pattern with 28 or more lines per inch is very impressive and attractive. But if the rifle can be expected to see lots of hard use in the field, then a coarser pattern will provide better adhesion when holding the rifle. Also, the coarser pattern will not tend to wear as quickly under field conditions.

TOKAREV REAMER

Q *I need a chamber reamer in 7.62x25mm for a Tokarev pistol. Obviously this is not something many people ever want or need so I have had no luck finding anyone listing it. Do you know where I can find one?*

A Dave Manson at Manson Precision Reamers can supply this chamber reamer as well as headspace gauges. The address is Manson Precision Reamers, 8200 Embury Road, Dept. SGN, Grand Blanc, Mich. 48439, telephone 810-953-0732. If you need a chamber reamer for almost any cartridge Dave can supply it and the quality of his work is top notch.

Matthews got most of the tough work down in Part 1. In this segment, he does some riveting, assembles parts and installs them in the Rapid Fire Vz-58 receiver.

BUILDING the RAPID FIRE Vz-58

By Steven Matthews

Part 2

He did most of the hard parts in Part 1 (7/20 issue). Now he's ready to complete assembly and test fire.

The gas piston and its return spring were the next parts to be installed. Unlike the AK-47, which has a tube surrounding the gas piston, the Vz-58 piston is exposed, with only the upper handguard covering it. The openings in the gas block/sight base are oval, so the gas piston and spring can be installed by tilting the front of the piston up to clear the front gas port block as the piston slides into place.

Once all the way back, the front of the piston is inserted into the front gas port block. Machining in the interior of the rear sight base/gas piston block limits rearward travel of the piston during use. Forward travel is limited by the small gas piston stop that I previously warned builders not to lose and to be sure to install before barrel installation.

The warning not to lose this part came because I did just that! Sometime between my original VZ-58 dummy gun build project and this project, I lost the very small gas piston stop. You just can't run down to the hardware store and get a new gas piston stop. In fact you usually can't even get one from surplus gun parts suppliers unless you buy a complete kit.

I had to use a small piece of high quality steel and handmake a new one. This added a couple hours to the project when you count the complete making and fitting process. Simply placing my parts in a small plastic bag rather than just throwing them in the parts drawer would have saved a lot of time and work.

During piston installation, some minor hand fitting and deburring of the holes was required to fit the piston correctly. The piston will seem to be loose in the gas piston block/sight base because of the oval holes. To prevent excess vertical play, the pin in the upper handguard will just clear the gas piston when it is installed.

The next items to be installed were the magazine release and the bolt hold-open device. The magazine release and its spring are installed in the bottom of the receiver and retained by a crosspin in the receiver. When I attempted to install this part, it would not fit.

Measuring indicated that the cutout in the receiver was .020" narrower than the magazine release. I don't know if the receiver was out of spec or the magazine release was oversized, I just knew it wouldn't fit. I had to thin the magazine release down until it would fit in its recess in the receiver.

I then moved on to installing the bolt hold-open device, along with its spring. While this part would fit in its recess, the fit was so tight that it wouldn't move easy enough for proper operation. This part required some thinning to allow for easy operation.

The bolt hold-open device is retained with the same crosspin that retains the magazine release. The crosspin that holds in the magazine release and the bolt hold-open device is retained by a small split shank retainer pin that extends down from the top of the receiver.

This pin just slides into its hole inside the receiver and snaps into place when the little protrusion on the end exits the receiver on the bottom.

With these two parts installed, magazine fit can be checked. There were some sharp burrs and edges that needed to be smoothed up to allow some of the magazines to seat fully, but this was not unexpected. I had several magazines and the size varied considerably. A little filing here and there was required to allow the magazines to seat and lock into place securely.

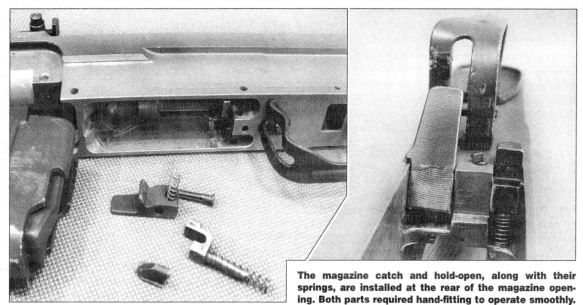

The magazine catch and hold-open, along with their springs, are installed at the rear of the magazine opening. Both parts required hand-fitting to operate smoothly.

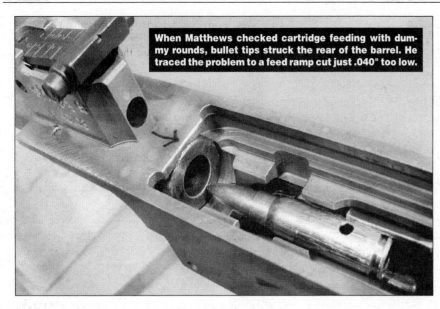

When Matthews checked cartridge feeding with dummy rounds, bullet tips struck the rear of the barrel. He traced the problem to a feed ramp cut just .040" too low.

Start by installing the small 3mm (about 1/8") rivet in the front of the trigger guard and then lay the assembly with the rivet through its hole in the receiver. The shank will extend into a recess in the inside and will be flared out with a punch.

Place a 3/4"x3/4" bar through the trigger guard to support the head of the rivet. Place the receiver and bar over the jaws of an open vise to support the assembly. Use blocks to prop the assembly up solidly so it won't fall off the vise while you are setting the rivet.

With the trigger guard fully seated against the receiver and the head fully supported by the 3/4" bar, use a long, thin punch down into the recess to flare out the rivet shank. Whenever riveting, check often to be sure that the parts are still seated tightly together. Be absolutely sure the head of the rivet is fully supported so that all hammering forces are applied to the rivet and not the trigger guard or receiver. Failure to support the rivet head can result in trigger guard or receiver damage.

Before you can install the rear rivet and the multi-function spring, the spring needs to be modified. The center leaf or finger right above the rivet hole needs to be removed. This leaf of the spring is used for tensioning the auto sear and will not be used in this semiautomatic project. Removal of this spring will also allow for easier access to the rivet head when setting it. I used an abrasive cutoff wheel in a Dremel tool to remove the finger.

The rear of the trigger guard will now be riveted in place, along with the multi-function spring. The holes in the receiver and trigger guard are sized at 3mm since that was the original size on Czech receivers. This required the use of a special shaped rivet and washer, since a standard 3mm rivet head would not properly secure the spring. The rivet supplied with the Rapid Fire compliance parts set is 4mm in diameter and the holes must be opened up to that size if you choose to use it.

I did not use the supplied 4mm rivet because the hole in the multi-function spring was vastly over 4mm. 4mm is roughly .160" and the hole in the spring was just over .200". This made for a very sloppy fit.

Instead I used a 3/16" (about .187") rivet instead. This made for a better fit in the spring hole. To use the larger rivet, I just drilled out the hole in the receiver and trigger guard to 3/16".

The rivet was set with nothing more than a steel block under the head and a ball peen hammer. With the round head of the rivet on the inside of the receiver solidly backed up and the parts fitted tightly together, the shank that extends out of the trigger guard was flared out and shaped with the hammer.

You should start with about 3/16" of rivet shank extending out of the parts, this will leave enough for head forming. First, you just use the flat face of the hammer to flare out the head.

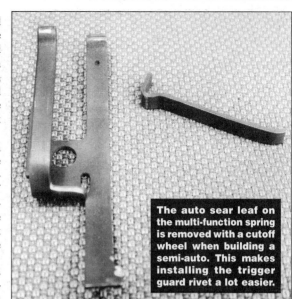

The auto sear leaf on the multi-function spring is removed with a cutoff wheel when building a semi-auto. This makes installing the trigger guard rivet a lot easier.

After the head is flared somewhat, start forming a rounded head by tapping around the edges of the flared head. This requires a lot of small taps, not a few heavy impacts. Remember solidly to support your workpiece so it doesn't fall over while you are riveting. Check often to be sure the parts are still fitted tightly together.

Now is the time to install the pistol grip screw nut. It just fits inside the square cutout in the receiver's bottom. To get it to stay in place, I used a center punch to place a couple dimples on the side. It's easier to install it now than after the fire control group is installed. Be sure to orient it at the correct angle for the pistol grip screw.

The Vz-58 features a "fixed" ejector that is mounted in the bottom of the receiver. The ejector is a small round stub that is affixed to a flange that is installed into a recess in the receiver's bottom. The ejector just slides into the groove and is staked in place to secure it. There is a small notch in the side to assist in staking.

The trigger guard can now be installed. It is riveted in place along with the multi-function spring. The rivet that holds on the rear of the trigger guard also retains the spring on the inside of the receiver. For reasons unknown to me, a lot of home builders balk at riveting (also known as setting rivets).

I simply can not understand this! I see on AK-themed websites that many AK-47 builders use screws for AK building because they are hesitant to rivet; that's harder than riveting! Riveting is nothing more than squishing the shank of a soft metal rivet so that it is tight and can't pull out. Rivets are low-tech fasteners that have been used for thousands of years. Beating the end of a rivet into shape is not rocket science, so don't be afraid to do it.

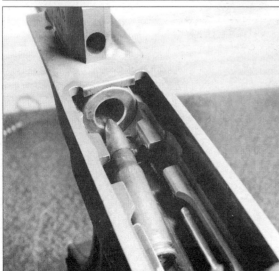

Matthews is a skilled welder, so he welded in and recut the feed ramp .040" higher, which immediately corrected the problem. Most of us would just return the receiver.

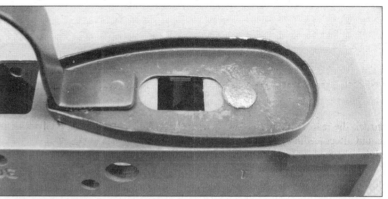

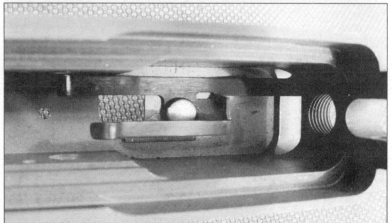

The trigger guard rivet retains the guard outside the receiver and the multi-function spring inside it. Matthews went to a slightly larger rivet for this spot.

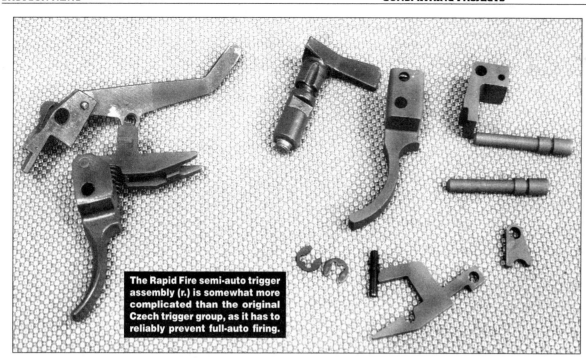

The Rapid Fire semi-auto trigger assembly (r.) is somewhat more complicated than the original Czech trigger group, as it has to reliably prevent full-auto firing.

At this point, I decided to check for proper cartridge feeding and ejection. The bolt assembly was reassembled and the bolt carrier, bolt, locking piece, top cover and springs were installed in the receiver.

I made up a dozen or so dummy cartridges to use in function testing. *Never* use live rounds for function testing, especially in this firearm.

When the bolt carrier assembly is cycled without the fire control group installed, the striker follows the bolt closed and can impact the firing pin with enough force to fire a cartridge.

I loaded up the dummy rounds in the magazine and pulled back the bolt and let it go just as if the gun was being loaded to fire. When function testing, you need to allow the bolt to go shut under spring force to duplicate real operation. Slowly operating the bolt doesn't replicate actual use and should only be used to troubleshoot problems.

At this point a *major* problem arose. Even with magazines properly loaded and installed, the gun would not chamber a cartridge. It would strip a round out of the magazine correctly, but the bullet points would not enter the chamber to allow for complete feeding. I found the bullet points would strike the barrel face about 1/16" to 3/32" below the chamber and immediately cause a jam.

It made no difference if it was the right or left round, all struck the rear of the barrel low. I checked everything that could affect feeding and everything was fine except for one thing, the feed ramp on the receiver. As the rounds rode up the feed ramp, they were not being raised high enough for the bullet points to enter the chamber.

At this point I decided to check the Vz-58 forums on the internet to see if others were having this problem with their builds. I found that several others were having the same problem, though however most claimed their guns fed fine.

A couple of builders had posted pictures of original Vz-58 feed ramps and it looked as if the originals were slightly higher. Further research located a Rapid Fire-supplied machinist drawing with feed ramp specifications. This drawing specified a 45° angle on the feed ramp and a depth of .040". Measurements on my receiver indicated the correct angle but the depth was twice as deep, .080" instead of .040".

This overly deep feed ramp was not lifting the rounds high enough to clear the edge of the barrel and easily enter the chamber. This is not a problem than can be easily overcome by most home builders. The only way for most hobbyists to deal with this major problem would be to return the receiver to Rapid Fire for replacement for one with a correctly machined feed ramp.

I'm sure Rapid Fire would have replaced this defective receiver with a good one if I had requested one since they have stood behind their products when engineering defects are found in new products. If returned it, however, all my past work on this project would have been for nothing.

Since my hobby gunsmithing shop is well equipped and I had the necessary skills, I decided to correct the problem myself. I welded the feed ramp up and then recut it to the correct depth. In fact, I made it just few thousandths higher just to be sure it was high enough.

The locking lugs were far enough away that the heat from the very small MIG weld would not affect heat treating and weaken the receiver. The weld was very small and would not damage the receiver due to heat distortion or annealing.

I also slightly chamfered the edge of the chamber to assist in smooth feeding. While I was at it, I polished up every point inside the receiver where rounds would contact the receiver. Once the feed ramp was recut, rounds fed and ejected as they were supposed to without striking the barrel low.

This incident should prove that gunwriters (at least this one) don't get specially prepared products. It is my opinion that this problem was the result of the receiver not being set in the machining fixture correctly or a cutting tool was not in the tool holder to the correct depth.

Only a few people have reported this problem on the internet, so I believe it is an isolated incident. Regardless of the cause, Rapid Fire should monitor the problem closely since too many incidents like this can kill a product's reputation.

While my fix did correct the problem, I do not recommend other hobbyist gunsmiths attempt fixes like this unless they are fully skilled in this kind of work. If one is skilled, this fix is very easy, but for those without the proper skills and judgment, attempts to repair problems like this could result in a ruined project.

Now that the chambering problems were corrected, I decided to install the fire control group. The original full-auto Vz-58 fire control group is replaced with Rapid Fire's U.S.-made semiautomatic components. The only original fire control parts to be reused are the previously installed multi-function spring, the safety/selector lever, and one spring.

The Rapid Fire semi auto fire control group is very simple in operation. A striker for the firing pin extends out of the rear of the bolt carrier. This striker is caught by a sear as the striker passes over. A spring loaded arm (the disconnector) allows the trigger to pull down the sear to release the striker.

As the bolt carrier reciprocates, the carrier presses down on the connecting arm (the disconnector) between the trigger and sear and disconnects the sear from the trigger. Before another round can be fired, the trigger needs to be released to reset the trigger and sear. These parts are small and appear a lot less robust than other military rifle fire control components, but apparently the design is solid and has been extensively tested and the parts perform as they should.

The Rapid Fire fire control group comes disassembled and has to be put together by the builder. The first thing one needs to do is to salvage the pivot pin and a spring from the original trigger. This pin and spring will be installed in the new trigger and will tension the disconnector when it is installed.

The spring is installed in the pocket in the new trigger and the disconnector is installed over the spring. The salvaged pivot pin will secure them together. Once installed, this pin needs to be secured to hold it in place if it is loose like mine was. I just staked it in place on the top and end to keep it from coming out under use.

The spring-loaded disconnector must move freely under spring tension or it won't work right. Once the trigger is assembled, it is installed in the receiver with a trigger pin supplied by Rapid Fire. This pin is retained in the receiver with an "E" clip. The safety lever can now be installed. It just slides into the side of the receiver and passes between the upper and lower arms of the disconnector. You will have to press down the multi-function spring to get it in place.

The pistol grip is retained by a long screw through the grip and into an angled nut inside the receiver. The grip is made of wood chip-impregnated plastic resin.

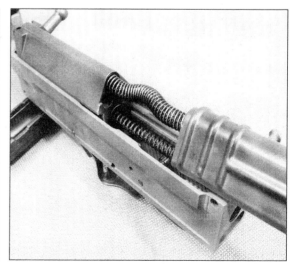

The top cover houses the recoil and striker springs. The striker must be in the forward position to install the top cover and springs. A pin at the rear retains it.

You will now have to install a pin in the new sear. Rapid Fire supplies a roll pin in the parts set that is to be used for this purpose. The trigger bar/disconnector pulls on it to operate the sear. While Rapid Fire found this inexpensive roll pin adequate for the job, I thought it was just plain cheap!

The Rapid Fire semi auto parts are well made and I felt there was no reason to use this cheap and flimsy pin in what otherwise appeared to be a quality fire control group. If you want to use it by all means do but I wanted something better and stronger.

I made a solid pin out of a small piece of drill bit shank that was just a few thousandths over original pin hole size. I machined a step on the shank to fit in the existing hole and then after pressing it in place I flared the other end into a slight countersink on the back side so it wouldn't come out.

This pin needs to extend out of the left side of the sear about 1/8" to 5/32". The sear now needs to be installed into the receiver, along with a small part known as a safety lock. This lock will secure the safety in the receiver. Rapid Fire includes a sear axis pin to secure the sear and safety lock in the receiver.

These parts can be a little tricky to install. Start by installing the sear axis pin a little way into the side of the receiver. Place the open end of the safety lock into the groove in the safety shaft and then push the axis pin through the hole in the safety lock only far enough to hold it in place.

Now place the sear down over the spring and wiggle it into place so that the small pin in the side of the sear is in the notch machined in the disconnector. Once it's positioned and depressed slightly under spring tension, you can push the axis pin all the way through. You may wish to use small needle-nose pliers to install these parts since the receiver is very small for fingers.

Once the pin is pushed in all the way, it is retained by an "E" clip. With all parts installed, check for smooth operation; there can be no binding. With the safety in the fire position (horizontal) pulling the trigger should pull the sear down. With the trigger in the safe position (vertical and extending over the pistol grip) the trigger should still pull but it should not pull the sear downward.

This is where I had a small problem. When I had the safety in the fire position and pulled the trigger, it would only pull down the sear a small amount before the disconnector would slip off the pin on the sear. This problem was traced down to the salvaged spring that I had installed in the trigger to tension the disconnector. It was too weak to keep the disconnector engaged with the pin on the sear. I replaced the spring and it corrected the problem.

After the fire control group appeared to be working properly I reinstalled the bolt carrier assembly (bolt, carrier, locking piece, striker, etc). I cycled the bolt carrier and verified that there was no binding of parts.

I then installed the top cover and the springs. The striker needs to be in the forward position to install the top cover and springs. I cycled the action under spring tension to verify correct fire control function. With the safety in the fire position cycling the bolt cocked the gun. Pulling the trigger correctly released the striker.

If I cycled the bolt with the trigger still pulled rearward, the gun would re-cock and the trigger had to be released to reset it for the next shot. This indicated proper disconnector function. When the safety was placed in the safe position and the trigger pulled the gun would not fire, indicating proper safety function.

You have probably wondered what was going to hold the top cover pin in place. A small pin/plunger extends down through the rear of the receiver and rests on the multifunction spring. The top of this pin will engage grooves in the top cover pin to hold it in place.

You just drop it into its hole in the receiver and then depress it slightly to allow the top cover pin to pass over it.

The buttstock easily installs on the Vz-58 with a long screw through the rear of the stock. The head is deep in the stock and you will need a long screwdriver to reach the head. Once the buttstock is installed, the buttplate and sling swivel can be installed. The screw in the buttstock passes through the sling swivel that fits in the side of the stock.

When installing the buttplate, be sure to install it in the right direction since the screw hole is made for fitting in just one direction. If you install the buttplate in the wrong direction you will deform the hole and buttplate when you tighten the screw. If you haven't done so already, install the pistol grip.

At this point all parts and assemblies should have been installed and fitted. You can now do some final function testing before going on to live fire testing. With your gun completely assembled, use your dummy rounds to be sure everything works with all assemblies installed and functioning.

STEEL + RAPID FIRE = Vz-58 RECEIVER,
A Closer Look at Rapid Fire and Their Vz-58 Semiautomatic Receiver.

These days it seems that very little is made in the USA. Many traditional "American" name-brand products are made nowhere near the United States. Many of these products are totally made in other countries or assembled in the U.S. from all imported parts.

The Rapid Fire receiver, while based on a 50-year-old Czech design, is totally made in the USA. This U.S.-made product provides jobs for American workers. There are foreign-made versions of the semiautomatic Vz-58 receiver, but in these times of U.S. workers jobs being lost to foreign competition, I prefer to buy American.

Rapid Fire receivers as are machined on site at Rapid Fire's facility in Troy, Ohio. Several Rapid Fire employees set up and operate large CNC machining centers to fabricate their Vz-58 receivers.

Operators set eight blocks of 4140 steel into machining fixtures in the machining centers. These computer-controlled machining centers then begin the long process of carving a Vz-58 receiver out of a block of steel.

Each machining center performs several operations on the receiver blanks. Other than loading and unloading, the CNC machines run without human assistance. Controlled by complex computer programs, they decide what tool is needed to do each operation and automatically change tools for the next operation.

Each machining station performs several operations and then the part is indexed to the next position for continuing machining. These machines can even self-diagnose many problems such as a broken or dull tooling. As each operation is completed, the computer program instructs the machine to change to the next needed tool.

If a major problem arises, the machine can alert a human operator for assistance. I have watched many machining centers operate and it's just amazing to see the machine quickly and accurately machine materials. As all operations are completed on each machining center, it shuts down and waits to be unloaded and reloaded by the operator.

The partially machined receivers are moved to another machining center for more precise machining. Since these CNC machines run without human operators, one worker can "supervise" several machines as they run more or less unattended.

Between machining centers, the parts are randomly checked for quality of machining. To make a Vz-58 receiver the "old fashioned way" with a single operator running one milling machine, it would take days to carve out a receiver and the price would be excessively high due to labor and machine time cost.

After all machining is completed, the receivers do have some minor marks that are removed by a surface finishing process after heat-treating, and the resulting receiver is nice and smooth. The Rapid Fire Vz-58 receiver when completed features a matte steel-colored finish.

This smooth surface means that little preparation is required for final finish application. The Rapid Fire Vz-58 semi auto receiver is well-made but it will need some hand fitting of parts, thanks to the tolerances encountered in the 50-year-old parts sets. Every manufactured part is made to a tolerance range and one cannot make a mating part that will fit several sizes of parts perfectly.

Rapid Fire has done a good job of duplicating the long-out-of-production Vz-58 receiver. Many parts will need to be hand fitted but this is preferable to the receiver being made so oversized that many parts fit sloppily.

The receiver featured in this article was the 349th in the Rapid Fire's first production run and did have some "issues." With the exception of the feed ramp error, the problems were easy to overcome. Any new product will have some glitches that have to be worked out and I'm sure Rapid Fire will address any issues that arise. All in all the Rapid Fire semiautomatic receiver is a pretty decent product for the home firearms builder. ◉

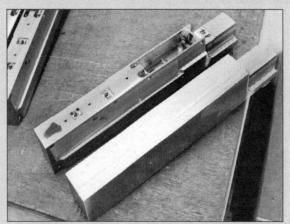
The Rapid Fire receiver starts out as a block of 4140 steel, and then they cut away anything that's not a Vz-58. It's an expensive, but authentic, way to make it.

Eight receiver blanks at a time are fixed into a "tombstone" fixture that presents them in turn to the cutting tools. Dozens of machining operations follow.

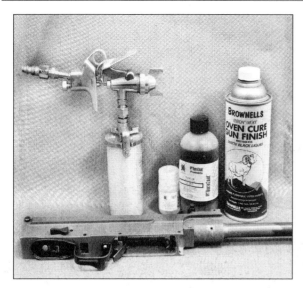

Why choose? Matthews used both Lauer DuraCoat and Brownells Teflon-Moly. He says the VZ-2000 DuraCoat spray almost exactly matches the original gray metal finish.

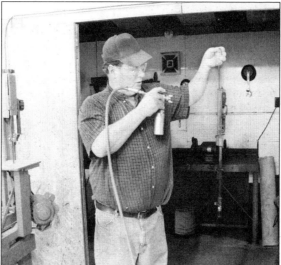

Matthews used an automotive touch-up spray gun to apply Lauer DuraCoat. Airbrushes are OK for pistols, but something a little bigger was called for here.

I decided to go with a two tone finish on my project. I had some matte black Brownells Teflon-Moly Oven Cure Gun Finish left over from a past project and decide to use it for the top cover, bolt carrier, rear sight and trigger. This finish is sprayed on and then baked at 300° for 30 minutes. Once it cools, it is ready to use and is extremely hard and durable.

The parts that I was going to DuraCoat were removed and lightly abrasive blasted. You don't have to abrasive blast parts prior to applying DuraCoat, but adhesion will be greatly increased if you do. Blasting was followed by cleaning/degreasing with lacquer thinner to remove all traces of oil or other contaminants.

After mixing the DuraCoat as per LCW's instructions I sprayed the DuraCoat with a small automotive type spray gun known as a touch-up gun. Airbrushes can be used on projects like handguns and small parts, but for larger projects like rifles a slightly larger sprayer works best.

After spraying the parts, I set them aside for a couple days to dry fully. Brownells Teflon-Moly Gun Finish applies differently. While abrasive blasting is optional with DuraCoat, it is mandatory with the Brownells product. Brownells Teflon-Moly Gun Finish must be applied to an abrasive-blasted surface or it will easily chip and scratch. If applied to properly prepared surfaces, it adheres so well it can only be removed by more abrasive blasting.

Once I had the parts abrasive blasted and cleaned, the finish was sprayed per Brownells' instructions with an airbrush. The parts were then baked at 300° for 30-60 minutes. Once the parts come out of the oven and cool, they are ready to use.

Both finishes have their pluses and minuses, their proponents and their opponents. I have found both finishes to be good products and I can recommend either to the home gunsmith. I use both on a regular basis depending on my needs.

Today's gun stocks usually come in two options, wood or plastic. In the 1950s, Czech designers decided to use a combination of both. The stock material on the Vz-58 is a mixture of wood chips and plastic resin. It looks very much like construction grade OSB particle board.

While it may look odd, it does seem to work well. The stock on my project was almost 50 years old and still looked decent. All that was needed was a light sanding and a couple coats of spray lacquer to return them to almost new appearance.

Once the gun was refinished, it looked as good as new. Due to the good mechanical condition of the surplus parts, the good Rapid Fire receiver, the Rapid Fire semi auto parts and careful assembly, it also worked as good as new. Total cost, which will vary according to supply and demand as well as the political situation, was about $550. This was a savings of over $700 compared to some other factory-made semiauto versions of the Vz-58.

This is a very good price for a unique and high quality gun such as the Vz-58. If this sounds like your kind of project why not give it a try? ◉

Never use live rounds for function testing. Load up a clip and cycle the action and verify that everything works right with dummy rounds. If things don't work right with dummies, things certainly won't work any better with live ammo. If and only if everything works right, you can move on to live fire testing.

When doing live-fire testing on homemade semi-automatic firearms, only load one round into the clip when doing the first live-fire test. If one round fires correctly the next test can be done with two rounds, followed by three rounds and so on.

The reason for this is safety. If you haven't got the build right or a part breaks in the first few shots, it's better to have a minimum number of rounds in the clip. You don't want to find out you have a runaway full auto malfunction with a 30-round magazine in the gun. If you have any problems, correct them before going on to finish application.

One nice thing about home building guns is that your choice of finish is almost unlimited. One can go with common spray paint, bluing, Parkerizing, sprayed-on polymers, plated finishes or anything you want. You can even pick your own colors. If you want a purple, yellow and green gun, then you can have it that way! My choice was, however, more conventional.

Original Czech Vz-58 guns were finished with a dark gray paint. This color did however vary a little over the production life of the gun. Lauer Custom Weaponry offers its DuraCoat sprayed-on finish in a color that is called VZ-2000. This color was a very close match for the original color that was on my parts set.

DuraCoat is a two-part sprayed-on firearms finish that applies as easily as spray paint. DuraCoat is a very durable no-maintenance finish that is available in dozens of colors. It can be easily applied by the home gunsmith with a small spray gun or airbrush.

When finished, the Vz-58 looks as good as new. From a distance, there's no telling it from an original. It makes for an interesting alternative to the AK-47.

Semi-Auto Suomi from scratch

Part 1: The Receiver

He's written about some easy projects lately: here's one that will be a real challenge. If you have the skill and patience, you can build an unusual semi-auto carbine for $200.

By Steven Matthews

He's written about a lot of projects you can do with hand tools, but this one is for those who can weld and have access to major power tools like a lathe or mill.

This project started a while back when I did a Finnish Suomi M31 display gun (1/20/08). Since I appreciate well-built firearms designs, I decided I needed a functional Suomi for my military arms collection.

Federally registered full auto versions are very rare and priced well out of my income range. I knew of no manufacturers offering semi-auto rifle versions of this rather obscure firearm.

The only remaining option was to build a semi-automatic version to BATFE guidelines. I did some internet research and found there were several others building semi-auto Suomis. Some of these designs were very good, but I wanted one that was all my own.

So I set out to design and build a unique version. My design is certainly no better than others; it's just different.

My main design criteria were ease and economy of build. I deleted some original features to save buying parts. This would result in a project that looked pretty much like a Suomi M31, but it would not be an exact copy.

No semi-automatic carbine can exactly copy the original SMG, since BATFE insists on significant differences to prevent easy conversion to full-auto. The closer it gets to original configuration, the closer you get to a prohibited full-auto gun design.

The design featured in this article will be built to BATFE guidelines for building semi-auto firearms. It will also meet what is known as U.S. compliance issues.

As always, don't consider this story a complete how-to guide. Use it strictly as a starting point for your own ideas. This is a complex project that requires skill and experience; don't try it unless you have them.

Here's the starting point–a Suomi parts kit from Cope's Distributing, AR-15 parts from Brownells and some 4130 steel tubing. These will come together to make a gun.

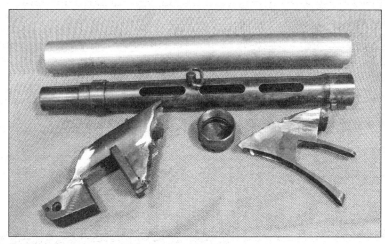

The receiver is torch-cut before it can be imported. From the mangled frame Matthews salvaged the magazine housing and the tangs for the rear of the receiver.

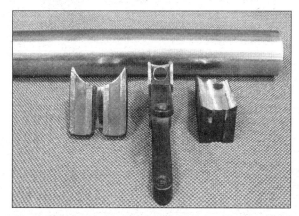

The original Suomi receiver wasn't a pure tube, so the salvaged components must be correctly contoured to fit the new receiver tube, which is perfectly cylindrical.

I ordered a couple Suomi M31 parts sets from Cope's Distributing. These were priced at $59.95 and were in great condition. Suomi kits are one of the few remaining parts kit bargains on the ever-changing surplus parts market. I decided to use a U.S.-made fire control group, and ordered DPMS AR-15 fire control components from Brownells. I needed an AR-15 hammer, trigger, disconnector and their springs and pins, as well as an AR-15 firing pin.

I had used a highly modified M31 bolt and AR-15 fire control in a previous project for a SGN article, the SGN-9 (4/20–7/20/08), so I was confident I could use it in the Suomi project.

To start the design process, I laid out the demilled receiver sections and barrel in approximate original configuration and then laid out the bolt and AR-15 fire control group on top of it to see if there appeared to be room to fit it in.

This was the first "oh crap" situation. With the trigger in approximately the original location, I was about 1/2"–3/4" short of having enough room to fit the fire control group behind the closed bolt. I studied this for a couple hours before the solution finally dawned on me.

I finally noticed that the rear portion behind the disconnector spring of the AR-15 trigger and disconnector did not have to be as long as stock, since the last 3/8" or so did nothing. If I cut off the unneeded portion I would gain 3/8"–1/2".

I then decided that I could shorten the rear of the bolt about a quarter-inch to gain some more space. When the shortened bolt was closed, it was a little too far rearward, so I decided simply to move the barrel about 1/4" forward. Once all these items were repositioned, there was just enough room to fit in an AR-15 fire control group in a new self-made semi-auto receiver.

While the Suomi appears from the outside to be of "tube gun" construction, it is not. The round tube part is just the top of the exposed portion of the receiver.

A lower portion that houses the fire control group is actually machined along with the upper portion. To ease the construction process, I decided to use conventional tube-type construction for the upper receiver and fabricate a new trigger housing that would attach to the trigger guard which in turn would be attached to the new tubular receiver.

The rear stock tang assembly and the rear of the magazine housing would secure the receiver in the stock, and the trigger guard with the new trigger housing would attach between those points.

Once I had the basic layout decided, I looked at the barrel setup. The original Suomi barrel was only about 12.5 inches long, and so would not meet the BATFE

mandated minimum length of 16 inches. An extension would need to be fabricated and permanently attached to the barrel to meet or exceed the 16" regulation.

The original Suomi design also featured an easily removable/quick change barrel system. This is fine on a factory-built gun but is unnecessarily complicated to duplicate on a home build semi-auto project. I therefore decided to go with a simple barrel bushing into which the barrel would be inserted and cross-pinned as is common on many firearms designs.

This bushing would be plug-welded permanently in place once the proper position was determined. The permanently installed 16-inch barrel would also help alleviate any BATFE concerns about easily installing a prohibited short machine gun barrel on the completed project.

At this point, I had a basic idea of how I would build the project. The hard part would be actually making and locating the parts correctly for proper operation. There was going to be extensive amounts of parts fabrication and hand fitting of those parts since this was pretty much a "from the ground up" project, there were no plans for this endeavor.

If you choose to do this project be warned that virtually every single part will need to be hand-fitted. This is not a kit gun assembly project. It is gun making with your own self-made parts, combined with some factory made parts. This should not discourage potential builders, hand making and fitting parts is all part of advanced hobby gunsmithing.

One of the appealing aspects of this project was going to be cost. The Suomi parts sets were inexpensive. The AR-15 fire control group is widely available and relatively inexpensive. A few dollars worth of gunsmith quality springs will be needed. A couple pieces of 4130 tubing will be needed and aren't all that expensive.

Even counting miscellaneous supplies such as finishing supplies, screws and small pieces of steel, the cost should be under $200. The largest expenditure on this project will be labor. If one doesn't mind trading labor for cost savings like I do, then this may be your kind of project.

Demilled Receiver Parts Salvage

For this project, only a few of the Suomi M31 parts from the parts set will be used. Several items need to be salvaged off of the demilled receiver sections so they can be used to construct the new semi-auto receiver. You will

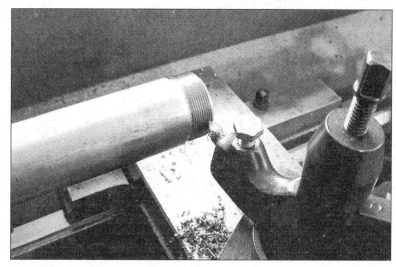

Here's where a lathe is essential. No common dies fit the receiver tube, so it must be threaded at the rear by lathe turning. The end cap must fit securely here.

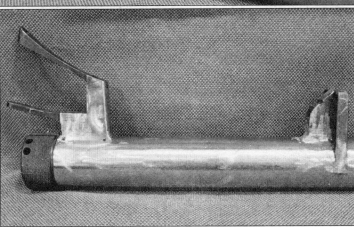

Carefully align the magazine housing and tang and weld them to the receiver tube. Getting them precisely in line with the tube and each other is essential here.

need to remove the stock tang assembly and the front and rear magazine housing portions.

One question people unfamiliar with the M31 Suomi may ask, is where are the sides of the magazine housing? There aren't any! The magazine on the M31 was supported only by the front and the rear of the housing. Ribs formed on the magazine body interfaced with grooves in the front and rear portions to secure the magazine in place. This method is unusual but it does work.

Remove the tangs and magazine housing parts by cutting them out of the old receiver with a saw or grinder. Cut out the portion of receiver tube they are a part of. The round portion of receiver tube can be removed after the parts are separated from the demilled receiver sections.

The old receiver portion needs to be carefully removed so that the salvaged parts will fit the new receiver just as they did the old one. This is important to maintain the correct height of the salvaged parts. Use files or grinders to remove the old receiver tube sections. Do not overgrind or -cut since you need to maintain the same contour as the originals.

Receiver Fabrication

The "tube" portion of the new semi-auto receiver will be made from a section of 4130 chrome-moly seamless tubing that is available for steel suppliers and aircraft parts suppliers. I used 1.5"x.187" wall tubing. Depending on size tolerances at manufacture, you will have an internal diameter of 1.125 to 1.130 inches. A piece 12⅜ inches long was used for the receiver tube.

I chose this size tubing for two reasons. First, the external size was approximately correct but the second and most important issue was the internal size. Under BATFE regulations, you cannot make a semi-auto Suomi receiver that will accept the original diameter full-auto bolt.

There is an exception to this rule but we aren't using that construction method here. In our case the semi-auto receiver must only accept a smaller diameter semi-auto bolt specifically made for this semi-auto project.

The 1.5" tube is slightly larger than the original external size of the Suomi receiver. The original size was 1.460". The tube can be used full-size if you choose but some dimensions and fits will need to be modified to fit the slightly larger size. Since I had a lathe, I turned the tube down to 1.460". I also squared up the ends.

The bolt and buffer assembly of an M31 are retained in the receiver by an end cap that threads onto the rear of the receiver. The tube must be threaded to fit the cap.

The threads are standard "V" type threads and set at 20 threads per inch. The threads must be cut on a lathe, since there are no dies available for the odd 1.460x20 TPI thread size. Lathe cutting threads is very easy if you know how to do it but is *extremely* unforgiving on mistakes. One little mistake can ruin a threading job, so proceed with caution. Cut your threads and use the end cap as a guide for the correct fit.

To complete the receiver, the salvaged portions need to be attached and grooves and cutouts need to be made. The order to do these operations can be varied to suit the builder, but this is the order I did them in.

The first thing I did was to attach the tang section to the new receiver tube. To allow room for fire control group installation the front side of this tang was cut so that all that remained was the pocket to which the trigger guard will attach. The hole that previously allowed the charging handle to pass though the tang was welded shut.

The top radius of the tang assembly was shaped so that the tang was flush against the receiver when it was installed in the stock. The front to back position was determined by leaving enough clearance for the end cap to be installed later.

The tube and tang were clamped together, then removed and MIG welded. Square fit is important here, so be sure the parts don't shift during removal or welding. I placed narrow beads along all sides and then ground off the excess so that they wouldn't interfere with stock fit.

The M31 receiver is held in the stock by a combination of the rear tangs and the front of the stock interlocking with the rear of the magazine housing. This housing also contains the magazine catch assembly. The receiver and tang assembly were fitted in the stock and the rear of the magazine housing was fitted to the front of the stock.

The top of the housing must be contoured to fit the receiver tube. It also must be sized so that it will be in the same up and down position as originally on the old receiver so that the magazine will be located at the correct height when retained by the magazine catch. It must fit squarely in all directions.

I made spot welds at the top edges of the housing to lock it in place before removing the receiver and finishing the welding. The back sides of the housing were then welded to the receiver tube. Use weld techniques here that will limit heat distortion. Grind the welds smooth with the receiver so they don't interfere with stock fit.

Before the front of the magazine housing was welded in place, I cut out the magazine opening in the receiver tube. I used the previously installed rear housing to align a magazine with the receiver and then drew a line around the magazine on the receiver to mark a rough location for the opening.

I then cut well inside this line. I then used a magazine as a guide to finish the opening to size. I cut the opening very close to size so that the side would help support the magazines. This opening needs to be sized for the types of magazine you will be using.

The shape of this opening is slightly different for drum and stick magazines. Since I am not a big fan of drum magazines, I cut the opening to accept stick magazines only, but you may decide to fit it for both types.

Once the opening is sized correctly, the front of the housing can be installed. On the original Suomi M31, the

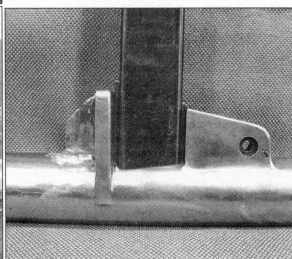

The Suomi magazine is supported only at the front and back. Before installing the front housing piece, cut and opening for the magazine into the receiver tube.

The ejection port in the receiver must align precisely with the extractor slot in the bolt. Start by cutting the port undersize, then cut it to final dimensions.

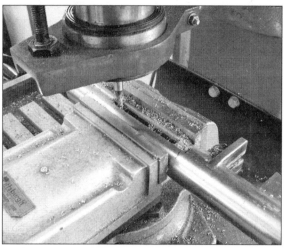

Here's one you won't want to try with the Dremel. Matthews used a milling machine to cut a 5/16" handle slot. Later, it can be widened for precise fitting.

Cut a hammer slot in the underside of the receiver tube just in front of the tang support, allowing hammer to pass into the receiver and impact the firing pin.

rear half of the housing was part of the forward receiver. The front half contained a groove that allowed the barrel shroud to slip between the housing and receiver.

Since I eliminated the removable barrel feature, this housing needs to be contoured along the full length of the top to fit the new receiver. Once shaped it can be MIG welded to the receiver tube along its sides and front. Use a magazine installed between the front and back housings to align the front section. Be sure the housing is square and that the magazine is square in the receiver before welding.

Clamp it in place, making sure to allow enough clearance to allow for easy magazine removal. Use narrow welds here to limit heat distortion of the receiver. Once they're welded, smooth up the welds for appearances.

With all the parts welded on the tube, the remaining cutouts can be made. A clearance slot needs to be cut in the bottom of the receiver to allow the hammer to access the bolt. This 7/16" wide by 2¼" long slot was cut right in front of the tang.

The original M31 featured an unusual method for operating the bolt. A handle that extended out of the rear of the tang section internally engaged the bolt. It looked like a little bolt-action rifle handle. Since this would interfere with our centrally mounted AR-15 hammer, this feature was eliminated.

This modification also removed one regulated foreign part from the project. For this reason, and to ease the build, I went with a more conventional bolt handle that would extend through the left side of the receiver. A 5/16" wide "starter slot" was cut in the side of the receiver.

This was to allow for opening the slot to full size later to maintain precise bolt alignment. This was another area where I made a small mistake and cut the slot way longer than needed. It should start about 3¾ inches from the rear of the receiver and extend about 4 inches forward. This slot size can be increased later to allow for full bolt travel.

An ejection port needs to be cut in the right side of the receiver. This port must be centrally aligned with the extractor on the correctly positioned bolt. This cut out was also cut in a "starter size" well under finish size to allow for final fitting later.

The finished cut out will be about 1⅝ inches long and about 5/8" wide. This cut should begin even with the front edge of the rear magazine housing. I located the starter cut at about the 1:30 position around the receiver tube. Once the bolt is fitted, the ejection port can be opened up on which ever side is needed to maintain correct alignment with the bolt and extractor.

In Part 2 (4/20 issue), Matthews will go to work on the barrel.

Ask the Gunsmith
By Reid Coffield

DRY-FIRING CENTER-FIRES

Q *Why is it considered improper to dry-fire a center fire rifle? The firing pin is obviously not contacting the chamber or anything. I can understand the problems you might have in dry-firing a .22 rimfire but I just don't get it with saying you shouldn't do this with a center fire. What gives?*

A You are right in that with a center-fire you don't have to worry about the firing pin hitting the chamber rim or wall. However, in many cases there is an internal stop or shoulder for the firing pin inside the bolt or breechblock. When the firing pin is thrust forward, it is abruptly stopped by this internal mechanical feature. That places a stress on the firing pin and can lead to damage or breakage of the firing pin.

Also in some firearms, the firing pin will be designed with enough taper on the tip that it may stick forward in the bolt or breechblock. Then when a live round is chambered and the bolt is closed, the round will be fired. Finally, the firing pin can swage out the area around the firing pin hole as it batters the inside of the hole. This raised area can then lead to feeding problems or even prevent the closure and lock up of the bolt.

When a live round or a snap cap is chambered, the firing pin is cushioned and the amount of travel or movement is limited. This puts less stress on the firing pin and inhibits the damage to the bolt or breechblock.

NOBLE STOCK

Q *I recently bought a .410 pump shotgun at a local yard sale. The gun is in fairly good shape but the buttstock is cracked and missing a large piece of wood where it joins the receiver. It is a Model 70 made by Noble. I checked with a local gun dealer and he told me that the company went out of business many years ago. Do you know where I can get a replacement buttstock? The shotgun was very cheap so I do not want to spend a lot of money on it.*

A Noble Arms was in business from 1946 until around 1971 when it closed its doors. However, parts including the buttstock can still be purchased from Numrich Gun Parts Corporation, P.O. Box 299, West Hurley, N.Y. 12491, telephone 866-686-7424.

MAUSER HSc

Q *I have a .32 Mauser HSc pocket pistol that was given to me by a friend whose father picked it up in Germany during World War II. It is a very streamlined design and I have thought about using it for concealed carry. Do you know of any mechanical problems related to this handgun?*

A Over the years I have worked on just a few of these pistols. In a couple of cases I have seen broken firing pins, but these were easily replaced. If you plan on carrying this pistol I would encourage you to first have a gunsmith check it out. Following that, you really should do a fair amount of shooting with it. It is much better to have a mechanical problem show up at the practice range than later in a more serious situation.

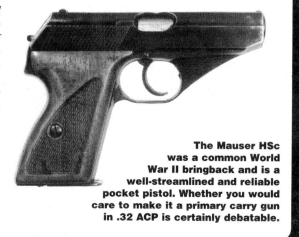

The Mauser HSc was a common World War II bringback and is a well-streamlined and reliable pocket pistol. Whether you would care to make it a primary carry gun in .32 ACP is certainly debatable.

Semi-Auto Suomi from scratch

Part 2: The Barrel and Bolt

Having gotten a good start on the receiver last month, Matthews turns this time to the barrel and bolt, where some accurate measuring will be required for good results.

With the receiver well under way, Matthews turns this time to the barrel, its shroud, and the bolt, getting to the halfway point of this big project.

By Steven Matthews

The first thing required here is to bring the stock 12½-inch Suomi barrel up to the BATFE-mandated minimum length of 16 inches. To be on the safe side, I went with 16.5 inches. This I did by brazing on a 4-inch (finished size) long extension to the barrel. I used a 6-inch piece of 3/4" O.D. by .120" wall 4130 tubing for the extension.

I turned the last 1.5 inches of the muzzle end of the barrel down to 9/16". I then bored one end of the extension tube 9/16" diameter and 1.5 inches deep. This allowed the extension tube to overlap the barrel by 1.5 inches and make for a more rigid assembly.

I turned a groove in the barrel at the seam between the barrel and extension. This seam was brazed permanently to secure the extension to the barrel. Use very even heating to prevent warping the barrel when brazing. I slowly turned the assembly on a lathe while brazing to prevent warping. Anti-scale compound will limit scaling in the bore.

The BATFE rules state that this extension must be *permanently* installed by arc welding, blind pinning or brazing. Set screws or low temp soldering are not approved methods. After brazing, the joint was worked down smooth with the barrel and the extension shortened to the desired length.

To ease the build process and to prevent a short sub-gun barrel from being easily installed, I fitted the barrel with a bushing permanently welded in place. I used a piece of 1¼-inch 4130 chrome-moly rod to fabricate a bushing. My receiver internal diameter was 1.130 inches, so I turned a 3-inch bushing to that size.

This bushing must be a snug fit in the receiver. I then bored out the center of the bushing to 3/4". About 1¾ inches of this bushing will be inside the receiver tube and the rest will extend out the front and be an attachment point for the barrel shroud. The last 1¼ inches of this

Matthews made a barrel bushing to align the barrel in the receiver tube. He used a temporary solder joint for test fitting, allowing for later changes if necessary.

A V-shaped feed ramp helps guide rounds past the bushing and into the chamber, which came from the factory in Finland with a much more modest feed ramp of its own.

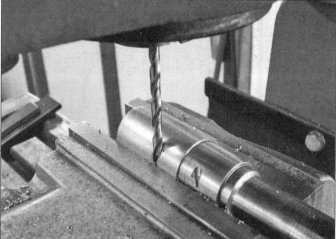

After feed testing, join the barrel and bushing permanently by crosspinning. Start out by milling a flat spot at the drilling point so the bit won't be deflected.

bushing can be turned to fit a shroud bushing or can be left full size, depending on how you are going to size the rear end of the barrel shroud.

The rear end of the Suomi barrel is just a little over 3/4" (.750"). This end must be machined to fit the hole that was bored in the bushing. A very light press fit or very tight slip fit should be fine. Getting this close fit can be tricky, so take it slow; once you have gone too far the material can't be put back on.

When the bushing and barrel are fitted together, you want the bushing to extend past the end of the barrel about 1/4"–5/16". This portion will form a small feed ramp to help the bullet slide up into the barrel.

This feed ramp can be made before or after assembling the two pieces. I tried two different styles of feed ramps. The first was simply a lathe-turned 45° chamfer all the way around the bushing.

Later testing indicated that it would work, but I thought another type might perform better. Since the Suomi magazine is of the dual feed type where rounds feed alternately from either side, I wanted a feed ramp that would guide the off-center rounds into the chamber a little better.

What I came up with was a wide V-shaped groove at the bottom of the bushing at about a 45° angle. I beveled and polished it to promote smooth feeding. This setup seemed to guide the rounds better, so that's what I used. Whichever feed ramp you use, the bushing and barrel need to be attached.

As a preliminary method, I soldered the barrel and bushing together. This would allow me to make changes in the location of the barrel and bushing if necessary later. This is only a temporary attachment method and is unsuitable for actual use.

Once you have determined the correct fitting of the barrel and bushing during feed testing, you can permanently join them. The positioning of the barrel and feed ramp can greatly affect feeding, and changes may need to be made later for reliable operation.

After testing, you can secure the bushing to the barrel by crosspinning at the seam line and bushing with 3/16" pins. I used two crosspins, but four would not be too many. If you crosspin, be sure to smooth the pins down so the bushing will easily slide into the receiver without binding.

Crosspinning is the easiest method and is used on many firearms, but you could thread the barrel and bushing if you prefer. Just be sure to secure the barrel from screwing out under use with a crosspin or set screw that can't come loose.

The barrel assembly will not be installed at this time, as the correct position will be determined later during final assembly.

Barrel Shroud Modifications

The original M31 barrel shroud was retained by interlocking lugs on the receiver and on the inside of the barrel shroud. This was part of the removable barrel system that has been removed here. There are two styles of shrouds commonly found on the Suomi. Both feature elongated slots along the sides.

One style stops just behind the muzzle and leaves only a small stub of barrel extending out the end.

The other features a large muzzle brake on the end of the shroud that extends past the end of the barrel. Whether a muzzle brake is needed on a 10+ pound 9mm subgun is debatable, but the kits I received had this feature and it does look very "military."

Since our semi-auto features a 16-inch barrel and the muzzle brake is about 2½ inches long, only about 1½ inches of barrel extends out of the shroud. This does give a more pleasing look to the gun, since an overly long barrel is not sticking out the front. The muzzle end of the stock M31 barrel is just a little under 3/4" in diameter, and the hole in the shroud is sized for the stock barrel.

The hole will need to be opened up to slightly over 3/4" to slide over the barrel. I drilled the hole to 13/16" to leave plenty of room for the barrel to pass through without the shroud resting on the barrel. The receiver end of the shroud will need to be modified to fit the extending barrel bushing.

I ground out the interlocking lugs, which leaves the shroud oversized to fit the barrel bushing. I then machined a bushing to match the shroud to the barrel bushing. The fit needs to be very tight if you want the shroud to free-float on the end of the barrel.

I silver soldered the bushing into the shroud with Brownells High Force 44 silver solder. I then drilled and tapped two holes for 10-32 set screws to lock the shroud in place. Once a final position has been determined for the shroud, at final fitting a dimple can be drilled slightly into the barrel bushing to make for a more secure set screw lock.

Takedown Lever Installation

Since I deleted the removable barrel feature, the takedown lever will now be strictly cosmetic. I simply inserted it into its hole and plug-welded the back side on the front magazine housing, then ground the weld smooth.

Bolt Modifications—Part 1

Like many submachine guns, the Suomi has a fixed firing pin. It must be converted to moving firing pin configuration to meet BATFE guidelines. The bolt also must be reduced in diameter to fit the new semi-auto receiver.

Rather than doing all the bolt work at once, I decided to split the work up into two parts. First, the fixed firing pin needs to be removed and discarded. Before removing the firing pin, I recommend removing the extractor so it won't get damaged when working on the bolt. It removes easily by prying up the front and then sliding it forward.

The fixed firing pin can be very easy or quite difficult. It rests in a hole in the bolt face, where it is crosspinned in place.

This pin is positioned vertically about 3/4" back from the front of the bolt and extends all the way through it. It is about 3/32" in diameter and can sometimes be hard to see, since the bolt was final finished with it in place.

The shroud hole at the muzzle needs to be drilled out to 3/4" to allow the extended barrel to pass through. The barrel extends only about 1½ inches beyond the muzzle.

The bolt is quite hard and must be annealed to allow machining. Matthews lathe-turned it down to 1.120 inches to fit the new receiver and to meet BATFE guidelines.

This small crosspin must have been installed with a sledgehammer! The best case situation is to start it moving with a strong stubby tool like as a nail set punch and then using a standard short pin punch to move it the rest of the way.

A long thin punch will tend to bend before you get the pin to start moving. I have had some pins absolutely refuse to move no matter how big the hammer and how strong the punch I used. The only option then is to drill it out.

Once the crosspin is out, the firing pin can be driven out with a long thin punch through the end of the bolt. The first hole in the bolt body is about 7/16", but it only extends about halfway through the bolt.

This hole then drops down to a smaller size. On some bolts, the hole drops immediately to about .090" and extends to the rear of the fixed firing pin. On others, the hole drops to an intermediate size an inch or two deeper before dropping to about .090".

The whole problem here is if the firing pin is very tight, you cannot get it out with a spaghetti-thin long punch.

I used a piece of small music wire as a punch. The thin punch may bend before the pin moves. Most will come out but I have had some in past projects that simply wouldn't budge and I had to drill out the firing pin.

Once you have the fixed firing pin out, throw it away. You have no need for a machine gun firing pin on this semi-auto project and don't want to be in procession of what could be considered a machine gun conversion part.

The Suomi bolt is alloy steel and heat treated for maximum durability. It is extremely hard. Before the bolt can be easily drilled or turned on a lathe, the bolt will have to be softened slightly by annealing. As received, the bolt would probably gauge about 50 on the Rockwell C scale. To be soft enough to machine, it needs to be brought down to about 25-30C.

This can be done by heating the bolt to a certain temperature and allowing it to cool slowly. Since most don't have 1000-1200° thermometers, this was done by color. In a dimly lit area gently and evenly heat the bolt to a very dull red color. This needs to be done in a dim area so you can observe when the bolt just begins to turn red. This dull red color will be hot enough to anneal the bolt down to a machinable level.

After reaching the right temperature, I recommend maintaining the heat for two or three minutes and then gradually withdrawing the heat to slow the cooling process. It is very important to heat the bolt evenly, since hot spots will over-soften the bolt and cool ones will leave the bolt too hard to work. The bolt needs to be softened just enough to be easily worked and no more.

When all your bolt work is done, you could have it professionally heat-treated if you want maximum durability but I do not think this is necessary.

It should last for thousand of rounds even though it has been softened. I *do not* recommend you attempt to heat-treat the bolt yourself. In this case, if the bolt is too hard it would be more of a danger than if it were soft.

Once the bolt has cooled, it can be lathe-turned to fit the new semi-auto receiver. My receiver was sized at 1.130 inches, so I turned my bolt to 1.120 inches so I would have about .010" running clearance. The bolt was contoured just like the original, with a reduced diameter in the middle. This is done to reduce binding of the bolt. Be sure you turn the bolt on center.

I used a live center in the 7/16" hole in the body and chucked up the thin forward portion where it was round and had no grooves against the lathe chuck jaws. All edges were then chamfered for smooth operation. While doing the main body turning, I also took 1/4" off the rear of the bolt to shorten it and leave more room to fit the fire control group in the receiver.

The next operation done to the bolt concerns what is known as the feed lips on the bolt. This is the protruding portion on the lower half of the bolt face that allows the bolt to strip cartridges out of the magazine.

On fixed firing pin designs, these lips extend far enough forward to allow the cartridge to slide up past the fixed firing pin as the rim slides up and onto the bolt face. As the round is chambered, the firing pin then can strike the primer squarely, rather than dragging against the cartridge base.

BATFE guidelines recommend removing these on semi-auto conversion projects so the bolt face is flush on the bottom, since it considers the feed lips to be a full auto feature.

The bolt face needs to be chamfered or beveled on the sides to allow the off-center cartridges in the dual feed Suomi magazines to slide over and center themselves on the bolt face when the round is stripped out of the magazine.

This is best done with small needle files or a carefully operated Dremel-type grinder. Just remember you can't put removed material back on after you take it off, so proceeded with caution. Considerable hand fitting and polishing will be required to get it just right and to feed well.

Here's one quick note here about feed testing. Do not check for smooth feeding of cartridges with the firing pin hole open, as the large hole will catch the rims and cause a jam.

Next, drill the bolt for a temporary bolt handle. The handle slot in the receiver, the bolt handle hole in the bolt body and bolt handle itself will all affect the alignment of the bolt in the receiver. All these were made undersize to begin with to allow for final precise fitting later. I recommend doing things this way to allow for slight repositioning if things get out of alignment during the fabrication process.

If they're not aligned properly, the bolt and receiver can be ruined. It's better to get close and then hand fit things until they are just right.

I placed the bolt in the receiver and aligned it so the bottom was square with the magazine. The feed lips on the magazine body should be equal distances from the magazine lip relief grooves in the bolt. You want the bolt to be centered between the sides of the magazine.

When the bolt was aligned correctly, I marked a location for the handle hole on the side of the bolt through the handle slot. I located the handle about .600" back from the front of the bolt body. A 5/16" hole was drilled for a temporary bolt handle.

This hole was drilled all the way through the left side of the bolt. This hole must be drilled squarely or the bolt handle will extend out of the receiver at an odd angle.

A piece of 5/16" rod can be used for a temporary handle. I accidentally let the bolt move slightly during drilling and mine was off a little—another one of those oh crap moments! If the hole is off too far, you can widen the slot on one side and then make an oversized handle to get correct alignment.

Once the bolt was realigned, a new temporary handle made and the groove widened, I ended up with a 3/8" handle and slot, which was about what I wanted to end up with anyway. A self-made and contoured bolt handle will be made later as a final handle after all fitting is complete. Several more operations will be done to the bolt but I decided to take a break from bolt work.

Next month (5/20 issue): Trigger assembly. ◎

The original bolt (r.) has feed lips on the bottom face that need to be removed, per BATFE. The finished bolt face (l.) is smooth from top to bottom and so is legal.

Drive out the vertical retaining pin to allow removal of the fixed firing pin. Matthews says the retaining pin can be tough to drive out and even hard to locate.

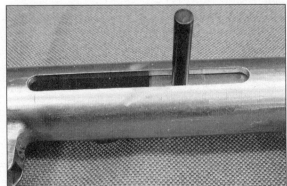

Matthews made a "starter" bolt handle using a 5/16" rod. This allowed him to make adjustments to the handle and slot to get the bolt well aligned in the receiver.

Semi-Auto Suomi from scratch

Part 3: Trigger Guard and Housing

He's gotten the barrel and receiver squared away; now it's time to build the trigger mechanism and a semi-auto bolt. There will be some careful machine work here.

In Part 2 (4/20 issue), Matthews modified the barrel and bolt. Now he builds a semi-auto fire control group.

By Steven Matthews

As required by BATFE regulations, the Suomi M31 needs to have a semi-automatic fire control group fabricated and installed. I made a housing to contain the fire control group and attached it to the original trigger guard. The fire control group on the original Suomi was located in a combined trigger guard and trigger housing.

I cut off the trigger housing part of this combined part, leaving only the trigger guard portion. The full-auto parts previously used in the trigger housing were discarded. The only part to be saved other than the trigger guard was the safety lever at the front.

I fabricated a trigger housing from a 2½-inch piece of 1x1½x3/32" rectangular tubing. This I cut to a height of 1¼ inches, which removed the top side and formed a U-shaped channel. The AR-15 fire control group is about .690" wide, so the channel was cut lengthwise and enough material removed to obtain a width of .690"–.700".

I then welded the channel back together and drilled 5/32" hammer and trigger pin holes in the housing. The trigger pin hole was located .700" from the rear and .350" up from the outside bottom. The hammer pin hole was located .314" above and .843" in front of the trigger pin.

The .314"/.843" hole spacing needs to be very close to these specifications for proper fire control group function. An oval hole also needs to be cut in the bottom of the housing to allow the trigger to pass through.

A hammer stop can be added to keep the hammer from going all the way forward. I placed a 5/32" roll pin 5/16" down from the top of the housing and 3/16" back from the front. When locating and drilling these holes, be absolutely sure they are square to each other and the housing walls. Pins running off at slight angles can seriously affect operation.

You can now install the components in the housing. Use shortened hammer and trigger pins to retain the

The original Suomi trigger housing that contained the full-auto fire control group was cut away, leaving only the trigger guard portion. Throw away full-auto parts.

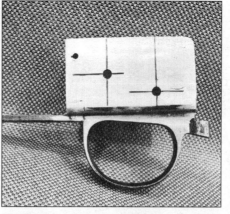

The housing must be drilled for hammer and trigger pins. Precise location and squareness of the holes is mandatory for proper function. Measure twice, drill once.

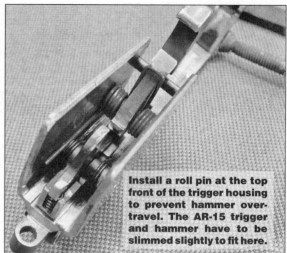

Install a roll pin at the top front of the trigger housing to prevent hammer over-travel. The AR-15 trigger and hammer have to be slimmed slightly to fit here.

The new trigger housing, made from rectangular tubing cut and rewelded to the desired width, will fit between the trigger guard and the newly made receiver tube.

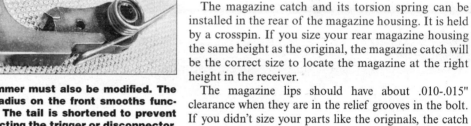

The hammer must also be modified. The larger radius on the front smooths functioning. The tail is shortened to prevent it contacting the trigger or disconnector.

parts. After widening the slot in the trigger guard, I attached the housing to the trigger guard with several small spot MIG welds. The housing was located as far back as possible while still allowing room behind the trigger for full travel.

The AR-15 trigger and disconnector need to be shortened to fit. I cut off the extra length behind the disconnector spring. Be sure to leave enough material to retain the spring in its recesses. The hammer needs to be modified by making the radius on the top front larger.

I shortened the tail of the hammer so it wouldn't press down on the trigger or disconnector when pushed back all the way by the bolt. In this design, the hammer is pushed back and down farther than normal and it may bind if not modified.

I decided to install a very basic trigger-blocking safety. I cut off part of the original safety and attached a long thin bar that would extend back under the front of the trigger. I formed a small lip on the front of the bar to engage shallow detent grooves that I filed in the trigger guard.

A slotted hole in the bar and safety would allow a spring-tensioned screw to pass through the safety assembly and the detents would keep the safety in position. A secondary screw farther back locked the safety and bar together.

When the safety is pushed rearward, the bar slides under the front of the trigger, blocking its travel. When pushed forward, the bar clears the trigger and allows normal movement. This is a simple little assembly to build and the sizing of all parts can be determined by the builder.

This semi-automatic trigger housing/trigger guard needs to be attached to the receiver. The stub on the rear of the trigger guard will fit in the small pocket in the tang section and be retained by the original screw.

The front, however, needs to be modified to be secured. I secured the front to the receiver by drilling a 3/16" hole down through the block on the front of the trigger guard. The top of the block was contoured to fit against the receiver at the correct height.

I then installed a 10-32 screw through the block and into a threaded hole that was formed in the receiver wall. This threaded hole needs to locate the housing correctly (centered between the stock sides) so be sure of the location before you drill and tap the hole.

Since the new trigger housing is wider than the original, the stock will have to be opened up to allow installation of the new trigger guard/housing. File out enough material only where the housing is located to allow for a good fit.

Along the rest of the sides of the trigger guard, there will be gaps about 3/32" wide, since the original Suomi receiver extended down around the trigger guard. I filled these gaps with thin strips of steel spot MIG-welded to the sides of the trigger guard. Spot welding is required here; if you welded all along the sides it would severely warp the trigger guard.

The magazine catch and its torsion spring can be installed in the rear of the magazine housing. It is held by a crosspin. If you size your rear magazine housing the same height as the original, the magazine catch will be the correct size to locate the magazine at the right height in the receiver.

The magazine lips should have about .010-.015" clearance when they are in the relief grooves in the bolt. If you didn't size your parts like the originals, the catch will have to be shortened or lengthened later when doing test fitting. Depending on how the old receiver was demilled, there may be gaps around the magazine catch lever and the trigger guard. These gaps need to be filled in with small pieces of steel spot welded to the trigger guard. When I filled in these small gaps, I also installed the stubby magazine lever guard.

Bolt Modifications—Part 2

It was now time to finish converting the bolt to semi-automatic operation. The slot was cut from the back and extended forward until it was about 1¼ inches from the front of the bolt body. This slot must be sized so that

A slotted hole allows the safety to slide back and forth by about 3/8". The spring allows the lip at the left end to engage two shallow grooves for a detent action.

Matthews modified the safety by trimming its slide and attaching a thin steel bar at the top. Its thickness will depend on clearance between trigger and housing.

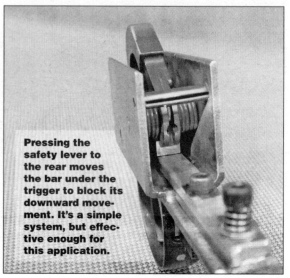

Pressing the safety lever to the rear moves the bar under the trigger to block its downward movement. It's a simple system, but effective enough for this application.

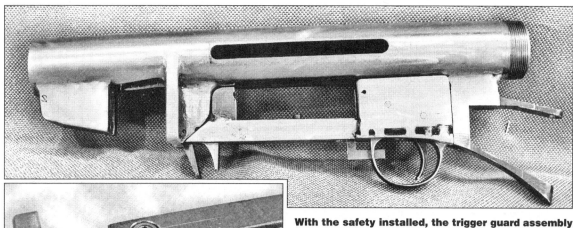

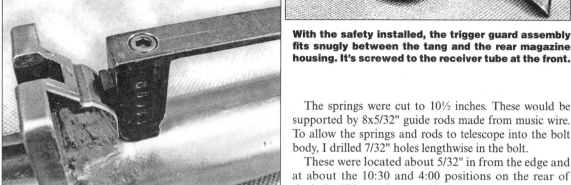

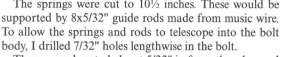

With the safety installed, the trigger guard assembly fits snugly between the tang and the rear magazine housing. It's screwed to the receiver tube at the front.

The magazine catch and torsion spring are installed in the rear magazine housing. Matthews salvaged the catch guard and installed on the new trigger guard.

when the bolt reciprocates and pushes the hammer down, the both the trigger and disconnector engage the hammer and hold it. The disconnector must also catch the hammer even if the trigger is pulled and held rearward. This is necessary to obtain semi-automatic operation.

A complete understanding of how an AR-15 fire control group operates is mandatory for proper fitting and functioning of the bolt and fire control components. Failure to fit these parts correctly could result in automatic fire. Fit and check parts over and over until you are absolutely sure they are working right.

The BATFE has expressed an opinion that they consider a malfunctioning semi-automatic firearm firing full-auto to be an illegal machine gun. Failure to fit your fire control system properly could put you in violation of federal firearms laws. Get it right and be legal!

Next, I fabricated a dual recoil spring system to replace the original single-spring system. This was necessary since the gun now features a hammer where the original recoil spring was located. The gunsmith quality springs I obtained from Brownells as part of one of their gunsmith spring kits, No. 1-OD. The springs were .215" diameter x .025" wire with about 12 coils per inch.

The springs were cut to 10½ inches. These would be supported by 8x5/32" guide rods made from music wire. To allow the springs and rods to telescope into the bolt body, I drilled 7/32" holes lengthwise in the bolt.

These were located about 5/32" in from the edge and at about the 10:30 and 4:00 positions on the rear of the bolt. This spacing would allow the hammer to pass between the springs. The holes were drilled to depth about 1/4" from the front of the bolt body. The remaining depth was drilled to about .165" to allow the 5/32" rods to pass through easily.

These holes must be drilled straight and parallel to prevent drilling through the side of the bolt or into the center hole. The left side hole must also be positioned so that it misses the bolt handle hole. When I drilled the left hole, Murphy decided to rear his ugly head! My left spring hole was located about 1/32" too close to the handle hole and I just skimmed the hole as I reached the depth of the handle hole.

This required that I use a slightly shorter spring and guide rod on the left side to prevent the spring from interfering with later bolt handle installation.

The guide rods need to be secured in a backplate assembly. This part was made from a 1⅛-inch diameter by 1⅛-inch long piece of 4130 rod. I drilled 7/32x3/4" deep holes in the part to allow the springs to telescope. The remaining depth was drilled all the way though 5/32" to allow the guide rods to pass.

To secure the guide rods in the backplate, I drilled a shallow counterbore on the rear of the plate. The rear of the guide rods were flared out by heating and hammering and then sized to slip into the counterbores.

The ends of these rods were then silver-soldered in place with Brownells High Force 44 solder.

These guide rods must be mounted straight and square or they will bind during use. The holes for the guide rods in the backplate must also exactly match the locations on the bolt. I made some little transfer punches that fit in the holes to get the holes matched in each piece.

A clearance hole must be drilled in the front center of the backplate to allow firing pin head clearance. I drilled the hole 15/32" diameter and 1/2" deep. The backplate and guide rods must stay aligned with the bolt when operating. They may or may not self-align, so I machined a groove in the top of the backplate. A screw through the end cap and receiver will interface with this slot and keep the backplate aligned with the bolt.

To soften impact of the bolt against the receiver end cap when it reaches its most rearward position, I made a buffer out of soft neoprene rubber. I located this buffer behind the backplate rather than in front as is the usual position of buffers. If I located it in front, I would have to drill clearance holes for the springs and firing pin head and I thought this would weaken the buffer disc and it would quickly fall apart.

Matthews welded steel spacers on either side of the trigger guard and housing to fill the gap between them and the stock. The original receiver extended into the wood.

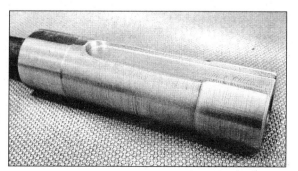

Matthews cut a shallow hammer slot .450" wide and .125" deep in the bottom of the bolt. This is needed since a full diameter bolt would push the hammer down too far.

When drilling the deep spring pocket holes in the bolt body, precise alignment is necessary. Matthews used a dial indicator to align quill travel with the bolt.

Matthews made short transfer punches to mark the hole locations on the back plate. The holes in both pieces must be precisely aligned to prevent spring binding.

The guide rod heads are fitted into recesses in the back plate. A screw through the receiver engages a groove in the back plate to prevent that part from rotating.

With the dual guide rods and the coil springs installed, the Suomi's transformation from a fixed firing pin to a hammer-operated system is well underway.

Firing Pin Assembly Fabrication and Fitting

It was now time to make the moving firing pin that is require by BATFE rules for the bolt. I decided to use a two-part setup rather than one long bolt-length pin. This would be less critical on alignment issues. This is where I made many design and fabrication mistakes. My original design featured several small holes that needed to be precisely drilled and aligned in the interior of the bolt to work right. There was little room for error or misalignment.

Unfortunately the existing holes drilled 70+ years ago in the Suomi bolts I had were drilled slightly off-center and did not precisely align with each other.

When I tried to drill my precisely located small holes, the bit would be deflected by the existing off-center holes and end up where it wasn't supposed to be, resulting in ruined bolts.

This was in addition to the fact that all my bolts were not the same. On some, the interior holes were drilled to two sizes and on others they were drilled to three, all of which were misaligned with each other by as much as a 1/16".

This resulted in three ruined bolts before I decided to go back to the drawing board. I figured if I couldn't get it right this way then my readers wouldn't be able to, either.

I came up with something eventually that was easier to make. I started by drilling the existing fixed firing pin hole from the front all the way through the bolt until it reached the 7/16" hole that was drilled from the back.

This I did on a lathe to maintain the best possible alignment. It was drilled to the existing size, which was between .177"–178" (#15 or #16 drill depending on drill size tolerances). This hole was then tapped with a 12-28 tap to a depth of about 5/8" deep. This was also done on a lathe with the tap aligned in the tailstock for best alignment, because if tapped crooked or off center things will not fit and operate smoothly.

The tapping depth of this hole may be adjusted later to get proper firing pin bushing depth. I should include a quick note here about thread fit tolerances for those less experienced builders. Taps and threaded materials can vary several thousandths in size depending on the tolerances to which they were made.

This firing pin bushing needs to be fitted very tightly. You don't want to use a bolt for the bushing that is greatly undersize and a tap that cuts way oversize. This will result in a sloppy fit and poor alignment of parts. The taps and threaded material I had varied as much as .004" each, which could result in .008" of "slop." I sized my materials and taps for the tightest fit, which was still looser than I wanted, but short of cutting a new oversize screw, it was as close as I could get.

The bushing would be made from a high quality (Grade 5 or higher) 1-inch (thread length) 12-28 machine screw. Do not use screws made from "butter grade" low quality steel. The screw was chucked up in a lathe (head outward) and a 5/64" (.078") hole was drilled through end to end. This hole must be centered on both ends; if it's off more than a couple thousandths, make another one until you get it right.

A shallow shear groove was cut right under the head so its head could be snapped off and filed down flush with the bolt face after installation. The screw was turned over and the 5/64" hole in the threaded end was enlarged to .105". It was drilled to a depth of about 11/16". The edge of the hole was chamfered.

This will result in a bushing that, when installed, will have about 1/4" of the 5/64" firing pin hole remaining for the firing pin point to extend through. Once you have well-centered holes in your bushing, it can be installed in the bolt face. Screw it into the bolt and snug it down. Do not tighten it enough to break off the weakened head at this time.

You want the shear groove to be about 1/32" above the bolt face. If it is far from the face, use your tap to deepen the threads. Once you have the right depth, the bushing can be permanently installed. For a tight fit, slightly deform some of the threads in the middle with a flat point punch and use high strength threadlocker on the screw.

Install it and tighten it down very tight. Either cut or break off the head and file the bushing flush with the bolt face. The edge of the firing pin hole can be *very lightly* chamfered for smooth operation. When finished, you should have a bushing with a well-centered firing pin hole.

Do not, however, be confused by appearances. When you cut a threaded part flush with an existing surface, things can look a bit off, since the exposed part may show the edge of the cut-off threads rather than the actual edge of the part.

The first step in fitting a firing pin bushing is to tap the bolt. Supporting the tap with the lathe tailstock will help maintain precise alignment for smooth function.

Matthews used a 12-28 machine screw for the bushing. He cut a shear groove under the head to allow it to be broken off. Then he could file it flush to the bolt face.

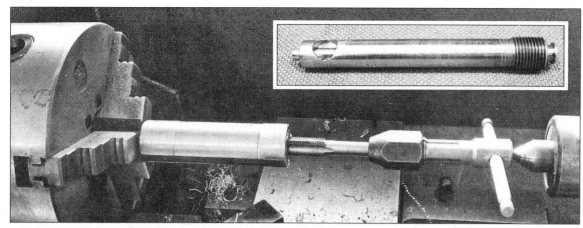

The rear end of the bolt must be bushed for the firing pin extension. The bushing was made from a Grade 5 bolt and the firing pin extension from 3/16" music wire.

Drilling small holes through 3 inches of steel can be tricky. Both parts were set up and drilled the same way, but the drill was deflected on the right-hand workpiece.

The .177" hole that remained behind the installed bushing was then drilled out to 3/16" This allowed me to install a 3/16" return spring on the firing pin. The rear portion of the 3/16" hole will need to be opened up to 7/32" to allow the head of the firing pin to pass. I recommend drilling this hole later after the firing pin is made. It will be drilled to a depth that allows for full firing pin extension.

A custom-made firing pin now has to be fabricated and fitted to the semi-automatic bolt. An AR-15 firing pin was used as raw material. The pin is heat-treated, so you will need sharp lathe tooling to cut the thin and flexible pin.

The shape of the pin will be changed extensively. The basic principle is to have a profile that will fit in the interior holes with plenty of support, yet still move freely. The first thing I did was to turn the head down to .215" so it would slide easily in the .218" hole in the bolt.

Then I drilled a small shallow hole (about 1/16") in the head, so it could be run on a live center. The pin was set up

between the live center and chuck and the 5/32" portion ahead of the firing pin head was turned down to .125" to allow the 3/16" firing pin return spring to fit over it.

The length of this portion was about .950". Ahead of this .125" portion, the pin was turned down to .100" for a length of about .750". The next portion was turned down to .072" so the point would pass through the .078" hole in the bolt. The length of this part was about .350".

All these lengths combined resulted in an overall length of roughly 2⅝ inches. These sizes can be adjusted somewhat to ensure smooth operation of the pin. The remainder of the pin was cut off and the end of the firing pin was given a rounded profile. The pin was then fitted to the bolt.

Variations in hole size and alignment mean considerable fitting and adjusting the sizes of the pin and holes may be needed. The firing pin must extend fully out of the bolt face and also easily retract about 1/16"–3/32" back into the bolt face under spring power. There can be no dragging or binding of the pin, it must move freely with adequate clearance.

Failure to fit the firing pin properly could result in an illegal and unsafe automatic fire malfunction. The head of the firing pin should be almost completely inside the 7/32" hole that was drilled in the bolt.

A hole drilled and tapped in the side of the bolt will allow the firing pin to be retained in the bolt body with a set screw. Locate this set screw so it is in the groove in the head of the firing pin. It should be set so that it limits firing pin retraction into the bolt face to about 1/16" to 3/32". The set screw cannot contact the shaft of the firing pin or it will bind. Set the depth so it clears the firing pin.

After all test fitting and disassembly is done, the set screw can be locked at the proper depth with threadlocker and by staking the threads.

Next month (6/20 issue): Finishing the semi-auto Suomi.

Ask the Gunsmith

By Reid Coffield

CHAMBER BURRS

Q *I have an older Colt revolver in .38 Spl. The gun is in fairly good shape. The finish is a bit worn but it is mechanically very tight with almost no movement in the cylinder when it is locked in place. My problem is ejection. After I fire the gun I have a problem ejecting the cases. Any ideas as to what is going on with this old gun? How can I fix it?*

A I would first encourage you to carefully examine each of the individual chambers. Look closely inside each for rust pits, burrs or scratches. Even a single pit, burr or scratch of significant size can cause an ejection problem. Upon firing the brass case, which is somewhat elastic, will expand to seal the chamber. The brass, under considerable pressure, flows out and is only stopped by the chamber walls. If there is a pit or deep scratch, the case will flow out and into this depression.

Once the gas pressure drops the case will contract a bit. It doesn't normally go all the way back to the size it was prior to being fired but it will be close. However, if the case expanded into a pit or scratch, it may not contract enough to come completely out of that depres-

If you look closely you can see scars on these cases from burrs in the chamber. This caused major extraction problems. Coffield says there's not much you can do about very severe chamber pitting.

sion. That spells trouble when you try to eject it from the cylinder.

The small bit of brass still protruding into the pit may lock the case in place. In many instances you have

to actually shear this protruding brass off the case before it can be ejected. Needless to say, this makes ejection a real bear.

Right now I have a Russian Nagant revolver on my bench with that problem. Six of the seven chambers are just fine, but one of 'em has a few pits and some burrs. When fired, the cases eject easily from the six good chambers but you have to use a cleaning rod to remove the case from the seventh chamber.

Sometimes it is simply impossible to fix or repair a pitted chamber. I don't know of any practical way to fill pits inside a chamber. If the chamber was cut to absolute minimum dimensions or less, you can sometimes get very lucky and use a chamber reamer to open it up a bit to normal dimensions. As you open the chamber you may cut out the pits or at least lessen their depth. Another possibility is to hone or polish the inside of the chamber. This may, just may, make it a bit easier to eject the fired cases as the pits will not have as much of a tendency to cut or shear off brass.

Another option is to experiment with different brands and types of brass. Sometimes nickel-plated cases will function better in situations where you have a rough chamber. You might want to try this. If all else fails and you have only one or two chambers that are pitted, simply load the good chambers and leave the bad ones empty. It's not ideal, but it will allow you to continue to use the gun.

Finally, as a last resort you may simply have to replace the cylinder. If you need a cylinder, check with the folks at Numrich Gun Parts Corporation, Box 299, Dept. SGN, West Hurley, N.Y. 12491, telephone 866-686-7424. By the way, a replacement cylinder will generally have to be fitted and for this you may need the services of a knowledgeable, experienced gunsmith.

Semi-Auto Suomi from scratch

Part 4: Finishing the Gun

In Part 3 (5/20 issue), Matthews made a semi-auto trigger group. In this installment, he finishes and tests this unusual carbine.

By Steven Matthews

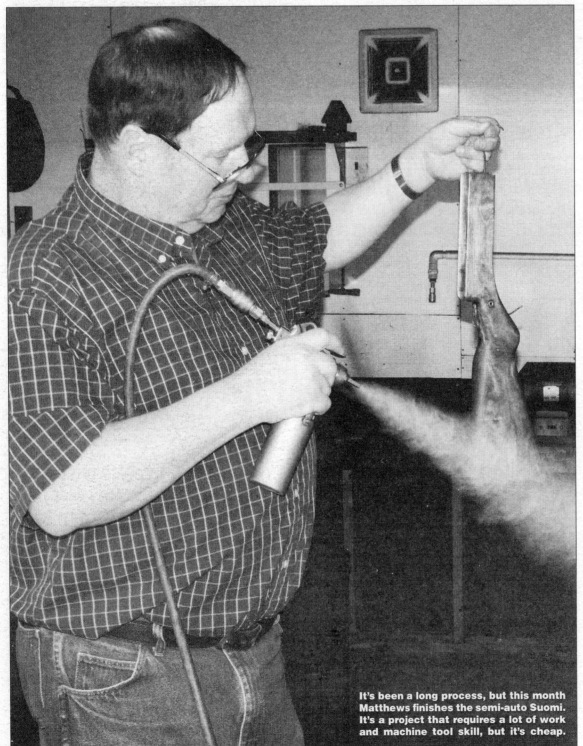

It's been a long process, but this month Matthews finishes the semi-auto Suomi. It's a project that requires a lot of work and machine tool skill, but it's cheap.

After the firing pin is fitted and operating smoothly, an extension needs to be fabricated. This will allow the hammer forces to be transferred from the rear of the bolt to the firing pin that is housed deep inside. I made it using 3/16x4½-inch music wire and a piece of tool steel for a cap. It was made overlong and then fitted later to obtain the desired .045" to .055" firing pin protrusion out of the bolt face. The cap was shaped like a screw head with a 3/16" hole drilled in one end so it could slide over the pin.

The smaller portion of the cap was sized at 1/4" while the rounded head was sized about .330-.340". The cap was then brazed to the pin. This extension will also feature a return spring, and the spring was sized at 3/4" long by 1/4" diameter and was made of .028" wire. After all sizing was done, I hardened the cap and the point of the pin for durability.

This extension pin must be housed in a bushing that will fit the 7/16" hole that is in the bolt body. This bushing was made from the shank of a 4½-inch long 1/2"-20 Grade 5 bolt. The first step was to drill a 3/16" hole all the way through the length of the bolt. This hole needs to be fairly well centered on both ends.

I started the hole on the threaded end of the bolt shank. Once the hole was all the way through, I supported the shank end with a live center in the 3/16" hole and turned the smooth shank down to 7/16" (check your hole size and adjust the size to fit). About 17/32" of threads were left on the end so the bushing could be retained in the bolt body when the end was tapped.

The threaded end of the 3/16" hole was enlarged to 1/4" diameter so the return spring and cap would fit inside. The 1/4" portion was drilled about 5/8" deep. This bushing will be overlong and will need to be fitted so that the edge is just under the rear edge of the bolt.

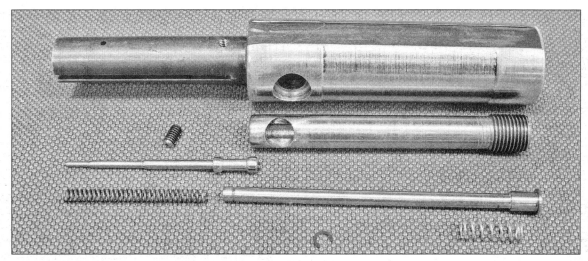

The new semi-auto bolt consists of the bolt body, firing pin, firing pin return spring, extension bushing, extension with rounded head and the extension return spring.

The head of the firing pin extension needs to extend only past the rear of the bolt body by about 3/32" to 1/8". Total extension travel will only be about 3/16".

Carefully drill and tap the rear of the bolt to 1/2"-20. Thread in about 5/8" to 3/4". To keep the bushing from turning out of its threaded hole during use, I drilled the bolt hole handle a little ways into the bushing. The installed bolt handle will extend into the bushing and lock it in place.

The extension pin needs to be securely retained in the bushing. My first attempt to retain the pin was by using

The bolt handle has a 1/2" diameter protrusion to fit into the bolt body. This serves to retain the handle in the receiver, and is removed through the takedown notch.

snap rings on the pin shaft, which failed in short order. The force of the firing pin being driven forward and then retracted by a spring quickly destroyed the snap ring and the pin fell out, Oh crap!

I eventually went with a 1/8" crosspin through the bushing body which ran through a clearance groove formed on one side of the extension pin. The crosspin was located about midway along the bushing's length. This set up was durable and is similar to methods found on some manufactured guns.

Some more knowledgeable builders may ask about the weight of the highly modified bolt. Bolts for blowback firearms need to weigh a certain amount to function properly. Fortunately, with the new firing pin setup housed in the interior of the bolt the weight was within a couple ounces of a standard Suomi bolt.

Bolt handle Fabrication and Fitting

Once you're sure the bolt is correctly aligned with the temporary handle, a permanent handle can be made. I had a 3/8" handle and a 3/8" (with about .005" running clearance) handle slot. I drilled a 1/2" diameter by 3/16" deep recess into the upper edge of the handle hole in the bolt body.

This would allow a 1/2" protrusion on the new bolt handle to fit down inside the bolt body and retain the handle inside the receiver, since the slot was smaller. A 1/2" takedown notch at the rear of the handle slot will allow removal during disassembly.

Do not cut the takedown notch yet, it must be about 3/4" beyond the maximum bolt handle travel and must only allow the handle to extend that far when the end cap is removed. I lathe-turned a handle with a 3/8" shank, followed by the 1/2" protrusion that would fit in the recess. The section that extended through the receiver wall was 3/8". I added about another inch of length and put a little head on the handle.

Ejector Fabrication and Fitting

I used a fixed ejector in the M31 just as the original, but mine was shaped differently. It was simply a small right triangle with the two points flattened. It was made out of a 3/32" thick piece of tool steel and then welded into the side of the receiver.

The ejector was sized to fit in its groove in the bolt. You want some clearance here so the bolt doesn't drag on the ejector. A small slot cut in the receiver wall would allow it to be welded flush to the outside of the receiver. Before I welded it in place, I hardened the side that contacts the cartridge rim for wear resistance.

I located it in the receiver wall so that the front of the ejector was about 3/4" in front of the rear edge of the ejection port. Be absolutely sure it is aligned correctly before you weld. The heat of welding may harden the ejector and make it too brittle to bend into the correct position.

Rear Sight Installation

On the original Suomi, the rear sight was riveted in place. It was also retained by a long lug on the bottom of the sight that extended into the receiver wall. I decided to remove the lug and simply attach the sight with 6-48 scope base screws through the sight and receiver.

Since the semi-auto Suomi receiver is so thick, there is plenty of room to tap 6-48 threads. I aligned the sight on the top of the receiver and marked the hole locations. They were then drilled and tapped. The screws were sized so they would not extend into the receiver interior and were coated with thread locker during installation.

Barrel Fitting

The barrel/barrel bushing assembly must be fitted to the receiver. This is where you learn something about feed geometry. For proper feeding, the round must be at the correct height to be stripped from the magazine, and the barrel must be at the right location for the round to make the transition from magazine to chamber.

There are many factors that affect how the round feeds. The location of the barrel, magazine and bolt all affect functioning. The angles and shapes of the bolt face, magazine lips, feed ramp, chamber size and a host of other

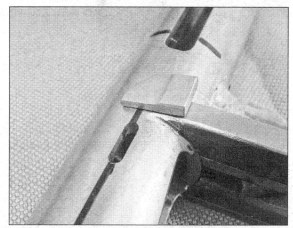

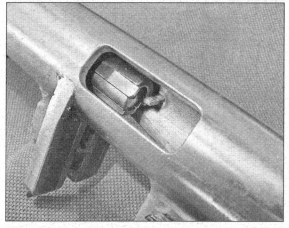

Matthews made an ejector from a piece of tool steel, then welded it in place unto a slot in the receiver wall. Be sure to size it to prevent dragging on the bolt.

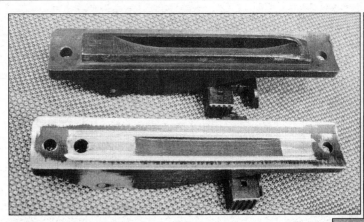

Matthews had to grind the bottom of the rear sight to make it fit the new receiver tube. Then it was aligned and secured in place with 6-48 scope base screws.

things all affect feeding. The bolt face, feed ramp and chamber are already done, so the location of the barrel in the receiver will now probably be the deciding factor for good feeding. Since this was a military style gun, I only set it up to feed full metal jacket ammo reliably. I had no interest in getting it to feed hollow-points or anything else.

I slid the barrel assembly into the receiver and the extractor was aligned with the extractor relief cut in the rear of the barrel. You'll need 10-15-FMJ-shaped dummy rounds to test feeding. Never use live ammo for testing purposes. Make sure the dummy rounds are easily distinguishable from live rounds.

I speak from experience on this issue: 20+ years ago I was testing my first self-made NFA registered MAC-10 open-bolt submachine gun with homemade dummy rounds. I got one live round mixed in during function testing. I got quite a surprise when one of the "dummy" rounds went bang! After yelling OH %$#*&^& and making sure I hadn't shot anyone, I found nice .45 cal. holes in my wall, closet, bed and tool box!!

With dummies in the magazine, operate the bolt by hand and see if the rounds will chamber. This needs to be done at a speed similar to actual operation to simulate actual functioning; don't try to ease them in slowly.

If the barrel is too close to the front of the magazine, you will have jams because the feed angle is too steep. If you get the barrel too far away, you run the risk of having the rounds completely out of the magazine before they are even close to chambering.

The best position allows the round to be pushed forward a ways in the magazine and then have the nose guide the round into the chamber without binding or getting stuck on anything. Considerable experimentation may be needed to get things just right. Small changes may need to be made on the bolt face or feed ramp, even when the barrel is positioned about right.

Different bullet profiles will sometimes affect feeding, so keep that in mind while testing. Once you find the correct location for good feeding, the barrel can be permanently installed in its bushing by the previously mentioned crosspinning, don't forget to do this!

The barrel/bushing assembly needs to be permanently installed in the receiver. Be *absolutely* sure the barrel is still located in the right position for good feeding before welding; once it's welded in place it would be very difficult to change.

I drilled 3/8" holes through the receiver wall and slightly into the bushing and these holes were then plug-welded to secure the barrel assembly in the receiver. You need to be sure to get good weld penetration into the bushing but not to overheat the barrel.

To prevent overheating, I plug welded about half the depth of the hole and then allowed it to cool before welding the rest of the hole shut. I placed these plug welds on each side and one on the top. After welding, the welds were dressed down smooth with the receiver tube.

Barrel Shroud Fitting

After the barrel was installed, I fitted the shroud. The rear of the shroud was a good tight fit on the remainder of the bushing that extended out of the front of the receiver. This allowed its front hole to free float and not to contact the sides of the barrel. Since the shroud will be secured with set screws, it can be adjusted for good sight alignment.

I placed the receiver in a vise and bore sighted at an object about 100 yards away. The shroud was then rotated until the front sight and rear sight were aligned with the bore sight view. The set screws were installed to lock the shroud and sight in place.

Once you're absolutely sure the shroud is positioned right, a shallow dimple can be drilled in the bushing under the set screw for the screw point to engage for a stronger connection.

Final Checks

Since the project is nearing completion, several items need to be checked or completed. The bolt handle removal notch can be cut at the end of the handle slot.

A complete function check should be done with all parts installed. Use the dummy rounds and cycle

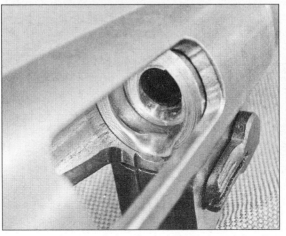

Correct barrel placement is vital to making the semi-auto Suomi feed. Use a screw to lock the barrel in place temporarily while function-testing with dummy ammo.

Be sure to align the extractor relief cut in the rear of the barrel with the extractor to prevent damage to the latter. The depth of the barrel assembly is critical.

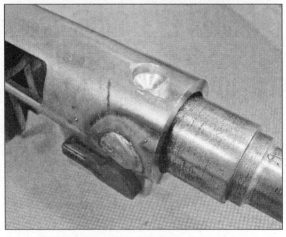

Once the final barrel position is determined, the barrel can be permanently installed by plug welding the bushing. Do this only when you are sure of the position.

A collar that slides over the bolt will act as a stop and roughly set headspace. Weld it in place once the correct setting is determined, avoiding heat distortion.

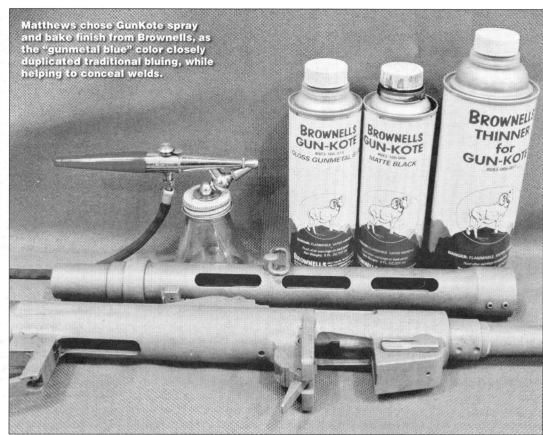

Matthews chose GunKote spray and bake finish from Brownells, as the "gunmetal blue" color closely duplicated traditional bluing, while helping to conceal welds.

them through the action. They should chamber and eject properly. Each cycle of the bolt should cock the hammer. The hammer must be held by the trigger or disconnector, depending on whether the trigger is pulled or released.

Disconnector function should create only semi-automatic operation, the trigger must be released for each shot and allow the trigger to reset. The bolt should move freely in the receiver with no binding or drag.

The recoil springs must return the bolt to the closed position with enough force to strip rounds out of the magazine easily and still have sufficient energy to close the action. The safety should be tested for proper operation.

Verify that everything works with dummy rounds before advancing to live fire testing. Believe me, adding 35,000 psi of pressure to the equation will not make anything work better. If things don't work with dummy rounds, they won't work with live rounds.

Once I was sure everything worked, I advanced to live fire testing. Be sure to wear safety equipment such as a full face shield, heavy gloves, hearing protection, etc. when testing new unproven firearms One round

was loaded into the magazine, chambered and test-fired. All worked well and the fired cartridges showed nothing abnormal.

Next, two rounds were loaded and the test was repeated. Semiautomatic operation was being performed by the fire control group. More rounds were loaded and checked to verify reliable operation. If you have any problems, correct them before going on to final finishing. Everything on my project appeared to be working, so I disassembled everything for finishing.

Marking the Project

Although BATFE regulations do not require home-made guns to be marked like manufactured firearms, the BATFE "highly recommends" marking them with the builder's name, address and self-assigned serial number. This is really a good "cover your butt" policy for the home builder. If the gun is lost or stolen, this does give some identifying information for possible recovery.

It also prevents the gun from being mistaken by law enforcement in some future encounter as appearing to be an untraceable firearm that has had the serial number

illegally removed. Law enforcement may not believe you made the gun and that you were not absolutely required to mark it since most law enforcement personnel are not up on the rules for home building firearms. A set of imported hand stamps can be purchased from suppliers like Harbor Freight for a few dollars and you can mark to gun as you please.

Final Finishing

The original Suomi M31 guns were very well finished for military arms. The surfaces were free of excessive machining marks and they were hot tank blued. I wanted my project to look as good as an original, so I smoothed up any surface defects such as scratches, machining marks or unsightly welds.

Projects with many arc welds into different alloys can sometimes cause bluing problems. The different welds and alloys can end up different colors, so I decided not to blue my project. I did however want it to look blued. Brownells offered a solution in the form of their GunKote firearms finish in the color of "gun blue."

Brownells GunKote is a sprayed on and baked finish that is extremely durable. It is one of my favorites.

The completed semi-auto has a few visual differences from the original full-auto Suomi, but effectively capture the essence of the subgun so effective in the Winter War.

The side charging handle was not an original feature; the Suomi had a small rear bolt handle. The muzzle brake is non-functional with the longer barrel, but looks good.

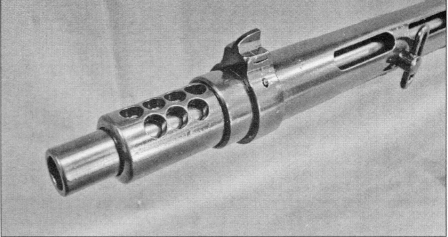

It is easy to apply and is relatively inexpensive for the hobbyist who can apply it himself. Brownells offers instructions with GunKote, but the basic procedure is to abrasive blast, clean, spray and bake at 300°. Once cool, the parts are ready to assemble, no need to wait for a week or more for the finish to cure like some finishes.

The wood on the Suomi stock was lightly sanded, stained and coated with a couple thin coats of satin lacquer.

Once it was finished and assembled, I was very pleased with the results. While the project was very labor intensive, cost was very low. It was well worth the labor investment to get a reasonable representation of this unique and interesting firearm.

I wound up with more than 150 hours in this project, thanks to all the design work and experimentation. Builders using this article as a very rough guide will have less time invested than I did. Just remember this article is just how I did the project and you may find better or easier ways.

Hobby gunsmithing is all about doing things your way and I encourage people to experiment to find interesting and unique ways to build a project. Just as I did, you will make mistakes and have to correct them, but that's all part of the hobby. If you are a reasonably skilled hobbyist gunsmith who likes military arms and like bargain priced projects, this project may be for you. Give it a try!! ◎

Material Sources
Semi-automatic Suomi 9mm Carbine

Suomi M31 Parts Sets
Cope's Distributing
Box 70, Dept. SGN, Pitsburg, OH 45358
1-866-775-9466, www.copesdist.com

Firearms / Gunsmithing Supplies
Brownells
200 S Front St., Dept. SGN, Montezuma, IA 50171
1-800-741-0015, www.brownells.com

4130 Chrome-Moly Tubing and Rod
Wicks Aircraft Supply
410 Pine St., Dept. SGN, Highland, IL 62249
1-800-221-9424, www.wicksaircraft.com

The Legal Side

When the hobbyist gunsmith builds a project based on a foreign military design, legal issues need to be addressed. The first of these is known in the hobby as U.S. Compliance or 922(r) Compliance. Under federal firearms regulations, a semi-automatic rifle cannot be built or assembled with more than 10 foreign or imported parts out of a list of 20 specified parts.

If more than 10 of the specified parts are used, the gun is considered to be a foreign-made semi-automatic rifle that would be un-importable and therefore is illegal under current rules. If fewer than 10 or less of the specified parts, then the gun is considered to be a legal U.S. made semi-automatic firearm. The 20 specified parts are as follows. 1) frames or receivers, 2) barrels, 3) barrel extensions, 4) mounting blocks (trunnions), 5) muzzle attachments, 6) bolts, 7) bolt carriers, 8) operating rods/charging handles, 9) gas pistons, 10) trigger housings, 11) triggers, 12) hammers, 13) sears, 14) disconnectors, 15) buttstocks, 16) pistol grips, 17) forearms or handguards, 18) magazine bodies, 19) magazine followers, 20) magazine floorplates.

Note that not all rifles have all 20 of the specified parts in their designs. The Suomi based semi-automatic rifle featured in this article contains the following foreign-made parts—magazine body, magazine follower, magazine floorplate, barrel, buttstock, bolt, handguard, and possibly trigger housing (this depends on if the trigger guard is still considered part of the trigger housing). This results in a foreign parts count of 7 or 8. This is less than

the 10 imported parts limit and therefore the project is considered to be a U.S.-made and legal semi-automatic firearm.

The second and most important issue deals with what actually defines a legal semi-automatic firearm verses a prohibited fully automatic firearm. Semiautomatic firearms based on or resembling prohibited fully automatic firearms must be built a certain way to be legal.

To be legal the firearm must differ considerably from its parent full-auto design. The BATFE has some general guidelines that need to be observed to maintain legality. These guidelines can vary somewhat on different firearms designs. The guidelines for this Suomi-based project were obtained from internet published copies of correspondences between the BATFE and other semi-automatic Suomi project builders. The guidelines in paraphrased form are as follows:

1) The receiver should be of substantially smaller diameter to prevent the use of an unmodified full auto Suomi bolt.
2) The protruding feed lips on the bottom half of the bolt face should be removed.
3) An open-bolt firing system featuring a fixed firing pin cannot be utilized.
4) A hammer or striker firing system that incorporates a positive disconnector that creates reliable semi-automatic fire should be used.
5) The sear mechanism needs to be modified or removed so that a full-auto sear mechanism cannot be used in the firearm.

6) The firing system should be designed with a conventional moving firing pin as is common on semi-automatic designs.
7) The barrel for a rifle must be at least 16 inches in overall length.

The design of this project incorporates these guidelines and features. Many mass produced firearms based on military designs are sold with something called a BATFE approval letter. This letter is simply a statement from the BATFE stating that the firearm or design was evaluated and found to meet their guidelines.

While this project was built to the listed guidelines it was not submitted to BATFE for an official approval letter since it was made to the guidelines and it was not for commercial manufacture.

If you want an official classification for your own project, you'll need to submit a completed sample to the BATFE for evaluation. The BATFE will not approve paper designs, they require an actual firearm. For more information on how to make home built firearms to BATFE guidelines or submit a sample for evaluation, contact the BATFE at BAFTE Firearms Technology Branch, 244 Needy Rd., Martinsburg, W. Va. 25401.

The builder should also be aware that many states or localities prohibit certain types of firearms that may be Federally legal in other locations. It is the builder's responsibility to verify that any home build project is legal in his locality before starting construction. ◎

Ask the Gunsmith

By Reid Coffield

REMINGTON 11 HAMMER

Q *I have an old Remington Model 11 12 gauge that I have had since I was a kid. It was an old used gun when I got it and I have shot it for more than 25 years. Although it is worn and shows its age, I have never had any problem with it up until now. I took it out to shoot some clay birds with a buddy and it doubled when I pulled the trigger. Fortunately I only load it with two shells but still it is a problem. What is wrong and how do I fix it?*

The hooks on the Remington Model 11 shotgun trigger can wear or break, leading to doubling or firing multiple shots. This is a dangerous situation which must be corrected, preferably by replacement with a new part.

A More than likely the problem is caused by wear or damage to the hammer hooks on your trigger. Check the hooks closely to see if the surfaces are worn, broken, or rounded on the tips. It's also a good idea to check the corresponding hooks on the hammer that mate with the trigger hooks. Again look for wear or damage.

Even if you don't find damage, the spacing between the hooks on the trigger is critical. The hammer hooks must pass between the trigger hooks yet a little, and here I am talking about a few thousandths, excess clearance can cause the hammer hooks to fail to engage. If that happens, the gun will double.

I would not recommend trying to build up these hooks by welding unless that is an absolute last resort. Instead, I would suggest you contact the good folks at Numrich Gun Parts, Box 299, Dept. SGN, West Hurley, N.Y. 12491, telephone 866-686-7424. They normally have an extensive supply of Remington Model 11 parts and can probably help you with either a hammer or trigger or both if needed.

TOKAREV REAMER

Q *I need a chamber reamer in 7.62x25mm for a Tokarev pistol. Obviously this is not something many people ever want or need so I have had no luck finding anyone listing it. Do you know where I can find one?*

A Dave Manson at Manson Precision Reamers can supply this chamber reamer as well as headspace gauges. The address is Manson Precision Reamers, 8200 Embury Road, Dept. SGN, Grand Blanc, Mich. 48439, telephone 810-953-0732. If you need a chamber reamer for almost any cartridge Dave can supply it and the quality of his work is top notch.

SW99 GRIP INSERTS

Q *I have the option of buying a Smith and Wesson Model SW99 9mm pistol from a friend. The price is very attractive and the pistol is in excellent shape. My problem is that I have heard that these guns have been discontinued by Smith and Wesson. Is that true? Also, if the guns have been discontinued, where can I get parts? I am especially interested in getting the grip inserts that allow you to adjust the grip for different size hands. My friend misplaced the extra grip inserts and right now it is set up for large hands. My hand is smaller so I want to be able to adjust the grip for a better fit.*

The SW99 has been out of production for several years, but parts are still available from S&W. Coffield says keeping accessories like grip inserts with the gun makes for a better sale later.

A Yes, the SW99 was discontinued by Smith and Wesson around 2004. However, Smith and Wesson still has lots of parts for this very fine pistol. To obtain the parts you need just give the folks at Smith and Wesson a call. The telephone number is 1-800-331-0852. While you are at it, I would suggest that you purchase both the small and medium inserts. If you ever sell the pistol, it will make it much easier and a more attractive purchase for the buyer to have a complete set of grip inserts with the handgun. Accessory parts like this are often misplaced or lost but they definitely make the handgun more desirable.

STUCK COMMANDER MAGAZINE

Q *I recently traded for a used Colt Commander in .45ACP. The pistol came with two magazines so I picked up four more at a local gun show. My problem is that two of the magazines stick in the frame. I have gotten the magazines mixed up so I do not know if any of the ones that stick came with the pistol. In any event, how can I fix this problem? Is it due just to the magazines?*

A It could be the magazines but it could also be due in part to the pistol. Certainly, you could have some magazines whose sides are bulged and these could be dragging on the inside of the frame. This could be checked easily enough by simply measuring the width of each of your magazines in several places and comparing the measurements.

It's also possible that you are getting contact on the sides of the magazines from the inside ends of one or more grip screws or grip screw bushings. If your magazines are a close fit in the frame, it wouldn't take much to have the bushings or screws bind the magazines.

Another possible point of interference is the magazine catch. If it is slightly out of spec, it could drag on the

front of some of the magazines even when pushed all the way over into the "open" or release position. You can easily check this by just removing the magazine catch and trying each of your magazines.

STERLING GRIP SCREWS

Q *I was given a Sterling .25ACP pistol that I understand is no longer in production. My problem is that the grip screws are missing. Can you tell me what the thread size is for these screws? If I get this information I could probably have someone make them for me.*

A The Sterling .25 auto uses a grip screw with 40 threads per inch and a major diameter of about .108". While you certainly can make these screws, you might find it a lot easier and less hassle to just give the folks at Numrich Gun Parts, Box 299, Dept. SGN, West Hurley, NY 12491, a call at 866-686-7424. They list these screws on page 969 of their #29 catalog. They show the price at only $1.95 each. At that price, I don't see how it would be worthwhile to make 'em or have 'em made.

EXTRACTOR MODIFICATION

Q *I am having extraction problems with my old Remington 513 .22 rifle. I noticed that the extractor does not actually fully engage the rim until the case has moved back out of the chamber a bit. My thought was to recut the bevel on the side of the chamber so the extractor was fully engaging the rim before the bolt was pulled back. Any problems with this?*

A Yep, there sure is! If you modify the angle of the extractor groove in the face of the barrel by making it deeper and exposing a portion of the case above the rim, you will not be fully supporting the side of the case at that point. That could lead to the case bulging or rupturing when the round is fired. Needless to say, that could be a major problem and safety hazard.

I would suggest you look at other possible reasons for the extraction problems. You could have a rough chamber, a worn or poorly fitted extractor, a collapsed extractor spring, etc. I think it is most likely something like this that is the root cause of the problem.

The Remington 513T was the mainstay of youth shooting programs in the 1950s and 60s. Coffield says that cutting the extractor groove deeper is no way to correct extraction problems.

RUGER .22 BARREL DIAMETER

Q *I plan on rebarreling an old Ruger .22 auto pistol I picked up as a project gun. I have a buddy with a lathe and he will thread my barrel blank. My question is do you know what the barrel thread is on this pistol? I measured it but I wanted to check with someone else before I started work on my barrel.*

A The Ruger .22 auto pistol has a barrel shank with a major diameter of .810" and threaded with 20 "V" threads per inch.

I Want My

You can have one with a Browning 1919A4 semi-auto kit from Ohio Ordnance and a bit of patience and careful work.

Photo by P. Kristopher Kuhn

Part One—

Belt-Fed!

By Steven Matthews

Receiver Assembly

If you are a military arms collector as I am, you probably have the same problem that I do; my wants exceeds my income. Living on a blue-collar income means that you have to be very frugal in your spending on firearms.

Like most collectors I started with inexpensive bolt-action military rifles. As time went by I moved up to semi-auto military guns. As I got older and had a little more money to spend, I began to look at the possibility of moving up to NFA-registered full-auto guns.

In order to do this, I had to limit myself to the very low end of the market and also sell off some other parts of my collection to finance this move up. Before 1986, full-auto guns were only priced about 50% over the cost of the semi-auto versions.

As we entered the 1990s, prices for legal full-autos began to escalate at a very rapid rate due to the law change in 1986 that froze the number of transferable machine guns. I had always wanted a Browning 1919A4 belt-fed machine gun and decided that I had better get one before the prices went beyond my means.

The Browning machine gun was designed by firearms genius John Moses Browning in the early part of the 20th century. It is considered by most firearms experts to be one of the best medium belt-fed guns ever made. Adopted in 1919, it served for decades until replaced by the M60 in the late 1950s. It was still in limited use in the Vietnam War. I bit the bullet so to speak and sold off a couple AR15s to finance the purchase. To keep cost down, I decided to take the build it yourself route.

I ordered a registered sideplate and a parts set from Ohio Ordnance Works and put in motion the paperwork process associated with obtaining legal full-auto guns. After a couple months of waiting for paperwork to clear and an expenditure of $1600, I was the proud owner of a "machine gun in a box". Once it was assembled, I was in machine gun heaven. Over the next few years the prices steadily increased to the point that I now had a $6-7,000 gun.

Unfortunately a bout of illness and surgery required something to be sold to cover the lost time from work and the Browning was history. After selling it, I knew that high prices meant I would never be able to afford another one. About this time (late 1990s) a small company in the western U.S. began offering a semi-auto version of the 1919A4 BMG. I couldn't afford this gun either, but figured that if they could build it, perhaps I could also if I could score some cheap parts.

I found a 1919A4 parts set and a blank sideplate for $335 and $85 respectively. At this time, there were no plans available for this project and no semi kits were available. I had to figure out how to make it semi-auto and meet all BATFE regulations.

I had to design, build and test several systems to get a working and legal semi-auto. BATFE regulations required extensive redesign of the internal workings to be legal. I probably put in 200 hours trying to figure it out before it was completed.

Ironically, the system I came up with is almost identical to the most common semi-auto 1919 operating system used in most versions today. If I had waited a couple years, I could have bought the parts ready made and avoided all the design work and associated headaches.

So where is all this going? Well if you have been reading SGN for the last couple years, you may have read some of my home gunsmithing articles and are aware that anytime I can do a project myself and save money, I take the do-it-yourself route.

I decided that I wouldn't mind having *another* Browning 1919 to write up as a build project article. I didn't, however, want to expend the same amount of work making all my own parts as I had years before.

What I needed was one of the widely available semi-auto 1919A4 kits on the market today. While not as inexpensive as the home-built and -designed one I made earlier, they can be had for about $1,000. This is only little more than many of the AR-15s on the market and puts it into the price range that many can afford today.

Ohio Ordnance Works offers a complete 1919A4 Semi-auto Browning kit for $950. It contains all the semi-auto conversion parts plus all the other parts needed to build a BATFE legal semi-auto version of the Browning Machine Gun.

So just what do you get for your $950? You get military specification 1919A4 parts from a real U.S.-made (they were sold to Israel then sold back to the USA) Browning Machine Gun. The semi-auto specific parts are made by OOW and are of the same high quality as the military parts. The semi-auto parts consist of a new manufacture semi-auto sideplate and a semi-auto fire control group.

Everything is included, even the rivets with which to assemble the receiver. The original 1919A4 parts are in used condition with a little finish wear but are functionally fine. The new semi-auto sideplate is made from 4140 steel, is completely machined to the proper size and has all holes and cutouts located properly. It is "in the white".

The new manufacture semi-auto fire control components are nicely machined and finished with Parkerizing.

The actual build process for this gun is fairly simple. You just assemble the new right sideplate to the top and bottom frame components and the front trunnion. The receiver of a BMG is basically just a heavy steel box that contains the internal parts.

The left sideplate on the parts kit I received was still installed, so I didn't have to assemble it to the other parts. Once the receiver is assembled, several subassemblies are inserted through the rear of the gun to complete it. These subassemblies are very easy to install because they are just parts that are removed for cleaning, maintenance and adjustment.

To assemble the receiver you need to install and set about 20 rivets. This is where a lot of potential builders balk. For some

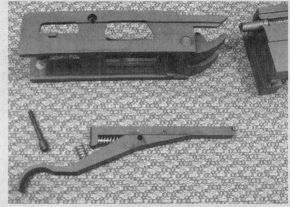

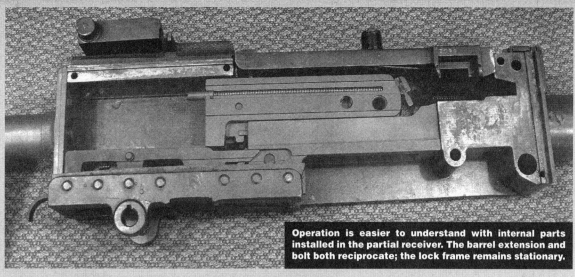

Operation is easier to understand with internal parts installed in the partial receiver. The barrel extension and bolt both reciprocate; the lock frame remains stationary.

The bolt, barrel extension and lock frame have all been modified to meet BATFE regulations. These assemblies have all been well Parkerized by Ohio Ordnance Works.

reason, people think that riveting is beyond their abilities. It is not difficult to set rivets. Rivets have been used for centuries and even relatively unskilled people can master the skill if they want to learn it. For more on this subject, see my story on building an AK in the September 20, 2005 issue.

Setting rivets with only basic hand tools such as punches, hammers and backing blocks is fairly easy, it's just slow doing it by hand. But we are not in any hurry in this case. It should be noted than many of the most durable and strongest military guns made feature riveted construction. The AK-47, FN MAG and Maxim machine guns are just a few that feature this type of construction.

Besides your basic hand tools such as hammers, files, small hand grinder, punches, etc., you will need a strong bench vise and several heavy pieces of steel for backing blocks.

One item that you will need is not a tool but is still an absolute necessity for building, owning and operating a 1919A4 BMG.

You need U.S. Army field manual number FM 23-55. This booklet explains in great detail how a Browning 1919A4 operates. It also explains how to set headspace, assemble, disassemble, and properly maintain the gun.

This booklet was printed for the soldier who would bet his life on his machine gun, so it is very complete in explaining almost everything an operator needs to know. It can be purchased from military manual dealers or can sometimes be downloaded off the internet. Even though it was written for the full-auto gun, it is very applicable to the semi-auto.

The assembly of the receiver is very easy to figure out. This article will just give you a basic overview of the build process. It should not be considered a step-by-step build tutorial. If you need a more detailed description of the process, a great one is available from American Gunsmithing Institute (1325 Imola Ave. W., Suite 504, Dept. SGN, Napa, Calif. 94559) titled *Browning 1919-A4 Machine Guns*.

Before you can rivet on the new sideplate, you need to remove the remnants of the old sideplate that remain on the bottom frame piece. When these guns were demilled, the restricted right sideplate was crudely cut off with a metal saw rather than removing the individual rivets. To remove them, just grind off the heads and punch out the shanks.

Once you have removed the old rivets, you can begin installing the new sideplate. The sideplate interlocks with the bottom section. You line up the holes and insert the rivets and then set them. This is best done one rivet at a time to ensure that each one is backed up solidly when forming the heads.

In order to set the rivets (set just basically means hammering an appropriate head shape on the remaining shank) you must

solidly support the head on a strong steel block on the inside of the receiver. I support one end in a strong vise and the other with a block on the workbench.

For a backing block I used a large piece of steel I had laying around. If you need to buy a piece, I recommend a piece 1/2" x 1½" x 2 feet long.

Whatever you use, be sure the head of the rivet you are forming is solidly against the backing block so that it tightly secures the parts being riveted together.

Always clamp your parts securely, since you will be hitting the rivets pretty hard and things will move if not secured well. You have two options in hand-forming rivet heads. You can form flush heads which require countersunk holes on your parts or you can have exposed heads. If using countersunk holes, just hammer the rivet shank down into the countersink and then grind off any remaining material

On exposed heads you can make them rounded or flattened, it's your choice, both look fine on this type of gun.

I used a combination of both depending on the look I wanted. Having some rivet heads showing tends to look more authentic. If you want round-head rivets use a punch with a relief cut into the end to form the head. If you want a flat head, just flatten the heads with a hammer or punch. Whichever type you do you will have to determine the correct amount of shank to have extending out of your work. If you have too little, you won't have enough material to completely form a head and if you have too much. it will look poor.

I used the flattened head here and about 3/16" extension was about right. I know I said it before, but it bears repeating: be sure the heads are solidly backed up and your parts are secured tightly. Failure to heed this advice will result in rivets that are incorrectly formed or are not tight after they are set.

Once you have set the rivets in the bottom of the new right sideplate, it is time to move to the top of the gun. The top receiver piece contains the top cover latch and holds the tops of both plates together. The front rivet extends through both sideplates, while the rear has an individual rivet on both sides, since a sin-

Gently heating the shank of the rivet will ease the forming process. It is, however, vital to heat only the shanks and to avoid heating the surrounding metal.

A hammer, punches, clamps, and back-up blocks are needed to rivet the receiver. Approximately 20 rivets need installation to build the receiver. It's not a hard job.

Some ingenuity may be required in setting up your back up blocks and propping up other parts of the rifle. Solidly supporting the rivets when forming is imperative.

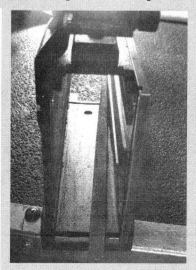

The rivet heads on the inside of the receiver must be filed flush to allow installation of internal parts. A hand file is the right tool for the job here.

The two largest rivets that retain the trunnion are the hardest to set but are easier than you would expect. These were set with nothing more than a hammer and block.

gle rivet here would interfere with internal parts. Clamp your parts together securely, install the rivet, support it solidly and then form the head.

Now it is time to move to the front rivets. *Before* you set the rivets through the trunnion, you must attach the D-shaped spacer at the bottom front of the plate. Only two rivets are set at this time because the third one passes through both plates and the trunnion. These two rivets will be countersunk, since they need to be flush when completed. Install the rivets, back them up, set them and then grind the heads off flush.

The front top rivet must be ground flush to allow installation of top cover components. The front cartridge stop is riveted in the feed tray on the inner right.

Be especially sure you grind the heads inside flush because the sideplate must be tight against the trunnion when it gets assembled. Now slide the front trunnion down into the grooves in the left and right sideplates. Locate it so that the two large and one small rivet holes line up and then securely clamp things together. Start with the small diameter rivet that extends through the sideplates and trunnion. Back the head up solidly and form the head.

The next rivets are hardest to set. These two large rivets are over 3/8" in diameter and thus it require considerable force to form the heads. The top front rivet will have to be a flush head so be sure to countersink the holes on both sideplates. The heads have to be countersunk to allow for other parts to be installed later.

Insert the large rivet and place the head solidly against a backing plate. It is especially important to have everything secured well on these two rivets because you will really be hitting them hard. Since this rivet is so large and hard to form, I have found that it really helps to heat up the end to be formed red hot with a fine tip torch before forming the head.

Be sure to *heat only the end* and do not heat the surrounding parts (heating the end like this also helps with the smaller rivets also). I use a ball peen hammer to form the head. Since the front rivet is countersunk, just hammer it flat till it fills the countersink.

After forming, grind off any remaining head so that it is smooth. For the rear rivet, I chose a slightly rounded head. This is easily formed by first flattening the head and then tapping repeatedly around the edges to round over the edges. This may sound difficult but really isn't, it just requires patience and a little work.

Two more rivets need to be set before the receiver is finished. The front and rear cartridge stops need to be installed. Just rivet them in as the others. I used a flush head on one and a rounded head on the other. Once these two are completed, most of the hard work is done and the receiver is almost complete.

One last item needs to be installed before the receiver is done. The bolt locking cam needs to be installed in the bottom of the receiver. This part locks the bolt in place when the gun is fired. It fits in the bottom of the receiver and is held in with a screw. This screw should be installed with high strength thread locker plus staked in place after installation. This is one part you never want to come loose. If this part fell out the results would probably involve flying debris and injury when the gun is fired!!

At this point I turned to finishing work. I deburred all sharp edges and smoothed up any rough spots. Although the finish on the parts set I received was pretty good, it got roughed up a lot in the building process and would benefit from refinishing. The semi-auto sideplate was also unfinished, so I decided to Parkerize the complete receiver and all exterior parts.

I used manganese phosphate Parkerizing from Brownells. I have covered this process for the hobbyist in past issues of SGN (October 10, 2005) if you want to read about it. This finish replicates the original finish and it pretty easy to do if you have the equipment.

Assembly of the receiver is done easily with basic hand tools. Specialty rivet forming tools are not needed unless you plan to go into gun manufacturing full-time.

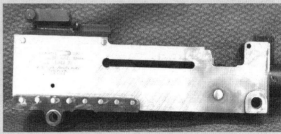

The right sideplate is now assembled to the other frame components. The internal parts can now be installed. Only five rivets need to be installed in the left sideplate.

In the photos for this article you can see that once finished, the gun looks as good as an original-issue Browning 1919A4. If you do a high-quality job your work will be as good as a factory built gun. Observant readers will notice that one item is missing from my gun, the front sight.

When I assembled the gun, I had misplaced the front sight since it wasn't being refinished and didn't find it till after I tested the gun and took photos for this article. Keep your parts organized to avoid embarrassing incidents like this!

Once refinished it time to install the parts into the receiver, and I'll cover that next month.   ◎

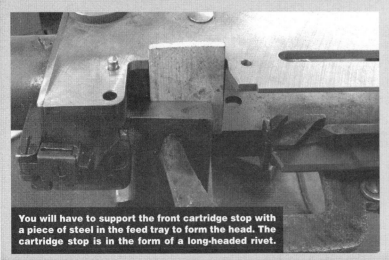

You will have to support the front cartridge stop with a piece of steel in the feed tray to form the head. The cartridge stop is in the form of a long-headed rivet.

Once Parkerized, the new semi-auto receiver looks just like the original 1919A4 receiver. There is no outward indication that it's an easily transferable semi-auto.

Ask the Gunsmith

By Reid Coffield

DRY-FIRING BURRS

Q *I have a .22 revolver that has been dry fired extensively. One of the consequences of this is a number of burrs on the rim seats that project into the chambers. This makes loading and extraction very difficult. I considered using needle files to remove these burrs. Is that the correct procedure?*

Coffield often uses this Menck tool to repair damage to .22 rimfire chambers. It is a specially ground, hardened swage that allows you to push the burr back into place. Don't file this area!

A Nope. Just filing away those burrs could create other problems. Keep in mind that the metal that was swaged or moved by impact from the firing pin was a part of the rim support. If you cut or file it away, you have lost that portion of the rim support.

A much better technique is to simply swage the metal back into its original position. Brownells Inc. offers the Menck .22 Chamber Ironing Tool which I have used for years for this type of job. The tool, which sells for a little less than $22, is a specially ground, hardened swage that allows you to push the burr back into place. It's fast, easy, and it avoids removal of metal that is of critical importance in supporting the rim of the .22 cartridge case.

WHAT'S WAC

Q *I found a set of old pistol grips in my grandfather's shop and I am puzzled as to what gun they were used on. I am sure the grips came off a pistol rather than a revolver and the only markings are the letters W, A, and C in a nice scroll superimposed on top of one another. A friend told me it stood for Winchester Arms Company. Any ideas?*

A Since Winchester did not produce any semiauto pistols, I doubt that your friend is correct. Instead, I think your grips might have come from a Warner Arms Company pistol. They made a little .32 auto and these grips might have been used on that handgun.

BROWNELL CHECKERING CUTTERS

Q *Where can I obtain W. E. Brownell checkering cutters?*

A The address is W. E. Brownell Tools, 9390 Twin Mountain Circle, Dept. SGN, San Diego, Calif. 92126, telephone 858-695-2479.

BORESCOPES

Q *I have been gunsmithing as a hobby for about three years. Not long ago I traded for a number of take-off military Mauser barrels. Among them was one that looked really nice. When I first checked it the bore seemed bright and shiny. When I got it home, I discovered that beneath the gunk in the chamber was a large pit. Since the barrel was ruined I decided to slice open the barrel just to look at the throat and the bore. I was amazed by how rough and pitted the bore was once I hacksawed the barrel into two parts. It was really bad. My question for you is how can you accurately determine the condition of a barrel? Again, when I first looked through it, it looked good.*

A If the tops of the lands in a barrel are not pitted, the barrel can look pretty darn nice and can easily fool you. You get a lot of light reflection off the tops of the lands and that can hide problems that exist in the grooves. Your only real shot at an accurate appraisal of the barrel bore is the area right near the muzzle which you can see from the outside. However, for the rest of the barrel, you are up the creek even if you use a bore light or mirror.

The only tool I have found that will allow me to see the true condition of the entire length of the bore is a Hawkeye Borescope made by the Gradient Lens Corporation, 207 Tremont St., Dept. SGN, Rochester, N.Y. 14608, telephone 800-536-0790. This is a fiber optic device incorporating a tiny angled mirror on the end of a long, slender hollow shaft that allows me to look directly at the side of the bore at any point in the barrel. I can actually look directly down into pits or other surface blemishes in the barrel.

Coffield uses a Hawkeye Borescope to inspect the bore on a Martini Cadet rifle. He says that borescopes are great for inspecting barrels, but are very expensive for the average hobbyist to buy.

A small Mini Maglite is attached to the device to provide illumination and this is focused directly where I look. There is normally no problem with glare hiding features I want to see. The only problem is that like most high quality tools, the Hawkeye Borescope is not cheap. In fact, it is pretty pricey. I had to wait for years before I could afford to invest in one. Generally you are looking at prices beginning in excess of $600 and up.

Unless you are going to do a lot of barrel work and can justify the expense, I doubt that it would be practical for the average hobbyist. However, if you can afford it, the Hawkeye Borescope is available from any of the gunsmith supply houses such as MidwayUSA, 5875 W. Van Horn Tavern Road, Dept. SGN, Columbia, MO 65203, telephone 800-243-3220, and is a wonderful tool.

CUT DOUBLE BARRELS

Q *Is there a quick way of determining if the barrels of a side-by-side shotgun have been cut?*

A Look at the muzzles and note the position of the tubes in relationship to one another. Uncut barrels will come together or even touch one another right at the muzzle. If you see a gap between the barrels, even one that has been filled with solder, it is quite likely that the barrels have been cut back from the original length.

Side-by-side shotgun barrels should touch at the muzzle. If they don't, the barrels likely have been cut, with predictable effect on the chokes. There's not much way to hide this modification.

ACTION SPRINGING

Q *I have a Mauser sporter based on a Model 98 action. My concern is with bending or springing the action. I have been told that unless my inletting is virtually perfect under the action, it can be bent. Is this true? If so, how can I avoid this?*

A If the inletting under the action is not even or level, it is possible that the action can be bent when the guard screws are tightened excessively. However, this can be easily prevented by simply bedding the action with one of the many modern synthetic bedding compounds. The bedding will conform to both the underside of the action as well as to the stock inletting and form a perfect interface between the two. With a properly done bedding job, you will not have any high or low spots under the action to allow it to bend.

BRITISH BULLDOG PARTS

Q *I have a British Bulldog revolver I want to use in cowboy action side matches. The gun is quite old and I need to replace some internal parts. Where can I find parts for this gun?*

A There were hundreds of different styles and makes of "British Bulldog" type revolvers built in England as well as Belgium in the latter part of the 19th century. Most were virtually handmade and the parts would not interchange even if you were to find parts. This is one of those cases were you will probably have to have a gunsmith make and fit any parts you need for this gun. ◎

I Want My Belt-Fed!
Part II: Final Assembly

The hard part was done in the last installment. Now it's time to assemble the internal parts, test and get to the fun part!

By Steven Matthews

In the first installment (9/20 issue), Matthews riveted together the receiver and installed the barrel trunnion assembly. Now he goes to work on the internal parts.

Before we start installing the internal parts perhaps we should discuss how the original Browning 1919A4 machine gun was modified to be a legal semi-auto rifle. The original BMG had no provision for semi-auto fire. When the trigger is pulled, it releases the sear, which fires the gun and causes to bolt to recoil.

As the bolt recoils, it pulls a cartridge out of the belt with the extractor on the front of the bolt. As it is pulled rearward, the extractor follows a track inside the receiver wall and pulls the round down into the slot in the front of the bolt face and aligns it with the chamber. As the bolt moves forward, it chambers the round, the extractor releases the round, the extractor moves up to snap the over the next round in the feed tray.

Before the bolt is all the way forward, the beveled front of the trigger engages a matching bevel on the sear and fires the gun just as the bolt is closed and locked in battery. This continues till the trigger is released.

BATFE regulations mean this trigger system is not acceptable for a semi-auto. The trigger and sear have been redesigned so that after each shot the trigger must be released and reset for the next shot. (This defines semi-auto operation.) On the semi-auto, if the trigger is kept pulled the sear just pushes it out of the way when the bolt closes. The spring loaded trigger has to snap up over the sear before it can release it again.

Matthews designed his own semi-auto 1919A4 a few years back, and says he could have saved a lot of annoyance if Ohio Ordnance's kit had been available at that time.

This is only one of the modifications needed for legality. The new manufactured right sideplate has to be thicker to prevent the use of the original full-auto parts and the semi-auto internal parts are modified to fit in the new receiver. Excluding these modifications to create semi-auto operation, the rest of the gun is identical to the original, so parts interchangeability is high.

Without shooting or disassembling the gun, there is no outward clue as to its mode of operation. The assembly of the internal parts is fairly easy. In my OOW kit all the subassemblies were pre-assembled. I will briefly explain the assembly procedure, but the military manual (FM23-55) can explain it in much greater detail and supply more pictures than can be included in this article.

The top cover contains the belt feeding mechanism and needs to be installed on the top of the receiver. It pivots on a bolt that extends through the receiver and has spring-loaded detents that hold the cover open for loading. Since this gun is chambered for 7.62 NATO (308 Win.), it requires spacers in the feed tray to compensate for the size difference of about a half-inch from the original .30-'06 caliber (other caliber conversions are available).

All the internal parts insert through the rear of the receiver. A preliminary headspace setting is done before inserting, it will need to be checked again later.

The bolt is the last part to be inserted into the receiver during assembly. You may have to depress the trigger to allow the bolt to clear as it slides into the receiver.

Mounting Your Browning 1919A4 Semi-auto on a Budget

Their weight means medium machine guns are designed to be used on some form of a mount. These can be of the "tripod" type with traversing and elevating mechanisms that limits their motion or a flexible mount that allows movement in any direction. Genuine military mounts with T+E mechanisms are very expensive. If you don't require a military mount, this is a very economical alternative for the "do it yourself" types out there.

The base of the home-built mount is made from 2"x 2" square tubing in a "Y" configuration. Matthews found filling the base with concrete increased stability.

Since my Browning 1919 shooting is basically high priced plinking at tin cans, junk, rocks, etc. I didn't want to spend big bucks on a mount. I also wanted to be able to rapidly change directions and shoot at various targets, so a flexible mount was the way to go for me. Whether it's because I'm resourceful or just cheap, I decided to make my own flexible pedestal type mount. I spent about $50 making mine and if you have a welder, drill and basic hand tools you can also.

The top section is easily made (if you can weld, of course) from angle iron and flat stock. A threaded couple welded to the bottom will allow the unit to swivel.

This is a very easy project so I won't go into great detail in how to build it, I will just describe how I made mine and you can use that as a starting point for your own. Depending on the materials you have available, you can modify the design to suit your needs.

You start by building a base. I welded three pieces of 2-inch square tubing together in a "Y" shape for the base with a 1½-inch threaded pipe coupler welded in the middle

The back plate retains all the gun's internal parts. You will need to press the top cover latch forward to allow the back plate to slide into its final position.

The front spacer is installed over the front cartridge stop. The rear spacer is installed at the rear of the feed tray. Both are retained by a pin that extends through the side of the feed tray and the belt holding pawl. The bolt assembly, barrel, barrel extension and lock frame are installed through the rear of the receiver. Be sure to open the top cover before you try to install the internals.

The barrel will extend through the front of the receiver and be supported by the barrel shroud at the front. Before installing the barrel, a preliminary headspace setting should be done. This is explained in the field manual. A final headspace setting will be done after assembly.

The barrel, barrel extension and lock frame will go in all in one piece. The fingers in the lock frame extend into the grooves in the barrel extension and the accelerator needs to be set against the spring loaded plunger.

This may sound complicated but isn't after you view the pictures in the field manual. These parts are pushed in till the spring loaded detent in the lock frame snaps into a hole in the sideplate.

After these parts are in all the way, the bolt can be inserted (with the extractor installed) on top of the other parts through he rear of the receiver. A tongue and groove arraignment aligns the parts properly.

You may have to pull the trigger to allow the bolt to pass over the trigger. Before the bolt is in very far, insert the bolt handle into the bolt through the slot in the sideplate. Once all the parts are inserted, the back plate can be installed. It slides down between the sideplates in the grooves.

You will have to push the top cover latch forward to allow the back plate to go in. Once all the way down, release the latch and it will retain the back plate.

Pull the bolt to the rear and you will see a screw head extending through the upper right of the back plate. While holding the bolt handle, rotate the screw while pushing forward to release the recoil spring. It is fairly strong, so hold onto the handle tight. Slowly allow the bolt to go forward.

Since the top cover spring is not pushing on the extractor, you may have to position the extractor in the proper grooves on the side of the receiver to get it all the way forward. Cycle the action to verify that everything is installed correctly and operating smoothly.

Now that all the internal parts are installed, check and set the headspace as instructed in manual FM23-55. While cycling the action, check to see if the fire control group is working correctly. Pull the trigger and keep it pulled. You should hear the firing pin drop. Pull the bolt to the rear and let it go forward.

After the bolt is in battery, release the trigger and it should reset for the next cycle. It is not uncommon for the triggers of semi-auto Brownings to be somewhat stiff and need to be pushed up till the parts smooth up by "wearing in."

Carefully polishing the front of the trigger and sear contact surfaces before assembly can alleviate this problem since freshly Parkerized parts are somewhat gritty and don't slide well till smoothed up with use.

The extractor on the front of the bolt pulls the cartridge out of the belt, then slides it down into a T-slot in the bolt face. It is aligned there with the chamber.

With the bolt all the way forward and the belt feed slide all the way inside the top cover, gently close the cover. Be sure the cam on the feed lever engages the groove in the bolt. The top latch should hold it closed.

After function-testing with dummies, the gun is ready to test-fire. Even though it is legally classified as a semi-auto rifle, its appearance screams "machine gun."

This mount is set up for standing shooting. A shorter upright section can be used for a sitting position. It's just the thing for those belt-fed plinking sessions.

For best results, a belt loading machine is required properly to load cloth belts. When adjusted right, this machine will load a 250-round belt in a few minutes.

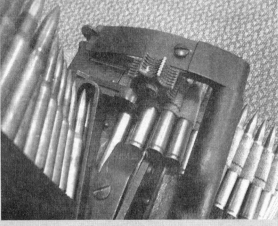

The belt loader will insert rounds into the advancing belt at a very fast rate if set up properly. The belt loader is adaptable to several calibers with modifications.

Cycle the action a few times to verify that the slide is moving right and left each time the bolt cycles.

Make up or buy 10-20 *dummy* (inert) cartridges. Insert them *correctly* into a belt or links. Belt or link loading is covered later in the article. Insert the dummies into the feed tray with the top cover closed and pull the belt through until it clicks and engages the belt holding pawl. Cycle the action *one time*. This should line up the first cartridge with the front of the bolt. Cycling the bolt now will pull out a cartridge and take it through the feeding cycle. Each time you cycle the bolt it should pull out a round, chamber it, and eject one dummy out of the bottom of the gun.

This sounds very complicated, but if the gun is assembled correctly, it will operate extremely well. Due to the excellent design by John Browning this action is performed flawlessly and at great speed. *If and only if* everything works right, it's time to move on to test-firing. This is *if* you have a means to load links or belts!

Unlike magazine-fed guns the Browning 1919A4 requires either belted or linked ammo. These belts and links cannot be easily assembled by hand. The cartridges need to be placed in the links or belts in the correct positions to ensure proper feeding and reliable operation.

The most common method of loading them is to use the Browning Belt Filling Machine Model 1918. This machine is a hand cranked device that feeds cartridges out of a chute and inserts them into a cloth belt as it advances through the machine. Once set up properly (they can be temperamental sometimes!) you can load a 200-round belt in a few minutes. There is only one problem with these machines, cost!

When I bought mine more than 12 years ago, the cost was about $75. Demand was low and supplies plentiful. These machines have not been made for decades. Now with all the semi-auto 1919s out there, the demand is high and the supply low which has resulted in a going rate of $500-$1000 today. If I could have only bought a truck load of the $75 loaders 15 years ago I could retire in style!

of the legs. I also welded on 2x3x¾ pads on the ends of each leg for feet. I also filled the legs with concrete to add weight for stability.

To attach the gun at the top I made a "U" shaped bracket out of three pieces of ⅛x2 flat stock welded together. A 9/16" hole through the sides will allow a pin to be inserted through the gun and mount for a pivot point.

On the bottom of this U-shaped bracket I welded on *another* 1½-inch threaded coupler. To hold the ammo can on the mount, I made a shelf out of 3/4-inch angle iron and welded it to the coupler with a strong bracket. It must be positioned correctly to allow the belted ammo to enter the feed tray as straight as possible.

The top and bottom are connected with a section of 1½-inch pipe threaded on the ends. You can make different lengths of pipe to allow for sitting or standing shooting positions. I also welded on a couple of handles to allow for tightening the pipe when assembling the mount.

Making a base, top section and upright pipe section that thread together makes it easier to store than if welded into one whole unit. The pipe should be screwed together tight at the base but left a turn or two loose at the top to allow the gun to rotate. Once you have it all welded up and checked out, paint it the color of your choice.

While it may not look like a military mount, it will cost hundreds of dollars less and work as well. If you are on a tight budget as I am, this is the way to go. ◉

There is, however, a lower-cost alternative. For about $250, you can get a belt linking machine. They are available from OOW and several other sources. These machines operate by

A carry handle is a desirable accessory for the 30-pound Browning 1919A4. You'll quickly find the barrel gets way too hot to touch during those long firing bursts.

Spade Grips
A Desirable Option

When originally designed, the Browning 1919A4 was intended to be used on a mount that securely held the gun in position. Since the mount held the gun on target, the pistol grip was only there to allow the operator to more easily pull the trigger. When used in a flexible mount this single grip doesn't leave much for the user to grasp and move the gun from target to target.

A more secure hand hold is required, and spade grips are the answer to this problem. These allow a two-handed hold for much better control. Most medium machine guns feature spade grips, even though they were on fixed mounts and it is a mystery to me why they weren't originally put on the 1919. Fortunately new manufacture spade grips are available for the Browning 1919A4. The ones I have seen are usually priced in the $400 range.

Of course if you have read many of my gunsmithing articles you know I won't pay my hard earned cash for something I can make myself for little expense. Call me cheap or resourceful, but the way I see it for every dollar I save making my own stuff it's a dollar I can spend on something I can't make myself.

Shown in these pictures are the grips I made myself for a total expense of $40. I bought a short back plate assembly that was originally designed for 1919s that were fired remotely by solenoids since it is smaller and would allow more room for my fat hands. You can also use the original back plate by cutting off the pistol grip if you want, it just sticks out more in back.

This design is pretty flexible as far as design and materials go, so I won't specify any dimensions. Basically all you are doing is making handles and brackets to attach to the rear of the gun and making a trigger with linkage to the gun's trigger to actuate it.

Besides offering better control of the gun, Matthews thinks spade grips just look more appealing. They can be easily made by the hobbyist gunsmith or purchased.

The handles and brackets can be welded or screwed on to the back plate. The trigger part is simply a lever system that pivots on short screws threaded into the buffer tube. An appropriate sized roller at the bottom will move the trigger of the gun for firing. Some experimentation will probably be needed to get the right linkage length and roller diameter to allow full movement of the trigger for firing and resetting. I have built a couple of these and varied the design considerably just to see what works.

The ones pictured were for my first semi-auto 1919 and were considerably different than the ones I made for my NFA full-auto. When I get around to making some for this new semi-auto, I may change the design somewhat again. Something that I haven't tried to make yet but may try is a hand crank design that allows for faster firing.

There are some commercial spade grips that feature this design, I believe they are marketed under the name of "M.O.A.T" (mother of all triggers). They are available from Tanstaafl Machine Tool Service (804) 932-3713. Once you

The "grip" part is simply brackets and handles mounted to the back plate. The "trigger" part is a lever and roller system that actuates the gun's regular trigger.

have used spade grips, you will never want to go back to the single grip. Besides the greatly increased control, spade grips just feel more like machine gun grips should !

---

placing 20 rounds and links in a grooved tray and pulling a lever to insert them to the proper location. While nowhere near as fast a belt filling machine, they are affordable. Its just like cars, the faster you want to go, the more it costs.

The Browning 1919A4 is not a light weapon at 30 pounds unloaded. It needs a mount and just like the loading machines there are two options. The expensive option is to by an original or reproduction GI-style tripod. These also feature a mechanism called a T+E mechanism which solidly holds the gun on a target. These can be relatively costly with an original going for $1,000-1,200 and reproductions somewhat less. There are also some mounts adapted from non- Browning guns at about half the price.

There is, however, a very inexpensive option. I built a flexible pedestal-type mount that can be swiveled in any direction for only about $50 (see sidebar). For plinking this is the most convenient type of mount. I made mine for shooting in the standing position, but it can be adapted to sitting position if you want. A little work here can save lots of money.

If you have a mount and loader you are ready to try out your new creation. If you have built your gun correctly, it should operate properly from the beginning., at least mine have. This is not due to my building skill but to the

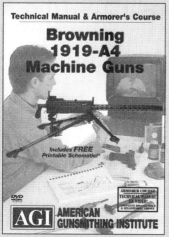

Technical Manual & Armorer's Course
Browning 1919-A4 Machine Guns
Includes FREE Printable Schematic!
DVD
AGI AMERICAN GUNSMITHING INSTITUTE

If you are interested in 1919A4s, whether full or semi-auto, one of the best information sources is AGI's Technical Manual and Armorer's Course, available on DVD.

excellent designed in reliability of the Browning 1919A4 design.

If you have problems, refer to FM23-55 since it has a troubleshooting section that covers most of the common malfunctions. There are also internet discussion forums with many hobbyists willing to help you out.

Once up and running correctly I have only found one problem with owning and shooting a Browning 1919A4 semi-auto. You will burn up ammo at an unbelievable rate!! With belts of 200-

250 rounds hanging off the gun and a gun designed for high volume firepower, you just can't stay off the trigger.

Even a semi-auto gun can fire at a rate of 200 rounds per minute if you have a fast trigger finger. It is not unusual to burn up several hundred rounds in a shooting session with one of these guns. The larger your pile of brass is, the more fun you will be having!!

Ohio Ordnance Works A Brief Overview

Who or what is Ohio Ordnance Works ? It was established in 1981 as an outgrowth of his gun collecting hobby by Robert Landies. OOW is housed in a discreet building in an industrial park in Chardon Ohio. Their primary focus is to buy, sell, manufacture, rebuild, and repair antique and modern legally registered automatic weapons.

Recognizing that not everyone can afford the expensive automatics, they have made available several semi-automatic versions of famous military arms. They offer semi-auto versions of the 1918 BAR, 1928 Colt-Browning water-cooled machine gun and the Czech VZ 58. They also offer kits for these guns.

They don't offer a complete 1919A4, but do sell a kit. This kit contains all the parts need to for the hobbyist gunsmith to build a legal semi-auto copy. Selling for $950, it is a real bargain for the home builder. Since it is a complete gun kit, it must be ordered through a FFL holder, so there may be a little more expense to pay your local FFL holder to order it for you. Complete 1919A4s in my area are hard to find and priced at about $1,400 so this can be a real money saver if you have the skills to build it yourself.

In addition to these kits and guns, they offer semi-auto AK-47/74 receivers, parts sets for several military firearms and military gun parts and accessories.

Their manufacturing facility is filled with modern metalworking equipment and skilled employees. They manufacture many of the parts themselves on site. Their facility is a military firearms collector's dream come true with dozens of classic military arms in stock. It should be noted that for security purposes their facility is not open to the public.

While there to pick up my 1919 semi kit, I was privileged to see one of their latest creations. I was asked not to reveal the exact nature of this new gun, since its design is awaiting BATFE approval. What I can tell you is they have taken one of the most reliable and well-respected man-portable machine guns and converted the design to semi-auto operation.

They have tested it with literally thousands of rounds fired without malfunction, the semi-auto is just as reliable as the full-auto version. It is a real beauty! When it has been approved for sale this impressive gun will be offered to the public, so keep watching their ads for its debut.

Contact Info:
Ohio Ordnance Works, P.O. Box.687, Chardon, Ohio, 44024, 1-440-285-3481, www.ohioordnanceworks.com

Building the Poor Man's Browning Belt Loader

By Steven Matthews

If you built Matthews' M1919 semi-auto, you may by now be wondering how to keep it supplied with belted ammo. Here he shows how to do it for about $35.

There's just no shooting a Browning 1919, even the semi-auto version, if you try to load the belt by hand. Matthews's homemade loader makes the job really easy.

Several months ago (9/20/06, 11/20/06) I wrote a pair of articles for SGN on building the Ohio Ordnance Works semi-auto Browning 1919A4 belt-fed. This kit-built gun project allowed the military firearms collector to advance into belt-fed guns for a very reasonable price. With a kit price of under $1,000, it put it within the reach of many shooters.

The relatively low cost of this kit is not, however, the only expense in owning and shooting a belt-fed Browning. The gun requires a mount and vast amounts of ammo. All that fun to burn up ammo needs to be loaded on cloth belts or metal links.

During its years of military use the "in the field" method of filling those cloth belts was the Browning Belt Filling Machine Model of 1918. This hand-cranked machine featured a tall chute that was filled with cartridges. By cranking a handle, it would insert a round in the belt and then advance the belt for the next round.

With one man filling the chute and another cranking the handle, a 250-round belt could be loaded in only a couple minutes. Unfortunately for Browning shooters today, these long out of productions antique belt loaders today can cost $1,000 if you can find one. Fortunately, I bought mine more than 20 years ago for less than $100.

A less expensive option is to buy a commercial hand-operated linking machine and use metallic links. These machines can be found for about $300. These machines feature a flat tray that holds about 20 cartridges and links and a lever that presses the rounds into the links.

While it is much cheaper than a cloth belt loader, it is still slow, since one has to lay out all the links and cartridges. Either option still requires the expenditure of $300-$1,000. Belts can be hand-loaded by individually inserting rounds and measuring to be sure they are located correctly. This is incredibly slow and tedious, which quickly affects the "fun factor" of owning one of these guns.

What is needed is an *inexpensive* belt loader for the hobbyist. I thought this made a fun project. To be practical for the DIY types, it would have to be easy to build with minimal tools. Well, I scratched my head and set forth to design and build an economy belt loader. What I came up with is fairly easy to make and while not as fast as a $1,000 loader, it is vastly easier and faster to use than doing the belts by hand.

More importantly, it is very inexpensive. Total cost for materials is only about $35! This loader is made for inserting .308 Win./7.62 NATO rounds into cloth Browning belts, which is the most popular and inexpensive version to shoot. Since both of my Browning guns are chambered for .308/7.62 I made no efforts to adapt it to other calibers such as .30-'06 or 7.92 mm Mauser.

The .308/7.62 rounds are much easier to insert in the belts since the rounds aren't set as deeply in the belt as the other sizes. With design changes, this loader may be adaptable to other sizes but I can't say for sure, so if you want to build one for other calibers you're pretty much on your own.

The only special tools needed beyond basic hand tools are a drill press and possibly an arc welder if you don't farm out the small welding job to make the handle. A hand drill is not accurate enough for drilling your holes, so don't even think about trying this project without a precise method for accurately drilling holes.

Although I did use a milling machine to make some of the pieces to speed up the build process, that's not essential. All the parts can be made with saws and files as long as the builder has the skill.

As a hobbyist, it doesn't matter if the parts are made in 10 minutes on a milling machine or if they take an hour to make by hand. It's all about the quality of work, not the time expended. About 25 parts will have to be made. Some are very easy to make, while others will require a certain amount of precision work.

Precisely locating and accurately drilling holes is the biggest issue. The holes need to be very squarely drilled, not running off at odd angles. The dimensions given will be in fractional measurements but decimal equivalents will promote greater accuracy. What I have listed is a rough guide to the materials that the builder will need at the end of this article.

Many of the parts I made were made from 6061 T6 aluminum to ease manufacture. For maximum durability, steel would be a better choice but it is a lot harder to work with than aluminum.

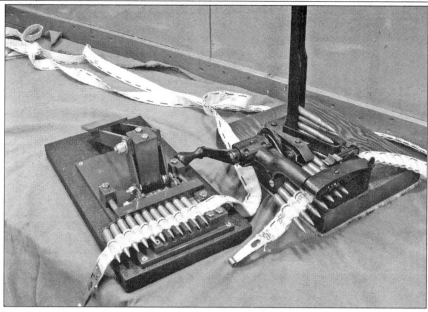

The M1918 Belt Filling Machine (r.) gets the job done quickly, but it will cost almost as much as a semi-auto 1919. Matthews' design is slower, but a lot cheaper.

Base Unit

Since considerable force will be applied to the handle to insert the rounds in the belt, the unit needs a solid base. All functioning parts will be bolted to a steel plate and this plate in turn will be attached to a wood base. I used a piece of 3/8x6x12 flat steel and a piece of 1x8x16 particle board to make the base.

The purpose of the particle board is to have a wide, lightweight base that can be placed on a table or countertop without the risk of damaging the table.

I screwed the steel plate down tight against the wood, since I drilled and threaded all mounting holes for the parts. If you wish, you can put spacer blocks between the steel and wood to leave space for nuts on the ends of the parts mounting bolts, it's your call.

Feed Tray

I made a feed tray out of a piece of 1x4x4 aluminum. In the center of this block I drilled six half-inch holes 3½ inches deep, spaced 17/32" apart. Once these holes were drilled, I then cut the block in half with a hacksaw. This resulted in two pieces of feed tray, but only one will be used.

I thinned this feed tray to 3/8". The last 1⅛" across the solid end was then thinned down to just a little under 5/16" to allow for belt thickness. Holes were clearance drilled and countersunk for 8-32 flat head screws in each corner to mount it on the steel plate. The feed tray will be located in the middle of the steel plate about 1" back from the edge.

Belt Stop Plate

The belt stop plate is made from a piece of 3/4x1x4 aluminum. This plate will allow the bullets to pass through the belt but hold back the cloth belt. Since .308/7.62 case necks don't extend past the edge of the belt as they do on .30-'06 belts, a clearance hole of only 2¼" needs to be drilled in the plate.

These holes are centered on the 1-inch side of the plate and drilled at the same spacing as the feed tray, 17/32". Once these

The belt stop is made from an aluminum bar with holes drilled at the same spacing as the feed tray. Saw and file out the grooves to create a comb-shaped part.

holes are drilled, take a saw and cut out slots on one side of the holes to form grooves in the plate. Cut under hole size and then file to final size. After the slots are cut, thin the top of this piece down to about 3/4". On one end continue to thin the last section down to a half-inch thick. Drill a quarter-inch mounting bolt hole in each end. The hole on the short end will need to be countersunk to allow a socket head screw to be flush with the top to allow easy passage of the loaded belt.

Pusher Bar

The pusher bar is made from a piece of 3/4x1x5¾" aluminum. This bar will have to have 3/8" (.375") holes drilled all the way through in each end. These holes will be for the guide rods to pass through and must be precisely sized and drilled squarely to allow for smooth function. Failure to drill these holes properly will cause parts to bind.

I first drilled 3/16" pilot holes, continued with a 23/64" drill and then finally used a 3/8" (.375") drill. Drilling in steps like this will allow the last bit to drill more closely to its specified size. Starting right out with the 3/8" drill will likely result in a hole several thousandths over the desired size and slightly off location.

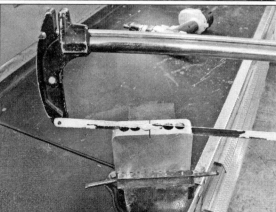

The feed tray starts out as an aluminum block. Then you drill six evenly-spaced holes and saw the block in half among its long axis. Measure carefully here!

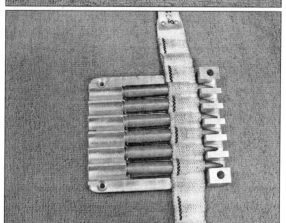

The holes, when cut in half, will form feed tray grooves. The groove spacing is determined by the loaded belt. The belt shortens as cartridges are inserted into it.

The pusher bar requires holes that are precisely sized and aligned for smooth operation. The clearance cut in the bottom will allow it to pass over the feed tray.

The left guide rod assembly features a belt guide in the front block, while the right assembly's front block has a low profile to allow the belt to pass over it.

The feed tray is attached to the metal base plate. The belt stop is mounted directly in front of the tray. The belt guide attaches to the side of the assembly.

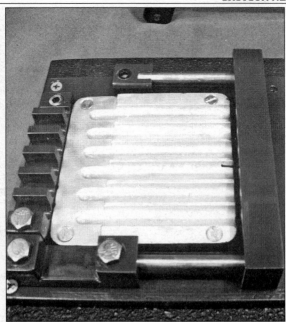

Proper guide rod alignment is a key to smooth operation. Use the pusher bar as an aid to determine proper location of the loader's front and rear mounting blocks.

These 3/8" holes are drilled in the 1-inch side and are located 3/8" in from the ends and 5/16" up from what will be the bottom. A relief cut will later be made on the bottom to allow the bar to pass over it.

Guide Rod Mounting Blocks

Three mounting blocks will be made from pieces of 3/4x1x1" aluminum. In the 3/4"x1" ends of all three blocks, drill a 3/8" (.375") hole 3/8" deep. The holes will be located 3/8" in from the sides and 5/16" up from the bottom. These holes must be square and accurately sized. Drill a quarter-inch hole through the top of the opposite end for a mounting bolt hole.

Take one of these blocks and thin it down to a height of about a half-inch to allow the loaded belt to pass over it easily. An additional block will now be made but this block will have a belt guide incorporated into it. Use a piece of 3/4"x1"x2¾" aluminum for this part.

Drill a guide rod hole in one end just as the other blocks, 3/8" in from the side and 5/16" up from the bottom. At a point 3/4" back from the front, cut out a groove for the belt to pass through. This groove needs to be 1³⁄₁₆" wide and cut to a depth of roughly 11/16". You want the bottom of this groove to be flush with the feed tray groove. Once this groove is cut out, shorten the whole piece to 3/4" high. Drill a quarter-inch mounting hole in each end of the piece. On the end that has the guide rod hole drilled in it be sure to locate the hole so that it doesn't pass though the guide rod hole.

Guide Rods

Since your pusher bars must slide easily over the guide rods, they need to be

The L-shaped handle/actuator is made from 3/16x1 flat stock. The arms must be identical, as must be the bolt spacing. The pivot block is 1½-inch square stock.

a couple thousandths of an inch smaller than the holes drilled in the bar. The easiest way of getting this size of rod is to buy a couple 3/8x6" Grade 5 bolts. The bolts will be just a few thousandths under the specified 3/8" size. Just cut off the heads and threads and you have rod. You will need two pieces 3¼ inches long for guide rods.

Pivot Block

This loader will feature a "L" shaped handle that will operate the pusher bar. This handle will pivot on a 3/8" bolt in a block. I used a piece of 1½x1½x3⅜" steel for a pivot block. A 3/8" hole was drilled through the side centered and a half-inch down from the top. Two quarter-inch holes were then drilled from top to bottom for mounting bolts.

Handle/Pusher Bar Actuator

This part is made from 3/16x1 steel. Cut two pieces 10 inches long and two pieces 3⅜ inches long. Overlap and clamp one short piece and one long piece together to form an "L" shape. The long piece should be on what will be the inside. Clamp up the other pieces in the same shape but this one needs to be a mirror image of the other so that the long part will be on the inside when mounted.

These two parts need to be identically shaped when welded together. To keep them identical, I clamped them together and aligned them to each other, then welded them. I also left them clamped together when drilling their holes to be sure the hole to hole dimensions stayed the same on both pieces.

At the top intersection of the two 1-inch pieces, I drilled a 3/8" hole centered in the 1-inch stock. The bottom hole is sized at a quarter-inch. It is centered on the material and a quarter-inch up from the bottom. Place a piece of scrap material between the two legs so that they don't flex and get out of alignment when they are drilled.

Take these two handle sections and bolt them to the pivot block and align them exactly parallel to each other. On the end of the handle weld on a piece of 3/16x3x3 steel to form a pad to push on when operating the handle.

Pusher Bar Brackets

Make these brackets out of 3/4" angle iron. Cut two pieces 5/8" long. Use a file to square up the legs on the inside since angle iron legs aren't flat all the way to the bottom of the legs. Drill a quarter-inch hole in each leg, centered and 5/16" in from the end of the leg.

Link Levers

Two small levers must be made to connect the brackets on the pusher bar to the handle. Two pieces of 1/8x5/8x1½ steel can be used for these parts. Drill a quarter-inch hole centered on the links and quarter-inch in from each end. This will result in a 1-inch center-to-center hole spacing.

Assembly

Now that all the parts are made, it's time to assemble them. This is where good alignment and proper location of the parts will make the difference between a smooth operating machine or one that binds. How accurately you made your parts will determine how much hand fitting is required to get things working properly.

All parts will be attached to the steel base plate. Locate and secure your parts in their proper places and then use long transfer punches through the bolt holes precisely to mark the drilling location. This is much easier than measuring out the hole locations.

If you are going to tap the holes in the base for ¼-20 bolts, you will be drilling the holes with a 13/64" or #7 drill. If you are going to drill clearance holes, use a quarter-inch drill bit.

Locate the feed tray squarely and centrally on the base plate about and inch back from the front. Use a transfer punch to locate the drilling location. Drill holes for a # 8-32 flat head screw, either a clearance hole or a tap hole size. Once the holes are complete, mount the feed tray.

The pivot block is mounted directly behind the pusher bar when it is all the way to the rear. It must be precisely parallel to the pusher bar for proper results.

The links connect the handle/actuator to the pusher bar. At the pivot points, the bolts need to be full diameter. Never rotate parts on the threaded bolt section.

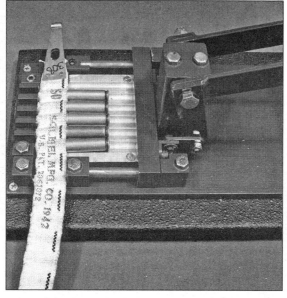

To load the belt, place it in the tray and start the cartridges. Then operate the handle to press them in until the bullets stick out the front side of the belt.

The pusher bar seats the rounds in the belt. Within reason, Matthews says, consistent depth is more important for reliable firing than the exact depth measurement.

The belt stop plate attaches directly in front of the feed tray. Center the grooves in the feed tray with the slots in the belt stop plate. Drill your holes and attach the plate.

Take the guide rod mounting block that has the belt slot in it and locate it along the side of the feed tray. Be sure you orient the guide rod hole to the rear. Align the slot in the block with the slot in the feed tray. Secure the block in place, mark your holes and then drill them. Attach the block with 1/4-20 bolts.

Insert one of your guide rods into the pusher bar and then place the end of the rod in the already mounted block. Slide the pusher bar up to the feed tray and mark the pusher bar for a clearance cut to allow it to slide over the tray. Remove the material in the clearance groove. You want there to be just enough clearance for the bar to slide over the feed tray without dragging.

Once you have this clearance cut made, remove about 1/64" to 1/32" from the remaining legs so that they don't drag on the base plate when installed on the rods.

When the pusher bar is complete, reinstall the guide rods in the pusher bar. Install the remaining guide rod mounting blocks on the rods. Insert the remaining guide rod end in the previously mounted block and locate the assembly over the feed tray.

Align the assembly so that it is square across the feed tray. Start with the side that has the already mounted block and locate the rear block on that side and mark it for drilling the bolt hole. Bolt this side in completely before doing the other side.

Tight tolerances mean the other guide rod assembly needs to be exactly parallel to the first one. Using the pusher bar as a locating aid, mark the locations of the mounting block holes. Be sure you have the blocks on each side aligned square with each other so that when at the end of the pusher bar stroke the bar stops at the same place on each side.

Although the loader has six grooves in the feed tray, you only load five at a time. The sixth groove is a dummy that allows proper belt alignment during loading.

If the blocks don't stop the bar at the same point, it will cause the bar to bind. You may have to drill the mounting block holes a little oversize to give some room for adjustment. Note that when testing this assembly you will need to press evenly on each side of the bar to move it, it will bind if you press more on one side than the other.

Once the pusher bar and guide rod assemblies are mounted, it is time to mount the pivot block. When the pusher bar is all the way to the rear, the pivot block will mount directly behind it. Locate the block so that it is centered behind the third groove (third from the left side guide assembly) in the feed tray. Mark holes, drill and attach it. Be sure it is aligned squarely behind the bar so that the handle will push evenly and squarely when installed later.

Mount the handle/pusher bar actuator to the pivot block with a 3/8" Grade 5 bolt. Be sure the unthreaded shank extends through the pivot points. Never rotate parts on the threaded portion of a bolt. Use a lock nut to hold the bolt in place. Remove any excess threaded portion of the bolt.

Tighten the bolt to remove any side play but leave it loose enough for free movement. With the handle mounted, you should have enough room between the lower arms and the pivot block for the bolt heads that will attach the links. If you don't, then just thin the heads before you install them.

Pre-assemble the link levers to the pusher bar brackets. I used pieces of quarter-inch bolts and cotter pins, since there isn't room for nuts to retain the bolts.

Attach the link levers to the handle with bolts and lock nuts. Be sure you have smooth shanks at all pivot points, remember no threads on moving parts.

Orient the brackets so that the legs face outward. Push the handle down and place the brackets against the pusher bar and use transfer punches to locate the holes for drilling.

These holes will be for a #7 or 13/64" drill bit, since the holes will be tapped for 1/4-20 bolts. Be sure when locating the brackets that they are aligned squarely and evenly.

Your loader should now be complete. A certain amount of tweaking will probably be required to get things operating smoothly. Slightly repositioning the guide rod assemblies can make a big difference in how easy the pusher bar moves. You may wish to paint your loader any color of your choice at this time. Do not paint the guide rods. Lubricate all moving parts, especially the guide rods.

Operation of Loader

Even though the feed tray features six grooves, you will only be loading five rounds at a time. The sixth groove is just for aligning the belt with a previously loaded round. Lay your cloth belt into the feed tray and roughly align the spaces in the belt with the grooves in the feed tray and belt stop bar.

At this point you may notice that the spaces in the belt don't align very well with the grooves in the feed tray. This is because the belt shortens in length as rounds are inserted into it. The spacing on the feed tray is for a loaded belt, not an empty one.

The belt changes length so much as it is loaded that about five rounds is the maximum that can be loaded without everything getting out of alignment.

Take five rounds and insert them into the pockets as far as they will easily go by hand. Push the handle down to seat the rounds to the correct depth. You want about 1⅛ inches of cartridge sticking out of the rear of the belt. This dimension will allow the belt to pass through the gun without dragging on the frame. This measurement can be varied somewhat.

On a Browning 1919, consistent cartridge depth in the belt is more important than the actual depth (within reason). As long as the belt feeds properly and the belt doesn't drag, everything is usually alright. To get the same depth each time you operate the handle, make up a stop block of the correct height and mount it under the end of the handle.

Once five rounds are fully seated, lift the belt up and move it over five spaces. Place the last round in the sixth groove to help align the belt. Keep repeating the procedure until the belt is full.

If built accurately and set up properly, this loader will do a fine job. Granted, it is not as fast as Model 1918 Belt Filling Machine, but considering that it cost more than $900 less, most can live with the slower speed. The huge cost savings make it well worth building. The $900 you save can be spent on ammo, other firearms or accessories. It's easy to build, so give it a try! ◉

Material List

1"x8"x16" piece of particle board

3/8"x6"x12" steel plate

1"x4"x4" aluminum or steel plate

3ft.- 3/16"x1" steel flat stock

3ft.- 1'x3/4" aluminum or steel bar

2 - 3/8"x6" grade 5 bolts

1½"x1½"x3⅝" steel bar

3/16"x3"x3" steel flat stock

1/8"x5/8"x6" steel flat stock

2" of 3/4" angle iron

Assorted quarter-inch bolts- 3/4", 1", 1 quarter-inch, 1½", 4"

2- quarter-inch lock nuts

2 -quarter-inch dia. x3/4" long socket head screws

2- quarter-inch x3/4" socket head screws

1- 3/8"dia.x3½" grade 5 bolt with lock nut and flat washer

4 - #8 X 1½" drywall screws

4- 8/32x1" flat head screws

2- 1/16" cotter pins

2- quarter-inch flat washers

What Can You Do with a Drill Rifle?

By Reid Coffield

Part 1

The army deactivated thousands of M1903 Springfields for ROTC units. Now you can buy them, but what do you do with one? Coffield shows how to make one into a bolt-action .22.

Coffield compares his drill rifle with an old M2 .22 Springfield. The M2 is a collectors item that is getting hard to find, thus this rimfire conversion project.

The 1903 Springfield is an American icon. It was the last and best primary issue bolt-action rifle used by the U.S. military. It saw use in virtually every part of the world in two World Wars and countless smaller affairs. It was carried by countless numbers of soldiers, sailors and marines.

Since it was replaced by the Garand in the late 1930s, it has become one of the most popular firearms among collectors. An original, full military 1903 Springfield will currently bring as much as $1,000 or more, depending upon the date of production and condition.

Over the years I've owned a number of Springfields. The one I use the most is a 1903M2 .22 training rifle. While mine is not a pristine collectable, it's a great shooting rifle and a lot of fun to use on the range or in the field. Since the M2 came with a sporter-style stock and receiver target sights, it never had the full "military" flavor of a standard 1903 .30-'06. From time to time I thought I'd really like to have a full military .22 Springfield.

Several months ago a friend of mine in Florida, Roger Deeks, sent me some photographs of a .22 Springfield he'd built. Roger used a 1903 Springfield drill rifle as the basis for this conversion. The drill rifle had been purchased from DuPage Trading Company through an ad here in SHOTGUN NEWS.

The moment I saw the photographs of Roger and his rifle, I knew I had to have one too! I immediately contacted Jim Yocum at Dupage Trading Company, Box 1274, Dept. SGN, Chandler, Ariz. 85244, telephone 480-664-2226. Dupage Trading Company was offering 1903 Springfield drill rifles for about $250. I thought that was a great deal so I made arrangements to get one for myself. In fact, a friend also wanted to get in on this deal so I ended up with two.

These drill rifles are basically complete, though they cannot be fired. The U.S. government deactivated the rifles by welding up the firing pin hole in the face of the bolt, welding a rod in the chamber, and welding the bolt stop or magazine cutoff in place so the bolt could not be removed from the receiver.

In addition to all this, a channel or groove approximately 3/8 inch deep and 3/4 inch wide was cut in the underside of the chamber area of the barrel about one inch ahead of the receiver. The barrel was also welded in one spot to the receiver to prevent or at least hinder removal and installation of a new barrel. And, just to further deactivate the rifle, the tip of the firing pin was cutoff. Even with all this, because it is possible to "reactivate" these rifles (with a heck of a lot of work!) an FFL is required for transfer.

I later learned that SARCO, another SHOTGUN NEWS advertiser, is also offering Springfield drill rifles. However, SARCO has gone one step further to modify their rifles so an FFL is not needed for purchase.

The folks at SARCO have milled out a section of the bottom of the front ring of the receiver. This effectively makes their Springfields "non-guns" so no FFL is required. At this time I do not know if the SARCO guns with this further modification could be modified to .22 rimfire.

While I can appreciate the liability concerns of the Army, I still look at the deactivation of these fine old rifles as an unfortunate waste. These were great, well-made, historic rifles and I just hate to see them mutilated like this. At least with the .22 rimfire modification, these old girls will once again live to be shot and enjoyed.

Almost all of these rifles had been used by high school and college ROTC units. Consequently, the stocks are often a bit rough and, I am told, some may even have minor wood

These 1903 Springfields were deactivated by extensive welding and used for years by high school and college ROTC programs. DuPage Trading and SARCO have them.

Note how the magazine cutoff/bolt stop was welded to the receiver as part of the deactivation. This was to prevent removal of the bolt by inquisitive cadets.

The magazine cutoff has been removed, but there is still enough weld extending into the receiver to prevent removal of the bolt. Here's where a set of files pays.

Coffield found that it's helpful to have an unwelded Springfield available to determine just how much weld needs to be removed without damaging the receiver.

The firing pin hole in the face of the bolt was also welded shut. No problem here, Coffield intends to cut off the bolt head anyway and install a new assembly.

repairs. However, for my purposes, this was not all that important. Besides, a little wood work with this project would not be a problem.

The rifle I received was a high number Springfield, #1411xxx, made in 1933. The barrel had a later date of August, 1942. This indicated that the rifle was rebarreled during World War II when a lot of older military small arms like this were refurbished. At some point still later in its life it was converted to a drill rifle.

Overall, the rifle was in reasonably good condition, though it was evident that it had seen a *lot* of use on the drill field. The buttplate was especially well worn. The only missing parts on my rifle were the magazine follower and follower spring.

My buddy's rifle was a bit more interesting. It was a low number Springfield, #200xxx, made in 1906 at the Rock Island Arsenal. Like my rifle, his was also rebarreled but this had been done in September, 1911. His stock was in pretty rough shape but he had wanted to replace it and put a pistol grip, "C" type stock on it. I also got the new "C" stock from Dupage Trading Company, but more on that later.

Before getting into this project, I need to comment on a couple of subjects. First I want to address the issue of the safety of reactivating these rifles. I would not recommend returning these rifles to .30-'06 or any similar high pressure cartridge. The rifles have been welded in a critical area; specifically the front ring of the receiver.

You and I have no way of knowing anything about the skill of the welder, how hot the front receiver ring got or how long it was subjected to this heat. It may or may not have sustained extensive damage and had the strength and heat treatment of the receiver compromised. You and I have absolutely no way of knowing for certain short of a very sophisticated and costly analysis by a metallurgical laboratory.

The best and most prudent course of action is to simply not do anything with these rifles that would stress the receiv-

ers. A .22 rimfire conversion, on the other hand, would not in any way compromise the safety of these rifles.

Keep in mind that most bolt-action .22 rimfire rifles lock the bolt body forward with nothing more than the shank of the bolt handle. More often than not the bolt shanks are quite small and frequently just a press fit into the bolt body. Our conversion will use the safety lug of the Springfield bolt. This lug is quite massive and more than adequate to contain the pressure and stress of a .22 rimfire cartridge.

I should also point out that my particular rifle is a "high number" Springfield. This simply means that it was produced after a major change in the heat treating process at Springfield Armory. In 1918 at or around serial number 800,000, the process for heat treating the receivers was changed to one that resulted in a more consistent and stronger receiver.

The change in the process at Rock Island Armory, which was also producing 1903s, was done in 1918 beginning with the receiver with the serial number of 285,507. Receivers

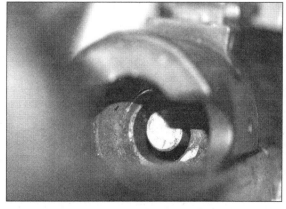

The further to ensure that the rifle could never be fired, a steel rod was placed in the bore extending into the chamber and secured in position by a large weld.

made with serial numbers below these are suspect and can sometimes fail. I definitely would not recommend that any low-number Springfield 1903 ever be fired with even a standard .30-'06 load. In fact, I do not recommend firing any low number or early Springfield with any centerfire cartridge. A .22 rimfire is OK in my opinion, but anything else could lead to safety problems.

Another issue that needs to be addressed is whether or not this conversion is "ruining" a collectable. In one sense, it is. When viewed as a historical artifact, the fact that these Springfields had been converted by the U.S. government to drill rifles does not in any way diminish their theoretical value as a collectable. After all, their use as drill rifles is just one part of the story and history of these rifles. The fact that you can't fire the rifle is really insignificant. I would venture to say that most antique "collectable" firearms are never fired anyway.

Unfortunately, the reality is that few if any collectors care about or want these drill rifles. That is all too evident by the current market price. A functioning 1903 Springfield will go for close to $1,000 or more. These drill rifles are selling for $250 or less. There's a message here. At this point in time, these rifles have little or no value to collectors.

So...if you want to preserve these rifles in their current condition, go for it! On the other hand, if you want to join me in making one 'em into a more desirable and useable firearm and one which will definitely have greater value than $250, join me in this project! Check the ads in SHOTGUN NEWS, buy a rifle, and build a great plinker. You'll definitely have a most unusual .22 rifle and it'll be a lot of fun to build and use!

My first step was to completely disassemble the rifle. To keep track of the parts once they were removed, I put them in a plastic stackable parts tray for storage. I use a separate labeled tray for each gun. Since I'm working on two 1903s at the same time, it's important to keep the parts separate and identify the gun they are from. There was no major problem in most of the actual disassembly. It was a little unusual to remove the firing pin assembly from the bolt while the bolt was still in the receiver. I'd never done that before.

After looking the guns over, the next step in the project was to remove the bolt stop or magazine cutoff. This had to come out in order to remove the bolt body. The cutoff had been welded in place in the receiver.

The Rock Island gun had a bit more weld here than the Springfield, so I started with it. The cutoff is normally held

The Springfield's barrel was welded to the receiver. In addition, a slot was ground into the barrel and a steel rod was welded into bore and extended into the chamber.

Coffield used his action wrench to try and twist the receiver off the barrel. To his surprise and relief, the weld broke and permitted the removal of the barrel.

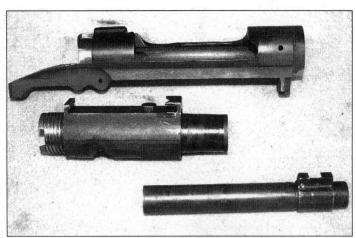

This is a tedious, messy job that can take quite a while. Again, it all depends on your welds and how good (or bad depending on how you look at it!) they are. Go slowly and do your best to avoid cutting or nicking the receiver. You may be tempted to remove the lever or "handle" for the cutoff immediately. After all, it's the largest part of the cutoff and easy to get to.

Don't! That part of the cutoff needs to be left in place as it gives you a gripping surface for pliers or vise-grips. Once you have cut away the vast majority of the weld, you can sometimes move the cutoff just enough to get the weld to crack. This can make removal of the cutoff a lot easier and certainly will save time.

Don't get excited if once you have the cut-off removed you still can't take the bolt out of the receiver. With both of these rifles, I found there were small amounts of weld inside the receiver, further blocking the removal of the bolt. It required a bit of careful file work with needle files as well as my carbide cutters to remove this material.

It's easy to get frustrated and to try to work too fast at this point. Take your time. If you start to get a bit PO'ed at the gun and that blankety blank son of a gun that welded it up; stop. Put your work away and let it set overnight. The next day the work will go faster and once that is done, the bolt can finally be removed.

I know I probably sound like a broken record (that sure dates me, do they still make records?!) but you absolutely have to go slow with this work. If you get frustrated and then get in a hurry, you'll have problems. If there's a "secret" to good gunsmithing it's simply taking your time and being careful.

Once you get the bolt out of the rifle, take a look at it. The face of both of my bolts had been welded up, closing off the firing pin hole. That was not a major problem since the bolt will be shortened and the front of the bolt will be cutoff.

With both of my rifles, the welding around the cutoff left some depressions in the steel of the receivers. While I could just leave this as it is, I will use my TIG welder to build these areas back up and reshape them to the original contours. However, before I do that, I want to do a bit more work on the barrels.

On both rifles the barrels had been tack-welded to the receivers. I used some files and later a sanding belt to cut down these welds. It appeared that the welds were just on the surface and did not penetrate deeply. However, I would not count on that, as appearances can be deceptive. While I would prefer to remove the barrel to be able to do more work on it, I spent a lot of time trying to figure out how I could do this with the receiver still attached.

My basic plan is to cut the barrel in two locations; about an inch and a half or so in front of the rear sight base and about 5½ inches to the rear of the muzzle. I'll be cutting away the center 13½ inches of the old .30 cal. barrel. I then plan on reaming out the rear portion of the barrel to a diameter of about .687" or 11/16".

The shorter front segment of the barrel will be reamed to .500" or 1/2". I'll then take a .22 barrel and turn it down so that it fits into the rear and front sections of the old barrel. In effect, the .22 barrel becomes a liner. By doing it this way, I can keep the original rear sight base in place. I can also preserve my front sight as well as the barrel marks when I use that shorter piece of barrel that I cut behind the muzzle.

Since the barrel had been welded to the receiver, I thought I might have to make a mandrel to support the receiver in my lathe when modifying the barrel. This mandrel is nothing more than a 10" long piece of mild, hot rolled steel turned to a diameter of about .694". This would serve as a good tight, sliding fit in the receiver. The rear of the mandrel would be placed in my three-jaw chuck supporting the barreled receiver.

However, before starting on the mandrel, I decided to put the barreled action in my barrel vise and apply a bit of pres-

With the barrel removed and severed between the sight bases, Coffield used an 11/16 inch drill to drill out the barrel stub for installation of the .22 barrel.

Coffield wanted to avoid having to remove the front and rear sight bases, so used a lathe to cut the barrel off about an inch in front of the rear sight base.

in place by a cutoff pin or spindle. This in turn is secured by a cutoff screw. If at all possible, remove the cutoff screw and pull the spindle out of the receiver. On some guns you can do this; on others you can't. It all depends on just how enthusiastic the welder was when he did your rifle!

The tool I used primarily was my Dremel, along with a number of different carbide cutters. These super hard cutters can go through the weld fairly easily. It's important to take your time, be careful, and if at all possible have another receiver handy so you can tell exactly where the original surfaces were located. The globs of weld can make things pretty confusing at times.

As you use these carbide cutters, you're throwing off tiny shards of metal so be sure to wear appropriate eye protection. All it takes is one tiny little particle of steel to seriously injure your eye. It's not worth the risk of losing your sight, so always wear safety glasses of some type when doing work like this.

sure to the barrel. Who knows, I might get lucky and the darn thing would turn off!

In order to avoid damage to the receiver, I used an action wrench I made years ago while working at Brownells. The unique aspect of this wrench is that it provides uniform, full contact to the curved surface on the top of the receiver. Traditionally many action wrenches had only two small contact points on the top of the receiver.

Using this older style action wrench I've seen a number of receivers that were dented or had flat spots pressed into them. This type of damage is something that you definitely want to avoid. Currently Brownells sells a version of the full contact action wrench with interchangeable heads for a variety of different receivers.

The outside of the barrel was cleaned with a solvent to remove any traces of oil or grease. It was then placed between two oak blocks which I had dusted with rosin to help them hold the barrel more firmly. The barrel and oak blocks were then positioned under the hydraulic jack in my barrel vise. A few pumps with the jack handle and about two tons of pressure was brought to bear to hold the barrel firmly in place.

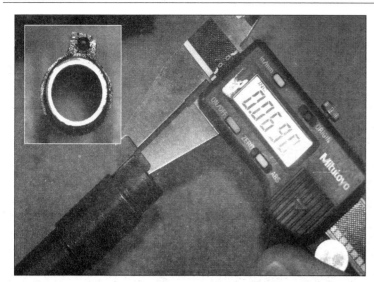

Once the front section of the barrel was drilled out, the remaining barrel wall was very thin. The barrel wall thickness at the muzzle end measured only about .069".

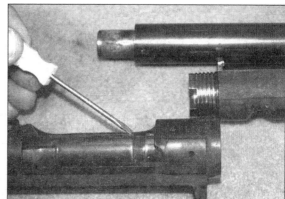

Coffield will shorten the Springfield bolt by cutting it at the rear of the extractor retainer groove. The new .22 barrel will extend back into the receiver.

I added a "cheater bar" or extension to my action wrench handle and carefully applied pressure to the receiver.

No one could have been more surprised than I when the darn barrel broke lose from the receiver! Evidently the weld had not penetrated to any significant depth. So much for government welding! Since the Springfield barreled action came apart so easily, I immediately set up the other barreled action made at Rock Island and pulled the barrel from it as well. Keep in mind I had filed and ground down the welds before applying any pressure. Also, while these actions separated easily, others might not.

With the barrel out of the receiver, I set it up in my lathe. The threaded shank of the barrel was held in a three-jaw chuck and the muzzle supported by a live center in the tail stock. I used a parting tool to cut it about 1" in front of the rear sight base.

The threaded shank of the barrel stub was left in the three-jaw chuck and a steady rest was used to support the barrel stub just ahead of the sight base. I had been tempted to cut the barrel closer to the sight base, but I realized that I would need at least an inch or so of the barrel for the steady rest.

A steel rod that extended from the chamber into the barrel had been welded in place. On the off chance that it might break loose, I had tried to drive it out with a long punch, but it was soon obvious that it was not going to move. The only way to get it out would be to use a drill.

Since the rod was smaller than the rear of the chamber, it would tend to flex a bit if I had attempted to drill it out from the breech end. Because of this, all my drilling to remove this rod was done from the muzzle end of the barrel stub.

I started out with a 5/16" diameter drill which was just a bit over bore size. I used this drill so it would not "wander" and would stay in line with the axis of the bore. My ultimate goal was to drill the stub out to a finished diameter of 11/16" or .687". This would be the diameter of the portion of the barrel that would extend back through the front ring of the receiver.

The first pass with the 5/16" inch drill was relatively easy and trouble free. The steel rod was freed and dropped out of

the barrel stub. I then moved up to a larger 3/8" inch diameter drill. That's when the trouble started!

I don't know what was used when the barrel was slotted and the steel rod welded into the bore. Whatever it was, it was harder than woodpecker lips! I finally cut through the welded area with a 1/2" drill and followed that up with a 1/2" carbide reamer. I then used an 11/16" drill to open up the barrel stub to the final diameter.

Or rather, I should say I tried to use an 11/16" drill. That darn weld just would not cut. I ran the 11/16" drill in as far as possible from the muzzle end and then reversed the stub and drilled in for the breech end. This left a web about 3/8" wide inside the stub.

I first tried a coarse rat-tail file and it would not even touch that darn weld! I then used small abrasive stones mounted on an extension powered by a hand drill to grind down most of the web. I followed this up with abrasive stones in my Dremel tool. To say that it was a royal pain in the you-know-what is an understatement of the first order.

I finally got the darn web ground out but it took forever, or so it seemed. The lesson to be learned from this is that you should check hardness of the weld before you start drilling. This can help to save time, damage to drills, and allow you to use a more efficient approach. In looking back on this, I should have just ground out as much of the weld as possible from both the inside and outside of the barrel and then removed the remaining web with abrasive stones.

Once the barrel stub was opened up with a uniform 11/16" diameter hole, I made sure the face of the stub on the muzzle end was smooth and square. I made a cleanup pass on the lathe and then smoothed it up further with a file.

A section approximately 5⅜ inches long was cut off the muzzle end of the barrel. This was done so I could preserve the barrel markings and the front sight base. I then used the 5/16" drill to open up the barrel bore. This was followed by a 1/2" drill. The result was a fairly thin sleeve. At the muzzle this barrel sleeve measure only about .069" or so thick. I again squared the rear end of the sleeve and cleaned up the muzzle end with a smooth file.

The next step in the process will be to turn down the .22 cal. target barrel so that it will fit into the barrel stub and extend back into the receiver. By the way, I got my .22 barrels from the folks at Numrich Gun Parts, Box 299, Dept. SGN, West Hurley, N.Y. 12491, telephone 866-686-7424. I needed a barrel that was at least 26 inches long.

Sure enough, they checked around and had some old take-off barrels from some European target rifles that were just perfect. If you need a barrel, check with the folks at Numrich. They can probably supply just what you need.

We'll also make sure the muzzle portion of the .22 barrel is turned to 1/2" so the front portion of the old Springfield barrel can be installed right over it. Keep in mind that we'll want to keep our modified barrel the same overall length as the original Springfield .30-'06 barrel. The original barrel measured right at about 23 inches long from the front face of the receiver to the face of the muzzle. We can be off a few

thousandths in this regard but we sure don't want to miss it much more than that. Remember, everything has to fit back into an original, unaltered stock.

Also, I have to allow for an extension of the .22 barrel into the receiver. I'll be cutting and shortening the bolt at the rear edge of the extractor retainer groove. This means that the .22 barrel will have to extend back from the front face of the receiver just a hair over 2 inches. Again, I can be off a few thousandths as I can make some adjustments to the bolt and to the rear of the .22 barrel. I will go into this in greater detail the next time we get together.

You might wonder why I'm bothering to run the rear of the .22 barrel so far back into the receiver. This is to compensate both for the shortening of the bolt and to allow easier loading and unloading of the small .22 cartridge. If the barrel were of normal length, it could be pretty difficult to chamber a cartridge.

I'll also hopefully take care of fitting the .22 barrel with an extractor and modifying the Springfield bolt by installing a new bolt head. Remember that we'll be changing this from a centerfire bolt to a rimfire. Yep, that should be fun!

If you've stuck with me this far and you want to join me in this project, give Jim Yocum at Dupage Traders a call and pick up one of these old Springfields. It's a lot of fun and you could end up with a very unique and distinctive .22 rifle.

Until next time, good luck and good gunsmithing! ◉

Converting the Springfield drill rifle into a .22 rimfire is one of the most interesting and challenging projects Coffield has undertaken in quite a few years.

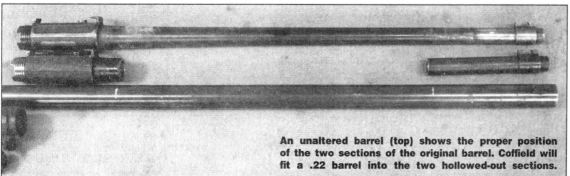

An unaltered barrel (top) shows the proper position of the two sections of the original barrel. Coffield will fit a .22 barrel into the two hollowed-out sections.

What Can You Do with a Drill Rifle?

By Reid Coffield

Part 2

In Part 1 (4/10 issue), Coffield unwelded the action and installed a .22 cal. barrel. Now he goes to work on the bolt.

This month, Coffield works on the barrel and bolt operations for his Springfield .22 drill rifle. Accurate measurements are essential in making this unusual conversion.

In the first installment of this series, I spent most of my time and effort in just taking the darn rifles apart. While I could remove the trigger guard and pull the action out of the stock by removing a few screws, everything else required a lot of cutting and grinding of welds.

The hardest part to remove was the magazine cut-off as it had been welded on three sides to the receiver. Fortunately with the use of a Dremel tool, abrasive cut-off wheels, and some carbide burrs, I was able to remove the magazine cut off with very little damage to the receiver. In fact, most of the damage that will need to be repaired was done by the welding.

While it's possible to do the necessary modification work on the barrel with it in the receiver, I knew it would be a lot easier and faster if I could separate the barrel and receiver. I wasn't at all sure if I could do this as there was a line of weld along the underside of the barrel shoulder where it joined the receiver.

I initially ground down the weld and then on a hunch, I put the barrel in my barrel vise, clamped an action wrench to the receiver and applied a bit of pressure. I didn't expect the barrel to turn off the receiver as I thought the weld was fairly deep. Fortunately I was wrong! The barrels on both receivers turned off with very little pressure. While the welds were certainly big and impressive, they obviously weren't very deep. There was very little penetration with the original welding.

After I pulled the barrel from the receiver I placed it in my lathe and cut it in two different locations. I first made a cut right at 4½ inches ahead of the barrel shoulder. I then repositioned the forward section of the barrel and cut it again about 5⅜ inches back from the muzzle.

The rear section of the barrel was then drilled and bored out to a diameter of 11/16". While doing this, I was able to remove the section of steel rod that had been welded into the chamber. By the way, this may not be the case with any other drill rifles but what ever it was the fellow doing the welding used on my barrel, he left a weld that was harder than woodpecker lips. I had a heck of a time cutting and grinding my way through the darn weld.

The muzzle section of the barrel was much easier to deal with, as all I had to do was drill it out to a diameter of 1/2". Keep in mind I'm doing this so I can slide a .22 rimfire barrel into this portion of the barrel and preserve the original sight and barrel markings. My goal is to have the ol' Springfield look like it's still in the original .30-'06 caliber.

The .22 barrel I'm using is one I got from the good folks at Numrich Gun Parts, 226 Williams Lane, Dept. SGN, West

Hurley, N.Y. 12491, telephone 866-686-7424. It's a bull barrel with a muzzle diameter of about .900" and an overall length of 26¾ inches. Evidently it came off of a European target rifle of some sort. While the outside was a bit rusted and worn, the bore looked perfect. If you need a .22 barrel for your rifle, by all means, check with the folks at Numrich. Goodness knows what they might have. I'm sure they can come up with something that you could use at a very reasonable price.

I needed a fairly long .22 barrel since I planed on turning it down so it would fit inside both the rear and forward portions of the Springfield barrel I had bored out. At the same time, I had to have enough barrel length to end up with a finished barrel the same length as my original .30-'06

The muzzle end of the .22 target barrel must be turned down to .500" inch diameter. Coffield got the barrel from Numrich Gun Parts, his go-to source for parts.

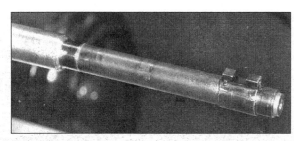

While the .22 barrel is still in the lathe, Coffield checks the fit with the bored-out section of the .30-'06 barrel. Dykem shows the part that needs turning down.

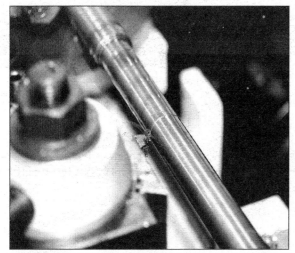

Once the muzzle end of the .22 barrel was fitted, Coffield reversed it in his lathe and fit it to pass all the way through the rear barrel stub. He countoured it smoothly.

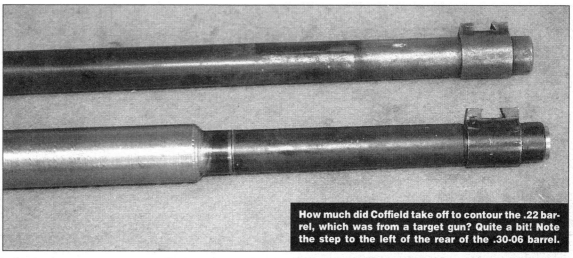

How much did Coffield take off to contour the .22 barrel, which was from a target gun? Quite a bit! Note the step to the left of the rear of the .30-06 barrel.

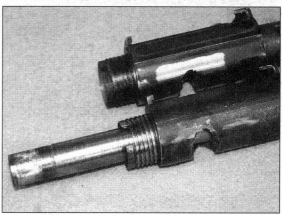

Coffield purposely left the breech end of the .22 barrel too long while he conceptualized his bolt design. Better to have too much length here than not enough!

Springfield barrel. The .30-'06 barrel measured right at 23¼ inches from the barrel shoulder to the muzzle. Fortunately, the barrels I got from Numrich were just about perfect.

In turning down the .22 barrel on my lathe, I first reduced the diameter of the entire length to about .900". This was the outside diameter of the front of the rear barrel stub. Once that was done, I turned down the muzzle end of the barrel to a diameter of .500". This was extended back a distance of 5⅜ inches.

My objective here was to ensure that the .22 barrel would fit inside the muzzle section of the Springfield barrel. I also wanted to use no more of the barrel length than absolutely necessary. If I had any extra barrel length left, I wanted it on the rear or breech end. If I screwed something up in

modifying and fitting the bolt, I wanted as much wiggle room as possible! That extra barrel length at the breech was insurance.

With the muzzle end turned and checked for fit with the Springfield barrel, I next turned down the breech end. Here the barrel had to fit into the rear barrel stub, which had been drilled out to 11/16".

As soon as I got close to this dimension, I began to check the fit of the barrel stub frequently. Once I had the .22 barrel turned down to allow a close sliding fit, I checked to make sure it would fit into the receiver as well. I had a slight bit of misalignment with the bore of the rear barrel stub as I had to take a bit more metal off the portion of the .22 barrel that extended into the receiver. It wasn't much; just a few thousandths.

Once both the front and rear parts of the Springfield barrel had been checked for fit on the turned down .22 barrel, I began removing a lot of metal from the center portion of the barrel. I needed it to be a reasonably close match to the diameter of the front of the rear barrel stub and the rear of the muzzle section of the old Springfield barrel.

My objective was to have a reasonably smooth taper from the rear of the barrel to the front. Keep in mind that since all of this is covered by the stock handguard, you could do away with any taper and just have the barrel turned to a uniform diameter with a step or two. However, esthetically I just couldn't do that. I wanted it to look like a normal, tapered barrel. It was a bit more work but in the end, I think it was worth it.

Once the barrel was shaped, I was able to remove the original chamber area at the rear of the .22 barrel. I had left this on as a precaution in case I needed extra length at the breech end. Fortunately this was not needed.

With the barrel shortened just a bit, I next shortened the bolt. I used a Dremel tool with a cutoff wheel as well as a hacksaw. My cut was made in the groove for the extractor collar. Once the front of the bolt with the locking lugs was removed, I positioned the bolt in my lathe. The rear of the bolt was supported by a plug I made years ago. This allowed me to use my three jaw chuck to hold the rear of the bolt while the front of the bolt was supported in the steady rest. This arrangement allowed full access to the front of the bolt to square it up and prepare it for a new plug or bolt head.

When shortening the bolt I ended up with a small web due to the smaller diameter needed for the firing pin. This was removed by using a 13/32" inch diameter drill. The drill was inserted from the rear of the bolt. The through hole that runs the length of the bolt body actually helped to ensure that the drill was properly centered. Once that was done I was ready to start on the bolt head.

Keep in mind that it's necessary to convert the bolt from a centerfire to a rimfire and this means that I'll need an off center firing pin. However, before modifying the firing pin I'll need to make a new bolt head. I had a piece of standard 4140 steel that was 3/4" in diameter and I wanted to use it. 4140 is very good steel and is commonly used for barrels and other firearm parts.

My biggest problem was determining just how the bolt head was to be shaped. I had cut the original firing pin. The

The modified .22 barrel (bottom) is shown with an unmodified .22 barrel directly above it. At the top is an original .30-'06 Springfield barrel. Extensive lathe work needed!

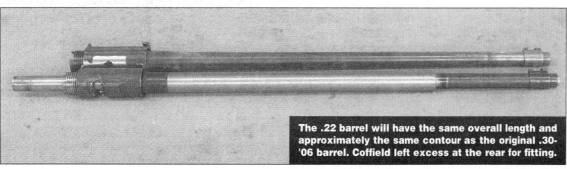

The .22 barrel will have the same overall length and approximately the same contour as the original .30-'06 barrel. Coffield left excess at the rear for fitting.

Coffield started the bolt shortening process by using a hacksaw and a Dremel cutoff wheel to cut the demilled bolt near the rear of the extractor collar groove.

Here's the front of the bolt after it was squared up in the lathe. The web of steel that was left actually provided convenient support for drilling the through hole.

shank of the pin was cut immediately ahead of the base that attached to the firing pin rod.

I then assembled the bolt body with this modified firing pin and measured from the front end of the bolt to the top or front of the stub of the firing pin with a depth micrometer. Using this measuring device, I determined that the stub of the new bolt head should extend approximately .175" deep into the bolt. Any more than that and the firing pin body would strike the rear of the bolt head. I didn't want that as it would eventually distort the rear of the bolt head or possibly drive it off the bolt body.

I also needed to determine approximately how long the new bolt head would extend from the front of the bolt body. To help figure this out, I used the firing pin I had selected for this project. I have no earthly idea where the firing pin came from or the gun that it was originally intended for. As a gunsmith, I always save any firing pins I run across.

The body of this pin was only .154" diameter and the overall length was right at .552". Since I wanted the firing pin to be enclosed in the body of the new bolt head, this meant that the bolt head had to be right at .500" long. As the bolt head extended back into the bolt body .175", the shoulder of the bolt head extending forward from the end of the bolt would therefore be only about .325".

Some may be thinking that I'm making this far too complicated. Why not just solder an offset pin into the front of the cut off firing pin base? That would sure be simpler.

Yes, it would be simpler but there's a problem with this. The Springfield firing pin base can move or rotate on the firing pin rod. If you have an offset rimfire pin projecting from this base, all it has to move or rotate is a few thousandths either to the right or left and it will miss the firing pin hole in the bolt head. By using an independent firing pin

secured in the bolt head, that will never be a problem.

Using my lathe, I turned the 4140 rod down to form a "T"-shaped plug for the new bolt head. While my bolt head measured a little more than .500" from front to back, yours may and probably will be different.

You have to adjust the dimensions of your bolt head based on the firing pin you'll be using, the specific length of your bolt body, and the location of the breech end of your barrel. Keep in mind this is one of the reasons I have not yet cut the rear of the .22 barrel to its finished length. I want to keep my options open to make any adjustments necessary to ensure proper bolt to barrel contact. My plan is to complete the bolt and then adjust the barrel to fit the bolt.

You might be worried about where to position the new firing pin. At first, this does look difficult to determine. Actually, it's not all that hard. First just determine the center of the face of the bolt head. From that center, measure out approximately .090".

Depending upon the diameter of your firing pin, that point should be the center of your new firing pin hole. Remember, you don't want to center your firing pin on the edge of the cartridge rim. If you do, half of the impact of the firing pin will be wasted.

You want to deliver the maximum impact to the inside of the rim where the priming compound is located. My firing pin had a diameter of about .085", so a location of .090" from the center of the bolt head positioned it just where I wanted it.

Also, another consideration you have to keep in mind is making sure the body of the firing pin will fit into the bolt head extension. If the body is too large a diameter, you may have difficulty positioning it so that the side of the hole in the bolt head does not extend beyond the side of the bolt head extension.

The diameter of the body of my firing pin was only about .154" diameter, so I had no problem. Keep this in mind if you make your own firing pin or use one you've salvaged from another gun.

Once I had the firing pin hole located on the face of the bolt head, I drilled it out with a #43 drill. I then reversed the bolt head and opened up the hole with a #22 drill for the firing pin body.

By the way, a quick and easy way to make sure you're absolutely centered when opening up a hole like this is to leave the smaller drill in your drill press chuck after drilling the first hole. Change the position of your part, in this case the bolt head, and position it so that the smaller drill moves easily up and down in the hole while it's still in the drill press quill. If it does, the hole is perfectly centered under the drill. Now remove the smaller drill and install your larger drill which will also be perfectly centered. Quick and easy!

When drilling for the body of the firing pin, I had to be careful not to drill too deeply. I went in right at .430" or so.

Coffield checks the fit of the cut bolt to get a rough idea as to how long to make the new bolt head. You can never check your work too often in a project like this!

This allowed the body of the firing pin to be fully seated in the bolt head. I did later need to adjust it just a bit deeper. I did this by placing the #22 drill in a large pin vise and turned it by hand. I could remove just a few thousandths at a time and there was little or no danger of going too deep.

I ended up with a firing pin protrusion of right at .0365". Generally the maximum firing pin protrusion you will want on a rimfire is .038". Any more than this and you run the possibility of the tip of the firing pin striking the edge of the chamber and damaging the pin or the chamber.

As I worked on fitting my firing pin in the bolt head, I used a broach carefully to open up the firing pin tip hole. A broach is a little known tool that looks a lot like a four sided ice pick. It is really handy for cleaning up holes and for opening up receiver sight apertures. By the way, I picked up my broach set from Brownells.

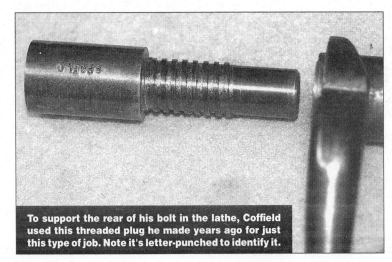

To support the rear of his bolt in the lathe, Coffield used this threaded plug he made years ago for just this type of job. Note it's letter-punched to identify it.

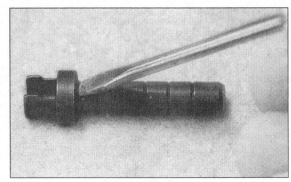

Coffield will cut the original firing pin at this point as part of the rimfire conversion. The separate rimfire pin will be retained inside the bolt head itself.

Coffield drilled the front of the bolt head for the rim-fire firing pin, then reversed it and made sure the hole for the firing pin tip was centered under the drill.

To remove any metal chips from the hole, I used a pipe cleaner. I keep some of these on my bench just for this type of application. You might want to start keeping some on your bench as well. They are great for cleaning out short, small-diameter holes.

Once the firing pin was installed, I needed to do something to keep it from falling out of the bolt head and back into the bolt body. I opted for a small 2x64 threads per inch screw. The screw was located in the side of the bolt head and extended down until it engaged a slot in the side of the firing pin body. While it would keep the firing pin from falling out of the rear of the bolt head and into the bolt body, it would not interfere with the free back and forth movement of the firing pin.

Since the firing pin moved very easily back and forth in the bolt head, I didn't need a firing pin return spring. I was delighted as this made the project a bit simpler.

I decided to use two of the small 2x64 screws to attach the bolt head to the Springfield bolt body. Using screws would

Coffield then installed the larger drill needed for the firing pin body hole *without* moving the bolt head. The larger diameter drill was now perfectly centered.

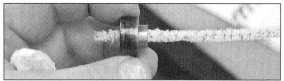

Pipe cleaners are often ideal for cleaning small holes, while if you need to open up a small hole, a broach like this will do the trick! Firing pin hole must be smooth.

allow the bolt head to be easily removed for cleaning, replacement, etc.

Before I started on this I wanted to make darn sure I could actually drill and tap the end of the bolt body. Remember that the lugs and front of the bolt are extremely hard. I wasn't 100% sure the bolt body would or could be easily drilled.

To test it, I used the front portion of the bolt I had removed earlier. I placed this in my drill press with the cut side up and drilled a small hole with the #50 drill I would later use for the attaching screws. The drill went in with no problem, so I was pretty darn sure I could drill and tap the bolt body as well.

The two screws were to be inserted from the front of the bolt head. I located the position of my first screw, which was roughly at 9 o'clock. The spot was marked and struck with a spring loaded automatic center punch. If you have to be very precise, always use a center punch before you drill. The small crater you create with the punch will help to keep the drill bit from walking or moving to the side.

Since the side of this hole was only about .020" or so from the side of the bolt head, it had to be precisely located. Once that hole was drilled, I coated the front of the bolt body with Dykem.

I positioned the bolt head on the end of the bolt and, using a small scribe through the hole in the bolt head, I marked the position of the hole for the screw.

This hole also had to be carefully positioned, as it was very near the edge of the hole that ran through the bolt body. Once it was drilled, I tapped or threaded it with a 2x64 taper tap.

The bolt head was countersunk with a #29 drill for the head of the 2x64 screw. I wanted to make sure the screw head was positioned below the face of the bolt head so it would not contact the rear of the barrel.

After that, it was just a matter of duplicating this same sequence of work to drill the bolt head and tap the bolt body for the second screw. I tried to make sure that this second

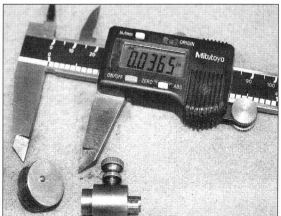

A caliper and firing pin protrusion gauge easily measure the projection of the firing pin tip from the face of the new bolt head. At .0365" it was just about ideal.

The new bolt head (l.) beside the original welded Springfield bolt head. No locking lugs on the rimfire bolt. The firing pin is held in place by a small screw.

The slotted screws in the bolt face hold the rimfire bolt head in position in the cutoff Springfield bolt. The screw on the side of the head retains the firing pin.

screw was located directly across from the first screw. This was both for esthetic reasons as well as to provide maximum even support for the bolt head.

This was a tedious part of the project and I had to be very careful that my screw holes were properly located. There was very little margin for error and it would have been awfully easy to drill out the side of the bolt head or bolt body. If you decide to use screws as I did, be *very careful* when you lay out and locate your holes!

That pretty well completed the work on the bolt. There will be one more item, as I will later add a stop to the bolt to prevent it from being pulled from the receiver as it's being used. Remember the left locking lug served as a bolt stop originally. Of course, the lugs had been cut off when I removed the front of the bolt.

In the next installment (6/10 issue) I'll be making and fitting an extractor. Once that has been done, there'll be a bit of cosmetic work on the receiver and then the barrel can be chambered and installed. I'll also need to do a bit of repair work on the stock. Years of use as a drill rifle left a lot of dings and dents that really need to be removed.

If you're at all interested in making up your own .22 rimfire Springfield, give the folks at Dupage Trading Company, Box 1274, Dept. SGN, Chandler, Ariz. 85244, telephone 480-664-2226 a call. I'm sure they'll be happy to fix you up and I'd be delighted to have you join me in this project. The more of those ol' Springfields we can resurrect, the better!

Until next time, good luck and good gunsmithing! ◎

What Can You Do with a Drill Rifle?

By Reid Coffield

Part 3

In Part 2 (5/10 issue), Coffield removed the original barrel and installed a target .22 barrel. In this installment, he finishes and test-fires his rimfire Springfield.

Just another guy with an '03 Springfield? Check the ammo! Coffield's home-brewed drill rifle conversion was definitely the most unusual and unique .22 rifle on range!

The 1903 Springfield is a beautiful rifle. In fact, I'd go so far as to say it's the most attractive military bolt-action rifle ever made. Aside from the skill and workmanship that went into building this rifle and its long and glorious history, it has always been very special to me and thousands of other Americans as well. Like the eagle and the flag, it's a symbol of America.

Countless gun owners have at least one 1903 or 1903A3 Springfield in their collections. In fact, so many people want Springfields that the prices have grown to an amazing level in the last few years. Now days, it's not at all unusual to see nice Springfields selling for more than $1,000.

I've been fortunate to own a few good Springfields over the years, and one that I have especially enjoyed was an M2 Springfield in .22 cal. This variation of the old 1903 .30-'06 Springfield was produced in .22 rimfire for training purposes. It has a sporter type stock and looks more like a civilian rifle than a military arm in many respects. I often wanted to have a more "military" .22 rimfire Springfield but that just never happened.

That is until I heard from a friend, Roger Deeks, who showed me some photographs of a 1903 Springfield drill rifle he converted to .22 rimfire. I was hooked! That was just what I wanted and I had to have one. Very shortly I contacted Dupage Trading Company,. Box 1274, Dept. SGN, Chandler, Ariz. 85244, telephone 480-664-2226 and obtained a demilled drill rifle just like the one Roger had. In fact, I ended up with two of 'em. One was for me and one for a buddy who also wanted a .22 Springfield.

In the first part of this series I covered how I initially cut through the many welds and disassembled the rifles. In the second part, I removed the barrels and cut a 5-inch or so section from the front and from the rear. This was done for two reasons. It allowed me to retain the original sights and barrel markings. Each section was then bored out for a liner made from a .22 bull barrel. I also modified the bolts and converted them to rimfire.

The only remaining tasks are to fit and chamber the barrel, install an extractor, fit a bolt stop to the bolt body, repair one or two areas on the receiver caused by the original welds, and repair and fit the stock. That's quite a bit of work! However, once it's completed we'll have a truly unique .22 rifle.

The first order of business was to repair a couple of places where original welds to demil the rifle had left some pits. There was also one spot on my rifle where I had accidentally cut a bit too deep as I removed the weld around the magazine cut-off. I used my Miller TIG welding outfit to take care of these problem areas. Once I had a deposit of weld to a sufficient depth, I allowed it to cool and then shaped it with some carbide cutters in my Dremel tool. This was followed up with a coarse abrasive wheel.

I discovered that whatever welding rod the welder had used, the darn stuff would not blue! It may have been some type of stainless steel. In any event, I have a small spot of nice shiny metal behind my magazine cut-off. It will not take a color from any cold blue I've tried thus far. It's not a big deal, but it's just one more of the many surprises you'll run into in a project like this.

With the welding completed, the next task was to fit the barrel and bolt. In turning down the .22 bull barrel I obtained from Numrich Gun Parts, I left the rear section of the barrel too long. This was deliberate. I

wanted to be sure I had plenty of barrel length to work with in fitting the bolt.

Initially I didn't know exactly how long the bolt would be, as I had never done a project like this. Whenever you're experimenting like this, always err on giving yourself extra material to work with. It's easy to cut away extra steel but it's the devil's own work to add it when you don't have enough!

To determine the appropriate length of the .22 barrel shank that extended into the receiver, I first installed the rear section of the original barrel in the receiver. Just a note of caution: *never* screw a barrel into a receiver without *always* applying a grease or lubricant to the barrel threads. If you

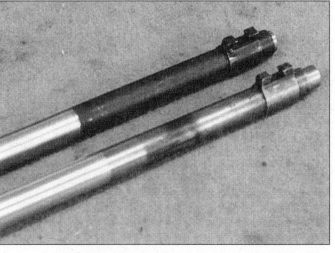

Numrich Gun Parts was the source for Schultz and Larsen .22 barrels that were turned down and fitted into sections of the original barrels at both the muzzle and breech.

Rooting out the demilitarizing welds is a messy job. Note the damage to the rifle's receiver above the slot for the magazine cut-off. This will have to be repaired.

fail to do this you run a great risk of galling the threads and ruining your barrel and possibly the receiver as well.

I use Hi-Slip Grease from Sentry Solutions Ltd., Box 214, Dept. SGN, Wilton, N.H. 03086, telephone 800-546-8049. This is a very effective grease and it comes packaged in a syringe for easy use. I have never had any problems with galling when using this product.

When installing the rear section of the original barrel, it's important to make sure it's properly aligned so the rear sight will not be canted. Fortunately, there is a witness mark on the left side of the receiver. All you need to do is line this mark up with the horizontal "ledge" on the midpoint of the rear sight base. When these two are lined up, the rear sight base will be level and the barrel shank firmly in place on the receiver.

I then slid the .22 barrel in the barrel stub and receiver. The bolt was put in the receiver and locked in place. When I

did this, I moved the barrel forward, creating a gap between shoulder of the front of the rear barrel shank and the matching shoulder on the .22 barrel. All I needed to do was measure this gap.

That was the amount of material I needed to remove from the end of the .22 barrel to fit it to the receiver. It wasn't all that much. It was only about .1205". Once that material was removed, the bolt would just contact the rear of the barrel shank when it was fully locked.

By the way, the .22 barrel I used to make my insert is a used Schultz and Larsen .22 target barrel which had been pulled from some type of match rifle. These barrels have the length you need for this project along with plenty of "meat," so you can duplicate virtually any outside contour.

Best of all, these barrels are inexpensive. They sell for only $41.95 and are listed in the latest #31 Catalog Product Supplement from Numrich. If you need a barrel or just about any other part for an obsolete gun or for a one-of-a-kind gunsmithing project, give Numrich a call at 866-6896-7424.

With the barrel fitted, I moved on to making and installing an extractor. All I wanted with this extractor was something to pull or push the cartridge case far enough out of the chamber to allow me to grab it with my fingers. I didn't need all that much.

I opted for a simple "L" shaped extractor. I started with a piece of .156" drill rod and a strip of 1/8" thick flat mild steel. I turned down about 1/8" of the end of the rod to a diameter of about .090". I then drilled a matching hole in the flat stock. Brownells High Force solder was used to join the two. By having this small projection and shoulder, I was able to get a lot more surface area between the pin and the flat stock for the solder. It makes for a very strong joint.

After the soldering was completed, I cut the flat stock. My extractor is relatively small with completed dimension of about .215" wide by .290" high. It only needs to be the width of the .22 rimfire cartridge base. Of course, I initially cut it out a bit larger to allow for fitting to the slot in the barrel. The round shank of the extractor was only about 1½ inches long at this point.

I drilled a hole parallel to the chamber that was 5/32" in diameter to match the shank of the extractor. This hole was

Only a .1205" gap remained between the .22 barrel shoulder and the '03 barrel stub when barrel contacted bolt. Removing .120" from the barrel gave a perfect fit.

about 2 inches deep. I wanted to have enough depth to allow for a spring to power the extractor.

After drilling this hole, I laid out two lines marking the width of the extractor slot. This was deepened with both needle files and the judicious use of a cut-off wheel on my Dremel. I had to be very careful to keep the bottom of the slot flat and at 90° to the chamber. The sides also needed to be vertical and parallel.

Fitting the extractor was next, and this was a very slow and tedious operation. You absolutely have to have your extractor properly fitted to the slot. I often coated the extractor with Dykem to check for contact as I worked. The important thing to keep in mind is to go slow and work carefully. I believe it took me about two hours or so to fit the extractor.

After fitting the extractor, I chambered the barrel by hand. With a .22 rimfire, you really aren't taking all that much material out of the barrel to form the chamber. You can easily turn the reamer by hand when doing this.

I did make sure the barrel was positioned vertically so the reamer would naturally follow the axis of the bore. Lots of cutting fluid was used and the chips were removed from the reamer frequently. As soon as the reamer began to cut the rim recess, I started checking depth and headspace.

After TIG welding to fill the damaged spots and careful reshaping of the welds, there was very little evidence of the original damage. This requires patience and skill.

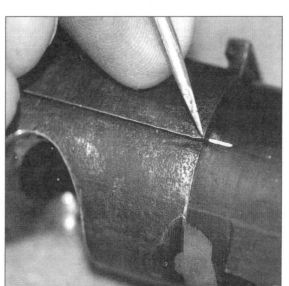

Note how the witness mark on the receiver's left side aligns with the horizontal ledge on the rear sight base. With proper alignment, the rear base will not be canted.

To fit the extractor shaft, Coffield made a hole parallel to and under the chamber with a 5/32" drill. There's not much room for error in this drilling job!

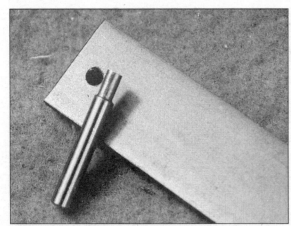

To make an extractor, Coffield turned down the end of this pin, drilled a matching hole in the 1/8" flat stock, soldered the two together and cut out the extractor.

The reamer cuts the chamber as well as the rim recess on the new extractor. This process is why it's very important that the extractor fit its barrel slot perfectly.

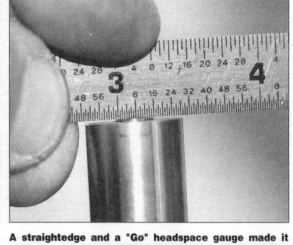

A straightedge and a "Go" headspace gauge made it easy to cut the cartridge rim's recess to the proper depth. If he could see light, he needed to keep on cutting.

This was easily done by placing a "Go" headspace gauge in the chamber and then setting a straightedge on the base of the gauge. If there was light between the straightedge and the end of the barrel, that indicated that I needed to continue deepening the chamber.

Once I had the straightedge in contact with the end of the headspace gauge and the end of the barrel, I was good to go! Remember that our bolt fits flush against the rear of the barrel.

With the barrel chambered and a rim recess cut in the extractor, I drilled and tapped the barrel above the extractor shaft for a 10-32 plug screw. This screw would serve as a retainer for the extractor. Once that was done, I installed the extractor in the barrel and marked the location of the plug screw hole on the extractor shaft.

Coffield carefully filed a slot into the rear face of the barrel and then fit the extractor to it. Note the close fit between the extractor and the sides of the slot.

The extractor was removed and a slot was filed to about half the width of the shaft for the screw. By extending this slot further to the rear of the shaft, I could control the projection of the extractor from the barrel. Initially, I set the extractor up to extend about .175". I can always increase this if necessary.

I had originally planned to epoxy the barrel into the rear barrel stub, but since I wanted to have the capability of adjusting the extractor, I changed my mind. Instead, I drilled and tapped the underside of the rear barrel stub for two 6-48 screws that extended into the .22 barrel. This will allow me to easily remove the barrel insert if I need to make any future adjustment to the extractor.

Once the barrel was fitted to the receiver, I reassembled the rifle. In putting the rear sight together, I used a new tool I obtained from Numrich which is a copy of an original U.S. ordnance tool for the Springfield rear sight. This sight crank allows you to quickly and easily turn the windage knob of the sight making installation very easy. Also, if your sight is a bit "sticky," use of this tool makes it very easy to "wear it in" by moving it back and forth from one side to the other.

The front section of the barrel was glued in place using five-minute epoxy. The front sight blade was installed to help ensure the barrel section was not canted to the right or left. You can visually spot even a very slight cant simply by looking from the back of the rifle over the rear sight. Your old Mark 1 eyeball is a darn good measuring tool!

If you do end up with the barrel canted it's not a big problem. All you need to do is heat the front barrel section with a propane torch until the epoxy softens and then adjust as needed.

The barrel insert was purposely allowed to extend a bit beyond the end of the front barrel section. This was then cut back and crowned. I used a crowning tool from Dave Manson Precision Reamers for this operation. Unlike other hand crowning tools, this one uses small carbide files to remove metal. It makes for an incredibly smooth, even crown. There is no doubt in my mind that this is the finest hand crowning tool made.

If you want more information about it, contact Dave Manson Precision Reamers, 8200 Embury Road, Dept. SGN, Grand Blanc, Mich. 48439, telephone 810-953-0732. It's a great tool and one you'll never regret adding to your shop. I've had mine for several years and it has performed flawlessly. A great tool!

At this point, I completed the reassembly of the rifle. Since I had to cut the old magazine cut-off out of the receiver, I needed a replacement, along with the spindle, plunger, plunger spring, and screw. All that took was a call to Numrich Gun Parts. If you need *any* for a Springfield or just about any other obsolete firearm, they have more of 'em than any other outfit in the nation. Give 'em a call and they'll fix you up.

The last step was to come up with some type of bolt stop. Remember that on a normal 1903 Springfield, the left bolt lug is stopped by the magazine cut-off to prevent it from coming out of the receiver. Since I cut off the front of the bolt, I no longer have anything to keep the darn bolt in the rifle!

However, that can be changed. I again turned to my friend Roger Deeks and used a technique he employed on his rifle. I turned a groove around my bolt body that was approximately .300" wide and .055" deep. This groove was located right at .465" ahead of the front face of the safety lug. Once it was completed, the extractor collar was installed.

I then took an old damaged extractor and cut out the center section. This was *reversed* and slid on to the extractor collar. By reversing this cut off section, it could not come off the bolt when it hit the bolt stop/magazine cut-off. It's a simple, elegant solution to a tough problem.

By the way, I had to do a fair amount of fitting to get the bolt to move smoothly in the receiver with this section of the extractor in place. It was just a matter of putting Dykem on the extractor section and noting where I had contact. Basically, it was just a tad bit too thick. My belt sander was used to remove the extra steel quickly and easily.

The spring-loaded extractor was held in position by a single 10-32 plug screw. This arrangement is commonly used in inexpensive single-and double-barrel shotguns.

Coffield used this copy of an old Springfield ordnance tool offered by Numrich to assemble and fit the rear sight windage screw. It saves lots of finger wear and tear.

Once the modified extractor was in place, the metal work was just about finished. As I mentioned earlier, the stock on my drill rifle had a lot of dings, dents, scratches, and assorted other scars from years of being tossed around by kids on a drill field. In addition, it had been refinished at some point and was heavily coated with a varnish-like material.

I could also see where the stock had been cracked in a number of places and repaired. While this certainly isn't the best stock, it'll do for the time being. I can always replace it on down the road. It's basically sound and will definitely be more than adequate for a .22 rimfire. It just needed a lot of TLC.

The first step in the process of salvaging the stock was simply to clean the wood. By cleaning away the surface finish as well as the accumulation of years of dirt and oil, the pores of the wood fibers would be opened and exposed. That's essential for a later step when I'll try to steam out most of the dents.

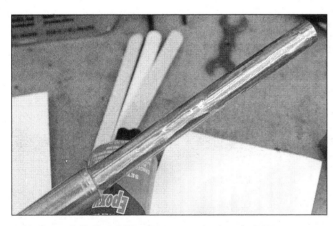

Coffield coated the .22 barrel with epoxy before installing the front section of the Springfield barrel. You can see the excess epoxy being pushed up as is seated.

To clean the wood, I used a product called Citristrip. This biodegradable paint stripper will, as far as I can tell, not harm or damage the wood as will some more aggressive strippers. While I definitely want to clean the wood, I certainly don't want to use any product that will in any way damage the wood fibers. Citristrip seems to meet this requirement. By the way, you can pick this up at most good hardware stores.

Using this product is pretty darn simple. It's an aerosol spray, so you just spray it on the stock and let it sit for about 30 minutes. After that, I washed the stock down with turpentine to remove the Citristrip residue. Again, I wanted to use products that would not harm the wood.

Turpentine is a natural wood byproduct made from pine rosin. It's a pretty good solvent and for years it was a used by painters for cleaning paint brushes. As far as I know, when used to wash down the stock it would have no negative effects on the wood.

Complete removal of the heavy coating of varnish took repeated applications of Citristrip; it was just so darn thick in several areas. I would be willing to bet the finish was applied by some kid with a paint brush and the emphasis was on getting a glossy finish, not necessarily an even one.

After the last application of Citristrip, I used paper towels to dry it. At that point I was better able to see for the first time the true condition of the wood. There were numerous dents and dings from rifles being piled together. You could easily spot places where the distinctive Springfield front sight of other rifles had been jammed into the stock!

There were also a number of cracks that had been repaired in the past. The good news was that I found one or two old ordnance marks or stamps I had not been able to see earlier. I definitely want to preserve these marks as I did my work.

Wood is composed of bundles of hollow cellulose fibers. When the surface of the wood is dented as so often happens when the rifle is dropped; the wood fibers collapse or are pressed together. To repair or raise these dents, I'll need to expand those collapsed wood fibers. It's kinda like inflating a flat tire.

This can often be done by using steam. The steam temporarily softens the wood, enters the hollow fibers, and expands or raises the compressed fibers. Once this has been done, the wood will often move back to its original position before it was dented.

The process is deceptively simple. A wet cloth is placed over the dent and then a hot iron is pressed against the wet cloth. The heat from the iron converts the water in the cloth to steam. Since the wet cloth is already in contact with the stock, the steam is forced into the wood and into the compressed wood fibers.

Generally, dents where the wood fibers have not been broken or cut can be raised fairly easily. Some people contend that if the fibers have been cut, the dents are harder

The Manson barrel crowning tool uses three tiny carbide files smoothly to remove metal from the muzzle. The smooth, chatter-free recessed target crown is complete.

to raise. I haven't always found that to be the case. Generally if I will stick with it long enough, sooner or later the dent or damaged area of the wood will rise. I think folks who have problems with this often just don't keep at it long enough.

While you could use your wife's iron, I wouldn't encourage this. In doing this work you'll inevitably stain the bottom of the iron or get some sort of gunk on it. If it's your iron; no sweat. If, on the other hand, it's your wife's iron, you could be in deep trouble! Believe me, I know from experience! It's a lot better to pick one up at a yard sale or the local discount house.

Several years ago I was in a hobby shop and bought an iron model airplane builders use to heat the plastic covering they use for airplane wings. It's really just a small iron on a handle. It works like a charm and is much handier than a full size clothing iron. I would encourage you to check your local hobby shop for something similar to this. It's a darn handy tool to have in your shop and it sure helps maintain domestic tranquility.

I was able to raise most of the major dents but I purposely left many smaller ones. My objective was not to make the stock look new. In fact, I believe that would be impossible; it had seen far too much use and abuse. Instead, I just wanted it to look its age, be reasonably clean, and not detract from the gun.

Besides, leaving some of the minor dents and dings will help to disguise any work I had done on the stock. One of the things I often notice is that many folks tend to do too much when cleaning or repairing an older firearm. Remember, age and use are part of the history of the gun. If you remove all traces of this honest wear, you're also removing part of the gun's past. I didn't want to do that.

Coffield cuts a slot for the extractor collar on his modified bolt. The collar will support the new bolt stop, which he made out of the center section of an old extractor.

Once the stock had been prepped, I rubbed in a coat of tung oil. Originally the 1903 stocks were simply dipped in vats of linseed or tung oil and allowed to drip dry. That's all the finish that was applied! Once I had rubbed in a coat of finish I put the stock in my drying cabinet and left it there until I was ready to assemble the rifle.

The second rifle I'm working on, which belongs to my buddy, was produced at Rock Island. The stock that came with his rifle at first appeared to be in pretty rough shape and he originally wanted to replace it with a newly made "C" or pistol grip stock. However, after I cleaned the stock, it turned out to be in very nice shape.

It was an original Rock Island stock with a number of arsenal marks still visible. Because of this, we changed plans and decided to keep the original stock on the rifle. Now we'll have a good low number Rock Island rifle with an original Rock Island stock and that's kinda special.

When working on projects like this you often find you'll want to change your plan based on new discoveries. Neither of us would have thought his stock was worth saving until it was cleaned and inspected. Needless to say, that was a very pleasant surprise.

The "C" stock, which came from Dupage Trading Company, is a beautiful, newly made replica. We'll just set that aside for some future project. If you need one of these stocks, by all means, give Jim Yocum at Dupage Trading Company a call. He'll be more than happy to fix you up with one.

With the rifle completed and assembled, I headed for the local range to see how it would shoot. Since I was using a Schultz and Larsen barrel, I was pretty optimistic about how it would perform but you never really know until the bullet meets the paper.

I set up on the smallbore/handgun range with my target at 75 feet. After bore sighting the rifle, I shot a number of groups with some mixed brand ammo. The groups were very good and gave an indication of potentially great performance. I then changed over to some Federal Gold Medal match ammo for some serious shooting. The rifle really liked it!

I got five-shot groups with iron sights that measured only .575" center to center. Most of this dispersion was vertical and I'm sure that was me. Four of the shots were .367" center to center. In short, this rifle is a shooter!

In addition, everyone that saw it seemed to think it was quite a trick. I have to admit that I do enjoy owning and using one-of-a-kind firearms and especially when I did the work myself. If you've followed along this far, I bet you're the same way!

I'm very pleased with how this rifle turned out. I ended up with a unique and unusual .22 that's a delight to shoot, and I may have saved a great old rifle from being broken up for parts or maybe even being made into a lamp! It wasn't easy or fast, but it was challenging and I learned quite a bit while doing it. When you think about it; that in and of itself is a great reason to do almost any gunsmithing project.

The next project on the list is to put together a replica M1D Garand. Like a lot of folks, I've enjoyed reading David Fortier's articles on various sniper rifles and especially the older ones used during World War II and Korea. Unfortunately, there is absolutely no way I'll ever be able to afford an original. So, since I just want a shooter, I think I'll put together a replica of one and you might want to do that as well.

Until next time, good luck and good gunsmithing!

Ask the Gunsmith

By Reid Coffield

DRY-FIRING CENTER-FIRES

Q *Why is it considered improper to dry-fire a center fire rifle? The firing pin is obviously not contacting the chamber or anything. I can understand the problems you might have in dry-firing a .22 rimfire but I just don't get it with saying you shouldn't do this with a center fire. What gives?*

A You are right in that with a center-fire you don't have to worry about the firing pin hitting the chamber rim or wall. However, in many cases there is an internal stop or shoulder for the firing pin inside the bolt or breechblock. When the firing pin is thrust forward, it is abruptly stopped by this internal mechanical feature. That places a stress on the firing pin and can lead to damage or breakage of the firing pin.

Also in some firearms, the firing pin will be designed with enough taper on the tip that it may stick forward in the bolt or breechblock. Then when a live round is chambered and the bolt is closed, the round will be fired. Finally, the firing pin can swage out the area around the firing pin hole as it batters the inside of the hole. This raised area can then lead to feeding problems or even prevent the closure and lock up of the bolt.

When a live round or a snap cap is chambered, the firing pin is cushioned and the amount of travel or movement is limited. This puts less stress on the firing pin and inhibits the damage to the bolt or breechblock.

NOBLE STOCK

Q *I recently bought a .410 pump shotgun at a local yard sale. The gun is in fairly good shape but the buttstock is cracked and missing a large piece of wood where it joins the receiver. It is a Model 70 made by Noble. I checked with a local gun dealer and he told me that the company went out of business many years ago. Do you know where I can get a replacement buttstock? The shotgun was very cheap so I do not want to spend a lot of money on it.*

A Noble Arms was in business from 1946 until around 1971 when it closed its doors. However, parts including the buttstock can still be purchased from Numrich Gun Parts Corporation, P.O. Box 299, West Hurley, N.Y. 12491, telephone 866-686-7424.

MAUSER HSc

Q *I have a .32 Mauser HSc pocket pistol that was given to me by a friend whose father picked it up in Germany during World War II. It is a very streamlined design and I have thought about using it for concealed carry. Do you know of any mechanical problems related to this handgun?*

A Over the years I have worked on just a few of these pistols. In a couple of cases I have seen broken firing pins, but these were easily replaced. If you plan on carrying this pistol I would encourage you to first have a gunsmith check it out. Following that, you really should do a fair amount of shooting with it. It is much better to have a mechanical problem show up at the practice range than later in a more serious situation.

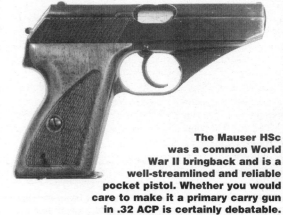

The Mauser HSc was a common World War II bringback and is a well-streamlined and reliable pocket pistol. Whether you would care to make it a primary carry gun in .32 ACP is certainly debatable.

Ask the Gunsmith

By Reid Coffield

WHITNEY SHOTGUN

Q *Can you tell me anything about a Whitney shotgun with an unusual safety? A friend said he saw a Whitney with a grip safety. I never heard of such a thing on a shotgun.*

The Whitney shotgun has a grip safety that must be depressed to allow firing. Coffield says this one was restocked in pine at some point; hardly a conventional stock wood choice!

A Some time ago I had a friend bring in a shotgun that belonged to his grandfather. He said it was unusual and wanted me to take a look at it and tell me anything I could about the history of the gun. I was so taken with its unusual nature that I made some photographs of it. It was a Whitney and just as your friend said, it had a grip safety.

The shotgun was marked as being made by Whitney Safety Firearms Company in Florence, Mass. It is a side-by-side 12-gauge boxlock with concealed hammers. It has twist steel barrels and an extractor rather than ejectors. What is so unusual and unique about this shotgun is the presence of a grip safety! You may have thought that John Browning developed that idea with the 1911 Colt .45 ACP but the basic concept predates the Colt 1911 by many years!

The shotgun functions as normal in that the top lever is pushed to the side, the barrels drop open and the gun is loaded. Once the barrels are locked back in place the user must squeeze the safety lever located behind the trigger guard in order to allow the gun to fire. If the safety lever is not pulled into the pistol grip, the gun will not fire. Very interesting!

Whitney Safety Firearms Company was in business for a relatively short time. One source said that it operated from 1887 until 1894 while another source indicated that it was only in business from 1891 until 1894. In either case, it didn't last long. I believe the owner was William H. Whitney. He obtained a couple of patents relating to firearms including one, #451,191 assigned to Whitney Safety Firearms for a safety lock.

The old shotgun shown in these photographs has certainly seen some hard use over the years and at one point the owner restocked it with a homemade buttstock made of pine. It is an interesting and unique firearm and one that proves that many of the design concepts we think of as originating with a particular firearm may well have had much earlier origins.

DON'T SKIP GRITS

Q *I am planning on refinishing an old Model 97 Winchester shotgun. The gun is very rough with lots of pitting. I know that I will have to do some draw filing in order to get to the bottom of the pits. My question concerns sanding or polishing. Just how important is it for me to go through every graduation of grits as I work my way up to a 400-grit surface polish? As I look at the number of grits from say 100 to 400 it looks like a lot of sanding that may not be necessary. Going from 200 to 240 does not seem like all that big a jump. Why not just go on to 280 and save some time?*

A First of all you could skip some grit graduations but believe me; you'll pay for that in terms of time and labor. If you go from one grit to the next, say 200 to 240, you don't have to spend as much time polishing to remove the previous grit marks. If you skip 240 and go to say 280 or 300, you'll find that it takes a lot more time to get all those 200-grit marks out of the steel. It can be done but you'll waste a lot of time, energy, and use a lot more abrasive! In truth, if you make the smallest possible jump in grits you'll be amazed how quickly and what little effort it takes to remove the previous grit marks. Your polishing will go much, much faster in the long run.

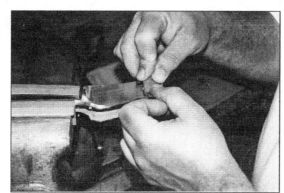

Coffield cautions against skipping grits when polishing if you want to do your polishing as quickly and efficiently as possible. If you skip grits, the finer paper won't remove scratches easily.

SQUIRES BINGHAM PARTS

Q *I have an old .22 rifle that a friend gave to me. It is a Squires Bingham .22 auto. Is the maker still in business? No one I asked could give me any info on it. Also, where can I get parts for it?*

A The maker is still in business. The address is Squires Bingham International, Inc., 179 Boni Serrano Road, Brgy. Socorro, Quezon City 1109, Philippines. For parts here in the U.S., I would suggest you check with Numrich Gun Parts Corporation, Box 299, Dept. SGN, West Hurley, N.Y. 12491, telephone 866-686-7424.

Another source here in the U.S. which is associated with Squires Bingham is Armscor Precision, Inc., 150 N. Smart Way, Dept. SGN, Pahrump, Nev. 89060, telephone 775-537-1444.

WEBLEY "WINGS"

Q *I was at a gun show and was looking at some old British military handguns. I noticed on some of the Webley revolvers there was a wedge shaped piece right in front of the cylinder. What is the function of this piece? A friend told me that it was to help deflect gas as it escaped between the cylinder and the rear of the barrel.*

A The reason for that wedge is not nearly so complex or involved. It was added to the gun simply to keep the face of the cylinder from hanging up as the gun was inserted into a holster.

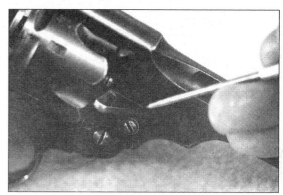

These "wings" on the cylinder retainer of Webley and Enfield revolvers were designed to make holstering the gun easier. They kept the face of the cylinder from hanging up on the holster.

SHOOT DAMACUS BARREL?

Q *As a 30-year subscriber to SGN I wish to ask my first question. I have an extra barrel assembly to my Winchester 97 Takedown shotgun that appears to have a Damascus design to the finish on the barrel. I know that smokeless powder was in for a while when this gun was produced. Is the barrel safe to use and was the finish done for appearances only?*

A Your Damascus barrel was probably produced between 1898 and 1914 when the production of Damascus barrels was discontinued. As for using this barrel today, I would not do so. I fully realize that numbers of folks will disagree with this but I just do not think that it is worth the risk to fire modern shotshells in a barrel that could easily be more than 100 years old. In addition, there is no way short of having the barreled action checked with an X-ray to determine if there is a fault, void, or crack within the wall of the barrel that would not be visible on the outside or in the bore. Even test firing the barrel with a high pressure proof load would not necessarily ensure that the barrel was safe. It might hold together for the test load but fail on the very next shot! I would set the Damascus barrel aside as an interesting and unique collector's item.

CARTRIDGE CARBON BUILDUP

Q *When I shoot my .223 bolt-action rifle, the cartridge case necks have a black deposit around them. Is this an indication that my chamber is not properly cut?*

A Probably not, as most cartridge cases will have some degree of carbon buildup on the case neck after firing. In order to determine if your chamber is oversize or not cut to standard dimensions you will need to make a casting of the chamber. That is the only way I know of to accurately determine the critical dimensions of a rifle chamber. ◎

Gunsmithing isn't all lathes and milling machines. The trusty hacksaw is a basic tool for this project of sporterizing an 8x56mm Austrian Model 95 Mannlicher rifle.

Straight-Pull Sporter

By PAUL MAZAN

Mannlichers are available at "good old days" prices, but what can you really do with one? Mazan shows how to make a beater into a classy hunting arm.

As we get older, we all seem to long for "the good old days." Those longed for days may refer to any number of things. Muscle cars, 50¢ packs of cigarettes, or 30¢ a gallon gas. In this case I'm talking about the good old days when you could buy a surplus Mauser for $25 or so and spend the winter months customizing it into your vision of the perfect sporter.

For years Williams Gun Sight Co. had a booklet out on how to sporterize military rifles, but I no longer see it listed on their website. I spent many a winter night learning to gunsmith on a surplus Mauser and turned several $30 surplus Mausers into sporters worth $25 by replacing the sights, sporterizing the military stock, fitting a recoil pad, drilling and tapping for scope mounts, bending the bolt, etc.

Back then, "sporterized" Mausers were almost literally a dime a dozen. Today there are many more accessories and replacement aftermarket parts available but, alas, the $25 Mauser is history, in fact a $100 Mauser is pretty hard to find in shootable condition.

What I have been seeing a lot of recently are Steyr M95 carbines. At first I didn't think much about them. The design is unusual in that it is a straight-pull bolt and the caliber is weird, using an 8x56R Hungarian rimmed cartridge.

I tried to ignore them but they are being offered online for as little as $69.99 on the auction sites and they just wouldn't go away. Like most guys, I work on anything that comes walking in the door and as I was cleaning the cosmolene off one of the carbines I started to take it much more seriously.

If you correct for inflation, a Mannlicher at $69.95 costs about the same as a Carcano cost in 1964. That makes sporterizing one a paying proposition for the hobbyist.

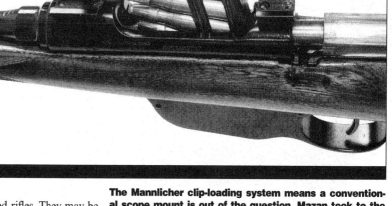

The Mannlicher clip-loading system means a conventional scope mount is out of the question. Mazan took to the Internet to find a Weaver pivot mount that got it done.

The stock is European walnut and is only a couple of inches short of the muzzle. By removing the military sights and adding a forearm tip, I figured it would make a nice Mannlicher-style sporter. The barrel is a light sporter weight and the action functions about as well as any military Mauser.

By this time I was hooked and started to look the gun over to see how difficult a project it might be, how to handle the problems I could identify, and what aftermarket accessories might be available. The first thing I addressed was the ammo. I knew there was surplus military ammo available, but it was World War II vintage with Berdan primers and military ball bullets.

That would be OK for plinking, but not for hunting. I then discovered that Hornady is making bullets and cases for these guns, so factory loads and reloading were both an option. Even better, the gun can be converted to 7.62x54R simply by fitting a barrel.

Why is that good news? Because although the original guns chambered in 7.62 Russian took a bullet about .312", the newer guns chambered in this caliber use .308" bullets and with the popularity of .30 caliber rifles, your selection of bullets is huge.

With the caliber question resolved, my next question was how I could put a scope on the rifle. The Mannlicher design takes a clip that holds the cartridges during feeding and then drops out the bottom of the magazine.

With a scope mounted over the action, there is no clearance for the clip to be inserted to load the gun and you're stuck with a single-shot.

One possible answer is to put a long eye relief scope mounted to the old rear sight base. That would solve the problem of how to load the gun, but I would prefer the traditional scope arrangement if possible. I'm a dyed-in-the wool traditionalist and I just don't like the looks of the scout-scoped rifles. They may be all the rage and handy as a roll of duct tape, but I just don't want one.

I seemed to remember that Weaver made pivot mounts where the scope actually pivoted on a hinge so the shooter could use the rifle's open sights should the scope become fogged or broken. They would be just the ticket for this project. Unfortunately, I also discovered that Weaver had discontinued the pivot mounts several years ago and they were no longer available.

Back in the "Good old days" I would have been out of luck but today we have something called the Internet and lots of auction sites where people try to sell off their old junk to folks that think that junk is a treasure.

I put in the keywords Weaver Pivot into the search engines of Gunbroker, Auction Arms, and the gun hating e auction site and got a list of bases and rings for sale at really cheap prices. The only thing missing was a fits chart to tell me what bases I needed.

Digging through old Brownells catalogs (I keep mine forever for reference, don't you?) I found a chart that listed the pivot bases but, nothing was ever made for the M95.

Measuring the front and rear rings, I found that they were the same diameter as the rings on the small ring Mauser. The only problem was that the rear ring on the Steyr is flattened.

With the bases priced at $1.99 each, I went ahead and ordered a set of pivot bases, The front is Weaver #146 and the rear is Weaver #155. The front fit like it was made for the gun but I had to flatten the underside of the rear base with a file to get it to fit the Steyr rear ring.

This may mean it will have to be shimmed to get the scope zeroed but bore sighting shows there to be more than enough adjustment to bring the crosshairs on target. I ordered a pair of Weaver pivot rings at the same time and paid $10 for them. These were the prices in early spring when I was doing this project and there were a lot of bases and rings available. Keep in mind that prices and availability on these discontinued items may vary and if you are planning to try this yourself I would advise that you look for rings and bases before you start the project.

My experience with the scope mounts was typical of everything else I looked for in the aftermarket. Nobody makes a replacement stock, so you will have to work with the military one. There are no aftermarket triggers, bottom metal, large head safeties or anything else for these guns, so you're going to have to be a bit creative.

I removed the barrel bands and sling swivel, stripped the military stock, degreased it with oven cleaner, raised the dents, fitted a rubber rifle pad, plugged the holes for the barrel bands in the forend and the sling swivel at the wrist.

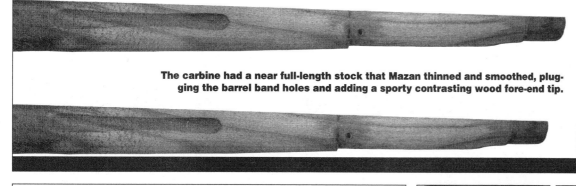

The carbine had a near full-length stock that Mazan thinned and smoothed, plugging the barrel band holes and adding a sporty contrasting wood fore-end tip.

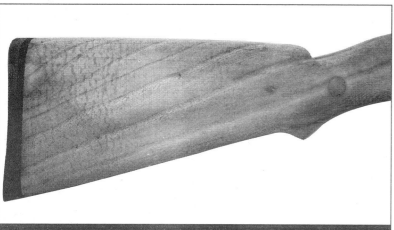

Mazan added a rubber pad to the butt to tame the 8x56 recoil and then rasped off the vestigial pistol grip, making the stock into a straight-gripped English style.

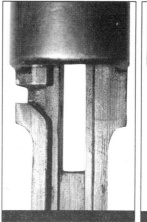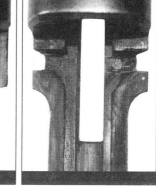

The cut for the reversed safety is made by duplicating the original cut from the left side of the bolt. This was done with a hand file. Action symmetry is handy here.

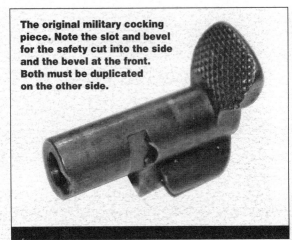

The original military cocking piece. Note the slot and bevel for the safety cut into the side and the bevel at the front. Both must be duplicated on the other side.

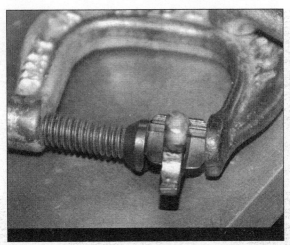

Modifying the safety for left-hand use required metal to be added with a TIG welder. The addition then had to be shaped very carefully. This was the tough part.

Mazan welded a turned-down sporter-style bolt handle to the left side of the bolt. Remember to allow room to clear the stock, since the bolt doesn't rotate for clearance.

Here's the partially modified cocking piece. The thumbpiece has been removed and filed and the safety slot is cut. It still has to be polished and the front bevel cut.

Taking a cabinet rasp, I removed about a pound of wood from the back end of the stock, slimming it down to a sporter contour. There is a little bump pretending to be a pistol grip that I rasped out, but you could flatten the area and glue on a piece of walnut and shape it into a pistol grip if you prefer.

With the butt slimmed down (I wish I could slim my own down as easily) I turned my attention to the forearm. Once again using a cabinet rasp, I tapered the wood from the front of the receiver to the tip, removing the steps for the barrel bands and the finger grooves.

Squaring the tip of the stock on a sander, I installed two pins into the fore-end and drilled matching holes in the walnut tip and glued the tip to the stock. If you don't like the Mannlicher style stock, it can simply be cut off and rounded it to the contour you do like.

I also discarded the upper handguard and removed the military sights from the barrel. If the carbine is to be left as a right handed gun, all that is left is finishing the wood and metal and reassembly. All pretty standard stuff and the final outcome is pretty much dependant on your ability with a wood rasp and sandpaper.

I would also suggest the addition of a bolt handle, as the military handle sticks straight out and has a ball on

the end you could almost play golf with. Next comes the fun part.

I confess to being a militant left-hander. You know the kind of guy that walks into your shop looking for a left-handed bolt action, semi automatic, chainsaw. Yep, that's me, but my endless search for a left-handed chainsaw is a story for another time.

When you show me a left-handed Remington, Ruger, or Winchester, I immediately want to know why I should have to pay more to get the same gun just because it's left-handed.

No, I won't buy a right-handed gun and make do. If you want my money, sell me something made for me to use like you do for your right-handed customers.

If you do this conversion you're going to have the price of the gun at $75 to $100 and the cost of a barrel into it and all the rest is shop time. Converting the Steyr 95 to left-hand operation is not too difficult and it will put something

Get That M1903 Mannlicher Back in Action!

By John Enright

It's a great-shooting gun, but at $2.50 a round, it's hard to justify a long range session. Here's how to cut that ammo cost: convert to 7.62x39.

The magnificent 1903 Mannlicher-Schoenauer rifle (to be referred to as the MS) and its classic caliber, the 6.5x54, have long since ascended to legendary status. The legend was carved out by famous hunters of yore such as "Karamojo" Bell and Ernest Hemingway, to name but two.

The rifle was first made as the Model 1900, based on an improved version of Germany's Model 1888 military rifle. Ferdinand Ritter Von Mannlicher then combined the new action with an improved rotary magazine designed by Otto Schoenauer, factory manager of the Austrian Arms Works, Steyr. The Model 1900 was first made in small numbers as a military rifle.

In 1903 Greece adopted the Mannlicher Schoenauer in 6.5x54 as its military rifle. The same year the MS was

first made and sold as a sporting rifle. The first caliber chambered was the 6.5x54, with others added later. Both the sporting and military models were henceforth known as the 1903 Model.

The 1903s became available on the surplus market during the glory days of the 1960s, where they were sold as complete rifles, carbines, or as barreled actions. The vast majority that I saw had badly worn or eroded barrels, mute testimony to use, and the effects of corrosive priming. The question arises as to what to do with them. Obviously, if the bore is good, keep them as they are. The 6.5x54 is a very good cartridge.

If the barrel is beyond redemption, the actions are well worth converting. However, problems arise, or, more correctly, magazine problems arise. The splendid magazine

has been made for the original 6.5x54, and that is the cartridge it works superbly with. I have heard of one converted to .243 Win. and I've seen them converted to .257 Roberts and 7x57, but it is extremely difficult and there are no guarantees. Each individual billet must be machined with, usually, some final handwork. The job is both arduous and extremely expensive.

Another alternative is to convert the rifle to a wildcat cartridge, based on the 6.5x54 case. The late Morris Rawlings, a Newcastle, NSW, gunsmith did just that. He necked the 6.5 case to .22 and made up a reamer to chamber it. The cartridge fed and worked quite well, giving a velocity very close to the .22-250.

In Vol. 2 of *Handbook For Handloaders*, P.O. Ackley mentions this cartridge and also the 6.5/.243, where the parent case was necked to 6mm. I have never seen this conversion.

These cartridges work, if you want to go the wildcat route. Not everyone wants to obtain the custom dies and commence case forming, though. There is another difficulty. To my knowledge, no major manufacturer loads the 6.5x54, or makes cases for it. The last to do so was RWS but, the cartridge is no longer available. The round is available from Old Western Scrounger (www.ows-ammo.com) and Shell Reloading (www.obsoleteammo.com) but otherwise, they're pretty thin on the ground.

So, the 1903 military MS looks, at first glance, too difficult and expensive to convert to another caliber. I originally thought so until, around 20 years ago, I came up with a fairly easy solution. If longer and wider cartridges

unique on your gun rack that the discount stores won't have. What makes this conversion both easy and quick is that the bolt and receiver are very symmetrical. In other words the left and right sides are dimensionally the same.

Mazan uses a "shoeshine" technique with abrasive cloth to polish the welded area of the bolt. Neat welding helps keep down the amount of this work you have to do.

To remove the bolt from the gun, simply push the trigger forward and pull the bolt to the rear. It should come free of the receiver with little effort. To modify the bolt, you will first need to disassemble it. The straight-pull action has a bolt within a bolt.

As the bolt assembly is removed from the gun, the inner bolt with the locking lugs is extended and must be compressed. To compress it, put the head of the bolt on your bench top and push down. Keeping it compressed, pull the cocking piece to the rear and rotate the safety under it to serve as a stop.

When properly installed, the safety occupies a position 180° from its original spot. Getting it correctly shaped and fitted is essential to proper rifle operation.

You can then unscrew the cocking piece and remove the inner bolt by reversing the bolt and pressing the threaded end of the firing pin against the bench until the bolt head extends from the outer bolt body. Once the bolt head and extractor move upward, you can grasp them and remove them from the bolt.

If it still won't come out, use a brass punch and gently tap on the back of the firing pin until it moves forward and out. The safety is removed simply by removing the screw at the back of the bolt. Removal of the firing pin isn't necessary for making the conversion, but you will probably want to clean it.

All that is necessary is to control the pressure of the expanding firing pin spring as you unscrew the firing pin spring retainer from the back of the bolt head. As always, be very careful when removing the firing pin spring retainer. It is un-

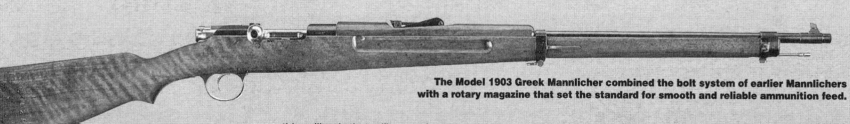

The Model 1903 Greek Mannlicher combined the bolt system of earlier Mannlichers with a rotary magazine that set the standard for smooth and reliable ammunition feed.

require so much work to convert the magazine, why not look for an alternative?

Obviously, for a cost-efficient conversion to utilize the action and magazine as is, a shorter cartridge having the same profile or width is required. It was around this time that the Chinese SKS 7.62x39 semi auto rifles arrived on the market here in Australia. The rifles were sold at almost giveaway prices, as was their military ammunition. They continued to be sold until 1996 when the Australian Government, in a well-documented knee-jerk reaction, banned the sale, possession and use of all semi auto rifles and shotguns.

A little experimentation revealed that the 7.62x39 cartridge is a perfect fit in the 6.5x54MS magazine. It presents from the magazine to be controlled during its very smooth feeding. Its profile and its length of 39mm, some 15mm shorter than the 6.5 MS, means that no machining or milling of the magazine cartridge billets is necessary to ensure feeding.

The 7.62x39 cartridge feeds "as is," without any alteration or adjustment to the original magazine being required. On my rifle, feed from magazine to chamber is like running a knife through water. A great advantage to

this caliber is that military and commercial ammunition is universally available.

The next part of the conversion was rebarreling and just what bore diameter to use. The caliber/diameter is not always understood. The standard .30 caliber is .300" measured on the bore lands, the highest point of the rifling. The bore groove diameter (the rifling's deepest point) for that caliber is .308. The .303 land diameter is .303", and the groove diameter is .311". The 7.62x39 military bullet diameter is .311", as is some of the commercial ammunition. Other commercial ammunition is available with a .308" diameter.

If you intend to use only military ammunition, the barrel may be better with a .311" groove size bore. Unfortunately this bore size is by no means as easy to obtain as the popular and more common .308" groove diameter. One alternative is a custom bored barrel, whether having a worn .308" barrel rebored or having a new one bored to that diameter. Neither avenue would be inexpensive but, there is a cheap alternative.

As mentioned, bore size of the .303 British cartridge is .303" land depth, and .311" groove depth. An ex-military barrel with the shank cut off, a new 7.62x39 chamber reamed and new correct sized threads cut would screw

straight in. The only drawback is that the .308 commercial ammunition will not be able to be accurately utilized.

There is a simple answer. The best solution seems to be to use a .308 bore size. A 7.62x39 reamer, made by the well-known Clymer company is used to cut the new chamber. The Clymer reamer has a long, tapering leade. The leade area is probably best described as that section of the barrel, just in front of the chamber but before the rifling commences, which is also known as freebore. The difference here is that, where the freebore is the same diameter, the leade tapers.

A .311" diameter projectile fired through the tapering leade is swaged down to .308" and is safe to use with no diminution in accuracy. Naturally, the .308" diameter projectile passes through the leade with no effect.

The Clymer reamer gives the shooter the best of both worlds as they are able to safely use all available 7.62x39 ammunition. Not only can they use all ammunition types but they can do so without any loss of accuracy due to bullet size.

If desired, the original military stock can be cut down and remodeled. My rifle came as a barreled action so that option was denied. If a new stock is required, it is not so hard to obtain. The MS sporter was made in a variety of

The sporter bolt handle flows perfectly toward the trigger for fast and easy retraction and is perfectly in keeping with the straight grip and Mannlicher fore-end.

The rather low comb gives plenty of clearance for the thumb when cycling the bolt. You don't want to get pinched here when doing some fast firing of the rifle.

der tension from the firing pin spring and unless controlled will either fly into the deepest, darkest, most inaccessible corner of your shop never to be seen again, or "you'll shoot your eye out, kid."

The trigger unit is removed from the receiver by pushing out the sear pin and allowing the trigger and the sear lever to drop free of the receiver. Your bolt is now disassembled for conversion

You will notice that there is a cut on the left side of the receiver rail just behind the rear ring. You must duplicate that cut on the right side to reverse the safety. The job can be done with a file and will go easier once you have cut through the case hardening.

A grinding wheel can be handy to cut through the case hardening, but be careful, try to make it a mirror image of the cut on the left side. That is the only modification necessary to the receiver, so now we will move to the bolt and the cocking piece.

The first step is to measure the distance from the edge of the cocking piece hole in the bolt body to the left edge of the bolt. Duplicate that measurement on the right side of the bolt and cut the bolt handle off, leaving the left and right sides of the back of the bolt the same size.

Once the bolt handle is removed, take a file and contour the right side of the bolt to match the left. Once the contour is the same, you can duplicate the cut for the safety with the side of a file. Work slowly and match both the width of the cut as well as its depth and angle.

Then carefully measure, drill, countersink and tap the hole for the safety screw. The screw that came with the gun is a metric thread, so I simply substituted a 6-48 screw because I don't have any metric taps. First drill the hole to depth with a #31 drill. Leave the bolt fixtured in your drill press, replace the # 31 drill with a #25 clearance drill and redrill the hole through to the slot you cut for the safety.

Once again, leave the bolt in place and put your 6-48 tap in your drill chuck and pass it through the top part of the hole that you just drilled through with the clearance drill. Turn the drill press chuck by hand and tap the bottom of the hole from the front of the safety slot to depth.

Back the tap out by again turning the drill chuck by hand, remove the tap and replace it with a drill the size of the head of the screw or a 6-48 countersink and countersink the hole so that the head will fit flush with the bolt when screwed down. Using one setup and using the drill chuck as a tap guide insures that all the holes line up straight and the tap follows the hole precisely.

The cocking piece is next and once again you will see a cut on the left side of the piece that must be duplicated on the right so the safety will clear the cocking piece when in the off position and lock it when on. Again, this can be done with hand tools if you don't own a mill.

large calibers. This necessitated that the rotary magazine cartridge billets were made wider, according to case size.

Stock width was kept to roughly the size of the smaller calibers or case width by making the wood surrounding the magazine thinner. Sometimes they crack, sometimes not, but this is the reason most aftermarket stockists or suppliers of semi-finished stocks can supply one to fit a MS. I contacted Geoff Slee and purchased a replacement stock. I thought of the full length carbine style but elected to take a conventional type.

The bolt handle can be turned down or, if required, swept back. A bolt handle can also be made up to duplicate the famous MS "butterknife" style in keeping with the rifle's lineage. The bolt handle is integral with the bolt

Although no modern rifle would have the bolt handle so far forward, the Greek Mannlicher can be made into an attractive sporting rifle with exceptionally smooth feed.

body, which should not pose too many problems with alteration or replacement. If iron sights are to be used, the bolt handle can be left as is, although most will want to alter it. If any scope except a long eye relief "Scout" type is contemplated, the bolt handle will have to be altered.

There may be aftermarket triggers available, but, I couldn't locate one. Instead, the heavy, two-stage military trigger was altered to single-stage, and the pressure lightened. It is now a crisp, creep free trigger breaking evenly at 3.5 pounds (1.3kg). This is not a job for an amateur and should be left to a qualified gunsmith.

If it is desired to fit a scope, the split bridge precludes the use of many scope mounts. A side mount of the correct dimensions can be fitted and will give good results. An alternative is to use the single mount system as made B Square company and currently by Lynx. This type mount consists of a rigid bridge, which is attached to the front of the receiver only. The rest hangs suspended across the action but does not make contact with it.

My rifle has a rechambered 24-inch (600mm) .308 Omark target barrel, turned down to sporter profile, bedded and floated. The barrel may be a little long for some preferences but to each his own. I want to see what ballistic advantage is gained by this length. Currently a Tasco 1.5 -5x40 scope is fitted. I obtained 7.62x39 factory loaded cartridges made by PMC and Norma. I also obtained Lee 7.62x39 reloading dies, and Sierra .308 125-grain spitzer bullets.

The rifle was sighted over a bench rest, then shot for accuracy. The results were better than anticipated. Three-

The rotary magazine is the key to the 03 Mannlicher's smooth operation. These have been seen in Steyr bolt guns, the Johnson and the Savage 99, but not many others.

shot groups shot with Norma factory loads came in at 1.45 inches. The worst was 2.25 inches, with a called flier. The average group size was a fraction under 2 inches. I think I can do better with reloads, but I'm not disappointed with the factory average. For a rifle that won't be used on game beyond 150 yards, that's perfectly adequate. It won't see much use on targets at more than 200 yards.

I believe this rifle is unique in the Southern Hemisphere and, perhaps the world. I do know that the MS conversion to 7.62x39 is extremely practical. I do know that, depending on how far the owner wants to go, a financially viable one in terms of rifle and cartridge. ◎

What had been a sad-sack surplus rifle is now a classy German-style sporter that will stand out in any company. There's a lot of work here, but not really much expense.

Measure its depth and width and locate the front edge by measuring from the front of the cocking piece to the edge of the cut. Match that measurement on the right side and duplicate the cut. It was nice of Mannlicher to provide us such a symmetrical design and handy patterns to duplicate when converting his design for the lefty. I'm sure that wasn't his intent but it certainly makes things easier.

The last thing to consider with the cocking piece is that huge checkered thumb piece used to recock the gun in the case of a light primer strike or defective primer. If you like it, you can leave it as is, modify it or remove it entirely.

Personally, I see no need for all that added mass so I cut it off and rounded the cocking piece. In a sporter a light strike or hard primer will simply be ejected and a new cartridge chambered. Most modern guns like the Remington 700, Winchester Model 70 and for that matter, the 98 Mauser, don't have them and it seems to be a relic of the 19th century.

Now we are off to the welders. A new bolt handle needs to be welded on the left side of the bolt after the original safety slot and screw hole are filled. We can use a much more elegant replacement bolt handle and weld it on at a downward angle so it isn't sticking straight out.

Do be careful not to make it lie too close to the stock, because you will want to be able to get under and behind it when operating its straight-pull action. Take the safety lever itself to the welders because you will notice there is a camming surface on the end of it that will need to be reversed. It is there to cam the safety, and you may have enough metal on yours to cut the opposite side without adding any metal but I did have to add metal to mine.

The fitting of the safety is probably the most difficult job of this entire project, and it will help to have a spare on hand to look at as you try to duplicate a reversed version of it. Angle of the cut, height of the bolt stopping face and height of the camming surface itself are all critical to get the safety to function properly.

My first attempt led to a safety that, when on, would allow the bolt to move just enough when the trigger was pulled to fire the gun when taken off safe. I had to have it rewelded and start over before I got it right.

I would recommend assembling the gun and taking it out for a session at the range before polishing and finishing just to be sure you are happy with the function of the bolt and safety.

The result of all this work is a light, handy, easy-to-carry carbine length firearm with plenty of punch for deer-sized game. I added a long triangular checkering pattern to enhance the long sleek lines of the Mannlicher design and am delighted with the result.

Maybe in this case those good old days we were discussing when a guy could sporterize an old military rifle for a reasonable price are back. If you can weld, or have a friend who can, your only costs are the rifle, the mounts, and the bolt handle. That puts it at around $100, and just over $200 if we add a new barrel. Not at all a bad deal in today's economy. ◉

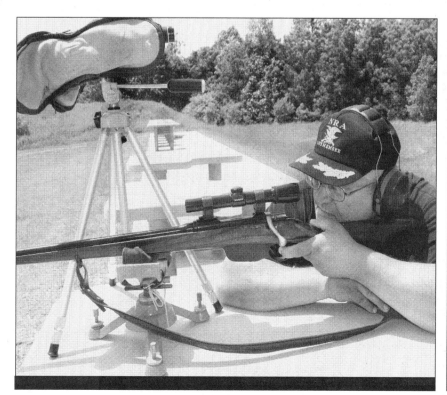

The 8x56 is a relatively hard-kicking caliber, so you're not going to turn this gun into a target rifle, but it makes a perfectly usable sporter for deer or elk hunting.

Straight-pulls are an acquired taste, but offer some variety in a world of turn-bolt actions. With Mannlichers available at very low prices, why not try one?

A Mosin-Nagant? Sporter?!?

By Reid Coffield

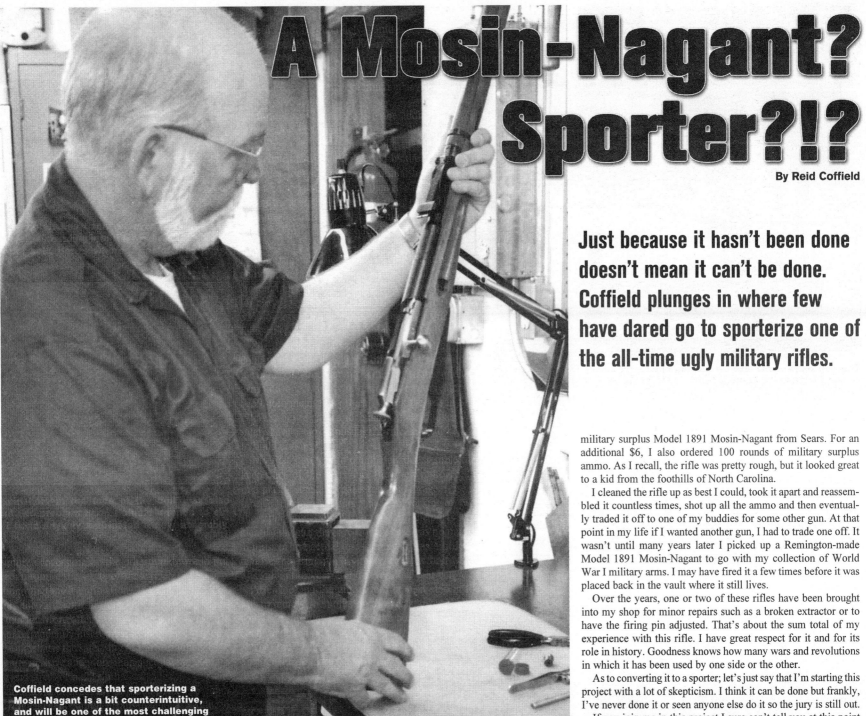

Coffield concedes that sporterizing a Mosin-Nagant is a bit counterintuitive, and will be one of the most challenging gunsmithing projects he has ever taken on.

Just because it hasn't been done doesn't mean it can't be done. Coffield plunges in where few have dared go to sporterize one of the all-time ugly military rifles.

military surplus Model 1891 Mosin-Nagant from Sears. For an additional $6, I also ordered 100 rounds of military surplus ammo. As I recall, the rifle was pretty rough, but it looked great to a kid from the foothills of North Carolina.

I cleaned the rifle up as best I could, took it apart and reassembled it countless times, shot up all the ammo and then eventually traded it off to one of my buddies for some other gun. At that point in my life if I wanted another gun, I had to trade one off. It wasn't until many years later I picked up a Remington-made Model 1891 Mosin-Nagant to go with my collection of World War I military arms. I may have fired it a few times before it was placed back in the vault where it still lives.

Over the years, one or two of these rifles have been brought into my shop for minor repairs such as a broken extractor or to have the firing pin adjusted. That's about the sum total of my experience with this rifle. I have great respect for it and for its role in history. Goodness knows how many wars and revolutions in which it has been used by one side or the other.

As to converting it to a sporter; let's just say that I'm starting this project with a lot of skepticism. I think it can be done but frankly, I've never done it or seen anyone else do it so the jury is still out.

If you join me in this project I sure can't tell you at this point where we'll end up, but I can guarantee that we'll both learn somethin' on the way. So…let's get started.

The first thing we need to do is get a rifle. There are lots of Mosin-Nagants out there and finding one shouldn't be any trouble at all. Almost any gun shop or gun show will have 'em. If you can't find one locally, then just check the ads here in SHOTGUN

Why? Why in the devil would anyone want to even attempt to sporterize a Mosin-Nagant rifle? Unlike the 98 Mauser or 1903 Springfield, the Mosin-Nagant does not offer the gunsmith hobbyist the smooth, flowing lines that ultimately allow him to build a sleek, elegant-looking sporter.

The action is not easily rebarreled or even converted to any other caliber. However, the Nagant does offer the hobbyist something perhaps just as important. It's inexpensive. In fact, it's darn cheap and it's available in huge numbers! It is currently the most inexpensive military bolt-action available to the American gun owner.

Century International Arms, Inc., 430 South Congress Dr., Suite 1, Dept. SGN, DelRay Beach, Fla. 33445, telephone 800-527-1252, has imported these rifles by the shipload and is currently offering them at incredibly attractive prices. Just check the ads here in SHOTGUN NEWS for Century as well as many other wholesalers.

Prices on various models of bolt-action 7.62x54R Nagants in excellent condition are more often than not well below $100. In fact, not more than a week or so ago I ran across a dealer that was selling M1944 carbines for less than $65 each. These were not worn-out junkers. They were wartime production guns that had been rebuilt at the end of the war and then placed in storage.

With prices like these and what seems like an unending supply, the gunsmith hobbyist simply can not afford to ignore this rifle. There's no denying it, the design of the rifle does pose some challenges. In fact, "challenges" might not be a strong enough word to describe what you'll face!

When Bob Hunnicutt, my boss here at SHOTGUN NEWS, suggested I look at a series on sporterizing the Mosin Nagant, I honestly thought he was kidding! He wasn't. Editors seldom have a sense of humor for some reason or other. But the more I thought about it, the more interesting the project became and the more I found myself challenged by the idea of turning what must be one of the world's most unattractive military bolt-action rifles into an acceptable sporter.

My first contact with the Mosin-Nagant took place when I was 16. As I recall I saved up the princely sum of $12.95 and ordered a

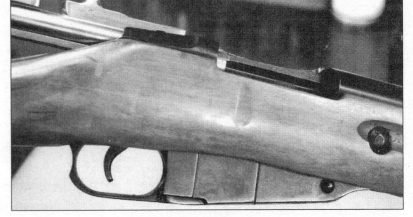

The Mosin's protruding fixed five-round magazine gives the rifle a very distinctive look and makes it very difficult to give it the smooth, clean flowing lines of a sporter.

The bolt handle was fine for kicking open with an ice-covered boot on the Eastern Front, but is located too far forward. Dealing with this will be a major challenge.

NEWS. Of course you can do like I did, and contact the folks at Century International Arms. They have 'em and will be more than happy to fix you up with a good one.

Before we get deeper into picking a rifle, I darn well better say something about collectables or I will be on the receiving end of numerous nastygrams from military rifle collectors. There are folks that collect Mosin-Nagants and there are some that are truly collectable you don't want to convert. Right off hand I'm thinking of Mosin-Nagants that were made by Remington and Westinghouse (Yep, Westinghouse made Russian rifles during World War I, as did manufacturers in France and Switzerland).

There are also Mosin-Nagants that have unusual markings indicating use by the Germans during both World Wars. Then of course, there are authentic Mosin-Nagant sniper rifles. If you run across any of these, they might make a great investment but you sure don't want to convert it into a sporter. Stick with common run-of-the-mill rifles.

If you pick one up in a local gun shop or at a gun show you will have a chance to look it over before you buy. There are a few things you might want to look for. First you need to be aware that late World War II production Mosin-Nagants can be really, really rough. The Russians needed guns by the hundreds of thousands and by 1943 they were not at all picky about metal finish or fit. All they were interested in was whether or not it would fire.

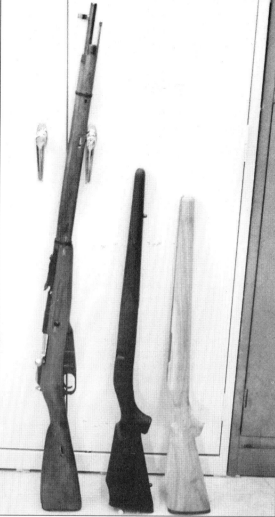

Shown with an issue Mosin-Nagant are two aftermarket stocks. Advanced Technology makes a handy synthetic version, while Boyd's offers a more traditional walnut stock.

Right now in my shop I have several Model 91/30 Mosin-Nagants. One is early war-dated 1940, another is dated 1942, and one is late-war dated 1943. The 1943 rifle is rough as a cob and that's being kind in terms of the description.

The 1943 rifle has incredibly deep machine marks all over the receiver. In addition, the top of the receiver was evidently cut on a milling machine using two contour cutters to give it a nice radius. The problem was that one of the cutters was worn more than the other. Consequently there is a "step" that runs the length of the front receiver ring right dead center at 12 o'clock.

It would be the devil to clean this receiver up. You would be faced with hours of file work and polishing. Because of that I would encourage you to try to find one that was made in 1942 or earlier. That'll save you a lot of work.

Also, check the bore. It would be a waste of time and energy to spend the hours that we'll need for this project on a rifle with a shot out, corroded bore. While you're at

Given the extensive modifications he plans to the Mosin's metal parts, Coffield decided a wood stock as made by Boyd's offered better flexibility for this project.

it, check the face of your bolt as well. On rifles that have been used a lot, the corrosive gas from the primer will erode the face of the bolt around the firing pin. This can be severe. I would pass on a rifle that had an eroded bolt face as that usually indicates a lot of firing with corrosive primers. Normally if the bolt face is bad, then the barrel is pretty bad as well.

If you see a lot of pitting on the outside of the rifle, pass on it. More than likely, there is pitting under the stock that you can't see.

Don't worry too much about the wood, as we will discard the stock. At the same time, though, the condition of the stock is probably a darn good indication of how much use or abuse the rifle has had. If the stock is beat up, cracked, oil soaked, and basically just in terrible shape, then there is a darn good chance that the steel parts are just as bad.

Currently a lot of rifles coming into the country are in very good shape. The three I have all appeared to have been rebuilt or reconditioned by the Russians after World War II before they were put into storage. If you have a chance to get one, these are probably the best rifle for our project. Again, Century Arms as well as many other dealers who advertise here in SHOTGUN NEWS have these rifles.

I've thought a bit about this rifle and what I would like to do to make it as attractive as possible. I envision a rifle with a wood

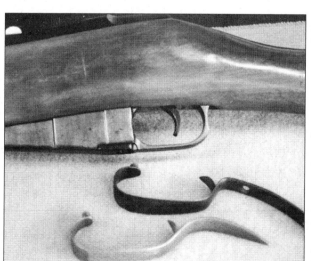

As he did with the Mauser 98, Coffield will use a shotgun trigger guard instead of the military guard. Getting it to mate with the rifle's action will be the fun part.

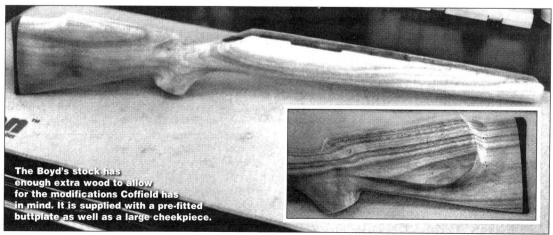

The Boyd's stock has enough extra wood to allow for the modifications Coffield has in mind. It is supplied with a pre-fitted buttplate as well as a large cheekpiece.

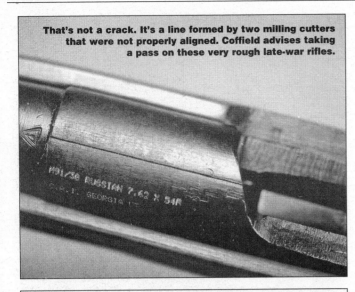

That's not a crack. It's a line formed by two milling cutters that were not properly aligned. Coffield advises taking a pass on these very rough late-war rifles.

Take a look at the rough machine marks on the receiver of this late-war rifle. They can be removed with hand tools, but it will take lots of time and elbow grease.

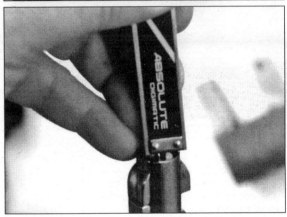

Place the end of the caliper over the tip of the firing pin and open the jaws. A rod will project downward until it contacts the face of the bolt. That's your measurement.

stock. The bottom metal or trigger guard and magazine box assembly spoil the lines of the gun. It's bulky and blocky and extends below the stock. I want to modify that and this will probably entail converting the rifle to a blind box magazine.

At the same time I will fit a shotgun style trigger guard as I did on the Mauser 98 project some time back. For my money that is one of the best ways to give the rifle a sleek, sporter appearance.

When undertaking a project like this where I will be doing a lot of work to a gun, I believe it's always best to make a list of the major jobs or parts of that project. Also, it's a darn good idea to list those jobs in the order that they will be done.

This bit of paperwork serves a couple of functions. First, it helps us to approach the project in an orderly and systematic manner. It will hopefully keep us for doing somethin' and then realizing that we shoulda done somethin' else before that and now we have to redo part of our work. That's a royal pain in the tush and somethin' I just hate to do. And yes, I've done exactly that more than once. So...let's make a list.

#1. Carefully inspect the rifle. Check the bore, headspace, firing pin protrusion, locking lug contact, etc. We absolutely do not want to get halfway through the project and find out that our receiver is cracked or some other major problem.

#2. Select an aftermarket stock. While it would be possible to cut a stock out from a blank piece of wal-

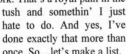

In your preliminary check of the rifle, be sure to check the firing pin protrusion. It needs to stick out enough to ignite the primer, not enough to pierce it.

nut, there are some commercial alternatives that will make stocking this rifle a lot faster and easier. By the way, there are some good serviceable synthetic stocks available but we'll pass on those and I'll tell you why when we get to selecting our stock.

#3. Cut and crown the barrel. We need to make the barrel proportional to the stock we will use. One of the simplest ways to enhance the looks of a sporterized military rifle is to simply have the length of the barrel properly proportioned to the stock. Later I'll give you a simple rule of thumb to do this.

#4. Remove the original military rear sight. Later we will want to install some good commercial sights on the barrel. Even if we set the rifle up for a scope, it never hurts to have a set of backup iron sights.

#5. Inlet and bed the action in the stock.

#6. Fit and modify the bottom metal.

#7. Shape the stock. One of the great features of the stock we will be using is that it has extra wood. It will allow us to do some custom modifications to make it more attractive and functional.

#8. Install a recoil pad. The older I get, the less I like recoil and the 7.62x54mm cartridge is no wimp by any means! A good 1-inch pad will make shooting a lot more pleasant and the more comfortable a rifle is to shoot, the more it will be shot!

#9. Install sling swivel studs.

#10. Modify the bolt handle. In addition to the bottom metal, the extreme forward placement of the bolt handle gives the Mosin-Nagant a very unique and not very pleasing look. With most sporters, the handle is just bent down or a new one is welded to the original handle stub. We'll try something very different! I've never done this and it might not work. If it doesn't then I might be buying another bolt from Numrich Gun Parts!

#11. Install commercial iron sights on the barrel.

#12. Drill and tap the receiver for a scope mount.

#13. Sand and finish the stock.

#14. Prepare metal for refinishing by polishing, bead blasting, etc.

#15. Refinish the metal. Normally I like to blue my metal but with this rifle I might just want to go with one of the bake on finishes.

#16. Checker the stock. While we're at it we might as well do a bit of checkering. It's not all that hard and even a simple, conservative pattern can make a sporter look really nice.

#17. Reassemble the rifle and head for the range! By the time we get to this point we will definitely be ready to do some serious shooting and hopefully we'll have a pretty nice and very unique sporter.

OK, let's get started. We have our rifle so let's take it apart. If you are not sure how to do this or you need a disassembly manual I would highly recommend the *NRA Firearms Assembly Guide for Rifles and Shotguns.* You can get this from the NRA or from just about any of the book dealers that advertise in SGN. Another great book on the Mosin-Nagant is *The Mosin-Nagant Rifle* by Terence W. Lapin. This is a North Cape publication and you can find their ads here in SGN as well.

It's important to check the uniformity of contact by the locking lugs. A lot of folks wouldn't bother to do this but it's important for both safety and functioning. We definitely want both lugs to engage the lug seats in the receiver.

When the cartridge is fired, a tremendous amount of pressure is built up in the chamber. Both lugs should bear against the lug seats and share the burden of containing that pressure. If only one is doing all the work, then there is always a good possibility that lug might just fail or crack. In addition, if only one lug is carrying the load, then when the gun fires the bolt head will twist out of alignment with the chamber. This can lead to extraction as well as accuracy problems.

Checking this is dirt simple. Just coat the rear surfaces of the bolt locking lugs with Dykem or machinist layout fluid and let it dry. Now insert the bolt into the receiver, pushing the handle all the way forward and then down, locking the bolt.

Open and then close the bolt at least half a dozen times. Remove the bolt from the receiver and inspect the rear of the locking lugs. You should have a considerable amount of the

Dykem removed from both lugs and that would indicate that both lugs were seating.

If your lugs do not seat evenly, my first option would be to replace the bolt head. These are available from Numrich Gun Parts Corp., 226 Williams Lane, Dept. SGN, West Hurley, N.Y. 12491, telephone 866-686-7424. The other option would be to lap in the lugs, but this would require pulling the barrel from the receiver. A few bucks for another bolt head is a lot less hassle!

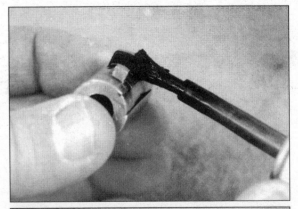

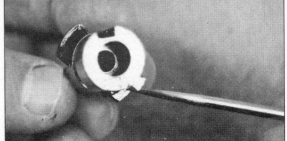

Coat the back of the locking lugs with machinist layout fluid. After cycling the bolt, you should see evidence of contact between the lugs and their seats in the receiver.

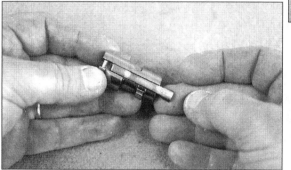

To check headspace on a Mosin-Nagant you should remove the bolt head from the bolt body. Coffield also advises removing the extractor from the bolt head when headspacing.

Firing pin protrusion is also important. If the protrusion is not enough, the rifle will not fire or will not fire reliably. If it is excessive, the firing pin can pierce the primer and release hot gases under great pressure into the shooter's face. Not a good thing!

Insert the headspace gauge into the chamber with shop tweezers. Then move it forward and rotate into a locked position with shop tweezers or bent needle-nose pliers.

While there are some military gauges around for checking firing pin protrusion, I prefer to use one that I made up years ago in gunsmithing school. All you need to do is pull the bolt from the rifle, then move the cocking piece to the left or counterclockwise. The firing pin will protrude through the bolt head. It can now be measured.

If you don't have a special tool for this, you can use the back end of a dial caliper. I believe that high power rifles should have a firing pin protrusion of about .064" plus or minus .002". These are the figures that Roy Dunlap used and they've worked well for me over the years.

If your firing pin protrusion is excessive, it can be corrected easily. The Mosin-Nagant has a unique feature in that the firing pin screws into the cocking piece. If protrusion is excessive, just disassemble the bolt and turn the firing pin clockwise to decrease the protrusion. If you need more protrusion, turn it counterclockwise.

There are flats on the firing pin body that allow you to put a wrench on it to turn it. Note that there are witness marks on the rear face of the cocking piece. Make sure the slot in the rear of the firing pin is aligned with these marks.

To check the headspace, you will need a set of headspace gauges. I think any of the reamer manufacturers such as Manson Precision would be able to supply these. The set I have is an old Clymer set that I got years ago.

Once you have the gauges, clean the chamber and the face of the barrel. Remove any grease or dirt that might have accumulated over the years. Next disassemble the bolt and remove the bolt head. Use a punch to drive the extractor to the rear and out of the bolt head. You need to remove the extractor so you don't get a false reading with the headspace gauges.

Be sure to clean the bolt head of any grease or dirt as well. Insert your Go gauge in the chamber and then insert the bolt head. Use some curved needle nose pliers or tweezers to rotate the bolt head into the fully locked position. If it won't, then your rifle does not have minimal acceptable headspace. If it does, remove the Go gauge and repeat the exercise with the No Go gauge. Here the bolt head should not rotate in to the locked position. If it does, you have excessive headspace.

You might be able to correct this by installing a new bolt head. The only other option would be to pull the barrel and refit it on a lathe by setting back the chamber. That last option is not a good one as far as I'm concerned. If I could not correct the problem with a new bolt head from Numrich then I would get another rifle!

While you have the bolt out, run a number of patches through the barrel. Ideally you want to have a smooth, unpitted bore. Most of the rebuilt Model 91/30 Nagants I've seen had darn good bores. If you find your bore is anything less than satisfactory I would suggest getting another rifle.

It might shoot well with a rough bore but odds are it won't. Again, we will be putting a lot of work into this rifle so if the barrel is bad, now is the time to get another rifle. I sure would.

With these checks completed, let's look at stocks. As I mentioned earlier, there are a number of synthetic stocks available. I have an Advanced Technology stock for the Mosin-Nagant that I got from the good folks at MidwayUSA, 5875 W. Van Horn Tavern Road, Dept. SGN, Columbia, Mo. 65203, telephone 800-243-3220.

This is a glass-filled nylon stock that has some very attractive lines. If you are looking for a quick way to stock your rifle and if you want the durability and ruggedness of a synthetic, this stock might be just what you are looking for. With a MSRP of only $69.99, it is certainly affordable.

My problem with a synthetic stock such as this is that you can't really alter it. I want to change the length of the forearm, alter the lines at the pistol grip, and modify the rifle to a blind box. Unfortunately, this nice synthetic stock just won't allow me to do that.

Instead I have opted for a walnut stock as supplied by the folks at Boyd's Gunstock Industries, Inc., 25376 403 Ave., Mitchell, S. Dak. 57301-5402. In terms of the wood, it's just a good solid piece of plain American walnut. Nothin' fancy but just about ideal for this project. With a MSRP of only $79.62, you get a lot of stock for the money.

When the bolt head is locked in place, the stud that engages the guide bar will bear against the right side of the receiver. Just use a magnet to remove the gauge.

The stock is supplied "semi-finished" and would require just a bit of inletting work along with some sanding on the exterior. I want to do more! There is plenty of wood for me to modify the forearm length, change the comb line, alter the cheekpiece, add a recoil pad, and improve the lines of the stock at the rear of the receiver.

Although the stock comes with a perfectly fitted and totally satisfactory black plastic buttplate, I intend to add a Pachmayr recoil pad. This will allow me to make any adjustment to the length of pull and pitch that I might want. Also, since this is walnut, I can checker the stock after it's finished.

For the hobbyists, it's really hard to beat a good walnut stock for these do-it-yourself projects. If you need a wood stock for a military rifle or for an older civilian rifle for that matter, give the folks at Boyd's a call. They probably have just what you need.

I'm runnin' a bit long so I'll wrap this up. If you want a challenge, grab a Mosin-Nagant and a Boyd stock and join me in this adventure. I'm not quite sure where we'll end up but I can guarantee that it'll be quite a trip!

Until next time, good luck and good gunsmithing!

Sporterizing the Russian Mosin-Nagant Rifle Part 2

By Reid Coffield

If all goes well, this Model 1891/30 Mosin-Nagant rifle will soon become a very nice and inexpensive sporter. Coffield found new and unexpected challenges in this one.

Here Coffield shortens and crowns the barrel, removes the rear sight base and starts the stock inletting for this unusual project.

Without a doubt, the Russian Mosin-Nagant rifle is currently the most common and least expensive military bolt-action available in the U.S. One quick look at any issue of SGN will confirm this. Because of this, it offers great opportunities for the gunsmith hobbyist in developing gunsmithing skills.

While you may not produce a sporter with the classic lines of a 98 Mauser or a 1903 Springfield, you can still do a lot of work with this old warhorse and gain some very valuable experience with very little expense or concern that you are ruining a valuable collectable.

While I've been a professional gunsmith for close to 30 years and did a lot of gunsmithing as a hobbyist for many years before entering the trade professionally, I've never attempted to sporterize a Mosin-Nagant. I grew up during the "Golden Years" of military surplus imports when you could pick up 98 Mausers for $25, '03 Springfields for $35 or so and 1917 Enfields for a few bucks less.

Those great rifles were plentiful, cheap, and it seemed everybody was sporterizing them. Those were the rifles I first converted to sporters. Some of those early conversions were good; some weren't so good but I learned something from all of 'em.

The Mosin-Nagants were available at that time; mostly imports from Finland and Spain. They were normally in pretty rough shape from service during the Spanish Civil War and World War II, and very, very inexpensive. Would you believe less than 10 bucks? Back in the '60's almost no one bothered to work on 'em. Why should they? There were all those boatloads of

wonderful Mausers, Springfields and Enfields coming into the U.S. Those were the rifles of choice.

Today we face a very different situation. The Mosin-Nagant is just about the only really inexpensive military bolt-action rifle currently available for the beginner to work on and develop his gunsmithing skills. Because it's so inexpensive, even if you make a mistake and possibly ruin the rifle, you haven't lost all that much. Even then, you will still have learned valuable lessons from the experience and that will pay off in your next project.

Since it's here and it's cheap, I think it's worth a shot! So...let's get on with it!

I've selected a Mosin-Nagant made in 1942. It's technically a Model 1891/30. I got my rifle from the good folks at Century International Arms Inc., 430 South Congress Ave., Suite 1, Dept. SGN, Delray Beach, Fla. 33445, telephone 800-527-1253, www.centuryarms.com. Century offers some great deals on various models of the Mosin-Nagant as well as many other military surplus as well as civilian arms. If you haven't checked out their ads here in SGN and on the web, be sure to do so. It'll be well worth your time.

In Part 1 of this series, I began by making a list of the major steps in this project. A list like this always helps me to stay on track and, most importantly, to do the work in a logical, systematic manner.

Failure to have a work list or plan and follow it can often lead to doing work out of sequence and then later having to redo all or part of that work. If you start a gunsmithing project that involves a number of steps, I would strongly encourage you to get into the habit of making a work list or plan.

The steps listed were as follows:

1. Inspect rifle (done)
2. Select aftermarket stock (done)
3. Cut and crown barrel
4. Remove military rear sight
5. Inlet and bed action in stock
6. Fit and modify bottom metal
7. Shape stock
8. Install recoil pad
9. Install sling swivel studs
10. Modify bolt handle
11. Install iron or open sights on barrel
12. Drill and tap receiver for scope mount
13. Sand and finish stock
14. Prepare metal for refinishing

The date on the receiver indicates that this rifle was produced in 1942. Coffield notes that the early war rifles are better finished than those produced later.

An American walnut stock from Boyds' will soon replace the military stock. Coffield says it's not a drop-in stock, but that alterations to it should be minimal.

Though the rifle can be seated in the stock as received, Coffield found that he still had quite a bit of hand fitting to do. Fortunately, the stock is made a bit oversize.

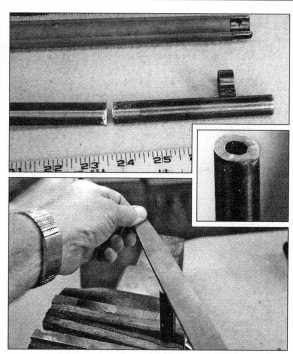

Quite a bit of the barrel was cut off. The hacksaw left the muzzle very rough and at a slight angle; a flat file was used initially to flatten and smooth the muzzle.

15. Refinish metal
16. Checker stock
17. Reassemble rifle

I checked the rifle for headspace, bolt lug contact, firing pin protrusion, bore condition, and overall condition in Part 1. It is *always* a darn good idea to carefully check any rifle you are going to do extensive work on *before* you begin your work. Nothing is more frustrating than spending hours and hours of work on a rifle, only to discover the receiver is cracked or the guard screw threads are stripped out or some other major problem. If you check your project rifle before you begin the work, you will almost never have an unpleasant surprise later.

With the rifle checked out, I began by taking the barreled action out of the military stock. The stock, barrel bands, cleaning rod, and handguard would not be used but they sure wouldn't be thrown away. A gunsmith *never* throws away gun parts! You never can tell when you might be able to use some of 'em. If nothing else, you might be able to trade 'em for somethin' you do need.

I decided to use a Boyds' walnut stock for my Mosin-Nagant. Boyds' Gunstock Industries, Inc., 25376 403rd Ave., Dept. SGN, Mitchell, S. Dak. 57301, telephone 605-996-5011, www.boydsgunstocks.com, offers one of the few walnut stocks available for the Mosin-Nagant.

The stock I received is just about ideal for this project. While it's unfinished, it requires just a modest amount of hand work to make it ready to drop in the action. However, I have some ideas I want to incorporate in this project that will entail a bit of alteration to the stock.

While it comes with a nicely fitted hard rubber buttplate, I plan on installing a nice thick Pachmayr recoil pad. In addition, I want to give the stock a more classic look by removing the Monte Carlo cheekpiece. I will also alter the length and shape of the forearm. Fortunately the Boyds' stock has rather generous dimensions and easily lends itself to these alterations.

The first order of business is to shorten the barrel. The standard issue barrel is about 29 inches long. In my opinion this is far too long for a nice looking sporter. I believe the barrel should not extend more than 22 or 23 inches beyond the front of the receiver.

This will give us a barrel long enough to make for pleasant shooting, a good sight radius, and yet short enough to be handy in the field. While a lot can be said for the advantages of short barrels, a short barrel will increase muzzle blast and that can make shooting downright unpleasant.

There is one other factor that needs to be considered before shortening a barrel, and that is the length of the forearm ahead of

the receiver. The barrel and forearm should be proportionally complimentary. If the barrel is too long and the forearm too short, the rifle looks awkward; it looks like something wasn't finished. If the barrel is too short and the forearm too long; the rifle will look fat or stubby.

In general it has been my experience that the forearm, measured from the front of the receiver to the forearm tip, should be approximately one-half the length of the barrel, less 1 inch. If the barrel measures 22 inches in length from the front face of the receiver, then the forearm should measure about 10 inches from the face of the receiver to the fore-end tip. This is just a guide and you can certainly vary this a bit, but for me it will more often than not produce a very proportionally pleasing rifle.

Since the Boyds' stock has a forearm that is 10½ inches long measured from the face of the receiver, I initially cut the barrel at the 23-inch mark. I'll be reshaping the forearm tip just a bit, so it'll probably end up being closer to 10 inches long. This will put the barrel a bit on the long side but not excessively so. Oldtime gunwriter Col. Charles Askins favored 23-inch barrels for his custom rifles, so the dimension is hardly unheard-of.

If you're working with a military rifle such as this and you're not sure as to the barrel or forearm length, leave the barrel a bit on the long side. You can never really make a mistake as you can always shorten the barrel after you have completed shaping the forearm.

I initially measured the barrel from the face of the receiver and marked it at 23 inches with a white grease pencil. Since this does not include the shank of the barrel inside the receiver, the actual length will be about 24 inches or so.

I secured the barrel horizontally in a padded vise and used a cleaning rod to position a tight-fitting patch in the bore just below where I planned to make the cut. This patch is used to prevent steel chips from the hacksaw getting into the receiver.

I then cut the barrel with an ordinary hacksaw. By the way, if you want to make your hacksaw blades cut faster, cleaner, and last longer, just apply a bit of cutting fluid as you make your cut. A lot of folks think you only need cutting fluid if you're using a drill press, mill, lathe or some other powered machine to cut steel. In reality, even the lowly hacksaw will benefit from the application of cutting oil. Try it and you'll become a believer!

The hacksaw left a pretty ragged, uneven cut with lots of burrs extending into the bore. Because of this I used a flat, second cut mill file to square up and smooth the end of the barrel. It wasn't necessary to get the muzzle perfectly flat; I just wanted it to be a bit more even as that would make crowning a lot easier and faster.

The next order of business was to crown the barrel. The bore of the barrel must terminate at the muzzle with no irregularities, burrs, or unevenness. When the bullet exits the bore, all points around the base of the bullet should break contact with the bore at precisely the same moment.

If the end of the bore is just the least bit canted or uneven, some part of the bullet base will still be in contact for just a millisecond after the rest of the base has cleared the bore. This permits the uneven escape of gas around the bullet. This can and often does

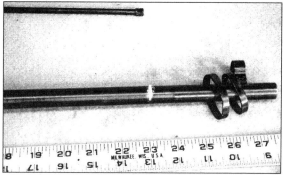

Based on the length of the forearm, Coffield decided to cut the military barrel at a point approximately 23 inches ahead of the receiver; a hacksaw is all you need.

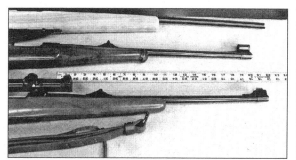

Coffield's rule of thumb is to make the forearm approximately half the length of the barrel for a properly proportioned rifle. Too short or long will look peculiar.

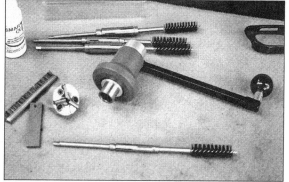

With the muzzle smoothed up by filing, Coffield was ready to use his hand crowning tools from Manson Precision; he thinks they are the best crowning tools available.

Manson makes use of an expandable pilot to ensure cutters are properly centered and aligned. Cutting is by three small carbide files rather than rigid fixed blades.

lead to a slight tipping or canting of the bullet just as it leaves the bore resulting in inaccuracy and larger groups on the target.

The key to preventing this is a good crown. If you have a lathe, it's relatively simple to crown a barrel with precision. Unfortunately my Jet lathe happened to be down for a few days. I was in the process of fitting a new quick-change tool post holder and the lathe could not be used quickly.

Since I wanted to move along on this project, I pulled out a crowning tool I acquired some time ago from Dave Manson, Manson Precision Reamers, 8200 Embury Road, Dept. SGN, Grand Blanc, Mich. 48439, telephone 810-953-0732. I used this same hand crowning tool in an earlier article on the Nagant revolver.

Even though it is a hand tool, it allows me to cut a crown quickly and precisely in a matter of minutes. In fact, even if my lathe had been available, I could not have gotten it set up to crown the Mosin-Nagant rifle barrel as quickly as I could with the Manson hand tool.

If you are not familiar with this tool, it has several unique features. First, it uses expandable pilots to guide the cutters. The pilot is positioned in the bore and expanded with a special wrench to the point that it allows for no perceptible horizontal movement of the cutter, which sits over an extension of the pilot.

The cutter is also unusual as it consists of a housing that holds three small carbide file blades. Rather than cut the muzzle as you do with a traditional tool, the Manson cutter literally files steel from the muzzle. The chips from these carbide file blades are fine, almost like hair. This results in an extremely smooth, even surface.

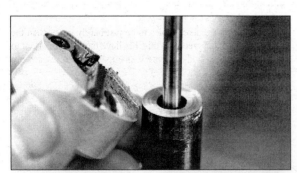

On the 11° target crown cutter, the carbide files are angled to cut a shallow recessed crown. The cup-shaped cutter slightly bevels the outside edge of the muzzle.

Before removing the rear sight base, this easily-missed screw must be removed. Then use a standard propane torch to melt the solder that secures the base to the barrel.

I can say without hesitating that I know of no other hand-held crowning tool that will provide as smooth and precise a crown as the Manson tool. To make it even better, chatter has never been an issue when I've used this tool.

Manson provides two primary cutters; one allows you to cut a flat 90° crown and the other an 11° recessed target crown. I used the 90° cutter first and followed it up with the 11° cutter. At that point I had a beautifully even and smooth crown. I could easily start using the barrel just as it was, but I was not through yet.

The outside edge of the barrel muzzle was very sharp due to the precise cutting of the 90° crowning tool. This edge had to be chamfered a bit, or I'd bleed every time I touched the muzzle!

I used a special cup type cutter that Manson also produces. All of these cutters were guided by the rigid, expandable pilot. There was no, I repeat, no chatter. That, my friends, is unusual for a hand-held crowning tool. With all cutting complete, the cutter was removed and the pilot loosened and withdrawn from the muzzle. In a matter of no more than 15 minutes or so, I had gone from a raw, hacksaw cut barrel to a nicely crowned muzzle.

If you are interested in this tool, by all means, give Dave Manson a call. The price for the tool will vary from about $300 to over $600 depending upon how many pilots and cutters you want. It's not a cheap tool but the results are consistently first-class.

With the barrel crowned, I checked the barrel length. The technically correct method of measuring a barrel is to close the bolt and insert a cleaning rod from the muzzle so that it rests on the face of the bolt. The rod is then marked even with the end of the muzzle and then withdrawn. A tape can now be used to measure the distance from the end of the cleaning rod to the mark on the rod. In this case, the barrel "officially" measures just a hair over 24 inches long.

The reason I brought this up is a lot of folks mistakenly think rifle and shotgun barrels are measured from the face or front of the receiver. I assure you the method I described is correct and

Whoever installed the base back in 1942 put solder only on one side, which made it easy for Coffield to pop it back off again, using only heat from a propane torch.

Coffield found that the rear face of the recoil lug was tapered rather than being perpendicular to the bottom of the receiver. A few file passes fixed the problem.

most importantly, it's the method the ATF uses for measuring and checking barrel length as well.

Now that the barrel has been shortened and crowned, the next step is to remove the military rear sight. The sight leaf is removed by first driving out a horizontal pin on which the sight leaf pivots. With the sight leaf removed, the leaf spring can be grasped with pliers and pulled up and forward out of the sight housing. There are two additional pins that secure the sight housing to the barrel. These should be driven out with a 3/32" flat pin punch.

When these pins are removed the rear sight housing should fall off, right? Nope. It normally won't move as it's also soldered in place. In addition, there's a small slotted positioning screw at the rear of the sight base. I believe this screw was used to hold the sight base in place before it was soldered to the barrel. The slot for the screw is very small so I had to alter one of my Wheeler Engineering screwdriver bits to fit it. The screw was then removed.

I used a regular propane torch to heat the base and melt the solder. It didn't take much heat in this case, as it appears that the solder used was a simple low-temperature lead solder. Whoever was doing the initial work only soldered one side of the base. Maybe he was pushin' hard to make his quota so the local commissar would stay happy. In any event, once the solder was melted, all it took was a few gentle taps with a brass hammer to drive the base forward and off the barrel.

Once the base was off, I found that there was a flat milled into the barrel to help secure the base. That, along with the two transverse pin holes, will need to be dealt with as it would look terrible and very much out of place to leave as is. I had no idea I would run into this, but that's just part of working on these old rifles. You often run into surprises and interesting challenges.

Another "surprise" that will cause a bit more work is the condition of the exterior of the barrel. When I first looked at the rifle I had not paid all that much attention to the exterior of the barrel other than to check for rust or pitting. Upon closer examination,

The inletting black is deposited on the wood at those points where there is wood-to-metal contact. Note limited contact at the bottom rear of the receiver tang.

Carefully manipulated scrapers remove the high spots as indicated by the inletting black. It's important to cut and try repeatedly; don't remove too much!

Coffield uses a rat-tailed file to open up the guard screw holes in the stock. He thinks some are too obsessed with a close fit between the screws and the stock.

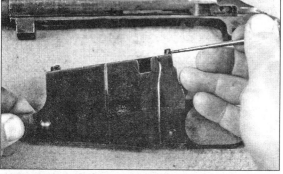

These tabs at the front and rear of the magazine box must fit into the magazine well cut in the receiver. Take special care not to bend them during the fitting process.

it was apparent that the machine marks on the outside of the barrel would have to be removed.

While the machine work on this rifle is not as rough as on rifles produced later in the war, the barrel does have pretty deep machine marks where it was turned on a lathe during production. In order to get a nice-looking sporter, these machine marks will have to be removed.

This will necessitate some draw filing as that is about the only practical way of smoothing the barrel without using my lathe. I can remember doing this frequently with old 1903A3 Springfield barrels years ago. If you are not familiar with draw filing this'll be a good opportunity to learn more about it.

I also noticed the rear of the recoil lug on the receiver was not square or at 90° to the bottom of the receiver. Instead, the recoil lug was slightly tapered from the point where it joined the receiver. This meant that recoil forces would tend to push the receiver up and away from the stock.

I used a small machinist square to check the rear face of the recoil lug and then a flat, 6 by half-inch Nicholson "O" cut file to true up the lug quickly. It didn't take more than a dozen light strokes with the file to do this. While this was a bit unusual, it's a darn good idea to check the face of any recoil lug to make sure it's perpendicular to bottom of the receiver. You never can tell; like me you may have to do a bit of file work.

The next step was to check the inletting and fit of the barreled action and bottom metal to the stock. The Boyds' stock comes with a pretty good inletting job. The barreled action would with just a bit of pressure seat into the stock. However, that didn't tell me just how well the metal fit the wood.

To find out I coated the receiver, the bottom metal, and the lower portion of the barrel with inletting black. Inletting black is just as the name implies, a black paint-like material. A small fiber brush was used to apply a coating of inletting black to the metal, which was then carefully pressed into the stock.

At any point where the metal contacted the wood, there was a trace of the inletting black, which is easily seen against the natural light color of the walnut.

Keep in mind that the goal is not to have complete and perfect contact between wood and metal at this time. Right now we just need to make sure that the receiver is seating fully to the proper depth. Basically we want the bottom half of the barrel to be down in the forearm as well as about half of the receiver.

The rear tang of the receiver should seat below the surface of the wood stock. If the metal extends above the stock, that would look just terrible. It would look like we had sanded away too much of the stock. Ideally we want a nice smooth surface with the top of the tang and the top of the wood on the same plain though it is acceptable to have the wood a bit "proud" or a few thousandths higher than the metal.

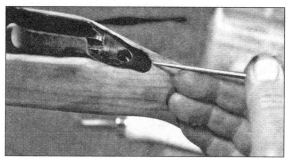

Coffield contends that it is very important to have the rear tang well below the surface of the stock. If sticks up high, the stock looks shrunken or even oversanded.

I discovered that only the bottom rear tip of the receiver tang was contacting the stock. This was due to the fact that the rear tang is angled down slightly. The bottom of the tang was not flat but the inletting for the tang was. This quickly showed up with the inletting black.

By using a number of small chisels, I was able to remove some of the excess wood and obtain more contact with the tang. This also caused the receiver to drop down into the stock a bit further. I could have taken out more wood but I stopped when I saw that the tang had dropped below the surface of the stock.

As I worked the receiver into the stock, I also checked the barrel channel in the forearm. The channel on this stock is actually a bit large for this barrel. Also the gap between the barrel and the sides of the barrel channel in the forearm is uneven.

There is a larger gap between the left side of the barrel and the forearm than on the right side of the barrel. Unfortunately when faced with a situation like this, you don't have very many options. In this case, I think I will just have to use bedding material to fill the gap. That's not the ideal solution but the only other option would be to splice in some wood.

Once the barreled receiver had been fitted to the stock, the next step was to check the fit of the trigger guard/magazine housing or bottom metal. The inletting for the bottom metal was very tight. In fact, you really could not get the bottom metal to seat fully into the wood.

As with the receiver, I had to break out the inletting black to check my points of contact. Once I saw where the bottom metal was binding against the wood, I used a variety of small scrapers, chisels, and gouges to relieve these pressure points. I had to be very careful not to get in a hurry doing this, as it's darn easy to take out too much wood. While inside the stock that can be hidden, if it's at the surface of the stock, say alongside the trigger guard, it'll stand out like a sore thumb.

By the way, I completely stripped the bottom metal by removing the follower, floor plate catch, and the follower pivot pin. The pivot pin, which is held in place by large rounded heads on either

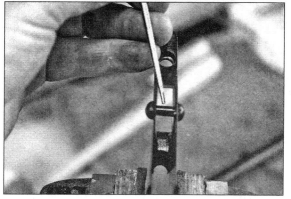

The follower mechanism will have to be relocated, as the magazine box is to be shortened by almost half. Its screw is permanently affixed to the magazine box.

end, must be cut to be removed. I used a Dremel tool with a cut-off wheel to do this. Since the bottom metal will be cut down, a substitute for this pin will be relocated inside the stock where it is not visible.

As I worked with the bottom metal, I used a plastic-faced hammer carefully to tap the underside of the metal to seat it in the stock. I also used a quick clamp to hold the barreled action in the stock. Keep in mind that the bottom metal must not only go into the stock, it must also seat properly into the underside of the receiver. There are two little tabs on the magazine; one on the front and one on the rear. Both of these tabs must seat into the magazine well cut into the receiver.

These tabs, by the way, are not all that substantial and are easily bent. If you have to use a hammer to seat the bottom metal, *be very careful!* It doesn't take much to bend the front tab. I know!

As you seat the bottom metal, check not only the traces left by the inletting black but look through the magazine well into the receiver. Note how the bottom metal is positioned and where it needs to go. The gun will give you clues as to what you need to do; you just need to be aware of those clues and act on 'em.

I noticed the bottom metal was not lining up with the guard screw holes in the stock. As I checked further, I discovered that the holes were both a bit too small and were not in alignment with the screw holes in the receiver and bottom metal. This was easily corrected with a rat tail rasp.

Some folks want screw holes to be just barely larger than the screw shanks. I disagree with this. I believe that it's important to have clearance around the screw shanks. The screws are not designed to take recoil. That's the job of the recoil lug. I have seen a number of stocks cracked where the screws shifted under recoil and literally pounded the stock until it split. I have also seen screws bent under recoil. A modest amount of clearance around the screw shanks will prevent this.

As I continued fitting the bottom metal, I found that the inletting needed to be opened up on the right side. This sort of thing is not all that uncommon on semi-finished stocks. The key to dealing with it is just to take your time, note where you are getting contact, and carefully take out a very small amount of wood. Don't get in a hurry and don't take out more than just a couple of thousandths of wood at a time.

Once I had the bottom metal seated, I used a yellow grease pencil to trace a line along the bottom metal to give me a rough idea as to where I needed to cut away excess metal. I also began to look at how and where I would be relocating the magazine follower.

I had hoped to be a bit further along but as I mentioned earlier, I've never sporterized a Mosin-Nagant. As my grandfather used to say, "We're plowin' new ground!" Next time, we'll continue with the modification of the bottom metal, bedding the barreled action, and hopefully doing a bit of shaping to the stock.

Until next time, good luck and good gunsmithing!

Sporterizing the Russian Mosin-Nagant Rifle Part 3

By Reid Coffield

Coffield could have gone with a synthetic stock, but he chose wood for its looks and ease of shaping. A good glass-bedding job will yield dividends in improved accuracy.

Making this old warhorse into a show pony has proven to be a very interesting project. Here Coffield glass-beds the action and prepares for some significant metal work.

This series on sporterizing the Mosin-Nagant has elicited more comments from readers than I expected. I've gotten several letters and have even had folks at the local range and gun shop comment on this project.

Everyone was very kind and supportive but the basic message was, "You're nuts!" At times with this project I have to admit I would totally agree with this assessment. Sporterizing what has to be one of the world's least attractive military rifles does pose major challenges.

However, that's one of the reasons I wanted to do it. Can you, as my grandfather used to say, turn a sow's ear into a silk purse? Well, maybe. We may not get a silk purse out of this but I believe we can make the Nagant into a reasonably attractive rifle.

The Mosin-Nagant is currently the most readily available bolt action military rifle on the market and certainly the least expensive. Numbers of dealers that advertise here in SHOTGUN NEWS offer some incredible deals on Nagants. I got mine from Century International Arms, Inc., 430 South Congress Dr., Suite 1, DelRay Beach, Fla. 33445, telephone 800-527-1252.

If you want to join me in this project, by all means, check the ads here in SHOTGUN NEWS and order a Nagant (or two!). It won't cost you an arm and a leg and it'll provide you with a great opportunity to do some gunsmithing and try something different. If you join me, I'll just about guarantee you'll be doing some things you've never done before!

In Parts 1 and 2 the rifle was inspected and checked. You always want to give any project gun a very detailed initial inspection to make sure you don't get halfway through the project and then find out there is a major problem such as a cracked receiver. The barrel was cut back to 24 inches and the military sights were removed.

The barreled action was then fit into a Boyds' walnut semi-finished stock. By the way, Boyds' Gunstock Industries, Inc., 25376 403rd Ave., Mitchell, S. Dak. 57301, telephone 605-996-5011 is the only supplier I know of still offering a walnut semi-finished stock for the Nagant. If you need one of these stocks or a stock for some other obsolete military or civilian rifle, give the folks at Boyds' a call. More than likely, they'll have a suitable stock.

With the barreled action fully seated in the new stock, the next step is to glass bed it. I am a firm believer in the use of synthetic bedding in situations like this. The bedding compound, which depending on the brand can be fiberglass, epoxy, or a nylon based material, serves several functions.

First of all, it ensures that you have absolutely perfect mating of the metal and stock. It also strengthens the stock and helps it withstand and absorb the recoil of the rifle.

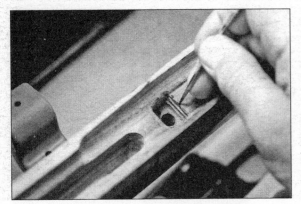

Coffield always grooves bearing surfaces to give the bedding a better purchase. Here he used a rotary cutter to make grooves in the stock recoil lug seat for the bedding.

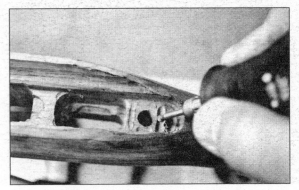

He cut similar grooves under the rear tang to ensure space for bedding. He advises always leaving a bit of clearance so that the bedding has somewhere to flow.

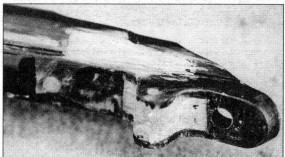

Any holes such as this must be filled with modeling clay to prevent locking the barreled action in the stock. Bedding will flow into any open space, causing big problems.

Use release agent liberally to keep the action from seizing. A Q-tip dipped in release agent is used to make sure that the guard screw threads are properly coated.

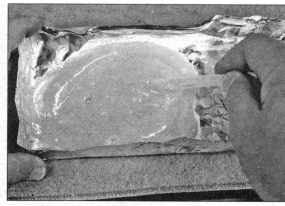

Coffield uses tin foil to make mixing containers for his bedding. These can be made to any size quickly and easily. When he's finished, they go into the trash can.

Another important feature of the bedding is that it helps to seal the wood in the inletting around the action. The wood in this critical area is highly susceptible to damage from excess oil or cleaning solvents typically used on guns. The bedding can serve as a barrier between these harmful chemicals and the wood.

Before mixing up the bedding compound I used a Dremel tool along with a small rotary burr or cutting tool to remove a bit of wood on the rear or back face of the recoil lug seat in the stock. This is to make sure there is a place for the bedding. If you have perfect wood to metal fit, there won't be any space for the bedding.

I just rout out a few grooves about 1/16" deep. I then do the same on the flat behind the recoil lug and under the receiver rear tang. In fact, it's a good idea to cut in a few grooves for the bedding any place that you intend to place the bedding.

Following this I use common, ordinary kid's modeling clay to fill in any slots, screw and pin holes, or other openings in the receiver into which the bedding might flow. If you don't seal off

these areas, bedding compound can flow into them. Once the bedding hardens or sets up, your action would then be mechanically locked into the stock. In other words, you're up the creek without a paddle! About your only option will be to drive the barreled action out of the stock and hope you don't damage the gun or ruin the stock in the process. More than likely, the stock will be damaged.

It was not at all uncommon to get two or three guns in my shop each year that had the action stuck in the stock because of bedding getting into places it shouldn't. This can easily be avoided by just using the modeling clay to fill those holes and slots. No big deal at all. Also, after the action has been placed in the stock and before the bedding sets up, take a few minutes to inspect the action and remove any excess bedding you spot. With the bedding still soft, this can be easily done and it can save a lot of work and hassle latter.

Once the clay had been used, I took a bit of plastic electrical tape and placed some on the front and sides of the recoil lug. I also placed a piece on the bottom of the recoil lug. This bottom piece had to be cut out to allow the front guard screw to seat in the recoil lug.

Just a little work with a razor knife after the tape was in place was all that was necessary. The tape serves a couple of functions. First the tape on the front and sides of the recoil lug makes putting the action in and out of the stock without damaging the bedding much easier.

The little piece on the bottom of the lug allows for a bit of compression of the wood over time. Otherwise the receiver might end up with the bottom of the lug in contact with the stock and cause the receiver to be canted and not bear evenly against the stock. Ideally the bottom of the receiver will always bear evenly and uniformly against the stock and bedding.

By the way, I also place a bit of tape on the vertical surface of the rear of the top tang. This allows a bit of space, just a few thousandths, between the end of the receiver tang and the stock.

Have you ever seen stocks that had a crack running from the back of the receiver tang? Bet you have.

This is normally caused by the receiver moving backwards under recoil and literally splitting the stock. True, the bedding we install will help to prevent this but a space of just a few thousandths will also help to prevent this from occurring. We don't want a large noticeable gap like you see on some older military rifles. A space the thickness of a piece of electrical tape is plenty.

With the tape installed, the next step is to apply release agent. Just about every bedding kit comes with some sort of release agent. Most are basically just wax. The important or critical element here is that you use it and you make darn sure that you coat every bit of metal that just might come in contact with the bedding. Check and then recheck to ensure that you have coated all the appropriate surfaces with release agent.

We have already covered mechanical locks where bedding gets inside slots or screw or pin holes, sets up, and holds the action in the stock. You can also stick the action in the stock by failing to apply release agent. The bedding compound is in one sense just really thick glue and like any good glue it'll bond to both wood and metal. Many folks have accidentally glued their actions into the stock. It's normally not as bad as a mechanical lock but it can ruin a stock and certainly will ruin your day!

With this project I'm using the release agent supplied with the Bedrock kit. If you ever find yourself without release agent, a darn good substitute and one that I used for years is regular old auto body paste wax. It'll work like a charm.

No matter what type of release agent you use, make a point of applying it to the metal *before* you even mix the bedding. By doing this, you'll not be rushed to get the bedding and barreled action into the stock. Again, apply the release agent to all the appropriate components *before* you even mix the bedding compound.

I also took the time to apply some strips of masking tape along the top rails of the stock around the receiver. I did this so any bedding that squished out would go on to the tape rather than the

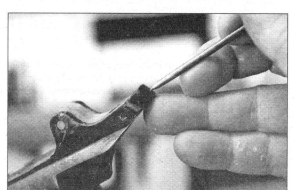

Electrical tape placed at the rear of the top tang ensures a space between the stock and the tang after the bedding sets up. The recoil lug gets the same treatment.

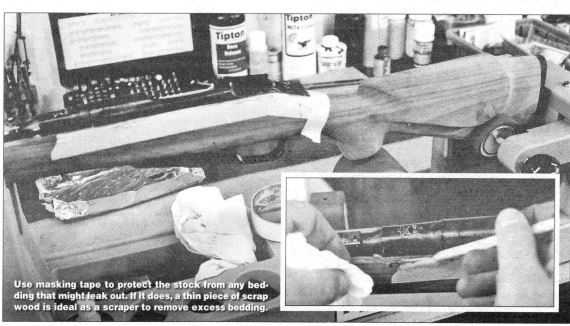

Use masking tape to protect the stock from any bedding that might leak out. If it does, a thin piece of scrap wood is ideal as a scraper to remove excess bedding.

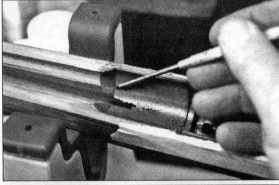

Though Coffield has bedded hundreds of rifles, there will still be occasional voids and drips that need to be filled or removed for a truly professional bedding job.

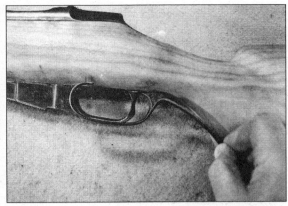

When compared with the Mosin-Nagant trigger bow, the shotgun bow, sized for double triggers, is about 3/4" longer and will have to be shortened to fit properly.

wood. True, the stock will still need to be shaped and sanded but this is something that I always do with finished stocks and it just makes clean up easier even on unfinished stocks as well.

I used Bedrock, a Battenfeld Technologies product sold by MidwayUSA, 5875 West Van Horn Tavern Road, Columbia, Mo. 65203, telephone 800-243-3220. This is a two part epoxy bedding material that is a simple one to one mix of hardener and resin. Any time I have to use a bedding compound, I always try to get one that is just a one-to-one mix by volume.

It is so much easier to use than some of the old bedding products that were four-to-one or three-to-two mixes. The simpler the process, the less likely I am to screw it up! It's important to keep in mind that even though you have a simple one-to-one mixing ratio of hardener to resin, you still need actually to measure out the components. I know lots of guys contend that they can "eyeball" it and get the right mix. Don't believe it and don't do it!

I always measure out my components as per the manufacturer's instructions. That may make me look old-fashioned but at the same time I don't have bedding compound that doesn't set up properly. After all the time and energy you expend in prepping the metal and the stock, why take a chance of messin' it all up? It just makes sense to measure the bedding components. 'Nough said about that.

If you're like me, you never seem to have a suitable mixing container when working with bedding or epoxy. After years of using bits of cardboard or plastic food containers I finally figured out how to deal with the problem. I now keep a roll of heavy duty tin foil in my shop. Any time I need a mixing container, I just tear off a piece and after folding it over a couple of times, make a shallow tray. I can make it any size I need and once I have used it, I just throw it in the trash. Fast, easy, and always available.

A question that frequently comes up has to do with how much bedding you should mix. I used to struggle with this and it seemed I always ended up with not enough. Now, I just say to heck with it and always mix up twice as much as I think I'll need.

Yep, I do waste bedding. I sure won't argue with that but what is much more important to me is that I never end up not having enough. Believe me, trying to mix up additional bedding in the middle of the process and still get it just as thick and the same color is no fun at all! To me it's penny wise and pound foolish to worry about an extra spoonful of resin and hardener. Getting a good bedding job is a lot more important.

Some bedding compounds like the Bedrock allow you to add material to thicken the bedding. I prefer to make my bedding thick enough so it won't run or drip through the stock. Some of the older compounds were like water and you ended up with as much on your bench and down the front of your pants as you got in the stock. If your bedding allows for a thickener, by all means, use it and be sure to use it before you add your dye.

Once the bedding is mixed, I add a brown dye to help color it. I tend to make the bedding darker than would seem to be appropriate at first. However, if the bedding is too dark I can always darken the wood a bit with a stain to lessen the contrast with the bedding.

This is a lot better than having the bedding too light, as there is nothing you can do about it after it has set up. Of course, you don't want the bedding to show any more than absolutely necessary, but on many of these older military rifles you'll often have gaps in the stocks that you just have to fill with bedding.

A trick I have used for years to avoid bubbles or air pockets in the bedding is to place bedding in the stock and on the receiver. I take special care in putting a bit of bedding on the rear of the recoil lug and bottom of the receiver in front of the magazine well. If you are going to get an air pocket, that's where it'll happen. Putting bedding on both the receiver and stock will help to avoid that.

While some folks will hold the barreled action in place with clamps or surgical tubing, I prefer to use the guard screws. I think this helps to ensure the receiver and bottom metal are properly aligned. If you do this, be sure you put plenty of release agent on the guard screws as well as the bottom metal. After all, bedding material can and probably will contact those components.

Holding the stock while preparing it, then later applying the bedding, and finally installing the barreled action can be very awkward. You really need three or more hands. I use a Tipton Gun Vise that I've had for quite a few years. I got it from MidwayUSA.

It'll hold the stock securely in a horizontal position without any danger of damage to the stock. On more than one occasion, I've seen stocks cracked when clamped a bit too tight in a standard bench vise. I let the stock and barreled action set for 24 hours while the bedding cured.

While it's possible to pull the action from the stock sooner, I didn't have any real need to do so. If you pull an action too soon, you can easily damage the bedding, so it's best to just give it enough time to set up properly. You do, however, want to remove any extra bedding that has seeped out from between the stock and action. The more you can remove now, the less cleanup you will have to do later.

Also, excess bedding can often make removal of the barreled action harder and more difficult. Just take a Q-tip or small piece of wood and scrape away the bedding. Once that is done, you can move on to another aspect of the project.

While the stock bedding was setting up, I started work on the trigger guard. In order to make the lines of the Mosin-Nagant

rifle more attractive, I felt I had to do something about the military magazine and trigger guard. The issue guard projects beyond the bottom of the stock and gives the gun a very distinctive appearance. There is no mistaking a Mosin-Nagant. You can spot one across a room and one reason for that is the magazine and trigger guard.

By altering the magazine and trigger guard, we can go a long way towards giving the rifle a slimmer, sleeker appearance. I will be cutting off everything that projects below the bottom line of the stock but while the bedding is still curing, I can go ahead and work on the old shotgun trigger guard that will be used to provide protection for the trigger.

The shotgun guard I selected is typical of those used on older, inexpensive side-by-side shotguns. You'll find bunches just like it in junk boxes on tables at any decent gun show. The only problem with this guard is that the bow is a bit too long. It was designed for double triggers and our Nagant will only have one trigger. If the guard is not shortened, it will look far too big.

By simply comparing the width of the shotgun guard to the issue Mosin-Nagant guard, I could tell that the shotgun guard bow was about 3/4" longer than needed. I used Dykem machinist layout fluid to coat the outside of the bow and marked off a 3/4" segment, then used a hacksaw to cut this out.

I then welded the two halves back together, making the bow considerably shorter. I won't kid you, welding this bow was a major pain. It was more like cast iron than steel and it did not weld easily. On the other hand, I have had numbers of other guards over the years that were made of better material and were super easy to weld. In this case, I just happened to get a bad guard. Such is life!

Once the weld had cooled, I used files to remove excess metal and to blend sides of the trigger guard bow into a smooth even surface.

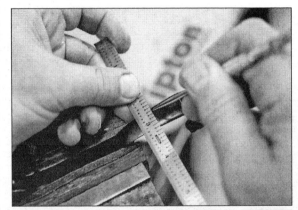

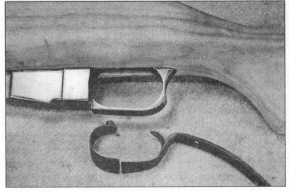

Coffield marked the cut points with a scribe, then used a hacksaw to cut away the excess material in the trigger bow, making the shotgun bow quite a bit shorter.

After welding the shotgun trigger bow, a process he found tedious because it was made of low-grade metal, Coffield removed excess metal and shaped the bow with a file.

By the way, don't get in a hurry and decide to try to bend the tang of the newly welded guard. First of all, you still have to shape the stock and the pistol grip so you don't really know what the final shape or curvature of the tang should be. Also, if you try bending the tang of the guard cold or without heat, you'll most likely break it where you have holes for the attaching screws.

When it comes time to bend and fit the guard tang, you absolutely have to heat the tang to get it to bend without cracking. We'll cover that later on. Right now just getting the trigger guard bow welded and shaped is all that's necessary.

The next day I pulled the barreled action from the stock. I first loosened the two guard screws about two turns each. I then used a large brass punch and small hammer to tap the head of each screw. All I wanted to do was to get the bottom metal to separate from the receiver. Once I saw a bit of movement I completely removed the two guard screws and the magazine/trigger guard.

With that out of the way, I then secured the stock and pulled the barreled action straight up and out of the stock. A common mistake is to lift up on the barrel and pry the barreled action out of the stock. This will almost always lead to damage to the bedding and to the stock, especially around the rear tang. Generally a large chip of wood will be knocked loose. You can avoid this by just pulling the barreled action straight up. I grab the barrel just ahead of the tip of the fore-end with one hand and the rear of the receiver with the other hand.

If you have trouble grabbing the receiver, slide the bolt into the receiver an inch or so and use the bolt body as a handle. Avoid the temptation to wiggle the barreled action back and forth or side to side. Pull it straight up and it will come out.

Once the stock and the metal have been separated, check the bedding for damage, as well as voids or air bubbles. You can fill in voids by mixing additional bedding and carefully filling each void. The trick is to put in just enough bedding to fill the void without having so much that it flows out over the "good" bedding.

In this case, the bedding looks pretty good. I used my trusty Dremel tool along with a razor knife and some small chisels to remove any bedding that went where it shouldn't have. The longer you wait, the harder the bedding will become and the more difficult cleanup will be.

Some folks don't bother too much with the appearance of the bedding inside the stock. After all, you can't see it when the rifle is assembled. I disagree with this, as the bedding is as much of an indication of your workmanship as the stock or metal finish. Sooner or later, someone will see it, so clean it up and make it

Here's where it gets interesting. Coffield marked the magazine box with the bottom line of the stock to prepare for shortening the magazine flush with the stock.

look neat. Where the bedding stops under the barrel for example, make sure you have a nice straight line. It just takes a few minutes with a chisel or gouge to do this and it sure makes your work look better.

The Boyds' stock has several lightening cuts in the barrel channel and one is back under the chamber section of the barrel. Some bedding flowed into this area as expected. In order to clean up the bedding and make it look nice, I used my Dremel to cut out this excess bedding so I had a nice clean line of bedding along the edges of the lightening cut. Again, it's not something you have to do but it will make your job look a lot more finished and precise.

I guess the bedding gods were not with me on this job as I also got a void behind the rear guard screw under the tang and on the right side of the receiver. I'll have to mix up a bit of bedding to fill in these holes.

Next time we'll cut and modify the trigger guard, fill some holes in the barrel, drawfile some machine marks out of the barrel, install a recoil pad, and begin shaping the stock. That's a lot of work but if we do just a bit at a time we can do it. So...finish up your bedding and have your shotgun trigger guard ready.

Until next time, good luck and good gunsmithing! ◎

Ask the Gunsmith

By Reid Coffield

such as Brownells, 200 South Front St., Dept. SGN, Montezuma, Iowa 50171, telephone 800-741-0015.

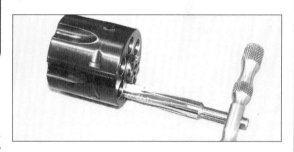

Shooting lots of .38 Spl. in a .357 Mag. revolver may leave a ring of fouling in the cylinder that will prevent chambering .357 ammo. Use a lead-removing reamer like this to scrape out the fouling.

MAUSER EXTRACTOR

Q *I do most of my shooting of old military rifles from a bench and single-load the cartridges. I have one 98K Mauser that will not allow me to load the cartridge in the chamber and close the bolt. Is this normal and how can I change it?*

A First of all, that is normal. The 98 Mauser was designed to be loaded from the magazine. However, it is generally possible to modify the extractor to allow it to pop over the rim of the cartridge. All you need to do is modify the angle of the bevel on the extractor hook. Be careful when doing this that you don't shorten the engagement of the extractor hook. The original Mauser system is often referred to as controlled-round feeding, and is much favored for dangerous-game rifles, as it helps prevent double-feeds.

To enable the Mauser extractor to override the rim of a chambered cartridge, this bevel must be polished and the angle adjusted. Purists object to this change to the controlled round feed.

.357 MAG. FOULING

Q *When I first bought a .357 Mag. revolver, I fired it a lot with .38 Spl. ammo. When I tried to use .357 ammo, I had problems. On four of the chambers, the .357 shells would go in, but the other two would not let the shells go in all the way. Did the factory screw up and only cut four chambers for .357?*

A That's not very likely. What is much more likely is that the .38 Spl. ammunition built up fouling in the chambers. This fouling, which starts right at the end of the .38 Spl. case, is preventing the full seating of the longer .357 Mag. cases. The problem can easily be solved by a good through cleaning of the chambers. Once you have removed the fouling, you will be able to fully seat the longer .357 rounds.

If the fouling is so severe that you cannot remove it with normal cleaning, you may have to take the revolver to a gunsmith. Generally a gunsmith will use a special tool that will just cut the fouling and will not in any way change the dimensions of the chambers. These special tools are available from companies such as Manson Precision Reamers, 8200 Embury Road, Dept. SGN, Grand Blanc, Mich. 48439, telephone 810-953-0732 or gunsmith supply houses

CARCANO CONVERSION?

Q *I know this sounds crazy but I am thinking of using an Italian Carcano rifle as the basis for a sporter conversion just to prove to a buddy that it can be done. Can you give me a suggestion of a caliber to use that would be more or less compatible with this action?*

A I would suggest you consider barreling and chambering your rifle for .300 Savage. With some slight modifications to the clip and the feed ramp, you can generally make this round work in that action. It will be a challenge but that can be one of the most rewarding and enjoyable aspects of gunsmithing. It can be a rush to successfully complete a project that you have been told "can't be done." Good luck with that Carcano! ◎

Sporterizing the Russian Mosin-Nagant Rifle

Part 4

By Reid Coffield

Coffield plows on in a task many might have regarded as impossible. This time he works on the stock and bottom metal.

Coffield says this Mosin project is now "over the hump" and headed for successful completion. What you do at this stage will make or break the rifle's appearance.

Every major gunsmithing project has a point at which you can look at your work and realize you're "over the hump" and well on your way to completing it. By the time we finish up a few more tasks, we'll definitely be there and in the home stretch with this Mosin-Nagant sporter.

Whenever I start a project such as this or even an extensive repair, I always try to make a list of the basic steps I plan on taking. This keeps me on track and helps me to do the various jobs in the proper sequence. Years ago I had a project involving a single barrel shotgun. It belonged to a customer who was a card shooter and used the gun for local turkey shoots.

Part of the project was to back bore or open up the diameter of the inside of the barrel up to the choke. I was also to polish the bore to a mirror like finish. You guessed it; I forgot about the back boring and spent several hours polishing the bore. I did a great job but then realized I still needed to back bore the darn thing. All that time and effort polishing was totally wasted.

I bored out the barrel and then once again had to polish the bore. By the time it was all said and done, there was absolutely no profit or money made on that job. It was a tough lesson for a young guy just starting out, but one I never forgot.

Your plan doesn't have to be elaborate or fancy. It can be as simple as a list on the back of an index card you keep with the gun. Just be sure to keep one and check it as you work on your project. When you've completed a task or stage just mark it off or line through it.

Keep in mind that a simple list will not itemize every action you'll need to take. As you work you'll run into problems that

need to be corrected or modifications that will add to the overall quality of the job. Go ahead and do 'em and just continue on with the list. Again nothing fancy or elaborate is required but something like this would have saved me several hours of tedious work.

Work plan for Mosin-Nagant sporter.
1. Inspect rifle (done)
2. Select aftermarket stock (done)
3. Cut and crown barrel (done)
4. Remove military rear sight (done)
5. Inlet stock and bed action (done)
6. Modify bottom metal
7. Shape stock

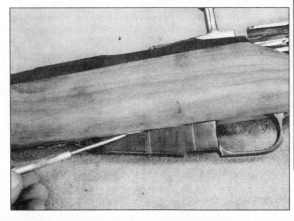

The first step in cutting the bottom metal is to draw a line with a grease pencil on the magazine along the outside of the stock. Then clamp it carefully in a vise.

Careful manipulation of a hacksaw with fresh blade severs the magazine box. Note how much metal was removed! This will really change the appearance of the old warhorse.

8. Install recoil pad
9. Install sling swivel studs
10. Relocate and modify bolt handle
11. Install iron sights
12. Drill and tap receiver for scope
13. Sand and finish stock
14. Prepare metal for finish
15. Refinish metal
16. Checker stock

So much for paperwork! Now let's get back to the rifle and get this project done. In the last installment the barreled action was bedded. With that completed I could reassemble the rifle and note exactly how much the magazine protruded from the bottom of the stock. As part of this project I will try to alter the lines of the rifle so it looks less like a Mosin-Nagant and more like a regular sporting rifle. A major part of that is to alter the characteristic projecting magazine.

With the barreled action and trigger guard in the stock, I used a yellow grease pencil to draw a line along the magazine flush with the stock. Everything below that line had to go! The magazine was then removed from the stock and clamped in my vise. Be careful when you do this as you can easily crush the thin walls of the magazine. There are a couple of solid points behind and in front of the magazine where you can safely clamp it.

I used a standard hacksaw to cut away the excess metal. Once that was done, the raw cut was cleaned up with a file and the magazine installed in the stock. I had been careful to make sure I didn't cut too much so the metal protruded above the line of the wood. This was expected. I just clamped the stock upside down in my vise and filed the metal down flush with the stock.

It may still be necessary to make adjustments in the height of the magazine as the stock is shaped and contoured. The rear trigger guard screw will need to be shortened a bit, which is no real problem. Also, there are gaps in the inletting around the magazine box. That's not really a problem either. All I need to do is to make the floorplate wide enough to cover these gaps. A number of high dollar commercial rifles do the same thing!

When the magazine was taken down to the level of the stock, I took the modified shotgun trigger guard and positioned it against the magazine. I got a surprise I should have anticipated. The rear of the guard will need to be below the wood to a depth equal to the thickness of the shotgun trigger guard tang. No prob-

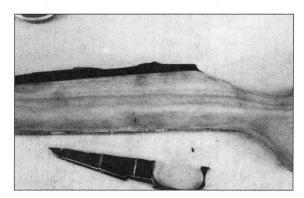

The characteristic lines of the magazine and trigger guard are eliminated. As Coffield intends to install a shotgun-style trigger guard, he cut off the issue guard.

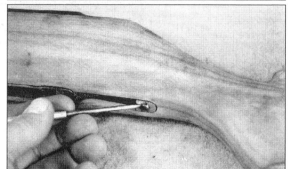

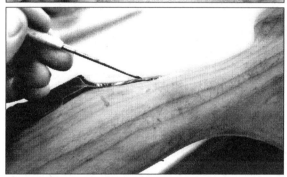

Big work with a big file: first take the bottom metal down flush with the stock. The rear guard screw will need to be shortened. Then blend the tang into the buttstock.

lem there, as you definitely don't want the shotgun tang to be sitting on top or above the surface of the wood.

That means it has to be inletted and the rear of the Mosin-Nagant bottom metal lowered as well. But that's not all! My shotgun guard is a bit narrower than the Mosin-Nagant bottom metal so I had to carefully file a slot in it the width of the shotgun guard tang. If I hadn't, I would've had a gap between the tang and the stock. That would have looked really bad.

After I filed the magazine down I also took the time to begin modification of the rear tang of the receiver. It also projects above the stock. By taking the metal down a bit, I can make the lines of the stock in the critical pistol grip area much more pleasing and also remove some unneeded metal. If you recall, I did basically the same thing with the Mauser 98 sporter project by reshaping and thinning the rear tang.

The unaltered tang has a couple of points that need to be corrected. First, and most importantly, the top of the tang is dead flat. That's fine for a military rifle but on a civilian sporter the tang must be slightly rounded in order to avoid any sharp angles or edges in the pistol grip wrist. The pistol grip should be rounded or oval shaped for a good, comfortable feel. Sharp angles will make it feel blocky and awkward.

I used a fairly coarse cut flat file along with a smooth cut half round file to do the shaping of the tang. I also made sure the files were coated with regular blackboard chalk to keep bits of metal from packing into the file blades. If this happens, these metal chips will cut deep grooves into the surface of the tang. Those grooves would be a heck of a headache to remove later, so it's best to avoid making 'em from the start. I also made sure I used a file card to clean out the chips every few strokes. A clean, chalked file will always cut cleaner and more efficiently.

The tang got quite a bit of attention, but even though it looked like I had done all that was needed, I'm pretty sure at this point

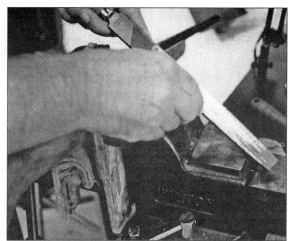

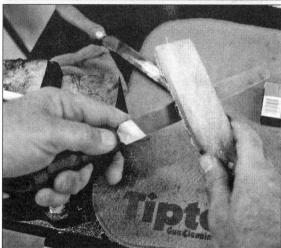

Anytime you are doing lots of filing be sure to chalk the file for a clean cut. A card file used frequently will clear any metal chips that adhere to the file surface.

I'll probably still have to come back and do a bit more work. As the stock is further reshaped I might well find the tang still needs a bit of tweaking. Also, when the bolt handle is relocated behind the rear ring or bridge of the receiver, the tang may need further work. As you know, I've never done a conversion of a Mosin-Nagant before so I'm not quite sure what I'll run into or have to do at that point.

Once the tang was reshaped, I began work on the stock cheekpiece and comb. If you're not sure how you want to shape or modify your stock, a great way of getting inspiration and guidance is to use another rifle stock as a guide. I think the Ruger Model 77 or No. 1 stock is very attractive and well proportioned.

When shaping my Nagant stock I pulled out an old 77 I've owned for 30+ years and laid it on the bench to use as a guide. If you don't have a gun you can use, check with your buddies. I'd bet you could borrow a gun for a few days to use as a guide.

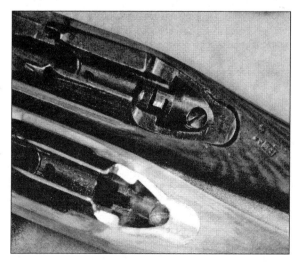

The top gun has an unaltered tang, while the bottom rifle shows the results of skilled work with a file. Nice tight inletting is the sure sign of a professional.

Coffield chose the Ruger Model 77 as the pattern for his stock, so he used a coarse rasp to carve away the Monte Carlo-style cheekpiece on the Boyd's walnut stock.

I can't say enough good things about the Boyd's stock. As far as I know these folks are the only ones still producing a real walnut stock for the Mosin-Nagant and for the hobbyist, this stock is almost ideal. Unlike some stocks, this one is a bit on the large size, so folks like me have enough wood to alter the lines, reshape, or personalize it.

For example, I really don't care for a Monte Carlo comb and cheekpiece. Lots of folks like 'em and the Monte Carlo cheekpiece does provide support for the shooter's face. However, I tend to prefer a more classic look. Because of that I removed the cheekpiece and altered the comb.

When doing this I first used a coarse cut rasp to take off the cheekpiece on the left side of the stock. As I was doing this, I was very careful to maintain a level straight line from about the middle of the pistol grip to the center of the side of the buttplate. You definitely don't want any low or dished areas behind the pistol grip. As you work, check your progress with a straightedge and only work on the high spots. As you look under the bottom edge of the straightedge, you'll not have any trouble seeing light if there's a gap or low spot between the straightedge and the wood.

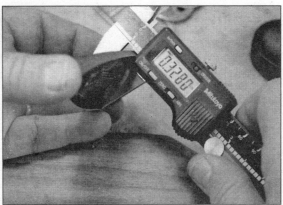

The first step in cutting the stock for a recoil pad is to measure the thickness of the original buttplate. Coffield carefully marks the stock prior to cutting it.

As I got closer to the final surface, I switched over to a fine cut rasp and checked my work even more frequently. Again, it's important for a good job to have a straight level surface on both sides of the buttstock between the center of the pistol grip and the center of the buttplate. To help with this, I made a mark with a marking pen in both of those spots. I then positioned the ends of the straightedge on these spots each time I checked for high or low areas.

If you think I'm harping on this too much, just take a look at the photograph of an old Springfield sporter I have in the shop.

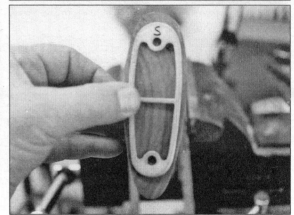

Pachmayr recoil pad templates show the dimensions of the metal liner to determine the proper size pad. The medium pad's too big; the small size is just right.

Note how the builder overcut the area behind the pistol grip. Not only is there a heck of a low spot, it makes it look like the buttstock was added on as an afterthought to the pistol grip. Oh yeah, that doesn't do any good for the strength of the stock either. Enough of that, no need to beat a dead horse!

Once the cheekpiece had been removed, I began work on the comb. To help in keeping me from removing too much wood, I used my straightedge to draw a line with a magic marker from the front tip of the comb to the heel of the stock. Again I started out with a coarse rasp and then followed up with a fine cut rasp and then later with a smooth cut file as I got nearer to the final surface. I also used my straightedge to check and ensure that my surface was level.

Here's how not to do it. Excessive thinning of the buttstock behind the pistol grip marks this as an amateur job. The finish is not much better, explaining the price.

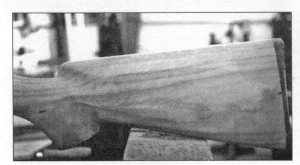

The buttstock is now basically shaped in a classic configuration, though Coffield will still have some detail work to do, especially around the point of the comb.

A simple trick Coffield uses to level the stock is to use a deck of cards. Adding or removing cards allows for subtle adjustments to the setup for the stock.

The cards enable Coffield to raise or lower the stock in minute increments to be sure that the butt is at 90° to the surface of the bandsaw blade for a straight, even cut.

The template can also be used to locate accurately the screw holes for the recoil pad. In this case, the original buttplate screw holes will have to be plugged.

After cutting the stock, a few strokes on some sandpaper over a piece of plate glass will ensure that the butt is perfectly flat, an important part of good installation.

With the cheekpiece removed and the comb rasped down, all that was left to do was to blend in the sides of the buttstock for a nice, even smooth surface. As always, I made frequent use of my straightedge to avoid low spots or dips.

While it's important to visually examine the stock as you work on it, I find it's even more helpful just to run my fingers over the surface of the stock. Your sense of feel is much more acute than most folks realize. You can feel and detect very subtle differences in the angle and height of the surface; some so minute that you wouldn't see 'em. Trust your fingers!

A common mistake is to leave the stock behind the point of the comb too thick. There is no hard and fast rule you have to follow. Of course you don't want the top of the comb to be as thin and sharp as a knife, but you also don't want the darn thing to be fat! Look at other commercial stocks such as the Ruger for guidance. As an old fellow I worked with once told me, just take off wood until you think you've taken too much, then you've probably got it right.

While I have 90% of the wood removed from the comb and the sides of the buttstock, I'll still have some more shaping to do. The angle of the front of the comb and how it flows into the wrist is not what I want, so I'll do a bit more work on that. The forearm will also need a bit of work and the tip of the forearm especially. Right now the tip is kinda square and makes the forearm look too deep or thick. By rounding the tip, it'll be possible to make the forearm look a bit thinner. But that will have to wait just a bit.

The next item on the list is the installation of a recoil pad. The 7.62x54mm cartridge can pack a good punch and I long ago decided that heavy recoil is to be avoided. Consequently, I'll be installing a nice thick Pachmayr recoil pad in place of the hard

Dowels are used to fill the original screw holes, which were first opened up with a quarter-inch drill. The protruding ends then are cut off and the butt sanded.

The new pad is on the stock and ready to be sanded down to match the lines of the stock. Note the use of a generous portion of masking tape to protect the stock.

After the pad has been sanded down, the lines of the toe and the heel continue straight through the pad. Making the angles match is a big part of how the pad looks.

plastic buttplate furnished with the Boyd's stock. Since the recoil pad is considerably thicker than the buttplate and I don't want to extend the length of pull, I'll need to cut the stock.

The first step is to determine the thickness of the recoil pad. In this case it's 1 inch. After removing the buttplate from the stock, I drew a line parallel with the end of the stock. The line was spaced about .672" from the butt of the stock. That was the thickness of the recoil pad minus the thickness of the buttplate, which was right at .325" thick.

I used my bandsaw to cut the stock. When cutting a stock, it's important to keep the stock level and the surface of the end of the buttstock at 90° to the bandsaw blade. A trick I use to set the stock up is to take a deck of cards and use them as a spacer under the forearm. By adding or removing cards, I can precisely position the stock so the butt is cut almost perfectly square or at 90° to the saw blade. Believe me, that's a lot better and more effective than trying to hold it steady with just your hands.

Once the stock had been cut and smoothed up, I needed to determine what size pad I would use. I know it'll be a 1 inch thick pad but will I need a small, medium or large pad? That is a pretty important issue. If you use a Pachmayr pad that is too large, you will grind through the rubber as you fit the pad and cut into the inner metal liner. That looks awful and even though some folks will just hide the metal that shows through the side of the pad with black paint, I always considered it a ruined pad and replaced it.

Some time back Pachmayr started offering a set of the metal inserts they use in the various pads for gunsmiths to use as guides. I bought a set from the folks at MidwayUSA. This set of guides sells for only about $10. Believe me, the first time you save the cost of a ruined pad, these guides will be worth every penny you spend on 'em.

Use of the guides is dirt simple. Just pick out one and lay it on the face of the buttstock. If the sides of the metal guide touch or are very darn close to the edge of the stock, move on to the next smaller guide. The guides are marked small, medium, large, and magnum, just like the pads. In my case, this stock will require a small pad.

With the proper size pad selected, the next step is to locate the attaching screw holes. Seldom does it ever work out for me that

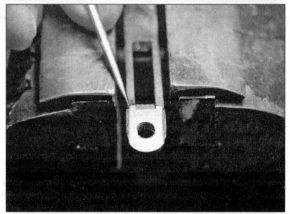

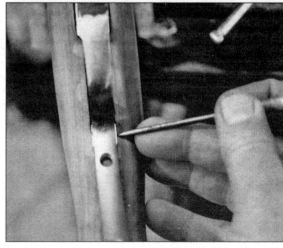

Coffield discovered that he needed to file a relief for the shotgun trigger bow in the rear of the bottom metal. A small tab of metal will be left on either side.

the existing screw holes will match the location of the pad screws. If any of the existing holes are anywhere near the new locations it's best to drill 'em out and glue in some quarter-inch inch dowel. Once the glue is dry, cut the dowel off flush with the stock. Now check the pad screw locations one more time and then drill 1/8" pilot holes.

These pilot holes are important. Admittedly you can turn in the attaching screws without pilot holes but you run the very real risk of cracking or splitting your stock. Believe me, my friends; I have seen more than one stock split when the owner tried to attach a pad without drilling pilot holes.

My first step in preparing the pad is to make sure the base is flat. The bases on most pads are a bit uneven or curved. I suspect this is due to warpage as the pad is pulled from the mold. It's no big deal, as all it takes to make sure it's flat is a few strokes across a sheet of abrasive laid on a piece of safety glass.

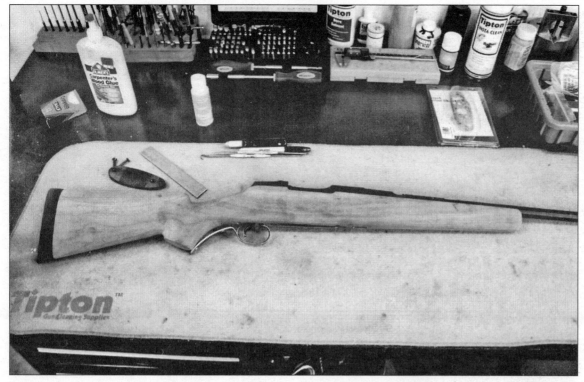

Over the hump! The Mosin-Nagant is really beginning to look like a sporter. There's still a lot of work to be done, but Coffield sees light at the end of the tunnel.

By the way, a trick to make pad installation easier is to put a bit of beeswax or soap on the screw threads before you turn the screws into the wood. This lubricates the screw and helps it to cut through the wood. Also, turn the screws into the wood at least once *before* you attach the pad. It'll make the final seating of the screws a lot easier.

The face of the pad is solid so it has to be cut for the attaching screws. I take a flat punch and insert it in from the back of the pad until the rubber of the face is stretched quite thin. I then use a razor knife to carefully slit the stretched pad over the punch. Finally, before I insert the screws, I put a drop of liquid soap over the slit. This helps to allow for insertion of the screws and screwdriver blade without further tearing of the face of the pad.

If you are careful, you should be able to install the pad without any evidence that anything was forced through the pad face.

You definitely want to avoid having a pad with screw holes that look like they were chewed on by a rat.

With the pad in place, I applied a strip or two of masking tape to the stock next to the pad. Some folks use their disk or belt sander to take the pad down to the stock and don't worry at all about hitting or sanding into the wood. After all, they'll be sanding the stock when they finish it, right?

I don't care for that at all. Disk sanding marks can be darn deep and add a lot of extra unnecessary work. I think it's best to treat the unfinished stock as though it were already finished when cutting down the recoil pad. I try to be super careful and stop when the disk or belt kisses the tape. This'll leave the pad a few thousandths high but that will sand right down to the stock very quickly.

When sanding down the pad, I pay special attention to the toe and heel lines. These lines should continue straight through the pad. This makes the pad look like it really is a part of the stock; not just something added on later. Also frankly, this is a darn good visual indication of good technique and gunsmithing practice.

Installing recoil pads is a pretty common job and one which isn't very glamorous but how you do it is important. An old gunsmith many years ago commented that he could tell more about the skill and ability of a gunsmith by looking at one of his recoil pad installations than by any other means. Good gunsmiths make good pad installations; unskilled gunsmiths don't. So…take your time and do a good job with your pads. You never know who will be looking at it and judging you and your work!

I didn't get quite as much done as I had hoped, but the rifle is beginning to look like a true sporter. It has certainly lost many of the characteristic Mosin-Nagant lines. I've had to modify my schedule a bit as I will reshape the fore end and then install the sling swivel studs. Also next time I'll finish up the bottom metal by making and installing the floorplate and hopefully moving the bolt handle. That will be a project!

If you are also working on a Nagant, hang in there! We gonna make these old warhorses look good! Until next time, good luck and good gunsmithing! ◉

Ask the Gunsmith

By Reid Coffield

LUBE THAT BARREL

Q *I wanted to test the fit of a Mauser barrel to the receiver by screwing it in by hand. I did not apply a lot of pressure to the barrel, but now it won't come out. Even a barrel vise and action wrench wouldn't budge it in either direction. What can I do?*

A My friend, you have a major problem. What has happened is that when you screwed your barrel in the receiver there were some tiny burrs or irregularities in the barrel thread. This is *very normal* and I doubt that the barrel was in any way defective. This did not cause a problem as the barrel was turned into the receiver, but when you attempted to remove it, the burrs acted almost like tiny fish hooks and grabbed on to the metal of the receiver threads. Some metal pulled loose and now you have this jamming the threads. This is often referred to as *galling*.

The way to prevent this is *always* to lubricate the barrel threads before turning the barrel into a receiver. This applies even to "testing" the barrel to receiver fit with just hand pressure. I always use a grease on my barrel threads. Right now I have a syringe of grease from Sentry Solutions Ltd., Box 214, Dept. SGN, Wilton, N.H.

03086, telephone 800-546-8049, on my bench just for this purpose. Even if I'm just "checking" the barrel to receiver fit, I'll lubricate the threads. It does take a bit of extra time and I do use a lot of grease over the year but I never have a galling problem.

As for what you can do now, I'm afraid you're up the proverbial creek without a paddle. More than likely, the threads on both the barrel and receiver are damaged. I would not be at all surprised if the receiver is not ruined. About the only way you'll be able to remove the barrel is by cutting it out on a lathe. That is a very time-consuming and difficult job, and the value of your receiver may not justify the cost if you have to pay someone to do this.

Failure to lubricate the barrel threads with a grease can and often will result in galling and damage to the barrel or receiver or both. Coffield says never spare the grease on this job!

ACCURACY KEY

Q *What is the most important component in an accurate rifle?*

A I believe the barrel is by far and away the most important part of an accurate rifle. With a good barrel you can still get great performance even if the action is less than ideal or if you have a mediocre trigger. On the other hand, if you have a bad barrel, even the world's best action or the finest trigger won't allow the gun to shoot accurately. The barrel is the heart and soul of a good rifle. If you are going to spend extra money on any component, the barrel is the place to make that investment.

GAS VS. BOLT GUNS

Q *On a gas operated semi-automatic rifle, will the gas loss needed to operate the mechanism make a significant difference in velocity? I have an AR varmint rifle and recently got into a discussion with a friend who uses a bolt-action rifle in the same caliber. We were wondering if his rifle would perform better because it did not have the gas loss.*

A The difference would not be at all significant. Many years ago, the N.R.A. did some testing with M14's and found that the gas loss was such that the difference in velocity was only a few feet per second. You would probably see more variation than that caused by differences in barrel length, bore dimensions, temperature, etc. ◉

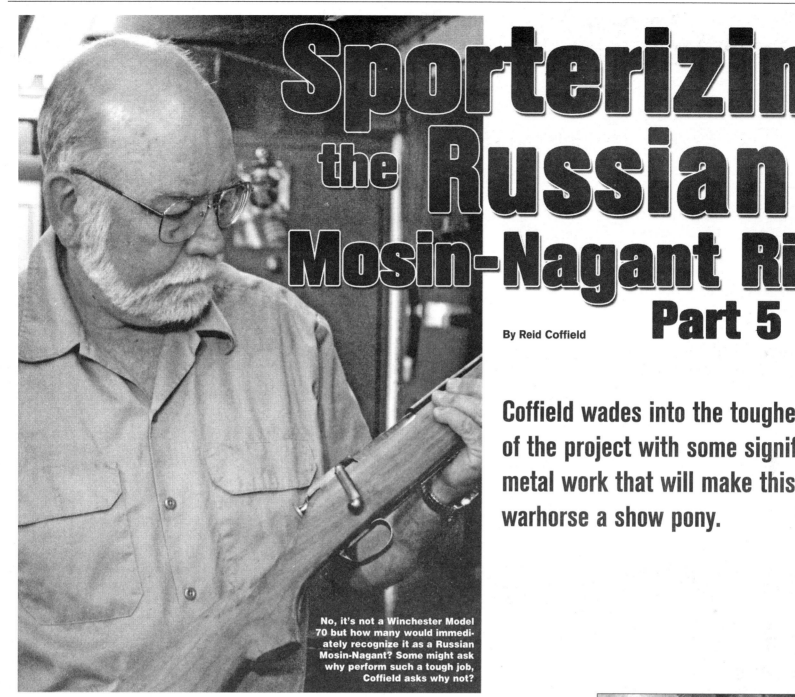

Sporterizing the Russian Mosin-Nagant Rifle Part 5

By Reid Coffield

Coffield wades into the toughest part of the project with some significant metal work that will make this old warhorse a show pony.

No, it's not a Winchester Model 70 but how many would immediately recognize it as a Russian Mosin-Nagant? Some might ask why perform such a tough job, Coffield asks why not?

The 7.62 x 54Rmm Russian Mosin-Nagant bolt-action rifle is one of those firearms most folks either love or detest. To some it's a fantastic rifle that can often prove to be extremely accurate and at the same time as rugged and tough as a rock. Perhaps equally important, currently the rifle and ammo are dirt cheap.

To others, no matter how inexpensive or serviceable these rifles are, they're one of the world's ugliest, most awkward bolt-action rifles. They're seen as crude and inferior to almost any other European or U.S. military bolt-action.

I have never been a real fan of the Mosin-Nagant; to me it was just one of those strange 19th century European rifles that were kinda interesting. It certainly had a lot of historical significance but it never had the romance of a Springfield, an Enfield, or a Mauser. Also, as a gunsmith I never saw anyone really spend a lot of time working on 'em.

Many, many years ago when I was a student at the Colorado School of Trades, we did a lot of work on surplus military bolt-actions. The students who, like me, were almost always strapped for cash brought in inexpensive military rifles to use as the basis for their projects.

While I remember a number of Arisakas, Schmidt-Rubins, and maybe even a Carcano or two being used as well as lots of Mausers, I don't remember anyone ever working on a Mosin-Nagant.

That was unfortunate. As I've learned while working on this Mosin-Nagant project, you can do some very interesting things with this old warhorse. It can be quite a challenge to alter its appearance and give it a real sporter look. I've a lot of respect for this ol' girl and for the potential it offers to the gunsmith hobbyist.

I started this project with a standard Model 1891/30 Mosin-Nagant I obtained from the folks at Century Arms International. Century, whose ads you'll often see here in SHOTGUN NEWS, is by far and away the largest importer of surplus military and police firearms in the country. If your interest has been piqued by this project and you want to try it, contact the folks at Century or one of the many other dealers in surplus arms that advertise here in SHOTGUN NEWS. Any of these fine folks will be more than happy to fix you up with a Mosin-Nagant or two or three!

In the earlier parts of this series (5/10, 7/10, 9/10, 11/10), I cut the barrel back, bedded the rifle in a Boyd's walnut sporter stock, fitted a Pachmayr recoil pad, reshaped the receiver tang, cut off the magazine box and trigger guard bow, and modified a shotgun trigger guard to replace the military trigger bow.

After cutting off the trigger bow and filing down the magazine so it was flush with the bottom of the stock, the next step is to install a shotgun trigger guard. In an earlier series on sporterizing a military surplus Mauser (available on CD at www.shotgunnews.com) I also utilized an old discarded double barrel shotgun trigger guard.

These guards are often very slender and nicely shaped. They add a custom touch to an old military warhorse and they offer good protection for the trigger. On the Mauser, I installed double set triggers, so the large guard from an old double-barrel shotgun was just the right size. Unfortunately, this Mosin-Nagant has just a single trigger and the guard was much too long.

Coffield compares an issue Mosin-Nagant with the project rifle. There's quite a difference! Getting from the one configuration to the other is no small task, of course.

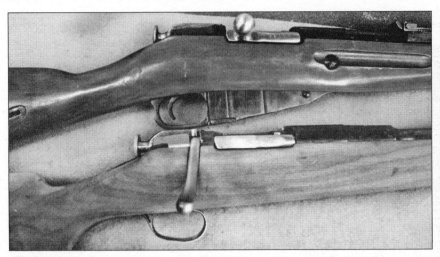

Moving the bolt handle rearward and installing a shotgun trigger guard revolutionizes the appearance of the homely Mosin-Nagant. Worth it? You can decide.

In Part 4, I cut a section out of the middle of the trigger guard bow and welded it back together. This made the guard bow much shorter and more appropriate for this project.

In order to install the modified guard, I needed to determine just where it would be located. There is a threaded stud on the front of the guard, and that can be used as the primary attaching point. Unfortunately in positioning the guard on the modified Mosin-Nagant bottom metal, I found there was not enough metal to support the stud.

At the point where it needed to be located, the metal on the Nagant was milled away as part of the inside of the old trigger bow. Also, there was a quarter-inch or so diameter hole for the spring that retained the original magazine floorplate.

My first order of business was to fill the spring hole. That was relatively simple. I just took a piece of mild steel quarter-inch diameter rod, cut it just long enough to fill the hole, and welded it into place. No sweat, no problem!

Next, I needed to build up some metal ahead of the trigger slot to permit positioning of the trigger bow stud. That was more of a chore. I used a TIG welder to deposit enough metal to provide the support needed for the threaded stud.

I wish I could claim that I was so good a welder that I did it all in just one sitting, but that wasn't the case. I first built up the metal, then filed it down to shape.

At that point, I found a couple of small pinholes or voids. Because of those, I had to go back to the welder and lay in a bit more steel and then file that back to shape. Finally, it was done!

Before moving on with installing the new trigger guard, I went ahead and took care of moving the bolt handle on the Mosin-Nagant. This is definitely the hairiest part of the project. No matter how you slice it, a Mosin-Nagant is darned hard to make look like a sporter with the military bolt handle. Even if you bend down the handle, it looks awkward. There are some commercial screw-on bolt handle kits that help, but in my opinion, even these fall short of the mark. The bolt handle is just too far forward.

Several months ago I saw an article in SGN by David Fortier in which there was a photograph of highly modified Mosin-Nagant being used in a rifle match in Europe. What grabbed me was the fact that the bolt handle had been moved back on the bolt body. I had thought of doing that but I wasn't sure about the idea until I saw that photograph. I knew then that I could do it and definitely would move that darn handle.

My first step was to turn down a 4-inch piece of half-inch steel rod to about 3/8" or .375" for about an inch. I then contoured the end of this smaller diameter section so it matched the curvature of the bolt body. This rod would serve as a base for my new bolt handle.

Next, I determined where my new bolt handle base would go on the body. In this case, it was right at .500" directly behind the existing safety lug/handle base.

The new base was then TIG welded to the bolt body. I had to use TIG since the new base was so close to the angled cam surface on the rear of the bolt. If I had tried to use my oxy-acetylene outfit, I am certain I would have ruined that cam surface since I was only about .100" from it! The heat from the weld had to be controlled and applied in a very precise manner. TIG was the only way I knew to do that.

Once the new bolt base was welded on, I cut off the excess material, leaving a stud about a half-inch high. With the original bolt handle still in place, I installed the bolt in the rifle action and began to cut a new bolt handle slot in the rear of the receiver.

Coffield TIG-welded a support base or stud for the new handle on the bolt body, then removed excess metal by hacksawing, filing and judicious use of a Dremel tool.

This was probably one of the hardest parts of the project. I noted where the new base was located against the receiver, and carefully began to cut a slot with a grinding stone on my Dremel tool. The slot ended up being about .400" wide.

The important thing to keep in mind here is that the new slot must be cut at a slight angle initially from the rear forward. It is not at 90° to the bolt ways. As the bolt turns and locks into place, it is drawn forward by the angle of the bolt lug seats, and you must take this into consideration as you cut the new slot. It is tricky!

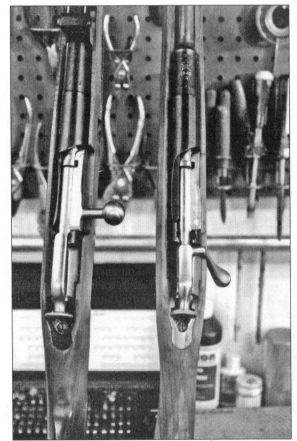

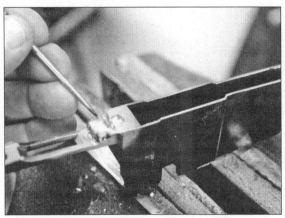

As you can see, the extension on the cocking piece of the project rifle has been cut back by almost 1/2" to provide needed clearance for the base of the bolt handle.

Coffield had to TIG weld a plug into the bottom of the magazine and fill a slot by welding to provide a position for the attaching stud for the new trigger guard bow.

The base for the original handle also serves as a safety lug. Even after the new bolt handle is in its place, the base will still perform this important function.

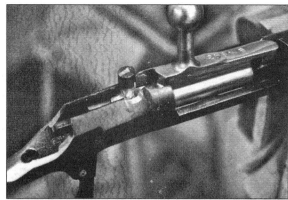

Here Coffield has begun to grind a slot in the receiver for the new bolt handle support base. Go slow when cutting or grinding in your new slot. Check fit often.

In cutting the bolt handle slot I initially cut too much on the top rear of the slot. In fact, I had to TIG weld that portion of the slot back up and recut it. I could have left it but there would have been a very unsightly gap. So, it was back to the welding bench to add on a bit of metal which was then dressed down.

After cutting the new slot, the next operation was to weld on a handle. Since this is a very European rifle, I felt it would be best to use a European-looking handle. I happened to have a butter knife handle in my supply of bolt knobs that looked like it would match.

I honestly don't know where I got this handle. It was picked up years ago somewhere along the way. You can probably find other

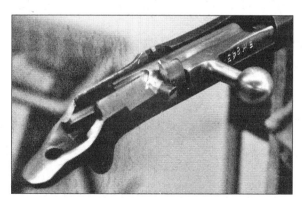

You will know you have completed the new slot when the bolt will lock fully into battery. Don't go too far, or you'll have to weld fresh metal onto the work and reshape.

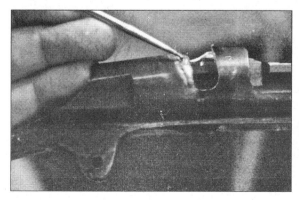

Even old gunsmiths make mistakes! Coffield mistakenly ground away a bit too much metal and had to build up the top rear portion of the bolt slot with TIG welding.

Here the slot has been repaired. How often do you see a bolt with two handles? Then he removed the original bolt handle, leaving only the new sporter handle in place.

butter knife handles that would also work at either Brownells or MidwayUSA. The important thing for me was that the handle was long enough to place the end of the knob right above the trigger bow. Also, I wanted a shank long enough to be bent back so it would be fairly close to the trigger.

Finally, there was an aesthetic consideration. The Mosin-Nagant action is fairly "deep," that is, the width from the top of the receiver to the bottom of the stock is rather large. The bolt handle had to be long or it would look awkward terminating in the middle of this expanse of wood on the side of the stock. The nearest comparison I can think of is the old Schultz and Larsen rifles that were imported years ago.

The handle was TIG-welded to the new bolt stud. The weld was then roughly filed to shape and the bolt checked for fit in the action. When I saw that everything appeared to work, then and only then did I cut off the original handle.

This was done with a hacksaw and then the base/safety lug was roughly filed and ground to shape. By the way, the shank of my military handle was quite soft but the base/safety lug turned out to be harder than woodpecker lips.

The barreled action was installed in the stock so the inletting for the new bolt handle shank could be completed. This was relatively simple. I just coated the underside of the handle with inletting black and noted where I got contact with the stock when the bolt was lowered as far as it would go. I used several different coarse round files for the inletting as well as my trusty Dremel tool.

All I needed to do was remove wood until the bolt could close completely. It was important to have the slot in the stock no wider than was absolutely necessary and properly angled for the bolt shank.

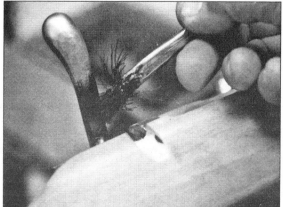

It's messy, but Coffield used inletting black to determine the shape and location of the bolt handle slot in the stock. Note the small contact patch at right.

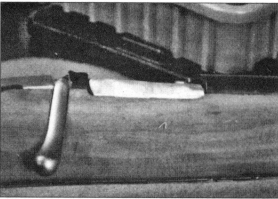

The new bolt handle is now in place and the stock cut to accept the bolt handle shank. Coffield says this part of the job represented a foray into new territory.

The next step was to modify the cocking piece. The cocking piece, which also serves as the safety, has an extension that projects forward along the top of the bolt. This projection must be cut back or it will block the movement of the new bolt handle base as the bolt is opened.

Before cutting the cocking piece, look at the underside of this extension. Note that there is a small raised stud. This stud engages the angled cocking cam on the rear of the bolt and draws the firing pin back when the bolt handle is raised. *Do not cut into that stud!* If you do, you'll be buying a new cocking piece from the good folks at Numrich Gun Parts!

I used a Dremel cutoff wheel to remove approximately .500" of metal from the end of the front of the cocking piece. This metal is extremely hard and a hacksaw would not even touch it. Once the metal was cut off, I used a belt sander to round the square end of the cocking piece to give it a nice smooth radius.

Before and while doing this, I checked several times by installing the cocking piece back on the bolt to ensure there was clearance for the bolt handle base. Fortunately, everything worked just fine.

With the bolt taken care of, I went back to work on the new trigger guard. I located, drilled and tapped the hole for the trigger bow stud. The stud on the trigger guard is threaded 1/4-24. This required a No. 6 drill for the hole. Fortunately I did have an appropriate 1/4-24 tap, even though it is a rather odd thread.

By the way, if you plan on doing gun work, whenever you get a chance to pick up unusual or odd taps and dies for anything

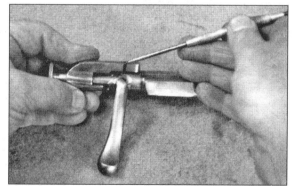

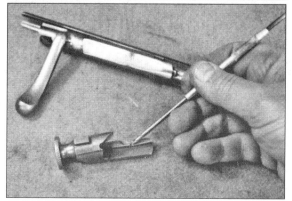

The front of the projection of the cocking piece had to be cut away, but the little part Coffield indicates here must not be altered or damaged. Be very careful!

The cocking piece is hardened, so the only way to cut it is with an abrasive cutoff wheel. This is not the part of the project where you want to be in a hurry.

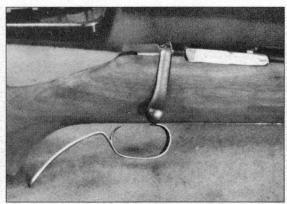

Once the bolt handle was in place, Coffield returned to work on the trigger guard. Note how the curvature of the guard tang does not match the curvature of the stock.

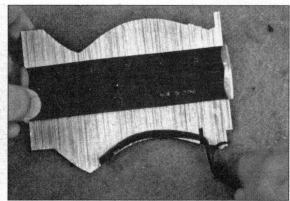

As Coffield worked with the trigger guard tang, he checked it against the contour gauge frequently. Making the bend correct is vital to getting a good fit.

There's still a bit of cosmetic shaping to do, but the basic length is correct. The bolt handle can be lifted and will clear the cocking piece as it is cammed back.

under 3/8" diameter, do so! You will be amazed how often you will run into a need for an offbeat, odd tap or die.

With the hole for the trigger bow stud drilled and tapped, the guard was turned into place but would not seat fully due to the curvature of the tang. The tang was bent for some long forgotten shotgun stock. It didn't come even close to matching the contour of the front of the pistol grip on my Boyd's stock.

I needed to modify the guard tang but I could not simply bend it, as this would surely break it. If you have to bend anything other than the thinnest pieces of metal it is almost always best to heat the metal and have it red hot when you reshape it.

Another problem I faced was getting just the right contour. You definitely don't want to try holding a red hot piece of steel against a wood stock! Yeah, it would make inletting faster as it burns in, but it sure wouldn't do the stock much good. Believe me; burning in your metal work is generally not a good idea!

The challenge is to get the tang bent to match the curvature of the inside of the pistol grip. A great tool to help do this is a contour gauge as used by carpenters and wood workers. You've probably seen this tool at hardware stores. It has a flat 6-inch long body which holds hundreds of tiny, moveable steel wires laid side by side.

You just press the ends of the wires against any irregular surface and they move precisely to form to that surface. This gives you a pattern that you can easily transfer or in this case, duplicate.

I used the gauge on the inside of the Boyd's stock pistol grip. I then had a model I could use when bending my tang without danger of damage to the stock. I used a propane torch to heat the tang to a red color. While the metal was glowing red, I carefully bent it using two pliers. By the way, you have to be very, very careful when working around the screw holes in the tang. These are weak points and you can easily break the tang at these holes.

I always made sure I had one of the pliers over the hole closest to where I was doing my bending. The wide face of the pliers kept the tang from bending at the hole.

It took about 20 minutes to get the tang where I wanted it. My curvature was not a perfect match to my gauge, but it was pretty darn close. With the tang reshaped, I could now inlet it into the stock.

I first installed the trigger guard and with a sharp pencil drew lines along either side of the tang as it lay against the inside of the pistol grip. Following that I turned the guard aside and used a small, very sharp chisel to make a series of cuts straight down

along the two lines. I did not attempt to make any cuts at the very end of the tang at this point, though I did note where the end of the tang would be located.

I used several small chisels and gouges to remove wood inside the two chiseled lines. I took extra care to make sure I didn't cut outside those lines. I cut away the wood to approximately two-thirds the thickness of the tang. With this done, I was ready to get dirty!

I don't know about you, but for me inletting black is a pure pain in the you-know-what. I can open a container of that stuff, stand on the other side of the room, and *still* get it all over me! OK, maybe I exaggerate a little but I do tend to get the stuff all over me when working with it. Unfortunately, I've not found anything else that works as well for me in spotting the contact points when inletting metal into wood.

The bottom and sides of the trigger guard tang were coated with the inletting black and then the tang carefully placed into the newly cut recess. The inletting black left a trace only where

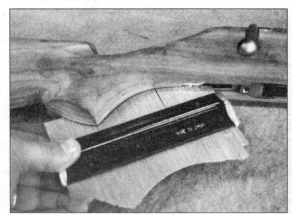

A carpenter's contour gauge is used to duplicate the inside curvature of the stock's pistol grip. The gauge has a profusion of wires that are free to move left or right.

The new trigger guard is now fully inletted into the stock and secured with two No. 8 wood screws. Using the shotgun trigger guard gives the gun a sporting look.

When it's all put together correctly, the cocking piece will be fully retracted as the bolt handle is fully lifted. Keep testing until it works just like this.

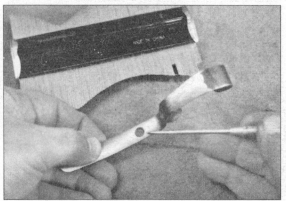

When bending the tang, be especially careful around the screw holes. The metal is weakest there and can easily break at those points. Support the tang with pliers.

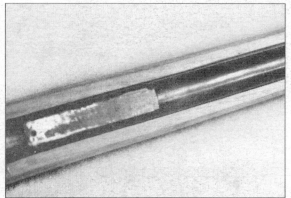

The only part of the Boyd's walnut stock design Coffield says he didn't like was the wide barrel channel, which he was easily able to correct with synthetic bedding.

To ensure clearance between the bedding and the barrel when correcting the barrel channel, Coffield placed a layer of plastic electrical tape along the barrel.

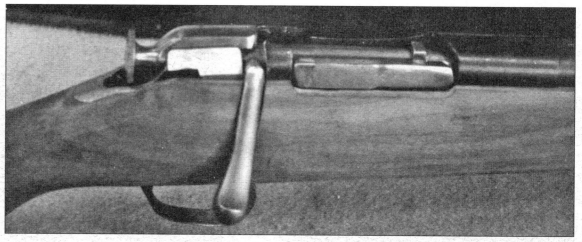

With the bolt modified, the hardest single part of the conversion has been completed. The project has been a big one, but Coffield says the end is now in sight.

there was metal to wood contact. It was just a matter of cutting away these contact points until the tang was fully inlet into the wood.

I had to be a bit careful with the very end of the tang. If you're not careful, you'll end up with a slight gap at the point. Since the inside of the grip is curved as well as the tang, the end of the tang will tend to pull away from the initial contact point on the grip.

Keep that in mind as you do your inletting, otherwise you'll end up using a bit of bedding compound to fill the resulting gap.

A trick to make your inletting easier is to file a slight angle on the sides of the tang. Instead of having the sides straight up and down, put a few degrees of taper on them so the base or bottom of the tang is narrower than the top. This'll help avoid unsightly gaps in your inletting.

Once the tang was fully inletted, I installed a couple of inch-long No. 8 steel wood screws to secure it in the stock. I used the existing screw holes in the trigger guard tang. As always when installing screws into wood, I drilled pilot holes for the screws.

In this case I used a 7/64" drill for the threaded portion along with a 11/64" drill for the short unthreaded section directly under the screw head.

With the wood screws in place, I used some files to do a bit of shaping to the tang and the surrounding wood. This was just to dress it up a bit and make sure my screw heads blended with the tang.

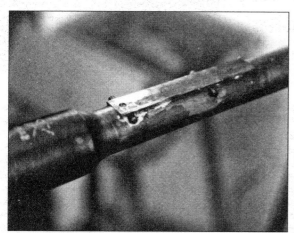

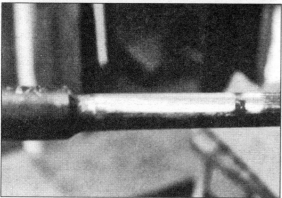

The holes for the pins that secured the rear sight base were filled by soldering in the original pins and then filing the pins flush with the surface of the barrel.

I had hoped to get more of the metal work done by this point. We still have to finish the magazine and make and install a floorplate. With the bolt taken care of, those are or should be relatively simple tasks. We'll take care of that next time.

In a project like this there are always some little jobs you need to take care of as you move along. For example, when I removed the military rear sight, I found two holes drilled through the top of the barrel for pins securing the sight base. With the base removed, these holes stood out like a sore thumb. The solution was pretty simple. I took the same two pins I had removed earlier and soldered them back into place in the holes. I then used a flat bastard file to reshape barrel where the sight base had been located.

At this point I didn't need to get a super smooth finish, I just wanted to make sure that portion of the barrel was round, reasonably smooth, and blended into the rest of the barrel.

Another job had to do with the barrel channel in the stock. As you know, I'm using a Boyd's semi-finished walnut sporter stock. It's a darn good stock and most importantly for me, it had lots of wood to allow shaping and modification. Lots of other

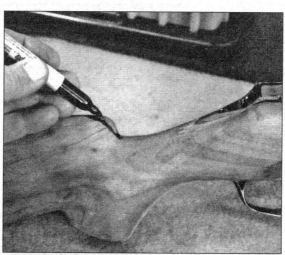

Coffield found the nose of the comb to be too angular. He drew in a more curved nose with a marker, then quickly reshaped the nose of the comb for a much better look.

stocks I know of just don't give you enough wood to allow for changes in style or dimensions but the Boyd stock does.

The only real criticism I have of the stock is the oversized barrel channel. Initially I thought I might be able to go with it, but the more I worked with this project the more I realized that I wanted to do something about that. Fortunately, the resolution is really simple.

I started by applying two layers of plastic electrical tape to the bottom half of the barrel, beginning just ahead of the chamber. After the tape was applied, I coated it with release agent.

I then applied a couple of strips of masking tape to the forearm alongside the barrel channel and coated them with release agent as well. This tape was simply to help make cleanup a bit faster and easier.

I mixed up some Bedrock bedding compound from MidwayUSA, which I had used earlier to bed the action. This I applied to the inside of the barrel channel and then the barreled action was secured in the stock. The next day after the bedding had cured, the barreled action was removed from the stock.

After cleaning up the excess bedding, I removed the tape from the underside of the barrel. When I then placed the barreled action back in the stock I had a nice uniform gap between the bedding and the barrel equal to the thickness of the tape. This gave me the free floating barrel I wanted while at the same time it filled the unsightly gap in the barrel channel.

Another "quickie" job I could have left until later dealt with the nose of the comb. The Boyd's stock had a rather pronounced, angular nose. I prefer a smoother, more radiused or curved nose. To modify the nose I used a pencil to draw in the outline of the nose I wanted on the stock.

If you do this, take your time and don't hesitate to erase your work and try other shapes and angles. Once you have the shape you like, go over the drawings with a black marker. Then just take a coarse file or rasp and remove the excess wood.

Keep in mind there is no "one way" or "required" shape for your stock. This is *your* rifle and you can darn well do it any way that pleases you!

As a friend who was an acknowledged expert on wines once told me, "Reid, if you like it, it's a good wine no matter what it cost or what other people think or say. If you don't like it, for you it's garbage and to heck with what other people think!"

I like that attitude! This is *your* rifle and *your* project. If you like the results, that's all that really matters.

Next time we get together, we'll finish the magazine and floorplate and do something about sights and the trigger. At this point, I honestly don't know for sure just what I'll do with that trigger! Remember, I told you I'd never done a Mosin-Nagant sporterization! We'll also finish up shaping the stock. After that we'll sand it and start applying finish. At the same time we'll prep the metal for a finish.

I'm still up the air about a metal finish. I might blue it or I might go for one of the bake-on finishes. We'll see what happens when we get there.

By the way, I would like to thank all the folks that have written about this project. It has stirred up a lot more interest than I had anticipated and that's great! The more folks that are working with guns, the better, and I hope you are enjoying this project as much as I am. Until next time, good luck and good gunsmithing! ◉

Sporterizing the Mosin-Nagant

Part 6

By Reid Coffield

He's done the major surgery; now Coffield is ready to get to the fine points of the facelift that will turn this hag into a princess.

Coffield's closing in on completion of his epic sporterizing project on the Mosin-Nagant rifle. A double-ended caliper helps avoid removing too much stock wood.

The Russian Mosin-Nagant is definitely not the world's greatest bolt-action rifle from a mechanical or design standpoint nor is it the most attractive. Even among diehard collectors, few if any would argue that it is. For the hobbyist or home gunsmith, the Mosin-Nagant offers many opportunities to practice gunsmithing techniques, hone skills, and solve challenging problems in converting this rifle into a useable and attractive sporter. As the most commonly available and least expensive military bolt-action rifle, it can serve as a tremendously valuable learning tool.

If you're interested in a true gunsmithing challenge, check out the ads here in SHOTGUN NEWS or contact the folks at Century International Arms, Inc., 430 South Congress Dr., Suite 1, DelRay Beach, Fla. 33445, telephone 800-527-1252. All of these dealers have lots of Mosin-Nagants and would be delighted to sell you one for your gunsmithing project. Try it! It's fun and it's challenging!

Before we get into working on the Mosin-Nagant, I need to bring you up to date on a couple of things. I've had several inquires from readers about wooden sporter stocks for the Nagant. When I started this project, I got my walnut stock from Boyd's Gunstock Industries, Inc., 25376 403rd Ave., Mitchell, S. Dak. 57301, telephone 605-996-5011. The stock was one of many carried by Boyd's and readily available at that time. Since then the folks at Boyd's have literally been buried with demand for their stocks. That's not surprising; they produce a good product at a reasonable price.

Anyway, the demand has been so great that they've had to temporarily cut back on the number of different stocks they could produce. Unfortunately the Mosin-Nagant stock was one of those temporarily pulled from production.

When I learned of this, I called and was assured the Mosin-Nagant stock would be back in production this fall. So if you need a Boyd's stock, you'll be able to get one, but it'll probably be fall before they're available. In the meantime, if you're interested in one of those stocks give Boyd's a call or drop them a note to let 'em know this is something you plan on ordering. That'll also help them to gauge the demand and better plan their production. As those of you who have been following this series know, I really like my Boyd's stock and highly recommend it for this project.

In the course of my research on the availability of wood Mosin-Nagant sporter stocks, I found Richards MicroFit Stocks, Inc., Box 1066, Sun Valley, Calif. 91352, telephone 800-895-7420, is also listing a stock for this rifle. I called them and was assured that they do indeed offer this stock, but because of demand they're also running several months behind.

As I understand it could take 60 to 90 days or more for them to fill an order for a Mosin-Nagant stock. I've not seen or used one of these stocks so I don't know anything about it. However, this may be another possible resource you might want to check out.

On a side note, I think it's interesting in this day of synthetic stocks that two of the companies producing traditional wood

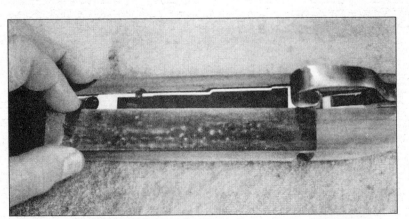

Coffield uses a 1-inch wide piece of 1/8" thick steel to make a floorplate. Be sure it's plenty long enough to reach between the action screw and trigger guard.

The rear notch for the trigger bow is made with repeated cuts with a hacksaw. This "straddle" style for a floorplate has long been popular with custom gunmakers.

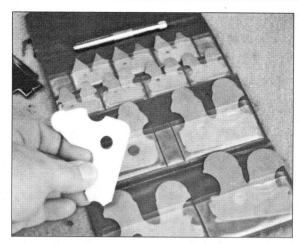

Radius gauges are useful for laying out curved lines when fabricating parts. These are tools used in cabinet-making to create standardized decorative features.

Coffield used a radius gauge to scribe in matching curved lines. Selecting a pleasing curve is crucial in making the floorplate an organic part of the rifle design.

stocks evidently can't keep up with the demand. Maybe there's a lot more of us who like wood stocks than we thought!

O.K., let's get back to work on that old Russian warhorse! The first thing I need to do is to make a floorplate for the magazine. Prior to this I had cut quite a bit off the original military magazine. In fact, anything that projected below the bottom of the stock was cut off! This drastically changed the lines and appearance of the rifle.

The way in which the military magazine projects below the stock is so unique and distinctive that it immediately identifies the rifle as a Mosin-Nagant. Nothing else in the world looks like it and, if I do say so myself, it looks bad!

You might think that instead of making the floorplate, it would be best to alter the follower assembly at this time. Nope. You gotta take care of that floorplate first. The reason is the Mosin-Nagant has a leaf spring attached to the original military floorplate by a single screw. This spring helps to power or raise the follower assembly. You have to attach this to the new floorplate before you can modify and adjust the follower assembly to work properly.

With a flush magazine and a slender, modified shotgun trigger guard, the appearance of the rifle is already very different.

However, I have to cover the bottom of the open magazine and provide a platform for the follower spring.

I started with a piece of 1/8" thick mild steel approximately 6 inches long by about an inch wide. I needed it to be wide enough to cover some gaps in the inletting and at the same time look nice. I wanted the floorplate to look as much as possible like any other floorplate you see on a commercial Mauser, Winchester, or Remington.

Initially I laid the strip of steel alongside the magazine opening to determine my actual length. The front of the floorplate needed to extend almost to the front guard screw. I already knew I would be using a screw to attach that portion of the floorplate to the magazine. The rear of the floorplate had to extend back to and on either side of the trigger bow. This is kinda like a "straddle" floorplate that custom gunmakers often use.

This was important for two reasons. First, it helped to cover some gaps in the inletting on either side of the magazine. Second, and most important, the trigger bow serves as an anchor to the rear of the floorplate. The bow would actually support and secure the rear of the floorplate.

I coated the steel flat with Dykem and laid out the outline of the finished floorplate. There were really only two critical dimensions. The first was the front end or tab that extended up to the front guard screw. This portion needed to be long enough to accept a screw and yet it also needed to be no wider than the magazine. I made mine right at .465" wide for a length of about a half-inch.

I then used an 8mm radius gauge to scribe in a curve to merge the narrower front end tab with the full width of the floorplate, which was about .860" wide. Once the outline was scribed in, I used a hacksaw to cut away excess metal. This was followed up with various files to smooth everything and remove metal down to the scribe marks.

The large slot at the rear of the floorplate was also cut with a hacksaw and then cleaned up with files. My slot was about .400" wide by about .300" deep. You'll want to base the width and depth of your slot upon the size of your trigger bow. It's very important that the floorplate fit snugly so there's no movement either side to side or up and down when it's in place. Don't forget to put a slight taper or bevel on the top of the front of the slot so it "wedges" under the curvature of the trigger bow as tightly as possible.

With the outline of the floorplate taken of, the next step was to taper the bottom. Remember this floorplate is made of 1/8" thick steel. If you leave it as is, it would be blocky and very uncomfortable when you held the rifle in the action area. Almost all floorplates have a curved surface to blend with the stock.

To achieve this, I scribed a line about .040" above the bottom along the sides of the floorplate. It was then a simple matter of tapering from the center of the floorplate out to these lines with files. This was followed up with a bit of work on a belt sander. You really don't have to remove a lot of metal to get the right "feel" for the floorplate.

Once the shaping was done, the next step was to drill and countersink a hole for the primary attaching screw. I started to use a 6x48 screw and then realized it just looked too darn small so I went instead with an 8x40. It's a little bigger and more substantial though I doubt there will ever be enough stress on the floorplate to matter. The location of the screw is not all that critical. Just make sure it's centered and it is located on the tang ahead of the mag well.

To make sure the floorplate is tight against the trigger bow, drill the hole in the floorplate first and use it to locate the hole on the magazine tang. Before you drill the magazine tang, move your hole location back just a few thousandths towards the trigger bow. This will ensure you have pressure on the trigger bow and your floorplate is nice and snug against the trigger bow when secured. After the hole is drilled and tapped, check the floorplate for fit.

With the floorplate complete, the next step was to install the follower assembly. The original assembly consists of a follower and follower carrier. The follower carrier is attached to the original floorplate by a small pin. The

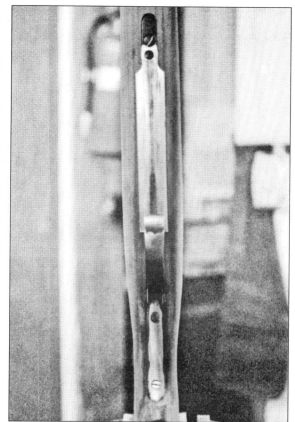

Once the floorplate was cut out and filed to the proper size, Coffield rounded the bottom to give it a more finished look and feel. Note the floorplate is not hinged.

floorplate and follower carrier assembly are held in the magazine by a hinge pin in the front of the magazine box and a spring catch located at the rear of the magazine box.

The design is really remarkable. The follower carrier and magazine floorplate clamp over the hinge pin. That hinge pin is the key to modifying the follower assembly. I removed the hinge pin and then in shortening the magazine, cut through the hinge pin hole. A small portion of that hole is still visible and it served as an aid in locating the new pin.

The military floorplate was removed from the follower carrier by driving out a small pin. I then laid the follower carrier on the outside of the magazine and moved it around a bit until I could determine the best location for the new hinge pin. The location was just above and to the right of the original hinge pin.

I already had a hole in the follower carrier which was about .099". This was equal to a #39 drill. I then just used a #39 drill to put a hole in both sides of the magazine box. The follower carrier is not as wide as the magazine box, so I had to take the military floorplate and cut off the two forward projections of the floorplate that originally extended on either side of the follower carrier. These projections had a small hole for the pin that joined the follower carrier to the floorplate.

Once the projections were cut off, I ground them down and made two small spacers. These spacers were placed on either

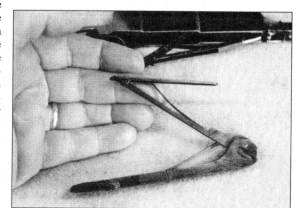

The complexity of the Mosin-Nagant follower makes modification to the magazine much more challenging. This is no mere W-shaped spring with a follower on the top.

Don't forget to put a bevel on the front of the trigger bow notch to allow it to seat fully and securely. With the floorplate in place, gaps around the magazine are hidden.

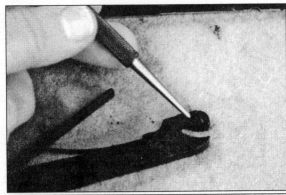

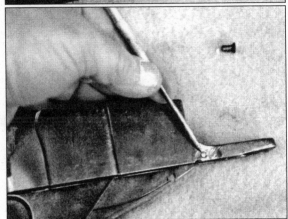

This hole on the follower carrier will be used for the new pivot pin. Note the pivot pin location just slightly above and to the right of the original pivot pin.

side of the follower carrier when it was pinned in place in the magazine.

Once that was done and the follower carrier positioned so the follower was level with the top of the magazine, I noticed that the lower end of the follower carrier extended below the level of the magazine box. With the new floorplate in place, this would have prevented the follower from going as high as needed for proper positioning of the cartridges.

I then removed the follower carrier and ground off the excess metal. It was placed back in the magazine box and checked again with the floorplate. The new floorplate now served as a "stop" for the follower carrier.

All that remained was to locate the follower carrier spring. Here I really lucked out. In examining an unaltered magazine I noticed that the screw for the follower carrier was in direct line with the rear folds in the side of the magazine box. All I had to do was mark the location of those folds on the side of the new floorplate and then scribe a line across the floorplate connecting those marks. The screw would be located at the midpoint of this scribed line.

The location of the spring is important. If it's too far forward or too far to the rear, it will not engage the follower carrier properly. However, using the folds in the side of the magazine box as locators basically solved that problem.

The spring was attached to the inside of the new floorplate with a small 6x48 screw. I had to open up the hole in the spring just a tad to provide clearance for the screw. Other than that, it was pretty straightforward.

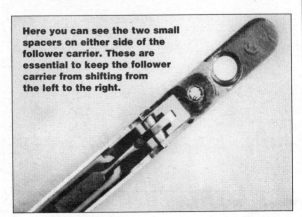

Here you can see the two small spacers on either side of the follower carrier. These are essential to keep the follower carrier from shifting from the left to the right.

I decided to go with a Huber trigger for this rifle. As far as I know, Huber produces the only aftermarket trigger for the Mosin-Nagant. I got my trigger from MidwayUSA, 5875 W. Van Horn Tavern Road, Dept. SGN, Columbia, Mo. 65203, telephone 800-245-3220. This trigger is adjustable in that it allows you to control the amount of engagement between the sear and cocking piece. The amount of sear engagement in this rifle plays a major role in determining the weight of trigger pull.

Basically, all you do is just install the Huber trigger in place of the existing trigger. Nothin' special is required to do that. Once the trigger is in place, you use a small Allen wrench supplied with the trigger to adjust the protrusion of a metal ball inside the trigger that bears against the sear. By turning the Allen screw clockwise, it will force the ball to move and push the sear down and away from the engaging surface on the bolt cocking piece. You have to be careful you don't adjust the ball protrusion too far. Huber cautions that you should have a minimum of .015" sear engagement.

When you have the trigger pull adjusted to your satisfaction you *absolutely must* test the sear engagement. Huber suggests dropping the butt of the rifle to the ground from a distance of at least 12 inches. You want to make darn sure the sear notch on the cocking piece will not slip off the sear and release the firing pin. Again, you have to check this thoroughly to make sure you've not created an unsafe condition with your rifle.

After installation of the Huber trigger I discovered I had a problem. The trigger was contacting the inside of the trigger bow and the return. The return is that small, tapered piece of metal that curves back and inward inside the trigger bow. As far as I can tell, it has no real function other than looking nice and giving the trigger bow a more elegant, finished look.

The problem was easily resolved by simply doing a bit of file work on the tip of the return and shortening it up a bit. I also shortened and reshaped the lower portion of the trigger. Neither job took very long but it is something you want to watch for when you modify or replace the trigger bow or even just use an aftermarket trigger.

Following this I assembled the rifle. I had to do a little work on the bedding to provide clearance for the interrupter/ejector. That took just a few minutes with my Dremel. Once that was done, the rifle was put together.

With the bolt out of the rifle, I loaded the magazine to see just how many rounds it would hold. I knew I would be able to get at least two rounds in the magazine. I was pleasantly surprised to find that the modified magazine would hold three rounds. That is plenty for me for most hunting applications. If I had to, I could always have three in the magazine and one in the chamber but I don't really see the need for that. After all, lots of folks hunt with single-shot rifles! Three rounds are plenty. If I miss more than three times, I've got a major problem and it's not lack of ammo!

The next order of business was to do a bit more shaping to the stock. While I have taken a lot of wood off the stock already, it's still a bit thicker and blockier around the forearm than desirable. Before I start removing wood, I have to determine just how much wood I have on the bottom of the forearm. The stock has a slot routed along the bottom of the barrel channel. I imagine this was to make the stock a bit lighter. My problem is that I don't know how thick the wood is below the bottom of this slot.

Fortunately I have a 7-inch double-ended caliper I bought some time ago from the folks at Woodcraft, Box 1686, Dept. SGN,

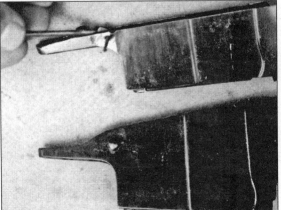

A portion of the carrier follower will have to be removed to allow the follower to rise to the proper height to ensure feeding of the last cartridge in the magazine.

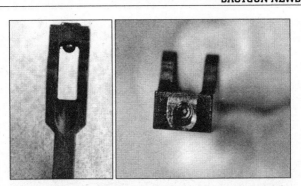

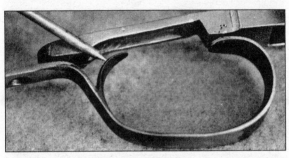

The Huber trigger for the Mosin-Nagant uses a moveable ball inside the trigger to control the height of the sear by turning a small Allen screw in the top of the trigger.

The return on Coffield's trigger guard was a bit too long and had to be shortened to allow full movement of the trigger. Rifle triggers may not fit shotgun guards.

Parkersburg, W. Va. 26104-1686, telephone 800-225-1153. A double-ended caliper is ideal for this situation. If you are going to do stock work I would strongly encourage you to add something like this to your tool inventory.

Though Woodcraft sells primarily to woodworkers, they do offer a number of tools and various supplies gunsmiths will find useful. If you don't have one of their catalogs; give 'em a call and get one. I think you'll find it very helpful.

By the way, by using my double-ended caliper, I found I had just a hair over a half-inch of wood between the bottom of the slot and the underside of the stock. I could easily remove a significant amount of wood without danger of cutting into the slot. That was a relief to know. There are few things worse in stock work than cutting into a lightening slot or the inletting when shaping the exterior. It can truly ruin your day!

As I've mentioned before, the Boyd's stock is designed with plenty of extra wood and it allows each user to custom shape it to his own specifications and desires. For me, one of the most frustrating aspects of working on some semifinished stocks is finding I have no way to modify or change the shape or lines of the stock. That is certainly not the case with this stock!

Earlier I cut away the cheekpiece and did some major reshaping of the buttstock. I also shortened the stock, discarded the hard rubber buttplate and installed a Pachmayr recoil pad.

There are still three areas I want to modify. The end of the forearm is very blocky and needs to be rounded. The forearm itself is too deep and should be made a bit thinner. And finally, the rails or top portion of the stock alongside the action and barrel are too wide. This should be thinned a bit and given a bit of taper so the stock has a more rounded feel. Right now it feels blocky.

I believe a good stock design uses a series of interrelated curves with very few flat surfaces. A well-designed stock almost seems to flow from forearm tip to the butt and when you hold it, you never feel any angular surfaces or flat spots. Sure, we're not going to make this Mosin-Nagant into anything that would get us into the Custom Gunmakers Guild, but we can make it look and feel pretty darn good.

At this stage in the final shaping of the stock, I find it very helpful to pencil in some guidelines. On the top rails, for example, I drew in lines that were approximately .100" outside the barrel channel and receiver inletting. These would help to keep my wood removal even and uniform.

As for tooling for this work, I used a 10-inch Nicholson half-round cabinetmaker's rasp. This is much finer than the least aggressive standard rasp I normally use. By using it, I will save a considerable amount of time sanding out residual rasp marks. This cabinetmaker's rasp will move wood, but it leaves a much smoother surface. The less damage you do to the wood now, the easier your sanding will be later.

I started by narrowing the rails along the top of the stock. As I did this, I constantly checked my work by running my fingers over the sides of the stock. I wanted to make sure that I had a nice, flowing surface with no sharp angular ridges or lines.

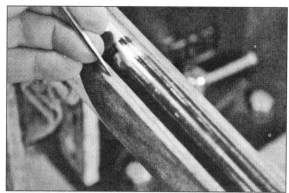

The rails along the top of the stock are much too wide for Coffield. He will cut these down to give the stock a better feel and look, checking with a straightedge.

Once the rails were completed, I then started work on the bottom of the forearm. Keep in mind there is a lightening groove cut into the bottom of the forearm barrel channel that extends to within a half-inch of the bottom of the forearm. I have to be careful that I do not cut into this groove.

As I did this work, I tapered the stock from around the front guard screw to the tip of the forearm. I was careful to keep this line level, with no dips or ripples. During the work, I checked the forearm with the edge of a ruler to make sure I was not accidentally cutting too much in one area and not enough in another. I also used my double-ended caliper to make darn sure I didn't even come close to cutting into that lightening groove.

Since I was removing so much wood on the bottom of the forearm compared to what I removed on the rails, I started with a coarse rasp followed by a medium and then a fine cut rasp. I then finished up with my cabinetmaker's rasp. I was surprised at how little wood I had to remove to shape the forearm. I thought I would really have to hog off the wood but I ended up taking a little less than .100". I didn't even come close to cutting into that lightening groove in the bottom of the barrel channel.

With the forearm tapered and shaped, the last step was to round the tip of the forearm. There's certainly no law that says you have to round the forearm tip. Heck, if you want to make it angular or flat, you can do that. After all, it's your stock! For myself, I think a round forearm tip is attractive and suitable for this stock.

Now, getting the darn thing perfectly round can be a challenge. Some folks can do it perfectly just by eyeball. I wish I could claim to be one of those guys but I'm not. I need help.

The help I'll use is a simple template cut out of an index card. I start by measuring the width of the forearm tip. In this case it's about 1.4 inches. I then draw a straight line on the index card and mark off 1.4 inches. That is now the diameter of my circle with the midpoint, also marked, at .7".

A compass is set up with the center at the midpoint and a circle is drawn passing through the two outside marks. I used scissors to cut the circle in half along the original line. The inside of one of the half circles was then cut out to form the template. That's all there was to it!

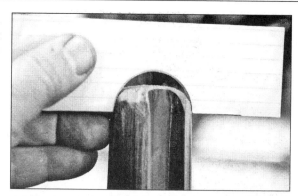

Solutions can often be very simple. Coffield used this template made from an index card to round the forearm tip. At this point he still has a lot of wood to remove.

With the template, it was just a matter of holding it over the end of the forearm tip and rasping away wood until it fit. As you do this, be sure to rotate the template around the tip of the stock for a smooth, uniform surface. Also, keep in mind the center of the forearm tip should be just slightly below the bottom of the barrel channel.

Well, that's about it. As always it seems, I didn't get as much accomplished as I had hoped. One thing you learn in gunsmithing is that most jobs take longer than you anticipated. No matter whether it's a simple repair or a major project like this Nagant, you always run into something that was unexpected. That just seems to be the nature of the beast. For most of us, it's no big deal. After all, we're gunsmithin' and havin' fun!

The next time we get together I'll sand, seal, and finish the stock. I'll also start workin' on the metal. If you remember, the outside of the barrel is extremely rough with deep machine marks. Because of that, we'll delve into the magic and mysteries of draw filing. Finally, if all goes well, I'll cover the selection and installation of sights. That's a lot and I might not cover it all but I'll sure give it my best shot.

Until next time, good luck and good gunsmithing!   ◎

Ask the Gunsmith

By Reid Coffield

ORTGIES CYCLING

Q *I have a German-made Ortgies .25 cal. semiautomatic pistol. It seems to be a fine quality little gun. The problem is that I can load the clip and fire the first round. It ejects and throws another round in the chamber. I then pull the trigger and nothing happens. I can pull back the slide and throw another round in the chamber and then it will fire. It seems like it is not cocking itself. Could the sear be the problem? It's an old gun made in the 1920s.*

A It sounds to me like your Ortgies is short cycling. The fact that it functions properly when you manually pull the slide back would seem to indicate that the sear is working correctly. However, when you fire the pistol, the slide may not be moving far enough to the rear to allow the striker/firing pin to engage the sear. In any event this problem should be correctable.

Any knowledgeable, competent gunsmith should be able to repair this pistol. If you cannot locate a gunsmith in your area to do this work, you might want to contact John Treakle, Hi-Caliber Gunsmithing, 2720 E. Hwy. 101, Dept. SGN, Port Angeles, Wash.

98362, telephone 360-417-6847. John is a very gifted and talented gunsmith and I know him well. We worked together on the tech staff at Brownells for many years. Give him a call and I'm sure he'll be able to help.

Ortgies pistols were very common World War II souvenirs, though they were without the cachet ascribed to the Walther PP or Mauser HSc. They were made in both .25 ACP and .32 ACP versions.

LUGER HOLD-OPEN

Q *I am having trouble with a Luger pistol that was given to me by a relative. From what I understand, the bolt is supposed to lock back after the last shot. Mine will do that. The problem is that the bolt will not lock back when the magazine is not in the gun. There is no gunsmith in this area so I am on my own. Can you help?*

A There is no problem with your Luger. The hold-open latch is pushed into position to block the movement of the breechblock by a button on the right side of the magazine. The button is attached to the magazine follower. As the follower rises, the button moves up, eventually contacting the bottom of the hold-open latch. When the last round is fired the magazine button will push the hold-open latch up far enough to block the forward movement of the breechblock. If the magazine is not in place, there is nothing to activate the hold-open latch.   ◎

This button on the Luger magazine follower activates the breechblock hold-open latch. If you look closely, you can see the bottom of the breechblock hold-open latch located above the magazine button.

Sporterizing the Mosin-Nagant
Part 7

It's been a long process, but Coffield is rounding into the home stretch. Here he finishes the stock and installs iron sights and a scope mount.

By Reid Coffield

If you've been working along with me on your Mosin-Nagant, we've come a darn long way towards making an old warhorse into a pretty decent sporter. This series started in the 5/10/07 issue and has run every other month since. When it's completed in the 7/10/08 issue, you'll be able to buy the whole series on CD from the SHOTGUN NEWS website. Not many folks would even consider the Russian Mosin-Nagant a candidate for sporterization. In its original military form, it certainly doesn't look like it could be made into a sleek, attractive sporter.

However, I think the modifications we've made have transformed the rifle into at least a pretty decent sporter. Sure, we won't make it into the Custom Gunmakers Guild with our Nagants, but we've had a lot of fun with 'em and we're going to have even more fun in the future. I just can't wait until I take the completed rifle out to the range and someone looks at it and obviously can't tell what the heck it is! That will be a hoot!

One item I need to give you a heads up about is the interrupter/ejector. The interrupter, which is a unique part of the Mosin-Nagant, puts downward pressure on the cartridges that remain in the magazine when the top round is chambered by the bolt. This takes pressure off the bottom of the bolt and makes feeding easier and smoother. The ejector is connected to the interrupter as part of a single assembly. That's all well and good. The problem you may encounter is having enough clearance inside the stock for the interrupter/ejector.

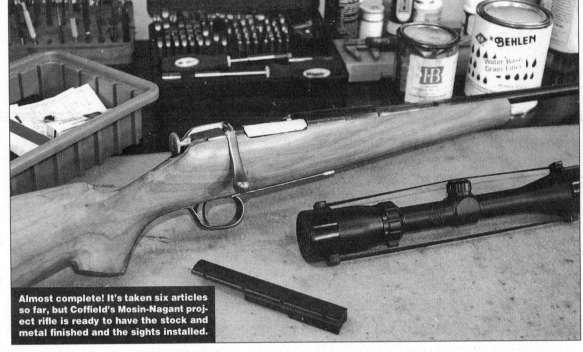

Almost complete! It's taken six articles so far, but Coffield's Mosin-Nagant project rifle is ready to have the stock and metal finished and the sights installed.

When the bolt is cycled, the interrupter/ejector, which is basically a spring, must flex outward away from the receiver. You absolutely have to have clearance for this to happen. If you don't, the receiver will be pushed upward out of the inletting and/or the bolt will be darned hard if not impossible to operate. It'll feel like there's pressure or drag on the side of the bolt preventing its movement.

I thought I felt a bit of excessive tension as I was working my bolt and sure enough, the interrupter/ejector was the problem child. It was easy enough to confirm by simply putting a bit of inletting black on the interrupter/ejector, placing the action in the stock, and cycling the bolt.

Upon removal of the barreled action, the inletting black from the interrupter/ejector was visible where it touched the stock. A bit of work with a sharp chisel and a scraper, and the problem was solved. It can be a head-scratcher if you run into this problem, but a bit of inletting black applied to the parts will tell the tale.

Let's get to work and get this ol' rifle finished. Most of the hard work has been completed. It's just a matter of doing a bit of touchup on the stock and then taking care of the sights and working on the finish for the metal and wood.

Earlier I had done quite a bit of shaping to the Boyds' stock. Boyds' Gunstock Industries, Inc., 25376 403rd Ave., Dept. SGN, Mitchell, S. Dak. 57301, telephone 605-996-5011, provided a darn nice walnut semi-finished stock. Like most stocks of this type, there was plenty of extra wood to enable folks to customize the stock to their personal tastes. I cut off

the Monte Carlo cheekpiece to give the stock a more conservative, traditional appearance. I also discarded the plastic buttplate provided with the stock and installed a soft Pachmayr recoil pad.

I also reshaped the forearm, making it much more slender. Originally the stock had a bit too much depth in the forearm. As part of the forearm modification the tip of the forearm was also reshaped to give it a more rounded appearance.

The interrupter/ejector, essentially a spring on the left side of the receiver, can cause problems if its movement is hindered by incomplete inletting.

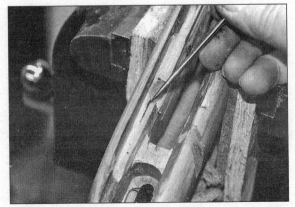

A trace of inletting black in the stock inletting indicates contact by the interrupter/ejector. This will make bolt movement difficult or even impossible.

Coffield reshaped the pistol grip to be flat and shorter. When reshaping the grip cap, he made sure its bottom line was aligned with the heel of the buttstock.

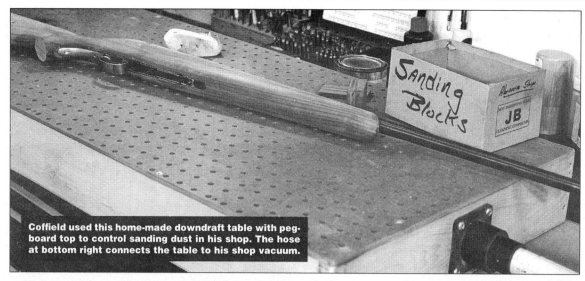

Coffield used this home-made downdraft table with peg-board top to control sanding dust in his shop. The hose at bottom right connects the table to his shop vacuum.

Coffield says it's important to resist the temptation to sand with the fingers. Always put your paper on some sort of block, whether homemade or commercial.

A perfect recoil pad fit results from sanding the pad and stock as a single unit. There's really no way around it, Coffield says, if you want a seamless fit.

The one area I still wasn't quite happy with was the pistol grip. It still looked a bit blocky and frankly, just a bit too long. The end of it seemed to stick too far out beyond the bottom of the stock. It was a simple matter just to rasp wood from the grip cap. When doing this, I was careful to keep the flat surface of the end of the grip at an angle, so if a line were run from the grip cap it would intersect the heel of the stock. This is a fairly standard convention among stockmakers and I think it has merit. It certainly helped make the pistol grip on this stock look a lot nicer as far as I was concerned.

Once the shaping had been completed, I was ready to do the initial sanding. I will be the first to admit I don't like to sand stocks. Because of this, I want to get it over with as quickly as possible while still doing a good job. Over the years I've discovered a few tricks to make the work faster and at the same time, produce a better job.

I learned long ago from an old friend that it's best to have a systematic plan for sanding a stock. If you don't, you'll probably waste a lot of time sanding some parts of the stock too much and others not enough. I know I sure did!

The trick is to make a list of the various parts of the stock, post it where you'll be doing your sanding, and then follow the list as you sand. My list is as follows:

1. Comb of buttstock
2. Toe line of buttstock
3. Right side of buttstock
4. Left side of buttstock
5. Right side of pistol grip
6. Left side of pistol grip
7. Front of pistol grip
8. Top of pistol grip
9. Bottom of pistol grip
10. Right side of forearm
11. Left side of forearm
12. Bottom of forearm
13. Tip of forearm
14. Top rails of stock

You can make your own list with the sequence in any order you like. The important point is that you're systematic and that you sand every part of the stock as much as needed but no more than needed.

The folks at MidwayUSA, 5875 West Van Horn Tavern Road, Dept. SGN, Columbia, Mo. 65203, telephone 800-243-3220, offer a very nice stock refinishing kit that includes a great chart with a diagram of a stock and a similar sequence for sanding. To my mind, that chart alone is worth the price of the kit.

When sanding I always use a backer for my sandpaper. These backers are just sanding blocks range from a simple 1/4" thick flat piece of wood about 3 inches long by 1¾ inches wide to pieces of hard felt that have been glued to bits of plywood. I also have various rubber sanding blocks as well. The importance of a sanding block is that it'll ensure your sanded surfaces are level. It will bridge the natural hard and soft area or high and low spots in the wood.

The next time you're at a gun show, check out some older rifles and shotguns with refinished stocks. Hold 'em up to the

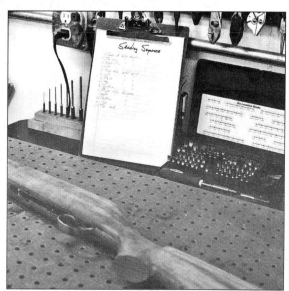

Coffield keeps his sanding sequence list readily available for quick reference as he works. Checking each area off with each grit used prevents missing a spot.

light and look along the surface of the stock. Don't be surprised if you find lots of dips and ripples. Some of those stocks look like a storm at sea! This results from the finisher just holding sandpaper in the hand rather than backing it with a sanding block.

Sanding blocks also show their value in preserving the sharp edges around the barrel channel, pistol grip cap, buttplate, and the inletting. If you have a cheekpiece, a sanding block will help to avoid rounding over the edges of the cheekpiece and having it look more like a wooden lump or growth on the stock than something designed to support your face!

I also learned long ago to leave the recoil pad or buttplate on the stock while sanding. I sand both the stock and the sides of the recoil pad or buttplate at the same time so I have a perfectly level, smooth joint between it and the end of the buttstock. If you don't, you can almost definitely count on the recoil pad or buttplate not matching the sides of the stock after you're finished. Generally, the wood will be narrower than the buttplate or recoil pad.

Because I've used a modified shotgun trigger guard with a long tang inletted into the stock, I did most of the sanding with this metal in place. As with the recoil pad, leaving the tang in place will ensure the wood around the tang is not over-sanded and the match between the wood and metal will be perfect. This also applies to the rear tang of the receiver. The wood and metal should be the same height after sanding. It does make sanding a bit more challenging but the results are more than worth it.

When sanding it's important always to sand in the direction of the grain. For gunstocks, this simply means having your sanding strokes run lengthwise along the stock. If you look closely at your stock you'll see elongated pores or holes in the wood. Those are created when the cellulose fibers of the wood are cut open during the shaping of the stock. These openings form a pattern commonly referred to as the "grain" of the wood.

By sanding lengthwise along the grain, the tiny scratches left by the sandpaper are hidden or disguised by the wood pores. If you sand across the grain, your sandpaper scratches would show up like a sore thumb. So…always, always sand with the grain and it'll make you stock finishing look a lot nicer.

Another thing you can do to make your work faster and more efficient is to use the proper grits of sandpaper and to use 'em in sequence. I start out with 80-grit. This may seem to be too coarse, but it makes quick work of removing all rasp and file marks left from my alterations to the stock. I'm very careful to sand every inch of the stock and not allow any portion of it to be missed. In addition, I make darn sure that I when I finish there are no marks on the stock other than those left from the 80-grit paper.

I then use some 150-grit paper and again follow my list as I sand each and every part of the stock. When I finish, I will have removed all the earlier 80-grit marks. After this sanding, I wipe the stock down with a damp cloth. I just want to dampen the stock. I sure don't want it so wet that water runs off the wood. I then dry the stock with a hot air gun.

As the stock dries, small bits of wood fiber or "whiskers" that have been lying on the surface are raised. Some folks call this "raising the grain". I then sand the stock again with my 150-grit sandpaper. Some folks would go on to the next higher grit but I like to repeat with the same grit when cutting off those whiskers. Again, I follow my standard routine of going by my list to make sure no parts of the stock are missed. I then raise the grain once more and then sand with 220-grit paper. This is followed by raising the grain and then sanding again with my 220-grit paper. This may be overkill, but I never have to worry about "whiskers" popping up after the finish is applied.

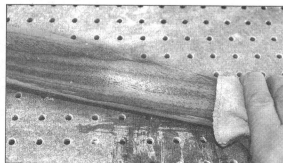

Use a wet cloth between sandings to dampen the wood and help raise the grain. When grain no longer rises with the cloth, the surface is ready for stains and finishes.

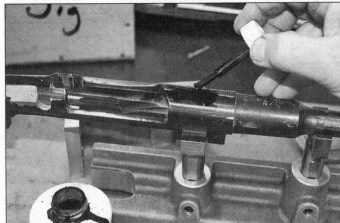

Coffield began scope mounting by applying Dykem to make scribed lines on the receiver readily visible. The scope base should be flush with the front of the receiver.

Unless you do the work outside, you'll make a mess of your shop with sanding dust. If at all possible, I try to sand outside. If I can't, then I use a home made down draft table. This is really just an elongated wooden box with holes in the top surface. My shop vac is hooked up to a port on one side of the box. As I sand the stock over the box, the vac sucks the majority of the sanding dust through the holes in the top of the box and into the vac. It's not perfect but it really cuts down on dust in my shop.

Once the stock has been sanded, the next step is to seal it. The function of sealing is to provide a barrier between the interior of the wood stock and the outside elements. You can use all sorts of things for sealers. A lot of folks just take their regular finish and thin it and then use it as a sealer. For this stock I decided to use some Laurel Mountain Stock Sealer. I've used both the sealer and finish for years and found it to be quite good.

To apply the sealer, I took a small paintbrush and brushed on the sealer until the stock would absorb no more. I was especially careful to make sure that I applied plenty of sealer to the inlet-

ting and to the wood under the recoil pad. Hobbyists will go to great lengths to seal their stocks and forget about the wood under a recoil pad or buttplate. To me it's kinda like locking all the windows in your house and then leaving the front door wide open. Unsealed wood under a buttplate will absorb moisture like a sponge. So be sure to seal every bit of exposed wood.

With the wood sanded and sealed, I set the stock aside in my drying cabinet. This is nothing more than a long, rectangular box with door and controlled heat and air movement. I use a small Golden Rod positioned at the bottom of the cabinet to provide heat. The cabinet has two openings for air and each has an air filter over it to keep out dust. As the air is heated, it rises and moves out of the box through the top vent. Fresh air is then automatically drawn into the cabinet by the bottom vent hole.

If you don't have a drying cabinet, I'd urge you to consider building one. It not only helps to cure your stock finishes faster and in a cleaner, more dust free environment, it also just helps to protect your stock finishing projects. I used to hang my stocks from the ceiling in my shop, dust would settle on them and every now and then I would accidentally hit one or even drop it! Believe me, a stock drying cabinet, no matter how small or simple, is the way to go!

Originally, I planned on having only iron sights on this rifle. However, the reality is that I'm 62 years old and I just cannot see iron sights as well as I once did. Now I will still put iron sights on this rifle if for no other reason than to have an emergency backup to my scope. As a gunsmith I can absolutely assure you that scopes can and do fail and often at the worst possible moment. Having iron sights as a backup is cheap insurance and can some times save your hunt. I well remember once hunting in Alaska when my scope fogged up to the point of being totally useless. Iron sights allowed me to keep hunting and to bag a darn nice caribou.

The scope base I choose is a one-piece Weaver style mount made by Advanced Technology Inc., 102 Fieldview Dr., Dept. SGN, Versailles, Ky. 40383, telephone 859-873-9877. This mount is made of a single piece of black anodized aluminum. It's mounted on the front ring of the receiver with two 10-32 screws and extends back over the bolt and the rear ring of the receiver. Our project rifle has had the bolt handle cut off and mounted behind the rear ring but this mount is still very appropriate.

Ideally I would want the scope base supported at both the front and rear. On a sporter such as this, I doubt there will be any significant loss of accuracy or movement of the scope using a base attached to only the front ring. Besides, this base is pretty darn massive and the two 10-32 screws will provide ample support.

The unit comes with very complete instructions showing how to mount the scope base without using any fixtures or jigs. While

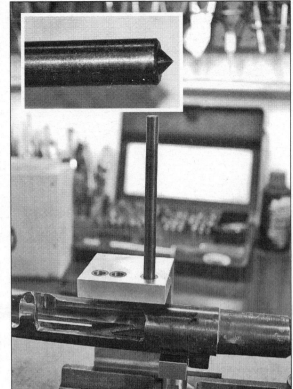

A transfer punch is used to help locate the overarm of the Forster Sight Fixture. This is an essential tool for accurately locating scope base screw holes.

you can certainly do that, I prefer to use a fixture when at all possible. In this case, I used a Forster Sight Mounting Fixture that I've had for more than 30 years. To me, this is the finest sight mounting fixture available and it will last a long, long time given proper care. These fixtures are still available at any of the gunsmithing supply houses such as Brownells or MidwayUSA.

One of the reasons the Forster Fixture is so darn good is that the barrel is held between two "V" blocks. This goes a long way towards ensuring that the receiver is positioned so the holes for the scope base or bases are properly located. In one sense, the scope base indexes off the barrel rather than the receiver. Consequently if the barrel is even just a bit angled off the axis or center of the receiver, the scope base is positioned to compensate for that. The fixture can even be used to mount iron sights on the barrel with a special adapter, but we'll get into that in a bit.

The first thing I did after placing the barreled action in the Forster Fixture was to coat the top of the receiver with Dykem. This enabled me to see what I was doin' when I made some locat-

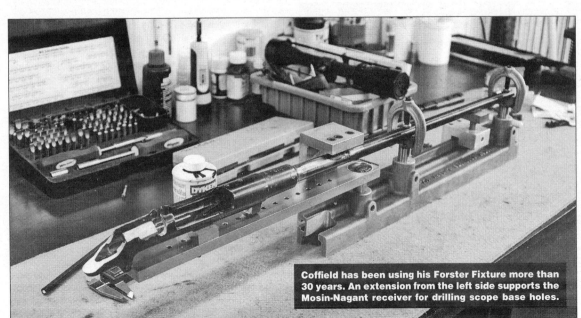

Coffield has been using his Forster Fixture more than 30 years. An extension from the left side supports the Mosin-Nagant receiver for drilling scope base holes.

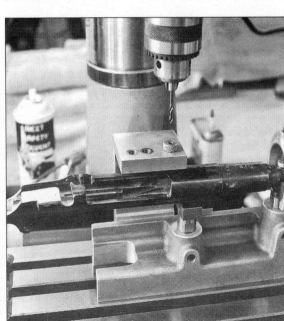

With a proper bushing installed in the overarm, Coffield has the Forster Fixture set up in his mill/drill ready to drill the first scope mount base screw hole.

Coffield says an easy way to set depth is to use drill bit shanks as gauges to set the depth stop on his mill/drill. The #38 drill has a shank diameter of .100".

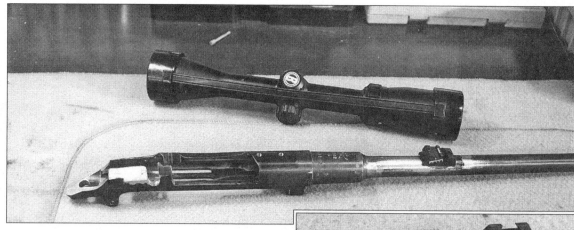

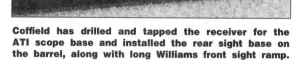

Coffield has drilled and tapped the receiver for the ATI scope base and installed the rear sight base on the barrel, along with long Williams front sight ramp.

ing marks. Next, the scope base was placed on the front ring of the receiver. The front of the base should be even with the front of the receiver. Make sure the base is reasonably level and then use a scribe inside the rear screw hole to mark the location of the hole on the top of the receiver.

The overarm of the Forster Fixture is attached to the Fixture and positioned over the location of the rear scope base screw hole scribed on the receiver. A transfer punch was inserted in the overarm and tapped lightly. The overarm was then removed and the location of the transfer punch mark compared to the scribed circle. The location of the overarm may often have to be adjusted to center the transfer punch in the scribed hole. It's important to be as precise as possible, because this will determine the location of the scope base.

Once the overarm had been located, a #31 drill bushing was installed in the overarm. I then moved the Fixture over to my mill/drill and, using a #31 drill, drilled the first hole in the receiver. The drill bushing made sure the hole was exactly where it was needed. Following this, I used a larger drill bushing and #22 drill for the final hole diameter. One way to ensure accuracy in drilling holes is to start out with a smaller diameter than required and then open it up to the final desired diameter. Also, using a fixture with hardened bushings for the drills makes it just about impossible for the drills to move off center as they cut.

After drilling the first hole, I tapped it using the 10-32 tap supplied with the scope base. The base was then attached to the receiver with one screw. I used a scribe to mark the location of the front attaching screw hole on the receiver. Drilling and tapping this last hole was done in the same manner as the first hole. All in all, mounting this base using the Forster Fixture was very fast and easy. After I finished mounting the scope base, I

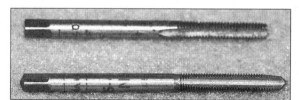

The bottoming tap (top) has cutting threads all the way to the tip. The regular tap (bottom) is made with the cutting threads gradually tapering into a point.

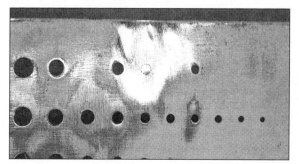

Thread scope or sight base screws to be shortened into a screw plate, then grind down flush to the plate, shortening the screw without damage to the threads.

checked to make sure my screws didn't extend too far into the receiver. If they did, they would interfere with the movement of the bolt. If that ever happens, just shorten the screws as needed.

With the scope base installed, the next part of the project was to install the iron sights. You have an almost infinite variety and combination of sights, both front and rear, to consider. I based my selection on a recommendation from an old Williams Gun Sight Company book, *How to Convert Military Rifles*. In this book Williams recommended using a 7/16" front sight ramp along with a .281" high front sight insert or bead.

The recommendation for the rear sight was a Williams WGOS-M along with a 3/8" blade. These sights are suggested for a military barrel that had been cut to 22 inches. The barrel on the project rifle is a bit longer, 23 inches, but that shouldn't have any significant effect on the sights. In actually mounting these sights I found that the WGOS-M was a bit too large. Instead, I used the WGOS-S, which was a better fit for the curvature of this particular barrel. Both the WGOS-M and WGOS-S are the same height; only the bottom radius of the base is different.

The rear sight was mounted first approximately 4¼ inches ahead of the receiver. The barrel at that point is .755" in diameter. That number is important as it'll determine how deep the screw holes can be drilled. To determine the safe depth of the screw holes, I subtracted the bore diameter, which is about .310", from .755", the diameter of the barrel. This gives .445" which is then divided by 2, which equals .222". That is the basic wall thickness of the barrel at the point where the rear sight is to be installed.

I can drill the holes approximately .100" deep with no danger of drilling into the bore. Ideally, I would like to have the depth of the holes equal to the diameter of the screw, which would be .134". However, .100" is more than adequate and will provide plenty of support for the threads of the two sight base screws.

Again, I used Dykem to mark where I wanted to position the sight. Then, as with the scope base, I used a scribe to indicate the approximate location of the rear screw hole. I placed the barreled action in the Forster Fixture, except this time, I used an extension for the Fixture. This enables the Fixture to be used to mount rear and front sights without repositioning the barreled action. Unfortunately this extension, which was not made by Forster, may no longer be available. I got mine years ago. However, if you want something like this, the photographs will give you a pretty good idea of how it's made and how it works.

The sight attaching screws are 6-48s which are just about the standard thread for sights. The drill required for the 6-48 screw is the #31. The only critical problem is just making darn sure I don't drill too deep and into the bore. With the rear sight, the hole depth can be as much as .134" though I will opt to just drill .100" deep. That will still provide plenty of purchase for the sight screw threads.

The way to keep from drilling too deep is to use the drill stop on the drill. Setting that for the proper depth is very easy. I took a #38 drill with a shank diameter of .100" and used that as a spacer under the drill stop when adjusting it. Your drills, as in this instance, can often serve as gauges as well as cutting tools.

As with the scope base, I drilled one hole for the rear sight base and then tapped it. The sight base was installed and then the front hole was located with a scribe. It was then drilled and tapped. This may seem like a lot of extra work rather than just drilling both holes at the same time but it ensures that the hole spacing is absolutely correct. Believe me; nothing will make you feel sicker than having a sight screw hole improperly located.

The front sight ramp is held on by just one screw, which again is a 6-48. The barrel diameter at the point where it'll be located is .622". Subtracting the bore diameter of .310" results in .312". This is then divided by 2, which equals .156". The total depth of the metal under the screw is no more than .156".

I will still drill to a depth of .100" since that leaves me with a wall thickness under the screw of .056". That sure doesn't sound like much, but it'll be plenty. The Forster Sight Fixture really comes into its own when you have to drill absolutely precise holes. There is no way you could do this freehand.

Since all these sight holes are so shallow, standard taper taps don't work too well. There is just too much lead or taper at the point of the tap. The front end of the tap will often contact the bottom of the hole before it can begin to cut threads. For this reason you will need to use a bottoming tap. A bottoming tap has less lead so the threads are cut closer to the bottom of the hole. With these holes, I used a modified bottoming tap where I had ground virtually all the lead off the tap. This gave me the maximum number of threads in my holes.

When fitting the screws to the sights, it's often necessary to shorten the screws. This is especially common when using shallow holes as I did. A simple method of shortening a screw without damaging the threads is to turn the screw into a screw plate so that just a bit of the threaded portion protrudes out the back side of the plate. You then hold the screw head with a screwdriver and grind off the part of the shank that sticks through the plate. A belt sander is ideal for this. Once the screw is shortened, turn it out of the plate. The threads will be perfect, right up to the grind point. Screw plates such as the one I used are available from both MidwayUSA and Brownells.

Keep in mind that the ramp is held on with just one screw. When installing the front sight bead, it's imperative that the ramp be supported. If you just clamp the barrel in your vise and drive in the bead, I'll almost guarantee the ramp will be loosened. Again, support the ramp as the bead is installed.

One last thought about iron sights. As I mentioned earlier, I used a combination of sights recommended by Williams for this rifle. I could have done the math to calculate the specific height of both the front and rear sight. Even if my numbers were absolutely perfect or the information from Williams is right on the money, when I finally get to the range the rifle could still shoot high or low.

Tables of recommended sights or formulas and calculations will never be able to account for internal stresses in the barrel, incorrect fitting of the barrel to the receiver, or other invisible factors. Always be prepared to change the height of the front bead or insert or in this case, the height of the rear sight blade. Some times, you just have to do that.

I had hoped to get the metal prepped for finishing but I just flat ran out of time. Next time we get together we will finish this old beast!

Until next time, good luck and good gunsmithing! ◉

Sporterizing the Russian Mosin-Nagant Rifle

Part 8

By Reid Coffield

Sometimes he wondered if it ever would end, but in this installment Coffield reaches the end of the line and takes his handsome sporter to the range, where it performs like a champ.

Coffield was very well pleased when two fellow shooters couldn't identify his rifle as a Nagant. Neither Michael, on the left, nor Blaise could identify the rifle.

We're definitely near the end of the road with this project! If you were with me when we started, one of the goals I had was to modify the rifle in such a way that at least from a distance it didn't look like a Mosin-Nagant. With all the work that was done modifying the magazine, relocating the bolt handle, and fitting a new walnut semi-finished Boyd's stock; I think we've done it!

The last time we got together, the barreled action was drilled and tapped for a scope mount. Iron sights were also installed. As I mentioned at that time, I am a strong believer in having back-up sights. You never know when a scope will be damaged or put out of action. That happened to me once and it really made a lasting impression. Having iron sights will ensure your hunt can continue. Nothing is more worthless than a rifle without sights!

The Boyd's semi-finished walnut stock was shaped, sanded and sealed. This stock has been pretty drastically altered. As with many semi-finished stocks, it had a lot of extra wood. By this, I mean the dimensions were very generous. This is good, as it allows the user to customize or personalize the stock to his individual tastes.

For example, the stock came with a Monte Carlo cheekpiece. That's fine if you like 'em. However, I prefer a more traditional look in my stocks so I just took a few minutes with a rasp and re-shaped the comb, removing the Monte Carlo cheekpiece. I also shortened and thinned the forearm. This is one of the great advantages of using a semi-finished stock. You can often alter it to fit your needs and tastes. Many times that just isn't possible with a pre-finished stock.

Earlier, I had sealed the stock using Express Oil Sealer from Brownells. The reason for sealing a stock is to create a barrier in the wood to prevent the absorption of moisture. Moisture will cause wood fibers to swell. This in turn can cause major problems with the bedding as the wood shifts and bends under the barreled action. A forearm is normally especially prone to warpage. Use of a sealer will not necessarily provide a 100% guarantee this won't happen, but it sure will help!

After sealing the wood, the next step was to fill the pores or open grain. Having an open grain was important and necessary in order to allow the sealer to penetrate deeply into the wood. Once the sealing process had been completed, those same pores needed to be filled. There are a couple of reasons for this. First, the filler will aid the sealer in creating a barrier to moisture. Secondly, by filling the pores it will make getting a smooth, even finish on the wood a lot easier and faster.

The wood stocks on many commercial rifles in the past were never filled. I have seen lots of Winchesters with porous, open-grained stocks. I've also seen a good many high dollar British doubles and sporting rifles with unfilled stocks. However, to me it just doesn't make sense not to fill the grain. It's not all that difficult, it's a mark of good craftsmanship, and it helps in getting a good looking finish.

One of the hardest things for a working gunsmith to do is try new techniques and products. That probably sounds strange and perhaps even flat-out wrong but bear with me for a minute. As a working gunsmith, your primary focus in life is to get the darn job done as quickly as possible and out the door.

You have to feel that way! You won't get paid until the job is done and you will always need the money. Consequently you normally just don't have time to experiment and fool around with this or that new product or technique.

You tend to use the procedures and products you learned as you got started. They work and as my Dad used to say, "If it ain't broke, don't fix it!"

The hobbyist is in an enviable position most professional gunsmith could only wish for. He has the luxury of time to experiment and try new things. Money for the rent or to keep the lights on is not dependent on when he gets this or that repair job finished.

Since this was my own project, I was not saddled with time and money constraints. This allowed me to try a new product for filling the Boyd's Mosin-Nagant stock. It's a water-based filler sold by Woodcraft I found in their catalog. It's sold under the H.

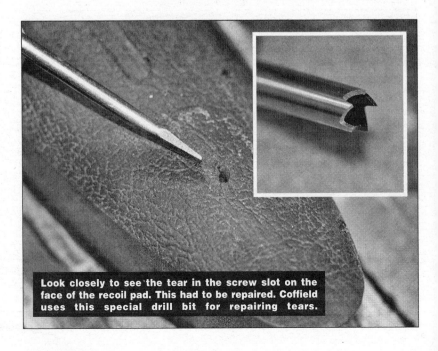

Look closely to see the tear in the screw slot on the face of the recoil pad. This had to be repaired. Coffield uses this special drill bit for repairing tears.

A drill press is used to turn the bit, intended as a screw extractor, into the face of the pad. The results are clean, symmetrical holes that look factory original.

Behlen brand and is a brown filler #B744-0026. It was listed for walnut and was touted as a quick drying product. In addition, the catalog description indicated that it filled the pores easily. Having never heard of it or even seen it, I decided I'd give it a shot.

When I got the material and opened the can I almost decided not to use it. It was black as pitch and had a very oily look. However, after stirring it turned a light brown color. I used a bit of paper towel to put some on the stock and then wiped it across the grain. It did dry very quickly. In fact, it may dry just a bit too fast for me. I had a little trouble getting it to spread out on the stock without building up on the surface.

Although the directions said it could be sanded in two hours, I put the stock back in my drying cabinet and didn't sand until the next day. I then went over the stock with 220 grit sandpaper. My objective was just to remove the extra filler on the surface of the wood. I didn't want to sand into the wood as this would open up more pores.

Once this sanding had been completed, I wiped the stock down with a tack rag to remove any remaining sanding dust. Tack rags are basically just pieces of lint free cloth that have been treated with various types of finish. You can find 'em at any paint or wood working shop.

Like the filler, I opted for a finish I'd never used. The product is Gun Sav'r Custom-Oil Gunstock Finish, Hunter Satin. It's a urethane/oil aerosol made by Chem-pak, Inc. in Martinsburg, W.Va. I was familiar with the company and had used some of their other

products, but I had never used this one. It was touted as a fast and easy finish so I decided to give it a shot.

Basically you apply it just like any other spray finish. It dries very quickly and seems to be resistant to runs. Since this Nagant is destined to be a hunting rifle, a satin finish made a lot of sense. This old rifle will probably get some rough use so a satin finish will tend to look better over a longer period of time and, of course, it won't reflect light like a high gloss finish. This product, by the way, is available from various suppliers. Both Brownells and Midway stock it.

I applied my first coat at 1:30 in the afternoon, followed by a second coat at 9:45 the next morning. A third coat was applied the next day at around noon. I gave the stock a fourth coat the following day and finished with a fifth coat the next day. In five days, the Gun Sav'r finish gave me a nice even, completely filled finish.

The total time involved could not have been more than 30–45 minutes or so. In fact, I probably spent more time shaking the aerosol can than I did actually applying finish!

All in all, the resulting finish is quite good. There was only one run which was entirely my fault. In making a pass with the aerosol can I paused over the stock when I should have kept the can in motion. Even this was easily sanded out and hidden with the next coat. With a satin, low gloss appearance, this finish is ideal for hunting rifles or guns that will get a lot of use and hard knocks. I will definitely use this product again. In fact, I will be getting a can of the high gloss finish as well. This product is easy to use and saves a lot of time. In a gunsmith shop, that's about as good as it gets! If you have a stock finishing project, try it. It may be just what you're looking for.

While the application of the stock finish took only a few days, I wanted to allow it to cure for at least a week before checkering. When working with the stock, I had a problem with the recoil pad. When I removed it from the stock to apply the finish, the slots I had cut for the attaching screws in the face of the pad were torn. I'm not sure what caused it but it really looked bad. I was faced with coming up with a means of correcting the problem or replacing the recoil pad. I decided to make a repair and it's one you might want to try if you ever have a damaged recoil pad.

I used a 1/4" screw extractor I purchased. from Woodcraft. It's a hollow cutter designed to drill around the shank of a wood screw whose head has been broken off. While I have used it for that purpose, I found that it's great for cutting clean, neat screw holes in the face of recoil pads.

You just chuck the screw extractor in your drill press and drill around the damaged screw slot in the face of the pad. The result is a pad with two perfect holes that most folks think are factory original! It's a great way to salvage a damaged pad.

I then began work on the metal in preparation for finishing it. This ol' Mosin-Nagant was produced during World War II in 1942 when Russia was under tremendous pressure from the Germans. Rifles and guns of all sorts were in short supply. When manufacturing small arms, the primary requirement was production; getting as many out of the factories in as short a time as possible.

One of the first things to be sacrificed was finish. It really didn't make a rifle shoot or function any better to have a smooth, even metal finish on the barrel or receiver. If it had deep lathe or machine marks on the outside, so what! The rifle would still function. This rifle was a great example of that and had lots of deep machine marks all over the barrel and receiver.

I could have left 'em but this is now a hunting rifle and I've already spent a lot of time working on it. It just doesn't make sense to leave it looking rough and crude. Those machine marks had to go!

There are a number of ways of dealing with this. You could simply break out the cloth backed abrasive and start sanding. You would eventually remove all those machine marks. However, the operative word is "eventually!" It would take hours and hours of darned hard work. If you're like me, and I bet you are, you have a life and other things to do, so why waste all that time sanding. There has to be a better, quicker way of solving this problem.

Some folks would just step over to a buffing wheel loaded with a very coarse abrasive and have at it. That will definitely remove the roughness but there are potential problems. First you have to have a buffer and a number of buffing wheels. Most hobbyists don't have these and really don't need 'em.

Secondly, unless the buffing is done by a very skilled individual, you'll almost always end up with dips, ripples or other irregularities on the surface. If you don't believe me, take a look at any number of refinished guns at your next gun show. Hold the rifle or shotgun up to the light and sight down the side of the barrel. I'd be willing to bet some of those barrels will look like a storm at sea with lots of waves and ripples! Buffers are great time savers but in the hands of an inexperienced or careless user, they can cause a lot of problems and easily ruin a gun.

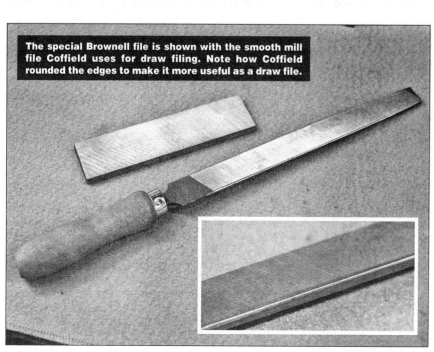

The special Brownell file is shown with the smooth mill file Coffield uses for draw filing. Note how Coffield rounded the edges to make it more useful as a draw file.

Nothing hard about draw filing: it just takes time. Each flattened spot must be overlapped with the next so material is removed evenly from all sides of the barrel.

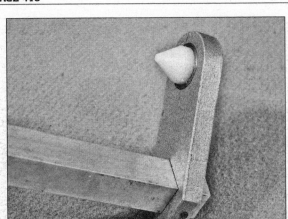

Each of the two uprights on the Clymer Barrel Spinner has a tapered Delrin insert to support the barrel damage-free as it is pressed against the abrasive wheel.

Traditionally when faced with a rough surface, either from machine marks or rust pits, gunsmiths would use a technique called draw filing to prep the metal. In draw filing, a file is held horizontally against the surface and pulled or pushed sideways along the length of the work piece. One hand is placed on each end of the file to provide control as the file is moved. Repeated, overlapping strokes are made until the machine marks, pits or irregularities are removed. It's a lot faster than sanding and it has the advantage of enabling the gunsmith to avoid dips and ripples in the surface.

Technically just about any file can be used for draw filing. I've found that a single cut file tends to work best for me. Having teeth in just one direction rather than two rows that cross tends to make the file easier to clean and avoid embedded metal filings.

Brownells actually offers a special draw file designed specifically for this purpose. I have one but more often than not I just use a 10-inch single-cut smooth mill file I modified for this purpose years ago. I ground the sharp edges off the sides of the file so it wouldn't dig into curved or tapered areas like the "fences" at the front and back of Winchester Model 12, 97, and 94 receivers.

As you draw file you must constantly check the file to make sure filings don't stick in the teeth. If they do, they'll create deep lengthwise scratches that'll be the devil to remove. In draw filing you make small, narrow flats the length of your barrel.

You then overlap your strokes so these flats are as narrow as possible. Once you've completed draw filing and have removed all machine marks, the next step is to remove all those tiny flats you made. This is done more often than not by hand polishing with an abrasive. We're back to that and yep, it does take time!

Years ago I discovered a couple of tools that really are time and labor savers when it comes to metal polishing and preparation.

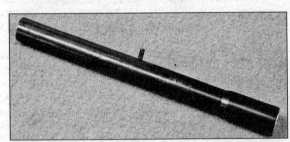

Coffield made this simple mandrel from a scrap barrel to support the receiver. The mandrel fits in the receiver and serves as a seat for one end of the Barrel Spinner.

Coffield secures the Mosin-Nagant barreled action in the Clymer Barrel Spinner. This allows the barrel to spin as it is sanded, preventing ripples and flat spots.

The first is the Scott Murray drum. Nope, this isn't a musical instrument! It's an expandable, rubber faced wheel for holding sanding belts. The one I have which I got from Brownells many years ago is 8 inches in diameter and 2 inches wide. This takes standard 2x25½-inch sanding belts.

The real beauty of the Scott Murray drum is that it enables you to change grits in a heartbeat. With traditional muslin wheels, you either had to have a row of several buffers all set up with wheels loaded with different grit polishes or you had to stop your buffer and change wheels when you wanted to change grits. That, my friends, took a lot of money and space for equipment. If you were working with just one buffer, you would waste a lot of time as you changed wheels. With the Scott Murray drum, you just cut off the buffer, remove the old belt and slip on another one and you're back in business. Fast and easy!

Now there is a downside to the Scott Murray drum. You have to be darn careful using it. Once you have the drum mounted on your buffer, never allow it to be turned on without a sanding belt

The Scott Murray Sanding Drum is one of Coffield's favorite tools. It saves him a lot of time and labor. Abrasive belts are quickly and easily removed and replaced.

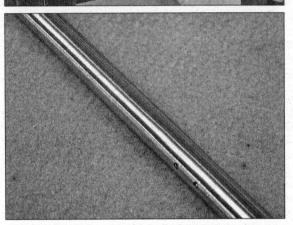

By varying the angle of barrel and drum, Coffield can easily control the amount of material he removes, leaving a smooth, even surface on the barrel in just minutes.

in place on the drum. If you do, you have problems! The drum is fairly soft rubber that expands as it turns. If the rubber is not confined by the belt, it will literally be torn off the metal base as the wheel spins. Since it runs at 1,700 rpm or so, those flying pieces of rubber can cause serious injury. So…never, never allow a Scott Murray drum to spin without a belt in place.

The other time and labor saver is a Clymer Barrel Spinner that I got from Brownells. For a long time, a lot of gunsmiths have used the lathe to polish barrels. They would set the barrel between centers in the lathe, turned on the lathe and use strips of abrasive to polish the surface. It works and it's a lot faster than using a buffing wheel.

The problem with this is you have to have a lathe; a darned expensive piece of equipment. Also, this really isn't a good practice as it deposits abrasive grit and crud on a precision piece of equipment. In one shop where I worked we used an old, worn out lathe just for polishing. Nothing we did could damage that old junker and woe be unto the guy caught polishing on one of the good lathes!

Clymer solved the problem for all of us by providing a tool that does the same thing as the lathe at a lot less cost. The tool consists of a bar with two uprights containing ball bearing bushings. These bushings allow the barrel to spin between adjustable Delrin centers. You just set the barrel up between the centers, then hold the barrel against the buffing wheel, polishing belt, or, in my case, the Scott Murray drum. The barrel will spin as it's polished, helping to reduce the possibility of ripples or flat spots.

You might have expected rust bluing, but Coffield selected a ceramic-based auto engine block paint as a metal finish. He wasn't sentimental after a very long project.

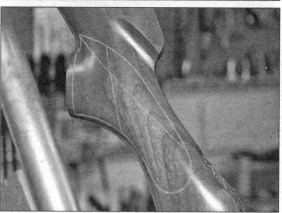

The first step in checkering is drawing an outline of the panel on the stock. Then make a light cut around the outline and scribe two intersecting master lines.

Once the barreled receiver was set up in the Clymer Barrel Spinner, it didn't take long to remove the deep machine marks along the length of the barrel. In fact, using the coarsest 60-grit belt, all machine marks and deep scratches and dings were eliminated in less than 15 minutes. Try doing that by hand! This was followed by 80 and 120 grit. I didn't go any higher as I had decided on using paint for the metal finish.

I admit my preference for metal finishing is with a traditional caustic salt or hot blue. Though I like that type of finish I have to admit that it really isn't all that resistant to rust. Hot blues are primarily a cosmetic finish. Any significant rust resistance is due more often than not to oils applied after bluing.

The toughest, most rust resistant finishes are various forms of plating followed by, believe it or not, paints. Various paints for firearms have been offered for years and all those I've used have worked just fine. There are two problems I see with 'em. First, many require baking in an oven to cure the paint. That's fine if you're working on a handgun or small parts but what happens when you have a full length rifle? Most of us don't have anything large enough to work with these long barreled actions.

The second problem for me is cost. Like so many specialty products, these gun paints tend to be kinda pricey. With the price of so many things going up, I'm always looking for a way to save a few bucks.

The first time I finished an aluminum receiver on a .22 rifle years ago I used some paint I had picked up at an auto parts supplier. Thinking back on that, I headed over to the local O'Reilly Auto Parts store. For a total of $6.44 I bought a can of Dupli-Color High Heat Ceramic engine block paint. In reading the label it sure looks like some of the more expensive gun paints and yet can be used without an oven. It looked good so I decided to try it.

Use of the Dupli-Color paint is pretty straightforward. It is important to make sure the work surfaces are clean and free of all oil, grit, and polishing residue. Also, any screw holes should be plugged or filled so paint doesn't get into the threads. The bolt raceway was covered with tape as paint here would inhibit the slick and easy manipulation of the bolt. Finally, don't forget to cover the opening into the barrel at the breech and muzzle.

By varying the angle of engagement between the barrel and the wheel, you control the amount of material you remove. Holding it perfectly horizontal across the face of the wheel will remove the least material; increasing your angle towards vertical increases the aggressiveness of the polishing belt.

The Barrel Spinner is just fantastic for plain barrels, but our Mosin-Nagant barrel is attached to the receiver. Because of this, I had to make a mandrel that extended into the receiver and provided a support for Barrel Spinner. This was a relatively simple job. I used a 7¾-inch piece of a junk Mauser barrel. One end was drilled with a center drill to accept the Delrin center of the Barrel Spinner while a roll pin was installed to act as a stop. The stop keeps the mandrel from turning inside the receiver. Nothing at all fancy about this.

Small parts such as the trigger guard and floorplate were hung on pieces of coat hanger. Screws were stuck into a piece of pasteboard with just the heads exposed. Light, even coats of paint were applied every 10 minutes until I had the coverage I wanted. The parts were then hung in my stock drying cabinet to cure. This paint dries to the touch in about an hour and can be handled within three hours.

While the metal parts were curing, I went back to the Boyd's stock. The only thing left to do was to checker it. I realize that

Coffield likes to try new products such as the Behlen wood filler and Gun Sav'r gunstock finish. It's not easy for a working gunsmith to experiment with new products.

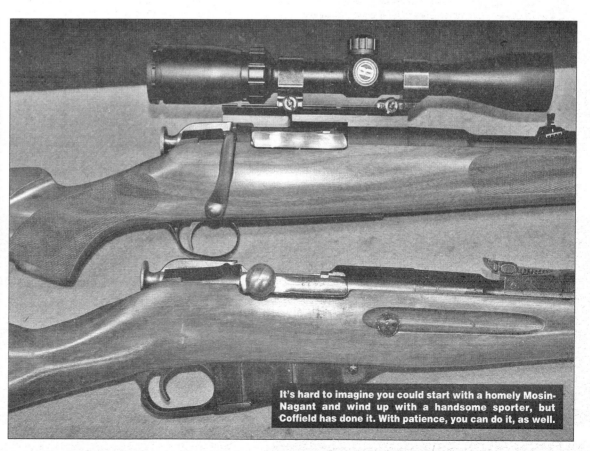

It's hard to imagine you could start with a homely Mosin-Nagant and wind up with a handsome sporter, but Coffield has done it. With patience, you can do it, as well.

It wasn't a sensible project economically, but meeting the challenge of turning a famously ugly military rifle into a good-looking sporter made it all worthwhile.

The first three shots landed in a tight group at 100 yards with Coffield having only bore-sighted the rifle! This was tribute to accurate installation of the scope.

most folks don't checker and have never even tried to checker. I would strongly encourage you to at least try it. Checkering is not all that difficult and it can give your projects a more finished, complete look.

There's lots of material out there on how to checker so I won't go into detail on this. I would suggest if you're interested that you spend a lot of time practicing on scraps of wood before attempt-

ing any work on a good stock. It's a waste of time trying to checker a stock if you can't first do a good job on a plain, flat piece of wood.

Most of the wood you and I use is simple American black walnut. Because it's so open-grained and porous, it will seldom accept checkering finer than 20 lines per inch. If you get finer with more lines per inch, the points or tops of the diamonds will tend to break off. The wood is just not dense enough to form the individual diamonds. As in the case with this stock, I normally opt for 18 lines per inch. That sounds kinda coarse but it really isn't. It looks and feels good and provides a solid, durable griping surface.

One of the most important and yet difficult aspects of checkering is making sure the pattern for the checkering panels match the stock and overall look of the gun. If you have a simple, plain stock it just doesn't make sense to have some sort of ornate, complex pattern with fleur de lies, ribbons, and other ornamental

touches. If it's a simple stock, it should have a simple checkering pattern.

I used grease or wax pencil to draw in the outline of the pattern. With the grease pencil you can easily erase and change the lines of the pattern until you get one that's appropriate. I believe this is much better than trying to use a pattern copied from some other stock. The dimensions are never the same on the two stocks and copied patterns never seems to fit.

Once the pattern was laid out, I scribed the two master lines in place. From then on it's just a matter of cutting grooves! This was definitely the most tedious and time-consuming part of the entire project. It took me a good four days. I would do just one panel each day and then have time to do some other work as well. I've found that it's best for me not to rush my checkering. If I try to do too much or get really tired I'll start making mistakes. My lines will start wandering and then I'll really have a mess.

After the checkering was completed, the rifle was assembled. As with any project of this type, I found a few spots I needed to touch up, but for the most part it all came together as planned. Once the rifle was assembled and the scope mounted, I headed for the range. Since this was planned as just a deer rifle, I didn't expect minute of an angle groups or bench rest accuracy. I just hoped it would be a decent shooter.

I had a variety of ammo to use. This included some old reloads I had made up almost 10 year ago. I also had some 180-grain Wolf Gold soft-point as well as some 203-grain soft point ammo I had obtained from Century Arms International. I was very pleased to discover that the rifle handled all of this ammo quite well.

The rifle shot much better than I had expected. In fact, with the Wolf Gold ammo, I got groups with five shots in 1½" at 100 yards. Over the years I've worked with many commercial rifles costing hundreds of dollars more than this old Nagant that wouldn't do near as well. The accuracy was more than adequate for most deer hunting situations. I was delighted and I would not be at all reluctant to take this ol' warhorse into the field this fall for deer.

While I was pleased with the results of this project, the most satisfying aspect of it all occurred after the shooting was finished. A couple of young fellows I knew, Blaise Parker and Michael Seabaugh, happened to be at the range doing a bit of shooting. They came down to my bench to visit and see what I was up to. As I handed them the rifle, Blaise remarked, "What kinda rifle is this? I've never seen one like this before." I could not have been more pleased!

Until next time, good luck and good gunsmithing!

Would you immediately identify Coffield's sporter as a Mosin-Nagant? If so, count yourself an expert. Most who saw it never suspected its humble Russian origins.

Ask the Gunsmith

By Reid Coffield

CHOKE TUBE INSTALLATION

Q *I do a little gunsmithing on the side as a part time business and find a lot of guys want me to convert older shotguns with fixed chokes to screw-in choke tubes. What are some of the problems I could run into if I start doing this work? My friends describe the work as simple and easy, but if it is so easy, why isn't everybody doing it?*

A I like your last statement! It reminds me of a comment a friend of mine made years ago that no job is easier than that which is done by somebody else. If you do gun work you will often have friends and customers encourage you to buy tooling and do this or that type of specialty work. More often than not it's because they have a gun that needs that work done. As far as they are concerned, "everybody" will also need to have this work done as well and according to them, you will make money hand over fist.

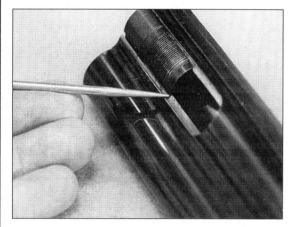

The most critical aspect in choke tube installation is the seating of the choke tube skirt on the internal shoulder. If there's a gap, debris can build up until the tube is blown out the muzzle.

Well, the reality is often not quite like that. I would strongly encourage you to take your friends' comments with a grain of salt. Don't ignore it but do some research on your own. In the case of this shotgun work, is there a real market for that work in your area? Check with the owners of your local gun shops and the operators of local ranges. These folks can often give you some useful feedback.

Next look at the cost of the tooling and how much tooling you will need. As you figure the size of your investment, look at the potential market and how long it might take to pay for the tooling. Even though this is a part-time business, you can't afford to pay for expensive tooling that will just gather dust on a shelf. Besides, you could use that same money to buy tools and supplies for rifle or handgun work.

As for things to watch out for when doing screw-in choke work, the most important to me is the fact that not all shotgun barrels are thick enough to take all types of screw-in chokes. Because of this you may be faced with having to have two or three different sets of tooling and that can run into big money really fast!

A second important factor for me is the critical nature of proper choke tube installation. Good installation work is really very precise. You must make sure that the axis of the choke tube is in almost perfect alignment with the axis of the bore. The rear end or skirt of the choke tube must seat firmly on a perpendicular shoulder cut into the barrel.

If there is a gap between the skirt and the shoulder this can allow gas, carbon, or parts of the wad to be forced under the choke tube. In some cases this can literally blow the tube out of the gun and ruin the barrel. Finally, bore diameters in shotguns are not all the same and some guns have bores that are too large to permit the use of standard choke tubes.

As you can see, there is a lot more to choke tube installation than simply taking a reamer and tap to the muzzle. It can be very profitable work in the right market. However, I would encourage you to go slowly, very slowly in making a decision to start doing this work. Don't let your friends, no matter how well-meaning they may be, rush you into this. After all, it's your money and your investment!

S&W STRAIN SCREW

Q *I was told that I can adjust the tension on the hammer spring of my Smith and Wesson to get a smoother, lighter pull. I tried it and it seemed to work. Is there something about this that I am missing?*

A Yep, there sure is! The screw you are talking about is called a strain screw and it has two functions. First, it keeps the mainspring or

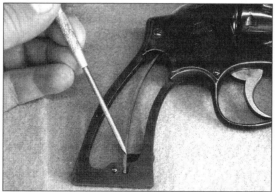

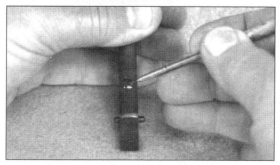

Note how the strain screw secures the mainspring and pushes it back away from the hammer. The strain screw should always be fully seated in the frame. It is not really a means for adjusting the revolver's trigger pull.

hammer spring securely in place in the frame. Next, it also places pressure on the mainspring forcing it back away from the hammer so that it can properly transfer energy to the movement of the hammer when the gun is fired.

The screw should always be fully seated in the frame. If it is not, it could further loosen to the point that the mainspring could shift or move within the frame or fail to provide enough energy to fire the revolver. If you wish to have a lighter trigger pull you would be much better off to simply replace the mainspring and rebound spring with lighter versions as offered by the various gunsmith supply houses.

7.35 CARCANO

Q *I have a sporterized Italian Carcano. I shot this gun years ago and would like to again do some shooting with it. Ammunition has been the problem as it is in 7.35mm. Where can I get ammo for it?*

A The first outfit I would contact for 7.35 Carcano ammo is Buffalo Arms Company, 660 Vermeer Court, Dept. SGN, Ponderay, Idaho 83852, telephone 208-263-6953. The last time I checked they were offering some newly loaded 150-grain soft-point ammo in boxes of 20 rounds for $34.

SGN contributor Bob Shell also offers 7.35 Carcano ammo. His address is Shell Reloading 1485 S. Lawson, Dept. SGN, Apache Junction, Ariz. 85220. His website is www.obsoleteammo.com.

I would also suggest you check with The Old Western Scrounger LLC, 219 Lawn St., Dept. SGN, Martinsburg, W. Va. 25401, telephone 304-262-9870. The folks at Navy Arms bought out Dave Cumberland who for years was the leading source for odd and unusual ammo and moved his business to West Virginia. They might have some 7.35mm Carcano ammo. It would be worth a call.

The much more common 6.5 Carcano ammo is available from SGN advertiser Graf & Sons (www.grafs.com).

MUZZLE BRAKE

Q *I want to install a muzzle brake on one of my centerfire rifles. How much clearance should I allow for the bullet as it passes through the muzzle brake? Also, do you have any suggestions on making the installation? This will be my first attempt. I have a lathe and will be doing the work myself.*

A First of all, you want to allow approximately .020" between the side of the bullet and the bore of the muzzle brake. If your bullet is .308", then you would want the bore of the muzzle brake to be approximately .348".

In making your installation, make sure that the threads for the muzzle brake are concentric with the barrel bore. Many barrels have a bore that is slightly off-center, so don't rely solely on the exterior of the barrel. When you set the barrel up in the lathe, make sure you index off the bore rather than the exterior or outside of the barrel. Also, make sure that your muzzle brake is not canted or angled. If this occurs, the bullet might strike the inside.

Be sure to check for bullet clearance and angle of the muzzle brake by using a rod about 6 inches long that will just slide into the bore. With this in place in the muzzle, any irregularity in the position or angle of the muzzle brake will be evident. ◉

This month, Matthews starts his most ambitious project yet; making a semi-auto Bren from a parts kit and raw materials. It won't be easy, but it'll be cheap!

Build Your Own
BREN GUN!
■ Part 1— Getting Started

Full-autos cost as much as a luxury car, and even semi-autos aren't cheap.
But if you have $350, a good set of tools, about 100 hours work time and
a lot of patience and ingenuity, you can have your own semi-auto Bren.

By Steven Matthews

The Bren light machine gun was fielded by the British and Commonwealth forces from just before World War II until as late as the Persian Gulf War.

Many military firearms authorities like SGN's own Peter Kokalis consider it the finest magazine-fed light machine gun ever made.

I have wanted a Bren for my collection of military arms for many years. There are NFA registered and transferable examples, but at today's highly inflated legal machine gun prices they are out of the reach of most blue collar working class stiffs like me, as they can run up to $50,000.

Much cheaper is a semi-auto replica of the Bren. There are several small manufacturers making them, but even those can run $2,500+. This price is fine for those with a fair amount of discretionary income, but not for those of us who have been hit hard by the current economy.

I lost my 33-year industrial job during the economic downturn, and health issues have made it hard to find new high-paying employment. I'm sure there are many SGN readers who are as financially challenged as I am. There is just no way we can drop $2,500 for a new toy.

There is one last low-cost option for some resourceful readers: home-build a semi-auto version. It may be hard to believe, based on retail prices of manufactured Brens, but you can build a semi-auto Bren for about $350. Of course, this low-cost option does have some big conditions. You have to do all the work yourself. If you buy the required U.S.-made parts and semi-auto parts, the price will escalate quickly. If you have to pay others for their labor, the cost will also go up fast.

This project is very labor-intensive, but material cost is extremely low. Any hobbyist gunsmith with a small hobby machine shop should be able to complete the project under the quoted $350 cost. A milling machine, metal lathe, MIG welder, bandsaw, torch and a few metalworking hand tools are required to complete it.

You can get by without some of the machine tools if you have the skill and endurance for a lot of tedious hand work. With the major machine tools, you can expect to put about 100 hours into this project. I had many more hours involved, but most of my time was engineering the project and testing concepts that I came up with (including many that didn't pan out!).

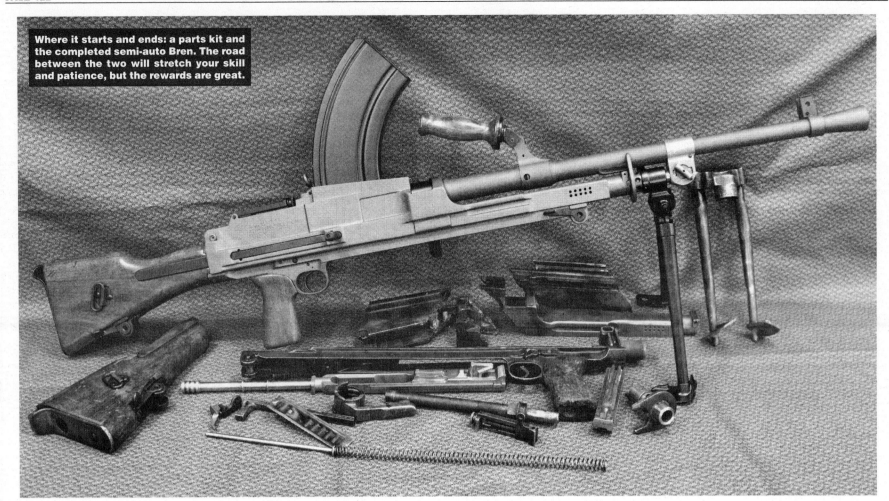

Where it starts and ends: a parts kit and the completed semi-auto Bren. The road between the two will stretch your skill and patience, but the rewards are great.

Any time you build a semi-auto firearm based on a foreign full-auto, there are legal issues to take into consideration. U.S. law and BATFE regulations forbid building a full-auto Bren gun. Since 1986, the BATFE has prohibited the manufacture of new full-auto guns for private individuals.

Illegally building or possessing an unregistered full-auto firearm is punishable by a $10,000 fine and a prison sentence of up to 10 years in a Federal penitentiary. One of my coworkers had a son who thought this law didn't apply to him, and he spent a few years in the pen when it became well known that he had illegal machine guns.

You might think that torch-cut receiver pieces like this would be good for nothing more than doorstops or trot line weights. Not if you're Steven Matthews!

Take this advice to heart, build only *legal* semi-auto guns! Semi-auto versions of many full-auto guns are legal but they must not be "readily restorable" to machine gun status. If a gun is considered by the BATFE to be "readily restorable" to machine gun status, it makes no difference if it only functions as semi-auto, it is still in their eyes a machine gun, and therefore illegal.

The BATFE has in the past issued what is known in the gun business as approval letters for semi-auto Bren designs. These letters state that if a gun is built in a certain way, it is considered to be a legal semi-automatic firearm rather than an illegal full-auto. These letters have been issued to small manufacturers and individuals.

Copies of these approval letters can be found on several semi-auto Bren building websites. While there are several letters and designs posted on the internet, all of them feature certain design parameters for the legal construction of a semi-auto Bren. One can also contact the firearms technology branch of the BATFE and seek technical advice concerning legal methods to building a semi-auto Bren.

The most common and economical way of making a semi-auto Bren receiver is to use the pieces of a properly destroyed Bren LMG receiver. This destroyed receiver has to have been torch-cut to BATFE specifications. To be legal under BATFE regulations, the reconstructed receiver must be made so it cannot accept several original full-auto Bren internal parts.

It should be noted that at no time during reconstruction can the receiver ever be in machine gun configuration, not even for five minutes! As the receiver sections are being reconnected by welding, they must always be in semi-auto only

configuration. You cannot reconstruct a full-auto receiver, then convert it to semi-auto; to do so would be illegal. This is a vitally important point that must be observed. When we get to receiver construction, these issues will be talked about in more depth.

Besides not allowing certain unmodified full-auto parts in the receiver, several Bren parts need to be modified to semi-auto only configuration. The bolt, bolt carrier, lower receiver and fire control group will need to be modified to semi-auto only configuration. These modifications should be done before making the receiver, so there is no doubt that you are working on a semi-auto project.

Having a completed semi-auto receiver plus unmodified full-auto internal parts could be a touchy legal issue, since the full-auto parts could conceivably be modified to fit the semi receiver and create full-auto fire out of a semi receiver.

To be legal, the basic operating system of the Bren must be changed. The Bren is an open-bolt design and the BATFE has ruled in the past that open bolt operation is purely a machine gun feature, and therefore not legal for semi-auto guns. The operating system of the new semi-auto Bren must be changed to closed-bolt operation. This will require making several new parts and modifying several old ones.

One last legal concern is about what is known as U.S. compliance or 922r compliance. Several years ago firearms laws were changed to prevent the importation of certain semi-auto military-style firearms. The law also specified that these firearms could not be assembled in the U.S. with *more than* 10 foreign parts out of a published list of 20 specified parts.

In a nutshell, the law says that certain firearms such as this project cannot have more than 10 of the listed foreign parts. 10 or fewer is legal but more than 10 is illegal. 10 or fewer parts make it a legal U.S.-made firearm, more than 10 make it an illegal imported gun.

In this article, several foreign-made parts will be replaced by self-made U.S. parts. Some of these U.S.-made parts can be purchased from semi-auto Bren parts suppliers, but if you make them in your own workshop, they are inexpensive and certainly U.S.-made.

This project comes in right at the limit. It has 10 of the specified foreign parts. Since the law says 10 or fewer, this project is a legal U.S.-made gun. Do not delete some of these U.S. parts, because that would put the parts count over 10 and change the legal status of the project.

■ PARTS ACQUISITION

The first thing you need for this project is a military surplus Bren parts set. Most of these parts sets include all parts for a Bren minus the barrel. A destroyed Bren receiver is normally included.

These receivers have been torch cut to BATFE specifications, and are now considered nothing more than scrap metal. Under federal law, these parts sets are unrestricted, but check your local and state laws. Bren parts kits are available from several SGN advertisers at several prices.

I frequent a web site known as weaponeer.net that is a website for firearms builders. Weaponeer had made arrangements with Military Gun Supply of Ft. Worth, Texas to offer discounted Bren kits through the Weaponeer site. These kits were offered for $185 plus shipping.

Since these were so inexpensive, I ordered two of them. While you can get by with one parts set, I wanted one for a semi-auto gun and another for a non-functional display gun. Since the dummy gun wouldn't have any internal parts, the leftovers could be used for the semi project if needed. Having extra parts on hand is convenient if you mess up a part when modifying it and need a replacement.

The parts kits I received were in pretty good shape. They showed a lot of finish wear but were functionally fine. Just keep in mind you are buying 65-year-old used parts and they aren't going to look new. All parts for this project will eventually be refinished, so finish condition is unimportant; all that matters is that they are functional.

These parts sets came without the barrels. Fortunately, Bren barrels are available and very inexpensive right now. I bought two barrels since I had two projects. I ordered a new-condition barrel from Omega Weapons Systems for $75. When I received it, the barrel was just as advertised; it looked like it had been made yesterday.

The other barrel I ordered was slightly cheaper, since it was going to go on a dummy gun. SGN advertiser I.O. Inc., of Monroe N.C., had what was advertised as good condition Bren barrels for $59. What I received from I.O. Inc. was still in pretty decent shape, even though it was less expensive. It showed a fair amount of finish wear, but the bore was very good. Either barrel would be fine for this project.

■ MAGAZINES

Neither of my parts kits came with magazines. Fortunately, Bren mags are very inexpensive. I got my magazines from I.O. Inc. These magazines were only $48 for 12 magazines or $6 each for singles. This is a real bargain for military grade 30-round magazines. My research also found them at similar prices at Numrich Gun Parts and Omega Weapons Systems.

■ MISCELLANEOUS MATERIALS

This project will require some materials for parts fabrication, namely springs, 4130 steel tubing, 4140 bar stock and a few other miscellaneous pieces of steel. These needs will be addressed as the parts are made.

■ WARNING

Before I start describing how I made this project, a couple things need to be made perfectly clear to those who are considering doing one. This article is only a rough description of how I built this project. I am not a professional gunsmith or firearms engineer. I am simply a hobbyist who is sharing my building experiences with others.

While this article can be used as a very rough guide, it does not contain all the information one needs to complete this project. Anyone using this article to help in building this project will have to supplement this information with his own gunsmithing skills and knowledge.

This project is *advanced* hobby gunsmithing and requires extensive metalworking skills and firearms knowledge. Many parts, especially the receiver, must be fabricated with excellent workmanship to function safely and correctly.

You must *completely understand* how a Bren gun operates. You should do considerable research on how a Bren gun functions. Reference materials on Bren gun operation such as *Small Arms of the World* by Smith and Smith or an older edition of *Jane's Infantry Weapons* should be consulted, along with Peter Kokalis' article in SGN (9/20/07).

You need significant gunsmithing knowledge to determine if the self-made parts fit and function correctly. I cannot overstate this: this project is not simple kit building, it is making a gun and parts. I will only be giving some general dimensions for the parts being made in this project since parts fit will vary somewhat between individual guns and also depend on the skill of the builder.

It is up to the potential builder to determine if the parts are correct and function properly. You are the builder, I'm just showing what worked for me; your results may be different.

Neither SGN nor the author accept any responsibility for the safety or legality of this project. The builder/reader is totally responsible for his own project. If you choose to do this project you and only you are responsible for the results.

If you have the skill and patience, however, you'll find this a fascinating and challenging project requiring little cash but a lot of ingenuity. ◉

Next month (8/20 issue): Making the compliance parts.

Here's the payoff: taking the firing line with an unusual and historic gun you've brought back from a pile of scrap metal. You'll be one of the very few.

The piston is one of the parts Matthews will recreate to provide the proper number of U.S.-made components in his semi-auto Bren gun building project.

Build Your Own
BREN GUN!
■ Part 2 — Compliance Parts

By Steven Matthews

He's gathered the parts and supplies (7/20 issue); now Matthews starts by crafting the U.S.-made parts that will be required to make a legal semi-auto Bren.

■ SEMI AUTO PARTS

Several of the original full-auto Bren parts will be reconfigured as semi-auto parts. Some parts will be extensively modified while others will only need slight modifications. Many parts will function the same as before but be modified to fit in the semi-auto receiver.

You may wonder why these parts need to be modified. The answer is simple: because the BATFE says so!

The BATFE approval letters approve a certain method for making a legal semi-auto Bren gun. Any significant change in the approved design may be illegal.

While exact dimensions are not specified in approval letters, the basic operating system must be maintained. If you want to go your own way on this project, contact the BATFE and get the new methods approved.

■ U.S. COMPLIANCE (922r) PARTS

You can't make a gun that is not importable entirely out of foreign parts. You have to combine it with enough U.S.-made parts to qualify it as a domestic product. I made all the regulated U.S. parts myself, namely the receiver, striker, trigger, gas piston, pistol grip, magazine floorplates and op rod. The need for a U.S.-made op rod is debatable due to how parts are named. Many sources call the rod that drives the bolt carrier forward an op rod. Op rods are on the BATFE list of regulated foreign parts, however none of the approval letters I read called this part an op rod.

A new op rod/recoil spring assembly will be made so either way it will be a U.S.-made part. These six or seven (if the op rod is counted) parts will result in a regulated parts count of 10 or less to maintain legality on the U.S. compliance issue.

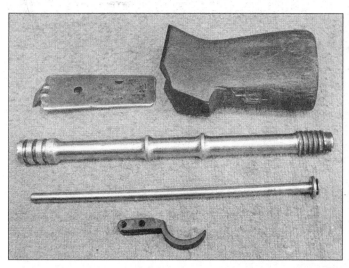

Matthews replaced these five parts with self-made "U.S. compliance" parts. BATFE regulations limit how many foreign-made parts can be used on this project.

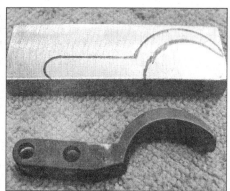

A new U.S.-made trigger is started by tracing the outline of the old trigger on a piece of alloy steel. Remove excess material with files and hand grinders.

Replacement U.S.-made floorplates start as tracings on a sheet of 4130 steel. Matthews made a pattern for them by unfolding an original Bren floorplate.

PISTOL GRIP FABRICATION

I started by making the easiest part first by duplicating the original pistol grip. You could make it any shape you please. I started by cutting out a chunk of rectangular wood out of an old military gunstock. I traced out the shape of the original grip and then cut out the shape with a bandsaw.

I drilled the grip screw hole through the rough cut grip. This hole is at a 90° angle so it is easy to drill right. I cut the recess in the top with a milling machine, but you could also form it with a router or Dremel tool.

To complete the grip, I simply shaped it to original form with a rasp and sandpaper. Once it was completed, I stamped it with my initials and USA to identify it as a U.S.-made part.

TRIGGER FABRICATION

Next, I made a new trigger. It is identical to the original trigger; its whole purpose was to add to the U.S. parts count. I drew the outline of the original trigger on a piece of O-1 tool steel that was the correct thickness. You could use 4140 or any other high strength alloy steel.

I cut the shape out with a bandsaw and then used a hand grinder to shape it like the original. Once the outside shaping was done, I stamped the part with my initials and USA to identify it as a U.S. part. I then clamped the old and new triggers together and used the original trigger as a drill guide to drill the new pin holes.

I cut the slot in the top with a hacksaw and then filed it to final shape. Since my O-1 tool steel was heat-treatable, I heat-treated the trigger to increase its strength.

The slot in the trigger can be formed with nothing more than a hacksaw and file. Stamp the new trigger with USA and your initials to identify it as a U.S. part.

While many hobbyists simply guess on temperature, there is a simple way of getting the right temperature before quenching the part. A liquid known as Tempilaq, available from Brownells, is available in several heat ranges.

Since the correct heat-treat temperature for O-1 tool steel is 1475-1525°, I obtained 1500° Tempilaq. Simply brush it on the part and then heat. When the applied dried Tempilaq melts and flows out, the right temperature has been reached. The quenched hardness of O-1 is about 60 on the Rockwell C scale, too hard for this part. To temper the part to a less brittle state and lower hardness, I floated the part on some molten lead in a bullet casting pot. I used 700° Tempilaq to gauge temperature and annealed the part for one hour. This brought the hardness down to about 44 Rc, about right.

MAGAZINE FLOORPLATES

Magazine floorplates add U.S. parts count and are very easy to make. Using simple sheet metal forming techniques will let you make them for less than $1 apiece. I used 4130 sheet steel in .035" thickness. I obtained 6x12-inch pieces from Aircraft Spruce (www.aircraftspruce.com) for a few dollars each.

I made a pattern for the floorplate blanks by unfolding and flattening an original. I laid it on the sheet steel, traced the outline and then cut out the floorplate blanks with a saw. I cleaned up the rough-cut blanks with a hand grinder.

I scribed a fold line on the sides in the same location as the originals. Then I clamped the blanks in a vise at the fold line and used a hammer and piece of steel to bend the edges over to 90°.

Blanks are bent along a scribed line. Use a vise and a steel bar to bend the sides evenly. The bent blanks should fit over the bottoms of the magazines.

To fold the 90° edges over to grip the lip on the bottom of the magazine body, I just made a forming guide out of a piece of the 4130 stock. This guide was sized to represent the shape on the bottom of the magazine.

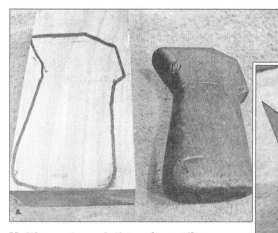

Matthews traced the grip outline on a piece of scrap walnut, then cut away the excess wood and used a milling machine to inlet the top to fit on the receiver.

Drill holes in the floorplates, then bend the end tabs and mark them as U.S.-made. These completed U.S.-made floorplates cost Matthews less than $1 each.

A replacement piston was made from precision ground O-1 drill rod stock, since that is what Matthews had in stock. The original is made from stainless steel.

The piston has 8 tpi square threads that will have to be cut on a lathe. Square threads may intimidate home machinists, but are no harder to cut than V-threads.

The new gas piston is simply a U.S.-made duplicate of the original. The piston head diameter is the most critical dimension; if it's off, the gun won't run.

The piston interior is hollow for most of its length. This must be carefully drilled on a lathe to prevent drilling out through the side of the workpiece.

I placed the guide on a partially formed blank and hammered the edges over. The guide was tapped out of the floorplates and then I used a thin putty knife to pry the bent edges up a little for an easy fit on the magazines.

The end tab was bent to duplicate the angle of the originals and I drilled a hole in the bottom, just like you'd find on the issue mag. The floorplates were then stamped USA.

■ GAS PISTON

The U.S.-made gas piston will duplicate the original. The fabrication of this part is fairly easy. The one process that may intimidate some amateur machinists is cutting square threads. Rather than using standard V-threads, the Bren designers opted for square threads, since they take impact forces better than V-threads.

The threads are at a pitch of eight per inch. With a proper lathe setup, these are really not that much harder to cut than regular threads.

Square thread dies are expensive and hard to find, so it's a lot easier and cheaper to cut them on the lathe. The original Bren gas piston is made from stainless steel. I did not have any suitable stainless in stock, so I opted for a piece of precision ground O-1 drill rod that I did have.

O-1 does have some degree of corrosion resistance, plus I figured I would spray it with GunKote when finished. The first thing I did was to turn a stub, the same size as the original, for the threads. The gas piston is supposed to be a loose fit in the carrier, so don't think the original is worn out because it is loose.

My first step in cutting square threads was to grind a square point at the front of a cobalt tool bit. This point was the same width as the square thread grooves. I set the lathe up for eight threads per inch and set the spindle on the lowest speed.

Unlike V-threads that are cut at an angle, I cut these threads at 90°. I then started to cut the threads at a rate

of a few thousandths of an inch per pass. I used plenty of lube and checked the size often. Cut the threads deep enough to have the slightly loose fit like the original.

Once the threads were cut, I drilled a shallow centering hole in the end to support the workpiece while I turned the remainder of the part. With the part supported between the chuck and live center, I turned the rest of the part to approximate the original.

Make sure you duplicate the piston head diameter precisely, since the gun won't function properly if the piston is not sized properly. I removed the part from the lathe and stamped it USA.

The original Bren gas piston is hollow. If left solid, it will add extra weight to the reciprocating mass of the carrier assembly and possibly cause functioning problems. Drilling an 8-inch deep hole precisely, even on a lathe, is no easy chore.

Drill your hole undersized and check that the bit hasn't run off center before you drill up to full size. You don't want to drill through the side of the part you just spent all that time making!

I actually drilled my hole under size by about 1/32" just to be on the safe side. This resulted in a gas piston that weighed about a half-ounce more than the original, but I figured it would still work OK.

The last machining operation was to cut the groove for the crosspin that locks the piston in place. Since this was a heat-treatable steel, I hardened the head of the piston for wear resistance. I used 1500° and 700° Tempilaq to get the right hardness and temper.

■ OP ROD/TELESCOPING RECOIL BUFFER

The new semi-auto Bren required a spring driven striker, so the op rod/buffer system had to be redesigned. The system I came up with is of my own design and is not compatible with any purchased semi-auto Bren parts.

I needed two springs behind the bolt carrier, one for the carrier and one for the striker, operating independently. Unfortunately, these need to occupy the same limited space behind the bolt carrier.

Add to this the fact that they would be long, skinny springs that would need to be supported so they didn't kink. I tried several setups and scratched my head for several days with no success.

Finally, one night while lying in bed unable to sleep, the answer just popped into my head. What I came up with was a telescoping tube system that featured an internal spring for the recoil buffer and an outer spring for the striker. This assembly would take the place of the original op rod and recoil spring and would count as a U.S.-made part.

I will explain how I made this part but there is one variable that may affect your results that is beyond my control: spring strength.

While I will specify the sizes of springs I used, not all springs of a given size are the same strength. Due to spring temper and the material used, the same size springs can vary considerably in strength. I obtained my springs from McMaster Carr Co. of Cleveland Ohio (mcmaster.com).

I started with some 4130 seamless tubing for the telescoping tubes. I got it from Wicks Aircraft of Highland, Ill. For the outer tube, I used 6¾ inches of 1/2 (.500" O.D.)x.065" wall thickness. This tube had an internal diameter of .370". For the inner tube, I used 10¼ inches of 3/8" (.375")x.028" wall thickness. This tube had an internal diameter of .319".

Do not be surprised if your tube diameters vary somewhat. To get the

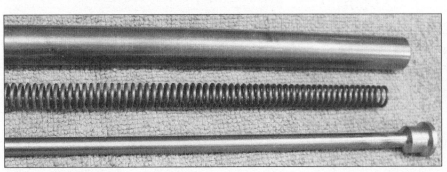

The rear section of the new U.S.-made telescoping op rod is made from a piece of 4130 tubing. A guide rod in the tube prevents the recoil spring from kinking.

Drill vent holes in the op rod to prevent it from acting as an air spring when being compressed. A couple holes in the buffer tube will also help vent air.

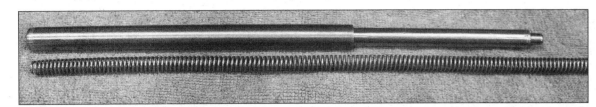

The completed telescoping op rod contains the recoil spring on the interior. Fit between the inner and outer rod needs to be close to prevent binding the unit.

The original Bren trigger group will be used in modified form. A U.S.-made trigger will be installed and full auto features will need to be removed.

.375" O.D. tube to fit in the .370" I.D. tube I had to ream out the larger tube and polish a couple thousandths off the smaller. You need to have a couple thousandths running clearance between the tubes so they slide together easily.

The next part I needed was a recoil spring. The spring I bought was 5/16"x.048" wire at 12 coils per inch (#9662K42). I used 18 inches of this bulk length spring. This spring must slide easily inside the small tube. If it doesn't, take a couple thousandths off its diameter by sanding it with it supported on a rod spinning on a lathe.

The part of this spring that fits in the larger tube must be supported with a guide rod to keep it from kinking when it is being compressed during recoil. I made a short bushing with a thin lip on the end that would be brazed into the end of the larger tube. Overall length of this bushing was about 3/8".

This bushing had a hole in it for a 7/32" guide rod that would be made from heat-treated music wire (available at hobby shops). The spring must slide easily over this guide rod, so you may have to alter the guide rod's diameter for smooth operation. Be sure to round the end for smooth operation. The guide rod must be centered in the tube to operate correctly so pay attention to this when brazing (or welding) the bushing or rod in place.

You'll need to make a cap with a small stub for the front of the smaller tube. This stub will fit in the back of the bolt carrier. I made the stub .240" diameter and 5/16" long. The bottom of the cap was sized to fit in the end of the tube and was only about 1/8" long.

With the spring installed, the tubes should slide together easily when compressed. To prevent this close fitting telescoping assembly from functioning as an air spring, drill vent holes in the ends of the tubes to allow the air to escape and refill quickly. I drilled six 1/8" vent holes in the last 1/2" of the large tube and three 1/8" holes in the last 1/4" of the small tube. These were spaced at about 120° intervals around the circumference of the tubes. When in use, the tubes and springs should be lightly lubricated.

While it is not needed yet, I will specify the size of spring I use for the striker spring that will slide over the smaller tube. I used a .480"x.041" wire at eight coils per inch (#9637K81). These springs are 11 inches long but will be stretched out to 13-15 inches later. The rear of the spring will bear against the large diameter tube and the front will fit in the rear of the striker.

■ **LOWER RECEIVER MODIFICATIONS**

The lower receiver needs to be modified to fit the upper receiver. The fire control group must also be converted to semi-automatic operation. The first operation is to grind off about 1¼ inches of the rails on the front portion of the lower receiver. These rails fit in grooves in the upper receiver and allow the upper receiver to slide rearward about 1/4" during recoil.

The new semi-auto Bren receiver will have shorter grooves to prevent a full-auto lower from being installed. I simply ground the rails off smooth with the sides of the receiver with a small hand grinder.

Since the new semi-auto Bren was going to be striker fired, the original fire control group (except for the replaced trigger) could be utilized if modified for semi-automatic operation.

The original Bren trigger group provided both full-auto and semi-auto operation. The full-auto feature must be permanently removed. The Bren trigger group consists of the trigger, disconnector, sear, safety/selector lever and associated springs.

The way the original group provided both firing modes was very simple. When the trigger is pulled, it pulls on the disconnector, which engages the sear. There are two protrusions on the disconnector and two engagement surfaces on the sear.

The bottom portion creates full-auto fire by pulling down the sear and keeping it held down till the trigger is released. Semi-auto fire is created when the selector/safety lever allows the disconnector to engage the top portion of the sear.

In semi-auto mode, the disconnector rides higher in the lower receiver. As the bolt carrier reciprocates, a protrusion on the bottom of the carrier assembly disengages the disconnector from the sear. Since the lower full-auto portions of the sear and disconnector are not needed, they will be removed.

I ground off the full-auto catch on the bottom of the disconnector flush with the bottom of the disconnector. The lower engagement surface on the sear was ground away. These parts are rather hard, and files may not be hard enough to remove the surfaces. If not, use a Dremel tool with grinding wheels. When removing the lower engagement surface on the sear, be careful not to damage the upper semi-auto section, as they are very close together.

To smooth disconnector operation, the top surface of the disconnector was radiused slightly. This will allow the bolt carrier and striker to slide over the disconnector easily. Do not change the overall height or it will not function right.

Before the new U.S.-made trigger was installed, I removed the trigger spring from the disconnector and clipped off 1½ coils to reduce tension on the trigger and disconnector.

To prevent the safety lever from rotating into the full-auto position, I made a safety lever stop from a # 8 fillister head screw for a stop. I drilled and tapped a hole for the screw and installed it. I let a short section extend into the receiver and placed a small weld on the end to secure the screw permanently to the receiver.

To allow the new telescoping buffer assembly to fit in the buffer tube, I opened up the hole in the end to 1/2" to allow for clearance of the new buffer assembly and striker spring. The buffer tube can be removed for drilling by unscrewing. There is a stiff spring inside it, so be careful when you remove the tube. ◉

Next month (9/20 issue): Bolt and bolt carrier.

The bottom full-auto notch on the rear of the Bren's disconnector and the lower full-auto notch in the gun's sear are removed for semi-auto only operation.

The original Bren gun trigger group consisted of the trigger, disconnector, selector lever, and sear. It provided both full- and semi-auto firing operation.

Radius and polish the top of the disconnector so the striker will slide over it easily. Do not alter its overall height, however, as that is a vital dimension.

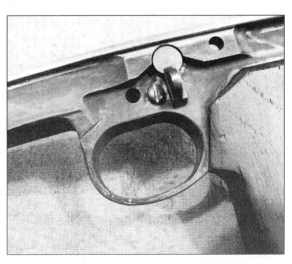

Install a safety lever stop to keep the safety from rotating into the full-auto position. A permanently installed screw works fine and is easy to install.

Build Your Own
BREN GUN!
■ Part 3—Bolt Assembly

He has acquired parts and materials and made the required U.S. compliance parts (7/20, 8/20 issues). Now it's time to work on the bolt and carrier.

By Steven Matthews

The bolt carrier steel is very hard and carbide tooling should be used to machine its rear to remove the full auto sear notch (r.) to meet BATFE rules.

The bolt cam (r.) needs to be modified to clear the firing pin extension. It will be reduced in both height and width. Hard tools are used to cut hard steel.

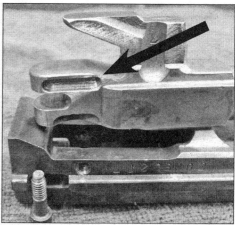

A groove for a locking screw (arrow) is machined in the side of the bolt cam. The carrier will need to be spot annealed to allow drilling and tapping.

Grind the locking screw head flush to permanently lock the semi-auto bolt cam into the carrier. Use thread locker and stake to make installation permanent.

The original bolt grooves (l.) need to be extended all the way to the bolt face to allow for clearance of denial pins that will be installed in the receiver.

The bolt carrier needs to be modified for semi-auto operation. The first thing I did was remove about 1 inch of rail on each side at the front of the carrier. This is so the carrier will fit in the new semi-auto receiver, whose grooves are shorter to meet BATFE guidelines.

These are intended to prevent a full-auto bolt carrier from being installed. Installed at the center rear of the carrier is a part that performs several functions. It features an angled cam that engages the bolt. The front of this cam also functions as a hammer to impact the firing pin on the original full-auto design.

On the bottom of this cam is a protrusion that engages the disconnector for semi-auto operation. Add to all this a sear notch for the open bolt full-auto operation. This piece is called a "bent" in British manuals. Since most of the former full-auto features are going to be removed from this piece, I will just refer to it as the bolt cam.

The first thing I did to meet BATFE guidelines was to remove the full-auto sear notch. I milled both the

bolt cam and the center of the carrier down to the depth of the original sear notch.

Mill up to the edge of the sear notch but do not go any further forward. The width of the cutout was made to match the rest of the carrier. These parts are hardened steel and you'll need a carbide cutter. The machining can be done with the parts assembled if you cut carefully, but they may be cut separately.

The bolt cam is held in place by an extremely stiff spring. To remove the cam, push the cam forward and then slide the charging handle catch sideways and out of the carrier. Then push the cam forward and downward to remove it from the carrier. This is best accomplished by pressing the cam up against a solid support with a lot of body weight; the spring is very strong.

The top of the cam needs to be reshaped for semi-auto operation. The front of the cam functions as a hammer for the firing pin in the original full-auto configuration, and this feature must be removed to meet BATFE guidelines. Removal of the contact point between the hammer and firing pin will also make room for a new semi-auto firing pin assembly.

The top of the bolt cam angles upward towards the front. The angled top needs to be milled down flush with the rear edge of the cam. Mill it down until it is just down to the radius on the rear of the cam. Do not go any deeper, since that could cause the cam to hang up on the bolt rather than to smoothly cam the bolt down.

This milling operation will remove most of the contact point between the hammer and firing pin on the front of the cam. Some more material needs to be machined off the front to allow for clearance for the new firing pin assembly.

I just guessed on how much and ended up taking off way more than necessary. The picture shows the general shape of this additional machining but the picture is of the first part I made and is about 1/16"—3/32 too deep. I had to re-machine a replacement cam once I found out my notch was too deep.

You may want to forgo this machining till you make the firing pin extension, and then use it as a guide to see how much needs to be removed. Retain as much of the rounded portion just under the firing pin contact point as possible, since this rounded portion engages the bolt and drives it forward. The width of the cam needs to be reduced so a firing pin extension can pass over the cam. I thinned the cam down evenly to a width of .320".

I wanted to prevent an original full-auto cam/hammer from ever being installed in the new semi-auto carrier. I considered welding in some denial blocks in the cam/hammer raceway but decided against it due to concerns about welding on the hardened steel carrier.

"The first thing I did to meet BATFE guidelines was to remove the full-auto sear notch."

◆

Eventually, I decided that instead of preventing a full-auto cam/hammer from ever being installed I would permanently install the semi-auto cam so it could not ever be removed. I machined a shallow groove in the right rear side of the cam that would allow full movement of the cam when installed.

I spot annealed a location for a retaining screw that would feature a smooth unthreaded round end that would fit in the groove in the cam. The hole was threaded in a fine pitch thread since the steel, even when spot annealed, was still quite hard. I installed the cam and spring and turned in the screw until the smooth portion touched the bottom of the groove.

I then backed off the screw enough that the cam could slide freely when in operation. The screw was then cut off flush with the side of the carrier so it could not ever be removed. When the screw is installed, use some permanent

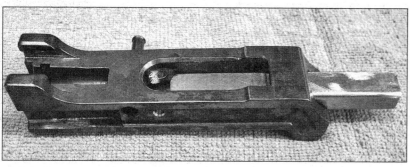

The firing pin extension is a long rectangular bar sized to fit in the recess in the bottom of the bolt. It must slide freely, but without excessive clearance.

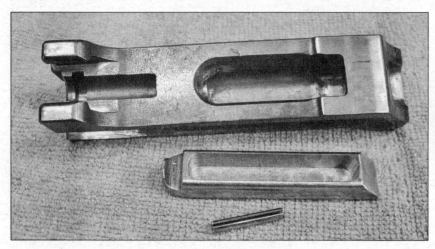

The rear of the firing pin extension should only extend out of the rear of the bolt about .055" when it is in its rearward position. It doesn't travel too far.

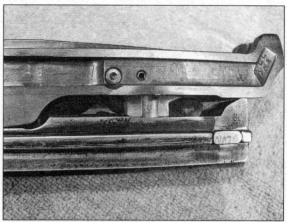

The firing pin extension will surround the bolt cam when it is installed. There must be clearance all the way around the cam when the bolt is in all positions.

A clearance pocket needs to be machined into the bottom of the firing pin extension. A crosspin and groove will retain the extension in the bolt.

To reduce weight, Matthews drilled four holes in the top of the firing pin extension. The sides are also machined a little shorter to reduce weight.

thread locker to secure it in place followed by staking the edges of the flush screw shank. Do *not* permanently install the cam in the carrier till you are sure all machining and test fitting is done.

■ BOLT MODIFICATIONS

The Bren bolt needs to be modified to fit in the new semi-auto receiver. It also needs to be fitted with a firing pin extension, since the new semi-auto Bren design is going to feature a striker behind the bolt. Later, when the new semi-auto receiver is made, it will feature denial pins (per BATFE guidelines) to prevent an original full-auto bolt from fitting in the receiver.

To allow the semi-auto bolt to clear these denial pins, grooves will be cut in the side of the bolt. The original bolt already features grooves in its sides, but these terminate before they reach the bolt face. These grooves need to be continued until they are flush with the bolt face. The Bren bolt is extremely hard, and these grooves will need to be cut with carbide tooling or ground with abrasives.

Before the next part can be made, the firing pin needs to be removed from the bolt. A crosspin pushes out the side and releases the firing pin. The bottom of the Bren bolt features a rectangular opening that extends from the back of the firing pin all the way to the rear of the bolt.

The bolt cam operates in this opening and a new firing pin extension will also fit in the opening. The firing pin extension will fit around the cam and extend out of the rear of the bolt where the striker can impact it.

This extension needs to be made from tool steel for strength and durability. The extension will need to be heat treated. I used a piece of O-1 tool steel, but you could also use a piece of 4140. I measured the opening and machined a piece of steel to fit in the opening.

This piece needs to be about 1/4" longer than the bolt opening to allow for final fitting. The front of the extension needs to be radiused to match the rounded front of the opening in the bolt. The extension needs to fit in the opening with only a few thousandths clearance. It must slide freely without excessive play.

The rear of the extension will be supported by the rectangular opening at the rear of the bolt, but the front must be supported with a crosspin. Mark a location for a slot at the front of the extension that is about .100" back from the front. Use an 1/8" ball end mill to machine a 1/8–9/64" deep slot across the extension.

Make this slot about 1/4" wide to allow for movement of the extension. I located my slot only about .060" from the front and this turned out to be very thin. If I do it over later, I will move back to .100" but decided to try the thinner size. This thin lip on the front will retain the extension in the recess.

Before the crosspin hole that retains the extension can be drilled, the firing pin needs to be modified. At full extension, the Bren firing pin extends out the front of the bolt face about .060–.065". The rear of the firing pin needs to be shortened so that when the extension is bottomed out against the rounded end of the recess, the firing pin extends out the front of the bolt face about .050–.055". This will give about .010" clearance so the pin is not bottoming out when struck.

Now comes the hard part—a hole for the crosspin needs to be located and drilled in just the right location to allow the extension to move forward and back about .075–.090". The hole needs to be located so that it allows the extension to contact fully the rounded end of the recess when pressed in all the way and then retract far enough to allow the firing pin to retract back into the bolt face.

My Bren bolt was hard as a rock, I estimate it was about Rockwell 60c. This was too hard to drill with the tooling I had. To bring the hardness down to a level that would allow drilling, I had to anneal the bolt slightly. I placed the bolt in my kitchen oven and baked it for one hour at 575°. This brought the hardness down to where it was just soft enough that it could be drilled with good hard tooling. This slight annealing will not greatly affect the strength of the bolt, since it is vastly stronger than necessary. The hardness is more for wear resistance in full-auto fire.

The bolt will wear a little faster but will last for many thousands of rounds fired. I certainly won't be shooting "military" quantities of ammo at today's ammo prices. Once the bolt is softened, the hole can be drilled. You will have to decide your location, just be absolutely sure it's right before you drill, because you only get one chance per bolt!

The groove and crosspin set up when located correctly should allow the extension to push the firing pin out of the bolt face about .055". The groove should be wide enough to allow the firing pin to retract back into the bolt face at least .032" when the extension is in the rearward position.

The rear of the firing pin extension can now be trimmed. The extension needs to be flush with the rear of the bolt when the extension is pressed all the way forward. The lower portion of the extension will need to be trimmed at an angle to allow clearance when the bolt is moving up and down during lockup and unlocking.

Form a pocket in the bottom of the firing pin extension to allow the bolt cam to fit inside with adequate clearance. This pocket will leave only about .070–.075" of material on the top and sides of the extension. You want to remove as much material as possible for clearance and light weight, yet keep enough for adequate strength.

> *"Later, when the new semi-auto receiver is made, it will feature denial pins (per BATFE guidelines) to prevent an original full-auto bolt from fitting in the receiver."*

Check for adequate clearance by test fitting the bolt, carrier and firing pin extension. The cam cannot contact the extension at any point during the bolt's travel forward and back or up and down.

Once I had the extension all formed, I decided it was still a little heavy. I drilled some lightening holes in the top and also trimmed down the sides where it was unsupported by the bolt. It is important to keep the extension as light as possible to prevent slam fires when the bolt reciprocates.

Once I had the bolt, firing pin and its extension sized right it was time to heat-treat the extension. If not heat-treated it will quickly deform during use. I heated it to 1500° with the use of Tempilaq and then quenched it in oil. As quenched, hardness is about Rockwell 60c, which is too hard for this part. I used 700° Tempilaq to gauge tempering heat which brought hardness down to about Rockwell 45c. ◉

Next month (10/20 issue): Starting the receiver.

Ask the Gunsmith

By Reid Coffield

ENFIELD BEDDING

Q *How and where do you bed the action on a Number 4 Lee Enfield? I have bedded a couple of 98 Mausers but this is the first time I have ever been asked to bed an Enfield and I am stumped. Can you help?*

A Bedding the British Number 4 Enfield is a bit different. Keep in mind that the rear of the socket into which the buttstock is fitted actually serves as the "recoil lug." While many folks do not do this, I bed the buttstock in the socket. This ensures that the stock bears fully and evenly against the receiver. It also helps to prevent any cracking or splitting of the buttstock at that point. You will often see older Enfields with cracks in this area.

I also bed the rear of the fore-end where it contacts the front of the socket. In addition, I bed the rear of the lug to which the sear is attached. Finally I bed the bottom of the front half of the receiver from the barrel on back approximately half way. The chamber area of the barrel is bedded and then the rest of the barrel is free floated. I certainly don't claim that this is the absolute "best" way to bed the Enfield but it's the method I've used for many years and it's worked quite well for me. Good luck with your Enfield!

REMINGTON 11 BUFFER

Q *I have an old Remington Model 11 shotgun that has been in the family for many years. Last fall after shooting it I noticed some pieces of what looks like leather fell out of the action. I am not a gunsmith so I did not take the gun apart. Do you have any idea what is going on with this old gun?*

A Sure do. What you saw were pieces of a fiber recoil buffer that is normally located in the rear of the receiver. It helps to dampen the impact of the bolt when it contacts the back of the inside of the receiver. The fiber buffer or cushion is normally riveted inside the receiver and most folks are never even aware that it's there. On many older Model 11s this buffer is worn or even missing. I would

strongly encourage you to take the gun to a gunsmith and have it checked out. More than likely you will need to have the buffer replaced. If the buffer is missing you could damage the gun by shooting it.

CASE AGE

Q *I am enclosing some empty .223 cases that I would like for you to look at. You will note that the necks are split. In one instance, the neck separated from the case upon firing. Is this caused by a bad chamber?*

A As best I can tell, your chamber is probably fine. The cases were not dimensionally oversize at all. What struck me was the age of this brass. Some of these cases are well over 30 years old! I believe your problem may well be related to the age of the brass. If you are going to reload .223 brass, by all means, try to use new commercial brass or at least use military brass that is less than 10 years old. Unlike fine wine or good whiskey, cartridge cases do not get better with age!

Use of old, brittle brass can result in case failure upon firing. Coffield recommends sticking to fairly new brass when handloading; advancing age is no friend to cartridge case brass.

RUBY PARTS

Q *Where can I get parts for a Spanish Ruby .32 pistol?*

The number of different makers and mechanical variations mean that correct parts for a Spanish Ruby pistol can be hard if not impossible to find. Numrich and others have them, but hand-fitting may be required.

A Check with the folks at Numrich Gun Parts Corporation,. Box 299, Dept. SGN, West Hurley, N.Y. 12491, telephone 866-686-7424. Now keep in mind that there were at least 30 or more manufacturers of "Ruby" pistols in Spain during and after World War I. They all look pretty much the same and are all basically blowback .32 autos. However, the internal parts and even the magazines will not necessarily interchange. Because of that, it can become quite a chore to find parts for the repair on one of these handguns.

BERETTA SILVER SNIPE SPRING

Q *I have an old Beretta Silver Snipe 20-gauge over-under that I bought at a yard sale (believe it or not!). It is in pretty good shape but one of the hammer "V" springs is broken. I contacted Beretta and they could not help me. Do you know where I could find a replacement spring?*

A Check with the good people at Bob's Gun Shop, Box 200, Dept. SGN, Royal, Ark. 71968, telephone 501-767-1970. They generally have a pretty good supply of parts for the old Beretta Silver Snipe and Gold Snipe over-unders.

MEASURING PITCH

Q *How can I measure the pitch of my shotgun? Also, what is the effect of pitch?*

A Pitch is basically determined by the angle of the butt of the shotgun relative to the axis of the bore. It can be easily measured with nothing more than a ruler. Place the butt of your shotgun on the floor next to a wall with the toe of the stock pointing away from the wall. Slide the gun towards the wall until the receiver touches the wall. Now take the ruler and measure the distance from the wall to the top of barrel at the muzzle. This distance is the pitch.

If the pitch is quite small, you may find that the gun will tend to slide down your shoulder when it is fired. This sometimes also leads to shooting high above the target. On the other hand, if the pitch is excessive, the gun could literally slip up your shoulder when it is fired. This could lead to shooting below the target. It could also enhance felt recoil as the stock presses against your cheek.

The best way to determine optimal pitch is by shooting against a patterning board and noting both where your shot concentration is located and your comfort with the shotgun. Pitch can have a significant effect on your use of a particular shotgun.

CLEANING FOR CAST BULLETS

Q *I am just getting started using cast bullets in some of my rifles. I have been told that before switching from lead bullets to jacketed bullets I should thoroughly clean the bore. Since I always clean my rifles after shooting anyway, why should I clean the bore when switching from cast to jacketed or jacketed to cast bullets? I often shoot both types of bullets in the same gun during a trip to the range.*

A With either cast or jacketed bullets, you get fouling or traces of the bullet material left in the bore. Lead fouling tends to have a negative impact on the accuracy of jacketed bullets and fouling from jacketed bullets has a detrimental impact on lead bullet accuracy. Consequently most authorities encourage a through cleaning of the bore when switching bullet types to ensure the best possible performance of the rifle. ◉

The recoil-operated Remington Model 11 has a fiber recoil buffer at the rear of the receiver that keeps the bolt assembly from battering the interior. Over time these dry up and fall out, and should be renewed.

Get out your heavy gloves and welding helmet for this one. These destroyed receiver sections will be reconstructed into a semi-auto Bren receiver.

Build Your Own
BREN GUN!
■ Part 4 — Receiver Fabrication

By Steven Matthews

Matthews has made a good start (7/20, 8/20, 9/20 issues). This time he gets into the meat of the project: rejoining the cut receiver sections. This one will test your welding skills!

Now comes what many would consider the hardest part of the build, making the receiver. BATFE allows you to use the destroyed Bren receiver sections as raw material for the construction of a new semi-auto receiver.

It must, however, be built to semi-auto specifications and at no time can it be in full-auto configuration. Re-welding torch-cut receiver sections is not the ideal way to make a new receiver, but it's the only economical option. To machine a Bren receiver out of a block of steel would take a huge amount of time and cost hundreds, if not thousands, of dollars.

In some cases, rewelding receivers is not advisable and is flat-out unsafe. Fortunately the Bren receiver is designed in such a way that it is a good candidate for rewelding. First off, the Bren receiver is massive. It is much larger and stronger than necessary to contain the forces of firing the .303 British cartridge.

The steel in the receiver is not heat treated to any great extent; in fact, it is rather soft compared to most receivers. This will allow it to be welded with common welding steels and the welds will not "self heat treat" and become brittle. It also can be heated and straightened if it warps without seriously affecting its strength.

While these characteristics do make it a good candidate for rewelding, the process requires experience and skill. All welds must be completely fused with the surrounding metal with no voids or cracks. All welds

The jagged torch-cut seams must be cleaned of all slag in preparation for welding. Any remaining slag can affect the strength of the new welds.

A long machined bar will serve as a fixture to align the bottom of the cut receiver sections for welding. A machined mandrel will align the barrel socket.

must penetrate 100%: just laying welds on the surface is unacceptable since they will be ground flush.

Since at least a quarter-inch of metal was removed at each cut, the equal amount of weld must fill in the gaps. Large gaps must be filled, you can't just butt the pieces up and then weld, as this would result in the receiver dimensions being wrong.

The alignment fixtures will align the sides of the two receiver sections, but correct length spacing must be determined by careful measurement by the builder.

Two big variables must be taken in to consideration: weld-induced warping and weld contraction. The heat of welding can easily cause the receiver to warp and straightness will be an issue. The weld heat also causes the weld to shrink some as it cools. This makes maintaining exact dimensions challenging. The welder of a Bren receiver must completely understand these issues and know how to compensate for them.

My choice of welding equipment was a 220 volt/175 amp mig welder. If you have the skill, a stick welder could be used, but this will make the job much harder, due to slag issues. A TIG welder would be a good option, but most hobbyists don't have TIG welders. I found the MIG welder to be completely satisfactory with the use of common ERS-70 wire.

■ DESTROYED RECEIVER SECTION PREPARATION

To meet BATFE destruction guidelines, the old fullauto receiver was destroyed by torch-cutting with at least 1/4" of metal removal per cut. This in itself is bad enough, but most receivers appear to have been cut by drunken monkeys.

Rather than nice straight cuts with little slag, most cuts were excessively large and featured tons of slag. All slag must be ground away for good welds. I used a 4½-inch electric grinder and a small air grinder with 2-inch discs to clean up the cuts. I used a small Dremel type tool for the tight spots.

Once the slag was ground out, I laid the sections in order on the workbench to see just how much welding would be required. This was not going to be an easy job!

■ WELD FIXTURES

As the receiver sections are being welded back together, they must be precisely aligned and measurements must be maintained. A fixture must be used to keep parts in position. Commercial Bren reweld jigs are available, but they are pricey. I just took a bar of steel and machined grooves on the top to match the inside dimensions of the old receiver.

The receiver sections will slip over the top of the bar and maintain correct alignment and spacing. The receiver sections will be securely clamped in place during welding. While this jig will keep the bottom aligned, there is one other area of vital importance, the barrel socket.

The receiver welds should be a series of short welds that alternate from side to side to limit receiver warping from heat. The welds need to be at 100% depth.

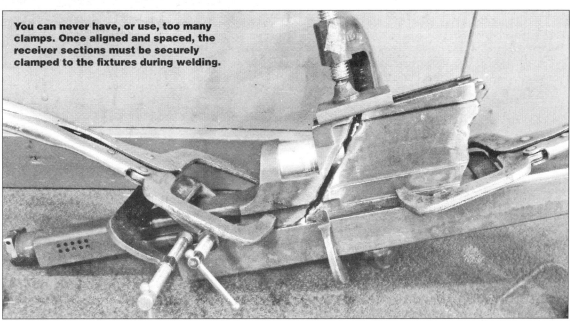

You can never have, or use, too many clamps. Once aligned and spaced, the receiver sections must be securely clamped to the fixtures during welding.

The gaps in the barrel socket will have to be filled in with weld and then ground down flush. Accessing this small area may be prove to be difficult.

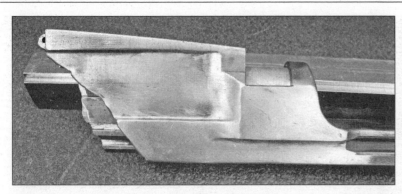

All weld seams will need to be ground smooth. Any shallow welds will need to be filled to full depth from the inside. There can be no gaps in any of the seams.

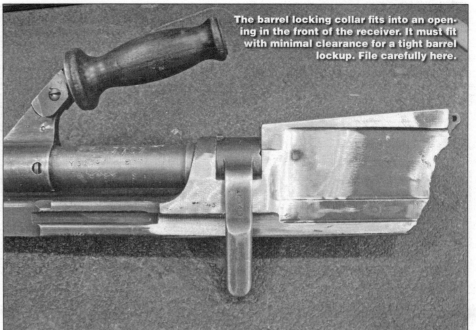

The barrel locking collar fits into an opening in the front of the receiver. It must fit with minimal clearance for a tight barrel lockup. File carefully here.

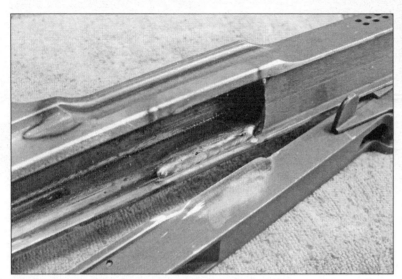

Fill in the front portion of the lower receiver grooves with weld to prevent an unmodified lower receiver from being installed in the semi-auto upper receiver.

BATFE destruction regulations specify a cut right through the barrel socket. Both pieces of the barrel socket must be precisely aligned during welding. I turned an alignment fixture out of a piece of aluminum.

One section was sized to fit the large hole in the front of the receiver just in front of the socket. The other section was sized to fit in the barrel socket. The barrel socket section must be sized precisely so that the barrel will slide easily into the socket but have only a couple thousandths clearance.

■ RECEIVER SECTIONS 1+2 REWELD

I started the rebuild by welding the first two forward pieces of receiver together. I placed the sections on the jig and installed the barrel socket fixture. These two pieces must be spaced to replicate the original receiver dimensions to allow the barrel to install correctly. Observe remaining receiver features such as ledges, protrusions, shoulders, etc., to gauge the correct spacing.

Once the correct spacing is set, use several C clamps to secure the parts in place. When the parts are spaced correctly, there will be large gaps to fill with weld. Place several large tack welds in each gap to maintain spacing while welding the remaining gap.

Fill in the gaps by working back and forth across the gaps. Only weld about an inch or so, then go to the same section on the opposite side of the receiver and weld there. Working back and forth using small welds will limit warping. You need 100% penetration on the welds, but this can be hard to do working from one side.

Weld as best as you can from the one side, any shallow welds on the inside can be rewelded from the inside once the parts are removed from the fixture.

Once all exterior welds are made, the barrel socket alignment fixture can be removed and the gaps in the socket welded. The fixture will probably have to be hammered out of the socket. All gaps must be welded up to obtain adequate receiver strength. Some spots will be hard to access but they must be done.

After all welds are done, the excess weld must be ground flush with the surrounding metal. This is especially important in the barrel socket so the barrel will fit correctly. Use the barrel and barrel locking collar to determine fit. The barrel must slide easily into the socket without excessive play and the barrel locking collar must be able to rotate easily without having excessive front to back play.

Once the barrel fits the receiver and the locking collar rotates smoothly, a notch needs to be cut in the side of the receiver to allow the locking collar latch to lock in place.

All interior welds need to be smoothed down flush and weld that is in the interior grooves needs to be removed. A dremel tool with stacked abrasive wheels is good for grinding out the grooves.

At this time, no more receiver sections can be reconnected until the two forward sections are modified to semi-auto configuration.

Weld needs to be placed in the forward sections of the interior grooves for the lower receiver and the bolt carrier so that an original full-auto lower receiver and full-auto bolt carrier cannot be installed in the new semi-auto receiver.

Add an amount equal to the amount of rail removed previously on both these parts. This is to meet BATFE guidelines for a semi-auto receiver. When welding in these grooves, use low weld heat and a series of short welds to limit warping. Check for straightness after welding and straighten if necessary.

The next thing I did was to weld 1/4" hardened denial pins (I used hard dowel pins) in both sides of the receiver so a full-auto bolt cannot be installed. This is also per BATFE guide lines. These pins need to be located so that they align with the grooves in the sides of the bolt. I located the pins so they would be about 1/2" back from the bolt face when the bolt was in it's forward position. These pins must not contact the bolt in any way so leave enough clearance (.025" or so) under the pins and along the sides.

■ RECONSTRUCTION OF RECEIVER SECTION 3

Now that the front sections have been turned into a semi-auto configured receiver, the rest of the sections can be joined. The third section must be more precisely aligned and spaced than the others, because it contains the locking shoulder and recess that sets headspace.

The bolt carrier must slide easily in the reconstructed Bren receiver sections. All interior grooves must be reworked after welding and must be straight.

Install denial pins in the receiver sides to meet BATFE guidelines. They must be positioned so the grooves in the bolt pass over them with adequate clearance.

The denial pins must be permanently installed by welding to meet BATFE guidelines. Counterbore the holes and then fill the gaps when welding them in.

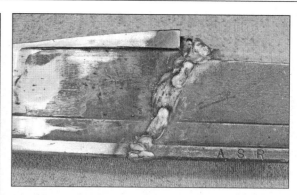

The seam is highly stressed since section 3 contains the locking shoulder recess. Weld with short alternating full depth welds to minimize warping.

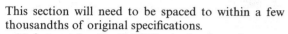

The locking shoulder is installed in what is left of the locking shoulder recess in receiver section #3. If it has been destroyed, the recess must be rebuilt.

Spacing of sections 2 and 3 is critical to maintain correct headspace. Approximate headspace will be determined by fitting the parts before welding.

This section will need to be spaced to within a few thousandths of original specifications.

Unfortunately, the BATFE-mandated receiver cuts went right through the locking shoulder recess in the receiver section. This recess would have to be rebuilt. I used an improvised method to set rough headspace and then after the spacing was set I rebuilt the recess, since enough of the recess did exist for an initial setting.

In order to locate this receiver section correctly, you must be already familiar with headspacing procedures; now is not the time to learn headspacing. According to the Bren headspace specifications that I downloaded from the weaponeer.net website, minimum headspace for the Bren is .064". Maximum spec is .070" and field reject is .074".

Since there may or may not be weld contraction when these sections are joined, I decided to go with a mid-range setting of .068". At this setting if there was no contraction it would be fine, if there was contraction of a few thousandths the locking shoulder could be modified to get the correct headspace setting.

Rather than buy a headspace gauge I improvised one with an empty cartridge (new or resized so it fits the chamber) and a shim, since the .303 headspaces on the rim. I simply cut a round shim and taped it to the base of the empty cartridge with double-face tape.

I sized this improvised gauge to .068". Make sure your gauge inserts fully into the barrel's chamber so that the rim is flush with the edge of the chamber and not extending out due to shoulder contact.

To locate section 3 and to set rough headspace, I securely clamped the two front sections to the fixture. The barrel was installed in the receiver and locked in place with the locking collar.

The .068" improvised gauge was inserted fully into the clean chamber of the barrel. I inserted the bolt carrier and the bolt (with extractor and firing pin removed) into the two front sections and pushed them all the way forward until the bolt face was tight against the gauge.

The bolt needs to be cammed upward into its locked position. The locking shoulder was installed in what remained of the locking shoulder recess in the third section. Then I slid the third section onto the alignment fixture.

It was pushed all the way forward until the locking shoulder was tight against the rear locking surface of the bolt. This section was then securely clamped in place. Make sure nothing moves during the clamping. After everything was secured, the barrel, locking shoulder, bolt and carrier were removed.

I placed several large tack welds in the gaps and then welded up the gaps using the same methods as before to limit warping and weld contraction. I rebuilt the locking shoulder recess by welding in all the gaps and then machined the excess weld out of the pocket. After all welds were done and ground down flush, I reinstalled the parts and checked headspace.

It turned out that my welds did cause some shrinkage because my .068" headspace gauge would not allow the bolt to close. An improvised minimum gauge of .064" would only allow the bolt to begin closing. I then ground about .005" off the rear of the locking shoulder to allow it to fit back further in the locking shoulder recess.

This locking shoulder reworking must be done with a precision surface grinder and be set up exactly square, you should not attempt to rework locking shoulders by hand grinding. I filed the locking shoulder screw hole a little to allow the shoulder to sit back further in the recess.

Once these modifications were done, I rechecked headspace. The bolt would just close on the .068" gauge, but would not close on an improvised .070" gauge. This indicated that headspace was within specifications.

■ RECEIVER SECTION 4 REBUILD

The last receiver section was located and welded in place using the same methods as before. Spacing of this section was just by guesswork, since its location is not as critical as the other sections. On my project, the torch-cut went right through the takedown pin hole in the rear of the receiver.

I aligned the receiver section so I had approximately the correct diameter hole. To keep from welding in the hole I used a hole-sized aluminum pin. This gave an approximate location and it's where I welded it together.

■ INTERNAL RECEIVER CLEAN UP

The receiver interior needs to be smoothed up so that all internal parts slide freely. Any ridges or high spots need to be removed. This is especially important for the grooves in which the bolt carrier and lower receiver ride. A long thin flat file works well in these grooves. A large flat file works for making the inside walls completely flat. If you have any warping, it needs to be straightened now. ◉

Next month (11/20 issue): Magazine well rebuild.

The locking shoulder is installed in the rebuilt recess in the receiver. Once it's fitted for correct headspace, the screw should be securely staked in place.

The bolt cams up to bear against the locking shoulder. Variables in receiver reconstruction mean the locking shoulder may need to be resized by grinding.

If the locking shoulder needs to be resized it must be done precisely with precision equipment. Exact angles and dimensions need to be maintained.

Forget the files and Dremel tools for this part! There's no substitute for a milling machine when you're cutting long, deep slots and need best accuracy.

Build Your Own
BREN GUN!

■ Part 5 — Magazine Well Rebuild

In the four previous installments (7/20, 8/20, 9/20, 10/20), Matthews made compliance parts, assembled the bolt and rebuilt the receiver. Now he rebuilds the magazine well and fabricates a striker.

By Steven Matthews

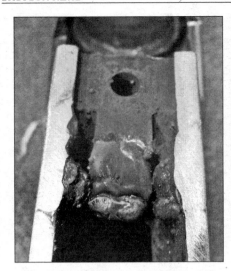

The missing catch at the front of the magazine well must be rebuilt by welding in material and then reshaping it to approximate the Bren's original form.

Matthews recut the sides of the rebuilt front magazine catch with abrasive discs on a hand-held air grinder. The remainder was then filed to its final shape.

Bren magazines rock into place much like AK-47 magazines, though upside down. The front catch in the well engages a tab at the front of the magazine box.

I added some reinforcements to the outside of the receiver at the seams between sections 1 and 2 and 2 and 3 since these were the sections under the most stress. I formed some thin steel plates and plug welded them over the seams.

I did use some long welds, but I used low heat and short welds to reduce weld heat-induced warping. I shaped the reinforcement plates so they would look like they were part of the original receiver rather than just some plate slapped on to the sides. All welds were dressed down smooth so they did not show.

The BATFE-mandated torch cuts went right though both the front and rear portions of the magazine well on my receiver. The front magazine catch was completely gone. The rear mag catch/ejector recess was partially destroyed as well.

Both sections would have to be completely rebuilt. There was little original material remaining. The only option was to place weld material where there used to be steel and then reshape the weld steel to the shape of the original parts. While this sounds difficult, it really isn't that bad.

I started by cleaning up what remained of the mag well so that a magazine could be inserted easily to full depth. A tab at the front of the magazine well interlocks with a protrusion on the front of the magazine to hold it in place.

The magazine just slips under the tab and then is rocked into place, in similar fashion to the AK-47, except it's upside down. I welded up the area, then reshaped the material to roughly replicate (pure guesswork here since nothing remained) the shape of the original tab.

This I did with nothing more than a file and an air-powered hand grinder with an assortment of abrasive discs. Several test fits and reshaping of the material resulted in what I think replicated the original tab. It functioned as well as the original, at any rate. At this time, I also recut the thin grooves in the magazine well walls that retain the magazine well cover, even though I eventually decided not to install the cover.

The destroyed rear section of the magazine well was much harder to repair. The rear magazine catch and the ejector are a combined assembly that slides into a machined pocket and held there by the pivot pin. Very little of this pocket remained. I used my welder to fill in the missing material.

To keep molten steel from running into what remained of the pocket, I clamped thin blocks of copper (you could use aluminum) to the inside wall of the pocket. This would allow welding right up to what used to be the side of the pocket and reduce the amount of material that needed to be cut out later.

Once all welding was done, I reshaped the exterior portion to something that resembled the original shape. I then set the receiver up in the milling machine and cleaned up the inside of the pocket with a common straight mill.

The thin slot in the bottom had to be re-cut but I had no size of T-slot cutter (or Woodruff key cutter) that was thin enough. I took one of my Woodruff key cutters and ground the cutting edge down to the correct thickness and then recut the thin slot. Use caution when using cutting tools that are this thin on the edges.

When reworking this recess, be sure to keep it centered in the receiver. If it's off-center, the ejector will not align with the ejector slot in the bolt. After a lot of test fitting, I finally had a pretty good fit and drilled the pivot pin hole in the sides. This locks the mag catch/ejector assembly in the pocket.

■ CHARGING HANDLE SLOT

All demilled Bren kits will probably feature a torch cut though the charging handle slot. The Bren charging handle is in the shape of a fat letter T. This handle rides in thin grooves that are cut in the sides of the receiver. A weld will probably fill in part of these grooves.

These thin grooves must be recut along with the wider portion that allows the handle to slide back and forth. The wide part can be reshaped with a file. The thin grooves can be cut with stacked abrasive discs on a Dremel. An opening at the rear of the slot allows the handle to pass through from the inside before it is slid forward.

This opening should only be just wide enough to allow the handle to pass through and no larger. In use, the handle must be installed before the bolt and carrier are inserted into the receiver.

■ OPTIONAL RECEIVER REINFORCEMENT

The Bren receiver is rather large and has a very thick cross-section. Many Bren builders just weld up the seams and gaps with 100% weld thickness and grind off the excess smooth. This is probably adequate but I'm kind of a strength nut when it comes to firearms parts, and wanted a little more safety margin on receiver strength.

■ RECEIVER MARKING

While BAFTE regulations do not require homemade guns to be marked, it is good idea to mark them anyway. This is especially important on any project that looks like a machine gun. Guns like this seem to draw unwanted attention from any law enforcement officers at the range when you are shooting.

Many law enforcement people have the "if it looks like an illegal machine gun, then it must be an illegal machine gun" attitude. Many also expect all firearms to be serial numbered, and missing serial numbers shout "illegal" to many law enforcement personnel.

Besides marking a serial number, maker's name and address on the receiver, I also marked the project as "semi-

To keep weld steel from running into the recess, clamp thin pieces of copper to the inside. You then can weld right over the copper without clogging things up.

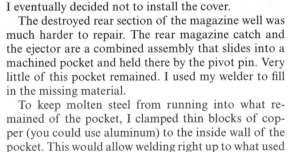

The rear magazine catch recess was almost completely destroyed during the demilling process. The missing material will have to be replaced by welding.

The thin slot in the bottom of the mag catch recess can be recut with a modified woodruff key cutter. The delicate tooling must be operated with great caution.

The ejector slides into the recess in the rear of the magazine well. It must be well centered so that the ejector aligns with the ejector groove in the bolt.

The magazine catch and pin will retain the combined ejector/mag catch assembly in the receiver. Very careful alignment of these parts is essential for function.

The reconstructed rear of the magazine well should look as good as the original if you do skillful work. Machine tools, sharp tooling and patience are required.

Optional reinforcement plates can be added and plug welded at the section 2 and 3 weld seams for strength. Use smaller plates between sections 1 and 2.

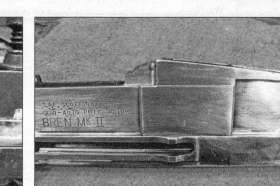

The reinforcement plates should be shaped to look as original parts of the receiver. A tight fit is required to make the plate seams unnoticeable.

The striker will also engage the disconnector to create semi-auto operation. A protrusion on the bottom of the bolt cam will also engage the disconnector, so this gun will in effect be double disconnected. This will be a double redundant disconnect of the trigger on each cycle of the bolt group.

I choose to use a piece of 4140 steel for this part that I bought from McMaster-Carr. I needed steel that could be hardened but not get so hard it would become brittle. I felt 4140 would be hard enough after heat treatment but be able to take sustained impacts without cracking.

Other steels could be used if you know what type of steel to select, I just choose this type because it was well suited for the job and I felt others would be familiar with it. I had to buy a 1-foot piece of 1¼-inch square 4140 bar, since even the suppliers of small quantities of steel have a 1-foot minimum purchase. This steel comes in the soft state and it will be hardened after fabrication.

I started with a piece 1x1.850x1.180 inches. I machined away the steel on the 1.180-inch sides to form rails that would ride in the receiver grooves. These rails were .100" tall and .190" wide. You will need to measure your specific grooves and make your parts to fit your receiver, since there will probably be some variation.

You will also need to measure the top to receiver groove distance and fabricate accordingly. Be sure to leave a few thousandths running clearance on the striker so it slides easily in the receiver.

Bevel all sharp edges to promote smooth operation. Once the basic block is formed and fitted, a clearance notch needs to be made in the top rear of the striker. This will allow the block to slide under the receiver if it would happen to hit the spring-loaded buffer with enough force to compress it. My notch was .300" deep and .750" tall.

The telescoping recoil spring assembly will pass through the striker, so a clearance hole will have to be made in the striker. Determine its location by measuring off the hole in the back of the bolt carrier. Once the location is determined, you can drill a 7/16" hole to allow clearance of the 3/8" rod of the spring assembly.

Drill this hole all the way through. Its front needs a shallow counterbore to allow for clearance of the raised portion around the hole in the back of the bolt carrier. The back side needs counterbored 1/2" diameter to allow the recoil spring to fit in the rear of the striker.

Leave about 1/4" of 7/16" hole between the two counterbores. Bevel all sharp edges so the recoil assembly doesn't get scratched during operation.

Two bevels need to be formed on the bottom of the striker. The rear portion needs to be beveled from the

auto rifle" to emphasize the fact it was not a machine gun. A $10 set of hand stamps is all that's needed to mark the project. If you stamp the info on the gun, be sure to back up the stamping area with a heavy steel block so you don't bend the receiver when hammering the stamps.

■ RECEIVER STRESS RELIEVING

Once all welding, machining and reworking the receiver is completed, one last operation needs to be done, stress relieving. All the welding on the receiver has induced a lot of stress into the receiver. To partially reduce them,

the receiver needs to be heated while solidly secured to a strong straight fixture.

I used my weld/alignment fixture for this job. The receiver was clamped to the fixture, then I placed the whole works in the kitchen oven and baked it at 450–500° for an hour and a half. Be sure to remove all traces of oil before you bake, or it will really stink up the house. It might also be a good idea to do this when the spouse is gone for the afternoon!

■ STRIKER FABRICATION

The heart of this semi-auto conversion is the striker-fired fire control group. While the original sear, modified disconnector, and duplicated U.S.-made trigger can be used, a new striker will have to be made from alloy steel. The new striker will ride behind the bolt and carrier in the bolt carrier grooves.

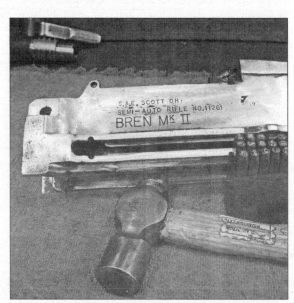

Although BATFE doesn't require it, Matthews recommends that all home-built guns be marked. It may save you a confrontation with a cop at the shooting range.

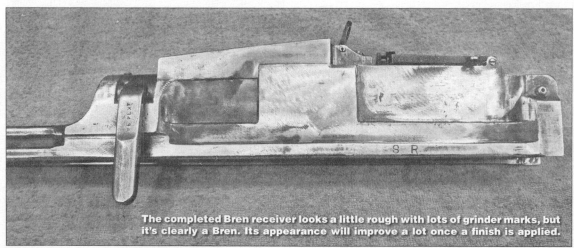

The completed Bren receiver looks a little rough with lots of grinder marks, but it's clearly a Bren. Its appearance will improve a lot once a finish is applied.

The receiver can be stress-relieved by clamping the receiver to the straight weld fixture, then baking at 450° for an hour. A kitchen oven works fine here.

back edge to about 2/3 of the way forward. This bevel will allow the striker to slide easily over the sear when the bolt carrier pushes the striker rearward during recoil.

A short bevel needs to be formed on the front of the striker. It should be angled to match the angle on the front of the sear. This short bevel will be the sear engagement surface and also will engage the disconnector as the striker moves forward to strike the firing pin. The lower sides of the striker need to be beveled to match the shape that is on the bottom of the bolt carrier

To verify that the striker operates smoothly, you will have to set the parts up in the lower receiver and operate them manually. The sear should retain the striker until the trigger is pulled. When the trigger is pulled, the striker should be released and slide over the sear and disconnector.

When the striker is being moved rearward, as in recocking, it should easily slide over the disconnector and sear and be caught by the sear again. The trigger should have to be released for resetting. Everything must slide easily for proper functioning. Considerable hand fitting and polishing may be required.

The striker must slide over the disconnector on the forward stroke easily enough that it does not slow the striker down any great amount, or it will have insufficient force when it impacts the firing pin.

At this point, the striker is overly heavy. There is a limit on how heavy a striker can be before it affects functioning of the recoiling bolt and carrier. A spring strong enough to push a heavy striker would cause short-stroking of the recoiling parts. An overly heavy striker can also effect functioning, since it increases reciprocating mass.

I machined several pockets and holes in the striker to reduce its weight. Depth of these lightening cuts were just a little under 3/4" deep. I also drilled lightening holes in the top and sides. Finally I stamped the striker USA to identify it as a U.S. part.

After you have done all fitting and testing, the striker needs to be heat-treated. The striker will be heated to 1500° (I used Tempilaq to verify temperature) and then quenched in oil. Maximum as quenched hardness of 4140 steel is about Rockwell 40c. This is fine for the majority of the part but the bottom that rides over the sear and disconnector needs to be harder for wear resistance.

To caseharden the bottom up closer to the range of Rockwell 60c, I used Brownells steel hardening compound. I applied this material to the red-hot steel before the part was quenched as per the instructions on the can. Once the bottom was treated, it was so hard that a file would just slide across without cutting. After the striker was heat-treated, I polished it for smooth operation. Then I wrapped it in aluminum foil and baked in the oven for one hour at 450° for stress relief. ◎

Next month (12/20 issue): Finishing the Bren semi-auto.

BUILD YOUR OWN BREN GUN! Part 5 – Magazine Well Rebuild

Ask the Gunsmith

By Reid Coffield

BLUING SALTS

Q *What chemicals are used in bluing salts? I asked my local gunsmith and he either did not know or would not tell me!*

A Most commercial hot bluing or caustic bluing salts are made up of sodium nitrate, sodium nitrite, and sodium hydroxide. The various commercial brands that are available are just variations on this basic mix with a little more of this or a little less of that.

HOW MUCH SANDING

Q *Just how smooth do I need to sand a stock? How high a grit should I go with my sanding before I start to apply the finish?*

A At a minimum for a regular sporter stock I would not consider sanding to anything less than 220 grit. That would be my bottom line. Normally I sand to a higher grit than that but 220 will give you a darn nice finish.

FLINTLOCK TOUCH HOLE

Q *I am working on a flintlock and need some help in locating the touch hole. Where should I put it and what diameter should I make it?*

A In regard to the location and site of the touch hole for a flintlock, let's first deal with the location. First you want to make sure that the touch hole is

For the most reliable ignition, the touch hole should be located in line with the top of the pan vertically and the front of the breech plug horizontally. Fire should touch the base of the charge.

located ahead of the end of the breech plug. Ideally, the back edge of the touch hole would be just even with the face of the breech plug. The idea is to direct the flame from the priming to the rear of the powder charge in the barrel.

In relationship to the pan, the touch hole should normally be located in the center of a line drawn on the side of the barrel across the top of the pan. The idea here is to allow the flame from the priming to immediately access the touch hole. If the touch hole is located near the bottom of the pan, the priming must burn down before the flame can get into the touch hole and reach the barrel charge. This will lead to slow ignition. Also, as fouling builds up in the bottom of the pan, it could block a low touch hole and lead to misfires.

As for the diameter of the touch hole, generally you can get by with using anywhere from a 1/32" drill bit to a 1/16" diameter drill. You might want to start off with the smaller 1/32" drill. If you have problems with ignition, you can always open it up to the larger 1/16" diameter.

TRASH THAT BARREL

Q *I have a major problem. I bought a nice 98 Mauser sporter in .270. I got a really good deal on the gun because it only had open sights. I thought I could drill and tap it for a scope. I borrowed a scope base drill jig from a buddy and in drilling the front base holes I drilled one all the way into the barrel. How can I fix this? Have I ruined the barrel?*

A Yep, you've unfortunately ruined the barrel. The only solution to this problem is to replace the barrel. ◎

The work's been done and payday has arrived. It was a marathon job that taxed Matthews' skills and determination, but now he's enjoying a semi-auto Bren gun.

Build Your Own
BREN GUN!
■ Part 6 — Finishing the Rifle

In the five previous installments (7/20, 8/20, 9/20, 10/20, 11/20), Matthews did some labor and machine-intensive work that will challenge any home gunsmith. This time he gets to the payoff.

By Steven Matthews

■ BARREL LOCKING COLLAR DETENT INSTALLATION AND FEED RAMP POLISHING

A couple of small jobs need finishing before you assemble the gun for bench testing. The barrel locking collar has a detent to hold it on place in the receiver. In your parts set should be two small pins with beveled grooves on their sides, plus a spring that is the size of the larger pin.

One pin goes in the small hole in the front of the receiver and the larger pin and spring go in the larger hole in the top of the receiver. The beveled surfaces allow the pins to operate each other under spring tension. I had to re-drill the holes for my detent pins since they were partially filled with repair welds.

The other job that needs to be done is to recut or smooth up the feed ramps. The double groove feed ramp is right under the front of the magazine catch.

These grooves need to be filed out to original shape if they were damaged during reconstruction and polished for smooth feeding.

■ WORK BENCH FUNCTION TESTING (NON-LIVE FIRE TESTING)

Assemble all the parts of the gun and begin what I call work bench testing. This is where one finds out if all the parts operate correctly when they interact. The first thing is to verify that all parts reciprocate smoothly with no binding when the charging handle is pulled and released. If parts operate smoothly, one can go to checking the operation of the fire control group. Check to verify that the striker releases when the trigger is pulled and it moves forward with enough force to set off the primers. This can be done by using primed cases with *no bullet or powder.* If the strike hits hard enough, you will get a loud bang

when the primer goes off. The Bren gun features a very wide firing pin and requires considerable force to set off the primer. Verify that the trigger is disconnected during each cycle of the bolt, carrier and striker.

Everything may appear to be working right on the bench, but there is a simple test that needs to be done that may not be apparent. I missed this detail till I was doing test firing and was having cycling problems. The Bren is a gas operated firearm with a rather short gas time acting on the gas piston. It is designed to operate with a certain weight of reciprocating mass and spring tension. More mass has been added to this semi-auto gun and the spring tension increased since a striker spring needs to be compressed along with the recoil spring. While the gas system is adjustable, the adjustments may not be able to compensate for the higher re-

The barrel locking collar is retained by a spring loaded detent in the front of the receiver. Beveled surfaces on the detent pins cam the pins in and out.

The dual feed ramps under the front magazine catch should be polished for smooth feeding. The ramps may have to be reconstructed due to receiver demilling.

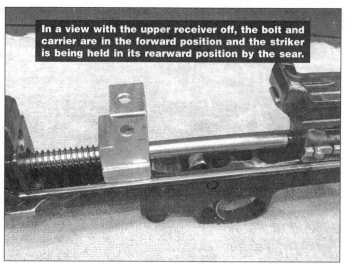

In a view with the upper receiver off, the bolt and carrier are in the forward position and the striker is being held in its rearward position by the sear.

After the striker is released by the sear, it must slide easily over the disconnector. If it drags, it will not have enough force to set off the primer.

The striker has been released and has moved forward to impact the firing pin extension. Striker spring tension will need to be adjusted for proper operation.

The bolt, carrier and striker are fully rearward. The parts are driven forward by the recoil and striker springs that have telescoped into the buffer tube.

ciprocating weight and spring tension. This caused my gun to short stroke during live fire testing. I suspected this as a cause of my malfunctions, so I did some testing. The springs mentioned in this article are what eventually worked, but were not the ones I used at first. To measure spring tension, I bought a $5 fishing scale at WalMart. I installed the original Bren springs and measured spring tension. The original spring required about 7 lbs. of force to begin rearward movement of the charging handle and 22 lbs. of force to maintain the bolt in rearward position. I then installed the new telescoping recoil spring assembly and checked it. It measured just slightly less, so this was not the problem. Unfortunately, when I installed the striker spring and rechecked my force at full

rearward position, it was several pounds over the stock measurement. This was retarding the reciprocating bolt carrier group and causing short stroking. Adjustment of the gas system could not compensate for the excessively heavy striker spring. I had to replace the striker spring with a lighter spring. The 11"x.480"diameter x.041" wire spring was just a little too weak for reliable ignition. To increase its strength, I just stretched it out to 12½–14" and reinstalled it. This was just enough to make it work 100%. Not high tech but it did work! Keep this in mind, you will probably have to do some tinkering with spring tensions to get everything working right because the exact springs are not available. The Bren is supposed to operate normally on gas position #2. Due to the additional spring required to drive a striker and the slightly heavier reciprocating parts, I needed to run mine on position #3 for 100% functioning.

Once the preceding testing results in good operation, one can go on to function testing with self-made *dummy* rounds (*empty* of live primer and powder, but with a bullet installed) or purchased action prov-

ing dummy rounds (available from Brownells). Use the dummy rounds to check that the gun will chamber and eject rounds properly. *Never use live rounds for testing.* Load several dummy rounds in the magazine and cycle the action vigorously by hand. My project worked fine on the work bench, so I decided it was time to go on to live fire testing. On your project, make sure everything works right before going to live fire. If it won't work right on the bench with dummy rounds, adding 45,000 psi of firing pressure to the equation is not going to make things work better.

■ LIVE FIRE TESTING

When setting up for live fire testing, set the gas system on position #2 to begin with. If the gun will not cycle reliably at setting #2, you can go to position #3. Do not set the gun on position #4, as this will overwork the action and probably open the bolt too soon and result in bulged cases. If the gun doesn't work right on position #2 or #3, you need to do some trouble shooting and find out where you made a mistake or need to do some adjustments.

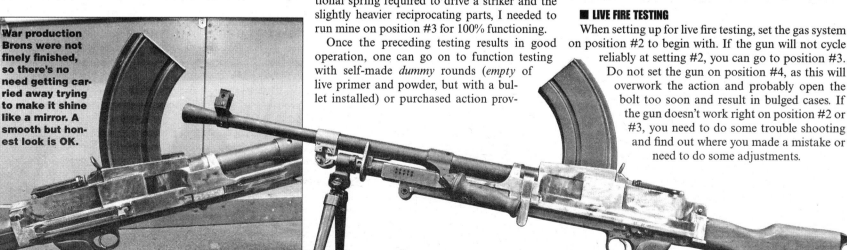

War production Brens were not finely finished, so there's no need getting carried away trying to make it shine like a mirror. A smooth but honest look is OK.

The semi-auto Bren gun is complete and ready for function testing, if still pretty ugly. Once functioning is correct, the project can have a finish applied.

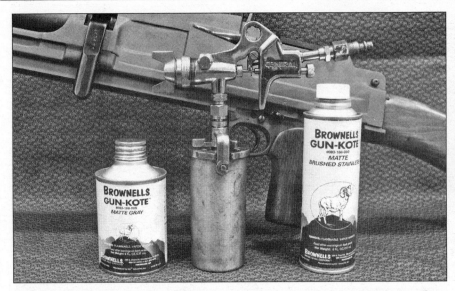

Spraying Brownells GunKote firearms finish over an abrasive blasted surface makes the gun look better than when new. GunKote is durable and easy to apply.

The scuffed up magazines were sprayed with Lauer Custom Weaponry's Dura-Coat firearms finish. DuraCoated surfaces do not have to be blasted or baked.

When live fire testing any homemade semi-auto firearm, you should only load one round in the magazine for the first shot. If one round chambers, fires, and ejects right, then you can go to two rounds for the next shot. The rounds in the magazine can be increased by one round for each subsequent test. This is for safety reasons. If you have a malfunction or you did not make a part right and have a full-auto runaway malfunction, you want as few rounds as possible in the gun.

Once the previously mentioned short stroking problem was fixed, my gun worked fine. It chambered all rounds smoothly and fired and ejected without a hitch. In fact, it worked so well that I shot up a lot more of the expensive .303 British ammo than I had intended. I could see right then and there I was going to have to find a source of inexpensive .303 ammo, because this

gun was fun to shoot! I did—and you may have to as well—run the gun on gas setting #3. The extra weight of the semi-auto striker and the tension of its spring required extra gas to reliably cycle the action.

The Bren's combat sights are set at the lowest setting of 200 yards, so expect rounds to hit a little high at 100 yards. My sights needed a little windage adjustment and this was done by driving the front sight sideways in it's dovetail slot with a hammer and punch. Remember when adjusting a front sight, you move it opposite of what you would move a rear sight. Accuracy with my new condition Bren barrel installed was pretty reasonable for this type of gun, about 3 to 4 inches at 100 yards. Remember, this is a combat grade machine gun, not a target rifle. It's made more for area fire than precise target grade shot placement.

■ FINISHING

Now that this old warhorse was working well, it was time to give it a new finish. Original Bren guns were blued, parkerized and I believe some were even painted in what was referred to as "war finish." I wanted to duplicate the appearances of a parkerized finish, but this project was not a good candidate for parkerizing. Firearms with a bunch of welds on them do not parkerize evenly. The welds will show up as slightly different in color and texture. To duplicate the appearance of zinc phosphate parkerizing, I used Brownells GunKote in the color of Matte Gray (#083-166-009). If you want the color darker, like manganese phosphate parkerizing, add a little black GunKote to the mix. I used the matte gray for most of the gun, but used matte black on several pieces to give it some highlights. This

Fired cases may or may not be reloaded depending on individual barrels. Bren chambers are at maximum size to promote reliability but this is hard on brass.

sprayed and baked finish is extremely durable if applied correctly. The parts are cleaned, abrasive blasted, cleaned again, sprayed with GunKote, then baked in an oven at 300° for 1 hour. When cool, the parts are ready to use. There is no need to wait for days for full hardness like some finishes. After finishing, the gun was reassembled, lubed and was ready to go.

The surplus Bren magazines I had were a little rough from years of storage and handling, so I decided to refinish them as well. I really did not feel like abrasive blasting them and applying GunKote. For an easy-to-apply finish on the magazines, I just degreased them and sprayed them with Lauer Custom Weaponry's DuraCoat firearms finish in the color of Matte Black.

■ FINAL THOUGHTS

The modified firing system for this gun is based on a military firearm. The gun is a military gun that has been repurposed/recreated for recreational use. All ammo used in this firearm should be military spec ammo with military hardness primers that are crimped in place. Commercial or re-loaded ammo may not function correctly and could cause malfunctions and be unsafe.

This gun should not be fired fast enough to duplicate full-auto fire, such as fanning the trigger. The disconnector and trigger system are not made for operation of that speed. If one tries to run the gun faster than the design limit, the striker may follow the bolt down and fail to fire a cartridge before complete lockup. This is a semi-auto gun—do not try to turn it into a machine gun with your trigger finger!

This project was very labor intensive, but also very inexpensive. If you can do all the work yourself like I did the cost will only be about $350, which is quite the bargain. Anyone who is a skilled hobbyist machinist and hobbyist gunsmith should be able to build this project. One just has to take their time and pay attention to the details. For those of us that don't have a lot of money, this build-it-yourself option is a great way of obtaining a rather expensive firearm at low cost. If this sounds like your kind of project, why not give it a try? ◉

The completely finished Bren project cost a fraction of a manufactured Bren. Those with equipment and skills can build the semi-auto Bren for less than $350.

BUILD YOUR OWN BREN GUN!   Part 6 – Finishing the Rifle

■ BREN PROJECT RESOURCES

BREN PARTS SETS
Military Gun Supply, 2901 Cravens Rd., Dept. SGN, Fort Worth, TX, 76119, 817-457-6000, www.militarygunsupply.com

BREN BARRELS AND BREN MAGAZINES
Omega Weapons Systems, 2918 E. Ginter Rd., Dept. SGN, Tuscon, AZ, 85706, 520-889-8895, www.omega-weapons-systems.com

I.O.Inc./Royal Tiger Imports LTD, Box 1977, Dept. SGN, Indian Trail, NC, 28079 888-968-4437, www.royaltigerimports.com

4130 TUBING AND 4130 SHEET
Wicks Aircraft and Motor Sports, 410 Pine St., Dept. SGN, Highland, IL, 62249, 800-221-9425, www.wicksaircraft.com

Aircraft Spruce, Box 4000, Dept. SGN, Corona, CA, 92878, 877-477-7823, www.aircraftspruce.com

SPRING STOCK AND 4140 BAR STOCK
McMaster-Carr, Box 94930, Dept. SGN, Cleveland, OH, 44101, 330-995-5500, www.mcmaster.com

FIREARM FINISHING SUPPLIES
Brownells, 200 S. Front St., Dept. SGN, Montezuma, IA, 50171, 800-741-0015, www.brownells.com

Lauer Custom Weaponry, 3601 129th St., Dept. SGN, Chippewa Falls, WI, 54729, 800-830-6677, www.lauerweaponry.com

Ask the Gunsmith

By Reid Coffield

DON'T LOSE PINS

Q *When I take guns apart, I seem to always have a problem losing small pins. The smaller the pin, the easier it seems for me to misplace or lose it. How do you keep from losing little pins?*

A I had that same problem for years and years. I finally started doing two things that have pretty much taken care of the situation. First, I use plastic parts boxes or trays to hold the parts when I disassemble a gun. These trays are molded from one piece of plastic, so there is no seam or gap in the bottom that will allow a pin to get lost. In addition, I take a piece of masking tape and place the small pins on the sticky side of the tape and fold over an identical length of tape. This makes a nice little holder for the pins and I can even make a note on the tape as to what pins are held in it. Since I have been doing this I have not lost any pins, even some really tiny ones used in some gun sights.

The secret to keeping track of tiny pins is masking tape! Just place the parts on the tape, fold it over, and you have a secure, easily seen package. You can mark the outside with the locations.

STUCK CHOKE TUBE

Q *I have seen a number of shotguns at my club that have stuck choke tubes. What is your advice to keep from having a choke tube stuck in the barrel?*

A In most of the cases I have seen, the owner never cleaned or lubricated the threads of his choke tubes. In some cases this leads to rust developing in the threads of the tube and/or the barrel. In other cases I have seen the threads gall or deform because of the lack of lubricant.

I believe that you should remove the choke tube after each shooting session. The threads on both the tube and the barrel should be cleaned to remove any carbon or fouling that may have leaked around the choke tube. Once cleaned, a good grease or tube lubricant should be applied to the threads. Then when the tube is installed no more pressure should be used than the minimum necessary to ensure that the tube is fully seated. I have seen several tubes that were damaged by excessive seating force.

It is also a good idea to periodically check the seating of your choke tube. If you do need to retighten the choke tube, make darn sure the gun is unloaded before you begin work on the muzzle end of the barrel. ◉

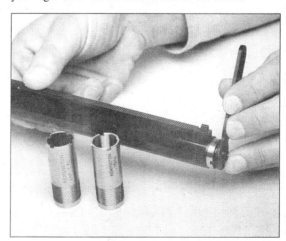

There's a reason choke tube tools are made of plastic or thin metal; you don't want to over-tighten the tube in the bore. Turning too tight can damage the tube or jam it in position.

101 Gunsmithing Projects on One Gun?

You don't need a safe full of junkers to learn gunsmithing, Coffield says. A single gun can be the test bed for a variety of skill-building projects.

By Reid Coffield

One of the great things about being a gunsmith, besides having the perfect excuse for being kinda crotchety and cantankerous, is that you get to talk to a lot of gun owners about workin' on guns. I really do enjoy being around gun people. They're among the finest folks you could ever want to meet, but you know that! As for spending time talking with 'em about my favorite subject; well, that's a real treat.

Over the years I've had the opportunity to help a good many men and women get involved in gunsmithing at various levels. At the minimum, most of the gun owners I've known have wanted to be able to take care of their own guns. I guess its part of that spirit of self-reliance that's so common among gun owners and so lacking among the rest of the population.

It's just a short step from being able to provide basic maintenance to being able to do other tasks as well. Sooner or later, most gun folks I've known have wanted to take that step. In talking with 'em, one of the things I've always emphasized is the idea that, if at all possible, you should not practice gunsmithing on your favorite gun.

If you're gonna learn a new skill, you need to do it on something other than your most prized or favorite firearm. The reality of any learning situation is that we all make mistakes when we start out. That's normal and to be expected. In fact, it's a necessary part of learning. If you haven't made any mistakes, you haven't learned anything! And yes, based on the number of mistakes I've made, some folks would definitely contend that I should've learned a *lot* over the years!

Coffield says there's nothing like an old military rifle like this Turkish Mauser with mixed numbers and low collector value as the basis for learning gunsmithing.

Most will buy into this idea that you need to practice to develop gunsmithing skills. No problem there. In fact, a lot of the folks I've worked with have gone out and bought guns just for that purpose. More than one person I've known has ended up with one heck of a collection of "project guns".

By the way, that term is often just a polite way of saying "junk". Now, there's nothing wrong with this if you're OK with a bunch of ol' beaters cluttering up your shop and taking up space in your gun safe. It's also fine if you're willing and able to spend the money.

The reality is that most of us just don't have either the money or the space to accumulate these project guns. The space is especially an issue for me and one that my wife, for whatever silly reason, seems to be kinda sensitive about. I guess it might have something to do with finding two old shotguns under the couch several years ago. Oh well, you live and learn!

Don't get me wrong; it's important to have a gun you can work on, experiment with, and test your skills. Where I think many folks miss the point is that you don't really need a lot of these project guns. In fact, you would be absolutely amazed at what you can do with just *one* project gun!

What follows is a list of tasks that can be performed on a typical centerfire military surplus rifle. There are still lots of these guns out there that are ideal candidates for the hobbyists at very modest prices. These are not and should not be "collector grade" guns.

For gunsmithing practice you want a real beater. If it looks like it's been drug behind a pickup over five miles of gravel road, that's fine! In fact, that may be the ideal gun. You're definitely not going to hurt anything working on something like that and no one can accuse you of "ruining" a rare collectable.

By the way, Century International Arms, Inc., 430 South Congress Dr., Suite #1, DelRay Beach, Fla. 33445, telephone 800-527-1252, www.centuryarms.com, which advertises here in SHOTGUN NEWS, often has some "well used" or slightly damaged guns for sale that would be ideal. I would definitely encourage you to check their web site to see what they might have as their inventory is constantly changing.

Do you really need a pile of junkers like this to develop gunsmithing skills? Coffield doesn't think so. He lists 101 projects you can perform on a single gun.

Also keep in mind that there are some tasks that are gun specific. You can't modify a fixed choke shotgun barrel on a Mosin-Nagant rifle or reshape a rimfire firing pin on an old 8mm Mauser. If your interests lay more with shotguns or .22s, some of these projects will not be relevant. On the other hand, if you're just interested in rimfires, get a beater .22 rifle for your work. Again, the vast majority of these projects will still be relevant. Of course, this applies to shotguns as well.

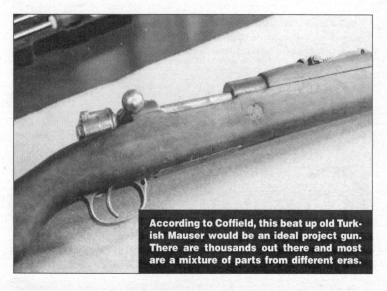

According to Coffield, this beat up old Turkish Mauser would be an ideal project gun. There are thousands out there and most are a mixture of parts from different eras.

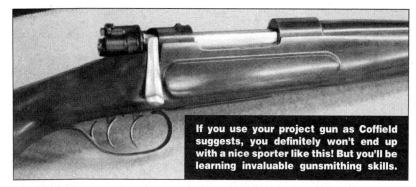

If you use your project gun as Coffield suggests, you definitely won't end up with a nice sporter like this! But you'll be learning invaluable gunsmithing skills.

You can learn a lot making a Mosin-Nagant into a sporter but you still won't learn as much as you would if you use the same gun as a test bed for many projects.

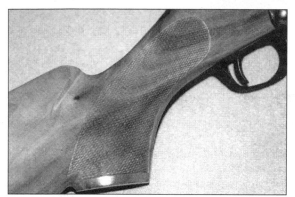

A simple checkering pattern like this is a great first step in learning to checker. Doing it on an inexpensive stock makes the inevitable mistakes bearable.

Finally, you'll need to stay very detached from your project gun and that can be hard to do. Once you've put a bunch of hours into repairing the stock, raising the dents, and applying a gorgeous finish, it's darn hard to strip it all off just so you can try another type of finish. You may find yourself wanting to "save" the gun and make it into a showpiece.

That's fine but you'll miss the opportunity to practice and learn more. Ideally at the end of the project you'll find yourself with a rifle receiver, a bunch of parts, and some scrap wood. But you'll also have gained a wealth of experience that far outweighs the value of that one gun.

What follows is a listing of 101 gunsmithing projects or tasks. You can do all of 'em or only a few. The more you do, the more you'll learn and gain through experience. The projects are more or less listed in sequence for maximum utilization of the rifle. In this case, I've assumed that we have a typical military Mauser based on the common Model 98 action. Of course, other rifles could be used.

One last thought before getting into the list; don't get in a hurry to complete any particular project. Take your time and do the very best work you can. This is a time and opportunity to learn, experiment, and develop your skills. Later when you're working on other guns there'll often be plenty of pressure to get the work done quickly. For now, go slow, relax, and enjoy it!

1. Disassemble the rifle.
2. Learn the proper name and function of each part. (That knowledge alone can be of great value when later diagnosing malfunctions or just ordering replacement parts.)
3. Clean and reassemble the rifle. (Work to develop a fast and efficient technique.)
4. Remove all dirt, grime, grease, and oil from the wood. (Try different methods with an emphasis on materials that do not damage or harm the wood finish.)
5. Use headspace gauges to check the headspace.
6. Determine the amount of contact between the bolt lugs and the lug seats in the receiver.
7. Measure firing pin protrusion.
8. Chemically strip the old stock finish.
9. Raise any dents in the stock.
10. Repair all gouges or cracks in the stock.
11. Refinish the stock with a military type oil finish.
12. Remove all rust from the metal components.
13. Clean the barrel bore.
14. Determine the rifling twist rate.
15. Lap the bore.
16. Make a chamber cast, measure it and compare with SAAMI chamber specifications.
17. Check for barrel erosion at the throat and muzzle.
18. Make a bore cast and determine the bore diameter and depth of the rifling.
19. Cut back the stock and reinstall the stock fittings or furniture to make a carbine or short rifle out of a full size rifle.
20. Cut the barrel and duplicate the original crown.
21. Reinstall the original front sight.
22. Make and install a post front sight insert.
23. Shorten and reshape the fore-arm.
24. Fill in the cut out for the sling swivel base with wood from the forearm.
25. Refinish the stock with Tru-Oil.
26. Add a pistol grip to the stock.
27. Add wood to the butt stock to raise and reshape the comb.
28. Add a cheekpiece to the buttstock.
29. Install a commercial buttplate.
30. Install a fore-end tip.
31. Refinish the stock with tung oil.
32. Install commercial sling swivels.
33. Checker the right pistol grip panel with a simple fill in pattern.
34. Stipple the left pistol grip panel.
35. Install a wood pistol grip cap and match the existing finish.
36. Cut a basket weave pattern on the right side of the fore-end.
37. Make and install a contrasting wood inlay on the left side of the fore-end.
38. Glass bed the action.
39. Polish the bolt ways of receiver.
40. Polish all machine marks from the bolt and receiver.
41. Streamline and reshape the military trigger guard.
42. Convert the military two-stage trigger to a single-stage trigger.
43. Recontour the military trigger.
44. Install a simple commercial trigger such as a Boyd's or Timney that does not utilize an integral safety.
45. Weigh and adjust the trigger pull to a specific pull weight; i.e., 3½ pounds.
46. Make and install a lever for the magazine floorplate release.
47. Adapt and install a shotgun type trigger guard.
48. Install commercial double set triggers.
49. Install a low scope safety.
50. Remove and reinstall the military barrel.
51. Cut the barrel behind the existing front sight.
52. Crown the barrel with a hunter or commercial crown.
53. Cut the barrel back 1/4" and make a recessed target crown.
54. Cut the barrel back 1/4" and make a 5° target crown.
55. Remove the military rear sight without damage to the sight or the barrel.
56. Make the measurements and calculations to determine the proper height of commercial sights such as those sold by Williams or Marbles.

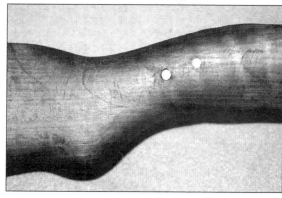

Even an old stock like this one can provide lots of good practice. Reworking this old armorer wrist repair could provide some darn good woodworking experience.

Mosin-Nagants are cheap and plentiful. Some that have been especially well used would be good project guns. Generally speaking, they aren't sought by gun collectors.

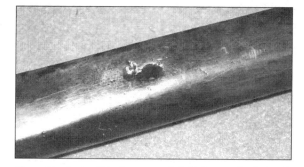

The pinhole in this forearm definitely needs help. It would be a great learning project. Coffield says friends and relatives will often give you junker project guns.

Installing a skeleton grip cap is a challenging task. It will test your skills in measuring, layout, carving and shaping. And it gives the project rifle a classy touch.

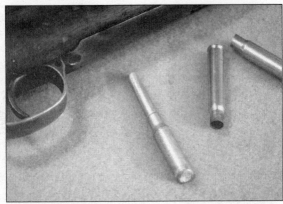

Making a chamber casting is often the only sure way of evaluating the condition of the chamber and barrel throat. Sporterized military guns often were rechambered.

As you can see with this list, there are many things you can do with just one gun. In fact, you can do even more than this! This list of 101 projects is by no means definitive. The number of projects you can do is limited only by your imagination.

OK, so now you have an idea of what can be done. More than likely you want info on how to do many of these tasks. Fortunately the information is readily available through a number of darn good gunsmithing books. I've listed many of these books along with a brief comment or two. Some may be out of print but they can often be found on Amazon.com or through some of the many book dealers that advertise here in SHOTGUN NEWS.

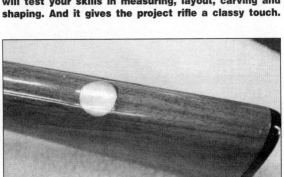

Inletting an initial shield into the buttstock requires patience and careful work. The stock of your project rifle is the perfect to place to learn to do this.

74. Install the barreled action into a semi-finished stock.
75. Shape the semi-finished stock.
76. Sand the stock to 300 grit.
77. Stain the wood. (Experiment with various stains; i.e., oil, water based, alcohol, etc.)
78. Install a metal pistol grip cap.
79. Make and install a cartridge trap in the buttstock.
80. Finish the stock to a high gloss with a hand rubbed oil finish.
81. Checker the pistol grip and forearm with an appropriate pattern.
82. Install Model 70 Winchester type sling swivels.
83. Remove the barrel and install a commercial, pre-threaded, short chambered barrel.
84. Extend the chamber and headspace the barrel.
85. Reshape the rear of the receiver ring and remove the charger clip guide.
86. Reshape the upper receiver tang.
87. Inlet the barreled action into a stock blank.
88. Fit a commercial curved metal buttplate.
89. Install a hollow metal grip cap.
90. Install an exotic wood fore-end cap.
91. Make a band type front sight ramp.
92. Check or serrate the front sight ramp.
93. Install the band front sight ramp.
94. Install a European type express rear sight.
95. Make and install a metal buttplate cartridge trap.
96. Finish the stock with a low gloss oil finish.
97. Checker the stock with an intricate pattern.
98. Polish the metal to 500 grit.
99. Blue the metal using caustic salts.
100. Stamp the caliber on the barrel.
101. Install an initial shield in the toe line of the stock.

1. The *Official NRA Guide to Firearms Assembly, Rifles and Shotguns*
2. *The Official NRA Guide to Firearms Assembly, Pistols and Revolvers*
3. Brownells Gunsmith Kinks Volumes 1-4
4. *Do-It-Yourself Gunsmithing by Jim Carmichel* (out of print but a great source of info)
5. *Gunsmithing* by Roy Dunlap (an older gunsmithing book but still in print and a very good source of information)
6. *Hobby Gunsmithing* by Ralph Walker (out of print but packed with good basic information)
7. *Checkering and Carving of Gunstocks* by Monty Kennedy
8. *Professional Stockmaking* by David L. Wesbrook (*the* definitive book on building a rifle stock)
9. *The NRA Gunsmithing Guide–Updated* (may be out of print but used copies can be found)
10. *Gunsmithing Tips and Projects* by Wolfe Publishing

There are a couple of catalogs you need to have available before you begin these gunsmithing projects. I strongly encourage you to contact the folks at Numrich Gun Parts Corp., Box 299, Dept. SGN, West Hurley, N.Y. 12491, telephone 866-686-7424. Numrich is the largest supplier of gun parts in the world and if you work on older guns, you'll definitely need their latest catalog. Also, give the folks at Brownells Inc., 200 South Front St., Dept. SGN, Montezuma, Iowa 50171, telephone 800-741-0015 a call and ask for their latest catalog.

Brownells offers the most extensive line of gunsmithing tools and equipment in the country. They not only can sell you the tools you need, they also have a staff of gunsmiths who'll be more than happy to talk with you and answer any gunsmithing questions you have.

57. Drill, tap and install a commercial rear sight such as a Williams Guide Open Sight.
58. Drill, tap and install a commercial ramp front sight.
59. Soft solder a front sight ramp to the barrel.
60. Silver solder a front sight ramp to the barrel. (Use a low temperature silver solder.)
61. Make and attach a sling swivel band to the barrel.
62. Forge and reshape the military bolt handle.
63. Cut off the military bolt handle and weld on a commercial bolt handle.
64. Drill and tap the receiver for scope bases.
65. Mount a scope.
66. Reshape and checker the bolt release lever.
67. Checker the bolt handle knob.
68. Polish the bolt body to a mirror like finish.
69. Jewel the bolt body.
70. Remove the metal finish from the barrel and receiver and hand polish to 400 grit.
71. Blue the metal with a traditional rust blue process.
72. Install a recoil pad on the buttstock without damaging the wood finish.
73. Fit and install a commercial trigger that has a side safety.

There you have it. The projects listed have ranged from very simple requiring only a few hand tools to those more involved requiring the use of a lathe or welding equipment. Try as many as possible and don't worry if the results are not perfect. After all, the objective is to learn and improve your skills and ability. Remember, the more you do, the more you'll learn and the greater your level of gunsmithing skill and expertise.

Good luck and good gunsmithing!　◎

This old Arisaka was picked up at a garage sale. The cracked wrist is an excellent repair project. Thousands of military arms are crammed in attics and basements.

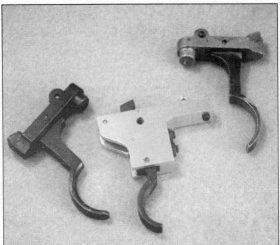

The only way to learn to install an adjustable trigger is actually to do it! A project rifle provides the perfect platform for this combination of wood and metal work.

Do you really want a safe full of junkers like this? Coffield says that doing many projects on a single gun saves your storage space for more desirable firearms.